# SCOTTISH EDUCATION
# FIFTH EDITION

Edited by T. G. K. Bryce, W. M. Humes, D. Gillies
and A. Kennedy

*Section editing by*
Tom Bryce
Janis Davidson
Donald Gillies
Tom Hamilton
George Head
Walter Humes
Aileen Kennedy
Ian Smith

EDINBURGH
University Press

Edinburgh University Press is one of the leading university presses in the UK. We publish academic books and journals in our selected subject areas across the humanities and social sciences, combining cutting-edge scholarship with high editorial and production values to produce academic works of lasting importance. For more information visit our website: edinburghuniversitypress.com

First edition published 1999
Second edition published 2003
Third edition published 2008
Fourth edition published 2013

Edinburgh University Press Ltd
The Tun – Holyrood Road, 12(2f) Jackson's Entry, Edinburgh EH8 8PJ

Typeset in Ehrhardt by
Servis Filmsetting Ltd, Stockport, Cheshire
and printed and bound in Great Britain by
Ashford Colour Press, Gosport, Hants

A CIP record for this book is available from the British Library

ISBN 978 1 4744 3784 4 (paperback)
ISBN 978 1 4744 3785 1 (webready PDF)
ISBN 978 1 4744 3786 8 (epub)

# Contents

# The Contributors

**Robert Anderson** is Professor Emeritus of History in the School of History, Classics and Archaeology at the University of Edinburgh. He has written extensively on the history of education, in Scotland and elsewhere. His most recent books are *Education and the Scottish People, 1750–1918* (1995), *European Universities from the Enlightenment to 1914* (2004) and *British Universities Past and Present* (2006). He is joint editor of *The Edinburgh History of Education in Scotland* (2015).

**Rowena Arshad, OBE** is Head of the Moray House School of Education/Co-Director of the Centre for Education for Racial Equality in Scotland, University of Edinburgh.

**Will Barlow** is a Lecturer in the School of Education at the University of Aberdeen.

**Jean Barr** is Emeritus Professor of Adult and Continuing Education in the University of Glasgow.

**Anna Beck** is a Lecturer in Teacher Professional Learning in the School of Education at the University of Strathclyde.

**David Bell, CBE** is Professor of Economics at the University of Stirling.

**Alan Britton** is a Senior Lecturer and Director of Internationalisation in the School of Education at the University of Glasgow.

**Terry Brotherstone** is an Honorary Research Fellow in History at the University of Aberdeen. A former Honorary President of the University and College Union Scotland, he was a member (2009–10) of the General Council of the Scottish Trade Union Congress (STUC) and the STUC nominee on the Scottish Government Advisory Panel on Higher Education Governance, chaired by Professor Ferdinand von Prondzynski (2011–12).

**Derek Brown** is Head of Education at Fife Council.

**Tom Bryce** is Emeritus Professor of Education, University of Strathclyde in Glasgow. A former Vice-Dean for Research, his interests are principally concerned with Scottish teacher education and science education.

**Charles Byrne** was, until recently, a Senior Lecturer in the School of Education at the University of Strathclyde.

**Nicola Carse** is a Lecturer in Primary Education in the Moray House School of Education at the University of Edinburgh.

**Claire Cassidy** is a Senior Lecturer and Course Leader for the Postgraduate Certificate in Philosophy with Children in the School of Education at the University of Strathclyde.

**Beth Christie** is a Lecturer and Programme Director for the Learning for Sustainability programme in the Moray House School of Education at the University of Edinburgh.

**Annette Coburn** is a Lecturer in Community Education at the University of the West of Scotland.

**Laura Colucci-Gray** is a Senior Lecturer in Science and Sustainability Education at Moray House School of Education, University of Edinburgh.

**Do Coyle** is a Professor of Languages Education & Classroom Pedagogies in the Moray House School of Education at the University of Edinburgh.

**Hazel Crichton** is Lecturer in Modern Languages in Education in the School of Education at the University of Glasgow.

**Kirsten Darling-McQuistan** is a lecturer in Primary Education in the School of Education at the University of Aberdeen.

**Janis Davidson** is a Lecturer in the Learning Enhancement and Academic Development Service at the University of Glasgow.

**Stephen P. Day** is a Senior Lecturer and year one Leader for the Professional Doctorate programme at the University of the West of Scotland.

**Andrew Dickie** is Head of Expressive Arts, Paisley Grammar School.

**Peter Donaldson** is Lecturer in Computing Science and Education and a member of the Centre for Computing Science Education in the School of Education at the University of Glasgow.

**Anne Donovan** is the author of the novels, *Buddha Da* (2003), *Being Emily* (2008) and *Gone Are the Leaves* (2014), and the short story collection *Hieroglyphics* (2001), a set Scottish text for Scottish Qualifications Authority examinations. A former teacher, she writes curricular materials, speaks at conferences and regularly visits schools. She is a Cultural Fellow at Glasgow Caledonian University.

**John Edward** is Director of the Scottish Council of Independent Schools. He is a Member of the Curriculum and Assessment Board and a Trustee of the Scottish European Educational Trust.

**Sue Ellis** is a Professor of Education in the School of Education and Co-Director of the Centre for Education and Social Policy at the University of Strathclyde.

**Ashley Fenwick** is a Lecturer in the Faculty of Social Sciences at the University of Stirling.

**Morag Findlay** is a Teaching Fellow in the School of Education at the University of Strathclyde.

**Larry Flanagan** is General Secretary of the Educational Institute of Scotland, a member of the Organisation for Economic Co-operation and Development's Trade Union Advisory Committee on Education and Training, and also an Executive Committee member of the European Trades Union Committee on Education.

**Joan Forbes** is an Honorary Professor in Education at the Centre for Child Wellbeing and Protection at the University of Stirling.

**Ruth Forrester** is a Lecturer in Mathematics Education in the Moray House School of Education at the University of Edinburgh.

**Leonardo Franchi** is Course Leader for Theology in Education and Curriculum Leadership in Religious Education at the University of Glasgow.

**Trevor Gale** is Professor of Education Policy and Social Justice and Head of the School of Education at the University of Glasgow.

**Hugh Gallagher** was, until recently, a Lecturer and Course Director of the Professional Graduate Diploma in Education in the School of Education at the University of Strathclyde.

**Donald Gillies** is Dean of the School of Education at the University of the West of Scotland. Previously he was Professor of Education Policy at York St John University.

**John Gould** is Curriculum Quality Leader at New College Lanarkshire.

**Shirley Gray** is a Senior Lecturer in Physical Education in the Moray House School of Education at the University of Edinburgh.

**Deirdre Grogan** is a Senior Teaching Fellow in the School of Education at the University of Strathclyde.

**Tom Hamilton** is an Honorary Professor at the University of Stirling and formerly Director of Education, Registration and Professional Learning at the General Teaching Council for Scotland.

**Juliet Hancock** is Director of Professional Learning in the Moray House School of Education at the University of Edinburgh.

**Linda Harris** was, until recently, a Lecturer in the School of Education at the University of Strathclyde. She was involved in a Europe-wide literacy project and went on to develop techniques for classroom discussion with colleagues in Denmark.

**George Head** is a Senior Lecturer in the School of Education at the University of Glasgow and former President of the Scottish Educational Research Association.

**Henry Hepburn,** a Reporter for the *Times Educational Supplement Scotland*, has been covering Scottish education for more than ten years and won Feature Writer of the Year Prizes at the Scottish Magazine Awards in 2014 and 2015.

**Allan Hewitt** is Senior Teaching Fellow and Deputy Head of School, School of Psychological Sciences and Health at the University of Strathclyde.

**Peter Higgins** is Professor of Outdoor and Environmental Education and Director of the United Nations Recognised Regional Centre on Education for Sustainable Development (Scotland) in the Moray House School of Education at the University of Edinburgh.

**Andrew Horrell** is a Lecturer in Physical Education and Director of the MA (Hons) Physical Education Programme in the Moray House School of Education at the University of Edinburgh.

**Ian Hulse** is a teacher of Mathematics at Harris Academy, Dundee.

**Walter Humes** is an Honorary Professor in the Faculty of Social Sciences at the University of Stirling. Prior to retirement in 2010 he held professorships at the universities of Aberdeen, Strathclyde and the West of Scotland.

**Gary Husband** is a Lecturer in Professional Education and Leadership in the Faculty of Social Sciences at the University of Stirling.

**Douglas Hutchison** is Depute Chief Executive and Director for People at South Ayrshire Council.

**Cristina Iannelli is** Professor of Education and Social Stratification at the University of Edinburgh and Co-director of the *Understanding Inequalities* project, an interdisciplinary research programme that aims to explore the causes, consequences and policy implications of social inequalities, funded by the Economic and Social Research Council (ESRC). Prior to that she was Co-director of the ESRC-funded centre AQMeN (Applied Quantitative Methods Network).

**John I'Anson** is an Associate Dean for Learning and Teaching in the Faculty of Social Sciences at the University of Stirling, and is Convenor of the Research on Children's Rights in Education network at the European Conference on Educational Research.

**Mike Jess** is a Senior Lecturer and Director of the Developmental Physical Education Group in the Moray House School of Education at the University of Edinburgh.

**Divya Jindal-Snape** is Professor of Education, Inclusion and Life Transitions and Director of the Transformative Change: Educational and Life Transitions (TCELT) Research Centre at the University of Dundee.

**Aileen Kennedy** is a Senior Lecturer in Education and Programme Director for the MSc in Transformative Learning and Teaching at the University of Edinburgh.

**Andrew Killen** is a Lecturer in the School of Education at the University of the West of Scotland.

**Vic Lally** is an Associate Director and Research Professor of the Centre for Computing Science Education, and a member of the Centre for Research and Development in Adult and Lifelong Learning, University of Glasgow. He is also Professor of Interdisciplinary Learning, Education, Technologies and Society in the School of Education at the University of Glasgow.

**Diarmuid McAuliffe** is a Lecturer in Art Education and Programme Leader for the MEd: Artist Teacher in the School of Education at the University of the West of Scotland.

**Lisa McAuliffe** is Programme Leader for the MEd in Inclusive Education in the School of Education at the University of the West of Scotland.

**Velda McCune** is a Senior Lecturer and Deputy Director of the Institute for Academic Development at the University of Edinburgh.

**Ann MacDonald** is a Senior Lecturer in Primary Education in Moray House School of Education at the University of Edinburgh.

**Brian McGinley** is an elected member of South Ayrshire Council and a former Lecturer in Community Education at the University of Strathclyde.

**Chris McIlroy** is a Visiting Professor at the University of Strathclyde and works with education authorities across Scotland as a consultant. He was previously headteacher of Yoker Primary School and chief inspector for primary and pre-school education in Her Majesty's Inspectorate of Education.

**Agnes Macintosh** is a Teaching Fellow (Home Economics) at the University of Strathclyde.

**Tom Macintyre** is a Senior Lecturer in the Institute of Education, Teaching and Leadership within Moray House School of Education, University of Edinburgh.

**Tommy MacKay** is Director of Psychology Consultancy Services and a Visiting Professor in the School of Education at the University of Strathclyde.

**Stephen J. McKinney** is a Professor in the School of Education at the University of Glasgow. He is the leader of the Research and Teaching Group: Pedagogy, Praxis and Faith.

**Susan McLaren** is Senior Lecturer Design and Technology in the Moray House School of Education at the University of Edinburgh.

**Susan McLarty** is a Senior Teaching Fellow in Mathematics in the Moray House School of Education at the University of Edinburgh.

**Margery McMahon** is Professor of Educational Leadership and Policy in the School of Education at the University of Glasgow.

**Joan Martlew** is a Visiting Fellow in the School of Education at the University of Strathclyde.

**Yonah Matemba** is a Senior Lecturer in Social Sciences Education in the School of Education at the University of the West of Scotland.

**Murdo Mathison** has been Policy and Communications Officer for the University and College Union Scotland, since 2014. A graduate of St Andrews University, he previously worked in various policy and campaigning roles in the third sector, public sector and politics.

**Ian Milligan** is International Advisor in the Centre for Excellence for Looked-After Children in Scotland at the University of Strathclyde.

**James Morgan** is a Head of Service at the Scottish Qualifications Authority.

**David Morrison-Love** is a Lecturer and Joint Programme Leader in Technological Education in the School of Education at the University of Glasgow.

**Lio Moscardini** is a Senior Lecturer and Course Leader of the MEd in Inclusive Education in the School of Education at the University of Strathclyde.

**Danny Murphy** is an Honorary Fellow of the University of Edinburgh. During his forty-year career in Scottish education, he was headteacher of three secondary schools: Crieff High School, McLaren High School and Lornshill Academy.

**Mark Murphy** is a Reader in Education and Public Policy and Co-Director of the Robert Owen Centre for Educational Change in the School of Education at the University of Glasgow.

**Robbie Nicol** is a Senior Lecturer in Outdoor Environmental Education and Co-Depute Head of School in the Moray House School of Education at the University of Edinburgh.

**Liz Niven** is a Scottish poet. Collections include *Stravaigin* (2000) and *The Shard Box* (2010). She has held writing fellowships across Scotland and has participated in international literary festivals across the world. Educational materials for the Scots language include Mercator's dossier for the European Bureau of Lesser Used Languages. She is an honorary Fellow of the Association for Scottish Literary Studies and a PEN executive board member.

**Patrick O'Donnell** is a Research Coordinator at Perth College, University of the Highlands and Islands.

**Stephen Parker** is Research Fellow in Education Policy in the School of Education at the University of Glasgow.

**Mark Priestley** is Professor of Education and Deputy Dean of the Faculty of Social Sciences at the University of Stirling. His research interests concern the school curriculum and curriculum development. He is a Co-Convener of EERA Network 3 Curriculum Innovation and Director of the Stirling Network for Curriculum Studies.

**Eileen Prior** is Executive Director of the Scottish Parent Teacher Council.

**Sarah Proctor** is a Teaching Fellow in Social Studies in the School of Education at the University of Strathclyde.

**Andrew Pyle** is Consultant Headteacher of Kilquhanity Children's Village (part of Kinokuni Children's Village Trust – Japan), formerly Kilquhanity House School, a free school located in Castle Douglas in Dumfries and Galloway where Andrew was educated.

**Ann Rae** is a Lecturer in Primary Education and Co-Deputy Head of the Institute for Education, Teaching and Leadership in the Moray House School of Education at the University of Edinburgh.

**Jackie Ravet** is Director of Equality and Diversity and Director of the Autism & Learning Masters Pathway in the School of Education at the University of Aberdeen.

**Morag Redford** is Head of Teacher Education at the University of the Highlands and Islands.

**Sheila Riddell** is Professor of Inclusion and Diversity and Director of the Centre for Research in Education Inclusion and Diversity in the Moray House School of Education at the University of Edinburgh.

**Margaret Ritchie** is a Lecturer in Education at the School of Education, University of the West of Scotland.

**Ian Rivers** is Professor of Education for Social Change and Head of School at the University of Strathclyde.

**Anne Robertson** is Head of Services and User Engagement, EDINA, at the University of Edinburgh.

**Boyd Robertson** was Principal of Sabhal Mòr Ostaig and a Professor at the University of the Highlands and Islands from 2009 to 2018.

**Judy Robertson** is Professor of Digital Learning in the Moray House School of Education at the University of Edinburgh.

**Lynne Robertson** is Senior Education Officer, Social Studies, Education Scotland.

**Leon Robinson** is Programme Leader for Religious and Philosophical Education in the School of Education at the University of Glasgow.

**Janys M. Scott QC** is a member of the Faculty of Advocates and the author of *Education Law in Scotland* (2nd edition 2016).

**Daniela Sime** is a Reader in Education and Social Policy in the School of Social Work and Social Policy at the University of Strathclyde.

**Raymond Soltysek** is a former Lecturer in Initial Teacher Education. He is an education consultant and National Coordinator, Scottish Association for the Teaching of English.

**Ian Smith** is a Professor of Education at the University of the West of Scotland, where he was Head and Dean of the School of Education from 2000 to 2009. Since 2010, a major focus of his work has been on international educational consultancy for the Council of Europe, including partner projects funded by the European Union.

**Joe Smith** is Lecturer in History Education in the Faculty of Social Sciences at the University of Stirling.

**Edward M. Sosu** is a Lecturer in the School of Education at the University of Strathclyde.

**Jennifer Spratt** is a Senior Lecturer and Programme Director for MEd in Inclusive Practice in the School of Education at the University of Aberdeen.

**Christine Stephen** is an Honorary Research Fellow in the Faculty of Social Sciences at the University of Stirling.

**Jonathan Tevendale** was a student at Mallaig High School at the time of writing Chapter 97 and is now a student at Oxford University. He won the Scottish Schools Young Writer of the Year Award in 2016.

**Deirdre Torrance** is an Honorary Fellow of the University of Edinburgh. Until recently, she was a Senior Lecturer in the Moray House School of Education, University of Edinburgh. She was also Director of Teacher Education Partnerships; Director of the Masters in Educational Leadership and Management; and Co-Director of the Masters in Leadership and Learning.

**Claire Wallace** is Depute Headteacher at Kilmarnock Academy, East Ayrshire Council.

**David Wallace** is a Lecturer in Community Education at the University of the West of Scotland.

**Elisabet Weedon** is an Honorary Research Fellow at the Centre for Research in Education Inclusion and Diversity in the Moray House School of Education at the University of Edinburgh.

**Iain White** is Principal of Newlands Junior College, an independent school in Glasgow which emphasises vocational education and personal development. He was formerly a secondary school headteacher for twenty years.

**Jacqueline White** is a Business Education Teacher at St Mungo's Academy, Glasgow.

**John Winter** is a Teaching Fellow in Education with responsibility for Mathematics in the Professional Graduate Diploma in Education at the University of Strathclyde.

# I

# AN OVERVIEW OF CONTEMPORARY EDUCATION IN SCOTLAND

# 1

# *Scottish Education, Fifth Edition*: Its Nature, Purpose and Structure

*Tom Bryce and Walter Humes*

This book provides a detailed, informed and critical account of contemporary education in Scotland. As for previous editions, it examines in depth each of the main sectors (early years, primary, secondary, further, adult and higher education) and tries to explain 'how it all works'. Four important perspectives are also scrutinised carefully – the historical, the cultural, the political and the socio–economic dimensions within which schools, colleges and universities operate. Each of the chapters was commissioned from specialists who have drawn upon up-to-date research and professional analysis to give fresh insights into educational developments – in particular during the period from the referendum of 2014 (when the Scottish populace determined not to opt for independence from the rest of the UK), through the uncertainties of the post-Brexit years. Political conflict between the Scottish (SNP) and the UK (Conservative) governments has dominated this period. With respect to education, the analyses in this text combine several 'insider' perspectives, where material has been written by educationists with first-hand experience of their own areas or organisations, and 'outsider' perspectives (the majority of the chapters), where researchers and analysts have provided independent, reflective commentary. All were asked to combine concise description with critical analysis – to give, in addition to basic information, an outline of the more contentious debates among the professionals concerned with each area in focus. Thus, what is contained in this text is what Scottish educators think about their own educational system; the writers have revealed its strengths and its weaknesses, their pride in it and their concerns for it. An effort has been made to 'tell it as it is', to provide clear description and penetrating analysis, in contrast to the rhetorical prose so prevalent in much of the documentation issued by central government and the agencies associated with it.

## THE FIRST EDITION: 1999

The first edition of *Scottish Education* was published to coincide with the end of the millennium and the reinstatement of the Scottish Parliament in 1999. It was reasoned that an understanding of education at that time, appropriately contextualised, would be important to the evolution of educational policy and practice in the future. The main target audience was both student teachers and experienced teachers engaged in professional development and learning. Sharing the broad spectrum of thinking which relates to policy and action is part of becoming an effective teacher or of extending one's field of influence and competence. Understanding the characteristic features of education in Scotland was

| SE1 Scottish Education | 1999 | Eds Bryce and Humes |
|---|---|---|
| SE2 Scottish Education: Post-devolution | 2003 | Eds Bryce and Humes |
| SE3 Scottish Education: Beyond Devolution | 2008 | Eds Bryce and Humes |
| SE4 Scottish Education: Referendum | 2013 | Eds Bryce, Humes, Gillies and Kennedy |
| SE5 Scottish Education: Fifth Edition | 2018 | Eds Bryce, Humes, Gillies and Kennedy |

considered essential. That said, not everything about Scottish education is distinctive. Rather an attempt was made to provide a wide range of material which would allow others to make their own judgements as to what is unique; what is similar but different; and what is indeed comparable to practices elsewhere in the UK, in Europe and beyond. In the final analysis, it would be for the reader to weigh things up and form judgements in the light of the evidence.

The first edition was well received by both academics and students. Reviewers in many journals commended the authors for their informed and well-researched accounts: the content was both authoritative and critical in setting out what matters to educators. Student teachers and postgraduates (teachers and other professionals pursuing higher degrees as part of their continuing professional learning) alike welcomed the accessibility which the text brought. A considerable amount of relevant material had been covered in one volume, pleasing students and education course directors alike. It was heartening also to learn of how many others, researchers, organisations, individuals in central and local government, journalists, and even some politicians, found the text to be a useful source of essential information.

## THE SECOND EDITION: 2003

| SE1 Scottish Education | 1999 | Eds Bryce and Humes |
|---|---|---|
| SE2 Scottish Education: Post-devolution | 2003 | Eds Bryce and Humes |
| SE3 Scottish Education: Beyond Devolution | 2008 | Eds Bryce and Humes |
| SE4 Scottish Education: Referendum | 2013 | Eds Bryce, Humes, Gillies and Kennedy |
| SE5 Scottish Education: Fifth Edition | 2018 | Eds Bryce, Humes, Gillies and Kennedy |

Four years on, a second edition was judged to be required and *Scottish Education: Post-devolution* was published in 2003. The first years of the Scottish Parliament had witnessed more changes than predicted, many but not all of them deriving from the operations of the Parliament itself. New departments of central government had introduced reform and local government continued to evolve, despite fears that centralisation of educational control might quickly result. Key bodies had changed or merged. Important initiatives had been brought about through the passing of the Parliament's first Act in 2000 (fittingly an Education Act). Primary, secondary and tertiary education had all encountered major shifts, particularly secondary and further education, with the implementation of National Qualifications (known initially as Higher Still). Universities had struggled with ever-increasing student numbers and related financial difficulties. Scottish education had survived its worst ever crisis with the Scottish Qualifications Authority exam debacle of 2000. The second edition reflected education post-devolution, tracking the effects of new parliamentary thinking and organisational change and brought everything up to date. Crucial gaps were filled and nine new topics were added in response to helpful feedback from readers. Some forty-two new authors were involved, many of the original team having changed field or retired.

The second edition continued to enjoy the popular and critical acclaim of its predecessor. Students and teachers, as well as reviewers and colleagues who work in teacher education throughout Scotland, said that the text was a unique source of vital information and ideas, helpful to their study and work, not least by what it locates in one accessible volume. Like their forerunners in the first edition, the authors of the 2003 *Post-devolution* edition had produced authoritative material and sharp reflective commentary. Along with commendation came an expectation that there should be future editions; that a book of this kind, updated as required, would be required from time to time to ensure shared understandings and common concerns throughout the profession.

## THE THIRD EDITION: 2008

| SE1 Scottish Education | 1999 | Eds Bryce and Humes |
|---|---|---|
| SE2 Scottish Education: Post-devolution | 2003 | Eds Bryce and Humes |
| SE3 Scottish Education: Beyond Devolution | 2008 | Eds Bryce and Humes |
| SE4 Scottish Education: Referendum | 2013 | Eds Bryce, Humes, Gillies and Kennedy |
| SE5 Scottish Education: Fifth Edition | 2018 | Eds Bryce, Humes, Gillies and Kennedy |

Five years on, the third edition, *Scottish Education: Beyond Devolution*, was published in 2008, the title signalling that the coverage concerned educational thinking and practice firmly contextualised in the by then familiar setting of devolved government – indeed with debate about independence on the increase (more of which later). The rapid developments in education between 2003 and 2008 could not be put down simply to devolution per se. The Labour/Liberal Democrat coalition which lasted until May 2007 continued to recognise the financial pressures on (post-school) students and adhered to its commitments to student support (for example, through not introducing top-up fees), though the consequences for the institutions themselves were demanding and complex. The school sector saw the beginnings of major curricular change with Curriculum for Excellence offering greater prospects for flexibility and 'bottom-up' initiatives to shift the system away from the constraining effects of 5–14. Some teachers became enthused and helped to bring about fast-changing developments, particularly in the primary sector; others awaited persuasion and change, such was the legacy of years of an *over*-specification of content and targets. Both primary and secondary schools had worked with new legislation concerned with learning support and, throughout both sectors, there was increasing recognition of the real benefits of formative assessment, a matter which sat (and continues to sit) uncomfortably alongside formal grading and the domination of the later stages of schooling by examinations and certification. As the third edition was going to print, the promised consultation on the upper school curriculum and assessment had just begun.

Significant political change was heralded, however, by the elections of May 2007, returning a Scottish National Party (SNP) minority government under the leadership of Alex Salmond. In education, some changes were immediately signalled, such as a reduction in class sizes, beginning with the early years of primary school, and the abolition of the graduate endowment tax. A 'rebranding' of the political framework took place in the autumn of 2007 when the new administration changed 'Scottish Executive' to 'Scottish Government'. It was thought that other, more significant, changes would be predicated upon successful financial management at national level, particularly in the lead-up to the proposed referendum on independence which, at that time, was set to take place in 2010. It was anticipated that the government would not shift significantly on many matters of educational policy, but it was hoped that the consultation on examinations and certification would result in speedy, firm direction for the future of the upper secondary stages of schooling (which it did not).

Thus, the commissioning of the authors for the third edition of *Scottish Education* took place during a period marked both by complex change and hesitant expectations on several fronts. There is never a time when something like education stands still, permitting it to be described as 'in place': there is always a need for its fast-evolving complexity to be critiqued in order that participating professionals, and other stakeholders, can regain focus and, hopefully, impetus. Some forty new authors were commissioned for the third edition, testimony to the extent of change among personnel in schools, universities and government organisations. A few topics were dropped, and/or relocated and combined differently, and three new topics were added, one on Citizenship Education, one on the Social Sciences in the secondary curriculum, and one on Multi-Agency Working. There was also a new, final section devoted to the Future of Education in Scotland.

As for the first two editions, SE3 received positive commendations from pre-service student teachers, from teachers studying for post-initial qualifications and degrees, and from reviewers in academic journals. It was pleasing to see that *Scottish Education* had become so established, an essential source text or guide to the educational system, spelling things out through critical appraisals of what goes on.

## THE FOURTH EDITION: 2013

| SE1 Scottish Education | 1999 | Eds Bryce and Humes |
| SE2 Scottish Education: Post-devolution | 2003 | Eds Bryce and Humes |
| SE3 Scottish Education: Beyond Devolution | 2008 | Eds Bryce and Humes |
| SE4 Scottish Education: Referendum | 2013 | Eds Bryce, Humes, Gillies and Kennedy |
| SE5 Scottish Education: Fifth Edition | 2018 | Eds Bryce, Humes, Gillies and Kennedy |

Not long after the publication of SE3 in 2008, the financial crisis affecting all of the developed world economies began with the calamities in banking. Public sector pay freezes were quickly put in place in Scotland, as elsewhere in the UK, directly affecting the income of teachers and lecturers and restricted budgets throughout the sector began to affect staffing, services and commitments. During the years between the third and fourth editions of this book,

Scotland's economy was managed well by the SNP minority administration and the education sector fared no worse than in the other parts of the UK. Nevertheless, financial difficulties continued everywhere with little sign of improvement. During that period, a variety of different problems arose in education, not all caused directly by economics, though the financial ones were the most challenging. Universities, largely driven by cost considerations (but also with an eye to the state of research and what particular institutions chose to prioritise) one by one took decisions to restructure themselves and to reduce their staffing, particularly in education. Redundancies and non-replacement of lecturers resulted. There was a massive loss of experience and expertise across the seven institutions concerned with initial teacher education: faculties of education were reduced to 'schools' within larger structures. In further education, similar retrenchment took place and college mergers were accelerated as a result. At the time of writing the fourth edition, plans were in place to reduce Scotland's forty-one colleges to twenty-eight in number. In local authorities, restructuring led to the loss of many of the staff supporting teachers in various capacities, with reduced budgets necessitating shared arrangements across schools. Schools themselves had to endure significant budget constraints and losses in staffing, particularly auxiliary staff in various categories.

Politically, the national election in 2011 resulted in a sweeping victory for the SNP under Alex Salmond perhaps due, in part, to perceptions of some government prudence in the preceding four years: the electorate had considered that public services had been administered competently. Educationally, the Cabinet Secretary, Mike Russell, had several significant matters to contend with. The fallout of the UK Government's 2010 Browne Report into the funding of higher education (with universities raising fees dramatically and students being required to repay loans at the cost of borrowing to government) led to significant differences between Scotland and the rest of the UK. With regard to the school curriculum, the national consultation on assessment and certification saw government setting a timescale for the replacement of Standard Grade and Intermediate 1 and 2 Awards by National Awards at levels 4 and 5, though that proved to be difficult for many authorities and schools. It was coupled with the continuing slow implementation of Curriculum for Excellence in secondary schools and protracted debates about the specifications offered in respect of curriculum content and delays in consequence. How long a 'broad general education' should last in secondary schools (one, two or three years, three being the preference of government) became a matter of serious debate for it determines when National level 4 and 5 courses should commence.

Thus, the commissioning of authors for a fourth edition of *Scottish Education* took place at a time of even greater challenges for all involved in education. Political machinations ensued between the SNP administration and the Conservative/Liberal Democrat Coalition Government of the UK formed in 2010, regarding the date for the long-promised referendum on independence. At the time of writing that book, 2014 looked like the probable date, hence the choice of subtitle for it and our decision to publish the fourth edition in the preceding year. More than sixty new authors were required, once more reflecting how many of the previous editions' writers had departed from their posts throughout the various sectors, not least from university faculties/schools of education (for the reasons described above). New topics were added: on learning in Scottish schools; alternative forms of schooling; education and the law; sustainable development education; the Scottish approach to school improvement; from adult learning to lifelong learning in Scotland; poverty and schooling in Scotland; the financing of Scottish education; and an additional chapter on the 3–18 curriculum in Scotland.

Once again, we are pleased to record, *Scottish Education* had been well received, particularly by students and staff involved in teacher education, and by researchers and journal reviewers. Readers appreciated the location of well-informed, concisely expressed, critical appraisals of what goes on in one accessible paperback – and again expectations were raised for another edition in five years' time. Two new general editors (Donald Gillies and Aileen Kennedy) were involved in the production of the fourth edition. The original editors (Tom Bryce and Walter Humes) had both reached retirement age and felt that the perspectives of younger academics would enhance the new edition, as well as ensuring continuity for the future.

## THE FIFTH EDITION: 2018

| | | |
|---|---|---|
| SE1 *Scottish Education* | 1999 | Eds Bryce and Humes |
| SE2 *Scottish Education: Post-devolution* | 2003 | Eds Bryce and Humes |
| SE3 *Scottish Education: Beyond Devolution* | 2008 | Eds Bryce and Humes |
| SE4 *Scottish Education: Referendum* | 2013 | Eds Bryce, Humes, Gillies and Kennedy |
| SE5 *Scottish Education: Fifth Edition* | 2018 | Eds Bryce, Humes, Gillies and Kennedy |

The referendum result on 18 September 2014 proved a failure for the SNP's campaign for independence; the YES vote was 44.7 per cent, the NO vote was 55.3 per cent (on an 84.6 per cent turnout). Being a devolved matter, education rarely featured in debates concerned with the referendum. It did, however, figure prominently in public discussion thereafter. The reasons were many and varied, with school education not faring well during the years between the publication of the fourth and this fifth edition of *Scottish Education*. Important issues included: (a) the continuing constraints on school staffing and support for teachers from the long-standing freeze on council taxation imposed by central government (and only relaxed in 2017); (b) increases in workloads, partly in consequence of that, but also due to continuing implementation pressures associated with Curriculum for Excellence, particularly in relation to assessment changes for National Qualifications at the upper stages of secondary; (c) the publication of national and international surveys of pupil attainments which showed that standards were falling in Scottish schools; combined with (d) ever mounting pressures for the raising of attainment in schools serving disadvantaged communities; (e) the growing insufficiency of support staff in mainstream school settings for pupils with additional needs due to spending cuts (numbers increased from 102.2 pupils per 1,000 in 2010 to 248.7 per 1,000 in 2016, according to the Scottish Parliament's Education Committee report in 2017); (f) growing concerns that Education Scotland's combined roles for both curricular implementation *and* inspection might not be in the best interests of developing the nation's schools and its teachers; (g) differential student fee structures and resulting intakes to Scottish universities from applicants across the UK; and (h) the effects of amalgamations and regionalisation on the morale of lecturers in further education colleges.

Throughout the period, political desire for centralisation of control has become increasingly apparent in several quarters in Scottish life: police operations and fire services being two obvious examples. Another illustration of this trend has been the government's attempt to form one overarching board to incorporate the Scottish Funding Council, Scottish

Enterprise, Highlands and Islands Enterprise, Scottish Development International, Skills Development Scotland (and others), under the control of a government minister. All parties that have enjoyed an extended period in office, with a relatively weak opposition to hold them to account, tend in the direction of increased authoritarianism. Arguably the most significant instance of this in education arose with the arguments that ensued with the publication of the government's governance review in June 2017 (Scottish Government, 2017). The proposed establishment of up to seven 'regional improvement collaboratives' to support schools instead of the current thirty-two local authorities, combined with increased statutory powers for the raising of standards to be given to headteachers, provoked dismay, with a Convention of Scottish Local Authorities (COSLA) spokesman stating: 'The simple truth is that there will be no meaningful local democratic accountability for education in Scotland' (Freeman, 2017, p. 1). In addition to political considerations, it should be recognised that financial savings have also been a driver for more centralisation during the years since the banking crisis commenced a decade ago. Matters like these, and many more besides, all of them affecting education in different ways, are analysed in the sections contained in this book. The chapters explain how teachers, in all sectors and at all levels, are operating during difficult times, endeavouring to maintain the quality of education in Scotland.

## BRINGING THIS TEXT TO FRUITION; ITS STRUCTURE AND PRESENTATION

With each new edition of this book we have sought to make changes, partly to reflect the evolving nature of educational policy and practice, but also in response to feedback from readers and contributors. Each edition of *Scottish Education* has been essentially a new book in its own right; such is the pace of change in education as well as the necessary choice of new authors. In that context we should admit that we do not always get everything right. For example, in the fourth edition Anne Donovan's name was omitted as one of the co-authors of the chapter on 'The Scots Language in Education'. We wish to offer our sincere apologies to Anne for this error and are delighted that she has agreed to update the chapter for this latest edition (once again working with Liz Niven). More than sixty-seven new authors were required to bring about SE5, yet again reflecting how many of the previous editions' writers had departed from their posts throughout the various sectors, especially from university schools of education. A number of topics have been combined in this new edition and several new ones added – on poverty, class and inter-generational disadvantage; digital education in schools; children's rights; governance reforms in the universities of Scotland; educating migrant and refugee pupils; and lesbian, gay, bisexual, transgender and intersex (LGBTI) issues in schooling. There are also new chapters in the final, future section and these will be mentioned in due course.

## SECTIONS AND SECTION EDITING

Like the first four editions, this volume would not have seen the light of day had it not been for the good efforts of those friends and colleagues who shared the editing with diligence, patience and care, in some cases taking material from rough first draft, through several revisions, to the final published version contained in the text. Ian Smith has now worked with us over two editions; three people were new to the task – Tom Hamilton, Janis

Davidson and George Head. They all tackled the work with energy and flair and we express our sincere personal gratitude to them. The section editors were:

| | | |
|---|---|---|
| I | An overview of contemporary education in Scotland | *Ian Smith* |
| II | The historical and cultural context of Scottish education | *Walter Humes* |
| III | Governance and direction in Scottish education | *Tom Bryce* and *Walter Humes* |
| IV | Management, organisation and learning in schools | *Donald Gillies* and *Aileen Kennedy* |
| V | Curriculum areas: early years and primary | *Aileen Kennedy* |
| VI | Curriculum subjects: secondary | *Donald Gillies* |
| VII | Cross-sectoral and interdisciplinary issues | *Tom Hamilton* |
| VIII | Assessment, certification and achievements | *Tom Bryce* |
| IX | Further and higher education | *Janis Davidson* |
| X | Scottish society: Education for all? | *George Head* |
| XI | Teachers and teacher education | *Aileen Kennedy* |
| XII | Looking forward: the future of education in Scotland | *The Editors* |

It should be noted that the sectioning in this book differs somewhat from that of the fourth edition, two new groupings here being Section IV: Management, organisation and learning in schools, and VII: Cross-sectoral and inter-disciplinary issues. Taking the sections in turn, the following paragraphs briefly preface their contents and give our rationale for the structure of SE5, thus providing a guide as to how the text might be read.

## Section I

Section I gives an overview to each of the education sectors (early years, primary, secondary, further and higher education). First, there is a description of the statutory provision across these sectors (Chapter 2), with up-to-date data and trends in pupil/student and teacher numbers, together with brief commentary on relevant policy initiatives. Chapters 3 and 4 introduce the primary and secondary sectors respectively, describing their philosophies and practices. Readers interested in them should read these chapters prior to the relevant detail contained in Sections IV, V, VI and VII where what is taught in schools, the pedagogies used by practitioners, the management of pupils and their learning, and the prevailing debates among the professionals concerned, are looked at closely. The small, but not insignificant private school sector, dealing with some 4 per cent of the pupil population, is considered in Chapter 5. The part played by the Scottish Council of Independent Schools (SCIS) representing some seventy schools is acknowledged. Scotland's further education (FE) colleges provide post-school education. They have been run independently of local authorities since 1993 (the year of 'incorporation') on the basis of a block grant from the Scottish Funding Council and are quite diversified. Chapter 6 provides an introduction to this sector, and analyses the development of FE before and following the watershed year of 2012 when colleges faced up to the 'regionalisation' instigated by central government. The chapter demonstrates the very significant blurring of the further education/higher education divide. The character and provision of tertiary education in Scotland is described in Chapter 7. Scottish universities have had to face up to very serious pressures in the last decade, not least financial ones, and government pressures associated with widening access. The chapter analyses the extent to which traditional academic values are under threat as institutions change to position themselves globally in respect of their research and teaching. The final chapter (8) in Section I examines the political context of the statutory provision of education in Scotland. It explains (and questions) official versions of the policy agenda in the years of devolved government and explores the roles of the various stakeholders in negotiating change. The chapter also looks at how educational issues are viewed and understood by politicians, not least the priorities of the Scottish National Party in government, as well as the present domination of all political debate by efforts to bring about equitable access to education at every level.

## Section II

Section II deals with the historical and cultural contexts within which education takes place. The long and interesting history of public education up to post-war times is dealt with in Chapter 9. Chapter 10 takes up developments since devolution in 1999. Analysis of the claimed distinctiveness of Scottish education features in both of these chapters. Chapter 11 considers that further and in some depth, endeavouring to get behind the myths and traditional claims that Scottish education is superior and 'special'. The argument contextualises distinctiveness at a time of debate and decision making about continued devolution or independence. The next three chapters examine three significant (and very different) features of schooling in Scotland. The first of these, Chapter 12, analyses the effects of intergenerational, social disadvantage on pupils' achievements in school, the evidence for which underpins present-day national concerns about 'the attainment gap' amongst communities and current priorities for government. On a quite different note, Chapter 13 looks at the contemporary position of education in denominational schools. It is 100 years since, by the 1918 Act of Parliament, Catholic schools 'became part of the "official" educational discourse in Scotland' (to quote the author). The final perspective offered in this section, in Chapter 14, is that of 'progressive' schools (of which there are few in Scotland) and, separately, the 'home education' that a minority of parents choose for their children.

## Section III

Section III is entitled 'Governance and Direction in Scottish Education'. It embraces six chapters concerned with how the educational system operates and is managed at several levels. Chapter 15 commences this section with an examination of how Scottish law affords the administrative framework for educational provision. The original Act of 1980 has been much amended and there are various statutes concerned with school education, amounting to what the author calls 'an unwieldy hotchpotch'. She provides a lucid guide to the laws affecting schools, authorities, teachers and parents. Chapters 16 and 17 examine the administration of education at central and local government levels respectively. With governance being the subject of a national review, published in June 2017, there are now serious challenges to the ways in which education operates and teachers' work is controlled (giving lie to the traditional belief that in Scotland 'education is centrally governed and locally administered'). The issues involved are further examined in the next two chapters. The national and local curriculum support that is provided for teachers is explored critically in Chapter 18. How schools and teachers are inspected is scrutinised in Chapter 19. Writing from her position in the Scottish Parent Teacher Council, the author of Chapter 20 closes this section by describing how parents can and should be involved in the education of their own children, that being a crucial means of improving positive outcomes for young people.

## Sections IV–VII

Detailed consideration of the school curriculum in Scotland is provided in Sections IV–VII. How teaching is organised and how pupils (and teachers) are managed in both school sectors are dealt with in Section IV. Two chapters provide complementary analyses of how early education and childcare are ensured (Chapters 21 and 22), with early schooling being the focus of Chapter 22. How learning can be conceived and distinguished from the teaching that purports to bring it about in primary and secondary schools is explored in Chapter 23. The ethos, behaviour and discipline of pupils are considered in two chapters: in primary schools in Chapter 25 and in secondary schools in Chapter 29. The latter is augmented by the discussion in Chapter 28 of the personal support and guidance which is provided during the teenage years. Two chapters deal with leadership issues and the organisation of teachers and their management – in primary schools in Chapter 24 and in secondary schools in Chapter 27. Transitions for pupils, both as they move from nurseries to primary schools around five years of age, and from primary to secondary around twelve years of age, are analysed in Chapter 26.

Sections V and VI deal with what is taught in schools: the curriculum areas of early years and primary school featuring in V and the traditional subjects of secondary in VI. The latter are presented in alphabetic order. All of these twenty-eight chapters highlight the relevant content of the Scottish Curriculum for Excellence as that is realised in schools, together with details of the pedagogies currently used by teachers, what they assess of pupils' learning, how they do that, and the key matters of contention among the practitioners concerned. The teaching of Science as part of S1/S2 broad general education, and Environmental Science at national and higher levels, are both discussed in the Biology chapter.

Following these sections is one that looks at topics and issues of relevance to *both* the primary and secondary sectors of school education, these being described as either cross-sectoral or interdisciplinary in character (Section VII). Chapters 58 and 59 respectively consider literacy and numeracy across learning, considerable efforts having been made in recent decades to counter the fragmentation that often prevails in conventional arrangements for school instruction. As we all know, modern technologies impact significantly on how young people acquire their understandings, thus Chapter 60 focuses on digital education in schools. Health and wellbeing (Chapter 61) and citizenship (Chapter 62) are matters of serious concern to life in modern Scotland, as elsewhere, and these figure as designated parts of Curriculum for Excellence. The authors look critically at what has been, and remains, challenging in schools as teachers tackle these across the curriculum. It is increasingly recognised that learning outside school yields significant benefits for young learners, albeit that outdoor activities make for awkward demands on management and timetables in the traditionally highly structured curriculum. The authors of Chapter 63 set out the 'experiential, adventurous and interdisciplinary' focus of contemporary outdoor learning. With the publication of the United Nations Convention on the Rights of the Child (UNCRC) in 1989, children's rights assumed great significance in all walks of life, not just in education. Chapter 64 sets out the distinctive legal and policy context for this in Scotland and explores the main issues arising from the translation of children's rights from legal text into practice in schooling. 'Learning for Sustainability' (LfS) is the title of Chapter 65 and its authors trace the evolution of the values and educational concerns associated with this movement. They emphasise that the revised professional standards issued by the General

Teaching Council for Scotland (GTCS) in 2012 expect every teacher and education professional to demonstrate LfS in their practice, and they stress how much more needs to be tackled in each sector of Scottish education. The last two chapters of Section VII are concerned with language: the Scots language and the Gaelic language. The educational stance on Scots language is rather more uncertain than the position on Scots literature (for which there is widespread support) according to the authors of Chapter 66. They conclude that 'there is still unease about the encouragement of spoken Scots in education and in formal society'. Writing from his position as Principal of Sabhal Mòr Ostaig (loosely referred to as the Gaelic College in Skye, more correctly it being an independent Academic Partner of the federal University of the Highlands and Islands), the author of Chapter 67 examines the renaissance of the Gaelic language over the last forty years – though it is spoken by only 1.1 per cent of the Scottish population (some 57,600 people). The chapter addresses the issues affecting the language for each sector of education and for a number of communities throughout Scotland.

## Section VIII

The four chapters in Section VIII deal with assessment, certification and achievements, each with a rather different focus. The opening chapter (68) looks at assessment in Scottish schools, and commences with the very considerable differences between formative and summative forms of assessment and the somewhat complex relationships between the two in practice. The former has an everyday focus in teachers' day-to-day work; the latter plays a very significant role in everything associated with pupils' educational progress (or not). Thereby it is bound up with judgements of 'abilities', 'aptitudes' and/or 'efforts', and – increasingly in a world dominated by accountability – the perceived competence of schools and teachers to achieve the standards expected. A full explanation is given of the national examinations and qualifications sat recently and currently by secondary pupils. Chapter 69 examines the work of the Scottish Qualifications Authority (SQA), the body responsible for awards and qualifications (other than degrees), the best known of which are the National Qualifications (Nationals, Highers, Higher National Certificates and Higher National Diplomas). Detailed attention is paid to recent criticisms of the Authority's operations by parliamentary committees. Chapter 70 follows this chapter and reveals the national attainment levels obtained by pupils and students in recent years. Written by the Head of Research, Policy, Standards and Statistics at SQA, the chapter sets out the achievement trends, bearing in mind the changes in course arrangements for the earlier Standard Grade awards, which were then replaced by Intermediates, then National Awards, as well as the newly developed forms of the Higher and Advanced Higher Qualifications. The final chapter (71) critically examines the recently devised National Improvement Framework (NIF), published by Scottish Government in 2016, and the proposed use of national standardised testing to improve standards in schools. The NIF was developed to improve the strategic management of educational change with a prime focus on reducing the disparity in attainments between socially advantaged and socially disadvantaged young people, an attainment gap which is proving difficult to close. Despite government rhetoric to the contrary over several years, the planned use of standardised tests means the return of national tests, as the writer plainly states.

## Section IX

Section IX is devoted to Further and Higher education in Scotland and has five chapters. The first one, Chapter 72, looks at the knowledge, skills and pathways in FE, that is on what is taught in colleges of this 'amorphous' sector, to quote the author. His analysis unpicks the crisis of identity and prestige currently facing FE post-regionalisation, despite that sector's long tradition of successfully supporting industry and the country's economy.

The chapter following this (Chapter 73) looks at the teaching and learning which takes place in further and higher education, sectors where the perceived levels of student support are traditionally viewed rather differently. Aptly entitled 'Higher education in turbulent times', Chapter 74 tracks the recent and current troubles facing universities in Scotland (and elsewhere in the UK for that matter), these being inextricably bound up with funding, purpose and accessibility, post-Indyref and post-Brexit. The authors share Cambridge University's Stefan Collini's (2011) regret that government policy means the substitution of the collective social aspiration to have 'an educated population' by a crudely economistic demand for 'an employable workforce'. Widening access to higher education (HE) has been a concern for many years, of course, and Chapter 75 examines that carefully, looking closely at related matters regarding the efforts of both FE and HE to retain students who gain entry to colleges and universities, or for students to progress successfully (or not) between the two. The author admits that the actions of the newly appointed Commissioner for Fair Access (in 2016) will require considerable, coordinated support across the sectors. The final chapter in Section IX (Chapter 76) emphasises the significance of the shift from past conceptions of 'adult education' to present-day reckonings of 'adult and lifelong learning', the latter embracing the learning provisions that stand outside the compulsory education system and are targeted on learners aged 16+.

## Section X

Entitled 'Scottish society: education for all?', Section X contains chapters concerned with the inclusiveness of education, in the face of the challenges presented by young people or their circumstances, by the rigidities or inflexibilities in what the system provides, by the perceptions and prejudices of society (and/or through ill-informed practitioners), and by the significant changes in society as a whole. The chapters look at the nature of these challenges, at the operation of agencies working to overcome barriers to the progress of individuals (in and out of schools and beyond), and at how practitioners in all fields must act themselves. The chapters vary in focus, the common thread being the support and assistance that is or can be available in the face of diverse forms of adversity.

Chapter 77 opens the section by examining the concept of inclusion itself, looking especially at definitions which underpin the Additional Support for Learning Act of 2004 (amended in 2009 and 2010) and which figure in policy documents like *Getting It Right for Every Child* (GIRFEC) and *How Good is Our School? Version 4* (HGIOS4). The analysis considers the various barriers to inclusion and the extent of real progress in making schools genuinely inclusive. The nature of additional support needs (ASNs) are examined in Chapter 78, the term 'additional support' being defined in legislation as something 'additional to, or otherwise different from provision (whether or not educational provision) made generally for children', as the author notes. Authorities are required to identify and keep under review the adequacy of any support provided for individuals with ASNs. The author warns against the persistence of any continued and narrow focus on normative categories for pupils which result in ASNs being used as a proxy for 'special educational needs'. The uniqueness of Scottish educational psychology services is described in Chapter 79, along with their impact on local and national policy. The contribution of psychologists to efforts to reduce the attainment gap and address the wellbeing of young people referred to them by schools is discussed in detail. Social work services and community learning and development are the subjects of Chapters 80 and 81 respectively. The former are statutory services run by local authorities and vital in the support they provide for individual families. While not a statutory requirement of local authorities, the latter are vital to present government priorities in respect of social justice and community empowerment. The information and argument provided in these chapters succinctly express what teachers need to know about the crucial support services provided by social workers and community educators. The writers firmly underline the gaps between rhetoric and practice in the face of severe budgetary constraint. In the introduction to Chapter 82, the author recognises that multi-agency working or 'Co-working across child sector agencies and professional groups has become a central tenet in governance, policy and practice in Scotland, other UK countries, and internationally.' The chapter untangles the issues and challenges facing professionals concerned to 'join up' their actions in the face of policy and legislation, to prevent exclusion and bring about positive outcomes for individuals who are at risk. 'Disaffection with Schooling' is the title of Chapter 83 and here the author unravels the links between disengagement in learning, non-participation, non-attendance or truancy, and exclusion – the latter being used by authorities and government to quantify the extent of disaffection. The author of Chapter 84 provides an understanding of the effects of family migration on young people's everyday experiences in Scottish schools, especially in the light of the recent increases in refugee numbers entering the country, here as elsewhere in the UK and throughout Europe. She explores how schools can best support the pupils and families affected. Gender inequality (both the normally understood extent of opportunity and bias in favour of males, but increasingly the extent of male *under*achievement) is analysed in Chapter 85. The authors widen the scope to take into account social class, research having shown that in terms of school attainment, 'girls from disadvantaged backgrounds are doing much worse than their more advantaged peers, and only marginally better than boys from similar backgrounds'. The writer of Chapter 86 provides an overview of the research on the experiences of LGBTI young people in Scotland. The text examines the policies that underpin inclusion in schools and looks at the support being given to schools which are tackling bullying of a homophobic, biphobic and transphobic nature. The topic is completely new to this fifth edition of *Scottish Education*. 'Race' equality, more correctly now expressed as 'ethnicity' equality, is analysed in Chapter 87, both in the 'assimilationist' thinking and strategies of pre-devolution Scotland, and in the educational attempts post-devolution to be more proactively 'anti-racist' in policy and practice. The author welcomes the fifteen-year Race Equality Framework published by Scottish Government in 2016 and speculates on 'whether the aspirations are converted into clear action targets with deadlines'. The final chapter in Section X, Chapter 88, spells out the extent of the religious intolerance – or sectarianism – in Scottish society and in Scottish schools. It examines the historical basis of it in anti-Catholic bigotry, contemporary views and experiences of sectarian discrimination, and recent research attempts to monitor sectarian attitudes and activities. The chapter stresses the importance and value of appropriate educational initiatives in all schools. In the light of increasing religiously aggravated crime (directed at several faiths, including

Muslims and Jews), the writer concludes that it may be time to reconceptualise sectarianism as one manifestation of a wider issue – religious intolerance.

## Section XI

Section XI is devoted to discussion of teachers and teacher professionalism, including both their initial preparation and the post-initial advancements considered necessary as essential requirements of professionalism in the twenty-first century. The roles of the GTCS and teachers' professional bodies (unions) figure also in this section, as do research by and on the work of teachers. Following a brief overview of the history of teachers and their education, the opening chapter (89) scrutinises the present position, including the composition of the workforce in respect of gender, age, ethnicity and language, together with current interests and concerns regarding university intake requirements. Chapter 90 examines initial teacher education in depth, in particular the nature and level of the academic demands thought suitable for qualifications to teach, the status and workings of post-Donaldson partnerships with schools in the preparation of teachers, and an exemplification of the emerging arrangements at one university. The next chapter (91) carefully traces the evolution of post-initial teacher education from 'in-service education', through 'continuing professional development' (CPD), to 'professional learning'. It acknowledges the similarities of developments in Scotland and elsewhere, largely through the influences of the Organisation of Economic Co-operation and Development (OECD) internationally. The authors conclude that the balance between externally imposed accountability and teacher initiated accountability needs to be reconsidered in order to better drive future professional learning activities. According to the author of Chapter 92, underpinning many of the reforms in education over recent decades has been the focus on 'the teacher as leader, as an educational professional who leads learning within and beyond their classrooms, for pupils and colleagues'. She considers leadership and standards determined for it before, during and following the Chartered Teacher initiative; the operations of the Scottish College for Educational Leadership (SCEL); the thinking derivative from the OECD report of 2015 on Scottish education; and present day analytical research which emphasises 'more collegial, collaborative, democratic and shared' forms of teacher leadership. The General Secretary of the Educational Institute of Scotland (EIS) discusses the teaching unions (or professional associations) in Chapter 93. Almost all teachers belong to one of the several which exist in Scotland. The GTCS, established in 1965 and granted independent status in 2012, is the subject of Chapter 94. Its author was formerly its Director of Education and Professional Learning and therefore well placed to describe its operations and powers as an independent body; to analyse the impact of developments upon its thinking within the Scottish educational context; and to identify the challenges immediately ahead. The final chapter in this section (Chapter 95) charts the historical and political evolution of educational research in Scotland. It looks at both research on and research by teachers; notions of 'evidence-based' practice; the effects of survey findings on pupil attainment; and critically examines the relationships between policy and research – a relationship which is all the more complex with the government's priorities for the improvement agenda.

## Section XII

The last section of this book is prospective in nature and entitled 'Looking Forward: The Future of Education in Scotland'. It provides focused thinking about the challenges and difficulties immediately ahead. In their very different ways, the writers say how various problems should be conceptualised and what has to be tackled. Chapter 96 provides an insightful contrast between the complexity in the design of Curriculum for Excellence, its requirements for inspirational teacher engagement and (what he crucially contends) its only *partial* implementation to date. He argues for robust forms of teacher engagement, given the complex of reasons for the current state of affairs – problems which he sees as largely organisational, managerial and political in nature. On a quite different turn, and for the first time in this book, a pupil's view of school education is offered in Chapter 97. While it is but one pupil's perspective and therefore cannot be claimed to be representative, it is remarkably frank and written by someone schooled by a lived experience of Curriculum for Excellence. It was commissioned from the young man when he was a pupil at Mallaig High School (in Lochaber on the west coast of the Highlands) and by the time this book appears in print he will be a student at Oxford University. Student teachers and in-service teachers will find his candid remarks particularly interesting. Newlands Junior College (NJC) in Glasgow is a recently opened initiative which 'exists to help young people aged 14 to 16 who are disengaged from education to re-engage and make a success of their lives, while contributing positively to society' (to quote the author of the next chapter, 98, and the Principal of NJC). It offers an alternative vocationally oriented programme for pupils identified by local schools (on the south side of Glasgow) who have become disengaged from regular schooling, have been absenting themselves from school, and show little enthusiasm for traditional forms and loci of learning. Another innovation in this edition is a journalist's perspective (Chapter 99), written by a man who has been covering Scottish education in the *Times Education Supplement Scotland* for many years. The chapter offers further frank observations of the teaching force in troubled times. The direction of post-school education and several post-devolution initiatives are critiqued in the hard-hitting analysis of Chapter 100. The writer considers that 'signs do not augur well for ... devolved, responsive local provision in Scotland'. This has echoes in the international perspective provided in Chapter 101, one largely framed by the first writer's experiences of education in Australia. The co-writers of the chapter note that, given the extent of economic dis/ advantage in this country, the future of education is here already and 'not very evenly distributed'. Chapter 102 is about the funding of education in Scotland and reviews recent decisions by government, how the system has operated, as a whole and in its parts, and considers the future prospects for viable, financially practicable options. The final chapter (103), written by the editors and informed by the perspectives provided in the book as a whole, gives our own view of the current scene, not least what might happen in education depending on changing governments north and south of the border.

## The Glossary

The professional shorthand shared by educationists, a profusion of abbreviations and acronyms, is no different from the discourse prevailing elsewhere in Europe. We have endeavoured to have these spelled out within each chapter where they are first encountered – for example, Education Scotland (ES) – but an additional glossary of terms and abbreviations has been supplied at the end of the volume. This lists all of the items found in the text and is included in addition to the conventional index.

## REQUESTS MADE TO AUTHORS

We asked contributors to maintain the tone and quality of previous editions, requiring them to give a clear account of current provision but also to have to an eye to the future. Among other recommendations, we asked that:

- Chapters should take account of recent research findings relevant to the topic.
- Reference should be made to recent policy initiatives and their implementation to date.
- Where there are areas of debate or controversy these should be explained and analysed.
- Chapters should not be simply descriptive but should offer a critical perspective on key issues.
- End of chapter references should be limited to ten. These should direct the interested reader to key texts should they require further material.
- Chapters should be of 5,000 words (the main chapters) or 2,500 words (notably the subject/curriculum chapters, but also several others).
- The text should be readable by a wide audience but without over-simplification of complex issues: the overuse of professional jargon should be avoided wherever possible. The readership would consist mainly of student teachers and teachers undertaking various forms of continuing professional development, but the text would also be consulted by a wide range of researchers, administrators and policymakers.

## CONFLICTING PERSPECTIVES

As before, it should be recognised that with so many contributing authors there are some conflicts and a few tensions evident in the text itself: it would be unreasonable to expect complete consistency of view and interpretation from everyone. In some instances, the editors do not share the line taken by the author, nor would we expect to do so. Many issues in education are highly contestable and a healthy system requires vigorous debate. The individual writers were certainly encouraged to express their own reasoned position for the stances they take.

## ACKNOWLEDGEMENTS

While we have endeavoured to provide a *fifth* definitive text on contemporary Scottish education, we have done so in recognition of the very considerable contributions by numerous researchers over many decades. As we wrote in previous editions, scholarly writing about Scottish education did not begin with the opening of the new Scottish Parliament in 1999: it was alive well before that but until the 1970s much of it was uncritical and reflected the official views of policymakers. This volume provides a range of perspectives, informed by evidence, analysis and interpretation: it includes new contributions not only by experienced Scottish writers but also by younger academics and practitioners who are less well known. We are indebted to all of them for accepting the invitation to contribute to this latest edition.

Others are due our thanks. Tom Malone created the cover for this and the earlier editions. His good efforts have sustained a recognisable brand. And we must thank staff at Edinburgh University Press, in particular Nicola Ramsey. Her support throughout the production of all five editions has been steady and encouraging. Jen Daly was the commissioning editor for this fifth edition; she, and her maternity cover, Adela Rauchova, worked cheerfully with the editorial team, as did Joannah Duncan, the managing desk editor and Naomi Farmer in her role as marketing manager. Barbara Eastman, the copy editor, negotiated final corrections with us courteously and carefully. The comprehensive index, which will be of great use to readers, was compiled by Lisa Scholey who deserves our warm appreciation. There are others without whose help the book would not have been produced but formal acknowledgement must stop somewhere. As we concluded our acknowledgements for previous editions, we should like to thank the many pupils, students, teachers and colleagues who have, over the years, taught us about Scottish education and for whom this book might be seen as an expression of gratitude.

## REFERENCES

Freeman, T. (2017) 'John Swinney announces "sweeping" education reforms with another consultation', *Holyrood*, News, 16 June.
Scottish Government (2017) *Education Governance: Next Steps*. Edinburgh: Scottish Government. Online at www.gov.scot/Resource/0052/00521038.pdf

# 2

# Educational Provision: An Overview

*Ian Smith*

## INTRODUCTION: STRUCTURE AND SECTORS

During the last quarter of the twentieth century, public discussion on Scottish educational provision would often centre initially on the period of compulsory education from age 5 to 16. This was provided by Scottish local authorities through the primary school sector until age 11, and the secondary school sector from age 12. However, twenty-first-century discussion of Scottish educational provision has more quickly included the significant contributions of other sectors, including preschool provision, special education, post-school provision involving further education colleges and universities, and community education. Changes in the position of these other sectors within the overall Scottish educational structure have been more marked and complex in recent years. There has been an increasing emphasis upon the importance and expansion of preschool education. Particularly significant changes have taken place in special education, with developing philosophies of approach in this area. Further and higher education have been required to engage with complex issues on the nature of provision and organisational structure. More broadly, Scottish administrations have placed a greater emphasis on 'lifelong learning', defined as the overall learning activities undertaken by the Scottish population from age 16 onwards. This chapter will reflect the relative structural stabilities of sectors within Scottish educational provision by initially covering primary and secondary school provision, before moving to other sectors. On the other hand, as will be mentioned subsequently, there has been much emphasis in recent Scottish Government policy on establishing approaches which cross the divisions between sectors. In particular, Curriculum for Excellence (CfE) is progressing curriculum development for ages 3–18, covering aspects of the preschool, primary, secondary and further education sectors (see https://www.education.gov.scot/scottish-education-system/policy-for-scottish-education/Policy-drivers).

Scottish educational provision is largely a state-funded service. The vast majority of primary and secondary schooling is provided by Scottish local authorities (of which there are currently thirty-two). While independent schools can report very high levels of pupil attainment and school leaver entry to higher education, the size of this sector is limited. In 2016, only 29,647 pupils attended independent schools in Scotland, just over 4 per cent of all Scottish pupils. While Scottish universities and further education colleges can draw upon other funding sources, both rely heavily for core funding upon public money received through the Scottish Funding Council (the SFC, created in 2005 by a merger of the previously separate Scottish Higher Education Funding Council and Scottish Further Education Funding Council). In 2013–14, further education colleges had an overall income of £487.7 million, with public money providing £346.2 million (71 per cent) of this directly from SFC grants, and making other contributions to the 18 per cent from tuition fees and educational contracts. In 2014–15, higher education institutions (HEIs) had an overall income of £3,484 million, with public money providing £1,130 million (32 per cent) of this directly from SFC grants, and making other contributions to the 27 per cent from tuition fees and educational contracts, and 22 per cent from research grants. In total, the SFC distributed £1,646.6 million in 2015–16, £568.6 million to colleges and £1,078 million to HEIs (these figures including capital funding). Finally, although both the publicly funded primary and secondary school sectors include 15 per cent of schools which are Roman Catholic denominational, these are managed by the local authorities, with certain rights for the Roman Catholic Church embedded in statute, for example regarding approval of teachers.

This chapter is concerned with the overall structure of provision between various sectors of education, including relevant statistics which illustrate the development of trends within this structure: broader policy implications will also be considered. Statistics quoted are principally from Scottish Government or SFC sources, with some use of additional statistical sources which are indicated in the references at the end of the chapter. Statistics for current and recent provision largely refer either to session 2015–16, 2014–15 or 2013–14 (the most recent full sets available at the time of writing vary depending on the aspect of educational provision). School statistics generally refer to publicly funded schools, although relevant independent school figures are also included.

## PRIMARY SCHOOL PROVISION

In 2016, there were 396,697 pupils in 2,031 publicly funded primary schools in Scotland. An additional 10,416 pupils were in forty-four independent primary schools. Pupil numbers for the first quarter of the twenty-first century indicate a primary school sector in which year-on-year variations in size have been relatively minor, and on a manageable scale. The number of pupils in publicly funded primary schools dropped from 390,260 in 2005 to 366,000 in 2011, then rose again to the 2016 figure. This number is projected to rise slightly to 400,000 in 2017, 401,000 in 2018, returning to 400,000 in 2019, and to 397,000 in 2020.

Scottish primary schools are relatively small, certainly compared to the general size of secondary schools. The overall average reflects provision for accessible schooling in sparsely populated parts of the country. In 2016, the average size of publicly funded primary schools was 195 pupils. In 2016, the average number of teachers in primary schools was twelve. Issues of primary–secondary transition are complex, and the size of primary schools may well be entirely appropriate to local social needs. However, differences in size between primary and secondary schools are part of the context for pupils' experiences of primary–secondary transition (see Chapter 26). Similarly, given the extent to which primary school staffing complements are smaller than secondary school, it may be questioned whether Scottish policy discussion on school leadership and management distinguishes sufficiently between the two sectors. For example, collegial approaches may be more readily applicable and easily achieved in primary schools.

In total, there were 23,920 teachers in publicly funded primary schools in 2016. The vast majority of these were generalist classroom teachers, who may teach all aspects of the curriculum. Only 871 teachers identified their main activity as more specialist (these were either teachers of art and design, music, and physical education, or teachers working in support for learning and additional support needs). These figures indicate the current context for any future debate about the further development of specialist teaching in primary schools, for example by generalist primary teachers achieving specialist professional recognition through continuing professional development, or by primary/secondary specialists emerging as part of general developments in primary–secondary transition.

In publicly funded primary schools, the pupil/teacher ratio fell continuously from 2000, dropping from 19.0 in 2000 to 15.7 in 2008. It then began to rise from 2009, reaching 16.8 in 2014. The ratio has dropped slightly since then, to 16.7 in 2015 and 16.6 in 2016. While there has been some reduction in average primary class sizes between 2000 and 2016, this has been relatively limited. Average primary class sizes for all classes moved from 24.4 in 2000 to 22.5 in 2009 and 2010, but rose again to 22.7 in 2011 and 2012. Since then, there have been continuous small rises, with average primary class sizes standing at 23.5 in 2016. For independent schools, the Scottish Council of Independent Schools (SCIS) does not publish separate figures on primary class sizes and pupil/teacher ratios. However, SCIS traditionally emphasises that independent schools have low pupil/teacher ratios across both the primary and secondary sectors.

Class sizes in the first three years of primary (P1–P3) in publicly funded schools have been of particular political significance. The Scottish National Party (SNP) election manifesto in 2007 had included a commitment to reduce class sizes in P1–P3 to a maximum of eighteen 'as quickly as possible'. Soon after that election, Fiona Hyslop, the then SNP Cabinet Secretary for Education and Lifelong Learning, called for flexibility on this target. Some attempt was made to adopt the eighteen pupil maximum in these classes for at least 20 per cent of the country's pupils. However, in October 2010, the SNP Government introduced a legal limit of twenty-five for P1 with effect from the 2011–12 school session. Mike Russell, Fiona Hyslop's successor, described this as a 'stepping stone' towards the target of the eighteen maximum. Certainly, regarding P1, 12.8 per cent of pupils were in classes exceeding twenty-five in 2010, but only 1 per cent in 2011 (although this figure still stood at 1.2 per cent in 2016). On the other hand, the P1 proportion at eighteen or lower, which was 30 per cent in 2010, dropped slightly to 29 per cent in 2011 and 27.75 per cent in 2012, then dropped significantly to 20.9 per cent in 2013, reaching 19.6 per cent in 2015. The slight recovery in 2016 has only been to 20.4 per cent. The proportion of P1–P3 overall in classes of eighteen or less (including classes of thirty-six covered by two teachers) was 12.7 per cent in 2006, and had certainly risen to 21.6 per cent in 2010. However, this proportion then began to decline, to 20.2 per cent in 2011 and 18.8 per cent in 2012, followed by much more substantial decline to 13.6 per cent in 2013, with decline continuing to reach 12.2 per cent in 2015, and the proportion only rising very slightly to 12.7 per cent in 2016. Political debate about class sizes in these years continues.

A description of the Scottish primary school sector may suggest a relatively stable and self-contained part of national education provision. However, there are complexities to this. The primary school system faces constant challenges in taking forward assessment and curriculum change, especially within the overall context of the development of CfE and the specific recent introduction of the new Achievement of Curriculum for Excellence (CfE) Levels returns, which collect data each year for all pupils in P1, P4 and P7, and the forthcoming proposed use of new national standardised assessments on reading, writing and numeracy for these (see Chapters 71 and 102). Beyond this, there are deeper issues in the relationship between primary provision and the adjacent sectors. The connection with preschool education will be explored later in this chapter. The challenges and complexities of primary–secondary transition have been the focus of much thought within Scotland over a number of years, with issues at best partially resolved (see West et al. 2010, and Brown et al. 2017, for fuller recent analyses). New teaching qualifications which cross the traditional primary/secondary divide have not yet been established in Scottish initial teacher education (although at the time of writing 'the development of teachers able to work in both primary and secondary' is included among the Scottish Government's aspirations for new routes into teaching, and there is the example of the University of Edinburgh's new Master of Science (MSc) in Transformative Learning and Teaching, fully accredited and offered for 2017–18, which provides a qualification across the primary/secondary transition – see www.ed.ac.uk/education/graduate-school/taught-degrees/transformative-learning).

## SECONDARY SCHOOL PROVISION

In 2016, there were 280,983 pupils in 359 publicly funded secondary schools in Scotland. An additional 17,786 pupils were in thirty-seven independent secondary schools. Pupil numbers for the first quarter of the twenty-first century indicate a secondary school sector which had been declining in size until 2016, with projections to show stability in 2017, with some slight increase in size subsequently, but on a scale likely to be manageable. The number of pupils in publicly funded secondary schools is projected to stabilise at 280,000 in 2017, before rising from 2018, to reach 296,000 by 2020.

In 2016, the average size of publicly funded secondary schools was 783. This means that the size of secondary school staffing complements significantly exceeds the primary school equivalents. The average number of teachers in these secondary schools in 2016 was sixty-four. These primary/secondary size differences have already been highlighted as potentially relevant for primary–secondary transition, and for approaches to leadership and management between the two sectors.

In total, there were 22,957 teachers in publicly funded secondary schools in 2016. The pupil/teacher ratio in secondary schools fell from 2000, dropping from 13.0 in 2000 to 11.6 in 2007. The ratio then rose again, reaching 12.3 in 2011. The ratio has subsequently stabilised at 12.2 from 2012 to 2016. A ratio as low as this had already been achieved in the early 1990s, for example the ratio was 12.2 in 1990. However, when compared with higher education where student/staff ratios in many disciplines and institutions may well have risen significantly during the same period, this underlying stability in pupil/teacher ratios can be presented positively as an indication of public resource commitment to the secondary sector. On independent schools, SCIS only publishes an overall pupil/teacher ratio covering both the primary and secondary sectors, which was 8.6 for 2016.

In 2009–10, 35.5 per cent of school leavers obtained three awards or more at Scottish Credit and Qualifications Framework (SCQF) Level 6 (Higher) or better. This proportion then rose gradually to reach 42.6 per cent in 2014–15, with relatively small increases each year (except for a small drop of 0.5 per cent between 2011–12 and 2012–13). However, the annual increase was never more than 3 per cent. For example, the increase between 2013–14 and 2014–15 was 1.1 per cent. The total increase over six years was only 7.1 per cent. In 2009–10, 22.2 per cent of school leavers obtained five awards or more at SCQF Level 6 or better. This proportion then also rose gradually to reach 28.6 per cent in 2014–15, with relatively small increases each year (except for a small drop of 0.3 per cent between 2011–12 and

2012–13). However, the annual increase was never more than 2.9 per cent. For example, the increase between 2013–14 and 2014–15 was 0.5 per cent. The total increase over six years was only 6.4 per cent. In 2009–10, 15.6 per cent of school leavers obtained at least one award at SCQF Level 7 (Advanced Higher). This proportion then also rose gradually to reach 18.8 per cent in 2014–15, with relatively small increases each year (except for no increase between 2011–12 and 2012–13). However, the annual increase was never more than 1.4 per cent. For example, the increase between 2013–14 and 2014–15 was 0.5 per cent. The total increase over six years was only 3.2 per cent. (See further details on attainments in National examinations in Chapter 70.)

The proportion of school leavers entering full-time further or higher education was 63.4 per cent in 2010–11. This then rose gradually to reach 66.4 per cent in 2014 15. The annual increase was never more than 1.1 per cent (the increase between 2013–14 and 2014–15). The total increase over five years was 3 per cent. Taking higher education separately, the proportion entering higher education was 36.3 per cent in 2010–11. While this stood at 38.8 per cent in 2014–15, this was only a total increase of 2.5 per cent over five years, and entry actually dropped 0.7 per cent between 2011–12 and 2012–13 and 0.2 per cent between 2013–14 and 2014–15. The annual increase was never more than 1.9 per cent. Taking further education separately, the proportion entering further education was 27.1 per cent in 2010–11. While this stood at 27.6 per cent in 2014–15, this was only a total increase of 0.5 per cent over five years, and entry actually dropped 1.4 per cent between 2012–13 and 2013–14, and 0.5 per cent between 2010–11 and 2011–12. The annual increase was never more than 1.3 per cent. On the other hand, the proportion of those entering employment rose continuously from 19.2 per cent in 2010–11 to reach 21.7 per cent in 2013–14, before dropping back slightly to 21.4 per cent in 2014–15.

This statistical analysis may suggest that public examination results, with consequent rates of entry to higher and further education, have essentially plateaued at a level consistent with underlying cohort attainment capacity relative to existing public examination standards, and with underlying cohort aspirations to continue in education. This raises interesting issues about how public policy debate should now proceed, especially if some may question the appropriateness of continuously targeting ongoing increases in upper secondary levels of attainment and the proportion of school leavers entering higher education. However, it can be argued that further increases can be delivered if relative underachievement in areas of deprivation is addressed, and this should be the focus of policy. For example, the Scottish Government has analysed school leaver qualifications in relation to the Scottish Index of Multiple Deprivation (SIMD), which uses a range of indicators to measure relative deprivation on a geographical basis across Scotland. Among 2014–15 leavers, 41.2 per cent of the 'most deprived' leavers achieved one or more awards at SCQF Level 6 or better, compared to 80.3 per cent of the 'least deprived'.

The preceding analysis is based upon pupil attainment in publicly funded secondary schools. Certainly, levels of attainment are proportionately higher in independent schools. Statistics for 2015–16 provided by SCIS, derived from Scottish Qualifications Authority (SQA) data, indicate that SCIS candidates comprised 7.4 per cent of all Highers entries and 16.2 per cent of all Advanced Highers entries. The A–C pass rate for Highers at SCIS schools was 92.3 per cent, compared to 77.2 per cent at all schools. The A–C pass rate for Advanced Highers at SCIS schools was 93 per cent, compared to 81.7 per cent at all schools. However, because of the relatively small numbers involved, such statistical variations are not significant enough to alter the analysis of relevant public policy issues already presented.

As with the primary school sector, a description of the Scottish secondary school system may suggest a sector which has a relatively stable place within national educational provision. Again, however, there are complexities to this, in addition to the points about attainment levels and leaver destinations already discussed. Internally, the secondary system has to engage constantly with assessment and curriculum change. As well as national developments which also affect primary schools, such as progression within CfE from second level (to the end of primary 7) to third and fourth levels (secondary 1 to 3), secondary schools have had to address specific issues such as those relating to the development and implementation of the new National 4 and 5 courses and assessments to replace the former Standard Grades (General and Credit) and Intermediates (see Chapter 68). However, perhaps more fundamentally, secondary schools face a continuing twenty-first-century debate about the place of their traditionally subject-based curriculum within overall Scottish educational provision. For example, if there is an effective limit to the proportion of school leavers who see entry to higher education as the next step in their personal and career development, will the secondary school system have to move even further beyond the subject-based curriculum than currently envisaged by CfE, with its greater emphasis on cross-disciplinary learning and teaching? Will engagement with vocational education, however this is defined, also have to move further than the current proposals under CfE, which include continuing development of 'skills for work' approaches and collaboration with further education colleges?

## PROVISION FOR ADDITIONAL SUPPORT NEEDS

Discussion of the role of special schools within overall Scottish educational provision has to be placed in the current context of the broader approach to additional support for learning (ASL) and additional support needs (ASN). Terminology in this area has developed continuously since the 1970s, and the careful and sensitive use of language is particularly important in this aspect of educational provision (see details in Chapter 77). Following the publication of the then Scottish Executive Education Department (SEED) report *Moving Forward! Additional Support for Learning* in 2003, and the Education (Additional Support for Learning) (Scotland) Act 2004 (www.legislation.gov.uk/asp/2004/4/contents), policy and practice is based upon the overarching concept of ASN. This progresses the commitment to mainstream inclusion contained in the Standards in Scotland's Schools etc. Act 2000. Pupils who would formerly have been identified with 'special educational needs' are now more positively described as entitled to 'additional support for learning'. Official statistics moved to reporting on the Coordinated Support Plan (CSP) targeting the ASN of young people receiving coordinated support, which would be developed from the Individual Educational Plan (IEP) these pupils generally have. The 2004 Act was supplemented by the Additional Support for Learning (Scotland) Act 2009 (www.legislation.gov.uk/asp/2009/7/contents) and the Education (Scotland) Act 2016 (www.legislation.gov.uk/asp/2016/8/contents/enacted), both of which strengthen the rights of children with ASN.

At the time of the introduction of the 2004 Act, the number of pupils in publicly funded special schools was projected by the then Scottish Executive to fall in line with the anticipated decrease in the number of children of school age, but also to account for the potential impact of mainstreaming of pupils with ASN. From a total of 7,100 in 2005, the number of pupils in publicly funded special schools was projected to fall to 5,200 in 2024. However, the number of pupils in publicly funded special schools broadly plateaued between 2012 and 2015, with 6,976 in 2012 and 6,920 in 2015, before dropping slightly to 6,735 in 2016.

More widely, in 2005, 34,577 pupils in publicly funded schools (4.8 per cent of all pupils) had a Record of Needs or IEP. Of these pupils, 27,540 (80 per cent) were in mainstream schools. They made up 3.9 per cent of mainstream school pupils. In 2011, numbers had risen to 98,523 pupils (14.7 per cent of all pupils) with an additional support need recorded. Of these pupils, 91,550 (93 per cent) were in mainstream schools. They made up 13.8 per cent of mainstream pupils. Since then, numbers have continued to grow very significantly. By 2016, 170,329 (24.9 per cent of all pupils) had an additional support need recorded. Of these pupils, 162,034 (95 per cent) were in mainstream schools. They made up 23.9 per cent of mainstream school pupils. These increases in numbers can be associated with widening in the way information on ASN has been collected since 2010. A new category of 'other' has been added, and also child plans (introduced in 2011, these are single or multi-agency plans based on an assessment guided by the *Getting it Right for Every Child* National Practice Model). In 2016, 'Other' type of support involved 131,042 pupils, and 'Child Plans' involved 25,095 pupils, while the longer-established categories of 'Coordinated Support Plan [CSP]' involved 2,385 pupils, and 'Individualised Education Programmes [IEP]' involved 37,733 pupils. There have been six extra 'Reasons for support for pupils with Additional Support Needs' introduced since 2012: communication support needs; young carer; bereavement; substance misuse; family issues; risk of exclusion.

Inclusion brings challenges for mainstream staff, and such statistics place the scale of inclusion in context. Policies based upon positive responses to ASN will clearly be central to the continuing development of educational provision in twenty-first- century Scotland.

## PROVISION FOR EARLY LEARNING AND CHILDCARE

Preschool provision has developed significantly in recent years, and this is reflected in some complexity in the language used for this sector. Traditionally, the term nursery education, or even nursery schooling, may have been used specifically to refer to education for 3–4 year olds. Then, the terms preschool education or early education may have been adopted, on some occasions referring to the 3–4 age range, on others to the under-3s also. At other times, the term preschool or early years care has been used, referring to provision for 0–4 year olds which is less formally educational. Most specialists will now stress the integration of early years education and childcare, particularly around the concept of learning, with the term early learning and childcare (ELC) being used (see Chapter 21). Use of this term was confirmed in the 2014 Children and Young People (Scotland) Act (www.legislation.gov.uk/asp/2014/8/contents/enacted).

The internal complexity of the ELC sector, in comparison to the structural coherence of the primary and secondary sectors, can be seen when current provision is summarised. From 2002, part-time preschool education (normally five two-and-a-half-hour sessions per week for thirty-three weeks each year) was provided free for 3- and 4-year-old children in Scotland, should their parents wish it. This was subsequently increased to 475 hours entitlement per annum (equivalent to thirty-eight weeks at twelve-and-a-half hours). Then, the Children and Young People (Scotland) Act of 2014 increased provision to 600 hours (five three-hour, ten minute sessions per week over thirty-eight weeks, although daily provision within the total can range from 2.5 hours to 8 hours). The Scottish Government has 'pledged' to increase provision to 1140 hours per year (thirty hours per week over thirty-eight weeks) by 2020, for 3 and 4 year olds, and eligible 2 year olds. Education authorities provide preschool education places in their own nursery classes and schools and also in partner settings such as playgroups and private nurseries. In September 2016, 96,961 children were registered for ELC local authority funded places. Of 3 and 4 year olds, 99 per cent were registered, and 9 per cent of 2 year olds (although around 25 per cent of 2 year olds are now eligible for funded ELC). In December 2015, of the 2,434 nurseries registered with the Care Inspectorate, 60.4 per cent were local authority, 32.4 per cent were private, and 7.2 per cent were voluntary/not-for-profit. There were 5,530 registered childminders in December 2015, 100 per cent private, with 32,660 children attending childminders.

The involvement of private provision indicates that, while free part-time early years provision has expanded greatly, parents continue to face challenges in accessing and funding wider ELC in twenty-first-century Scotland. Costs of private provision are significant and continue to rise. For example, a Family and Childcare Trust survey in 2017 (https://www.familyandchildcaretrust.org/childcare-survey-2017) indicated that parents in Scotland spent an average of £111.37 per week for twenty-five hours nursery care per week for a child under 2, and £105.25 for the equivalent childminder care.

The complexities of this sector are also reflected in the staffing position within preschool provision. Only some of the staff working in the preschool sector are fully registered school-teachers. At September 2016, there were 1,775 General Teaching Council for Scotland (GTCS) registered teachers employed or working peripatetically in local authority and partnership ELC centres. On the other hand, the overall daycare sector workforce was 33,460 in 2015. There has been considerable focus on the overall ELC workforce, and the development of its qualifications. The Scottish Government commissioned *An Independent Review on the Early Learning and Childcare (ELC) and Out of School Care (OSC) Workforce*, chaired by Professor Iram Siraj, from March 2014 to April 2015 (Scottish Government, 2015). This review's wide-ranging report included the key first recommendation that the Scottish Government convene 'a strategic group to oversee a maximum 15-year vision and development plan for workforce reform'. There were also more specific recommendations, such as requiring pre-registration training for childminders, further developing the role of qualified teachers within ELC, and introducing specific early years initial teacher education programmes and qualifications. In responding to the independent review in December 2015 (www.gov.scot/Resource/0049/00490358.pdf), the Scottish Government accepted the recommendation on a strategic group, setting up an Early Learning and Childcare Strategic Forum, and asked the Care Inspectorate to scope a framework for an induction programme for childminders. In October 2015, the government had already announced that it would ensure all nurseries in the most deprived areas in Scotland would have an additional graduate working with children by 2018, whether this is a teacher with early childhood expertise or a graduate holding the BA Childhood Practice degree. On the other hand, the government did not accept the recommendation on specific early years initial teacher education programmes and qualifications.

However, the Scottish Government continues to work at the development of the sector. In October 2016, the Scottish Government issued *A Blueprint for 2020: The Expansion of Early Learning and Childcare in Scotland* (Scottish Government, 2016a), which explored a range of approaches associated with the doubling of entitlement to free ELC by 2020, including the associated training and recruitment of staff required to deliver the expansion. The document repeated that all staff working in daycare children services need to be registered with the Scottish Social Services Council (SSSC) or another regulatory body such as the GTCS, except childminders who need to register with the Care Inspectorate. In particular, the document stressed that care workers in supporting roles are required to hold or be working towards a relevant practice qualification at SCQF Level 6/Scottish Vocational Qualification (SVQ) Level 2 (e.g. National Certificate) or above (an estimated 15 per cent of the daycare workforce). Care workers in roles with more responsibility are required to hold or work towards at least a relevant qualification at SCQF Level 7/SVQ Level 3, or comparable (an estimated 67 per cent of the daycare workforce). Managers of daycare services need to hold or be working towards the Bachelor of Arts (BA) Childhood Practice degree (an estimated 19 per cent of the daycare workforce hold or are working towards a relevant degree). In January 2017, the Scottish Government announced an additional £1.5 million to recruit more teachers and graduates for nurseries in deprived areas in Scotland, with an extra 435 graduates to be in place by 2018. This was described as the 'first step' in realising the commitment to ensure nurseries in the most deprived areas benefit from an additional graduate by 2018. Of course, this still leaves staffing of this sector much less clear than its primary school neighbour. The twenty-first-century Scottish ELC workforce has still not become an all-graduate profession.

## FURTHER AND HIGHER EDUCATION PROVISION

### Further Education

Although publicly funded, Scotland's further education colleges have been independent bodies since 1993 (except that education authority control was retained for the two colleges in Orkney and Shetland). In 2009–10, there had been forty-three SFC-funded further education colleges. By 2016, after a process of mergers within regionalisation (as described in Chapters 6 and 72), there were now twenty-six further education colleges in Scotland, twenty incorporated and six non-incorporated, within thirteen college regions. Ten of these colleges were part of the University of the Highlands and Islands (UHI). The colleges deliver a range of provision, including vocational and non-vocational courses at further education (FE) level (i.e. at SCQF Level 6 or below), and courses at higher education (HE) level (mainly Higher National Certificate (HNC) and Higher National Diploma (HND), i.e. SCQF Levels 7 and 8). In 2015–16, the colleges had 5,324 full-time equivalent (FTE) teaching staff, and 5,480 FTE non-teaching staff.

In 2014–15, 221,660 students were studying at the twenty incorporated colleges. Student numbers peaked in 2007–8 and declined by around 41 per cent between 2007–8 and 2014–15. The decline has principally been in the number of part-time students which fell by 48 per cent between 2007–8 and 2014–15, from 321,281 to 165,853. The number of female part-time students fell at a steeper rate than male part-time students (53 per cent for women compared to 43 per cent for men). The number of part-time students aged twenty-five years or over fell by 54 per cent. All of this can be associated with SFC funding changes requested by the Scottish Government, which aimed to focus funding on courses most likely to lead to employment, with consequently less funding for courses not leading to qualifications or which were less than ten hours in duration. Although the number of part-time students has declined, the majority of the sector's enrolments remain on part-time FE courses (FE college figures refer to enrolments on each separate course taken, and therefore may be higher than the total number of students in the system). In 2015–16, 65.9 per cent of the sector's 281,051 enrolments were part-time FE students. However, part-time enrolments declined even more than part-time student numbers. The 185,133 part-time

FE enrolments in 2015–16 represents a reduction of more than 50 per cent of these types of courses since their peak in 2007–8. In particular, the reduction in very short (less than ten hours) programmes and non-recognised qualifications accounted for 70.7 per cent of the total reduction of all FE enrolments between 2007–8 and 2015–16. On the other hand, between 2007–8 and 2014–15, the number of full-time FE students increased by 18 per cent, from 66,534 to 78,318. However, between 2014–15 and 2015–16, full-time FE enrolments dropped by 1,152 (2.4 per cent). Part-time enrolments had fallen further between 2014–15 and 2015–16, by 15,980 enrolments, or 7.9 per cent (see discussion in Chapter 72).

The overall number of HE students in Scotland has generally increased in recent years, but this increase has largely been in the HEIs rather than the FE colleges. HEIs accounted for 82.5 per cent of all students enrolled in HE in Scotland in 2015–16, with the remaining 17.5 per cent studying at colleges (and 72.4 per cent of these were studying at HNC/HND level). However, between 2014–15 and 2015–16, HE enrolments in colleges, both full- and part-time, had increased, full-time increasing slightly by 341 (1.1 per cent), and part-time more substantially by 831 (5.1 per cent). In 2015–16, HE full-time activity accounted for 41.6 per cent of all full-time activity in colleges, which is the highest in all eleven years since 2005–6. Despite this, the reduction in FE enrolments outweighed the increase in HE enrolments, leading to an overall decrease in college student enrolments between 2014–15 and 2015–16, with enrolments falling by 15,960, a reduction of 5.4 per cent.

While the Scottish FE sector faces challenges in maintaining and developing its provision in twenty-first-century Scotland, this is more likely to involve constantly adjusting to increasingly complex requirements, rather than simply 'downsizing' in response to declining demand for its provision.

### Higher Education

In 2015–16, there were 285,450 students in HE in Scotland, an increase of 4,165 (1.5 per cent) from 2014–15, and mainly reflecting an increase at first degree level. Specifically at HEIs, the number of students increased by 2,995 (1.3 per cent) to 235,565, of whom 179,460 were full-time and 56,105 were part-time. The nineteen HEIs, members of Universities Scotland, comprise Scotland's fourteen campus-based universities, the UHI, the Open University in Scotland, Scotland's Rural College (SRUC), Glasgow School of Art, and the Royal Conservatoire of Scotland. All HEIs are self-governing, although in receipt of public funding through the SFC. The 2015–16 student total includes the 14,665 Open University students in Scotland.

HE comprises three main levels: sub-degree (principally HNC, HND), first degree and postgraduate (see Chapter 7 for fuller details and discussion). HEIs generally will be more concerned with first degree and postgraduate work, and the universities almost exclusively so. Sub-degree work is more likely at FE colleges. While the total number of students was 285,450 in 2015–16, which represented an increase from the 281,285 of 2014–15, the total for 2010–11 had been 290,000, which then dropped to 281,630 in 2011–12, 278,745 in 2012–13, before recovering to 279,495 in 2013–14. From 2014–15 to 2015–16, the number of first degree students increased by 4,075 (2.6 per cent) from 154,420 to 158,495; the number of research postgraduates increased by 385 (3.1 per cent) from 12,525 to 12,910; and the number of taught postgraduates increased by 125 (0.3 per cent) from 43,675 to 43,800. At sub-degree level, the number of HNC/HND students increased by 295 (0.7 per cent) from 40,765 to 41,060, whereas the number of other sub-degree students fell by 720

(2.4 per cent) from 29,905 to 29,185. The decline at other sub-degree level continues the downward trend evident from 2008–9. The majority of students at HEIs (66.8 per cent) were studying at first degree level.

However, as the overall student numbers above indicate, there is evidence of a plateauing in entry to HE, and this is especially so with entrants from Scotland. After consultation in 2011, the Scottish Age Participation Index (API) was discontinued and the preferred measure then became the Higher Education Initial Participation Rate (HEIPR). It roughly equates to the probability that a 16 year old will participate in HE by the age of thirty. The Scottish HEIPR is a measure of all initial entrants aged between 16 and 30 (inclusive). It was 55.6 per cent in 2009–10, remained at 55.6 per cent in 2010–11, rose slightly to 56.1 per cent in 2011–12 and then dropped to 55.0 per cent by 2013–14. While Scottish HEIPR has increased to 55.4 per cent in 2014–15, and 55.9 per cent in 2015–16, this is still only 0.3 per cent higher than it was in 2009–10, and less than it was in 2011–12.

Any overall growth in student numbers can be associated with recruitment from outwith Scotland. From 2000, the proportion of students entering HE in Scotland from outwith Scotland grew continuously, from 13.8 per cent of entrants in 2000–1 to 26.2 per cent of entrants in 2012–13. In contrast, Scottish domiciled entrants declined from 86.2 per cent in 2000–1 to 73.8 per cent of entrants in 2012–13. These proportions remained the same in 2013–14, with very small further declines in the proportion of Scottish domiciled entrants in 2014–15 and 2015–16. In 2014–15, there were 133,660 entrants, of whom 97,790 (73.2 per cent) were Scottish domiciled, while 26.8 per cent were from outwith Scotland. Of the 135,090 entrants to HE in Scotland in 2015–16, 98,575 (73.0 per cent) were Scottish domiciled, while 36,515 (27 per cent) were from outwith Scotland. Of these, 10,290 (7.6 per cent) were from the rest of the UK, 8,885 (6.6 per cent) were from the 'Other EU', 995 (0.7 per cent) were from 'Non-EU European', and 16,345 were 'Non-European' (12.1 per cent).

Issues also persist on the wider access aspects of entry to HE from Scotland. The overall percentage of Scottish-domiciled entrants to HE from the 20 per cent most deprived areas in 2015–16 was 16.1 per cent, which shows that people of working age from these areas were under-represented among HE entrants by -3.2 per cent. There has been very little movement in these figures since 2006–7. The overall percentage of Scottish-domiciled entrants to HE from the 20 per cent most deprived areas, with the associated under-representation, for 2006–7 was 15.0 per cent (and -4.4 per cent). Therefore, over a ten-year period, the proportion of entrants from the most deprived areas only rose by 1.1 per cent. In terms of institution type, in 2015–16 22.9 per cent of HE entrants to colleges were from the 20 per cent most deprived areas, with this figure 15.3 per cent for 'Scottish post-92 institutions', 13.8 per cent for the Open University in Scotland, 12.1 per cent for 'Newer universities in Scotland' (those established in the 1960s), 11.4 per cent for 'Specialised HEIs in Scotland' (such as Glasgow School of Art), 8 per cent for 'Ancient universities in Scotland' and 7.4 per cent for 'Universities outside of Scotland'. Therefore, entrants from the most deprived areas are least likely to attend the 'highest ranking' 'Ancient universities', and most likely to attend 'post-92' universities, or FE colleges. For example, taking young (i.e. under 21) Scottish-domiciled entrants to full-time undergraduate courses at Scottish HEIs for 2015–16, 20.9 per cent of entrants to the University of the West of Scotland came from the 20 per cent most deprived areas, but only 4.3 per cent of entrants to the University of St. Andrews.

## PROVISION FOR LIFELONG LEARNING, COMMUNITY LEARNING AND DEVELOPMENT

### Lifelong Learning

A policy emphasis on lifelong learning has been set since 2003, when the Scottish Executive produced *Life through Learning through Life*. This defined lifelong learning as about 'personal fulfilment and enterprise; employability and adaptability; active citizenship and social inclusion' (p. 7). Such definitions seem broadly consistent with academic conceptualisations of the learning society, for example as summarised by Lyn Tett, who identifies three relevant models of the learning society: learning for work; learning for citizenship; learning for democracy (Tett, 2010, p.35, drawing upon Ranson, 1998; see also Chapter 81 in this book). Of course, it may be suggested that policy detail focuses heavily on 'learning for work'. For example, the Scottish Executive's lifelong learning vision emphasised 'the best possible match between the learning opportunities open to people and the skills, knowledge, aptitudes and behaviour which will strengthen Scotland's economy and society' (Scottish Executive, 2003, p. 6).

This emphasis on 'lifelong learning' for work has been sustained in recent Scottish Government policy documents such as *Developing the Young Workforce: Scotland's Youth Employment Strategy: Implementing the Recommendations of the Commission for Developing Scotland's Young Workforce* (Scottish Government, 2014a). The foreword emphasises that 'this is about ensuring a work relevant educational experience for our young people' (p. i). The focus includes averting 'the risk of young people becoming unemployed' (p. ii). A target is set of 'reducing 2014 levels of youth unemployment by 40 per cent by 2021' (p. iii), which reflects the Scottish Government's particular concern with continuing numbers of 16–19 year olds Not in Employment, Education or Training (NEET) (the NEET proportion dropped from 12.7 per cent in 2012 to 8.4 per cent in 2014, but had risen again to 10.7 per cent in 2016). The document develops very comprehensive and detailed sets of 'Key themes and milestones' for the contributions of schools, colleges, Modern Apprenticeships and employers, specified for each year from 2014–15 to 2020–1, and linked to a range of eleven key performance indicators (KPIs).

For example, *Developing the Young Workforce* indicates that the number of Modern Apprenticeships (MAs) has increased from over 21,000 in 2010–11 to over 25,000 in each of years 2011–12, 2012–13 and 2013–14, with a commitment to year-on-year increases to reach 30,000 per year in 2020. Within MAs, Advanced Apprenticeships, now called Graduate Level Apprenticeships, will be developed at universities, providing work-based learning opportunities up to Master's degree level for employees, and created through partnership with industry and the FE and HE sectors. They are part funded by employers, and will initially focus in 2017 on Information and Communication Technology (ICT)/ Digital, Civil Engineering and Engineering. More widely, from October 2017 the Skills Development Scotland (SDS) Individual Learning Accounts (ILAs) are to be renamed Individual Training Accounts (ITAs), with the Scottish Government's intention that the new scheme will make it easier for job seekers and low paid workers to gain access to qualifications and skills training, specifically courses which result in industry recognised qualifications. Other schemes include Getting Ready for Work, which is targeted at young people, and Training for Work, which is targeted at adults who have been unemployed for three months or more.

## Community Learning and Development

As with lifelong learning, the conceptualisation of 'community learning and development' (CLD) requires consideration. From 2002, this term was adopted by the Scottish Executive to replace the former term 'community education'. In *Working and Learning Together to Build Stronger Communities* (Communities Scotland and Scottish Executive, 2004), the national priorities for CLD were identified as 'achievement through learning for adults; achievement through learning for young people; achievement through building community capacity' (p. 1). Policy commitment to such approaches has been sustained by the Scottish Government.

A key recent document is *The Requirements for Community Learning and Development (Scotland) Regulations 2013: Guidance for Local Authorities* (Scottish Government, 2014b). This relates to the implementation of *The Requirements for Community Learning and Development (Scotland) Regulations 2013* ('the CLD Regulations' www.legislation.gov.uk/ssi/2013/175/pdfs/ssi_20130175_en.pdf), which place duties on local authorities to audit the need for CLD and to consult and plan for it at local level. The 'Guidance' document emphasises that CLD 'includes both programmes with an explicit learning focus and other types of activity that are designed with participants and promote their educational and social development', as well as 'activities that develop communities' (p. 8). Each local authority is required to develop a CLD three-year plan (p. 13). The 'Guidance' document also relates to the policy document *Strategic Guidance for Community Planning Partnerships: Community Learning and Development* (Scottish Government, 2012). The Scottish Government sees this as 'renewing its commitment to Community Learning and Development (CLD)', which matters 'because building a learning culture is central to the well-being, resilience and dynamism of our communities' (p. 2). Momentum is also sustained with the document *Community Learning and Development Plans 2015–18: Planning for Change in Scotland's Communities* (Scottish Government, 2016b). This report 'focuses on the plans published under the CLD Regulations in September 2015' (p. 2). It highlights that 'Almost all plans make reference to workforce development' (p.6), and 87 per cent of plans 'have either priorities or actions explicitly contributing to improving employability' (p. 19). This emphasises the continuing link between lifelong learning and CLD around 'learning for work'.

## CONCLUSION: TWENTY-FIRST CENTURY CHALLENGES

As indicated in the introduction to this chapter, the structurally most stable parts of Scottish educational provision remain the primary and secondary school sectors. However, even these sectors face significant challenges as Scottish education moves further forward in the twenty-first century. The relationship between the primary school sector and the adjacent early years and secondary school sectors continues to require specific consideration. Transition from the primary to the secondary school remains a particular issue. Within the secondary sector, the underlying challenge is judging whether CfE will sufficiently reform the current subject-based curriculum and assessment which may have reached some kind of systemic limit in overall levels of attainment, especially for progression to HE, and in meeting young people's aspirations outwith HE, particularly in areas of multiple deprivation.

Other sectors face challenges which may be even more directly structural. The fullest, most inclusive response to ASN may have reduced the role of special schools but increases the demands on mainstream school staff. Policy on ELC must address the extent of free provision and the cost implications for parents if they have to move beyond free provision, and the nature of the workforce, especially levels of qualification, status and pay relative to schoolteachers. For HE, there are challenges on whether recruitment from within Scotland has plateaued, unless wider access from school leavers and lifelong learners from areas of multiple deprivation is achieved, or whether further growth will depend on recruitment from beyond Scotland. FE faces the continuing challenges of regionalisation, and the need to clarify its role in a complex set of potential relationships, including partnerships with secondary schools, HEIs and employers. Lifelong learning and CLD present a particular challenge for the Scottish Government to give substance to its broader aspirations in these areas.

## REFERENCES

Brown, J., Croxford, L. and Minty, S. (2017) *Pupils as Citizens: Participation, Responsibility and Voice in the Transition from Primary to Secondary School.* Edinburgh: Centre for Research in Education Inclusion and Diversity, University of Edinburgh.

Communities Scotland and Scottish Executive (2004) *Working and Learning Together to Build Stronger Communities.* Online at www.scotland.gov.uk/Resource/Doc/47210/0028730.pdf

Ranson, S. (1998) *Inside the Learning Society.* London: Cassel Education.

Scottish Executive (2003) *Life through Learning through Life: The Lifelong Learning Strategy for Scotland.* Online at www.scotland.gov.uk/Resource/Doc/47032/0028819.pdf

Scottish Executive Education Department (2003) *Moving Forward! Additional Support for Learning.* Online at www.scotland.gov.uk/Resource/Doc/47021/0023972.pdf

Scottish Government (2012) *Strategic Guidance for Community Planning Partnerships: Community Learning and Development*, June. Online at www.gov.scot/Resource/0039/00394611.pdf

Scottish Government (2014a) *Developing the Young Workforce: Scotland's Youth Employment Strategy: Implementing the Recommendations of the Commission for Developing Scotland's Young Workforce.* Online at www.gov.scot/Resource/0046/00466386.pdf

Scottish Government (2014b) *The Requirements for Community Learning and Development (Scotland) Regulations 2013: Guidance for Local Authorities.* Online at https://www.education.gov.scot/Documents/cld-regulations-la-guidance.pdf

Scottish Government (2015) *An Independent Review on the Early Learning and Childcare (ELC) and Out of School Care (OSC) Workforce.* Online at www.gov.scot/Resource/0047/00477419.pdf

Scottish Government (2016a) *A Blueprint for 2020: The Expansion of Early Learning and Childcare in Scotland.* Online at www.gov.scot/Resource/0050/00507518.pdf

Scottish Government (2016b) *Community Learning and Development Plans 2015–18: Planning for Change in Scotland's Communities*, March. Online at https://www.education.gov.scot/Documents/cld-plans-2015to18.pdf

Tett, L. (2010) *Community Education, Learning and* Development, third edition. Edinburgh: Dunedin Academic Press.

West, P., Sweeting, H., Young, R. (2010) 'Transition matters: pupils' experiences of the primary-secondary school transition in the West of Scotland and consequences for well-being and attainment', *Research Papers in Education*, 25 (1), 21–50.

## Websites

Audit Scotland, especially for FE College statistics, at www.audit-scotland.gov.uk

Care Inspectorate, especially for ELC statistics, at www.careinspectorate.com

Higher Education Statistical Agency, especially statistics, at www.hesa.ac.uk
Scottish Council for Independent Schools, especially statistics, at www.scis.org.uk
Scottish Funding Council, especially statistics, at www.sfc.ac.uk
Scottish Government statistics at www.scotland.gov.uk/Topics/Statistics

# 3

# Scottish Primary Education

*Claire Cassidy*

In 2015 the Organisation for Economic Co-operation and Development (OECD) published its report Improving Schools in Scotland: An OECD Perspective, a review of education policy that had been commissioned by the Scottish Government with

> The agreed purpose [being] to inform the ongoing development of education policy, practice and leadership in Scotland, by providing an independent review of the direction of the Curriculum for Excellence (CfE) and emerging impacts seen in quality and equity in Scottish schooling. (OECD, 2015, p. 3)

This chapter reflects on the evolution of CfE as featured in the report, with its focus being on Scottish primary education. In doing so, it considers the primary education reforms that led to CfE. There have been many influences on Scottish education, and Paterson (2003) offers a comprehensive analysis of the political and historical shaping of Scotland's educational system in the twentieth century, so this chapter does not attempt to give a complete historical account of the topic. Rather, it reflects on the links between and across the three key Scottish educational reforms in our most recent past: *A Curriculum for Excellence* (Scottish Executive, 2004), the 5–14 Curriculum, *The Structure and Balance of the Curriculum* (see Scottish Education Department, 1993 and the revised version, Learning and Teaching Scotland, 2000) and *Primary Education in Scotland* (Scottish Education Department, 1965), commonly known as the *Primary Memorandum*.

Scotland began working through a period of curricular reform in 2004 with *A Curriculum for Excellence* (Scottish Executive, 2004). The document by that name (ACfE), grew out of the 2002 National Debate on Education, a Scottish Executive consultation exercise open to pupils, parents, teachers, employers and others interested in education. The debate was designed to explore the state of school education in Scotland, revealing that, while there was perceived value in much of Scottish education, there was also a need and desire for improvement. Consequently, a Curriculum Review Group was established in 2003 'to identify the purposes of education 3 to 18 and principles for the design of the curriculum' (Scottish Executive, 2004, p. 7). The Group was charged with taking into account developing technologies and future demands and patterns of work in the global context, while also maintaining a view of children's development and the role of adults working with children in a range of educational settings. Ironically, the result was a document not far removed from the educational reform of 1965, *Primary Education in Scotland* (Scottish Education Department, 1965).

## THE *PRIMARY MEMORANDUM*

*Primary Education Scotland* (Scottish Education Department, 1965) was designed to share best principles and practice at philosophical and pedagogical levels. Teachers, administrators and others with responsibility for primary education were urged by William Ross, the then Secretary of State for Scotland, to use the *Primary Memorandum* to 'stimulate thought and constant reappraisal of our own work' (Scottish Education Department, 1965, p. iii). From the outset, the need to focus on active participation of children in their own learning and the role of the child at the centre of learning is clear. The *Memorandum* asserted that teachers should pay due attention to the natural development of the child, allowing them to learn through experience, stating that teachers 'must appreciate the stages through which the child is passing in his development towards adulthood, and attempt to provide for him the environment, experiences and guidance which will stimulate progress along natural lines' (Scottish Education Department, 1965, p. 3). While acknowledging the role of the child's environment, the *Memorandum* saw the goal of education as being one that must 'concern itself with fostering in him [the child] the qualities, skills and attitudes which will make him useful to society and adaptable to the kind of environment in which he will live as an adult' (ibid., p. 17).

It was important that children were furnished with the tools to investigate for themselves, and that they would be encouraged to find answers to the questions they set themselves. Following not only from Rousseau, but also from Dewey, the *Memorandum* was clear that children learn best when motivated by the area of study and that, therefore, learning and, by implication, teaching should be developed from interest. The authors eschewed the practice of a subject-based curriculum in favour of purposeful activities that would be more meaningful to the child as a consequence of being responsive to his interests. Not by accident is the first chapter of the *Memorandum* centred on 'The Child'. Step-by-step, the chapter sets out considerations with regard to the child: growth and development; the primary-school years; the needs of the child; the need for security; the need for guidance; the need for freedom; the need to understand; and the need for the 'real' and the 'concrete'. Each section explicates the key factors in relation to the child and his education. Teachers are guided towards supporting the child with advice on how best to think of children's development. The text takes this further to consider the child's environment. The global and societal environment is considered before reflection on the school environment and how it engenders positive learning experiences. These learning experiences, while initiated by the child, are facilitated by the staff of the school, and the *Memorandum* explores the roles of the headteacher, the class teacher, the specialist teacher and the ancillary staff in the child's education. The school is seen not simply as a location where children are placed to be acted upon, but as a whole environment where an ethos is generated that is conducive to children's interests and, therefore, their learning.

The *Memorandum* discusses a range of methods and organisational approaches considered to be conducive to child-centred learning, as these children would also 'grow up to be citizens of the future" (Scottish Education Department, 1965, p. 53). These learning experiences would occur by virtue of a curriculum influenced by the 1956 Schools (Scotland) Code, which set out the key aspects for instruction. The *Memorandum* expanded upon the Code's designated areas of spoken and written English, arithmetic, music, art and handwork, nature study, physical education, geography, history and – for girls – needlework, to create more open and versatile opportunities for teachers to create links across the subject areas. The *Memorandum*'s authors recognised the limitations of the Code and put extra emphasis on a more holistic approach that was more relevant for pupils without generating an overloaded curriculum. Integration of curricular subjects was viewed as essential. There was a place in environmental studies – the new collective term for arithmetic, history, geography and science – where teachers were urged to find applications for language and mathematics skills. Drama and music could also come together, and art and craft would be a merger of handwork and needlework that would be available for boys as well as girls. Further, time allocations were not seen to be helpful, and it was not anticipated that each child would have the same experiences in every class in every school; it was for headteachers and their staff to decide what best suited their children in their contexts in judging what to include in the curriculum, which now revolved around the main headings of Language Arts, Environmental Studies, Art and Craft Activities, Music, Physical Education, Health Education, Handwriting, Gaelic and Modern Languages. However, this was, in some ways, an ideal.

The 1980 Her Majesty's Inspectorate (HMI) report *Learning and Teaching in Primary 4 and Primary 7* surveyed 152 schools (6 per cent of the primary schools in Scotland), where 'They evaluated what teachers were doing and assessed what pupils were achieving' (ibid., p. 5). The survey took account of what was happening in P4 and P7, the rationale being that, by P4, children could read and count, and that P7 was the year before children migrated to secondary school. The survey showed that, far from the possibilities presented by the *Memorandum* to engage in a wide variety of activities through a range of curricular areas, teachers were themselves constricting the learning of pupils by 'concentrating on a very narrow span of activity' (ibid., p. 46) with a determined focus on 'basic skills' to the detriment of other learning opportunities, 'with such conviction that it requires to be examined as a fundamental issue' (ibid., p. 46). It was not the curriculum that was failing pupils but, the report asserted, teachers' attitudes. The report went on to conclude that there was 'the need to preserve breadth in the curriculum; and the importance of maintaining and supporting a teaching force of quality and imagination' (ibid., p. 55).

## 5–14

It was this that the 5–14 programme worked to address. To anyone who has been teaching in a Scottish primary school since 1991, the 1965 curricular areas will not be new. In fact, for at least twenty years in Scotland, teachers very much held to the areas suggested above, but, under 5–14, in an arguably more prescriptive manner. The consultation paper *Curriculum and Assessment in Scotland: A Policy for the 90s* was issued in 1987 (Scottish Education Department, 1987) and heralded the advent of the 5–14 programme, addressing what was identified by the Secretary of State as 'a need for clearer definition of the content and objectives of the curriculum; the establishment of satisfactory assessment policies in all schools; and better communication between schools and parents, including reporting on pupils' progress' (Scottish Education Department, 1993, p. 1).

Following the review of the existing curricular advice by the Scottish Consultative Council on the Curriculum, guidelines covering curriculum and assessment were set for children aged between 5 and 14. Between 1989 and 1993, proposals relating to curriculum content and programmes of study were scrutinised and developed under six key areas: English Language, Mathematics, Environmental Studies, Expressive Arts, Religious and Moral Education, and Personal and Social Development, with Gaelic and Modern

Languages coming later. There were also groups considering Assessment and Testing, and Developing the Whole Curriculum. Like the *Primary Memorandum*, the subject areas incorporated subgroups of subjects: for example, Expressive Arts comprised art, music, drama and physical education, while Environmental Studies was a composite of science, history and geography (later known as social subjects, science and technology); but different headings were used, such as People in the Past; People in Place, Earth and Space; and Living Things and the Processes of Life. Also, just as the *Memorandum* advocated working from children's knowledge, experience and interests to create learning opportunities for society's future citizens, the authors of the 5–14 programme saw the task of education as satisfying 'the needs of the individual and society and to promote the development of knowledge and understanding, practical skills, attitudes and values' (ibid., p. 3).

Interestingly, the document *The Structure and Balance of the Curriculum* was revised in 2000 (Learning and Teaching Scotland, 2000) to take account of what had been recognised as good practice under the terms set out by Her Majesty's Inspectorate of Education (HMIe); but the focus remained on equipping children with the necessary skills, knowledge and attitudes that would lead to 'a personally rewarding life, productive employment and active citizenship' (ibid., p. 3). This document directs teachers to a 'structured continuum of learning' (ibid., p. 4) for their pupils. While the *Memorandum* was open-ended, and teachers and headteachers had liberty to make use of the curriculum to fit contexts in which they found themselves and their pupils, the 5–14 programme did not work in the same way. The programme laid out the governing principles of the 5–14 Curriculum: breadth, balance, coherence, continuity and progression. However, the application of these principles was much more rigid in practice than in theory. The philosophy behind the programme was such that it should allow for integration and cross-curricular opportunities while building upon children's experiences, while also ensuring a comprehensive range of curricular areas to learn about and to draw from. In practice, what tended to happen was that there was much focus on the balance of the curriculum.

The *Memorandum* had shied away from setting timetables, since this was seen as inflexible and led to rigid timetabling that would be too closely related to the teaching of discrete subjects as opposed to curriculum integration; it would ultimately lead to children disengaging with the topic under investigation, since neither their individual needs nor their interests would be taken into account. Significantly, in an attempt to ensure provision for a range of learning experiences and the attainment of high standards, the 5–14 programme recommended time allocations. A minimum time allocation for each curricular component was recommended for each of the five areas in an attempt to protect parts of the curriculum other than Language and Mathematics, following the earlier criticisms that these two areas dominated classroom practices. Mathematics and Language were each allotted 15 per cent of the timetable, with the Expressive Arts sharing 15 per cent. Environmental Studies was given 25 per cent of the timetable, and Religious and Moral Education had 10 per cent. There was provision for 20 per cent flexibility time which schools were allowed to use for an emphasis of their own choosing, such as whole-school activities, pastoral care or cross-curricular activities. It is important to note that the 5–14 guidelines and its recommended time allocations very quickly became viewed not as guidelines, but as mandatory strictures that were fully enforced across the primary school sector.

Consequently, the curriculum became more and more fragmented, with class teachers teaching the curriculum in discrete subjects with limited evidence of cross-curricular activities or integrated approaches to learning, despite the principle of coherence which was originally designed to facilitate the linkages between one area of knowledge and skills and another. This was contrary to the stated intentions of the 5–14 programme. The guiding principles of breadth, balance and coherence were intended to go hand-in-hand with continuity and progression, and these latter two aims were supposed to work for the benefit of individual children.

## ATTAINMENT AND ASSESSMENT

Continuity meant that teachers would try to build on children's previous experiences while also taking into account their abilities and attainment. Progression, similarly, allowed children to work towards goals that were set within the guidelines. The programme put in place a set of five attainment levels, ranging from level A through to level E, with the later addition of a sixth level, level F, to account for, and to allow provision for, more able children. It was intended that children would progress through each level, beginning at level A, following a programme of study set out under specific strands within each curricular area. For instance, within the English Language document, children would experience Reading, and within this there would be several related strands that ran across the levels: for example, reading for information, reading for enjoyment, reading to reflect the writer's ideas and craft, and so on. This allowed teachers a common language to share with colleagues and parents. Children would be expected to attain certain levels at certain stages throughout their primary school career and into the second year of their secondary schooling. In order to progress from one level to the next, teachers would monitor and assess performance against the criteria set out in the strands.

Should teachers consider a child to have completed and grasped the work within the strand pertaining to a specific level, they would move on to the next. In maths and language, however, there were National Tests that children had to pass in order to progress to the next level. While the progressivism of the *Memorandum* denounced formal testing, particularly in the early years, in favour of observation or diagnostic testing, the 5–14 programme lauded it as good practice. What resulted was exactly what the *Memorandum* warned against: teachers limiting their content to 'teach to the test', or that the time-consuming activity would provide no more information on the children's learning than what the teacher had already observed in everyday teaching and interaction. Often the pressures on children and teachers resulted in teachers 'helping' the children to pass tests at the expense of their understanding, ability or readiness to move to the next level. An initial protest from teachers and parents over the tests and their implementation was relatively short-lived. The 5–14 National Tests were later replaced by National Assessments, which were, to all intents and purposes, the same as National Tests but under a new and different name to reflect the work initiated in 2002 by the Assessment is for Learning (AifL) development (see Chapter 68).

With perhaps the exception of the formal National Assessments that seemed little improved from the National Tests in terms of actual practice, the philosophy of assessment in Scottish primary schools appeared to take a more positive turn in supporting teachers' assessment practices. Teachers began to employ more formative assessment strategies in their teaching than may be implied by the summative National Assessments. The principles of AifL became embedded in the CfE with *Building the Curriculum 5* (Scottish Government, 2011a). An online National Assessment Resource was also made available to support practitioners in developing a common understanding of assessment and in sharing good assessment practice, though this has recently been overtaken by newer developments and advice, notably relating to the Scottish Government's National Improvement Framework (www. gov.scot/Resource/0049/00491758.pdf; see Chapters 68 and 71).

## CURRICULUM FOR EXCELLENCE

The goal of ACfE was to ensure children develop as: 'successful learners', 'confident individuals', 'responsible citizens' and 'effective contributors' (Scottish Executive, 2004). This document aims to 'establish clear values, purposes and principles for education from 3 to 18 in Scotland' (Scottish Executive, 2004, p. 3). It is worth noting that the original title, *A Curriculum for Excellence*, has since changed to *Curriculum for Excellence* (CfE). It is not clear why, or when exactly, this changed but in losing the '*A*', the implication is that this *is* the curriculum that will ensure excellence rather than being one of several that *might*.

As mentioned earlier, CfE evolved from five National Priorities for Education that grew out of the National Debate on Education. The National Priorities of Achievement and Attainment, Framework for Learning, Inclusion and Equality, Values and Citizenship, and Learning for Life were pulled together to create cohesion across the ages and stages when children are expected to undertake some form of education or formal schooling. It was anticipated that these five priorities could be targeted through the four capacities that CfE aims to foster. The document clearly, though not uncontroversially, states that 'It is one of the prime purposes of education to make our young people aware of the values on which Scottish society is based … Young people therefore need to learn about and develop these values' (ibid., p. 11). While the National Debate demonstrated where there was agreement over positive aspects of the 5–14 programme, perhaps there was an intention to provoke engagement with the reform due to the focus on values and the use of ambiguous phrases such as 'To enhance opportunities and allow greater personalisation of learning' (ibid., p. 15), or the curriculum 'must be inclusive, be a stimulus for personal achievement and, through the broadening of pupils' experience of the world, be an encouragement towards informed and responsible citizenship' (ibid., p. 11).

CfE retains something of the focus on experiential learning as promoted in the *Memorandum* but with a renewed push to develop cross-curricular approaches and an integrated curriculum through the principle of relevance and purpose. The principles for curriculum design hold onto the notions of breadth, progression and coherence, but these are enhanced by once more suggesting that there should be enjoyment and challenge for children, while also offering personalisation and choice. Indeed, planning more responsively to accommodate children's interests has been welcomed by many teachers, particularly in the early years. CfE proposes that children be encouraged to learn in a range of meaningful contexts rather than the rigid attainment levels previously advocated. The learning contexts are still, however, subject-specific: expressive arts, health and wellbeing, languages, mathematics, religious and moral education, sciences, social studies and technologies, with the suggestion that schools decide for themselves how they organise learning. The stages are perhaps broader than those created under 5–14 but the experiences and outcomes, framed by the prefix '*I can …*', are somewhat vague. Indeed, where 5–14 was very explicit, CfE remains rather oblique in terms of progression through the stages.

Those designing CfE perhaps missed a huge opportunity to overhaul and rethink what happens in Scotland's schools under the guise of curriculum. The curriculum in Scotland at the beginning of the twenty-first century could have fallen under headings such as Creativity or Thinking or Rights, if headings were needed at all. Perhaps an approach such as this might have encouraged teachers to think beyond curricular areas and make stronger integrated links that would enable them to move away from what Paterson calls 'the peculiarly Scottish version of child-centredness' (Paterson, 2003, p. 116), where controls and freedoms of children come into conflict. Such a move away from a direct curricular focus may have been a more appropriate way of viewing the new curriculum, since the emphasis is not just on formal content but on the overall ethos within the school and preparation for life as citizens in Scotland.

It is a concern that teachers are, in fact, not clear about the notion of 'responsible citizenship', nor are they any wiser about the other 'capacities' and what it means to be an 'effective contributor', 'successful learner' or 'confident individual'. The documentation fails to clarify this, resulting in trite mantra-type use of the phrases, with children not being any clearer than their teachers. Interestingly, the language of these four capacities, presented as lists in the structure of the curricular areas in the experiences and outcomes does not shed any greater light on what the capacities might mean (see https://www.education.gov.scot/Documents/All-experiencesoutcomes.pdf). The OECD (2015) report authors also identify the lack of alignment between the experiences and outcomes and the 'four capacities' and the need for a stronger narrative to be established in order to take children's learning forward. This recommendation makes teachers central in taking the agenda further, with the suggestion that a 'strengthened middle' (p. 10) is required to develop networks and collaborative partnerships to enhance practice and, therefore, pupil learning.

March 2007 saw the first of sixteen 'roadshows' concerned with CfE. During the roadshows, teachers, headteachers, local authority education personnel, members of the CfE writing team and other education stakeholders engaged with the first draft of the learning outcomes; these related to science. Worries emerging from these early discussions appeared to be that the core skills within language and maths would be lost, and requests were expressed for more structure and a desire to know what *exactly* teachers would be expected to do. Notably, and perhaps in contrast to the dilemma of needing to know precisely what teachers were expected to implement, general discussion among some of those present suggested disappointment over the lack of innovation being presented. Additionally, there were concerns from those attending the roadshows about the difficulties in gaining an overview to avoid duplication in either the topics covered or the learning and teaching approaches used to meet the curriculum. There were also concerns about the potential for increased workload, a fear that seems to have been realised as teachers are currently engaged in a workload campaign (see, for example, www.eis.org.uk/Campaigns/Teacher_Workload_Campaign.htm). The OECD (2015) report again parallels teachers' initial misgivings, with the recommendation that innovation must not be 'stymied' (p. 21) by the burden of a bureaucratic workload that teachers seem to be experiencing.

While the philosophy of teacher autonomy and opportunities to be creative were generally welcomed, in some ways CfE has not moved far from 5–14 as teachers consider there has been a lack of guidance about curriculum content. Perhaps, though, in making these criticisms, there is a danger one overlooks that under 5–14 there was scope for integration and cross-curricular topics; that there was good practice. Indeed, the message is clear: teachers are seen as 'agents of change' but they demand structure, support and some form of 'meaningful engagement' in order that they do not simply resort to familiar old practices (Priestley, 2010, p. 34), or to prevent CfE from being perceived as promoting vagueness through autonomy rather than affording autonomy through vagueness. Indeed, the OECD's (2015) report makes clear that CfE has led teachers to focus too much on systems and the curriculum rather than on children's learning, resulting in claims that bureaucracy for teachers needs to be reduced.

## NEW FOCUS

In many respects, CfE resonates soundly with the 1965 *Primary Memorandum*. In fact, were today's student teachers encouraged to read the *Memorandum*, they would find that there is little difference in the stated philosophy of Scottish education in 1965 from that of today. Had 5–14 not ignored the very positive but now much neglected *Education 10–14 in Scotland* (Consultative Committee on the Curriculum, 1986), the development from the *Memorandum* need not have taken as long to reach the principles and philosophy of CfE. The 10–14 document built very much on the tradition of pupil experience being essential to learning. The curriculum design for this programme used helpful phrases that will be recognisable in the ethos and principles of CfE, for instance, 'learning to learn', 'physical development and wellbeing', 'social competence through active involvement in school life and activity', 'living together in a community and a society', and so on (Consultative Committee on the Curriculum, 1986, p. 47). Further, the document called for greater continuity and liaison between primary and secondary schools. It also had as its axiom that 'a young person's experience of education should be coherent, continuous and progressive' (ibid., p. 5) and that, if these characteristics were missing, there needed to be 'sound educational reasons for their absence' (ibid., p. 5).

Certainly, teachers now work in ways that promote inclusion and require liaison with integrated services and the wider community to meet the needs of all children. While teachers may embrace CfE and its approaches to learning and teaching, social deprivation, poor parenting, and a lack of resources for schools and those working with children will make this challenging. Teachers and those working with them must battle hard to meet the philosophies or principles underpinning CfE; they work to help children learn and learn for themselves, but what needs further consideration is that, to create any kind of meaningful educational reform, commitment is required and not solely from those working in schools. The political agenda, as ever, impacts on school practices and policies, with the SNP taking control of the Scottish Parliament in 2007 and retaining it in the 2011 and 2016 Scottish elections; their attention is on CfE and its impact, notably focusing on closing the attainment gap between the most and least disadvantaged and reducing inequality in Scotland's schools.

Informed by the OECD (2015) report, the Scottish Government published its *National Improvement Framework for Scottish Education* (2016a) with a view to 'achieving excellence and equity', quickly followed by their *Delivery Plan* (Scottish Government, 2016b). First Minister, Nicola Sturgeon, introduces the first of these documents by making clear that: 'the Framework will provide a level of robust, consistent and transparent data across Scotland that we have never had before, to extend our understanding of what works and to drive improvements across all parts of the system' (Scottish Government, 2016a, p. 1). Controversially, this requirement involves the introduction of national standardised testing in literacy and numeracy at primaries one, four and seven, with teachers' judgement being central (see Chapter 71). The aim, though, is *Getting it Right for Every Child* (GIRFEC; see Chapter 77) by taking account of children's needs and working towards fairer outcomes for all children. On this, there appears to be agreement, though teachers' anxiety around 'A Relentless Focus on Closing the Attainment Gap' (Scottish Government, 2016b, p. 4) relates to the very quick time frame to realise the goal. With money being ploughed into Scottish schools 'with the greatest intensity on children living in poverty' (ibid, p. 5) through the 'Attainment Challenge' and with proposals to shift school governance more directly to headteachers, it will be vital that teachers are able to focus on children's learning, as exhorted by the OECD. The controversial issue of primary school testing will potentially distract primary teachers from this task, with the likes of the organisation Upstart Scotland advocating changing the school starting age to seven in order to retain the focus on early learning through play or, as Samuelsson and Carlsson (2008) refer to it, 'playing learning', arguing that children should not experience failure through testing and that the attainment gap will not be addressed unless social-environmental factors are taken into account.

The language of commitment and creativity in addressing the future of Scottish education has been used in the McCormac report *Advancing Professionalism in Teaching* (Scottish Government, 2011b) in tandem with the need for teachers who are academically able and imaginative through the Donaldson report on *Teaching Scotland's Future* (Scottish Government, 2011c). This drive towards creativity and commitment is aligned with a need for collaboration, continuing professional development and practitioner research. The OECD (2015) advocates that 'There is need now for a bold approach that moves beyond system management in a new dynamic nearer to teaching and learning' (p. 10). Caution must, therefore, be exercised to ensure that primary education in Scotland is driven by the child and the child's needs being situated in the centre of all considerations and developments. Teachers must be free to engage with learning, both children's and their own, in order to address the very clear demands of delivering 'quality and equity in Scottish schools'. The OECD authors suggest that CfE is renamed, proposing the likes of *Raising Achievement and Attainment for All* or *Curriculum for Excellence and Equity*. Renaming and, therefore, repositioning the curriculum may well be conducive to refining the philosophy required to advance Scottish primary education.

## REFERENCES

Consultative Committee on the Curriculum (1986) *Education 10–14 in Scotland*. Dundee: Consultative Committee on the Curriculum.

Her Majesty's Inspectorate (1980) *Learning and Teaching in Primary 4 and Primary 7*. Edinburgh: Scottish Education Department.

Learning and Teaching Scotland (2000), *The Structure and Balance of the Curriculum*. Edinburgh: Scottish Executive.

OECD (2015) *Improving Schools in Scotland: An OECD Perspective*. Paris: OECD.

Paterson, L. (2003) *Scottish Education in the Twentieth Century*. Edinburgh: Edinburgh University Press.

Priestley, M. (2010) 'Curriculum for Excellence: transformational change or business as usual?' *Scottish Educational Review*, 42 (1), 23–36.

Samuelsson, I. P. and Carlsson, M. A. (2008) 'The playing learning child: towards a pedagogy of early childhood', *Scandinavian Journal of Educational Research*, 52 (6), 623–41.

Scottish Education Department (1965) *Primary Education in Scotland*. Edinburgh: HMSO.

Scottish Education Department (1987) *Curriculum and Assessment in Scotland: A Policy for the 90s*. Edinburgh: Scottish Education Department.

Scottish Education Department (1993) *The Structure and Balance of the Curriculum*. Edinburgh: Scottish Education Department.

Scottish Executive (2004) *A Curriculum for Excellence*. Edinburgh: Scottish Executive.

Scottish Government (2011a) *Building the Curriculum 5: A Framework for Assessment*. Edinburgh: Scottish Government.

Scottish Government (2011b) *Advancing Professionalism in Scottish Teaching: Report of the Review of Teacher Employment in Scotland*. Edinburgh: Scottish Government.

Scottish Government (2011c) *Teaching Scotland's Future: Report of a Review of Teacher Education in Scotland*. Edinburgh: Scottish Government.

Scottish Government (2016a) *National Improvement Framework for Scottish Education: Achieving Excellence and Equity*. Edinburgh: Scottish Government.

Scottish Government (2016b) *Delivering Excellence and Equity in Scottish Education. A Delivery Plan for Scotland*. Edinburgh: Scottish Government.

# 4

# Scottish Secondary Education

*Tom Bryce and Walter Humes*

Scottish secondary education continues to be fairly uniform in nature across the country, the vast majority of the pupil population (some 95 per cent) attending state comprehensive schools where traditional subjects dominate the curriculum. These are taught by subject specialists and the upper years still tend to have more influence upon what is taught in the lower years than do the primary years which precede them – despite national efforts to enable better progression from primary to secondary through the curricular reforms of 5–14 then Curriculum for Excellence (CfE). Debate about how far into secondary schooling 'broad general education' should extend is largely over: the government's preference for a 3 + 3 model of the six years of secondary featuring conspicuously in official documentation; that is, with early specialisation emphatically discouraged (as can be read in the CfE briefing paper, https://www.education.gov.scot/Documents/cfe-briefing-1.pdf). That said, and echoing the national ambitions to raise attainment and achievement, the briefing does concede that: 'Most learners will also progress into the fourth curriculum level in many aspects of their learning before the end of S3.' The upper years of secondary schooling retain subject choices and specialisation focusing on what young people will tackle subsequently in further or higher education or on entry to the world of work. At the time of writing it was, however, still unclear how many secondary schools commence specialised choices of study for National Qualifications at the beginning of S3 or S4.

Members of the general public have always reasoned that secondary education should help young people to make choices suited to their varied aptitudes and that good prospects are linked to natural ability. Sociologists have argued about how pupils' destinations are strongly governed by their social background. Educators have stressed access and flexibility, with Paterson emphasising how comprehensives have successfully widened achievements (Paterson, 2003). However, politicians in Scotland now face evidence that standards are falling (according to international survey data, as well as teachers' assessments of CfE level attainments, both of which are detailed in Chapter 68), thus raising questions about whether secondary schooling requires radical change.

Earlier remarks about the relative constancy of what goes on in post-primary education are not to say that *no* changes have occurred since the first edition of this book was published (nearly two decades ago). The visitor to any secondary school today would be struck by several things, not least the number of adults other than the class teacher working in classrooms; the amount of learning and teaching involving group activities; the use of advanced technologies (like iPads), school intra-networks and the Internet – for pupil research and investigation, as well as instruction; the increased movement of pupils in and out of schools (at further education (FE) colleges, work placements and so forth); and the growing number of coordinated, inter-subject activities, sometimes with whole-school learning events. Also noteworthy is the sheer amount of 'bureaucracy' and regulation which patently invades the lives of pupils and teachers, the seemingly necessary database entering being seen as a drudge, as for those who work in other professions. Most of the educational changes have come in the wake of national initiatives and programmes intended to widen access to courses suited to pupils' needs and to make learning more challenging across the ability range. Conspicuously, they all accompany the drive for efficiency and higher rates of attainment, the pervasive 'philosophy' which means that everyone, not least teachers, must do better at what they have always been doing: practice is determined by success rates, for which schools and teachers are held accountable.

## COMPREHENSIVE EDUCATION? SCOTLAND'S DEMOCRATIC TRADITION

The uniformity of secondary, comprehensive provision can be viewed in at least three ways: as an expression of social unity tied up with Scottish identity; as a reflection of democracy and communal solidarity (schools should serve their neighbourhoods); and as a demonstration that opportunities to succeed should be available to all. Social unity is usually interpreted as applying to class, gender and ethnic background but it is notable in Scotland that it does not apply to religion, where the principle of separate education has been accepted and endorsed in law since 1918. In West Central Scotland in particular there is widespread provision for children to attend Catholic primary and secondary schools. These exist alongside non-denominational schools. Other chapters in this volume provide detail of this significant aspect of Scottish education (see Chapters 13 and 88 in particular).

Historically, it is well documented that secondary education was class based and elitist up until the 1930s. It only became a statutory right in 1936. The idea of formal schooling being a sorting device or, in the words of the psychologist Sir Godfrey Thomson, 'a succession of sieves, sorting out pupils into different kinds' (quoted in Paterson, 1983), continued in the period after the Second World War when the junior/senior secondary system became formalised. Junior secondary schools were designed for pupils who had 'failed' the qualifying examination at age 11/12, while senior secondaries were for those who had 'passed'. The authors of this chapter went to senior secondary schools following their successful passes in the qualifying examinations at the end of their primary schooling. In the 1950s some 35 per cent of the secondary school population in Scotland gained similar admission to senior secondary schools. In England during the same period only 20 per cent of pupils gained places at grammar schools (the equivalent of Scottish senior secondary schools). Thus Scotland could claim to be relatively democratic in its provision. Furthermore, in small towns and rural communities, where numbers could not justify the creation of separate schools, 'omnibus' schools catered for the full ability range but with strictly demarcated courses for those who 'passed' and those who 'failed' the qualifying examination. Official claims that junior and senior secondary schools were accorded parity of esteem were never convincing and sociological evidence indicated that there was a strong social class factor in selection. Despite the Scottish Advisory Council on Education's recommendation in 1947 that a comprehensive system, together with a common curriculum core and a common examination, should be put in place, it was not until 1965 that the Scottish Education

Department formally decided to implement such a system. That was more than fifty years ago, underlining the constancies referred to at the start of this chapter.

Nevertheless, the development of comprehensive education within secondary schools since the late 1960s has been rather uneven, certainly during the years of the Conservative Government (1979–97) where there were instances of policy change consistent with the concept of social unity (e.g. 'mainstreaming' of pupils with additional support for learning needs) but rather more where policy change was designed to counter it (e.g. parental choice of schools). To an extent what pupils encounter in secondary schools varies with the relative affluence or poverty of the neighbourhood setting, and in the conurbations of the central belt there is probably more variation amongst schools than elsewhere in the country. The parental choice legislation of the 1980s served to distort the intake of individual schools, such are the powerful perceptions of the examination results achieved and of the potential behavioural disruption of pupils in particular areas. The Labour–Liberal Democrat coalitions following the re-establishment of the Scottish Parliament in 1999, and the Scottish National Party (SNP) administrations since 2007, brought about no major changes to the structure of schools. Considerable efforts were made to construct new buildings and effect mergers between schools where pupil numbers have fallen, although inferior constructions such as those featuring in the 2015 Edinburgh school building fiasco have blighted the actions of some local authorities. This has been happening in an increasing number of authorities according to reports made public in 2017. A BBC investigation reported on 13 April 2017 that 'at least 72 more schools in Scotland were found to have similar defects to Edinburgh schools judged to be unsafe'. Efforts have also been made to alter how schools are managed through changes to the personnel and promotion structure involved; and to bring greater coherence to the curriculum and to qualifications obtainable by the end of the secondary years. During this period, we have also seen a greater devolution of (financial) management to headteachers from local authorities. In June 2017, the Scottish Government published a series of proposals which would further reduce the role of local authorities. Headteachers would be given the power to appoint their own staff but they would also be held responsible for closing the attainment gap. New 'regional improvement collaboratives' would be established which would have an important role in supporting curricular and staff development. At the time of writing, many of the details of these proposals are unclear. What can be said is that they have proved controversial, with critics arguing that they would undermine democratic accountability and supporters claiming that they would free schools from bureaucratic constraints.

Over the last twenty years or so, there have been efforts, of differing kinds, to modify secondary school education, to depart from the 'one-size-fits-all' approach. These have included the development of the National Qualifications (NQs) framework, covering both traditional academic subjects and vocational subjects, with increasing flexibility of attendance at school and college; the varied ways in which additional support needs are catered for; and the several specialisms available in some schools. However, Scotland has stopped well short of the level of diversity in England (the continuing expansion of free schools and academies) and it is fair to say that the 'Scottish comprehensive principle' has been subject to adjustment but not in ways that undermine its fundamental tenets. Indeed it received considerable public endorsement during the National Debate of 2002 which preceded the CfE programme. What can be said is that there is now greater awareness of the elusiveness of equality as a social and moral principle. 'Equal' treatment may not mean 'the same' treatment (equality of *process*) as in the case of children with disabilities. Nor is equality of *access* to educational provision enough to guarantee desired educational benefits for all. And despite the proliferation of qualification levels, few if any would claim that we have achieved equality of *outcome*. A more credible claim might be that we are trying to operate on the basis of equality of *consideration* for all pupils – a form of equality that recognises differences (of needs, interests and abilities) among pupils and tries to make appropriate, and fair, provision accordingly. The grounds for differential provision must, however, be adequately justified if adherence to a (modified) version of the comprehensive principle is to remain credible. Against this background, what evidence is there about the success of current Scottish secondary education?

## OFFICIAL VIEWS: INSPECTORS' REVIEWS AND THE OECD PERSPECTIVE

The three most recent reports by Her Majesty's Inspectorate of Education (HMIE) on the performance of the education sectors in Scotland were published in 2009, 2012 and 2017, drawing from inspections carried out across consecutive periods. Titled slightly differently these were: *Improving Scottish Education: A Report by HMIE on Inspection and Review 2005–2008* (HMIE, 2009), *Quality and Improvement in Scottish Education: Trends in Inspection Findings* 2008–2011 (Education Scotland, 2012) and, most recently, *Quality and Improvement in Scottish Education* 2012–2016 (Education Scotland, 2017). Summary comments in the 2009 report by the Senior Chief Inspector of Schools (Graham Donaldson) indicated that in secondary schools, performance in national examinations remained good (but could be improved further) and that a wider range of accreditations were being gained through various youth award schemes and school–college partnerships. 'Overall, pupils in S1/S2 are still not sufficiently challenged' and 'Boys continue to perform consistently less well than girls' (HMIE, 2009). Summary comments in the 2012 report by the chief executive of Education Scotland (Donaldson's successor, Bill Maxwell) indicated that 'much progress has been made in embedding new, improved approaches in every-day educational practice'; and that there had been 'steady progress in the implementation of Curriculum for Excellence'. 'Focus is still needed in the first years of secondary to maintain the earlier gains in primary school' (Education Scotland, 2012). Writing as HM Chief Inspector of Education in the 2017 report, Maxwell stressed the numerous strengths in the quality of professional practice and provision across the system, inspectors having 'observed many examples of outstanding and innovative practice which are securing very positive outcomes for children and young people', but that it was 'equally clear that there are also important areas where leaders' and practitioners' efforts to improve need to be more focused' (Education Scotland, 2017).

Table 4.1 lists the 'strengths of secondary schools' and the 'aspects for improvement' in the 2009 and 2012 reports. The shading identifies those features essentially common across that six-year period of inspectorate observations, despite the different wording used. (The aspects have been reordered to place the commonalities at the top of the lists, though the originals were not ranked.) It is notable that, while pupils' final achievements, both academic and non-academic, were deemed to be more than satisfactory, and that pupil–teacher relationships were of 'high quality', inspectors had concerns about the consistency of teachers' efforts to help all learners; and how good practice in monitoring and progressing individuals could be improved in schools. Elsewhere in the 2009 report, and cross-referring to the Organisation for Economic Co-operation and Development's (OECD's) 2007 report on the *Quality and Equity of Schooling in Scotland*

Table 4.1 'Strengths of secondary schools' and 'aspects for improvement' identified in the HMIE reports of 2009 and 2012

| 2009 | 2012 |
|---|---|
| **Strengths of secondary schools** | |
| The overall quality of teaching and staff commitment. | Teacher–pupil relationships which are high quality and ensure learning takes place in a positive climate. |
| The performance of many young people at the point when they leave school. | Young people who are gaining achievements in a range of activities both in and out of school. |
| Recognising and promoting achievement. | Young people's learning and achievement is being supported through a wide range of partnerships with schools. |
| The quality of leadership of headteachers and increasingly of others in leadership roles. | Headteachers and senior managers show quality of leadership and have high expectations for their schools and young people. |
| Curriculum innovation focused on improving the quality of learners' experiences and meeting the learning needs of individuals. Pastoral care for young people, positive ethos, and staff and learner relationships. Levels of satisfaction of stakeholders, particularly parents. | Young people who are polite, courteous and friendly and show a positive attitude to learning. Schools provide high quality support, care and welfare to young people. Staff demonstrate commitment to the life and work of the school and in improving the outcomes for young people. |
| **Aspects for improvement** | |
| Consistency in the quality of teaching and learning including building on good practice and focusing staff development on how young people learn and how they develop learning skills. | Schools now need to ensure high quality and consistency in learning and teaching, and ensure that good practice is shared. |
| Meeting the learning needs of every young person, especially by monitoring and tracking progress and ensuring coherent programmes with skills-based and applied learning. | There is room to improve tracking and monitoring of young people's progress and achievements to ensure improved attainment, particularly for those young people who are at risk of missing out. |
| Raising achievement particularly by building on prior learning and ensuring challenge for each individual young person, especially those at the early stages, boys and vulnerable groups such as children who are looked after at home. | Approaches to self-evaluation need to impact on young people's learning and achievements, including their attainment. |
| Engaging all young people actively in learning, giving each a sense of personal responsibility for their own learning and encouraging them to think independently and creatively. | Develop the curriculum with better progression pathways in order to meet the needs of all learners. |
| Focusing self-evaluation on improving outcomes for young people, with clear lines of responsibility and accountability for innovation and improvement. | Schools' approaches to meeting learning needs in order to improve support and challenge in learning should be developed further. |
| Pursuing an ambitious, strategic vision for improvement including mobilising leadership at all levels. | |

(www.oecd.org/edu/school/reviewsofnationalpoliciesforeducation-qualityandequityofs-choolinginscotland.htm#3), it is stated that 'in comparison with most OECD countries, the Scottish school system is high performing and highly equitable in respect of both learner outcomes and school quality' (HMIE, 2009). This is not said in the 2012 report and, in the years since, there has been a decline in Scotland's standing internationally according to the Programme for International Student Assessment (PISA) surveys of assessments in reading, mathematics and science (fully discussed in Chapter 68 of this book). The 2017 HMIE report (Education Scotland, 2017) doesn't set out 'strengths' and 'aspects for improvement' in the same way as before, the text referring instead to 'improvements' and what should be 'focused on' (so a further tabulation of points made is not really possible). However, the text makes clear that, with respect to secondary education, there is 'a con-tinued need to focus on improving young people's attainment and achievement ensuring, for example, the curriculum provides suitably flexible pathways to meeting young people's individual learning needs'. The inspectors stress that the quality of learning had improved; overall pupils were motivated and had positive attitudes to their learning. Nevertheless, there was much variation within and between schools. During the CfE level 3 period (of broad general education), there still needs to be a better, shared understanding by teachers of standards to be reached by pupils.

It is relevant therefore to note the 2015 OECD report, *Improving Schools in Scotland: An OECD Perspective*, for the period of their observations overlapped with that of the Scottish Inspectors cited in the 2017 report. The OECD report was commissioned by Scottish Government to provide an independent appraisal of the direction of CfE and emerging impacts on quality and equity, specifically picking up on pupils' broad general education (up to 15 years of age). OECD commented on many positive developments in Scottish education, highlighting upward trends in attainments and destinations, inclusivity, pupil attitudes, and drops in risk habits (smoking and alcohol) and disruptive behaviour in schools. Explicit recognition is made of life expectancy and mortality rates being worse here than the OECD averages, with the disparities between advantaged and deprived areas, and their impact on public services, being of serious concern. There were

> particular challenges confronting secondary schools. Liking school drops sharply among sec-ondary students and [the] reported [sense of] belonging in school among Scottish teenagers has dropped since 2003. National surveys show a higher incidence of low achievement against expected levels among secondary pupils than previously.

The OECD considered that CfE management, nationally, required a bolder approach, driven by a focus on teaching and learning rather than simply system management. The gap between high- and low-performing local authorities required particular attention. And, echoing the points made in the inspection reports outlined above, insufficient use was being made of formative assessments. The OECD report stated that Scottish education should: 'Strike a more even balance between the formative focus of assessment and develop-ing a robust evidence base on learning outcomes and progression', as argued in this volume in Chapter 68. Overall, it concluded that Scottish education was at a 'watershed moment' and called for 'a new narrative' for CfE.

## The Backgrounds of Pupils

The social background of schools, both primary and secondary, has always been acknowledged as an important influence on pupils' aspirations and educational outcomes. Recent concerns of government are to counter the adverse effects of poverty and deprivation and to put in place measures which might give support to schools – hence the interest in present efforts to 'close the attainment gap'; in leadership qualities; augmentation of learning support staff; and so forth. The extent of the disadvantage, and indications that inequity can be countered, is contained in a recent study initiated by the Scottish Commissioner for Children and Young People (SCCYP), the ScotCen (2015) report on *The Identification of Effective Secondary Schools in Challenging Circumstances*. This statistical work looked at the 365 secondary schools in Scotland, finding that 141 of them (two fifths) were in areas of deprivation. However, twenty-four of them were performing better on Scottish Qualifications Authority (SQA) attainments than expected, that is, better than statistical prediction from indices of Scottish Index of Multiple Deprivation (SIMD) and Free School Meals (FSM) measures. A follow-up study of this research is anticipated. The attainment gap will not be easy to tackle, not least because of the intergenerational effects in social circumstances. According to the OECD *Trends Shaping Education Spotlight 8* paper, 'a key driver of inequality is the intergenerational transmission of advantage' (OECD, 2016) – for example, the influences of parental/grandparental education on successive generations. Among the many international trends and comparisons in the OECD paper, there is discussion of the tendency for more experienced teachers to move during their careers to more advantaged schools, thereby having the effect that younger/less-experienced teachers often populate schools in less advantaged circumstances. The data for the UK as a whole show that effect to be notably greater than the overall international average. Effects like these give support to political arguments about the need for local determinations of staffing resources in schools and increased power to be given to headteachers on that score. The Scottish Cabinet Secretary for Education announced in February 2017 that extra funding (to be known as the Pupil Equity Fund) and amounting to £1,200 per pupil receiving free school meals would be given to schools in disadvantaged areas. Glasgow would be the biggest 'winner', given its relatively high levels of poverty, and set to receive £21.6 million of the total of £120 million. To cite one school, St Andrews Secondary in Carntyne, Glasgow, would receive additional funding of £354,000, according to the *Times Educational Supplement Scotland* (TESS) of 1 February 2017.

## OTHER PERSPECTIVES

The official account of the strengths and limitations of Scotland's secondary schools, outlined above, drawing on inspectorate reports, is written by senior staff with responsibility for maintaining standards. Their judgements are based on substantial evidence but they cannot be regarded as entirely neutral observers. They enjoy narrative privilege in the sense that they are able to write their own version of events and, in some respects, they are assessing the success of policies that they have been responsible for developing and promoting. It is necessary, therefore, to look at other sources of evidence.

In recent years, the views of teachers have been canvassed by surveys carried out, or commissioned by, their professional organisations, such as the EIS and the Scottish Secondary Teachers' Association (SSTA). These too present a partial picture, but deserve to be set against official accounts. An EIS report (www.eis.org.uk/Teacher_Workload/survey_ stress.htm) of a survey of some 7,000 teachers in 2014 found significant levels of concern about the number and speed of changes. Many staff complained about excessive workload and the effect it was having on their health and wellbeing. They also reported issues with school management. More positively, they said that their main professional satisfaction came from contributing to the progress and achievements of pupils. Nevertheless, only 33 per cent of respondents said they were generally satisfied with their working life. Another EIS survey (www.eis.org.uk/CfE/CfE_survey_Final_results.htm) found that secondary teachers were unhappy with various aspects of the implementation of the senior phase of CfE. These included resources, information and support, timescale and workload. A similar survey in 2015 by the SSTA (https://ssta.org.uk/national-qualifications-reducing-teacher-workload/) reported a lack of confidence among teachers about their ability to deliver and assess the new courses developed as part of the CfE reforms. The Association claimed that their representations to Scottish Government had been ignored. These comments give a flavour of the tensions that can exist between officialdom and classroom teachers when changes are being introduced.

Another important perspective is that of pupils. A small survey reported in Murphy et al. (2015, Chapter 3) was carried out in 2014 by the Centre for Educational Sociology at Edinburgh University in conjunction with the secondary headteachers' organisation School Leaders Scotland (SLS). Among the points to emerge was a feeling that schools did a good job for able pupils and those destined for university but perhaps could do more for the less academically gifted. Even high achievers felt that there was perhaps too much emphasis on examinations and that more attention should be given to preparation for life after school. The quality of relationships with both staff and other pupils was seen as crucial in relation to whether school was an enjoyable experience. Several respondents referred to bullying as an issue that deserved to be taken more seriously. Although most schools now have anti-bullying policies in place, it is evident that the topic is one that concerns many pupils. There have been a few tragic cases where youngsters have taken their own lives because they have been victims of bullying. On the positive side, many respondents to the survey expressed appreciation for the opportunities to engage in a variety of extra-curricular activities (see below).

The Murphy et al. (2015) study is a vital source for anyone seeking to understand the evolution of the comprehensive secondary school in Scotland. It covers key principles (equality, fraternity and liberty) and asks a series of challenging questions. These include:

- What counts as an educated 18-year-old in this day and age?
- How should a democratic state schooling system balance the diverse needs, values and interests of different individuals with the broader social, economic and cultural needs of the nation as a whole?
- Who should be responsible and who is accountable for delivering the system?
- How do we know if our schooling system is achieving its purposes? (pp. 47–8)

The book also presents important evidence about the persistence of social class as a factor in educational achievement and about the changing relationship between secondary schools and further and higher education. With regard to the first point, one conclusion is that, despite improved opportunities for all, 'middle class parents have been able to maintain the positional advantage of their children through the comprehensive system' (p. 135).

## BEYOND THE FORMAL CURRICULUM

Media attention on secondary schools tends to focus on exam performance and changes to the curriculum. But headteachers would stress that schools are about more than formal learning and staff make strenuous efforts to provide a wide range of social and cultural opportunities for pupils. These include dramatic and musical performances, sporting activities, charity events, outdoor expeditions, foreign exchanges and community involvements. Pupils attest to their enjoyment and value and often recall them as memorable parts of school life. They help to develop confidence and maturity, qualities that can have a positive impact on learning. Headteachers also see these wider activities as important ways of building a sense of community, where people support each other, learn to work as part of a team and develop positive attitudes. The climate of most secondary schools nowadays is very different from earlier perceptions of them as rigidly disciplined examination factories.

There are other ways in which the formal curriculum, with its increasing focus on examinations in the upper school, is broadened. Schools are concerned to promote ideas such as global citizenship, environmental awareness and economic literacy. These topics encourage interdisciplinary thinking, drawing on the expertise of teachers in different departments. They can help to develop problem solving and critical thinking about topical issues. The aim is to make connections across learning, rather than to think of knowledge as consisting of a series of separate units. The subject of interdisciplinary learning is, however, highly contested (see Humes, 2013).

All schools also have social education programmes, where sensitive topics such as alcohol, drugs, sexual behaviour and the risks of social media are addressed. Pupil responses to these tend to be mixed, some claiming that the coverage is embarrassing, out of date or ill-informed. Again, health and wellbeing is regarded as a policy priority but, despite sustained efforts over a number of years, Scotland's record in reducing obesity among youngsters is poor. Mental health has recently attracted a great deal of attention. Figures from Policy Hub Scotland (see www.policyhubscotland.co.uk) suggest that over 50 per cent of mental health problems start by the age of 14 and 75 per cent by age 18. There is strong evidence that depression and other mental health issues are much higher in areas of social deprivation, according to the Mental Health Foundation (2016) report, Mental Health in Scotland: Fundamental Facts 2016. One school, St Paul's High in Pollok (one of Glasgow's more deprived areas), started a pilot programme in 2016/17 for parents, S4 pupils and staff on how to cope with stress and anxiety. It involved the expertise of a clinical psychologist from the National Health Service (NHS). Initial results appear to be encouraging.

Schools continue to have a 'hidden curriculum'. This term refers to the values that are conveyed through rules and rituals (timetabling, assemblies, punishments, etc.) and the relationships that exist amongst the staff and between staff and pupils. The culture or ethos of schools can vary according to how the hidden curriculum messages are conveyed and received. For a minority of pupils, the hidden curriculum may be more powerful than the formal curriculum, in some cases encouraging disaffection and disengagement from learning. This reminds us that institutions can produce effects other than those intended. Some studies have suggested that the most alienated youngsters reverse the professed values of the school, seeking status among their peers by breaking rules, not conforming and resisting attempts to include them in positive activities.

## THE FUTURE OF SECONDARY EDUCATION

In their review of the last fifty years of Scottish comprehensive education, Murphy et al. (2015, Chapter 11) draw a number of lessons which should inform future developments. Most significantly, they say that comprehensive secondary schools need a clear vision that is 'holistic, shared and transparent' (p. 199). What do they mean by these terms? It is not sufficient to see secondary education in isolation. How that sector relates both to primary schools and to post-secondary destinations is important. The vision needs to be shared with all the stakeholders, principally pupils, parents and teachers, but also others with an interest in schooling, such as employers. On the question of transparency, Murphy et al. observe: 'The leaders of Scottish education have often found it convenient, for political and pragmatic reasons, to allow ambiguities in how they define the goals of reforms and the strategies for achieving them' (p. 200). This may account for the rather shaky journey of CfE, where teachers have expressed uncertainty about what is expected of them.

The authors go on to set out the principles which should be observed as the system moves forward. There should be an attempt to 'achieve a fair balance between uniformity and diversity' (p. 201). Too much uniformity can lead to a static culture, in which there is a reluctance to innovate. But too much diversity could lead to unfairness and uneven quality of provision. Furthermore, 'the wider determinants of inequality' (p. 201) need to be recognised. In an unequal society, there are external constraints on what schools can achieve. That is not to say that they should cease to strive to raise aspirations and encourage upward social mobility, but schools on their own cannot compensate for powerful economic, structural and cultural inequalities.

With regard to the content of education, Murphy et al. state that the comprehensive secondary school 'should be clear about the knowledge, skills and understanding it expects all of its learners to develop': 'Less-advantaged and lower-attaining pupils should have access to the powerful knowledge of academic disciplines and subjects, just as more advantaged young people need access to less academic types of learning' (p. 202). The implication of this is that two of the central concepts of CfE – personalisation and choice – should not be allowed to dominate. All pupils deserve to experience a common curriculum: the development of separate tracks or pathways, with different statuses, undermines the comprehensive principle. Furthermore, teachers as well as learners should be empowered to make a real contribution to policy and practice. Their voices need to be heard, not as a token gesture during carefully managed 'consultation' exercises, but as a regular part of their professional work, contributing to the evolution and improvement of the system as a whole. Finally, the authors stress that 'A sound knowledge base and capacity for independent scrutiny are essential to a successful comprehensive system' (p. 203). They call for 'systematic data collection and analysis, transparency and peer review' (p. 204) and contrast such an approach with that of the 'positional authority' of the inspectorate, which has been a major influence on policy in the past.

Taken together, these recommendations would not lead to a radical transformation of secondary schooling in Scotland, but they would help to refine and improve a system that has been slow to adapt and disinclined to think critically about its underlying purposes. It would be wrong to place the main responsibility for this on conservative teachers, resistant to the demands of CfE. Greater responsibility should be attributed to the leaders of the educational policy community in Scotland (politicians, bureaucrats, professionals), who too often have failed to engage with challenging questions of meaning and purpose, and have proceeded without proper regard to the substantial body of evidence relating to learning, curricular innovation, professional development and institutional change.

## REFERENCES

Education Scotland (2012) *Quality and Improvement in Scottish Education: Trends in Inspection Findings 2008–2011*. Online at http://dera.ioe.ac.uk/14912/7/QISE_tcm4-722667_Redacted.pdf

Education Scotland (2017) *Quality and Improvement in Scottish Education 2012–2016*. Online at https://education.gov.scot/Documents/QuISE_full_2012_16_web.pdf

HMIE (2009) *Improving Scottish Education: A Report by HMIE on Inspection and Review 2005–2008*. Online at http://dera.ioe.ac.uk/8777/7/ise09_Redacted.pdf

Humes, W. (2013) Curriculum for Excellence and interdisciplinary learning. *Scottish Educational Review*, 45 (1), 82–93.

Mental Health Foundation (2016) *Mental Health in Scotland: Fundamental Facts 2016*. Online at https://www.mentalhealth.org.uk/file/1750/download?token=TGrdFSpM

Murphy, D., Croxford, L., Howieson, C. and Raffe, D. (2015). *Everyone's Future: Lessons from Fifty Years of Scottish Comprehensive Schooling*. London: IoP Press/Trentham Books.

OECD (2015) *Improving Schools in Scotland: An OECD Perspective*. Online at https://www.oecd.org/education/school/Improving-Schools-in-Scotland-An-OECD-Perspective.pdf

OECD (2016) *Trends Shaping Education Spotlight 8. Mind the Gap: Inequity in Education*. Online at www.oecd.org/edu/ceri/spotlight8-Inequality.pdf

Paterson, H. (1983) 'Incubus and ideology: The development of secondary schooling in Scotland 1900–1939', in W. M. Humes and H. M. Paterson (eds.), *Scottish Culture and Scottish Education, 1800–1980*. Edinburgh: John Donald.

Paterson, L. (2003) *Scottish Education in the Twentieth Century*. Edinburgh: Edinburgh University Press.

ScotCen (2015) *The Identification of Effective Secondary Schools in Challenging Circumstances*. Online at http://scotcen.org.uk/media/563157/effective-schools-summary.pdf

# 5

# The Independent Sector

*John Edward*

## INTRODUCTION

Scotland's independent schools are, as a recent Cabinet Secretary for Education put it, part of the 'rich tapestry' (www.journalonline.co.uk/News/1007992.aspx#.WigOV0tpGi4) of the Scottish education system. Some schools can trace their origins to the early centuries of the Scottish kingdom. Others are the products of mercantile philanthropy in the seventeenth and eighteenth centuries, some of the classical and progressive thinking of the Enlightenment and Victorian times. Yet more are the products of post-Second World War changes in education, particularly those of the 1970s. All retain the same commitment to autonomy, diversity and choice: whether single-sex or mixed, day or boarding, all-through or preparatory, urban or rural, selective or not. As a result, the independent sector of education cuts a particular path in Scotland. It does not correspond to the pattern or structure of state education, divided across local authorities, nor is it confined to one geographical area. Indeed, many pupils will cross school authority boundaries every day. It provides preschool, primary, secondary and additional support needs education for young people aged 3–18 across Scotland. The membership of the majority of independent schools of the Scottish Council of Independent Schools (SCIS) has helped to sustain a corporate sense of identity and participation, common purpose and shared professional development in Scotland.

The change that Scottish school-age education has undergone in the last decade, while not unprecedented, is all-encompassing. In part, this is the natural result of the devolution of parliamentary power to Scotland in 1999, but it is also an indication of the pace of change in education worldwide. While autonomous in their teaching, learning and governance, independent schools have felt the impact of all of these developments. Some, like the review and design of the new National Qualifications by the Scottish Qualifications Authority (SQA), have been met with engagement well beyond the proportionate size of the sector. However, schools have also had to deal with additional developments specific to them, including the creation of the Office of the Scottish Charity Regulator (OSCR) and its specific testing of public benefit in independent schools; recent General Teaching Council for Scotland (GTCS) requirements for the registration of teachers qualified outside Scotland; or the introduction of a points-based 'tiered' immigration system which affects both boarding school pupils (Tier 4) and teachers and other school staff from outside the European Union (EU) (as of 2017).

## THE INDEPENDENT SECTOR IN DETAIL

The definition of an independent school was formally established in the Education (Scotland) Act 1980 (www.legislation.gov.uk/ukpga/1980/44/pdfs/ukpga_19800044_en.pdf) as 'a school at which full-time education is provided for pupils of school age (whether or not such education is also provided for pupils under or over that age), not being a public school or a grant-aided school', and subsequently amended by the School Education (Ministerial Powers and Independent Schools) (Scotland) Act 2004. All independent schools in Scotland are required, in accordance with the 1980 Act, to be registered with the Registrar of Independent Schools. The Registrar, originally an official of the Scottish Government appointed by the Scottish ministers, is now a post within Education Scotland, the public agency established in 2011 by bringing together the responsibilities of Her Majesty's Inspectorate of Education (HMIE) and Learning and Teaching Scotland.

Data from the school year of 2016–17 shows there are 29,647 pupils in independent schools in Scotland (www.scis.org.uk). SCIS represents around 97 per cent of those pupils in more than seventy schools which are located in twenty-two of the thirty-two education authorities in Scotland. Scattered and diverse though the sector may be, its pupils place the sector numerically between the seventh and eighth largest education authorities in Scotland. They therefore represent a significant proportion of young people in school education in Scotland. Independent schools are particularly prevalent in the City of Edinburgh (where they represent at least 25 per cent of the total pupil population at secondary level), in the cities of Glasgow, Aberdeen and Dundee, and in Perth and Kinross, with the remainder mostly in other areas in the central belt (see SCIS website). There are no independent schools in the local authority area of Highland or the Western and Northern Isles of Scotland, while small Additional Support Needs (ASN) schools are often located in more rural locations.

The geographical diversity of the sector is matched by the diversity of types of schools. The independent sector offers parents not only an alternative to education authority schools but also a range of choice within the sector. A large majority of the schools are co-educational, reflecting the long-standing tradition of co-education in Scotland; there remain several girls-only schools and one boys-only school. Most of the schools are all-through schools, offering education from age 3 to 18, whilst some are senior or junior. In recent years, consistently 10 per cent of the pupils in independent schools are boarders – over twenty mainstream schools offer boarding provision, while more than ten ASN schools, catering for physical, behavioural, emotional and social support, offer residential care.

## DIVERSITY OF SCHOOLS

Scottish independent schools have many ideals in common. The sector has a strong tradition of academic attainment, positive leaver destinations ($c.90$ per cent go on to higher education), individual pupil focus, sound discipline and a commitment to a wide range of sporting, cultural and extra-curricular activities. Many of the schools combine their own long-established traditions with modern approaches, in an effort to prepare young people to become active and useful members of society, or – to use the language of Curriculum for Excellence (CfE) – 'responsible citizens' and 'effective contributors'. The blend of the traditional and modern approaches is often reflected in the physical environment of the schools, many of which are located in (at times challenging) historic buildings, which house more modern and high-tech facilities.

Pupils in independent schools are encouraged to discover and develop their talents and to pursue new interests through clubs and societies, sport, music, drama, outdoor pursuits, and community and voluntary activities. They are encouraged to undertake community and voluntary work to support those who are less fortunate and to play an active part in their local community. They are also encouraged to become 'global citizens' through international education programmes, supported by exchange opportunities, visits abroad and programmes such as the Model United Nations – an educational simulation of diplomacy, international relations and the United Nations.

It is interesting to speculate why these schools, some of which have been providing education for hundreds of years, have managed to thrive and are still so popular in the twenty-first century. One key aspect is that independent schools are just that – independent – and thereby in autonomous control of their own resources and able to plan strategically for the future, to raise the resources needed and to implement those plans directly. Being independent of local and central government gives the schools the freedom and flexibility to adapt to changing circumstances, the ability to respond to new initiatives, to develop specialist and school-specific expertise, and to use their resources to meet the needs of current generations while anticipating the needs of learners yet to come.

Although the independent sector can be seen as a group and sector distinct in itself, it is important to recall that each school has its own character and ethos. Some will be based on the principles of founders or past school leaders; others may draw on a more specific faith or philosophy. In choosing an independent school for their child, it is essential for parents and pupils to visit several schools, to meet pupils and staff, and to understand the rhythms and approaches of each school. First-time parents often seek advice from SCIS and from the London-based associate body, the Independent Schools Council (ISC), about choosing a school and about questions to ask when they visit (see ISC website). Websites and open days have all but replaced the traditional prospectuses that schools used to produce.

## FEES

Although average fees at primary, secondary and boarding are lower than elsewhere in the UK, they remain a significant demand on parental and wider family income (see SCIS website). Undoubtedly parents do much soul searching before they make the commitment to paying fees, possibly for as long as thirteen years (or more if using a school nursery), or often for the six years of secondary education, while some will opt for the initial seven years of primary education after which they will review and assess the position. Most families tend not to break the commitment once a pupil has settled happily into school. At one end of the spectrum, there will be parents who can afford fees due to their high earning capacity; at the other end of the spectrum significant and growing numbers of young people receive means-tested free or assisted places. Although some means-tested fee assistance is offered to pupils in junior or primary schools, most awards tend to be offered at the stage of entry to the senior school, and in many schools an increasing percentage of secondary pupils will be in receipt of means-tested fee assistance. Likewise, at every school there will be large numbers of parents who do not ask for help but who make personal sacrifices themselves, use their savings or those of the wider family, take advantage of fee planning services and make difficult choices in order to afford an independent school for their child. Consistent pupil numbers and school results suggest that fees represent value for money in the eyes of the families who have chosen this route. The costs are broadly comparable to the cost of educating a child in an education authority school (see SCIS website). It can be argued that parents are thereby paying twice for education, through the taxation system and through school fees. Nevertheless, a child's education can be seen as possibly the most important investment that a family can make.

## BURSARY PROVISION AND CHARITABLE STATUS

Most independent schools are charities and many have long histories, with some founda-tions stretching back several hundred years. The oldest schools, still bearing the names of their founders, were set up to help those for whom education was not accessible before a national education system was established in the late nineteenth century. Even when there was an entitlement to a state education for every child, the independent foundations continued, dependent on endowments, raising fee income or government grant. Individual school histories record the history of independent education, the interesting factor being the schools' ability to survive change and to adapt to new situations. In the latter part of the twentieth century, independent schools again found themselves in the position of becoming fully independent when grant-aided and direct grant status was discontinued in the 1970s, followed by the termination of the Assisted Places Scheme by the Labour Government after 1997. Once again the schools were required to reassess their position and almost immediately embarked on fundraising initiatives to support children of parents who would not otherwise be able to pay the fees. These efforts have enabled the schools to maintain their communities of pupils from diverse social backgrounds, with a wide cultural, social and ethnic mix.

Independent schools are not restricted to taking pupils from a predefined catchment area and can use their endowment and other funds to award bursaries to those for whom the fees would be out of reach. During the debate on the Charities and Trustee Investment (Scotland) Act 2005, on the reform of charity law in Scotland, it became clear that inde-pendent schools wished to retain their charitable ethos in tune with the purposes for which they were originally founded. The debate in the Scottish Parliament on the passage of the preceding Bill produced some sharply divided views about the nature of independ-ent schools. Some took the view that independent schools were a 'dis-benefit' to society because they perpetuated inequalities and their benefit was restricted to those able to pay fees. Supporters of independent education took the opposite view, namely that the schools enrich society, that in a democratic country parents have the right to choose the school that is best for their child and that public benefit was demonstrable. The debate reflected the fact that objections to independent education tend to be on political or social grounds rather than on educational grounds. The Charities Act confirmed that the advancement of education was a charitable activity, the new factor being that charities were required to demonstrate that they provide public benefit. Under the legislation, all charities, including independent schools, were required to meet a charity test in order to remain on the Charity Register, overseen by the OSCR. In 2005, the funds distributed in scholarships and bursa-ries by independent schools were worth an estimated £12.5 million a year and, taking into account the savings to the public purse of educating 31,500 children, figures compiled by SCIS for the independent sector in Scotland estimated that they saved the exchequer over thirty-five times as much as they received in non-domestic rates reductions and other relief (estimated at £4.5 million a year in 2005). By 2016, the amount of overall financial assistance provided by schools was in excess of £40 million, the majority of that being means-tested fee assistance, as demonstrated to OSCR in the individual reports on each school charity. In addition, a substantial amount of other public benefit is derived from the sharing with local authority schools and other bodies of school staff and resources, subject teaching, teacher support for national examinations, and the wide-scale provision of school facilities at little or no public cost.

The analysis of comparable costs with education authorities reflects similarities in the way that schools are structured, whether fee-paying or otherwise. School costs are labour dominated and salaries and wages form almost 70 per cent of the overheads, with utilities an increasing and fixed cost. Teachers in the independent sector are paid either in close relation to the national salary scales (Scottish Negotiating Committee for Teachers) or a modest percentage above the national scales, particularly in boarding schools where pastoral and extra-curricular roles are combined with classroom teaching. One key difference between independent and local authority schools is the pupil–teacher ratio which is favourable in the independent sector. SCIS statistics show that the average pupil teacher ratio across all independent schools in 2016 was 8.6:1, while the Summary Statistics for Schools in Scotland published by the Scottish Government in 2016 show the average pupil teacher ratio across all local authority schools was 13.7:1. In the independent sector, salaries, wages and all other costs have to be met from fees, whereas published education authority costs exclude a number of factors, including costs met centrally by the authorities such as support for learning and transport, and the very significant cost of capital building programmes.

## STRUCTURE OF EDUCATION

Although distinctive, most independent schools in Scotland reflect the structure of education authority schools, offering seven years of primary and six years of secondary education. As indicated earlier, many also have an integrated preschool department, thereby offering education to pupils from age 3 to age 18. The educational agenda in independent schools is not likely to differ significantly from the agenda in other schools, as the majority of pupils still sit the same SQA National Qualifications as other pupils in Scotland. The national priorities of literacy and numeracy, interpersonal skills, citizenship, enterprise, child protection and wellbeing, ecology and information technology feature in all schools.

For the most part, independent schools in Scotland present pupils for the Scottish system, in particular National 4 and 5, Highers and Advanced Highers. The Advanced Higher qualification has proved popular in Scotland and its increasing recognition south of the border has helped to strengthen the rigour of the Scottish sixth year, when pupils can develop independent learning skills and prepare for further and higher education. In independent schools, over 80 per cent of pupils stay on for a sixth year, which means that a disproportionate number of presentations for Highers and Advanced Highers come from the independent sector. Statistics produced by SCIS and by the SQA indicate consistently good results from independent schools at the key stages of S5 and S6. In 2016, 92.3 per cent of candidates achieved A–C passes at Higher, compared to 77.2 per cent in all Scottish schools; and 55.3 per cent of all Higher entries were awarded an A. In the same year, the number of pupils achieving A–C pass rates in National 5 reached 94.6 per cent of entries, compared to 79.4 per cent across all schools. Of that number, 68.1 per cent achieved an A grade. Of all Advanced Higher entries, 16.2 per cent came from SCIS schools, with a pass rate of 99.3 per cent, and 53.3 per cent achieving an A grade. It could be argued that the figures are not comparing like with like, given that independent schools can select their pupils and are not restricted to a specific catchment area. Whilst comparisons between local authority and independent schools in the same area also favour independent schools, the focus on the individual learner's development is as important to families as academic results alone.

Some of the most well-known independent schools in Scotland are boarding schools, which enjoy a worldwide international reputation – necessary to compete in what is now a fully global market. Whilst the popularity and demand for boarding education has declined in recent years, there will always be a need for boarding schools by parents who frequently move location and who are seeking security and stability for their child in a family atmosphere. More recently, boarding has become popular with families where both parents have significant work and other commitments. Scottish boarding schools also attract international boarding pupils from around the world seeking a British education. The structure in mainstream boarding schools in Scotland tends to reflect the independent school system in England and many of the Scottish boarding schools offer the English system of examinations, at General Certificate of Secondary Education (GCSE) and A level; some also offer the International Baccalaureate. Comparable Scotland-wide analysis of International Baccalaureate, A Level and GCSE results is not available although individual results for each participating school are. Each year the ISC releases A Level and International Baccalaureate results and Scottish independent schools are included in the data produced, although not disaggregated specifically at a Scottish level (see ISC website).

## SCHOOL PHILOSOPHY

Independent schools regularly review their curriculum, with a view to offering an intellectual challenge that is appropriate to pupils' abilities, alongside an education that can teach social, moral and emotional values. Independent schools are not swayed by current trends in education and will, for example, choose to retain subjects such as Classics, if they can justify the value of learning and teaching such disciplines. To date, independent schools are resisting the fall in presentations for Scottish qualifications in subjects such as physics, chemistry, biology, economics and, in particular, modern foreign languages, which they recognise are crucial to the broadest possible career choice and to a vibrant, dynamic economy. Independent schools will, wherever possible, offer subjects that are considered to be important to society and relevant to current needs, as well as providing the broadest possible subject choice for diverse pupils.

Contrary perhaps to public perceptions, independent schools do not just cater for the most academic children. Very few independent schools are fully academic selective. Testing forms part of the application process, especially for those schools with strong waiting lists, but test results are used as much to be sure that schools can meet each individual child's educational needs and to decide how those needs can best be met. When selecting their pupils, the schools are looking as much for potential as for ability, both academically and in areas such as sport, art, music and debating, so that talents can be encouraged and developed. Many of the mainstream schools offer substantial learning support and many have their own style of curriculum, for example schools modelled on the Kurt Hahn philosophy, or Rudolph Steiner schools or specialist schools for music.

The most popular entry stages tend to be at nursery (ages 3 and 4), at ages 5 and 11 (day schools) and at ages 13 and 16 (boarding schools). Although most children in Scotland start school in the year when their fifth birthday falls between 1 March and 28 February, each independent school has its own policy. Applications for entry at the start of a new school year (late August for day schools and early September for boarding schools) are made during the autumn months of the previous year, to give schools sufficient time to process applications and organise entrance assessments. Assessments and interviews are usually held in the spring term and, although this varies from school to school, schools in the same city or region will generally seek to coordinate dates for open days, entry offers and so on.

There are growing numbers of independent special schools in Scotland, mainly residential over fifty-two weeks of the year, that cater for young people with specific disabilities (such as autism, visual or hearing impairment) and for young people with emotional, social and behavioural difficulties. In most cases, although not all, these pupils are referred to the school by the local education authority or by social services and are funded by their local authority. The special independent schools' community provides a valuable service for families of young people who are not suited to mainstream schooling, despite the shift in recent years to mainstream students with particular needs.

## PUBLIC POSITION

A survey for the ISC by Populus in 2011 (https://www.isc.co.uk/media-enquiries/news-press-releases-statements/more-parents-than-ever-favour-independent-education/) indicated that approximately one third of parents in Scotland would send their child to an independent school if they could afford the fees, while approximately one half said they would not. This figure remains consistently lower than that for England and Wales where almost 50 per cent said they would send their child to an independent school if they could afford the fees. There have always been a smaller proportion of independent schools in Scotland than in England and the absence of independent schools in many parts of Scotland eliminates the choice for families in those areas.

There are undoubtedly parents in Scotland who can afford to pay school fees and who choose not to, either because they are against fee-paying education in principle, perhaps because they have no experience of independent education, or because they choose to spend their money differently. A YouGov survey for *The Times* in 2016 (https://www.theti mes.co.uk/article/private-schools-should-lose-tax-breaks-and-charitable-status-7rh6tx8jc) showed that over 40 per cent of Scots thought independent schools should no longer be classed as charities, while 7 per cent of those polled thought such schools should be banned altogether. There are also parents who may choose an independent school reluctantly, as it goes 'against the grain', but they consider it to be in the best interest of their child.

It is important for independent schools, individually and for the sector as a whole, to be aware of, and responsive to, the complex reasons why parents may choose an independent school. SCIS questionnaires to parents have shown that examination results, facilities and social networks come low in considerations; rated below the individual attention given to a child, small classes, good discipline, clearly defined values and realisation of the child's potential. Around 50 per cent of parents are 'first time buyers' of independent education, not having attended an independent school themselves. Parents indicate that they value a close partnership with their child's school and seek a core set of values or an ethos that will reflect and support their particular family environment. At the same time, the nature of the relationship between school and family, reinforced by the presence of parental contracts signed prior to admission, binds all parties to seeking actively the successful academic, extra-curricular and developmental outcomes for the pupils concerned.

Education Scotland inspection reports comment not only on academic standards but also on climate and relationships, on expectations, on promoting achievement and equality, leadership, and on the quality of the school's partnership with parents and with the local community. The approach of early engagement and a focus on attainment that is currently being promoted in Scotland is familiar in the independent sector for pupils with a broad range of learning outcomes. A caring pastoral environment is particularly important for schools with residential provision where children are away from home either because of family circumstances or because they have been referred to the school by their local authority as children with particular additional support needs.

## TEACHING IN THE INDEPENDENT SECTOR

The ethos of achievement that is prevalent in independent schools extends beyond the pupils and their families to the teaching and support staff. Teachers in independent schools are required to have a university degree and a recognised teaching qualification. Schools attract well-qualified, highly skilled and talented teachers who are subject to the necessary safe recruitment checks prior to appointment and thereafter. As a result of the passage of the Education (Scotland) Act in 2016, all teachers in the independent sector will in due course require to be registered with the GTCS. The Scottish Council of Independent Schools has worked with schools and the GTCS to ensure staff are supported in meeting those requirements through specific professional learning. Although the independent sector is not part of the national Induction Scheme for probationers in Scotland, many newly qualified teachers welcome the opportunity to undertake their probationary year in an independent school on the same basis as teachers in the Induction Scheme. In many cases, this will lead to an offer of employment within that school.

Teachers in the independent sector in Scotland are supported through their probationary year and throughout their professional career by the extensive SCIS programme of professional learning and development (see SCIS website). The SCIS professional learning programme encourages teachers to keep their skills up to date, to work closely with teachers from other schools and to share good practice across the sector. Around eighty workshops, seminars and conferences, designed for both teaching and support staff, take place annually at venues around Scotland. Topics cover a broad range of educational management, teaching, care and welfare, and administrative areas. One of the strengths of independent schools is the quality and commitment of the staff who readily contribute to the wide programmes of extra-curricular activities offered during the school day, after school, in the evenings, at weekends and sometimes during the holidays. Teachers are supported by highly skilled and committed administrative and care staff for which a similar extensive Continuing Professional Development (CPD) programme is offered.

Teachers from the independent sector make a significant contribution to the work of national educational bodies in Scotland such as the SQA and other organisations. The recent design and review of CfE and National Qualifications saw the involvement of a disproportionate number of independent school teachers. Teachers move between the independent and education authority sectors continuously and maintain contact with colleagues through subject associations, national working parties and other professional groupings.

The teaching and support staff in schools also establish close inter-agency links with health professionals, social workers, Police Scotland and other community bodies, especially given the growing requirements of national programmes including *Getting it Right for Every Child* (GIRFEC), the delivery of school-age immunisations such as seasonal influenza and Human Papilloma Virus (HPV), or 'Prevent' – a duty placed on schools by the Counter-Terrorism and Security Act 2015 on preventing children and young people from being drawn into terrorism.

## REGULATION AND INSPECTION

Independent schools have to be registered with the Registrar of Independent Schools, a position appointed by Scottish ministers that now sits within Education Scotland. Unlike England and Wales, schools are subject to the same inspections by HMIE, located within Education Scotland, as local authority schools. In addition, given the substantial diversity and autonomy within the sector, independent schools now receive Quality Improvement and Professional Engagement (QUIPE) visits from Education Scotland. The Care Inspectorate inspects the care provision for preschool and after-school activities and for pupils in schools with residential accommodation, as School Care Accommodation Services. Care Inspectorate reports are public documents and reflect the ethos and high standards generally found across the sector. The schools have their own quality assurance systems and receive advice and guidance from SCIS and from the professional associations to which their heads, bursars and governors belong – updated with each successive change in regulation, guidance or primary law such as the Children and Young People Act of 2014 (www.legislation.gov. uk/asp/2014/8/contents/enacted). As most of the schools are charities, they are required to prepare and submit accounts according to the recommended practice laid down for charities and the requirements of the Office of the Scottish Charities Regulator, as mentioned earlier. The schools are primarily accountable to the pupils and their parents with whom they develop close relationships through the head, the teachers, the guidance system, the school council and parental liaison groups. The importance to schools of the autonomous governance provided by school boards – acting as charity trustees as well as directors of the limited company, and employers – cannot be underestimated and, unlike in England, there is no equivalent in local authority schools.

## CONCLUSION

It is interesting to reflect on the position of the independent sector in Scotland since devolution and on whether the perspective towards the independent sector has changed. Numerically the sector is remarkably stable having had 30,000–32,000 pupils for almost two decades. Within the sector there have been occasional changes, mainly in the form of closures of small proprietor-owned schools, which found it difficult to meet the challenge of providing an increasingly diverse curriculum across a broad spectrum of academic ability, together with rising costs and the increasing burden of regulation.

Qualitatively, the independent sector is highly regarded by educationalists in school, further and higher education, employers and other professionals. Despite varying views on fee-paying education, the sector appears to be widely respected and accepted across the political spectrum as part of the Scottish education system. This is reflected in an outward-looking approach. Independent schools are now represented on bodies such as the Scottish

Qualifications Authority Advisory Council, the Curriculum for Excellence Management Board, the GTSC and the Scottish Teachers' Pension Scheme Advisory Board, along with a range of other working groups.

Independent schools, both mainstream and ASN, are always willing to cooperate and work in partnership with local authorities, individual schools and pupils, and the Scottish Government. A key feature of all of schools is that independence for them indicates autonomy, but not distance or isolation from teaching and learning in Scotland – the advancement of which is the shared objective of the Scottish Government, Parliament and all the independent schools in SCIS. A review of the independent sector published on the SCIS website in 2014 restated the view that the independent sector neither would nor should shrink from the policy questions and challenges that lay ahead, nor should it be a silent presence in any discussion about children and young people in Scotland. Just as for the country itself, the relative size of the sector does not make it any less diverse, opinionated or multiform.

## WEBSITES

Care Inspectorate at www.careinspectorate.com/index.php/index.php/care-services/
Charities and Trustee Investment (Scotland) Act 2005 at www.legislation.gov.uk/asp/2005/10/contents
Charities and Trustee Investment (Scotland) Bill at www.parliament.scot/parliamentarybusiness/Bills/25928.aspx
Education Scotland at https://education.gov.scot/what-we-do/inspection-and-review
Education (Scotland) Act 2016 at www.legislation.gov.uk/asp/2016/8
Independent Schools Council at www.isc.co.uk
OSCR review of schools at www.oscr.org.uk/charities/managing-your-charity/reviews-of-charitable-status/charitable-status-reviews-schools
Scottish Council of Independent Schools at www.scis.org.uk
Scottish Government at www.gov.scot/Topics/Education/Schools/Parents/independentschools
Summary Statistics for Schools in Scotland, No: 7-2016, at www.gov.scot/Publications/2016/12/9271

# 6

# Scottish Further Education

*Patrick O'Donnell and Mark Murphy*

## INTRODUCTION

Scottish further education (FE) can never be accused of being unyielding and monolithic. Over the last two decades, FE colleges in Scotland have continually been responding and realigning themselves (in both similar and idiosyncratic ways) to the emerging socio-economic policies, challenges and markets and through this process they have become complex and multilayered institutions. They have evolved to become key agents in developing the skills base of the economy by providing vocational programmes for new entrants to the labour market and by integrating with leading employee programmes, both of which help to modernise the skills of the workforce. The sector has long been recognised as central and effective agents in the delivery of lifelong learning and social inclusion objectives. It has been proactive in realising the policy aspirations outlined in Curriculum for Excellence (CfE, although admittedly at the time of writing there is a lacuna in research on the scope and nature of the relationship between FE and CfE). However, in recent years the nature and character of Scottish FE has been challenged. In July 2012, the Scottish Government (2012a) report *Reinvigorating College Governance: The Scottish Government Response to the Report of the Review of Further Education Governance in Scotland* outlined a radical new structure for the Scottish FE sector and, within a year of this announcement, its overall impact had been unparalleled, creating seismic changes. The transformations can be viewed as a response to a range of separate and intersecting factors, including global, socio-economic and political pressures and agendas. However, the core message from government rhetoric is that the sector should be fully comprehensible in terms of role, identity and accountability. The newly emerging paradigm for FE governance – a reform process referred to as 'regionalisation' – has clearly overturned previous structural and governance arrangements, reconfiguring the Scottish FE landscape into thirteen regions, each with its own FE provider. The restructuring has led to the number of incorporated colleges decreasing from thirty-seven in 2012 to twenty in 2014–15 (Auditor General, 2016). The overall transition from operating as separate autonomous FE institutions to operating within a larger regional collective is now complete; however, the performativity scripts and accountability measures are still evolving and embedding within the newly structured sector.

The policy rhetoric advancing the need for reform offers a clear sense of a radical 'modernising project' for the Scottish FE landscape. The newly emergent policy agenda is linked to a drive to improve accountability, efficiency and effectiveness with the need to reduce duplication (rationalisation) being singled out. Considering the history of Scottish FE, the drive for better efficiency and effectiveness is not new, but what is innovative is how the prescribed policy solution breaks with traditional privileges through the adoption of regional architecture aimed to give far more centralised control. Under the regionalisation paradigm, the Scottish FE sector is better placed, so the argument follows, to develop highly skilled and flexible human capital as well as enhancing social capital. This modernising project for the Scottish FE sector can be seen as part of a larger transnational scheme involving Scotland's sense of national identity and place in the European context. The reforms are underpinned by the argument that a sustainable economic future for Scotland can only be achieved through collective wisdom, collective effort and shared vision on the challenges ahead, and the role FE will play in ensuring Scotland's social and economic successes. The need to foster flexible and well-educated citizens to cope with rapid economic and technological development and change has been stressed repeatedly within the policy rhetoric.

This chapter offers an exploration of the recent developments unfolding within the Scottish FE sector, and placing them against a backdrop of previous governance developments taking hold from the early 1990s. It considers the main driving forces and legitimising discourses behind the current restructuring of the Scottish FE sector and argues that the reform process commonly referred to as 'regionalisation' will help to create a unifying narrative for the sector through new and tighter levels of centralised control. It is argued that by recognising and unpacking the political drivers and discourses we come to see how they reconstruct and delineate FE. However, although the regional architecture is now clearly visible, the unfolding cultural shifts and adjustments taking place mean that any contemporary readings and analysis of the Scottish FE reforms can only be a partial account. As such the following is simply a snapshot of a newly evolving sector enacting new policy reforms and imperatives.

## POST-INCORPORATION GOVERNANCE: CREATING CONDITIONS FOR DIVERSITY

To grasp the magnitude of the regionalisation agenda, one has to place it against the cultural and structural changes ushered in under the 1992 Further and Higher Education (Scotland) Act. Under that Act, the Scottish Office took overall responsibility for and control over colleges from local authorities. This process, known as 'incorporation', ended a period of almost five decades of local authority control resulting in individual colleges becoming self-governing institutions responsible for managing their own affairs (from April 1993). Under the aegis of incorporation, colleges were said to be set free, liberated from the suffocating constraints of local authority control – a relationship that was seen to strangle innovation in the FE sector – and become independent corporate bodies with considerable freedoms to decide their future trajectories. However, these freedoms were accompanied by new and intense levels of accountability and performativity measures. New funding arrangements designed to both reward and punish institutions according to their ability to meet certain predefined performance criteria were established, meaning that in many cases colleges confronted each other in a quasi-market where they were required to do more with less resources. The approach was rooted in an overarching neo-liberal agenda of opening up public services to market forces and private enterprise.

During the post-incorporation years, FE colleges' core mission was hence reconceptualised in terms of the market ethos, with strategic planning foregrounded. FE colleges appointed their own boards of governors and new senior management positions were created to govern – human resources management, estate management and accounting functions. Naturally, as the sector has attuned itself to its individual 'corporate identity', value for money and the need to see direct benefits to the organisation became more acute. Significantly, reforms under incorporation created fierce competition between Scottish colleges. As a consequence, the drive in diversifying revenue sources intensified. The concept of commercial enterprise increasingly found a foothold in the FE mindset. Incorporation was unlike any other change imposed upon Scottish FE in the past and, with the endless importation of non-contextualised business and commercial practices, it was inevitable that patterns of disharmony would emerge. Strategic planning increasingly focused on a formalised agenda wherein efficiency targets were prioritised at the cost of staff industrial relations. This was exacerbated when colleges moved away from national bargaining, leaving college senior managers to negotiate directly with staff. Significantly, the removal of national bargaining opened the way for more diverse and fragmented working practices to unfold within the sector. Arguably, this period witnessed an erosion of the more traditional unifying narratives on the role and purpose of the Scottish FE sector.

From the late 1990s onwards the political rhetoric on education started to mutate with the election of New Labour in 1997 and its Third Way politics. While neo-liberalism rested on a belief in the benefits of the free market, competition, individual freedom and, significantly, a minimal role for state intervention, 'Third Wayism' was more interested in creating conditions where equity and social justice were reinvigorated and combined with competitiveness and market policies. However, the extent to which 'Third Way politics' departed from the neo-liberal policies of the early to mid-1990s is much debated. As Ball (2007) notes, there have been both continuities and ruptures between neo-liberalism and the Third Way. What is clear is that New Labour policy reflected the importance of the post-compulsory sector contributing to Britain's competitive edge in the global market by producing and disseminating economically productive knowledge. Also from the late 1990s, the overarching mission and rhetoric of lifelong learning policy started to form part of the overall legitimising discourse of the requirement for the sector to expand learning opportunities and be more accessible to non-traditional learners, becoming more flexible in terms of developing qualification frameworks that meet the needs of individual learners, employers and industry. Significantly, there was a renewed emphasis on the need for post-compulsory education to become even more entrepreneurial by engaging in collaborative ventures with other agencies. Indeed, under New Labour Third Way politics, partnership became a powerful discourse in mobilising change. In many respects, colleges evolved (although in different ways and at different rates) to become more discursive, taking on a certain operational plasticity which meant that they were more receptive to repeated nuanced rebranding. The post-incorporation era (particularly under New Labour) can be seen as having ushered in a new entrepreneurial spirit, with FE increasingly delivering a range of higher education (HE) courses and collaborating more and more with universities on a range of access courses and degree delivery. Against New Labour commitment to opening up HE to more diverse groups of students and widening participation, the boundaries between FE and HE became more porous than at any other time in the past. This blurring was a significant contributory dynamic to the growing diversity and complexity of the Scottish FE sector.

When the Scottish National Party (SNP) formed a government in May 2007, the policy for post-16 education increasingly emphasised the importance of 'skills utilisation for economic growth' – perceived as one of the central pillars for underpinning the future goal of an independent Scotland. However, as Gallacher (2009) points out, the Scottish National Government policy trajectory for post-16 education from 2009 to 2012 did not focus solely on instrumental and utilitarian elements: the importance of the wider aspects of lifelong learning were also acknowledged and promoted. Thus, some of New Labour's key themes and imperatives continued to feature within FE under the SNP.

## TIME FOR CHANGE: SUPPLANTING THE OLD ORDER AND CONSTRUCTING A NEW LANDSCAPE

In January 2012, Professor Griggs (review chair) submitted his 113-page report, *Report of the Review of Further Education Governance in Scotland* (known within the Scottish context as the Griggs Review), to the Scottish Government (Scottish Government, 2012a). The review's remit was twofold. First, to consider whether current institutional governance arrangements in the college sector in Scotland deliver an appropriate level of democratic accountability; and secondly, to examine the structure of college governance and make recommendations for sector-wide change that would support the role of colleges in economic and social development. The report delivered across-the-board evaluation of the governance of the Scottish FE sector and incorporated the central messages articulated in the consultation documents *Putting Learners At The Centre: Delivering our Ambitions For Post-16 Education* (Scottish Government, September 2011) and *College Regionalisation: proposals for implementing 'Putting Learners at the Centre'* (Scottish Funding Council, November 2011).

To gain legitimacy and traction, the regionalisation agenda instinctively sought to call into question the established equilibria, habits, values, behaviour patterns and procedures of FE governance and management set in motion in the 1990s. Within the policy discourse outlining the new reforms for Scottish FE, we can detect explicit claims that the old governance order was outdated and below expectations in terms of sector accountability and coherence. The Griggs Review identified that the 'individualisation of colleges' had created 'inequalities and differences across Scotland' that are 'haphazard and not controlled or managed in any way' (Scottish Government, 2012a, pp. 18–19). Significantly, the Review highlighted how the review team found the Scottish FE sector 'not fit for purpose, and in need of fundamental reform'. As Griggs states (ibid., p. 60): 'Given the discontinuity and disharmony in the sector across many issues we believe that this report and its recommendations give a solid and consistent base that can form the foundation on which other things can and will evolve.'

In July 2012, the government published its response to the Griggs Review in a document called *Reinvigorating College Governance: the Scottish Government Response to The Report of the Review of Further Education Governance in Scotland* (Scottish Government 2012b). The signifier 'reinvigorating' evokes the idea that old FE governance arrangements set in place almost two decades ago were in need of an overhaul and a large infusion of vitality to meet the perceived social and economic challenges ahead. The report (ibid., p. 1) was explicit in its position: 'current governance arrangements are fundamentally flawed because they lack public accountability'.

The themes and overall policy trajectory outlined in the Scottish Government's response document are now very familiar to the FE sector and the regionalisation architecture is now fully embedded. The underpinning logic is clear: regionalisation aims to create conditions of coherent planning, collaboration and partnerships rather than diversity of vision and mission and fierce competition between institutions. Developing regional college provision was said to reduce duplication and increase efficiency through larger and more focused and networked colleges. FE provision would be delivered more effectively at a regional level through new partnership arrangements between other educational providers (schools and universities), local employers and other agencies and stakeholders including Scottish Funding Council (SFC) and government. Under the regionalisation hegemony the Scottish FE landscape has been radically changed, divided up into thirteen regions. The new paradigm has seen existing incorporated colleges reformed into two types: 'regional colleges' representing a merger of existing FE colleges and located within what is referred to as 'single-college regions', and 'assigned colleges' representing two or more colleges collaborating together to provide FE provision within what is termed 'multi-college' regions. At the time of writing there are ten 'single-college regions' and three 'multi-college' regions: see the regional map of FE in Appendix 2 of the Auditor General's (2016) report.

Each region has an overarching single body: the Further Education Regional Board (FERB). This is the focal point of engagement with FE regional partners and performs a number of activities including: planning FE provision strategically across the region; entering into the 'regional outcome agreement' with the SFC; and deciding how funding should be allocated and how efficiencies should be secured. Each FERB will have a chair who will be appointed by and report to government as well as negotiate with the SFC. Broadly speaking, the outcome agreements (operating on a three-year cycle) contain a number of commitments that seek to reflect national priority areas while also addressing specific regional needs. This approach – framed across both micro and macro measurable objectives – is intended to dissolve the multifaceted nature of the sector which has developed over the last two decades, while at the same time achieve more meaningful and intimate relationships between colleges and key stakeholders in advancing a range of imperatives. These include: increased accountability and confidence in the allocation of resources, ensuring that resources are concentrated where there is the greatest need; and continuous improvements to maximise college impact on the learner, the employer and the economy.

Each region has been allocated an outcome agreement manager (employed by and appointed by the SFC) who is tasked with coordinating linkages with all policy areas, ensuring all data and priority areas are accurately reflected within the outcome agreements. In ethnographical terms, the outcome agreement managers are firmly embedded within their allocated region, perceived as critical friends and having the authority to interpret policy imperatives for their regional board. On a wider horizon, they will work collectively with others, including Education Scotland and the College Development Network, to support development and disseminate good practice. What we have here is departure from the competitive, Darwinian survival of the fittest temperament and atomistic educational arrangements that characterised Scottish FE under incorporation. What we have now is a shift towards more universalistic and collective orientations. Under the regionalisation agenda, college principals and their respective boards no longer operate as single autonomous entities. Instead they now work with their respective regional board in devising strategy and responding to the outcome agreements. Consequently, the underlying reform is that the locus of power has shifted from college principals to the Scottish Government, via the FERBs. The logic is that the transformations stemming from the regionalisation agenda will create the governing architecture and networked conditions for a more cohesive, manageable and responsive FE sector to emerge.

Generally speaking, education is a deliberate, purposive activity aimed at the achievement of a range of ends which include the realisation of economic and social goals benefiting the individual and the community and nation. With respect to the criteria of being 'fit for purpose' we know from the regionalisation paradigm what the FE landscape will look like in terms of governance and structural arrangement. However, it is perhaps necessary to pose the question, 'What will the topography of the FE landscape look like in terms of overarching educational goals and imperatives?' In other words, 'What are the newly emerging mandates for FE in terms of developing and nurturing social and human capital?' With respect to identifying the evolution of overarching strategies, it is important to note that since 2012 a number of new reports have been published both augmenting and developing the vision already set out in *Putting Learners at the Centre: Delivering our Ambitions for post-16 Education* (Scottish Government, 2011). Currently, the FE outcome agreements are informed by the government response document, *Developing the Young Workforce – Scotland's Youth Employment Strategy* (Scottish Government, 2014a), which sets out how the Scottish Government will implement the recommendations from an earlier publication, *Education Working For All! Commission for Developing Scotland's Young Workforce Final Report* (Scottish Government, 2014b) (commonly called the Wood Report). This Developing the Young Workforce (DYW) strategy sets out a seven-year national plan which looks to improve the options on offer for young people, and reduce youth unemployment to the levels of the best-performing countries in Europe. Significantly, the strategy will also be pivotal in helping to re-establish a core narrative on the purpose and identity of the Scottish FE sector.

In July 2013, the Post–16 Education (Scotland) Bill was passed which provided the necessary legislative underpinning for the wider reforms to post-16 education currently being pursued, including the process of regionalisation. The emerging education policy in Scotland offers a discursive space for blending economic and social imperatives. On one level, the aspirations set out in the policies reflect an inward-looking gaze, focusing on shaping social and cultural life. The aspirations reflect a clear social–ethical dimension, seeking to foster and strengthen the bonds of a more civil and fairer society with closer communities – encapsulated in policy rhetoric on the need for better social cohesion, a 'better and fairer Scotland'. This inward-looking focus has been informed by the central threads of social capital theory which relates to the social interactions, values and networks that facilitate a sense of shared core understandings and collective action for mutual benefit. However, running in parallel with this we can see an outward-looking dynamic focusing on ensuring the Scottish education system is able to respond effectively to the multilayered and dynamic economic challenges created by globalisation. This response involves producing highly skilled and flexible human capital.

## EMERGING DISCOURSES

There is a strong case to argue that the Griggs Review publication and subsequent government response documents and statements created a pathologising effect. In these documents and reports the sector was depicted as 'infirm and unwell' and in need of urgent and drastic treatment. Within the regionalisation agenda there is an undeniable sense of a 'modernising project' unfolding, with the demand for better alignment, accountability, fairness and transparency surfacing to occupy a dominant position within the discourse framing discussions on the restructuring of the governance of the sector. There are overarching future-focused discourses, too: the sector needs reinvigoration to operate effectively in a new future where sector agility and responsiveness looms large. Naturally, there are other drivers and imperatives at play here. Within the policy discourse, the search for better accountability, fairness and transparency are accompanied by a stress on 'partnership', 'efficiency', 'resourcefulness' and 'effectiveness', with the latter being defined as the need for the sector to be more responsive to the emerging economic and social–cultural transformation. Human capital and social capital formation are certainly intimately embroiled, with policy discourses projecting a range of aspirations such as: 'responsible citizens', 'flexible workers' and 'self-actuated and self-directed lifelong learners' able to make connections between their own learning and its broader social, economic and global context.

The current reforms for governance have found the legitimacy to jettison old structural arrangements and radically reconfigure the boundaries by discursively employing a range of familiar policy imperatives and drivers to the FE sector. Policy steering has also been achieved by a number of recognisable levers to mobilise change, such as the allocation of funds on a sanction and reward basis and associated performativity scripts. The whole approach, especially where the outcome agreements are concerned, is participatory, inclusive and affirming the different actors within a network of new obligations and relations. In broad terms then, it is a discourse of economic sustainability and advancement, mixed with ethical undertones of fairness and egalitarianism, discursively employed to legitimise deep-rooted structural changes to the sector and in many instances simply underscore and buttress the trajectory of changes already set in train over the last two decades, such as the focus on student experience, widening access, and closer links with universities, schools, industry and employers. Indeed, the policy rhetoric on the role for post-16 education – in combating poverty, social exclusion through the creation of new pathways for educational success, and creating engaged, informed and responsible citizens – clearly draws on the ethical discourse underpinning social capital theory advanced by New Labour 'Third Wayism'. Moreover, notions of partnerships and collaboration have been a focal point within the current reconfiguration of post-16 education.

The restructuring of the sector involves the creation of new networks as well as the enforcement of new sources of power and legitimacy. Under the regionalisation template, universities, colleges, schools and other stakeholders will have a new synergy, cast in the role of 'interdependent delivery partners', operating within set geographical locations – what Coffield et al. (2007, p. 735) refer to as 'local ecologies'. Within this partnership and collaboration notion, we can detect an underlying mix of humanist and communitarian discourses at play, emphasising cooperative practices between educational organisations and rejecting what they perceive as the corrosive effects of working in isolation and in competition where the self-interest of individual leaders can dominate. Within the political sphere, however, 'partnership' is defined in a rather nebulous way, loosely seen within the realm of education as 'community of actors, stakeholders and organisations', blissfully striding towards achieving shared goals and common purpose. As Cardini (2006, p. 396) suggests: 'partnerships function as a magic concept; a concept that because of its links with other notions such as "networks", "cooperation" and "trust", sounds modern, neutral, pragmatic and positive'. Perhaps we need a cautionary note here, or even be a bit sceptical. As Arnott and Ozga (2010, p. 339) remind us: 'Discourse, in effect, creates and recreates that world by eliminating some possibilities and focusing on others.' This foregrounding and restricting strategy has been picked up by Cardini (2006) who argues that within the political discourse advocating partnerships and collaboration (often conflated), there resides a somewhat naive assumption that individuals within partnership arrangements meet as equals in a collaborative democratic decision-making process. In accepting Cardini's sentiments, it is inevitable that partnerships, especially newly formed multi-partnerships, can at times be characterised as a process of struggle for dominance among differing groups competing over the legitimisation of values and maps of meaning. In such cases, group members cannot be perceived as mere automatons, but agents within their own ideological, social and economic frameworks; as Fay (1996, p. 67) argues: 'Agency is a relative trait ... some people are more "agential" than others by virtue of their place in the social order, their social aptitudes, their disposition.' Thus, within these newly evolving FE partnerships created through regionalisation, old institutional mindsets, meanings and values, together with biographical and political differences amongst the main actors, are likely to surface to become crucial dynamics determining the sustainability for both the partner and the partnership. Indeed, when we contemplate the potential mechanisms able to deliver a broad synchronisation of the sector, the newly evolving partnership arrangements will be amongst the most compelling.

So where are we with the practicalities of regionalisation? At the time of writing, each of the thirteen FE regions is (re)forming new sensibilities that will help to shape a new operational culture and structure, one that embeds responsiveness and flexibility, resourcefulness and efficiency in meeting local, national and global imperatives and challenges. In terms of seeking new levels of vitality and coherence, FE colleges will inevitability be jettisoning old mindsets and anchoring new thinking and approaches to their cultural and operational practices. However, as stated earlier, although the regionalisation architecture is now a visible entity, the cultural and operational changes and associated challenges are still unfolding. As a recent Auditor General's (2016, p. 1) report on Scotland's colleges highlights: 'The college sector has continued to exceed activity targets but colleges are still adjusting to substantial changes that affect how they operate.' And yet, this is not the only challenge for the programme of reform. The report also noted certain oversights with reference to the government having in place transparent and robust measuring technologies and systems to assess and report all expected benefits from its programme of reform. Thus, there is (at the time of writing) evidence to suggest more work needs to be done in assessing and articulating the policy goals associated with regionalisation and mergers.

## CONCLUSION

During the post-incorporation years, the evolving Scottish FE sector has been dynamic in its outreach and outlook, constituted by expansive rhetoric, terms and signifiers such as, 'transformation(al)', 'competitiveness', 'partnership', 'flexibility', 'collaboration', 'networking', 'international reach' and 'enterprise and entrepreneurism'. Such terms have been deployed to describe and legitimise the organisational activities, as well as to mobilise new changes. Significantly, over the first decade of the twenty-first century, the dynamics of entrepreneurialism, partnership, collaboration and competition coexisted within the sector in a rather convoluted, paradoxical and open-textured way. Consequently, diverse contexts of practices, visions and missions have flourished, making it increasingly challenging to detect a clear consensus on the actual role and identity of the Scottish FE sector during this period.

Against the historical backdrop, regionalisation seeks to infuse new levels of coherence and unity through the construction of new geographical boundaries. Constructing new geographical boundaries or 'local ecologies' (Coffield et al., 2007) has taken place through the combined approaches of new levels of centralised control and accountability systems including newly evolving performativity scripts in the form of national and local outcome agreements. In many ways the newly emerging regionalisation agenda is cloaked in the familiar rhetoric of economic imperatives that was used to promote incorporation. But what is different is that the emphasis and focus of attention is now towards partnership and collaboration rather than individualisation and competition. Within this discourse, the collective identity construct of regionalisation is towards homogeneity and this sits starkly contrasted to the diversity of the FE sector created under incorporation. What is emerging here is a new architecture of governance and although it is radical and progressive in that it re-scales the sector and overturns traditional power relations, at a deeper structural level and in terms of continuity with the past, it is a structure that still embraces a concern with prudent fiscal control. As such, regionalisation also equates to rationalisation, saving in expenditure, reducing duplication and purging those elements that do not contribute effectively to the new overarching vision and mission. Consequently, despite the reported omissions (highlighted in the 2016 Auditor General's report), levels of surveillance, guidance and control loom large in the new governance paradigm and will be likely to grow and mutate to capture more and more data on activities. One intriguing aspect of the new structure is the way it brings together a multiplicity of actors and forms of managerialism within one domain. Given the scale and pace of change, operational tensions will materialise, especially where the pursuit of progress may depend upon a paradoxical intertwining of compulsion and consent by means of the allocation of funds on a sanction and reward basis.

## REFERENCES

Arnott, M. A. and Ozga, J. (2010) 'Education and nationalism: the discourse of education policy in Scotland', *Discourse*, 31 (3), 335–50.
Auditor General (2016) *Scotland's Colleges*. Online at www.audit-scotland.gov.uk/report/scotlands-colleges-2016
Ball, S. (2007) 'Leadership of academics in research', *Educational Management, Administration & Leadership*, 35 (4), 449–77.
Cardini, A. (2006) 'An analysis of the rhetoric and practice of educational partnerships in the UK: an arena of complexities, tensions and power', *Journal of Educational Policy*, 21 (4), 393–415.
Coffield, F., Edward, S., Finlay, I., Hodgson, A., Spours, K., Steer, R. and Gregson, M. (2007) 'How policy impacts on practice and how practice does not impact on Policy', *British Educational Research Journal*, 33 (5), 723–51.
Fay, B. (1996) *Contemporary Philosophy of Social Science*, London: Blackwell.
Gallacher, J. (2009) 'Higher education in Scotland's colleges: a distinctive tradition?', *Higher Education Quarterly*, 63 (4), 384–401.
Scottish Funding Council (2011) *College Regionalisation: Proposals for Implementing 'Putting Learners at the Centre'*. Edinburgh: Scottish Funding Council.
Scottish Government (2011) *Putting Learners at the Centre: Delivering our Ambitions for Post-16 Education*. Edinburgh: Scottish Government.
Scottish Government (2012a) *Report of the Review of Further Education Governance in Scotland*. Edinburgh: Scottish Government.

Scottish Government (2012b) *Reinvigorating College Governance: The Scottish Government Response to the Report of the Review of Further Education Governance in Scotland*. Edinburgh: Scottish Government.

Scottish Government (December 2014a) *Developing the Young Workforce – Scotland's Youth Employment Strategy*. Online at www.gov.scot/Publications/2014/12/7750

Scottish Government (June 2014b) *Education Working For All! Commission for Developing Scotland's Young Workforce Final Report*. Online at www.gov.scot/Publications/2014/06/4089

# 7

# Scottish Higher Education

*Walter Humes*

This chapter is divided into four sections. The first offers an overview of the higher education sector in Scotland, including its institutions and student numbers. The second section describes the teaching and research work of universities. In the third part, an attempt is made to relate current provision to earlier accounts of, and ongoing debates about, the contribution of higher education to the social and cultural life of Scotland. Finally, some topics which are likely to remain on the policy agenda for some time will be discussed. For a more detailed perspective on important policy issues (notably funding and governance), readers should consult the chapters in Section IX.

## INSTITUTIONS: HISTORY AND DIVERSITY

The higher education (HE) sector in Scotland consists of nineteen institutions: fifteen universities, the Open University in Scotland, Glasgow School of Art, the Royal Conservatoire of Scotland (previously the Royal Scottish Academy of Music and Drama) and Scotland's Rural College (previously the Scottish Agricultural College). Edinburgh College of Art was a separate institution until August 2011 when it merged with the University of Edinburgh. A significant proportion of work at higher education level is also offered in some further education (FE) colleges, often as part of an arrangement which allows students to transfer to degree courses at universities. Provision of this sort offers an important route for those students from 'non-traditional' backgrounds who may have left school with limited qualifications but who wish to re-enter education at a later stage.

Of the fifteen universities, four are 'ancient' dating from the fifteenth and sixteenth centuries: St Andrews (founded in 1411), Glasgow (1451), Aberdeen (1495) and Edinburgh (1582). The prestige of these institutions is reflected in their architecture (buildings represent an important symbolic statement), in their many distinguished graduates, and in the significant sources of income which they enjoy from endowments and donations. Following the Robbins report of 1963, which began a massive expansion of higher education across the United Kingdom, another four universities were created, three of these developing from existing institutions. Both Strathclyde in Glasgow and Heriot Watt in Edinburgh had strong prior histories, particularly in the fields of science, engineering and technology. Queen's College, Dundee, which became Dundee University, had been an integral part of St Andrews University before gaining independent status. One entirely new university (Stirling) was established in 1967, initially with an emphasis on liberal arts but gradually acquiring a broader portfolio of courses. A further phase of expansion took place three decades later, leading to a group often referred to as the 'post-1992' universities: Robert Gordon (Aberdeen), Glasgow Caledonian, Edinburgh Napier, Abertay (Dundee), West of Scotland (UWS – formerly the University of Paisley) and Queen Margaret (Edinburgh). All of these 'post-1992' universities developed from existing colleges and central institutions (the Scottish equivalent of English polytechnics). Starting in the same period, teacher education, which until then had taken place in specialist colleges of education, was gradually merged with the university sector: for example, Jordanhill College became part of Strathclyde University, and Moray House joined with Edinburgh University. The University of the Highlands and Islands (UHI), granted full university status in 2011, deserves particular mention. It consists of a partnership of thirteen colleges and research institutions covering a wide area in the north of Scotland, supported by seventy learning centres designed to make higher education available to students in remote areas.

Detailed statistics relating to UK higher education are compiled by the Higher Education Statistics Agency (www.hesa.ac.uk). These include information about age, gender, school (state/independent), level of study (undergraduate/postgraduate), mode of study (part/full-time), place of origin (home/overseas) and post-qualifying destination. The figures for 2014/15 show that in the UK as a whole, 2.3 million students were studying for a qualification or credit at 162 HE providers. In Scotland, there were 288,770 students (232,570 undergraduate and 56,200 postgraduate). These figures include students from Scotland, the rest of the UK, the European Union and other parts of the world. There was considerable variation in the size of student populations attending different Scottish universities. The largest were Edinburgh (28,800), Glasgow (26,815) and Strathclyde (21,210). These figures can be contrasted with those at Abertay (4,220), Queen Margaret (5,270) and UHI (7,850). A notable feature of the smaller institutions was that they had relatively few students studying at postgraduate level.

All of these universities have a collective voice through Universities Scotland and receive public funding from the Scottish Funding Council (SFC). Universities Scotland was founded in 1992 and describes itself as 'a membership organisation working for the Principals and Directors of Scotland's 19 higher education institutions' (www.universities-scotland.ac.uk). Its interests extend to 'all aspects of higher education activity in Scotland, from teaching and employability to research and knowledge exchange, from widening access to issues of internationalisation, funding, efficiency and government'. Universities Scotland operates as an autonomous national council of Universities UK (www.universitiesuk.ac.uk).

The SFC was established in 2005 with a remit to act as the national strategic body for funding teaching and learning, research and innovation in both the university and college sectors (www.sfc.ac.uk). It is responsible for investing around £1.5 billion of public money each year. In 2017, the Scottish Government sought to reduce the independence of the SFC by proposing that the SFC board should be dissolved and the work of the council subsumed under a single national board covering a number of economic agencies (Highlands and Islands Enterprise, Scottish Enterprise and Skills Development Scotland). This move was seen as a centralising 'power grab' which would reduce the capacity of those allocating HE funds to act as a buffer between the Scottish Government and individual universities. Following a lively debate in the Scottish Parliament, the proposal was rejected. It seems likely, however, that some form of overarching agency will be set up to coordinate the strategic direction of institutions with important economic functions. The SFC already attaches considerable importance to economic targets when negotiating 'outcome agreements' with universities. These agreements set out what colleges and universities are expected to deliver in return for the funding they receive. Critics argue that not all academic work should be valued in this way. They maintain that intellectual and cultural life will suffer if universities are only seen in terms of their economic output and their production of graduates for the workplace. Moreover, it is claimed that if government control of higher education increases, there may be negative implications for democracy.

It would be hard to maintain that all Scottish universities enjoy equal status. Their reputations depend on a number of factors: standards of admission and competition for places; the quality of teaching and research, as judged by the Quality Assurance Agency and the Research Excellence Framework (see below); their ability to attract and retain leading academics; the percentage of students gaining 'good' degrees (first class or upper second) and securing employment in graduate occupations; the number of students pursuing postgraduate courses; the facilities available to staff and students (accommodation, libraries, laboratories, information technology, social facilities, etc.). Universities have different 'missions', some giving more emphasis to academic excellence in traditional disciplines and professions (medicine, the law, religion), others defining themselves more in relation to the needs of commerce and industry, producing graduates with technical, entrepreneurial and managerial skills. It is not a uniform picture, however, and the profile of a university may show strengths in certain fields without being able to reproduce that quality across all subject areas. Moreover, as new areas of knowledge gain importance, universities develop courses in response to demand: for example, the field of business and management education has expanded from modest beginnings to become one of the most popular areas of study for both undergraduates and postgraduates.

Institutional variation is also evident in the differing drop-out rates of universities. In 2016, some 8 per cent of Scottish students left their courses at the end of the first year, compared with a UK figure of 7.2 per cent. The average figure concealed significant differences between universities. The ancients, particularly St Andrews, had very few students dropping out. By contrast, figures for newer universities (Abertay, Robert Gordon, Queen Margaret, UHI and UWS) were all above average, with UHI and UWS both over 14 per cent. Newer universities tend to be more flexible about entrance qualifications and take greater numbers of students from disadvantaged backgrounds, which may partly explain the variations. The reasons for dropping out may be financial and social as well as academic. Universities do provide support services in an attempt to improve retention figures but clearly there is scope for further work in this area.

The different priorities of universities are reflected in the fact that some have chosen to align themselves with UK-wide groups representing particular interests. Thus Glasgow and Edinburgh are both members of the 'elite' Russell Group which represents twenty-four leading UK universities that are 'committed to maintaining the very best research, an outstanding learning and teaching experience and unrivalled links with business and the public sector' (www.russellgroup.ac.uk). Another UK-wide grouping, consisting of twenty-six universities, is MillionPlus, also called the Association of Modern Universities. Four Scottish universities (Abertay, Edinburgh Napier, UHI and West of Scotland) are members. MillionPlus states that it is 'driven by a strong commitment to robust research and evidence in policy decisions in order to support a successful and flourishing UK higher education system, which can rise to the global economic, social and cultural challenges of the 21st century' (www.millionplus.ac.uk). It is evident that there is considerable overlap between the mission statements of the Russell Group and MillionPlus, both emphasising research, economic importance and social engagement. This suggests that the groupings may be more about (self) perceptions of status than anything else. Boliver (2015) has argued that the 'elite' claims of the Russell Group are simply about reinforcing old hierarchies of self-interest. However, the very existence of these groupings raises questions about the unity and coherence of the higher education sector as a whole. They seek to make representations to government and the funding councils promoting their particular interests, suggesting a level of institutional tribalism that makes it difficult for the Scottish and UK governments and the UK funding councils to develop policies that can apply to all universities.

There is, however, one important respect in which all universities have been moving in the same direction, albeit to varying degrees. Starting in the 1980s, there has been growing pressure for all public sector organisations to develop modes of operation that had been employed for many years in the private sector. This process has been described in various ways, often using terms such as managerialism, marketisation, performativity and account-ability. Mechanisms for monitoring targets, quality and staff performance are now standard practice, as well as tighter financial control and a sharper focus on measurable output. The older culture which allowed for a considerable measure of relative autonomy, professional judgement and self-regulation – implying a high degree of trust – has been replaced by one which requires clear evidence of achievement and value.

This shift is manifest in various ways. The relationship between academic departments and centralised 'service' departments has changed significantly, with the former having to conform to the bureaucratic requirements of the latter. Central directives from departments of finance, planning, human resources, recruitment, marketing and public relations limit the degree of autonomy which academic departments once enjoyed. A much more 'corporate' approach to management has developed, reflected in a proliferation of policy documents and strategic plans, promoted by an expanding cadre of senior staff at vice-principal level, each with a specific managerial remit. All this has changed the culture of universities, some more than others, and has led to a degree of discontent among academic staff who feel that their efforts in teaching and research represent the 'core' work of universities, and that the ascendancy of what they regard as a bureaucratic mindset has undermined the true purpose of higher education (see Bailey and Freedman, 2011; Collini, 2012). A number of surveys of staff morale (e.g. those reported in *Times Higher Education* on 4 February 2016 and 16 February 2017) have suggested a reduction in job satisfaction and a lack of trust in university management. The setting up of a committee in 2011 to review the governance of Scottish universities, with the aim of making them more democratic, transparent and accountable, proved controversial, leading to more modest reforms than were recommended in the committee's report (Scottish Government, 2012). (See also Chapter 74.)

## TEACHING, RESEARCH AND KNOWLEDGE EXCHANGE

The main activities of universities can be described under three headings. First, there is the teaching of students across a wide range of disciplines and using a variety of methods: as part of this, the quality of students' learning is regularly assessed. It is expected that the content of teaching will draw on the latest knowledge in the relevant field. The standard of teaching is subject to scrutiny on a UK-wide basis by the Quality Assurance Agency (QAA, 2017): its principal aim is to 'enhance the quality and secure the standards of UK higher educa-tion wherever delivered in order to maintain public confidence' (www.qaa.ac.uk). QAA has a Scottish office in Glasgow which has devolved responsibility for the work of QAA in Scotland: it claims that there is a distinctive Scottish approach to quality with a strong emphasis on partnership between a number of agencies, including the Scottish Higher Education Enhancement Committee (SHEEC) (QAA Scotland, 2016). There have been tensions between UK and Scottish approaches to teaching quality. A Teaching Excellence Framework (TEF) was introduced by the UK Government in 2016 with the aim of recognising and rewarding excellence in teaching and learning. Scotland, however, has favoured a process of enhancement-led institutional review (ELIR) which focuses on arrangements for improving the student learning experience. A number of Scottish universities decided not to participate in the TEF exercise carried out in 2017. Those who did performed well, with three gaining gold awards (Dundee, Robert Gordon and St Andrews) and two silver awards (Heriot-Watt and Abertay). The debate about the best approach to teaching quality remains complex and unresolved.

An important element in efforts to maintain parity of standards in teaching and learning between universities is the UK-wide system of external examining, whereby academics from one university monitor the work of students in other institutions and take part in examination boards to decide on the level of final awards. The Higher Education Academy (HEA), another UK-wide agency, which has an office in Edinburgh, is also concerned to develop and improve teaching and learning: it describes its function as 'improving learning outcomes by raising the status and quality of teaching in higher education' (www. heacademy.ac.uk).

The second area of activity is research. Universities are expected to generate new knowledge, advancing understanding in the disciplines they teach. The new knowledge may be 'pure', concerned with theories and principles which alter the way in which problems are framed or issues conceptualised, or it may be 'applied', having implications for the way in which practices in a wide range of fields (medicine, engineering, economics, government, law, etc.) are carried out. Funding for research comes from a variety of sources but the most prestigious awards, which attract strong competition, are made by the various UK Research Councils (e.g. for medicine, engineering and physical sciences, arts and humanities). The quality of research is assessed against national and international standards on a UK-wide basis through the Research Excellence Framework (REF; last carried out in 2014). The next REF is planned for 2021, following the recommendations of the Stern Report (Department for Business, Energy and Industrial Strategy, 2016) and a subsequent consultation exercise by the UK funding councils. Greater emphasis will be placed on the 'impact' of research. The concept of impact is highly contested. It can be variously defined in terms of the economic and social value of knowledge, its instrumental capacity to shape legislation and influence policy, or its potential to build capacity and enhance expertise.

Academic staff have come under increasing pressure to secure research grants and publish the findings of their work in leading academic journals. This has led some critics to argue that teaching is in danger of being undervalued. In the *Times Higher Education* survey of teaching in 2017, a majority of respondents said that research was more highly valued than teaching by their institution and that promotion depended more on research income and output than on high quality teaching (*Times Higher Education*, 2017). It used to be the tradition in Scotland that teaching of first-year classes would be undertaken by a professor, on the grounds that they deserved to hear leading scholars in the discipline. This is less common now, as senior staff are often recruited principally for their research expertise and may have very limited teaching commitments. Other critics argue that the heavy emphasis on research undermines the role of universities as democratic institutions, lessening their contribution to the public good (Bailey and Freedman, 2011).

The third area of activity, knowledge exchange, has gained in significance in recent years as government wishes to see economic benefit from the large public investment in higher education, and universities wish to demonstrate that they are not remote ivory towers but are engaged with the wider community. According to Universities Scotland, 'Knowledge exchange with the public, private and third sectors has been a priority for Scotland's universities for many years' (www.universities-scotland.ac.uk). It can be seen as one way of demonstrating the capacity of universities to make a positive impact not only on business and industry, but also on policy development and public services. An important part of this has been the setting up of a number of joint innovation programmes between universities and the private sector, which involve sharing expertise, facilities and equipment. In some cases, this has involved negotiating complex contractual agreements, covering intellectual property rights and commercial spin-offs. Universities Scotland states on its website that it 'supports the Scottish Government's ambition that Scotland should become a world-leading entrepreneurial and innovation nation'. It also reports that since 2013 eight specialist innovation centres have been established in sectors believed to have strong research and growth potential: these include industrial biotechnology, oil and gas, aquaculture, construction and imaging systems. It is predicted that such collaborative working between the academic and business worlds will help to solve problems, create new products and give a boost to the economy. Targets are ambitious: it is hoped that the innovation centres will generate £1.4 billion and create 4,000 jobs over five years.

It is fair to say that while knowledge exchange has been energetically promoted by government and university senior management – both seeing it as a source of additional revenue as well as evidence of social engagement – some academics remain uneasy about what it means for the aims and values of universities. Commercial companies are understandably concerned with the confidentiality of new products or processes and this can come into conflict with traditional academic impulses to make new knowledge available in the public domain as soon as possible. Furthermore, tricky ethical issues can arise when dealing with companies working in sensitive fields, such as pharmaceuticals, oil exploration or renewable energy. This raises questions about the objectivity of the 'knowledge' that is generated. Critics of knowledge exchange see it as the commodification and commercialisation of knowledge, which they fear may run the risk of compromising the role of the academy as a guardian of truth (see Collini, 2017).

## TRADITION, IDENTITY AND CHANGING CHARACTER

In Chapter 82 of the previous edition of this volume, George Kerevan raised a number of important issues about the changing character of Scottish higher education. He drew attention to the historic appeal of the notion of the 'democratic intellect' as characterised in George Davie's celebrated work (Davie, 1961). This emphasised the intellectual breadth, philosophical grounding and social commitment of traditional Scottish university courses: they sought to promote a conception of the good life and the good society. They also provided a route into the professions and career advancement for individuals, but within a context that emphasised public responsibility and a sense of national identity. Davie's thesis that these characteristics had been progressively weakened in the course of the nineteenth and early twentieth centuries, through academic specialisation and anglicisation, has been subject to criticism but it remains a powerful statement of an influential reading of Scotland's educational history.

Kerevan went on to suggest that over the last fifty years the civic role of Scottish universities has been subject to a range of pressures which have led to a questioning of their role as open, classless and independent guardians of national culture. The most powerful pressure has come from the massive expansion of the sector. At the start of the 1960s there were 18,500 students in four universities. By the end of that decade there were 38,000 students in eight universities. Following the granting of university status to the 'post-1992' institutions, by the year 2000 the number had increased to a massive 144,000. As indicated earlier, that figure had doubled to nearly 290,000 by 2015. According to Kerevan, Davie's celebration of generalist higher education had been transmuted by this expansion into a form of mass vocationalism.

Even if this interpretation is not accepted without qualification, the pattern of growth over a period of fifty years represents a significant shift in the educational and cultural profile of the population. One of the striking features of improved educational provision is that it creates further demand: parents who are themselves graduates want their children to have the same opportunity. Furthermore, a mass system of higher education creates new expectations and leads to new priorities. Governments unsurprisingly wish to see social and economic benefits from the additional resources they have to provide. They expect courses to equip graduates with the skills that are needed in the job market. The notion of learning for its own sake, unconnected to extrinsic rewards, begins to seem something of a luxury. At the same time, dependence on state funding creates fears of state control and a loss of academic freedom. That is why those universities which have the capacity to do so have sought to reduce their financial dependence on government through commercial activities, overseas recruitment and charitable giving by alumni and other benefactors. The larger ancient universities, Edinburgh and Glasgow, simply by virtue of their output of graduates, many of whom have gained distinction in their chosen fields, are advantageously placed to attract donations from former students.

Prior to 1992, funding for all UK universities was disbursed through the Universities Funding Council (UFC), which reported to the Department for Education in London. Growing nationalist sentiment, and a feeling that the UFC was not always sensitive in its dealings with Scotland, Wales and Northern Ireland, led to the creation of separate funding councils for the four jurisdictions. It was perhaps hoped that this arrangement, reinforced by the devolution settlement of 1999 and the creation of a Scottish Parliament, would resolve some of the tensions about resource allocation. That has proved optimistic. As well as arguments about the fairness of funding regimes in the further and higher education sectors – the further education sector has felt disadvantaged by recent settlements and a substantial reduction in student numbers following restructuring – questions are sometimes asked about the precise nature of the relationship between the Scottish Funding Council and the Scottish Government. To what extent are SFC decisions subject to formal and informal pressures from government officials? Again, if university principals were to speak out publicly – as distinct from making discreet behind-the-scenes representations – against particular proposals, what consequences might follow? In post-devolution Scotland, some observers perceive a centralist drift and feel that it is difficult for academics to fulfil a radical intellectual role of the kind that may have been possible in the past.

Furthermore, university leaders face something of a dilemma in terms of positioning their institutions within the current political context. Given that context, they want to project their distinctive Scottishness and to appeal to the strengths of the Scottish educational tradition. At the same time, they are acutely conscious that they will be compared with other universities in the UK and beyond. Increasingly, all UK universities, and especially members of the Russell Group, see themselves as international institutions, keen to compete for the best scholars and brightest students across the globe. For a country of its size, Scotland continues to do fairly well on both a national and international scale. There are various 'league tables' of universities, using a range of criteria, but no universally agreed system of measurement. According to the rating system used by the journal *Times Higher Education* in 2017, within the UK Scotland has three universities in the top twenty: Edinburgh was ranked sixth, Glasgow eleventh and St Andrews fouteenth. Oxford and Cambridge came out top. In terms of world rankings, five Scottish universities featured in the top 200: Edinburgh was placed 27th, Glasgow 88th, St Andrews 110th equal, Dundee 180th equal and Aberdeen 188th equal. Dundee's position has been steadily rising, thanks partly to its global reputation in biomedical sciences. The USA and the UK have dominated these lists for some time but this may change: China, India and many smaller countries have made huge investments in higher education and many new institutions are moving up the international tables.

## DISCUSSION

One topic that is likely to remain high on the agenda for some time to come is access to university education, particularly for those students from the most socially disadvantaged communities. In 2014, the First Minister of Scotland, Nicola Sturgeon, stated:

> I want us to determine now that a child born today in one of our most deprived communities will, by the time he or she leaves school, have the same chance of going to university as a child born in one of our least deprived communities. (Quoted in Scottish Government, 2016, Foreword)

A Commission on Widening Access was set up in 2015 and reported in 2016. Its philosophy was summed up in four propositions: 'Equal access is fundamentally about fairness … is a social good … is compatible with academic excellence … is an economic good' (Scottish Government, 2016, p. 7). These principles can be seen as consistent with the Scottish democratic tradition in education, albeit expressed in modern terms, emphasising the economic as well as the personal and social benefits. Two of the key recommendations were the appointment of a Commissioner for Fair Access and a set of clear targets to be achieved by specific dates.

The Scottish Government moved swiftly to act on the Widening Access report and remains committed to maintaining free tuition for home-based undergraduates – in contrast to the situation in England – as an important part of its strategy to reduce social-class differences in access to higher education. However, some studies have questioned whether this would automatically lead to fairer representation of all those with disadvantaged backgrounds. One study (https://www.suttontrust.com/research-paper/access-in-scotland/), using figures from the Universities and Colleges Admissions Service (UCAS), has shown that targeting the poorest 20 per cent of postcodes has led to an encouraging increase in students from those areas but a much smaller increase from those just outside the target zones identified under the Scottish Index of Multiple Deprivation. Riddell (2016) has criticised both politicians and senior managers in ancient Scottish universities for being 'unaware of the evidence which shows that university participation in Scotland continues to be organised along social class lines, reproducing rather than disrupting social inequalities in the labour market and in the wider distribution of wealth' (Riddell, 2016, p. 28: see also Riddell et al., 2016 and Chapter 85 in this text). In other words, all the efforts that universities already make to encourage applications from schools in socially disadvantaged areas and to provide summer schools and other forms of support for 'non-traditional' applicants may not be enough to counteract the deep structural impediments which have their roots outside educational institutions.

Another challenging issue facing Scottish higher education arises from the referendum decision of the UK electorate in June 2016 to leave the European Union (EU) The implications for EU nationals working in Scottish universities and for access to major sources of funding are considerable. According to the website of Universities Scotland, some 16 per cent of academic staff working in the higher education sector are from the EU, a figure that rises to 23 per cent for research-only staff. Moreover, the same source states that in 2016 there were around 24,000 students from the EU enrolled on undergraduate and postgraduate courses in Scotland. Funding from EU sources – some £88.8 million a year – has made a vital contribution to research programmes across a range of disciplines (www.universities-scotland.ac.uk/). The potential loss of this income and uncertainties about future recruitment of staff and students from the EU is a serious source of concern to university leaders.

The political aspects of this have been intensified by the fact that, although the UK vote was to leave, Scotland voted strongly in favour of remaining in the EU. The Scottish Government has made robust representations to London, seeking to protect the national interest, but these have not led to any special concessions and the final outcome remains unclear. Continuing uncertainty about Scotland's constitutional position within the UK is also a complicating factor. The possibility of an early second referendum on Scottish independence has receded, following the inconclusive outcome of the 2017 UK general election. But the Scottish National Party (SNP) leadership has indicated that it will await the result of the Brexit negotiations before deciding when, and if, a second referendum is to be held. If a vote in favour of independence were to be achieved, it might enable Scotland to remain in the EU – though that would certainly involve a lengthy negotiation process – but it would have complicated consequences for relations between Scottish higher education and the rest of the UK. At present, arrangements for admissions and research assessment are conducted on a UK-wide basis. If Scotland became fully independent, would it be necessary to establish separate bureaucratic bodies to carry out these functions? To date, there is no indication that these matters have been thought through.

Policy decisions in any field depend crucially on reliable evidence. In the course of the enquiry into the governance of Scottish higher education referred to above (Scottish Government, 2012), members of the committee found that relatively little independent research had been undertaken on the subject. The report pointed out that, if future policy is to be genuinely 'evidence-informed', the research base needs to be strengthened. Accordingly, it recommended that the Scottish Government should 'instruct' the Scottish Funding Council to establish a Centre for Higher Education Research in a suitable institutional setting. This could serve as an important resource for future strategic decisions about the form and function of the sector. To date, there has been no sign of movement on this recommendation. Some individual academics carry out research on aspects of Scottish higher education but the potential to build capacity that would benefit the whole system has so far not been realised. There is also a need for a stronger knowledge base in relation to the economics of education: few people in Scotland have a good understanding of the rationale behind resource allocations to the various sectors. Such knowledge would, however, open up areas of controversy as arguments over the apparent privileging of higher education at the expense of the further education sector have shown.

Scottish universities seek to uphold a number of principles that are hard to reconcile: academic excellence and social equity; community engagement and global reach; maintenance of valued traditions and openness to change; intellectual freedom and commercial realism. There remains a strong commitment to the notion that universities should be public institutions accessible to all who have the ability to benefit from higher learning. But economic pressures are likely to make it harder to maintain standards, especially when the funding regime south of the border gives English universities some advantages. In England, there is one well-established independent university which receives no state funding – the University of Buckingham – though students there are able to access public funding through the student loan scheme. It is also the case that a small number of other institutions in England have recently been granted 'private university' status. Any suggestion that a Scottish university should seek independent status would be highly controversial, not least because it would seem to run counter to the cultural and historical values associated with Davie's notion of the democratic intellect. One Scottish university, St Andrews, probably has the capacity to do so, partly because of its success in recruiting fully fee-paying students from overseas, particularly from the United States. In the current political climate, however, it is unlikely that such an idea would be floated publicly. It seems fair to predict that, given the ongoing debates about Scotland's place within the UK and Europe, in a context of funding constraints, the shape and direction of the higher education system will continue to be a focus for robust exchanges about national identity, institutional mission, economic value and intellectual purpose.

# REFERENCES

Bailey, M. and Freedman, D (2011) *The Assault on Universities: A Manifesto for Resistance*. London: Pluto Press.

Boliver, V. (2015) 'Are there distinctive clusters of higher and lower status universities in the UK?' *Oxford Review of Education*, 41 (5), 608–27.

Collini, S. (2012) *What Are Universities For?* London: Penguin.

Collini, S. (2017) *Speaking of Universities*. London: Verso.

Davie, G. E. (1961) *The Democratic Intellect*. Edinburgh: Edinburgh University Press.

Department for Business, Energy and Industrial Strategy (2016) *Building on Success and Learning from Experience* (the Stern Report). London: UK Government.

QAA (2017) *Building on World-Class Quality: Strategy 2017–20*. Gloucester: QAA.

QAA Scotland (2016) *Annual Report 2015–16*. Glasgow: QAA Scotland.

Riddell, S. (2016) 'Scottish higher education and social justice: tensions between data and discourse', *Scottish Educational Review*, 48 (1), 13–29.

Riddell, S., Weedon, E. and Minty, S. (eds) (2016) *Higher Education in Scotland and the United Kingdom*. Edinburgh: Edinburgh University Press.

Scottish Government (2012) *Report of the Review of Higher Education Governance in Scotland* (the von Prondzynski Report). Edinburgh: Scottish Government.

Scottish Government (2016) *A Blueprint for Fairness: Final Report of the Commission on Widening Access*. Edinburgh: Scottish Government.

*Times Higher Education* (2017) 'The Teaching Survey 2017', 16 February.

# 8

# Policy and Politics in Scottish Education

*Donald Gillies*

This chapter explores how education policy in Scotland is made and reviews the nature of recent policy changes. It also examines the central role of politics within education and the different political pressures which come to bear on the policy process and on the system itself. The principal focus will be on the schools sector. Issues relating to other sectors can be found in Chapter 21 ('Childcare and Early Education') and across Section IX ('Further and Higher Education'). Schooling is political both in its creation and its control and so it is inevitable that public education in Scotland today has a strongly political edge. While education policy is set by politicians, whether at national or local levels, the key role of practitioners, and school communities more broadly, should not be forgotten in terms of how that policy is enacted in particular settings. In this regard, Ball et al. (2012) are among a number of policy theorists who have moved away from the notion of 'policy implementation' towards that of 'policy enactment', this latter term being preferred as one that captures better the notion and significance of professional agency (Priestley et al., 2015).

A further revision of older notions of policy analysis is that which focuses on policy as a 'process' rather than a 'thing' and so a much more fluid and messy phenomenon than that considered in traditional models which viewed it in simple, linear, 'stagist' terms with initial discrete activities such as 'problem identification', leading straightforwardly to 'implemented solutions' (Sabatier and Weible, 2014). However, conceiving policy neither as text (for example, a document) nor as process (policy activity), but as 'discourse', allows for understanding how specific discursive perspectives – ways of viewing and positioning the social world – define problems and shape the possible responses to them. Thus, the problems which policy is created to address are not natural phenomena: they are only made problematic by the dominant discourse or ideology held by those with the power to initiate policy change (Adams, 2014, p. 32ff.). In other words, identifying a 'problem' is dependent on the perspectives of those reviewing a policy area. A further helpful concept in this context is that of 'social imaginary' (Rizvi and Lingard, 2010, p. 8) which refers to the expected outcomes of policy, the alternative, 'better' situation which policy is intended to create. Such outcomes, again, are not common sense: they are what a particular discourse envisions and selects as its preferred future. One should also note that 'policy' covers a wide range of instruments and must not be seen as synonymous with legislation. Indeed, a parliamentary act tends to be a rare form of education policy, and much more policy activity is centred around guidelines and circulars, whether at national or local government level. While legislation is prescriptive, educational policy in Scotland, even that surrounding Curriculum for

Excellence, is much more commonly advisory or hortatory rather than imperative. In this particular chapter, it will be more the policy process at national level which is considered. This may be seen as appropriate since the role of local authorities in relation to education in Scotland is something that has been in contested flux in recent times.

## POLICY, POLITICS AND DEMOCRACY

The policy process in Scotland needs to be viewed within the broader context of modern Western democratic practice. There has been a tradition within this model that simple majority rule is insufficient and that a much more open form of 'government by discussion', as the liberal philosopher John Stuart Mill termed it, is what should mark parliamentary democracy. Certainly in the early days of the devolved Scottish Parliament there was great stress laid on mass consultation on education policy: the process leading to the passing of the first piece of education legislation – the Standards in Scotland's Schools etc. Act 2000 – and the conduct of the National Debate, which preceded Curriculum for Excellence, involved major exercises in public engagement. This approach to governance, including a commitment even to pre-legislative consultation, has not been maintained and current practice tends to be limited to online questionnaires on government proposals where prospective respondents are guided to specific issues on which comment is deemed welcome. Nevertheless, even within the previously ostensibly pluralist model, the extent to which the process had any significant influence is questionable. The passing of the Standards in Scotland's Schools etc. Act 2000, for example, was marked by, at best, 'enlightened elitism' (Gillies, 2001), where power and influence lay in very few hands even although a wide range of disparate voices had been encouraged to contribute during the legislative process. On the other hand, while 'government by discussion' may appeal to democratic ideals, the electoral system does deliver power into the hands of the executive, and exercising it as they alone see fit, albeit in line with manifesto principles, is entirely legitimate.

A further development within parliamentary practice at Holyrood has also served to compromise the quality of legislation. Without a second revising chamber, a key role in scrutinising legislative proposals rests with the committee system at Holyrood. Under the Scottish National Party (SNP) Government, the independence and muscle of the system has been questioned, with the government increasingly being seen to 'pack' such committees with their own Members of the Scottish Parliament (MSPs) and to enforce considerable party discipline in their operation. The need for party discipline may be particularly pressing for the SNP, it could be argued, since for many years, on the margins of Scottish politics, the Party entertained a considerable number of maverick figures and a wide divergence of political stances. With power has come the need for much more rigour in terms of maintaining a political line but opponents see, as a consequence of this, the stifling of debate and an absence of forensic scrutiny at the committee stages of the legislative process. Some problematic aspects of recent legislation such as the Offensive Behaviour at Football and Threatening Communications (Scotland) Act 2012, and the 'named person' provision in the Children and Young People (Scotland) Act 2014 (see Chapter 10), are adduced as symptomatic of a weakened parliamentary committee role.

One development in the policy process which could be seen as an alternative form of scrutiny and consultation has been the use of inquiries or policy reviews, and resultant reports and proposals, as the basis for policy developments. On key education issues, government has set up reviews chaired by non-parliamentary figures to develop ideas and draft proposals. Since devolution this has been seen, for example, in relation to the McCrone report on pay and conditions, *A Teaching Profession for the 21ˢᵗ Century* (Scottish Executive, 2001); the development of *A Curriculum for Excellence* (Scottish Executive, 2004); the Donaldson report (2010) on teacher education, *Teaching Scotland's Future*; and the McCormac review of teacher employment, *Advancing Professionalism in Scottish Teaching* (Scottish Government, 2011). In addition, the government has called in the Organisation for Economic Co-operation and Development (OECD) on two occasions to review and report on Scottish education, first in 2007 on quality and equity (www.oecd.org/edu/school/reviewsofnationalpolicies-foreducation-qualityandequityofschoolinginscotland.htm), and later in 2015 on the overall improvement agenda (www.oecd.org/education/school/Improving-Schools-in-Scotland-An-OECD-Perspective.pdf). The government has also set up panels of international 'experts' to consider key policy areas, in education this being focused on the attainment challenge.

The democratic process of consultation and discussion, therefore, tends to be channelled through this structure. The process can be thorough and transparent, but when, as has happened on two key occasions, government accepts the emerging proposals and moves immediately to implementation, due parliamentary scrutiny and full consultation with the teaching profession can be sacrificed. This was the case with both Curriculum for Excellence and the Donaldson Review and, certainly in the former case, the results have been problematic. In addition, with both of the OECD reviews and the involvement of panels of experts, government, through its capacity to construct the official version of events ('narrative privilege'), is in the powerful position of interpreting and synthesising their views for public consumption. Thus, government tends to look for any evidence supporting its actions and its plans, and that is what is often given most prominence in their reactions. Overall, this method of externalising policy development can be seen to be in sympathy with the values of pluralist democracy through consultation and engagement, and commendable in seeking expert views and professional knowledge to support policy change. However, it remains an inconsistent form of governance and its relationship to Parliament and parliamentary committee processes uncertain. On a more cynical view, this approach can be seen to serve government well, in terms of realpolitik, as a way of limiting political opposition, deflecting culpability and extracting objective endorsement.

## THE POLICY PROCESS AND THE POLICY COMMUNITY

Humes (1986) was amongst the first to challenge the concept of the 'policy community', a loose assemblage of various interested groups (now typically known as 'stakeholders'), who contributed to some kind of extended, democratic conversation and discussion as policy was developed and settled. Humes instead suggested that there was 'a leadership class' within Scottish education – a seam of individuals of similar social backgrounds and profiles positioned across professional bodies, government and civil service – which wielded power in what could be seen as essentially conservative and protectionist ways. Whether or not such a thesis still applies today is open to debate but Scotland is a small country and key education agencies and committees are often populated by the same people, occasionally in different guises, but still representing a very small cross section of the educational, far less the wider, population of the country.

Apart from appeals to democratic principles, the notion of the policy community was also championed for practical reasons: the wider the range of informed individuals and groups who contributed to policymaking, the better the prospects of that policy being appropriate, and the greater the chances of it attracting commitment and so having effect. This form of consensual politics very much marked the opening years of the Scottish Parliament when government, the teaching unions and the local authorities worked closely together. That began to unravel during the SNP-led administrations, from 2007, when considerable strains emerged between central and local government, largely related to the council tax freeze and subsequent difficulties for local authorities in balancing budgets and fulfilling their duties. In most cases, central government has managed to maintain effective relationships with the teacher unions, although that too has faltered around issues of workload. The difficulties which arose between government and local authorities led to a breakaway in 2015 by four Labour-run local authorities from the Convention of Scottish Local Authorities (COSLA), the umbrella body responsible for collective representation of local authorities in Scotland. This weakening of local authority unity made the 'governance review' (www.gov.scot/ Topics/Education/thegovernancereview), initiated by Cabinet Secretary John Swinney in 2016–17, all the more apposite, it could be said, as the associated proposals indicated a preference for 'regional educational collboratives', cutting across current local authority boundaries, and a move towards greater empowerment of individual schools and headteach-ers. It is not entirely clear from government policy as to why the role of local authorities in public education, which has been in place since 1929, should now be so ill-favoured. Given the stated Scottish Government antipathy toward the academy and free school movement developing in England, which rests on the removal of local authority involvement, it seems inconsistent for what appears to be a similar trajectory to be initiated in Scotland.

The policy community, whatever its contested nature in Scotland, is an important group to explore. At the apex, as one would expect in a parliamentary democracy, stand government politicians, advised by civil servants and key education personnel, such as Her Majesty's Inspectorate of Education (HMIE). The somewhat awkward marriage of Learning Teaching Scotland with the inspectorate, forming Education Scotland, thus uniting curriculum development and support functions with those of inspection, has prompted the perception that the role of HMIE in policy development has diminished over recent years. Nevertheless, they still have a key role in informing government policy and in drafting policy documents. A former Senior Chief Inspector, Graham Donaldson, was tasked with the review into teacher education; a former Chief Inspector, Ken Muir, is Chief Executive of the General Teaching Council for Scotland (GTCS); and another, Bill Maxwell, was Chief Executive of Education Scotland from 2011 to 2017, so their influence could still be viewed as extensive, at least by proxy. However, a parliamentary committee inquiry in 2016 into the roles of Education Scotland and the Scottish Qualifications Authority (SQA) was anything but sympathetic and so there does remain the sense that there is government concern about these two bodies' positions.

The GTCS, in place since 1965, but from 2012 an independent, self-regulatory body, has been an influential member of the policy landscape. While largely tasked with setting and maintaining teaching standards and codes of conduct, and, more recently, with supporting and encouraging continuing professional learning, it does carry weight generally when contributing to policy discussion. The governance review of 2017 indicated that it would give way to an expanded Education Workforce Council covering a much broader spectrum of those employed in the education sector. In its current configuration, most of the elected teacher members of its council are drawn from the main teaching organisation, the Educational Institute of Scotland (EIS), and it too has a strong voice in education policy. It has been largely cooperative with government in a number of areas of recent policy development but has differed over such issues as workload and some aspects of curriculum reform. The Scottish Secondary Teachers' Association (SSTA) is a much smaller organisation but has been more vocal about these matters, although weakened in recent times by leadership turnover.

On the employers' side, the umbrella body, COSLA, as has been noted, has also been weakened through internal divisions and breakaways, but it still possesses influence, especially so if local council elections continue to give power to the SNP. This sets up the prospect of some difficult times for the SNP national government if their own SNP local government colleagues resist and challenge policy direction. Groups representing directors of education (the Association of Directors of Education in Scotland, ADES), headteachers (School Leaders Scotland, and the Association of Headteachers and Deputes in Scotland, AHDS) and parents (the Scottish Parent Teacher Council, SPTC) are also prominent in voicing policy views but, as with all those external to government, the degree to which their opinions affect policy is by no means clear.

The role of research in policy development is also somewhat opaque. Government has largely bypassed Scottish academia in commissioning the little research it does and tends to rely on the private sector, or its in-house analysts, for this form of evidence. This has been much more of a quantitative nature rather than in-depth qualitative studies of educational problems. At times this can give the impression that complex social and educational challenges can be reduced to simple numerical data. Some other research, such as that from the Joseph Rowntree Foundation on poverty and the attainment gap (https://www.jrf.org.uk/sites/default/files/jrf/migrated/files/education-attainment-scotland-full.pdf), has been given some prominence in the media but the extent to which it influences policy is questionable. In any event, the nature of the relationship between research findings and policy formulation within a democracy is by no means uncontested. While much has been made of evidence-based, evidence-informed or evidence-led policy, all research findings need to be judged in the light of prevailing moral values, democratic sensibilities and political rationality. This differs significantly from scientific rationality and the idea that research findings can be mapped simply onto consequent policy is both fanciful and dangerous. In a democracy, one would expect that such findings, and their possible implications, would be subject to rigorous democratic discussion and filtered through numerous value positions. Perhaps the most that can be expected is that policy be 'evidence-aware' (Gillies, 2014). This would mean that policymakers were at least cognisant of the relevant research evidence when making decisions, even if choosing to ignore the evidence were to be the final option. This is not as illogical as appearance would suggest. For example, research evidence may show that school attainment results would rise sharply if certain pupils were excluded from the system. Acting on such research evidence, however, would be undemocratic, unfair and immoral. Choosing to privilege political rationality over this sort of 'scientific' research evidence would not be perverse or baseless. It is what democratic decision making always entails: making judgements based on a number of competing and compelling reasons.

Of groups within the policy community whose influence has waned, one such would be the churches. Although there are still allocated places for church representatives on local authority education committees, their influence has weakened considerably, in line with their reduced national profile. If anything, it is the humanist or secular movement which has grown in public visibility and they have been vocal in criticising the denominational sector, in challenging the continued place of religious observance in schools, and in promoting children's rights (to withdraw) in this regard.

The influence of the business sector tends to fluctuate. There are perennial protestations from business leaders about young people's lack of readiness for the workplace and, while these may represent genuine concerns, this is a script that has remained unaltered for generations and is not matched by any complementary self-reflection on the quality of in-house training and induction offered to recruits from school. Some business leaders have taken a more direct role in educational matters: the entrepreneur Tom Hunter has been active in seeking to influence aspects of Scottish education, and Jim McColl, an engineering millionaire, has founded a college for secondary pupils aimed at improving skills for work, and life chances (see Chapter 98). On the other hand, Scottish Government policy documents are replete with emphasising the major role of education in economic development and, indeed, at times it reads as if that is the main purpose of the school system.

## THE SCOTTISH POLITICAL LANDSCAPE

The rise to power of the SNP has been the dominant political development in Scotland since devolution. In 2003, it took under 24 per cent of the vote in the Scottish parliamentary elections and, two years later, polled less than 18 per cent in the UK general election. Yet, by 2007 it took 33 per cent of the Scottish parliamentary vote, enough to take power as a minority government, and in 2011 it achieved an overall majority in Parliament on the back of 45 per cent of the popular vote. This percentage was increased marginally in 2016 but the party lost seats and so slipped back into a minority government position. Despite losing the Scottish independence referendum vote in 2014, it took all but three of the fifty-nine Westminster seats the following year, winning 50 per cent of the vote overall. That proved to be a peak and in the 2017 council elections it polled 32 per cent, and in the general election of the same year 37 per cent, losing twenty-one of its fifty-six seats.

Since 2007, therefore, the SNP has had overall control of, and responsibility for, education in Scotland. While its main goal is that of political independence, it has developed a policy position on education which was very much in line with the broad consensus that marked education policy since devolution (Arnott, 2016; Arnott and Ozga, 2016). Thus there is a strong commitment to education within the public sector, concerns about inequality, and resistance to the situation in England which has weakened local authorities, introduced academies and free schools instead, and diluted the role of universities in teacher education. A number of policies have been introduced to improve the lot of the disadvantaged, albeit with varying degrees of success: free school meals; reduced class sizes; increased nursery and childcare provision; and pressure on higher education to widen access.

The Labour Party has attacked government on the failure of these schemes to achieve the desired ends of more educational equality, and on cuts to education budgets. Their policy position is in alignment with much of what the SNP has been aiming to do and they assert their distinctiveness merely by promising to be more effective in addressing these challenges. Their 2016 manifesto did promise increased, unannounced school inspections as a means to drive up standards, and also suggested a return of a form of the Chartered Teacher Scheme, which had been designed to support the development of teachers committed to the classroom rather than management. The Labour Party also committed to increasing taxes to fund educational investment, not a position which the SNP has favoured in recent times.

The Liberal Democrat position in 2016 also supported increased taxes to boost education spending and championed a more local approach to governance, rejecting what was seen as centralising SNP tendencies. They had opposed the introduction of testing and their mani-festo favoured more teacher autonomy in respect of professional judgement. Their electoral weakness, however, has deepened seriously in recent years: they were part of a coalition Scottish Executive as recently as 2007 and yet the party won only one Scottish seat in the 2015 UK general election. In the Scottish parliamentary election in 2016 they took less than 8 per cent of the vote and won only 5 seats out of the 129 at Holyrood. Typifying their plight was the case of Carole Ford, a former head of School Leaders Scotland, and a regular, outspoken critic of the SNP generally and its education record particularly. Standing in the Glasgow Kelvin constituency, she took but 3.7 per cent of the vote and lost her deposit.

This experience tends to substantiate the emergent situation in Scottish politics where the constitutional issue seems so dominant that it overshadows all other area of policy and government activity. It means that voters appear currently to vote in each election, whether at UK, Scottish or local council level, as if it were a rerun of the independence referendum. Education, health, welfare, transportation, and even the economy and defence, become subordinate to this overarching question.

The Conservative Party has reaped considerable electoral benefit from this, by appear-ing to garner much of the unionist, or anti-independence, vote. They emerged consider-ably strengthened from the 2016 election, gaining 22 per cent of the vote and increasing their Holyrood group by sixteen seats to thirty-one. In what would have seemed an impos-sible scenario but a few years ago, they overtook the Labour Party and became the largest opposition group in the Scottish Parliament. Their education policies tend to be quite distinct, unsurprisingly, from the left-of-centre consensus. Their 2016 manifesto stressed once more their keenness on empowering headteachers and weakening local authority and central government involvement, but also called for more, and flexible, childcare, and for an increased focus on vocational education. They proposed the possibility of clusters of schools operating independently of local authorities and of the desirability of introducing the Teach First scheme which recruits graduates directly into classrooms – 'training on the job' – rather than through university teacher education courses. They also favoured a form of graduate tax and a boost to the further education (FE) sector. Their recovery was cemented by taking 25 per cent of the vote in the 2017 council elections, and following that with 29 per cent in the general election a month later, increasing their Westminster seats from one to thirteen.

The Green Party, despite scoring less than 1 per cent in the Scottish Parliament election of 2016, gained four extra seats to finish with six, thanks to the system of proportional rep-resentation employed. Their policy platform differs from the main parties in its espousal of local democratic decision making rather than a focus on leadership and headteachers. They support a range of policies aimed at tackling inequality in education, such as on widening access, and on closing the attainment gap. They promote progressive, learner-centred ideas on education with little enthusiasm for any focus on testing and grades. While they promote themselves as 'radical', their 2016 education manifesto was relatively subdued, backing away, for example, from a previous suggestion to end denominational schooling.

Other parties, such as various socialist groupings, have polled poorly in recent years, schism and disarray marking their decline since 2003 when they has six MSPs elected to Holyrood. The UK Independence Party (UKIP) did win a seat in Scotland in the European Parliament election of 2014 but has had, otherwise, little profile in Scottish politics.

Since mid-2016 when a series of poor results in relation to the performance of Scotland's school pupils began to emerge (see Chapter 68), education has proved to be a ripe source of political advantage for the opposition parties at Holyrood. This has made the sector the focus of considerable negative attention, with government and professional bodies called to account regularly and the subject of harsh political and media criticism.

## GLOBAL POLICY INFLUENCES

Over the last decade, it could be argued that Scotland represented a challenge to global trends in state education. It had resisted market pressures, maintaining a state comprehensive system administered by local authorities; it had eschewed high-stakes testing; and it remained committed to rejecting tuition fees for higher education. In recent years, however, that has started to shift. First came the commitment to national assessments throughout primary school, then the querying of local authorities' roles and the mooting of increased autonomy for headteachers. Free tuition fees has been retained as a policy position but the research which demonstrates that this has not widened access for disadvantaged students but has instead represented a considerable subsidy to middle-class families has started to put that commitment under pressure, especially at a time of falling government tax revenues and austerity generally. What can be said, however, is that Scotland has moved more recently towards global norms in education policy terms. Apart from these policy revisions, the Scottish Government has relied on one of the key global powers in education, the OECD, to evaluate its work and to populate its advisory group on education, and so it is not surprising to see Scottish education policy now begin to conform with international policy trends.

It is possible to identify several significant ideological drivers which are influencing current education policy internationally. Of most importance are neo-liberalism, human capital theory, new public management and total quality management, elements of all of which can be seen within what Sahlberg (2011) calls the 'global education reform movement' (GERM). Neo-liberalism covers a very wide range of ideological positions but they can be seen to coalesce around several central common beliefs, which have become dominant throughout the capitalist world: the primacy of the market; deregulation; privatisation; lowering taxes through cuts in public spending; and, a focus on the individual rather than community or society. The most strident manifestations of neo-liberal policy are not evident in Scottish education but one can see constituent elements such as the effects of the council tax freeze and the use of the private sector in the tendering processes for various aspects of educational provision, most notably in new school building construction.

Human capital theory is a very strong theme in government thinking and several recent Scottish policy documents, including those around the attainment challenge, demonstrate this outlook by positioning education as an investment which later repays society and the individual in terms of economic output and income levels. While the theory has some specious attractiveness for politicians in its simple input–output model, it presents education not as an intrinsic good but as merely instrumental for the economy. It is also hard to square with the inclusion agenda, particularly for those children with the most complex needs. To seek a 'return' on the costs involved in supporting such youngsters would be viewed as repugnant by most in education.

New public management has been an important development across the public sector, essentially importing private sector practice so that terminology such as 'customers' and 'clients' become common, 'efficiency' a key issue, and educational institutions seen much more as 'businesses' and their heads as chief executive officers. A major effect of this is heightened focus on management, and particularly leadership, as the key factors in securing desired school outcomes. Its associated concept of managerialism sees educational problems as more susceptible to being solved through management strategies, initiatives and policies, rather than as complicated and confounded by fundamental societal phenomena. The recent focus on leadership in Scottish education can be seen as typical of this approach and a central plank of the current drive on attainment is that the effects of poverty within education can be managed out of the system through effective educational leadership, rather than as a prime subject for socio-economic policy. Total quality management has had significant impact on Scottish education over the last two decades and its language and effects can be seen across the system whether in the form of local authority 'quality' personnel or in the standards and competencies models for teacher roles and others. Its focus on high standards and consistency is hard to resist but at times it can involve an overly mechanistic and formulaic approach to complex social and relational issues, and take an insufficient account of contextual factors.

All of these ideological trends are summarised by Sahlberg's (2011) concept of GERM, whose main components are standardisation; a narrowed curriculum; prescription around learning, and around learning goals; corporate management models; and test-based accountability. For some time, much of this seemed distant to Scotland but there is no doubt that evidence of its presence in Scottish education is more visible now and may increase if the pressures from the Programme for International Student Assessment (PISA), the Scottish Survey of Literacy and Numeracy (SSLN) – now replaced by national assessments – and elsewhere, narrow the curriculum, and testing becomes more high stakes. Finland, however, has shown that another way is possible and it will be intriguing to see if the Scottish Government of the next few years has either the confidence or principled vision to follow such a different course.

The uncertainty around what will result from Britain's withdrawal from the European Union, and the prospect of a second Scottish independence referendum thereafter, mean that constitutional issues, albeit fused with economic concerns, will continue to dominate political debate. The Conservative politician, Rab Butler (1902–82), described politics as 'the art of the possible'. While that is disappointingly constrained for those with radical or revolutionary ideals, there is no doubt that all of the policy ambitions and political aspirations circling around Scottish education today are dependent wholly for their realisation on the economic context within which such activity exists. In the current economic situation, there seems little prospect of public finances being sufficiently healthy to allow for anything other than the reshuffling of limited funds to support whatever becomes the next priority. Changes in culture, in commitment and in philosophy are not reliant on tax revenues and it is perhaps in addressing these areas that the best hopes for a better educational world for our children and young people lie.

## REFERENCES

Adams, P. (2014) *Policy and Education*. Abingdon: Routledge.

Arnott, M. (2016) 'Governing strategies and education policy: the SNP in government, 2007–2016', *Scottish Affairs*, 25 (1), 45–61.

Arnott, M. and Ozga, J. (2016) 'Education and nationalism in Scotland: governing a 'learning Nation'', *Oxford Review of Education*, 42 (3), 253–65.

Ball, S., Maguire, M. and Braun, A. (2012) *How Schools do Policy*. Abingdon: Routledge.

Donaldson, G. (2010) *Teaching Scotland's Future: Report of a Review of Teacher Education in Scotland*. Online at www.gov.scot/Resource/Doc/337626/0110852.pdf

Gillies, D. (2001) *The Scottish Parliament and Educational Policymaking.* Unpublished masters thesis, University of Strathclyde, Glasgow.

Gillies, D. (2014) 'Knowledge activism: bridging the research/policy divide', *Critical Studies in Education*, 55 (3), 272–88.

Humes, W. (1986) *The Leadership Class in Scottish Education.* Edinburgh: John Donald.

Priestley, M., Biesta, G. and Robinson, S. (2015) *Teacher Agency: An Ecological Approach.* London: Bloomsbury.

Rizvi, S. and Lingard, B. (2010) *Globalizing Education Policy.* Abingdon: Routledge.

Sabatier, P. and Weible, C. (2014). *Theories of the Policy Process*, third edition. Boulder, CO: Westview Press.

Sahlberg, P. (2011) 'The Fourth Way of Finland', *Journal of Educational Change*, 12 (2), 173–185.

Scottish Executive (2001) *A Teaching Profession for the 21st Century: Agreement Reached Following Recommendations Made in the McCrone Report.* Online at www.gov.scot/Publications/2001/01/7959/File-1

Scottish Executive (2004) *A Curriculum for Excellence.* Online at www.gov.scot/Resource/Doc/26800/0023690.pdf

Scottish Government (2011) *Advancing Professionalism in Scottish Teaching: Report of the Review of Teacher Employment in Scotland.* Online at http://www.gov.scot/Topics/archive/reviews/reviewofteacheremployment

# II

# THE HISTORICAL AND CULTURAL CONTEXT OF SCOTTISH EDUCATION

# 9

# Historical Perspectives

*Robert Anderson*

Scottish education has been characterised by a peculiar awareness of its own history. Since 1707 its distinctness has been a mark of national identity to be defended against assimilation with England, and its supposed superiority has been a point of national pride. Two achievements were especially notable: the early arrival of universal or near-universal literacy, and a precociously developed university system; on these was founded the 'democratic' myth of Scottish education, often traced back to John Knox, and expressed in the literary and popular image of the 'lad o' pairts', the boy of modest social origins from a rural or small-town background climbing the educational ladder to the ministry or school teaching. Like other national myths, this idealises reality, but has a core of truth, though most historians would agree that it represented an individualist form of meritocracy, rather than reflecting a classless society. For all the virtues of the rural parish school, the chief features of modern Scottish education were created in the few decades following the Education (Scotland) Act 1872, and as a pioneering urban and industrial country, Scotland was deeply marked by the class divisions of the nineteenth century. The 1872 Act was a political and administrative landmark, but (as we shall see) the basic task of schooling the new working class had already been largely overcome, and the increased intervention of the state was not so much a reaction against the previous dominance of religion and the churches, as a modernised and secular form of an ideal of 'national' and public education, aimed at imposing cultural uniformity.

## THE PARISH SCHOOL AND LITERACY

The leaders of the Scottish Reformation had an unusually clear vision of the role of education in creating a godly society. The *First Book of Discipline* of 1560 sketched out an articulated educational structure, from parish school to university, and sought to provide basic religious instruction and literacy in each parish. Achieving this was the work of several generations, but it is today generally agreed that, by the end of the seventeenth century, the network of parish schools was largely complete in the lowlands, though not in the highlands. The Act of 1696 passed by the Scottish Parliament, which was strengthened in 1803 and remained the legal basis of the parish schools until 1872, consolidated this structure. The landowners (heritors) were obliged to build a schoolhouse and to pay a salary to a schoolmaster, which was supplemented by the fees paid by parents; ministers and presbyteries were responsible for the quality of education and the testing of schoolmasters. This was a statutory system, but one run by the church and the local notables rather than the state.

Schooling did not become compulsory until 1872, and attendance in the early modern period depended partly on the perceived advantages of education (which were greater for boys than girls), and partly on the pressure of landowners, ministers and community opinion. Attendance was clearly not universal, and recent studies of literacy have challenged the traditional optimistic picture. Houston (1985, pp. 56–62) estimates male literacy (defined as the ability to write a signature rather than making a mark) at 65 per cent in the lowlands in the mid-eighteenth century, and female at no more than 25–30 per cent. This put the Scottish lowlands among the more literate areas of Europe, but was not a unique achievement. As elsewhere, literacy varied regionally (the borders and east central Scotland being the most advanced), was higher in towns than in the countryside, and was correlated with occupation and prosperity, reaching artisans, small merchants or farmers before labourers, miners, factory workers or crofters.

It is very likely that the early stages of the Industrial Revolution, with the accompanying phenomena of urbanisation and migration from the highlands and Ireland, worsened overall rates of literacy. But exact figures are lacking until the official registration of marriages was introduced in 1855. At that time, 89 per cent of men and 77 per cent of women could sign the registers – compared with 70 per cent and 59 per cent, respectively, in England. But signature evidence may underestimate the basic ability to read, for writing was taught as a separate skill, with higher fees, and many children, especially girls, did not advance beyond reading. Taken as a whole, the evidence on literacy suggests that by 1800 Scottish lowland communities had made the fundamental transition to written culture. Illiteracy survived, but was stigmatised and deplored by the church and the secular authorities, and the ability to read was broad enough to support the beginnings of a tradition of working–class self-education and self-improvement.

None of this applied to the highlands, where attempts to create schools suffered from adverse economic and geographical conditions, the slow penetration of the church's basic parochial organisation and the resistance of an oral Gaelic culture. After the Jacobite risings of 1715, and even more after 1745, church and state combined to enforce loyalty and orthodoxy, and it was axiomatic that this must be through the medium of English. Parish schools were supplemented by those of the Society in Scotland for Propagating Christian Knowledge, founded in 1709, but the refusal to teach in Gaelic (except initially as an aid to learning English) created a formidable cultural barrier between family and school. Nevertheless, by the early nineteenth century conditions in the more prosperous parts of the highlands and islands were not so different from the lowlands, though usually with scantier resources, and illiteracy was being driven into its last redoubts in the Western Isles.

A notable feature of the parish school was its connection with the universities. Schoolmasters were expected to have some university experience, and taught enough Latin to allow boys to pass directly into university classes. This system had evolved to encourage the recruitment of ministers, and there were bursaries to give promising pupils financial support. This was the origin of the tradition of the 'lad o' pairts', and though in practice most such boys came from the middle ranks – the sons of ministers, farmers and artisans – rather than the really poor, the educational opportunities offered in the countryside made Scotland unusual.

## BURGH SCHOOLS AND UNIVERSITIES

The parish school legislation did not apply in burghs. It was normal for royal burghs to maintain burgh schools, whose existence can be traced back into the Middle Ages. Originally these were grammar schools, teaching Latin with an eye to the universities, but town councils began to appoint additional teachers for modern and commercial subjects, and by the late eighteenth century there was a move to consolidate the various schools in an 'academy', usually housed in impressive new buildings. The expanding middle class of the towns was thus well catered for, and outside the big cities the burgh schools and academies were open to both sexes, an unusual feature at the time. But town councils had no statutory duty to provide education for the mass of the population, and most basic education in the towns was given by private teachers. Although Scotland has a strong tradition of public education, private schools once had a vital role, in rural areas as well as in the towns, being squeezed out only in the nineteenth century by competition, from churches and charitable bodies as well as the state. These schools have been underestimated as they left few traces in historical records. They ranged from the 'dame school' where a woman taught reading to young children in her own home, through the 'private adventure' school which at its best could give the same sort of education as a parish school, to expensive boarding and day schools in the cities, training boys for the university or a commercial career, or 'young ladies' in the accomplishments expected of a middle-class bride.

The vigorous state of urban education by 1800 reflected the prosperity of the age of improvement, as did the striking success of the universities, of which Scotland had five. Three were founded in the fifteenth century (St Andrews, Glasgow and King's College Aberdeen), and two after the Reformation (Edinburgh and Marischal College Aberdeen), but the Reformation did not change their fundamental character, as inward-looking institutions teaching arts and theology, whose core task was the training of the clergy. The political and religious upheavals of the seventeenth century were damaging, but after 1700 the universities embarked on a notable revival culminating in the age of the Enlightenment, when Scotland was for a time in the van of European thought. The lecture-based curriculum had a broadly philosophical approach, embracing modern subjects like science and economics, and directly expressed enlightened ideals of politeness, improvement and virtue. The universities could thus offer a liberal education to the social elite, while simultaneously developing professional training, most fully at Edinburgh, in law and medicine. Medical education was especially important in securing the universities' reputation and attracting students, as was to remain the case in the nineteenth century. Socially, the fact that all the universities except St Andrews were situated in large towns kept them in touch with contemporary demands and made them accessible to the new commercial and professional classes; the sons of the aristocracy and gentry, no longer sent abroad to universities like Leyden, rubbed shoulders with a more modest and traditional contingent aiming at the ministry or school teaching.

## THE INDUSTRIAL REVOLUTION AND MASS EDUCATION

Scottish educational traditions evolved within a predominantly agrarian society, dominated by its traditional elites, and committed to religious uniformity. Industrialisation, the appearance of modern class divisions, the rise of political democracy and the growth of religious pluralism posed formidable challenges, and required far-reaching adaptations. The working of the Scottish system had not been affected by the union of 1707, but the practical and political response to industrialisation was inevitably similar in Scotland and England, and required legislation which brought them closer together.

The problems of educating the new urban working class were first tackled around 1810, initially by philanthropists advocating the 'Lancasterian' method of monitorial instruction, but mainly by the church. Supporting schools became a standard activity for church congregations, and there were many religiously inspired committees and societies which promoted special types of school – infant schools, schools in the Highlands, schools for girls, schools for the 'ragged' children of the streets, evening schools for factory workers. These activities were coordinated locally by the church's presbyteries, and nationally by the General Assembly's influential Education Committee. But hopes of a continuing partnership between church and state were shattered by the Disruption of 1843, after which the Church of Scotland was a minority church. Shortly afterwards, in 1846, state aid to education (which had started in the 1830s with building grants, and was supervised from 1840 by a Scottish inspectorate) was reorganised to give annual grants to schools which followed the state's curricular 'Code'. The grant system encouraged the professional training of teachers through the 'pupil-teacher' system of apprenticeship, linked with the 'normal' or training colleges run by the churches. In dispensing its grants, the state did not discriminate between denominations. The new Free Church threw itself into an ambitious educational programme, while Episcopalians and Roman Catholics concentrated on providing for their own adherents. The growth of Catholic schools, especially in Glasgow and the west, was fuelled by Irish immigration, and state support was especially important because of the poverty of the Catholic community. The Catholic system also had distinctive cultural features such as teaching by religious orders, and separate boys' and girls' schools.

There thus developed a dual public system: the statutory parish schools, still limited to rural parishes, and a very diverse sector of denominational and voluntary but state-aided schools. Attempts to merge the two systems and achieve a more rational use of resources preoccupied politicians for many years, but always foundered on the rocks of party-political and religious dissension. The 1872 Act was thus a considerable achievement. It created a 'state' system by giving control of most schools to an elected school board in each burgh and parish, and persuaded the Presbyterian churches to hand over their schools to the boards. This contrasted with the situation in England and Wales, where the Education Act of 1870 inaugurated a bitter rivalry between board and church schools, requiring further legislation in 1902 and 1944.

The 1872 Act created two new agencies which, in different forms, were to share the direction of education thereafter. The school boards gave new scope to local opinion. They were elected by a form of proportional representation, and the franchise included women if they were independent property-holders; women could also be members of the boards, and made a distinctive contribution in the larger towns. School boards lasted until the Education (Scotland) Act 1918, when they were replaced by ad hoc education authorities on a county basis; only in 1929 was education transferred to the all-purpose local authorities. The second creation of 1872 was the Scotch Education Department (SED: not renamed Scottish until 1918). From 1885 the SED was attached to the new Scottish Office, and its early secretaries Henry Craik (1885–1904) and John Struthers (1904–23) turned it into a powerful bureaucracy, giving Scotland a more centralised and uniform state system than England. The balance between central and local control was weighted from the start towards the SED, since school boards and local authorities, despite their powers to raise local taxation, still depended on state grants and had to meet the conditions laid down centrally.

## BEFORE AND AFTER THE 1872 EDUCATION ACT

The creation of state systems of popular education was a general feature of the nineteenth century, related to broader movements of democratisation (the franchise was extended to urban workers in 1867), to the needs of a developing economy, and to the rise of the nation state and national rivalries. Legislation reflected the desire of the state to control a vital agency of citizenship and national efficiency, as much as to promote mass literacy. In fact both school attendance and literacy were already at a high level in Scotland, as the reports of the Argyll Commission in 1867–8 revealed. The practical significance of the 1872 Act was that it established common standards and filled the gaps which the voluntary system had been unable to reach.

The first gap was between men and women. In 1870, 90 per cent of bridegrooms could sign their names, but only 80 per cent of brides. The idea that girls needed a less complete schooling than boys lingered, but in the mid-nineteenth century there had been a growth of separate schools for girls, which probably helped to accelerate female literacy. It was associated with the rise of the woman teacher, and although it was well after 1872 before women outnumbered men in the profession, the training colleges offered women a significant path to independence and social mobility. After 1872, most school boards abolished the small girls' schools, and mixed education became the norm. By 1900, when formal literacy was virtually complete, there was only one point between men (98 per cent) and women (97 per cent), and girls stayed slightly longer at school than boys (Anderson, 1995, pp. 234, 305).

A second gap was within the working class. Under the voluntary system, skilled and 'respectable' workers, who could afford to pay the standard school fee of about threepence a week, had access to schools of reasonable quality, and their children could stay long enough to master the basics, as did nearly all children in the rural lowlands. But the urban poor usually had access only to inferior schools, charging a penny a week or giving a charitable free education. In factory and mining districts, and in the big cities, child labour was a major disincentive to education. Factory legislation, as well as compulsory schooling, progressively removed this obstacle, and though school fees were not abolished until 1890, school boards offered an education of equal quality to all their constituents. The huge urban schools which remain the symbol of the Victorian era in education became part of the homogeneous working-class experience which had evolved by 1900.

A third gap was between lowlands and highlands. The Argyll report revealed the poverty and backwardness of education in the Western Isles, Skye and some mainland districts, though these conditions were by now untypical of the Highlands as a whole. For some years Highland school boards were to struggle with inadequate resources, but the problems were overcome within a generation. Part of the price was a further retreat of Gaelic. The 1872 Act has often been blamed for this, and it is true that official policy made only minor concessions to the language; but there was nothing new in this, for Highland educational initiatives had always insisted on the primacy of English. It was not until after 1945 that serious efforts were made to promote bilingualism.

A fourth gap, which the 1872 Act did not remedy, was the situation of Catholic schools. Illiteracy persisted in the Catholic community, and helped make the western counties a problem area. The religious settlement of 1872 was not accepted by Catholics or Episcopalians, and they continued to receive direct state grants, which covered running costs but not capital expenditure. The Episcopalian schools stagnated and eventually withered away, but the Catholic sector expanded, from 65 schools in 1872 to 226 in 1918; about an eighth of all Scottish children were in Catholic schools. Lack of resources meant that schools were under-equipped, teachers poorly paid and secondary education underdeveloped. This was increasingly felt as an injustice, and the 1918 Act transferred Roman Catholic schools to the education authorities, to be supported on the same financial basis as other schools, with safeguards for religious instruction and the denominational affiliation of teachers. Protected and promoted by the hierarchy, often in alliance with the new Labour electorate, Catholic schools soon acquired an entrenched position in the public system.

The 1872 Act made education compulsory from five to thirteen, raised to fourteen in 1883. But this was theoretical, as children could leave earlier if they had mastered the 'three Rs'. From 1901, however, fourteen was generally enforced as the effective leaving age, and by then the elementary curriculum included subjects like history, geography, elementary science, physical training and some semi-vocational elements: woodwork for boys, cookery and 'domestic economy' for girls. Once every child passed through the school, governments also saw its value as an agency of social welfare: school meals and medical inspection were put on a statutory basis in 1908. The daily routines of the elementary school were not to change fundamentally thereafter until the 1960s.

## THE REMODELLING OF ELITE EDUCATION

While elementary education developed on its own lines, having an essentially working-class character which contrasted with the lack of sharp social differentiation in the old parish schools, secondary schools and universities were remodelled to meet the needs of the expanding middle class for professional qualifications and examination credentials. The movement for university reform began early, and was often controversial. There were royal commissions of inquiry in 1826 and 1876, and reforming Acts of Parliament in 1858 and 1889, which overhauled both constitutions and curricula. In the early nineteenth century the universities had no entrance examination, and although there was a recommended curriculum, many students stayed for only a year or two, chose which lectures to attend and took no examinations – formal graduation had become the exception. But this no longer suited the needs of the age, and the outcome of reform by the 1890s was a standardised pattern of graduation, with the arts curriculum offering a choice between three-year Ordinary and four-year Honours degrees. Specialised courses, including separate faculties of science, replaced the old Master of Arts (MA) curriculum with its compulsory Latin, Greek and philosophy. The typical age of entry rose from fifteen or sixteen, as it still was in the 1860s, to seventeen or eighteen, and free entry gave way to an entrance examination equivalent to the school Leaving Certificate introduced by the SED in 1888. These changes were only possible because secondary schools had also been reformed and given an extended academic curriculum.

A secondary school system was constructed from disparate elements. The 1872 Act transferred the burgh schools to school boards, but otherwise did little for secondary education. Resources were found instead from endowments, and in the 1870s and 1880s many older endowed schools, including the former residential 'hospitals' like George Heriot's in Edinburgh, were modernised. Further gaps were filled by 'higher grade' schools, founded by school boards as extensions of elementary schools, especially in Glasgow. In 1892 the first state grants for secondary education appeared (ten years earlier than in England), and were used to build up schools in smaller towns as well as to strengthen existing ones. The result was that although schools differed in prestige and legal status, they formed an effective national network able to prepare both for the universities and for business careers. The Argyll Commission in the 1860s had identified 59 public secondary schools with 14,879 pupils. By 1912 there were 249, with 38,312 pupils (19,611 boys and 18,701 girls). Of these, 143 gave a full five-year course, and 106 a three-year or 'intermediate' one; 171 of the schools charged no fees (Anderson 1983, pp. 134, 243–6). This pattern was to change little until the 1940s.

Two points were especially significant. First, though Scotland was not a pioneer in university education for women – because of legal obstacles, their admission was delayed until 1892 – mixed secondary education became firmly established, at least outside Edinburgh, Glasgow and Aberdeen, where high schools and endowed schools remained single sex. Middle-class parents now had as good a choice of education for their daughters as for their sons, and this was reflected in the percentage of women students at the universities, which was high by contemporary standards: 23 per cent by 1914, rising to 34 per cent in the 1920s, though it fell again in the 1930s to 26–7 per cent.

Second, the schools served a wide social range. The road to the university now lay only through the secondary school, but analysis of the social origins of university students suggests that opportunities for mobility were not narrowed. Although Scotland had a few English-style 'public schools', like Fettes College, and some exclusive day schools, like Edinburgh Academy and its equivalents in Glasgow, the Scottish middle class were generally content to use their local schools. At the other end of the social scale, accessibility was wide because many secondary schools charged no fees, and bursaries were fairly widely available. Transfer from elementary to secondary schools around the age of twelve became an accepted if still limited phenomenon. The 1918 Act required education authorities to make free secondary education available to all, though they could and did retain fee-paying in designated schools.

## THE TWENTIETH CENTURY: TOWARDS AN INTEGRATED SYSTEM

By 1900, the extension of the elementary curriculum and the increasing number of children staying at school after age twelve raised the question of relations between the two sectors. The SED was now using the term 'primary' for the early stages of education, but the underlying social conception was still that true secondary education was only for an academically gifted minority, and it was official policy (formalised in 1903) to draw a sharp distinction between secondary and advanced elementary education. A 'qualifying examination' at twelve identified the exceptional talents who might climb the educational ladder (a favourite image of the time), but the majority stayed on in the primary school and took 'supplementary courses'. After leaving school, they were encouraged to attend evening 'continuation' classes, mostly vocational. The reforming mood created by the First World War raised hopes of an end to this dualism, especially as the 1918 Act proposed raising the leaving age from fourteen to fifteen. But financial crisis suspended this provision – and also plans for compulsory continuation classes for adolescents – and the SED resisted pressures for 'secondary education for all', continuing to insist that the different types of course should be rigidly separate. Its controversial regulations of 1923 renamed the supplementary courses 'advanced divisions', but these were denied secondary status, and most had only a two-year curriculum.

In practice the interwar years saw a blurring of the distinction between courses. In smaller towns, both types were given in 'omnibus' schools which took all older children, and elsewhere the authorities usually grouped advanced education in 'central' schools, replacing all-age schools with a redistribution at age twelve (the 'clean cut'). The Education Act of 1936 proposed raising the leaving age to fifteen in 1939, and although this was postponed because of the war (until 1947), the SED finally accepted that all post-primary courses should be called secondary, divided where necessary between 'senior' (five-year) and 'junior' (three-year) schools. This system was consolidated and developed in the 1940s. Most senior secondary schools were old-established secondaries, with superior buildings, equipment and staffing, while junior secondaries were either former central schools or new foundations. All-age primary schools finally disappeared except in remote rural areas. Thus apart from places served by bilateral omnibus schools, Scotland now had a selective secondary system based on the 'twelve-plus' examination, given new scientific authority by the intelligence testing developed in the 1930s.

Secondary schools were the most dynamic sector of Scottish education between the wars: numbers rose to about 90,000 by 1939. But low birth rates and the collapse of traditional industries had a generally negative and depressing effect. Despite a few initiatives like the creation of the Scottish Council for Research in Education in 1928, official thinking remained conservative. There was, for example, no vigorous promotion of scientific and technical education, of a kind which might have helped revive the Scottish economy. The Second World War changed this, directly by underlining the importance of science and advanced education, indirectly by creating long-term social aspirations which broke the fetters of the selective system. Even for the political left, selection seemed acceptable after the war as an expression of equality of opportunity, and the more idealistic vision expressed in the 1947 report of the Scottish Advisory Council on Education was rejected by the SED. But the breaking down of the old industrial economy, with its relatively small elite and its mass working class, undermined the assumption that academic education and examination qualifications could be reserved for a quarter or a third of the population. There was also a fundamental change in the career expectations of women. Thus by the 1960s there was an increasing demand to stay on at school, and to gain qualifications which the junior secondaries were unable to offer. One response was the introduction of the Scottish Certificate of Education in 1962, with a Higher Grade which was less university-oriented than the old Leaving Certificate, and a new Ordinary Grade offering a wider range of subjects for fourth-year pupils.

These pressures paved the way for the eventual raising of the leaving age to sixteen in 1973, and more immediately for the abolition of selection in 1965, a policy which aroused some controversy at the time, but which soon achieved wide acceptance, as it failed to do in England. The pattern of mixed, six-year comprehensives was almost universal in Scotland. Difficulties arose chiefly in the cities, where it meant the end of the remaining fee-paying schools run by councils, and where residential segregation strongly influenced the character and achievement of schools. A further consequence of the policy, also concentrated in the cities, was the withdrawal of the state's direct grants to old-established endowed schools, which now passed with their middle-class clientele into the independent sector.

The organisation of secondary schooling and its relation with primary schools was the most politically sensitive issue in Scottish education for much of the twentieth century. But primary education had its own revolution after 1945. An expanding birth rate, and the shift of the population from central districts to suburbs and new towns, required a massive programme of new building and teacher training. So did the introduction of more child-centred educational methods, and the SED's Memorandum *Primary Education in Scotland* of 1965 gave these official sanction?

Expansion was also marked at the post-secondary level. Government policy after 1945 accepted the need for more students in both traditional universities and technical colleges, and the Robbins Report of 1963 only endorsed a trend already well under way. A new university opened at Stirling, and Strathclyde and Heriot-Watt universities were created from existing advanced technical colleges. Technical colleges and art schools had their roots in the nineteenth century, and the leading ones had been financed directly by the SED as 'central institutions' since 1900. Now full-time and degree-level work was encouraged, and local technical and adult education were combined in a network of 'further education' colleges. The old teacher-training colleges, renamed colleges of education in 1958, were also encouraged to expand their remit and award degrees. By 1980, therefore, the concept of a 'tertiary' education of which traditional universities were only one part was well accepted, and it attracted more than 15 per cent of the age group; but the general extension of full university status came only in the 1990s.

## CONCLUSION

The growth of secondary and higher education since 1945 can be seen as the latest stage in a continual expansion of education, and of its place in the lives of individuals, which began in the mid-nineteenth century and shows no sign of coming to an end. At its outset most working-class children, if they attended school at all, left at ten or eleven, while middle-class children, apart from a small minority who went to the universities, left at fourteen or fifteen. By 1980, the age of leaving full-time education, though still conditioned by social class, ranged from sixteen to twenty-two or more. In responding to the problems created by the Industrial Revolution, Scotland was given a good start by its tradition of national education and by a cultural disposition, with religious, political and social roots, to value educational achievement. But as other countries caught up, Scotland ceased to be so exceptional, though some indicators (notably the rate of participation in higher education) remained very favourable. Many historians would argue that while the system promoted meritocracy, and allowed individual Scots to move upwards into both Scottish and British elites, the education offered to the ordinary child was less impressive. The structure of schooling which developed after 1872 reflected class divisions in Scotland much as elsewhere, and twentieth-century progress towards greater equality of opportunity, though perhaps made smoother by an idealised conception of the educational past, had still to contend with social inequalities which the formal integration of educational institutions achieved by the late twentieth century could not itself remove.

## REFERENCES

Anderson, R. D. (1983) *Education and Opportunity in Victorian Scotland: Schools and Universities*. Oxford: Clarendon Press.

Anderson, R. D. (1995) *Education and the Scottish People, 1750–1918*, Oxford: Oxford University Press.

Anderson, R., Freeman, M. and Paterson, L. (eds) (2015) *The Edinburgh History of Education in Scotland*. Edinburgh: Edinburgh University Press.

Houston, R. A. (1985) *Scottish Literacy and the Scottish Identity: Illiteracy and Society in Scotland and Northern England, 1600–1800*. Cambridge: Cambridge University Press.

Humes, W. and Paterson, H. (eds) (1982) *Scottish Culture and Scottish Education, 1800–1980*. Edinburgh: John Donald.

Paterson, L. (2003) *Scottish Education in the Twentieth Century*. Edinburgh: Edinburgh University Press.

Withrington, D. J. (1988) Schooling, literacy and society. In T. M. Devine and R. Mitchison (eds), *People and Society in Scotland. I. 1760–1830*, Edinburgh: John Donald.

# 10

# The History of Scottish Education since Devolution

*Donald Gillies*

'The Scottish Parliament, adjourned on the 25th day of March in the year 1707, is hereby reconvened.' With these suitably dramatic words from Winnie Ewing at the opening session on 1 July 1999, political power formally returned to Scotland under the devolution settlement. Winnie Ewing's role was probably apt because, in some ways, it was her Scottish National Party (SNP) victory in the Hamilton by-election of 1967 which can be seen as the source of the subsequent decades of struggle for devolution and home rule for Scotland. While the referendum of 1979 had resulted in a narrow majority in favour of devolution, the margin was insufficiently wide to meet the electoral requirements of the time. The election of the Labour Government in 1997 produced a further referendum which resulted in a convincing victory for those supporting devolution: 74 per cent voted in favour of devolution, with 64 per cent voting in favour of the second question on tax-varying powers.

While the devolution settlement marked a significant shift in political structure, it should be remembered that Scottish education – along with the church and the law – had never been integrated into a British system, remaining separate for the duration of the union of Parliaments. However, what did alter hugely was that, rather than be the subject of policy and legislation at Westminster, where Scottish Members of Parliament (MPs) were always a small minority, Scottish education would now be governed from a Scottish Parliament in Edinburgh. As one of the two key devolved areas alongside health, education became a major focus for political debate and public engagement and it was significant that the first Act of the new Scottish Parliament should be focused on education: the Standards in Scotland's Schools etc. Act of 2000.

Since 1999, the Scottish Parliament has had only two forms of government, essentially: the elections of 1999 and 2003 saw the formation of a Labour–Liberal Democrat coalition 'Executive'; the election of 2007 resulted in a minority SNP Government, followed by a majority one in 2011, but returning to a minority government from 2016. There has been, therefore, some degree of continuity and, as the nature of coalition and minority government would suggest, a relatively conservative agenda throughout. There have been two major changes only during the whole period as far as school education is concerned: the first was the development of Curriculum for Excellence (CfE) from 2004, and the second the introduction of the National Improvement Framework from 2015. Other education issues which have had the biggest impacts are the increasing role and scale of nursery and early years' provision, the inclusion agenda, the mergers of further education colleges and the continued commitment to free tuition fees in the tertiary sector.

## CURRICULUM CHANGE

At the advent of devolution, the school curriculum was somewhat fragmented with the 5–14 arrangements guiding primary and lower secondary years; Standard Grade for S3 and S4; and a range of courses governing the upper secondary: Access, Intermediate, Higher, Advanced Higher. In the private sector, A levels and the International Baccalaureate featured highly. Prior to 1999, provision for early education and childcare was not subject to national curriculum guidelines, a situation that was to change markedly in the decades since.

A number of factors combined which led to the creation of proposals for a 3–18 curriculum. There was dissatisfaction from various groups, including parents, at the lack of cohesion and consistency across the different ages and stages: at 5–14, grading was from A to E (Level F was a later addition); at Standard Grade it was from Level 7 to Level 1; while in the upper school the grading was ranked from D to A. In addition to the lack of structural coherence, there was concern about the 'cluttered' nature of the primary curriculum, the lack of connections across learning, about the role and power of assessment and certification within the system, at problematic variations introduced by secondary schools and local authorities where courses for older students were adapted for earlier use, and at the perennial issue of giving due place to vocational courses. In 2002, the then Scottish Executive launched a National Debate on education which had a wide range of public engagement opportunities and, in its wake, created a review group to identify the purposes of education 3 to 18 and principles for the design of the curriculum (Scottish Executive, 2004, p.7).

The somewhat chequered progress of Curriculum for Excellence has been catalogued in previous editions of *Scottish Education*. However, from a current perspective it is possible to identify three principal factors which contributed to its uneven and contested implementation or enactment. The first, and most damaging, factor was that the original proposals were never subject to professional consultation: the Scottish Executive of the day approved the proposals immediately in their entirety without there being any further public or professional engagement. Thus, teachers, upon whose commitment and expertise the success of the development depended, were never involved until such time as expected to bring it to life in the classroom. Secondly, it seems clear now that there was insufficient professional advice, development and support for practitioners as they grappled with what was a significant shift in curriculum philosophy and design. The recent dips in performance identified in the Scottish Survey of Literacy and Numeracy (SSLN) may well be linked to problems at the outset of implementation such as those around the interpretation of 'active learning' and related uneven practice (Drew and Mackie, 2011). The fact that the curriculum was implemented piecemeal from the early years onward, also meant that secondary teachers were relatively detached for some years, and the teacher workforce as a whole never fully engaged collectively with the development. The third damaging factor was that the original review group was only tasked with identifying principles and purposes of the curriculum: curriculum content and assessment were not considered at this point. Instead, the eight 'curriculum areas' emerged unheralded in the months following, while the assessment arrangements, certainly for secondary schools, took years to be outlined. This created a fractured and unsatisfactory model (Priestley and Humes, 2010).

Some revision of the detail of Curriculum for Excellence took place in the light of teacher unrest over workload. In the summer of 2016, the Cabinet Secretary, John Swinney, brought forward with Education Scotland and Scottish Qualifications Authority (SQA) proposals to streamline the use of experiences and outcomes documentation – notoriously extensive – and to reduce internal assessment at the senior phase of the secondary school. In the light of concern about SSLN results, however, the government had already produced proposals for national assessment to be introduced at P1, P4, P7 and S3 stages. As these form part of the National Improvement Framework, these issues will be considered in more detail below.

Given the traditional gestation period for curriculum development in Scotland and the truncated lifespan of policy once eventually implemented, one can assume that within the next five years another major revision will be forthcoming.

A further feature of curriculum since devolution has been its ever-expanding nature. Schools have increasingly been seen as sites where all issues of social welfare can be addressed and so, in addition to the curricular areas of CfE, have also come a whole number of other issues requiring teacher attention. This can be seen at the most strategic level with the importance given to health and wellbeing within the curriculum itself, but also have come expectations that schools will address such issues as healthy eating, physical activity, two extra languages, bullying, drug and alcohol abuse, racism, social cohesion, cyber safety and personal hygiene. All of these can be seen as worthy and important but, as it is rare for the inspectorate or local authorities to tell schools to drop anything from the curriculum, it is becoming increasingly difficult for schools to find the time to cover all that is required of them. While imaginative approaches to interdisciplinary activity can assist, it still remains a challenge for schools to give due attention to all that is expected of them.

## LEGISLATION

The history of educational legislation enacted in Scotland since 1999 follows a trajectory which reveals an increasingly specific and outcomes-based approach to schooling. Earlier legislation could be said to be more about strategic issues and general principles, whereas recent legislation has been much more focused on operational matters and named goals and targets (see Redford, 2005–present). The main reason for this shift has been an effective opposition attack on the SNP's record on education and an oddly reactive response to this. The main plank has been that the SNP has been so obsessed by the constitutional question that they have neglected their oversight of education, an argument which, as a matter of perception, is difficult to substantiate. Two other lines of attack have been over standards of literacy and numeracy which, according to the SSLN, have evidenced slippage, and over the 'attainment gap' which has shown a continuing gulf between attainment levels reached by socially advantaged groups and those of others. This has been a deep-set problem in Scotland since records began and so the culpability of the SNP Government for this is, at least, a shared one with all who have gone before. A more confident and effective government, and specifically Cabinet Secretary for Education, could perhaps have withstood such attacks, given their limited basis. Instead the government launched a series of hasty, reactive initiatives which were pushed through to official policy with minimal consultation. This was compounded by the First Minister putting her political reputation on the line in saying she would be judged on her record of closing the attainment gap (Scottish Government, 2016, p. 1). While narrowing the attainment gap may be a legitimate political goal, the prospects of closing it are minimal, in a country with such levels of child poverty as Scotland, and such a scale of social immobility. The whole political venture, while worthy in its social goals, seems based on limited understanding of the nature of the attainment gap, the factors which support it, and the massive socio-economic and cultural overhaul required to address it (Murphy, 2014).

The pressure on the SNP Government regarding pupil attainment was compounded by the Programme for International Student Assessment (PISA) 2015 results for Scotland which were released in late 2016. The results showed a continued downward trajectory both in terms of achievement and as relative to other countries – thus in criterion-referenced and norm-referenced terms. While the results were based solely on attainment in reading, mathematics and science, and so reflective of only a small part of the curriculum, there was little other room for consolation. The PISA results for Scotland have been in gradual decline since 2000, despite a minor, unexplained, improvement between 2006 and 2012 in reading attainment. Nevertheless, several critics identified Curriculum for Excellence, the blueprint for which only emerged in 2004, as the culprit, while another laid the blame at the 1+2 Languages Policy, only launched in 2012. A more judicious response would be that the decisive factors remain unknown and so it is impossible to tell if Curriculum for Excellence has slowed, increased or had no effect on, this rate of decline. The PISA results for 2018 may give better evidence on this matter as the 15 year olds involved then will certainly have had all their schooling under the Curriculum for Excellence model. Meanwhile, it may be that the introduction of national assessments, if properly implemented, at least will produce data to allow for informed decisions to be made about adjustments to the curriculum and classroom practice to address any issues which arise regarding pupil attainment.

The first education act of the re-established Scottish Parliament, the Standards in Scotland's Schools etc. Act (2000) covered a range of disparate issues, most prominent amongst which were giving children the right to an education, it having previously merely been the duty of a parent to provide such; stipulating the purpose of school education, this being lifted from the United Nations Convention on the Rights of the Child (1989); making school development plans, and consulting on such with school pupils, a requirement; and making 'mainstream' schooling the default position for all, except where this was deemed unsuitable for the child, for other children or where associated costs proved prohibitive. These last two legal changes were the most fundamental and far-reaching: the first set in motion a continuing trend towards the empowerment of children and young people in relation to their own lives and education, at least in terms of their 'voice' being heard; and, with the latter, a continuing move towards 'inclusion' of all children within the school system, and a vast reduction in 'special' school provision. The system and its workforce took considerable time to adjust to this significant change and many struggled to cope with the consequent challenges in relation to including those with additional physical, and particularly cognitive or behavioural, needs. Compounding this development was a perceived lack of resources, material and human, to support the educational system in coping with this change, although over time local authorities did come to employ considerable numbers of pupil support assistants, albeit poorly paid and not always well qualified. As will be seen, extensive further legislation around children with additional support needs was to follow as the inclusion agenda gathered momentum.

The Education (Additional Support for Learning) (Scotland) Act 2004, and amended in 2009, superseded legislation dating from 1980 which had addressed 'special educational needs' through the use of a Record of Needs for those children deemed eligible. It may be surprising that it took over twenty years for legislative change to be enacted, given the increasing importance of the inclusion agenda over the decades prior. The new legislation introduced the concept of 'additional support needs' which was both a less harsh term and a broader categorisation to reflect wider social and contextual factors which may affect children's needs. This was in tune with the dominant political discourse, largely associated with the emergence of New Labour in the 1990s, which had given high priority to addressing social exclusion and so viewing the inclusion agenda as not solely restricted to issues of cognitive or physical impairment. In the wake of this legislation came the *Getting it Right for Every Child* (GIRFEC) policy guidance in 2008 which took a similarly comprehensive approach, aimed at a much more integrated multi-agency approach to children and their needs. While progress towards this goal has been fitful, and its effectiveness exposed by a number of distressing cases involving failures in child protection, many local authorities have attempted to align better the whole range of children's services, and key school personnel are much more likely now to be working with many different agencies focused on child welfare, even if coordinating and optimising this model can be complex and problematic.

This proactive approach to child welfare issues, again highlighted in the prominent place given to health and wellbeing within Curriculum for Excellence, has not been without opposition. This emerged most strongly in relation to the Children and Young People (Scotland) Act 2014 which had aimed to give statutory status to aspects of the GIRFEC approach. One of the provisions was to provide a 'named person', such as a health worker, headteacher or pastoral care teacher, to offer support or advice to children and their parents, if requested. The proposed role was not entirely clear, however, with it sometimes being described as that of 'monitoring' a child's welfare, and of permitting state access to confidential data and interaction with children, without parental knowledge or consent. This brought a flurry of complaints from a range of interest groups who argued that it was undermining the role of parents, an unwarranted intrusion into family life, and a breach of privacy and human rights, with the 'named person' being seen as an ugly mix of state snooper and Big Brother. In 2016, the UK Supreme Court ruled in favour of the complainants and necessitated government revision of the proposed scheme.

This development can be seen as evidence of two issues affecting Scottish education in recent years: inadequately drafted legislation, exacerbated by weak parliamentary committee scrutiny; and a government reluctance, or timidity, surrounding targeted, as opposed to blanket, intervention. The Scottish Attainment Challenge, for example, initially was focused on schools in the areas of most deprivation but the associated policy was termed 'excellence and equity', presumably so that it would be seen to embrace everyone in education and not just those deemed to have most need. Successive governments have lacked the courage, and perhaps understanding, to embrace proportional equality when most relevant, and have instead stuck with simplistic numerical equality which can, of course, increase divisions between the 'haves' and the 'have nots'. Croxford (2003, p. 744) explains how early intervention schemes which are not targeted, and so not deliberately exclusive, lead, perversely, to widening the gap between advantaged and disadvantaged groups. Whitty (2002, p.111) similarly argues that universal 'excellence' in provision will increase the attainment gap rather than narrow it. Evaluation of the Pupil Premium initiative in England suggests that the greatest impact comes where resources, material and human, are explicitly targeted at those unambiguously identified as being in most need (Demie and Mclean, 2015). Blunter approaches such as 'increased staffing' do not have the same traction. The risk is evident, therefore, that a policy aimed at 'excellence and equity' may lack required clarity of purpose and precision of focus.

## THE NATIONAL IMPROVEMENT FRAMEWORK

The National Improvement Framework for Scottish Education was launched in January 2016 after a very limited consultation period both in terms of extent and time. The exercise had suggested a somewhat rushed response to the disappointing SSLN figures of the previous summer and an urgency born of forthcoming Holyrood elections. By this stage, the First Minister had all but overshadowed the Cabinet Secretary, Angela Constance, in terms of the education portfolio and it was no surprise that the minister did not survive the post-election reshuffle. The main surprise of the policy was the return to national assessments in primary school, and it was significant that the consultation exercise had specifically omitted reference to this aspect of the proposals. It was clear that the government was determined to introduce this measure but, in any case, the opposition to it turned out to be somewhat muted. The actual nature of the 'national assessments' remained imprecise for some time, again giving the impression that this was about policy headlines and public perception much more than detail and substance.

Revised in December 2016, the framework was focused on raising attainment, closing the poverty-related attainment gap, children's health and wellbeing, and employability. Amongst the stated 'drivers' for improvement, it was no surprise to see leadership given a prime role. This had been a continued mantra of government and of policy discourse, and had seen tangible expression in the creation of the Scottish College for Educational Leadership in 2014, and the development of associated qualifications for headship, spurred by the Donaldson Report of 2010.

The framework itself had been predated by the Scottish Attainment Challenge launched in February 2015 which had earmarked £100 million for targeted support to selected local authorities with the highest incidence of socio-economic disadvantage and on named primary schools elsewhere in similar circumstances. The proposals were further developed over the years following, with the headline figure being increased to £750 million, although there was some opposition to the suggestion that this be redirected finance already allocated to local authorities from Holyrood.

The flurry of activity around the attainment gap, and these related policy initiatives, have certainly become a strong narrative in Scottish educational discourse but it will take some time before the impact can be evaluated. When allied to doubt about the governance arrangements in relation to local authorities and education, and the evident preference in Cabinet for more devolution of finance and responsibility to schools, there is a lack of stability within the system which makes prospects of major improvements here questionable.

## GOVERNANCE

The devolution settlement of 1997 marked the biggest change in the administration of Scottish education, but since then the overall picture within the state system has been relatively static. The key role in terms of provision remains with local authorities, whose shape has been untouched since the reforms of the 1990s which saw the end of the larger regional authorities. There has been continued, if low level, dissatisfaction with these governance arrangements in that significant economies of scale remain lost since the demise of the larger regions, such as Strathclyde. While some smaller local authorities have tried to pool resources, this has not proved successful. The governance review (Scottish Government, 2017), initiated by the new Cabinet Secretary for Education, John Swinney, aimed to address these issues with the proposal to move to 'regional improvement collaboratives' but, again, issues over democratic control arise and it is hard to see how this model could coexist with current local authority boundaries. In addition, the related government suggestion of more powers and resources being given directly to headteachers, thus bypassing local authority involvement altogether, would again create even greater issues about economies of scale. This is particularly acute in relation to additional support needs: while local authorities have the necessary scale to provide central support this would not be the case if such responsibilities were devolved to individual schools where piecemeal provision would be inevitable.

One common feature of governance since devolution has been the tendency for merger of educational bodies. For example, Her Majesty's Inspectorate of Education, which had been reformed in 2001 as an 'executive agency' and so more distanced from government, was merged in 2010 with the curriculum development and support body, Learning and Teaching Scotland, to become a new body, Education Scotland, tasked more directly with the improvement agenda. Learning and Teaching Scotland had itself been formed of a merger of the Scottish Consultative Council on the Curriculum and the Scottish Council for Educational Technology in 2000. The new body, Education Scotland, has had numerous internal reformulations since 2010 and it has been subject to criticism from various quarters, whether for the quality of its resources, or for the number and nature of school inspections completed. While this merger did resurface the problems of the inspectorate being seen to inspect and evaluate what they themselves promote and support, it did also send out a signal about the increasing role of self-evaluation in schools, where schools and teachers have been encouraged to develop their own systems of quality assurance, supported by the *How Good is our School?* series of publications.

The Scottish Qualifications Authority was another offspring of merger, this time uniting the Scottish Examination Board and the Scottish Vocational Education Council from 1997. This merger sent out a signal about the intended parity of esteem between academic and vocational qualifications but was also symptomatic of the growing 'skills' agenda within education where the deemed needs of the economy became much more prominent in relation to educational provision and assessment. Vocational qualifications were very much the domain of the further education sector, and it underwent massive reorganisation on regional lines in 2013, following a government consultation exercise in 2011. The restructuring was controversial and protracted, with pay-offs, resignations, funding shortfalls, reduced college places and staff unrest being the subject of considerable media and political interest. A similarly controversial merger of Scottish police forces met with widespread disapproval and was seen by some as evidence of a strong centralising tendency within the SNP Government. The querying in the governance review of 2017 of the continued role of local authorities in education would tend to give support to this impression of government preference.

## THE CHANGING CLASSROOM

Developments in technology have probably been the single biggest influence on schools and the classroom over the past two decades. This has had considerable impact on school administration and on pedagogy, although teachers are often unsatisfied with how the system has kept up with the pace of change. The national intranet, Scottish Schools Digital Network (GLOW), has attracted repeated criticism and it rarely appears in the educational press without the word 'clunky' in close attendance. Technology has brought easier access to more and better data for schools and teachers and, where used judiciously, can assist decision making and planning. Otherwise, however, it has added to increased paperwork and workload stress. Technology, particularly in its social media manifestation, has brought a number of challenges to schools and young people, in particular. Cyberbullying and sexual harassment have become common and the relatively hidden nature of this activity makes it hard for schools to support and protect those who experience it. Teachers, too, have found themselves subject to online abuse and as the Internet becomes increasingly beyond regulation it is difficult to see how these trends can be reversed.

The continuing gender imbalance in the teaching workforce is changing steadily the nature of schools. The 2016 figures show that 90 per cent of primary teachers and that 63 per cent of secondary teachers are female. The number of male teachers in primary has actually grown slightly from 8 per cent to 10 per cent in the last decade but the trend toward a feminised profession continues in the secondary sector with the percentage of males in the secondary sector declining in the last sixty years from 58 per cent to 37 per cent. The number of primary headteachers who are female has remained static over the last decade at 86 per cent but in secondary schools this has risen from 29 per cent to 41 per cent. Whether or not the gender of the teacher is significant for the learning experience is inconclusive but the changing profile of the headteacher is at least coming more to reflect the overall gender profile of the teaching workforce, although concerns about female representation within promoted posts persist.

The perennial issue of rewarding effective teachers who wish to remain in the classroom rather than move into more formal management and leadership posts has not been resolved. The McCrone report of 2001 created the post of Chartered Teacher, with increased pay and related qualifications, but this role was then removed in the wake of the McCormac review of 2011. In primary schools, the introduction of principal teacher posts has given some opportunity for teachers to take on more responsibility, often related to curriculum, without having more formal administrative roles. However, these posts quite often exist in the absence of deputy headteacher posts and so the duties of that role fall to principal teachers. In secondary schools, the introduction of faculty heads, responsible for a number of subject areas, has become widespread. This development suits an age of austerity but does reduce the promotion prospects for teachers.

Changes to the school estate have been considerable over the last decades, largely making for more pleasant and suitable accommodation. The financial arrangements for this development have attracted widespread public and political criticism and the quality of the finished work has also been queried as a result of building decay, such as wall collapses and roof damage, within Edinburgh's new school estate. As these new builds age over the coming years, even more problems will arise as significant debt still needs to be paid off, making it even more difficult for local authorities to contemplate the costs of future modernisation.

Government has also been exercised about teacher shortage in certain geographical areas in Scotland and in certain subject areas, particularly in science, technology, engineering and mathematics (STEM). In 2016, universities and the General Teaching Council for Scotland (GTCS) were encouraged by government to look at new ways to attract and retain teachers.

Several innovative routes to teaching were developed, albeit amid some concern about retaining quality. In difficult economic times, however, teachers' pay remains stagnant and there must be concerns both about the capacity of the profession to attract new recruits and about the prospects of future trade union action on pay and conditions.

## FUTURE

The recent history of Scottish education has been marked by its very high public profile since devolution but also as a growing site of political dispute. Opposition parties have had success in attacking the SNP Government record and this success will only encourage more of the same. While democratic accountability is vital, the risk is that education becomes subject to more and more revision, change and tinkering to suit short-term political needs. The opposition parties' approach has created a common discourse of negativity about Scottish state education and, should this continue, it becomes even harder for teachers to approach their work with confidence and any degree of satisfaction. As the 2016 Scottish election showed, however, because the constitutional issue remains so dominant within Scottish politics, opposition success in attacking the government record on education has not translated into any electoral reward. Indeed, during the 2014 referendum on Scottish independence, the issue of education rarely arose at all, certainly in relation to the compulsory sector. Organisations representing higher education did become more involved in the debate but this was not observable elsewhere in the system.

It seems certain that change will come in two areas in the coming years. The evidence from the SSLN and PISA results will continue to put pressure on the curriculum. The introduction of national assessments will have an effect on classroom practice but, even so, it seems likely that a more formal revision of the curriculum will be instituted. The second area is likely to be in terms of governance with the role of local authorities changing and new arrangements favouring increased local headteacher empowerment within a more regional approach to educational provision.

For Scotland itself, the unresolved constitutional issue in relation to independence, and the continuing repercussions of the UK vote to leave the European Union (EU), make for a very unsettled and polarised political landscape and not the optimum context within which to expect educational success to blossom. Society owes its young people the prospects of a better future and their concerns need to be become more prominent if the education system is to support their development as it should.

## REFERENCES

Croxford, L. (2003) 'Baseline assessment in Scotland', in T. Bryce and W. Humes (eds), *Scottish Education, Second Edition: Post-devolution*. Edinburgh: Edinburgh University Press, pp. 740–5.

Demie, F. and Mclean, C. (2015) 'Context and implications document for: tackling disadvantage: what works in narrowing the achievement gap in schools', *Review of Education*, 3, 175–8. doi:10.1002/rev3.3053

Drew, V. and Mackie, L. (2011) 'Extending the constructs of active learning: implications for teachers' pedagogy and practice', *The Curriculum Journal*, 22(4), 451–67. http://dx.doi.org/10.1080/09585176.2011.627204

Murphy, D. (2014) *Schooling Scotland: Education, Equity, and Community*. Edinburgh: Argyll Publishing.

Priestley, M. and Humes, W. (2010) 'The development of Scotland's Curriculum for Excellence: amnesia and déjà-vu', *Oxford Review of Education*, 36(3), 345–61. http://dx.doi.org/10.1080/03054980903518951

Redford, M. (2005–present) 'Education in the Scottish Parliament', *Scottish Educational Review*, vol. 38 onwards.

Scottish Executive (2004). *A Curriculum for Excellence*. Edinburgh: Scottish Executive.

Scottish Government (2016) *National Improvement Framework for Scottish Education*. Edinburgh: Scottish Government.

Scottish Government (2017) *Education Governance: Next Steps*. Edinburgh: Scottish Government. Online at www.gov.scot/Resource/0052/00521038.pdf

Whitty, G. (2002). *Making Sense of Education Policy*. London: Paul Chapman.

# 11

# The Distinctiveness of Scottish Education

*Walter Humes and Tom Bryce*

Education has traditionally been identified as one of the three institutions which mark the social and cultural life of Scotland as distinctive, especially when compared to England. (The other two are the law and the church.) With the establishment of a Scottish Parliament in 1999, and particularly after the election of a minority Scottish National Party (SNP) administration in 2007, followed by SNP victories in 2011 and 2016, a new focus for the political identity of Scotland has been created. And despite the electorate's rejection of complete independence at a referendum in 2014, the status of Scotland as a nation remains at the forefront of constitutional debate. Throughout the post-devolution period education has been high on the agenda of all parties and there has been much reflection on the particular contribution which the educational system has made and continues to make to national life. This chapter attempts to address this issue in a number of ways. It first looks at one influential account of the Scottish educational tradition, before going on to examine its formal distinctiveness as reflected in key educational institutions. It then attempts to uncover the values and principles which underlie the formal structures, noting the views of critics of the dominant Scottish tradition. Finally, it considers possible future directions, taking account both of developments elsewhere in the UK and international pressures which make it difficult for educational systems to diverge markedly from global trends.

A useful reference point for the discussion that follows can be found in James Scotland's two-volume history of Scottish education, published in 1969. In his final chapter, Scotland attempted to define the Scottish tradition in education. He summed up his interpretation in six propositions which, he suggested, encapsulated the essence of Scottish attitudes towards education:

- education is, and always has been, of paramount importance in any community;
- every child should have the right to all the education of which he is capable;
- such education should be provided as economically and systematically as possible;
- the training of the intellect should take priority over all other facets of the pupil's personality;
- experiment is to be attempted only with the greatest caution; and
- the most important person in the school, no matter what theorists say, is not the pupil but the (inadequately rewarded) teacher. (Scotland, 1969, p. 275)

Much has changed in the period since this list was drawn up and a few of the items no longer seem persuasive, but some at least (the first three?) would still receive widespread endorsement. And although the pride which Scottish people traditionally have had in the quality of their educational system is now held less confidently, belief in the importance of education, its value both for the individual and for society as a whole, remains unshaken. Thousands of Scots, many from modest backgrounds, can testify to the power of education to enrich (in some cases, transform) their lives, and even those who have not themselves done particularly well at school are often anxious that their own children should take advantage of the improved opportunities now open to them.

These attitudes, whether laudatory or qualified, help to ensure that the position of education in the national consciousness remains strong. Moreover, belief in the worth and purpose of education is linked to the sense of national identity which is regularly invoked to draw attention to the differences between Scottish and English society. This takes the form of a story or 'myth', shaped by history but not always supported by historical evidence, to the effect that Scotland is less class-conscious than England, that ability and achievement, not rank, should determine success in the world, that public (rather than private) institutions should be the means of trying to bring about the good society, and that, even where merit does justify differential rewards, there are certain basic respects – arising from the common humanity of all men and women – in which human beings deserve equal consideration and treatment. Taken together, these features can be summed up in the phrase used by George Davie for the title of his famous book, *The Democratic Intellect* (1961). To describe the democratic intellect as constituting a 'myth' is not to dismiss it as untrue. Gray et al. (1983, p. 39) make the point that a myth is a narrative that people tell themselves for two reasons – 'first, to explain the world and, second, to celebrate identity and to express values'. The extent to which the values are actually achieved in practice is a matter for analysis and interpretation. So too is the question of who promotes the myth and who benefits from it. These are crucial issues that will be revisited later in the chapter.

At this point, however, it is necessary to ground the discussion in some factual information about those features of the day-to-day workings of the Scottish educational system which mark it out as distinctive. How are the differences between Scottish and English education reflected in the experiences of pupils, teachers and parents? What is the significance of these differences? And how do they connect with broader questions of consciousness, identity and values?

## FORMAL DISTINCTIVENESS

Perhaps the most potent expression of the distinctiveness of Scottish education is the separate legislative framework which sets out the nature of provision and the agencies responsible for its delivery. Chapter 15 provides full detail of Scottish Law as it pertains to education but some preliminary points may be noted here. Legislation is framed by the Scottish Government and formal responsibility for the system as a whole rests with the First Minister. Prior to devolution, Scottish legislation often (but not always) post-dated statutory provision in England, but it did not always follow an identical pattern. A clear example was the legislation relating to parental choice of school enshrined in the Education Act of 1980 (England and Wales) and the Education (Scotland) Act of 1981. Legislative differences were also evident in the arrangements for school boards in Scotland compared to governing bodies in England, devolved school management in Scotland compared to local financial management in England, and the circumstances which required the opening and maintenance of a Record of Needs for children requiring special educational provision in Scotland compared to the Statement of Needs in England. Subsequent amendments to all of these provisions did not lead to greater uniformity in Scottish and English practice.

One of the first Acts of the Scottish Parliament was the Standards in Scotland's Schools etc. Act 2000. It introduced a new school improvement framework, one part of which set out five national priorities for education under the following headings: achievement and attainment; framework for learning; inclusion and equality; values and citizenship; learning for life. The emphasis on inclusion and equality has been a consistent feature of policy throughout the post-devolution period. Provision for pupils with disabilities and additional support needs has been improved, partly through better diagnosis and programmes catering for diverse requirements of individual pupils. The role of learning support teachers and classroom assistants, working in conjunction with classroom teachers, has also been important. While it was left to schools and authorities to implement the national priorities, the legislative framework required them to formulate improvement and development plans accordingly. This can be seen as a familiar Scottish combination of firm central direction of policy alongside delegation of responsibility for implementation to local government in the interests of democratic accountability.

Evidence of Scottish distinctiveness can be seen in the separate institutional apparatus which maintains the system. There is one national examination body, the Scottish Qualifications Authority (SQA), whereas in the rest of the UK there are several examination boards, ostensibly serving different parts of the country though schools are not confined to entering candidates in the board located in their geographical area. Other important bodies expressive of the separate character of the Scottish system include Education Scotland (ES), which since 2011 has had full responsibility for work previously carried out by two predecessor bodies (Learning and Teaching Scotland and Her Majesty's Inspectorate of Education) and the General Teaching Council for Scotland (GTCS). ES advises the First Minister on all matters relating to the curriculum as they affect the age range 3–18 and has a particular responsibility for leading and supporting the implementation of Curriculum for Excellence (CfE). Unlike in England, there is no formally prescribed national curriculum though, in practice, most schools follow closely the recommendations contained in national documents such as those deriving from CfE. Other areas of activity for which ES has responsibility include: evaluating the quality of educational provision at school, local authority and national levels; encouraging innovation, particularly in the use of educational technology; increasing the system's capacity for self-evaluation and self-improvement; and promoting high quality professional learning and leadership. Following a consultation on the governance of Scottish education in 2015–16, rather to the surprise of some observers, who had expected that the inspection and curriculum advisory functions of ES might be separated, the organisation was given a 'renewed and revitalised' role, with enhanced powers (Scottish Government, 2017). The governance review was a response to growing concerns about the quality and direction of Scottish education. Although ES emerged intact, the role of local authorities was reduced: new 'regional improvement collaboratives' were promised to provide support for teachers and schools. At the time of writing, many of the details of the reforms have still to be fleshed out.

The GTCS, established by statute in 1965, is the body which controls entry to the profession, accredits initial training courses for teachers, and has responsibility for assessing whether probationary teachers can proceed to full registration. In April 2012 GTCS changed from being an advisory non-departmental public body (NDPB) to a fully independent, self-regulatory body under The Public Services Reform (General Teaching Council for

Scotland) Order 2011. Among its main areas of activity are setting standards and codes of conduct for teachers, reviewing the training appropriate to teachers, providing opportunities for professional update, and conducting inquiries where there are concerns about teacher competence or misconduct. The GTCS's existence is testimony to the relative status of teaching as a profession in Scotland, compared to England. An English GTC was not established until 1998, with powers that were significantly weaker than those enjoyed by the GTC in Scotland, and only lasted until March 2012, following a decision by the UK Conservative/Liberal Democrat coalition to abolish it.

One of the striking characteristics of Scotland's educational policy community is that it is relatively small, with many of the key players (in SQA, ES, GTCS and local authorities) meeting on a regular basis and forming overlapping networks. This perhaps makes it easier to reach a consensus than in a larger, more anonymous system. There is, however, a downside. 'Groupthink' can develop, leading to complacency and a failure to question existing practices in a fundamental way. This may help to explain the relative conservatism identified by James Scotland as an element in the Scottish educational tradition.

A significant feature of Scottish education for which claims are made in respect of distinctiveness is the breadth of the curriculum available to pupils in schools, and it would be fair to say that all the national programmes – Standard Grade, 5–14, Higher Still and CfE – have sought to preserve breadth of study. The replacement of Standard Grade and Intermediate courses by National level 4 and 5 awards has not diminished that breadth. Also, as Chapters 3, 4 and 103 indicate, from the primary and secondary perspectives, it is predicated on a recognition that greater diversity and flexibility should be encouraged – to a much greater extent than heretofore – within nationally prescribed guidelines. That said, the descriptors of the four levels of CfE have a somewhat traditional feel for what should be taught in the years of compulsory schooling – though the mantra of a 'broad general education' is used for the years up to the end of S3, rather than S2 (as discussed in Chapter 4). The principles of challenge, enjoyment, personalisation, choice and relevance imply that curriculum balance should be construed in terms of individual children rather than in terms of time allocation for subjects. While developments on that front seem modest, and rather varied by school and authority, more opportunities may be seized by teachers throughout the country. The potential for difference from England's more prescribed curriculum remains quite significant.

Compared with the school system, the formal distinctiveness of Scotland's universities is less clear-cut. For most of the twentieth century Scottish universities were seen primarily as United Kingdom institutions and the body responsible for their funding – originally the University Grants Committee (UGC; later the University Funding Council) – was accountable to the Department of Education and Science (DES) in London. This position was reviewed from time to time but the consistent message from Scottish university principals was that they were against the Scottish Office taking over responsibility. Part of the explanation was a desire to retain international standing and a fear that the Scottish Office might try to interfere with academic freedom. These attitudes began to change in the 1980s when, following a major financial exercise involving severe cutbacks, in which there was a feeling that the UGC's understanding of, and sympathy for, the Scottish dimension was deficient, demands for the establishment of a separate Scottish subcommittee of the UGC were voiced. These were initially rejected but the climate had altered and it was only a matter of time before the funding arrangements were revised. In 1992 the Scottish Higher Education Funding Council (SHEFC) became responsible for distributing grants for teaching, research and associated activities in all Scottish higher education (HE) institutions. In 2005 SHEFC was replaced by the Scottish Funding Council under the provisions of the Further and Higher Education (Scotland) Act which brought together funding arrangements for both further education (FE) colleges and universities. Matters relating to quality assurance in universities, however, continue to be administered on a UK-wide basis under the direction of the Quality Assurance Agency (QAA), a body established in 1997. Similarly, research is assessed on a UK-wide basis with the results having important implications for the funding of universities (though the detailed allocation of funds is decided by each country's funding council). During the last few years, Scottish universities have come under public scrutiny following debates about student fees (see below), cutbacks on staffing, the threatened closure of courses and concerns about a serious divide between management and academic staff. This led in 2011 to a review of the governance arrangements and recommendations designed to increase democracy and accountability. Successful lobbying on behalf of university principals, however, meant that reforms were limited.

Two particular HE issues are likely to be highly sensitive over the next few years. The first relates to the number of students enrolled at Scottish universities, in particular the consequences of maintaining the principle of free tuition for home-based students. This has had an effect on applications from both the European Union (EU) and the rest of the UK. Since it is illegal to discriminate against people from another EU state, the benefit of free tuition resulted in a steady increase in European applications (from 4.5 per cent of the Scottish university population in session 2002/3 to 8.7 per cent in 2012/13). The capping of free tuition places by Scottish Government creates a quota, one which necessarily cannot discriminate against European states. Hence universities like Glasgow, Edinburgh and Dundee have reported that their recruitment of Scottish students has been falling and the proportion of EU students has been rising, both in quite significant numbers – meaning that Scottish candidate numbers are being squeezed from abroad. The Universities and Colleges Admissions Service (UCAS) has also admitted that applicants to Scottish universities from England were 15 per cent more likely to be offered a place than Scots. At this stage, it is unclear what will happen in respect of EU students when the details of post-Brexit arrangements become apparent.

The second point relates to the proportion of university students from relatively disadvantaged circumstances, concerning which Scottish Government set up a Commission on Widening Access. Its final report, *A Blueprint for Fairness*, was published in spring 2016 (Scottish Government, 2016). The first of thirty-four recommendations in that document was that a Commissioner for Fair Access should be appointed to lead cohesive and system-wide efforts to drive fair access in Scotland, acting as an advocate for access for disadvantaged learners and holding to account those with a role to play in achieving equal access. Professor Sir Peter Scott was appointed and among his first public statements was the warning that a university place should not be seen as a 'reward' for working hard; he condemned the 'sense of entitlement' among pupils who achieve good grades – a statement which many commentators found disconcerting. It remains to be seen what detail will be fleshed out by 2018 when a 'Scottish Framework for Fair Access' is due to be published.

Teacher education in Scotland is now part of the university sector – previously there were separate colleges of education – but the distinctive character of provision remains strong. Whereas in England the Office for Standards in Education (Ofsted) and the Teaching Agency (previously the Training and Development Agency for Schools) exercise considerable control over matters of supply, funding and curriculum content, these agencies have no counterparts in Scotland. Here a partnership model operates, strengthened by the recommendations of the 2010 Donaldson Report, involving university schools of education, Scottish Government, local authorities and the GTCS. That is not to say that there is complete satisfaction with the system – critics complain that the prevailing model of teacher education is too conformist – but there is certainly no desire to follow the English pattern.

## UNDERLYING VALUES

The extent to which the various manifestations of formal distinctiveness embody a particularly Scottish vision of the nature and purpose of education is a matter of continuing analysis and debate. G. E. Davie (in *The Democratic Intellect*) argued that the special character of Scotland's educational system has been progressively weakened by a process of assimilation to English norms, notwithstanding the separate legislative framework. According to Davie, the Scottish university curriculum, with an emphasis on curricular breadth and philosophical enquiry, was steadily weakened during the nineteenth century by a narrow English empiricism which led to specialisation and fragmentation of knowledge. This process was aided by the introduction of English-style examinations and the appointment of English candidates to key university chairs in Scotland. Secondary schools were required to adapt to the changes in order to prepare candidates for university entrance and so the anglicising tendencies gradually entered the whole system. One manifestation of the trend was the disparagement of Scots and Gaelic as legitimate forms of language for learning.

The pessimism of Davie would now be challenged. Gaelic language and culture is strongly promoted by the Scottish Government. Similarly, it is possible to point to the development of curricular materials with a strong Scottish flavour across a range of subjects in primary and secondary schools. Scottish history is well established as a field of study in schools and universities, and the use of Scottish texts in drama and literature courses is widespread. The teaching of Scottish Studies is now compulsory for all secondary pupils. Although this provoked some hostility from critics who feared that it represented an attempt to politicise the curriculum in favour of the SNP's independence agenda, it attracted strong support from a wide cross section of academics, artists, writers and poets. Add to this the wider cultural renaissance in Scotland, which includes art, music and media, and the argument that Scottish society and Scottish education are dominated by English values and institutions seems hard to sustain.

It is, however, not a simple either/or issue, with the 'purity' of Scottish values being set against the 'contamination' from south of the border. A significant number of Scots feel themselves to be both Scottish and British (and in some cases European as well) and they want the next generation to enjoy the freedom to enter different cultural worlds. They certainly want Scottish identity and culture to be given proper recognition within the curriculum but they also want their children to be able to cope with the globalisation of knowledge. The international character of many areas of learning and the employment markets associated with them (e.g. technology, computing, economics, banking, law, government) is now recognised. These are cross-national trends which cannot be resisted. To the extent that any educational system must try to prepare young people for the future, Scotland cannot afford to construct a curriculum on the basis of romantic retreat to an imagined golden age of the past. Scottish distinctiveness has to be shaped and redefined in a way that is compatible with the realities of the modern world.

Furthermore, self-confidence about one's own national identity should not be incompatible with tolerance of diversity in other people. That is a mark of cultural maturity. A useful first step would be recognition of the diversity inside Scotland itself. There has always been considerable cultural variation within Scotland – between Highlands and Lowlands, Edinburgh and Glasgow, cities and rural communities, Catholics and Protestants. This diversity has sometimes been submerged in a standardised and idealised model of Scottish life which, with staggering improbability, manages to combine elements of Knox, Burns, Hampden, Red Clydeside and a kailyard version of community life. Stripping away these internal mythologies may serve to counteract the easy recourse to demonising the English. Blaming England for Scotland's ills prevents the hard thinking that is needed now that Scotland has assumed greater responsibility for its own affairs. And if independence were to become a reality, the scope for excuses and attributing blame to others would be further diminished.

## CRITICS OF THE SCOTTISH TRADITION

One way of extending the demythologising process is to examine what critics of the Scottish educational tradition have had to say. The accounts of that tradition which receive greatest attention and which help to shape popular consciousness tend to be those which are written by members of the educational establishment. It is not surprising that interpretations coming from such sources should give more prominence to the achievements of the system, rather than its shortcomings. However, there is a counter-tradition – albeit a minor one – of radical twentieth-century criticism which casts interesting light on the cherished principles invoked by officials. It is an interpretation, moreover, that raises important questions about the relation between schooling, society and values.

A. S. Neill (1883–1973) became a key figure in the progressive movement, not only in Britain but internationally, attracting enthusiasm and notoriety in almost equal measure for his school, Summerhill. Neill left Scotland because he disagreed fundamentally with the emphasis on discipline and authority, and the centrality of the teacher rather than the pupil. Strongly influenced by Freudian psychology, he based his school on the principle of freedom and saw modern society as hostile to individuality and creativity. Summerhill continues to the present day (currently under the headship of Zoe Readhead, Neill's daughter) having defeated an attempt to close the Suffolk school following an adverse inspection report. The High Court ruling was described by one observer as acknowledging that 'the school's duty was not to the nation but the child'.

Neill was an important influence on two other Scots, John Aitkenhead (1910–98) who founded Kilquhanity House, a small independent school in south-west Scotland during the Second World War, and R. F. Mackenzie (1910–87), who worked in the state sector. Aitkenhead's philosophy and practice is described in Chapter 14 of this volume. Mackenzie tried, ultimately unsuccessfully, to establish a regime within the state system which challenged traditional ideas on curriculum content and pupil learning. His efforts led to his suspension and subsequent dismissal as head of a comprehensive school in Aberdeen. In retirement he wrote a 'Manifesto for the Educational Revolution' which, though inspiring and visionary, was never likely to overturn the powerful structures and practices of mainstream Scottish education (Humes, 2011). Like Neill, Mackenzie (1977, p. 6) saw attitudes to schooling as symptomatic of wider social attitudes: 'The crisis in Scottish schools is a crisis in Scottish life ... Scotland's schools are at the centre of Scotland's perplexity, one of its main causes.' He believed that for many Scottish youngsters the experience of schooling was largely negative. They were given few opportunities to explore and enjoy learning in creative ways that connected with life outside school; they were constantly reminded of their inadequacies and failures; and they were ill-equipped to meet the challenges they would face as adults. These deficiencies, Mackenzie believed, helped to explain the cultural malaise from which he felt Scotland suffered – a malaise evident in a lack of drive and initiative, a passivity in the face of officialdom and an impoverished sense of life's possibilities. It is a bleak picture of institutional failure and missed opportunities.

The current generation of teachers and headteachers would certainly disagree with the critics and claim that modern schools are much less oppressive places where pupil achievements are celebrated and the richness of learning in all its forms is recognised and encouraged. That may be so – though it would be a matter for debate – but it does not diminish the responsibility to confront past practices and to reflect on their significance for the present and future. The value attached to schooling in Scotland makes it doubly important to consider its wider social impact and here the need to confront uncomfortable truths remains strong. In a statement which resonates powerfully with the critics, the historian T. C. Smout comments:

> It is in the history of the school more than in any other aspect of recent social history that the key lies to some of the more depressing aspects of modern Scotland. If there are in this country too many people who fear what is new, believe the difficult to be impossible, draw back from responsibility, and afford established authority and tradition an exaggerated respect, we can reasonably look for an explanation in the institutions that moulded them. (Smout, 1986, p. 229)

Even if the radical educational philosophies of Neill, Aitkenhead and Mackenzie are not accepted, it is possible to recognise the validity of what Smout is saying about Scottish society. The situation may have improved, but it is a slow process. Resistance to change in working practices, reluctance to take on new challenges, unwillingness to accept leadership roles, reticence in the face of professional and bureaucratic authority – these are still recognisable features of life in Scotland. They are by no means universal but they are sufficiently widespread to have attracted the attention of social commentators. In the Thatcher years they led to the phrase 'dependency culture' being coined, a concept that implied an expectation that the state would provide when personal responsibility failed. Under New Labour an attempt was made to address the problems associated with passivity and defeatism through an emphasis on civic involvement, entrepreneurship and creativity – all designed to reduce dependence on state benefits and encourage people, particularly young people, to become active citizens, contributing not only to personal advancement and the economic life of the country but also to attitude sets in families and communities.

The Scottish Parliament certainly has the potential to promote significant economic, social and cultural reform. For that to happen on the scale that is needed, however, would require a major transformation encompassing not only education but a wide range of other public and private services as well. The capacity of children to benefit from schooling is profoundly affected by issues of housing, employment, poverty and health. It is in the interconnection of these forces that solutions to the sort of cultural defects which Smout describes must be found. A major test of the Scottish Parliament, therefore, has to be its success in tackling these problems in an innovative and coordinated way – in other words, in showing that 'joined-up government' can make a difference. Prior to the reorganisation of local government in 1996 some of the larger regions (notably Strathclyde and Lothian) tried to coordinate social strategy on a multidisciplinary basis but, with the fragmentation of services involved in the creation of thirty-two councils, some ground was lost. The importance of developing policies which locate educational provision in the context of broader social issues is, however, now well understood by both politicians and professionals. Integrated community schools, serving as focal points for a range of services, not just schooling, were promoted strongly in the immediate post-devolution period, but inter-professional working has proved difficult to operate and effective integration of services is more of an aspiration than a reality. The squeeze on local authority budgets means that simply maintaining existing provision now takes priority.

## COMPETING INTERPRETATIONS

In earlier sections of this chapter a contrast has been drawn between celebratory interpretations of the Scottish educational tradition (such as James Scotland's) and critical interpretations (such as R. F. Mackenzie's). To polarise these inevitably oversimplifies the forces at work, not least by failing to take account of the particular circumstances at any given time in the evolution of the tradition. Lindsay Paterson has claimed that an analysis of the ways in which Scottish education has been subject to reform suggests that a highly complex blend of traditional and radical thinking can be detected at various points in recent educational history (Paterson, 1996). He argues that it is misleading to interpret the development of Scottish education in terms of a crude dichotomy between control and liberation. Depending on the circumstances of the time, different educational philosophies were mobilised in a variety of ways. Referring to the introduction of comprehensive education, he states that 'the single act of abolishing selection [was] a real victory for progressive educational thought' and that its radical effect can be seen 'in the slow revolution it has brought about in the educational aspirations of the whole community'. Significantly, however, the switch to comprehensivisation was not a peculiarly Scottish development, though it is often claimed that comprehensive schools had their roots in the old 'omnibus' schools found in small towns and rural communities in Scotland. This claim ignores the extent of selection and streaming within omnibus schools. Nevertheless, evidence from public consultation as part of the National Debate on the future of Scottish education carried out in 2002 indicates continuing support for the comprehensive principle, however defined.

Paterson's analysis highlights the 'negotiated' character of Scotland's educational distinctiveness; that is, the extent to which cherished principles – expressive of 'the myth' – have to be redefined in response to changing social and economic pressures. Here there are some very interesting tensions. At one level, the establishment of a devolved government and the continuing possibility of complete independence points in the direction of a more robust assertion of Scottish distinctiveness in education (as in other fields). At the same time, however, Scotland – like England – is subject to global pressures which are tending to push educational systems in similar directions. These global pressures are political, economic, cultural and technological in character. They involve international comparisons of educational attainment on a range of measures; analyses of future requirements in terms of workforce planning and skill needs; interpretations of the impact on educational systems of migration within Europe and from further afield; the expectations of multinational companies in respect of infrastructure support and human resources; and above all, the shift from an economy based principally on heavy industry requiring limited education in the workforce to one which is knowledge based and requires high levels of basic skills, regular retraining and flexibility. If Scotland wishes to be taken seriously on the international stage it cannot afford to ignore these trends. Its educational system has to respond to them and this may involve adjusting and redefining aspects of its educational tradition. The hard task is to negotiate this process skilfully, taking account of external realities while remaining true to values and principles that have important social, cultural and historical resonance. Following concerns about whether standards of education in Scotland were falling, the Scottish Government in 2016 appointed an International Council of Education Advisers, indicating the need to take account not only of traditional values but also of the global pressures referred to above.

Assessments of how devolution has affected the distinctiveness of Scottish education offer varying emphases. Thus Arnott (2005), writing before the SNP assumed power, suggested that Labour administrations chose 'to pursue a largely conservative agenda which [was] shaped by the myths and traditions associated with the social democratic consensus' (p. 257). At the same time, she noted that there were elements of both convergence and divergence in educational policy between Scotland and England. Given the global influences deriving from economics, technology and the requirements of the labour market, it is not surprising that many countries are adapting their educational systems in similar ways, while trying to explain and justify the changes in terms which resonate with familiar discourse. Arnott and Menter (2007) suggest that neo-liberalism, in the form of New Public Management, has influenced educational policies in both countries but stress that 'while globalization may be a convergent force, nationalism is (and always has been) a divergent force. In the new settlement since devolution, it is important to Scotland, if not to England ... to "carve its own furrow"' (Arnott and Menter, 2007, p. 261). In another paper, Arnott and Ozga (2010) argue that 'nationalism – as an idea – is being used as a discursive resource in policy-making by the new Scottish government' (Arnott and Ozga, 2010, p. 347), promoting a sense of national identity (e.g. through the emphasis on citizenship education). At the same time, the international emphasis on competitiveness, skill development and employability tends to limit the scope for national distinctiveness. A slightly different emphasis is offered by Ozga and Lingard:

> For the most part, devolution seems to have enabled the continuation of Scottish distinctiveness, while simultaneously beginning to open up some of its more traditional aspects including, perhaps, the academic bias and the caution about experimentation ... It may also have enabled change in the traditionally rather hierarchical nature of schools and of the teaching profession. (Ozga and Lingard, 2007, p. 74)

All this helps to bear out Paterson's point about the complexity and malleability of traditions. The story of the distinctiveness of Scotland's educational tradition can be told in more than one version. New 'myths' can replace the old ones and the task of deconstruction is never-ending. What can be said is that the claims made for the quality of Scottish education, past and present, have been substantial and that they have sometimes led to an unjustifiable degree of complacency. The value attached to education, both by policymakers and by ordinary Scots, remains high but the ideals expressed in the official discourse need to be constantly tested against the realities as experienced by pupils, teachers, parents and employers. As the Scottish Parliament grapples with these challenges, Scottish education needs both its advocates and its critics.

# REFERENCES

Arnott, M. (2005) 'Devolution, territorial politics and the politics of education', in G. Mooney and
    G. Scott (eds), *Exploring Social Policy in the 'New' Scotland*. Bristol: Policy Press, pp. 239–61.

Arnott, M. and Menter, I. (2007) 'The same but different? Post-devolution regulation and control in
    Scotland and England', *European Educational Research Journal*, 6 (3), 250–65.

Arnott, M. and Ozga, J. (2010) 'Education and nationalism: the discourse of educational policy in
    Scotland', *Discourse: Studies in the Cultural Politics of Education*, 31 (3), 335–50.

Davie, G. E. (1961) *The Democratic Intellect*. Edinburgh: Edinburgh University Press.

Gray, J., McPherson, A. and Raffe, D. (1983) *Reconstructions of Secondary Education*. London:
    Routledge.

Humes, W. (2011) 'R.F. Mackenzie's "Manifesto for the Educational Revolution"', *Scottish
    Educational Review*, 43 (1), 56–72.

Mackenzie, R. F. (1977) *The Unbowed Head*, Edinburgh: Edinburgh University Student Publications
    Board.

Ozga, J. and Lingard, B. (2007) 'Globalisation, education policy and politics', in B. Lingard and
    J. Ozga, *The Routledge Falmer Reader in Education Policy and Politics*. London: Routledge,
    pp. 65–82.

Paterson, L. (1996) 'Liberation or control: what are the Scottish education traditions of the twentieth
    century?' in T. M. Devine and R. J. Finlay (eds), *Scotland in the 20th Century*. Edinburgh:
    Edinburgh University Press, pp. 230–49.

Scotland, J. (1969) *The History of Scottish Education*, vol. 2. London: University of London Press.

Scottish Government (2016) *A Blueprint for Fairness: The Final Report of the Commission on Widening
    Access*. Online at www.gov.scot/Publications/2016/03/1439

Scottish Government (2017) *Education Governance: Next Steps*. Edinburgh: Scottish Government.
    Online at www.gov.scot/Resource/0052/00521038.pdf

Smout, T. C. (1986) *A Century of the Scottish People 1830–1950*. London: Collins.

# 12

# Poverty, Class and Intergenerational Disadvantage

*Edward M. Sosu*

Familial poverty and social class have a direct effect on children's future prospects in Scotland. On average, children from affluent households attain better grades in school, are more likely to go to university, occupy more prestigious positions and earn higher income than their counterparts from poorer families. In other words, inequality in income during childhood results in unequal opportunities and outcomes in later life. Previous and contemporary government policies have attempted to break this cycle with varying degrees of success. The current chapter describes the nature of poverty, social class and 'intergenerational' disadvantage. First, it examines contemporary definitions and measurements of poverty and social class, as well as rates of poverty in Scotland over time. Second, it examines the concept of intergenerational disadvantage and the mechanism by which experiences of poverty in childhood lead to poverty in adulthood. It draws on evidence from Scottish data in advancing this argument. Finally, it briefly considers some contemporary policy responses in Scotland to breaking this cycle of disadvantage.

## DEFINING POVERTY AND SOCIAL CLASS

Poverty is a complex construct and its definition has been hotly debated over the years. The British sociologist Peter Townsend proposed a relative approach to defining poverty. According to him:

> Individuals, families and groups in the population can be said to be in poverty when they lack the resources to obtain the types of diet, participate in the activities and have the living conditions and amenities which are customary, or are at least widely encouraged or approved, in the societies to which they belong. Their resources are so seriously below those commanded by the average individual or family that they are, in effect, excluded from ordinary living patterns, customs and activities. (Townsend, 1979, p. 31)

The above definition is termed *relative poverty* and is currently the most widely accepted definition. It suggests that what is considered as poverty varies from one country to another due to differences in needs, social norms and time period. For instance, essential needs might vary from one county to another depending on variables such as weather. As such, what might be essential goods for survival in a colder climate (e.g. heating and clothing) might be different from those required to survive in warmer climates. Poverty has also been defined in absolute terms. According to the United Nations (1995), *absolute poverty* refers to 'a condition characterised by severe deprivation of basic human needs, including food, safe drinking water, sanitation facilities, health, shelter, education and information. It depends not only on income but also on access to services.' The practical implication of this definition is that eliminating poverty requires comprehensive changes to several institutional systems that determine the distribution and access to different forms of resources such as income, food, housing, education, services and information. Further complexity around the definition of poverty extends to whether individuals have or are experiencing *short- or long-term poverty*, *income volatility*, and the *time at which they experience poverty* in their lives. More recent discussion has also been focused on *income inequality* and the Scottish Government, as part of its performance targets, has committed to reducing income inequality (Scottish Government, 2016a). These different forms of poverty have recently been shown to have an impact on children's educational and employment outcomes (e.g. Schoon et al., 2011; Hardy, 2014). Fundamentally, the way poverty is defined determines what governments and societies consider a problem, and the actions needed to reduce levels of poverty.

In the UK and many other countries around the world, poverty is measured, and by default defined, using household equivalised income. Equivalised income refers to total household income plus the value of any state benefits received minus taxes (income tax, national insurance and council tax). This is the income that is available to buy goods and services. It is then adjusted to take into account the size of the household. Governments using this approach set the poverty 'threshold' at 60 per cent of median household income. Median income is the income in the middle point if you arrange all incomes from the lowest to the highest. The poverty 'threshold' is therefore any income that is 60 per cent lower than the median income. In Scotland, individuals are said to be in *relative poverty* if they are living in households whose equivalised income is below 60 per cent of UK median income in that year. For instance, in 2015/16, the median income in Scotland was £24,400. After housing costs are taken into account, the poverty threshold was set at £12,900, which means that individuals with equivalised income below this amount were living in relative poverty. Scotland also produces figures for *absolute poverty* which takes into account inflation (see Scottish Government, 2017 for discussion on how this is computed). One of the main criticism of this approach to measuring poverty is that the 60 per cent threshold is arbitrary and simply a proxy measure which needs to be validated using direct measures of people's actual living standards (Serafino and Tonkin, 2014; Mack, 2016). However, research using these thresholds of poverty has indicated that they are directly correlated with poorer outcomes such as low educational attainment of children (e.g. Schoon et al., 2011). Advantages of this approach are that poverty rates can be tracked over time and comparisons can be made between countries (Mack, 2016).

Alternative measures of poverty have focused on the income needed for maintaining 'physical necessities' of living; these began with the work of Seebohm Rowntree in 1899. Using information from families in York and studies on the nutritional needs of prisoners in Scotland, Rowntree argued that poverty is when 'total earnings are insufficient to obtain the minimum necessaries for the maintenance of merely physical efficiency' (cited in Townsend, 1979, p. 33). He set out to determine a poverty threshold by estimating the average nutritional needs of adults and children, translated these needs into quantities of different foods, and then into cash equivalent. He also added minimum costs for clothing, fuel and household essentials and used the total cost to estimate the 'poverty line'. Those without sufficient income to afford these basic needs were classified as primarily poor. This approach of estimating poverty underpins the *consensual method* and the *minimum budget standards approach*, which are current alternative measures of poverty (for further details see Mack, 2016). It also informs decisions on minimum income support rates that governments around the world provide to those living in poverty.

One of the key constructs that is directly linked to discourses of poverty in the UK is *social class*. Like poverty, social class is a complex concept that entails an individual's economic position, power, social status or prestige and culture. According to Townsend (1979, p. 370), 'class may also [refer to] segments of the population sharing broadly similar types and levels of resources, with broadly similar styles of living and some perception of their collective condition'. The acknowledgement of social class by the government in the UK dates back to 1911, when the social positions of individuals were graded based on their occupations. A variant of this approach of measuring social status nationally is still being used. Currently the Office for National Statistics in the UK provides classifications of status based on the conditions of an individual's occupation such as career prospects, autonomy, mode of payments and period of notice. Eight different social classifications are produced using this approach known as the National Statistics Socio-Economic Classification (NS-SEC). These are: higher managerial and professional occupations; lower managerial and professional occupations; intermediate occupations; small employers and own account workers; lower supervisory and technical occupations; semi-routine occupations; routine occupations; never worked and long-term unemployed.

Another way in which *social class* has been measured is by asking individuals about their own social positions. Research in the UK (Townsend, 1979) suggests that people either place themselves in one of three main social classifications (i.e. upper, middle and working class) or a finer grouping of classes (i.e. upper, upper middle, lower middle class and so on). In 2011, the BBC in collaboration with academics undertook a survey of over 160,000 people in the UK. To determine social class, they examined people's income and assets, cultural interests and activities, and the status of their friends and business contacts. They proposed seven classes based on this study. These are elite; established middle class; technical middle class; new affluent workers; traditional working class; emergent service workers; and precariat (Savage et al., 2013). Irrespective of the type of classifications used, there is a strong correlation between social class and levels of income. Thus, the majority of those living in poverty tend to come from lower social classifications, or tend to identify themselves as working class.

## HOUSEHOLD AND CHILD POVERTY RATES IN SCOTLAND OVER TIME

Recent data indicates that about 20 per cent of the population in Scotland (1.05 million people) were living in relative poverty in 2015/16 after accounting for housing cost (Scottish Government, 2017). As can be seen in Figure 12.1, rates of poverty have fluctuated in the 1990s but fell from 25 per cent in 2000 to about 20 per cent in 2005. It remained unchanged between 2005/6 and 2009/10 before falling to 16 per cent in 2011/12. However, since then the rates have gradually risen to a current level of 20 per cent in 2015/16.

With respect to child poverty, figures in 2015/16 show that one in four children (26 per cent) were living in relative poverty after accounting for housing cost. This

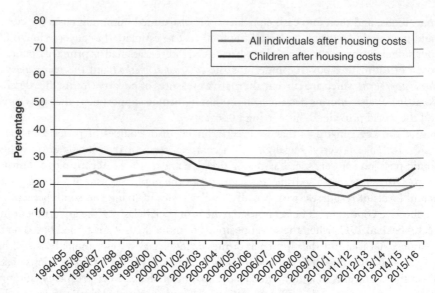

**Figure 12.1    Relative poverty (below 60 per cent of UK median income in the same year) in Scottish households, 1994/5 to 2015/16**

Source: Data based on households below average income (HBAI) data set, Department for Work and Pensions (DWP) (Scottish Government, 2017, Table A1)

represents a total of 260,000 children. The trend is similar to the trajectory observed in the general population. Child poverty rates have decreased from 30 per cent in the 1990s to about 25 per cent in 2005. They remained stable until 2009/10 before falling to 19 per cent in 2011/12. However, rates of child poverty have gradually risen since then to 26 per cent in the most recent year.

One of the important points to note is that the 60 per cent of median approach used in defining poverty rates means that changes in poverty rates are directly linked to relative changes in the income of those at the bottom and those at the top. Poverty rates therefore increase when there are increases in the amount of income going to top earners and a relative fall in the earnings of those at the bottom. This explains recent rises in poverty rates in Scotland. For instance, income inequality rose by three percentage points from 2014/15 to 2015/16. This was largely driven by increases in the amount of income going to top earners at the same time that income for those at the bottom were falling, mainly due to changes in the amount of income support provided by the government (Scottish Government, 2017).

A widely debated issue within the UK is why people are in poverty. Some political and media discourses in the UK often describe those living in poverty as individuals who are 'workless' or 'work-shy', and to some extent portray them as being responsible for their own plight. While it is the case that families where no adult is working are at a higher risk of poverty, existing data equally indicates that an increasing proportion of children and adults living in poverty are in working households (Figure 12.2). For instance, 70 per cent of the children in Scotland who were living in poverty in 2015/16 were from households where at least one person was working. According to the Scottish Government, this upward trend in in-work poverty reflects increases in the number of working households in low paid and

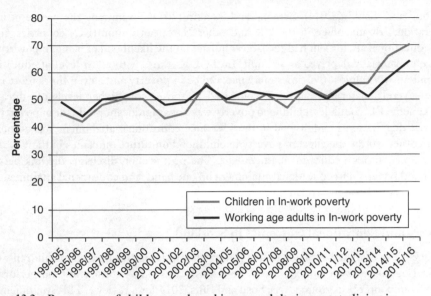

**Figure 12.2    Percentage of children and working age adults in poverty living in households with at least one adult in employment (after housing cost)**

Source: Data based on HBAI data set, DWP (Scottish Government, 2017, Table A7)

part-time jobs. This, combined with decreases to the level of state support provided to families on low income, explains this increasing trend in in-work poverty.

## POVERTY AND THE INTERGENERATIONAL TRANSMISSION OF DISADVANTAGE: THE ROLE OF EDUCATION

There is significant evidence to suggest that parental income is one of the best predictors of a child's future life chances (d'Addio, 2007; HM Government, 2014). Blanden and Gibbons (2006) found that in the UK, teenagers who experienced poverty were almost four times as likely to be in poverty as an adult compared to their peers who were not in poverty as teenagers. Studies examining the effect of poverty in childhood on future outcomes indicate that the UK has a relatively low level of earnings mobility, meaning that there is a strong relationship between the economic position of parents and the amount of income earned by their children (d'Addio, 2007). This persistence of disadvantage across generations (i.e. from parent to child) is termed *intergenerational transmission of disadvantage* and has been the focus of interest among academics and policymakers. It examines the degree to which children born into poor families grow up to become poor adults (Serafino and Tonkin, 2014). It is important to note that advantages are equally transmitted from wealthy parents to their children. A report published by the Social Mobility and Child Poverty Commission (2015) found that the majority of the elite in the Scottish public sector were privately educated and attended a handful of highly selective universities, key indicators of parental wealth.

The mechanisms by which intergenerational transmission of disadvantage occurs have been the subject of research. Studies of high-income economies like Scotland suggest that the impact of parental income on future poverty acts mainly through children's educational attainment (d'Addio, 2007; Rundiza and Lopez Vilaplana, 2013; HM Government, 2014;

Serafino and Tonkin, 2014). Serafino and Tonkin (2014), examining the nature of inter-generational disadvantage in the UK and other European Union (EU) countries, found that educational attainment had the largest impact on the likelihood of being in poverty and severely materially deprived as an adult. In the UK, those with a low level of educational attainment were almost five times more likely to be in poverty and eleven times more likely to be severely materially deprived, compared to those with higher levels of education. Unlike some EU countries, childhood poverty was not a significant predictor of poverty and material deprivation in adulthood in the UK once educational attainment was accounted for. In other words, the effect of poverty in childhood on future outcomes in the UK oper-ated mainly through educational attainment. The next section discusses the link between childhood poverty and educational attainment on one hand, and educational attainment and income in adulthood in Scotland.

### Poverty and Educational Outcomes in Scotland

There is clear evidence in Scotland that poverty has a significant impact on children's edu-cational outcomes with students from the richest households consistently outperforming those from poorer backgrounds (see Sosu and Ellis, 2014 for a review). This attainment gap starts before children begin formal schooling with children from high-income households about six to eighteen months ahead of low-income peers in vocabulary and problem solving by the time they are 5 years of age. Subsequently, this attainment gap widens as students' progress through the school years. For instance, data on academic attainment in numeracy at key stages of primary to secondary school in 2011, 2013 and 2015 (Figure 12.3) shows that pupils from the least deprived postcodes outperformed those from the most deprived households at all stages of measurement. The gap in attainment starts at primary 4 (P4) and widens by the time children get to the second year of secondary school (S2). At S2, pupils

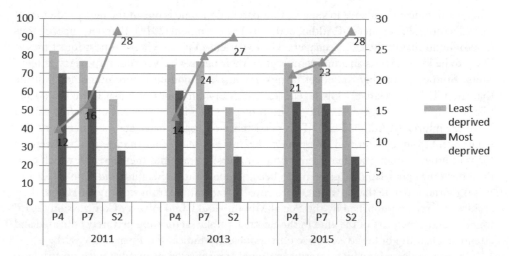

**Figure 12.3   Percentage of pupils performing well or very well by deprivation**

Source: www.gov.scot/Topics/Statistics/Browse/School-Education/
ScottishSurveyOfLiteracyNumeracy

living in areas of low deprivation were more than twice as likely to be assessed as performing well, or very well, than those in areas of high deprivation.

Attainment at the end of compulsory education (S4) equally indicates similar impacts of poverty, with students from the least deprived background consistently outperforming low-income peers by a substantial margin (Sosu and Ellis, 2014). The impact of poverty on attainment is given further credence by international attainment surveys such as the Programme for International Student Assessment (PISA) which indicates that attainment in Scotland is notably stratified by students' socio-economic backgrounds (OECD, 2013; Scottish Government, 2016b).

Poverty leads to poor educational attainment through several mechanisms, some of which are outlined below (see for example Boaler et al., 2000; Conger et al., 2010; Yoshikawa et al., 2012). First, low income restricts parents' ability to invest in resources and services that matter for children's educational outcomes. Such investments include extra tuition, books, trips to museums and so on. Second, there are substantial differences in the amount and quality of 'educational interaction' that children experience at home and these differences are correlated with class and poverty intergenerationally: a telling example would be the variation in the preschool experience of children whose parents read to them every night and those who do not. Third, low income is thought to affect attainment through poor health. Children from low-income households suffer greater health problems associated with poor housing and nutrition, and exposure to environmental hazards. This increases levels of absenteeism, making them miss out on learning. Fourth, school-related factors such as ability grouping exacerbates the effect of poverty on outcomes. As indicated above, gaps in attainment begin before children enter formal schooling. This means that teaching strategies based on ability place these children in lower ability groups. Lower ability groups usually have less exposure to complex and challenging ideas required in assessments. Additionally, children are likely to construct negative identities of themselves as learners when they are identified at a very early stage as 'weak learners' resulting in a self-fulfilling prophecy. Finally, poverty affects attainment through impact on family stressors. Low-income parents experience greater levels of stress with resultant negative parent–child relationships. For instance, they are more likely to use harsh discipline, and experience relationship conflicts that negatively affect their children's welfare and learning. In other words, experiences of poverty hinder children's attainment through multiple mechanisms. Breaking the link between poverty and educational outcomes therefore requires attention to these multiple mechanisms of effect.

## Educational Outcomes and Earnings in Scotland

Evidence indicates that higher levels of educational attainment are associated with better employment prospects and higher earnings, leading to a reduced risk of poverty (e.g. Smith and Middleton, 2007). Grundiza and Lopez Vilaplana (2013) found that across the EU, an adult with poor qualifications is more likely to be in poverty than one who is highly educated. In Scotland, educational attainment is linked to post-school destinations, labour market outcomes and future earnings. The majority of students from affluent backgrounds end up in university while those from the most deprived backgrounds end up in further education colleges due to differences in entry grade requirements (Sosu and Ellis, 2014). These differences in destination have a direct influence on future incomes, with students from affluent backgrounds more likely to benefit from a 'graduate wage premium' over the course of their working lives (Browne et al., 2010). Studies in Scotland have also found a direct relationship between educational attainment and future employment, occupational status and earnings (Howieson and Iannelli, 2008). Educational attainment at the end of compulsory education (S4) significantly predicts several labour market outcomes at the age of 22–3. Low attainers are more likely to be unemployed (12 per cent versus 4 per cent), working part-time (12 per cent versus 6 per cent) and earning less (differences of £23.45 and £44.94 per week for men and women respectively). Low attainers on average are also more likely to be in low-status positions in their jobs (Howieson and Iannelli, 2008). The conclusion from both international and Scottish studies is that household income during childhood mainly impacts future life chances through the educational attainment of the child, resulting in intergenerational transmission of disadvantage.

## POLICY RESPONSES TO POVERTY AND INTERGENERATIONAL DISADVANTAGE IN SCOTLAND

Governments in Scotland over the years have introduced a range of legislation, policies, strategies and frameworks to reduce poverty and the intergenerational transmission of disadvantage (see Sosu and Ellis, 2014). Within the context of this article, these policies can be categorised into: (a) those aimed at ameliorating the impact of poverty and promoting poverty reduction in general, and (b) those aimed at improving educational attainment in order to prevent intergenerational transmission of disadvantage through education. Recent flagship policies aimed at poverty reduction include the *Child Poverty Strategy for Scotland*, and *Getting it Right for Every Child* (GIRFEC) which promote a child-centred, multi-agency approach to tackling economic disadvantage and improving outcomes for all children. These policies aim to encourage different agencies within health, education and social services to work together in providing the appropriate support at the right time to children, young people and their parents. They are conceived as a national approach to supporting all children with emphasis on early intervention and prevention so that families do not fall into poverty. A combination of universal approaches such as free hospital prescription charges, free school meals for all children from primary 1 to primary 3, as well as targeted approaches such as family income support is provided. Fundamentally, these goals are to be achieved through more specific initiatives such as the Early Year Framework; Achieving Our Potential; Equally Well; Parental Involvement Act; the Early Years Collaborative and many others. Over the years, greater emphasis has been placed on these general poverty reduction policies, all which have the potential to reduce the transmission of economic disadvantage.

The second sets of policies are those specifically targeted at improving educational outcomes for children from low-income households. Until recently, such policies have only hinted at improving educational attainment and evidence of their impact has been limited (see Sosu and Ellis, 2014 for a review). However, since 2015, the government has put in place specific policies and associated funding to close the attainment gap associated with poverty. Recent flagship policies include the launch of the *Scottish Attainment Challenge* in 2015 which committed £750 million during the term of the Parliament to improve educational achievement of pupils in selected local authorities with the highest concentrations of deprivation. The initial tranche of funding was, however, only targeted at primary schools in nine out of thirty-two local authorities, and selected secondary schools. In February 2017, the government extended the coverage of schools with £120 million of the money allocated for *Pupil Equity Funding* to be directly given to schools to help tackle the attainment gap. Around £1,200 per pupil was allocated to schools based on all pupils from primary 1 (P1) to third year of secondary (S3) who are eligible and registered for free school meals. Three main policies were to underpin improvements associated with the above funding. These are a *National Improvement Framework* published in 2016 which sets out the vision and priorities for improving attainment for children from low-income households; *Curriculum for Excellence* which is the national curriculum covering education from preschool to secondary; and GIRFEC which is a national multi-agency approach for improving outcomes for all children. A key test of the success of these policies will be the extent to which they lead to improvements in the educational attainment of children from low-income households, and by extension reduce intergenerational transmission of disadvantage in Scotland.

## CONCLUSION

Scotland is a high-income country with comparatively significant levels of poverty. Several Scottish governments over the years have committed to reducing levels of poverty through several intervention programmes. There is also a greater recognition that poverty reduction requires comprehensive structural changes in not one but several institutional systems, in particular the role played by education. As discussed above, education is one of the important mechanisms by which economic disadvantages persist across generations. Breaking this cycle will require attention to improving educational outcomes for children from low-income households. The evidence so far suggests that there has been no significant improvement in the inequalities in educational attainment in Scotland. Recent policy focus on this particular issue offer some hope. However, consistent monitoring of the impact of these policies is required to ensure that it achieves its set goals.

## REFERENCES

Blanden, J. and Gibbons, S. (2006) *The Persistence of Poverty across Generations: A View From Two British Cohorts*. York: Joseph Rowntree Foundation.

Boaler, J., Wiliam, D. and Brown, M. (2000) 'Students' experiences of ability grouping – disaffection, polarisation and the construction of failure', *British Educational Research Journal*, 26 (5), 631–48.

Browne, J., Barber, M., Coyle, D., Eastwood, D., King, J., Naik, R. and Sands, P. (2010) *Securing a Sustainable Future for Higher Education: An Independent Review of Higher Education Funding and Student Finance*, (the 'Browne Report'). Online at https://www.gov.uk/government/publications/the-browne-report-higher-education-funding-and-student-finance

Conger, R. D., Conger, K. J. and Martin, M. J. (2010) 'Socioeconomic status, family processes and individual development', *Journal of Marriage and Family*, 72 (3), 685–704.

D'Addio, A. C. (2007) *Intergenerational Transmission of Disadvantage: Mobility or Immobility across Generations? A Review of the Evidence for OECD Countries*. Paris: Organisation for Economic Co-operation and Development (Working Papers No. 52).

Grundiza, S. and Lopez Vilaplana, C. (2013) *Intergenerational Transmission of Disadvantage: Is the Likelihood of Poverty Inherited?* Online at http://ec.europa.eu/eurostat/statistics-explained/index.php?title=Intergenerational_transmission_of_disadvantage_statistics&oldid=164494

Hardy, B. L. (2014) 'Childhood income volatility and adult outcomes', *Demography*, 51, 1641–65.

HM Government (2014) *An Evidence Review of the Drivers of Child Poverty For Families in Poverty Now and For Poor Children Growing Up To Be Poor Adults*. UK: Williams Lea Group.

Howieson, C. and Iannelli, C. (2008) 'The effects of low attainment on young people's outcomes at age 22–23 in Scotland', *British Educational Research Journal*, 34 (2), 269–90.

Mack, J. (2016). *Income Threshold Approach*. Online at www.poverty.ac.uk/definitions-poverty/income-threshold-approach

OECD (2013) *Programme for International Student Assessment (PISA)*. Online at www.oecd.org/pisa/aboutpisa/

Savage, M., Devine, F., Cunningham, N., Taylor, M., Li, Y., Hjellbrekke, J., Le Roux, B., Friedman, S. and Miles, A. (2013) 'A new model of social class: findings from the BBC's Great British Class Survey Experiment', *Sociology*, 47 (2), 219–50.

Schoon, I., Jones, E., Cheng, H. and Maughan, B. (2011) 'Family hardship, family instability and children's cognitive development', *Journal of Epidemiology and Community Health*. doi:10.1136/jech.2010.121228

Scottish Government (2016a) *Purpose Target: Solidarity*. Online at www.gov.scot/About/Performance/scotPerforms/purposetargets/solidarity

Scottish Government (2016b) *Programme for International Student Assessment (PISA) 2015: Highlights from Scotland's Results*. Edinburgh: Scottish Government.

Scottish Government (2017) *Poverty and Income Inequality in Scotland: 2015/16*. Edinburgh: Scottish Government.

Serafino, P. and Tonkin, R. (2014) *Intergenerational Transmission of Disadvantage in the UK and EU*. London: Office for National Statistics.

Smith, N. and Middleton, S. (2007) *A Review of Poverty Dynamics Research in the UK*. York: Joseph Rowntree Foundation.

Social Mobility and Child Poverty Commission (2015) *Elitist Scotland?* London: Social Mobility and Child Poverty Commission.

Sosu, E. and Ellis, S. (2014) *Closing the Attainment Gap in Scottish Education*. York: Joseph Rowntree Foundation.

Townsend, P. (1979) *Poverty in the United Kingdom*. Harmondsworth: Allen Lane and Penguin Books.

United Nations (1995) *Report of the World Summit for Social Development*. Copenhagen 6–12 March. Online at www.un.org/documents/ga/conf166/aconf166-9.htm

Yoshikawa, H., Aber, J. L., Bergman, L. R. and Beardslee, W. R. (2012) 'The effects of poverty on the mental, emotional, and behavioral health of children and youth', *American Psychologist*, 67, 272–84.

# 13

# Catholic Education in Scotland

*Stephen J. McKinney*

This chapter on Catholic education focuses on the contemporary position and continued existence of state-funded Catholic schools in Scotland. It begins by briefly exploring a variety of issues concerning the discussion of Catholic schools: explaining terminology, and arguing that debates about Catholic schools are not conducted within a cultural and historical vacuum and that, within the discussion, the identification of various *critical positions* is imperative to understand the complexity and the limitations of the debate. This initial section includes a summary of the most recent census findings on religious affiliation in Scotland. The chapter then provides an overview of denominational schools in Scotland and locates Catholic schools within a broader examination of the contemporary faith schools debate that has emerged in England and Wales. It continues by offering a brief sketch of the history of Catholic schools, discusses the contemporary rationale for Catholic schools as articulated by the Catholic Church, and examines the current provision of Catholic schools and Catholic support systems. Finally the chapter discusses the contemporary challenges and opportunities that have emerged for Catholic schools: the changing nature of the pupil population; opposition to Catholic schools; the historical abuse reported in Catholic residential schools; and the recruitment of Catholic headteachers.

## PRELIMINARY REMARKS

The history of contemporary Catholic schools and the closely associated history of the Catholic community in Scotland are complex, and nomenclature can be ambiguous and confusing. For the purposes of this chapter, the expression the 'Catholic community' will refer to all those who claim some link or allegiance to Catholicism in Scotland but who will have a wide variety of interpretations of Catholic identity, that may consist of religious, national, cultural and even secular elements, or combinations of these elements. One of the interesting features of Catholic schools in Scotland is that, apart from key celebrations in Catholic churches, the Catholic school may be the main, if not the only, meeting point for the full range of the Catholic community.

An important feature of the discussion and study of Catholic schools in Scotland is the status of those engaged in this discussion. The majority of academics writing about Catholic schools in Scotland, particularly those supporting Catholic schools, come from, or are associated with, the Catholic community in Scotland (e.g. Fitzpatrick, 1999; 2003; McKinney, 2011; O'Hagan, 2006). This means that they have insider status, and can be considered by others to share certain preconceived views, be uncritically supportive of Catholic schools and possibly defensive of the position of Catholic schools in Scottish education and society. However, these 'insider' academics are the academics most likely to have the impetus and interest to research Catholic schooling in Scotland in any depth and hence add to the body of knowledge concerning this highly relevant topic for Scottish education and society. Arguably, some of the academics who challenge the continued existence of Catholic schools (e.g. Brown, 1970; Bruce, 2003) also have some form of insider status, coming from a particular educational, sociological or philosophical perspective that has its own internal dialogues or discourses, shared opinions and degrees of conformity to accepted norms of beliefs. Therefore the notions of insider status and insider views are useful in that they challenge us to be critically aware of our preconceived views and intellectual standpoint as we engage with the subject of Catholic schools in Scotland.

The questions surrounding Catholic schools in Scotland are discussed, like many debates concerning Scottish education, in a variety of arenas and are frequently the object of media attention, often presented as a 'controversial' issue in the press. This is disappointing as the debate touches on complex interconnected issues of religion, philosophy, education, culture and society that gain nothing from being trivialised or sensationalised. The academic discussion, while following the media debate closely, has a responsibility to pose deeper questions and to engage with the complexity of issues that emerge from these questions and, where appropriate, challenge the media debate to discuss the topic accurately and fairly and to engage in a more nuanced manner.

The census results from 2011 indicate some important changes in the religious landscape in Scotland since the 2001 census. The census question asked: 'What religion, religious denomination or body do you belong to?' There was a noticeable decrease in the percentage of people who claimed to belong to the Church of Scotland, the largest Christian denomination (42.4 per cent to 32.4 per cent) and a noticeable increase in the number of people who claimed to have no religion (27.8 per cent to 36.7 per cent). Surprisingly, the percentage of people who claimed to belong to the Roman Catholic Church, the second largest Christian denomination, has remained stable at 15.9 per cent (841,000) since 2001. This statistic can be contrasted with the figures provided by the Catholic Church for the same period. These statistics indicate that the Catholic population in 2012 was 637,454 and national average weekly mass attendance for 2011 was 160,867. This indicates a marked distinction between religious affiliation and religious practice, with only 25.2 per cent actively participating in the principal form of worship.

## CONTEMPORARY FAITH SCHOOLS IN SCOTLAND

Catholic schools are not unique to Scotland, because there are Catholic schools in England and Wales and in many other parts of the world. There are various models for funding Catholic schools in other parts of the world including partial state funding and independent funding. State-funded Catholic schools in Scotland are unique in two senses: they are fully state-funded and, with very few exceptions, they are the only form of state-funded faith schooling in Scotland. According to the Scottish Catholic Education Service (SCES) website, there are 366 Catholic state-funded schools in Scotland. There is also a Jewish primary school (Calderwood Lodge) in East Renfrewshire and a small number of Episcopalian schools. At the time of writing, Calderwood Lodge is about to relocate to a newly built, faith school campus, shared with a local Catholic school. The links between the

Episcopalian schools and the Episcopalian Church appear tenuous, apart from small grants from the church to support the provision of Religious Education. Arguably, these other forms of faith school, despite being constantly referenced for the purposes of academic accuracy, seldom feature in the faith school debate in Scotland in any meaningful way. Ironically, the debate over the *possibility* of establishing a state-funded Muslim school in Glasgow generates more interest and publicity.

The public and academic debates on state-funded faith schools in Scotland, then, have become focused, understandably, on Catholic schools. This focus contrasts with the focus in England and Wales, where the wider variety of state-funded faith schooling and the continued expansion and extension of faith schooling enables a more sophisticated and more complex academic engagement. The debate in England and Wales, for example, is not simply focused on one form of Christian faith schooling (and limited questions associated with divisiveness and sectarianism) but is focused on a variety of Christian faith schools (e.g. Church of England, Catholic, the Emmanuel Schools Foundation) and a variety of other faith schools (e.g. Jewish, Muslim and Sikh), and this religious and cultural diversity means that the debate does not easily lend itself to generalisations, categorisation and, importantly, stereotyping (see McKinney, 2011, for a discussion of contemporary faith schools in the UK).

## BRIEF HISTORY OF CATHOLIC SCHOOLS IN SCOTLAND

The Catholic population of the south-west of Scotland was increased in the late eighteenth and early nineteenth centuries by the arrival of Irish seasonal workers and some of these workers settled in the area. Irish Catholics and Highland Scottish Catholics who moved to the city to seek employment increased the Catholic population of the city of Glasgow. It is important to note that the Catholic population of Scotland was to be further augmented in the nineteenth and twentieth centuries by patterns of migration that drew Italian, Polish and Lithuanian Catholics. The Irish Catholics, however, were by far the largest national–cultural group to emerge in Scottish Catholicism and provided the critical mass of Catholics that were required for the establishment of Catholic schools. The number of Irish Catholics in Glasgow, for example, increased from 450 in 1805 to 15,000 in 1822. A key point in the development of Catholic schools was the establishment of the Catholic Schools Society in Glasgow in 1817. The society was overseen by a board of fifteen Catholics and fifteen Protestants and was chaired by the well-known Glasgow merchant, and Protestant, Mr Kirkman Finlay, MP. The schools were ostensibly established to educate the children of poor Roman Catholics, though no religion was to be taught (this was to change shortly afterwards). The Catholic school system grew throughout the nineteenth century, coming under considerable pressure as the numbers of Catholic Irish immigrants rose quite dramatically as a result of a series of potato famines in Ireland (1845–9).

A variety of forms of schooling, and of varying quality, had emerged in Scotland by the mid-nineteenth century, including other church schools such as Episcopalian and Presbyterian. While all statistics from this era should be treated with caution, there were thirty-two Roman Catholic schools reported to be in existence in 1851. The Argyll Commission, which called for a greater rationalisation and state involvement in schooling throughout Scotland, reported that there were sixty-one Roman Catholic schools in 1864. The Catholic community declined the invitation to incorporate the (then) sixty-five Catholic schools into the state school system at the time of the 1872 Education (Scotland)

Act, concerned that the Catholic ethos, the right to appoint Catholic teachers and the Catholic religious instruction available in Catholic schools would be jeopardised. Catholic schools continued to be independently funded by subscription but struggled to maintain adequate standards both in terms of resources and building infrastructure. The recurring narrative from writers from the Catholic tradition is that the Catholic community had to pay for education twice: for the state schools through local rates and for the maintenance of the voluntary Catholic schools. A more complex narrative indicates that the Catholics were also paying for the construction and interior decoration of churches and contributing funds to the St Vincent De Paul Society (SVDP). The SVDP is a Catholic charitable organisation that enabled the poorer Catholic children to attend school by providing clothing, school materials, meals and assisting with the small fees that had to be paid (McKinney, 2017). The number of Catholic schools grew: 127 in 1880; 163 in 1890; 189 in 1900; 220 in 1910; and 226 in 1917. The negotiations surrounding the 1918 Education (Scotland) Act brought the Catholic schools into the state system as fully state-funded and ensured that denominational status, the right to appoint Catholic teachers and to retain Catholic religious instruction were preserved. One of the effects of the 1918 Act was that Catholic schools became part of the 'official' educational discourse in Scotland.

A number of Catholic religious orders and congregations (e.g. Jesuits, Marists and Notre Dame Sisters) had a key role in Catholic schooling throughout the late nineteenth century and much of the twentieth century, and, in the case of the Notre Dame Sisters, in the education of Catholic teachers. Catholic schools continued to grow and develop throughout the twentieth century and aided the social mobility of members of the Catholic community. They were able to benefit from major changes in socio-economics and education in Scotland after the Second World War. These included: the decline of (a perceived) structural sectarianism; the rise of the multinationals providing employment opportunities for young people free of any religious bias; free access to higher education; the demise of junior and senior secondary schools and the inauguration of comprehensive education; and the replacement of the Scottish Leaving certificate with the Ordinary and Higher grade certificates. The numbers of Catholic schools, like non-denominational schools, experienced a post-war boom in the 1960s and 1970s and the 1970s and 1980s were marked by the withdrawal of the religious orders and congregations from schooling and the recognition of the emerging importance of the 'lay' Catholic teacher. The 1990s and early 2000s were to witness the increased success of Catholic schools as measured by Her Majesty's Inspectorate of Education (HMIE) reports and the cruder indicators of the 'league tables'. The 2000s were also a period of unprecedented public support for Catholic schools from the Scottish National Party (SNP) government.

## CONTEMPORARY RATIONALE FOR CATHOLIC SCHOOLS

The international scope of Catholic education is very broad and varied and is rooted in the concept of Catholic education as a lifelong process, or journey, to Christian maturity and includes formal and informal education, education of both children and adults in primary, secondary and tertiary modes. The attempt below to summarise the Catholic rationale for Catholic schools is problematic in that, like all such attempts, it is open to the criticism that it lacks conceptual depth and is a poor substitute for the development of a contemporary distinctive philosophy of Catholic education. The reader is referred to the Vatican website for a more detailed explanation and development of this rationale in a series of documents. Among the key documents are the following: *Christian Education* (1965); *The Catholic School* (1977); *Lay Catholics in Schools: Witnesses to Faith* (1982); *The Religious Dimension of Catholic Schools* (1988); *Catholic Schools on the Threshold of the Third Millennium* (1998); *Educating Together in Catholic Schools* (2007); and *Educating Today and Tomorrow: A Renewing Passion* (2014). These primary sources are augmented by secondary texts from major contemporary writers on Catholic education: John Sullivan; Gerald Grace; Graham Rossiter and Tom Groome (see McKinney and Sullivan, 2013).

Catholic schools are perceived by the Roman Catholic Church to be a faith-formational approach to education and, where they exist, an integral component of the lifelong process of Christian formation. This Catholic formation is sometimes conceived as a dynamic relationship between evangelisation (call and recall to faith) and catechesis (deepening of faith). The Catholic Church states that the role of Catholic schools is to assist parents (the primary educators) to educate children in the Christian faith and to provide an effective general education that will enable the children to contribute actively to society as good citizens and as mature Christian men and women. Catholic schools provide a context for the pursuit of a synthesis of faith and reason and should be engaged in dialogue with contemporary culture and life. The Catholic school aspires to be a Christian community that is founded and operates on 'Gospel values' (values such as love, equality, compassion, inclusion), and these should be manifested in the daily activities of the school and in mutually respectful relationships. The Catholic school aspires to be a community that has prayer and liturgical life at the heart of its daily operation. Religious education in Catholic schools is considered to be rooted in this vision of faith formation and an important part of the primary and secondary school curricula. This education in Christian faith is constructed as an invitation and all documentation prohibits coercion or any suggestion of indoctrination. Catholic schools are encouraged to interact with other non–Catholic schools to engage in dialogue with them.

The visitor to the Scottish Catholic school would observe that there are Christian symbols and iconography on open display (McKinney, 2011). These take the form of statues, pictures and crucifixes in public spaces and in the classrooms. The day in the Catholic school in Scotland is characterised by prayer, at least a shared prayer in the morning and often a prayer in the afternoon. There are further opportunities for prayer in the school day, especially in the primary schools. There are also opportunities to celebrate the seasons of the Christian year (e.g. Advent, Christmas, Lent and Easter) through liturgies and celebration of the Eucharist. Where a Catholic primary school is in close proximity to a Catholic Church, there are opportunities to pray and celebrate the Eucharist in the church as well as in the school. The local priest is the chaplain to the Catholic primary school and usually a frequent visitor. This strong partnership is epitomised in the shared preparation in the Catholic primary school for the reception of three Sacraments (Reconciliation, Eucharist and Confirmation). A designated priest, layperson or a team ministry provide chaplaincy services to the Catholic secondary school. There are opportunities for interdisciplinary learning activities that incorporate religious themes, especially Christian themes, related to subjects such as History, English, Science and Modern Studies.

One of the claims of the Vatican documentation on education is that the Catholic Church has a mission to educate the poor. This is articulated in *Christian Education* (1965) and is revisited in subsequent documents, most recently in *Educating Today and Tomorrow* (2014, section 5): 'Those who find themselves in greater difficulties, who are poorer, more fragile or needy, should be at the centre of schools' attention and concerns.' Grace (2002) has referred to this as the 'Catholic schools principle of preferential option for the poor' and has perceived this as a key feature of the historic mission of Catholic schools in Scotland and the wider UK, serving a community that was primarily at the lower end of the socio-economic scale (see also O'Hagan, 2006 and McKinney, 2017). While the continued existence of three independent Catholic schools in Scotland may temper these claims a little, there is evidence that the state-funded Catholic schools in Scotland continue to exercise this principle (McKinney et al., 2013; McKinney, 2014).

## CONTEMPORARY CATHOLIC SCHOOLS IN SCOTLAND AND CATHOLIC SUPPORT SYSTEMS

There are fifty-three secondary, 310 primary and three additional support needs (ASN) state-funded Catholic schools in Scotland. There are also three independent Catholic schools, two in Glasgow and one in Perthshire. The state-funded Catholic schools, like all other state-funded mainstream schools, are comprehensive and co-educational (with the exception of Notre Dame High School for Girls in Glasgow). Approximately 120,000 children attend Catholic schools accounting for 20 per cent of the overall school population. Catholic schools tend to be located primarily in the post-industrial west-central belt where many of the Irish immigrants and their descendants had worked and settled, but there are a small number of Catholic secondary and primary schools in Dundee, Perth and Edinburgh, and primary schools in Aberdeen, Inverness, parts of the Highlands and the Borders (for the full geographical extent of Catholic schools and regular updates see the SCES website).

As part of the state school system, Catholic schools have full equal access to local and centralised support systems. They have access, for example, to local authority curriculum advisors and are invited to send delegates to meetings for all new initiatives. Catholic schools, however, have other tiers of support established to focus on the 'Catholic' aspects of Catholic schools or to review general educational initiatives and their implications for Catholic schooling. The Scottish Catholic Education Commission (CEC) sets national policy on all educational matters on behalf of the Catholic bishops of Scotland. The creation of SCES (the operational arm of the CEC) and the appointment of Michael McGrath as full-time director in 2003 have had a significant impact on the profile and development of Catholic schooling in Scotland. Mr McGrath was succeeded as director in 2016 by Barbara Coupar. SCES has created a mission statement (*A Charter for Catholic Schools in Scotland*, 2004) and policy documents designed to enhance Catholic Education. SCES has also led and overseen the creation of Called to Love (2008) and God's Loving Plan (2014) (programmes of relationships and moral education for the secondary and primary levels, respectively) and provides a wide variety of resources on its website. In addition, SCES provides continuing professional development (CPD) for Catholic teachers and supports the work of the religious education advisors employed by the Catholic Church and the organisations that represent the Catholic primary and secondary headteachers (Association of Catholic Primary Head Teachers in Scotland, CHAPS; and Catholic Head Teachers Association, CHAS). Recent significant achievements have included the launch of the national syllabus for Religious Education in Catholic schools, *This is Our Faith* in 2011. This syllabus encompasses primary one to S3 in secondary school. This has been enhanced by the introduction of a Senior Phase version in 2015. SCES has also introduced two highly successful award schemes that aim to put faith into action: the Caritas Award (for secondary schools) and the Pope Francis Award (for primary schools). SCES has also consolidated Catholic representation at various levels of local and central government and has worked collaboratively with partners in Catholic Education throughout Europe including the European Committee for Catholic Education (CEEC)

The majority of Catholic teachers are trained in the School of Education, University of Glasgow, primarily following the Master of Education with Teaching Qualification (Primary) (MEduc) programme, the Professional Graduate Diploma in Education (PGDE) Secondary and PGDE Primary courses. The MEduc programme has superseded the Bachelor of Education (BEd) programme and continues to prepare students for teaching in Catholic schools within a post-Donaldson Report framework. The student intake on the initial teacher education (ITE) courses in the School of Education is not exclusively Catholic, but the main ITE courses are funded by the Scottish Funding Council for the training of Catholic teachers for the Catholic sector, and the School has a responsibility to undertake this task. In 2016, the role of the School of Education was expanded to provide a Catholic Teacher Certificate at the Universities of Strathclyde and Edinburgh for an initial trial period. This is taught as blended learning (a combination of contact and distance learning). This was introduced to serve the large number of Catholic ITE students who attend the University of Strathclyde and who wish to teach in Catholic schools, and in response to the needs of the Catholic schools on the east coast. This trial may be extended to the Universities of Dundee and Aberdeen.

Any Catholic teachers wishing to teach in the Catholic sector are able to acquire a qualification, but not approval, to teach in the Catholic sector. Approval of 'religious belief and character' (for all teachers) to teach in a Catholic school comes exclusively from the bishops of Scotland and is separate from the function of the School of Education.

## CHALLENGES AND OPPORTUNITIES

State funding for Catholic schools in Scotland in 1918 meant that they became integral to the 'official' educational discourse and, as a result, there have been a series of historical and contemporary debates about the position of Catholic schools within the state-funded school sector in Scotland. These debates have questioned whether it is appropriate for Catholic schools to be funded by the state and have raised issues about Catholic schools in Scotland being perceived as divisive, as being related to sectarianism and as being anachronistic (see McKinney, 2013, and McKinney and Conroy, 2015, for fuller discussion). Those who advocate state funding for Catholic schools argue that these schools are highly valued by members of the Catholic community who are taxpayers, and the state, rightly in their view, is supporting their choice of school education for their children. This is a choice that appears to be increasingly exercised by the wider non-Catholic community in Scotland. From one perspective, this is a measure of the perceived success and attractiveness of Catholic schools, in terms of academic attainment and achievement, the social environment and the faith context. The increased numbers of non-Catholic children, while requiring balance between inclusion and retaining a Catholic identity, creates opportunities for dialogue between faith and cultures and different religions. A further challenge for Catholic schools is the increasing number of children from the Catholic community whose family links with Catholic Christianity may be tenuous (as measured by the falling church attendance discussed above), and whose understanding of the aims and practice of Christian life may be somewhat limited.

Catholic schools have recently faced challenges from some political parties, notably the Green Party. The Green Party, in its 2007 manifesto, stated that the party 'will move towards the integration of state-funded religious schools into non-denominational education'. This aim did not appear in the 2016 manifesto nor does it appear in their education policy on their website. However, when challenged by representatives of the Catholic Church, a Green spokesperson publicly stated that this remained one of the aims of their education policy. As the vast majority of religious schools in Scotland are Catholic schools, the aim is to effectively phase out Catholic schools and the small number of other faith schools. In an interview with the *Scottish Catholic Observer* (13 February, 2015), Patrick Harvie stated that the Green Party 'supports an integrated secular education system' and that 'children have the right to a neutral education'. This position is consistent with the policy of the Green Party of the United Kingdom. It is acknowledged that these are reported sound bites but there are, nevertheless, serious academic questions to be raised about the meaning of an 'integrated secular education system' and a 'neutral education'.

The National Secular Society and the Humanist Society Scotland oppose faith schools in Scotland (and the UK) and question and challenge the continued existence of Catholic schools in Scotland. These organisations respect the right to freedom of religious expression and belief, enshrined in human rights legislation, but they argue that this should be consigned to the private sphere and should not impinge on the public sphere. They argue that the state should not fund any form of faith schools because the state and organised religion should be separate. Faith schools, therefore, are perceived to be an unwelcome and formal link between the state and religion by the secularists and the humanists. At the same time, the continuing existence of state-funded faith schools (whether Catholic, Church of England or Jewish) indicates that the state recognises the importance of faith in some forms of schooling, or, at least, is prepared to tolerate this form of schooling. This link was confirmed, and even celebrated, by the Cardinal Winning lecture in February 2008 at the University of Glasgow, delivered by Alex Salmond, the then Scottish First Minister. Mr Salmond expressed his unequivocal support for Catholic schools. This incident highlighted that the debate on Catholic schools in Scotland is undertaken against the backdrop of the uneasy coexistence between the secularist agenda of the separation of the state and religion and the twenty-first-century agenda of accommodation of a multicultural, multi-ethnic and, importantly, multi-religious Scotland.

One very serious issue that has received increased attention has been the continuing inquiries into historical incidences of physical, mental and sexual abuses in residential Catholic schools. The former Benedictine school, Fort Augustus Abbey School (and its preparatory school in East Lothian) is one of the most widely publicised examples. The Fort Augustus Abbey School was closed in 1993 but in 2013 a number of ex-pupils reported physical and sexual abuse by the monks. This prompted legal action against a number of former staff and an apology by Bishop Hugh Gilbert of Aberdeen on behalf of the Catholic Church in Scotland. Another example is the Smyllum orphanage that was run by the Daughters of Charity of St Vincent De Paul from 1864 till 1981. It has emerged that deceased children were buried in unmarked graves in Lanark and there are accusations of physical and psychological abuse towards children. These and other cases, some outwith the Catholic Church, prompted the Scottish Government to charge the Scottish Child Abuse Inquiry with the investigation of the abuse of children in care in Scotland. The inquiry identified seven Catholic religious orders and congregations that were to be part of the investigation. The hearings began in late May 2017. These inquiries are creating opportunities for dozens of victims to voice their experiences and more may come forward. This is resulting in legal action against perpetrators and support and compensation for victims and, crucially, the generation of safeguards for the future.

A recurring issue is the requirement for approval to teach in a Catholic school. This refers to the requirement for any teacher who is to be appointed to a post in a denominational school to be approved in regards to their religious belief and character by the denominational body. This is affirmed in the 1980 Education (Scotland) Act section 21(2) (i) and, from the perspective of the Scottish Catholic Church and schools, helps to retain the Christian integrity of Catholic schools. This has been challenged in recent years as an equalities issue on a number of grounds: as a form of discrimination against those who are not Catholic in the selection of staff (though there are many non-Catholic teachers working in Catholic secondary schools) and as a form of advantage for Catholic teachers as they can teach and assume leadership roles in both denominational and non-denominational schools. Non-Catholic teachers have perceived this situation as both unjust and unfair. In 2006, David McNab was prevented from applying for a promoted post in pastoral care in St Paul's Secondary School, Glasgow, because he is an atheist. An employment tribunal decided that there had been discrimination in this case and ruled in his favour. Nevertheless, the tribunal upheld section 21(2)(i) of the 1980 Education (Scotland) Act. Since then, there have been several calls for the Scottish Government to review this legislation, most recently in late 2016 from the Equality and Human Rights Commission.

Over the last few years there has been publicity about the crisis in recruitment of qualified Catholic teachers and headteachers for Catholic schools. Some of the initiatives to recruit more Catholic teachers have been discussed above. These challenges are not unique to Scotland and are shared with many other countries (for example, England and Wales, Australia and New Zealand). The challenges in recruiting Catholic headteachers are, in some ways, similar to the challenge of recruiting headteachers for non-denominational schools. Headteachers have been charged with a greater range of duties and responsibilities and liaison work with a wider group of stakeholders. The *ADES Paper on the Recruitment of Head Teachers* (Robertson et al., 2013) identified three major additional challenges for the recruitment of Catholic headteachers: a smaller pool of potential candidates for this role in Catholic schools; potential candidates working in non-denominational schools (possibly easing some of the tensions and feelings of injustice mentioned above); and some who may feel they would not acquire Church approval. There have been moves to address all three of these issues by: identifying suitable candidates for headship in a Catholic school; discussing ways to facilitate easier transition for candidates located in non-denominational schools; and seeking greater clarity on the conditions for church approval and consistency in the application of the conditions. The University of Glasgow and SCES are both planning to contribute to the new Scottish Government qualification, 'Into Headship', and this should provide an invaluable opportunity to prepare Catholic leaders for the future.

## CONCLUDING REMARKS

State-funded Catholic schools in Scotland reach their centenary in 2018. The centenary year is an opportunity to celebrate the position and value of Catholic schools and evaluate their continued contribution to Scottish education and society. This includes scholarly revision of different aspects of the history of Catholic schools in Scotland. There is a rich, multilayered historical and contemporary rationale for Catholic schools: religious formation of a minority; preferential option for the poor; and promoting social mobility and inclusiveness and openness to others. Catholic schools will, of course, continue to attract opposition in the public arena and the arguments of opponents deserve to be counter-argued in a rational and

148  SCOTTISH EDUCATION

measured way. There is ample scope for further and deeper research into Catholic schools and the effects of Catholic schools and this can contribute to wider international debates about the position of Catholic schools and faith schooling in contemporary societies.

## REFERENCES

Brown, W. E. (1970) *Can Catholic Schools Survive?* New York: Sheed and Ward.
Bruce, S. (2003) 'Catholic schools in Scotland: a rejoinder to Conroy', *Oxford Review of Education*, 29 (2), 269–77.
Fitzpatrick, T. A. (1999) 'Catholic education in Scotland', in T. G. K. Bryce and W. M. Humes (eds), *Scottish Education*. Edinburgh: Edinburgh University Press.
Fitzpatrick, T. A. (2003) 'Catholic education in Scotland', in T. G. K. Bryce and W. M. Humes (eds), *Scottish Education, Second Edition: Post-devolution*. Edinburgh: Edinburgh University Press.
Grace, G. (2002) *Catholic Schools, Mission, Markets and Morality*. London: Routledge.
McKinney, S. J. (2011) 'The contemporary faith school debate in the United Kingdom', *Education Today*, 61 (2), 11–18.
McKinney, S. J. (2013) 'Religious intolerance: sectarianism', in T. G. K. Bryce, W. M. Humes, D. Gillies and A. Kennedy (eds), *Scottish Education, Fourth Edition: Referendum*. Edinburgh: Edinburgh University Press, pp. 883–92.
McKinney, S. (2014) 'The relationship of child poverty to school education', *Improving Schools*, 17 (3), 201–16.
McKinney S. J. (2017) 'Catholic schools in Glasgow and caring for the needs of those who are poor', in S. Whittle (ed.) *Vatican II and New Thinking about Catholic Education*. London: Routledge.
McKinney, S. J. and Sullivan, J. (eds) (2013) *Education in a Catholic Perspective*. Ashgate: Farnham.
McKinney, S. J. and Conroy, J. C. (2015) 'The continued existence of state-funded Catholic schools in Scotland', *Comparative Education*, 51 (1) 105–17.
McKinney, S. J., Hall, S., Lowden, K., McClung, M. and Cameron, L. (2012) 'The relationship between poverty and deprivation, educational attainment and positive school leaver destinations in Glasgow secondary schools', *Scottish Educational Review*, 44 (1), 33–45.
McKinney, S. J., Hall, S., Lowden, K., McClung, M. and Cameron, L. (2013) 'Supporting school leavers in areas of deprivation into initial positive school leaver destinations', *Improving Schools*, 16 (1), 67–83.
O'Hagan, F. J. (2006) *The Contribution of the Religious Orders to Education in Glasgow during the Period 1847–1918*. Lampeter: The Edwin Mellen Press.
Robertson, B., Christie, J. and Stodter, J. (2013) *An ADES Paper on the Recruitment of Head Teachers in Scotland. October 2013*. Online at www.gov.scot/Publications/2016/09/2138/8

### Websites

Humanist Society Scotland at https://www.humanism.scot/
National Secular Society at http://www.secularism.org.uk/
Scottish Catholic Education Service (SCES) at http://sces.org.uk
The Holy See at http://w2.vatican.va/content/vatican/en.html
*The Innes Review*, the best source of scholarly articles on the history of Catholic schooling in Scotland, at https://www.euppublishing.com/loi/inr?expanded/=&

# 14

# 'Progressive' Schools and Home Education

*Andrew Pyle*

This chapter falls into two sections. In the first, an account is given of the life and work of one of Scotland's leading progressive educators, John Aitkenhead (1910–98). Whereas the work of other Scottish teachers in the progressive tradition, such as A. S. Neill and R. F. Mackenzie, is well-documented (see Chapter 11), relatively little has been written about Aitkenhead. This account draws on the present author's access to unpublished papers relating to Kilquhanity House, the school founded by Aitkenhead, and to correspondence and other material which explains the development of his thinking. The second section of the chapter describes the choice exercised by some parents to make provision for their children's education outside the state system, which many of them regard as too formal and regimented and unable to cater adequately for individual needs and interests. In contrast to the extensive sources used in relation to Aitkenhead, here there is a dearth of material to draw on. Official information, where it exists, is thin and out of date. Moreover, organisations which support and promote home education are keen to protect the confidentiality of parents, some of whom have had negative experiences in their dealings with various forms of officialdom. Taken together, however, the two sections provide some insight into a small, but significant tradition in Scottish education – one that values freedom more than conformity, and questions the priority of academic studies over other forms of learning.

## JOHN AITKENHEAD AND KILQUHANITY HOUSE SCHOOL: A HUMAN JOURNEY

'I would die a happy man if there was a Parliament in Edinburgh and a school like this in every part of Scotland' (John Aitkenhead speaking on camera in 1968). Unfortunately, John Aitkenhead did not live to see either. This short statement encompasses the man and his vision. Students of education considering 'alternative education' in Scotland are commonly directed to the two names, A. S. Neill and R. F. Mackenzie, both pioneers and activists in progressive educational ideas and practice. Mackenzie worked in the state sector, as headteacher in Braehead Secondary School in Fife and in Summerhill Academy in Aberdeen, where he was allowed to pursue his experimental approach for a time, but where the authorities later made significant efforts to destroy his practice (see Murphy, 1998). Neill's independent school Summerhill (the name is coincidental) acquired an international reputation, attracting both supporters and critics, but remained south of Hadrian's Wall.

He regarded Scotland as too imbued with the spirit of Calvinism to embrace a philosophy of freedom and self-expression (see Croall, 1984).

Aitkenhead's school, Kilquhanity House, was founded in 1940 and managed to survive for fifty-seven years on the same site in the picturesque Urr Valley a few miles from Castle Douglas in rural Galloway. The small country estate continues to this day in the guise of Kilquhanity Children's Village, the Scottish centre for the Japanese group of schools under the name of Kinokuni Children's Villages founded by Shinichiro Hori, a former Professor of Education and passionate advocate for the work and practice of Aitkenhead, Neill and the American philosopher John Dewey.

Aitkenhead, born in 1910, the son of a carpenter working in the Clyde shipyards, was raised in Glasgow and moved to Ardrossan in 1920. In 1922 his father sought work in New York when employment dried up in the shipyards during the depression years, returning to Ardrossan in 1928. Aitkenhead's mother refused to accompany her husband to America and kept house in Ardrossan where John, even as a schoolboy, would find manual work to contribute to the family income. He attended the local high school in Ardrossan where his natural academic ability and sporting prowess, especially in rugby, made him popular amongst his peers. In 1928 he attended the university in Glasgow, where he studied English and Classics. After graduation, he trained as a secondary teacher at Jordanhill College but also maintained his link with the university by undertaking postgraduate studies in Education.

Glasgow University had at this time recently started a degree course in Education. Aitkenhead attended lectures on the History and Theory of Education from October 1932 until May 1933, with William Boyd as lecturer. Boyd, known for his translation of *Emile*, by the French philosopher Jean Jacques Rousseau, was to become a significant influence on Aitkenhead's thinking about education and politics. It is notable that Aitkenhead kept his lecture notes from Boyd's course for the rest of his life. In his own notes to the first lecture given by Boyd, Aitkenhead wrote:

> The province of pedagogy is the upgrowing and upbringing of the human being. More compre-hensively Education is the whole process of determining human behaviour.
> Education in the first instance, is a practical business, also in the last.
> People do first and think afterwards. By doing things we learn.
> Unfortunately, our education today for the most part puts the cart before the horse – teaching in the hope that people would do.

These notes reflect the philosophy of pragmatism as applied to education, set out fully in Dewey's highly influential book *Democracy and Education* (1916). The Boyd lectures introduced Aitkenhead to a plethora of ideas and questions on psychology, philosophy, and aesthetics. The list of Examination Topics for 1932–3 indicates the range of thought about education to which Aitkenhead was introduced:

1. What every educated person should know about education.
2. What every educated teacher should know about education.
3. Learning for school and learning for life.
4. Child-centred education.
5. Man made a rational being by society.
6. The organic basis of rational education.
7. Fundamental and necessary skills.

8. Animal behaviour and human behaviour.
9. The formation of sentiments.
10. Conflicting tendencies in human life.
11. The making of moral personality.
12. The nature of intelligence.
13. The development of intelligence by training.
14. Knowledge as potential intelligence.
15. The mind of rediscovery in learning.
16. The relation of organic, moral, intellectual and spiritual education.

It would be interesting to compare this curriculum with that of trainee teachers in the university today and the thinking and direction given to Scottish education by the flagship policy of Curriculum for Excellence.

Boyd's influence in Aitkenhead's development went beyond the walls of the university as Aitkenhead is known to have regularly accompanied Boyd as a volunteer to help run the 'soup kitchens' on Clydeside to provide some support for the unemployed and impoverished during the Great Depression when some 30 per cent of Glaswegians were out of work. At the same time, Aitkenhead was running Boy Scout Groups:

> I was one of his first students, and I was one of the first who took the complete education degree. But education that I was involved in was in the Boy Scout movement. I was running two or three Scout meetings a week. And that was freedom of attendance. Nobody ever forced a boy to join the Boy Scouts. But if you join the Boy Scouts, you have to learn to pass various standards in practical things, you see? And then you learn by doing, by going to camp, you know? So I was really being an educator at night. (Aitkenhead, 1966)

William Boyd deserves a biography in his own right as a significant contributor to the development of Scottish education and for his role within the Education Institute of Scotland (see Humes, 2015).

Boyd and Aitkenhead developed a friendship and relationship that would last until Boyd's death in 1962. Boyd gave a little financial and a lot of moral support and encouragement to Aitkenhead. Writing in 1959 to Aitkenhead, he said:

> My dear John, I have pleasure in sending a contribution to your building fund. … I have been thinking over your very interesting undertaking [Kilquhanity] and am wondering if you are getting all the value out of the experiment that you might. It is good to have a school like yours where some children get a real chance to grow into a good personality and way of life. But I would like to have a distillation of the experience for everybody wanting a better kind of education. In a word, I want to have the ideas that have come to you and that are still coming presented in a form that will set more folk thinking. Have you done any writing about Kilquhanity? … But without some exposition of your principles you have only done half of your job. … Any way John, you have my best wishes for the success of your efforts to meet the demands of the Department [Scottish Education Department's new registration requirements]. While I see the need for some kind of national control on educational institutions I greatly feel that it is going to make the experimentation that is needed to ensure growth and real progress very difficult.

Aitkenhead read A. S. Neill's book *Is Scotland Educated?* in 1936. By 1938 he had read all of Neill's books published to date and he wrote to Neill requesting a visit to Summerhill. He visited for two weeks and was 'bowled over' by what he experienced. By this time

Aitkenhead had signed the Peace Pledge Union and was committed to pacifism. He visited Summerhill a second time specifically to discuss the opening of a similar school in Scotland. Neill's reply was that Scotland was 'too benighted' and any such school based on Summerhill would fail.

Then, world events took over. In 1918 Aitkenhead had witnessed the homecoming of the wounded and emotionally troubled soldiers returning to Ardrossan from France and the distressed families mourning their slain. The 'war to end all wars' was to be overtaken by the events in Germany from 1933 onwards and the declaration of war on 3 September 1939. Neill was to change his mind and now encouraged Aitkenhead telling him the time was right before 'freedom goes out the window'. By this stage, Aitkenhead had been working for three years in state schools in Argyll and Ayrshire, becoming progressively more disenchanted with what he saw as an oppressive and ill-conceived system.

Aitkenhead was now the sum of his parts: a pacifist, a poet, a socialist, informed and passionate about alternative ways of providing education, a nationalist, a practical man with a brain. He found premises in Galloway and on 18 October 1940 he drove down to Kilquhanity with his wife Morag and their four-month-old baby. It was a bold, some would say foolhardy, step to take for a young man of thirty. There he was, opening an alternative school in Scotland, with very little finance, at the start of a major war, renting a seven-and-half-acre country estate with a big house and small farm steading.

In that first year (1940) the only commercially printed brochure about the school was produced (Figure 14.1). Thereafter all brochures and information, apart from the 1959 appeal leaflet, were produced on a Gestetner (a hand cranked, duplicator machine).

How did the theory transfer into practice? It is true to say that over the fifty-seven years of Kilquhanity's existence the practice and methodology both evolved and adapted to the participants in the community, both staff and pupils; to pressures from outside – the inspectorate; and to cultural changes in world. Throughout the life of the school, however, certain things remained constant.

The idea of self-government was cultivated and managed through the council meeting. The existence of 'school councils' will be familiar to some in the state sector but the format at Kilquhanity will not be common practice. The meeting was held weekly, attended by all, with one vote each, chaired by an older pupil and scribed by a pupil. The meeting was the place for points to be raised, discussed and decided upon: specific requests for alterations to weekly routine – trips and outings, agreements to postpone or extend certain lessons, late bedtimes, weekend activities. The meeting also served to be the means of 'justice' for the community. Grievances were brought up, bullying discussed and resolved, upsets and misunderstandings dealt with by the whole community, not by an adult in 'authority'. This has led some spectators and commentators to think this was a place where 'anything goes': this view could not be further from the reality. The guiding principle was that 'with freedom comes responsibility', which involved accepting that your actions should not impair the freedom of others: this requires practice and involves learning of a challenging kind. The process also meant that agreements and new rules made at one meeting might often be renegotiated at a later date – the competence of the 'scribe' was important to be able to refer back to decisions made previously. Justice was by general agreement, clemency was often shown, punishment was rare as an 'undertaking' by the perpetrator of an offence would be monitored by all and reviewed at a subsequent meeting.

The daily routine of useful work complemented the council meeting. This was a period of about forty minutes of every weekday when everyone would participate in

---

## A NEW SCHOOL IN A SAFE AREA
## A SCHOOL FOR YOUNG CITIZENS OF THE NEW EUROPE

Kilquhanity a refuge in a war, a training for peace.

Freedom – Today, freedom of mind is at stake in the world; Kilquhanity champions it. This world reflects the Scots love of freedom as well as the educational ideal that Scotsmen have been content to boast about since the days of John Knox. Attendance at class is voluntary. The pupils have their own government and share with the adults the responsibility of running the school.

| | |
|---|---|
| 'A! Fredome is a noble thing! | Freedom is a noble thing. |
| Fredome mayss man to haiff liking; | Freedom gives man a choice. |
| Fredome all solace to man Giffis, | Freedom gives all men comfort, |
| He levys at ess that frely levys!' | He who lives at ease lives freely.' |

[This is a quotation from the fourteenth-century Scottish poet, John Barbour.]

Safety – Perhaps even more than sound education, physical safety is the concern of parents today. Kilquhanity is at the centre of one of the safest areas of Britain.

Health – The men and women who planned Kilquhanity believe that a healthy child is a happy child. Meals are planned for nutrition and enjoyment.

Education – Aiming, as it does, at a balanced community, Kilquhanity is co-educational. The fullest scope and encouragement are given to all artistic expression – music, dancing, painting, handwork and gardening. At the same time the staff is fully qualified to prepare pupils for examinations up to University entrance standard. International in outlook, Kilquhanity welcomes children of any nationality.

Ages – from 3 years up.

Fees – For boarders, from £30 to £40 per term, according to age. For day pupils, about one third of that.

---

**Figure 14.1  Kilquhanity House brochure**

tasks that were of benefit to the whole community. Chopping firewood, clearing out fire grates, setting fires, peeling potatoes, preparing the morning 'piece' of marmalade or honey, coffee, tea and hot chocolate, sweeping communal areas, cleaning bathrooms and toilets. The school did not employ domestic staff apart from a cook. If individuals failed to carry out their task this could be brought up at the council meeting, discussed and resolution sought. Often this would be an agreement to swop duties with another person, adult or pupil, in a similar situation. Learning that we are all in it together and society relies on the action of the self and others was an important life lesson in Kilquhanity.

The third element, in addition to the council meeting and useful work, that remained consistent throughout was some aspect of agriculture and horticulture. The school was part of the seven-and-half-acre estate that included: a small dairy herd of three or four cows, often with one in calf; farrowing pigs, chickens and ducks; and 'John's Garden' in one corner of the estate where potatoes were a regular crop, along with fruit and vegetables nurtured by pupils with Aitkenhead's guidance. He said:

> I count myself lucky that I grew up learning the old-fashioned dairying skills like hand-milking and butter-making, and I believe skills like these have frequently been of more value in the work I have chosen with children than a couple of honours degrees.

And talking of the farm: 'This is real fun for children, but of far more importance, these activities, in my opinion lay the foundation, the curiously elusive yet all important foundation, of mental health. They are the old art, the old magic, the real recreation.' The reference here to mental health shows that, in some respects, Aitkenhead was well ahead of his time as it is only now that this issue is receiving serious attention in state schools. Attendance at classes was not compulsory but the expectation was that pupils would attend. For older pupils, there would be a degree of negotiation as to what was studied in the art room or science lab. As class sizes were very small, certainly less than ten children, choice and individual ideas could be pursued. And age was not a criterion for attendance as a class might have a representative of all the teenage years up to sixteen. The reality was that attendance in class was high as to be absent was often to miss out on the fun and excitement in what was in the main part practical activity. Even in non-practical lessons, like English and Mathematics, physical activity would be brought in through drama or learning geometry by going outside to look at and measure aspects of the estate and its buildings.

Learning through 'hands-on', practical activity was the key for Aitkenhead in children's learning:

> In fact, I am prepared to say we practice education through art, and would go so far as to claim that the rare and rewarding sense of community, enjoyed by staff and pupils and former members of the school, reflects the extent to which the spirit of the arts permeates school life. Someone has said that real culture unites people, whereas the academic culture of today divides and separates them. I think I agree with that, and I imagine that in any school where all the arts are cultivated – dance, drama, painting, pottery and music – so long as these are really enjoyed and creatively used … In such a school, we have glimpses of the kind of order, organic unity, that could unite society again. Anyway, whatever the theories behind it (and many of us in schools must admit to success by the use of methods we don't wholly understand) the participation in art undoubtedly provides for the human needs of many kinds – the need to express oneself in music or movement or patter; the very basic need to create, to compose. (Aitkenhead, 1961)

The school ran an appeal for funding in 1959. This occurred as a result of the introduction of new legislation requiring all independent schools to be registered. Registration would be achieved following successful inspection of the education and premises by Her Majesty's Inspectors. The majority of independent schools at that time achieved registration within the first six months of the legislation being introduced. It is to be noted that Aitkenhead and Kilquhanity took fourteen years to finally be registered. It is a myth, however, that there was a constant battle between Aitkenhead and the inspectorate. Indeed, it is recorded in the Scottish Education Department papers that the education inspectors felt that Kilquhanity was an 'important experiment to be supported'. It was, in fact, officials who inspected the premises who disliked Kilquhanity and often sought closure through appeal to the minister or by the issuing of letters demanding upgrades to the buildings and health and safety measures, which Aitkenhead could ill-afford. The school was run on a financial 'shoestring' and was often in debt or seeking additional financial support from parents or others. Aitkenhead had, in the first instance, used his teacher's pension from only five years' service to provide the money to pay the first year's rent of Kilquhanity and start the school. It was only in the mid-1960s and early 1970s that the school was financially viable and then only just. By the mid-1990s some of the buildings were dilapidated and dangerous and pupil numbers were dwindling. At this time Aitkenhead's health was deteriorating and the school closed in 1997.

Aitkenhead would often quote 'education is the generation of happiness'. He attributed this statement to Herbert Read, when it was in fact originally part of an essay written by William Godwin, the 'father' of anarchism:

> The true object of education, like that of every other moral process, is the generation of happiness. But as in society the interests of individuals are intertwisted with each other and cannot be separated, it is also necessary to train him to be useful, that is, virtuous. To make a man virtuous we must make him wise. ... He who would be eminently useful, must be eminently instructed. But wisdom is not only directly a means of virtue; it is also directly a means to happiness. The man of enlightened understanding and persevering ardour has many sources of enjoyment which the ignorant man cannot teach. (Godwin, 1797)

Enjoyment in learning, learning real things, learning through practical creative activity, children and adults learning together – these tenets reflect the man whose childhood was spent in Ardrossan in the interwar years; the man whose political allegiance switched from the Scottish Liberal Party to the Scottish National Party (SNP) with its campaign for an independent Scotland; the man who made friends with the like of Christopher Grieve and Naomi Mitchison, and who became a poet in his own right.

Aitkenhead was a dominie whose view of education and of his school is encompassed in this quotation:

> The ancient popular cultures are more or less dead. The educated literary cultures have failed the masses. ... The commercial cultures are debasing, their chief aim the exploitation of the now wealthy young worker. Yet somewhere these are speaking to the condition of their customers in a way most schools are failing to find. For myself I have been trying to establish a school where at all school ages, the programme speaks to the condition of the pupil. Baden Powell put it nicely once: 'if you want to catch a fish you must put on the hook what the fish like.' Children like to feel as if they are in charge. Curiously enough, being in control of yourself is being free. Kilquhanity is not a school where you do what you like, or do as you please, regardless. If a child has a chance to do well the things he likes doing, he will gather the wherewithal to master the things he so far does not like doing, provided he sees them as worth his time and pains. (Aitkenhead, 1961)

## SCOTLAND'S HOME EDUCATORS

No school committed to Aitkenhead's philosophy of freedom is available to Scottish children today. For something similar in outlook, we have to turn to those individual parents who choose to withdraw their children from the state system and make educational provision for their children at home. Here immediate difficulties are encountered arising from the limited data available and the lack of independent research evidence. In 2009 the Scottish Government's published figures for all thirty-two local authorities showed a population of 755 children registered as home educated. This showed an approximate 10 per cent growth on the previous year; a trend which had continued for several years. A Freedom of Information (FOI) request by the present author to the Scottish Government for an update of data received a referral to: 'Analysis of Education (Schools) Statistics Survey September 2010'. This stated:

> Following consideration of the views expressed through the consultation the Scottish Government will carry out the proposal to discontinue the National Statistics collection of data on:
>
> • Children Educated Outwith School, Placing Requests, Teacher and Educational Psychologist Vacancies, Expenditure on Schools and the Independent School Census. (www.gov.scot/Topics/Statistics/Browse/School-Education/scotstat/NatStatsCollection/ StatsSuvrey2010)

Thus, there is no centralised data available from 2010 onwards. A FOI request in 2016 to all thirty-two individual local authorities revealed a further increase of approximately 16 per cent across the nation of children registered as home educated, but the overall numbers remain small in relation to the total school population. Reasons for withdrawing a child from school are varied. Parents may be committed to a philosophy of freedom in education and see formal schooling as too formal and restrictive; they may be concerned that their child is unhappy or that the school has not dealt adequately with allegations of bullying; they may feel that the child's particular learning needs are not being catered for; in a few cases, they may wish their child to be brought up in accordance with a particular faith tradition and consider that the school does not make provision for this. The authorities are no longer required to ask of parents/carers reasons for removing a child from state provision so information on this is sparse as some authorities do ask the question, but others do not. There is, of course, an unidentified number of children who are unknown to the authorities as their parents have never registered them for schooling.

Following on from further enquiries, a Scottish Government representative informed the present author: 'you may also be interested to know there are plans to take forward a refresh of the statutory home education guidance in due course. The guidance will be updated to reflect any changes to education policy relevant to home educators' (email communication, 30 August 2016). As the previous document was issued a decade ago (Scottish Government, 2007), there is certainly a need to take account of more recent developments. In that publication, home education is described as 'a key aspect of parental choice' and as 'an equally valid choice alongside the option to send a child to school'. However, it also states that 'Home education is a right conditional upon the parents providing an efficient education suitable to the age, ability and aptitude of the child.'

In Scotland today the relationship between the home educator 'families' and the local education authority is hard to describe. Individual local authorities take responsibility for interacting with families who have withdrawn their child from state education. However, within each authority different departments take responsibility for family liaison – an education officer, an educational psychologist, family support worker and so on. This may be influenced by the identified needs of the family or administrative convenience for the authority. The law states that a child who has never been registered with a school need not be registered with the authorities as being home educated. A child who is removed from the state sector in the transfer period between primary and secondary education also does not require to be registered with the authorities as being home educated. (See also Chapter 15 regarding the law pertaining to home education.)

This situation has both its supporters and critics. Some home educators maintain that it is their right, in law, and they are simply exercising their right. In a free society, state compulsion might be seen as anti-democratic and oppressive. But the situation could also be regarded as a source of concern: an unknown number of children may be spending their critical years without any systematic check on their progress and development. Some will certainly be receiving an education programme that could be considered to be ethically and morally appropriate. Others might be abused, indoctrinated, radicalised or allowed to run wild – who knows?

An Internet search on home education in Scotland provides references to a number of sites. The registered charity Schoolhouse, founded in 1996, is identified by the Scottish Government as an appropriate organisation from which to seek advice and support. Schoolhouse's home page states that it is 'Scotland's national home education support charity' and the website provides information on a wide range of questions that parents considering home education may have (www.schoolhouse.org.uk/). These cover legal and financial issues, curriculum resources, recommended reading and support groups in different parts of the country. The stated aims of the organisation are to:

- support and enable the education of children and young people outwith school
- support and enable parental involvement in their children's education
- encourage children to take responsibility for, and participate in decisions about, their education in accordance with their own wishes
- promote community interest in children's education
- provide independent information and support.

Other useful sites are Education Otherwise (https://www.educationotherwise.org/) and Home Education UK (www.home-education.org.uk/).

'Flexi-schooling' is a combination of home education with some days attending school (either state or private). One family interviewed for this chapter started home education on a full-time basis; then when their child reached age 7 they applied to local schools for a two-day per week placement. This has worked well for both the school and the family with the child benefiting from being with a small number (twelve) of other children in a class-based learning situation, whilst enjoying benefit from his home education for the other three days. For this family, education is the 'pursuit of pleasure' and is not time limited by 'bells' and their child is not taught against his will. The education provided at home is 'relevant in the moment' and is 'owned by the child'. This family does consider that basic numeracy is essential and that as their child has a hearing impairment, reading and literacy are of the utmost importance. Their mantra is the A. S. Neill (1968) statement: 'I would rather see a school produce a happy street cleaner than a neurotic scholar.' However, they do regard their situation as a luxury most people cannot afford.

Economically advanced countries have become obsessed with ideas about the school curriculum meeting the needs of a wealth producing, globally competitive market. If, as a nation, we are to satisfy the expectations of the population in terms of health care and support services we are obliged to find that finance from 'production'. But the nature of 'production' is changing rapidly and traditional forms of education may not produce the skills and attitudes that are required. Some commentators emphasise the importance of creative and social skills. Others stress that, in future, many routine tasks will be undertaken by computers but that analytical skills will be in high demand. Those who have been schooled in traditional subjects and styles of learning may be at a disadvantage. By contrast, those who have been encouraged to explore their interests in a free-ranging, interdisciplinary way, drawing on both the arts and sciences as appropriate and testing their ideas through experience, may have the edge.

The alternative educators at Kilquhanity and Kinokuni, alongside some of the home educators, are champions for freedom of mind and creativity. They represent a different set of values from the mainstream. Education Acts from 1944 until today by both UK and Scottish Governments have persistently taken childhood out of education to the detriment of individual development and the development of society. Education ministers obsessed by value for money, attainment and statistics continuously introduce change to state schools with no positive benefit to Scottish society. The term 'balance' in education is often touted as the way forward – a balance between the formal academic curriculum and development of the individual. Education is not about balance: it is about how society interacts with the individual child, what type of society people really aspire to develop in Scotland, and what we wish to give to our children to enable them to become contributing members of that society.

John Aitkenhead knew what childhood is about: some of the home educators know, too. For the state, childhood is integral to capitalism – developing units of production. Schools like Kilquhanity and some of the home educators are curators of childhood in the same way that a curator in a botanic garden saves and protects seeds and plants for the future benefit of humankind.

## REFERENCES

Aitkenhead, J. (1961) 'Kilquhanity House', *The New Era in Home and School*, 42 (7).

Aitkenhead, J. (1966) Talking of Kilquhanity. Transcribed text of video-tape interview by Shinichiro Hori at Kilquhanity House School, 20 September.

Croall, J. (1984) *Neill of Summerhill: The Permanent Rebel*. London: Ark Paperbacks.

Dewey, J. (1916) *Democracy and Education*. New York: The MacMillan Company. Reprinted by Dover Publications in 2004.

Godwin, W. (1797) The Inquirer: Reflections on Education, Manners and Literature. Part 1, Essay 1: Awakening of the Mind. London: G. G. and J. Robinson.

Humes, W. (2015) 'The educational achievements of a "Great Visionary": William Boyd (1874–1962)', *Scottish Educational Review*, 47 (2), 37–58.

Murphy, P. A. (1998) *The Life of R. F. Mackenzie: A Prophet Without Honour*. Edinburgh: John Donald.

Neill, A. S. (1968) *Summerhill*. Penguin: Harmondsworth, p. 22.

Scottish Government (2007) *Home Education Guidance*. Edinburgh: Scottish Government.

# III

# GOVERNANCE AND DIRECTION IN SCOTTISH EDUCATION

# 15

# Education and the Law

*Janys M. Scott*

Scotland has, and has always had, its own distinctive system of school education. The law provides the administrative framework for education. The basic structure is to be found in the Education (Scotland) Act 1980, although this Act has been much amended since 1980 and now has to be read in conjunction with several other measures. The Scottish Parliament has passed no less than thirteen statutes principally concerned with school education. Not all the legislation has been brought into force. There are also numerous regulations. The result is an unwieldy hotchpotch. The courts are occasionally called upon to interpret and apply the law. The following is a brief guide, rather than a comprehensive statement.

## THE SCOTTISH MINISTERS AND EDUCATION AUTHORITIES

Oversight of education was devolved to the Scottish ministers by the Scotland Act 1998. They have the responsibility of securing improvements in the quality of school education.[1] Since August 2016 they have been obliged to exercise their powers with due regard to reducing inequalities of outcome for pupils who experience those inequalities as a result of socio-economic disadvantage. They must also publish a 'National Improvement Framework' setting out strategic priorities and objectives in relation to school education.[2] They are advised by Her Majesty's Inspectors of Education,[3] now as a matter of practice part of the agency known as Education Scotland. The Scottish minsters issue guidance in a number of areas of education.[4] This differs from statute and regulations that must be obeyed. Guidance may be departed from if there is good reason not to follow it.

Public education in Scotland is managed by councils operating as education authorities. Scottish legislation refers to a school where education is provided by an education authority as a 'public school', as opposed to a private school under independent management. Every education authority has a duty to secure that there is made for its area adequate and efficient provision of school education.[5] 'School education' means progressive education

---

[1] Standards in Scotland's Schools etc. Act 2000 section 3.

[2] Education (Scotland) Act 2016, inserting sections 3A and 3C in the Standards in Scotland's Schools etc. Act 2000.

[3] Education (Scotland) Act 1980 section 66.

[4] For example in relation to school attendance, exclusion from school, home education, relationships education and religious education.

[5] 1980 Act section 1.

appropriate to the requirement of pupils, regard being had to the age, ability and aptitude of such pupils. It includes early learning and childcare for children who are under school age, and the teaching of Gaelic in Gaelic-speaking areas.[6] As part of their general duty an education authority should ensure the availability of adequate facilities for social, cultural and recreative activities and for physical education and training for pupils attending schools in their area. Psychological services should also be maintained to advise parents and teachers on appropriate methods of education for children with additional support needs.[7]

An education authority making decisions of a strategic nature or considering what steps to take to implement such a decision must also have due regard to reducing inequalities of outcome for pupils who experience those inequalities as a result of socio-economic disadvantage.[8] An education authority is generally expected to provide school education free of charge.[9] Pupils provided with free education must also receive free books, writing materials, stationery, mathematical instruments, practice material and any other article necessary to take full advantage of education.[10] The authority may provide clothing for activities such as physical exercise.[11] Where ordinary clothing is necessary to allow a pupil to take advantage of education this must be provided.[12] The authority should make such arrangements as it thinks necessary for pupils' transport to school.[13] Food and drink may be provided in school, in which case it must be provided free of charge to pupils whose parents are in receipt of certain benefits. The availability of school lunches should be promoted.[14] Education authorities are required by law to observe certain nutritional requirements.[15] A teacher has no right to inflict corporal punishment on a pupil, but physical restraint to avert danger of physical injury or danger to property will not be treated as corporal punishment.[16]

Although there is, in effect, a national curriculum, which schools are expected to follow, the curriculum is not prescribed by law. There are some rules on the content of education, but these appear to reflect preoccupations of legislators at various points of time. Schools are required to continue religious observance and instruction, unless a local referendum permits discontinuance.[17] All public schools must be open to pupils of all denominations and any parent may withdraw a child from religious instruction and observance.[18] In 2000 a ban on the intentional promotion of homosexuality in schools was repealed and a positive duty imposed on education authorities to have regard to the value of a stable family life in

---

[6] Part 2 of the Education (Scotland) Act 2016 promotes the availability of Gaelic medium education, allowing parents to request an assessment of the need for such education in a particular area.

[7] 1980 Act section 4.

[8] Education (Scotland) Act 2016, inserting section 3B in the Standards in Scotland's Schools etc. Act 2000.

[9] 1980 Act section 3.

[10] 1980 Act section 11(1).

[11] 1980 Act section 11(2).

[12] 1980 Act section 54. When in force section 23 of the Education (Scotland) Act 2016 will add a new section 54A to the 1980 Act under which the Scottish ministers may pass regulations requiring payment of clothing grants.

[13] 1980 Act section 51.

[14] 1980 Act section 53 to 53B; amended by Education (School Meals) (Scotland) Act 2003, and prospectively further amended by section 22 of the Education (Scotland) Act 2016.

[15] 1980 Act sections 56A to 56E; Nutritional Requirements for Food and Drink in Schools (Scotland) Regulations 2008, SSI 2008/265.

[16] 2000 Act section 16.

[17] 1980 Act section 8.

[18] 1980 Act section 9.

a child's development and the need to ensure that the content of instruction is appropriate, having regard to the age, understanding and stage of development of each child.[19] The Scottish ministers may issue guidance about sex education.[20] Somewhat archaically, education authorities are required to

> ensure that care is taken to develop in pupils … reasonable and responsible social attitudes and relationships, to cultivate … consideration for others, and to encourage … the practice of good manners, good attitudes to work, initiative and self-reliance and habits of personal hygiene and cleanliness.[21]

Education authorities should endeavour to secure that schools are 'health promoting' by providing activities and an environment and facilities which promote the physical, social, mental and emotional health and well-being of pupils.[22] Pupils should be encouraged and assisted to take advantage of facilities for medical and dental treatment in school.[23] They should have access to careers advice.[24]

## PUBLIC SCHOOLS[25]

Free early learning and childcare must be provided for certain two year olds and for children broadly between the ages of 3 and 5,[26] for 600 hours in each year, over at least thirty-eight weeks of the year in sessions of more than two-and-a-half hours, but less than eight hours in duration.[27] Early learning and childcare may be provided for other preschool age children and children of school age who have not commenced attendance at school.[28] Parents may purchase additional hours or early learning and childcare for children who are not eligible for free hours.[29] They do not have to take advantage of free early learning and childcare for their children.

Parents do, however, have to provide education for children once they are of school age. A child will be of school age on the commencement date (usually the first day of the new school year) immediately following his or her fifth birthday. A child may start primary school at the age of 4, provided he or she attains the age of 5 before a particular date, usually at about the end of February.[30] Younger children may be admitted to primary school at the discretion of the education authority if the education provided is suited to the age, ability and aptitude of the child.[31] Primary education is designed to meet the needs of pupils up to

---

[19] Ethical Standards in Public Life etc. (Scotland) Act 2000 sections 34 and 35.
[20] 2000 Act section 56. See *Conduct of Relationships, Sexual Health and Parenthood Education in Schools*, December 2014. Online at www.gov.scot/Publications/2014/12/8526
[21] Schools General (Scotland) Regulations 1975, SI 1975/1135 regulation 11.
[22] 2000 Act section 2A, inserted by Schools (Health Promotion and Nutrition) (Scotland) Act 2007.
[23] National Health Service (Scotland) Act 1978 section 39(3).
[24] Employment and Training Act 1973 section 8.
[25] That is schools managed by education authorities.
[26] Children and Young People (Scotland) Act 2014, section 47 and Provision of Early Learning and Childcare (Specified Children) (Scotland) Order 2014 (SSI 2014./196) as amended by SSI 2015/268.
[27] Children and Young People (Scotland) Act 2014, sections 48 and 51.
[28] 1980 Act section 1(1C).
[29] 2000 Act section 33.
[30] 1980 Act section 32.
[31] 2000 Act section 38.

the age of 12.[32] A primary one class taught by a single teacher is generally limited to twenty-five pupils. Primary two and three classes may contain thirty pupils.[33] There is no legislative restriction on the size of upper primary classes, but teachers' contracts do not require them to teach more than thirty-three in a single year group class and composite classes containing pupils from more than one year group are limited to twenty-five.[34] Numbers in a class may be further limited by the size of the room in which pupils are being taught.[35]

Secondary education caters for children who have attained the age of 12.[36] Subject to the size of the room, the number of pupils in a class is limited by teachers' contracts to thirty-three in the first two years, and after that to thirty, save for practical classes where the limit is twenty. A child ceases to be of school age at about the age of 16 and may leave school at the beginning of the Christmas holiday or at the end of May, depending when his or her birthday falls. A pupil who attains the school leaving age does not have to leave school. A pupil over the school leaving age who has not attained the age of 18[37] is treated as a 'young person' and as such generally exercises his or her own decisions in relation to education, rather than having decisions taken by parents.

Denominational schools are public schools which have a link with a church or religious body. The existence of such schools is deeply rooted in Scottish history, particularly in the case of the Roman Catholic community.[38] These schools transferred to the control of education authorities after 1918,[39] or were established later as religious foundations and transferred to the public system.[40] An education authority has the power itself to establish denominational schools.[41] The education authority controls the curriculum and appoints staff, but teachers must be approved as regards religious belief and character by representatives of the church or religious body in whose interests the school is conducted. The time set apart for religious instruction or observance should be maintained. There should be an unpaid supervisor of religious instruction.[42]

If an education authority proposes to close a public school, or to effect other material changes in the provision of education, it must follow a procedure prescribed by law.[43] It must prepare a statement indicating the educational benefits of the proposal and a paper setting out the details of what is proposed. It must then consult with persons including the parent council of the school, the parents, the pupils, the staff and any trade union representing staff, and the community council. Her Majesty's Inspectors of Education should be asked for a report on the proposal. A public meeting should be held. The education authority should then prepare a consultation report. Special considerations apply to the closure of rural schools, where there are detailed and demanding requirements directing consideration

[32] 1980 Act section 135(2)(a).
[33] Education (Lower Primary Class Sizes) (Scotland) Regulations 1999, SI 1999/1080, as amended by SSI 2010/326.
[34] Scottish Negotiating Committee for Teachers (SNCT) Conditions of Service.
[35] Schools General (Scotland) Regulations 1975, SI 1975/1135, regulation 8.
[36] 1980 Act section 135(2)(b).
[37] Education (Scotland) Act 2016, section 19 and schedule 1 paragraph 21 removes the upper age limit of 18 in respect of young people with additional support needs who have remained at school.
[38] See Chapter 13.
[39] Education (Scotland) Act 1918 section 18.
[40] 1980 Act section 16.
[41] 1980 Act section 17(2).
[42] 1980 Act section 21.
[43] Schools (Consultation) (Scotland) Act 2010.

to the effect on the local community.[44] The Scottish ministers may call in a closure proposal if it appears that the education authority may have failed to comply with the requirements of the Act or failed to take account of a material consideration relevant to the decision to implement the proposal. If a call-in notice is issued, then the closure proposal will be referred to a Schools Closure Review Panel which may grant or refuse consent or remit the proposal back to the education authority for a fresh decision.[45] Changes affecting the provision of education in denominational schools will generally require the consent of the Scottish ministers.[46]

## EDUCATION OTHER THAN IN PUBLIC SCHOOLS[47]

Parents may choose to send their children to a private independent school. These schools are required to register with the Registrar of Independent Schools in Scotland. An application for registration will only be granted if the Scottish ministers are satisfied that efficient and suitable education will be provided and that the welfare of pupils will be adequately safeguarded and promoted. The proprietor and teachers must be proper persons to act as such and the premises must be suitable.[48]

There is one mainstream school in Scotland that is neither managed by an education authority, nor an independent school. Jordanhill School in Glasgow receives direct grant-aid from the Scottish ministers[49] and the reasons for this are historical.

Children may be educated at home by their parents, in which event there is no requirement to follow any particular curriculum or undertake any form of assessment of progress. If a child has attended public school, the consent of the education authority is required before the child may be withdrawn from school.[50] No consent is required for home education of a child who has not attended public school, or who has finished primary education but not commenced secondary education. An education authority has no duty to monitor home education, but if it becomes aware that a child is not receiving education suitable to age, ability and aptitude then notice should be served on the parent requiring information about the education being provided. Continued failure could result in an attendance notice requiring the child to attend a particular school.[51]

## PARENTS

Parents have a statutory duty to provide efficient education suitable to the age, ability and aptitude of their children either by causing them to attend a public school regularly or by other means.[52] If a child who has attended a public school subsequently fails without

---

[44] Schools (Consultation) (Scotland) Act 2010, sections 12 and 13 as amended and sections 11A, 12A as inserted, by Children and Young People (Scotland) Act 2014, section 80.

[45] Schools (Consultation) (Scotland) Act 2010, sections 17A to 17D2 and 13 as inserted, by Children and Young People (Scotland) Act 2014, section 81.

[46] 1980 Act sections 22C and 22D.

[47] Public schools are schools managed by education authorities.

[48] 1980 Act sections 98 to 103B, as amended by School Education (Ministerial Powers and Independent Schools) (Scotland) Act 2004.

[49] 1980 Act section 73.

[50] 1980 Act section 35(1).

[51] 1980 Act sections 36 to 41.

[52] 1980 Act section 30.

reasonable excuse to attend, the parent may be committing an offence.[53] No offence is committed if a child would be required to walk an unreasonable distance to school. For children under the age of 8 the 'walking distance' is two miles and for children of 8 and over it is three miles. Beyond those distances education authorities should provide transport. If the child attends a particular school as a result of a placing request by the parent, then the parent is responsible for getting the child to school whatever the distance. Where a child is unwell the parent does not have to send the child to school, although the education authority may seek a medical examination. Other circumstances may also provide a reasonable excuse,[54] but unreported bullying has been held not to exonerate a parent from sending a child to school.[55] There is controversy about the criminal liability of a parent who is not aware that the child is not at school. On one view such a parent could not be prosecuted.[56] A child who fails to attend school regularly without reasonable excuse may be referred to the children's hearing which may impose a compulsory supervision order.[57]

The corollary is the general statutory principle that, so far as compatible with the provision of suitable instruction and training and the avoidance of unreasonable public expenditure, pupils are to be educated in accordance with the wishes of their parents.[58] This does not, however, mean that parental wishes must in all cases prevail, as there will generally be other factors to consider.[59]

When the Education (Scotland) Act 1980 refers to a 'parent' this includes a mother and a father, provided she or he has parental responsibilities and parental rights or the responsibility to maintain the child. In practice all parents are likely to fall within this definition (unless the child has, for example, been adopted). Both parents remain responsible for the child's education, even if separated and even if the child lives with one and not the other. A step–parent who has accepted the child as a member of his or her family will be liable to maintain the child and so is treated as a 'parent' for the purposes of the child's education. A person who is actually looking after the child, such as a foster parent, should also be treated as a 'parent'. Persons who have parental responsibilities, or share the care of a child, may be of the same gender. All such persons will be parents for the purposes of legislation relating to education. Parents have a right of access to the educational records of their children.[60] In practice schools are increasingly being required to deal separately with parents who do not reside together, but who both have responsibility for their child.

The Scottish Schools (Parental Involvement) Act 2006 establishes two bodies to encourage parental involvement in schools.[61] Each public school has a 'parent forum' which is simply a collective term for all the parents of pupils in attendance at the school (other than a nursery school or class). A parent forum may be represented by a parent council. There

[53] 1980 Act section 35.
[54] 1980 Act section 42.
[55] *Montgomery v Cumming* 1999 SCCR 178.
[56] *O'Hagan v Rea* 2001 SCCR 178 *cf Barnfather v Islington Education Authority* [2003] EWHC 418 (Admin), [2003] 1 WLR 2318.
[57] Children's Hearings (Scotland) Act 2011 section 67(2)(o).
[58] 1980 Act section 28.
[59] *Harvey v Strathclyde Regional Council* 1989 SLT 612, HL.
[60] Education (Disability Strategies and Pupils' Educational Records) (Scotland) Act 2002 section 5; Pupils' Educational Records (Scotland) Regulations 2003, SSI 2003/581.
[61] Scottish Schools (Parental Involvement) Act 2006 section 5.

is no statutory blueprint for a parent council, but membership is restricted to parents and persons co-opted by the parent council. In the case of a denominational school, the council must co-opt at least one member nominated by the church or body with which the school is associated. A parent council is required to support the endeavours of those managing the school in the exercise of their statutory functions.[62]

## PUPILS

Education authorities have a duty to provide schools. Parents have a duty to provide education. Until comparatively recently there was no express recognition of the right of the child to receive education. Section 1 of the Standards in Scotland's Schools etc. Act 2000 now states the right of every child of school age to be provided with school education, either directly by an education authority, or through arrangements made by such an authority. Article 2 of the First Protocol to the European Convention on Human Rights gives a child the right not to be denied education. The weak negative formulation in the Convention has been interpreted by the European Court of Human Rights as a positive right for persons to avail themselves of the existing means of instruction provided by the state[63] but does not confer the right to attend any particular school.[64] The domestic formulation of the child's right to education is positive, and reflects article 28 of the United Nations Convention on the Rights of the Child.

Section 2 of the Standards in Scotland's Schools etc. Act 2000 is also self-consciously modelled on the United Nations Convention on the Rights of the Child. An education authority is required to secure that education is directed to the development of the personality, talents and mental and physical abilities of the child or young person to their fullest potential,[65] reflecting the right of the child in terms of article 29 of the United Nations Convention. In carrying out this duty, an education authority is required to have due regard, so far as reasonably practicable, to the views of the child or young person in decisions that significantly affect him, taking account of the child or young person's age and maturity.[66] This is consistent with the right of the child capable of forming views to express those views freely found in article 12 of the United Nations Convention.

The Scottish ministers are obliged to keep under consideration whether there are any steps which would or might secure better or further effect of the requirements of the United Nations Convention on the Rights of the Child.[67] The statutory structure of education law is gradually being amended to give effect to children's rights. Education authorities should give pupils the opportunity to make their views known when preparing annual plans.[68] Pupils should be consulted in relation to school improvement plans.[69] There are provisions for consulting pupils of a suitable age and maturity in respect of

[62] 2006 Act section 8.
[63] *Belgium Linguistics Case (No 2)* (1979 – 80) 1 EHRR 252.
[64] *Ali v Head Teachers and Governors of Lord Grey School* [2006] UKHL 14; *R (on the application of SB) v Denbigh High School Governors* [2006] UKHL 15.
[65] 2000 Act section 2(1).
[66] 2000 Act section 2(2).
[67] Children and Young People (Scotland) Act 2014, section 1.
[68] Annual plans now replace annual statements of improvement objectives, as the Education (Scotland) Act 2016 replaces section 5 of the 2000 Act with a new section 3F.
[69] 2000 Act section 6, as amended by Education (Scotland) Act 2016, section 3(3) and (4).

school closures or other significant changes that may affect them in respect of the structure of educational provision.[70] If a medical examination is required in connection with the child's education then it is a precondition of the examination that consent is given by the child, if he or she has sufficient understanding to give consent.[71] Children may ask to see their own pupil records, provided they have a general understanding of what it means to exercise this right.[72] Children aged 12 and over who have additional support needs have the right to express views, provided they have capacity and this will not adversely affect their wellbeing.[73]

Children attain capacity to take decisions in relation to their own affairs at the age of 16.[74] This is broadly reflected in legislation relating to education. Young persons over the school leaving age exercise their own rights to make placing requests and appeal against exclusion from school, in place of their parents.[75]

## PLACING IN SCHOOLS

Pupils are deemed to belong to the area in which their parents are ordinarily resident.[76] Each education authority will have general arrangements for placing children in their area in public schools. These arrangements should be published or otherwise made available.[77] As a matter of practice, education authorities will delineate a particular 'catchment area' for each school so that pupils living in that area will generally attend that school. Education authorities in Scotland do not practice academic selection of pupils. There is a legal requirement to publish information about schools, including basic general information about schools in the area, information relating to a particular school and supplementary information about arrangements for placing children in schools.[78] Information about a particular school is usually presented in the form of a school handbook and updated annually.

Parents are entitled to make a placing request for their child to attend a school other than the one in which the child would be placed under the authority's general arrangements.[79] The authority must have guidelines that it undertakes to follow in the event that more placing requests are received than there are places in a particular school.[80] The authority is entitled to reserve places for children moving into the area. Subject to this, the authority is only entitled to refuse a placing request on one or more of a number of grounds. The grounds include having to employ an additional teacher or extend the school accommodation, or if the capacity of the school would be exceeded. A placing request may also be

---

[70] Schools (Consultation) (Scotland) Act 2010 section 2 and schedule 2.
[71] 1980 Act section 131A.
[72] Data Protection Act 1998 sections 7, 8, 9A and 66.
[73] Education (Additional Support for Learning) (Scotland) Act 2004, as amended by Education (Scotland) Act 2016, section 19 and schedule 1.
[74] Age of Legal Capacity (Scotland) Act 1991 section 1.
[75] 1980 Act section 28G.
[76] 1980 Act section 23(3).
[77] 1980 Act section 28B.
[78] Education (School and Placing Information) (Scotland) Regulations 2012, SSI 2012/130.
[79] 1980 Act section 28A, amended by School Education (Amendment) (Scotland) Act 2002 to ensure that a placing request may be made for a primary one place for a child under 5.
[80] 1980 Act section 28B.

refused if admitting the child would be seriously detrimental to order and discipline or to the educational wellbeing of pupils.[81]

If the authority refuses the request the parent may appeal to an appeal committee.[82] This is a committee set up and maintained by the education authority.[83] Appeals should be dealt with promptly, and in accordance with rules of procedure.[84] The committee may confirm the decision of the education authority if satisfied that one or more of the grounds for refusal exists or exist, and that it is in all the circumstances appropriate to do so.[85] If decisions by the education authority, or the appeal committee, are not taken within prescribed time limits they are deemed to have been refused,[86] so that parents may proceed to the next step in the appeal process.

A parent whose appeal is refused by the appeal committee may appeal to the sheriff by way of a summary application.[87] The sheriff will hear evidence in private and may confirm refusal of the placing request if, on the evidence at the time of the hearing, one or more of the grounds for refusal exists or exist and it is in all the circumstances appropriate to confirm the refusal. The sheriff's decision is final, which means there can be no further appeal. If, however, the sheriff has exceeded his powers by, for example, misconstruing the legislation or trespassing into matters of policy that are for the education authority, the Court of Session may intervene in a petition for judicial review.[88]

## EXCLUSION FROM SCHOOL

An education authority should not exclude a pupil from school unless the parent refuses or fails to comply, or allow the pupil to comply, with the rules, regulations or disciplinary requirements of the school. A pupil whose continued attendance would be likely to be seriously detrimental to order and discipline in the school or the educational wellbeing of pupils there may also be excluded.[89] There is a prescribed procedure for exclusion. On the day that a decision is taken to exclude the pupil the parent must be told, orally or in writing, of the decision and given a date within seven days of the date following the decision, where the headteacher, other teacher, or official of the education authority will be available to discuss the decision. If the pupil is not readmitted within seven days, or if the parent has not indicated that there will be no appeal, then there must be written notice to the parent of the reasons for the exclusion, any conditions for readmission and of the right to appeal.[90]

A parent may appeal against exclusion and a young person over the school leaving age may appeal in place of the parent. A child under the school leaving age may also appeal if he or she has legal capacity.[91] The test of legal capacity is whether a child has a general

---

[81]  1980 Act section 28A.
[82]  1980 Act section 28C.
[83]  1980 Act section 28D and schedule A1.
[84]  Education (Appeal Committee Procedures) (Scotland) Regulations 1982, SI 1982/1736.
[85]  1980 Act section 28E.
[86]  Education (Placing in Schools Etc – Deemed Decisions) (Scotland) Regulations 1982, SI 1982/1733.
[87]  1980 Act section 28F.
[88]  See for example *Dundee City Council, Petrs* 1999 Fam LR 13, *Aberdeen City Council v Wokoma* 2002 SC 352.
[89]  Schools General (Scotland) Regulations 1975, SI 1975/1135, regulation 4.
[90]  SI 1975/1135 regulation 4A.
[91]  2000 Act section 41.

understanding of what it means to instruct a solicitor, with a presumption that a child of 12 or more will have such an understanding.[92] The legislation makes no provision for a conflict between the actions of a child and those of a parent in relation to an appeal.

An appeal against exclusion should be made to the appeal committee.[93] The rules of procedure are the same as for placing requests.[94] If the appeal is not determined expeditiously it will be deemed to have been refused.[95] Further appeal lies to the sheriff. There have been a number of conflicting approaches to appeal but, since a decision on judicial review in the Court of Session in 2004, the law on how a sheriff should approach an exclusion appeal has become more settled. The sheriff requires to be satisfied that the decision to exclude the pupil was justified in all the circumstances of the case. This means the court should look at the factual basis for the exclusion.[96]

## ADDITIONAL SUPPORT FOR LEARNING

A pupil has additional support needs where, for whatever reason, he or she is, or is likely to be, unable without the provision of additional support to benefit from school education. The statutory provision for such children is found in the Education (Additional Support for Learning) (Scotland) Act 2004.[97] Additional support in relation to children at school is provision which is additional to, or otherwise different from, the educational provision made generally by the education authority for pupils of the same age.[98] Every education authority should make adequate and efficient provision for such additional support as is required by the individual child or young person, and should also make appropriate arrangements for keeping the needs and adequacy of the support under review.[99]

Special schools and special classes exist to provide education specially suited to the additional support needs of children or young persons selected for attendance there by reason of their needs.[100] Education for pupils with additional support needs should, however, where possible, be provided in mainstream schools.[101] Only where mainstream education would not be suited to the ability or aptitude of the child, or would be incompatible with the provision of efficient education for other children, or would result in incurring unreasonable public expenditure, should a child be educated in a special school.

Certain children qualify for a coordinated support plan. These are children whose support needs are likely to have a significant adverse effect on their school education or whose needs arise from multiple factors which, taken together, would have such an effect. No support plan is required unless the needs are likely to continue for over a year, the education authority is responsible for the pupil's education, and significant additional support will be

---

[92]  Age of Legal Capacity (Scotland) Act 1991 section 2(4A) and (4B).
[93]  1980 Act section 28H.
[94]  Education (Appeal Committee Procedures) (Scotland) Regulations 1982, SI 1982/1736.
[95]  Education (Placing in Schools Etc – Deemed Decisions) (Scotland) Regulations 1982, SI 1982/1733 regulation 5.
[96]  *Glasgow City Council, Petitioners* 2004 SLT 61, approving *Wallace v City of Dundee Council* 2000 SLT (Sh Ct) 60, followed in *F v City of Glasgow Council* 2004 SLT (Sh Ct) 123 and *S v City of Glasgow Council* 2004 SLT (Sh Ct) 128. For exclusion arising as a result of discrimination, see below.
[97]  As amended by the Education (Additional Support for Learning) (Scotland) Act 2009.
[98]  2004 Act section 1.
[99]  2004 Act section 4.
[100]  2004 Act section 29(1).
[101]  2000 Act section 15.

needed from more than one source, whether within the local authority or by another agency as well as the education authority.[102] A coordinated support plan will set out the factor or factors from which the pupil's additional support needs arise, the educational objectives to be achieved taking account of those factors, the additional support required and the persons by whom the support should be provided.[103] It will also nominate the school the pupil is to attend. The 2004 Act makes provision for assessment and examination of pupils with a view to identifying those who have additional support needs and those who require a coordinated support plan.

Disputes relating to coordinated support plans may be referred to the First-tier Tribunal for Scotland Heath and Education Chamber.[104] The First-tier Tribunal operates in accordance with rules of procedure,[105] the overriding objective of which is to enable the tribunal, with the assistance of parties, to deal with references fairly and justly. Proceedings should be informal and flexible and avoid delay, in so far as is compatible with proper consideration of the issues. The tribunal may confirm or overturn the decision of an education authority in respect of the need for a coordinated support plan or the contents of the plan, or require the education authority to prepare a plan or review a plan or to amend its contents. The tribunal may also require the authority to rectify a failure to provide, or make arrangements for provision of, additional support identified in the plan.[106] An appeal lies on a point of law to the Upper Tribunal, with the permission of the First-tier Tribunal or the Upper Tribunal and thereafter on limited grounds to the Court of Session.[107]

Where a child has additional support needs there are separate provisions for placing requests.[108] A placing request may be refused on the same general grounds as those which apply to children who do not have additional support needs, but in the case of children with such needs a placing request may be made specifying a special school. This may be a school under the management of the authority, or it may be an independent special school in Scotland, or elsewhere in the United Kingdom, provided the managers are prepared to admit the child. If the specified school is not a public school, the education authority may refuse the request if they are able to make provision for the additional support needs of the child in a school other than the specified school, they have offered the child a place at the other school, and if it is not reasonable, having regard to the respective suitability and cost of the two schools, to place the child in the special school. Appeals in respect of refusal of a place at a special school are referred to the Additional Support Needs Tribunal, as are refusals for children with a coordinated support plan.

## EQUAL OPPORTUNITIES

The Equality Act 2010 applies in certain respects to schools in Scotland. This Act protects particular characteristics, including disability, pregnancy and maternity, race, religion and

---

[102] 2004 Act section 2.
[103] 2004 Act section 9; see also Additional Support for Learning (Co-ordinated Support Plan) (Scotland) Amendment Regulations 2005, SSI 2005/518.
[104] 2004 Act section 18.
[105] The First-tier Tribunal for Scotland Health and Education Chamber (Procedure) Regulations 2017, SSI 2017/366.
[106] 2004 Act section 19.
[107] Tribunals (Scotland) Act 2014, sections 46 to 50.
[108] 2004 Act section 22 and schedule 2.

belief, sex and sexual orientation.[109] If a person treats another less favourably because of a protected characteristic, this constitutes discrimination.[110] It is also discrimination to apply a provision, criterion or practice which puts a person with a protected characteristic at a disadvantage when compared to someone who does not have that characteristic, if this is not a proportionate means of achieving a legitimate aim.[111]

This Act bears upon education authorities, independent schools and grant-aided schools. The body responsible for a school must not discriminate against a person in its admission arrangements, the way in which it provides education, or gives access to a benefit, facility or service, or by excluding a pupil or subjecting a pupil to any other detriment.[112] However, these measures do not apply to anything done in connection with the curriculum.[113] With regard to religion or belief, these provisions do not apply to denominational schools, nor to anything done in connection with acts of worship or other religious observance organised by or on behalf of a school (whether or not forming part of the curriculum).[114] A body responsible for a school must not harass a pupil. Harassment occurs when a pupil is subjected to unwanted conduct related to a protected characteristic that has the purpose or effect of violating the pupil's dignity or creating an intimidating, hostile, degrading, humiliating or offensive environment for him or her.[115] A responsible body will be held responsible for discrimination or harassment by its employees unless it has taken all reasonable steps to prevent such behaviour.[116] Claims relating to contravention of the Equality Act 2010 are generally heard in the sheriff court.[117]

The Equality Act 2010 is of particular importance to pupils with disabilities. If a disabled pupil behaves in a particular way in consequence of his or her disability and as a result is treated less favourably, that is discrimination, unless the person accused of the discrimination can justify what he or she has done by showing that it was a proportionate means of achieving a legitimate aim.[118] The Act also imposes a duty to make reasonable adjustments in certain respects to avoid disadvantage to persons who are disabled.[119] There is a duty to take such steps as are reasonable to provide auxiliary aids and services to pupils who would, but for such aids and services, be put at a substantial disadvantage in comparison to pupils who are not disabled.[120] For example, an education authority was found to have discriminated against a diabetic pupil who could not attend school for a period because there was no one to manage his insulin regime and the school had failed to recruit support staff to assist him.[121] Complaints about disability discrimination in schools should be made to the First-tier Tribunal for Scotland Health and Education Chamber.[122]

---

[109] Equality Act 2010 section 4.
[110] 2010 Act section 13.
[111] 2010 Act section 19.
[112] 2010 Act section 85.
[113] 2010 Act section 89(2).
[114] 2010 Act section 89(12) and schedule 11 paragraphs 5 and 6.
[115] 2010 Act section 26 and 85(3).
[116] 2010 Act section 109.
[117] 2010 Act section 114, save in relation to disability discrimination, where claims are to the Additional Support Needs Tribunal.
[118] 2010 Act section 15.
[119] 2010 Act section 20.
[120] 2010 Act sections 20, 98 and schedule 13 paragraph 2.
[121] See Kissock, S. (2013) *GLC Scottish Test Case Win for School Child With Diabetes*, 11 July. Online at http://govanlc.blogspot.co.uk/2013/07/glc-scottish-test-case-win-for-school.html
[122] 2010 Act section 116 and schedule 17 paragraphs 7 to 12.

In addition to duties under the Equality Act, bodies responsible for schools are required to prepare accessibility strategies designed to increase the extent to which disabled pupils can participate in the curriculum, and improve the physical environment of schools to assist pupils with disability to take advantage of education and associated services.[123]

## CLAIMS AGAINST TEACHERS AND EDUCATION AUTHORITIES

It is not generally possible to sue an education authority for failure to carry out a statutory duty.[124] If an authority does not comply with its statutory duties a complaint may be made to the Scottish ministers who may order the authority to discharge its duty.[125] Education authorities are also vulnerable to complaints to the Scottish Public Services Ombudsman, if injustice or hardship has been suffered in consequence of maladministration.[126] The Ombudsman cannot investigate the giving of instruction, whether secular or religious, the curriculum or discipline in an educational establishment under the management of an education authority. Where no other appeal or review is possible, decisions of education authorities may be subject to judicial review by the Court of Session.

Teachers are, however, vulnerable to actions for damages, and education authorities and managers of independent schools may be liable in respect of the actions of their employees.[127] Teachers owe a common law duty of care to pupils. The standard of such care is sometimes seen as equivalent to the care that would be afforded by a reasonable parent.[128] The role of a teacher is in most cases more complex than that of a parent and the more modern test rests on the standard of a professional person.[129] A professional person who fails to act as a member of that profession with ordinary skill would do if exercising ordinary care is open to an accusation of negligence.[130] Such allegations may arise if a pupil is injured at school. Pupils injured as a result of bullying at school have made claims, but nearly all such claims have failed, mostly because it is difficult to show that injury has been caused by failure on the part of teachers.[131] Negligent failure to address a pupil's educational needs may give rise to a claim in damages, as where an educational psychologist negligently failed to diagnose a pupil's dyslexia, resulting in a failure to address her problems,[132] but such claims are rare.

## FUTURE LEGISLATION

The volume of education law is growing, but it is being developed piecemeal. It is becoming harder to identify and to apply the law. A prime example was the attempt to institute a

---

[123] Education (Disability Strategies and Pupils' Educational Records) (Scotland) Act 2002 sections 1 to 3.
[124] *X (Minors) v Bedfordshire County Council* [1995] 2 AC 633, HL.
[125] 1980 Act section 70. The Education (Scotland) Act 2016, section 24, will remove the right to complain to ministers in cases where the complaint may be made to the Additional Support Needs Tribunal.
[126] Scottish Public Services Ombudsman Act 2002.
[127] *Phelps v Hillingdon London Borough Council* [2001] 2 AC 619, HL.
[128] For example *Gow v Glasgow Education Authority* 1922 SC 260.
[129] *Beaumont v Surrey County Council* (1968) 66 LGR 580; *McPherson v Perth and Kinross Council* Lord Eassie, 26 January 2001, unreported.
[130] *Hunter v Hanley* 1955 SC 200. In the case of teachers the professional standards required by the General Teaching Council for Scotland will be relevant to a decision on whether ordinary skill and ordinary care have been exercised.
[131] See *Bradford-Smart v West Sussex County Council* [2002] EWCA Civ 7, [2002] ELR 139.
[132] *Phelps v Hillingdon London Borough Council* [2001] 2 AC 619, HL.

'named person service', which for school-aged children would involve a member of school staff advising, informing and supporting children and young people and their parents.[133] A central feature of the service was the sharing of information between different agencies involved with the child and family. The Supreme Court held that this part of the legislation imposed an unrealistic task on information holders in trying to work out when information should be disclosed and when there was an overriding duty of confidentiality. As a result the provisions were not consistent with article 8 of the European Convention on Human Rights.[134] The Scottish Government remains determined to implement the named person service in a revised form. It is part of a programme of reform aimed at the 'wellbeing' of children, assessed by reference to the 'SHANARRI' factors.[135] In pursuit of this aim the traditional divisions between different functions of the local authority are being broken down, in favour of a more holistic service for children. Local authorities and other service providers for children are to be involved in preparing children's services plans.[136] They will have duties to prepare plans to meet the wellbeing needs of individual children.[137] Education remains a political priority, but the emphasis is now on social change.

---

[133] Children and Young People (Scotland) Act 2014, Part 4.
[134] *Christian Institute v Lord Advocate* [2016] UKSC 51.
[135] As defined in the Children and Young People (Scotland) Act 2014, section 96. The acronym stands for 'safe, healthy, achieving, nurtured, active, respected, responsible and included'.
[136] Children and Young People (Scotland) Act 2014, Part 3.
[137] Children and Young People (Scotland) Act 2014, Part 5.

# 16

# Central Government and the Administration of Scottish Education

*Morag Redford*

When the previous edition of this book was published, the Scottish Parliament was led by the Scottish National Party (SNP), through a majority administration. Following the election in May 2016, the same party formed a minority administration. This period saw a major change in SNP education strategy as the government began to take a more direct role in the implementation of policy and legislation. This chapter presents an analysis of the political administration of Scottish education in the fourth session of Parliament (2011–16) and provides an introduction to the work of the administration in the fifth session (2016–present). Much of the detailed work of the Scottish Parliament is done in committees. The committees comprise a small number of Members of the Scottish Parliament (MSPs) with membership reflecting the balance of political parties: they take evidence from witnesses, conduct enquiries and scrutinise legislation. The records of the Education and Culture Committee (E&CC) of the fourth session present a government focused on implementing change in the governance of further and higher education; and using legislation to require local authorities to implement specific policies for children and young people. The work of the Education and Skills Committee (ESC) at the start of the fifth session shows a committee determined to maintain an overview of the work of the administration while addressing wider issues in education.

In the Parliament all areas of education – further and higher education, lifelong learning, schools, preschool care and skills – fell within the remit of the E&CC until 2016 and within the remit of the ESC from 2016 onwards. For the period of the fourth Parliament (2011–16) Stewart Maxwell (SNP) was the Convener with a series of Deputy Conveners: Neil Findlay (Labour) to September 2013, Neil Bibby (Labour) to December 2014, Siobhan MacMahon (Labour) to September 2015 and Mark Griffin (Labour) to the end of the fourth Parliament. At the start of the fifth Parliament in June 2016 James Dornan (SNP) was Convener and Johann Lamont (Labour) Deputy Convener.

The legislation introduced during the period under review was:

1. the Post-16 Education (Scotland) Bill, which received Royal Assent on 7 August 2013;
2. the Children and Young People (Scotland) Bill which received Royal Assent on 27 March 2014;
3. the British Sign Language (Scotland) Bill, which received Royal Assent on 22 October 2015;

4. the Higher Education Governance (Scotland) Bill, which received Royal Assent on 13 April 2016;

5. the Education (Scotland) Bill, passed by Parliament which received Royal Assent on 8 March 2016.

Scottish education was led politically by government policies, administered through Parliament and the civil service during the fourth session of Parliament. In 2013, Michael Russell MSP held the post of Cabinet Secretary for Education and Lifelong Learning, with Aileen Campbell MSP as the Minister for Children and Young People and Alasdair Allan MSP as Minister for Learning, Science and Scotland's Languages. Angela Constance MSP was appointed Cabinet Secretary in November 2014, when Nicola Sturgeon MSP became First Minister, with Aileen Campbell MSP and Alasdair Allan MSP retaining their roles. The appointment of John Swinney MSP as both Deputy First Minister and Cabinet Secretary for Education and Skills in June 2016 signalled an increased focus on school-based education by the government. The ministerial responsibilities also changed, with Mark McDonald MSP appointed as Minister for Childcare and Early Years and Shirley-Anne Somerville MSP as Minister for Further Education, Higher Education and Science.

The implementation of policy and legislation throughout this period was the responsibility of the local authorities and three non-departmental public bodies funded directly by the government: Education Scotland, the Scottish Qualifications Authority (SQA) and Skills Development Scotland (SDS). The role of Education Scotland at this time was to support quality and improvement in learning and teaching: this included the responsibility for school inspections and curricular development. Education Scotland was led, since it was established in 2011, by Bill Maxwell, due to retire from the post in June 2017. The SQA is the national body responsible for the development, accreditation, assessment and certification of qualifications other than degrees, and was led throughout this period by Janet Brown. SDS provided career guidance in schools and colleges and had a key role in supporting the implementation of government policies on education and training for young people aged 16 to 19. Damien Yates was chief executive from 2008. The Scottish Funding Council (SFC) is also a non-government public body, which contributes to the funding of teaching and research in Scotland's twenty-seven colleges and nineteen universities. Mark Batho was chief executive of the SFC to 2013, Laurence Howells to 2016, and John Kemp appointed as interim chief executive in early 2017. The nineteen universities are supported by Universities Scotland, which is the collective voice of the university principals.

In this administrative structure, each of the thirty-two local authorities reported directly to the government on their activities but the negotiations in relation to annual budgets, new legislation and government initiatives were led by the Convention of Scottish Local Authorities (COSLA), as the national voice for local government. COSLA and the government, along with representatives of the teaching unions, formed the Scottish Negotiating Committee for Teachers (SNCT) which negotiated the pay and conditions of service for teachers. The majority of teachers were represented by either the Educational Institute of Scotland (EIS) or the Scottish Secondary Teachers' Association (SSTA) both of whom took an active role in all aspects of education. The Association of Heads and Deputes Scotland (AHDS) represented primary school leaders, with School Leaders Scotland (SLS) representing the majority of secondary headteachers. Local authority education managers were represented by the Association of Directors of Education in Scotland (ADES). The General

Teaching Council for Scotland (GTCS) is the independent, professional regulatory body which maintains and enhances teaching standards in Scotland. Ken Muir has held the post of chief executive of the GTCS since 2013. All of these organisations took an active role in the discussion and development of education policy in Parliament, contributing papers and evidence to the E&CC and ESC. The education agenda from 2013 to 2016 focused on the governance of further and higher education; legislation to take forward the government policy on *Getting it Right for Every Child* (GIRFEC) and early years provision; and the national examination structure for Curriculum for Excellence. The period at the end of the fourth session and the start of the fifth session of Parliament focused on closing the attainment gap in schools.

## THE GOVERNANCE OF FURTHER AND HIGHER EDUCATION

The legislative focus of the Scottish Government between 2013 and 2016 was on two bills which changed the structure of further education (FE) provision in Scotland through the closure and amalgamation of colleges and attempted to introduce changes to the governance of higher education institutions to make them more inclusive and accountable to students and staff. The Post-16 Education (Scotland) Bill sat with the administration's reform agenda to promote economic growth through the provision of education and skills to support the workforce. Most significantly (and controversially), it imposed college regionalisation through legislation. It introduced new provisions in the way the government funded higher education through the SFC and caused considerable debate around a proposed code of governance for higher education. Each stage of the bill brought a large number of amendments and the government was pushed by the E&CC to respond directly to issues identified in their evidence sessions. The political strength and determination of Michael Russell forced the core content of this bill through committee as the government struggled to justify the regionalisation agenda for colleges. The depth of the Cabinet Secretary's commitment to making the changes can be seen his promise to the committee: 'I put on record my commitment to work with partners, including the Committee, on any differences and suggestions for improvement to produce the best possible piece of legislation that will deliver real benefits for learners' (Redford, 2013, p. 80).

It was Michael Russell's successor, Angela Constance, who oversaw the Higher Education Governance (Scotland) Bill which proposed legislation in place of the Scottish Code of Higher Education Governance, a voluntary agreement reached between the universities in 2013. As a newcomer to the education brief in Parliament, the Cabinet Secretary lacked the political strength of Michael Russell and struggled to lead the bill through the committee stages. The E&CC received 300 separate submissions in relation to the proposed bill and the Cabinet Secretary faced specific criticism in relation to the proposal to define academic freedom and abolish the role of rector in the ancient universities. The debate continued through the three stages of the bill with amendments proposed to ensure that the role of rector was unchanged. There was further opposition to the government proposal to redefine academic freedom from that in the 2005 Further and Higher Education (Scotland) Act. Liz Smith MSP (Conservative) argued that the amendment was not necessary and that the government should not be 'trying to legislate on academic freedom in relation to academic issues in institutions' (Redford, 2016). The SNP majority in the committee meant that a revised definition of academic freedom for research-active staff in Scottish universities was included in the Act.

## CURRICULUM FOR EXCELLENCE

The children and young people who began their schooling with the introduction of Curriculum for Excellence moved into the senior phase of the curriculum in 2014 and were the first to experience new national qualifications. The E&CC took a close interest in the introduction of these qualifications and held a series of evidence sessions in February and March of 2014 just before the first group of young people sat the new Higher examinations. Evidence sessions were a structure used by the committee to bring individuals and organisations into the Parliament to answer questions about an area they were leading or supporting. In holding evidence sessions on the curriculum, the committee was responding directly to issues raised in the press by parents and professional associations about the new examinations. There were specific issues about the timescale of the introduction and an increased workload for teachers as they worked with the SQA to prepare examinations. One local authority, East Renfrewshire, refused to implement the new examinations in 2014. The evidence sessions gave the professional associations the opportunity to raise queries from their members about the lack of curriculum notes, sample papers and national assessment bank materials. The evidence given to the committee demonstrated a gap between the website-based support offered by the SQA and limited school-based support work given by Education Scotland who had worked with ninety-two of the 367 secondary schools in Scotland. These discussions at committee raised the question of a delay in the introduction of the examinations. The government, through the Curriculum for Excellence management group, refused to delay the introduction. In response to the evidence sessions held by the E&CC, they introduced a new package of support measures through Education Scotland. The most the committee convener could do was to extract a promise from Alasdair Allan, the minister responsible, that the new examinations would be, 'implemented smoothly and successfully' (Redford, 2014, p. 93). There were problems with the implementation in May 2014 and it was Michael Russell who faced the committee that October to answer for the government. The work of the committee in October 2014 gave parents, teachers and local authorities a forum in which to describe the challenges of the new examination system and the committee called Education Scotland, the SQA and the government to answer questions about the evidence they had heard. The administration stood back from the questions at this point and announced a review of Curriculum for Excellence by the Organisation for Economic Co-operation and Development in 2015. It also asked Education Scotland to provide additional support for schools in the 2014–15 school year. The additional support was discussed by the E&CC in February 2015 when the professional associations challenged the success of the new support, but committee interest had moved on to the new Advanced Highers and the wider debate around the national examinations was closed.

## THE USE OF INQUIRY STRUCTURES

The E&CC made considerable use of parliamentary inquiries to explore topics of interest to committee members and to gather evidence relating to issues on which they wanted to challenge the government. Committee members usually made a series of fact-finding visits to directly inform the inquiry. The Scottish Parliament Information Centre (SPICe) summarised the information for the committee and presented it as a report that was then used to establish which organisations and individuals they wanted to invite to give evidence. The committee undertook a lengthy inquiry into the decision-making process for taking children into care in 2013. In this inquiry, the committee heard evidence from eight panels of witnesses including young people who had been in care, professionals and organisations working in the care system, and academic experts. The committee approach to this inquiry was praised by the Centre for Excellence for Looked after Children in Scotland (CELCIS) which said that bringing together all the organisations who worked in the sector 'was a unique and forward–thinking way to help us own the issues' (Redford, 2013, p. 85). The committee used the evidence from witnesses in this inquiry to question Aileen Campbell, Minister for Children and Young People, about the proposed content of the Children and Young People (Scotland) Bill 2014 and the enactment of the GIRFEC policy as legislation. The report published by the committee at the end of this inquiry directly informed the content of the 2014 bill. Other inquiries held by the committee during this period included a single evidence session on outdoor learning in December 2013 where they explored the difference between outdoor education and outdoor learning with the head-teacher of Beeslack Community High School and representatives of the Scottish Advisory Panel for Outdoor Education, the Scottish Outdoor Education Centres and Professor Peter Higgins from the University of Edinburgh. The range of knowledge and experience included in that panel illustrates the reach of the committee and one of the routes they used to explore topics of interest. This evidence session did not lead to a report beyond the record of the evidence session and no decision was made to take action or question ministers, but it did raise the profile of outdoor learning within the school curriculum.

The inquiry on the attainment of pupils with sensory impairment, held by the committee in May 2015, followed directly from their work on the British Sign Language (Scotland) Bill between February and April 2015. The content of the bill included a national plan for the language, with education as one of the key areas. The evidence collected by the committee as they worked on the bill raised questions about educational provision for pupils with sensory impairment: they began the inquiry with two evidence sessions from expert witnesses on visual and auditory impairments. The committee then visited the Dundee multi-sensory service at Craigie High School before taking further evidence from local authorities and schools for children and young people with sensory impairments. The evidence sessions and visits identified the following issues for the committee: lack of trained education staff; the level of qualifications needed as a teacher of visual or auditory impaired children and young people; limited college and employment opportunities; and the sharing of resources between local authorities. The committee took these issues to their final evidence session with Alasdair Allan, the minister responsible, supporting civil servants and a director of Education Scotland. In his opening statement to the committee Alasdair Allan acknowledged 'that there is still significant room for improvement' and commented on the different issues identified in the evidence sessions and recognised that 'there was work to do on the training of staff, inclusive education and transitions' (Redford, 2015, p. 118). The content of the opening statement to the committee demonstrated to the committee that the government had acknowledged the issues that required to be addressed in order to improve the services offered to children and young people with sensory impairments. Members of the committee then used the remaining time to ask the minister about the areas that were not acknowledged in his statement: the variation of support between local authorities; workforce planning in relation to specialist teachers; and employment destinations following college. Alasdair Allan acknowledged the issues but said in reply to questions that those areas were the responsibility of local authorities and colleges. The evidence session gave committee members the opportunity to ask the lead civil servant for inclusion about the numbers of specialist teachers employed. The reply that there were about fifty-eight specialist teachers of visual impairment and eighty teachers of hearing impairment in May 2015 enabled those figures to be put into the record of the session and the public domain. The committee had further questions about the lack of specialist staff and the level of British Sign Language (BSL) required to support children and young people with auditory impairments. The minister and supporting civil servants did not answer those questions directly and referred back to local authority responsibilities. The committee questions were designed to highlight the gap between government responsibility for workforce planning for education and local authority responsibility to employ teachers. This gap can be seen in Alasdair Allan's statement about specialist staff:

> There is no indication that local authorities feel that they cannot find teachers. There is a debate to be had about whether the right number of teachers is in the system, but there is no evidence that local authorities cannot find qualified teachers. (Redford, 2015, p. 119)

The committee also asked the minister about the level of BSL knowledge required by teachers of the deaf. At the end of this discussion the convener asked the minister to undertake to collect information about the number of teachers of the deaf who held BSL level 1 and the number who worked at a higher level. This is another tool that the committee used to require the government to collect and share information to support the work of the committee. The minister agreed to the request and that information was published in later committee records.

The E&CC also used the inquiry structure between March and June 2014 when they held an inquiry on Scotland's educational and cultural future prior to the independence referendum in September 2014. The education sessions in this inquiry addressed university issues, particularly possible changes to research funding, student fees and visas for international students.

The ESC committee used aspects of the inquiry structure at the start of the fifth session of Parliament in June 2016 and held a series of overview panels to collect evidence on: further and higher education; attainment; children's services; Curriculum for Excellence; and early years. They held only one panel for each area and included representatives of those responsible for or working in each area. As the previous committee had done, they met with the Cabinet Secretary to debate the issues raised in the panels. The ESC then used the evidence collected in the overview panels to establish their work plan for the parliamentary year. This innovative approach to establishing the work the committee wanted to focus on in their first year, linked their programme directly to the work carried out by the E&CC in the previous Parliament. This included a decision to maintain an overview of college mergers, to write to the Cabinet Secretary in relation to his commitment to undertake further scrutiny on additional support needs, and to undertake further work on the senior phase of Curriculum for Excellence and on children's hearings.

## CHILDREN, YOUNG PEOPLE AND EDUCATION

The policy focus of the SNP administration in the second half of the fourth session of Parliament was on raising attainment for all children. They led into this policy focus indirectly from 2014, through the Children and Young People (Scotland) Bill, and then more directly with the Education (Scotland) Bill in 2016. The first of those bills proposed legislation for the joint delivery of children's education and services through a focus on children's rights. This included changes to early years provision, permanence planning for looked-after children, regulations about the national adoption register and increased powers for Scotland's Commissioner for Children and Young People. This bill was led through Parliament by Angela Constance who again struggled to support the content through the committee stages, and aspects of the bill were dropped to ensure that Parliament passed key areas of the bill into legislation. The most controversial element was the proposal to introduce a 'named person' for each child from birth to 18 years old. Government faced considerable challenges from parents, health visitors, teachers and children's services staff about the role, the sharing of confidential information and the costs of introducing the policy. The government was forced to modify the proposal in the bill but still faced a legal challenge from a parental pressure group who felt that it impinged on parental rights. Angela Constance remained Cabinet Secretary for Education when the Education (Scotland) Bill introduced the 'requirement for education authorities and the Scottish ministers to attach greater significance to narrowing the attainment gap, making it a priority for all' (Redford, 2015, p. 114). This bill was the starting point for the work the administration was to develop throughout 2014–15 and introduce as their key education policy in August 2015. This was led by the First Minister, Nicola Sturgeon, who set two priorities for her administration: to raise standards for every pupil in the country and to 'close the gap in educational outcomes between pupils from the most and least deprived parts of Scotland' (Scottish Government, 2015). The priorities were actioned immediately through consultation on a policy document called the National Improvement Framework (NIF) while the E&CC was working separately with Angela Constance on the Education (Scotland) Bill. Although the Convener of the E&CC, Stewart Maxwell, was an SNP MSP, the committee was sidelined as the First Minister pushed closing the gap into a published policy in December 2015. Stewart Maxwell complained to the Cabinet Secretary, who apologised to the committee, but reminded them that content of the bill was about creating the reporting structure that would support the NIF. The remaining content of this bill introduced pieces of legislation that were needed to support the overall focus on raising attainment, such as the requirement for each local authority to appoint a chief education officer, who would be held responsible for implementing government policy. Parliament and the E&CC were held at a distance from the development of the policy, although the committee did ask the Cabinet Secretary about the use of existing data in local authorities and discussed the proposed development of national standardised assessments for pupils. This gap between the E&CC and government ministers widened at the start of the fifth session of Parliament when John Swinney was appointed Deputy First Minister and Cabinet Secretary for Education. John Swinney brought a new style of leadership to the post of Cabinet Secretary and an increased focus on educational improvement. The change in the name of the committee, dropping the word 'culture' and replacing it with 'skills' reinforced the point that a new managerial approach to policy development had arrived.

## EDUCATION AND SKILLS

The programme of the new SNP administration in June 2016 focused on equality in the education system and opportunities for all, supported by an economy with more jobs and what they termed 'fair' work. The priority of closing the attainment gap set by Nicola Sturgeon when she became First Minister in the previous Parliament now became the focus for her new administration: 'Our top priority is to raise standards in schools and close the attainment gap, delivering opportunities to our young people no matter their family background' (Scottish Government, 2016).

John Swinney began his tenure as Cabinet Secretary for Education and Skills by holding a round table discussion with all the organisations involved in school-based education in June 2016. He undertook an extensive range of school visits in his first few weeks in office and established an international advisory group for education. At the end of June 2016 he published: *Delivering Excellence and Equity in Scottish Education: A Delivery Plan for Scotland* (www.gov.scot/Publications/2016/06/3853). The plan had three key priorities: closing the attainment gap, ensuring the curriculum 'delivered for' children and teachers, and empowering teachers, schools and communities. This plan linked directly to the NIF published the previous year and connected to ongoing work on decluttering the curriculum and ensuring that teachers were free to teach. He followed this with a review of the governance of education in the autumn of 2016 through an online survey. The consultation process unsettled various layers of the school-based education structure in Scotland as government statements increasingly indicated that headteachers should have more ability to plan staffing and curriculum to suit their school community. Key pillars of Scottish education, the General Teaching Council, Education Scotland and the newer Scottish College for Educational Leadership were concerned about proposed changes to their roles, as was COSLA, the umbrella body for local authorities. The school year 2016–17 brought a closer focus on the challenge of recruiting teachers for rural schools and a direct challenge to the national workforce planning system for teacher education. The government worked directly with the Council of Deans of Education, the group that represented all of the Scottish institutions providing initial teacher education, to introduce new routes into teaching. This series of programmes were particularly focused on recruitment to mathematics and sciences, bringing career-changers into schools. The Cabinet Secretary announced changes to assessment in September 2016, with school-based unit assessments in National 5 and Higher programmes replaced by a stronger final exam and externally assessed coursework. The publication of the results of the Programme for International Student Assessment (PISA) in December 2016 brought the focus back onto attainment. Scotland's overall performance in PISA 2016 was lower than the results in 2012 for science and reading, but similar to the 2012 results for maths. Importantly Scotland's overall performance declined in comparison with similar countries and both Parliament and the press questioned the government on the gap in attainment. In his statement to Parliament about the PISA results, John Swinney acknowledged the poorer outcomes and used the opportunity to confirm his intention to introduce a national improvement plan for education with a continued focus on closing the gap and raising attainment for all.

In January 2017 the ESC announced an inquiry into teacher workforce planning. This inquiry followed concerns raised with MSPs about the challenge of recruiting teachers in rural areas, which was unexpected by the administration and interrupted their planned sequence of work. The ESC used the inquiry to engage directly with the Cabinet Secretary about the work the administration was doing to address teacher shortages and to explore initial teaching qualifications. The issues raised in committee were followed up in the debating chamber and the Cabinet Secretary responded by announcing a new structure for the teacher workforce planning committee and a tender for a new initial teaching qualification focused on recruiting the brightest and the best students. The work of the committee demonstrated their ability to follow their own agenda and require direct responses from the government and any organisations providing evidence. The ability of the administration to close the gap and raise attainment for all is likely to be held to account by the parliamentary committee for Education and Skills throughout the fifth session of Parliament.

By far the most contentious set of policy proposals introduced by John Swinney have been those relating to school governance. Following the consultation exercise in 2016, a document entitled *Education Governance: Next Steps* was published in June 2017 (Scottish Government, 2017). It proposed the setting up of regional improvement collaboratives which would reduce the role of local government in the provision of educational services. The precise function of these collaboratives, and how they would relate to other bodies, was not entirely clear, despite references to the importance of 'partnership'. Headteachers would have more freedom to make decisions based on the particular needs of their school community, but they would be held directly accountable for reducing the attainment gap. Education Scotland would be 'renewed and revitalized', a decision that surprised many as that organisation had been held partly responsible for the limited success of Curriculum for Excellence. Two new bodies were to be set up, a Scottish Education Council and an Education Workforce Council, leading some observers to suggest that the system would remain heavily bureaucratic, with schools being given greater responsibility but subject to centralised control.

The proposals were strongly attacked at the Scotland Policy Conference held in June 2017. Keir Bloomer, an independent education consultant (and former chief executive of a local authority), described the regional improvement collaboratives as 'top-down, authoritarian, unwanted and hierarchical'. Others suggested that structural reform would not necessarily address the challenges facing Scottish education, which were rooted in a compliant and conformist culture. John Swinney responded robustly to the critics. He described his proposals as serious and wide-ranging reforms designed to improve Scottish education, and accused opponents of indulging in invective and hyperbole. The scene is set for education to remain high on the political agenda for some time to come.

## REFERENCES

Redford, M. (2013) 'Education in the Scottish Parliament', *Scottish Educational Review*, 45 (2), 78–90.

Redford, M. (2014) 'Education in the Scottish Parliament', *Scottish Educational Review*, 46 (2), 90–104.

Redford, M. (2015) 'Education in the Scottish Parliament', *Scottish Educational Review*, 47 (2), 105–22.

Redford, M. (2016) 'Education in the Scottish Parliament', *Scottish Educational Review*, 48 (2), 108–21.

Scottish Government (2015) *A World Leader in Education*. Online at https://news.gov.scot/speeches-and-briefings/a-world-leader-in-education

Scottish Government (2016) *A Plan for Scotland: The Scottish Government's Programme for Scotland 2016–17*. Online at www.gov.scot/Publications/2016/09/2860

Scottish Government (2017) *Education Governance: Next Steps – Empowering Our Teachers, Parents and Communities to Deliver Excellence and Equity for Our Children*. Online at www.gov.scot/Publications/2017/06/2941

# 17

# Local Governance in Scottish Education

*Brian McGinley*

## POLITICAL TENSIONS AND THE CONTESTED EDUCATIONAL NARRATIVE

This chapter will explain the nature of governance and outline the current arrangements for local governance in Scottish education. It will then contrast Scottish educational developments with international trends and consider some implications of the politicisation of education. One of the biggest issues currently facing education today is finding the best way to govern the service to drive up standards and reduce the attainment gap. The chapter will therefore provide a critical assessment of the motivation for and potential impact of the Scottish Government's policy initiatives during 2016/17 and comment on the proposals finally outlined in *Education Governance: Next Steps* (Scottish Government, 2017).

One of the primary questions that may be usefully posited in exploring debate around local governance in education is: What is the nature and purpose of governance? Traditionally, the concept has been associated with the process of directing the implementation of government decisions through national and local planning and development processes. It gives impetus to the attempt by central government to steer social and economic development throughout the country. However, in more recent times, it has also been used to denote a mode of control different from a direct hierarchical model, through the involvement of stakeholders and stewards (Mason et al., 2007), especially in the international arena. A more egalitarian approach in the UK has been mainly associated with the influence of European Union policy on member states. In addition, outwith the governmental arena, the term is now used in the corporate world to describe institutional practices involving market principles and self-regulation (Mayntz, 2003).

The broader understanding of the role and importance of governance has come about due to significant and continuous policy failures of traditionally dominant autocratic and centralist approaches. Consequently, policy developers began to realise that policies would only be successfully implemented if they had the agreement of target groups at grassroots level: successful policy is not just about political will but also needs to consider citizens' understanding and reaction. Also, the conditions for good governance are predicated on a capable state that is accountable to its citizens, subject to the rule of law and conscious of the potential for unintended consequences of its decisions.

Education is a fundamental feature of Scottish life and identity, which may in part be due to the traditional myth that education in Scotland is more democratic than in other parts of the UK, given its history, roots and traditions. Also, its social function has tended to be uncritically accepted as a support for the importance of the democratic features in Scottish society. This historical and long-lasting belief was reinforced by situations where, for example, prior to devolution, education was used to resist right-wing Thatcherism ideology that heralded school opt-outs of local authority control and increased selectivity in England. Scotland seemed to accept comprehensive education with ease by having a greater concern for equity and social justice rather than promoting elitism and maintaining social advantage. Post-devolution, there was initially broad agreement among the main parties about the direction of Scottish educational policy, but over time disputes have arisen over the management and implementation of the major reform programme, Curriculum for Excellence (CfE). However, as a key devolved matter, education has been caught up in the broader New Public Management agenda of public sector reform while attempting to function successfully within an increasingly complex political relationship of local autonomy versus central control.

## LOCAL GOVERNANCE ARRANGEMENTS IN SCOTTISH EDUCATION

It would probably be fair to state that Scotland has historically promoted its education system as being distinct from other parts of the UK with its emphasis on breadth of learning. The teaching profession is governed by the General Teaching Council for Scotland and pupils' academic certification is awarded through the Scottish Qualifications Authority, which has suffered from increasing public criticism in recent years. The Scottish Parliament, since devolution, has overall political responsibility for national education policy, but each of the thirty-two local authorities, made up of elected councillors and other stakeholders, is the accountable body which runs schools under the watchful eye of the Care Inspectorate and Education Scotland. Further legislation is planned as part of the *Education Governance: Next Steps* document (Scottish Government, 2017).

However, currently the education function is discharged through councils as education authorities. Made up of councillors and religious representatives, these oversee the delivery of education to pre-5s and school age children. The legislative responsibility for this arrangement is contained in a broad range of Acts including the Education Scotland Act (1980) as amended; the Self-Governing Schools (Scotland) Act 1989; the Standards in Scotland's Schools, etc. Act 2000; the Education (Disability Strategies and Pupils' Educational Records) (Scotland) Act 2002; the Education (Additional Support for Learning) (Scotland) Act 2004; the Scottish Schools Parental Involvement Act 2006; and the Schools (Consultation) (Scotland) Act 2010. (See Chapter 15 for the law pertaining to education in Scotland.) From this legislative context, we can assert that local governance is directed from the centre in the standards that it sets, the consultations it conducts, the additional support that it provides where required and the ways in which it engages with parents. More specifically, the education authorities are charged with ensuring that educational provision is integrated and designed to meet the needs of children, young people and families and to enable investment in education, skills and training to enhance opportunities for self-development, social mobility and employment. The range and type of topics that local education authorities decide upon include: standards and quality, attainment, improvement planning, inspection reports, consultation outcomes, service evaluations and reviews, devolved school management policy and school catchment areas, pupil attendance and exclusion rates, as well as holiday arrangements. These functions currently benefit from local flexibility and accountability as decisions are tailored to meet community needs with local politicians being directly answerable for the decisions that they take.

## THE POLITICAL CONTEXT OF SCOTTISH EDUCATION GOVERNANCE

The actual extent to which Scottish education is distinctly different is open to question. Ozga (2005) argues that any difference is far from being an ideologically based stance or a cogently developed response to Scottish circumstances. Scottish education policies are susceptible to global and UK modernising developments and so there is a danger that 'travelling policies' collide with local practices, cultures and systems. This may mean that the imported ideas cause disruption and tension where the core local educational narrative is weak. It also makes for an ambiguous and contested political terrain. Funding priorities can reflect national or international trends rather than providing a targeted resource base to tackle locally identified needs.

Scotland, in some quarters, is regarded as one of the most centralised countries in Europe. Local representation has been largely eroded over the past fifty years with the number of elected local governments being reduced from 400 to just thirty-two (COSLA, 2014). Historically, there has been a continuous, if varying, level of tension between central and local government in most countries, including the UK, but in the past, there has been a general recognition and respect that both levels of government perform different functions. However, it is arguable that in Scotland, central government is undermining local governance through politically motivated initiatives as well as proposed changes to structures which seek to deal directly with individual schools and bypass local government. Through this, it seems that Scottish Government wants local government to be more accountable to it despite the democratic deficit this creates. The political context is one within which education is striving to increase standards at a time that services suffer from substantial resource cuts, diminished local government cash settlements, and are hampered by a lack of available trained teachers, teacher overload and unacceptable stress levels. Many of the core arguments for devolution of government to Scotland were made around Westminster being too remote, a lack of local accountability and a desire to bring decision making and representation closer to the people. However, since the establishment of Parliament in Edinburgh, there has been a creeping and unhealthy centralisation agenda which undermines a diverse range of contributory views on policy. This monocultural east coast view of the world is dominant in policy as it fails to take account of the different needs and practices across the country.

Local governance is important because it provides a check and balance to the imposition of national power. It also provides local accountability and enables local solutions and responses to local problems and opportunities. It would be fair to state that since the establishment of the Scottish Parliament, under different political parties, there have been continuous tensions and frustrations between the two levels of government. This rivalry has often been managed through negotiated agreement but at times has also resulted in reluctant cooperation and levels of mistrust. It could be argued, therefore, that policy development which proposes centralist structural change is more concerned with issues of influence, control and resource reduction rather than a reasoned effort to improve the quality of public services. Since the current government took over the running of Scotland ten years ago, centralisation has developed apace with regional police and fire forces being amalgamated;

national organisations being merged; and the further education sector being regionalised. In the last case, a reduction of colleges from forty-two, prior to 2012, down to twenty-five in 2016, with the loss of over 120,000 training places, indicates that there are agendas at work other than the presenting political rationale. Ultimately, the recent road to centralisation across Scotland is littered with individual sector cuts and reorganisations, with a cumulative effect on local power, influence and flexibility which appears to go unnoticed. In spite of the political rhetoric that espouses regionalisation of education to facilitate school innovation and community involvement, it could equally be argued that, fundamentally, Scottish Government views local government as a threat to its power and a barrier to its policy implementation. It is argued by some political and social commentators that the aim of the government in Scotland is to reduce the responsibility and impact of local services to providing 'bins, basketballs and burials'.

## GOVERNANCE REVIEW

The core current debate in education has been an ongoing battle to determine which governance process is best placed to offer schools appropriate levels of autonomy, control and regulation. In some respects, this debate has been concerned with the nature and extent of local government, and the services it provides, which was inevitable after the Scottish Parliament was established because the local governance systems were not altered to reflect the new arrangements. Structures have been continuously changed in a piecemeal manner and without a full public debate. An example of this 'sector by sector' change was the governance review which took place between September 2016 and January 2017. It sought views from all stakeholders on the ways in which education should be governed in Scotland and how funding could be made fairer. It also focused on finding ways of improving teacher and other school-based practitioner support.

The stated rationale for the consultation was predicated on a clear political commitment to raise standards and close the poverty-related attainment gap based on the principles of equity and excellence. However, controversially, the government claimed a range of successes in reforming the curriculum and the workforce but the veracity of this may be disputed if we consider the action plan required by the Organisation for Economic Co-operation and Development (OECD, 2015) report, which pointed essentially to a lack of a core educational narrative and poor central governance. Notwithstanding this, the government was committed to reviewing local governance arrangements but without acknowledging, nor proposing to deal with, the required actions set out in the OECD report.

In short, the articulated ambition here is to empower teachers, parents, the local community and other professionals to make decisions, not just about children's learning but their 'school life', a concept which remains unclear. Interestingly, in analysing the questions posed during the consultation, these were all concerned with structures, principles and professional roles; there were no questions about the role of parents or the local community, nor any opportunity to discuss an interpretation of excellence and equity, which were telling omissions. Also, questions were posed about the strengths and weaknesses of current governance arrangements, the key principles of education and the best funding formula. The problem with these types of questions is that they are aimed at professionals with current inside knowledge of the system, encouraging those with a vested interest and discouraging inputs from others who are not 'in the know'.

## THE PROBLEM WITH THIS REVIEW

Despite the consultation being publicly presented as a conversation and the claim that no decisions had yet been made, it appeared to the contrary: that the process itself and the answers being sought were from a singular perspective. To critics, three main issues seemed critical. First, the consultation document was predicated on an ideological belief as set out in the 2016 SNP manifesto: to give more power and resources directly to headteachers, and to place teachers, parents and community at the centre of school improvement (https://www.snp.org/manifesto_2016). Second, the proposals lacked robust research evidence that the plan to change the governance structures, as well as to increase the responsibility of individual headteachers, would add any significant value to tackling the pernicious attainment gap. Third, the questions asked in the consultation document were narrow, skewed and, to some, unintelligible: they appeared to be in favour of a preferred structural solution, although the extent and nature of the problem they purported to address had not been cogently identified.

Many stakeholders took the opportunity to make their views known on the proposals. It is worth outlining the responses to ascertain some of the main points being made. At the outset, it would be useful to note that responses can be grouped in at least two different categories. First, there are those who have a direct interest, knowledge, experience and involvement in the education sector, for example professional bodies. The second category includes those who have a more public interest in education such as social reform think tanks.

In the first category, one of the most telling responses about the effectiveness of this review was supplied by the Scottish Parent Teacher Council (SPTC) which indicated that their members were perplexed by the type of questions posed. It reported confusion among parents because of professional assumptions, the use of jargon and a lack of clarity which denied them the opportunity to contribute effectively. Many of their members provided negative feedback on the public information events which left attendees unable to make their voice heard. It could be argued this is contrary to section 28 of the 1980 Act which presumes taking cognisance of parents' wishes.

Education Scotland, in its offering, pointed to the excellent partnership work that currently exists, lauded the flexibility in the current system to meet local needs and the synergetic alignment of national and local initiatives. However, it also lamented the level of inconsistencies, the lack of tracking and other data as well as an inability to tackle underperformance and develop professional training. Most importantly it stressed the need for consensus in reform and underlined the centrality of local flexibility for pedagogical, curricular and self-evaluation reasons. It also recognised the possible unintended consequences that changing the governance arrangements would detract from a focus on the quality of teaching and learning and the needs of learners. It warned of the danger that changes in structure may lead to a stricter focus on educational achievements rather than a wider collegiate concern for child wellbeing. However, in its submission there was an assumption that regional improvement collaboratives would happen and the contribution sought to position the agency in terms of a national development role in the new set-up, giving some credence to the claim that Education Scotland operates symbiotically with government.

The response of the Association of Directors of Education in Scotland (ADES) showed that they were open to change but remained unconvinced that a cogent argument for fundamental alterations had been made. They were very clear that the acid test for any adjustment must be set in the context of positive improvements for young people. ADES also emphasised that amendments must build on best practice and collaborative endeavour. They were concerned that good work may be hampered in the process of structural change, especially in relation to other complementary policies, such as integrated children and young people service planning. ADES argued that the current system of national policies was clear and the challenge was to turn these aspirations into improved measurable outcomes.

Through their contribution to the consultation, the Scottish Secondary Teachers' Association (SSTA) teachers' union firmly stated that the review should not lead to major changes in the system. There had been concern in some quarters that the proposed move to hand headteachers more powers and relieve councils of local control would ultimately lead to schools 'opting out' of council control as in England. Scotland's association of council chief executives also advised against wholesale changes. Furthermore, the Society of Local Authority Chief Executives (SOLACE) were very clear in their statement that education would be best served through keeping an electoral-based system of local democratic control. They stated the importance of maintaining flexibility in the local structure to find local solutions to local problems. Also, they emphasised in their view that the most effective arrangement was a system which incorporated a national framework, to set the context, and a local delivery mechanism that had foundational local accountability strengthened through regional collaboration with the collegiate support of national agencies.

In the second category of responses, the Commission on School Reform, set up by think tank Reform Scotland, supported the notion that schools should be allowed to make all decisions about children's learning and school life which it believes will assist substantially a closure of the attainment gap. However, the veracity of this claim is questionable and lacks credible research. In fact, this assertion is disputed by the Educational Institute of Scotland (EIS) which unequivocally maintains that the biggest cause of the attainment gap is due to substantial and sustained underfunding of education over many years.

Again, in support of educational change, some political commentators and educational correspondents called for long overdue educational reform because of poor international rankings and claimed a public appetite for more school autonomy with teachers and parents having more influence. However, this type of social comment points to a superficial positioning that is largely unsubstantiated and panic driven. In fact, more credence should be given to the Chartered Institute of Public Finance and Accountancy's cautionary advice that acceding more power to headteachers could leave schools exposed to major financial risk and lead to a lack of direction, support and skills.

Finally, some concern was expressed that the Scottish Government was using the review process to quietly dump previous educational schemes and commitments, which have failed or are no longer the political 'flavour of the month'. For example, it was understood, through Education Scotland, that the Scottish Government had abandoned the three-year-old £700,000 initiative, the Scottish Improvement Partnership Programme (SIPP), which was supposed to drive up standards by twinning schools across council boundaries.

## TACKLING THE ATTAINMENT GAP IN SCOTTISH EDUCATION

After almost ten years in continuous government and three months prior to the Scottish Parliamentary election in 2016, the Scottish Government launched the Scottish Attainment Challenge to tackle the poverty gap in education, through the principles of excellence and equity. Scottish Government clearly state that 'Equity can be achieved by ensuring every child has the same opportunity to succeed' (www.gov.scot/Topics/Education/Schools/Raisingeducationalattainment). This assertion is debateable. If you provide the same opportunity to each child in a situation where inequality exists, then consequentially the gap will never be closed. Instead, what is required is a system of opportunities and interventions that meets identified and expressed needs of those who are disadvantaged. So, this status quo approach could be representative of a government that builds perceptions and sound bites rather than acknowledges hard analytical evidence. Excellence is an endeavour which breeds dissatisfaction with the present and puts learners on a constant journey of higher attainment which may not be supportive of good mental health. Constant striving to make results better can become an end rather than a means to an end. The importance of learning achievement, in a schooling system, is that it is coupled with clear and known purposes with a relevance that is articulated to an intended application. The attainment gap will only be closed if there is a comprehensive analysis and understanding of its underlying causes, which are addressed through revised social aspirations for fairness and inclusion. If the government continues to set out consultations and subsequent policies with a focus on local political structural change, preconceived ideas and pre-emptive solutions, then the types of young people who are currently unsuccessful in the education system will continue to be failed. Is the education system in Scotland too close to the Scottish Government to resist its centralist political will?

## EDUCATION GOVERNANCE: NEXT STEPS

On 15 June 2017, the Deputy First Minister and Cabinet Secretary for Education and Skills, revealed the government's plans for major governance reforms to the primary and secondary sectors in Scottish education. The reasons why such reforms were deemed necessary lay in part in the growing criticism of the Scottish Governments' handling of education's overarching policy, including Curriculum for Excellence. The First Minister had staked her political reputation on a promise to fix the inequality within education and to improve the country's international standing. Structural changes were therefore inevitable to demonstrate a national response to political opponents, draw more control to the parliamentary centre, create a narrative of inadequacy on the local education authority system and promise to empower teachers and parents.

### Summary of Reforms

The proposed changes include the Scottish Government setting up a Scottish Education Council, chaired by the Cabinet Secretary for Education and Skills, to oversee the performance of new national priorities for education. Furthermore, headteachers will be legally responsible for raising attainment and closing the attainment gap, a seismic policy shift with potential consequences for headteacher recruitment and accountability. They will also select and structure their own staffing and management arrangements for the school to help deliver these aims. Headteachers across Scotland will be supported by one of seven regional improvement collaboratives led by a Scottish Government appointed regional director. Also, the role and purpose of Education Scotland will be augmented with inspections having a refreshed focus on professional learning and leadership. Parents and pupil voices will be strengthened through legislation to enable further student participation and parental involvement in school decision making. Councils will remain directly responsible for providing school buildings, placing procedures, additional support needs, early learning and childcare, school staffing, including headteachers, and human resources. This is a split in operational functions that will mean a change in procedures and protocols, as well as changes in staff working conditions and responsibilities.

## Analysis and Comment

These organisational alterations ignore the grave concerns of the Convention of Scottish Local Authorities (COSLA) together with the opposition of many education stakeholders. However, the EIS teaching union has reportedly given the proposals a cautious welcome as the accompanying narrative is that these reforms will 'free teachers to teach' and 'empower headteachers' to address the poverty-related attainment gap and increase international education rankings. This guarded support is surprising, as the proposals do not contain any performance improvement targets, nor delineate the inevitable financial costs which will run into millions of pounds and come from an already depleted pot of public finances. Clearly, these alterations indicate a governmental drive for a firmer and consistent national direction with a more direct and assertive regional delivery. However, critics argue that such administrative modifications come at a price as these will adversely undermine local democratic control, and hamper local creativity and flexibility to meet local needs. It will place further burdensome pressures on individual schools that will detract from their emphases on pupil learning. In addition, the operational divide between 'local' and 'central' creates unnecessary confusion, separates learning pathways, and builds competing structures and processes that undermine the efficient and effective service delivery of education for learners. There is some concern that these adaptations relate *only* to the primary and secondary sector, thus dislocating the early years and additional support needs services. There is also a concern that direct lines of employee accountability for teachers will be blurred and disrupted, with potential clashes between the local authority as employers and Education Scotland as representatives of Scottish Government. Legislation will be required to implement these changes and a new Education Governance Bill will be introduced to the Scottish Parliament by June 2018.

So, underneath these headline radical reforms, there are many significant questions to be asked in terms of policy justification and clarification, as well as necessary considerations of the operational implications of expected outcomes, costs and unintended consequences. Ultimately, whether these organisational vicissitudes will bring the intended or stated outcomes remains open to question. When this regionalisation of the education improvement function is viewed contextually from a public policy perspective, it becomes evident that these moves are more about diminishing the role of local councils and increasing central control, rather than attempting to improve our children's educational experiences and their learning journey.

## CONCLUSION

The problem with the centralisation agenda pursued to date is that, at its core, it seeks the demise of local government as a political base and replaces local democratic control with national or regional non-elected bodies. The approach to minimise the impact and influence of local government has three strands: first, to move local services directly to the political centre or to non-elected quangos; second, to saddle councils with increased responsibility and cuts in its resource base; and third, to develop a narrative of community and organisational empowerment which bypasses local government influence, and lacks a solid resource infrastructure, robust accountability processes and independent scrutiny. We must be honest and recognise that local government funding for local services, including education, has been reduced significantly over the past ten years and the situation is now critical. Also, that historic responsibilities have been surreptitiously removed and the freedom to set local government taxes are being interfered with by national government. The central question is whether this creeping accumulation of power and control is adept governing or inept domination.

Ultimately, the main argument of this chapter has been that the Scottish Government's consultation on the future governance of Scottish schools was prejudged, partial and presumptive. Significantly, in the *Next Steps* document the government's response clearly ignored large parts of the response to the public consultation. The consultation appeared to be looking for answers to fit preconceived ideas to meet the political interpretations of circumstances. The move to creating regional improvement collaboratives and deal directly with schools inherently assumes that the current governance arrangements are somehow to blame for the attainment gap. This undeclared position lacks substance and credence. The attainment gap will only be closed if there are sincere, respectful and cooperative partnership arrangements between national and local government that enhance teaching and learning through teacher development and by placing the learner at the very heart of the process. It will not be achieved through preconceived structural alterations that are politically motivated and lack a substantive evidence base.

We would do well to heed the words of Rhodes (1999) that administrative reform breeds more cynicism than efficiency and effectiveness. There is clearly an argument that supports the idea that, in the absence of an agreed central narrative for CfE and without a clear mandate of local democratic control, the change to regionalisation may not achieve the stated intentions and have significant unintended consequences.

Clearly, significant challenges lie ahead for all public services, including education, as constrained finance continues to bite hard, with no realistic plan to fund services to the level they need. Scotland would benefit from a strong and relevant form of local government that meets the needs and aspirations of local people with its functions and responsibilities enshrined in law, as is the case in other countries. It would be very dangerous to sleepwalk into a single tier of government in Scotland, through a lack of debate, which ends up with government functioning through a plethora of unelected quangos and boards with no local control.

Finally, if the government fails to recognise the need for genuine partnerships among all education stakeholders, then this move to regionalisation will only serve to distance education provision from local communities and parents, with significantly reduced accountability, influence and agility to respond to local need. Crucially, no amount of direct additional resources will solve the attainment gap if the regionalisation measures are top down and political resolve is imposed on those who have a different perspective and contribution to make. We should work together on the persistent and unjust attainment problem for the maximum benefit of all our children and to build a progressive future for this country.

## REFERENCES

COSLA (2014) *Commission on Strengthening Local Democracy*. Online at https://www.localdemocracy.info/news/final-report/

Mason, C., Kirkbride, J. and Bryde, D. (2007) 'From stakeholders to institutions: the changing face of social enterprise governance theory', *Management Decision*, 45 (2), 284–301.

Mayntz, R. (2003) 'New challenges to governance theory', in H. P. Bang (ed.), *Governance as Social and Political Communication*, Manchester: Manchester University Press, pp. 27–40.

OECD (2015) *Improving Schools in Scotland: An OECD Perspective*. Online at https://www.oecd. org/education/school/Improving-Schools-in-Scotland-An-OECD-Perspective.pdf

Ozga, J. (2005) 'Modernizing the education workforce: a perspective from Scotland', *Educational Review*, 57 (2), 207–19.

Rhodes, R. A. W. (1994) 'The hollowing out of the state: the changing nature of the public service in Britain', *The Political Quarterly*, 65, 138–51.

Rhodes, R. A. W. (1999) *Control and Power in Central-local Government Relations*. Aldershot and Brookfield, VT: Ashgate.

Scottish Government (2017) *Education Governance: Next Steps – Empowering Our Teachers, Parents and Communities to Deliver Excellence and Equity for Our Children*. Online at www.gov.scot/ Resource/0052/00521038.pdf.

## Website

General Teaching Council for Scotland at www.gtcs.org.uk

# 18

# National and Local Curriculum Support

*Derek Brown*

This chapter places support provided by local authorities in the context of the histori-cal evolution of their role in Scottish education and explores the recent pressures on the system for reform in a context of austerity – a context which will have a number of consequences for provision of education across the system in future. Consideration is then given to how overlapping changes over time have contributed to the curriculum found today in Scotland's schools, and in particular to improvements in learning. This part examines some of the implications of Curriculum for Excellence and its relation to other national developments. The chapter then maps the kinds of local authority provision that exist in Scotland at the time of writing to support the development and improvement of the curriculum experienced by young people. Lastly, it considers the implications of recent planned changes to governance in education in Scotland and highlights examples of improvements which have been brought forward through the implementation of a number of key national strategies. These give some sense of the resource and other requirements needed to enhance future provision. Reference will also be made to teacher perceptions of the support they receive and the pressures that change over time has created. Fife is used as an illustration at times, to show how regional planning intersects with national policymaking objectives.

## THE HISTORY OF LOCAL AUTHORITY SUPPORT FOR THE CURRICULUM

In previous editions of this book, Alison Cameron gave a comprehensive account of the historical development of local authority support for schools in Scotland. Her account charted the role of curriculum advisors throughout the 1970s and onwards, professionals who could take forward support for school staff in region-wide planning, with a strong emphasis on the development of curriculum and pedagogy in both primary and secondary schools. The advisors were mainly subject experts who could take an authority-wide view of planning for development in specific subjects and could bring forward a strategic plan, for example, for literacy or numeracy. Following local authority reorganisations in 1996, and from 2000 onwards, with the new Standards in Scotland's Schools etc. Act, these advisors were increasingly replaced by Quality Improvement Officers (QIOs), who had a more general function in supporting school improvement, especially in relation to the new *How Good is Our School?* documents that came on stream around that point.

The legislation brought forward in the Standards in Scotland's Schools etc. Act (2000), was one of the most important early pieces of legislation by the new Scottish Parliament. Its principles have underpinned educational developments progressed in Scotland since then. The duties established for local authorities in the 2000 Act were described in the following terms:

- It shall be the duty of the [education] authority to secure that the education is directed to the development of the personality, talents and mental and physical abilities of the child or young person to their fullest potential.
- An education authority shall endeavour to secure improvement in the quality of school education which is provided in the schools managed by them ... with a view to raising standards of education.

This chapter focuses on the support for schools in planning and delivering curriculum improvements. Such processes, however, need to be seen in relation to the above statutory duties, which contain an element of regulation, or quality assurance, but also an explicit requirement to drive change and manage improvement. The interaction of the regulatory function and the improvement function has been a subject of ongoing debate in Scottish education over time and continues to resonate in the recent *Education Governance: Next Steps* report (Scottish Government, 2017b). The splitting off of improvement functions from local authorities is contrasted in that report with the stated intention of retaining both functions within an expanded Education Scotland.

With the advent of Curriculum for Excellence (CfE), and its broadly progressive, learner-centred philosophy, such duties have been challenged. Alison Cameron showed how the challenges involved in bringing forward the significant change envisaged within CfE actually helped to define more clearly the role of the local authority QIO. She highlighted the evolution of the middle sector of Scottish education – that is, the support systems lying between the policy framework and the day-to-day work of schools – during the complex period of implementation of CfE and warned about the tensions that were starting to fracture this middle at the very point that it was arguably most relevant to shaping the progress of the national education system.

> For many involved in education in Scotland, there has never been a time with greater potential to 'get it right'. If Curriculum for Excellence, despite the doomsayers, is to be the vehicle for achieving a major breakthrough in improving the learning experiences and the life chances of young people, the stakes are very high. As education directorates struggle with the unenviable task of offering up savings without damaging frontline services, quality improvement services are an obvious target. Elected members question the expenditure on what they view as highly-paid officers, who are not directly accountable to them and whose role is difficult to comprehend. (Cameron, 2013, pp. 207–8)

Cameron's text acknowledged the undoubted impact of fiscal austerity throughout the United Kingdom since the financial crisis of 2008, which are passed on to the Scottish Government through cuts in funding via the Barnet settlement, are then in turn devolved to local authorities, creating challenges in the oversight of local authority financial governance. She shows how, over time, and especially following the end of ring-fenced funding of education in 2007, this has led to an erosion of central education teams in local authorities, as front-line services are ostensibly protected by chief officers and senior politicians who have struggled to justify maintaining authority-based support for schools at the expense of actual school-based spend.

Cameron noted the stress some elected members felt in being between the twin pressures of having meaningful systems to enable rigorous local political oversight of education and an imperative to balance the books. As a result, officers who might have previously had roles closer to schools are often given a wider clutch of responsibilities, which can mean that their capacity to support, challenge or influence schools is diluted. Thus, councils increasingly delegate key authority-wide responsibilities to headteachers or operate on a short-term secondment basis to support specific developments. While there are examples of this being a success, there are also other examples of it leading to short-term thinking, discontinuity of planning and variability of provision. The overall effect of this has been to exacerbate the local unevenness of support for schools, which figures as an issue in a number of recent reports on Scottish education, including the evaluation report, *Improving Schools in Scotland* (OECD, 2015), and the *Education Governance: Next Steps* review, which states:

> Across Scotland the tailored education improvement support which local authorities are able to provide to schools has significantly reduced over recent years. Understandably resources available have focussed on frontline delivery. In a number of smaller local authorities there is no longer the critical mass to deliver the improvement support which schools need. (Scottish Government, 2017b, p. 34)

## OVERLAPPING PRIORITIES WHICH HAVE DRIVEN CHANGE

The National Improvement Framework (NIF; see Chapter 71) and the accompanying plan to implement it, entitled the *Delivery Plan for Excellence and Equity in Scottish Education*, have shifted the emphasis of curriculum support in recent times, with an increasing drive to focus on the NIF priorities and the outcomes expressed in a national 'scorecard' (Scottish Government, 2017a).

The four key priorities in the National Improvement Framework remain:

- health and wellbeing;
- developing the young workforce;
- attainment (literacy and numeracy);
- equity.

Broadly, these are underpinned by substantial pieces of national public policy documentation. The health and wellbeing priority draws lessons from the Christie Commission, and from various strands of activity related to *Getting it Right for Every Child*. Developing the Young Workforce substantially responds to the Wood Commission Report of 2014, *Education Working for All*. The work on attainment draws on lessons from the Donaldson report on initial teacher education, but also from the 2015 Organisation for Economic Co-operation and Development (OECD) report. And the equity agenda is rooted in studies on poverty and attainment, such as has been done by the Joseph Rowntree Foundation (Sosu and Ellis, 2014; and Chapter 12 in this text).

The implementation of each of these national priorities within the framework has presented different challenges to local authorities, since there are complex partnership networks which have to function effectively in local contexts to deliver them, and each of these is affected in different ways by proposed changes of governance (see below). Arguably, in addition, as the expert panel assembled by Scottish Government highlighted in its most recent report, the scorecard approach utilised within the NIF (with an express focus on outcomes) and its relationship with the progressive child-centred approach advocated within the Curriculum for Excellence documentation.

> the Council was concerned that, in the drive to deliver clarity of purpose for all those involved in Scottish education, there was a risk that education policy was moving away from the 'whole child' approach of CfE towards a more specific, measureable approach as required by the NIF. (Scottish Government, 2017c)

Indeed, of the four priorities, *attainment*, for the broad pupil population, is probably the only one which predominantly can be addressed by taking a schools-focused approach. This is the one most directly in control of education professionals. The others demand a wider perspective and partnership infrastructure.

The health and wellbeing agenda is squarely retained as a local authority responsibility. This is probably due to the fact that significant emphasis has been given to local authority implementation of health and wellbeing-related developments within the recent Children and Young People's Act, which sought to legislate to ensure that the principles of *Getting it Right for Every Child* were established in all parts of the country and for all children. This Act gives local authorities responsibilities for delivering 1,140 hours of early learning, with some flexibility, from the age of 2 for some children. It also makes local authorities responsible for named person services (at the time of writing legislation is expected on this). Since the objectives relating to both of these areas of national priority are complex and challenging to deliver, it is difficult to see how the government could have taken these away from local authorities without significant change to primary legislation which had only recently been brought forward, in some cases in the face of a particular set of responses from key stakeholder groups. However, once these two areas of public policy are implemented, the need for local authority improvement of them will undoubtedly reduce. One of the main challenges to the system in recent years has highlighted the gap in wellbeing and attainment experienced by children at the age of 5 in Scotland. The Growing up in Scotland website and work in early years collaboratives triggered cross-cutting improvement activity that galvanised partnerships. In Fife, there have been documented improvements in wellbeing and literacy due to such an approach, showing that there is hope that such gaps can be identified and closed. But, there is still a job to do in reaching parents.

The equity agenda, in contrast, is being pursued through the specific mechanism of direct funding of schools, as part of the new 'powers' to headteachers. However, in this area, the governance report highlights the importance of partnerships with parents and other agencies, which reveals a tension between the challenge of empowering headteachers with greater autonomy and that of creating local infrastructure that is implicit in the local authority approach taken in the Children and Young People's Act. Resolving these tensions will involve careful local authority planning in future and high-quality leadership, including that of headteachers. Direct funding may allow a thousand flowers to bloom; however, the *Next Steps* report makes it clear that the local authority is still responsible for financial governance around this issue.

Developing the Young Workforce (DYW) is perhaps the most challenging initiative to progress across the country. On a system-wide basis, the variables are multiplied when consideration is given to the local partnerships which need to be in place to enable this strategy to be fully successful. In short, system elements in different parts of the country are uniquely different from those found in other areas. Partnerships need to be formed by the newly established business-led DYW boards (of which there are twenty-one) with over 2,000 headteachers across the country; a range of economic development services in local authorities (and their business engagement teams); the recently established regional colleges (all of which are at different stages of improvement themselves); the local employers (whose attitudes and capacity to engage are critical); the local and national agents of Skills Development Scotland (SDS) and similar third-sector agencies.

DYW has implications for education and economic development, and bringing these elements into line will require joined-up partnership working by national agencies on a scale which is unprecedented in Scotland. It is notable that in parallel to the governance review in education, a separate exercise was being conducted in the world of enterprise and skills, which encompassed SDS, the Scottish Funding Council (SFC) and Scottish Enterprise. In hindsight, it might have been helpful if these two pieces of work could have been more explicitly linked, so as to encourage more local interaction between education and economic development services and agencies. Those of us who work directly in this area are aware that funding mechanisms driving post-16 activity can impact positively on transitions. The young people most affected by this are still those most at risk of labour market marginalisation. In Fife we have improved positive and sustained destinations by over 3 per cent in the past three years, which stands favourable comparison with national figures. But, system improvements are required to further address the needs of the 7 per cent or so of young people falling out of the system on leaving school. These figures are based on annual reports done by SDS across the country and published on the Insight system: nationally, 93.33 per cent of pupils had positive destinations in 2015–16.

The Learner Journey Review (15–24), which is currently being conducted, attempts to address some of these issues, with both the Cabinet Secretaries for Enterprise and for Education recently making pronouncements on the subject. This review focuses on the efficacy of different system elements, such as those which seek to address the needs of those who do not achieve a positive initial destination from school in Scotland, placing their economic future at considerable risk. It also focuses on other system issues, such as progression through Scottish Credit and Qualifications Framework (SCQF) levels and articulation between system elements. Finally, it seeks to review the economic outcomes achieved in Scotland at the end of the period of the learner journey, as defined in the review.

In trying to address these issues, it is impossible to split off curricular planning from partnership working and explicit mechanisms to support learners as they progress through the system. A wider view is needed, with the curriculum being set in a broader economic context. As Andreas Schleicher of the OECD Education Directorate, in *The Case for Twenty-First Century Learning*, observes:

> We live in a fast-changing world, and producing more of the same knowledge and skills will not suffice to address the challenges of the future. A generation ago, teachers could expect that what they taught would last their students a lifetime … Conventionally, our approach to problems was to break them down into manageable bits and pieces, confined to narrow disciplines, and then to teach students the techniques to solve them. Today, however, knowledge advances by synthesizing these disparate bits. It demands open-mindedness, making connections between ideas that previously seemed unrelated and becoming familiar with knowledge in other fields. (www.oecd.org/general/thecasefor21st-centurylearning.htm)

While the NIF has four priorities, the challenges that there are in building partnerships to enable each of them run the risk of having them split off from one another, fragmenting into silos, rather than, as Schleicher recommends, synthesising. This is perhaps the greatest risk in the NIF. One thing that might help in this is if there were a bigger idea shaping the senior phase of education and beyond. Something which could bring about a clearer focus on developing a high-end knowledge economy in Scotland and this should be strengthened by a clear epistemological framework which shapes school, college and university provision from level 7 upwards. This might help to bring into line the different progression routes available from that point onwards in the system: Higher National courses, Advanced Highers, Higher National Certificates and Diplomas, college access courses and first year of university. The Theory of Knowledge element of the International Baccalaureate Programme is an example of how such an idea can underpin a senior phase curriculum and encourage the kind of questioning of knowledge by students that is currently not an explicit curricular requirement in Scotland.

## CURRENT SUPPORT FOR CURRICULUM BY LOCAL AUTHORITIES IN SCOTLAND

On the specific issue of the curriculum as it is currently found in schools, local authority support in taking forward planning for curriculum is best seen as being an aspect of the broad statutory responsibilities that were established for local authorities in Scotland, as part of the Standards in Scotland's Schools etc. (2000) Act. However, the precise ways in which these powers are delegated has been varied across Scotland, due to a number of national and local factors. Most of the national guidance around Curriculum for Excellence has provided delegated powers to 'schools and local authorities' to implement guidance. The *Next Steps* report highlights the differences of approach that this has led to being adopted across Scotland, with some local authorities stipulating clearly senior phase plans for an entire block of schools, and others delegating powers to headteachers. This has led to an element of public reaction around, for instance, the number of subjects young people are allowed to study in S4 and concomitant variances across schools in Scotland. A recent Reform Scotland report showed that some schools continue to undertake eight subjects in S4, whilst others follow a narrower curriculum of six subjects. Broadly speaking, many of the more academic schools in the country tend to continue with a wider subject provision in S4, although there are some notable exceptions.

However, this is perhaps best viewed as an example of an unintended consequence of an ambiguity in national guidelines leading to a pattern of variability across the country. In this context, OECD deemed the middle tier of Scottish education as requiring to be strengthened, but also suggested a simplification and clarification of national guidance. Interestingly, the *Next Steps* report supports this proposition, that local authority imposed models for curriculum design are seen as a barrier to empowering headteachers to make a difference to outcomes for young people.

Responses to the Governance Review consultation highlighted a lack of consistency in relation to school devolution across local authorities. This can have a significant impact on achieving excellence and equity; for example by taking a mandated approach to the number of subjects young people study in S4 across an entire education authority. This shuts down curriculum flexibility and decisions which should be taken for individual young people at school level. (Scottish Government, 2017b, p. 20)

The most recent *Quality and Improvement in Scottish Education* report from Education Scotland reflected on the state of the nation in relation to curricular provision, as seen in inspections undertaken between the years of 2012–16 (Education Scotland, 2017). It showed the extent of progress in shaping Scotland's curriculum, based on the existing frameworks for quality improvement. Broadly speaking it painted a positive picture, and yet the things that it suggested still need to be tackled indicate the limited extent of what has been accomplished through CfE as a national development. For example, approaches to literacy and numeracy were identified as requiring further attention, as was interdisciplinary learning:

> While there have been improvements in children's progress in literacy and numeracy, it is still too variable. (p. 14)

> Cameron, A. (2013) 'Local Opportunities for interdisciplinary learning, work-based learning, creativity and personal achievements were not always being planned well enough to ensure that all young people can apply their learning and progress with sufficient pace and challenge. (p. 21)

Since the 2013 edition of *Scottish Education*, in which Alison Cameron's chapter appeared, we have seen the report by the OECD (2015) *Improving Schools in Scotland* and the subsequent response from Scottish Government (2017a), expressed in the *National Improvement Framework* (NIF) and the *Delivering Excellence and Equity in Scottish Education: A Delivery Plan for Scotland* (www.gov.scot/Publications/2016/06/3853). The OECD report made some explicit remarks about the 'middle' tier of the system, sometimes seeming to use the term to mean local authorities per se and at other times more loosely to refer to middle leadership within the system. A key statement was this: 'We call for a strengthened "middle" operating through networks and collaboratives among schools, and in and across local authorities. We see leadership best operating not only *in the middle* but *from the middle* ...' (OECD, 2015, p. 19). The report highlighted issues around the complexity of advice to teachers concerning CfE but also noted some structural variability in practice, which is partly due to a lack of appropriate resource and the consequent fragmentation of local systems. This latter point is actually supported by the text of the *Next Steps* report, which was referred to above.

As Alison Cameron noted five years ago, the pressure on resources in Education Scotland led to a more 'proportionate' inspection model, with fewer school inspections being carried out. Similarly, local authority inspections have been less frequent in recent years than was true a few years ago. One recent inspection report emphasised the importance of consistently higher levels of support and challenge from central officers and elected members. It thereby showed how successful local authority inspection processes will feature effective local political oversight of education and highlighted the potential benefits. Future models of inspection for local authorities will draw on lessons from the recent Education Scotland reviews of attainment challenge authorities.

There have been other models for local authority scrutiny deployed as well, such as validated self-evaluation (VSE). According to Education Scotland, VSE 'is not inspection. It is a voluntary process which aims to support and challenge the work of local authorities to improve the quality of provision and outcomes for learners' (https://education. gov.scot/what-we-do/inspection-and-review/Validated%20self-evaluation). This model focuses on outcomes, systems and cultures within local authorities. It is backed by quality management in education documentation, which is about to be strengthened and updated.

As the OECD noted, practitioner-led inquiry and collaboration tend to be the most effective approaches to curriculum and staff development. These can enable greater professional understanding and organisational improvement at both school and local authority level. Practitioner-led inquiry has been a powerful mechanism for support, especially in literacy and numeracy in primary schools. In Fife, team activity has proven to be successful in supporting improvements in literacy, initially in primary schools, but increasingly focused on numeracy and secondary schools as well. This has been supported by research-driven approaches, built up in universities. There are other examples of universities supporting school improvement. For instance, the Scottish Attainment Challenge has brought with it a research-based attitude to engendering curriculum innovation. In addition, there has been widespread sponsoring in Scotland of the Education Endowment Trust resources, which are all supported by research analysis and meta-analysis. Such strategies have increasingly encouraged an evidence-based approach to curriculum planning and delivery across Scotland, for example around the justification of spending through the Pupil Equity Funding.

An issue for schools, and possibly a challenge for future regional improvement collaboratives, is that university research is not always straightforward to engage with. Different models of improvement are being promulgated by different academic approaches. How is a school to differentiate in its planning between 'improvement science', for instance, and 'collaborative inquiry'? Both of these approaches are different in focus, demand significant investment of time and potentially financial resources, and involve a different methodology for improvement. On a sliding scale between empirical and deductive, they are quite distanced from one another. One of the functions of the governance structure in future should be to bring together these strands of research activity into a clearer framework for schools to engage with, otherwise we run the risk of people embarking on programmes of improvement without a clear sense of final direction.

Each local authority has systems for managing its statutory obligations to improve the schools in its area. They are normally dependent on a process of school improvement planning which is subject to local authority scrutiny. The best of these plans concentrate on a few clear priorities and have widespread cultural buy-in across a school community. Any scrutiny process, normally overseen by a QIO, or equivalent officer, focuses on the rationale for planned improvement and checks that a rigorous process has been undertaken to ensure effective planning has taken place.

In addition, processes for overseeing the quality of performance through annual reporting by schools tend to involve local authority coordination and scrutiny. Support and challenge around this activity helps the process of managing the local authority's statutory responsibility, but can also enable more effective leadership development for headteachers, to ensure that longer-term school improvement is delivered and sustained. Such oversight is critical when leadership changes have to be managed in schools, both on a short-term temporary basis, but also on a longer-term basis. Typically, local authority systems involve processes of self-evaluation, attainment reviews, approaches to surveying the views of stakeholders and assessing the performance of local systems for managing the range of provision, all the way through from early years outcomes, attendance and exclusions, to leavers' destinations in particular areas.

## THE CHALLENGE AND COMPLEXITY OF SCHOOL IMPROVEMENT

This section considers the relative contributions of school leaders, local authorities and national bodies in driving forward the improvement agenda. For secondary schools, there is substantial scrutiny of attainment, normally in three phases:

- after the initial publication of Scottish Qualifications Authority (SQA) results (August);
- after the publication of Insight (September; Insight is an online benchmarking tool designed to help bring about improvements for learners in the senior phase of secondary school (S4 to S6));
- after the updated publication of Insight (March).

Insight provides a lot of data available at school and subject level around progression and the attainment of different groups of pupils (Scottish Index of Multiple Deprivation (SIMD), additional support needs, broad bands of attainment). Thus, there are a number of key lenses for use, which can help to identify the extent to which teachers and school leaders have been successful in identifying priorities for improving attainment and enabling this improvement through development, part of which is curriculum development. If anything, the breakdown of attainment by SIMD group and learners' needs has exacerbated questions about social inequity and educational outcomes. There is no simple answer to these questions and we need improved tools to inform school-based improvement. And, finally, the planning of schools in relation to Pupil Equity Fund spending has added an extra element for local authority scrutiny in relation to school based planning. The Pupil Equity Fund, which is directed to schools, needs to be governed by a plan, to be overseen locally. As this model builds up, local oversight of headteacher autonomy will have to evolve in relation to funding and governance.

In relation to managing performance, it is worth noting that along with the shift from subject advisors in local authorities to QIOs, there has also been a move in many local authorities to faculty management structures, which can see a middle leader responsible for a number of subjects within such a structure. Whilst these are often described as being in cognate groupings, the *Next Steps* review suggested that there can be an erosion of curriculum awareness in the system, with those with direct operational responsibility for overseeing the work of teachers, sometimes coming from a very different subject background. This can be especially challenging when implementing new qualifications.

A range of activities are planned on a local authority basis to support schools with curriculum implementation. In lieu of advisory services, professional networks of subject-based teachers tend to be organised on a regional basis to enable exchange of ideas and information. Recently, assessment of new qualifications has also been a predominant theme for local authority support for schools. This has required coordination of networks of teachers across local authorities to be charged with the implementation of new arrangements in local areas. These networks have been helpful to teachers in managing the recent changes to SQA National Qualifications. The changes required intense curriculum development, especially in relation to the purpose of enabling people to understand expectations with regard to arrangements and standards for the new courses. To accompany the implementation of new National Qualifications from 2013 onwards, there was a national drive, coordinated by Education Scotland and national partners, such as the Association of Directors of Education in Scotland (ADES), to build a National Assessment Resource Bank, which was instituted to enable sharing of resources across the country for new courses at Higher and National 5 levels in particular. Such networks have also been used recently to support the development and roll-out of new national benchmarks for attainment of levels for the broad general education phase of Curriculum for Excellence. A national group of Quality Assurance, Moderation of Standards Officers (QAMSOs) has been established across Scotland, which is working collaboratively with Education Scotland to develop materials to support the moderation of the new national standards.

In these approaches, effective practitioners are brought in to support national planning by SQA or Education Scotland and then to disseminate messages locally to others. However, these national cascade models, whilst enabling enthusiasts to make a useful contribution, do run the risk of missing out many staff. Of course, this is a perennial problem with any cascade model for improvement. They can also be workload intensive, with less engaged colleagues finding out halfway through programmes what has actually been required from the start.

The recent decision to remove units from National Qualifications over a three-year period is an illustration of the way in which the curriculum can become affected by different external forces (see Chapter 68). With the advent of Higher Still in the late 1990s, units were grafted into existing Higher courses and a new suite of National Qualifications. With the Curriculum for Excellence revision of these qualifications and the demise of Standard Grade, the unitisation of courses came under pressure. Practitioners commented on the challenges of implementing a more competency-based assessment regime implemented by SQA at high pace. Their trade union representatives painted a picture for ministers of high workload. However, there are no magic solutions to such problems. In responding to a policy intention rooted in reducing workload, and in moving away from unitised courses, there have had to be adjustments by SQA to coursework in National Qualifications and pupils will experience longer exams. Some trade unions now argue that this creates more workload.

This episode showed the challenges that exist in attempting to simplify a complex examination system, with national organisations being themselves subject to regulatory forces that can be powerful in their influence. In a local context, such changes require to be worked through. In Fife, this involved convening our subject teacher networks and enlisting the support of our secondary heads to engage with them. Managing such changes means that local authorities need high quality officers with high levels of understanding and skills. Maintaining trust with teaching staff in uncertain times is an issue, so it is important to secure agreement through local processes with representatives.

The role of Education Scotland in supporting local improvement activity is also worth mentioning. The process of overseeing the improvement of schools carried out by Education Scotland has traditionally involved Education Scotland Area Lead Officers who liaise directly with local counterparts, especially in relation to the local area strategic risk assessment process. These colleagues can be helpful to each other in providing context around school inspections. Specific inputs on curricular issues from Education Scotland Development Officers are included within the Education Scotland Improvement Plan, but such inputs tend to emphasise the scope of the activity being brought forward nationally, which can be difficult for schools to process. Development Officers tend to be seconded on a short-term basis to support particular strands of activity, which are connected to the overall strategic plan for the national agency, and these colleagues engage locally with colleagues across the country. This can lead to strong examples of support for local authorities, but it can also further increase the variability of provision.

## PROPOSED CHANGES TO SCHOOL GOVERNANCE

The central concern is how proposed changes to the governance of Scottish education, involving a reduced role for local authorities in improvement and more statutory powers given instead to headteachers, might affect the nature and quality of curriculum support. There are three key elements to this.

1. Critics have argued that what is proposed has the potential to reduce democratic account-ability by marginalising the contribution of local authorities (cf. Chapter 17).

   There will need to be a clear demarcation of roles to ensure that the type of local support and challenge for the system that is required to make it robust exists. The definition of the work of the collaborative and a requirement for local authorities to have a continued improvement function will be key to this, if only to manage the performance of the systems locally, includ-ing the impact of senior leaders in improving the systems as a whole. As the *Next Steps* report makes clear: 'At the moment the lines of accountability between local and national bodies are not clear enough' (p. 23).

   Clarification of this area should be the key purpose of the future legislation and guidance on such legislation that will be brought forward – as will a clear idea from Education Scotland about expectations of local authorities in terms of future performance.

2. Regional collaboratives will require to be staffed and will need to establish credibility relatively quickly, so as to ensure a seamless transition from one system to another.

   As noted above, the OECD review of Scottish education commented on the variability of the 'middle' of Scottish education, and while at times in the report the phrase, 'the middle', seemed to be used loosely to refer to system leadership at middle management level, at other times the report was clearly questioning the variability of local authority support for schools. Following the OECD review, a greater emphasis has been placed on more systematic collaboration between local authorities to support improvement and curriculum development. Increasingly, there are national drives in relation to science, technology, engineering and mathematics (STEM) and DYW which are necessitating learning across authorities, especially since some of the regional structures involve a number of local authorities. This point also applies to engagement with colleges and formulating planned school–college partnership activity. Building on such exist-ing experience of regionalisation, and of the lessons learned from such work, will be crucial. Most importantly, therefore, the regional improvement collaboratives will have to have a clear idea of the nature of the improvements that they are trying to engender and the tools required to enable this to happen. One of the biggest risks in this is that culturally there are potential ten-sions between collaboratives and local authorities. Therefore, high-quality system leadership is required and a very carefully framed national partnership approach.

3. Another important aspect will be the resources for this future regional improvement activity, as there will need to be some significant investment.

   To a considerable extent, finance and how it is controlled locally has shaped what has been possible in terms of local authority funding of schools. The *Next Steps* report acknowledged that local government budgets have been pressurised in recent times, concomitant with the austerity period that followed the 2008 financial crash. It also notes a concern about the lack of improvement provision in some local authorities, but also says that local authorities will be required to support collaboratives. The resource issue will have to be addressed as part of any planned development and will no doubt become part of the fairer funding debate: a more transparent and accountable set of systems must emerge.

What is proposed is both a policy and a structural change, which may be liberating for headteachers, but which may also run the risk of fragmenting further aspects of national public policy. There are clear tensions here, which the *Next Steps* review shows Scottish Government is aware of:

> However, an empowered system does suggest a clarified role for national government – for example, empowering teachers and headteachers to make decisions about curriculum content raises questions about the extent to which we can mandate or require certain elements of that curriculum. (Scottish Government, 2017b, p. 39)

There is also no doubt that in empowering head teachers, there will be a greater need to focus on attainment by those who lead schools. To achieve this, the wider priorities of the National Improvement Framework and its delicate relationship with the principles of Curriculum for Excellence need to be appreciated in the round by headteachers and those who oversee or measure their progress in future. Clarifying who is accountable for what and how they will be held accountable is the first and most important step to take. This sounds easy, but it is likely to become difficult, simply due to the complex governance arrangements that future legislation will require to unpick. This chapter has shown how complexity can be a major challenge. Describing clearly the evolving relationships between local authorities and regional collaboratives is also crucial, again requiring a carefully framed national partnership approach. Most importantly, there needs to be a clear vision of the system that we aspire to in Scotland. And if what the country ends up with is broadly what OECD recommended then we will be moving in a positive direction.

## REFERENCES

Cameron, A. (2013) 'Local authority support', in T. G. K. Bryce, W. M. Humes, D. Gillies and A. Kennedy (eds), *Scottish Education, Fourth Edition: Referendum*, Edinburgh: Edinburgh University Press, pp. 198–208.

Education Scotland (2017) *Quality and Improvement in Scottish Education 2012–2016*. Online at https://education.gov.scot/Documents/QuISE_full_2012_16_web.pdf

OECD (2015) *Improving Schools in Scotland: An OECD Perspective*. Online at https://www.oecd.org/education/school/Improving-Schools-in-Scotland-An-OECD-Perspective.pdf

Scottish Government (2017a) *National Improvement Framework and Improvement Plan for Scottish Education*, Edinburgh: Scottish Government.

Scottish Government (2017b) *Education Governance: Next Steps – Empowering our Teachers, Parents and Communities to Deliver Excellence and Equity for our Children*, Edinburgh: Scottish Government.

Scottish Government (2017c) *Report of the Initial Findings of the International Council of Education Advisers*, July. Online at www.gov.scot/Resource/0052/00522962.pdf

Sosu, E. and Ellis, S. (2014) *Closing the Attainment Gap in Scottish Education*, York: Joseph Rowntree Foundation.

# 19

# School Inspection and School Improvement

*Douglas Hutchison*

Since Scotland's first inspector was appointed in 1840, the role of inspectors has changed as the educational and political landscape has changed. In October 2010, the Cabinet Secretary for Education at the time, Mike Russell Member of the Scottish Parliament (MSP), announced at the Scottish National Party (SNP) annual conference that he would be merging Learning and Teaching Scotland (LTS) and Her Majesty's Inspectorate of Education (HMIE) to form a new organisation focused on quality assurance and quality improvement in education across the country. In July 2011 the new organisation known as Education Scotland came into being and, as well as LTS and HMIE, included two smaller teams which were the National Continuing Professional Development team and the Scottish Government's Better Behaviour Better Learning team. Education Scotland describes itself as 'the key national agency for promoting improvement in the quality and effectiveness of education' (Education Scotland, 2013). The organisation has now been in existence for some years during a period when education has become more highly charged politically. More recently, the future structure of Education Scotland itself was in question, with calls for the separation of the improvement function from the inspection function. However, the publication of Education Governance: Next Steps (Scottish Government, 2017) appears to have consolidated Education Scotland's position, with improvement and inspection remaining part of the same organisation.

Inspectors are part of Education Scotland and are involved in a broad range of inspection and review activities that cover early years, primary, secondary, special and residential special schools. In addition to school inspections, inspectors are involved in the inspection of community learning and development, careers information and guidance services, college reviews and the validated self-evaluation of local authority education services and educational psychology services. Since the Schools (Consultation) Scotland Act 2010 has been in force, an increasing amount of time is spent by HMI evaluating the educational benefits of proposals that require statutory consultation, including school closures. HMI also undertake roles such as Area Lead Officer, acting as liaison between one or more local authorities and Education Scotland. The functions described here are some of the main functions carried out by the inspectorate as part of Education Scotland, focusing mainly on their role inspecting schools.

The First Minister stated that 'the defining mission of this government will be education' in her statement to the Scottish Parliament on 'Taking Scotland Forward' following the Scottish Parliamentary elections in May 2016. The Deputy First Minister, John Swinney was appointed as the new Cabinet Secretary for Education and Skills in that month indicating the priority being given to education. John Swinney replaced Angela Constance MSP who had only been in post for eighteen months. It is in this context that the inspectorate operates and needs to define the purpose for its existence. This chapter first sets out briefly the recent history of the inspectorate and the main changes it has experienced. The approaches to inspection have also changed and will be described along with current debates about the future direction of inspection models. The announcement of the merging of LTS with HMIE in 2010 at the SNP's annual conference gives a clear indication of the influence of politics and politicians on the inspectorate. The very existence of the organisation remains a political choice and so the links with politics and politicians will also be explored. The strength and the future of the inspectorate, however, will more likely depend on the extent to which it can demonstrate that it is bringing about improvement. That question will be explored in the context of the limited literature available on the impact of inspections.

## RECENT DEVELOPMENTS IN THE INSPECTORATE

Inspectors have existed in Scotland since 1840 with the purpose of ensuring high-quality education for learners. The present day inspectors still bear the title HMI, Her Majesty's Inspector. They are approved by the Privy Council, a requirement which is believed to give them an element of independence. Since the start of the twenty-first century the inspectorate has seen a few changes. Following the disastrous implementation of a new national exam system then called Higher Still, resulting in the Scottish Qualifications Authority's (SQA's) examination results being delayed or sent to the wrong candidates, the inspectorate was moved out of government and no longer had a direct leadership role in education policy. The new agency, known as HMIE, was established in April 2001 and moved from Victoria Quay to headquarters in Livingston in 2003, outside Edinburgh. In the Scottish Parliament's Education, Culture and Sport Committee debate on Higher Still on 30 October 2000, then opposition MSP, Mike Russell (SNP), said to then Minister for Children and Education, Sam Galbraith MSP (Labour):

> Your opinion of HMI is not shared by others. One of the written submissions we have received states: 'It is disingenuous of Douglas Osler [Senior Chief Inspector] to claim … that HMIs do not make policy …'. On 9 October Mr Osler made an artificial distinction between national policy, for which you are responsible, and the detailed implementation of policy.

HMI were accused of being both responsible for the development of policy and for the inspection of policy, in this case, Higher Still being the 'policy'. The view was taken that they should only be responsible for one aspect and not for both and therefore their role was more clearly focused on inspection rather than on leading policy development.

Commenting on the crisis of 2000 that led to the establishment of HMIE as an arm's length agency of the Scottish Executive, Clarke and Ozga (2011) state that

> There was also, of course, an element of convenient scapegoating in this: the Inspectorate were seen to be too powerful by politicians who took advantage of the situation to blame them for a crisis for which they (the politicians) were largely responsible. (p. 9)

The same authors compare the Scottish inspectorate with the English system for inspecting. One of the main differences is in scale. In Scotland 'The inspectorate, policy makers and senior teachers occupy a partially shared milieu that implies a reduced social distance (and demands its negotiation as a shared space)' (ibid., p. 11). In England by contrast there is a larger social space and not the 'small society' that characterises Scottish political and policy culture.

Between 2001 and 2011, HMIE existed therefore as an executive agency which was independent but accountable to Scottish ministers for the effectiveness of the organisation. When Education Scotland was established, it was also established as an executive agency accountable to ministers. However, the same agency is once again responsible for the development and the implementation of major national policies, including Curriculum for Excellence. More recently, one of the strategic directors, who is also an inspector, has been playing a leading role in the development of the National Improvement Framework and the Scottish Government Delivery Plan for education. It appears that what was unacceptable in 2000 has within ten years become acceptable again.

Throughout the changes in structure from 2000 onwards, the recruitment of inspectors has remained broadly consistent. Adverts are placed periodically and a selection process leads to appointment as an inspector. This might seem like tedious detail, but it is worth emphasising that inspectors are selected from current education professionals representing the broad range of inspection activity undertaken by Education Scotland. Inspectors are from a teaching background in the main but also include, for example, people from community learning and development, educational psychology, further education and local authority officers. Education Scotland also includes a number of health and nutrition inspectors who evaluate progress on implementing the Schools (Health Promotion and Nutrition) (Scotland) Act 2007 and aspects of health and wellbeing within Curriculum for Excellence. Until 2011, the organisation known as HMIE also included inspectors from children's services, health and police backgrounds, but seven of these transferred to the Care Inspectorate in 2011 when the responsibility for inspection of children's services and child protection also passed to that organisation.

Education Scotland also uses a large number of associate assessors on inspections who are professionals currently working in the field being inspected. In addition, school inspections include lay members who generally represent the parent/carer voice on the team.

The total number of inspectors has varied over the past ten years peaking in 2006 at eighty-seven, falling to 57.3 in 2013 and settling at 66.45 full-time equivalent in 2016. The overall number of inspectors matters because it has a direct influence on the number of inspections that can take place. That figure has also varied and has been raised as a concern by opposition MSPs in the Scottish Parliament. Preschool, primary, secondary and special school inspections have varied between 314 in 2012–13 to 261 in 2015–16 and dropped as low as 191 in 2014–15. The number of inspectors and the number of inspections will also be influenced by the model of inspection, so at this point it is worth exploring the changing approaches to inspection.

## CHANGING MODELS OF INSPECTION

At the time Education Scotland was formed, the overall approach to inspection was one where self-evaluation was considered to be mature and well established. How Good Is Our School? was on its third iteration as a self-evaluation tool and focused much more on outcomes rather than on processes. Five quality indicators (QIs) were evaluated in school inspections and three of these contributed to the National Performance Framework. An evaluation of satisfactory or better on improvements in performance (QI1.1), learners' experiences (QI2.1) and meeting learners' needs (QI5.3) usually resulted in a positive inspection with no follow-through inspection. In addition to the three quality indicators mentioned, curriculum (QI5.1) and self-evaluation for improvement (QI5.9) were also evaluated on the six-point scale ranging from unsatisfactory to excellent.

The model of school inspection in operation was more flexible than previous approaches and aimed to take greater account of how well the school knew itself and how well it was performing for its children and young people. Professional dialogue lay at the heart of the inspection, with the school setting out its own self-evaluation at the start of the week. If the inspection team were able to determine that their findings were in line with the school's self-evaluation then it was possible to shorten the inspection process. Small changes, such as including a member or members of the school senior management team in the end-of-day team meeting, as well as shared lesson observations involving a member of staff from the school, led to greater openness in the process. From the time when the inspectorate first published the quality indicators used in school inspections, there has been growing openness and willingness to become increasingly transparent. The decision was also taken to shorten reports and share with the head teacher and the chair of the Parent Council the Record of Inspection Findings (RIF). The RIF was the summary of the inspection team's findings and was the professional document to be used by schools to help with their own improvement. In addition, the size of the team and length of inspection was proportionate to the size of the school, in particular taking account of small schools.

For a number of years, however, Education Scotland also issued Inspection Advice Notes which were also sometimes referred to as 'raised expectations notes'. As the implementation of Curriculum for Excellence progressed, expectations were raised in relation to what was accepted as leading to an evaluation of good or better. The raised expectations and other developments in education ultimately meant that How Good Is Our School? (HGIOS) needed to be revised again. Following a period of consultation How Good Is Our School? Version 4 (HGIOS4) was published in 2016. HGIOS4 had a greater emphasis on equity which had become a much higher priority for the Scottish Government from the point at which Nicola Sturgeon succeeded Alex Salmond as First Minister.

Along with a revised set of quality indicators, Education Scotland consulted on different approaches to inspection models and trialled some of these approaches during 2015–16. From the start of the academic session in August 2016, Education Scotland started rolling out new inspection models. With the publication of HGIOS4 came a new set of quality indicators used for evaluation during inspections. The QIs evaluated include leadership of change (QI1.3); learning, teaching and assessment (QI2.3); raising attainment and achievement (QI3.2); and ensuring wellbeing, equality and inclusion (QI3.1). In addition, the school or centre chooses a further quality indicator for evaluation, but the evaluation is not published. Parts of other quality indicators are commented on, such as curriculum and involvement of parents. One of the main changes is the reintroduction of the evaluation of leadership. It is clear that effective leadership is fundamental to how well children and young people progress in a school and therefore unsurprising that it has been reintroduced after being dropped in 2008.

In addition to a new set of quality indicators, the report to parents/carers was also changed. It is now set out as a very brief list of strengths and areas for improvement. From the start of the millennium, the report has gradually become briefer and more focused. The early reports were lengthy documents written in what many thought was formulaic and coded language which could only be understood by professionals. A briefer report was introduced in 2008 followed soon after by a letter to parents. The letter has now been replaced by a list of strengths and areas for improvement. A document known as the summarised inspection findings (SIF) is also published. The SIF is similar to the previous Record of Inspection Findings and is now being published rather than sent only to the headteacher, local authority and chair of the Parent Council. This move is more likely to make available the key messages emerging from inspections to anyone who has an interest in the outcome.

The full inspection model is broadly similar to the previous inspection model. Schools are given roughly two weeks' notice and the inspection begins with professional dialogue around the school's self-evaluation. The inspection team engage in lesson observations, analysis of data and documents and professional dialogue with staff, learners, parents/carers and partners who work with the school. Other changes to inspection models include changing the notice period to two days, short inspection, localised thematic inspection and a neighbourhood model of inspection. The thinking behind these changes can be found in Education Scotland's (2016) discussion paper on approaches to inspection. The paper asks some extremely relevant questions about inspection, but does not offer the answers. The different models of inspection, in some ways, provide the response. The questions include: to what extent does inspection encourage a 3–18 approach to curriculum planning? Inspections take place mainly in individual sectors rather than evaluating a cluster. The impact of poor practice in early literacy in an early years centre, for example, will have an impact on a primary school. In the same way, poor teaching of science in a primary will impact negatively on the secondary school.

A further question the paper explores relates to the added value of local education authorities. The inspection of local education authorities stopped partly in response to the Crerar Review (Crerar, 2007) and replaced it with a validated self-evaluation model. The weakness in validated self-evaluation is that there is no national benchmark and it is not possible to compare local education authorities using a consistent set of quality indicators. In addition to local education authorities, however, the paper also asks the very pertinent question of how it is possible to evaluate the extent to which the education system as a whole is improving across Scotland. Unlike England, Scotland has not been data rich during the years of 'broad general education' and only has consistent data relating to SQA examinations which can be used to make comparisons between schools and between local authorities. In addition, the reduction in the number of inspections at establishment level and at local authority level make it difficult for policymakers to evaluate the overall health of the system.

All of these questions need to be constantly balanced against the imperative to reduce the workload burden of inspection and scrutiny in general. The Care Inspectorate's approach to the joint inspection of services for children and young people continues to have an excessively large footprint and is extremely demanding of staff time, before and during the inspection. Overall, however, inspection works well and is less burdensome where self-evaluation is taken seriously and is well embedded in practice. Equally, where self-evaluation is for improvement rather than for inspection, it is more likely to result in improved outcomes for children and young people. The new models of inspection are aimed at addressing some of these questions and will include, as mentioned, thematic and neighbourhood inspections. The extent to which inspection actually leads to improvement, however, is a more fundamental question that is worth exploring.

## THE LINK BETWEEN INSPECTION AND IMPROVEMENT

The research evidence that school inspections lead to improvements is mixed. A significant amount of work focused on the impact of inspectorates across Europe has been led by Dr M. C. M. Ehren and published on the school inspections website (www.schoolinspections.eu). Ehren takes the view that school inspections are a key feature of school improvement but also have unintended consequences such as increased bureaucracy. The intended effects of inspections are broadly to set expectations; promote self-evaluation and as a consequence have a greater capacity for improvement; and finally, as a result of better quality education, arising partly from inspection, children and young people benefit from higher achievements. Klerks (2012) took the view that there is no clear evidence that school inspections automatically lead to the improvement of educational quality. Instead, 'research shows that in practice there is a complex interaction between different characteristics of school inspections and the inspector on the one hand and the school with its pupils, teachers and management on the other hand' (ibid., p. 2). The small number of schools which experience repeated follow-through inspections supports the view that inspection of itself does not automatically lead to improvement.

Inspection is a means of managing dispersed public services, where in effect, 'the threat/promise of inspections involves the authority of the state becoming temporarily present in the space of relative autonomy' (Clarke and Ozga, 2011, p. 5). What distinguishes inspection as a mode of governing are three key features: the first is that it involves direct observation; the second is that it is a form of qualitative evaluation involving the exercise of professional judgement rather than simply looking at statistics, 'judgement is at the core of the activity and thus raises questions about the articulation of knowledge and power' (ibid., p. 4); the third is that it is embodied evaluation, that is, the inspectors are present in person to carry out the evaluation. It is not difficult to conclude from these three key features why inspection exists in a contested space where the judgements and the evaluations of the inspector may be at odds with those of the professional being evaluated. The strength of the inspectors' judgement tends to lie in their ability to benchmark nationally rather than making a comparison with local schools.

At times, inspection is a contested space and the inspectorate works hard to ensure consistency and transparency. The emphasis on professional dialogue is central to the current approach to inspection. However, no amount of professional dialogue is likely to redress the power relationship between a school and an inspection team, given the high stakes nature of the inspection process (Clarke and Ozga, 2011). The extent to which self-evaluation is not robust and well embedded in a school is the extent to which there is likely to be tension or challenge in the outcome of an inspection. In their own analysis of trends in inspection findings, Education Scotland concluded that self-evaluation needs to improve and also needs to impact on the quality of learning and teaching, and on learners' achievements.

Education Scotland is responsible for accountability in the system but also for improvement. Godfrey et al. (2015) conclude in their evaluation of school inspections that accountability is in tension with improvement and more thought and effort is needed to translate inspection outcomes into improvements. Spicer et al. (2014) outline how accountability systems lead to organisational and system level outcomes. Principally, as mentioned already, their view is that it is by setting expectations and institutionalising norms. HGIOS4 sets out clearly in its features of highly effective practice what the expectations are in a particular aspect of the school's operation. Then, by providing feedback and consequences, systems of accountability build the capacity of educators and of local stakeholders. Godfrey et al. (2015) found in their review of the literature that the Scottish approach to inspection is the one which researchers find is most aligned with a learning approach as opposed to an inquisitional or audit focus. It is thought to be a system where self-evaluation and inspection complement each other, with the same language being used in both.

Inspection and the inspectorate, however, need to be about more than the inspection of individual establishments. In the same literature review, Godfrey et al. point to the work of Ozga and Lawn (2014) who examine the system-steering role of inspectorates and state that 'Inspectorates have a unique role in combining data and expert judgement into use by policy makers. As well as developing … knowledge about improvement, inspectorates hold governments to account, staying independent from them, evaluating their policies' (Godfrey et al., 2015, p. 9). The technical question of whether inspection leads to improvement is one that merits further empirical research in the Scottish context. Much of the research available relates to the Office for Standards in Education (Ofsted) and the Dutch inspectorate. However, the question of holding governments to account mentioned by Ozga and Lawn also merits further discussion and is the final aspect of the inspectorate to be examined in this chapter.

## POLITICS AND THE INSPECTORATE

From the beginning of Education Scotland, one of the challenges has been to ensure that the same people were not determining policy and then inspecting that policy. It has not been particularly clear how the distinction has been maintained. The issue came to the surface once again at an evidence session of the Education and Skills Committee of the Scottish Parliament on 30 November 2016, when the chief executive, chief operating officer and strategic director at that time were giving evidence during a two-hour session. The Conservative MSP Liz Smith took the senior team from Education Scotland to task on the issue of acting as both 'judge and jury', stating: 'Do you accept that in doing the job of delivery, with the responsibility you just outlined, and in also doing the inspectorate job, you are acting as judge and jury?' (Scottish Parliament, 2016).

The chief executive may have had a sense of déjà vu with the experience of 2000 repeating itself. However, the choice to form a single organisation was not a decision made by either LTS or HMIE, but a decision made by the Cabinet Secretary.

Another line of questioning at the same committee highlighted a related area of vulnerability in the current arrangements and that is 'political compliance'. Evidence submitted to the committee by the Educational Institute of Scotland (EIS), the main teaching union, stated that Education Scotland was failing to hold minsters to account, a view reported again in The Herald which stated:

> The union also attacked the politicisation of inspection and review body Education Scotland which is supposed to be independent and impartial from government. It said: 'Critical challenge to government policy would seem to be an obvious role for the main pedagogic body within Scottish education but it is not one the EIS sees as a strength of Education Scotland'. (The Herald, 6 January 2017, p. 2)

The committee of 30 November 2016 pursued the same issue from various perspectives. The senior team were asked about their role on the Curriculum for Excellence Management

Board and Johan Lamont MSP (Labour) challenged the senior team to 'give examples of where Government policy has changed as a consequence of your realising that something is not working on the ground and is in fact detrimental?'

Tavish Scott MSP (Liberal Democrat) tackled the chief executive on advice which had been sent to schools with title of chief inspector on the front page:

> the letter that you issued to schools about assessments was issued under your title of chief inspector, which means that they will treat it as a statement of absolute writ they had better follow or else. There is a clear conflict.

The letter being referred to did indeed have the title Chief Inspector of Education on the front page which was very likely a tactical error by Education Scotland. The title no longer appears on Education Scotland's organisational charts. The post occupied previously by the head of HMIE was senior chief inspector of education and a number of chief inspectors reported directly to the senior chief. The current post holder is titled chief executive of education Scotland and his current reporting team are strategic directors. This may appear to be a trivial matter, but it also may be an indicator of political influence. At the time Education Scotland was created, inspection appeared to be diminished along with the titles in use such as senior chief inspector, chief inspector and assistant chief inspector. The number of inspectors dropped significantly and the number of inspections dropped significantly. With the appointment of a new Cabinet Secretary, and a government who have asked to be judged on their success in improving educational outcomes, it appears that inspection has become more important. The governance review referred to at the start of this chapter reinforces the position of inspection within Education Scotland. The document states explicitly that 'Education Scotland will have a strengthened inspection and improvement function' (p. 8). The Scottish Government's Attainment Challenge, aimed at closing the poverty-related attainment gap, will amount to around £750 million over the lifetime of the Parliament. It is clear that inspection will form a central part of the Scottish Government's evidence gathering on the question of whether the money is, first of all being used wisely by schools and local authorities, and second whether or not it is making any difference.

In a United Kingdom context, Power (1994) talked about the explosion of audit and stated that

> the reinvention of government is informed by two opposite tendencies. On the one hand there are centrifugal pressures for the decentralisation and devolution of services … On the other hand there are equally powerful pressures to retain control over functions that have been made autonomous. (Ibid., p. 2)

Power takes the view that inspection becomes important because it appears to reconcile these two forces, on the one hand devolving power and on the other maintaining authority, thus allowing government to control an increasingly devolved and decentralised context. Once again, the policy direction of the Scottish Government, made explicit in Education Governance: Next Steps, is to devolve more budget and control directly to schools, bypassing local authorities. It is clear from Power's analysis why the inspectorate appears to be moving to centre stage again: to maintain the tension between central control and autonomous functions. Ironically, reflecting on significant failures of audit at the time, almost fifteen years ahead of the financial crisis of 2008, Power states that 'where audit has failed, the common response has been to call for more of it'. In a context where nationally we have failed to address the poverty-related attainment gap, where Programme for International Student Assessment (PISA) results show Scotland regressing to average from above average, the solution appears to be to increase the role of the inspectorate. Education Scotland is going into another period of change with a refreshed senior management team and further restructuring to incorporate the functions of the General Teaching Council for Scotland and the Scottish College for Educational Leadership. There will, no doubt, be fresh challenges relating to the question of having responsibility for policy and inspection. The main threat to Education Scotland's integrity, and by extension the integrity of the inspectorate, however does not come from this dual responsibility or restructuring. The main threat comes from trying to maintain the balance between following ministerial instructions and using professional knowledge and experience to influence government and avoid harming the educational chances of Scotland's children and young people.

Inspection has a role, not least because of the quality of some of the men and women who serve as inspectors. However, it needs to be much more clearly independent of government and ensure it has a robust evidence base. That evidence base will include evidence from inspections but also needs to include empirical evidence of improvement to learning, teaching and attainment of learners as a result of inspection.

## REFERENCES

Clarke, J. and Ozga, J. (2011) Governing by Inspection? Comparing School Inspection in Scotland and England. Paper for Social Policy Association Conference, University of Lincoln, July 2011. Online at www.education.ox.ac.uk/wordpress/wp-content/uploads/2013/10/Governing-by-Inspection-SPA-2011.pdf

Crerar, L. (2007) Report of the Independent Review of Regulatory, Audit, Inspection and Complaints Handling of Public Services in Scotland. Online at www.gov.scot/Resource/Doc/198627/0053093.pdf

Education Scotland (2013) Transforming Lives through Learning. A Guide to Our Corporate Plan 2013–2016. Online at https://www.education.gov.scot/Documents/ES-corporate-plan-guide.pdf

Education Scotland (2016) Discussions on Future Approaches to Inspection. Online at https://education.gov.scot/what-we-do/inspection-and-review/about-inspections-and-reviews/new-approaches-to-inspection/Discussions%20on%20future%20approaches%20to%20inspection

Godfrey, D., Ehren, M. C. M. and Nelson, R. (2015) Literature Review: Impact of Inspections on the Improvement of Schools and of Networks of Schools. Online at www.schoolinspections.eu/literature-review-impact-of-inspections-on-the-improvement-of-schools-and-of-networks-of-schools/

Klerks, M. (2012) The Effect of School Inspections: A Systematic Review. Paper present at the ORD, Wageningen, The Netherlands. Online at http://schoolinspections.eu/impact/wp-content/uploads/downloads/2013/12/ORD-paper-2012-Review-Effect-School-Inspections-MKLERKS.pdf

Ozga, J. and Lawn, M. (2014) Frameworks of regulation: evidence, knowledge and judgement in inspection. Sisyphus Journal of Education, 2 (1), 7–14.

Power, M. (1994) The Audit Explosion, DEMOS. Online at www.demos.co.uk/files/theaudit explosion.pdf

Scottish Government (2017) Education Governance: Next Steps. Online at www.gov.scot/Resource/0052/00521038.pdf

Scottish Parliament (2016) Official Report: Education and Skills Committee, 30 November. Online at www.parliament.scot/parliamentarybusiness/report.aspx?r=10664&mode=pdf

Spicer, D.E., Ehren, M., Khatwa, M. and Bangpan, M. (2014) Under What Conditions Do Inspection, Monitoring and Assessment Improve System Efficiency, Service Delivery and Learning Outcomes for the Poorest and Most Marginalised? EPPI-Centre. Institute of Education, University of London. Online at https://eppi.ioe.ac.uk/cms/Portals/0/PDF%20reviews%20 and%20summaries/System%20efficiency%202014%20Spicer%20protocol.pdf?ver=2014-07-24-154813-763

# 20

# The Parent Dimension in Education

*Eileen Prior*

If the most significant influences on the learning of children are their home circumstances and the engagement of families in that learning, the challenging questions for educationalists have to be: How do we understand, recognise, support and encourage families in the joint enterprise that is the education of children? In a system which has as its focus the education professional, where and how does the parent and wider family fit? When family engagement in children's education is one of the most significant mechanisms to improve outcomes for young people, what has to change? This chapter examines policy and practice around family engagement, looks at what structures are currently in place in Scotland, why parental engagement is recognised as being so important, the many different forms it takes and gives a perspective on how we are doing in Scotland. It also considers what may lie ahead.

## WHERE ARE WE NOW?

It is useful to reflect on the current position in Scotland. In terms of parental representation, the main driver is the Scottish Schools (Parental Involvement) Act 2006. The legislation created the possibility of a parent council (PC) in every school in the country as a means of involving the parents of all children at a school (termed the parent forum) in the life of the establishment. Under the 2006 Act, the parent forum (i.e. all parents and carers with children at the school) was given the right to have a PC, a right which is currently exercised in the majority of schools. In essence, the act established the PC as independent of both school and local authority, with the freedom and flexibility to work in whatever way it sees fit. The guidance produced by government places an emphasis on the PC as a representative body for the parent forum, encouraging partnership with the school and local authority to promote parental involvement and pursue areas of interest to parents.

Alongside PCs, schools in Scotland may also have a Parent Teacher Association (PTA) or similar body. PTAs have a long history in our schools going back to the 1920s, primarily as bodies which bring together staff and parents, organise fundraising and social events and generally build a community within a school. PTAs, like PCs, are independent of school and local authority and are constituted voluntary bodies.

Parent representation is not the whole picture, however. With increasing understanding of the importance of parental engagement in learning, there are an increasing number of programmes and projects to encourage and support this priority, for example Save the

Children's Families and Schools Together (FAST) and Partnership Schools Scotland. In addition to the parental involvement legislation, the important role of parents and families in education is also reflected elsewhere in policy and practice.

## THE NATIONAL PARENT BODIES

The longest-standing national parent body is Connect (formerly the Scottish Parent Teacher Council or SPTC), a charity and company limited by guarantee, which was formed in 1948 (see SPTC, 1998) and has been successful in sustaining its original purpose of promoting partnerships between schools and parents, and serving its member parent groups. A board of trustees drawn largely from its parent membership as well as nominated teachers leads the charity, funded through the membership of parent groups. Connect also provides professional updates to education professionals, and is active in the development of good practice in family engagement, through its Partnership Schools Scotland programme, the latter founded on the work of Dr Joyce Epstein's National Network of Partnership Schools at Johns Hopkins University, Baltimore.

The last part of the parental involvement jigsaw is a body which was also part of the Parental Involvement legislation of 2006. Within the Act, the government committed to develop a national parents' body that would take forward the 'parents as educators' agenda (more of this later). The result was the National Parent Forum Scotland (NPFS), which was formed by government in 2009 and is funded through government grant. The forum is intended to comprise one parent volunteer from each local authority area, nominated or selected by parent councils or local authority. The body's purpose is to provide parent councils – in fact all parents – with an opportunity to discuss and raise educational issues at a national level. Members of NPFS participate in many significant decision- and policy-making bodies in Scottish education, as well as producing a wide range of parent-friendly publications on the curriculum, qualifications and other elements of government policy and practice. The advent of the NPFS represented a sea change in government's approach to engagement with parents: parents have the opportunity to be at the policymaking table, instead of reacting to what flows from it.

## WHY PARENTAL INVOLVEMENT?

Historically, there has been substantial resistance in some quarters to any parental involvement which went beyond that of willing supporter at home. This resistance reflected the widely held view that parents will focus only on their own children and that only the sharp-elbowed middle classes are moved to be active, in order to promote their own agenda. In addition – and in common with other professionals – many in education believe they know what is best for a child, a position which inevitably leads to conflict with some parents. However, we have moved from a point where parents were given a duty to ensure their child was educated (the 1872 Education Act) to one where a child's attendance isn't enough – legislation and policy have followed the evidence, and there is a great deal of focus now on the necessity to engage parents both in the school community and in the process of learning.

Research began to emerge in the last quarter of the twentieth century which spoke of the influence of parental involvement in the attainment of young people. The 1980 Education Act – which created the precursor to PCs and school boards – was the first policy acknowledgement of that growing realisation: children whose parents are actively involved in their education do better at school. It was becoming clear that children were being substantially disadvantaged in their schooling by factors including poverty and socio-economic standing, but that parental expectation and parental involvement also play very significant roles in educational outcomes. Parenting, and engagement of parents, therefore began to appear on policy documents as a way of addressing the issue of young people who were, at best, not achieving their potential, and, at worst, leaving school with no qualifications and no prospect of gainful employment or training. Ultimately, the emerging policy imperative around parental involvement is about impacting on outcomes – both educational and social – and reflects a growing understanding of the interrelationship and interdependency of home and school when it comes to young people's learning. Despite this growing realisation, however, there has been relatively little research in the UK into the area of parental involvement: why does it make a difference, and what exactly are the strategies that work best?

One of the most significant figures has been Professor Charles Desforges (see Desforges and Abouchaar, 2003), whose analysis of the research up to that date led to the conclusion that there are two quite distinct types of parental involvement: the spontaneous engagement of parents because they are motivated to do so, and the interventions by professionals designed specifically to engage parents in their child's education or school. While the first category is well researched (though generally in the United States) the second is backed primarily by anecdotal evidence. What Desforges demonstrated, however, is that spontaneous parental involvement is not about to make radical changes to outcomes for the most disadvantaged youngsters any time soon. He showed that parents are more likely to be involved with their child's school where:

- They are middle to upper class.
- The mother has been successful in higher or further education.
- There is no deprivation, no significant ill health (particularly mental health) and both parents are together.
- The child is in his or her early years at school.
- The child is showing high levels of attainment.
- The child is skilled in mediating between home and school – in other words is playing a part in managing that relationship and expectations.
- The family is white and/or from a Western cultural background.

Should we be surprised by any of this? The parents who are likely to become engaged spontaneously with their child's education are also likely to become engaged with sporting, cultural and other interests because they often have the capacity, confidence, wherewithal and drive to do so. This contrasts sharply with those families who face significant barriers through poverty, health or social issues; where the parents' own experience of school may not have been good or they themselves have learning difficulties; or where there simply is not the capacity to take on the added role as partner educator. Increased globalisation also means that many schools in Scotland have a significant number of cultures and languages represented within the school community: while often academic aspirations are high for the children, in some cases the realities of poverty, language and different cultural backgrounds can lead to significant barriers. In short, where parents and families do not come from the same background or have the same advantages or education as the professionals in school, the barriers to participation are significant and require careful management if they are to be addressed.

One of the challenges is that although parental engagement with education is generally associated with better outcomes for young people, there continues to be significant debate about what is meant by engagement and how the dynamics of that leads to better outcomes (see Hills and Stewart, 2005; Feinstein et al., 2006). Parents have always been – and will always be – advocates for their own children. For most young people, the requirement to have parents as advocates diminishes as they grow and determine their own direction. However, it is worth highlighting the groups of young people who do not fit this general rule: young people with disabilities who continue to need extensive parental engagement with the education system to ensure their needs are met; and young people who are in care, who rarely have an adult who is passionately involved with their upbringing, and so have no one in the role of advocate in their education. These two groups of young people share something with the Not in Education, Employment or Training (NEET) group: positive educational outcomes and positive destinations are in short supply.

Desforges and Abouchaar (2003) cite 'at home good parenting' as having a significant positive effect on children's achievement:

> even after all other factors shaping attainment have been taken out of the equation. In the primary age range the impact caused by different levels of parental involvement is much bigger than differences associated with variation in the quality of schools. The scale of the impact is evident across all social classes and all ethnic groups. (p. 4)

If we are to accept this principle of 'at-home good parenting' as being of central importance to attainment at school, we have to be mindful that children from many different backgrounds benefit from a good home, and conversely recognise that poor parenting exists in both affluent and deprived homes.

Mongon and Chapman (2012) argue that nearly all parents have positive general aspirations for their children. However, Cuthbert and Hatch (2008, p. 3) state that 'it has been an act of faith for many school and children's service leaders to believe that *a closer connection with families* would lead to better outcomes for young people'. The evidence is more tenuous. *'Spontaneous' parental involvement* (in crude terms, a 'good home') is associated with positive outcomes. In contrast, the evidence from *'enhanced' parental involvement* (in crude terms, programmes to involve parents) is at best inconclusive, albeit showing high levels of appreciation from the adults involved (Desforges and Abouchaar, 2003). Desforges and Abouchaar conclude that this does not mean that parental involvement cannot be promoted: on the contrary, they write: 'if the best of what is known about parental engagement is applied then real progress is possible'. The introduction of parent forums and PCs in Scotland can therefore be seen as a response to the evidence outlined by Desforges and Abouchaar: these are deliberate strategies to engage all parents at a school based on that act of faith identified by Cuthbert and Hatch. It is indeed a leap of faith, placing on parents an expectation that they step beyond their traditional role as advocates for their own children, and take on a role of involvement with their child's school and, potentially, the country's educational policy.

It is worth noting that the mode of parental involvement we are now pursuing in Scotland is in marked contrast to the previous system of school boards, which gave parents a quasi-management role within schools – attracting, as a result, those parents who were able and willing to take on the workload and challenges of such a role. It was the eventual realisation that school boards were ineffective in engaging a wide range of parents – and therefore (possibly) impacting on educational outcomes – that led to their demise. There is a raft of research which examines the interplay between school and family, and the impact such interplay has on outcomes for young people.

## CLOSING THE ATTAINMENT GAP IN SCOTTISH EDUCATION

The report by this title, written by Edward Sosu and Sue Ellis and published by the Joseph Rowntree Foundation in 2014, contains key reflections around the question of parental involvement. These include:

- 'Effective parental involvement programmes that focus on helping parents to use appropriate strategies to support their children's learning at home rather than simply seeking to raise aspirations for their children's education' are proven to have a positive impact on reducing the attainment gap.
- While certain studies suggest that only parental involvement will close the attainment gap, there is a lack of clarity on what parental involvement actually is. Other research suggests it is not the quantity of parental involvement that has the most impact, rather the quality.
- Most effective is when parents use appropriate strategies to help their children learn at home. Parents from more deprived areas may have the same amount of time to help their children but their efforts are less effective. Strategies that are very effective include: providing a good space for homework, interesting books and effective strategies for tutoring their children.
- Approaches for parental involvement are strengthened when parents work with a qualified professional.
- Where programmes are highly structured, and provide parents with suitable materials and high levels of support, retention rates are high. Schools need to work with parents to ensure they feel supported in the programme.
- Studies show that parental aspirations have very little to do with closing the attainment gap – what matters is having the technical and social know-how to work effectively with their children.

(See also Chapter 12 in this book.)

Dr Joyce Epstein's School–Family–Community Partnership Model, proposed in the late 1980s, has become influential in parent engagement research (see Figure 20.1).

The model depicts the partnership of schools, families and communities as overlapping spheres. Each has a stake and influence in the education of a child. The overlap of the spheres conveys that the interests and influences of the stakeholders in a child's education are mutual. Two factors influence the degree of overlap: time and experiences. Time in schools, the age of the child, and the experiences of the child in the family and in school can influence the degree to which schools, families and communities have mutual interests

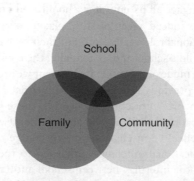

Figure 20.1   The Partnership Model (Epstein)

and influences on the child (Epstein, 2001; Epstein et al., 2002). The model illustrates the interpersonal relationships and patterns of influence that are most important in a child's education. According to this thinking, there are two types of interactions: those within organisations and those between organisations. Additionally, there are various levels of interactions. Standard, organisational interactions occur between families and schools. These include communication in the form of newsletters and reports about the school's activities and performance. Specific, individual interactions are those between parents and teachers. At the centre of this is the child, who interacts with schools and the family. The child is both changed by the interactions and produces change in others (Epstein, 2001; Epstein et al., 2002). The key concept that underlies both parts of the Partnership Model is that all stakeholders in a child's education have mutual interests and influences. The primary shared interest is a caring concern that the child be successful. Additionally, the model suggests that stakeholders' shared interests and influences can be promoted by the policies, actions, beliefs, attitudes and values of the stakeholders.

While this might seem like common sense, the model differs from earlier theories on school–family relationships. In particular, the Partnership Model revises previous concep-tualisations that viewed families and schools as existing in separate spheres, which entailed a view that they have separate responsibilities. It also revises conceptions of the school–family relationship as one that must be alternately sequential. In a sequential relationship, parents are expected to have more of a role than schools, and vice versa, in certain periods of a child's life.

While the Partnership Model acknowledges that schools and families often do have more or less influence at certain ages, it also suggests that the overlap between families and schools can be increased with concerted effort by one or more of the stakeholders (Epstein, 2001).

Another important aspect of overlapping spheres of influence is that schools and families share similar characteristics. Epstein uses the terms 'school-like families' and 'family-like schools' (Epstein, 2001) to explain the behaviours of families and schools that believe in each other's importance. In school-like families, parents encourage, support and develop their children's academic skills. They may assist with homework or introduce educational activities as part of their regular family activities. Similarly, they may use time in the same manner as the school or reward their children for accomplishments. These families teach their children to view school activities as part of the normal and natural rhythm of everyday life. Family-like schools, in a similar manner, take on the attitudes and characteristics of a caring family. Like families, they may individualise attention to meet the unique needs of each child. This could mean changing the standards or rules based on individual circum-stances. It can also mean striving to create more open and reciprocal relationships between teachers and students.

The Partnership Model emphasises the shared attributes of schools and families. It also suggests that behaviours and attitudes of schools and families can increase the degree of overlap between schools and families, resulting in many benefits for students. Epstein's research and practice has led to the definition of six types of involvement to describe the various ways in which schools, families and communities engage when they focus on student learning. Each is equally valuable and relevant, and may be more or less appropriate at different points in the school career of a young person:

- parenting;
- communicating;

- volunteering;
- learning at home;
- decision making;
- collaborating with the community.

## HOW IS PARENTAL INVOLVEMENT WORKING IN SCOTLAND?

If PCs and PTAs are now the primary formal mechanisms for parental involvement, are they living up to expectations and delivering greater parental involvement with other parts of the schooling endeavour and, perhaps, leading to greater parental engagement with the education of their children?

PCs have now been operational since 2007. Designed with a light touch so that each parent body had the flexibility to address the issues concerning them and their school, the outcome has been predictably variable. The non-prescriptive approach adopted in the legislation, while laudable in its objective of enabling flexibility, has left the door open to confusion as to the rights and responsibilities of PCs among parents themselves, school management and local authorities – and a tendency to opt for a tick-box or simplistic approach, where parental involvement with the school (perhaps seen as presence and involvement in PC or PTA) and parental engagement with learning remain confused and ill defined. The patchwork, and sometimes haphazard, nature of implementation can of course, in part, be put down to the nature of the parent body: parents (and therefore the PC) are a fluid group of individuals who come and go with little or no warning as their children change school and families move house, and as other roles and responsibilities become more pressing. Some PCs therefore struggle to sustain themselves and often rely on one or two willing individuals. In 2016 the National Parent Forum of Scotland commenced a review of the Parental Involvement legislation.

A further factor influencing their effectiveness has been the level of support enjoyed by PCs. While each local authority is charged with providing support to help the parent groups function, in reality this has been wildly different across the country. Parent officers, who were charged with helping to establish and sustain PCs, have often found their role has changed over the years, so that they are now responsible for many other areas of work – for example home schooling, school refusers, professional update and so on – and parental involvement is now a very small part of their role. In truth – as indicated earlier – the legacy of suspicion and lack of understanding of parents' roles and capacities continues to hold back parental involvement in our schools. Engaging with parents as partners in the education of children is variable and sometimes problematic. Information flow is often seen as a one-way process – towards parents – with a marked reluctance to hear, and act upon, those views from parents which come back up the chain. As for evidence of gains being made in pupil attainment as a result of greater parental involvement, there remains little evidence, though specific programmes which seek to engage families in learning (such as FAST and Partnership Schools Scotland) are showing promise. However, in the recently published study by Gorard et al. (2012), looking at a number of factors concerned with the impact of attitudes and aspirations on educational attainment and participation, the authors conclude that 'There is a reasonable case that parental involvement is a causal influence for their child's school-readiness and subsequent attainment' (p. 73).

## FOR THE FUTURE

Change is in the air in Scottish education. The introduction and implementation of Curriculum for Excellence, and its associated qualifications, continues to cause stresses and strains in the system. However, the greatest stress is that we continue to see a significant gap in attainment between young people from the most and least advantaged homes: most disturbingly perhaps is the fact that *some* schools demonstrate significant success in raising attainment for disadvantaged pupils, but we are unable to replicate that impact across the system. The raft of policy initiatives to address this is extensive and, perhaps most significant for the matter of parental involvement, increasingly recognises the important role of families. The National Improvement Framework, Helping to Improve our School, the review of the Parental Involvement legislation and the governance review all have a strong focus on involving and engaging families. Scotland has an opportunity to move away from the binary view of parental involvement (involved = visible; disinterested = not visible) to one which is a great deal more sophisticated, reflects the evidence and uses that evidence to harness the potential of family and community to help address the shameful reality of our attainment gap. Change seems inevitable in our system – the hope is that all our young people will benefit from changes in practice and values in parental engagement.

## REFERENCES

Cuthbert, C. and Hatch, R. (2008) 'Aspiration and attainment amongst young people in deprived communities: analysis and discussion paper'. London: DCSF, Cabinet Office Social Exclusion Task Force.

Desforges, C. and Abouchaar, A. (2003) 'The impact of parental involvement, parental support and family education on pupil achievement and adjustment: a literature review.' Research Report No 433. London: DfES.

Epstein, J. L. (2001) *School, Family, and Community Partnerships: Preparing Educators and Improving Schools*. Boulder, CO: Westview.

Epstein, J. L. and Sheldon, S. B. (2002) 'Present and accounted for: improving student attendance through family and community involvement', *Journal of Educational Research*, 95 (5), 308–18.

Epstein, J. L., Sanders, M. G., Simon, B. S., Salinas, K. C., Jansorn, N. R. and Van Voorhis, F. (2002) *School, Family and Community Partnerships: Your Handbook for Action*, second edition. Online at https://www.gpo.gov/fdsys/pkg/ERIC-ED467082/pdf/ERIC-ED467082.pdf

Feinstein, L., Sabates, R., Anderson, T. M., Sorhaindo, A. and Hammond, C. (2006) 'What are the effects of education on health?' OECD Copenhagen Symposium on Measuring the Effects of Education on Health and Civic Engagement. Online at www.oecd.org/dataoecd/15/18/37425753.pdf

Gorard, S., See, B. H. and Davies, P. (2012) *The Impact of Attitudes and Aspirations on Educational Attainment and Participation*. York: Joseph Rowntree Foundation. Online at https://www.jrf.org.uk/report/impact-attitudes-and-aspirations-educational-attainment-and-participation

Hills, J. and Stewart, K. (eds) (2005) *A More Equal Society? New Labour, Poverty, Inequality and Exclusion*. Bristol: Policy Press.

Mongon, D. and Chapman, C. (2012) *High-leverage Leadership: Improving Outcomes in Educational Settings*. London: Routledge.

Sosu, E. and Ellis, S. (2014) *Closing the Attainment Gap in Scottish Education*. York: Joseph Rowntree Foundation. Online at https://www.jrf.org.uk/sites/default/files/jrf/migrated/files/education-attainment-scotland-full.pdf

SPTC (1998) *50th Anniversary of the Scottish Parent Teacher Council 1948–1998*. Edinburgh: Scottish Parent Teacher Council.

# IV

# MANAGEMENT, ORGANISATION AND LEARNING IN SCHOOLS

# 21

# Early Education and Childcare

*Christine Stephen*

Early education and childcare signifies the out-of-home provision for children up to school starting age. This provision may in a group setting or in the home of a childminder. Scotland has one school entry point in August and children range from 4 years 6 months to 5 years 6 months on entry to school. This chapter is written from the perspective of a researcher, a role that confers particular benefits when tasked with reviewing an arca of educational provision. As a researcher I have had the opportunity to explore, observe and discuss practice with the adults and children in early education settings in Scotland for over twenty years. Early education and childcare in Scotland is characterised by diversity of provision, plurality in policies and contextualised practices. This chapter gives an account of contemporary policies and practices, acknowledging relevant historical antecedents and articulating implicit discourses. It considers key features of curriculum and pedagogy and reviews areas of strength and challenge.

## THE DEVELOPMENT OF EARLY EDUCATION IN SCOTLAND

If up-take of provision is any indicator of parental satisfaction then early education in Scotland has been a success story so far. Whether labelled as preschool education, early years education or nursery education, the provision made available to children before they begin school has become a taken-for-granted feature of their educational careers over the twenty years since 1997 when every child in Scotland became entitled to a part-day, government-funded place in an early education setting for the year before they began primary school. Prior to 1997 there had been some limited provision for young children in local authority settings (often restricted to free places for children considered to be at risk), in private sector establishments, and in playgroups typically founded by local action and managed by volunteering parents, most usually mothers. The advent of a 'free' place for every child brought profound changes to the early education landscape in Scotland. Government-funded places were made available in local authority settings, either nursery classes attached to a primary school or free-standing nursery schools, in voluntary sector settings and with private providers. Voluntary and private providers had to be nominated partners with their local authority to offer these places, and all settings, regardless of sector, were subject to an evolving system of inspection and regulation, including requirements about the qualifications of staff.

The initial entitlement to a free (government-funded) place for one year was quickly extended to two years before beginning school (1999) so that 3 to 5 year olds were offered a part-time place, typically 2.5 hours during the morning or afternoon on five days per week during the school term. By 2003, 83 per cent of 3 year olds and 99 per cent of 4 year olds were taking up their entitlement to a part-time place in an early education setting. In 2016, 99 per cent of 3 and 4 year olds were registered as attending a local authority early education or partner provider setting for their government-funded place (www.gov.scot/Publications/2016/09/8729/3). Early education settings are now predominantly located in permanent premises, increasingly designed or renovated specifically for young children. In some, though few, circumstances childminders have been accepted as partner providers offering government-funded part-time early learning and childcare places. More typically, children spend time with a childminder before or after their government-funded place with a local authority provider. Increasingly, where staffing and premises permit, local authority settings, like private providers, are offering places beyond the 'free' hours.

There has been very little interest in Scotland in the provision of the kind of 'nature' or 'outdoor' nurseries found in some Scandinavian countries but attention to the ways in which time spent outdoors can contribute to learning is growing. Early education is also available in Scotland through the medium of Gaelic in voluntary sector playgroups and local authority settings which can offer the same entitlement to government-funded provision as English medium settings and are subject to the same curricular expectations. There are particular pedagogic challenges when offering children early education in a language which they have little access to outside the educational setting (only a minority have access to Gaelic at home) but this provision has grown in popularity (Stephen et al., 2016).

In 2014 the annual entitlement was increased from 475 to 600 hours per year for each 3 and 4 year old and some 2 year olds considered to be vulnerable because of family circumstances. But increasing the length of time which children were able to spend in an educational setting was not the only change concerning policymakers at that time. In the Children and Young People (Scotland) Act 2014 they sought to tackle the ongoing differentiation between 'education' and 'childcare' and address the recognition that children younger than 3 would also benefit from time in an early years setting. The expectations about practice incorporated in the act and the accompanying statutory guidance (e.g. about the importance of relationships and nurture) were intended to apply to all aspects of a child's experience in an out-of-home setting, making it explicit that (a) education and care are not separate but 'indivisible and seamless', and (b) that learning is continuous and starts from birth (Scottish Government, 2014). Provision for children before they began school was relabelled as early learning and childcare.

A further policy initiative commenced in 2016 aimed at extending the annual hours for a government-funded place from 600 to 1,140 per year by 2020. Driven by a range of policy goals this expansion recognises that early education and childcare equips children well for later success in school and contributes longer term to the country's economic capacity. In addition, it is expected that having access to a government-funded place for 1,140 hours per year will reduce the cost to parents of education and care while they work and therefore contribute to increasing levels of economic activity. Furthermore, for children growing up in socially and economically disadvantaged households it is expected that investing in an expansion in the hours of early education and care provision will contribute to narrowing the attainment gap, a current political and policy imperative across the Scottish education system. This extension of provision will require almost twice as many practitioners as currently work in early education and childcare, and acquiring and equipping substantially more premises. In the preparation phase some alternative models of provision are being piloted and evaluated in an attempt to match what is offered to the needs and desires of all parents and children. At the time of writing this chapter we cannot know if the aims of this ambitious and resource intensive project will be achieved but it offers the prospect of another significant shift in the landscape of early education in Scotland.

## CURRICULUM, PEDAGOGY AND EVERYDAY PRACTICES

### National Policy and Guidance

Developing guidance on curriculum expectations, pedagogic approaches and everyday practices has been an iterative interaction between policy-driven necessities and articulating the values, understandings and principles that underpin the thinking of the providers, practitioners and advisors who are involved in the process. Formal guidance can then be seen as both an expression of the consensus on good practice and an influence on everyday experiences.

Earlier iterations of the early education curriculum were replaced in 2007 with the publication of guidance for the early level of the Curriculum for Excellence (CfE) (Scottish Executive, 2007). Extending from 3 to 6 years of age, the early level relates to the two years before children move to primary school and the first year of primary school. Whether the opportunities for continuity and progression offered by this span across early education settings and primary school have been fully exploited is a matter of debate but it is important here to note that, with the development of a national curriculum from 3 to 18, early education achieved recognition as an integral part of the education system. Although education before the starting age for school continues to be of non-statutory status and parents are able to take up or decline a place as they choose, the census figures shown above demonstrate that spending time in an early educational setting is now part of the experience of almost all children in Scotland.

With incorporation into the national curriculum came expectations that early education would work towards achieving the four headline goals for educational progress in Scotland under CfE –becoming successful learners, confident individuals, responsible citizens and effective contributors. These goals were readily aligned with existing values and purposes in the early education field, even if these had previously been largely implicit. Pedagogy too received more explicit attention with the championing of what is described as 'active learning'. This approach was familiar to and welcomed by early education practitioners and providers who were already engaged in providing opportunities for learning through 'spontaneous play', 'planned, purposeful play', 'investigating and exploring' and 'events and life experiences'. However, the expectation of 'focused learning and teaching' and 'sensitive intervention to support or extend learning' was more challenging for some early years practitioners. The early level of CfE includes, as it does for each level, a series of expectations and outcomes over eight curriculum areas for children's learning. The curriculum designers argued that these were both appropriate for an active learning pedagogy and supportive of a spiral conception of learning in which skills and knowledge are revisited and built on over time to enhance breadth, depth and progression.

Scotland has not developed a curriculum for children younger than 3 years old experiencing early learning and childcare, but guidance set out in *Pre-Birth to Three*, originally published in 2010, continues to shape understandings and practices. (The most recent documentation is given in the *Professional Learning Framework – Autumn 2017* from Early

Years Scotland, 2017). *Pre-birth to Three* aimed to shape the ways in which practitioners thought about the needs of the children for whom they were responsible and about their own role. It was not an expression of a pedagogic approach or a set of expectations and outcomes but articulated four principles to guide practitioners' actions and interactions. These principles were concerned with ensuring the rights of the child, nurturing relationships, responsive care and mutual respect. The influence of this focus on relationships and listening to and respecting children can be seen to be continued in the aims and pedagogic approach found in CfE and the national indicators of wellbeing developed to encompass the 'basic requirements' for any child to thrive (Scottish Government, 2008).

Following the developments set out in the Children and Young People Act (2014) with its emphasis on the blended nature of education, care and learning as a process that continues from birth, further practice guidance was compiled (Scottish Government, 2014). Scottish early education policy's enduring concern with child-centred practice, play and attending to and responding to the individual needs and desires of children feature strongly in this 2014 guidance, accompanied by aspects of practice that have emerged with greater recognition of the need to take account of the emotional conditions in which children thrive. This guidance prompts attention to the assets that children bring to any interaction, as well as the contribution of adults and the requirements of the United Nations Convention on the Rights of the Child for children to be respected, valued, listened to and have their needs addressed. It makes links with the values and principles underpinning CfE and *Pre-birth to Three* and is centrally concerned with what is needed to foster wellbeing, communication, inquiry, curiosity and creativity. Interestingly, it is the dispositional aspects of these areas which are given most attention, a circumstance which reflects a long-held understanding in the field of early education in Scotland that the prime focus should be on supporting children to become confident learners who are keen to explore, rather than on what is learned. Some justification for the guidance is given from research evidence, theory and policy positions, with particular attention paid to thinking about play and attachment. The significance of parental engagement in children's education is stressed, another enduring theme in early education in Scotland. Pedagogy is interpreted as being about the process of learning and the interactions and experiences that support this. Curriculum is seen as encompassing both the interests and curiosity that engage children and the experiences, knowledge and skills that practitioners seek to promote intentionally. The guidance is written around three developmental stages (baby, toddler and young child) and what is needed at each stage in terms of appropriate learning opportunities, interactions with adults, and the physical and material environment.

## Everyday Practice and Implicit Understandings

There is little evidence of everyday practices in Scottish early education settings being influenced by explicit theory about child development (particularly post-developmental thinking), learning or the purposes of educational provision. In the course of their initial professional education most practitioners will have been introduced to little beyond the work of Piaget and Vygotsky (Stephen, 2012). Piaget's thinking is evident in continuing notions of age and stage constraints and norms, the value placed on active or experiential learning and in the emphasis on providing a well-resourced environment. The influence of Vygotsky's theory on practitioners' understandings is typically found in ideas about learning being a social and constructive process. However, if there is little recourse to explicit theory to shape practice, there is a powerful and long-standing implicit consensus on appropriate practice among those who manage provision and those who work directly with children in the early education field in Scotland. This consensus is reflected in the everyday work of practitioners, national practice guidance, staff deployment decisions, the approach to planning and recording progress, and everyday routines and schedules.

Three features are central to this Scottish consensus on high-quality provision and practices. The first of these is a clear recognition of the importance of supportive or nurturing relationships between children and practitioners. Strengthened by the growing understanding of the rights of young children to be consulted and listened to, the second key feature of the consensus is usually referred to as 'child-centred practice', often characterised as 'following the children's interests'. This approach is made evident in the provision of an environment that offers opportunities for children to make decisions about the activities they undertake and the careful collection of observations of children and accounts of their conversations as they select and engage with playroom activities and resources. These records are used to shape practitioners' thinking about 'next steps' and 'extending choices' and to develop profiles of the young learners. The third key feature is a belief in play as the key medium through which children learn, a perspective also enshrined in each iteration of the national curriculum since 1997. This valorising of play as the way to learn retains its power despite debates elsewhere about the kinds of play that promote particular forms of learning and the alternative ways in which play is characterised and its relationship to learning is conceptualised (Brooker et al., 2014). Most children in Scotland experience a mix of what is known as free play and structured or adult-initiated play in their early learning setting, but there are, for example, questions about the cognitive challenge present in free play or whether activities structured or initiated by adults are perceived by children as play and can satisfy curiosity and promote learning in the same way as self-initiated activities. The label 'play' is applied to a range of diverse experiences such as physical or digital exploration, engaging in games with rules or in imaginative scenarios and acting out roles. Defining play remains elusive and bound by theoretical and philosophical positions and links between specific play activities and learning outcomes are more often asserted than evidenced.

The influence of the consensus on practice can be seen in the ways in which young children spend their time in Scottish early education settings and the activities which practitioners consider to be both normal and desirable. For the majority of the time children are engaged in activities and with resources that they have selected from the range prepared for them and made accessible to them by their practitioners. They may be engaged in an activity alone, with peers or be alongside others but not interacting with them. These activities range from painting at an easel, through construction with large and small blocks, pretend play in an area set up as a 'home' or other scenario (perhaps a hospital or shop), to climbing and bike riding or gardening outside. Children in many settings will also spend some time each day (perhaps ten to fifteen minutes) in a small group with one practitioner involved in activities designed to prompt exploration of concepts related to number, science or language and communication. In small or large groups they will listen to stories, sing, share news and explore feelings.

The playroom environments designed for young children have many common features across private, local authority and voluntary sector providers, for example the presence of a display of books, craft activities, small world resources, a pretend play area and appropriate dressing-up clothes, and some kind of construction equipment. However, the child-centred ethos of provision means that the range of options available in any one place on any one day will be distinct as practitioners aim to relate activities and resources to their observations of children's play and interests and their understanding about what is needed to support skill development and extend interests and emerging concepts. Additionally, the local context, for instance the nature of the premises, arrangements for mealtimes, and seasonal events will shape experiences in any one setting on any one day and individual children come to the setting with their own expectations and preferences. However, what is shared is the focus on presenting a range of play opportunities, designed to reflect children's interests and facilitate aspects of learning, in a nurturing environment that supports children's capacity to make choices and form relationships.

## REFLECTIONS ON EARLY LEARNING AND CHILDCARE IN SCOTLAND: OPPORTUNITIES AND CHALLENGES

The explicit recourse to key principles and values that has been a feature of curriculum, pedagogy and practice guidance in Scotland is to be welcomed. It offers direction when difficult choices have to be made, can shape the nature of relationships and ways in which children and adults' interactions are construed, and creates 'ideal' roles and objectives against which self-evaluation, external accountability and professional development can take place. But despite this care and the continuing development of curriculum advice and practice guidance, some challenges remain. For example, *Building the Ambition* (Scottish Government, 2014) makes the point well that children have their own notion of an appropriate and absorbing curriculum which has to be considered along with the intended curriculum of practitioners and the eight specified areas of the Curriculum for Excellence. While *Building the Ambition* acknowledges this multiplicity it offers less help with professional judgements about how to prioritise these alternatives or find a form of practice that alleviates potential tensions, particularly in settings where professional colleagues may not share the same perspectives on valued learning.

*Building the Ambition* (Scottish Government, 2014) also includes explicit mention of pedagogy, a long-overdue addition to national guidance in Scotland. But there is more that could be offered here to assist practitioners to move towards the kind of secure, professional knowledge and capacity to articulate pedagogic principles for their actions that is advocated. Elements of appropriate pedagogy remain largely implicit in the document, though they are a good fit with the consensus that exists about good practice in Scotland described above. However, there is little attention to the value of developing and sharing a repertoire of pedagogic practices and the ways of judging which pedagogic practices will support learning in which circumstances (e.g. effective action research). Practitioners make these kind of professional decisions 'on their feet' every day in the playrooms in which they work, but that does not deny the scope for further reflection and development to extend shared repertoires, challenge the assertions and expectations of others and avoid recourse to what is considered 'normal and desirable' or 'just what we do'.

Despite the bold statement in the Children and Young People Act that learning is to be seen as a continuous process from birth, structural, policy and practice divides remain. *Building the Ambition* is concerned with meeting the needs of children before they begin school – the early level covers children aged 3 to 6 years old – and it is widely recognised that moving to primary school continues to mean a shift to a different educational culture. The long-held desire to ensure that transition from early learning settings to primary school takes place without risking confusion over the expectations and norms of these different learning cultures remains unfulfilled. Ensuring that moving to school does not have a negative impact on the progression and disposition to learn of at least some children is likely to require the development of an appropriate pedagogic repertoire for all professionals (those with both teacher and early years qualifications) which articulates well with the child-centred, needs-based pedagogy advised in *Building the Ambition*, the active learning approach advocated for children in the early level, and the more transmission- and teacher-orientated perspective of the primary school tradition. Further work is needed to enhance the theoretical and empirical base for 'active learning' and find ways of supporting children as they move from what Vygotsky thought of as the shift from everyday to scientific or academic concepts (Fleer, 2010).

The inclusion of specific and explicit principles for practice as a valuable and distinctive feature of guidance for early education practice and policy in Scotland has been welcomed in earlier paragraphs of this chapter. However, particularly in a period of policy proliferation, this does not always remove the possibly of tension between goals and the likelihood that changes will bring benefits and drawbacks. The potential impact of the current expansion plans on the nature of the experiences of young children is a case in point. The contribution that early educational provision can make to a child's learning and educational achievement has been acknowledged in Scotland since the decision was made to offer a government-funded places at the end of the twentieth century. While these benefits are part of the case for the current initiative, politicians and policymakers are also keen to ensure that the changes are designed to maximise the potential of childcare provision to increase the economic capacity of parents. Specifically, the aim is to enhance flexibility in provision to meet the needs of working parents. However, little or no attention is paid to evidence that, for example, children benefit most from stable relationships with practitioners and peers, and that increasing the 'dosage' of early education is not necessarily a positive experience for all aspects of development for younger children (NICHD, 2002; Sylva et al., 2004). While flexibility over days and hours of attendance may be helpful for parents, there is the potential that children's experiences will be less positive when they are not able to build a familiar relationship with a small number of practitioners and are denied the emotional and social satisfaction they derive from being included in an established group of peers.

There is a similar potential for tension between goals around the policy desire to support the development of vulnerable children and close the attainment gap at the same time as improving the quality of provision and enhancing outcomes for all children. The history of efforts to scale up interventions, particularly those aiming at poverty reduction, is not encouraging. Nevertheless, to date the plan for Scotland remains largely one of meeting the needs of children who are experiencing particular disadvantages within universal provision. The success of these efforts remains to be seen, as does the expectation that change will extend to the home learning environment of vulnerable children.

Scotland has a variety of alternatives to universal group provision on which to draw for early intervention strategies and it is reassuring to note that some of these are included in the novel forms of provision being trialled in 2017 as part of the preparation for expansion. Community childminding is a bespoke service developed by the Scottish Childminding Association which offers highly responsive packages to children and their families at a time of particular need. Early Years Scotland provide a Stay and Play service which can also act as an alternative form of early intervention. Targeted at difficult to reach families or those who are experiencing difficulties and who are less likely to make use of existing group provision, Stay and Play sessions are led by a trained practitioner and aim to support children's development, stimulate their curiosity and playful exploration, and model positive interactions and ways of managing children's behaviour. In the context of group education settings an effective model of nurture group provision for children before they begin school has been developed in local authority nurseries in Glasgow.

The drive to reduce the persistent attainment gap that is a recognised feature of educational outcomes in Scotland brings increased political pressure to assess children's attainment at every stage of educational provision. This pressure is seen by many in the early years field in Scotland as a threat to their long-held understanding that young children's development should not be measured in a simplistic quantitative way or subject to comparison with arbitrarily set 'norms'. They continue to champion the focus on creating individual descriptive profiles that include accounts of strengths, weaknesses, interests and progression as being appropriate for a child-centred approach, for the aims and values of early learning, and for their understanding of the ways in which young children develop their knowledge and skills. Nevertheless, it seems likely that the early years field will have to address the challenge to what is seen as a valuable and distinctive feature of early education in Scotland. Given opportunities to engage with initiatives around assessment it may be possible for early years educators to negotiate changes that maintain the focus on professional judgements and evidence gathered in everyday playroom experiences.

Research evidence suggests that the most significant resource for any young learner is a sensitive and responsive practitioner (e.g. Bowman et al., 2000). However, the status of the early education workforce has long been a matter of concern and debate in Scotland and, with the need to significantly extend the workforce to meet the planned expansion in hours this continues to be a matter of pressing concern. Like the nature of early years provision in Scotland, the qualifications and training routes of practitioners is diverse. The workforce review published by Siraj and Kingston in 2015 acknowledged existing good practices and provision but was clear that there was a need to enhance the qualification levels of early education practitioners and make improvements to the content of initial and continuing professional development. Siraj argued strongly for the development of degree level qualifications for early education practitioners on a par with primary school teacher education and in addition to the currently available degree qualifications for managers of early learning and childcare settings. It seems difficult to disagree with recommendations that would result in a more highly educated and critically aware workforce, particularly as what little research evidence there is points to the value of targeted early education qualifications. Nevertheless, so far discussions about expanding the workforce have been dominated by seeking ways of recruiting staff with college-level qualifications. Suggestions that Scotland should move to a degree level qualification as the 'basic' professional educator grade in early education encounter some resistance and a lack of willingness to engage with the cost of employing more graduate-level practitioners. This is a situation which should be returned to if the quality and efficacy of early education is to be sustained and improved over time.

It is encouraging that the practice of consulting widely with representatives of practitioners, providers, parents and other bodies, and academics engaged in the early learning and childcare field, has continued into the twenty-first century in Scotland. But there has been an important reduction in government funding for research and evaluation studies and this, coupled with pressures in higher education institutions to target spending on income-generating courses, has left Scotland with a much reduced field of active research-ers. This is in some contrast to the situation in countries such as Australia, New Zealand and Norway where academic researchers (often working with practitioners) continue to be able to apply for and carry out robust studies that relate to local questions and to theoretical developments. The mutual benefit derived from government funding for research is illus-trated by the impact of two commissions early in the twenty-first century from Learning and Teaching Scotland. Stephen and Plowman were commissioned to carry out an initial literature review and an exploratory empirical study about learning with digital technolo-gies in the early years (Stephen, 2006; see also Stephen and Plowman, 2003; Plowman and Stephen, 2005). The findings informed the policy framework and practice guidance and professional development, raised Scotland's profile as a leader in research and practice with digital technologies for young children, and facilitated the research team's success in winning funding for further internationally acknowledged projects. If the academic study of early learning and development is to be sustained in Scotland, the current dearth of funding opportunities will have to be addressed.

One final global, rather than local, challenge is worthy of mention here. As the twentieth century progressed, the pace of transition to the digital era accelerated, a change that is now firmly and globally entrenched. This shift demands not only decisions about what digital resources to purchase for early learning and childcare settings. More importantly, it requires new thinking among early education professionals about what counts as valued knowledge, about the skills with technology that are developed at home and those which educators can enhance, about finding, storing and retrieving information, and new perspec-tives on literacy and the opportunities for creativity and problem solving that come with growing up in the digital age.

## CONCLUSION

This chapter reflects on some of the current challenges and tensions for early learning and childcare provision in Scotland. There is much that is positive about Scottish early educa-tion provision, pedagogy, the curriculum and the everyday experiences of young children in playrooms and the homes of childminders throughout the country. The continued focus on what is usually described as child–centred practices permits a responsive approach that makes space for individual interests and needs. There is concern for children and their families and the quality of the educational provision offered, a desire for further profes-sional development and working across the early level as children make the transition to school, and there are big policy ambitions to overcome the influence of social and economic disadvantage.

## REFERENCES

Bowman, B., Donovan, M. S. and Burns, M. S. (eds) (2000) *Eager to Learn: Educating Our Preschoolers.* Washington, DC: National Academy Press.

Brooker, L., Blaise, M. and Edwards, S. (eds) (2014) *Sage Handbook of Play and Learning in Early Childhood.* London: Sage.

Early Years Scotland (2017) *Professional Learning Framework – Autumn 2017.* Online at https://early yearsscotland.org/Media/Docs/Secure/EYS%20Professional%20Learning%20OC17.pdf

Fleer, M. (2010) *Early Learning and Development.* Melbourne: Cambridge University Press.

NICHD Early Child Care Research Network (2002) 'Early child care and children's development prior to school entry: results from the NICHD Study of Early Child Care', *American Education Research Journal*, 39 (1), 133–64.

Plowman, L. and Stephen, C. (2005) 'Children, play and computers in pre-school education', *British Journal of Educational Technology*, 36 (2), 145–57.

Scottish Executive (2007) *Building the Curriculum 2*. Online at https://www.education.gov.scot/ scottish-education-system/policy-for-scottish-education/policy-drivers/cfe-(building-from-the-statement-appendix-incl-btc1-5)/Building%20the%20Curriculum

Scottish Government (2014) *Building the Ambition*. Online at www.gov.scot/Resource/0045/00458455. pdf

Scottish Government (2008) *Getting it Right for Every Child*. Online at www.gov.scot/resource/ doc/1141/0065063.pdf

Siraj, I. and Kingston, D. (2015) *An Independent Review of the Scottish Early Learning and Childcare (ELC) Workforce and Out of School (OSC) Workforce*. London: Institute of Education, University College London. Online at http://dera.ioe.ac.uk/23083/1/00477419.pdf

Stephen, C. (2012) 'Looking for theory in preschool education', *Studies in Philosophy of Education*, 31 (3), 227–38.

Stephen, C. (2006) *Early Years Education: Perspectives from a Review of the International Literature*. Edinburgh: Scottish Executive Education Department.

Stephen, C. and Plowman, L. (2003) 'Information and communications technologies in pre-school settings: a review of the literature', *International Journal of Early Years Education*, 11 (3), 223–34.

Stephen, C., McPake, J., Pollock, I. and McLeod, W. (2016) 'Early years immersion: learning from children's playroom experiences', *Journal of Immersion and Content-based Language Education*, 4 (1), 59–85.

Sylva, K., Melhuish, E., Sammons, P., Siraj-Blatchford, I. and Taggart, B. (2004) 'The Effective Provision of Pre-School Education (EPPE) Project: findings from pre-school to end of Key Stage 1'. Online at http://dera.ioe.ac.uk/18189/2/SSU-SF-2004-01.pdf

# 22

# Early Schooling

*Deirdre Grogan and Joan Martlew*

## INTRODUCTION

In Scotland, Curriculum for Excellence (CfE) has attempted to ensure progression from the nursery curriculum and the first years of school by introducing one 'early' level, which covers children aged 3 to 6 years and encompasses the two contexts. This new approach tries to take the best elements of the old preschool *3–5 Curriculum* and develop it as a stronger element of the teaching and learning approach in the first years in primary school. The early level sets out experiences and outcomes within eight main subject areas in order to address progression in children's learning. These are Expressive Arts, Health and Wellbeing, Literacy and English (including Gaelic Learners), Numeracy and Mathematics, Religious and Moral Education, Social Subjects, Science, and Technologies.

In Scotland, children start compulsory schooling in the August nearest their fifth birthday, starting school between the age of 4 years 6 months and 5 years 6 months. All children in Scotland are entitled to nursery education from the age of 3 (see Chapter 21 for discussion of early years/preschool provision). A key current challenge for Scottish teachers is the changing philosophy and methodology of this new curriculum in relation to the primary school sector. The underpinning philosophy is based on the principles of active learning, increasing the ownership of children's choice and ensuring an appropriate level of challenge. In 2016, Upstart Scotland (www.upstart.scot) broached the question about what age children should start school in Scotland and whether children would benefit from starting at the age of 7. The question raised debate but the conclusion was that we need to revisit the pedagogy used in primary one and tailor this more explicitly to how young children learn.

In other parts of the UK, active learning is part of the guidance on effective practice in the early years, for example in England this is promoted as an appropriate pedagogy in the early years Foundation Stage. The guidance for children aged 3 to 7 years old (the Foundation Stage) in Wales refers to 'play/active learning' and 'active educational play' and argues that 'The value of play/active learning cannot be emphasised strongly enough" (Welsh Government, 2008, p. 7). Similarly, the Foundation Stage in Northern Ireland stresses the benefit of children being actively involved in their learning experiences. This chapter discusses the educational provision for 3–8 year olds in early education in Scotland and considers the impact of this new curriculum.

## THE ORGANISATION OF LEARNING

CfE has at its core seven key principles which are:

- challenge and enjoyment;
- breadth;
- progression;
- depth;
- personalisation and choice;
- coherence;
- relevance.

These must be taken into account when planning learning experiences for all children and young people. They apply to the curriculum at an organisational level, in the classroom, and in any setting wherever children and young people are learners. The environment should allow children to take ownership of their own learning and to set their own challenges.

Educational researchers consider play to be an integral element of a high quality provision for young children (Siraj-Blatchford and Sylva, 2004). Recent evidence suggests that play develops children's content knowledge across the curriculum and enhances the development of social skills, competencies and disposition to learn (Wood and Attfield, 2005), and is therefore considered to be an integral element of a high-quality provision for young children (Siraj-Blatchford and Sylva, 2004). While play is considered to be a vital component of an early years environment, many primary teachers are unsure of how to organise a play-based curriculum (Moyles, 2011). CfE in Scotland 'active learning' is defined as:

> learning which engages and challenges children's thinking using real life and imaginary situations. It takes full advantage of opportunities for learning presented by: spontaneous play; planned, purposeful play; investigating and exploring; events and life experiences; focused learning and teaching; supported when necessary through sensitive intervention to extend or support learning. (Scottish Executive, 2007, p. 5)

Therefore, if active learning is defined as being learning where the child or young person is responsible for initiating, planning and controlling their learning, these approaches are relevant at every stage within the primary school, not only in the nursery setting. Everyday practice should include the learner in planning experiments, testing hypotheses, discussing their ideas, establishing investigations, reviewing or revisiting their discoveries and undertaking creative work in the expressive arts.

However, the term can be interpreted differently by teachers. Martlew et al. (2011) found that play in some 'active learning' classrooms was peripheral, something that the children were engaged in during parts of the structured day rather than an integral element of the learning process. In order to develop this model of active learning, teachers need a sound theoretical knowledge of how young children learn and the importance of an environment which promotes and supports their learning. Children need to be allowed to focus on their own leaning and to become involved through motivating opportunities and experiences. Thus, the traditional classroom setting needs to be redesigned to afford children the freedom to make choices whilst still retaining the necessary balance between child-initiated, teacher-initiated and teacher-focused learning (Fisher, 2013). Teachers are now more involved in discussing pedagogy within the early level and local authorities are investing in training teachers, particularly in primary one, to support developments and also to reflect on current practice.

The design of the learning environment promoting a play-based pedagogy could incorporate specific learning bays with a limited number of desks and chairs; children given responsibility for the design and resource allocation of specific areas; and time allocated for consultation and reflection on learning by child and teacher.

## THE NATURE OF YOUNG CHILDREN'S LEARNING

Fisher (2013, Section 1 – Competent Young Learners) identifies the learning characteristics of young children as follows:

- Young children learn by being active.
- Young children learn by organising their own learning experiences.
- Young children learn by using language.
- Young children learn by interacting with others.
- Young children learn by interacting with others and their environment.

Therefore, careful consideration needs to be given by the teacher to the organisation not only of the classroom or nursery environment itself, but also to the structure of the day. Although the pedagogical approach in the primary classroom is to some extent building on the play-based learning seen in the nursery setting, it should aim to mirror and extend this type of pedagogy to enable progression in learning. On entry to nursery, children are encouraged to self-register, make decisions about the organisation of their day through deciding when to have snack, who to play with and what resources and experiences they will explore. This type of approach should span the early level where the educator will carefully observe, support and extend the children's learning. The adults should employ a variety of strategies to develop children's understanding and thinking. Within the primary one setting, children should be encouraged to organise their own day by collecting targets related to curricular areas on completion of their learning experiences. These should be appropriately differentiated to meet the varying needs and interests of all the children in the class.

An important factor in developing quality interaction is through sustained shared thinking (Siraj-Blatchford and Sylva, 2004) when the adult is with one or two children; this allows the adult to tune in to their thinking and to develop a deeper understanding. The importance of conversations and an appropriate use of questions is crucial to develop a shared understanding of the child's intellectual process. Research findings indicate that children who engage in sustained shared conversations are more likely to do well in school and in life. Various strategies have been developed in order to support the adult's role in this interaction; these encourage children to set their own questions and lines of enquiry. The teacher should take time to 'tune into' the children's thinking prior to asking questions or contributing any ideas or suggestions (Siraj-Blatchford and Sylva, 2004).

Bruner (1990) suggests that the most sustained and productive conversations come from children working together. This encourages discussion and the development of ideas which are not 'dependent' on adult intervention. These findings square with the work of Laevers (1994) who stated that children were more likely to be involved with their own learning if they were offered choices and ownership. He outlined a five point scale (the Leuven Involvement Scale) for assessing the child's level of involvement and engagement using

240                                                    SCOTTISH EDUCATION

five categories: (1) low activity, (2) frequently interrupted activity, (3) mainly continuous activity, (4) continuous activity with intense moments and (5) sustained intense activity.

Teachers working with children in the early stages of school must deliberately consider the ways in which young children learn. Young children are actively trying to make sense of the world around them, each discovery or solution leading to the child formulating new threads of learning. Children are curious, capable and persistent learners and, if this is respected by teachers, allows the child to reach new understandings through self-directed learning experiences.

Traditionally within the Scottish education system there have been separate curriculum guidelines for nursery and primary schools. This resulted in major differences not only in the dominant philosophies about how young children learn but also in pedagogies. The primary curriculum guidelines (or '5–14' as they became known) were introduced in the 1990s and contained broad statements of attainment outcomes within each strand of learning for each curricular area. Each strand had descriptors for each level A–E and children were tested at the appropriate level prior to moving onto the next level. This resulted in many teachers feeling that they were forced to 'teach to the test' and that the curriculum was becoming overcrowded. Packs were created to support teachers in the implementation of each level of the guidelines and the type of tasks within these packs were overwhelmingly written, worksheet based and were to be undertaken on one's own. Many teachers felt that the packs stifled their ability to shape the curriculum to meet the particular learning needs and interests of the pupils in their classes. Many also thought that the packs forced teachers into a particularly inactive pedagogy and that children's enjoyment of learning was being eroded.

One new and positive aspect of these 5–14 guidelines was that they were developed to support the child's education from the first class in primary school into their second year of secondary education. It was felt that children would benefit from a clearer progression of their learning; indeed primary–secondary liaison became much stronger with many upper primary teachers and secondary teachers taking more time to discuss children's next steps in their learning. At this time, some forward-looking education authorities saw the potential in viewing a child's education as a seamless process and so encouraged nursery staff to meet with primary early years teachers to discuss children's progress.

The first document designed to support the curriculum for children attending nursery was *Partners in Learning: 0–5 Curriculum Guidelines*, published by then Scottish Office Education and Industry Department (SOEID) in 1994, a guide developed to assist with planning and reviewing the nursery curriculum within the Strathclyde region in Scotland. It identified five broad curricular bands: Language and Literacy, Mathematical, Expressive and Aesthetic, Environmental, and Personal and Social, with each of these broad bands broken into key areas. The key components were learning processes, contexts and content with special emphasis on the child at the centre. There was also recognition given to the role of the parent as the 'prime educator'.

> Children learn through interaction with their environment and with the people in it. In nurseries and at home, adults and children form partnerships which support the children as they learn and develop. Adults carry the responsibility for ensuring that, as far as they can, the environment in which the child learns is used effectively for learning and that the interaction and conversations which take place between adults and children increase the competence of the children as learners and help children to value themselves as persons. The central role is that of a partner in learning. (Scottish Office Education and Industry Department, 1994, p. 123)

This first document proposing nursery curriculum guidelines was followed by a *Curriculum Framework for Children 3 to 5*, published by the SOEID in 1999, designed to support all nursery providers throughout Scotland. The guidelines were divided into key aspects with features of learning (outcomes) recorded for each area. Each key aspect was illustrated with examples from practice and supported with reflective questions. The curricular areas were similar to the primary curriculum except that mathematics was incorporated into environmental studies (Knowledge and Understanding of the World). Teachers used the guidelines to direct their planning and to assess children's learning:

> Effective planning establishes clear goals for learning that are designed to match the needs and achievements of children. Planning, whether long or short term should leave the staff clear, confident and well-prepared for what they are trying to achieve in children's learning. (Scottish Office Education and Industry Department, 1999, p. 4)

This document provided teachers with a clear explanation of how young children learn and the power of play in contributing to it.

Children's transition from the nursery setting to the more traditional classroom environment within the primary school became a crucial aspect to be reviewed in order to ensure a smoother and more natural development in children's experiences, thinking and learning. However, the 5–14 curriculum guidelines, despite their good intentions, were criticised by many teachers. Apart from the formal assessment practices that pressured children and overburdened teachers, many criticised the lack of a theoretical basis for the content of the levels. The lack of a focus on appropriate pedagogies was also deemed to be unsatisfactory and it became apparent that the curriculum in Scottish schools needed to be reviewed. A review group was established in 2004 to evaluate the existing curricula. This review offered the potential for radical change in the education of young people, placing a greater emphasis on learners and learning than there had been previously. The outcome of this review was the development of the first single curriculum which allowed for more depth in terms of the children's learning and more space for teachers to make decision about the focus of their teaching. This curriculum, the 'Curriculum for Excellence', addressed the learning and teaching of young people from 3 to 18. The current curriculum is now divided into curricular areas and has outcomes/experience at each level which the child has to achieve over a period of time. This singular curriculum replaced both the 5–14 and the 3–5 curriculum guidelines. An early level was introduced which specifically addresses the nursery stage but also includes the first class in primary thus signifying a new dawn in continuity and progression. CfE, with its seven principles of pedagogy aimed to develop active, experiential learning for all learners, not just for young children. The early level allows staff from different establishments, such as a nursery school and the infant department of a primary school, to jointly plan to ensure clear development for the children, and also focuses on meeting their needs, taking account of how young children learn. 'Building the curriculum' documents were devised to support teachers in their thinking, in particular the implementation of learning and the assessment of that learning. Active learning is paramount in both nursery and primary settings and teachers now do reflect on their current practice in order to improve their approaches. Her Majesty's Inspectorate of Education (HMIE) in a report on inspection and review 2002–5 (HMIE, 2006) identified this as a key theme for improvements in primary schools when they stated 'the quality of pupils' learning experience is still too variable and too often lacks relevance, engagement and excitement' (p. 4). Questions were included in the *Building the Curriculum 2* document (Scottish Executive, 2007) to encourage teachers to be reflective, to evaluate the opportunities planned for children's learning, and indicating that children could revisit their own work in order to achieve depth of learning. The early level should ensure an effective transition for young children as the methodology stated in the Curriculum for Excellence endorses active learning and children taking full ownership and responsibility both in nursery and in primary one. *Quality and Improvement in Scottish Education 2012–2016* (Education Scotland, 2017) highlights a positive picture in relation to outdoor learning and the engagement of young children in their own learning.

The principles that provide the pedagogical basis for the CfE guidelines are:

- depth;
- progression;
- personalisation and choice;
- challenge and enjoyment;
- continuity;
- breadth;
- coherence.

Scottish teachers who truly engage with these principles will be ready to embrace the true philosophy of CfE. Engagement with only the outcomes and experiences will not result in real changes in Scottish education.

## PLANNING FOR CHILDREN'S LEARNING

Responsive planning is common in the nursery environment in Scotland but has been less so in the formal school sector and is not supported by many of the planning frameworks commonly used in primary schools. CfE endorses this view of the child being actively engaged in their own learning by involving them in the planning process. Responsive planning closely links to the concept of the emergent curriculum; teachers need to be flexible and creative in their thinking in order to allow children to direct their own learning. Through scaffolding the learning and developing effective interactions, the child will be supported to make their own discoveries or to identify potential solutions to initial hypotheses. Teachers within the nursery environment are accustomed to the children designing and developing their curriculum; however, some primary school teachers find this approach to planning a challenge. The emphasis on planning for learning in the early stages has changed with the focus now strongly related to active learning and a play-based pedagogy. *Building the Curriculum 2* (Scottish Executive, 2007) outlines that the learner should be responsible for instigating, planning and managing their learning. Building the ambition (Scottish Government, 2014) further endorses this by focusing on early pedagogy and the role of the educator.

The focus on early learning being delivered through a more child-orientated method is also being given increasing emphasis elsewhere, with other parts of the United Kingdom and Europe also promoting this shift. The Welsh Government highlights the importance of play as a vehicle for children's learning:

> children being active and involved in their learning. Children learn best through first-hand experiences … The purpose of play/active learning is that it motivates, stimulates and supports children in their development of skills, concepts, language acquisition/communication skills and concentration. It also provides opportunities for children to develop positive attitudes and

to demonstrate awareness/use of recent learning, skills and competencies, and to consolidate learning. (Welsh Government, 2008, p. 54)

In Northern Ireland the revised curriculum for 4- to 5-year-old children (2000; The Enriched Curriculum) emphasises the importance of a play-based curriculum which provides the children with high-quality learning experiences as opposed to the more formal adult directed learning which preceded it.

Responsive planning has also been successfully implemented within Reggio Emilia preschools since the 1980s where the teacher is perceived as having an equal role with the child; both are viewed as learners. This is in line with the current policy direction as outlined in the Donaldson review of teacher education (Scottish Government, 2011a), where teachers are positioned as learners and enquirers. Within Reggio Emilia, the initial planning phase focuses on the child sharing their interests and possible questions of inquiry with the teacher. The teacher supports the child or a small group of children in co-constructing their knowledge through the identified interests of the children using the environment as 'the third educator' (Malaguzzi, 1995). This particular pedagogical approach has been welcomed by teachers in Scotland in the early years; however, its development needs to be supported for those teachers who require clarity and additional guidance to help them implement responsive planning in the primary school classroom. Fisher's model (2013) clearly outlines the elements required for the successful implementation of responsive planning which teachers could use as the basis for developing their own pedagogical stance in relation to the balance of child-led and teacher-led learning experiences.

Moyles (2011) develops this further and describes 'three major concepts of play and playfulness that need to be explored when considering an appropriate pedagogy' (p. 21). She identifies these as play, playful learning and playful teaching. She also stresses that time should be given so that children can evaluate and reflect on their learning. If these models are to be implemented successfully, teachers should plan on a weekly basis to ensure a balance of child-initiated, teacher-initiated and teacher-focused experiences. Modification of weekly plans in response to observations of children's learning, and consultation meetings where children discuss and record their ideas, can then drive the next week's learning experiences.

## THE OBSERVATION AND ASSESSMENT OF YOUNG CHILDREN'S LEARNING

The importance of observing young children in order to gain an insight into their thinking and learning takes considerable organisation in terms of time and methods of recording or documentation. Teachers must schedule time within their weekly planning to allow this important task to be undertaken. One method of documentation that is currently implemented within some nursery settings in Scotland is based on the Reggio Emilia approach: a method of recording children's involvement and learning using photographs, narrative and children's drawings (Malaguzzi, 1995). This method of recording children's learning allows the teacher to review and analyse further in order to set appropriate next steps in a child's learning. A further development of documenting children's learning has been devised by Carr (2001) who refers to this method of documentation as a Learning Story. As the name suggests, this documentation contains both narrative and photographic evidence.

Both methods allow children to comment on their own understanding through revisiting evidence of their prior learning. This evidence could include photographs, examples of emergent writing, narratives of conversations with the child, paintings and/or drawings, allowing the teacher and the child the opportunity to retell the story of the learning. Although this method of documenting is well established within the nursery sector, it is not widely used at the present time within the primary school. The demands of CfE require a shift in recording of children's learning. *Building the Curriculum 5* (Scottish Government, 2011b) states that the child should have regular time to talk about their learning; therefore traditional methods of assessment have little value as summative assessment material or test results cannot be revisited to develop a child's thinking or identifying next steps in learning. Goouch (2008) suggests that teachers, through their ongoing observations, should engage and support young children and help them to 'find meaning and sense in their play narratives' (p. 101). However, she states that the teachers must be confident and believe that cognitive development will occur without the need to 'hijack' the situation (ibid.). This should impact positively on the quality of both teaching and learning within the classroom.

## REFLECTIONS

In light of the recent changes in pedagogical approaches and curricular developments (from 2010–16), there is a requirement for those professionals working with children in the early years to reflect even more deeply on their own pedagogical stance. All early years teachers have knowledge of how young children learn; they need to consider how they use this knowledge and the impact that this will have on the organisation of the learning environment and the design of appropriate learning experiences. Early years teachers are aware that young children gain more in terms of knowledge and skills when the learning experiences take account of children's interests, therefore the teacher should ensure that this design allows children to take their own learning along exciting new threads. There is a current shift in the thinking of the role of the teacher; teachers need to be observers, responsive planners, scaffolders and extenders of children's learning. Recording children's learning through documentation allows both parties to revisit key episodes of learning and supports progression in consolidating key concepts and developing new knowledge and skills.

There are, however, perennial questions to think about. How can teachers be supported with this shift in thinking in the delivery of the curriculum for young children? Are teachers given time to debate pedagogical issues with their professional partners (nursery, primary teachers)? Is there a need for specialist teachers within the early years to promote and develop this particular and vitally important stage in educational provision? As stated in *Building the Curriculum 5* (Scottish Government, 2011b, p. 19), 'Learners do well when engaging fully in their learning, collaborating in planning and shaping and reviewing their progress.' It has been recognised in Scotland that this places a demand on early years teachers, in the context of the delivery of CfE, and new specialist qualifications were proposed in *The Early Years Framework* published by the Scottish Government in 2009: 'The Scottish Government will work with Teacher Education Institutions to develop courses which will offer more specialised early years teaching skills' (www.gov. scot/Publications/2009/01/13095148/10).

Through setting up productive networks, teachers can explore their own pedagogical processes through professional debate and exploration, enabling them to question and develop their own practice. This should result in deeper understanding of the child as a learner, and the creativity, competence and knowledge children bring to learning situations. The potential for Scottish education to be at the cutting edge depends on staff commitment, expertise and professional development both in nursery and in primary. The vision and understanding of the importance of this developing pedagogy relies not only on the teachers involved in implementing this approach within the learning environment but also relies on the leadership team within the setting understanding and putting mechanisms in place to support these developments.

Finally, teachers need to truly believe in this developing pedagogy otherwise the danger may be that they resort to a more traditional teaching methodology. Teachers and school leaders need to allow time to properly embed this child-centred pedagogy in order to see the long-term benefits of children's participation and engagement in their learning. Finally, it is equally important that Scottish Government supports and allows this to happen over a sufficient period of time before making a judgement on teacher effectiveness in the early years.


## REFERENCES

Bruner, J. (1990) *Acts of Meaning*. Cambridge, MA and London: Harvard University Press.

Carr, M. (2001) *Assessment in Early Childhood Settings: Learning Stories*. London: Paul Chapman.

Education Scotland (2017) *Quality and Improvement in Scottish Education 2012–2016*. Online at https://education.gov.scot/Documents/QuISE_full_2012_16_web.pdf

Fisher, J. (2013) *Starting from the Child: Teaching and Learning in the Foundation Stage*, fourth edition. Maidenhead: Open University Press.

Goouch, K. (2008) 'Understanding playful pedagogies, play narratives and play spaces', *Early Years*, 28 (1), 93–102.

HMIE (2006) *Improving Scottish Education: A Report by HMIE on Inspection and Review, 2002–2005*. Livingston: HMIE.

Laevers, F. (ed.) (1994) *Defining and Assessing Quality in Early Childhood Education*. Belgium: Laevers University Press.

Malaguzzi, L. (1995) 'History, ideas and basic philosophy: an interview with Lella Gandini', in C. Edwards, L. Gandini and G. Forman (eds), *The Hundred Languages of Children: The Reggio Emilia Approach to Early Childhood Education*. Greenwich, CT: Ablex

Martlew, J., Stephen, C. and Ellis, J. (2011) 'Play in the primary school classroom? The experience of teachers supporting children's learning through a new pedagogy', *Early Years*, 31 (1), 71–83.

Moyles. J. (ed.) (2011) *Thinking about Play: Developing a Reflective Approach*. Maidenhead: Open University Press.

Scottish Executive (2007) *A Curriculum for Excellence – Building the Curriculum 2 – Active Learning in the Early Years*. Online at https://education.gov.scot/Documents/btc2.pdf

Scottish Government (2011a) *Teaching Scotland's Future – Report of a Review of Teacher Education in Scotland*. Online at www.gov.scot/Publications/2011/01/13092132/0

Scottish Government (2011b) *Curriculum for Excellence. Building the Curriculum 5: A Framework for Assessment*. Online at www.gov.scot/resource/doc/341834/0113711.pdf

Scottish Government (2014) 'Building the Ambition: National Practice Guidance on Early Learning and Childcare. Children and Young People (Scotland) Act 2014'. Online at www.gov.scot/Resource/0045/00458455.pdf

Scottish Office Education and Industry Department (1994) *Partners in Learning: 0–5 Curriculum Guidelines*. Online at https://files.eric.ed.gov/fulltext/ED374885.pdf

Scottish Office Education and Industry Department/Scottish Consultative Committee on the Curriculum (1999) *A Curriculum Framework for Children 3 to 5*. Dundee: SCCC.

Siraj-Blatchford, I. and Sylva, K. (2004) 'Researching pedagogy in English pre-schools, *British Educational Research Journal*, 30 (5), 713–30.

Welsh Government (2008) *Play/active Learning: Overview for 3 to 7-Year Olds*. Online at http:// learning.gov.wales/docs/learningwales/publications/130215play-activeen.pdf

Wood, E. and Attfield, J. (2005) *Play, Learning and the Early Childhood Curriculum*, second edition. London: Paul Chapman.

# 23

# Learning in Scottish Primary and Secondary Schools

*Tom Bryce*

This chapter explores how learning can be conceived and must be distinguished from the teaching that purports to bring it about in schools. The topic of learning is broad and only the cognitive dimensions will figure here – thus attitudinal learning and skill acquisition have been set aside. All teachers hope that the learning of their students will be meaningful to them and so the main pedagogies currently encountered in Scottish classrooms are scrutinised in the light of that intent (the pursuit of *meaning*). Active forms of learning, collaboration and discussion amongst pupils are much encouraged in the Scottish curriculum and the chapter considers some recent research on how these may be managed and what can be achieved. The chapter also looks at some of the approaches which have been advanced by enthusiasts as alternatives to traditional teaching methods. Findings from recent advances in neuroscience are used to comment on these and on important issues like gender differences, giftedness, (so-called) multiple intelligences, and 'learning styles'.

## THE CONCEPT OF LEARNING

The real point to teaching is that it should bring about learning and the public has quite reasonable expectations that a significant amount of learning is taking place in schools. Leaving aside what should be learned (set out in the curriculum chapters of sections V, VI and VII) and the achievements and qualifications which pupils leave schools with (explored in Chapter 70), it is rather difficult to capture the amount and, more importantly, the quality of the actual *learning* that takes place in classrooms. We can portray aspects of *teaching* fairly easily; the methods that are used routinely by teachers can be described; the dynamics – or not – of schoolroom instruction can be revealed. But, when it comes to saying what is happening in the minds of learners, inferences are required to convey what we think is going on – and this is as true for observers as it is for the practitioners directly concerned. So much of learning is *mental* and therefore not directly observable. Pupils may be taught 'this' when in fact they learn 'something else', even where the words for 'this' and 'something else' are identical, with classroom discussion moving along on an assumption of mutual understanding which can so easily be unfounded. A young child, for example, might echo his teacher by saying say that *the Earth is round*, but if his teacher does not realise that, at this point, this particular child is envisaging a flat, disc-shaped island in a dark blue sea, their conversations are likely to go amiss and subsequent, connected understandings will fail. The child has *not* learned that the Earth is round (spherical), even though he may say it is. Or, turning to numeracy skills for a different example, pupils may be trained to calculate in primary arithmetic and become rather good at formulaic exercises using memorised tables. But should they fail to see where and when these algorithms can be applied to real world problems, their *mathematical* learning will not have been successful; they can't do maths. Perhaps that learning was sacrificed in favour of getting *the right answers* concerning the number facts? Research tells us that instruction only works when the tasks which pupils are trained in truly *problematise* the mathematics; where the learners are allowed to work out for themselves methods to complete the tasks; and where structured discussion requires pupils to routinely explain their thinking processes.

Generalising these ideas, we have to concede that we are essentially *theorising* when we try to represent those understandings which we think are taking place and the abilities which we believe are developing (or not) on a day-to-day basis. The language and vocabulary of this theorising is familiar to anyone who thinks about learning, pertinent questions being:

- Is the learning *deep* or superficial? Has it had any *impact*? Can students *use* their learning?
- Does that learning *transfer* beyond the illustrations used in the lessons? Or, was it just *rote* learning?
- How *meaningful* and long lasting will the learning be? Will these ideas stick in students' *memories*?
- Is the learning real and *authentic*?
- Fundamentally, what *motivates* young people to grasp ideas the way teachers do and realise their importance?

This last point concedes that very many questions about learning boil down to questions about motivation and interest.

## WHAT HAS BEEN LEARNED ABOUT LEARNING?

Turning to research on learning, it may be useful to summarise what is known about the psychology of school learning, for psychologists and educators agree, in broad terms, about how learning takes place, or at least under what conditions it occurs effectively. Adopting the now prevalent *constructivist* approach to learning, a brief summary of what has been learned about learning would be that:

1. Learning requires active involvement (people learn by constructing meanings on the basis of what they already know) and is primarily social in the everyday settings where people think and work together (*social-constructivism*).
2. Early-learned, preschool ideas – particularly local community knowledge and folklore – are often the source of partial understandings and misconceptions: these ought to be openly discussed and inconsistencies resolved as learning proceeds.
3. Learners benefit significantly by learning how to monitor their own learning and become familiar at working with feedback designed to take their learning forward; that is, when they get *feedforward* from their teachers (discussed further in relation to formative assessment in Chapter 68).
4. Learners need to see the relevance and use of what they are learning in the classroom activities in which they participate.

5. The focus of learning should be upon general principles and problem-solving strategies, rather than upon isolated factual detail.

6. Motivation to learn grows from working with motivated, expert teachers who are able to work alongside learners with a wide range of interests and capabilities.

See, for example, Ausubel (2000) and Cohen et al. (2010).

Developmentally speaking and in respect of point 2 above, research indicates that early-learned ideas persist well into the primary school years and beyond. To take one small example, Blown and Bryce (2017) report that the proportions of children giving *animistic* responses to questions asked about the causes of daytime and night-time (*The Sun goes to bed at night*; *The Moon sleeps behind the mountains during the day*; and so forth) are approximately 30 per cent in the 3–6 year range (unsurprising?); about 20 per cent in the 7–9 year range (interesting?); about 10 per cent in the 10–12 year range (worrying?); and about 5 per cent in the 13–15 year range (alarming?). It seems also that, even where correct scientific expressions are acquired, they *coexist* with everyday expressions, rather than replace them.

Some of the more recent curricular initiatives led by Scottish Government (or its agencies) do reflect the points listed above, though with varying degrees of consistency and impact upon practitioners. The whole thrust on more *active learning* which is embodied in Curriculum for Excellence's (CfE's) emphasis upon *challenge* and *interest* most certainly relates to points 1, 2 and 4. Statements about the making of *meaning*/providing *meaningful experiences*/setting *meaningful contexts* for learning and so on, permeate the experiences and outcomes descriptors throughout CfE documentation. Furthermore, the intention to *declutter* the curriculum in the move from 5–14 (the previous version of the national curriculum in Scotland) to CfE was consistent with point 5. The push for *collaborative learning* among pupils is evidently underpinned by points 1, 2 and 6 and the largely successful movement *Assessment is for Learning* (AifL) explicitly follows from point 3 (and is examined in detail in Chapter 68).

A number of rather different initiatives instigated by some enthusiastic teachers, and/or promoted by commercial programme developers, also connect with these points – notably so-called *brain-based*, or *neuro-scientific* approaches, or pedagogies said to be aligned with personal *styles of learning*, in particular to points 1, 3, 4 and 6. As we shall see, claims for the effectiveness of some of these 'fashionable' pedagogies are largely exaggerated. That said, there is no reason to suppose that the numbers of Scottish teachers who incline to these approaches to teaching are any different, proportionally, from those in other parts of the UK; perhaps in even smaller numbers, given the natural conservatism of the teaching profession in Scotland.

Whether 'mainstream' or 'fashionable', pedagogies which try to make pupils genuinely active in their learning are consistent with constructivism. The terms are not completely interchangeable, however, for constructivism is essentially 'mental' and some forms of activity, even when visibly dynamic, with pupils not left as passive receptors of information, may not lead to them being able to use their current state of understanding to grasp new ideas. Activity makes meaningful learning more likely; it does not guarantee it and rote methods are very much less likely to promote meaningful learning. This raises the alternative meanings of the term 'rote' as used by professionals and laymen and the quirkiness of language. Educational psychologists (e.g. Ausubel, 2000) and most teachers see 'meaningful' and 'rote' as the two ends of a spectrum concerned with the extent to which a learner can be helped to use his/her previous learning to grasp a new idea; in layman's language, 'rote' usually refers to repetitive/recitation strategies in order to '*make* one learn something' – like 'chanting the times tables'. Bluntly put, no amount of chanting makes one understand what the multiplications stand for. However, if one *has* learned what they mean in a deep sense through a variety of methods and examples, chanting may indeed be helpful to facilitate routine calculations. The methods which better ensure grasp of the process (the keys to understanding) may also help to offset the off-putting tedium of recitations – which so many adults attest to turning them off maths.

Nevertheless, and before we look further at some of these pedagogies, there is no getting away from the fact that some learning is an *individual* affair, no matter the amount of apparent activity. Pupils listen to teachers; they read texts and worksheets; they watch TV, recorded materials and iPad presentations; they often work on their own with (usually well-) developed schemes of activity, many commercially produced; and they carry out practical work. Though almost always with the guidance of their teachers, pupils typically make some sense of new material on their own, despite the conventional view being that pupils are told what to think and do. Didacticism is frequently characterised very negatively for reasons that we need to consider carefully. Clearly, on the other hand, much learning is social in the sense that working alongside others means that clarification, influence and stimulation arises from shared activity; the interpersonal context drives the learning which is taking place for many pupils. And, not to be neglected, some learning is incidental as far as individuals are concerned; they did not plan or expect to learn something, but it came about, either by virtue of the teacher's clever interjections during instruction or by peers' comments and reactions in the course of shared work and discussion.

Let us look now at the approaches which are in favour with teachers in Scotland, first one which figures in many primary classrooms and involves a blend of individual and group work and is much in tune with constructivism.

## STORYLINE: A POWERFUL PEDAGOGY FOUND IN MANY PRIMARY SCHOOLS

Storyline is a child-centred, topic-based pedagogical approach where pupils are encouraged to devise a setting, invent characters, and evolve a story with incidents and events in which these characters figure. The method recognises the value of the existing knowledge of the learner and the human element ensures that feelings, values and morals are integral to the classroom activities typically managed by the teacher and tailored to the children's inventions and the models they make. The tasks and artefacts usually vary, there being much scope for differentiation by ability. However, the ongoing 'story' enables the teacher to maintain a connecting 'line' and manage the class as a whole. The approach, which is popular in many Scandinavian countries as well as in its native Scotland, has been theorised in several ways, with Piagetian constructivism, Deweyian experiential learning and Vygotskian notions of language all figuring strongly (see Bell et al., 2007). MacBeath crisply captures the approach as one designed to

> enthuse and engage children in learning by making connections with the external world of their lived reality and the inner world of their creative imagination ... it is called storyline because all learning is a form of narrative quest for deeper meaning. (MacBeath in Bell et al., 2007, p. 17)

In Scotland, many educators see the Storyline approach as consistent with the curriculum advice advanced in *The Primary Memorandum* of 1965 and somewhat at variance with the subject or disciplinary emphasis of the 5–14 Guidelines which dominated the 1990s and early 2000s. Noting the centrality of shared learning and reflective learning, MacBeath observes that Storyline takes constructivism one stage further, 'exemplifying the interplay of doing and knowing, showing how children are able to construct new worlds, engaging the enactive in concert with the symbolic' (p. 18). Reflective learning occurs when children want to learn and it is important to recognise the fun and support which enthusiastic teachers give when working with Storyline; the partnership between learner and teacher is paramount and the affective dimension is vital. Many practitioners dedicated to Storyline attest to the fun they had themselves when they learned about the approach through the very active forms of in-service education organised by the originators, Fred Rendell, Steve Bell and Sallie Harkness. Teachers who wanted to learn how to teach with Storyline went through the methodology itself: sleeves up, model making, bringing their stories alive and so on. The theoretical aspects (mentioned above) were very secondary to the real acquisition of skills and know-how. With the shift from the 5–14 curriculum to Curriculum for Excellence, the focus upon more active forms of learning and explicitly *integrated* subject matter, Storyline came into its own again (though it never went away in Scandinavia).

## GROUP WORK

The term group work (sometimes written as groupwork) covers a multitude of approaches used by both primary and secondary teachers, including *Storyline*. The SPRinG project funded by the UK Teaching and Learning Research Programme (TLRP) provides advice to teachers regarding the management of groups. Six key points to guide the planning of group work can be found in TLRP (2007a). These include advice about the number of groups which seem to work well in typical classrooms; group size (4–6 pupils seems often best) and group composition; whether same or mixed ability, friendship, personality and working style; integrating those with particular needs or not; and so on. Many Scottish practitioners would not be surprised to read that 'the best form of mixing is probably putting high and middle ability pupils and low and middle ability pupils together' (TLRP 2007a). Additionally, the report stresses that group work is at its best when it enables pupils to think and talk together, explicitly about their understandings, and are encouraged to question each other and share ideas. It also notes that social skills in pupils need to be developed *first* before communication skills like taking turns to talk; active listening, questioning and explaining; summarising and persuading each other; and agreeing to group decision making. Subsequent attention to the learning of problem-solving skills is then possible. Both primary and secondary Scottish teachers use group work extensively, increasing the demands on pupils and upping the challenges as progress is made. Arguably, however, much more sharing of the advances made and the weaknesses still prevalent could be made between the two sectors in the interests of better pedagogy overall. However, it is pertinent to recognise that a group, irrespective of age, cannot learn *for* an individual – it is still the individual who must learn and this cannot be masked in group work. That said, and looking at the dynamic aspects of group work, takes us to what is commonly referred to as *collaborative learning*.

## COLLABORATIVE LEARNING

For some time in Scotland, there have been a number of authority-wide, professional learning (CPD) initiatives focusing on how teachers manage the work of small groups;

on how pupils can learn to collaborate or cooperate with each other in the course of their learning; and on how discussion can be made more effective. Perhaps the most popular model of cooperative learning stems from the original North American work in the 1980s and 1990s by Johnson et al. (1998). This model is known as *Learning Together* and has five characteristic components. It would be fair to say that very many Scottish teachers, whether knowingly or not, do manage their pupil groups with some adherence to these features, namely that in their teaching there is:

- positive interdependence (pupils need each other as they work and discuss issues – mutual goals are arranged);
- individual accountability (the teacher ensures that individuals do not 'float');
- face-to-face interactions (under various arrangements – pairing, sharing, etc.);
- social skills (good manners and thoughtfulness are emphasised)
- group processing (with the teacher assigning essential tasks).

In some situations the first of these requires considerable skill – and where discipline is wanting, unrelenting patience and effort – on behalf of the teaching staff to make progress. Research in Scotland by Stephen Day with science classes in S2 indicate the gains that can be made by determined staff who focus upon using cooperative learning to advance pupils' learning and develop scientific literacy. In the action research reported in Day and Bryce (2011 and 2012), three academic sessions figured in the work where the focus was upon the handling of controversial topic discussion (socio-scientific issues which have been prioritised in CfE science and crop up especially in the Topical Science strand). Conforming closely to the Learning Together model, the teachers devised tasks where:

1. pupils had to carry out activities and book/Internet-based research, both of which were required to find answers to challenging questions (in this case about global warming);
2. individuals were encouraged to explain and account for their reasoning to each other and to the teacher, sharing their views in open discussion within their groups;
3. the teacher pressed for steps to be completed efficiently and ensured participation by all, asking questions as appropriate and directing pupil activity where required;
4. the noise level within groups was held at a reasonable level to enable all groups to work in parallel without disrupting each other;
5. groups were required to report to each other on the completion of particular steps, turns being taken for individuals to act as spokesperson, with completed diagrams/findings/conclusions displayed appropriately in the laboratory/on computers;
6. the teacher ensured that alternative views on contentious aspects were aired clearly in accord with pupils' scientific knowledge as then understood (and left unresolved if necessary).

Full details of the findings of this research are given in Day and Bryce (2011 and 2012) but some of the main findings are worth noting here.

Cooperative learning proved useful in effecting a shift in the pattern of typical exchanges within science classroom discourse away from teacher-to-pupil (traditional teacher dominated discourse which is *didactic*) towards pupil-to-pupil and pupil-to-teacher interactions. However, the majority of these interactions indicated that more work needs to be done to slow down the interaction and to infuse more higher-order thinking questions into the mix. A possible reason for the high proportion of fast exchanges was that the pupils were young and unfamiliar with both the cooperative learning approach being used in the science context and unfamiliar with the style of teaching adopted by their science teachers. (A questionnaire finding indicated that some 73 per cent agreed that these lessons were different from normal.) However, as teachers became more comfortable with the cooperative learning approach and the materials used, the proportion of slow interactions increased. The pupils noticed that their teachers 'had taken a step back'. There had been a palpable sense of apathy regarding school science (not confined to lower ability pupils) across the S2 cohort in the first round of the action research which was not present in the second or third round cohorts.

The data certainly indicated that 'discussion lessons' can have an influence on pupils' opinions and attitudes towards issues such as climate change and global warming. Somewhat worryingly, 55 per cent of S2 pupils felt that they were not able to express their own opinions in the climate change and global warming discussion lessons. When asked why this was the case in follow-up interviews, the pupils reported a number of reasons. Some felt that their views differed from the majority of the class and did not want to stand out. Others did not feel comfortable expressing their opinions in a group where they did not know the other members well enough. Some said they did not feel that their view would be given proper consideration by other members of the group or by the teacher, which suggests that teachers need to get the classroom ethos right for these types of lesson before pupils will feel confident enough to offer their own opinions. Overall, we concluded that greater use of cooperative learning as part of the teacher's everyday practice should help to foster greater social cohesion within the class which might in turn lead to pupils feeling more comfortable in expressing their views more openly.

In another strand to this research we compared the views of the humanities and science teachers in that school regarding their use of discussion and what they thought it usefully achieved. Teachers of English, Religious and Moral Education, History and Geography as well as the science teachers were interviewed individually. There were detectable differences. The science teachers' emphasis upon discussion tended to stress social skills, communication skills and listening, thus providing practice for democratic citizenship (*discussion as an educational outcome*); the humanities teachers' emphasis was on reasoning skills and the exposure of pupils to multiple perspectives, thus conceiving of discussion more as open-ended inquiry (*discussion as a method of instruction*). We have no reason to believe that the school in question was untypical of Scottish comprehensives.

In turning to other, 'alternative' pedagogies, it might be useful to contextualise them in a particular way, by outlining what recent research on the human brain has to say about learning.

## MODERN NEUROSCIENCE AND MESSAGES FOR THE CLASSROOM?

Given the recent and rapid advances in the medical sciences, not least the variety of ways in which the human brain's workings can be scanned and monitored, there is growing interest in what neuroscience may offer to teachers. Unfortunately, there is rather more overblown enthusiasm in the extrapolations of what scientists can say to teachers than recent research actually offers. The Royal Society itself stated in 2011: 'We urge caution in the rush to apply so-called brain-based methods, many of which do not yet have a sound basis in science' (The Royal Society, 2011, p. v). This is echoed in a recent article in *The Psychologist* (Brookman, 2016) and in Owens and Tanner (2017). Few texts speak plainly but without exaggeration to practitioners, exceptions being Hall (2005), TLRP (2007b) and Geake (2009). With regard to abilities, intelligence(s) and learning styles, in many cases neuroscientists have been able to overturn or at least qualify some of the common assumptions of the last few decades. Before looking at these, let us first consider the question of gender differences and comparisons between more talented and less able pupils.

## The Intellectual Development of Boys and Girls

With advancing technologies, brain differences between men and women are known to be *greater* than previously understood, some of them affecting behaviour in unexpected ways. Women's brains are now known to be better interlinked with more parts involved in specific tasks, men's thinking taking place in more focused areas. Brain-imaging techniques reveal that different anatomical regions of the brain mature differentially in childhood, and typically by several years, for example favouring earlier development in girls for those areas which handle verbal fluency, handwriting and face recognition; favouring earlier development in boys for those which handle spatial and mechanical reasoning and visual targeting (see detail and sources in Bryce and Blown, 2007). At face value, these might suggest that gender differences would be apparent in the development of children's understanding of commonly encountered phenomena in their preschool and school years, and in what children acquire by way of general knowledge. Learning of this kind has the potential to relate to the scientific and other ideas they are taught in schools, either directly (in which case there might be conflicts with ideas prevailing in their local ethnic groups and communities), or indirectly through the influences of role models and expectations that are sometimes held differently for boys and girls. Our own research, using data about children's grasp of basic astronomy, shows clearly that gender does *not*, however, play an important part in such basic thinking. Boys' and girls' development and intuitive understandings are similar. This is important since significantly changed patterns of achievement in formal school learning have nevertheless been evident among boys and girls over recent decades, and these tell us about worldwide cultural change and improved professional expectations (and, arguably, account for what teachers have been able to do through more equitable instruction). The extent to which girls have overtaken boys in regard to achievements and the gender differences apparent in interests and attitudes in school, particularly in science, is reviewed in Bryce and Blown (2007) and across the wider range of achievements in Chapter 85 of this book. To put the point about gender differences more forcefully, there has been a reversal of educational disadvantage from female to male in recent years (just when there are declining proportions of male teachers – not just in Scotland, but worldwide).

## Gifted Individuals

The neurological evidence to date, according to Geake (2009), does indicate that the observed differences between academically gifted (or talented) pupils and their less able counterparts are indeed apparent from brain scanning technology. Differences are detectable in the thickness and density of the neurons of the cortex. In one study considering 'generic' giftedness, for example, 'the frontal cortices of the high IQ group were thinner when the children were young, but then grew rapidly so that when the gifted children reached adolescence, their frontal cortices were significantly thicker than average' (Geake, 2009, p. 82). Importantly, however, Geake is at pains to say that in drawing out implications educationally, it is crucial to note that, despite these anatomical/structural differences, 'the basic functioning of a gifted brain *when learning* is the same for all brains ... Thus it is an unfortunate *edu-myth* that gifted children can teach themselves' (Geake, 2009, p. 83, emphasis added). He goes on to argue that they need guidance and encouragement like any other children, hence advocating that educational programmes for the gifted should include:

- setting tasks with high working memory demands, e.g., tasks with multiple components which require extensive information selection;
- reducing the quantity of small tasks, e.g., repetitive basic examples;
- using challenging tests to evaluate prior knowledge (gifted children, like all children, learn extensively outside of school);
- designing assessment tasks with the higher-order Bloom's taxonomies of analysis and synthesis;
- using above-age learning materials;
- offering lessons on topics beyond the regular curriculum. (Geake, 2009, p. 84)

This naturally takes us to the question of how intelligence itself is viewed.

## Abilities and Intelligences

During the later decades of the twentieth century, it was (and probably still is) common to regard people as having *multiple* intelligences, rather than a certain level of *general* intelligence. Howard Gardner's original (1983) model of multiple intelligences (MI) splits human cognition into seven intelligences (linguistic, logical-mathematical, musical, bodily-kinaesthetic, spatial, interpersonal and intra-personal intelligence), postulating that people have a unique blend of these intelligences. Naturally these have had great appeal to educators, for the model implies that we need to attend to all intelligences during schooling. This has provided justification for increased variety and flexibility in the curriculum (see Gardner, 1999 and Smith, 2008). The evidence from neuroscience research however, according to Geake (2009), is not supportive. '[T]he more sober reality is that cognitive abilities tend to be correlated within an individual; hence, the increasing numbers of teachers' reports about not observing any long-term impact of applying MI theory in their classrooms' (Geake, 2009, p. 79). This means that the neuroscience is in line with earlier statistical research which revealed the intercorrelations among the various sub-tests of intelligence quotient (IQ) measures. In his discussion of the multiple intelligence argument, Geake widens the debate, noting that: 'With a couple of updates of terminology, Gardner's MI is Plato's curriculum' (Geake, 2009, p. 78). And emphatically that:

> as worthy as such a curriculum might be, does this imply that our brains process the specialized information of these subject areas completely separately from each other? No ... There are not multiple intelligences so much as there are multiple applications of general intelligence to various endeavours. (Geake, 2009, p. 78)

This is not hair-splitting, though, in practice, it perhaps turns on whether Gardner's theory is used to justify *restricting* what pupils get access to in order to promote their learning, or whether it is used to *broaden* what they need to tackle in order to promote their learning. School learning both reflects and contributes to individual cognitive differences and so, thinking of the typical Scottish school curriculum, the traditional stress has been on breadth rather than specialisation. On paper however, CfE allows schools to be more flexible in the curriculum offered to pupils and so a more restricted curriculum for some pupils could be considered to be an operational option of flexibility. It seems that significant degrees of variation between schools have not taken place to date. Will they now be *allowed to occur*, in the prevailing political climate of centralised control in Scotland, questions having been raised about the curriculum in the light of international comparisons about pupils' attainments (see Chapter 68 concerning the PISA 2015 findings reported in 2016)?

With regard to factors which determine human intelligence and age-old debates about nature *or* nurture, nature *and* nurture, nature *via* nurture and so forth, behavioural geneticists like Plomin have shown that (perhaps counter-intuitively) while there is certainly a significant genetic influence upon human intelligence, and environmental influences do significantly shape it, the heritable genetic contribution actually *increases* with age (see, for example, Plomin, 1994). That is, while environmental influences, including schooling, can give children more skills and knowledge, and therefore contribute to observable differences between individuals, learning also 'increases genetic influence by reducing random environmental effects. That is, learning enables us to reach our genetically mediated ceilings' (Geake, 2009, p. 89). Or, in the words of Ridley (2003), 'The older you grow, the less your family background predicts your IQ and the better your genes predict it' (p. 91).

### Learning Styles

A major review and analysis of research into learning styles was conducted in the early 2000s by TLRP in England. The findings were overall critical of what had been up until then a wide promotion of the idea that learners vary significantly in their preferred style of learning (there being very many ways of categorising these styles). In their recommendations, Coffield et al. concluded that pupils are more likely to gain from being trained in how to learn and develop themselves rather than in being assigned to a particular learning style: 'One of the main aims of encouraging a metacognitive approach is to enable learners to choose the most appropriate learning strategy from a wide range of options to fit the particular task in hand ...' (Coffield et al., 2004, p. 132). Regarding one line of thought about learning styles, TLRP (2007b) refers to an investigation into the effectiveness of different learning styles taking up the notion that learners might have visual (V), auditory (A) or kinesthetic (K) preferences. The TLRP reviewers noted that 'this study showed no benefit from having material presented in one's preferred learning style', concluding that:

> attempts to focus on learning styles were 'wasted effort'. Of course, this does not detract from the general value for all learners when teachers present learning materials using a full range of forms and different media. Such an approach can engage the learner and support their learning processes in many different ways, but the existing research does not support labelling children in terms of a particular learning style.

Scottish practitioners, on the whole, have never been extreme on this matter.

### FINALLY

At the start of this chapter it was conceded that learning is difficult to grasp conceptually, despite us all having firm *personal* understandings of what we variously do and do not understand as individuals – and equally strong views that we *are* capable of learning (we simply need the right kind of help). By exploring some of the main pedagogical approaches which are evident in modern Scottish classrooms (and probably, for the most part, elsewhere in the UK), the discussion has dwelt on approaches which are now part of the central educational landscape (like the *activity* so important to young people's advancement) and the strategies which teachers adopt in increasing numbers (like managing *cooperative learning* in groups). Exploring them critically has raised a number of related ideas and practical considerations. Necessarily, the discussion has also raised 'alternative' pedagogies, several originating in the work of particular teachers and programme enthusiasts – with some being doubted for their real efficacy. Usefully, at least in this writer's eyes, modern science has been able, and will continue to be able, to shed light on what is worth doing or needs to be better developed. Learning being what learning is, this chapter has, however, only scratched the surface of a very big topic.

## REFERENCES

Ausubel, D. P. (2000) *The Acquisition and Retention of Knowledge.* Dordrecht, The Netherlands: Kluwer Academic Publishers.

Bell, S., Harkness, S. and White, G. (eds) (2007) *Storyline. Past, Present and Future.* Glasgow: Enterprising Careers, University of Strathclyde.

Blown, E. J. and Bryce, T. G. K. (2017) 'Switching between everyday and scientific Language', *Research in Science Education*, 47 (3), 621–53.

Brookman, A. (2016) 'Learning from educational neuroscience', *The Psychologist*, 29, 766–9.

Bryce, T. G. K. and Blown, E. J. (2007) 'Gender effects in children's development and Education', *International Journal of Science Education*, 29 (13), 1655–78.

Coffield, F., Moseley, D., Hall, E. and Ecclestone, K. (2004) 'Learning styles and pedagogy in post-16 learning: a systematic and critical review', report no. 041543. London: Learning and Skills Research Centre.

Cohen, L., Manion, L., Morrison, K. and Wyse, D. (2010) *A Guide to Teaching Practice*, revised fifth edition. London: Routledge.

Day, S. P. and Bryce, T. G. K. (2011) 'Does the discussion of socio-scientific issues require a paradigm shift in science teachers' thinking?' *International Journal of Science* Education, 33 (12), 1675–1702, doi:10.1080/09500693.2010.519804

Day, S. P. and Bryce, T. G. K. (2012) 'The benefits of cooperative learning to socio-scientific discussion in secondary school science', *International Journal of Science Education*, doi:10.1080/09500 693.2011.642324

Gardner, H. (1999) *Intelligence Reframed. Multiple intelligences for the 21st century.* New York: Basic Books.

Geake, J. G. (2009) *The Brain at School: Educational Neuroscience in the Classroom.* Maidenhead: Open University Press.

Hall, J. (2005) 'Neuroscience and education. A review of the contribution of brain science to teaching and learning', SCRE Report No 121. Glasgow: The Scottish Council for Research in Education.

Johnson, D. W., Johnson, R. T. and Holubec, E. (1998) *Cooperation in the Classroom.* Boston: Allyn and Bacon.

Owens, M. T. and Tanner, K. (2017) 'Teaching as brain changing: exploring connections between neuroscience and innovative teaching', *CBE Life Sciences Education*, 16 (2), 1–9.

Plomin, R. (1994) *Genetics and Experience: The Interplay Between Nature and Nurture.* Newbury Park, CA: Sage Publications.

Ridley, M. (2003) *Nature via Nurture*. London: Harper Perennial.

Smith, M. (2008) *Howard Gardner, Multiple Intelligences and Education*. Online at www.infed.org/thinkers/gardner.htm

The Royal Society (2011) 'Brain Waves Module 2: Neuroscience: Implications for education and lifelong learning', RS Policy Document, 02/11. Online at https://royalsociety.org/~/media/Royal_Society_Content/policy/publications/2011/4294975733.pdf

TLRP (2007a) *Principles into Practice: A Teacher's Guide to Research Evidence on Teaching and Learning*. Online at https://www.yumpu.com/en/document/view/43747097/principles-into-practice-a-teachers-guide-to-research-evidence-on-

TLRP (2007b) *Education and Neuroscience: Evidence, Theory and Practical Application*. Online at www.tlrp.org/pub/documents/Neuroscience%20Commentary%20FINAL.pdf

# 24

# Leadership, Management and Organisation in the Primary School

*Deirdre Torrance*

## INTRODUCTION

In Scotland, we like to focus on what makes us culturally distinctive from other parts of the United Kingdom and indeed from countries further afield. In Scottish education, we like to focus on the consensual nature of policy formation and our discrete legislation that arguably protects us from the worst effects of UK policy implementation. However, many contemporary Scottish education policy themes bear a striking resemblance to global policy themes that pay no heed to borders or legislation as they circumnavigate the globe. 'Leadership' provides an excellent example of this phenomenon. Indeed, its positioning in the title of this chapter is illustrative of the manner in which leadership is currently positioned as a higher order term in relation to management and organisation/administration. The distinction often made between leadership and management has the potential for including a wider range of staff in collegiate leadership practices. Conceptualisations of educational leadership continue to evolve, often interpreted as involving a relationship of social influence, fluid in its practice across the school organisation, and responsive to context and purpose. Less often explored is whose influence and for what purpose?

This chapter begins with an exploration of the terms leadership, management and organisation, first in the global policy context, then in the Scottish policy context. It goes on to explore those terms in relation to key staff remits within the primary school in Scotland, before exploring some of the opportunities and challenges that the enactment of those terms present for school practice and policy.

The chapter concludes with a brief discussion of what is needed to turn the policy rhetoric into practice to enable all staff to contribute in distinctive and complementary ways to school leadership, management and organisation in Scotland's primary schools. The relevance of this discussion is brought into sharp focus, as policymakers and practitioners across Scotland work through the implications of the governance review and related proposals to reform the governance of schools. The review, entitled *Education Governance: Next Steps – Empowering Our Teachers, Parents and Communities to Deliver Excellence and Equity for Our Children* (www.gov.scot/Resource/0052/00521038.pdf), was published in June 2017. In Chapter 27 of this text, Danny Murphy discusses implications for leadership in detail.

## LEADERSHIP, MANAGEMENT AND ORGANISATION IN THE GLOBAL POLICY CONTEXT

Internationally, the discourse surrounding leadership, management and organisation (more often referred to as administration within the UK) has shifted significantly since the 1990s. This has occurred in response to many (but not all) education systems becoming increasingly preoccupied with school leadership as they chase the improvement agenda, in the belief that increased leadership capacity will translate into improved school achievement and pupil attainment. In order to compete in the global marketplace, education is placed under increasing pressure to deliver improved services to meet the needs of society. Traditional top-down change management strategies with heroic leaders at their apex were found to be largely ineffective in securing sustained school improvement. School improvement came to be understood as complex, requiring more than the management of systems and people; rather, a more sophisticated and nuanced relationship between members of the different strata of school hierarchies. The perception had developed of management as formal, structural and operational, with leadership heralded as a more inclusive, non-elitist, flexible, strategic and shared endeavour. The term organisation (or administration) came to be perceived as functional and not worthy of much attention.

Within this same time period, more and more responsibility for schools and their performance has been devolved to school level, as part of a 'glocalisation' movement, within which international and national policy themes are translated into local solutions, in theory at least. In more recent years, the recession experienced by many countries has led governments around the world to identify strategies to get more 'bang for their buck'. In so doing, higher expectations have been placed on staff in schools to engage with, and effectively take more responsibility for, the school improvement agenda. Arguably, the governance review with its proposals to reform the governance of schools is a natural response to such trends. This period has also seen the stripping out of strata with subsequent flatter models of school management being seen as desirable at the same time as raising expectations for what schools should deliver. A concomitant theme in international policy is the 'reprofessionalisation' of teachers. Torrance and Forde (2016) discuss the debate surrounding reprofessionalisation, both generally at an international level, and specifically at the national level in Scotland. Essentially, reprofessionalisation can enhance professional agency whilst deprofessionalisation can ensure compliance with externally mandated policies, resulting in a narrowing of the scope of professional decision making and practice.

## LEADERSHIP, MANAGEMENT AND ORGANISATION IN THE SCOTTISH POLICY CONTEXT

In Scotland, the global policy movement to enhance teacher quality can be traced through new and enhanced expectations for the teaching profession in Scotland, as apparent in the Donaldson review of teacher education (Scottish Government, 2011a), the McCormac review of teacher employment (Scottish Government, 2011b), the General Teaching Council for Scotland (GTCS) (2012) *Review of Professional Standards* and the governance review. The promotion of educational leadership forms one strand of those expectations. Arguably, the consensual policy development around its promotion was made possible by the publication in 2008 (revised 2010) of *The EIS and Leadership in Schools*. This long awaited policy statement (Educational Institute of Scotland, 2010), issued by the largest

Scottish professional body/teaching union, made a distinction between leadership and management, positioned leadership as intrinsic to the teacher's remit, and paved the way for an uncontested national reform strategy.

With its new independent status and enhanced position, GTCS subsequently revised in 2012 the full suite of professional standards. In 2014, GTCS introduced a five-yearly professional update requirement for all teachers, as Scotland's solution to alternative and unpalatable reaccreditation schemes adopted by other countries. This provided the mechanism for reform, through the implementation of key recommendations from *Teaching Scotland's Future* (TSF) (Donaldson, 2010, p. 16), a simultaneous attempt to reprofessionalise and deprofessionalise teaching, through the promotion of 'extended professionalism':

> This review endorses the vision of teachers as increasingly expert practitioners whose professional practice and relationships are rooted in strong values, who take responsibility for their own development and who are developing their capacity both to use and contribute to the collective understanding of the teaching and learning process.

In the standards, the GTCS explicitly aligns its expectations with the policy aspirations of TSF. Indeed, the standards have formed a key policy element in efforts to raise the quality of the teaching profession, with the GTCS asserting that,

> These revised standards support the creation of a reinvigorated approach to 21st century teacher professionalism, recognising the importance of teacher responsibility for, and ownership of, their professional learning. The teaching profession, working in partnership with other professions, has a moral imperative to secure the best learning opportunities and experiences for all learners in Scotland. (www.gtcs.org.uk/professional-standards/professional-standards.aspx)

One way of taking forward that policy aspiration – much in keeping with the Educational Institute of Scotland (EIS) (2010) policy – was the positioning of leadership across the standards:

> All teachers should have opportunities to be leaders. They lead learning for, and with, all learners with whom they engage. ... Different forms of leadership are expressed across the suite of Professional Standards including leadership for learning, teacher leadership and working collegiately to build leadership capacity in others. (www.gtcs.org.uk/professional-standards/professional-standards.aspx)

In this way, we can see that despite Scotland's unique cultural context, its (some would argue erroneous) historical belief in the standing of its education system, along with its separate school governance arrangements and education legislation, Scottish policy has followed the international trend of largely replacing management with leadership in its policy discourse in order to stimulate workforce reform and engagement with the school improvement agenda. Global travelling educational leadership policy has been mediated by embedded Scottish practices and cultures, negotiated through consensual policy networks resulting in little opposition. Indeed, Scotland has adopted the TSF (Donaldson, 2010, p. 2) uncontested mantra of: 'the two most important and achievable ways in which school education can realise the high aspirations Scotland has for its young people are through supporting and strengthening, firstly, the quality of teaching, and secondly, the quality of leadership'. This mantra is very similar to the global travelling policy theme identified in and propagated through a report by McKinsey & Company (Barber et al., 2010, p. 5). McKinsey & Company was commissioned (in collaboration with the then National College for Leadership of Schools and Children's Services in England) to compile a report, summarising findings from an international review of school leadership. The report quoted and promoted the view of Leithwood and colleagues that, 'school leadership is second only to classroom teaching as an influence on pupil learning' (Leithwood et al., 2006, p. 4). As discussed by Torrance and Humes (2015), that endorsement of school leadership shaped contemporary thinking and policy but was devoid of the nuanced argument crafted by Leithwood et al. over many years. They recognised the controversial basis for the claim, essentially making clear that it was not leadership per se, but rather its practice as a catalyst, that determined whether or not that mantra held true.

Despite the unique nature of its education system, contemporary Scottish education policy aligns itself to certain principles found in international rhetoric, including the core principle that leadership should form an integral feature of the remit of every qualified teacher. Expectations previously located within the now discontinued Chartered Teacher Standard have been repositioned to form new expectations for every teacher. In so doing, teachers are being increasingly expected to demonstrate that they are expert practitioners, with particular focus on (the somewhat conflated themes of) practitioner enquiry and teacher leadership, through engagement with and leading of curriculum development and the enhancement of pedagogy. Subsequent to the governance review, it will be interesting to see how the new Education Workforce Council for Scotland, which is to replace the GTCS, will take this policy agenda forward.

The inclusion of all teachers in school leadership represents an internationally prescribed distributed perspective on leadership, frequently referred to in Scottish policy as distributive leadership (propagated as more democratic), the term endorsed in the rhetoric of official inspectorate documents. Distributed leadership represents a government-endorsed performativity strategy providing 'subtle and clever ways to deliver standardised packages of government reforms and performance targets' (Hargreaves and Fink, 2009, p. 191), the assumption being that formal leaders at the apex of hierarchical management structures will engender the requisite culture, processes and practices to legitimise and enable informal leaders to focus on the leadership of learning, within the overall strategic direction of the school. This assumption is premised upon staff having a clear understanding of how their role might contribute to school leadership, and having the capability to lead. The challenges to such an assumption are discussed below.

## SUPPORT STAFF LEADERSHIP

In the fourth edition of *Scottish Education*, Carroll and Torrance (2013) explored the ways in which the role of support staff with the remit of supporting teaching and learning has evolved in response to changes in expectations of the teacher's position. The role has become increasingly complex in part due to: enhanced expectations placed on the teacher's position; efforts to free more of teachers' time to focus on teaching; the mainstreaming of pupils with more complex educational needs; and fiscal restraint with fewer teaching and support staff available. Support staff can find themselves in para-leadership roles, for example in supporting the educational needs of vulnerable pupils, or in the public spaces of the school and frequently in the absence of teachers. They perform this duty often with little or no pre- or in-service training or professional development, either for themselves or for the teachers with whom they work closely, learning on the job and responding to contextual expectations. As their role often requires them to switch between different aspects of their remit, they frequently work with a range of teachers, negotiating working relationships, different expectations of their role, and the boundaries between teaching and non-teaching roles, often with unclear line management arrangements.

Arguably, within a distributed perspective, there is the potential for support staff to have an influencing relationship within and beyond the school. The headteacher's or senior management team's endorsement of and encouragement for that leadership role within 'whole school' areas is key. However, even with that, support staff may not be perceived by teachers or indeed by themselves as having a leadership locus within the classroom. The exception to this may be in relation to pupil care, welfare and personal concerns for which support staff may have a legitimised leadership role, perceived as the expert in providing long-standing or in-depth support for pupils with additional support needs, both within and outwith the classroom context.

Despite their unique position and contribution, support staff can feel somewhat isolated as they negotiate their role according to each context, purpose and the colleagues that they work with. Clear line management and a defined support network, along with greater role clarity and more public acknowledgement of the contribution they can make to school leadership may help support staff with this. There are clear implications for both support staff and teachers in formal and informal leadership positions in relation to developing the school's capacity for leadership for learning.

## TEACHER LEADERSHIP

The teacher's leadership and organisational attention is focused largely on the classroom or learning context: the micro level. It is promoted as a strategy for engaging teachers in bottom-up, democratic school improvement processes. This strategy is located within a perspective that achievement and attainment can only be improved if the quality of pupil experience is enhanced by teachers themselves identifying areas for improvement through critical reflection in and on practice, taking professional responsibility for enacting changes to practice. Teacher influence is perceived as distinct from and complementary to formal management positions, exercised through relationships with peers, requiring power sharing through professional responsibility, mutual accountability and collaboration.

Despite various interpretations of, and conceptual confusion with, teacher leadership, two themes recur across a number of definitions: influence and pedagogic focus. In order to have leadership influence, teachers require to be perceived as effective practitioners. They also need to be: skilled in relation to the craft of pedagogy with a level of expertise in at least some area; skilled in working with adults as well as children; and motivated to continuously innovate and improve their own and others' practice to enhance the educational experience of pupils. Moreover, teachers' professional identity needs to incorporate a sense of agency beyond the semi-private context of their own classroom into the wider school context. Teacher leadership therefore involves teachers moving from the relative safety of their micro-level space(s) within the school organisation into other teachers' micro-level spaces, or to 'break cover' in their efforts to influence practice within the wider meso-level of the school.

Teacher leadership does not occur in isolation, being embedded within a distributed perspective, enabled and supported (or constrained) by a variety of factors including peers and those in formal leadership positions. Arguably, within a distributed perspective, teachers can be instrumental in transforming schools through school improvement efforts, exercising influence individually and collectively. Teacher leadership is therefore promoted as reprofessionalising teaching as pedagogic practice. As such, it is perceived as central to constructions of school leadership. Teacher leadership potentially: strengthens school organisation through developing a learning community; builds networks of support and expertise; enhances teachers' self-esteem and work satisfaction; and increases motivation, performance and retention levels. Central to teacher leadership is a developmental process focused on continuous professional learning for self and others, linked to a sense of agency to construct and contribute to school improvement.

However, despite such laudable claims, there is limited and mixed empirical evidence of the impact of teacher leadership either informally focused at classroom level or formally focused on wider school responsibility. Despite the rhetoric and policy endorsement, beyond classroom organisation and sound pedagogy – which could alternatively be perceived as a basic premise for teaching being regarded as a profession – it is questionable whether all teachers have the disposition or capabilities to enact a leadership role. Moreover, for those who do, their leadership potential may be constrained to more accurately represent delegated activities or tasks, since in reality, school improvement foci and policy is generally top down in nature within Scottish primary schools.

Teacher leadership involves teachers perceiving their role as central to progressing collaborative practices. The collaborative nature of the professional development process behind teacher leadership is recognised in the professional standards for non-promoted Scottish teachers (GTCS, 2012) but limited to expressions of building working relationships in the Standard for Full Registration. The Standard for Career Long Professional Learning provides a more developed form of teacher leadership, with the development of curriculum and pedagogy at its core, aligned to practitioner enquiry. However, in both standards, the construct of practitioner enquiry is limited to 'know how' rather than enact, with the absence of an articulation of autonomy and agency as facets of practitioner enquiry, and a corresponding absence of an articulation of the exercise of social influence related to teacher leadership (Torrance and Forde, 2016). As such, the promotion of teacher leadership in the standards is constrained, with a lack of guidance for its practice in engaging teachers in bottom-up, democratic school improvement processes.

## MIDDLE LEADERSHIP AND MANAGEMENT

The title of the role of middle leader is apt, as it is where the micro and meso-levels meet in the school's organisational structure. Middle leaders therefore have different areas of responsibility, including leadership of the curriculum, departmental leadership, pastoral care, additional support provision and school improvement initiatives. As members of the senior management team, middle leaders contribute to and lead aspects of the school improvement agenda, often including a focus on developing a learning culture, leading learning and leading change. In the exercise of their role, as well as budget and resource responsibilities, middle leaders may have line management responsibility for individuals or groups of staff. Indeed there is an emphasis on leading and collaborating with teams in the limited theory available, and in policy rhetoric, with an associated emphasis on motivating and leading people. Middle leaders in the primary school are generally principal teachers or depute headteachers. They commonly have a teaching commitment, which may involve at least partial responsibility for a class. Their middle leadership, management and organisational attention focuses both on the department level (infant, middle or upper primary stages) and the wider school context. The role is very much context specific and responsive to the needs of different primary school models across Scotland, be they small/large, rural/urban or deprived/affluent. Even within a school, a variety of roles may be classified as middle leaders. So, a middle leader in a large primary school could be one of several principal teachers or depute headteachers. In a small primary school, the principal teacher may be the only other member of the senior management team or, in a shared headship model, and may be the only continuously present promoted member of staff.

The role of the middle leader is complex, particularly within a distributed perspective, as incumbents mediate a range of different perspectives and needs, translating policy into practice. Day-to-day management and organisational priorities often supersede middle leaders' attention to the leadership dimensions of their role. Regardless, given the flatter management structures of schools and the reduction of promoted posts due to fiscal restraint, middle leaders potentially perform a crucial role in the leadership, management and organisation of the primary school. Perhaps surprisingly then, this role has been given scant attention in either policy or theory until relatively recently, perhaps explaining the dearth of structured professional development (career long professional learning) for middle leaders in Scotland until very recently. When the professional standards in Scotland were revised, a new Standard for Middle Leadership and Management was developed. Middle leaders may now draw from a range of professional standards (GTCS, 2012) to support different facets of their professional development and the professional development of colleagues, from the Standard for Full Registration, to the Standard for Career Long Professional Learning, to the Standard for Middle Leadership and Management. Indeed, in their preparation for headship, some middle leaders may also draw from the Standard for Headship (GTCS, 2012).

## HEADSHIP

The headteacher's leadership, management and organisational attention is, in theory at least, focused largely on the strategic aspects of the school and wider context, where the meso- and macro levels meet. That said, the nature of schools, community needs and human relationships often means that headteachers perceive the practice realities as focused more on immediate 'firefighting'. Moreover, in smaller primary schools, headteachers may have a regular teaching or class commitment, they may be teaching heads or hold one of the growing number of shared headships in rural communities, with their attention stretched across pedagogic, school and systems leadership. The influence of the headteacher's role in Scottish primary schools is both direct and indirect, working with and through others for strategic school improvement. The headteacher legitimises or constrains the leadership influence of others across the leadership continuum, their role being central to and omnipresent within a truly distributed perspective on leadership.

In Chapter 27, Danny Murphy discusses a range of challenges in the recruitment and retention of headteachers in Scotland and links this discussion to the governance review. Forde and Torrance (2016) also discuss those challenges, critically examining the policy expectations and demands placed on headteachers. They conducted an interrogation and textual analysis of successive sets of professional standards and the key purpose of headship with its articulation of the expectations of the role, and drew from an analysis of interview data relating to the lived experiences of headteachers. From this, they discuss tensions experienced by headteachers as they work to meet the increased expectations placed upon their role, including higher expectations for: their leadership of learning in the classroom context; development of a culture of improvement and a sense of community in the wider school context; and contributing to the educational system beyond the school context. They do so whilst working within clear limitations of their ability to shape those expectations. Such limitations include the multiple and competing accountabilities headteachers face, as well as the bureaucratic demands placed upon them, along with the domination of operational matters and administrative demands in contrast to their strategic leadership aspirations for the role. As an officer of the local authority, Scottish primary headteachers mediate the space between the professional autonomy of a senior manager and their accountability to others, with limited scope for major budgetary and staffing decisions, and the time-consuming paperwork required by central services.

This role complexity, regardless of type or size of school, is exacerbated by the sense of isolation experienced by many heads, compounding the emotional demands of the role. The headteacher is held accountable for the overall quality of learning across the school, as well as for the smooth running of the school, and held legally responsible for any incidents that occur within or indeed outwith the school. That accountability can be made very public through the publication of Her Majesty's Inspectorate of Education (HMIe) inspection reports and Care Commission inspection reports (for pre-5 education), as well as academic attainment levels, often perceived as very blunt instruments for measuring human endeavour or influence on young people and their communities. Not surprisingly, headteachers actively engage with and develop networks of support, through their relationships with the school's senior management team, with fellow headteachers, with parents' associations and with those within and beyond the school community that share their motivations and interests. They expend considerable effort in aligning strategic vision with school improvement efforts, motivated by the potential to enhance the learning experiences and life chances of both individual and large numbers of children. Indeed, headteachers are perceived as central to the improvement agenda in Scottish education, despite their generally limited engagement in teaching and learning. In recognition of this, newly developed national professional learning programmes have been designed both to prepare and support aspirant (Postgraduate Certificate of Education Into Headship) and newly appointed (Postgraduate Certificate In Headship) headteachers. The potential effect of the introduction of the mandatory headship qualification by 2018 on applications for headship will be of interest to employers across Scotland.

## OPPORTUNITIES AND CHALLENGES

Educational leadership, management and organisation continue to evolve in theory, policy and practice. As we approach the third decade of this millennium and explore alternative governance arrangements for Scottish education, it is opportune to take stock of the opportunities and challenges facing their practice in Scottish primary schools. The theory of educational leadership, management and organisation is still relatively young, originally borrowed from business models, and still establishing itself as its own field and drawing from contested assumptions. Although the pool of empirical research is widening and deepening, much of what is written is aspirational or normative. Through lack of investment, there is comparatively little quality research conducted in Scottish schools to ascertain the nature and extent of educational leadership, management and organisation. Given the expectations now placed upon all Scottish teachers to contribute to school leadership, Scotland provides a rich case study for exploration. In so doing, insights could contribute to international understandings, instead of Scottish policymakers borrowing prescriptions from other nations.

The positioning of leadership as a higher order set of processes to management and organisation is deliberate. However, for the claims made about the impact that leadership can have on school effectiveness and its outcomes, there needs to be a clear understanding of what leadership practices are required to be securely rooted in school organisations and cultures. We need better understandings of, and agreement about, who does what and how each discrete leadership and management contribution relates to and supports the others. If a distributed leadership perspective is indeed what the profession and its policymakers ascribe to – genuine educational leadership rather than performance leadership – then candid discussion is needed around power, influence and accountability. It is not enough for individual schools and teachers to interpret the aspirations of Scottish policy documents including those of the professional standards.

*Teaching Scotland's Future* (Donaldson, 2010, p. 5) proclaimed, 'There is an urgent need to challenge the narrow interpretations of the teacher's role which have created unhelpful philosophical and structural divides.' Subsequently, the professional standards in Scotland were designed as a policy tool for workforce reform (Torrance and Humes, 2015). However, the constructs of 'teacher leadership' and 'practitioner enquiry' underpinning the standards are complex, loosely articulated and not expanded upon (Torrance and Forde, 2016, p. 122):

> the challenges that occur in the space where teacher leadership and practitioner enquiry overlap need to be recognised and addressed, specifically the profession itself needs to ask: who owns the space where teachers' pedagogical expertise is recognised and collaborative processes are enacted?

Since the most recent version of the professional standards was published in 2012, it is now timely to consider how they might be reviewed and further revised. This time, the teaching profession could be actively and wholeheartedly engaged in the consultation and development processes with the intention to build understanding, consensus and agree expectations to underpin the standards, rather than using policy aspirations to try to drive reform. In so doing, the standards could be further utilised as an effective developmental tool to support professional learning and self-evaluation (Forde and Torrance, 2016). Such workforce reform as part of a wider strategy of modernisation will require teachers to regard themselves as experts in curriculum and pedagogy – not technicians implementing policies designed elsewhere – with a sense of agency and set of competencies to enable them to engage collaboratively in leading with and influencing others. If all teachers are indeed to be leaders then the focus of that activity and sphere of influence need to be clear. Similarly, the contribution that support staff can make to school leadership needs to be better understood and supported.

Within such new understandings, the roles of the middle leader and manager, and of headteacher, need careful consideration. Whilst the attractions of stripping out layers of school management staffing in search of less expensive and more collegiate structures is understandable, it is time to consider if the models of school management and organisation sufficiently meet the needs of schools as complex organisations, something that is beginning to be recognised through the governance review. Moreover, the adequacy of apprenticeship stages warrants further discussion to ensure that teachers are well prepared and properly supported in preparation for taking on senior management roles.

If the role of headteacher is indeed fundamentally important for the development of leadership capacity and for school improvement, then clearer expectations and parameters are required to enable headteachers to focus their efforts on impacting on 'leadership for learning' across a school community. Headteachers should then be better able to address the key purpose of headship as expressed in the Standard for Headship: focusing on teaching and learning. Again, the governance review recognises this need. In order for this workforce reform to be progressed, multilevel conversations are required to reach consensus over who is accountable and for what, who holds power and how this should be shared, and who should have influence and for what purposes – both within schools and across the wider system. In so doing, the demanding public role, the conflicting expectations and the multiple accountabilities that headteachers face, along with the multitude of operational matters that impede their ability to engage with strategic leadership and management priorities need to be addressed (Forde and Torrance, 2016).

## CONCLUSION

Arguably, Scottish policy around educational leadership has never been more clearly articulated or aligned. However, there is still a distance to go to ensure that the rhetoric becomes the reality, with support staff and all teachers, regardless of their remit, perceiving their role as making a valuable contribution to school leadership, management and organisation. In tandem with this is the need for further discussion of how various roles can make a distinctive and complementary contribution to school leadership. As part of that discussion, it would seem appropriate to return to the question of who is accountable, and for what, in the leadership and management of our schools. From that, the specific role contributions both within the school and across the wider education system can be better defined. As new models of governance are explored, if distributed leadership is to continue to feature as the endorsed model of school leadership, then collective responsibility will be key within fluid models of shared power and decision making.

The agency for, and practice of, educational leadership, management and organisation is socially constructed within school contexts. Educational leadership has the potential to empower members of a school's community to construct rather than merely implement policy. The questions requiring further exploration are: to what extent will that potential be realised, what will be required to support that process, and is Scotland ready to engage in challenging conversations around power, authority and accountability?

## REFERENCES

Barber, M., Whelan, F. and Clark, M. (2010) *Capturing the Leadership Premium: How the World's Top School Systems Are Building Leadership Capacity For the Future.* London: McKinsey & Company.

Carroll, M. and Torrance, D. (2013) 'Classroom management: working with school support assistants in the primary classroom', in T. G. K. Bryce, W. M. Humes, D. Gillies and A. Kennedy (eds), *Scottish Education, Fourth Edition: Referendum.* Edinburgh: Edinburgh University Press, pp. 413–22.

Donaldson, G. (2010) *Teaching Scotland's Future: Report of a review of teacher education in Scotland.* Edinburgh: Scottish Government.

Educational Institute of Scotland (2010) *The EIS and Leadership in Schools.* Edinburgh: EIS.

Forde, C. and Torrance, D. (2016) 'Changing expectations and experiences of headship in Scotland', *International Studies in Educational Administration*, 44 (2), 21–37.

GTCS (2012) *Review of Professional Standards.* Online at www.gtcs.org.uk/web/FILES/about-gtcs/statement-for-review-of-professional-standards.pdf

Hargreaves, A. and Fink, D. (2009) 'Distributed leadership: democracy or delivery?' in A. Harris (ed.), *Distributed School Leadership: Different Perspectives.* London: Springer, pp. 181–93.

Leithwood, K., Day, C., Sammons, P., Harris, A. and Hopkins, D. (2006) *Seven Strong Claims About Successful School Leadership.* Nottingham: National College for School Leadership.

Scottish Government (2011a) *Teaching Scotland's Future – Report of a Review of Teacher Education in Scotland.* Online at www.gov.scot/Publications/2011/01/13092132/0

Scottish Government (2011b) *Advancing Professionalism in Teaching: A Review of Teacher Employment in Scotland.* Edinburgh: Scottish Government.

Torrance, D. and Forde, C. (2016) 'Redefining what it means to be a teacher through professional standards: implications for continuing teacher education', *European Journal of Teacher Education*, www.tandfonline.com/doi/abs/10.1080/02619768.2016.1246527?journalCode=cete20

Torrance, D. and Humes, W. (2015) 'The shifting discourses of educational leadership: international trends and Scotland's response', *Educational Management, Administration and Leadership*, 43 (5), 792–810.

# 25

# Discipline, Behaviour and Ethos in Primary Schools

*Jackie Ravet*

Concern over standards of behaviour in schools is, arguably, one of the key educational issues of our times. It has simmered near the top of the government agenda for decades, fuelling public debate and stimulating the ongoing quest for the causes of troublesome behaviour and effective approaches to discipline in the primary classroom. Perceptions of behaviour in Scottish primary schools are therefore constantly evolving. However, there has been a significant shift over the past decade. This shift is linked to growing acceptance of the idea that pupil behaviour is inextricably linked to the development of a positive school ethos, the quality of teacher/pupil relationships and opportunities for child-centred, participatory learning as set out in the Scottish Curriculum for Excellence (Scottish Government, 2004). This trend has been supported by a policy emphasis on a range of dialogic and relational behaviour support strategies, such as restorative practice. These strategies, and their impact on teachers and pupils, have been systematically trialled, monitored and reviewed across Scottish schools via a series of national research studies, most recently by Black et al. (2012). Arguably, this cumulative research provides an evidence base for the Scottish Government claim that behaviour in Scottish schools is showing 'encouraging and sustained improvement … [with] fewer and fewer children being excluded' (Scottish Government, 2013, p. 1). In this chapter, the links between the concepts of discipline, behaviour and ethos within the Scottish educational context will be examined. This analysis will begin with an historical overview that will highlight the evolution of these concepts over past decades. The focus will then shift to recent policy initiatives and their implementation to date. Areas of controversy associated with policy implementation will be highlighted in order to provide a critical perspective.

## HISTORICAL CONTEXT

The way that terms like discipline, behaviour and ethos are understood and addressed in primary schools is inextricably linked to historical and sociocultural context, institutional context and, of course, to the specific context of individual classrooms. There is therefore an inevitable disjunction between the way that these concepts are constructed theoretically and the myriad of ways that they are interpreted in schools. They cannot, therefore, be treated as unitary concepts; this makes discussion problematic. Further, though it is useful for the purposes of this chapter to attempt to identify the broad trends that have, historically, shaped our understanding of discipline, behaviour and ethos, it would be a considerable oversimplification to suggest that there has been a neat, linear progression over past decades. The following overview should therefore be treated with a degree of caution noting that, inevitably, it is a construction and a selection.

Arguably, the notion of discipline that has dominated educational thinking until relatively recently has been broadly associated with the control and regulation of pupil behaviour by teachers in order to facilitate learning and socialisation. In the early twentieth century, this formulation was expressed as a harsh authoritarianism. Scottish schools at that time were highly formal places in which teachers transmitted knowledge didactically, and pupils were expected to be silent, still and learn – by rote where possible. Classes were large, authority was strict and control was maintained via rigid rules and routines enforced through the use of corporal punishments (Gavienas and White, 2003). Behaviour that flouted the rules or deviated from rigid teacher expectations was viewed as maladjustment and explained as a psychological or medical problem in the child, not as a problem linked in any way to school ethos, that is, the general climate of a school – its atmosphere, relationships and practices – and the values that underpinned them. Thus, attitudes reflected the wider values and morals of Scottish society with its expectations of deference, respect and conformity to authority.

The cultural upheaval of the 1960s, however, gave rise to some considerable questioning of notions of power and authority within Scottish culture and elsewhere, and triggered a period of significant educational change. Policy was influenced by liberal writers such as Montessori and Froebel, and by the research of Jean Piaget. The result was a substantial softening of many of the harsher realities of classroom life as child-centred education became the new orthodoxy as set out in the landmark report *Primary Education in Scotland* (Scottish Education Department, 1965). This report had a considerable impact on practice. For example, teachers were encouraged to make the school environment welcoming and stimulating, to adapt the curriculum to the needs and interests of primary-aged children, to grant pupils new freedom to learn through discovery, and to create an ethos that was positive, warm and supportive. The report argued that these reforms would help pupils to take more responsibility for their behaviour in the classroom.

Corporal punishment was reviewed for the first time during this period, and its use gradually waned throughout the 1960s and 1970s until it was finally abolished in state schools in 1981. However, sanctions such as verbal reprimands, detention and lines continued to be common currency in primary schools and constituted the main approach to low-level indiscipline in the classroom. Referral to the headteacher and exclusions were generally reserved for more serious misdemeanours such as verbal abuse, aggression or violence, whilst pupils considered too difficult to manage were often moved to special schools or units for what became known as pupils with social, emotional and behavioural difficulties (SEBD). This categorisation has always been vague (Macleod and Munn, 2004) and became a catch-all label for pupils whom teachers perceived as challenging and resistant to help. The implication of the label at this time was that such pupils had a psycho-medical problem requiring specialist input that was beyond the reach and remit of teachers in mainstream schools.

Though the use of physical force was no longer sanctioned, the teacher's singular power to shape and determine pupil behaviour continued unabated despite the advent of child-centred education. Indeed, Piaget's theory of developmental sequentialism was used to justify the view that young pupils are largely dependent on the expert guidance and protection of teachers, and incapable, by virtue of their age and developmental stage, of acting as independent agents who might contribute to discussions about behaviour. Thus, teachers were constructed as nurturers and protectors whose power over pupils was fully legitimised by society.

Parents, however, began to have more involvement in education as a result of the new child-centred policies of the 1960s. Educators recognised that parents might act as a useful bridge between home and school and had the potential to reinforce learning and standards of behaviour at home. Research indicated that there were clear benefits for pupils in terms of improved attainment, attendance and behaviour (MacBeth et al., 1984). Thus, by the 1980s it had become axiomatic that parents were 'welcome' in schools and that this should be integral to primary school ethos. However, the parental role was generally limited. Subsequent research suggests that parent participation at that time was, and arguably still is, predicated on the tacit understanding that they must work for, not against, teachers and schools, and act as willing conduits for the standards, values and norms advocated by them, especially in matters of behaviour (Crozier and Reay, 2005). The minority of parents who tried to question teacher decisions on discipline had little real power to bring about change.

In the 1970s, a new wave of sociological researchers began to question who was setting the school discipline agenda and whose purposes it served beyond the classroom. It was argued that discipline in schools reflected the values and beliefs of dominant groups within wider society and might be viewed as a form of social control that reproduced class hierarchies and perpetuated social inequality. Research into the curriculum and·the hidden curriculum, that is, the way that the curriculum is organised, taught and managed, explored this influence on pupil behaviour. There was evidence that teacher attitudes and labelling shaped pupil identity via the 'self-fulfilling prophesy'. These findings heralded a growing discomfort with the child deficit model and the exclusion of pupils with SEBD to special schools. Many of these concerns were highlighted in the Pack Report (Scottish Education Department, 1977), an influential government enquiry into truancy and indiscipline in Scottish schools.

Throughout the 1980s school effectiveness research appeared to confirm that the environment of the school could exacerbate, if not create, indiscipline. The ethos of the primary classroom therefore became a new focus for enquiries into the causes of pupil indiscipline, with the implication that teachers and schools could, and should, do something about it. In 1992, the Scottish Office acted upon this by distributing indicators to schools to enable them to review and evaluate the quality and effectiveness of school ethos. A significant feature of this new directive was the emphasis on prevention, rather than punishment, through the use of behaviourist approaches such as praise, points systems and other forms of reward for good behaviour. Supporting pupil self-esteem became an important aspect of school ethos. Positive, respectful relationships between teachers and pupils were also highlighted.

This initiative signalled a significant departure from the traditional approach to discipline outlined above, with its emphasis on problems in the child and reliance on punishments and sanctions. Within this new model, teachers were no longer constructed as the victims of pupil behaviour, but as the potential architects of discipline and indiscipline in the primary classroom. The then Scottish Office tried to support schools to address its new expectations throughout the 1990s via the Scottish School Ethos Network, the Promoting Positive Discipline Initiative, plus a plethora of teacher handbooks and resource packs designed to help schools bring about improvements in various aspects of ethos. It was hoped that these measures might also help to reduce rates of exclusion in primary schools in view of the sharp upturn that occurred in the mid-1990s.

Many teachers took advantage of these support mechanisms to improve their practice. However, the uptake of positive approaches was uneven across Scottish schools and also varied from classroom to classroom depending on the perspectives of individual teachers (Gavienas and White, 2003). This is linked to the problem, mentioned earlier, of the interpretation of definitions of discipline and behaviour. Thus, there was considerable variation in the way that policy was enacted, and little debate on the subject between or within schools. The result was a lack of a shared understanding of what, in practical terms, a positive school ethos meant, and how it could be created across the widely varying contexts, locations and catchments of Scottish schools. Some teachers felt that the focus on prevention rather than punishment undermined their authority and made the enforcement of school standards difficult. Thus, in some schools the emphasis on sanctions continued. A survey of primary teachers (Munn et al., 1998) revealed that low-level disruption such as talking, playing, wandering about and disturbing others were the behaviours of greatest concern to teachers at this time. Verbal abuse and violence were considered relatively rare, though bullying, for the first time, was considered to be a growing problem and tackling it became an educational priority in the late 1990s. The association of good discipline with positive ethos and prevention therefore had a gradual evolution across Scottish primary schools. However, the impetus for change gathered pace with the emergence of new legislation on pupil rights. This legislation has changed the landscape of Scottish education dramatically. Its impact on notions of discipline, behaviour and ethos will now be considered.

## CHILDREN'S RIGHTS AND DISCIPLINE IN THE PRIMARY SCHOOL

In 1989, the United Nations Convention on the Rights of the Child set out a framework for children's rights that included two articles, twelve and thirteen, calling for the creation of better opportunities for children to voice their thoughts, opinions and concerns, and to participate in decision-making processes affecting their lives. In 1995, this document gained legal status in Scotland via the Children (Scotland) Act. This was followed by a host of further acts and codes of practice that applied the spirit of the convention to the sphere of education. Importantly, this legislation was aligned to an emerging focus within Scottish educational policy on the inclusion of pupils with special needs within mainstream contexts, including pupils with SEBD. This rights-based, inclusive approach was set out in the Standards in Scotland's Schools etc. Act (2000).

Inclusive practice has since become the key organising principle for a new vision of schooling that places an unprecedented emphasis on learners' rights, especially learners with 'additional support needs' (ASN). The legislation expresses the presumption that these pupils will be included in mainstream schools rather than being taught separately in special schools and units (except in exceptional circumstances) thereby reversing, in theory at least, decades of segregation. Pupils with ASN and their parents have also been given entitlement to a say in educational decision making that is explicitly enshrined in law.

Decisions about such matters had traditionally been considered integral to the teacher role and dependent on their specialist knowledge and expertise. The fact that they are, potentially at least, being opened up to pupils and parents represents a considerable shift in thinking about the forms of knowledge that should influence classroom practice and behaviour management. However, current research into pupil voice provides an evidence-based rationale for enhanced pupil involvement. Researchers in this field suggest that, contrary to traditional assumptions based on the Piagetian developmental model, primary pupils are quite capable of reflecting upon various aspects of their schooling and contributing their ideas, views and opinions to strategic decision-making processes in schools (Ravet, 2007). It is argued that pupil perspectives have the potential to redress the adult bias that has traditionally dominated educational thinking, and can ensure that decisions about school improvement are accurately focused on matters of direct concern and relevance to those they are meant to benefit – the pupils themselves. What pupils repeatedly report is that problems within the teacher/pupil relationship and boredom with the curriculum are two fundamental causes of learning disengagement and low-level indiscipline in the primary classroom (Ravet, 2007). School-based enquiries into pupil involvement further reveal that where participation is genuine, as opposed to tokenistic, it can help pupils to develop the communication skills, social skills, metacognitive skills and problem-solving skills that underpin academic achievement and learning progress. Participation is also associated with enhanced learning ownership, improved engagement and, importantly, better behaviour in the classroom.

The relationship between behaviour, learning and ethos highlighted by research, and the principle of pupil involvement advanced by policy and legislation, were brought together in a landmark document, published by the Scottish Executive Education Department in 2001, entitled *Better Behaviour – Better Learning* (BB-BL). This was launched in response to concerns about widespread indiscipline in Scottish schools. It states:

> discipline policy cannot, and should not, be separated from policy on learning and teaching – the two are inextricably linked. Children and young people are more likely to engage positively with education when careful consideration is given to their learning and teaching. (p. 8)

BB-BL therefore emphasised the role of a positive learning environment in creating the conditions for positive discipline. It also highlighted the fundamental importance of positive and supportive relationships between pupils and teachers as a means of preventing indiscipline. Though the report acknowledged the continuing role of rules, rewards and sanctions in the classroom, it also recognised that causes of indiscipline are many and varied and that pupils, teachers and parents must work together to explore specific problems and identify appropriate solutions. Partnership with pupils, parents and other agencies was therefore given considerable emphasis, and a range of new approaches to support participation and social justice in the classroom were recommended for trial across Scottish schools, such as restorative approaches, solution-oriented approaches, nurture groups and approaches to emotional literacy. The report acknowledged explicitly the link between pupil participation and the reduced incidence of challenging behaviour.

This document clearly signalled a radical departure from the idea of discipline as the imposition of extrinsic control. According to the Scottish Government, behaviour in Scottish schools was now to be viewed essentially as a collaborative enterprise with its roots in positive relationships and positive learning. Subsequent policy developments, especially Curriculum for Excellence (CfE) (Scottish Government, 2004) and related guidance (e.g. Scottish Government, 2010), align with, and reinforce, the message of BB-BL. CfE lies at the very heart of the Scottish Government strategy to provide a broader, more flexible, child-centred and participatory curriculum that will foster a sense of pupil agency, involvement and control. It might be prudent, therefore, to consider how schools have responded to these policies, and to evaluate their impact.

## PROMOTING POSITIVE BEHAVIOUR: IMPLEMENTATION AND IMPACT

In 2012, the Scottish Government published the latest in a sequence of interim reports on behaviour in Scottish schools (Black et al., 2012), undertaken in consultation with school management, teachers, support staff and pupils. Building on previous research in 2006 and 2009, the report aimed to report on the impact of BB–BL and to provide 'a clear and robust picture of behaviour in publicly funded mainstream schools and of current policy and practice in relation to managing behaviour' (p. i).

The key findings were as follows (from Black et al., 2012, pp. i–v):

- the overwhelming majority of staff across all sectors saw all or most pupils as generally well behaved;
- the most frequently encountered negative behaviours were low-level behaviours such as running in corridors and talking out of turn in class;
- physical violence and aggression were considered rare and were more likely to be directed towards other pupils than at staff;
- verbal abuse between pupils was frequently encountered in primary schools, but only a minority of teachers and support staff experienced verbal abuse;
- overall, perceptions of behaviour, including positive behaviour, low-level negative behaviour, and serious indiscipline/violence have improved since the 2006 and 2009 surveys;
- the promotion of positive behaviour through whole school ethos and values was seen by staff as the most helpful approach. However, all schools used a multi-pronged approach combining social and emotional wellbeing programmes, reward systems, pupil participation, restorative approaches, peer mentoring, and solution-oriented approaches;
- there was a continued move away from more punitive methods (e.g. punishment exercises);
- teachers were more confident in their ability to promote positive behaviour and felt better supported;
- staff were far more inclined to refer to 'relationships', rather than 'behaviour management' or 'indiscipline' when talking about the ways in which they deal with negative behaviour;
- overall there was more recognition of the potential underlying reasons for challenging behaviour and the importance of a holistic approach;
- there was concern at the growing numbers of children entering primary school with nurture and attachment issues, mental health issues and conditions like attention deficit hyperactivity disorder (ADHD) and autism. Teachers found the behaviour of these pupils 'particularly challenging'.

The Scottish Government responded to the report by acknowledging the progress that had been made in embedding the values of BB–BL (Scottish Executive Education Department, 2001) over the past ten years. However, it recognised that disruptive behaviour, whether minor or serious, continues to have a significant impact on teaching and learning. They therefore issued new policy guidance entitled *Better Relationships, Better Learning, Better Behaviour* (BR–BL–BB) (2013, www.gov.scot/Publications/2013/03/7388). In this guidance, the Scottish Government emphasised the need to strengthen and develop current approaches to ensure they are fully embedded across Scottish schools. Next steps and priority actions were specified to support local authorities, practitioners and partners to further improve relationships, learning and behaviour.

## ISSUES ARISING FROM POLICY AND GUIDANCE

On the surface at least, the findings of the interim report indicate that a notable shift has taken place in schools. Where, in the past, the meaning of discipline and indiscipline was being prescribed and imposed by teachers and policymakers, now there are signs of progress towards a more participatory approach between teachers and pupils, where the meaning of discipline and indiscipline are negotiated. This is evidenced in the report by the decrease in use of sanctions and punitive approaches, and the increase in uptake of new approaches, like restorative practice and solution-focused interventions, that are, essentially, relational and dialogic. Teachers are clearly beginning to appreciate the power of school ethos in influencing pupil behaviour.

A change in underlying teacher understandings of behaviour is also evidenced by the increase in references to 'relationships'. Wider acceptance that the underlying causes of challenging behaviour can be complex, and that behaviour should be considered holistically, rather than being viewed purely as a deficit in the child, is also significant. These indicators are positive and encouraging, and suggestive of progress in the direction set out by the Scottish Government in BB-BL (Scottish Executive Education Department, 2001). However, there is some reason for caution.

## LIMITATIONS OF QUANTITATIVE METHODS

It should be noted that the research that underpins the 2012 interim report is largely based on the results of a quantitative survey of around 5,000 staff including headteachers, teachers and support staff. Though some qualitative interviews that included pupils were undertaken, these interviews did not focus on the issues raised in the quantitative survey but on three quite separate, specific themes: parental involvement, emotional wellbeing and transitions. This qualitative data does not, therefore, help to deepen our understanding of the survey results. This means that underlying questions about the findings cannot be answered. For example, although teachers report making more use of dialogic and relational approaches, the data do not reveal how faithfully such approaches are being implemented, nor how well they are adapted to include all learners, especially those with communication difficulties who might be disadvantaged by relational, talk-based interventions (discussed further below). We also know from the findings that teachers report school ethos to be important, but we do not know exactly what they mean by this and what aspects of ethos they value most. Equally, though teachers appear to appreciate the need for a more holistic approach to the analysis of behaviour that includes home and family background, we do not know how well teachers are taking classroom environmental factors into account, including the influence that they themselves exert as teachers. Further, from these data, we do not know what tensions school staff experience in implementing the policy or the barriers they encounter. It is therefore difficult to establish whether the changes that are arising are deep and gaining real traction in primary schools, or whether they are generally more superficial and tokenistic.

## PUPIL AND PARENT VOICE?

It is notable that there was limited pupil participation in the research underpinning the interim report. Pupils did not participate in the quantitative survey, only in the qualitative research strand. Their views are excluded in the executive summary and there is very limited reporting of pupil perspectives in the wider report. The pupil participants were also selected by their schools, which raises obvious problems of representativeness. Arguably, the minor role awarded to pupil voice in the report is surprising given the pupil-centred policy context from which the research arises. Pupil perspectives might be expected to lie at the very heart of such a study.

It would certainly be valuable to know more about how pupils directly affected by the new approaches and initiatives experience, engage with, and evaluate them. It is also important to gain insight into any barriers to participation pupils face. Research already indicates that barriers might arise because pupils lack the means or motivation to participate in decisions about their learning and behaviour, or because pupils continue to view discipline as the responsibility of the teacher and school (Ravet, 2007). Barriers may stem from the way that teachers mobilise participation in the classroom. For example, where teachers are not used to treating pupil contributions with the confidentiality automatically extended to adults, they may speak for, over and instead of pupils, rather than *with* them, without being aware of it. Teachers may also be unprepared to treat pupil contributions seriously and act upon them wherever appropriate. Such selectivity can subvert the participatory ideal and, of course, undermine inclusion. Arguably, it is also surprising that parent perspectives on behaviour are completely omitted from the interim report. CfE (Scottish Government, 2004) and subsequent policy documents referred to earlier in this chapter, emphasise that parents must play a key role in education and decisions about learning and behaviour. Research by Hartas (2011) emphasises that parents powerfully influence the 'human capital' that children bring to schooling and play a key role in helping to untangle the complex proximal and distal factors influencing the 'ecology' of behaviour in the classroom. There is therefore a pressing need to bring parents in from the margins of debate about behaviour so that their voice can be more clearly heard.

## ADDITIONAL SUPPORT NEEDS AND BEHAVIOUR THAT CHALLENGES

The final point in the interim report summary clearly indicates that teachers feel highly challenged by pupils who enter primary school with additional support needs that are social and emotional in nature. For example, the report specifies that teachers find the behaviour of learners with autism challenging. This is confirmed in the wider research (e.g. Emam and Farrell, 2009) which warns that behaviour that challenges in the classroom may be linked to the relationship between learners with autism and their teachers, to a lack of teacher awareness of the condition and to the strategies used to support them. Some teachers still view such behaviour as a problem 'in the child'.

Florian and Black-Hawkins (2011) provide a valuable framework for exploring this. They propose that 'inclusive pedagogy', a distinct approach to teaching, can enhance inclusion for all by focusing teacher attention on how they can respond more positively to difference. This requires teachers to become aware of, and avoid, the labelling and stigmatisation of different groups of learners arising from deterministic assumptions about what they can and cannot achieve. The authors advocate teaching strategies, such as choice-based activities and visual approaches, which can be used with all children, regardless of level of need, to reduce the barriers to learning that can trigger challenging behaviour. They highlight the importance of trust and collaboration between adults and learners within this model. Inclusive pedagogy has clear affinities with the relational and participatory principles underpinning CfE and may be a valuable way forward for teachers struggling with traditional attitudes and approaches.

## POLICY SHIFT

It is noteworthy that the latest Scottish Government guidance comes with a new title. The reference to 'better relationships' in BR–BL–BB clearly signals a strengthening of this element of policy. It establishes 'relationships' as a key aspect of behaviour support in triadic union with 'learning' and 'behaviour'. This aligns the guidance more closely with other policies, for example CfE. It also clearly resonates with the finding of the interim report in which teachers and support staff identify school ethos and relationships as 'the most helpful approach'.

It is also significant that the ordering of the words in the title of the guidance is the reverse of those in the BB–BL (Scottish Executive Education Department, 2001), so that the word 'learning' now precedes the word 'behaviour'. This may suggest acknowledgement that better learning is, in fact, a prerequisite for better behaviour, not the other way round (Head, 2007). Importantly, this reconstructs behavioural issues as potential 'learning difficulties' so that, rather than blaming the child and trying to 'fix' behaviour, it can be approached by reviewing the curriculum and pedagogy, as Florian and Black-Hawkins suggest. This squarely locates difficulties with behaviour within the sphere of teaching and the responsibility of teachers, and represents an evolution in the thinking that underpins the new policy.

## CONCLUSION

Since the publication of BB–BL (Scottish Executive Education Department, 2001) the Scottish Government has initiated a substantial, and arguably radical, programme of reform and development with the aim of promoting positive, child-centred, participatory approaches to discipline across Scottish schools. At the heart of this programme lies an emphasis on improving behaviour by improving relationships between teachers and pupils, by enhancing the quality of teaching and learning, and by fostering pupil and parent participation in matters of discipline. CfE reinforces the message that a positive, nurturing and pupil-centred school ethos is fundamental to pupil happiness, progress and positive behaviour. BR–BL–BB takes this a step further. These initiatives reflect the broader and more holistic understanding of discipline in schools that is emerging.

To date, there is clearly room for cautious optimism regarding the influence of these policies on schools, teachers and pupils. Black et al.'s report (2012) indicates that, although there is still evidence of low-level disruption, perceptions of behaviour have generally become more positive. More serious behaviours, such as violence and aggression toward others, continue to be perceived as rare. Government statistics also show that the numbers of pupil exclusions have been gradually falling since 2006 (Table 25.1).

Though it is not possible to pinpoint the range of factors that may have influenced this decline, it is not unreasonable to suppose that changes in schools as result of

Table 25.1   School exclusion numbers

| Year | 2006/7 | 2007/8 | 2008/9 | 2009/10 | 2010/11 | 2012/13 | 2013/14 |
|---|---|---|---|---|---|---|---|
| Exclusions total | 44,794 | 39,717 | 33,917 | 30,211 | 26,844 | 21,955 | 18,430 |

Note: Figures are not available for the year 2011/12.

Source: Scottish Government, 2016.

BB-BL have contributed to it. However, there is still much to do to help teachers and support staff make sense of the many complexities of the relational aspects of behaviour support that are now being emphasised – especially as they pertain to marginalised children. Links between relationships, learning and behaviour and their implications for pedagogy will require continued research, wider dissemination and effective implementation. A renewed emphasis on the inclusion of parents in a collaborative approach to behaviour seems overdue. A strong focus on qualitative research in schools is also required to enable a robust and methodologically rigorous focus on the pupil experience and the generation of data to evidence how learners make sense of new approaches. Such research and evidence can then be used to further challenge traditional thinking, stimulate restructuring, and facilitate a deeper transformation of ethos, behaviour and discipline in schools. Unfortunately, we are now in a period of challenging financial pressures on educational services and families. Funding and resourcing will therefore need to be prioritised if the promise of 'Better relationships, better learning, better behaviour' is to be fully realised.

## REFERENCES

Black, C., Chamberlain, V., Murray, L., Sewel, K. and Skelton, J. (2012) *Behaviour in Scottish Schools*. Edinburgh: Scottish Government.

Crozier, G. and Reay, D. (2005) *Activating Participation: Parents and Teachers Working Together Towards Partnership*. Stoke-on-Trent: Trentham.

Emam, M. M. and Farrell, P. (2009) 'Tensions experienced by teachers and their views of support for pupils with ASD in mainstream schools', *European Journal of Special Needs Education*, 24 (4), 407–22.

Florian, L. and Black-Hawkins, K. (2011) 'Exploring inclusive pedagogy', *British Educational Research Journal*, 37 (5), 813–28.

Gavienas, E. and White, G. (2003) 'Ethos, management and discipline in the primary school', in T. G. K. Bryce and W. M. Humes (eds), *Scottish Education, Second Edition: Post-devolution*. Edinburgh: Edinburgh University Press, pp. 352–62.

Hartas, D. (2011) 'The ecology of young children's behaviour and social competence: child characteristics, socio-economic factors and parenting', *Oxford Review of Education*, 37 (6), 763–83.

Head, G. (2007) *Better Learning, Better Behaviour*. Edinburgh: Dunedin Academic Press.

MacBeth, A., Corner, T., Nisbet, S., Nisbet, A., Ryan, D. and Strachan, D. (1984) 'The child between: a report on school family relations in countries of the European Community'. Brussels: European Commission.

Macleod, G. and Munn, P. (2004) 'Social, emotional and behavioural difficulties: a different kind of special educational needs?' *Scottish Educational Review*, 36 (2), 169–76.

Munn, P., Johnstone, M. and Sharp, S. (1998) 'Is indiscipline getting worse? Scottish teachers' perceptions of indiscipline in 1990 and 1996', *Scottish Educational Review*, 30(2), 157–72.

Ravet, J. (2007) *Are We Listening? Making Sense of Classroom Behaviour with Pupils and Parents*. Stoke-on Trent: Trentham.

Scottish Education Department (1965) *Primary Education in Scotland*. Edinburgh: HMSO.

Scottish Education Department (1977) *Truancy and Indiscipline in Scottish Schools* (The Pack Report). Edinburgh: HMSO.

Scottish Executive Education Department (2001) *Better Behaviour – Better Learning: Report of the Discipline Task Group*. Online at www.gov.scot/Resource/Doc/158381/0042908.pdf

Scottish Government (2004) *Ambitious, Excellent Schools – Our Agenda for Action*. Edinburgh: Scottish Executive.

Scottish Government (2010) *Building Curriculum for Excellence through Positive Relationships and Behaviour*. Online at www.gov.scot/Publications/2010/06/25112828/0

Scottish Government (2013) *Better Relationships, Better Learning, Better Behaviour*. Online at www.gov.scot/resource/0041/00416217.pdf

Scottish Government (2016) *Summary Statistics for Schools in Scotland*. Online at www.gov.scot/Publications/2016/12/9271/336283

# 26

# Transitions from Early Years to Primary and Primary to Secondary

*Divya Jindal-Snape*

This chapter focuses on transitions to primary and secondary schools in Scotland. It highlights the importance of understanding research-based conceptualisations to provide better support to children and significant others. Data are presented from research conducted in Scotland to provide insights into what is actually happening in Scottish schools and how this matches up with the relevant policy and legislation. The chapter then concludes with recommendations about key aspects of transition practice to support children, parents and professionals.

In Scotland, children normally move to primary school at the age of 5 and to secondary school at the age of 12 years. Children and families are usually aware of the school their child will be moving to, unless the move is based on placement request or meeting the additional support needs of a child (Jindal-Snape et al., 2006). Systems are put in place to familiarise children with the new context through open days, induction days, reciprocal visits and sharing of information about the child with the receiving organisation. The transition planning and preparation is influenced by national and local policy as well as how transition is conceived.

## CONCEPTUALISING TRANSITION AND THE IMPACT OF TRANSITION SUPPORT

It is important to understand what one means by transition, as that will inevitably have an impact on planning and preparation. There is no clear consensus amongst researchers and professionals regarding its significance. In an unpublished study (Jindal-Snape and Mitchell, 2014–16), a small sample of primary and secondary school staff from one secondary school cluster in Scotland were asked what transition meant to them. There was a mix of responses, with some seeing it as a one-off physical move from one stage to another with an explicit focus on education:

> Seamless move from primary to secondary with a clear focus on teaching and learning. (Head Teacher, Primary School, Female, 11–15 years professional experience)

> Any move between stages or establishment or settings or even classes. (Head Teacher, Primary School, Female, 20+ years professional experience)

The latter quote is useful in that it shifts the focus from moving schools to moving between classes within the same school. Some see transition as one-off or linked with 'big' moves focused on specific time points. However, others reported that transition is an ongoing process and involves several subtle as well as larger changes; with several such changes within the same day and in the same physical context. Further, some see transition as a physical or visible change; others see it as a process of experiencing change, for example in one's identity, the environment or others' expectations of the child (see also, Jindal-Snape and Foggie, 2008).

> Any change in learning environment or expectation. (Guidance Staff, Secondary School, Male, 6–10 years professional experience)

A few school staff focused on the holistic aspect of transition, one focusing on the impact of change and the other on adaptation,

> A period of change which can affect young people in a variety of ways (i.e., psychologically, socially, physically etc.). (Guidance Staff, Secondary School, Female, 11–15 years professional experience)

> Transition is physical, social and emotional adaption to new environments and stressors. (Guidance Staff, Secondary School, Male, 6–10 years professional experience)

It seems that there was a lack of shared understanding about transitions amongst staff (teachers, pupil support worker, guidance staff and deputy headteacher), even within the same school cluster. This seemed to have an impact on what they considered the start of transition support to be: spanning from starting in December before the move to secondary school in August to March/April immediately before the move, with long-term planning and preparation only cited when a child had a coordinated support plan in line with the Education (Additional Support for Learning) (Scotland) Act 2004 (ASL), amended 2009. This legislation places specific duties on local authorities with clear timescales for transition planning and practice for children and young people who are identified to have additional support needs. However, it can be argued that transition itself leads to additional support needs for some children and therefore it is important to be mindful of emerging additional support needs, rather than focusing simply on children with previously recorded needs. Although one professional said that it is an ongoing process with continuous support, a majority indicated that transition support lasted a few months once the child had started their new school.

However, there was evidence from this study that the impact of transition is not linear, and issues can arise at different times. Of the forty-one who responded at Stage 4 (S2, end of second year of secondary school), 32.5 per cent ($n = 13$) of children indicated that they had problems at the start of S1 (first year of secondary school) that had been resolved by the end of S1; 7.5 per cent ($n = 3$) said that they had problems at the start which had not been resolved; and, most importantly, 10 per cent ($n = 4$) said that they had no problems at the start but were experiencing problems at the end of S1. Similarly, 19.5 per cent ($n = 8$) of children said they had problems when they moved to S2 that had been resolved, 4.9 per cent ($n = 2$) said they had problems at the start that had not been resolved, and 12.2 per cent ($n = 5$) said they had no problems at the start but had some at the end of S2. One S2 child highlighted the perception that support is required only at the start of a new school:

> Nothing because they think we've settled in enough. (S2 pupil)

Another child, however, identified that there were ongoing support systems in place, albeit only through guidance staff.

Further, some pupils saw transition as a time of anxiety and concern, whereas others saw it as an exciting time with a sense of achievement and progression, a springboard to success and that children yearn for this change and the opportunity to 'move on' and 'move up' with increased choices (Jindal-Snape and Foggie, 2008). Also, the same aspects of transitions can worry or excite different children and the same child at different times (Jindal-Snape and Hannah, 2013). Our research suggests that most children make these transitions successfully and for some it involves adaptation over a longer period of time. Therefore, transition can be defined as (1) an ongoing process of psychological, social and educational adaptation, (2) over time, (3) due to changes in context, interpersonal relationships and identity, (4) which can be both exciting and worrying, and (5) requiring ongoing support. According to Multiple and Multi-dimensional Transitions (MMT) theory, every individual experiences multiple transitions at the same time, and these cause, and interact with, the transitions of significant others. The theory suggests that transitions are quite complex and that a holistic approach to understanding them and providing support is required (see Jindal-Snape, 2016 for detail).

For example, a child could be experiencing multiple transitions when starting school, such as moving house, birth of a sibling, starting a karate club and other age-related changes. In a Scottish primary school there can twenty-five to thirty such children in one classroom, with every child's various transitions interacting with others' transitions. Similarly, these transitions will have an impact on the significant others in each child's ecosystem such as their family and teacher. The significant others are most likely to be experiencing several transitions, along with the ones triggered by the child's transitions. For example, a parent might experience transition due to their child's developmental stage and starting primary school, such as going back to full-time employment, and a professional might be experiencing concurrent transitions, such as moving house, or undertaking part-time studies. The child will also be affected by the changes in their parents' or teacher's life, suggesting that they will experience transitions as a result of each other's transitions as well as their own concurrent transitions. Previous research has not looked at transitions of significant others. However, our study (Jindal-Snape and Mitchell, 2014–16) studied the MMT of all stakeholders. The next section considers two particular types of transitions: starting primary school and starting secondary school.

## EARLY YEARS TO PRIMARY SCHOOL TRANSITIONS

Most starting school research internationally is dominated by the readiness debate, primarily a child's readiness to start school (Maturational Approach), with some highlighting the need for the school to be ready and others the need for both child and school readiness (Interactionist Approach) (Jindal-Snape, 2016). Others have also highlighted the social and emotional readiness of the child; again a Maturational Approach with children with additional support needs being retained in nursery in one Scottish local authority if staff and parents do not consider them ready to start school, but without any specific planned programme of support in the retained year (Gorton, 2012).

Research suggests that starting school can be a significant transition for the entire family (Jindal-Snape and Hannah, 2013). Due to the developmental stage, children's patterns of interaction with parents/carers might change, with implicit messages given of being 'grown up' as a schoolchild. Similarly, there are implicit messages for parents with expectations that they should know the norms and culture of primary school. Parents used to the more open and accessible environment of the nursery, can find the primary school less accessible and find it frustrating to wait a few months before speaking with the teacher to find out how their child is settling in.

In Scotland, the Early Years Framework provides a policy context to inform the development of practice so that all children can develop to their maximum potential. During the policy development stage, the Scottish Government established four task groups, one of these focusing on the role of preschool experiences to prepare a child for the transition to school. They defined effective transition supports as: 'those where children feel "suitable", where they feel secure, relaxed and comfortable in their new environment' (Scottish Government, 2008, paragraph 98). This raises several questions regarding what is 'suitable' in practice. Are we asking children to fit into someone's notion of suitable? If we were to take a positive slant on this, we could see it as a good starting point for seeing successful transition as a sense of belonging and perhaps extended to feelings of wellbeing. They recommended features of effective transition programmes, namely: (1) partnership working between sectors with clearly defined induction arrangements; (2) in line with legal obligations, supporting children with additional support needs within a multiagency, child and parent partnership framework; (3) effective parental involvement and communication, including several formal and informal opportunities for parents and children to visit the new school; (4) effective curriculum planning to ensure continuity in learning based on thorough knowledge of each child; (5) effective leadership, ethos and shared vision in nurseries and schools to improve transitions for the child; and (6) implementing active learning approaches and encouraging children to have more agency for their learning (Scottish Government, 2008).

Jindal-Snape and Hannah (2013) used some of these themes to see whether, from the parents' perspective, the practice matched the policy. A total of 107 parents from eighteen schools in two very different (in size and geographical location) local authorities (LAs) participated in the study. Data were collected using a questionnaire with closed and open questions in term 2 of P1 (first year of primary school in Scotland). The findings suggested a fairly good match between practice within these two LAs and the policy; however, several areas were identified for development. The majority of parents (73.6 per cent) reported that the nursery and primary school had worked together to organise reciprocal visits and exchanges of information about their child. However, some parents (17.9 per cent) said that they were not always clear about what information was passed on about their child and when, highlighting the importance of transparent partnership and better involvement of parents in information sharing, especially as, during this change, a parent/carer might be the only constant in the life of the child. A large majority of parents (86.9 per cent) reported that the nursery and 94.4 per cent that the primary school had done all they could to support their child's transition. However, a slightly lower number reported that they had not been supported effectively as parents:

> Such a completely alien environment for both me and my child – child knew no other children in P1 and I knew no other parents. I had no familiarity or knowledge of the school and couldn't do anything to smooth the way with my child e.g., lining up in the morning, school lunches, gym … even the fact that notes would be put in with schoolbags. Sounds daft but if you've not had any experience of school and no ability to speak with other parents then lots of small concerns/questions/issues begin to mount up. (Parent of Primary 1 pupil)

Some others felt involved and valued in the transition process at home (good parent–child communication), nursery and school (good parent and professional communication):

> The school made you feel very secure and happy. They also had meetings to show you how they were going to teach your child and also how to help your child at home. (Parent of Primary 1 pupil)

However, the communication seemed to be one-sided with parents receiving information or attending an open day rather than a two-way dialogue. In Scottish schools, there seems to be a time lag between children starting school mid-August and the first parent contact evening in November. Normally there are no *formal* mechanisms for parents to communicate with their child's teacher about any other changes the child might be experiencing or finding out about how they can support the child at home. Some parents said that it was problematic:

> [I wish someone had] prepared me for the 'black box.' In nursery, you see the teachers and the classroom every day. At Primary, you drop off, pick up in the playground. You never see the classroom, only communicate through notes unless something bad happens. (Parent of Primary 1 pupil)

There was evidence of children's needs being considered by the schools; however, two parents reported that the assessments related to their child's additional support needs were not timely or accurate leading to problems for their child. Parents commented that the school induction visits for children and parents were very important in familiarising them with the new environment, especially when children were able to join their future class in the primary school before the move.

Most parents had proactively worked towards preparing their child for the move and were keen to be involved. However, some parents saw themselves as passive recipients of information, with some responding that preparing children for transition was the school's role. Parents responded positively about the preparation from the nurseries in terms of preparing the child through developing reading/writing skills and independence skills. One of the recurring themes from all parents was the importance of good and trusting relationships between child and teacher, parents and teacher, child and parents, parents and parents, child and child, nursery and school, and so on.

> I meet a teacher once in a large group and I'm supposed to trust her with my child why? Because it's socially accepted? This seems weird. (Parent of Primary 1 pupil)

Parents reported that trust had to be built over time through conscious effort on both sides. In most cases, transition support was put in place a few months prior to the move and then it stopped a few months after that, thereby suggesting that transition was viewed as a one-off event. However, in some cases, reciprocal visits started a year in advance.

What was also evident was that in all schools there were examples of good practice that had not been shared with other schools across the local authorities or even within school clusters. As a result of this study, some schools changed their transition practices, including the use of photographs of significant people and places in the new environment to enhance their familiarity, parents organising 'play dates' over the summer prior to the start of school, and a school organising a summer fair for new and current children and families to meet in a fun environment (Jindal-Snape and Hannah, 2013). Despite the importance of the secure attachments and meaningful relationships formed by a child with their nursery or primary school teacher, there is little, if any, focus in the literature on transitions experienced by the professionals when the children started with or left them.

Table 26.1    Things looking forward to/worried about prior to starting S1 and what was good about moving to secondary school/still worrying

| | | | | |
|---|---|---|---|---|
| Seeing old friends already in the secondary school | 35 | 32 | 3 | 1 |
| Several teachers | 22 | 23 | 7 | 0 |
| Travelling to school | 20 | 23 | 10 | 2 |
| Variety of sports | 30 | 30 | 2 | 0 |

Note: $n$ = 61; stage 2 data collected three-and-a-half months after starting S1; children could choose as many options as they wanted.

## PRIMARY TO SECONDARY SCHOOL TRANSITIONS

Primary to secondary school transition has been researched extensively internationally and has concerned policymakers and practitioners for some time, with several countries adapting their curriculum and educational stages (such as creation of middle schools) to minimise disruptions and discontinuities. Similarly, in Scotland the Curriculum for Excellence was introduced spanning ages 3 to 18, to support seamless transitions through school and post-school.

Although moving to secondary school signals progression and 'moving up', suggesting that most children would find primary–secondary transition to be satisfying and fulfilling (Jindal-Snape and Foggie, 2008; Galton, 2010), some children find this move to be stressful and challenging (Jindal-Snape and Miller, 2008). As can be seen from Table 26.1, in one local authority, data showed an increase in areas children were looking forward to and a reduction in areas they were worried about after the move (Jindal-Snape and Mitchell, 2014–16). In another local authority, despite the study being conducted nearly four years ago (2010–11) with three secondary school clusters, the trend for aspects which a majority of the P7 children were looking forward to (making new friends, different subjects) and were worried about (losing old friends) was similar (Jindal-Snape et al., 2011). In Jindal-Snape and Foggie (2008), children reported that this mismatch in expectations before and after starting S1 came, in part, from conversations they had had with older siblings/cousins.

Although support from primary and secondary schools is vital, it is important to be mindful of children's other support networks especially at home. For example, in Stage 2 of the study presented in Table 26.1, children indicated that the people they spoke with most about the move were their family (see Figure 26.1).

In Stage 4, towards the end of S2, this picture stayed unchanged in terms of people they were continuing to speak to about secondary school. Twenty-seven of the forty-one children from Stage 4 also gave examples of the type of support they received from their family, with the majority indicating that it was related to emotional, social and organisational support, with only four touching on academic aspects:

> there [sic] always there and everyday they ask me how school was and make sure ... there is nobody bullying me or being mean to me. (S1 pupil)

> they still help me now by asking me if I have any problems and make me fell [sic] I can share my feelings with them. (S1 pupil)

> My mum drove me to school for the first week which helped me because I didn't really know the way to school confidently. My brother who is in the older years of school also walked in with me so I wasn't alone. (S1 pupil)

> Helping with my subjects. (S1 pupil)

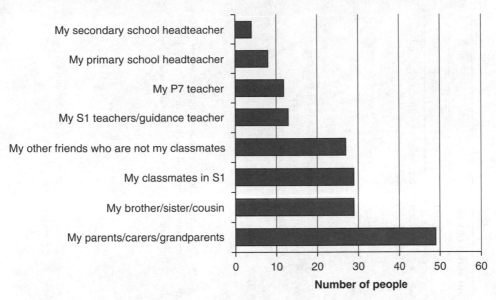

**Figure 26.1   People children spoke with most about the move to secondary school (Stage 1, start of S1)**

The importance of early primary–secondary transition planning has been highlighted repeatedly, with emphasis on high quality activities (e.g. Galton, 2010). Effective, planned and authentic communication is again seen to be vital:

> I feel that the process of some teachers visiting the Primary on a single afternoon (usually the teachers that are 'free' or available) to write down information is perhaps not the most effective way of sharing information. Information should be continually shared, especially in P7. (Guidance Staff, Secondary School, Male, 6–10 years professional experience)

In some Scottish schools the norm is for children to start visiting secondary school once a week two years prior to finishing primary school, for example, to use the swimming pool or science labs. This can help familiarisation with the physical environment as well as opportunities to get to know some secondary staff. In some Scottish LAs, teachers have been seen to work in each other's classes for a few days to facilitate continuity of pedagogical approaches and building on curriculum taught in P7 when children are in S1. However, these require time, goodwill and structural flexibility. Some local authorities also have all-through schools where children stay in the same physical location for their entire school career. However, there is no clear evidence to suggest that transitions are easier in all-through schools compared to when children move to different locations (Jindal-Snape et al., 2011).

In terms of practice for children with additional support needs, although studied in the context of post-school transitions, there is some evidence that the ASL Act has led to effective collaboration between professionals from different agencies, increased frequency of informal interactions taking place in non-school settings such as the child's home, and an improved active participation of young people in review meetings (Richardson et al., in press). This greater empowerment and agency of the children is also in line with Scottish policy directives such as *Getting it Right for Every Child* (GIRFEC).

Table 26.2   Aspects of effective transition practice

| Key aspect | Potential actions for, and by, relevant stakeholders | | |
| --- | --- | --- | --- |
| | Child | Family | Professional |
| Familiarisation | • Visits to the new school as early as possible, e.g. to use the swimming pool or other facilities<br>• Staff and children visiting new school<br>• Induction days<br>• Information pack including photos of significant people and places | • Informal visits for parents over time<br>• Induction visits | • Reciprocal visits to interact with children and other professionals over time |
| Opportunities to create friendship and support networks | • Through co-curricular activities with other nurseries and schools as well as in the community (to ensure multiple, stable support networks)<br>• Peer buddies from the same and new institution | • Formal parent networking events organised by schools<br>• Informal networking events organised by (and through) parents, parent councils and/or Parent Teacher Associations<br>• Adoption of a system of parent/family buddies | • Teacher buddies and shadowing across stages (potentially in the school cluster)<br>• Creation of transition teams |
| Secure attachment | • Portfolios or artefacts from previous school and/or home<br>• Building on existing secure attachments and support networks such as with parents, community clubs<br>• Opportunities for creation of non-stigmatised secure attachments with teachers, pupil support workers and guidance staff | • Valuing the role of parents in forming secure attachments and ensuring their involvement in the transition process<br>• Supporting parents' understanding of the role of secure attachments during transitions | • Sound school leadership from headteachers, supportive ethos and mechanisms for providing opportunities and support for staff |
| Continuous open communication and collaborative partnerships | • Discussions about what to expect<br>• Opportunities to talk about what they are looking forward to, or worried about | • Parents involved actively as partners | • Through reciprocal visits, intranet and sharing of information about the child |

|  |  |  |
|---|---|---|
|  | • Effective two-way communication (not just provision of information) with parents<br>• Parental input in the information that is shared about their child so as to include other aspects related to home/community and other transitions child might be experiencing<br>• Opportunities to meet with staff working with their child<br>• Understanding of legislative obligations of schools and local authorities and their rights, especially for children with additional support needs | ○ Information should focus on educational, social and emotional aspects<br>○ Parents and children should have opportunity to see the information and add to it<br>• Working together to bridge the gap between pedagogical approaches and curriculum<br>• Shared understanding of transition and best practice<br>• Opportunities to meet with parents and other staff<br>• Understanding of legislative obligations of schools and local authorities and childrens'/parents' rights, especially for children with additional support needs<br>• Working collaboratively with other agencies involved in the life of the child as relevant<br>• Early identification of support needs of child |
| Co-curricular activities | • School fair<br>• Residential trips (especially for older children)<br>• Clubs/activities in the community to foster sense of belonging |  |
| Training and support for transitions | • Rehearsing in a safe environment using creative approaches, such as creative drama, sketches, stories<br>• Increased understanding of own transition support needs | • Better provision of transitions training in qualifying programmes<br>• Enhanced continuing professional development (CPD) provision<br>• Increased understanding of own transition support needs and clear mechanism of organisational support |
| Active learning, participation and agency | • Opportunities to participate actively in their learning in preparation for transition to different educational stages<br>• Opportunities and ethos suitable to develop learner agency<br>• Active participation in all aspects of transitions and child's learning | • Peer education opportunities<br>• Opportunities and ethos suitable to develop professionals' agency |

In terms of parents' transitions, parents of these children were asked if they felt their child starting secondary school was their transition, too. Of the twenty-one who responded, sixteen said *yes*, two said *no*, and three that they *did not know*. They did not give reasons for their view despite having the option to do so. Three parents also reported that they had faced problems with the move but did not indicate what these were. Despite the small sample, the data suggest the importance of good partnership between professionals and families, and transition support for families. Families report feeling further away from the secondary school than they did in the primary school, with access to teachers perceived to be more limited (Jindal-Snape and Foggie, 2008), with the first parents' evening being conducted in different schools/local authorities at different times ranging from two to six months after the move. However, as all children have a named guidance teacher in Scottish secondary schools, access should theoretically be easier. Similar to parents, there was a mixed response from school professionals in this study with some indicating that children moving schools or classes had triggered their transition, whereas others said that it had not. As mentioned earlier there were gaps in their support and training. One professional responded: 'New pupils to know. Issues often the same but how they are resolved is often different ... my learning curve continues' (Pupil support worker, Secondary School, Female, 6–10 years professional).

## EFFECTIVE TRANSITION PRACTICE

Despite the different educational stages and the need to adapt the practice to suit an individual, based on international and Scottish research, existing good practice and policy recommendations, aspects of effective transitions practice can be summarised as shown in Table 26.2). In line with the MMT theory, practice has to consider transition support needs of the child and all the significant people in their environment. This can be extrapolated from Table 26.2 to apply to others. However, this is just a starting point and further research is required to understand the transition support needs and resources inherent in the child and the environment.

## CONCLUSION

As transition is a dynamic process, it is vital that transition support is provided *across* the educational lifespan rather than at a particular point. This support should be in line with an individual's specific needs and should consider the changes they are experiencing in different aspects of their life. As families and professionals are the most important support networks for the child and have their own transition support needs, they too need to be supported well so that they can support the child properly. Also, currently professionals are expected to support children's transitions without specific training and require further specific professional development. Finally, to be able to facilitate successful transitions and support wellbeing, it is important to conceptualise transitions as dynamic, multiple and multi-dimensional.

## REFERENCES

Galton, M. (2010) 'Moving to secondary school: what do children in England say about the experience?' in D. Jindal-Snape (ed.), *Educational Transitions: Moving Stories From around the World*. New York: Routledge, pp. 107–24.

Gorton, H. (2012). *'Are They Ready? Will They Cope?' An Exploration of the Journey From Pre-School to*

*School For Children With Additional Support Needs Who Had Their School Entry Delayed.* Doctoral thesis, University of Dundee, Dundee. http://discovery.dundee.ac.uk/portal/files/2112743/ Gorton_dedpsych_2012.pdf

Jindal-Snape, D. (2016) *A-Z of Transitions.* Basingstoke: Palgrave.

Jindal-Snape, D. and Foggie, J. (2008) 'A holistic approach to primary-secondary transitions', *Improving Schools*, 11, 5–18.

Jindal-Snape, D. and Hannah, E. (2013) 'Reconceptualising the inter-relationship between social policy and practice: Scottish parents' perspectives', in A. Kienig and K. Margetts (eds), *International Perspectives on Transitions to School: Reconceptualising Beliefs, Policy and Practice.* Abingdon: Routledge.

Jindal-Snape, D. and Miller, D. J. (2008) 'A challenge of living? Understanding the psycho-social processes of the child during primary-secondary transition through resilience and self-esteem theories', *Educational Psychology Review*, 20, 217–36.

Jindal-Snape, D., Baird, L. and Miller, K. (2011) 'A longitudinal study to investigate the effectiveness of the Guitar Hero Project in supporting transition from P7-S1'. Dundee: Report for Learning and Teaching Scotland.

Jindal-Snape, D., Douglas, W., Topping, K. J., Kerr, C. and Smith, E. F. (2006) 'Autistic spectrum disorders and primary-secondary transition', *International Journal of Special Education*, 21 (2), 18–31, https://files.eric.ed.gov/fulltext/EJ843602.pdf

Richardson, T. D, Jindal-Snape, D. and Hannah, E. F. S. (2017) 'Impact of legislation on post-school transition practice for young people with additional support needs in Scotland', *British Journal of Special Education*, 44(3), 239–56. doi: 10.1111/1467-8578.12178

Scottish Government (2008) 'Early years framework: final report from integrated services task group'. Online at www.scotland.gov.uk/Publications/2008/07/services-report.

# 27

# Leadership, Management and Organisation in the Secondary School

*Danny Murphy*

## INTRODUCTION

Throughout my career as teacher and headteacher, the core mission of those leading and managing secondary schools has remained essentially the same: to help create, in a very specific school community of diverse young people, each with a unique perspective and unique identity, the positive ethos, work environment and supportive systems that will assist each one to find and develop their best selves – skilled, knowledgeable and insightful – so they are ready to make a valuable contribution as positive, capable, committed citizens in their communities and in the rapidly changing world beyond.

The overall aim of this chapter is to stimulate thinking about how those leading and managing in our secondary schools, and the organisational structures of secondary education within which they work, can respond best to that challenge. The first section introduces some important issues in secondary school management and leadership. The second highlights the impact of contemporary adolescence on secondary schooling. The final section, in reviewing the current framework of secondary education, distinguishes between secondary *schooling* and secondary *education* and recommends that those leading and managing secondary education nationally should make further changes to its architecture. At the time of writing, the Scottish Government has just published its governance review (hereinafter 'the review') and related proposals to reform the governance of schools (Scottish Government, 2017). The far-reaching changes proposed will have significant effects on school leaders. Implementation of the proposals will take some time, and evaluation of the resulting changes even longer. However, some relevant discussion of the proposals as they stand has been incorporated into the text of this chapter.

## SCHOOL MANAGEMENT AND SCHOOL LEADERSHIP

School management, like most forms of organisational management, involves instructing and directing activities, communicating aims, setting up processes, receiving and giving reports on progress, allocating, and evaluating the use of resources. Good management provides order, predictability, efficiency and clarity. Management posts in Scotland's 359 (in 2015, www.scotland.gov.uk/Topics/Statistics) public sector secondary schools generally conform to a standard hierarchical pattern established by national agreement in 2001, on the remits and associated salaries of three levels of post: the headteacher who has overall responsibility, and the principal teachers (PT) and depute headteachers (DHT) to whom she or he delegates particular defined responsibilities. The review proposed that headteachers should have enhanced powers in appointments, though it is unclear how much room there will be for flexibility or innovation in changing school management structures, given that negotiations around pay and conditions continue to take place at national level. The leadership and management work of these 'promoted posts', particularly that of the headteacher, is the main focus of this chapter. The complementary chapter by Deidre Torrance (Chapter 24) provides more detailed insight into how leadership is exercised across a school.

Many local authorities of the 1980s and 1990s positioned headteachers as 'middle managers', with schools as local 'branches' implementing policy, and practice decided centrally. It has been widely recognised more recently (not least in the review) that distant micromanagement of schools has limited improvement capacity. The advice and prescriptions of the remote authors of detailed policy documents do not always work in particular schools in very specific contexts where, at the 'quantum level' of individuals, there can be considerable unpredictability, inefficiency, different understandings of purpose and priority and consequent levels of disorder. In school communities there are people who do not respond well to being managed or may have different purposes or values to those of the organisation as a whole. Sometimes the tight lines of 'efficient production' need to be disrupted and individual solutions sought – a pupil who is not learning, for example, is not merely an inconvenient obstacle getting in the way of efficient production, a faulty cog in an efficient machine to be rejected and replaced, but is a central concern of the enterprise. Responding to that student may involve inefficient uses of time and non-standard procedures. This is one of many reasons why, as outlined in Chapter 26, 'leadership', characterised as more flexible in concept and practice than management, has become increasingly important in educational thinking and in job specifications, a trend cemented by the Donaldson report (Donaldson, 2011) in which the terms 'leaders' and 'leadership' feature 149 times (management only seventeen times) and in the subsequent reframing of the Professional Standards for Scottish teachers. This is a generally positive discourse, aiming to empower teachers and school managers. However, improved leadership, though potentially very influential within a school community, is no 'silver bullet'. Many problematic issues of secondary education neither derive from, nor can be sorted, at school level, while sometimes poor policy may be the problem. 'Politicians find educational leadership an attractive concept because it places responsibility for success or failure largely in the hands of professionals: thus "failing schools" are presented as the victims of poor leadership (rather than ill-conceived policies)' (Humes, 2000, p. 41).

Leadership is related to, but different from, management. It involves complementary qualities of influence, inspiration, flexibility and situational judgement, rather than direction and control. Much of its power comes not from positional authority but from the willingness of others to follow. Leaders are found in every area of school life, wherever their language or behaviour rallies support, wherever others accept their ideas or follow their actions. Not every manager has leadership qualities. Nor is every influential leader in a school community a manager. This gives 'leadership' a potentially disruptive power. Consider the influence of a fourth-year boy who inspires others to challenge school authority, a teacher who drains energy from his colleagues with constant negative talk, or, more positively, a member of support staff who is unfailingly cheery – all are leading, but may be leading in contrary directions.

One of the challenges for school managers is to understand the flows of leadership power in their own specific school context and to try to harness it to a shared purpose. This requires credible, wise actions and judgements, which others (including teachers, parents and pupils) observe, respect and accept. This form of educational leadership involves making sense and sharing understanding of the sometimes complicated contradictory forces in a school community; it inspires hope and generates trust, key ingredients in a flourishing school. The task is more demanding in school communities where there are high levels of social mistrust, low levels of social and educational capital and/or significant socio-economic challenges in the wider community. However, even inspiring leadership is, on its own, never sufficient. While leadership can inspire followers to go up the hill with great enthusiasm, management is needed to ensure that the right resources are there to complete the tasks.

Headteachers, moreover, even with the enhanced powers proposed by the review, do not exercise power alone. They share responsibility for school management and performance with others. Currently, local authority directors can direct and instruct the activities of headteachers. National government and national agencies (such as Education Scotland and the Scottish Qualifications Authority) set priorities for school education which the headteacher is expected to implement. Local and national employer–union agreements limit school-level flexibility. In the review proposals, powerful new directors of the new 'regional improvement collaboratives' (RICs), reporting directly to the Chief Executive of Education Scotland, who is also responsible for inspection and reports directly to the Cabinet Secretary, will exert a powerful influence on how headteachers understand 'improvement', how it is to be measured and how their performance will be judged. This is a streamlining of the 'top-down' power of the system. In the local context of the school itself, parents and pupils also exert influence in the spaces where they can make their voice heard. The review recommends that their voices should be louder and more influential than at present, but their voices may not always agree with the professional voices of teachers or the policy voices of national agencies and politicians. They may not even agree with each other.

Ensuring that all these different, equally legitimate, voices and influences on school activity are respected is a challenging management task. Finding a way forward that commands widespread support demands skilled leadership. Good preparation for this complex work of school management and leadership has never been more needed.

The review proposes that responsibility for leadership development across Scotland (now subsuming 'management') is to be passed on to Education Scotland, working through the new RICs. At the time of writing, there has been no national evaluation of the impact of the leadership development programmes only recently developed and directed by the newly formed Scottish College for Educational Leadership, in partnership with local authorities and universities. These programmes will now require further change, not least to take account of the changes in headteachers' management responsibilities envisaged by the review. An independent evaluation of the current programmes should inform the development of any new programmes.

The recruitment and retention of school leaders, particularly headteachers, has been the subject of several recent studies (e.g. MacBeath et al., 2009; Draper, 2016) and is identified in the review as an important area for future action. The numbers applying for headships is worryingly low in some cases, while headship training programmes, though valuable, need to be supplemented by earlier career preparation for leadership and management and more 'in–post' support for serving headteachers. MacBeath and his associates found that teachers have limited opportunities to experience management responsibilities and only 8 per cent see themselves as future headteachers.

These and similar studies identify a number of current disincentives, dissuading some from seeking management positions in general and headship in particular. Headteachers have significant, and under the review will have even greater, financial responsibilities. They deal with the most difficult conflicts of school life. The expectations of schools being able to deliver on national priorities are high and headteachers can end up caught between the top-down requirements of national policy and local government requirements and bottom-up pressures from their community and its people. Time-consuming and important local challenges of which national government is unaware, such as an epidemic of gang violence or drug abuse in the local community, can spill into the school and force national issues onto the back-burner. The tensions and dilemmas that result from such conflicts of values and interests in the school community, and between local and national priorities, can have both emotional and relational costs for the headteacher, some of which can have a long-term impact. Some headteachers are 'broken by the job' (Murphy, 2013, pp. 25–6). MacBeath et al. (2012) summarise these pressures as experienced by the majority of headteachers and outline various 'coping strategies' headteachers adopt in response, on a continuum from 'dutiful compliance' through 'quiet self-confidence' to 'defiant risk-taking'. Given that both responsibilities and accountabilities will increase under the review's proposals, it seems unlikely that these tensions and dilemmas will reduce.

On the positive side, MacBeath (2009) found that 88 per cent of the headteachers felt their work was either satisfying or very satisfying despite such pressures, many describing it as a 'privilege', 'the best job in the world'. Valuable features included: professional autonomy; support from other members of their leadership team and from parents; having a positive influence in the school community; improving learning and teaching; exercising strategic leadership; and personnel functions, such as guiding the professional development of teachers. The encouraging increase in the numbers of female secondary headteachers (41 per cent in 2016 as opposed to 18 per cent in 2003, with 54 per cent of DHTs now female; www.scotland.gov.uk/Topics/Statistics) suggests that, for all its pressures, the job remains attractive. The review proposes to increase professional autonomy, particularly in relation to learning and teaching, and, in time, this may help to reduce some of the pressures of conflicting demands. The challenges of leading and managing contemporary secondary schools are further complicated by the rapidly changing character of adolescence, briefly sketched in the next section, and changing expectations of schools, explored in the concluding section of the chapter.

## THE CHANGING CONTEXT OF SECONDARY SCHOOLING

Young people grow up in very different circumstances. Their identity is profoundly affected by factors such as the physical, social and economic environment of their home, significant relationships in the family and their peer group, and the opportunities and constraints characteristic of their family circumstances. Secondary school, where, if they attend every day, they will spend less than a fifth of their waking adolescent years (12–18), helps young people locate that individual experience within a wider knowledge and understanding of the world. In the formal structured learning of the school curriculum, schools help pupils learn from the rigorously tested knowledge of academic disciplines and the practical and physical knowledge of the workroom and the gym. Research studies suggest that among the in-school factors which affect pupil learning, the overall impact of school leadership and management is second only to the quality of teaching, but there are many factors outside school that also affect how and what pupils learn, and even in schools much of the learning takes place outside classrooms.

Alongside cognitive and physical learning, schools are also expected to contribute to their pupils' moral and emotional development. Much of this learning takes place informally, in less structured settings. Schools teach, and those in them learn, not just through lessons, but through their character as mini-communities. The secondary school is perhaps the last occasion when young people are compelled to share time and space with a cross section of the population as a whole, many of whom they would never otherwise meet, and perhaps would never wish to meet, given their different interests and values. Through life and work in a secondary school, young people learn about where and how they fit, or do not fit, into wider society, and how to live and work alongside others. The experience of daily working life in a diverse secondary school community, its differing values and interests, its inequalities, its fair and unfair systems, can be positive and purposeful, but can also be negative and disempowering. This learning experience in school does not always connect with the life experience of the learner, or the often confusing and occasionally chaotic experiences of modern adolescence.

By age 18, young people will have been selected for different futures, in large part as a result of their performance in national examinations, will have become eligible to vote in elections, will have explored different leisure interests, will have made and lost friendships, observed or been subject to bullying, grown physically and matured sexually, being attracted to, and developed a sense of their relative attractiveness to, potential partners, becoming sexually active in the process (around a third experience first intercourse at age 14/15 and the median age is 16). They will have, in many cases, experimented with drugs or alcohol (over 50 per cent of 15 year olds report having been drunk at least once).

Rapid social and technological change also poses new questions and challenges for the 'informal' side of secondary schooling. Many young people now share their lives almost continuously through social media (such as Instagram, Twitter, Snapchat and Facebook) and engage with different aspects of an international media culture, much of which originates well beyond Scotland – an exciting culture of science, technology, music, dance, games and film, but also of pornography, drugs, abuse, misinformation and 'alternative facts'. Beyond the face-to-face community of locality and school are online communities, with very different worldviews. School education can contribute greatly to the quality of the conceptual framework, critical insight and personal skills needed to meet these and many other experiences of adolescence in the twenty-first century. The social identity young people form in the process strongly influences their future choices and chances.

To encourage and support these different kinds of learning going on in a school community – cognitive, physical, moral, emotional, informal – school leaders need not only to understand the different forces at work on the thinking and development of young people – whether from inside or outside the world of the school – but also to be able to give a credible account of how they should be met in the very specific setting of an individual school community, with its particular characteristics, personalities, relationships, cultural and socio-economic context; school leaders who not only know when the school should be the authoritative voice of learning and laws, but also when it should reach out and listen.

In a context of social experiences that are more fragmented, individualised and diverse than those of previous generations, contemporary schools seek to develop and share a range of common understandings and values that respect difference but also define what is shared. This task is not just for the classroom, but is taught, and learned, by the way the school community works. The school leader as educator is challenged to make sense of the experiences of school, formal and informal, fair and unfair, positive or negative, in relation to the overall development of the young person. This is a complicated educational task, made more difficult by tensions inherent in Scotland's secondary schooling that can create obstacles to the learning of some pupils. After reviewing some relevant issues of governance, the final section of the chapter therefore examines critically the organisation of secondary education and makes related recommendations for those who manage the system as a whole.

## WHERE NEXT FOR SECONDARY EDUCATION?

Governance concerns the provision, regulation and direction of a service or activity (Murphy and Raffe, 2015, p. 139). Some inconsistencies in provision, such as significant variations in school staffing and funding levels, are not in the review of governance, but subject to further consultation. The changes proposed, however, are wide-ranging and will affect every level of Scottish schooling – from individual schools to national agencies and government. The rhetoric seeks to empower teachers, headteachers and school communities, 'starting with a presumption that decisions about children's learning and school life should be taken at school level' (Scottish Government, 2017). To ensure that teachers and headteachers across Scotland are able to make contextually sensitive decisions, headteachers' powers will be enhanced and system capacity developed through more professional support and growing networks of professional knowledge. Given current inconsistencies across local authorities, many will welcome this emphasis on consistent support across Scotland.

However, though seeing many positives in the offer of increased autonomy, school managers may be wary of the message of school-level empowerment, given the number of powerful agencies and interests, and sometimes competing voices, jostling for influence. Inspectors, national officials and directors, including the new RIC directors, impatient to see *their* priorities, and the processes they recommend, given precedence at school level, may continue to exercise positional authority over school headteachers in any new system, limiting school-level decision making. Change may not be welcome if others continue to share in the responsibility, but headteachers acquire even more of the accountability.

Change also creates opportunity costs and unintended consequences. The 2015 Organisation for Economic Co-operation and Development (OECD) review emphasised the importance of the 'middle tier' between national and local levels, evening out disadvantages, providing support services and reducing schools' exposure to risk through quality assurance and safety nets of resources. Scottish local authorities have played this role since the 1920s, so change will bring much 'unpicking'. Setting up new systems takes time: negotiations, new bureaucracies, new professional and local rivalries, new structures and communication channels, new teams and partnerships. There may also be (small 'p') political tussles around the influence and power of the new RICs. Any impact of the changes on pupil attainment, particularly among the least advantaged pupils – the stated intention – is likely to be indirect and difficult to unpick from the impact of the many other factors involved, not least because the proposed changes are themselves multifactorial. Even if the attainment of the least advantaged is improved, some of the changes may not have contributed positively, they may even have had a contrary effect. Ranson, based on an analysis of governance changes in England, suggests that granting greater responsibility, and associated accountabilities, to individual school communities may further advantage schools supported by socially advantaged communities, leaving schools with less social, educational and financial capital struggling to keep pace (Ranson, 2008, p. 217).

There can be no doubt that the present Scottish system of governance muddles and mis-aligns responsibilities and accountabilities at different levels of leadership and management – school, middle tier and national-level agencies and officials (Murphy, 2014, p. 82ff.). It will be some time before it is clear whether the new system clarifies responsibilities and accountabilities or replaces one jumble with another one.

A further structural problem, with a bigger role in inhibiting further improvement, is Scotland's fragmented incoherent upper-secondary curriculum. Curriculum for Excellence outlines two discontinuous curriculum phases: the 'broad general education' (BGE), an educational entitlement to age 15 described in holistic integrated terms; and the 'senior phase' (SP) of 'individual pathways' – subject-based secondary school learning, college education, work-based training or employment. The different characters of BGE and SP represent in a very stark form the competing demands placed on secondary schools – first, to value and develop fully the capacities of every young person, and second, to prepare them for competitive selection for different roles in an unequal adult world. Educational progression for all surely requires equally valuable educational options for all, yet Scotland's paradoxical system, where some achieve 'Higher' and so others are necessarily 'lower', aims nonetheless to value all equally.

Although there is as yet limited evaluation, anecdotal evidence suggests that, despite the aspiration of Curriculum for Excellence, secondary schools, faced with the demands of the new examination system, have continued to place progression in subject learning at the heart of curriculum planning. Subject teachers, whose teaching identity is in part formed through their special subject expertise and who are held accountable for results in subject-based examinations, need to build from the earliest stages a foundation of concepts, information and skills on which later learning, and success in national examinations, can be built. This is particularly the case for subjects, such as Modern Languages, Mathematics or the Sciences, where progression in learning has a strong sequential character. In the absence of any other educational rationale, the selective character of senior phase, based around performance in subject-based examinations, thus inevitably washes back into planning and delivery of the curriculum in the earlier phases of secondary schooling.

Young people's experience reflects this trend. Before, and within, the senior phase, learning experiences diverge as different future pathways are blocked off or opened up according to performance in examinations. Those who can progress their education in school beyond the compulsory leaving age are motivated to perform in examinations and, along with some who go on to college, have ready access to a range of supports and services, and clear, well-understood educational pathways to post-18 work or continuing education. Others, aware from an early age that they cannot compete successfully with their peers in national examinations, easily lose motivation, may choose not to bother trying to learn and consequently fail to realise their potential as learners. After leaving formal education, these young people can then find themselves having to navigate a complex, sometimes confusing, territory of local provision, some of which lacks broad educational components, and where they are often less able to access available supports. Recently much good local work has been supported through the 'Developing Young Workforce' initiative, but this is inconsistent across the country, not well aligned with school systems, nor underpinned nationally by a clear educational rationale.

The selective function of the senior phase influences many aspects of a young person's secondary school experience – not least the value the young person places on school learning and on themselves as learners. How often have we heard young people say, 'I was no good at school', valuing their learning experience in terms of their examination performance? The inequalities of adult life thus cast a shadow over young people in school as selection for different possible future pathways comes nearer, and they see ahead of them many closed doors. This selective function dominates the systems and structures of secondary schools.

However, we now increasingly expect, with equal force, that our secondary schools should find and liberate the best within each of our young people. Our secondary schooling system struggles to achieve both of these valuable objectives, which, for some, particularly those who do not do well in examinations, seem to be in conflict. Lacking a clear educational rationale and framework to respond to this challenge, the senior phase is leading to worrying inconsistencies in provision and attainment, inconsistencies which may be on the increase (Scott, 2015).

The proposed changes in governance argue that enhancements in the capacity and autonomy of school-level professionals will 'close the attainment gap', but the proposals leave intact the underpinning competitive structures of secondary schooling and current unequal educational entitlements at 16+.

In *Schooling Scotland* (Murphy, 2014, p. 105ff.), I argued that we need a new educational vision for our secondary education system if we are to provide the best opportunities for *all* our young people, one that values a greater variety of secondary learning and offers more flexibility in the location and character of secondary education. This is not a job for individual schools. Major structural change in the school system has to start with a broad, agreed well-understood national vision, across the political spectrum. It is a leadership and management job at national level to develop that vision and make the necessary system changes.

In the absence of an educational rationale for senior phase, there is no current attempt to outline what an equal educational entitlement might look like, other than through equalising attainment; and no attempt to resolve the tension at the heart of secondary education between the vision of Curriculum for Excellence of an empowering education for all and the requirement of secondary schools to rank and select young people competitively for post-secondary destinations of unequal status and reward. Reforms in governance may improve implementation within the existing framework, but the framework itself is educationally limiting.

No young person should reach the age of 18 feeling they have failed in education, unsure of their potential and uncertain of their future. We need a new post-16 system to make that change, one which protects the quality of what schools can and are doing in subject-based disciplinary learning, but also recognises and values other attributes than those of the examination hall. Currently Scotland requires secondary *schooling* for all its young people to age 15 or 16 (depending on the month of their birth), a requirement which sees some short-changed in a fragmented post-16 system. It is long past time that Scotland gave all its young people entitlement to a full secondary *education* to age 18.

In a well-managed national system, all positive educational experiences in the senior phase, in or out of school, would be planned and their educational value recognised nationally. This is not to argue for any dilution of subject learning. Through academic disciplines, young people gain access to what Matthew Arnold in *Culture and Anarchy* (1869) called 'the best that has been thought and said' and consequently a better understanding of the world we live in. But constant failure to succeed in *competitive* learning is demotivating. Many of those who leave school before age 18 are already disadvantaged by their lack of achievement in school and are often doubly disadvantaged by ending their formal education early. If we are to motivate all our learners, we need to balance the rigours of classroom learning in a framework which values other skills, abilities and experiences, values what young people 'bring to the table', nurtures and rewards their best selves, while delivering a broad educational entitlement for all.

First, Scotland needs to make clear, as many developed education systems have (including England) that all young people should be entitled to six years of secondary education, an education that liberates their potential as well as grading and sorting them into 'higher' and 'lower' in terms of their academic success.

Second, the post-16 entitlement should be redesigned to recognise and value the variety of worthwhile educational experiences and outcomes, within but also outside schools and colleges. This entitlement needs a national structure, such as a process of graduation from secondary education, open to all at age 18. Too many of our current leavers leave their school building at the end of S4 or Christmas of S5 with a self-image of educational 'failure', with little formal public recognition of all they have done and all they can be. A broadly framed graduation certificate would define an entitlement to important educational experiences, a minimum threshold of competence in core learning areas and recognise and value a variety of talents and achievements including, but not limited to, national examination success (Murphy 2014, p. 115ff.). Secondary education to age 18 would thus be given an underpinning educational rationale and structure with the capacity to spark ambition and reward and value a variety of types and locations of learning, The broad definition of 'achievement' in such a framework would continue to include examination performance, an important and valuable indicator of learning and capacities, but also the many other qualities, skills and achievements young people develop in their adolescence and in college, work training and other learning environments beyond school. This framing would have a beneficial 'washback' effect into all of the secondary school experience, broadening the focus of the school learning experience in the way that Curriculum for Excellence intended, but has failed to achieve in the senior phase.

Individual schools can and do make an enormous difference to the life chances of individual young people, but are limited by our under-designed and unequal national educational entitlement at 16+. On the ground, teachers and headteachers have to make the present fragmented organisational structure, with its cluttered policy framework and poorly aligned sets of responsibilities and accountabilities, work as well as it can. But it is now a leadership and management task *at national level* to bring citizens, employers, teachers and school leaders, politicians and the officials who work for them, together to help *all* our young people 'find and develop their best selves' in the more flexible and responsive secondary education system – including, but not limited to, secondary schooling – that the challenges of our common future demand.

## REFERENCES

Donaldson, G. (2011) *Teaching Scotland's Future*. Edinburgh: Scottish Government.
Draper, J. (2016) 'Expectations and experiences in headship', in J. O'Brien (ed.), *School Leadership*, third edition. Edinburgh: Dunedin Academic Press.

Humes, W. (2000) 'The discourses of educational management', *Journal of Educational Enquiry*, 1 (1), 35–53.

MacBeath, J. (2009) *The Recruitment and Retention of Headteachers in Scotland*. Online at https://www.eduhk.hk/apclc/roundtable2010/paper/The%20Recruitment%20and%20Retention%20of%20Headteachers%20in%20Scotland_John%20Macbeath.pdf

MacBeath, J., Gronn, P., Opfer, D., Lowden, K., Forde, C., Cowie, M. and O'Brien, J. (2009) *The Recruitment and Retention of Headteachers in Scotland*. Edinburgh: Scottish Government.

MacBeath, J., O'Brien, J. and Gronn, P. (2012) 'Drowning or waving? Coping strategies among Scottish head teachers', *School Leadership and Management*, 32 (5), 421–37.

Murphy, D. (2013) *Professional School Leadership: Dealing with Dilemmas*, second edition. Edinburgh: Dunedin Academic Press.

Murphy, D. (2014) *Schooling Scotland: Education, Equity and Community*, Edinburgh: Argyll Press

Murphy, D. and Raffe, D. (2015) 'The governance of Scottish comprehensive education', in D. Murphy, L. Croxford, C. Howieson and D. Raffe (eds), *Everyone's Future: Lessons From Fifty Years of Scottish Comprehensive Schooling*. London: Trentham/Institute of Education.

OECD (2015) *Improving Schools in Scotland: An OECD Perspective*. Online at https://www.oecd.org/education/school/Improving-Schools-in-Scotland-An-OECD-Perspective.pdf

Ranson, S. (2008) 'The changing governance of education', *Educational Management and Leadership*, 36 (2), 201–19.

Scott, J. (2015) 'The governance of Curriculum for Excellence in Scottish secondary schools: structural divergence, curricular distortion and reduced attainment', paper presented in evidence to the OECD committee examining Scottish education. Online at headteachertp://www.academia.edu/20171586/OECD_Evidence_Paper_2015

Scottish Government (2017) *Education Governance: Next Steps*. Online at www.gov.scot/Resource/0052/00521038.pdf

# 28

# Personal Support (Guidance)

*Claire Wallace*

## HISTORICAL CONTEXT

To understand the role of Personal Support, it is beneficial to review some of its background and history. With the inception of comprehensive schools in the 1960s came an increased focus on the needs of individual pupils which might be beyond academic achievement. This led to 'Guidance' focusing on three main areas: personal support (for example, with any problems in school or at home); vocational support (for example, providing advice and support on careers/further education) and curricular support (for example, with subject choices and/or any issues with classes, teachers, courses).

By 1971 the Guidance role had largely evolved into a promoted post, allowing for 'management time', and usually involved teaching both a core curricular subject and Personal and Social Education (PSE). Although principal teachers of Guidance (PTGs) were a clear and identifiable point of contact for pupils, it was made clear by Her Majesty's Inspectors that all staff had a degree of responsibility for a pupil's personal, vocational and curricular needs – a familiar concept in today's Curriculum for Excellence. A major development in the role of the PTG came with the publication of *More Than Feelings of Concern* (Scottish Consultative Council on the Curriculum, 1986) which aimed to define the role and its objectives. Although this publication reaffirmed the importance of one member of staff as a point of contact who knew the pupil well, it also emphasised the idea of a caring school community where pupil welfare was the responsibility of everyone. Again, this idea is recognisable in today's approach to pupil wellbeing.

Perhaps the next major milestone in the development of Guidance was the McCrone Report and subsequent agreement in 2001 (Scottish Executive Education Department, 2001). Guidance was largely ignored and the only mention of it came in recommending that unpromoted teachers be involved in the pastoral care of pupils. The agreement removed the post of assistant principal teacher in every area and so, by implication, Guidance teams in schools became much smaller. Inevitably, this created a challenge for local authorities and could be described as the beginning of the idea of 'full-time Guidance' (a system where PTGs no longer taught subject classes at all and taught only PSE) – schools had fewer Guidance staff but the same number of pupils with the same needs. Therefore, local authorities and schools had to consider removing teaching subject classes from Guidance teachers to allow for more time to be dedicated to supporting pupils.

From this point to the present, local authorities have very much created their own structures for Guidance, and so there is a degree of variation across Scotland. In fact, there is even variation within local authorities with individual schools opting for the model which suits them best. Although it is more common than ever to find schools opting for full-time Guidance staff, there can also be variation within authorities on this matter with some headteachers opting to have their PTGs continuing to have a subject commitment. Indeed, many PTGs will openly say that they would not wish to lose their subject commitment. Perhaps the greatest degree of confusion comes from what principal teachers of Guidance are actually called. Some schools have kept the traditional 'Guidance' title while others are opting for 'principal teacher of Pastoral Support' or 'principal teacher of Personal Support'. To avoid confusion and for the purpose of consistency, from this point on this chapter will use the term 'Personal Support' or 'principal teacher of Personal Support' (PTPS).

Although many aspects of the traditional role still exist, huge changes have taken place in the support role over the years. The 2004 review into the Children's Hearing System, *Getting it Right for Every Child: A Report on the Responses to the Consultation on the Review of the Children's Hearing System* (Scottish Government, 2004), highlighted a significant increase in the number of identified children with multiple needs. This increase has clearly had a major impact on support in schools, in terms of how it is organised and how much time/resources it receives. As previously mentioned, many schools are now opting for full-time Personal Support staff while another approach has been the development of robust first-level personal support systems in response to this increase in need, whereby register/ tutor teachers take a more proactive role in supporting pupils. This idea supports recent professional dialogue which has re-emphasised that supporting pupils is everyone's respon- sibility and is also a way for unpromoted teachers to gain experience in Personal Support.

In terms of the structure of Personal Support, secondary schools are largely still opting for either a vertical structure, where PTs Personal Support are responsible for a house group, or a horizontal system, where the PTPS is responsible for a year group. Both systems have advantages. Some schools prefer the vertical structure because it allows all children from the same family to be grouped in a house with the same PTPS, thus allowing the parents/carers to liaise with one central person. However, other schools opt for the horizontal system because they like the idea of the PTPS following one group of pupils from S1 to S6 and one PTPS dealing with key calendar events such as options interviews. Although these traditional structures largely remain, there has been some experimentation with tutor groups and mentor groups whereby an unpromoted teacher (usually someone with an interest in Personal Support) will take responsibility for supporting a small group of pupils and work closely with them on pertinent issues such as attendance, behaviour and so on. Such staff will liaise closely with the PTPS and become part of the Personal Support structure in the school.

Another key part of the Personal Support structure is the line manager. Line managers for Personal Support tend to be depute headteachers (DHTs) with a responsibility for child protection. Their role is to be the senior leadership team link to Personal Support while also acting as the school's child protection coordinator. However, some schools, as well as grouping subjects into faculties, have opted for a 'Support Faculty' where Personal Support, Learning Support and Behaviour Support are grouped into a faculty with all of the principal teachers managed by a faculty head of Support. This is a relatively new and unusual approach but it is worth mentioning as it demonstrates yet another variation in this hugely diverse system.

As well as schools making changes to adapt to this greater need, the Scottish Government has implemented a number of policies and initiatives in response. These policies and initiatives have played a major role in reshaping both thinking and practice in Personal Support and have led to a number of changes in the role.

## GETTING IT RIGHT FOR EVERY CHILD

Getting it Right for Every Child (GIRFEC) is Scotland's national approach to improving outcomes and supporting wellbeing for all children and young people. Its origins were in the review of the Children's Hearing System and the GIRFEC approach has developed over a period of ten years, playing a major role in shaping Personal Support in schools.

With the initial Getting it Right for Every Child report recognising that there was a dramatic increase in children with multiple needs across the country, it was stated that a greater emphasis must be placed on joined-up working and on a child-centred approach to support. This led to the publication of A Guide to Getting it Right for Every Child (Scottish Government, 2008) which identified the key principles of GIRFEC:

1. *Support should be child-focused*. All supports must ensure the child or young person – and their family – is at the centre of decision making and the support available to them.
2. *Support is based on an understanding of the wellbeing of a child*. It looks at a child or young person's overall wellbeing – how safe, healthy, achieving, nurtured, active, respected, responsible and included they are – so that the right support can be offered at the right time.
3. *Support is based on tackling needs early*. It aims to ensure needs are identified as early as possible to avoid bigger concerns or problems developing.
4. *Support requires joined-up working*. It is about children, young people, parents and the services (e.g. education, social services, National Health Service (NHS), etc.) working together in a coordinated way to meet children's specific needs and improve their wellbeing.

The principles of GIRFEC are not new and as far back as 1986, in More Than Feelings of Concern (Scottish Consultative Council on the Curriculum, 1986), a proactive, joined-up and pupil-centred approach was advocated when supporting pupils. What was new was the language of GIRFEC. With Curriculum for Excellence's (CfE's) focus on Health and Wellbeing, principal teachers of Personal Support are more aware of emotional and mental wellbeing than ever before and this awareness has been cascaded to pupils. GIRFEC puts huge emphasis on all aspects of wellbeing and developed the now well-known indicators of wellbeing (more commonly known as SHANARRI) – all young people should be safe, healthy, achieving, nurtured, active, respected, responsible and included. These SHANARRI indicators have been embraced by both staff and pupils and, even in early years' centres, children can talk about SHANARRI.

The GIRFEC approach and the eight indicators of wellbeing have become part of daily practice for PTs Personal Support in schools and the associated tools, for example the Wellbeing Wheel, My World Triangle and the Resilience Matrix, are used to assess wellbeing, work with colleagues and access support for families.

## THE CHILDREN AND YOUNG PEOPLE (SCOTLAND) ACT 2014

The Children and Young People (Scotland) Act 2014 aimed to 'further the Scottish Government's ambition for Scotland to be the best place to grow up in by putting children and young people at the heart of planning and services and ensuring their rights are respected across the public sector' (Scottish Government, 2014). This is an ambitious pledge and has implications for schools and for the role of the PTPS in particular.

As well as placing a definition of wellbeing into legislation, the Act put in place a single planning process to support children who require more/extra support – the Child's Plan. Available nationally from August 2016, the Child's Plan is part of the GIRFEC approach in supporting and safeguarding the wellbeing of young people. The Child's Plan will be coordinated by the lead professional who is responsible for ensuring that it contains information about the child's wellbeing needs and the views of the child and their parent/carer. The plan must also detail action(s) taken and the service(s) involved in it and in providing support. Finally, each plan should have a clear outcome(s)/aim(s) and a review date. Clearly, there is a degree of expectation on the lead professional in activating, maintaining and reviewing the Child's Plan and this may well have implications for the daily workload of the PTPS as, inevitably, they will be required to undertake this role for some pupils in their caseload.

Perhaps the main implication from the Act on the PTPS is the *named person* role. The Act states that every child from birth to 18 (and beyond if still in school) must have access to a named person. The named person will be one point of contact for advice and support for young people and their parents and will also be a point of contact for other services if they have a concern. Additionally, the named person will be responsible for sharing information on a young person's needs and circumstances with other professionals as appropriate and with the knowledge of both the parent and child, apart from in certain circumstances, for example child protection. The named person must be a promoted member of staff and so for secondary school pupils, the PTPS will usually be the named person.

In many ways, PTs Personal Support are already fulfilling this role on a daily basis in schools – they are the central point of contact for pupils in their caseload; they work closely with pupils and parents, often on very personal, sensitive and confidential issues; they provide advice and support; and they refer to and liaise with other agencies as appropriate. The main change is that this role is now statutory as the Act places a duty on local authorities to provide this service, even during holiday periods and during sickness absence. The named person has caused a great deal of controversy and was subject to a legal challenge which resulted in a ruling stating that changes are required to the information sharing provisions of the Act to make the provisions compatible with Article 8 of the European Convention of Human Rights.

## WHAT IS INVOLVED IN PERSONAL SUPPORT?

If a group of local authorities, or even a group of secondary schools within a local authority, were asked the question, 'What do principal teachers of Personal Support do on a daily basis?', there would be a variety of answers. However, there are a number of tasks/roles which seem to be generic to Personal Support. Some roles are specific to particular year groups while some are relevant for all pupils. The following information is taken from one local authority's document on the roles and responsibilities of a principal teacher of Personal Support:

    Broad General Education S1 – S3
    – Primary/secondary liaison: liaising with primary staff, pupils and parents including visits and induction programme for P7 pupils; assisting with formulating class lists; supporting pupils in all aspects of transition;
    – S1 pupil interviews;

- S2 personalisation and choice subject choice interviews;
- S3 subject choice interviews.

Senior Phase S4–S6
- S4 subject choice interviews; careers/further education support; SQA [Scottish Qualifications Authority] presentation check;
- S5/6 subject choice interviews; careers/further education support; support with job/FE [further education]/UCAS [Universities and Colleges Admissions Service] applications; community involvement programmes; SQA presentation check.

All Year Groups
- A commitment to a pupil and parent/carer focus and supporting, advising, directing pupils as appropriate;
- Fulfilling the statutory duties of the Named Person;
- Responsibility for formulating, maintaining, reviewing and evaluating Child's Plans;
- Preparing reports/documents for appropriate internal and external meetings;
- Attending and contributing to internal and external meetings as appropriate;
- Responding to requests for information from other appropriate bodies;
- Overall responsibility for attendance monitoring, analysis and appropriate interventions;
- Overview of behaviour and attainment;
- A particular focus on meeting the needs and improving the outcomes of the most vulnerable pupils including, but not limited to LAC/LAAC [Looked After Children/ Looked After Accommodated Children], Young Carers etc.;
- Referring pupils to appropriate agencies for support, counselling etc.;
- Participating in the development, promotion and implementation of school policy and procedures in relation to meeting learners' needs, such as GIRFEC, Child Protection etc.;
- Maintaining pupil files/electronic records;
- Liaising and co-operating with the senior leadership team to develop new initiatives and drive school improvement;
- Promoting partnership working with professional and support staff, the senior leadership team, parents/carers and appropriate agencies;
- Liaising with associated primary schools/tertiary education establishments, other schools in the authority and external education providers to promote continuity, coherence and progression to and from secondary school.

This list is by no means exhaustive and many principal teachers of Personal Support also have additional remits within schools, for example responsibility for UCAS or responsibility for whole school ethos. A number of the duties on this list are confined to specific times in the school calendar, for example subject choice interviews, P7 inductions and SQA, and so they can be demanding of a PTPS's time at that particular point in the session but will not arise again until the next school year.

In contrast, roles such as attendance and behaviour monitoring can be considered as daily duties and can vary from relatively simple to extremely time-consuming tasks. For example, the daily monitoring of caseload attendance can be a relatively quick task which uncovers no issues. However, if this monitoring finds that a pupil is not in class as they should be, an investigation can begin which uncovers truancy. Inevitably, this involves calling parents/carers and, depending on the outcome, can result in meetings, referral to year head, involvement of subject teachers, involvement of outside agencies – the list is endless. This is often identified as a key issue by PTs Personal Support – the inability to plan because each day can depend on what happens with the pupils. Therefore, the role can be immensely varied but also hugely unpredictable.

## PASTORAL CARE

Arguably the most time-consuming parts of the PTPS role are the areas which involve pastoral care. PTs Personal Support spend an enormous amount of time dealing with highly sensitive and very personal matters and regularly support pupils affected by issues such as poverty, social deprivation, unemployment, mental health, substance misuse and family breakdown. With the current figure of one in five children living in poverty in Scotland, schools are dealing with more complex needs than ever before and it is not unusual for PTs Personal Support to deal with issues of neglect and/or child protection. Inevitably, pupils with this level of need require more support and one of the widely acknowledged issues in Personal Support is that staff spend most of their time on a very specific group of pupils. Obviously this can create a workload issue and it is not unusual to hear this concern raised in schools. Supporting pupils with such sensitive issues can often involve regular, and sometimes lengthy, sessions with pupils to offer support, advice and counselling and can result in the involvement of parents/carers and/or other agencies. One of the key remits of the PTPS is partnership working and it is fair to say that they have regular contact with a number of partners including social services, the NHS, psychological services, police and so on.

As well as liaising with external partners, the PTPS works closely with staff, both teaching and non-teaching, across the school. Information gathering is an integral part of the Personal Support role with PTs often asking teachers for feedback on pupil achievement, behaviour and wellbeing. This information can be extremely useful in making decisions and in providing the right support for young people. Similarly, the PTPS is often required to share information with colleagues. For example, if a pupil is experiencing a particularly difficult time due to a family circumstance, such as a bereavement, it may be agreed by the pupil, parent/carer and Personal Support teacher that this should be shared with subject teachers. It is also common for the PTPS to share with a young person's teachers the targets, strategies and supports agreed at support meetings with partner agencies. However, information sharing between Personal Support and the wider school can be a contentious issue. As Personal Support teachers often receive information which is highly confidential, not just about pupils but also about families, it is not always appropriate, or necessary, for it to be shared with class teachers. Such information is usually only shared on a 'need to know basis' to protect the confidentiality of young people and their families. While this is widely accepted in schools, it can lead to criticism of Personal Support and it is not unusual for subject teachers to state that they could support pupils better if they had more information. This is an issue which is unlikely to be resolved.

## PERSONAL AND SOCIAL EDUCATION/HEALTH AND WELLBEING

In most schools, PTs Personal Support are responsible for all aspects of the planning, delivery and quality assurance of PSE programmes. In the past, PSE has suffered from credibility issues and there are a number of reasons for this:

- It is compulsory.
- It is not certificated.

- It was, at times, taught by 'conscripts' such as teachers who had space on their timetable and were given PSE.

Therefore, it could be quite difficult to 'sell' to pupils, particularly those in the senior school who felt that their one period per week of core PSE could be better used for exam preparation rather than learning about the dangers of alcohol again. This is not said to be flippant or disrespectful but PSE programmes also tended to be old-fashioned and underdeveloped, largely due to a lack of time with PTs Personal Support juggling a subject commitment, PSE teaching and the needs of their caseload.

With the increase in schools opting for full time Personal Support staff, and the arrival of Curriculum for Excellence with its focus on 'Health and Wellbeing', an opportunity arose to create quality, relevant and modern programmes for pupils and many schools sought to completely overhaul PSE. According to the Scottish Government's (nd) guidance, Health and Wellbeing (HWB) should address the following:

- mental, emotional, social and physical wellbeing;
- planning for choices and changes;
- physical education, activity and sport;
- food and health;
- substance misuse and relationships;
- sexual health and relationships.

Obviously, most of these topics are 'traditional' PSE topics and so many schools have opted for a PSE/HWB hybrid with a greater focus on mental and emotional health which seems to be very topical at present. However, other schools have made more sweeping changes and have even rebranded PSE as Health and Wellbeing. Some of these programmes have also been developed in partnership with other subjects such as Physical Education (PE) and Home Economics on an interdisciplinary learning project basis. Many schools feel that this type of project-based work has given PSE a degree of credibility with pupils that it has never enjoyed before.

CfE's focus in the senior school on 'planning for choices and changes' as part of Health and Wellbeing seemed to create an opportunity for more relevant PSE. Many schools have opted for 'blocks' of PSE throughout S5/6, with PSE classes taking place at particularly relevant times of the school session, for example in the lead-up to the UCAS deadline. Another approach, perhaps to deal with the credibility issue for older students, has been to offer certificated options within the PSE/Health and Wellbeing umbrella. With a variety of SQA wider achievement qualifications available including Wellbeing, Leadership, Personal Achievement and so on, many schools are offering these qualifications, thus allowing pupils to gain further certification as part of PSE/HWB. Clearly, a great deal of change has taken place in PSE but there is huge variation across authorities and schools as to how much PSE has changed and how much it will continue to change. Many schools are happy to develop their own approach to developing PSE while others would be very grateful for further guidance.

## CURRENT ISSUES IN PERSONAL SUPPORT

Many of the current issues in Personal Support have always been, and will probably always remain as, relevant and potentially problematic matters. Time pressures, teaching commitment and school structures will always have to be considered when schools and local authorities are making decisions about Personal Support and will most likely always be discussion points for books such as this. However, certain issues are very much present at the moment for Personal Support staff and do impact on their daily work and on their planning for the future.

## The Named Person

Everyone is awaiting further guidance from the Scottish Government on how to proceed but this arguably impacts on PTs Personal Support more than most. Many PTs Personal Support are concerned about the statutory aspect of the role and are asking what this means for them in terms of conditions of service. In addition, there is concern about the holiday and absence cover for the named person – who will fulfil this role when a child's named person is on holiday or absent? How will information be shared securely about this young person and how much should be shared? As well as being concerned about the logistics of the role, PTs Personal Support are concerned about the implications for workload. It is argued that certain aspects of the role, for example the Child's Plan, will result in more time being spent working with partner agencies and on administration tasks. This has already been raised as a concern by the Educational Institute of Scotland (EIS), Scotland's largest teaching union.

## Pastoral Care

Probably most principal teachers of Personal Support would identify pastoral care as the most time-consuming, most important, most rewarding and most emotional part of their daily job. The pastoral care given to pupils in schools involves dealing with highly confidential, extremely sensitive and often very emotive issues. While this aspect of the role has always existed, it has changed hugely over the years mainly as a result of the increasing number of young people in schools with additional support needs. PTs Personal Support are dealing with an increasing number of pupils living in very difficult circumstances and, consequently, are spending more and more time supporting these pupils and ensuring they are safe. While the time spent with such young people is crucial, PTs are concerned about having less time for other roles as a result. Resources are also a concern because, while the numbers of pupils with needs is increasing, the resourcing available to support schools is not. This is extremely challenging for schools and can be a source of great concern for PTs Personal Support.

## THE FUTURE OF PERSONAL SUPPORT

The future of Personal Support, and the direction it will take, depends very much on the final guidance for the named person. If PTs Personal Support become named persons, then surely it can be expected that aspects of the existing role will have to change to accommodate this new and statutory responsibility? However, there may well be cause for optimism at present for Personal Support. With local authorities and schools having access to new types of funding, for example the Scottish Attainment Challenge and the Pupil Equity Fund, there is arguably the potential to respond to the increasingly complex issues faced by young people in schools. If local authorities and schools can commit more resources, it can be hoped that this will result in enhancing the quality of Personal Support across Scotland.

## REFERENCES

Educational Institute for Scotland (2016) *EIS Says Additional Resources Required for Named Person.* Online at www.eis.org.uk/public.asp?id=3397

Scottish Consultative Council on the Curriculum (1986) *More than Feelings of Concern.* Dundee: SCCC.

Scottish Executive Education Department (2001) *A Teaching Profession for the 21st Century. Agreement Reached Following Recommendations made in the McCrone Report.* Edinburgh: SEED.

Scottish Government (nd) *Health and Wellbeing in Curriculum for Excellence.* Online at www.gov.scot/Topics/Education/Schools/HLivi

Scottish Government (2004) *Getting it Right for Every Child: A Report on the Responses to the Consultation on the Review of the Children's Hearing System.* Edinburgh: Scottish Government.

Scottish Government (2008) *A Guide to Getting it Right for Every Child.* Online at www.gov.scot/resource/doc/238985/0065813.pdf

Scottish Government (2012) *A Guide to Getting it Right for Every Child.* www.gov.scot/resource/0039/00394308.pdf

Scottish Government (2014) Children and Young People (Scotland) Act 2014. Online at www.legislation.gov.uk/asp/2014/8/pdfs/asp_20140008_en.pdf

Scottish Government (2017) *Getting it Right for Every Child.* Online at www.gov.scot/Topics/People/Young-People/gettingitright

# 29

# Ethos and Behaviour in Secondary Schools

*Raymond Soltysek*

## DISTINCTIVE CONTEXTS

In September 2014, the Scottish Government extended voting in the Independence referendum to 16 and 17 year olds, a bold constitutional step that enfranchised 98,000 new voters. Two thirds of those eligible registered to vote and an estimated 75 per cent of those who registered turned out, and this engagement was enough to encourage the Scottish Government to continue the extension of voting rights for the 2016 Holyrood election. Some saw this as an expression of faith in the Curriculum for Excellence and its ability to produce 'responsible citizens' and 'effective contributors'; if schools were successful in achieving these aims, the argument went, then there was no reason why 16 year olds should not be prepared for the civic responsibility of the ballot box.

This radical change of electorate resulted in the amusing coincidence that on the day of the Holyrood elections, many 16 and 17 year olds were sitting their Higher English examination. The choice for the 'Reading for Understanding, Analysis and Evaluation – Text' element (a last minute replacement triggered by concerns of a breach in security) was a passage by an English journalist/commentator who argued against the extension of the franchise to under-18s. The resultant social media storm – which involved many of those who left the exam to go straight to the polling booth, trolling the author directly on Twitter – was perhaps evidence of a growing confidence in young people to challenge voices of authority and, ultimately, to engage and contribute.

This extension of voting rights to under-18s perhaps demonstrates a distinctiveness in Scotland's social, cultural and political values. While Scotland acknowledged the integrity of young people, the UK Parliament has consistently refused to extend voting rights to this group at the 2015 general election, the 2016 European referendum and the 2017 snap general election. The Prime Minister Theresa May has recently suggested that 16 and 17 year olds should instead take part in 'mock' elections to a powerless 'Youth Parliament'. This divergence in attitude is also apparent in the fact that while the Scottish Government enfranchised European Union (EU) and non-EU residents in the 2014 independence referendum while denying the vote to Scots who had chosen to live or work abroad, the Westminster government took an almost diametrically opposite stance for the EU referendum, with EU migrants who have made homes and careers in the UK being denied a vote, while UK nationals living abroad were balloted. Combined with the disparity of the result in this latter referendum – 62 per cent of those in Scotland voting to stay in the EU, while 52 per cent of those who voted in the whole of the UK elected to leave – the contrast in attitudes could not be more apparent. While political decisions to enfranchise certain groups or disenfranchise others must always be seen in the context of possible gerrymandering – independence and the EU are more popular amongst young people, while the Conservative Party polls better with a predominantly anti-EU, ageing demographic – there is some mileage in the belief that the extension of the vote to under-18s in elections in Scotland is a statement of confidence in the young people the education system produces and in the Curriculum for Excellence itself. Of course, whether that faith is justified is more pertinently discussed elsewhere, but if Curriculum for Excellence is indeed preparing young people for responsible roles in civic society, we would expect to see that reflected in the ethos of the secondary school.

## BEHAVIOUR AND ETHOS: THE STATE OF PLAY

The Scottish Government approach to behaviour management has been markedly coherent since Labour Education Minister Jack McConnell commissioned the *Better Behaviour – Better Learning* report (Scottish Executive, 2001) which has underpinned provision for the past seventeen years. It set an agenda of increased resources and training for behaviour management, increased curriculum flexibility to cater for the needs of all pupils – especially the most demotivated and disaffected – and, most importantly in terms of the relationship with Curriculum for Excellence, an increased awareness of all forms of pupil achievement in school, both academic and social. It reported on the issue in the context of general public anxieties over pupil behaviour, but was informed by a more professional debate led by work of academics that looked at the issue from a positive perspective, examining and celebrating efforts in schools around the country that were engaging with pupil behaviour in imaginative, strategic ways. Importantly, the 2004 *Better Behaviour in Scottish Schools: Policy Update* (www.gov.scot/Publications/2004/11/20233/46420) committed the government to major studies of behaviour in Scottish schools every three years, providing the most up to date data and rigorous analysis possible of behaviour issues in schools as perceived by teachers, managers, support staff and pupils.

At the time of writing (January 2018), the Scottish Government had just published the 2016 study (Scottish Government, 2017), and so a detailed analysis is not possible. What is clear, however, is that after a consistent – if slight – pattern of improvement in reported behaviour through the 2006, 2009 and 2012 reports, the results of the 2016 survey are more problematic. While the executive summary notes little overall change in low-level or serious disruption in secondary schools, the data suggests some trends that raise concern. Secondary teachers reported a decrease (albeit of less than 10 per cent) in five of eleven surveyed positive classroom behaviours, whereas in 2012, an increase had been reported in all of these. Meanwhile, an increase in low-level disruptive behaviour was noted in nine of eleven surveyed classroom behaviours, including an increase of more than 10 per cent in three – making unnecessary noise, hindering peers and late-coming. Thankfully, in the area of serious disruption, teachers reported only one as worse than 2012, a slight increase in the inappropriate use of mobile phones.

There are, of course, many positive trends to be celebrated, and pupils are still, on the whole, well behaved. Every headteacher (up 1 per cent on 2012) and 86 per cent of secondary teachers (down 2 per cent) noted pupils as 'generally well behaved' in all or most lessons; however, support staff were less enthusiastic, with only 54 per cent agreeing with this assessment, a drop of seven percentage points on 2012. Physical violence against teachers, while always a concern, is still very rare, with no significant change to the very low levels reported in 2012. In supporting behaviour and ethos in schools, there was a reported increase in restorative practices and nurture initiatives. A corresponding decrease in the use of punishment and detention was also reported, a finding that schools are adopting more supportive and less punitive styles of pupil management – a point perhaps reinforced by the exclusion figures for 2014–15. During this period, the 14,098 exclusions from secondary schools represented a decrease of almost 18 per cent on the previous 2012–13 reported period (17,106 exclusions), and a substantial 35 per cent decrease from the 2010–11 figures (21,688 exclusions) which were reported in the fourth edition of this book (Soltysek, 2013).

Generally, then, those who actually work in schools express a broad satisfaction with the ethos they encounter, but the 2016 report sees a slight but significant reversal in the upward trends noted since 2006. The reasons for this will undoubtedly prompt a great deal of debate. Whilst immediate press coverage has concentrated on 'disengagement' with the curriculum, particularly at National 4 level (e.g. Denholm, 2018), the report paints a worsening picture of behaviour in *primary* schools, and so it is unlikely that disenchantment with post-16 qualifications is the key factor. The report suggests behaviour 'is inherently bound up with the ethos of a school, with relationships in the classroom and around school, and with engagement in learning' (Scottish Government, 2017, p. 8). In addition, coming at a time of stretched resources, professional retention and recruitment problems, stagnant pay and limited promotion opportunities, and a growing sense of disquiet with Scottish Government policy regarding the curriculum and school governance, it may be that the report is indicative of a profession that is disinclined at the moment to be positive.

As noted in earlier studies, pupil-on-pupil indiscipline is more common than indiscipline towards or involving staff. While there are still issues around bullying and the use of social media to intimidate others, the staff in the 2016 report noted no significant change in these matters, but there has been considerable survey evidence recently that this is an area requiring urgent attention, most specifically for excluded and marginalised groups.

The ENABLE Scotland's 'national conversation' of 2016 (https://www.enable.org.uk/) highlighted revealing and worrying trends regarding the inclusion of pupils with learning disabilities. Involving some 800 children as well as parents, teachers and carers, the report makes for somewhat depressing reading. It stated that 60 per cent of children with learning disabilities feel lonely, around two thirds of young people who have learning disabilities and/or autism spectrum disorders reported being bullied, only 49 per cent believe they are achieving their full potential in the classroom, and 46 per cent feel socially excluded in the playground. While the report's main focus is to generate debate about the presumption of mainstreaming in the Scottish education system, it clearly raises questions of ethos. Similarly, the 2016 report by the organisation Time for Inclusive Education (TIE; https://www.tiecampaign.co.uk/publications) reported distressing figures regarding the inclusion of lesbian, gay, bisexual and transgender (LGBT) young people. The survey indicated that 90 per cent of LGBT people experience homophobia, biphobia and transphobia at school, while 64 per cent reported active bullying because of their sexual orientation or gender identity.

There are obviously training and resources issues involved in building an inclusive and supportive ethos in schools. The ENABLE report cites the *Teaching Scotland's Future* report (Scottish Government, 2011) suggesting that 98 per cent of teachers feel teacher training does not adequately prepare them to teach young people with learning disabilities, while the TIE report suggests 80 per cent of teachers feel they are not adequately trained to support young LGBT people (https://www.tiecampaign.co.uk/publications). A 2017 report by UNISON Scotland points to issues around falling numbers of staff, reduced funding and increased workload impacting on the ability to deal with behaviour in schools, whereas a BEMIS (2013) study, while acknowledging the goodwill of schools, points to deficiencies in their training and ability to deliver acceptable levels of human rights education, a factor which clearly impacts on ethos.

## CONCEPTUALISING BEHAVIOUR MANAGEMENT

Put simply, behaviour management is the management of behaviour. Every pupil in a school constantly 'behaves' during a school day, and, as we have seen, most pupils are perceived to behave 'well'. Therefore, if we accept that behaviour management is concerned with the management of behaviour and that most behaviour is satisfactory, then what teachers should be concentrating on most of the time is managing that satisfactory behaviour to ensure positive outcomes for the pupil(s) concerned. The purpose of behaviour management is often seen in terms of outcomes for *others* – such as maintaining an effective learning environment for *other* pupils, or preserving the authority of the teacher, or upholding the rules of the institution – but at a basic level, interactions which aim to change a young person should, ethically, have at their core the purpose of making that young person's life *better*.

Basically, schools do this through a variety of strategies which can be conceptualised with reference to main theories of learning. The 2012 survey (Scottish Government, 2012) notes that 'a wide range of different approaches are used in secondary schools to promote positive behaviour', which suggests a flexible, solutions-focused mentality is finding some currency. Whether consciously stated or not, schools adopt, to some extent or another, an 'eclectic' approach to behaviour management, using strategies and techniques which can be organised under three related theories of learning (Figure 29.1).

A *behaviourist* approach is concerned solely with ensuring one type of behaviour ('good') and preventing another ('bad'), and with modifying behaviour at the moment of occurrence; a pupil needs to be stopped from chatting in class, or bothering their neighbour or running across the road. It is an approach that is attractive for the school as an organisation

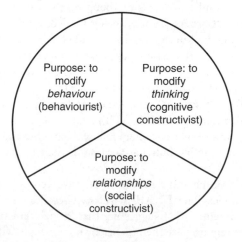

Figure 29.1  Behaviour management and learning theories

because it is a simple 'input–output' model where effort put in to consistently clarifying expectations, consistently recognising acceptable behaviour to ensure its repetition and consistently sanctioning unacceptable behaviour to ensure its eradication, results in a more productive classroom ethos. The teacher should focus more on acceptable behaviour, since this has the effect of promoting satisfactory behaviour in the classroom as a model. Just as we would praise, acknowledge or reward an outstanding pupil essay or drawing in order to exemplify best practice and establish what successful outcomes look like, we should do the same for behaviour. Spending time drawing attention to the satisfactory behaviour that we see from minute to minute in school, it is argued, helps children learn what acceptable behaviour is.

This is a fundamental principle of assertive discipline strategies of writers such as Lee and Marlene Canter and Bill Rodgers which underpins many school behaviour management policies (see, for example, Canter, 2010). Such strategies rest on the notion that pupils should be made aware of explicit expectations of acceptable behaviour, and then be encouraged to meet those expectations through explicit and consistent rewards for meeting them and sanctions for not meeting them. This is, of course, a system founded on behaviourist principles which are looked on suspiciously by some educationalists but, at a practical level, it has been adopted with wide success in many schools.

Such schools have developed sophisticated reward schemes which the 2012 Behaviour in Scottish Schools reports describe as 'in frequent use' (www.gov.scot/Publications/2012/10/5408). These may be based on 'merits' that can be awarded by individual teachers and tracked through computerised registration systems such as SEEMIS, and pupils are sometimes organised into 'houses' for which they can earn 'house points' that can translate into a range of rewards such as trips, social events such as discos, or activity days. Some schools have regular award 'ceremonies' that publicly celebrate 'good' behaviour. It is probable that individual teacher engagement with such reward systems is variable between schools or even within individual schools. For some teachers, rewarding pupils for acceptable behaviour has become part and parcel of the learning and teaching in their classes; for others, it may be seen simply as a bribe to keep children quiet, or a bureaucratic imposition. In addition, there is a great deal of current debate about the efficacy of rewards, with a body of opinion suggesting that a reliance on a reward culture builds dependence and discourages the development of intrinsic drivers – or what McLean (2008) terms 'motivational resilience' – to engage fully with learning and to behave in an acceptable manner in the classroom. However, there is a general acceptance of the notion that *praise* that is honest, specific and genuine is a key factor in building confidence and motivation in pupils, which in turn has a positive effect on their behaviour. The teacher who praises often and genuinely is likely to have a productive, well-behaved, positive classroom, and for such teachers, the assertive discipline catchphrase 'catch them being good' has become something of a mantra.

In dealing with unsatisfactory behaviour, the behaviourist approach again stresses the need for clarity and consistency. Key to this is a 'discipline hierarchy', and many schools have instituted such hierarchies as whole school policy. These consist of a series of 'stages' that are explicitly communicated to the pupils (often through a notice in the classroom and in clear assertive statements by the teacher) and which make it clear to them what the consequences of misbehaviour will be. What is noticeable is that more and more schools are rejecting written punishment exercises as an effective sanction and stress that the *consistency* of sanction is far more effective than the *severity* of the sanction: that is, if a pupil knows that misbehaviour *will definitely* earn a relatively innocuous sanction (such as a three-minute detention or an alert home), they will be less likely to 'misbehave', while in systems where severe sanctions are administered inconsistently, the pupil may decide to 'gamble'.

However, behaviourist approaches are extremely limited in their long-term efficacy because, as Fontana (1994) puts it, 'The behavioural approach concentrates upon what people actually do and upon the context and the consequences of their action rather than upon what goes on inside their heads' (p. 98), and a focus on this – modifying *thinking* – requires *cognitive constructivist* approaches. A pupil who has had positive experiences of school and the relationships therein will be predisposed to think, feel and react positively to future experiences. Conversely, a pupil who has had negative experiences will respond accordingly, and unless this is addressed, negative thought process, feelings and patterns of behaviour can be reinforced.

Pupils cognitively assess the tasks they are asked to perform, their ability to undertake those tasks and the feedback they receive on their performance. Pupils who judge tasks as too hard, too easy or irrelevant, who feel they cannot do what is asked of them or feel they will get nothing from it, and who feel that their performance will inevitably result in failure and frustration, develop repeated patterns of response which can cause difficulties; they may become hostile to the work they are asked to do and the individual asking them, or they may avoid tasks in any way they can. It is this cycle which must be addressed.

Cognitive constructivist strategies are utilised in secondary mainly with individual pupils who have social, emotional or behavioural difficulties (SEBD). Coaching, mentoring, counselling, emotional awareness building and cognitive behaviour therapy (CBT) are some of the methods used to make pupils more aware of their thought processes and resultant reactions. The purpose is to build resilience, to help pupils recognise the potential destructiveness of their thought processes and to offer them strategies to control their behaviour. It is probably fair to say that cognitive strategies in the classroom are more prevalent in the primary school, through circle time discussions or celebratory self-esteem boosting techniques such as 'class VIP' or 'class clap', but pupils' emotional wellbeing is also supported in secondary through nurture groups or activities such as drum therapy and the growing use of the explicit teaching of emotional awareness and the use of reflective behavioural correction or behaviour journals. In keeping with this developing awareness of the need to attend to pupils' *thinking*, there has recently been a great deal of publicity concerning the use of mindfulness techniques in schools. However, the evidence from a recent US study (Maynard et al., 2017) is highly sceptical of its claimed benefits for young people, suggesting that the evidence base for improved behaviour is weak, and even that 'contemplative practices' for which young people are not cognitively developed enough may actually 'worsen symptoms'.

Both behaviourist and cognitive constructivist approaches to behaviour management rest on individualist assumptions: that is, that it is the individual pupil who can be adapted, changed or worked on, to fit in with the accepted norms of the classroom, and many see this as essentially coercive. A more democratic *social constructivist* approach recognises that the individual operates in a socially interactive context, and that if behaviour is to change, it is the social interaction which must change, not the individual. Most schools now accept that building relationships with pupils requires more than basic behaviourist strategies: it is highly doubtful that young people develop an intrinsic sense of social responsibility – or of right and wrong – based solely on being rewarded and punished, and yet it is this intrinsic sense which is one of the aspirations of Curriculum for Excellence. Thus, social constructivist approaches seek to *modify relationships*.

Social constructivist approaches to behaviour management concentrate not on systems, procedures or rule books, but on solutions. These are often arrived at through strategies such as mediation or buddying, and there is a growing acceptance of restorative practices as a model for managing behaviour through collaboration and genuine discussion. Restorative practices see behaviour as an interactive circle, and seek to change that interaction, not the individual. These practices also accept the existence of multiple realities; in other words, whereas other behaviour management systems seek the 'truth' of an incident which usually lies in the teacher's interpretation of the events, all parties in an interaction have their version of the truth, all these perceptions have validity and all have the right to be heard. Thus, restorative practices look beyond the immediate context of an incident to the systems issues concerned; that is, what other factors lying outside the immediate context might have impacted on the interaction. Restorative practices also refuse to embrace a personal deficit model by apportioning blame, and seek the cooperation of all concerned rather than the coercion of an individual to achieve solutions that are flexible, realistic and neutral in response.

In the traditional model of discipline management, the key function was the apportionment of guilt; procedures attempted to find out what happened, who was to blame and what the appropriate punishment should be. Restorative practices, developed from reparative and restorative justice strategies in the criminal justice system, adopt an inclusive approach that involves an investigation of any event in order to prevent its reoccurrence. The key drivers of the restorative investigation include:

- What happened?
- Who has been affected and how?
- How can the harm be repaired?
- What has been learned to prevent it happening again?

The strength of such strategies is to allow the 'victim' to be central in any resolution of conflict arising in school, and offers a powerful way to deal with issues such as bullying which, as noted above, are of serious concern. Schools, in a highly structured and supportive environment and with the agreement of all concerned, can bring together the relevant parties involved (pupils, teachers, support staff, parents, etc.) to interrogate the circumstances of any conflict and find solutions which meet the needs of the 'victim', the 'perpetrator' and the institution.

Academic evaluation of restorative practices in schools in Scotland is somewhat sparse and out of date, but the *Restorative Practices in Three Scottish Councils* (Scottish Executive, 2007) report into pilot schemes is rightly optimistic about the capacity of restorative practices to create a positive, inclusive and empowering ethos. More and more schools are now embedding restorative practices as their 'default' behaviour management policy and developing sophisticated structures to enable it. However, it would be fair to say that most schools to a greater or lesser extent operate an eclectic 'mixed economy' of management approaches that can be characterised as behaviourist, cognitive constructivist and social constructivist; for instance, a school which has a foundation of positive assertive discipline will still engage pupils in emotional awareness strategies as necessary, while a school which prides itself on a democratic restorative ethos will still set rules. This is because no one strategy on its own is sufficient to manage all the facets of behaviour or to modify behaviour, thinking and relationships as necessary.

Table 29.1   Summary of behaviour management strategies

| Strategies | Advantages | Disadvantages |
| --- | --- | --- |
| Behaviourist | • Anecdotal evidence of effectiveness<br>• Widely used<br>• Is generally effective, at least in the short term<br>• Offers proactive means to prevent misbehaviour<br>• Systematic and strategic, offering support to practitioners | • Is a deficiency model<br>• Demands the pupil change rather than the context<br>• Is more about teacher's needs than pupil's<br>• No connection between discipline and learning<br>• Weak research evidence base |
| Cognitive constructivist | • Good research base<br>• Widely used<br>• Considers learning perspectives<br>• Is effective in the long term<br>• Offers proactive means to prevent misbehaviour<br>• Systematic and strategic, offering support to practitioners | • Is a deficiency model<br>• Demands the pupil change rather than the context.<br>• Demands high level of training<br>• Violates dignity of child by labelling them 'maladapted' |
| Social constructivist | • Growing research evidence base<br>• Widely used<br>• Encourages no-blame culture<br>• Has an effect on whole ethos of school<br>• Democratic and respectful of pupil rights<br>• In keeping with Curriculum for Excellence<br>• Works well with more serious cases | • Is reactive rather than proactive<br>• Depends on cooperation of all<br>• Demands high levels of training<br>• Relevance at ongoing classroom level not yet clear |

In conclusion, the main relative advantages and disadvantages of the various strategies used in schools might be summarised as shown in Table 29.1.

## DISTINCTIVE CONTEXTS REVISITED

With the fragmentation of local and national educational management structures in England – the development of free schools, academy chains, faith schools and a proposed new wave of grammar schools sitting alongside state schools – there has been a corresponding fragmentation of approaches to learning and to behaviour management, and a furious 'progressive versus traditional' debate figuring on social media through Twitter and teacher-authored blogs. There has been a definite move away from and against child-centred, skills-based approaches, and, using as justification the writings of Hirsch and Willingham on knowledge, a growing movement which values didactic teaching, content-led curricula and methodology and rote and rehearsal learning has developed (see the discussion in Christodoulou, 2014). While the perceived lack of importance given to content knowledge in the Curriculum for Excellence has been debated for many years, with writers like Lindsay Paterson of Edinburgh University and Mark Priestley of Stirling University making thoughtful contributions to the debate on the topic, the situation in England has been much more febrile and radical. Perhaps the flag bearer for this traditional approach has been the much-publicised Michaela Community School, a free school in Brent, London. The darling of the anti-educational establishment and of the Conservative Government (the headteacher famously derided state education at the Conservative Party conference in 2011), Michaela eschews much of the pedagogy which we would recognise in Scottish classrooms; for instance, it expressly prohibits the use of group work.

More than that, however, these pedagogical traditionalists also favour teacher-centred behaviour policies. Much is made of the 'Michaela ethos', with desks in rows, children forbidden to speak in corridors between lessons and frequent detentions for being late to school by one minute, for not having a pen or ruler or for forgetting to bring payment for school lunch. This 'no excuses' type of behaviour management policy denies the need for anything other than a behaviourist approach which ensures the acquiescence of children to the demands of the teacher and the institution; indeed, Michaela made national headlines when it advertised for a detention manager at a £35,000 salary who would be a 'sergeant major' and not a 'would-be counsellor'.

Once more, the difference in ethos north and south of the border could not be more marked. Encouraged by a curriculum that is child-centred and places social and emotional wellbeing at the heart of its principles, Scottish schools have developed a range of appropriate strategies that are nuanced in their purpose and flexible in their approach. There are possible threats to this on the horizon, however. The Scottish Government is considering funding arrangements that may give schools more autonomy (see Chapters 17 and 18 in Section III), and there are pressures from neo-liberal policy thinks tanks such as Reform Scotland to take a step further and free schools from local authority control entirely, which may allow space for the intervention of private enterprise and the creation of 'maverick' schools to develop. In addition, serious problems with teacher recruitment and retention have led to calls for work-based apprenticeship models along the lines of Teach First or Schools Direct in England. That this has led to a deprofessionalisation of the teaching workforce is undeniable – 30 per cent of Michaela staff are unqualified – and this in turn may lead to professional insecurity that makes a 'no-nonsense' approach to behaviour that gives primacy to the unquestioned and unquestionable authority of the teacher attractive and supportive, while placing the needs of the pupil far down the list of priorities.

However, for the moment, Scottish secondary schools, for all their difficulties with indiscipline, bullying and disengagement, take a much more strategic view of the issue, seeing the use of explicit, consistent and flexible strategies grounded in sound educational theoretical perspectives as a means of creating a productive ethos that encourages responsibility. Stressing the need to recognise pupils' positive contributions to the school, there has been a growing emphasis on including young people in the decisions which are made about their education through curricular initiatives, solutions-focused approaches to dealing with problems and organisational arrangements that offer pupils a say in decision-making processes. It is a distinctive way of approaching the relationship between young people, their teachers and their schools, and it is to be hoped that it can continue and improve.

## REFERENCES

BEMIS (2013) *A Review of Human Rights Education in Schools in Scotland.* http://bemis.org.uk/documents/BEMIS%20HRE%20in%20Schools%20Report.pdf

Canter, L. (2010) *Assertive Discipline*. Bloomington, IN: Solution Tree Press

Christodoulou, D. (2014) 'Minding the knowledge gap: the importance of content in student learning', *American Educator*, Spring, 27–33.

Denholm, A. (2018) 'Rise in pupil disruption blamed on 'disinterest' in curriculum', *The Sunday Herald*, 1 January. Online at www.heraldscotland.com/news/15800731.Rise_in_pupil_disruption_blamed_on__disinterest__in_curriculum/

ENABLE Scotland (2016) *#IncludED in the Main?! 22 Steps on the Journey to Inclusion for Every Pupil Who Has a Learning Disability*. Online at https://www.basw.co.uk/resource/?id=6825

Fontana, D. (1994) *Managing Classroom Behaviour*. Leicester: John Wiley & Sons.

McLean, A. (2008) *Motivating Every Learner*. London: Sage.

Maynard, B. R., Solis, M. R., Miller, V. L. and Brendel, K. E. (2017) 'Mindfulness-based interventions for improving cognition, academic achievement, behavior, and socioemotional functioning of primary and secondary school students', *Campbell Systematic Reviews*, Oslo, vol. 13, 10 March. Online at https://search.proquest.com/openview/78a665bf5147d14a213ffcf93a62af86/1?pq-origsite=gscholar&cbl=2040247

Scottish Executive (2001) *Better Behaviour – Better Learning: Report of the Discipline Task Group*. Edinburgh: Scottish Executive Education Department.

Scottish Executive (2007) *Restorative Practices in Three Scottish Councils*. Online at www.scotland.gov.uk/Resource/Doc/196078/0052553.pdf

Scottish Government (2011) *Teaching Scotland's Future: Report of a Review of Teacher Education in Scotland*. Edinburgh: Scottish Government.

Scottish Government (2012) *Behaviour in Scottish Schools 2012*. Online at www.gov.scot/Publications/2012/10/5408/0

Scottish Government (2017) *Behaviour in Scottish Schools Research 2016*. Online at www.gov.scot/Resource/0052/00526338.pdf

Soltysek, R. (2013) 'Ethos and behaviour in secondary schools', in T. G. K. Bryce, W. M. Humes, D. Gillies and A. Kennedy (eds), *Scottish Education, Fourth Edition: Referendum*. Edinburgh: Edinburgh University Press, pp. 403–12.

Time for Inclusive Education (2016) *Attitudes towards LGBT in Scottish Education*. Online at www.tiecampaign.co.uk/research

UNISON Scotland (2017) *Hard Lessons. A Survey of Scotland's School Support Staff*. Online at www.unison-scotland.org/library/20170109-Schools-Damage-Series.pdf

# V

# CURRICULUM: EARLY YEARS
# AND PRIMARY

# 30

# Expressive Arts

*Charles Byrne*

This chapter will examine the nature of Expressive Arts subjects in the Scottish primary curriculum and will explore some issues relating to teaching and learning in, and specific benefits associated with, the Expressive Arts. I will also suggest that participation in the Expressive Arts beyond school can have benefits for our young people, and for their lives as adults.

## WHAT ARE THE EXPRESSIVE ARTS?

In broad terms, the Expressive Arts can be defined as those areas of study which provide creative engagement and/or aesthetic experiences which enrich our lives including the ways in which we make sense of our world through visual, musical, dramatic and physical means. In practical terms, within the Scottish primary curriculum, the Expressive Arts are Art and Design, Dance, Drama and Music. Physical Education is no longer included although the Expressive Arts can and do also contribute to general health and wellbeing in many ways.

In the Scottish curriculum, all primary schools are expected to provide young people with opportunities to engage in the Expressive Arts. The previous 5–14 curriculum guidelines endeavoured to ensure that the Expressive Arts were included within the primary school and the early years of the secondary school. These guidelines defined set levels of performance in each area which most young people would be likely to achieve at specific stages in their school careers. Teachers would have been able to use the different levels and programmes of study to assess children's progress in each discrete area. However, our research (Wilson et al., 2008) found that few teachers were comfortable with teaching and assessing children's progress in subjects in which they themselves did not profess expertise. With the formal start of Curriculum for Excellence (CfE) in 2010–11, a new agenda for education for pupils aged 3–18 has been created, with one aim being that there will be more space for the Expressive Arts (Wilson et al., 2008). The language and levels of assessment have changed slightly although the expectation that each teacher will deliver all aspects of the Expressive Arts remains. The Expressive Arts are one of eight curricular areas in the broad general education phase of CfE, and the inclusion of dance redefines this area as indeed one for expressive communication and engagement. It places them on an equal footing with other curricular areas, giving a clear signal that the Expressive Arts should form an important part of the education of young people in Scotland. Through them it is expected that young people will develop a sense of their own identity, both socially and culturally, and appreciate the value of the arts in a national context and as part of developing global citizenship.

## THE BENEFITS OF THE EXPRESSIVE ARTS

Few who have experienced a meaningful education in any of the Expressive Arts areas would doubt the benefit that the arts bring to our lives and it is clear that policymakers and curriculum planners recognise their value and the positive effect they can have on the lives of young people in particular. Many claims are made for the Expressive Arts such as that children learn better when they are engaged in high-quality arts experiences or that the Expressive Arts are instrumental in developing some of the social and interpersonal skills required for working with others in collaborative settings. The skills of problem solving, creativity and the ability to communicate through a variety of media are also considered to be developed through engagement in the Expressive Arts. Several research studies have looked for a 'transfer effect' in each of the Expressive Arts whereby young people's academic abilities are improved or enhanced through them. Hetland and Winner (2001) found only one such effect among hundreds of studies, and that was in the use of language within a drama setting. These findings were controversial in that they seemed to indicate that there was, in fact, little or no benefit to be gained in studying and participating in the Expressive Arts, but an important clarion call was made – that we should not expect more from the Expressive Arts than we do from all the other subjects in the curriculum. Children should study and engage in the Expressive Arts because they have intrinsic value and not because of any side effects or ancillary benefits they may have. Studies which have found improved spatial–temporal reasoning after participants listened to a piano sonata by Mozart have been difficult to replicate (Rauscher, 2002). From this was coined the term the 'Mozart Effect', which in turn led to an interest in parents purchasing CDs of music to play to their youngsters in the hope of using the power of music to develop the mind and creative abilities of children. In the absence of any hard evidence which support the claims of the authors of related books and music compilations, we must assume that the parents' desire to seek support for developing their children's education potential may well be the cause of any effect on the children.

Each of the Expressive Arts usually requires many weeks or months, if not years, of practice in order to perfect the skills involved. So, the lifelong skills and capacities (in the true sense of the word) of determination, commitment to achieving long-term goals, application and organisation do come to the fore in the arts. If we only selected young people for each of the Expressive Arts based on some innate ability then few would develop beyond their first attempts. Aptitude is just as important as interest and motivation in determining success in the Expressive Arts. Dedication and hard work are also key ingredients of success and these are exemplified through the arts and implicitly understood by performers and artists. It is not that each of the Expressive Arts should be presented in an easy version for schools, but rather that children can engage in real, meaningful experiences from any age at a level that suits their developing skills and abilities.

### Musical Capacities

We know that babies acquire language at a rapid rate in the very early years and that our aural awareness and ability to distinguish tiny nuances of tone and pitch are key to our learning to understand the spoken word. This *musical* skill is common to most young children and, in fact, babies are born with the ability to distinguish the same words, spoken at varying pitches by different people. This acuity allows babies to understand both mothers and fathers who will normally speak at different pitch levels. While most humans lose this ability, some who go on to play musical instruments or to sing may retain this *perfect pitch*: the ability to know the exact pitch of any note played or sung.

Nursery rhymes, songs and games play a key role in developing language and the musical characteristics of the rhyming sounds and rhythms of speech can help babies and young children make sense of the sounds around them. The use of infant directed speech ensures that babies begin to recognise the rise and fall in words and the wonderful 'speech to song' illusion discovered by Dianna Deutsch when she realised that a short spoken phrase, heard repeatedly, appeared to be sung rather than spoken and could therefore be perceived as a melody.

## Drama and Dance Aptitude

In other arts areas, there is no doubt that the benefits of involvement in drama, musical theatre and dance activities can have huge and lasting benefits for young people. Ken Robinson, author, speaker and international advisor on the arts, relates the experience of a friend who, when a young girl, was taken to the doctor because her school had complained that she could not sit still and that she may have had attention deficit hyperactivity disorder (ADHD). The girl was left in the room with music playing on the radio, and the doctor observed that far from having anything wrong with her, she was, in fact, a dancer and she subsequently enrolled in a dance school, finding her true vocation in life. The author has many years' experience of working with young people in music theatre settings, where the skills and techniques learned in the Expressive Arts together create a vibrant and exciting performance. Many of the young people involved went on to further study and employment in the arts, but, more importantly, continue to be involved the arts and to use the valuable experiences and skills in their work and lives. The benefits of such experiences to the lives of young people are difficult to measure although it is clear that rehearsing, preparing and performing can generate what Csikszentmihalyi (2014) has described as '*Flow*' or '*Optimal Experience*', the feeling of effortless involvement and satisfaction when individuals are engaged in, usually, creative activities.

Wilson et al. (2008) noted that research in England found that pressure was exerted on schools to perform well in mathematics and language at the expense of subjects like the Expressive Arts. In Scotland, while there is no recognised measure of international comparison of schoolchildren's performance in the Expressive Arts, there is a perceived pressure on teachers to ensure that young people do well in these so-called 'core' subjects and we know that if planned drama or art activities are missed for any reason, teachers may make little effort to replace the missed session, which may not be the case for mathematics and language sessions. So, while many teachers would agree that the arts are important, it would seem that some subjects are more important than others (Bamford and Wimmer, 2012).

There is an aspiration that Expressive Arts will be accorded a level of importance in the education of our young people. Education Scotland's website outlines some of the value of studying Expressive Arts, suggesting that they help young people to explore and express their own and others' feelings. While the Scottish Government, through CfE, sets out broad areas for engagement in the Expressive Arts in the form of experiences and outcomes for each discrete area, schools will deliver this provision in different ways. Some may provide regular opportunities for young people to experience some of the Expressive Arts with a focus on specific ones, such as Dance and Drama, at specific times of the year (end of term assemblies, Burns night, etc.). Such an approach is consistent with the requirement to provide 'personalisation and choice', one of the seven CfE principles for a well-designed curriculum.

## APPROACHES TO TEACHING AND LEARNING IN THE EXPRESSIVE ARTS

There are two approaches which schools and teachers can adopt when teaching the Expressive Arts: teaching 'in' the arts, and teaching 'through' the arts. In some Scottish primary schools, each area is taught by a 'specialist' who may be a member of the school staff with a special interest in that area, or by a visiting specialist. Typically, music may be delivered by a specialist during that time of the week which is protected for planning and other curricular matters – so called 'McCrone time'. Since the subject specialist delivers the lesson while the class teacher is not present, there is little possibility of engaging in any form of staff development. The issue of teacher confidence is again relevant here as teachers often express concern, worry and even dread at the prospect of delivering the arts in a discrete way. Comments like 'I dread art lessons, I'm not artistic in the slightest' (Wilson et al., 2008, p. 42) are not uncommon among teachers. A lack of technical skill or curriculum knowledge in each of the Expressive Arts is a real source of worry. This teaching 'in' the arts approach is clearly not working for all.

Teaching 'through' the arts, or an 'infused' approach, involves teaching which makes use of the specific areas when working in another curricular area. For example, a class may be working on an aspect of language such as a short story. A drama in education approach could be deployed to enrich the learning experience by having some of the characters from the story develop some ideas and issues through the use of drama conventions such as the 'Mantle of the Expert' or 'freeze frame'. These would allow the pupils opportunities to explore and develop creative responses to the story and is an engaging and worthwhile addition to the original lesson.

An infused approach which can successfully integrate all four Expressive Arts areas might be found in Stravinsky's *Petrushka* ballet, which has as its central issue the nature of human feelings. This can be a vehicle for creating masks and puppets, singing and playing themes from the ballet, creating simple dances in response to the many folk-like tunes and exploring the characters through the use of drama conventions such as the use of masks or mimed activities (Dickinson and Neelands, 2005). In Scottish primary schools, Expressive Arts activity can also be complemented and supported by visiting arts organisations and artists who may focus on a specific theme or topic and provide advice and expertise in their own area. Examples of visiting artists would include a touring drama group raising specific issues such as good citizenship and anti-bullying, or a musical group who tackle a whole range of social issues through songs.

In terms of progression, it is hoped that pupil responses to each of the arts areas will become more sophisticated and advanced as they move through each stage of the primary school, although the level of support and exemplification provided by local authorities and others may not be enough to allow for high-quality work when learning through the arts.

## WIDER PARTICIPATION IN THE EXPRESSIVE ARTS BEYOND SCHOOL

Outside school many young people in Scotland are involved in the Expressive Arts in a number of ways. Instrumental lessons are popular and the growth of private music schools and weekend drama classes clearly fulfil a need for parents to seek to enrich their children's development through the arts. Most parents of young children have dutifully attended the annual dance display and, of the thousands who attend these classes for a few years or more, many go on to become dance teachers themselves and to provide tuition in tap, ballet, modern and traditional Scottish dancing. The popularity of television programmes which feature dancing has only added to the popularity of this art form.

Trinity College (www.trinitycollege.co.uk/site/?id=6), for example, now has graded examinations in music, pop and rock, dance, drama and speaking, and even offers an Arts Award at several levels which allows young people up to the age of 25 opportunities to develop their interest in 'any area ... from fashion to poetry, rapping to dancing, sculpture to film' (www.artsaward.org.uk/site/?id=64). Perhaps primary schools could tap into this system to provide a focus for the development of dance skills in the curriculum. It is recognised that initial teacher education courses cannot adequately prepare all teachers with the skills and aptitudes required in each of the Expressive Arts, and we know that aspects of good practice and teaching and learning approaches are covered, with some opportunities to develop expertise in at least one area. Schools and local authorities do invest in ongoing professional development on a range of issues, so it is worthwhile considering the role of the Expressive Arts in this career development. Engaging in some of the opportunities provided by external agencies in art and design, music, drama, dance and the arts in general, could be rewarding for staff and young people alike, while developing skills and abilities which can result in teacher confidence and belief in their own teaching abilities.

## REFERENCES

Bamford, A. and Wimmer, M. (2012) 'The role of arts education in enhancing school attractiveness: A literature review', European Expert Network on Culture Paper. Online at www.interarts.net/descargas/interarts2548.pdf

Barnes, R. (2002) *Teaching Art to Young Children 4–9*, second edition. London: Routledge.

Byrne, C. (2014) 'Creative engagement in and through music: the challenge for undergraduate and postgraduate students', in P. Burnard (ed.), *Developing Creativities in Higher Music Education: International Perspectives and Practices*. London: Routledge, pp. 151–62.

Csikszentmihalyi, M. (2014) *Applications of Flow in Human Development and Education: The Collected Works of Mihaly Csikszentmihalyi*. Dordrecht: Springer.

Dickinson, R. and Neelands, J. (2005) *Improve Your Primary School through Drama*. London: David Fulton.

Hetland, L. and Winner, E. (2001) 'The arts and academic achievement: what the evidence shows', *Arts Education Policy Review*, 102 (5), 3–6.

Perkins, M. and Goodwin, P. (2006) 'Play and planning: a sound pathway to pleasureable and purposeful reading', in M. Lewis and S. Ellis (eds), *Phonics: Practice, Research and Policy*. London: Paul Chapman Publishing.

Rauscher, F. (2002) 'Improving academic achievement: impact of psychological factors on education', *Educational Psychology*, 267–78

Scottish Government (2005) *Curriculum for Excellence: Building the Curriculum 3: A Framework for Learning and Teaching*. Edinburgh: Scottish Government.

Wilson, G. B., MacDonald, R., Byrne, C., Ewing, S. and Sheridan M. (2008) 'Dread and passion: primary and secondary teachers' views on teaching the arts', *Curriculum Journal*, 19 (1), 37–53.

# 31

# Literacy and English

*Sue Ellis*

The Literacy and English curriculum in Scotland is described in two key documents: one document, *Literacy and English Principles and Practice* (Scottish Government, nd a), outlines its rationale and scope, and another, *Literacy and English Experiences and Outcomes* (Scottish Government, nd b), provides a more detailed description of the sort of progression expected across the five levels of the Curriculum for Excellence (CfE) framework: Early (to be achieved by Primary 1 or earlier); First (to be achieved by Primary 4 or earlier); Second (to be achieved by Primary 7 or earlier); Third (to be achieved by S3 or earlier); Fourth (to be achieved by S6 or earlier). The experiences and outcomes for the curriculum are lightly specified and intended to be indicative rather than prescriptive. They are organised under the broad headings of: Listening and Talking; Reading; and Writing, which are further described under the subheadings detailed in Table 31.1. Because in Scotland every teacher is responsible for developing articulate and literate young people, the document uses italics to indicate those experiences and outcomes that are the responsibility of every teacher regardless of subject specialism. For ease of use, these are also reproduced in a separate document, *Literacy Experiences and Outcomes* (Scottish Government, nd c).

Some important points are worth noting from the *Literacy and English: Principles and Practice* document: first, it highlights the importance of ambitious, integrated and responsive language and literacy teaching to capture and build engagement and enthusiasm. For example, it emphasises the importance of teaching critical literacies that encourage children and young people to think about authorial intent and the reliability of information. Second, it underlines the importance of developing an appreciation of home literacies in the form of Scotland's literary and linguistic heritage, including the 149 indigenous home languages

Table 31.1 The organisational headings and subheadings for the Literacy and English curriculum

| Listening and talking | Reading | Writing |
|---|---|---|
| Enjoyment and choice | Enjoyment and choice | Enjoyment and choice |
| Tools for listening and talking | Tools for reading | Tools for writing |
| Finding and using information | Finding and using information | Finding and using information |
| Understanding, analysing and evaluating | Understanding, analysing and evaluating | |
| Creating texts | | Creating texts |

and dialects children bring to school (Scottish Government, 2016a). Such directions make it clear that the intention is to promote a socially and culturally situated vision of literacy rather than a narrow, basic-skills, 'autonomous' perspective on learning to read and write. Third, *Principles and Practice* embraces flexible and grounded teaching; the wide age range covered by each level accommodates the idea that learning does not always happen at a regular pace, and that applying learning in different contexts not only gives depth, breadth and meaning but offers different 'ways in' for children, allowing different learning pathways towards a common outcome.

The Scottish Attainment Challenge (SAC), launched in February 2015, brought a renewed focus on literacy attainment, particularly on raising the attainment of Scotland's poorest children and on closing the attainment gap between children in poverty and their better-off peers. It initially targeted seven local authorities with the highest percentage of children living in poverty (Glasgow, Dundee, Inverclyde, West Dunbartonshire, North Ayrshire, Clackmannanshire, North Lanarkshire) and in 2017 was extended to a further two authorities (Renfrewshire and East Ayrshire). A schools programme and an innovation fund launched alongside the attainment challenge widened the policy's reach to schools elsewhere who served deprived populations and wished to try innovative ideas. In 2017, a four-year Pupil Equity Fund was introduced. This allocates significant funding directly to schools, based on the number of pupils eligible for free school meals, and can be spent on any initiative to raise literacy, numeracy and health and wellbeing attainment. The attainment challenge and Pupil Equity Fund have prompted national conversations about research that matters and the nature of evidence. The value of theorised professional knowledge is slowly, through these, beginning to reassert itself.

## TEACHING AND LEARNING

The *Principles and Practice* document seems to envisage teachers as curriculum designers, having sufficient knowledge and agency to create a Literacy and English curriculum from first principles. This is different from the way that teachers are positioned by the national curricula in other parts of the UK which stipulate detailed teaching content and pedagogies and that use high-stakes national testing and school inspections as compliance mechanisms. In theory therefore, the principles and practices should make the implementation of Literacy and English in CfE quite distinct from the language and literacy curricula in the rest of the UK. Translating policy messages about the curriculum into practice is, however, a complex process and the reality is that many differences are smoothed out by the UK-wide resources and media reports on education. Almost all Scottish primary schools use commercially published materials for teaching reading, phonics, grammar, handwriting and punctuation, and a great many also use commercial schemes for teaching writing. Such literacy materials are usually written in England and designed primarily for that country, with activities cross-referenced to Scotland's CfE levels. Although in theory Scottish teachers have the freedom to determine how schemes are used, in practice many teachers simply follow the publisher's guidelines.

CfE emphasises enjoyment and engagement and many classrooms have book corners to promote reading for pleasure, although their quality and use varies. Schools and local authorities also use literature circles, paired reading and personal reading time in class, although sometimes over-regulation by teachers means they fail to create the open, social spaces for developing young people's personal identities as readers and writers.

It is unclear how, or whether, the formative assessment strategies of *Assessment is for Learning* introduced in 2002 (www.gov.scot/Publications/2005/12/0792641/26439) impacted on literacy attainment. Its legacy, however, is that it is now standard practice for teachers to share learning intentions and success criteria, to use pupil self-assessment and peer assessment, to inquire into pupil confidence levels using a 'traffic lights' or 'thumbs up' system, and to provide feedback framed as 'two stars and a wish', listing two things the pupil has done well and one thing to improve (see Chapter 68).

## MONITORING AND ASSESSMENT

The attainment challenge prompted renewed debates about monitoring and assessment. Assessment in CfE was originally underpinned by a belief that professional judgement need only be supplemented by a national survey giving general trends and did not require a national test yielding school-level and local authority-level data. However, the 2014 national survey data showed an unexplained fall in literacy attainment (Scottish Government, 2015). An independent report for the Joseph Rowntree Foundation (JRF) had argued that professional judgement was not sufficient and that independent, standardised, success measures were required, both to enable local educators to know and understand the equity gap in their own context, and to enable policymakers to determine which reforms should be scaled-up (Sosu and Ellis, 2014; Chapter 12 in this text). Rolling out successful reform is a central tenet of Scottish education policy and, as the report argued, identifying what to scale up, and where, is hugely problematic without any hard data to make comparative judgements about what worked, for whom and in which circumstances.

In 2016 the Scottish Government therefore proposed a national test as one element of the National Improvement Framework (NIF) and it amended the Education Act to require local authorities to monitor, and take steps to address, the attainment gap between rich and poor (Scottish Government, 2016b). There is disquiet amongst some educators about unintended 'toxic' consequences of testing and whether it will lead teachers to narrow the curriculum and 'teach to the test'. However, another view is that if teachers teach differently in such circumstances, it is a professional decision for which individual professionals and the profession as a whole, must be held accountable.

It is possible that having a more open system could lead to wider debate and better use of test data. Despite the CfE rhetoric on testing, twenty-seven of Scotland's thirty-two local authorities had contracts with private suppliers for standardised testing in primary schools (Audit Scotland, 2014, p. 17). These data are used in some schools and local authorities to set and stream children for literacy teaching, sometimes on entry to school aged 4–5 years (see 'Issues', below). The NIF could challenge such practices and help to ensure that data is used to interrogate the system rather than enshrine existing inequalities (see Chapter 71).

Internationally, literacy attainment in Scotland ranks in the middle group of Organisation for Economic Co-operation and Development (OECD) countries. The Programme for International Student Assessment (PISA) literacy data show that the difference between the averages of the top and bottom 25 per cent of attainers in Scotland is the equivalent of 5.5 years of schooling; and 16 per cent of Scotland's pupils performed lower than Level 2, the OECD baseline proficiency level for full participation in a democratic society. Scotland is below the OECD average on reading for enjoyment, with 47 per cent of pupils agreeing that they 'read only to obtain the information they need' and 26 per cent reporting that they believe 'reading is a waste of time'.

## HISTORICAL LITERACY AND LANGUAGE CURRICULUM DEVELOPMENT

Three distinct curriculum policy phases have characterised Scotland's language and literacy journey in the past sixty years. From 1960 to 1989, curriculum advice was developed by groups of teachers, inspectors and teacher educators working for the Scottish Committee on Language Arts (SCOLA) in the Primary School and reporting to the Committee on Primary Education. This promoted integrated methodologies such as Scottish Storyline (Bell et al., 2006; Chapter 23 in this text) but contained weak mechanisms to ensure implementation; the system was supposedly founded on debate followed by consensus, but schools had absolute power to determine both content and pedagogy, which led to wide differences in expectations and attainment.

The second curriculum policy phase was designed to address these continuity, breadth and progression problems. The 5–14 English language guidelines (SOEID, 1991) outlined key content to be inspected by Her Majesty's Inspectorate of Education (HMIE). This led to accountability, a clear knowledge progression and literacy got a distinct 'slot' in the curriculum. It also led to serious curriculum overload as every curricular area bulged with schemes and worksheets to provide evidence of coverage and progression, replacing more integrated, responsive and active approaches. The Scottish Storyline Method migrated to Scandinavia, where it thrived, while planning in the 5–14 curriculum focused on mapping activities to attainment targets rather than on identifying the priorities and contexts to give the best payoff for pupils. The overload and demand for coverage left few opportunities for literacy to be social, relaxing, contextualised, purposeful or self-directed.

Curriculum for Excellence (Scottish Government, 2004), as the third phase of language and literacy curriculum policy, was implemented in 2010/11 to address these problematic issues, and to put schools and teachers firmly in the driving seat. It deliberately left spaces for responsive, nuanced teaching but has been criticised as vague and not sufficiently directive.

The context of implementation for CfE was that local authority and HMIE staffing had been downsized across Scotland and most had shifted from curriculum specialist to generic responsibilities. In addition, initial teacher education courses had reduced the time for focused literacy teaching in their Primary Education degrees (Ellis, 2015). It is possible also that the curriculum advice provided by Education Scotland framed by the 'experiences and outcomes' encouraged teachers and local authorities to think about the literacy curriculum in terms of a series of 'good activities' at the expense of building a more substantive, theorised, body of knowledge.

In these circumstances CfE's appeal to abstract principles rather than to firmly grounded, specific content arising from theoretical and research knowledge about language and literacy development becomes particularly problematic. The differences are both subtle and important. For example, CfE places great emphasis on pupil engagement and choice, a focus that is supported by curriculum evidence. However, the experiences and outcomes translate this as ability to *justify* choice rather than the role of choice in promoting reader agency and reader identity, social and emotional empowerment. Choice in writing is presented as understanding the expectations of an audience rather than writing to fulfil one's intellectual and emotional needs, enhance social agency or effect change. Despite an emphasis on digital literacy, CfE implementation reflects fundamentally traditional, 'autonomous' understandings of becoming literate rather than a view of literacy as a cultural practice (Street, 1984).

## ISSUES

The lack of theorised content knowledge in CfE means that Scottish teachers are sometimes struggling to negotiate a coherent curriculum pathway, which can result in confused practices that directly contradict what one might consider its core principles. The challenge to make good, productive use of test data is an obvious one facing Scottish teachers. However, no less important is the challenge of designing a literacy curriculum that provides an effective bridge between school literacy practices and those practices pupils bring from home.

The challenge of using test data is complex. In Scotland it is common to find within-class attainment groups for reading and writing. Less common, but not infrequent, are school-wide 'ability-setting' systems for language work. These have been enabled, although not explicitly encouraged, by the unmonitored and unexamined ways that test data has been used/not used in local authorities and schools as well as by policies of building larger primary schools with more than one class at each stage. Setting and streaming are considered internal, educational decisions and the policies are not publicised to parents, the inspectorate or sometimes even the local authority. Some single-form entry schools may set children by putting different aged pupils into the same class, but this makes the policy more salient and tends to attract negative comments from parents.

Whilst setting and streaming simplifies the task of curriculum delivery for teachers (particularly where the curriculum is conceptualised as discrete programme delivery), it is unlikely to improve literacy learning. Instead it enshrines in a school system the inequality in children's home literacy experiences. In terms of teaching and learning, it downplays the learning potential offered by a socially mixed classroom environment and can impact negatively on teacher expectations and on the self-esteem and aspirations of children in lower sets. Importantly, it limits the flexibility that a class teacher has to spontaneously extend lessons when children are interested and to capitalise on wider class work as a specific and meaningful context for literacy learning. It makes a number of important primary pedagogical practices harder: the class teacher is less well positioned to 'seize the teachable moment', to link ideas across literacy learning contexts and to re-enforce literacy skills through other curricular work, and it becomes more difficult to prompt meaningful peer interaction across attainment bands. These aspects are all particularly important for the progress of pupils who struggle with learning to read and write.

National testing will open such regimes to public and academic scrutiny but may also introduce new, unintended, toxic consequences. Much depends on how it is implemented and on the political, professional and media conversations around the data generated. Learning to use any new tool takes time and educators and policymakers need some protected space to learn how to use the National Improvement Framework well to raise attainment. Research on the role of recognition heuristics in testing (Katz and Dack, 2014) warns us to attend closely to the professional knowledge base, to teachers' access to reliable research advice, and to everyone's awareness of what test results can and cannot explain.

Strong curriculum knowledge can provide the ballast that is required to keep conversations about test data grounded. Luke (2003), writing about the Australian curriculum, distinguishes between schools that provide 'balanced programmes' and those with 'shopping-list programmes'. Balance requires complex understandings of literacy as a decoding, semantic, pragmatic and critical endeavour, and an acceptance that there can be many pathways to achieving impact. Scottish teachers and policymakers need to adopt sophisticated understandings of what it means to be literate if they are to enact a curriculum that attends to differences in how literacy is 'lived' in school and in the community, and to research advice about how an effective curriculum can bridge these. This means they need to be directed to look beyond the narrow predetermined progression pathways of skills-based, autonomous models of literacy (Street, 1984). Only if they do this will they improve attainment and deliver educational equity. CfE is set up to allow this to happen but educators need the professional knowledge to enact literacy teaching that is effective, efficient, intellectually engaging and socially and culturally responsive. This is central to harnessing the intrinsic motivation of pupils from low-literacy backgrounds and empowering them through literacy.

The focus on Scotland's literary heritage also presents dilemmas about what is distinctively Scottish in CfE's literacy, language and literature frameworks. Modern Scottish authors are published by (largely American-owned) publishers aiming for profit maximisation in an international marketplace. Even the popular and quintessentially Scottish *Katie Morag* stories were changed to widen their international appeal so that Katie's original 'Grandpa Island' became a rather masculine 'Granny Island' to accommodate US sensibilities about young girls visiting old men. Clearly, forging a modern curriculum that is connected to our history, to the lives of Scotland's children, and to Scotland's aspirations for the future is a complex and demanding task at every level.

## REFERENCES

Audit Scotland (2014) *School Education: Accounts Commission Report Prepared by Audit Scotland, July 2014*. Edinburgh: Scottish Government. Online at www.audit-scotland.gov.uk/docs/local/2014/nr_140619_school_education.pdf

Bell, S., Harkness, S. and White, G. (eds) (2007) *Storyline. Past, Present & Future*. Glasgow: Enterprising Careers, University of Strathclyde.

Ellis, S. (2015) *Improving Literacy in Scotland: Four Policy Proposals*. University of Strathclyde International Public Policy Institute Policy Brief Series. Glasgow: University of Strathclyde. Online at http://strathprints.strath.ac.uk/53550/1/EllisS_IPPI_2015_improving_literacy_in_scotland_four_policy_proposals.pdf

Katz, S. and Dack, L. A. (2014) 'Towards a culture of inquiry for data use in schools: breaking down professional learning barriers through intentional interruption', *Studies in Educational Evaluation*, 42, 35–40.

Luke, A. (2003) 'Making literacy policy and practice with a difference: generational change, professionalisation and literate futures', *Australian Journal of Language and Literacy*, 26 (3), 58–82.

Scottish Government (nd a) *Curriculum for Excellence: Literacy and English Principles and Practice*. Online at https://education.gov.scot/Documents/literacy-english-pp.pdf

Scottish Government (nd b) *Curriculum for Excellence: Literacy and English Experiences and Outcomes*. Online at https://www.education.gov.scot/Documents/literacy-english-eo.pdf

Scottish Government (nd c) *Curriculum for Excellence: Literacy Experiences and Outcomes*. Online at https://education.gov.scot/Documents/literacy-across-learning-eo.pdf

Scottish Government (2004) *Ambitious, Excellent Schools – Our Agenda for Action*. Edinburgh: Scottish Executive.

Scottish Government (2015) *Scottish Survey of Literacy and Numeracy 2014 (Literacy)*, Chapter 2: Reading. Online at www.gov.scot/Publications/2015/04/7639/3

Scottish Government (2016a) *Summary Statistics for Schools in Scotland, No: 7-2016*. Online at http://www.gov.scot/Publications/2016/12/9271

Scottish Government (2016b) *National Improvement Framework for Scottish Education – Achieving Excellence and Equity*. Edinburgh: HMSO. www.gov.scot/Publications/2016/01/8314

SOEID (1991) *English Language 5–14: National Guidelines*. Edinburgh: SOEID.

Sosu, E. and Ellis, S. (2014) *Closing the Attainment Gap in Scottish Education*. York: Joseph Rowntree Foundation.

Street, B. (1984) *Literacy in Theory and Practice*. Cambridge: Cambridge University Press.

# 32

# Mathematics

*Susan McLarty and Ruth Forrester*

## INTRODUCTION: AIMS OF PRIMARY MATHEMATICS

In Scotland, mathematics occupies a central place in the primary curriculum. As in most education systems, it is seen as essential in preparing learners for everyday life, study and work and in satisfying the needs of society for mathematically educated citizens. In daily life, people are required to manage many mathematical demands. They may need skills to plan journeys, understand food labels or decide on a mortgage. They should have the relevant skills to understand data, critique their value and vote judiciously. In future study, students of medicine or social sciences, for example, may need skills to research correlations between diet and health. In work, some will be expected to use statistics intelligently to guide decisions about the siting of a new hospital or the balance of sources of renewable energy which will power the nation.

It is impossible to predict which learners will choose a career as a nutritionist or an engineer, nor to predict what mathematical problem solving such careers will entail in future. Additionally, the increasing availability of technology has made future mathematical needs even more unpredictable as the requirement for routine computational skills reduces. Nevertheless, it is clear that the mathematics curriculum will play a crucial role in preparing individuals for future problem solving. This has consequences for primary mathematics.

It is not enough simply to develop knowledge of a range of fundamental mathematical ideas. The knowledge needs to be useable and the learner needs to have sufficient understanding to adapt and apply it in unforeseen situations. Instrumental understanding (Skemp, 1976) may be adequate to solve textbook problems but may not be transferable to different contexts. Primary Mathematics must aim for the development of that deeper and more adaptable understanding which Skemp calls relational understanding and others call conceptual understanding.

## IS THE SCOTTISH CURRICULUM CONSISTENT WITH RESEARCH AND THEORETICAL PERSPECTIVES?

The Curriculum for Excellence (CfE) in Scotland acknowledges the broad aims of preparing learners for life, study and work. How is this reflected in the mathematics recommendations? The Mathematics curriculum is laid out in two documents entitled 'Principles and Practice' (https://education.gov.scot/Documents/mathematics-pp.pdf) and 'Experiences and Outcomes' (https://www.education.gov.scot/Documents/numeracy-maths-eo.pdf). These seem to support the aims of developing mathematical knowledge which is fit for the purposes outlined above. For example, the Principles and Practice document states: 'Mathematics is at its most powerful when the knowledge and understanding that have been developed are used to solve problems. Problem solving will be at the heart of all our learning and teaching.'

Instead of prescribing particular methods of calculation, Experience and Outcome MNU1-03a states: 'I can use addition, subtraction, multiplication and division when solving problems, making best use of the mental strategies and written skills I have developed.' The clear aim is to develop calculation skills which are understood in sufficient depth to be used in problem solving rather than focusing on practice of traditional standard algorithms.

The documents also set out a range of pedagogical approaches which should be used to support the learning of mathematics. These appear to be broadly anchored in research, draw on widely accepted theoretical ideas about mathematics teaching and learning, and adopt a constructivist perspective. Recommended 'experiences', such as investigating and exploring, are embedded in the experience and outcome statements. It is recognised that learners need to be mentally active, building conceptual understanding and making mental connections for themselves. This emphasis on helping learners to make connections within mathematics and across the curriculum is supported by research showing the value of connectionist teaching (Askew et al., 1997).

In contrast with traditional teaching approaches, social aspects of learning are recognised. Teachers should facilitate learning by scaffolding mathematical thinking. The call for learners to discuss mathematical ideas with each other is consistent with research findings which demonstrate the role of mathematical talk in helping learners to actively construct knowledge for themselves (Mercer and Sams, 2006). Misconceptions are seen as opportunities for learning, in keeping with the constructivist view that cognitive conflict can fuel the adaptation of conceptual structures necessary for deepening understanding (Swan, 2001; Chapter 23 in this text). Teachers are expected to build on 'the principles of Assessment is for Learning' (AifL), recognising research results which indicate the positive effects of formative assessment and meta-cognition on learning (Hodgen and Wiliam, 2006; also Chapter 68 in this text).

Problem solving is seen as a pedagogical approach, as well as an aim for the mathematics curriculum. Teachers are expected to build on 'relevant contexts and experiences', and to develop 'problem-solving capabilities'. These approaches echo the Dutch 'Realistic Mathematics Education' (RME) approach (van den Heuvel-Panhuizen, 2000), where carefully planned trajectories help learners to build on prior knowledge from familiar contexts and develop their understanding in the process of solving new problems.

Overall it can be argued that Curriculum for Excellence documents conform with the important aim of developing mathematics understanding appropriate for future problem solving. Implicitly at least, the intended curriculum concords with contemporary mainstream theory and research findings in mathematics education. Yet the intended curriculum may not be the curriculum experienced by learners. Much depends on the interpretation of curriculum documents and the ability of schools to put those ideas into practice.

## INTERPRETING THE CURRICULUM: SOME ISSUES

Concerns have been raised about weaknesses in the mathematical knowledge held by many primary teachers in Scotland. Many of these teachers were taught mathematics in a traditional manner, with emphasis on procedural calculation rather than problem solving and enquiry. Despite the requirement for all teachers to hold at least Scottish Credit and Qualifications Framework (SCQF) level 5 mathematics qualifications, their understanding may well be patchy. Even if they are convinced of the value of helping learners to develop relational understanding, many lack the necessary depth of knowledge to facilitate this. Limited instrumental understanding of mathematics leads to limited ability to support relational learning for the next generation – a cycle that is hard to break without adequate professional development. Changes to initial teacher education programmes in recent years have generally led to considerable reductions in time spent on mathematics education. As a result, student teachers have limited time to develop the profound pedagogical knowledge of mathematics they need in order to scaffold learners' conceptual understanding and foster the development of creative problem-solving skills.

There may also be varied interpretations of the intended curriculum. In particular, the CfE focus on problem solving and enquiry approaches may be interpreted in very different ways. Traditionally problem solving has been seen as learning about mathematics in the abstract, then later applying the mathematical ideas to real life situations (frequently presented as 'word problems'). Research highlights the difficulty that learners have with this traditional approach to problem solving and shows the lack of transferability of knowledge developed in this way (Nunes and Bryant, 1996). In contrast, a 'problem solving and enquiry approach' such as the Dutch RME approach involves learning *through* problem solving, giving understanding which is more transferable between varied contexts. Teachers who are unaware of the difference may simply interpret CfE statements about 'applying mathematical concepts to understand and solve problems in a traditional manner'.

## IMPLEMENTING THE CURRICULUM: DIVERSITY IN PRACTICE

There is diversity of practice within schools and across the thirty-two local authorities in Scotland. Schools have autonomy over their provision for mathematics in terms of:

- *resources* chosen to structure and support learning and teaching. Some select locally developed materials, others prefer commercial publications. Many use a combination of resources to support different aspects of mathematics.
- *organisation for learning* – whole class teaching, within class grouping, setting by attainment can all be found. There is anecdotal evidence that the prevalence of setting across classes is declining and flexible groupings are being promoted.
- forms of *assessment* used to track learning and to report on attainment of individuals and the school as a whole (but see discussion of recent policy developments below).

This creates both vulnerability and strength within the system. Vulnerability is most apparent when schools, or indeed local authorities, lack teachers with specialist expertise to take responsibility for mathematics. Consequently, there may be over-reliance on commercial resources, used undiscerningly and leading to instrumental teaching. There is frequently then an emphasis on the 'outcomes' of the curriculum, at the expense of the 'experiences'. Conversely, the strength of the system allows developments to arise at a local level, some of which attain significance and are more widely disseminated. Several local authorities have drawn inspiration from international approaches, using them to engage staff in professional development or to design their own local resources. Examples include the New Zealand

Framework for Mathematics; Western Australia's First Steps in Mathematics; Cognitively Guided Instruction (CGI) from the USA (Carpenter et al., 2015); and the Mathematics Recovery programme, originating in Australia (see in Wright et al., 2012). Each draws on a wide range of international research into children's development in understanding and learning of mathematical concepts and skills.

Mathematics Recovery, in particular, is proving influential in promoting teacher understanding in several areas of Scotland. With its associated Stages of Early Arithmetical Learning (SEAL; see, for example, one school's outline of the approach intended for parents at: http://elnumeracyandmaths.edubuzz.org/home, this has become established as the preferred model for teaching number in schools in several local authorities. It is favoured for its potential to provide both a structured framework for progression in numerical knowledge and understanding, and guidance on effective pedagogy. It promotes enquiry-based teaching which is aimed just beyond the edge of a child's current thinking, assessed through close attention to the child's knowledge and strategies for calculation or problem solving. Assessment is often carried out with individual children and videoed to provide opportunity for teacher analysis and self-development. The programme aims, moreover, for children to develop increasingly sophisticated reasoning and calculating strategies ('progressive mathematisation'). Consistent with much current research, it advocates building strong mental models and calculation strategies, and delays the introduction of algorithmic procedures for arithmetic operations until middle or upper primary stages. Mathematics Recovery is a demanding approach for teachers as it requires detailed knowledge of learning and teaching pathways in number. In some areas, this has been supported with extensive teacher professional development, which has proved effective in expanding teacher knowledge, expertise and enthusiasm. In other areas, probably due to restricted budgets for staff development, a cascade model of development has proved to be less effective.

## THE MATHEMATICS CURRICULUM IS WIDER THAN NUMBER

Most local developments have concentrated on improving teaching and attainment in number. It is hard to find similar levels of interest or initiative being shown in developing other aspects such as measure, shape and data handling. Three new strands in primary mathematics were introduced by Curriculum for Excellence. Teachers face the challenge of developing an appropriate pedagogy for these, and knowledge of what are reasonable expectations for younger learners.

- Developing *algebraic thinking* from an early age is considered by many to deepen and enhance learning and attainment across the whole Mathematics curriculum, and has been the focus of ongoing research (Fosnot and Jacob, 2010). Yet the rationale for its introduction has been poorly communicated to teachers, and for many this may appear to be an invitation to teach formal algebra in the primary years.
- *Probability* is unintuitive and experience shows that many adults lack sound concepts of chance and uncertainty. Including it in the primary curriculum may allow children to develop concepts which underpin the ability to assess risk in the future. Teacher professional development is essential if this topic is to be taught effectively.
- *Mathematics – its impact on the world, past, present and future*. This is a small topic in the curriculum, but one that promotes the study of mathematics in its cultural context. It provides opportunity for mathematics to be seen as a human creation, and as a way of making sense of the world around. It invites the study of innovation and of important figures in

the development of mathematics. How much importance teachers attach to this and how much impact it will make on children's perceptions of mathematics would be an interesting research study.

## RECENT POLICY DEVELOPMENTS AND THE WAY FORWARD?

One of the most significant recent educational policy documents is the *National Improvement Framework* (Scottish Government, 2016; see Chapter 71). With the laudable agenda of raising attainment and closing the attainment gap, it nevertheless controversially proposed to reintroduce national testing in primary mathematics. Such tests would be standardised, nationally set and externally imposed. The stated aim was to provide evidence to support teachers' judgement of when children 'achieved' a level of Curriculum for Excellence. Furthermore, data generated from these assessments would be used to assess not only individual children's progress but also how well schools and authorities were performing in raising attainment in mathematics.

Such high-stakes assessments run counter to the extensive work which has been ongoing to support teachers in using learner-centred assessment in mathematics, following 'Assessment is for Learning' approaches (see Chapter 68). Work on identifying 'significant aspects of learning' was developed throughout 2015 and was being used to build profiles of individual learners' achievements across all types of learning experiences in mathematics, including talk. These aimed to evidence children's achievements across the breadth, challenge and application of mathematical learning. Exemplars disseminated through Education Scotland showed portfolios of work annotated by both teacher and learner, to provide holistic pictures of achievement when transitioning from one curriculum level to the next.

The dangers of high-stakes externally imposed assessments are well known: limiting of experiences and narrowing of teaching, often leading to 'teaching to the test' – an instrumental focus on number facts and skills at the expense of other aspects of mathematics. To compound this move to standardised testing, 'benchmark' statements were hurriedly produced over the summer of 2016 for every experience and outcome in mathematics. Regrettably, they concentrated on the 'outcomes' of learning, rather than evidencing the 'experiences', and to the dismay of many teachers, especially those who had invested in developing new types of assessment and recording, appeared to signal a return to an atomised prescription of the curriculum (see also Chapter 68).

Teachers, schools and local authorities are vulnerable when accountability stakes are high. Having risen to the challenge of developing local mathematics programmes when offered the opportunity by the openness of Curriculum for Excellence, and having, in many cases, assumed responsibility for teachers' professional development in mathematics, it remains to be seen how resilient they will be in protecting these programmes from the straitjacket of national standardised assessment and the inevitable comparisons and accountability challenge of published attainment results.

## CONCLUSION: PRIMARY MATHEMATICS AT A CRITICAL JUNCTURE

This is a critical period for primary mathematics in Scotland. Curriculum for Excellence offers a curriculum consistent with contemporary international research and pedagogy. There are signs that many teachers have embraced this and are actively developing new grassroots programmes which stimulate deeper understanding and enjoyment of mathematics, and serve the secondary purpose of building teachers' professional pedagogical knowledge. However, these are not fully embedded in practice across the whole of Scotland, and the political influences of traditionalist testing and accountability measures may stifle their growth and ultimately lead a return to narrower, more limited mathematics learning. We would like to hope that teachers feel sufficiently empowered to maintain and develop CfE's emphasis on rich learning experiences with 'problem solving at the heart'.

## REFERENCES

Askew, M., Brown, M., Rhodes, V., Wiliam, D. and Johnson, D. (1997) 'Effective teachers of numeracy: report of a study carried out for the Teacher Training Agency'. London: King's College, University of London. Online at http://mikeaskew.net/page3/page4/files/EffectiveTeachersofNumeracy.pdf

Carpenter, T., Fennema, E., Franke, M., Levi, L. and Empson, S. (2015) *Children's Mathematics: Cognitively Guided Instruction*, second edition. Portsmouth: Heinemann.

Fosnot, C. T. and Jacob, B. (2010) *Young Mathematicians at Work: Constructing Algebra*. Portsmouth: Heinemann.

Hodgen, J. and Wiliam, D. (2006) *Mathematics inside the Black Box: Assessment for Learning in the Mathematics Classroom*. London: GL Assessment.

Mercer, N. and Sams, C. (2006) 'Teaching children how to use language to solve maths problems', *Language and Education*, 20 (6), 507–28.

Nunes, T. and Bryant, P. (1996) *Children Doing Mathematics*. Oxford: Blackwell.

Scottish Government (2016) *2017 National Improvement Framework and Improvement Plan for Scottish Education: Achieving Excellence and Equity*. Online at www.gov.scot/Resource/0051/00511513.pdf

Skemp, R. R. (1976) 'Relational and instrumental understanding', *Mathematics Teaching*, 77, 20–6.

Swan, M. (2001) 'Dealing with misconceptions in mathematics', in P. Gates (ed.), *Issues in Mathematics Teaching*. London: Routledge Falmer, pp. 147–65.

Van den Heuvel-Panhuizen, M. (2000) 'Mathematics education in the Netherlands: a guided tour'. *Freudenthal Institute Cd-rom for ICME9*. Utrecht: Utrecht University. Online at www.fi.uu.nl/publicaties/literatuur/2000_heuvel_panhuizen_mathematics_education.pdf

Wright, R., Ellemor-Collins, D. and Tabor, P. (2012) *Developing Number Knowledge*. London: Sage.

# 33

# Modern Languages

*Hazel Crichton*

It is now widely accepted that learning to communicate in another language brings a raft of cognitive, social and personal benefits to the learner. Similarly, the advantages that knowledge of another language brings to business as a result of globalisation are well documented. In addition, the enjoyment of interpersonal communication, skills development and increased intercultural understanding that language learning provides means that it is essential that children are encouraged to start learning another language as early as possible. The purpose of this chapter is to provide a comprehensive overview of current provision and the issues surrounding the teaching and learning of Modern Languages (ML) in the primary school in Scotland. It will set the context with a brief history of the development of modern languages in the primary school, since the first pilot studies of Modern Languages in the primary school in the late 1980s to the present day. Issues relating to language learning and teaching in the primary will be discussed as well as possible future implications. In the UK, Scotland has consistently led the way in teaching and learning ML in primary schools. The aim to realise a meaningful language learning experience for Scottish schoolchildren is driven by a combination of political will and programmes of professional development for primary teachers. However, there are a number of issues which ML in the primary school has faced from its inception and continues to face, which will be discussed later in this chapter.

## BACKGROUND

Modern languages in Scottish primary schools is currently well-established practice in P6 and P7 and this has since been extended by the Scottish Government-led policy, '1+2' (mother tongue, plus learning two other languages, starting from age 5; Scottish Government Languages Working Group, 2012), introduced in 2012. This bold move aimed to bring Scotland into line with other countries in Europe, where two foreign languages in the primary are the norm, as a result of the European Union (EU) Barcelona agreement (2002). Its goal was to engage the 450+ million EU citizens in lifelong learning and develop their skills to communicate with their neighbours, in at least two languages other than their mother tongue. Discussion of this initiative figures later in the chapter.

Prior to 2012, children in Scottish primary schools were usually taught a foreign language from P6 for the last two years of their primary schooling, most often a European language, with French, German and Spanish dominating. This situation had been prevalent throughout Scotland since the early 1990s after a series of pilot studies involving twelve secondary schools and their associated primaries, which after close evaluation had been deemed successful (Low et al., 1995). One of the factors which had contributed to the success of the pilot studies had been the close collaboration between the secondary and primary teachers, where, in all but one of the twelve pilot projects, the secondary teachers were involved in delivering the language provision to the P6 and P7 children, with support from the primary teachers. When it was decided that the vision of language learning in the primary school was to become a reality and was to be extended across the country, the model of the secondary specialist providing input was not adopted, however. Ministers instead decided that the primary teachers themselves would teach the foreign language to their P6 and P7 classes. The rationale for this decision was that primary teachers were in a better position to embed the language in their daily routine, thus giving pupils exposure to the language throughout their school day. A programme of training covering a total of twenty-seven days was set up and within five years from the conclusion of the pilots in 1995, over 5,000 teachers had undergone training, thus addressing the aim that all primary schools in Scotland would have at least one trained modern languages specialist, who would take the implementation forward. By 2004, 96 per cent of P6 pupils and 98 per cent of P7 pupils were learning a modern language in primary (Her Majesty's Inspectorate of Education, 2005).

From the start of the training programmes, it was 'not the intention to produce specialist linguists but instead to give the primary teachers sufficient linguistic competence within specific areas' (Tierney and Alonso-Nieto, 2001, p. 11). However, over time, as government devolved funding for training to the local authorities (LAs), the original twenty-seven-day training programme was cut considerably, with many authorities offering twilight courses of short duration for interested primary teachers with few further professional development opportunities. The issue of training is one which will be revisited as it can be considered a key factor to ensuring confidence and competence in Scotland's primary teaching force.

## CURRICULUM FOR EXCELLENCE

The introduction of Curriculum for Excellence (CfE) in 2010–11 meant that primary teachers could move away from the prescriptive content- and assessment-driven practices of the previous 5–14 curriculum. In CfE, broad levels of attainment act as signposts for progression from early to second level in the primary school. In ML the focus is on skills development, rather than ticking off items on lists of vocabulary or structures, which had become the norm within the 5–14 curricular framework. CfE allowed teachers to consider teaching and learning activities which were appropriate for their pupils and which addressed areas such as knowledge about language, and intercultural and communicative competence. The descriptions of the capacities relating to modern languages in the *ML Principles in Practice* paper underline the wider aspects of language learning:

- **successful learners**, who can reflect on how they have acquired and learned their first language and how this can assist them in further language learning;
- **confident individuals**, who, through experiencing success and support, can interact with others in real-life situations, talk about topics of personal interest and deliver presentations in their new language;
- **effective contributors**, who can work in individual, paired and group situations, and establish and maintain contact with other speakers of the target language;

- **responsible citizens**, who have a growing awareness of life in another society and of the issues facing citizens in the countries where their new language is spoken. (https://education. gov.scot/Documents/modern-languages-pp.pdf)

The emphasis in CfE on the role of ML in literacy development, intercultural enhancement and awareness, communication and interpersonal skills could be considered to play to the primary teachers' strengths. CfE also provides flexibility in terms of cross-curricular opportunities, allowing learners to explore social, geographical and cultural elements of the language they are learning and the countries in which it is spoken, thus giving them access to meaningful language contexts and culturally relevant language that can be used to communicate appropriately with speakers of the target language.

While the contribution that ML makes to Scotland's young people's intercultural awareness can be considered crucial, particularly given the increasing multicultural nature of their classrooms, it could also be argued that one of the biggest contributions that ML makes within the primary curriculum is to overall literacy development. Literacy is one of the three overarching themes which are the responsibility of teachers across all the areas of the curriculum (the other two being numeracy and health and wellbeing, both of which are also addressed by ML).

The study of another language in the primary school allows teachers to make links between languages, demonstrating the interconnected nature of certain language 'families' and also to explore differences in sounds, orthography and structure from their native language. In addition, the study of ML provides opportunities for pupils to develop a meta-language to describe, compare and contrast features of their own language and the language they are learning. Understanding how language 'works' at an early age enables pupils to become more articulate, with a greater understanding of how to use language effectively. A secure knowledge about language also supports learning of additional languages.

Progression through the different levels of CfE experiences and outcomes for subject areas within the primary school is indicated from 'Early' which includes nursery level and P1, through 'First' at the end of P4 to 'Second' at the end of P7. However, the ML experiences and outcomes originally had no 'Early' or 'First' level. This was because primary ML learning still reflected a P6 start, although the documentation acknowledged that many schools were starting to teach ML at an earlier stage, for example some LAs were starting to teach ML from nursery school. Within two years of implementing CfE, the Scottish Government announced a manifesto commitment to introduce and implement by 2020 the aforementioned model for language learning based on the European Union '1+2 model', that is, mother tongue, plus two foreign languages, for the whole of its school-age population. This initiative came into being as the result of a report from the Scottish Government Languages Working Group (2012) which had been set up in 2011, representing practitioners, policymakers, LAs, teacher educators, parents and business interests, to look at the future of ML teaching and learning in Scotland. The report made thirty-five recommendations, including Recommendation 1: 'that schools offer children access to an additional language from Primary 1' (p. 12) and Recommendation 4:

> that a second additional language (L3) be introduced for pupils at a later stage in the primary school. The time for introduction of the L3 language would be a matter for schools and Local Authorities to determine but no later than P5. (p. 17)

The Scottish Government accepted thirty-one of the thirty-five recommendations and partially accepted the other four. Crucially, Recommendation 23, which related to the training of in-service teachers, was partially accepted, the government stating that it was up to universities themselves to decide how they might collaborate to contribute to teachers' professional development. No clear steer or funding emerged from the government to the universities, responsibility for career-long professional learning having been devolved to LAs, who were granted £4 million in 2013–14, £5 million in 2014–15 and £7 million in 2015–16 to take language learning in the primary school forward. LAs were able to spend this money as they wished, most appointing Development Officers to work with and provide guidance and support to the primary schools. Government-funded organisations such as Education Scotland and the Scottish Centre for Information on Language Teaching (SCILT) were also tasked with developing the initiative. All these organisations have worked hard and enthusiastically to provide support for all the primary teachers tasked with taking the initiative forward. It is also important to note the professionalism of the primary teachers already in post and their commitment to making the initiative work; however, there are a number of issues which need to be addressed if a meaningful programme of language teaching and learning in Scottish primary schools is to be successful.

## CHALLENGES

It appears that the Scottish Government's motives for a devolved funding model to LAs were prompted by acknowledgement of the widely differing demographics, geography and educational provision in each of the thirty-two LAs. Thus, it could be argued, funding in each LA could be targeted appropriately. However, this has resulted in the adoption of a variety of training, events and support for primary teachers in different authorities, without a systematic overarching national framework for development.

Despite Education Scotland stating that 'In line with the guidance for teaching a first modern language in P1, primary practitioners do not have to be fluent in the language(s) they teach' (https://education.gov.scot/improvement/Documents/modlang12-1plus2approachMar17.pdf), those practitioners teaching the children in the later stages in primary are concerned about the demands made on them regarding teaching a second and/or third language at a more advanced level (Tierney, 2009). The difficulty many teachers face is their perceived lack of communicative competence and correct pronunciation which is seen as necessary in teaching ML, success in which requires good quality input and modelling by the teacher. Teachers' lack of confidence, which has always been an issue related to teaching ML in the primary school (Crichton and Templeton, 2010), appears to be compounded by a lack of a national strategy regarding both pre-service and career-long professional learning to ensure a minimum level of competence across the country with consistent quality assurance standards.

The apparent sidelining of the universities, arguably the most knowledgeable providers of professional development with regard to teacher education, has led to what might be considered a 'tips for teachers' approach to teaching languages, addressing neither the need for developing intercultural awareness through the foreign language(s), nor exploring opportunities for developing understanding about language structures in the children's own and the foreign language, leading to greater literacy development. Current approaches may also not benefit teachers wishing to achieve a deeper level of understanding in their own language learning.

It has been left to individual LAs and, in some cases, schools, to choose which languages will be taught as the first and second foreign languages. This has led to a number of issues relating to progression and transition. Primary schools experience great difficulty in training sufficient staff to ensure progression in each language from P1 to P7. There is also a problem if the language chosen as the first foreign language is not taught in the associated secondary school. Some primary schools have chosen Mandarin or Gaelic as one of the additional languages, in areas where there appear to be no or few opportunities to develop these languages further at secondary level. It cannot therefore be assumed that the language learnt in the primary is carried on in the secondary, despite the government's clear message of the need for progression to ensure a satisfactory level of language. By concentrating so much on ML in the primary school, the government may be missing what is happening in Scottish secondary schools. Issues of decreasing numbers studying languages for National Qualifications will be considered in Chapter 51 where modern languages in the secondary are discussed; however, it is important to stress here a lack of cohesion between both sectors regarding expectations and delivery of ML.

## CONCLUSIONS

It is clear that the situation in Scottish primary schools regarding ML teaching and learning from P1 is still evolving. The government hopes that by 2020, the 1+2 policy will be firmly established and all children will be on the way to becoming proficient in at least one foreign language, with most able to communicate competently in another. Primary teachers have embraced the initiative and are keen to make it work. However, they acknowledge that without adequate and appropriate training, they will feel insecure about their knowledge and understanding of the language(s) they are supposed to be embedding in the curriculum, with the subsequent effect on their confidence. While it is essential that LAs require flexibility to respond to the particular needs of their specific locality, this needs to be balanced by the development of a national modern languages framework with clear and realistic outcomes and a coherent continuous professional development programme across the country. This would seem to be the best way to address the rather piecemeal approach taken by LAs so far. Universities are already implementing action to ensure that initial teacher education programmes provide adequate preparation for future primary teachers. A national framework of consistent good quality career-long professional learning for primary teachers is essential to enable modern languages in the primary school to be meaningful for Scottish pupils in the years ahead.

## REFERENCES

Crichton, H. and Templeton, B. (2010) 'Curriculum for Excellence: the way forward for modern languages in Scotland?' *The Language Learning Journal*, 38 (2), 139–47.

European Council of Barcelona (2002) 'Presidency conclusions', Barcelona, European Council. Online at http://aei.pitt.edu/43345/1/Barcelona_2002_1.pdf

Her Majesty's Inspectorate of Education (2005) 'Progress in addressing the recommendations of "Citizens of a Multilingual World". Report for the Scottish Executive Education Department, 23 March. Online at https://www.languagescompany.com/wp-content/uploads/progress-update-CMW070306-tcm4-325627.pdf

Low, L., Brown, S., Johnstone, R. and Pirrie A. (1995) 'Foreign languages in primary schools: evaluation of the Scottish pilot projects 1993–1995. Final Report'. Stirling, UK: Scottish CILT.

Scottish Government (nd) *Curriculum for Excellence: Modern Languages Experiences and Outcomes.* Online at https://education.gov.scot/Documents/modern-languages-eo.pdf

Scottish Government Languages Working Group (2012) *Language Learning in Scotland: A 1+2 Approach.* Online at www.gov.scot/Publications/2012/05/3670

Tierney, D. and Alonso-Nieto, L. (2001) 'Modern languages in the primary school in Spain and Scotland', *Vida Hispanica*, 23, Spring, 9–12.

Tierney, D. (2009) *The Pedagogy and Implementation of Modern Languages in the Primary School: Pupil Attitudes and Teachers' Views.* Unpublished PhD thesis, University of Strathclyde.

# 34

# Physical Education

*Nicola Carse and Mike Jess*

Following its long-term place on the margins of Scottish primary education, the last decade has seen a change in fortune for physical education. With new curriculum guidance, considerably more curriculum time for all children, and a significant investment in primary teachers' professional development, physical education in Scotland is passing through one of its more positive and fruitful periods.

## POLICY BACKGROUND

In 2001, Her Majesty's Inspectorate of Education (HMIE) in Scotland published a report on the physical education curriculum, learning, teaching and resourcing within Scottish primary schools. Whilst some positive aspects were identified, that report raised numerous concerns about the quality of primary physical education and led to a number of reforms which were incorporated into the development of Curriculum for Excellence (CfE). Around the same time as this HMIE report, and in response to wider societal concerns about the nation's health and inactivity, the first Scottish physical activity strategy was published and identified the minimum level of daily activity required by young people to provide health benefits (Scottish Executive, 2003). To provide a physical education response to these developments, a Physical Education Review Group (PERG) was formed by the Scottish Executive and drew its membership from a range of bodies and individuals involved in education, physical education, and sport. The PERG report (Scottish Executive, 2004) proposed that the subject had a central role to play in the promotion of health and wellbeing and therefore was an aspect of the curriculum which required greater priority and should build the foundations for healthy and active lifestyles from an early age. PERG proposed three main aims for the future development of physical education in Scotland: more time for physical education; more teachers of physical education; and more choice in physical education. Taken together, the introduction of CfE and the recommendations from these key Scottish Government reports have had a significant impact on the physical education curriculum within Scottish primary schools.

## CURRICULUM OVERVIEW

With the introduction of CfE, physical education began to prosper as it was moved from the Expressive Arts to the new curriculum area of health and wellbeing. Consistent with the

United Nations Convention on the Rights of the Child, the health and wellbeing curriculum area sets out the right for all children and young people to have access to appropriate health services and to have their health and wellbeing promoted (Scottish Government, 2009). Importantly, health and wellbeing is viewed in a holistic sense with specific focus placed on mental, social, emotional and physical wellbeing. While physical education, physical activity and sport are presented as one area of health and wellbeing, each of these components receives individual attention within the CfE guidelines. As such, having played a somewhat marginal role within the Expressive Arts curriculum, the physical domain now holds a more prominent position within CfE, with physical education itself now recognised as holding a key role across the education, health and sport sectors. Indeed the overall aim for the experiences and outcomes which constitute physical education are to establish a pattern of daily physical activity leading to sustained physical activity in adult life (Scottish Government, 2009).

The frequency of physical education within the curriculum has been a main concern of the Scottish Government throughout the CfE implementation process. Following the PERG report in 2004, and with the introduction of CfE, the Scottish Government stipulated that schools should seek to provide every pupil with at least two hours of quality physical education every week. However, meeting this target proved problematic and since 2011 progress in this area has been more closely monitored with questions about physical education provision in schools included in the national annual healthy living survey. This data suggest that over the last five years, the number of primary schools reaching the two-hour target has risen steadily from 84 per cent in 2012 to 99 per cent in 2016 (Scottish Government, 2016). With the two-hour commitment seemingly in place, the government's focus is now on the quality of the physical education experiences received by primary school children.

In relation to assessment within physical education, the aim of the experiences and outcomes is to provide guidance for teachers in planning learning experiences that take into account what children can be expected to achieve at different points in their learning journey. Complementary to the experiences and outcomes, the significant aspects of learning (SALs) support teachers to provide progressive learning contexts by viewing physical education in a holistic sense. In this respect, the integration of four main areas is emphasised: physical competencies; cognitive skills; physical fitness and personal qualities (Education Scotland, 2014). The paper introducing the SALs states that the aim is:

> to help practitioners to make judgements as to the achievement of a level across all lines of development, to work with colleagues to create a shared understanding of standards and learners' progress and to identify key assessment opportunities and forms of assessment. (Education Scotland, 2014, p. 1)

Therefore, it is evident that the emphasis is on embedding assessment within teaching and using it to inform the learning process rather than on the measurement of learning (cf. Chapter 68). This emphasis on assessment as part of the learning process is also articulated in the focus on progression in learning within physical education through experiential learning which centres on promoting breadth, challenge and application within learning experiences. However, despite the seeming emphasis on trusting teacher judgement within assessment through CfE, this has been somewhat eroded in recent years with the Scottish Government placing renewed emphasis on standardised testing for assessment through the National Improvement Framework (NIF; see Chapter 71). In an attempt to 'close the attainment gap' the NIF has seen standardised testing introduced in Maths and Literacy, which raises questions over the place of curriculum areas not scrutinised by standardised testing, and in particular the core status of health and wellbeing within the curriculum.

## RESOURCING

At the heart of the developments in primary physical education, considerable amounts of money have been made available by the Scottish Government. Between 2006 and 2012 initial government funding in the region of £6 million was made available to devise and deliver postgraduate certificates in primary physical education that would help generalist class teachers develop a specialism in physical education. Offered by the Universities of Edinburgh and Glasgow these programmes attracted in excess of 1,000 teachers. Furthermore, to support participation levels and opportunities within and beyond physical education, the Active Schools programme was introduced in 2000 and has become embedded within Scottish primary schools. Funded by the Scottish Government and coordinated by sportscotland, the Active Schools programme operates through a network of local authority managers, school-based coordinators in primary and secondary schools, and volunteers who deliver activity sessions in schools and communities across Scotland. The Active Schools coordinators have a significant role in the integration of physical education, physical activity and sport by creating opportunities for children to be physically active before, during and after school, as well as in the wider community. Official reports on the effectiveness of Active Schools have emphasised the significant impact the programme has had on physical activity levels, particularly in primary school settings.

With these initiatives in place, the period from 2010 onward has seen the Scottish Government focus on supporting the quantity and quality of physical education within Scottish primary schools. In particular, sportscotland and Education Scotland have jointly invested £6.8 million and £4.8 million respectively across local authorities to develop a package of national initiatives to increase the support available to schools and teachers. The most significant initiatives in terms of resourcing have been employing local authority physical education lead officers (PELOs) and the core physical education fund, a grant initiative where individual schools or clusters of schools had the opportunity to apply for up to £3,000 of funding which could be used to improve the quality of learning experiences in physical education. A recent report evaluating these large-scale initiatives noted the positive impact that the PELOs have had on promoting the two-hour target and on teachers' learning and teaching practice, although it also highlights that physical space and resources continue to be a concern for schools and teachers, and a potential barrier, inhibiting efforts to promote physical education (Lowden et al., 2014). In terms of resourcing, overall the last decade has seen significant financial input into primary physical education developments.

## LEARNING PROGRAMMES

It would be misleading to suggest that there is a 'typical' learning programme or lesson for primary physical education in Scotland. However, as in many other parts of the world, many primary schools still deliver a multi-activity curriculum programme in which specific physical activities are sampled in 'blocks' of four to six weeks to reflect the structure of the school year. It is therefore common for two or more activities, particularly sports and games, to be taught within each term. However, the recent upsurge in more contemporary and in-depth professional learning for primary teachers across the country (e.g. the postgraduate certificates) has seen the dominance of this multi-activity approach increasingly being challenged, and more holistic, models-based and interdisciplinary practices introduced into schools (Carse, 2015). This transition towards more holistic approaches reflects the overarching aims of health and wellbeing (Scottish Government, 2009): the nationwide introduction of 'significant aspects of learning' (Education Scotland, 2014) and the complexity-informed core learning and basic moves (Jess, 2012) approaches that are common in many primary schools. These holistic approaches seek to help primary school children develop the interrelated physical, cognitive, social and emotional learning that acts as a foundation for successful engagement in physical activity within and beyond the school. In addition, more integrated and interdisciplinary physical education models have been introduced in primary schools; these different models include 'better movers better thinkers', sport education, cooperative learning, teaching personal and social responsibility, critical thinking and teaching games for understanding (TGfU).

With holistic, contemporary models and interdisciplinary approaches now more common, primary physical education learning programmes and lessons in Scotland are beginning to move beyond the skill technique and activity-specific sampling sessions of the multi-activity approach. Efforts to establish learning programmes that revisit and scaffold children's learning and also seek to connect physical education learning across and beyond the school are increasingly being reported in the literature (e.g. Jess, 2012; Carse, 2015). As a consequence, it is not uncommon for primary school children, particularly early years children, to work in different movement 'stations' over an extended period of time in a manner that is similar to their work in classroom settings.

Therefore, while primary physical education programmes in Scotland may still be dominated by the more traditional multi-activity approach in many places, there is a growing body of evidence to suggest that the recent introduction of more holistic and educationally focused developments are beginning to impact on practice.

## TEACHER EDUCATION

While the recent focus on primary physical education has resulted in increased professional development opportunities for primary class teachers, developments within initial teacher education (ITE) have unfortunately been less positive. While the ITE of primary teachers remains firmly rooted in Scotland's university sector, teacher education policy has moved towards a more academic focus, which means that the time allotted to curriculum subjects has been reduced during this introductory phase of professional learning. As such, although most undergraduate ITE programmes offer a physical education elective course for final year students, many of the global concerns that have long been reported about ITE in primary physical education appear to be a feature in Scotland.

Conversely, post-qualification professional development opportunities for primary school teachers in Scotland have been in evidence. As noted earlier in the chapter, in response to the PERG recommendations, the Universities of Edinburgh and Glasgow were both commissioned by the Scottish Executive in 2006 to develop, deliver and evaluate the impact of postgraduate certificates in primary physical education. These programmes had a specific aim of building the confidence and competence of primary teachers by helping them to develop a specialism in physical education. Teachers enrolling on these two–year, part-time, Masters–level programmes were offered an opportunity to engage with primary physical education in considerably more depth than traditional professional development courses. Instead of providing pre-prepared resources and lesson plans, these programmes helped the teachers explore key theoretical concepts. Consequently this encouraged the teachers to critically reflect on their beliefs, values and contexts and then explicitly design learning experiences in physical education aligned to the needs of the children in their classes (Carse, 2015).

Initial findings tracking the impact of these programmes reported increases in teachers' confidence and subject knowledge, and changes in their general approach to the teaching of physical education, particularly in relation to the assessment of children's learning, differentiating of physical education experiences, and personalisation of learning in the physical education context (Jess et al., 2012). Given the longer timescale of this professional development experience, many of the teachers began to develop physical education programmes that were contextualised within their individual school settings, while some began to adopt leadership roles in order to develop physical education learning communities reflecting contemporary innovation agendas (Carse, 2015). Interestingly, while the teachers acknowledged the positive impact of a supportive policy context, they also experienced considerable autonomy to experiment and develop their physical education ideas because of the ongoing marginal status of physical education within their schools. Conversely, a regular constraint was the feeling of isolation as teachers tried to collaborate with their colleagues and other physical education practitioners. In particular, the teachers reported how they struggled to overcome the traditional view of physical education as a multi-activity sport and games programme that was held by most of their colleagues and pupils (Carse, 2015). While the impact of these postgraduate programmes on the class teachers' physical education practice continues to be studied and reported, efforts are currently being made to explore the possibilities of practitioner inquiry as a form of professional development as academics and teachers seek to work, learn and research together.

## CONCLUSION

For primary physical education in Scotland, the last decade has been one of significant development across the political, professional and academic landscape. The initial driver for this change in fortune came at the policy level, as a complex mix of issues and recommendations were raised in the national health survey, the HMIE report, the national physical activity strategy and by PERG. Building on this encouraging political activity, we have seen a move to the new core curriculum area of health and wellbeing and almost all schools delivering two hours of physical education to all primary children. In addition, with significant investment to support primary teachers' teaching of physical education, we are now seeing the subject area in a very different position from what it was at the turn of the century. However, while these developments may have seen Scotland make 'inroads into history making education change as it relates to primary school physical education' (Petrie, 2016, p. 544), this last decade has only been the beginning, and there is still much to be done if primary physical education is to build on the exciting foundation that has been put in place across the country.

## REFERENCES

Carse, N. (2015) 'Primary teachers as physical education curriculum change agents', *European Physical Education Review*, 21 (3), 309–24, doi: 1356336X14567691

Education Scotland (2014) 'Professional learning paper: assessing progress and achievement in health and wellbeing – physical education'. Edinburgh: Scottish Government.

HMIE (2001) *Improving Physical Education in Primary Schools*. Edinburgh: HMSO.

Jess, M. (2012) The future of primary PE: a 3–14 developmental and connected curriculum', in G. Griggs (ed.), *An Introduction to Primary Physical Education*. London: Routledge, pp. 37–54.

Jess, M., McEvilly, N., Campbell, T. and Elliot, D. (2012) The Scottish Primary Physical Education Project Evaluation Report 2. *The Postgraduate Certificates in Primary Physical Education: Initial Impact on Teachers*. Edinburgh: University of Edinburgh.

Lowden, K., Hall, S., Watters, N., O'Brien, J. and McLean, M. (2014) 'Measuring the impact of the "Two Hours/Two Periods of Quality Physical Education" programme: final report'. Glasgow: Education Scotland.

Petrie, K. (2016) 'Architectures of practice: constraining or enabling PE in primary Schools', *Education 3–13*, 44 (5), 537–46.

Scottish Executive (2003) 'Let's make Scotland more active: a strategy for physical activity'. Edinburgh: HMSO.

Scottish Executive (2004) 'The report of the review group on physical education'. Edinburgh: HMSO.

Scottish Government (2009) *Curriculum for Excellence: Health and Wellbeing Principles and Practice*. Edinburgh: Scottish Government.

Scottish Government (2016) *Sport and PE in Schools*. Online at www.gov.scot/Topics/ArtsCultureSport/Sport/MajorEvents/Glasgow-2014/Commonwealth-games/Indicators/AiSch

# 35

# Religious (and Moral) Education

*Yonah Matemba*

## INTRODUCTION

In Scotland, Religious Education (RE) in state schools comprises two programmes, namely, Religious and Moral Education (RME) and RE offered in non-denominational and denominational (de facto Catholic) schools, respectively (Conroy, 2014). In the primary sector, RME offered in the country's 2,056 non-denominational schools is based on a Christian Protestant framework but with a strong multifaith and moral component. On its part, the Catholic sector – comprising 312 primary schools – offers catechetical RE, which, despite its Catholicity focuses some attention to 'other' religions. In addition to Catholic schools, there are other state-funded denominational primaries in Scotland (one Jewish and three Episcopalian) that use the RME curriculum (Matemba, 2015). An independent Muslim primary school established in 2011 in Glasgow (the first of its kind in Scotland), while in the main uses the Curriculum for Excellence (CfE) guidelines, does not teach either RME or RE, choosing instead to offer a stand-alone course on Islam within the context of the Islamic education offered by the school (https://qalam-academy.org/index.html). This chapter describes Scottish primary RE in state-funded public education for both non-denominational and denominational school sectors and hence, its rather unusual title: 'Religious (and Moral) Education'. To avoid confusion between these terms, the chapter will simply refer to 'RE', as the subject is commonly known.

## SOCIO-RELIGIOUS CONTEXT

How society and the educational establishment in Scotland has come to understand what RE should be and, more importantly, how it should be offered to children and young people in public education, is to a large extent a consequence of powerful sociocultural currents, such as secularisation, religious diversity, immigration and liberal educational policies, including post-Piagetian child-centred educational thinking and its impact on how religious knowledge should best be presented to children (see Fairweather and MacDonald, 1992; Conroy, 2014). Beyond the simplistic notions of a post-secular age, a nuanced understanding of the complex sociocultural context that has shaped the framing of Scottish primary RE is necessary.

As the recent (2011) national census highlights, despite the gradual decline in the number of people identifying themselves with Christianity (65.2 per cent (in the 2001 census) to 53.8 per cent) (Scottish Government, 2013), there is a growing visibility of religion (not belief in God, per se) in the public square. Although the number of people with 'no religion' has grown to 37 per cent from 27.8 per cent in the previous census, there is nascent interest in alternative religious/spiritual practice, an increase of 0.3 per cent from 0.2 per cent. In addition, while as a distinct community the number of Catholics has remained unchanged (15.9 per cent), Islam has seen a modest growth from 0.84 per cent to 1.4 per cent (Scottish Government, 2013). Thus, educational policy, curriculum reforms and school practice have aligned teaching and learning in RE in ways that attempt to address the educational needs of learners within the socio-religious context of a multi-cultural and inclusive Scottish society.

## LEGAL AND POLICY FRAMEWORK

RE in Scotland is guided by legislation created at the turn of the nineteenth century (1872 Act) as part of the educational reforms that engendered the present modern Scottish system of state-funded education. Initially reluctant to be part of a 'secularised' new system of education but without proper safeguards for the religious nature of their schools and the place of RE, the Catholic and Episcopalian Churches refused to be part of the 1872 educational settlement. In a landmark Church–State concordance (1918 Act), the Catholic and Episcopalian Churches were given judicial powers to manage their own schools, including for the Catholic Church, complete control over RE. The 1918 Act led to the creation of the bipartite system of state-funded public education we see today in Scotland: non-denominational (i.e. 'liberal–secular' in character) and denominational (i.e. Catholic but also including Episcopalian and Jewish) (Conroy, 2014).

Over the decades, the 1872 Act has been amended. The legislation that governs the current provision of Scottish RE derives from the 1980 Education Act, which as in all preceding legislation, imposes a statutory duty on schools to provide RE to *all* children in public schools, which was reaffirmed as a compulsory subject by the 1929 Local Government Act (Fairweather and MacDonald, 1992). The 1980 Act makes two exceptions: first, RE should be locally determined, and second, parents have the right to withdraw their children from RE (i.e. the 'conscience clause'). In practice, however, few parents ever exercise this right, in part due to a lack of knowledge that this right exists, but also because they want their children to engage in RE. In 2013, of the 12,185 pupils classified as absent, only 184 were as a result of parental withdrawal from RE, and in the majority of cases, they were children of Jehovah's Witnesses (Nixon, 2018).

Although legislation imposes a statutory duty on schools and local authorities to provide RE, it does not detail the *form* that this education should take. Through policy directives, the education department issues advice contained in policy letters on how schools and local authorities can meet the statutory obligations (see Scottish Government, 2011a). The current policy guidance (2011) issued in line with CfE and introduced in 2009, highlights the following key points: RE as a legal requirement in schools; Christianity as a key religion of study – on the account of history and national tradition; conscience clause related to parental right to withdraw from RE; right of education authorities and schools to decide the nature of RE in their areas; and interdisciplinary approaches to teaching and learning in RE (Scottish Government, 2011a). Compared to the previous policy guidance (1992), notable changes in the current policy letter relates to the absence of time allocation for RE in non-denominational schools, although for Catholic schools, a minimum of two hours of

RE a week has been retained. At a local level, each school is expected to have an RE policy, detailing how it will meet the legislative, policy and curriculum expectations, including specific areas of RE (i.e. material content) to be taught in the school.

## POST-MILLAR REFORMS AND CURRICULUM DEVELOPMENTS

By the late 1960s it was evident that, as a school subject, RE was in serious trouble and that if nothing was done, it was in real danger of disappearing from schools altogether, especially in non-denominational schools (Fairweather and MacDonald, 1992). The plight of RE was such that the Scottish Department of Education did not recognise it as a bona fide 'academic' subject; in fact, the government introduced (in 1965) new areas of study in the primary curriculum and RE was not classified as a distinct subject, with the suggestion that it should be integrated within other curricular areas. The Millar Report (SED, 1972), instituted by the government to examine to the fullest extent the plight of RE, engendered curriculum reforms in the subject: child-centred pedagogies, educational approaches and, importantly, ensuring that teaching in primary RE go beyond Christianity as *primus inter pares* in RE to include content from different principal religions and moral issues.

As a response to the recommendations in the Millar Report to improve RE, there emerged teacher professional committees (with government support), such as the Scottish Central Committee on RE (SCCORE), which had representatives from both denominational and non-denominational schools, an important first in Scotland. SCCORE produced a number of professional reports that provided practical ideas for RE teachers. For its part, the Scottish Joint Committee on RE (SJCRE), which had representatives from the churches (except Catholic), the Department of Education, local authorities and the Educational Institute of Scotland (EIS), produced a comprehensive RE handbook for primary schools, detailing (a) aims and objectives, (b) developmental psychology and religion in children, (c) pedagogical approaches and (d) thematic areas of study. Alongside these developments there also developed an 'advisorate', comprising a cadre of RE specialists who were deployed in each of the country's local education authorities to oversee RE; today, this important support mechanism for the subject is no longer available, but needed (see Matemba, 2015).

The educational reforms of the 1990s, leading to the creation of the 5–14 curriculum in 1992, provided an opportunity for important changes in RE in aligning the subject to post-confessional thinking towards the professionalisation of RE as an educational rather than religious activity. In 2009/10, the 5–14 Guidelines were replaced by the outcomes-based curriculum, CfE, covering learning from 3 to 18 years. RE within CfE in both non-denominational and denominational guidelines cover a plethora of issues contained in lists of 'experiences and outcomes' (Es and Os). As shown in Table 35.1, the non-denominational curriculum covers three main strands under 'Christianity', 'World Religions Selected for Study' and 'Development of Beliefs and Values' (drawn from religious and non-religious traditions and beliefs), while the Catholic guidelines cover two strands under 'Catholic Christianity' and 'Other World Religions' (the guideline CfE documents were first published in 2009, see Scottish Government, 2011b).

CfE is organised into five progressive levels (early, first, second, third and fourth) across the 3–18 age range, although in practice, learning in primary RE tends to cover early and first levels. CfE is an *open* curriculum that does not prescribe the content to be taught, nor the pedagogical approach to be used in RE, with teachers having autonomy to develop

Table 35.1    Strands in Scottish RE in non-denominational and denominational CfE
guidelines

| Strands within non-denominational RE | Strands within Catholic RE |
|---|---|
| Strand 1: Christianity | Strand 1: Catholic Christianity |
| • Beliefs | • Mystery of God |
| • Values and issues | • Image of God |
| • Practices and traditions | • Revealed truth of God |
| | • Son of God |
| Strand 2: World Religions Selected for Study | • Signs of God |
| • Beliefs | • Word of God |
| • Values and practices | • Hours of God |
| • Practices and traditions | • Reign of God |
| | |
| Strand 3: Development of Beliefs and Values drawn from Es and Os in: | Strand 2: Other World Religions |
| • Christianity and selected world religions | • Beliefs |
| • Non-religious views | • Values and issues |
| • Ethical and moral studies | • Practices and traditions |

curriculum at a local level in response to the recommendation that RE should be based not
only on tradition (Christianity as the religious tradition of Scotland) but, importantly, on
locality (i.e. religious and cultural composition of school and local community input) as
well. As such, to meet the expectations of CfE, teachers are required to have a high degree
of subject knowledge and pedagogical competence related to curriculum Es and Os in RE.

## TEACHING, LEARNING AND SCHOOL PRACTICE

In the post-Ninian Smart discourse on RE, a plethora of pedagogical approaches to and of
RE have emerged (Williame, 2007), although in Scotland, elements of the phenomenologi-
cal (emphasising dimensions common to most religions), neo-confessional (confessing to
one religion while recognising that others also have 'truth'), neutral ('non-judgemental'
approach in the study of religion), world religions (multifaith/comparative study of religions) and philosophical inquiry (technique involving critical thinking, reflection and analysis) can be found in non-denominational RE, while the confessional/doctrinal ('truth' lies
in the single religion studied) highlights common approaches in Catholic RE (see relevant
CfE documents).

The nature of CfE as an open curriculum coupled with the absence of specific guidance
for how and what to teach in RE means that – particularly in the non-denominational
sector – teachers adopt different pedagogical approaches and teach a variety of different
religions and topics, partly influenced by their philosophical orientation towards religion (or none), understanding of particular pedagogical approaches, subject knowledge
of various religions and viewpoints independent of religion. As such, across the nation
there is little uniformity of practice in non-denominational schools, with some RE classes
focusing on Christianity, others on religions selected for study, for example Islam, and, in
some cases, focusing on spiritual/non-religious issues, such as the 'Simpsons and morality', 'Australian Aborigines' and 'ancient Egypt' (Matemba, 2015). It is also common for

schools to focus on Christian topics such as Easter around the Easter period, and equally involve children in the nativity play to coincide with the Christmas period.

As subject 'generalists' in non-denominational schools, teacher orientation towards RE is guided by three principles, namely, (a) neutrality, (b) objectivism and (c) professionalism. While there are many teachers in non-denominational primary schools 'offering sophisticated accounts of religious practices and beliefs', there are others who often betray 'a naïve and modestly pious approach to the subject' (Conroy, 2014, p. 248). In Catholic schools a picture of uniformity of practice is evident, which ensures that as per the vision of the Catholic Church – as endorsed by the Bishops' Conference of Scotland (BCS) – an appropriate curriculum is being delivered. Alongside CfE guidelines, Catholic teachers use a Church 'approved' prescribed resource book entitled *This is Our Faith*. Catholic teachers are reminded that the 'Catholic faith is a great privilege and vocation ... [and that] it is in teachers hands that lies the task of transmitting the living faith of the Church from generation to generation' (BCS, 2011, p. 3).

In the non-denominational sector, the amount of time schools spend on RE varies, for example on average about one hour or less per week (Conroy, 2014). In some cases schools use Religious Observance, involving whole school collective worship (Scottish Government, 2017), as proxy for doing RE (see Matemba, 2015). The picture in the Catholic sector is different where schools spend no less than the mandated two hours a week in RE, thus ensuring adequate coverage of RE towards helping children grow into faith (BCS, 2011). As a pre-employment requirement, Catholic teachers undergo an additional certification programme (offered only by the University of Glasgow, www.gla.ac.uk/schools/education/standrewsfoundation) in which RE is a critical component. Most teachers in Catholic schools are, therefore, better prepared to offer RE as required by that particular sector.

In both non-denominational and Catholic RE, the teaching of (moral) values is emphasised, although in the non-denominational sector, moral issues are conceptualised as being a distinct form of knowledge, as evidenced in the title 'RME', while in Catholic schools moral issues are embedded within RE. In both school sectors, teaching and learning in RE emphasise pro-social values such as fairness, empathy, respect for self and others, and care of the environment (Conroy, 2014). As part of 'doing' RE, in many schools, classroom or indeed whole school activities aim to inculcate in children the value of being charitable and, as such, pupils are engaged in fundraising projects for local, national and international charities (Matemba, 2015).

## CONCLUSION

RE in the Scottish primary school sector – both non-denominational and denominational – promises to provide learners with a fulfilling learning experience towards achieving the overall expectations of the curriculum (i.e. CfE). However, across the non-denominational sector, 'adequate' time allocation is needed to ensure wider coverage of the curriculum if RE is to fully meet the long list of competing aims (eleven in total) for the subject within CfE, for example from 'recognising religion as an important expression of human experience' to making 'a positive difference to the world by putting my beliefs and values into action' (Clanachan and Matemba, 2015, p. 130). In non-denominational schools, to bolster teachers' confidence and increase material knowledge of different religions, additional career-long professional learning opportunities would be beneficial, 'although at a time of government cuts teachers might struggle to get the appropriate level of funding to attend such courses particularly for a less regarded school subject' (ibid.) known as RE.

## REFERENCES

BCS (2011) *This is Our Faith: Guidance on the Teaching of Religious Education in Catholic Schools*, Glasgow: SCES.

Clanachan, T. and Matemba, Y. H. (2015) 'Primary teachers' confidence in religious and moral education in Scottish non-denominational schools', *STeP Journal: Student Teacher Perspectives*, 2 (3), 121–33.

Conroy, J. (2014) 'Religious education at schools in Scotland', in Martin Rothgangel, Robert Jackson and Martin Jäggle (eds), *Religious Education at Schools in Europe: Part 2: Western Europe*. Vienna: Vienna University Press, pp. 234–60.

Fairweather, I. and MacDonald, J. (1992) *Religious Education*. Edinburgh: Scottish Academic Press.

Matemba, Y. H. (2015) 'Mismatches between legislative policy and school practice in religious education: the Scottish case', *Religious Education*, 110 (1), 70–94.

Nixon, G. (2018) 'Conscientious withdrawal from religious education in Scotland: anachronism or necessary right?' *British Journal of Religious Education*, 40 (1), 6–19.

Scottish Government (2011a) *Curriculum for Excellence—Statutory Guidelines for the Provision of Religious and Moral Education in Non-denominational schools and Religious Education in Roman Catholic schools*. Edinburgh: Scottish Government.

Scottish Government (2011b) *Curriculum for Excellence: Religious and Moral Education*. Online at https://beta.gov.scot/publications/curriculum-for-excellence-religious-and-moral-education/

Scottish Government (2013) *Scotland's Census 2011*. Edinburgh: Statistical Office.

Scottish Government (2017) *Curriculum for Excellence – Provision of Religious Observance in Scottish Schools*. Livingston: Scottish Government.

SED (1972) *Moral and Religious Education in Schools*. (The Millar Report). Edinburgh: HMSO.

Williame, J. (2007) 'Different models for religion and education in Europe', in R. Jackson, S. Miedema, W. Weisse and J. Williame, J. *Religion and Education in Europe*. Munster: Waxamann, pp. 56–66.

# 36

# Science

*Stephen P. Day and Andrew Killen*


## PRIMARY SCHOOL SCIENCE PROVISION: PAST AND PRESENT POLICIES

Under the 5–14 curriculum (1993–2010), every young person was entitled to experience science education during primary education, but under Curriculum for Excellence (CfE) this entitlement has shifted to the right of every young person to experience a broad general education (BGE), with the decision as to what constitutes a BGE being taken by the headteacher. The place of science education within the early years and primary curriculum was formally enshrined within the BGE phase of CfE in March 2006, when the curriculum review group published *A Curriculum for Excellence: Progress and Proposals* (Scottish Executive, 2006). In this document, the Science rationale (3–15) outlines the two main aims of science education as being the development of young people as scientifically literate citizens, able to hold and defend informed views on social, moral, ethical, economic and environmental issues related to science; and the preparation of young people for further, more specialised, learning by developing their secure understanding of the 'big ideas' and concepts of science.

This rationale was further elaborated upon in April 2009 with the publication of the CfE Science *Principles and Practice* and *Experiences and Outcomes* documents (Education Scotland, 2009a; 2009b). These documents place an emphasis on the Science curriculum beginning in the early years, progressing through the primary phase and on towards the secondary phase of education. Proportionately, fifty-five of the 123 Science E&Os sit within the early, first and second levels corresponding to the primary phase of education. Therefore, primary education has a vital role to play in Scottish young people's science education experience.

The Science E&Os are organised under the curriculum organisers: Planet Earth: *Biodiversity and Interdependence* (relating to biodiversity, photosynthesis and evolution); Biological Systems: *Body Systems and Cells* (relating to cell theory; biotechnology); and Inheritance (relating to reproduction, DNA and genetics). The E&Os are constructed in such a way that they have an associated aspect of knowledge, skills and practical techniques appropriate to the level. For example, SCN 0-01a ('I have observed living things in the environment over time and am becoming aware of how they depend on each other') has an associated skill – focused observation; a knowledge component – how plants and animals interact, perhaps as part of a food chain over time; and a practical technique – sampling. The related level 1 E&O SCN 1-01a ('I can distinguish between living and non-living things. I can sort living things into groups and explain my decision') extends this to include the ability to identify living from non-living things by pupils using the seven characteristics of life (the knowledge component) and their ability to classify living organisms into groups (the technique component) and their ability to justify their decision (the (communication) skills component).

## CONCERNS ABOUT PRIMARY SCIENCE

Through the Science and Engineering Education Advisory Group (SEEAG), a group of leading Scottish scientists focused political attention upon science educational practice across schools as well as in initial teacher education by raising concerns about weaknesses in science, technology, engineering and mathematics (STEM) teaching, particularly within primary education (SEEAG, 2012). However, these concerns are not new. For example, Harlen et al. (1995) reported that 'research shows that in Scotland, primary teachers' confidence about teaching science and technology is less than for almost all other curriculum aspects' (p. 195). More recently, the 2007 *Scottish Survey of Achievement (SSA): Science* (the report of which was published in 2008) suggested that almost all of the primary teachers surveyed taught science to their own classes, with around 90 per cent of the teachers being fairly or very confident teaching biology topics, but far fewer were confident about teaching chemistry (60 per cent) or physics (just over half; www.gov.scot/Resource/Doc/226080/0061213.pdf). However, there has been no research since 2008 that focuses on primary teachers' confidence when teaching science. In fact, there has been very little Scottish research focused on primary science practice. In part this is due to the fact that science education research has moved towards a focus on primary teachers' attitudes to teaching science, coupled with a lack of funding for research in this area.

Various studies (e.g. Palmer, 2004) show a general low level of scientific literacy among pre-service and in-service primary teachers, and that these teachers tend to have negative attitudes towards science with these negative attitudes often emerging from poor experiences during their own education. Unfortunately, these negative attitudes often persist during pre-service teacher education (Tosun, 2000; Palmer, 2001). Osborne and Simon (1996) suggest that there is a correlation between teachers who lack ability, confidence and enthusiasm for science (or any other subject) and their use of less stimulating, didactic methods, and that these teachers tend to not respond effectively to children's questions and are more likely to have pupils with a poor attitude towards science. However, what is not clear from Osborne and Simon's analysis is whether this means that these teachers negatively influence pupils' attitudes, or that they teach pupils who already have existing negative attitudes. Evidence suggests that many primary teachers have an incomplete understanding of science concepts (van Aalderen-Smeets et al., 2012).

These concerns have perhaps been exacerbated recently, in response to Scotland's reported position within international league tables of pupil attainment. Many European governments have focused their attention upon the results of transnational comparison studies such as the Programme for International Student Assessment (PISA), which assess science, mathematics and reading (see Chapter 68). In terms of Scotland's performance in science, as assessed through PISA, there has been a decline in science scores from above the Organisation for Economic Co-operation and Development (OECD) average (514 to 513 from 2003 to 2012) to similar to the OECD average in 2015 with a score of 497 (www.gov.scot/Resource/0051/00511095.pdf). While these results correspond to the science performance of Scottish 15 year olds, as opposed to those for primary pupils, the science education these pupils experienced coincides with the implementation of the Curriculum for Excellence (CfE) 3–15 Science curriculum from 2010 until the present day. So it is perhaps reasonable to ask, 'Is this decline real, or is it an artefact of changes to assessment practices? If the decline is real then why has there been a decline in science performance?'

This situation perhaps masks some deeper concerns with Scottish science education that have a longer history than that encompassed by the CfE reform of the Science curriculum. For example, as far back as 1994, in a report entitled 'Effective learning and teaching in Scottish secondary schools: the sciences', Her Majesty's Inspectorate of Education suggested that science was often neglected in primary schools and acknowledged that science teaching in primary schools had not been taken up in a systematic way. In their impact report, *The Sciences 3–18* published in 2013, Education Scotland suggested that in practice, primary school science is too often predominantly or exclusively delivered through an interdisciplinary approach which lacks sufficient planning to ensure breadth, or for the development of children's knowledge and skills in a progressive way. It was also suggested that the contribution of the science element in children's broad general education was not always being met. This suggests that a deficit view of science education is not a new phenomenon.

## SCIENCE WITHIN PRIMARY INITIAL TEACHER EDUCATION CURRICULA

The place of science within primary ITE programmes has changed considerably over the last four years and must be seen within the overall context of the reform to ITE as directed by *Teaching Scotland's Future* (Donaldson, 2011) published by the Scottish Government. In *Teaching Scotland's Future*, Graham Donaldson argued for the replacement of the existing Primary Bachelor of Education (BEd) degree with a new undergraduate degree combining the study of education with wider university study (see Chapter 90 for more detailed discussion).

That said, there are two main entry routes into primary teaching in Scotland: either through a four-year undergraduate degree or a one-year Professional Graduate Diploma in Education (PGDE). The proportion of pre-service primary teachers entering the profession via the PGDE route is higher than that from the undergraduate route. In a typical year between 2001 and 2010, 60 per cent of the intake to primary teaching and 75 per cent of the intake to all programmes was through the PGDE route (Gray and Weir, 2014).

According to Donaldson in *Teaching Scotland's Future*, the BEd's 'specificity of purpose can lead to an over-emphasis on technical and craft skills at the expense of broader and more academically challenging areas of study' (Donaldson, 2011, p. 39). However, if the PGDE route accounts for a majority of teachers entering the profession, then the question must surely be asked, 'Why did Donaldson pay almost no attention to the structure and content of PGDE programmes?'

Within primary ITE curricula, the amount of time primary education students spend learning about science teaching within the primary context is low. For example, within our own institution (University of the West of Scotland, UWS) under the old BEd programme, all students experienced three compulsory Mathematics and Science modules over the first three years of the programme, which equated to seventy-two hours of face-to-face science teaching. Under the new Bachelor of Arts (BA) programme this has reduced to one compulsory module in sustainable development. Students also have the opportunity to study optional modules with a science focus, but the number of students choosing these options is low. This situation is mirrored across the other ITE institutions in Scotland.

Within the PGDE Primary programmes, students' experience of primary science varies considerably. However, within UWS, PGDE Primary students receive approximately ten hours of dedicated face-to-face science teaching. It would be fair to suggest that, despite the increased political emphasis on science as a priority within the primary setting, initial teacher education curricula do not place a similar emphasis on the direct teaching of primary science. However, we acknowledge that similar arguments can be advanced for many other curricular areas.

## PRIMARY SCHOOL SCIENCE PRACTICE

Part of the problem in understanding what happens in practice is the dearth of research into what actually happens in the primary classroom with respect to the teaching of science. A combination of personal experiences of working in primary schools, numerous visits to primary schools supporting students in ITE, and regular communication with practising headteachers and class teachers reinforces the view that too often the teaching of science does not enjoy the status consistent with Education Scotland's view that 'recognises science as a priority ... [and that] quality provision must be evident *all the time*' (Scottish Government, 2014, pp. 4–7, emphasis added).

There are a number of reasons why the teaching of science may be either ineffectively taught or be subjugated within the curriculum. Experience indicates that, although there are many examples of excellent primary science teaching throughout Scotland, too often what transpires is that lessons are not engaging, sufficiently challenging or suitably situated within the life- of children, with an over-reliance on a whole school 'Science Week' approach. One potential reason for less than effective teaching of primary science is a lack of teacher subject knowledge. When asked directly about a lack of teachers' science subject knowledge, a number of headteachers expressed their frustration over the lack of science expertise in primary schools arguing that having at least one teacher with an appropriate science degree might address the situation. Entry requirements to primary ITE programmes in Scotland do not currently specify a need for a science qualification.

A UK-wide national audit reinforced this view, arguing that the teaching of science is better quality where primary teachers hold qualifications in science (Ofsted, 2010). Where science is less well taught, a recurring theme is the significant number of teachers who express concern over their own personal lack of confidence in teaching the subject. Teacher and subject knowledge confidence is crucial when teaching science and the Education Scotland (2013) *Sciences 3–18* report substantiates the point that there are significant levels of low confidence within the profession. In addition to the above concerns, headteachers have raised concerns over a lack of support and training for teachers in facilitating practical work in science. In a report published in 2014 (https://www.rsb.org.uk/policy/education-policy/school-policy/scottish-science-education), the Scottish Learned Societies Group found insufficient access to training and support for the delivery of practical primary science lessons. These factors continue to create an environment in many Scottish primary schools that is at odds with the Scottish Government's (2014) vision that 'Curriculum for Excellence is enabling new and exciting opportunities to make school science education stimulating and exciting for all pupils.' There is an independent evaluation currently being carried out on the Scottish Schools Education Research Centre's (SSERC) Primary Science Mentoring scheme which will provide useful insight into current practice.

As well as the challenges discussed above, other wider policy guidance is also impacting significantly on the teaching and delivery of effective science in primary schools. The Scottish Government's (2015) Attainment Challenge and Glasgow City Council's Improvement Challenge (2015) are examples of policy cited by headteachers as having an impact on the teaching of primary science. The purpose of the attainment challenge is to accelerate targeted improvement activity in literacy, numeracy and health and wellbeing in specific areas of Scotland, and focusing more heavily on these core subjects could result in science being taught less often in primary schools. Headteachers suggest that the focus on 'closing the gap' in these curricular areas is seen as the priority, and consequently, existing significant and exciting science development in their schools has been affected negatively.

## CONCLUDING REMARKS

It is clear that in practice, the teaching of science within primary schools is not occurring in a consistent and sustained manner nationally (despite there being some areas of excellent practice) and that often science is not taught as a discrete subject. If the quality and quantity of science teaching within primary schools is to improve, greater emphasis needs to be placed on the development of primary education ITE students' own science learning within pre-registration education. In addition, steps need to be taken to address the concerns of practitioners regarding the under-resourcing of primary science and the availability, access and variety of quality career-long professional learning opportunities in the area of primary science. However, it is critically important to remember that well planned and implemented science teaching has the potential to facilitate and support pupils' progression in terms of literacy, numeracy and health and wellbeing and, as such, provides an excellent context for learning which might help to narrow the attainment gap over the years ahead.

## REFERENCES

Donaldson, G. (2011) *Teaching Scotland's Future: Report of a Review of Teacher Education in Scotland*. Edinburgh: Scottish Government.

Education Scotland (2009a) *Curriculum for Excellence: Sciences: Principles and Practice*. Online at https://education.gov.scot/Documents/sciences-pp.pdf

Education Scotland (2009b) *Curriculum for Excellence: Sciences: Experiences and Outcomes*. Online at https://www.education.gov.scot/Documents/sciences-eo.pdf

Education Scotland (2013) *The Sciences 3–18*. Online at https://education.gov.scot/improvement/Documents/Sciences/SCI14_SciencesCurriculumImpact/sciences-3-to-18-2013-update.pdf

Gray, D. and Weir, D. (2014) 'Retaining public and political trust: teacher education in Scotland', *Journal of Education for Teaching: International Research and Pedagogy*, 40 (5), 569–87, doi: 10.1080/02607476.2014.956541

Harlen, W., Holroyd, C. and Byrne, M. (1995) 'Confidence and understanding in teaching science and technology in primary schools'. Scottish Council for Research in Education. University of Glasgow.

Ofsted (2010) *Successful Science: An Evaluation of Science Education in England 2007–2010*. Manchester: Ofsted.

Osborne, J. and Simon, S. (1996) 'Primary science: past and future directions', *Studies in Science Education*, 26, 99–147.

Palmer, D. H. (2001) 'Factors contributing to attitude exchange amongst pre-service elementary teachers', *Science Education*, 86, 122–38.

Palmer, D. H. (2004) 'Situational interest and the attitudes towards science of primary teacher education students', *International Journal of Science Education*, 26, 895–908.

Science and Engineering Education Advisory Group (2012) *Supporting Scotland's STEM Education and Culture: Second Report*. Online at www.scotland.gov.uk/Resource/0038/00388616.pdf

Scottish Executive (2006) *A Curriculum for Excellence: Progress and Proposals. A Paper from the Curriculum Review Programme Board*. Online at www.gov.scot/resource/doc/98764/0023924.pdf

Scottish Government (2014) *Improving STEM (Science, Technology, Engineering and Mathematics) Education*. Online at www.gov.scot/Topics/Education/Schools/curriculum/ACE/Science

Tosun, T. (2000) 'The beliefs of pre-service elementary teachers toward science and science teaching', *School Science and Mathematics*, 100, 374–9.

van Aalderen-Smeets, S. I., Walma van der Molen, J. H. and Asma, L. J. (2012) 'Primary teachers' attitudes toward science: a new theoretical framework', *Science Education*, 96 (1), 158–82.

# 37

# Social Studies

*Juliet Hancock, Lynne Robertson and Anne Robertson*

## INTRODUCTION

The evolving nature of Social Studies within the Scottish education context over the past decades, to its current position as a discrete curricular area, is well recognised, incorporating history, geography and modern studies (see Her Majesty's Inspectorate of Education, 2008; Simpson, 2013). The intention in this chapter is not to document detail that has already been covered elsewhere regarding this evolution. Instead, the chapter seeks to shine light on Social Studies in Scotland today, through considering its purposes and the possibilities inherent within Social Studies as a curricular area. The chapter exemplifies what it might look like to make Social Studies really *work* within early years and primary classrooms, and beyond, through one example of a historical event in Scotland's past. Some consideration is given to the current policy context in Scotland, insofar as it exerts an influence on practice.

## WHAT ARE SOCIAL STUDIES?

With the above in mind, it is pertinent to begin with the question of, 'What are social studies?' Authorities in the field have long debated the dimensions of an appropriate definition of social studies and differing perspectives are taken both nationally and internationally. The emphasis is variously placed upon nurturing civic competence, the development of pupils' understanding of societal contexts, to a non-statutory approach to citizenship learning and teaching in schools (DfES, 2012), and the correct use of social science terms, theories and methodologies in interpreting the world (Moos, et al., 2009). Social Studies are presented in Scotland's Curriculum for Excellence (CfE) through the themes People, Past Events and Societies; People, Place and Environment; and People, Society, Economy and Business. Education Scotland states that:

> Through social studies, children and young people develop their understanding of the world by learning about other people and their values, in different times, places and circumstances; they also develop their understanding of their environment and of how it has been shaped. (Education Scotland, 2013)

## A SCOTTISH APPROACH TO SOCIAL STUDIES?

Through the detailing of principles and practice within social studies, we perhaps come closer to defining a clear Scottish approach, whereby a significant purpose of social studies is that, alongside the development of understanding cited above, 'comes the opportunity and ability to influence events by exercising informed and responsible citizenship' (Education Scotland, 2013). In order to be active and engaged citizens, however, it has been argued that citizenship needs to be more 'explicitly connected with wider social and political action and with a view of democracy as requiring more than just active, committed and responsible citizens' (Biesta, 2008, p. 50). The issue has also been raised, albeit in the Canadian context (Gibson, 2012), that learners themselves say they are unaware that they are learning about citizenship, with the accompanying sense that, as a subject area, social studies lacked real relevance to their lives.

If social studies is to achieve its stated aim of promoting informed and responsible citizenship and also to build the understanding needed to influence and act on a wider social and political stage, then learners need to not only learn a body of knowledge, but also to be able to think and act responsively to issues in a diverse and interdependent world. These skills and abilities underlie good citizenship, and make social studies education part of a process of building informed, engaged and active learners. This, in turn, has the potential to develop the content of the Social Studies curriculum into the most inclusive of all school subjects (Ross, 2001, p. 19), as well as one of the most relevant and engaging. Social studies can directly support learners as they engage critically with classroom or school issues, or challenges in their local or wider community. Connections between current issues and the past are there to be made, whether learners are exploring sustainability, democratic processes, human rights, their own immediate communities, the distant or more immediate past, whether Scotland wide or on a more global arena. A reaffirmation of the contribution of social studies to learners' understandings of these and other issues must include needing to learn how to reflect critically on their place in the world and to consider what these issues mean to them.

## MAKING SOCIAL STUDIES WORK

Common across all three of the CfE Social Studies themes previously mentioned is the concept of place. Geographic information can be seen to have an intrinsic value in understanding place as it links location to people and events, creating place. Geographic information can visually illustrate what is happening, where, how and why, and can reveal the impact on people at that location. It can provide insight into what happened in the past, what is happening now and what is likely to happen in the future. The ability to use the properties of geographic information to communicate, reason and solve problems, or spatial literacy, encourages critical thinking and inquiry-based teaching, and is present as a concept, if not explicitly stated within experiences and outcomes, in the early years and primary stages of Curriculum for Excellence.

Large-scale mapping and aerial photography are types of geographic information that can assist learners to understand their sense of place. The detail represented within large-scale mapping can assist a young learner to identify familiar places, for example building footprints of their school, playground, local park, pathways and home. When different types of geographic information are captured digitally with the same geographic referencing system, powerful visualisations enable young learners to view different types of source information for the same place. They gain a deeper understanding through comparing and contrasting different digital geographic information, for example a modern conventional map, an aerial photography and a historical map. In addition, such technology often provides learners with the ability to add their own information (labels, marker points, photographs, graphs, lines, areas) reflecting their interpretation of the event or item studied. One of the essential objectives of the Digital Learning and Teaching Strategy is to ensure that digital technology is a central consideration in all areas of curriculum and assessment delivery. In the context of the Social Studies curriculum and its focus upon place, examining what this essential objective might look like within early years and primary helps to exemplify the potential connections which can make social studies work.

## EXPLORING WHAT THIS MIGHT LOOK LIKE IN PRACTICE

The sinking of the HMS *Iolaire* on 1 January 1919, with the loss of 205 young men returning from the First World War, remains one of the worst maritime disasters in British waters, and should qualify as a significant First World War event. A common approach to teaching such an event may focus upon a date–time recount of the event. However, place-based interpretations of the event afford learners a greater degree of critical thinking and self-interpretation. Figures 37.1a and 37.1b show different interpretations of the same event.

Could today's teachers, and learners, take a similar approach to leveraging geographic information and associated digital technologies when considering Social Studies topics such as:

- Past
    - Was our school the site of a poorhouse in the Victorian era? If so, where would I have gone to school?
    - Are there stories in my family about the local impact of the First and Second World Wars? Did the stories take place 'somewhere' and can that place be identified today?

- Environment
    - In our town, have people's homes or local shops been flooded? Why is flooding happening?
    - What wildlife likes our playground or school buildings? Does it live here, does it visit each day or only at certain times of year? Why?

- Society/economy
    - What facilities can our village/town/local place offer a Syrian refugee family?
    - What happened to the corner shop my grandparents remember, and why?
    - What journey does a pint of milk make to come to our school?

These examples of possible aspects for enquiry are not necessarily new in themselves. The manner in which they are explored within the classroom and the emphasis upon critical thinking is something which needs further attention. However, the approach allows us to move closer to Social Studies as a significant contribution to learners being able to think and act responsively to address issues in the diverse, interdependent and ever-changing world in which they not only learn, but in which they live. Are today's teachers able to take advantage of such approaches to enquiry and to integrate, in the pedagogical sense, the links

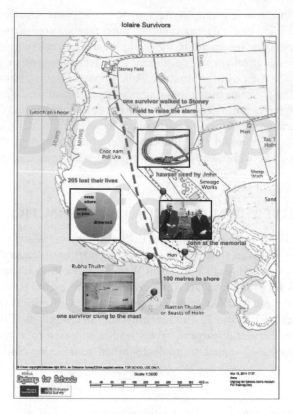

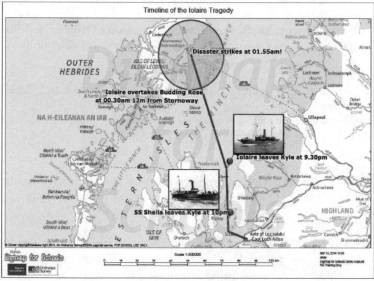

**Figure 37.1    Interpretations of the sinking of the HMS *Iolaire***

Source: Images produced using Digimap for Schools, contains OS data © Crown copyright and database right (2014).

and connections made within social studies? Dewey suggested that 'the increasing emphasis upon them [social studies] ought to be a means by which the school system meets the challenge of democracy' (Dewey, 2008, p. 185).

Having explored the above, it is useful to briefly comment on the current policy context within Scotland, which exerts its own influence upon thinking and practice within schools. This is significant, in part to the previous discussion of citizenship, but also in relation to defining the purposes of Social Studies, in order that as a curriculum area it is not just presented through what might be socially approved idea or norms (Ross, 2001).

## MAKING CONNECTIONS: THE POLICY CONTEXT

Whilst Curriculum for Excellence has continued to develop, the policy landscape in Scotland has itself been changing. The prevailing government has sought to highlight the issues of inequity in both the wider Scottish society and in educational attainment, between those from the most advantaged and least advantaged backgrounds. This would appear to present an opportunity for a significant contribution from Social Studies, given its focus on citizenship in the Scottish context and the potential for providing stimulating and relevant content for children and young people which can help them to engage in their learning.

Linked to the above, and launched in January 2015, the National Improvement Framework (NIF; see Chapter 71) set out four key priorities, one of which is to close the attainment gap between the most and least advantaged children. This has been prompted further in the wake of the independent Organisation for Economic Co-operation and Development (OECD) report into the Scottish education system, the findings of which included a focus on closing the gap and raising the bar, simultaneously. The launch of the attainment challenge coincided with the development of the NIF, with the stated aims of achieving equity in attainment outcomes and closing the poverty-related attainment gap. The challenge was accompanied by £750 million, targeted on supporting pupils in the local authorities of Scotland with the highest concentrations of deprivation. Linked to attainment, in September 2016, Scotland's Deputy First Minister launched the Digital Learning and Teaching Strategy. This aims to create the conditions to allow all of Scotland's educators, learners and parents to take full advantage of the opportunities offered by digital technology in order to raise attainment, ambition and opportunities for all. However, the OECD report, coupled with the NIF, have led directly to the commencement in 2017 of standardised assessments in literacy and numeracy for primaries 1, 4 and 7 and secondary 3. Together with the ongoing emphasis on literacy, numeracy, health and wellbeing, and science, technology, engineering and mathematics (STEM), this has potential implications for those curricular areas which are not seen as priority.

## CONCLUDING THOUGHTS

It would therefore appear timely, within the context of policy relating so specifically to issues of inequity, to reinvigorate discussion as to the potentially negative impact of privileging certain curricular areas above others. In doing so, the need for a stronger focus upon the merits of other curricular areas becomes very clear, in order to effectively address learning, both in the manner and for the reasons that current policy suggests. The sorts of complex questions and ideas rooted within Social Studies as a curricular area ideally situates them for the critical thinking which enables learners to be informed, to question their social and political world, to be able to consider a range of opinions, draw their own conclusions, consider themselves, their communities, the welfare of others and, ultimately, to be not just responsible, but active and engaged as citizens.

Just as differing perspectives exist in relation to the exact definition and purpose of social studies, so too are there different approaches to its interpretation and negotiation in practice across the sectors. However, where a clear purpose within the teaching of social studies does not exist, Dewey warned that 'the supposed end for which they [the social studies] were introduced – the development of more intelligent citizenship in all the ranges of citizenship – will be missed' (Dewey, 2008, p. 185), leading to learner perceptions of irrelevance as raised earlier. The disparate and yet intertwined content and process of the social enquiries that can be stimulated by social studies, as illustrated by the possibilities outlined, can present as a vibrant and vital part of the early years and primary curriculum in Scotland. They offer the opportunity for citizenship-focused education but also the opportunity to learn about how and why it is important to consider multiple perspectives, and to explore contemporary topics such as Islamophobia, conflict, challenges of migration, racism, and aspects of democracy and citizenship. Explicit connections and a focus on the development of critical thinking should therefore be placed at the heart of approaches to social studies which might be considered to 'work' best.

## REFERENCES

Biesta, G. J. J. (2008) 'What kind of citizen? What kind of democracy? Citizenship education and the Scottish Curriculum for Excellence', *Scottish Educational Review*, 40 (2), 38–52.

Dewey, J. (2008) 'The challenge of democracy to education', in J. A. Boydston (ed.), *John Dewey: The Later Works, 1935–1937*, Vol. 11. Carbondale, IL: Southern Illinois University Press, pp. 181–90.

DfES (2012) National Curriculum in England, Department of Education. Online at https://www.gov.uk/government/collections/national-curriculum

Education Scotland (2013) *Social Studies: Principles and Practice*. Livingston: Education Scotland.

Gibson, S. (2012) '"Why Do We Learn This Stuff"? Students' Views on the Purpose of Social Studies', *Canadian Social Studies*, 45 (1), 43–58.

Harris, R. and Foreman-Peck, L. (2004) '"Stepping into other people's shoes": teaching and assessing empathy in the Secondary History Curriculum', *International Journal of Historical Learning, Teaching and Research*, 4 (2), 1–14.

Her Majesty's Inspectorate of Education (2008) *Developing the Four Capacities through Social Subjects: Focussing on Successful Learners in Primary Schools*. Livingston: HMIE.

Moos, L., Krejsler, J. and Fibæk Laursen, P. (2009) 'Denmark', in J. Scheerens (ed.), *Informal learning of Active Citizenship at School. An International Comparative Study of Seven European Countries*. Dordrecht: Springer.

Ross, E. W. (2001) 'The struggle for the social studies curriculum', in E. W. Ross (ed.), *The Social Studies Curriculum: Purposes, Problems, and Possibilities*. New York: SUNY Press, pp. 19–41.

Simpson, F. (2013) 'Sciences, social studies and technologies', in T. G. K. Bryce, W. M. Humes, D. Gillies and A. Kennedy (eds), *Scottish Education, Fourth Edition: Referendum*. Edinburgh: Edinburgh University Press, pp. 470–4.

# 38

# Technologies

*Susan McLaren*

## INTRODUCTION

Since the introduction of Technology Education to the Scottish school curriculum twenty-five years ago, there have been various editions of national guidelines. The timeline includes:

- Guidelines for 5–14 Environmental Studies (SOED, 1993) providing a shared rationale for Science, Social Studies, Health Education, Information and Communication Technology (ICT) and Technology Education;
- Technology Education for Scottish Schools (SCCC, 1996) introducing the concept of Technological capability, the four mutually supportive aspects of technological sensitivity, technological creativity, technological perspective and technological confidence;
- *National Guidelines for 5–14 Environmental Studies: Society, Science and Technology Education* (Learning and Teaching Scotland, 2000);
- Curriculum for Excellence (CfE) Technologies (Scottish Government, 2009) encompassing: Technological Developments for Society; ICT to enhance learning, Business, Computing Science, Food and Textiles; and Craft, Design, Engineering and Graphics contexts for developing technological knowledge and skills; and currently
- CfE Technologies (Education Scotland, 2017) encompassing: Technological Developments for Society and Business; Digital Literacy; Computing Science; Food and Textiles; and Craft, Design, Engineering and Graphics.

Throughout the various iterations and reconfigurations, there has been some consistency regarding the kinds of technological experiences to which young people are entitled, that is, practical designing, making and appraising; exploration of technologies in the world as it is now; investigation of technologies past and future; and education for sustainability.

## TECHNOLOGIES IN THE EARLY AND PRIMARY YEARS: A SCOTTISH CONSTRUCT

Technology Education, or in current CfE nomenclature, Technologies, has been hampered by what appears to be a limited appreciation of what this area of learning involves and the contribution it offers. The Technologies impact review, published under the title *Building Society* (Education Scotland, 2015) identified 'building the technologies brand' as one of three most urgent actions required. Technology Education and/or Technologies, it seems, is all too often associated as being 'something to do with computers'. There have been several attempts at clarification. Efforts at appeasing the various traditional secondary school stake-holders and constructs of Home Economics and Technical Education, are evident. Initially, the 5–14 Environmental Studies guidelines, published by the then Scottish Office Education Department in 1993 (SOED, 1993) included ICT and Health Education, although the latter were removed in the subsequent reconfiguration which created *5–14 Environmental Studies: Society, Science and Technology* (Learning and Teaching Scotland, 2000). These three were to be considered as 'stand-alone' learning areas, bound by a common rationale, while promoting opportunities for interdisciplinary learning.

It can be argued that of all the eight learning areas of CfE, Technologies has proved to be subject to the most scrutiny leading to revision, redesign and reconfiguration. However, the underpinning philosophy of creating learning which nurtures habits of mind such as designerly and enterprising thinking remain at the fore. Teaching and learning seeks to develop curiosity and confidence in using, appraising and creating technologies for different needs and wants (i.e. systems, artefacts, products and environments). Technologies are very much to be rooted in real-time, real-world, creative and problem-solving contexts.

Generally, Technologies as a learning area within CfE continues the idea initially introduced in 5–14 Environmental Studies (SOED, 1993) of promoting the development of informed attitudes. Teachers are to help learners appreciate that although technological solutions may be acceptable to some, they may be unacceptable to others. A seminal publication in 1996 from the Scottish Consultative Council on the Curriculum (SCCC), *Technology Education in Scottish Schools*, describes four mutually supportive and interdependent aspects of technological capability as 'technological perspective', 'technological confidence', 'technological creativity' and 'technological sensitivity'. The last being a habit of mind which asks questions about, and reflects on, social, moral, ethical, aesthetic and environmental issues, as well as technical and economic aspects of all technological activity, past, present and proposed. This includes recognition of the provenance of resources and energy transfer used in design and make activities. Learners are to become more aware of the full life cycle of a product, for example from inception through manufacture, transportation, marketing, and use, and they should understand the differences between waste/disposal/reusing/repurposing and recycling. This thinking encourages learners to appreciate that all technological developments have consequences for people, society and the environment of the world. This has remained a core to learning through and about the Technologies over the past twenty-five years.

After different configurations, following political and factional debates, the Technologies (Scottish Government, 2017) currently has five organisers. These are intended to serve as guidelines to inform planning for technological-related learning, teaching and assessment for learners in early years through to third year of secondary school.

- Technological Developments in Society and Business:
    - awareness of technological developments (past, present and future), including how they work;
    - impact, contribution and relationship of technologies on business, the economy, politics and the environment.

- Computing Science:
  - understanding the world through computational thinking;
  - understanding and analysing computing technology;
  - designing, building and testing computing solutions;
  - exploring Computing Science concepts, processes and systems.

- Food and Textiles:
  - This 'shares' many aspects with food-related learning in Health and Wellbeing and specific technological attitudes, skills and knowledge only become clearer when referring to experiences and outcomes and the suggested benchmarks which are offered to support professional judgements about the achievements of a learner.

- Craft, Design, Engineering and Graphics:
  - designing and constructing models/products;
  - exploring uses of materials;
  - representing ideas, concepts and products through a variety of graphic media;
  - application of Engineering.

- Digital Literacy which, as its predecessor, ICT to Enhance Learning, is considered to be at the 'heart of all learning'. Whilst located in CfE Technologies (Scottish Government, 2017), Digital Literacy is a permeating responsibility throughout learning and not to be considered as a distinct context. The significant learning is planned around these aspects:
  - using digital products and services in a variety of contexts to achieve a purposeful outcome;
  - searching, processing and managing information responsibly;
  - cyber resilience and internet safety.

In summary, the principles underpinning the Technologies planning, teaching and learning are to enable children and young people to be informed, skilled, thoughtful, adaptable and enterprising citizens, and to:

- develop understanding of the role and impact of technologies in changing and influencing societies;
- contribute to building a better world by taking responsible ethical actions to improve their lives, the lives of others and the environment;
- gain the skills and confidence to embrace and use technologies now and in the future, at home, at work and in the wider community;
- become informed consumers and producers who have an appreciation of the merits and impacts of products and services;
- be capable of making reasoned choices relating to the environment, to sustainable development and to ethical, economic and cultural issues;
- broaden understanding of the role that ICT has in Scotland and in the global community;
- broaden understanding of the applications and concepts behind technological thinking, including the nature of engineering and the links between the technologies and the sciences;
- experience work-related learning, establish firm foundations for lifelong learning and, for some, for specialised study and a diverse range of careers (https://education.gov.scot/Documents/technologies-pp.pdf).

## VALUE AND PURPOSE: CONTRIBUTION TO LEARNING

Education through, for and about technologies provides a context for learning which is founded on the learner's observation of his or her surroundings and experiences, and broadening to a more global understanding of the role of technologies, the ways they are brought into being and the purposes they serve. Learners engage in real-world contexts and processes to develop the technological attitudes, skills and knowledge (T-ASK) necessary to reflect on, interpret, analyse and critique what they see, perceive and experience. Progression in terms of T-ASK enables learners to develop an increased awareness of the interdependency of people and the environment, and understand the relationships between social, economic, cultural, physical and technological factors. The potential of the Technologies curriculum lies in the contextualising and structuring of learning experiences to increase awareness of technologies, stimulate curiosity and encourage appraisal of the applications of technologies, and provide challenging, open-ended, design and/or problem-solving opportunities. This requires reference to the significant aspects of learning (Education Scotland, 2016b) and interpretation of the guidelines in practice. Technologies education is intended to offer opportunities for practical and active learning, for example when adopting a design, make and critique approach. At times, this results in successful learning being determined by the *completion* of an outcome (e.g. a product, system or environment). However, more important are the intellectual processes and creative endeavours through which valuable and authentic learning is achieved in the *journey* to completion. Confusion in purpose arises when 'doing' technologies dominates teacher thinking and planning. This can render technologies as 'tasks', 'activities' or, at worst, reduce technologies to 'constructing a model'.

Technologies offers opportunities for learners to engage with uncertainty, take ownership for their own ideas, make design decisions and engage in creative visualisation and modelling from their mind's eye through to a physical manifestation for others to experience, taste, test and review. However, learners should also experience 'making without designing' and 'designing without making', to complement 'designing and making', working solo, in pairs or in groups. Learners should be considering users, functions, needs and wants, and be involved in justifying, and communicating their ideas to different audiences, including 'client groups'. Learning can range from making toast for very specific personal tastes and preferences to proposing the siting of a wind farm to generate energy for a village. As such, Technologies lends itself well to 'elegant fit' interdisciplinary learning with maths, science, art and design, and social subjects. Currently a great deal of attention is given, nationally and internationally, to science, technology, engineering, and mathematics (STEM) education. Politically STEM is considered to be an economic driver, with numerous employment opportunities related to STEM education. The drive to increase interest and enthusiasm for STEM from early years through to training and graduate level is considered as urgent and high priority. However, all too often STEM has become shorthand for Science education, and Technology is conceptualised as computing or ICT. Indeed, government-funded teacher professional learning tends to focus on Science Education, Digital Literacy and Computing. Although there is great potential in planning for interdisciplinary learning through a STEM education framework, this needs to be underpinned with a well-informed rationale.

## PLANNING FOR TECHNOLOGIES

Jones and Moreland (2004, p. 123) caution that the 'construction of a knowledge base for teachers is pivotal for effective technology teaching'. They agree with Shulman's (1987) emphasis on the teacher requiring a secure understanding of what is to be learned, what is to be taught and skill in planning for development of new learning which is related to the prior knowledge. However, Fox–Turnbull (2012) identified difficulties in planning based on prior learning: each individual learner has their own personal, social capital related to the technologies, so too has the teacher. Teachers need to consider conceptual, procedural and emotional ways of knowing and also take into account of societal, cultural, ethical, technical, economic and environmental values. If teachers themselves are insecure with the technologies-related content and learning goals, then they will encounter difficulties in identifying authentic learning purposes, planning and scaffolding learner progression. Jones and Moreland (2004) discuss issues arising when teachers' interventions focus on the social and managerial aspects of technology tasks rather than offering prompts and feedback which enable learners to progress in their technological-related skills and knowledge, and conceptual and strategic understanding.

Planning for learning and teaching draws on a wide range of strategies; the more secure the teacher is with the underpinning technological content, the more appropriate and creative the pedagogical choices will be (Shulman, 1987). The approach(es) adopted (e.g. guided enquiry, apprenticeship, discovery; whole class, solo, paired or group) will also depend on the focus of specific learning intentions and the teacher's understanding of the funds of knowledge the learners bring to their learning. The aim is for learners to develop their repertoire of T-ASK through scaffolded experiences and applying their learning to increasingly complex and/or unfamiliar scenarios and design challenges. A useful planning model involves three different components: 'creative practical (*aka* Big) tasks, proficiency (*aka* Small) tasks and case study tasks' (SCCC, 1996; Barlex, 2011). A balance of these different types of tasks, from early years through to the time of transition to secondary school, will enable learners to develop an increasingly varied core of technological skills and knowledge which inform their design decision making and actions. Indeed, when planning for design-centred Big Tasks, teachers explicitly determine the design decisions which the learners are to make. These can be helpful to frame the learning and inform formative judgements and summative assessments on learner performance and achievement.

In addition to the five organisers, the large number of 'experiences and outcomes' and 'benchmarks' which cluster around the thirteen 'significant aspects of learning' there are cross-cutting aspects of learning for learners to develop and demonstrate:

- knowledge and understanding of the big ideas and concepts of the technologies;
- curiosity, exploration and problem-solving skills;
- planning and organisational skills in a range of contexts;
- creativity and innovation;
- skills in using tools, equipment, software, graphic media and materials;
- skills in collaborating, leading and interacting with others;
- critical thinking through exploration and discovery within a range of learning contexts;
- discussion and debate;
- searching and retrieving information to inform thinking within diverse learning contexts;
- making connections between specialist skills developed within learning and skills for work;
- evaluating products, systems and services;

- presentation and communication skills;
- awareness of sustainability.

Unsurprisingly, assessment against the various levels of CfE Technologies as illustrated by the current benchmarks (Education Scotland, 2017; see Chapter 68 in this text) is not without issue. The very nature of Technologies as a learning area could be undermined by a reductionist approach to assessment against atomistic 'benchmarks'. Such an approach to assessment is not conducive to the underpinning ideas on which Technologies is based. Learning thrives on creativity and encourages learners to cope with open-ended design challenges, seek resolutions and explore alternatives. Such learning encourages learner autonomy and informed decision making. The concepts of holism through systems thinking, designerly performance and practical action will be all too easily lost if teachers attempt to track progress against each and every benchmark. The advice offered is that the benchmarks are to ensure there are no major gaps in learning across the major organisers in each curriculum area and they exist 'to support holistic assessment approaches across learning. They should not be ticked off individually for assessment purposes' (Education Scotland, 2017, p. 2).

## CONCLUSION

The type of learning described here may prove to be too messy and too uncertain for some, challenging a teacher's sense of 'control'. Technologies education does not manifest widely in primary schools across Scotland and as yet the root cause remains elusive. The learning is often a mutual experience for the learner and the teacher where the only difference is that the teacher is more aware of the learning that may be encountered along the designerly journey. Learners are motivated to drive their own learning on a 'need to know', 'need to do', 'need to practice', 'need to ask' and 'need to think' basis (McLaren and Stables, 2008). When carefully planned and creatively presented, Technologies is well received and valued for the authentic learning it offers.

## REFERENCES

Barlex, D. (2011) 'Nuffield Design and Technology – a brief history', in Clare Benson and Julie Lunt (eds), *International Handbook of Primary Technology Education Sense*. Rotterdam: Sense Publishers, pp. 119–36.

Education Scotland (2009) *Curriculum for Excellence: Technologies Principles and Practices*. Online at https://education.gov.scot/Documents/technologies-pp.pdf

Education Scotland (2015) *Building Society: Young Peoples Experiences and Outcomes in the Technologies*, March. Online at http://dera.ioe.ac.uk/22403/2/TechnologiesImpactReport__tcm4-850866_Redacted.pdf

Education Scotland (2016a) *A Statement for Practitioners from HM Chief Inspector of Education*. Online at https://education.gov.scot/improvement/Documents/cfestatement.pdf

Education Scotland (2016b) *Professional Learning Paper: Significant Aspects of Learning. Assessing Progress and Achievement in the Technologies*, March. Online at https://blogs.glowscotland.org.uk/glowblogs/technologies/files/2016/06/TECHPLPMar2016_tcm4-746156.pdf

Education Scotland (2017) *Benchmarks: Technologies*. Online at https://education.gov.scot/improvement/Documents/TechnologiesBenchmarksPDF.pdf

Fox-Turnbull, W. (2012) 'Learning in technology', in P. J. Williams (ed.), *Technology Education for Teachers*. Dordrecht: Sense, Springer, pp. 55–92.

Jones, A. and Moreland, J. (2004) 'Enhancing practicing primary school teachers' pedagogical content knowledge in technology', *International Journal of Technology and Design Education*, 14 (2), 121–40.

Learning and Teaching Scotland (2000) *National Guidelines for 5–14 Environmental Studies: Society, Science and Technology Education.* Dundee: LTS.

McLaren, S. V. and Stables, K. (2008) 'Exploring key discriminators of progression: relationships between attitude, meta-cognition and performance of novice designers at a time of transition', *Design Studies*, 29 (2), 181–201.

SCCC (1996) *Technology Education in Scottish Schools: A Statement of Position.* Dundee: Scottish Consultative Council on the Curriculum.

Scottish Government (2017) *Curriculum for Excellence: Technologies: Principles and Practice.* Online at https://education.gov.scot/Documents/Technologies-es-os.pdf

Shulman, L. (1987) 'Knowledge and teaching: foundations of the new reform', *Harvard Educational Review*, 57 (1), 1–23.

SOED (1993) *National Guidelines: Environmental Studies 5–14.* Edinburgh: HMSO.

# VI

# CURRICULUM: SECONDARY

# 39

# Art and Design

*Diarmuid McAuliffe*

The following will try to 'story' the many narratives that have emerged within secondary art and design education since 2013. Questions such as what does it mean to be an effective art and design teacher in Scotland today and what will this generation of teachers bring to learners that will help to shape their futures well into this century? From the outset Henry Giroux's cautionary note is worth observing:

> No tradition should ever be seen as received, because when it is received it becomes sacred, its terms suggest reverence, silence, and passivity. Democratic societies are noisy. They're about traditions that need to be critically reevaluated by *each* generation. (Giroux, 1993, p. 156, emphasis added)

It could therefore be argued that Scotland has been far too 'sacred' around its school art and design traditions and complacent about the need for change and challenge. The narratives that I will draw on are informed by the profession in the following ways: (1) through their collective voice in the recently formed Network of Art Teachers Across Scotland (NATAS), and (2) through the Scottish Government in the form of the Scottish Qualifications Authority (SQA) and Education Scotland. The art teaching profession asserts through these networks that it needs time to reflect on the many changes that have occurred since 2013, some of which are listed below; and, whilst there is a call from teachers for a period of 'stability', there are at the same time clear fault lines emerging around Curriculum for Excellence (CfE), both within the subject and more generally, that now require attention. Yet many teachers are of the view that new national qualification courses are brilliant and that the freedom of broad general education (BGE) is achieving results. The Advanced Higher is now so experimental and exciting, but the pace of curricular reform is simply too slow and it may take a generation or two to see the same level of reform in S1–3. The following is a list of views that have been expressed by the profession in a recent public consultation exercise using both online and offline forums:

- less time afforded to art and design within the BGE phase;
- lack of advocacy in communicating the 'work relatedness' of art and design beyond the career route;
- increased 'gendering' of art and design;
- continued existence of formulaic practices in art and design;

- lack of engagement around the opportunities that interdisciplinary learning (IDL) offers such as the emerging STEM to STEAM strategy (see below);
- failure of the primary curriculum to engage pupils in enough art and design;
- poor pupil articulation around their art learning;
- continued existence of a single exam board;
- widening the creative scope within national and higher courses focusing on the quality of art and design work;
- lack of transparency from SQA in the marking of folios.

The reliability of the SQA Art and Design exam results along with the depletion of subject leadership in schools reflected the range of themes when the fourth edition of this book was published in 2013, but we are now in a different position with very few of the past certainties still in place. The 'direction of travel' for the subject is again available for the profession to determine and groups like NATAS are seizing the moment.

The time allocated to art and design in the S1–3 phase has diminished within the Expressive Arts subject cluster since CfE was first introduced and it is not uncommon for pupils to be now offered as little as one fifty-minute period per week. This reduction in time is primarily due to the increased pressure on schools to meet the physical educational requirements within Health and Wellbeing (HWB) set down by the Scottish Government. Ironically, Art and Design is not part of the HWB subject cluster (except for dance which sits between the two) and does not therefore benefit from the increased time allocation that this area has received, despite being a major contributor to pupils' health and wellbeing.

The failure of the primary curriculum to engage pupils in enough art and design is another cause of great concern to secondary art teachers and much now needs to be done at the primary level to find time for art and design making. This failure is due, I believe, to a crisis in communication. Historically, it has always been the case that one could almost gauge the 'health of a nation' by counting the resources it allocates to the arts. The subject in schools has always paid a heavy price at times of educational crisis, not least predicaments in literacy and numeracy, and the situation is no different today as we try to 'close the attainment gap' (see www.gov.scot/Resource/0051/00511513.pdf).

Making Thinking Visible (MTV) is a Harvard Graduate School initiative that has been adopted by the Scottish Government in its efforts to help close the 'attainment gap' and has been piloted throughout Ayrshire since 2016. It signifies the potential application of art and design visual methods to assist in the process of concept visualisation intended to aid learners' to 'see' resolution in their learning.

However, the notion of a broad general education in visual thinking has yet to be realised as children and young adults spend increasing amounts of time in the screen-based world and demands for more visual and multi-modal methods in teaching, learning and assessment are ever increasing. A good education in art and design should assist in helping pupils and young people to negotiate the visual world in a 'critical' way within and beyond the art department.

Poor articulation of pupils' own learning is commonplace within art departments and whilst learners may have had a wonderfully immersive and successful creative experience using materials and aesthetic ideas, they struggle at the end to verbally articulate this learning. This is one of the great challenges for the subject. Furthermore, the perception that art departments are the preserve of only those wishing to be artists or designers is

Table 39.1 Course entries and awards 2012–16

|  | 2012 | 2013 | 2014 | 2015 | 2016 |
|---|---|---|---|---|---|
| Advanced Higher | 1,415 | 1,494 | 1,393 | 1,450 | 1,422 |
| Higher | 7,019 | 6,494 | 6,392 | 4,125 | 5,500 |
|  | 21%M | 19%M | 18%M | 21%M | 19%M |
|  | 79%F | 81%F | 82%F | 79%F | 81%F |
| Standard Grade/ | 11,259 (SG) | 7,760 | 9,104 (N5) | 10,150 | 9,650 |
| National 5 (SG)/(N5) |  |  |  |  |  |
|  |  |  | 21%M | 21%M | 29%M |
|  |  |  | 79%F | 79%F | 71%F |

Note: M = Male; F = Female

Source: https://www.sqa.org.uk/sqa/80674.html

very misguided, as is the view that, if you 'cannae draw', there is little point in being there. Ask any S2

> why they are not continuing with art and design and they will talk about the lack of opportunity to do fun projects … the emphasis on drawing and on writing, the lack of ICT opportunities and the fact that they don't 'see' the point of the subject. (Coles, 2012)

## THE GENDERING OF ART AND DESIGN

According to the National 5 statistics, some 80 per cent of candidates taking Art and Design today are female (https://www.sqa.org.uk/sqa/80674.html; see Table 39.1). Boys have, for many years now, been abandoning the subject at a significant rate both in Scotland and across the UK (Coles, 2012). This has created an imbalance that would seem to suggest there is possibly an unconscious gender bias operating within art departments that is distorting the curriculum in favour of girls (manifest in the large concentration of fashion-related projects).

This gender split has become the norm for those studying an expressive arts subject; it is, however, particularly problematic when the same gender divide applies to those who teach the subject. Recruitment of males into Art and Design teacher education courses has become increasingly difficult with only one in twenty applicants succeeding to become teachers of art (according to UWS recruitment statistics). Yet, we do see a more equal gender distribution when we consider Higher Photography, which in 2016 had 58 per cent male candidates (ibid.). The use of new media and new technologies, engagement in three-dimensional work and the provision of different approaches to drawing seem to be strategies that interest boys and these are currently lacking in Scottish art and design departments. We continue to have an over-reliance on drawing and painting and 'linear methods of recording and outcomes which are cloned and similar' (Coles, 2012, p. 6). We should endeavour to make the curriculum more 'work related' – the use of design and craft can appeal to boys. Animation and film-making have clear pathways to careers in the creative industries, which may attract many more boys into the subject.

## NETWORK OF ART TEACHERS ACROSS SCOTLAND

The University of the West of Scotland (UWS) founded the Network of Art Teachers Across Scotland (NATAS) in 2016 (see https://natas.live/2016/08/16/network-of-art-teachers-across-scotland/). This group, which comprises over 400 teachers and gallery educators from throughout Scotland, was set up in order to provide a framework for subject-specific professional development and provide practice-based networking opportunities linked to the cultural sector, events, initiatives and festivals across Scotland. It is also intended to serve as a lobbying group on behalf of teachers that would voice their concerns to government and especially the SQA. The National Society for Education in Art and Design (NSEAD), a UK body, has partnered with NATAS on all of its public events thus far.

## HOW GOOD IS OUR SCHOOL?

The assessment matrix, *How Good is Our School? Version 4* (HGIOS4), has only recently had 'creativity' added to the list of indicators which Her Majesty's Inspectorate of Education (HMIe) now use when evaluating how good a school is doing (see https://education.gov. scot/improvement/Pages/frwk2hgios.aspx). This is undoubtedly helpful to the subject as management is now required to ensure that creativity as an attribute is embedded across the whole school and, whilst art and design does not have a monopoly in this area, we are in many ways ahead of others. Art and design teachers should therefore be taking full advantage of this opportunity in privileging creativity in subject teaching and discouraging formulaic outcomes. The SQA are fully behind this initiative and hopefully we will see this indicator as a potential 'game changer' for the subject.

## FROM STEM TO STEAM

There is growing interest across the developed world in using art and design thinking to help 'traditional mainstream thinking' associated with science, technology, engineering and mathematics (STEM) advance towards a more 'flipped' progressive approach of STEAM, which is STEM with the inclusion of art. Art gives visibility to STEM subjects but its development is regrettably in its infancy in Scotland. Evidence from the US and elsewhere suggests we should be seizing this opportunity to demonstrate the subjects' wider applicability to life and learning, giving new relevance to art and design in this very competitive and market-driven school environment.

## CONTEMPORARY ART, LIVING ARTISTS AND YOUTH CULTURE

The use of living artists and designers in projects can be transformative and make art more critical and relevant to learners' lives. We also need to connect our teaching to youth culture and this can be done effectively through contemporary art. Contemporary art and design practices provide a means of dealing very effectively with areas of current concern, such as ethnicity and sexual orientation to mention just two. Recently, the N5 question paper saw a helpful update suggesting that social and cultural influences could now be included. The privileging of female artists and designers over male ones can help to bring a level of criticality into the classroom. Widening the canon of artists and designers we refer to in schools to include black and ethnic minorities can extend the impact of our teaching beyond the classroom. As Susan Coles argues '[I]s it wrong to prefer Bansky over Monet? Whose life is it anyway?' (Coles, 2012). Mulgan and Warpole (1986) remind us of the alienating impact of ignoring the art of our time: 'Concentrating on pre-twentieth century forms inevitably means concentrating on cultural products that were originally created for a wealthy, minority audience' (p. 62).

## ANNUAL SQA COURSE REPORT AND ASSESSMENT

The format of the Annual SQA Course Report is being challenged as teachers see it as being too general and are again seeking more visual exemplars. The latter has in the past led to formulaic responses. The SQA give great importance to the Course Report in their overall feedback to teachers but despite this there is plenty of evidence to say that many teachers are simply not following the correct exam procedures. Tightly prescribed assessment criteria are not always adhered to, especially amongst ambitious young teachers. Over-subscribing to an area of assessment that does not carry more than a few marks, regardless of how well it has been attempted, is an all-too-common mistake. Better understanding of these and further training will ensure that teachers of art and design better inform young people taking the subject.

## REMOVAL OF UNIT ASSESSMENTS

The Scottish Secondary Teachers' Association (SSTA) N5 modification survey identified a trend across all practical subjects including art and design of an increase in teacher workload due to the unit assessments (see https://ssta.org.uk/wp-content/uploads/2017/02/February-2017-newsletter.pdf). Teachers have welcomed their removal, with the NSEAD reiterating the need for quality not quantity in relation to art and design. However, to maintain the integrity of the course, it is advised that the course assessments must be strengthened to qualify for twenty-four Scottish Credit and Qualifications Framework (SCQF) credits. The removal of the unit assessments frees artwork from the label of being 'exam work', resulting in a more integrated learning experience.

## EDUCATION SCOTLAND (2016) BENCHMARKS

The Expressive Arts Benchmarks published in March 2017 (https://education.gov.scot/improvement/Documents/ExpressiveArtsBenchmarksPDF.pdf) were designed to support practitioners' professional judgement, with succinct statements that bring the clearest expression to date on the purposes and principles of the subject. It is a welcome and progressive set of Benchmarks with few restrictions and a further indicator of the curricular affordances and permissions available to Scottish art and design teachers.

## REFERENCES

Bakhshi, H. (2016) 'Is art education running out of steam?' *The Guardian*. Online at https://www.theguardian.com/culture-professionals-network/2016/feb/16/art-education-running-out-of-steam-teachers-art-design

Coles, S. (2012) 'Where have all the boys gone?' *The National Society for Education in Art and Design magazine*. Spring, issue 4.

Education Scotland (2016) *A Statement for Practitioners from HM Chief Inspector of Education*. Online at https://education.gov.scot/improvement/Documents/cfestatement.pdf

Efland, A. (2002) *Art and Cognition: Integrating the Visual Arts in the Curriculum*. New York: Teachers College Press.

Fisher, E. and Fortnum, R. (2013) *On Not Knowing: How Artists Think*. London: Black Dog Publishing.

Giroux, H. A. (1993) *Border Crossings*. New York: Routledge.

MacDonald, S. W. (2006) 'The trouble with postmodernism', in Tom Hardy (ed.), *Art Education in a Postmodern World: Collected Essays*. Bristol: Intellect Press.

McWilliam, E. (2007) 'Unlearning how to teach', *Innovations in Education and Teaching International*, 45 (3), 263–9.

Mulgan, G. and Warpole, K. (1986) *Saturday Night or Sunday Morning: From Arts to Industry – New Forms of Cultural Policy*. London: Comedia Publishing Group.

Perkins, D. (2003) 'Visible thinking'. Online at http://www.pz.harvard.edu/vt

Ritchhart, R. and Perkins, D. (2008) 'Making thinking visible', *Educational Leadership*, 65 (5), 57–61.

# 40

# Biology

*Stephen P. Day*

Modern biology is an eclectic mix of subjects that evolved from traditional fields of botany, zoology, microbiology and physiology, with newer areas such as molecular and cellular biology, to name but two. Biologists use a wide array of analytical techniques found in other disciplines to push the boundaries of knowledge. Nowhere is this interdisciplinary approach more evident than in biomedical and life science, where knowledge gains over the last decade have been substantial, advances being driven by the ability of modern biologists to develop or adapt analytical techniques as new technology increases their ease of use. Biology's diversity is educationally problematic, particularly within the context of curriculum design and teacher recruitment. Fairly considerable tensions exist between proponents of differing content areas as to what knowledge ought to be taught. In addition, consideration must also be given to the moral, ethical and social perspectives which impinge on the use of biological knowledge, as well as which methods and techniques should be introduced to pupils to allow them to experience the subject's practical side.

## THE PHILOSOPHY OF BIOLOGY

Despite approving of T. H. Huxley's view of biology as 'a coherent subject with a coherent philosophy and … [providing] a firm basis for future study in a range of specialised disciplines', Slingsby (2006) noted that, as biology has grown, the addition and removal of content (to the biology curriculum) has been haphazard and without regard to the effect these revisions have on the overall philosophy of the subject. These curricular tensions were just as evident during the recent revision to the Highers in Biology and Human Biology as well as that of the new Advanced Higher Biology curriculum as part of the Curriculum for Excellence (CfE) reforms. According to Griffiths (2008), Biology's philosophy can be viewed from three distinct but related perspectives: (1) by looking to biology to test general theses within the philosophy of science; (2) by engaging with conceptual problems that arise within biology itself; and (3) by looking to biology for answers to distinctively philosophical questions in such fields as ethics, the philosophy of mind and epistemology.

The extent to which biology education reflects these perspectives lies at the heart of tensions that exist within the biology curriculum in Scotland. For example, the National 4, 5 and Higher Biology course specification documents make a number of bold claims for biology education: for example, that biology plays a crucial role in our everyday existence; is an increasingly important subject in the modern world; and, aims to find solutions to many of the world's problems. They also suggest (borrowing from the language of CfE) that all biology courses should encourage the development of skills and resourcefulness, which lead pupils to becoming confident individuals. Also, these documents suggest that successful learners in biology think creatively, analyse and solve problems with the aim of producing responsible citizens, through studying relevant areas of biology, such as health, environment and sustainability. However, what is neither recognised nor clarified by this rhetoric is the fact that the aim of developing scientific literate citizens is itself open to question and has long been problematic (Day and Bryce, 2011; 2013b).

Furthermore, the National 4 and 5 course specifications suggest that the purpose of the biology curriculum is to develop learners' interests and enthusiasm for biology in a range of contexts where the skills of scientific inquiry and investigation are developed by investigating the applications of biology. These should enable learners to become scientifically literate citizens, able to review the science-based claims which they will meet. While it is difficult to argue against such an optimistic claim, there is a lack of definition as to how biology teachers might consider what needs to be taught, in terms of knowledge, competencies and skills. This situation is nothing new given the tone of the science principles and practice documentation that underpins the CfE 3–15 Science curriculum (Day and Bryce, 2013b).

## UPTAKE AND SUCCESS IN SECONDARY SCHOOL BIOLOGY

Biology emerged from humble beginnings in the mid-1960s to become, by 2016, the third most popular subject taken by pupils in Scotland at National 5 when one adds together N5 Biology and Environmental Science. This trend continues at Higher when one adds together Biology with Human Biology and Environmental Science (SQA, 2016b).

Table 40.1 shows the total number of candidates for all biology courses over the transition from the old to the new CfE compliant National Qualification courses. These statistics can be interpreted in a number of ways depending on how you view progression. If we interpret the data from the perspective that candidates pick National 4 and progress to National 5 in S4, then this suggests that there has been decline in the total number of candidates by 19.6 per cent from 2013 to 2016. Interestingly, Table 40.1 indicates a decline in the total number

Table 40.1   Number of candidates sitting each course in biology

| | | | Middle School Upper School | | | | | | | | |
|---|---|---|---|---|---|---|---|---|---|---|---|
| Year | SG | Int 1 | N4 Bio | N5 Bio | N4 ES | N5 ES | Int 2 | HB | HHB | HES | AHB |
| 2010 | 20,570 | 5,718 | – | – | – | – | 7,354 | 9,308 | 4,078 | – | 2,177 |
| 2011 | 20,315 | 5,873 | – | – | – | – | 7,490 | 9,767 | 4,226 | – | 2,288 |
| 2012 | 20,336 | 6,358 | – | – | – | – | 7,995 | 9,581 | 4,410 | – | 2,417 |
| 2013 | 20,276 | 6,109 | – | – | – | – | 8,035 | 10,127 | 4,273 | – | 2,458 |
| 2014 | – | 578 | 10,092 | 16,146 | 145 | – | 7,013 | 10,328 | 4,156 | – | 2,518 |
| 2015 | – | 42 | 10,471 | 21,635 | 231 | 122 | 444 | 9,699 | 3,016 | 83 | 2,425 |
| 2016 | – | – | 9,929 | 21,208 | 298 | 194 | – | 7,492 | 5,990 | 392 | 2,362 |

Note: SG = Standard Grade; Int 1 = Intermediate 1; Int 2 = Intermediate 2; N4 Bio = National 4 Biology; N5 Bio = National 5 Biology; N4 ES = National 4 Environmental Science N5 ES = National 5 Environmental Science; HB = Higher Biology; HHB = Higher Human Biology; HES = Higher Environmental Science; AHB= Advanced Higher Biology.

of candidates taking Higher Biology (by 27.5 per cent) and an increase in the total number taking Higher Human Biology (by 44.1 per cent).

The increasing popularity of Human Biology presents a challenge to the traditional view that biology in the middle years of secondary provides a suitable platform for a progression pathway at Highers since the Human Biology content of the National 4 and 5 curriculum does not provide sufficient underpinning to the Higher Human Biology course. With the emergence of National 3, 4, 5 and Higher Environmental Science, the range of choice in terms of Biology-related National Qualifications has grown. Perhaps, the popularity of Environmental Science might grow further in the years ahead.

Despite this apparent popularity, a number of issues persist with the Biology curriculum: it is still content heavy, despite the promised decluttering of CfE, and does not allow sufficient time for the development of practical inquiry skills, or for the development of informed attitudes. More worrying is that the direct teaching of problem-solving skills seems to be undermined by the fact that, at National 4 and 5 level, questions are no longer clearly labelled as Knowledge and Understanding, and Problem-solving, but are holistically graded. At Higher Grade there are still too many topics which allows little opportunity for consolidation and remediation in the time available. In addition, there is growing evidence that the gap in the ability identified within the previous curriculum (Standard Grade Credit level and Higher Grade) has not shrunk between the new National 5 and Higher Biology qualifications.

## BIOLOGY IN THE SECONDARY CURRICULUM

### Science – Broad General Education

The broad general education (S1–S3) phase of CfE science contains sixty-nine experiences and outcomes (E&Os) covering both levels 3 and 4, of which twenty-four focus specifically on biology: eleven at level 3 (six relating to content knowledge and five to experimental skills); and thirteen at level 4 (six relating to content knowledge, five to experimental skills and two relating to socio-scientific discussion). These E&Os are organised under the curriculum organisers: Planet Earth: *Biodiversity and Interdependence* (relating to biodiversity, photosynthesis and evolution); Biological Systems: *Body Systems and Cells* (relating to cell theory; biotechnology); and Inheritance (relating to reproduction, DNA and genetics). Teachers are encouraged to deploy various active learning approaches such as cooperative learning and inquiry-based learning to enhance pupil engagement and enjoyment. However, within science teachers' practice, all-to-often the curriculum is dominated by *learning science* (the concepts and principles) and *the doing of science* (experimentation, investigations and inquiry), rather than the *learning about science* (how science interacts with society) (see Bryce (2010)). Despite the fact that this curriculum has been in place since 2010, there is still a distinct lack of emphasis on the discussion of socio-scientific issues as a means for developing scientific literacy. In practice, socio-scientific discussion is often poorly enacted, dominated by teacher-mediated discourse with little opportunity for pupils to develop opinions based on information derived from multiple perspectives that impinge upon the issues being discussed (and often reduced to a simple pro-versus-con dichotomy).

While the lack of meaningful socio-scientific discussion within the broad general education phase of Science may be lamentable, what is rather more worrying politically is the fact that Scotland has slipped for the first time in a decade in the latest Programme for International Student Assessment (PISA) rankings for Science literacy. The PISA Science assessment relates to three domains within scientific literacy: *Scientific competencies* which comprises explaining phenomena scientifically, evaluating and designing scientific enquiry, and interpreting and evaluating data scientifically; *Knowledge*, comprised of content knowledge, procedural knowledge and epistemic knowledge; and *Content areas*, which relates to knowledge but is classified according to the major scientific fields of physical systems, living systems and earth and space systems. In addition, the context of each test item can be calibrated within a personal, local/national and global level.

The PISA 2015 results suggest that the 2015 cohort of Scottish 15 year olds coped less well than their 2012, 2009 and 2006 counterparts. This has led some commentators to suggest that this decline is down to Curriculum for Excellence's emphasis on competencies and skill as opposed to knowledge. What is clear, however, is that questions need to be asked of the curriculum, the teaching of science content and perhaps the validity of the PISA assessment.

### Biology (National 4 and 5)

The Biology (National 4 and 5) course is designed to be practical, experiential and hopes to develop scientific understanding of biological issues. The published rationales for these courses suggest that the course covers a range of topics, from molecular through to whole organism and beyond. The course, so the rationale claims, allows flexibility and personalisation by offering choice in the contexts studied. Furthermore, the course aims to develop (within a biological context) learners' scientific and analytical thinking skills; investigative, experimental and problem-solving skills; understanding of biological issues; the acquisition and application of knowledge and understanding of biological concepts; and understanding of relevant applications of biology in society. Thus the courses should provide opportunities for pupils to become scientifically literate citizens, whilst developing their literacy and numeracy skills. However, a number of questions emerge from this rationale: In what way will true flexibility and personalisation be achieved in practice? Who decides what these relevant applications of biology are and how is the decision made? In what way are these applications applicable to society as a whole?

In terms of content, both Biology National 4 and 5 have three units of study: Cell Biology; Multicellular Organisms; and Life on Earth. All National 4 courses are internally assessed, with National 5 courses being assessed internally and externally. The reliance on internal assessment as the only evidence of competence at National 4 led some to question the value of this qualification to employers and universities. Both courses contain an Added Value Unit where pupils are expected to draw on and extend the skills they have learned from across the other units, and demonstrate the breadth of knowledge and skills acquired, in unfamiliar contexts and/or integrated ways. To achieve the Biology (National 4 and 5) course, the pupils must pass all of the required units, including the Added Value Unit.

In addition, the Added Value Unit in biology is assessed by a written assignment that is related to activities that further develop the skills necessary to conduct investigative/practical work in Biology. Also, the Added Value Unit allows learners to demonstrate their ability to research using the Internet. Pupils utilise the skills, knowledge and understanding learnt as part of the course to undertake an investigation into a topical issue in biology. Teachers are allowed to provide guidance to pupils on topics for study, taking into account their learning needs and the relevance to everyday issues.

In practice, the Added Value Unit in Biology reflects the biology concepts learned within the course related to pupils' everyday lives with regards to a topical issue. The SQA suggest the following topical issues such as the use of Factor VIII or other genetically engineered products for human use: the production of beer, wine, cheese and so on; gene therapy; pharming; commercial plant growing; conservation of endangered species; and habitat loss. However, teachers are free to steer pupils towards other topical issues as long as they conform to the assessments standards set by the SQA. While pupils are free to choose a topic to be investigated, it is reasonable for their choice to be one where the teacher has some expertise and has resources available to enable the learner to successfully meet the assessment standards. However, the quality and originality of the Added Value Unit in terms of pupils' effort is open to question.

The SQA verification report that focuses on the Added Value unit states that 'Much of the evidence submitted for verification was in the form of a written report, and in many instances it was clear that this had been produced to meet the requirements of a National 5 Coursework Assignment' (SQA, 2016a, p. 6). The report further suggests that this approach can be adopted at the discretion of the school, but that there are differences in emphasis in the assignment at each level. For example, it is not a requirement for candidates to compare the data from two sources at National 4 and that schools need to ensure that pupils are not disadvantaged by being expected to complete tasks that are not relevant to their level. This suggests that most schools are delivering the National 5 course to all pupils and differentiating by level in terms of assessment for each unit within the course. This has led to the over-assessment of pupils and to an increase in the workload of teachers.

### Environmental Science (National 4 and 5)

The new Environmental Science National Qualification course, which developed out of the Intermediate Two and Higher Managing Environmental Resources (MER) course, was introduced in 2013. As with all National 4 and 5 courses, it has three units: Earth's Resources (encompassing the study of Planet Earth, Earth's Materials, and Energy); Living Environment (encompassing the study of Ecosystems, Inter-relationships and Biodiversity); and Sustainability (encompassing practical and other learning activities related to natural resources and the impact of human activities on them). In addition, this unit covers the principles of sustainable development, resource use and abuse, and global environmental issues. It remains to be seen how popular this will be in the longer term. It is possible that Environmental Science might grow but it is more likely that it will end up following Biotechnology (as a niche subject) or even become non-viable over the longer term.

### Higher Biology and Human Biology

The new NQ Higher Biology course contains three units: DNA and the Genome (which explores the molecular basis of evolution and biodiversity); Metabolism and Survival (which considers the central metabolic pathways in cells and how they are controlled, as well as how cells are manipulated and modified in biotechnology); and Sustainability and Interdependence (which attempts to model and understand complex interactions between many interdependent entities, such as the human population's dependence upon sufficient and sustainable food production from the harvest of a narrow range of crop and livestock species).

The new NQ Human Biology course contains three units: Human Cells (which introduces stem cells as being capable of dividing and differentiating into specialised cells and emphasises central metabolic pathways and their control as well as the central role played by DNA to cell processes); Physiology and Health (which focuses on reproduction and the cardiovascular system); and Neurobiology and Communication (which emphasises the importance of the brain's structure in relation to its function).

It could be argued that the construction of the new range of National Qualifications (NQs) in Biology has paid little regard to the philosophy of biology, particularly in terms of biology's ability to provide a perspective on the interface between science and society, given the over emphasis on canonical content, problem-solving and investigations skills at the expense of socio-scientific discussion.

### Higher Environmental Science

The new NQ Higher Environmental Science course, which was introduced in 2014, has started small and is growing but it remains to be seen whether it will develop to the point where it might rival Higher Biology's and Higher Human Biology's popularity. The Environmental Science course is made up of three units. The first unit, Living Environments, is made up of three subunits: Investigating Ecosystems and Biodiversity; Interdependence; and Human Influences on Biodiversity. The second unit, Earth's Resources is made up of four subunits: Geosphere; Hydrosphere; Biosphere; and Atmosphere. The third unit, Sustainability, also has four subunits: Food; Water; Energy; and Waste Management.

### THE MANAGEMENT OF BIOLOGY IN SCHOOLS

The role played by principal teachers of biology in the management and development of the subject at school and local authority level has continued to be undermined as faculty heads subsume their roles. The move towards faculties of science is worrying since many faculty heads are physical scientists and many struggle to fully appreciate the philosophy of biology and its complexity. An uncomfortable perspective would be that many physics and (to a lesser extent) chemistry teachers privately question biology's place as a science and often see it as the least of the three sciences. Biology is a rapidly advancing subject that is as deep as it is broad, which naturally lies at the interface between science and society. This requires biologists with a clear view of how the subject at large is developing to be able to make decisions which will allow for the future development of secondary school biology over the coming years. Without effective autonomous leadership at local level, decisions about the future development of the subject risk being sidelined.

### Interdisciplinary Learning

Many controversial socio-scientific issues are biological in nature and biologists can potentially contribute to the interdisciplinary teaching of these issues. However, in the context of CfE, interdisciplinary learning (IDL) is conceptually ill-defined, despite Education Scotland issuing a briefing paper focused on IDL that makes some rather bold claims for the efficacy of it that are not substantiated by research. A number of questions remain regarding how biology teachers ought to engage with IDL. Do biology teachers teach the multiple dimensions themselves in the class context or does IDL require a team approach with each teacher contributing their particular specialism? The answer to this question is vital to the successful implementation of this pedagogical approach. Research into how science teachers can engage pupils in IDL using socio-scientific discussion is described in Day and Bryce (2011) and Day and Bryce (2013a) under the premise that one teacher presents all the perspectives rather than using a team approach.

## Fieldwork

There are many opportunities for fieldwork in biology particularly in the area of environmental monitoring. Recently, a number of Citizen Science projects have developed in conjunction with outdoor learning. These involve pupils in participating in the collection of environmental information that contributes to expanding our knowledge of the natural environment. At present, the educational benefits of pupil participation in such projects are unclear in terms of pupils' understanding of the nature of science, attitude to science, and the environment and science knowledge gains.

However, the opportunities to participate in practical activities in the newer areas of molecular biology are restricted by availability of equipment, cost of reagents and expertise. Many schools get around these concerns by making arrangements with further education colleges where pupils can visit and participate in experiments such as agarose gel electrophoresis, polymerase chain reaction (PCR) and enzyme linked immunosorbent assays (ELISAs).

## LOOKING TO THE FUTURE

In March 2017, Education Scotland issued the Science benchmarks for the broad general education phase of CfE. These benchmarks are meant to support teachers' professional judgement and help to provide evidence that can be used in professional dialogue, moderation and the monitoring of pupils' progress. However, the benchmarks risk being used as a bureaucratic tick-box exercise. At the draft stage, the Learned Societies Group criticised the benchmarks as being: riddled with misconceptions and inaccuracies; required to be refocused more on outcomes; lacked exemplification of how outcomes could be evidenced; and lacked clarity as to how schools might use the benchmarks to support their assessments. While many of these criticisms have been taken on board and inaccuracies dealt with in the final document, some of the criticisms remain valid and the changes do not go far enough. There are few benchmarks for those experiences and outcomes that deal with socio-scientific discussion. If the published benchmarks are to help support teachers' professional judgement and dialogue, then the questions are: How will these benchmarks be used in practice to support pupils' attainment and how will that attainment be measured? We will have to wait and see exactly how the final benchmarks will be implemented before we can judge whether they will lead to improved learning and attainment over the next few years, particularly since we have no standardised assessment in science that covers the broad general education phase of the science curriculum. Perhaps an improvement in the next round of PISA Science assessments in 2018 will provide evidence of progress.

## REFERENCES

Bryce, T. G. K. (2010) 'Sardonic science? The resistance to more humanistic forms of science education', *Cultural Studies of Science Education*, 5, 591–612.

Day, S. P. and Bryce, T. G. K. (2011) 'Does the discussion of socio-scientific issues require a paradigm shift in science teachers' thinking?' *International Journal of Science Education*, 33 (12), 1675–1702.

Day, S. P. and Bryce, T. G. K. (2013a) 'The benefits of cooperative learning to socio-scientific discussion in secondary school science', *International Journal of Science Education*, 35 (9), 1533–60.

Day, S. P. and Bryce, T. G. K. (2013b) 'Curriculum for Excellence Science: vision or confusion?' *Scottish Educational Review*, 45 (1), 53–66.

Griffiths, P. (2008) 'Philosophy of biology', in *The Stanford Encyclopaedia of Philosophy*. Online at http://plato.stanford.edu/entries/biology-philosophy/

Scottish Executive (2006) *A Curriculum for Excellence: Progress and Proposals. A Paper from the Curriculum Review Programme Board*. Online at www.gov.scot/resource/doc/98764/0023924.pdf

Slingsby, D. (2006) 'Biological education: has it gone anywhere since 1875?', *Biologist*, 53 (6), 283–4.

SQA (2012) Biology (National 4). Online at www.sqa.org.uk/files/nq/CfE_CourseSpec_N4_Sciences_Biology.pdf

SQA (2014) Environmental Biology (National 4). Online at www.sqa.org.uk/files/nq/CfE_CourseSpec_N4_Sciences_EnvironmentalScience.pdf

SQA (2016a) NQ Verification 2015–16 Key Message Reports N3 to Advanced Higher. Online at www.sqa.org.uk/files_ccc/VKMBiology2016.pdf

SQA (2016b) Annual Statistical Report. Online at https://www.sqa.org.uk/sqa/80674.html

# 41

# Business Education

*Jacqueline White*

The Business Education curriculum in Scottish secondary schools consists of four individual business subjects in the Senior Phase (S4–S6) – Accounting; Administration and IT (Information Technology); Business Management; and Economics. In recent years schools have moved from Standard Grade and Intermediate awards to the new National Qualifications (NQs). There are only a few Business Education departments in Scotland who have the capacity to teach all four subjects. Business Management is taught in almost all schools along with Administration and IT; however, larger secondary schools often include a third subject on their curriculum. When this is the case it tends to be Accounting rather than Economics that is chosen. Accounting is regarded as a subject that complements Business Management and in many schools young people study Accounting as a 'crash course' subject in sixth year.

The contribution that Economics can make to a young person's understanding of the world and their place within it is often underestimated. In an already 'cluttered' curriculum, Economics is in direct competition with other social subjects being taught in secondary schools. However, it remains a popular choice of study for young people within the independent sector in Scotland. It is part of a portfolio of subjects taught with the International Baccalaureate (IB), a qualification primarily taught in independent schools.

## BROAD GENERAL EDUCATION

An opportunity for change came with the introduction of Curriculum for Excellence (CfE). In business classrooms, teaching methods moved away from 'chalk and talk' approaches towards pupil-centred methods that enable young people to learn from engaging in practical business activities. Assessment procedures in classrooms changed with the implementation of Assessment is for Learning (AifL); this brought new assessment practices into business classrooms that supported young people in their understanding of business concepts. An increased emphasis was placed on the teaching of information and communication technology (ICT) skills and the use of technology to support and enhance learning and teaching in business education departments.

Business Education teachers make a significant contribution to the Technologies and Social Studies areas of the broad general education (BGE) in the early years of secondary. They provide breadth and depth to children whilst building the foundations for specialisation in the senior phase. Young people use ICT to research the 'real world', solve problems, make decisions and communicate findings to others. They are able to gain an insight into the economic and social dimensions of society and learn how to be successful learners and confident individuals who are able to contribute to society by becoming effective contributors and responsible citizens.

There are a variety of different BGE curriculum structures (S1–S3) within secondary schools in Scotland which can mean that children only receive one or two periods of technologies/social subjects per week. More often than not, the BGE curriculum allocation is shared with Computing Science, especially within faculty structures. The real challenge for Business Education across Scotland is to provide a continuum of learning within CfE in which the experiences and outcomes (E&Os) are consistently linked to the new NQs.

*Enhancing Learning and Teaching through the use of Digital Technology* (Scottish Government, 2016a) focuses on young people's digital skills and argues for a coherent plan to strengthen the digital skills of teachers. Business Education teachers have always had to keep up to date with technology in order to provide young people with the relevant learning experiences; nevertheless this document proposes that digital technology will soon be a requirement for every teacher under the General Teaching Council for Scotland (GTCS) professional standards. At the same time, Education Scotland has been in consultation with stakeholders on a strategy to refresh the CfE experiences and outcomes (Scottish Government, 2016b). They have recently produced a set of benchmarks for digital literacy (Education Scotland, 2017a) and the social sciences (Education Scotland, 2017b) that set out what young people need to learn in order to achieve each level of the CfE curriculum. These benchmarks should support moderation procedures and build consistency within teachers' professional judgements.

Business Education teachers need to work collaboratively with Computing Science teachers to create relevant learning experiences that prepare young people for the world of work and the digital age. Colbert et al. (2016) found that 'digital natives' entering the workforce often differ in their expectations of work and working practices. 'Digital Natives' is a term used by Prensky (2010) to describe young people today who have grown up with new technology at their fingertips, whereas some Business Education teachers might be described as 'digital immigrants' – adults who have adopted technology as it has become available. In some schools, 'digital immigrant' teachers are struggling to teach children who speak an entirely different language. Prensky (2010) suggests that what teachers need to know is how technology can be used by young people to enhance their own learning. He goes on to recommend that teachers should become experts at providing context, ensuring rigour, asking quality questions and evaluating the quality of young people's work.

## SENIOR PHASE

Young people's learning in the senior phase (S4–S6) should be active, engaging and enterprising. Business Education teachers should continue to build on the BGE pedagogy; however, these approaches to learning are not consistently applied across all schools in Scotland. The challenge for Business Education teachers is to provide relevant learning experiences that enable young people to make connections and to develop a deeper understanding through higher-order thinking skills. Senior phase characteristics include: learning independently; taking responsibility for learning; active learning; collaborative learning; and applying learning and skills development. The new qualifications reflect the aims,

Table 41.1  Qualifications in the Scottish Credit and Qualifications Framework

| National courses 2016–17 – SCQF levels | | | |
|---|---|---|---|
| 7 | Advanced Higher Business Management | Advanced Higher Accounting | Advanced Higher Economics |
| 6 | Higher Administration and IT | Higher Business Management | Higher Accounting | Higher Economics |
| 5 | National 5 Administration and IT | National 5 Business Management | National 5 Accounting | National 5 Economics |
| 4 | National 4 Administration and IT | National 4 Business | | |
| 3 | National 3 Administration and IT | National 3 Business | | |
| 2 | National 2 Information Technology | National 2 Business in Practice | | |

Source: www.sqa.org.uk

values and principles of Curriculum for Excellence and are intended to provide suitable progression from the BGE.

The Scottish Government (2016c) acknowledges that the quality of teaching is a key factor in improving children's learning and the outcomes they can achieve. They want to continue to improve the professionalism of teachers and the quality and impact of teacher professional learning. One step towards this is the removal of mandatory unit assessments for National 5, Highers and Advanced Highers on a phased basis over a three-year period from 2017/18, to reduce workload for teachers and young people.

The Scottish Credit and Qualifications Framework (SCQF) is Scotland's Lifelong Learning Framework that provides an agreed means of recognising and valuing learning across shared contexts in Scotland. Young people studying Business Education subjects can join at an appropriate level and continue to study such subjects up to Doctorate Level (SCQF 12). Table 41.1 demonstrates the options available to young people in secondary schools who wish to study Business Education subjects.

## ACCOUNTING

The National Qualification in Accounting is available at National 5, Higher and Advanced Higher. Learners develop their ability to use ICT as a tool for preparing and presenting accounting information through a choice of accounting contexts. Young people are required to use new international accounting terminology in their internal and external assessments and are expected to use digital technology to complete an accounting assignment.

It was anticipated that the number of potential candidates across Scotland would be much less than had previously been due to the fact that the new Accounting award would only be available from SCQF Level 5 upwards. This decision highlights the degree of difficulty encompassed within the Accounting curriculum. There was an increase (21 per cent) in

Table 41.2    Numbers of entries in Accounting, 2014–16

| Level | 2014 | 2015 | 2016 |
|---|---|---|---|
| National 5 Accounting (SCQF Level 5) | 777 | 938 | 895 |
| Higher Accounting (SCQF Level 6) | N/A | 585 | 1,364 |
| Advanced Higher Accounting (SCQF Level 7) | N/A | N/A | 39 |

Source: www.sqa.org.uk.

the number of National 5 candidates presented from 2014 to 2015; however, as Table 41.2 shows this has tapered off in 2016. On a more positive note there has been a substantial increase (133 per cent) in the number of candidates being presented at Higher Level from 2015 to 2016. Many candidates have taken on the challenge of upgrading their award from National 5 to Higher, with some candidates opting to study Higher Accounting as a crash course without prior certification at National 5 Level. Although there has only been one sitting of Advanced Higher Accounting to date, the presentation numbers are rather small across Scotland.

## ADMINISTRATION AND IT

The National Qualification in Administration and IT is available at National 3, National 4, National 5 and Higher. There are no plans to introduce Advanced Higher into the National Qualification Framework as this qualification was scrapped in 2011 because of low numbers. Administration and IT courses provide practical opportunities for learners to develop and apply their organisational and administrative skills. Young people use industry-standard software packages to research, create, communicate and summarise electronic information. They develop skills in problem solving and decision making that prepare them for careers in business and administration.

From 2014 to 2015 there has been an increase (31 per cent) in the number of National 5 presentations; however, as Table 41.3 shows, this has tapered off in 2016. There has been an increase (31 per cent) in the number of candidates being presented at Higher Level from 2015 to 2016. Again, there is a demand from S6 pupils in schools to study Higher Administration and IT as a crash course without prior National 5 Level certification. Administration and IT is currently running second in popularity to Business Management within business education departments. Young people see this course as an opportunity to improve their IT skills and make them better equipped for the modern workplace.

Table 41.3    Numbers of entries in Administration and IT, 2014–16

| Level | 2014 | 2015 | 2016 |
|---|---|---|---|
| National 5 Administration and IT (SCQF Level 5) | 4,267 | 5,619 | 5,448 |
| Higher Administration and IT (SCQF Level 6) | N/A | 3,025 | 3,965 |

Source: www.sqa.org.uk.

## BUSINESS MANAGEMENT

The National Qualification in Business Management is available at National 5, Higher and Advanced Higher. Young People in Scotland can study National 2 Business in Action,

Table 41.4 Numbers of entries in Business Management, 2014–16

| Level | 2014 | 2015 | 2016 |
|---|---|---|---|
| National 5 Business Management (SCQF Level 5) | 5,845 | 7,602 | 7,986 |
| Higher Business Management (SCQF Level 6) | N/A | 5,259 | 9,108 |
| Advanced Higher Business Management (SCQF Level 7) | N/A | N/A | 363 |

Source: www.sqa.org.uk.

National 3 Business and National 4 Business within the senior phase. This group of awards have no formal examinations and are internally assessed by teachers in schools. From 2014 to 2015 there was an increase (30 per cent) in the number of National 5 presentations; however, as Table 41.4 shows this has tapered off in 2016. There has been a significant increase (73 per cent) in the number of candidates presented at Higher Level from 2015 to 2016. As well as those candidates moving from National 5, there are young people again choosing to study Higher Business Management as a crash course without prior National 5 Level certification.

The introduction of Advanced Higher in 2016 has shown itself to be relatively successful with 363 candidates being presented across Scotland. Business Management has taken over from Administration and IT as the most popular subject within the Business Education portfolio. Learners combine theoretical and practical aspects of learning through the use of real-life business contexts. Young people study current business theory and practice and use this to research and analyse a real business organisation through the SQA assignment.

## ECONOMICS

The National Qualification in Economics is available at National 5, Higher and Advanced Higher. Although numbers are relatively small across schools in Scotland there is a definite positive trend within the presentation figures. Economics develops learners' understanding of the economic environment in which they live, by enabling them to understand economic concepts within a real-life context. From 2014 to 2015 there was a significant increase (69 per cent) in the number of National 5 presentations. This positive trend continued into 2016 with a substantial increase of 93 per cent (see Table 41.5). This continued on into Higher with a sizeable increase (212 per cent) in the number of candidates presented from 2015 to 2016. There might be two likely reasons for this increase: young people are opting to study Higher Economics as a crash course without prior certification at National 5 Level and the popularity of Economics in schools within the independent sector.

The introduction of Advanced Higher in 2016 has shown itself to be moderately successful with 96 candidates being presented across Scotland. The course highlights how

Table 41.5 Numbers of entries in Economics, 2014–16

| Level | 2014 | 2015 | 2016 |
|---|---|---|---|
| National 5 Economics (SCQF Level 5) | 89 | 150 | 289 |
| Higher Economics (SCQF Level 6) | N/A | 179 | 558 |
| Advanced Higher Economics (SCQF Level 7) | N/A | N/A | 96 |

Source: www.sqa.org.uk.

economic concepts, government policy and global trade affect our daily lives. Young people can develop an in-depth understanding of society's economic challenges and have the opportunity to consider possible solutions.

## CONCERNS AND CHALLENGES

The management structure of many Business Education departments has changed over the past decade. The idea of a principal teacher leading and managing Business Education is difficult to find in secondary schools today. Business Education teachers are likely to work under a faculty structure where the faculty head is either a Computing Science or a Business Education specialist. Some schools have gone down the route of a technologies approach to leadership where the Technology specialist is in charge. There are some advantages to a faculty system as it gives teachers the opportunity to collaborate and support each other around technology. A large faculty will have the capacity to offer a wider range of subjects; however, challenges can arise when a member of staff needs support and the manager does not have the relevant knowledge or skills to assist them. As school rolls decrease there is a propensity for in-house competition to exist within a faculty structure. School funding is dependent on the number of pupils who study a particular subject and any move towards another subject area whether positive or negative can impact on funding and resources within the faculty.

The core subjects in Business Education are Business Management and Administration and IT; however, Business Education teachers are required to register with the GTCS to teach all four subjects – Accounting, Administration and IT, Business Management and Economics. Teachers should keep abreast of these subject areas and be able to teach any one of them as required. Universities, through initial teacher education (ITE) programmes, have a responsibility to enrol student teachers who meet the General Teaching Council for Scotland (2013) entrance requirements. Applicants must have credits in Accounting, Economics, Information Technology and Business Management. The difficulty for selectors on the Professional Graduate Diploma in Education (PGDE) course is that there is no longer a specific undergraduate business course that fully covers all four subjects. Prospective applicants often require to study additional units so as to meet the GTCS's requirements. Universities should continue to maintain the quality of Business Education teachers, not only for the reputation of the Scottish teaching profession, but for the young people in Business Education classrooms.

The broad general education poses many challenges for Business Education teachers. There is a conflict between the contribution they can make to the digital literacy curriculum and the contribution they can make to the social studies curriculum, especially when timetable allocations in schools are so limited. Young people are often not receiving the necessary teaching time needed to enable them to move forward into the senior phase. Schools need to ensure that aspects of CfE relating to the use of digital technology and the development of digital skills are relevant, ambitious and forward looking (Scottish Government, 2016a). The challenge for Business Education teachers is how to develop and embed approaches to learning, teaching and assessment that make effective use of digital technology.

The senior phase continues to be a challenge for Business Education teachers. Are four subjects sustainable within the present structure? The future of Business Education is in the hands of teachers who have already demonstrated that they are equipped to solve the many challenges faced in secondary schools today; this is the reality of an ever-changing curriculum. There are rising expectations that young people should be learning within an innovative environment where twenty-first-century competences are taught by teachers who are confident in pedagogy, curriculum and assessment methodologies. In today's connected world, teachers should take the opportunity to extend their boundaries through partnerships that provide learning opportunities for themselves and young people. Collaborative professionalism is crucial to improving and innovating Business Education learning environments in Scottish secondary schools.

## REFERENCES

Colbert, A., Yee, N. and George, G. (2016) 'The Digital workforce and the workplace of the future', *Academy of Management Journal*, 59 (3), 731–9.

Education Scotland (2017a) *Benchmarks Technologies*. Edinburgh: Education Scotland.

Education Scotland (2017b) *Benchmarks Social Studies*. Edinburgh: Education Scotland.

General Teaching Council for Scotland (2013) *Memorandum on Entry Requirements to Programmes of Initial Teacher Education in Scotland*. Edinburgh: GTCS.

Prensky, M. (2010) *Teaching Digital Natives: Partnering for Real Learning*. Thousand Oaks, CA: Corwin Press.

Scottish Government (2016a) *Enhancing Learning and Teaching through the Use of Digital Technology: A Digital Learning and Teaching Strategy for Scotland*. Edinburgh: Scottish Government.

Scottish Government (2016b) *Delivering Excellence and Equity in Scottish Education – A Delivery Plan for Scotland*. Edinburgh: Scottish Government.

Scottish Government (2016c) *National Improvement Framework for Scottish Education: Achieving Excellence and Equity*. Edinburgh: Scottish Government.

# 42

# Chemistry

*Margaret Ritchie*

Chemistry is a major subject with a huge impact on the modern world. It consists of five major divisions: Organic, Inorganic, Analytical, Physical and Biochemistry. Further subdivisions of these categories include Forensic, Medicinal and Nuclear Chemistry.

- Organic Chemistry involves the study of compounds containing carbon including fuels, plastics, organometallic chemistry and drug development.
- Inorganic Chemistry involves the study of non-carbon containing compounds and incorporates Nuclear Chemistry, geochemistry, bioinorganic and industrial applications. Physics, Chemistry and Biology interconnect in Analytical Chemistry – both quantitative and qualitative.
- In Analytical Chemistry, spectroscopy is applied in environmental science, drug testing and Forensic Science.
- Physical Chemistry is linked to Physics through electrochemistry, thermochemistry, chemical kinetics and quantum mechanics.
- Biochemistry incorporates the study of chemical processes within a living organism, leading on to molecular biochemistry, clinical biochemistry, endocrinology and enzymology.

A knowledge and understanding of Chemistry at school helps to support the study of Physics and Biology and incorporates links to many other subject areas in the curriculum. Chemistry teachers often have a breadth of backgrounds and expertise for promoting topical aspects of the discipline and its application in everyday life. In Scotland, applicants for the secondary Professional Graduate Diploma in Education (PGDE) programme in Chemistry must demonstrate competence in the major areas of the subject and a minimum competency in English to Higher level, that is, Scottish Credit and Qualifications Framework (SCQF) Level 6. Scientists educated outwith the UK wishing to undertake a PGDE teaching qualification in Scotland may struggle to produce a formal English qualification despite being fluent in English. Of recent there have been concerns that the number of teachers in science, technology, engineering and mathematics (STEM subjects) in Scottish schools has been decreasing and recruiting student teachers in STEM subjects has become problematic (Seith, 2015). This may restrict opportunities for pupils to study these subjects resulting in a skills shortage in STEM subjects in the future workforce. From Table 42.1 it is clear that the replenishment rate in some subjects is not being met and there are serious shortages in the STEM subjects including Chemistry.

Table 42.1   Number of student teachers recruited into STEM subjects in 2015–16

| Subject | Target intake | Actual intake | Percentage of places unfilled |
|---|---|---|---|
| Biology | 88 | 81 | 8 |
| Chemistry | 69 | 57 | 17 |
| Computing | 37 | 20 | 46 |
| Mathematics | 146 | 76 | 48 |
| Physics | 54 | 38 | 30 |
| Technological Education | 58 | 35 | 40 |

Source: STEMEC, 2016.

## TRENDS IN UPTAKE WITHIN SECONDARY SCHOOL CHEMISTRY

Chemistry has remained the second most popular subject for pupils interested in the sciences. It is the second most popular science subject taken by pupils in Scotland at National 5 and at Higher (SQA, 2016). Table 42.2 shows the number of candidates sitting SQA examinations at each course level for the years 2005 to 2016. Combining the number of pupils studying Intermediate 2 and National 5 Chemistry in 2014 and 2015 shows a reduction in the number of pupils that proceeded to undertake Higher Chemistry. Furthermore, the trend continues and there was a further decrease in the number of pupils taking National 5 Chemistry in 2016. These results indicate a continuing reduction in the numbers of pupils preparing to undertake Higher Chemistry after 2016. The total number of entries for Higher Chemistry in 2016 was 10,077, down from 11,419 in 2014. The number of pupils sitting Higher Chemistry in 2016 was 7.49 per cent lower than in 2015. By contrast, Advanced Higher (AH) Chemistry continues to be the second most popular advanced higher qualification. Further analysis of the SQA results shows the percentage of pupils achieving A–C grade was 83 per cent, which is 3 per cent higher than 2015. While there was an initial increase in

Table 42.2   Number of candidates sitting each course in Chemistry

| | Middle school | | | | Senior school | | | |
|---|---|---|---|---|---|---|---|---|
| Year | SG | Int 1 | N4 | N5 | Int 2 | H | AH | Bac in Sci |
| 2005 | 20,896 | | – | – | | 9,411 | | |
| 2006 | 20,668 | 1,929 | – | – | 3,369 | 9,168 | 2,016 | |
| 2007 | 20,078 | 2,479 | – | – | 3,725 | 9,490 | 2,039 | |
| 2008 | 19,773 | 2,824 | – | – | 3,918 | 9,505 | 2,143 | |
| 2009 | 19,475 | 3,058 | – | – | 4,110 | 9,582 | 2,183 | |
| 2010 | 18,906 | 2,934 | – | – | 4,319 | 10,179 | 2,226 | 119 |
| 2011 | 19,021 | 2,987 | – | – | 4,565 | 10,293 | 2,472 | 138 |
| 2012 | 18,747 | 3,157 | – | – | 4,663 | 10,630 | 2,496 | 151 |
| 2013 | 18,785 | 3,031 | – | – | 4,708 | 10,656 | 2,545 | 142 |
| 2014 | – | 275 | 7,249 | 14,157 | 3,839 | 11,419 | 2,671 | 137 |
| 2015 | – | – | 6,396 | 16,659 | 464 | 10,893 | 2,783 | 94 |
| 2016 | – | – | 5,398 | 17,046 | – | 10,077 | 2,614 | 88 |

Notes: SG = Standard Grade Chemistry; Int 1 = Intermediate 1 Chemistry; Int 2 = Intermediate 2 Chemistry; N4 = National 4 Chemistry; N5 = National 5 Chemistry; H = Higher Chemistry; AH = Advanced Higher Chemistry; Bac in Sci = Baccalaureate in Science.
Source: SQA, 2016.

the number of pupils undertaking a Baccalaureate in Science after its introduction in 2009, the number has reduced significantly over the last few years. However, these figures do not include pupils being awarded an Interdisciplinary Project alone.

## CHEMISTRY IN THE SECONDARY CURRICULUM

### Science – Broad General Education

Curriculum for Excellence (CfE) is divided into two phases: the broad general education (BGE) and the senior phase. The BGE phase (Education Scotland, nd a) begins in early learning and childcare (age 3) and continues to the end of S3. Its purpose is to develop the knowledge, skills, attributes and capabilities of the four capacities of CfE. During the BGE phase, learners should: achieve the highest possible levels of literacy, numeracy and cognitive skills; develop skills for learning, skills for life and skills for work; develop knowledge and understanding of society, the world and Scotland's place in it; and experience challenge and success so that they can develop well-informed views and the four capacities.

The BGE phase is designed to articulate early years and primary learning with the senior phase, providing a seamless transition from age 3 to 18 for all pupils. S1–S3 phase of the BGE in Science contains sixty experiences and outcomes (E&Os) at levels 3 and 4. Pupils should have covered all level 3 E&Os by the end of S2. Outcomes are grouped into five organisers: Planet Earth; Forces, Electricity and Waves; Biological Systems; Materials; and Topical Science. Outcomes linked to Chemistry are present in Topical Science, Planet Earth: *Processes of the Planet* (relating to states of matter and climate change); *Energy sources and sustainability* (relating to renewable energy); *Earth's materials* (relating to soils, minerals and extraction of substances); *Properties and uses of substances* (relating to elements, compounds, extraction and separation techniques); and *Chemical changes* (relating to acids and bases, evidence of reactions, rates of reactions). Concepts in Chemistry may also contribute to Biology and Physics outcomes. During first and second year pupils may experience Chemistry, Physics and Biology as discrete subjects with some topics combining two or three of the sciences.

National courses are designed to start in S4. However, there are a variety of models of course structure in schools where S3 pupils prepare for national courses during the BGE phase after making a course choice in S2. There may also be an opportunity to change courses at the end of S3. Pupils then choose their subjects for further study at the end of S4.

A Science Progression Programme developed by Highland Council Education Department provides a model of transition through the sciences and demonstrates junior and senior phases linked through themes. Chemistry concepts are promoted through the organisers: Planet Earth (relating to water cycle and changes of state) and Materials (relating to dissolving, separation, water conservation, acids and alkalis).

Learning within the BGE phase can involve themed or project learning where pupils experience skills and knowledge applied in interesting contexts, often described as interdisciplinary learning. The GO4SET and Faraday Challenges involve partnerships with local business, colleges, industry and academia. Chemistry teachers can access a variety of resources to support delivery of courses and professional learning. Resources include those provided by the Royal Society of Chemistry (RSC), Royal Academy of Engineering, Scottish Schools Education Research Centre, STEM Central, Association for Science Education, Times Education Supplement Scotland and General Teaching Council for

Scotland (GTCS). RSC resources also support an understanding of Chemistry at primary level through fundamental topics including changing of state and properties of materials. These resources support early years through to second level with concept development in the sciences matched to RSC resources and are available on Learn Chemistry (see www.rsc. org/learn-chemistry).

A particularly useful initiative by the RSC is Chemistry at Work (CAW) which can support primary–secondary transition, the BGE phase and the senior phase in Chemistry (Royal Society of Chemistry, nd). CAW events emphasise what is happening in the local area. They aim to show a positive image of the chemical sciences and to present them as exciting, interesting and wealth-creating activities, which are worth considering as a career, while providing a basis for partnership development between a school and its community.

In Scotland, the basis of CfE involves the 'Building the Curriculum' (BTC) series, ranging from numbers 1 to 5 (Education Scotland, nd b). By implementing BTC4 – Skills for Learning, Skills for Life and Skills for Work, teaching staff may help young people to develop and apply enterprise and employability skills, engage with the world of work, and investigate the world of work locally, nationally and globally. Since CAW helps pupils to appreciate Chemistry in everyday life and the world of work, it satisfies the philosophy and recommendations associated with BTC4 and the BGE phase. A CAW template was created to help schools in Scotland engage with local businesses and expertise (Ritchie, 2014). The impact on pupils' awareness of Chemistry in everyday life has been reported as significant (Ritchie, 2014).

### Assessment – Introduction of Benchmarks

More recently benchmarks in Science have been introduced to clarify what learners need to know and be able to do to progress through the levels, and to support consistency in teachers' professional judgements (Education Scotland, 2017). Benchmarks have been developed to provide clarity on the national standards expected within each curriculum area at each level. They set out clear lines of progression in literacy and English and numeracy and mathematics, and across all other curriculum areas from early to fourth levels. All eight significant aspects for learning for sciences are clearly embedded in the benchmarks and provide the structure against which the benchmarks have been developed. Skills development is integrated into the benchmarks to support greater shared understanding. Benchmarks draw together previous assessment guidance (including significant aspects of learning, progression frameworks and annotated exemplars) into one key resource to support practitioners' professional judgement of children's and young people's progress across all curriculum areas.

## CHEMISTRY

### The Senior Phase

The senior phase, from S4 to S6 (ages 15 to 18), follows the BGE and builds on the E&Os achieved by the end of S3. Pupils can extend and deepen their learning and develop skills for learning, life and work, through qualifications and personal development (work placements and volunteering). Pupils can undertake N4, N5, H and AH Chemistry courses, which include assessment of an Added Value Unit (AVU). Availability of resources and support may affect pupil opportunities. Resources available at universities and colleges may help to support senior phase courses.

## N4 and N5 Chemistry

Both courses include the mandatory units Chemical Changes and Structure, Nature's Chemistry and Chemistry in Society as well as an AVU. All N4 units are internally assessed. The lack of external assessment has resulted in the qualification being undervalued. For N5, the AVU constitutes an assignment. N5 pupils complete an external assessment of the assignment and an external exam. A major challenge in delivering the national courses in Chemistry is bi-level, or, tri-level teaching where, because of lack of facilities and resources pupils with sharply differing abilities study together in the same classroom.

## H and AH Chemistry

The H Chemistry course incorporates Chemical Changes and Structure, Researching Chemistry, Nature's Chemistry, Chemistry in Society and the AVU. This includes controlling reaction rates and recognising underlying patterns. Collision theory, catalysts, the concept of electro-negativity and intra-molecular and intermolecular forces, are investigated. Learners undertake research in Chemistry, develop key skills in collecting information, and plan and undertake a practical investigation related to a topical issue. The course includes Organic chemistry, the chemistry of food and everyday consumer products, soaps, detergents, fragrances and skincare. Chemical processes, percentage yield and atom economy of processes are also covered. Learners use Analytical Chemistry to determine purity of reagents and products.

The AH Chemistry course (SQA, 2015) incorporates Inorganic and Physical Chemistry, Organic Chemistry and Instrumental Analysis, Researching Chemistry and an AVU. This course develops principles and concepts of Inorganic and Physical Chemistry including electromagnetic radiation and atomic spectroscopy. Learners gain an understanding of physical and chemical properties of transition metals and investigate chemical equilibria. They develop an understanding of feasibility of chemical reactions and research structures of organic compounds, including aromatics and amines and the use of spectroscopic techniques. They also study the use of medicines and drug interactions. Learners experience different practical techniques and related calculations. Learners identify, research, plan and safely carry out a chemistry practical investigation. For pupils completing a H and AH course, external assessment involves both the added value and an exam. At H and AH, the added value is assessed in the course assessment and must address the key purposes and aims of the course by addressing one or more of breadth, challenge or application. Challenges associated with H and AH Chemistry courses include lack of equipment and resources and pupils who have poor numeracy skills.

## LOOKING TO THE FUTURE

It is arguable that the Baccalaureate in Science programme has not been fully utilised because pupils studying AH Chemistry fail to deepen their research skills. Pupils not studying an AH can complete an Interdisciplinary Project and therefore have the opportunity to develop research skills. More recognition of the Baccalaureate in Science and the Interdisciplinary

Project by the SQA, universities and colleges would be useful. The Baccalaureate in Science Interdisciplinary Projects may also be used to help support interdisciplinary learning while helping to develop sustainable school–community partnerships that promote awareness of the role of science and Chemistry in society to staff and pupils (Ritchie, 2012).

## REFERENCES

Education Scotland (2017) *Curriculum for Excellence Benchmarks*, March. Online at https://education.gov.scot/improvement/Pages/Curriculum-for-Excellence-Benchmarks-.aspx

Education Scotland (nd a) *Broad General Education*. Online at https://education.gov.scot/scottish-education-system/Broad%20general%20education

Education Scotland (nd b) *Building the Curriculum*. Online at https://www.education.gov.scot/scottish-education-system/policy-for-scottish education/policy-drivers/cfe-(building-from-the-statement-appendix-incl-btc1-5)/Building%20the%20Curriculum

Ritchie, M. R. (2012) 'The Donaldson Review and Scottish baccalaureates – a model for implementation in schools', *School Science Review*, 93 (345), 99–108.

Ritchie, M. R. (2014) 'Chemistry at work – a model of school-community partnership', *Education in Science*, 256, 22–3.

Royal Society of Chemistry (nd) Chemistry at Work. Online at https://www.stem.org.uk/elibrary/resource/36047

Seith, E. (2015) 'Shortage fears intensify as trainee numbers falter'. Online at https://www.tes.com/news/tes-magazine/tes-magazine/shortage-fears-intensify-trainee-numbers-falter

SQA (2015) *Advanced Higher Chemistry Course Specification*. Online at www.sqa.org.uk/files/nq/AHCourseSpecChemistry.pdf

SQA (2016) Statistics 2016. Online at https://www.sqa.org.uk/sqa/80674.html

STEMEC (2016) STEMEC report. Online at www.gov.scot/Topics/Education/Schools/curriculum/STEM/STEMEC/Report/FinalSTEMECReport

# 43

# Computing Science

*Vic Lally and Peter Donaldson*

## INTRODUCTION

More than six years have now passed since the centenary in 2012 of Alan Turing's birth. At that time one of the important things to say about Computing and Information Systems education in Scottish Schools was that it was on the cusp of change. Alan Turing, the 'father' of modern computing, was a little known British genius, who is commemorated in one of the leading schools of informatics in the UK, at the University of Edinburgh (the Turing Room). Turing's contributions to the country's future, both as a computer scientist of genius, and a wartime code-breaker, are seminal. Yet, despite this, it continues to be the case that his reputation does not extend far beyond Computer Science. In a way, a similar fate has befallen Computer Science education itself. As an area of study, it continues to be somewhat neglected beyond the universities, yet there remains little doubt that the skills of Computing Science (CS), Computing education and computational thinking more broadly are of considerable and increasing importance for Scotland's economic and scientific futures. Therefore, it is crucial that new curriculum developments in this field support and enhance the talents and abilities of all Scotland's young people.

## ACHIEVEMENTS AND CHALLENGES FOR COMPUTING SCIENCE EDUCATION

Any account of the situation and progress of Computing Science in schools must be seen in the context of the broader changes within Scottish education since the introduction of a Curriculum for Excellence (CfE) into Secondary schools in 2010–11. The CS Exemplification project, supported by the British Computer Society (BCS), the Royal Society of Edinburgh, and Education Scotland, heralded changes from the 5–14 Information and Communication Technology (ICT) curriculum to the new Computing Science in the Technologies curriculum of CfE. Starting in 2011, and ending in 2013, it helped to exemplify exciting new approaches to teaching Computing Science concepts and programming skills in the later years of the broad general education. It made use of many new visual programming environments for novices, such as Scratch, Snap and AppInventor, and emphasised a creative approach to teaching CS.

During the first Computing at School Scotland (2014) conference in Microsoft's Edinburgh Office, many Scottish Computing teachers gathered together to examine the project outcomes, and new learning and teaching materials. Subsequent conferences in Glasgow, Dundee and Edinburgh Napier University brought together a growing number of Computing education initiatives. Recognising a pressing need for further professional learning to support Computing teachers, the Scottish Government funded a national programme of professional learning and networking for computing (PLAN C) between 2013 and 2015. During this project, over fifty lead teachers worked together with two national project officers to develop an understanding of research-informed teaching practices specifically for CS. They then shared this by establishing twenty-four PLAN C hubs across Scotland where colleagues in local areas could meet, share their own experiences and explore the new approaches to learning and teaching.

In 2015, Skills Development Scotland launched a skills investment plan for Scotland's ICT and digital technologies sector. Their Digital World campaign helped to raise wider public awareness of the opportunities enabled by studying CS. The pace of developments accelerated further still in 2016 with Education Scotland's release of *How Good is Our School?* which highlighted the underpinning nature of Computing Science for digital skills focusing on 'Increasing Creativity and Employability' (Education Scotland, 2016). In the same year Computing at School Scotland and BT launched the Barefoot project for primary schools in Scotland, and Education Scotland, together with Hewlett Packard and Intel, started the Digital Schools Award for primary schools.

Finally, some five years after Turing's centenary, Education Scotland released revised experiences and outcomes and benchmarks for the Technologies curricular area. The Centre for Computing Science Education was also established at the University of Glasgow. This will eventually become a central hub for the development of innovative approaches to Computing Science teacher education, a key focus for other strategic initiatives to support CS education, and a place where people can come together to help shape the future of the subject in Scotland.

Notwithstanding these developments, the greatest challenge presently facing the subject is teacher supply. The recent report by Computing at School Scotland (2016) has provided much insightful analysis that helps in understanding this issue.

In terms of Computing Science as a specialism, the most significant parameter is that the number of full-time equivalent (FTE) Computing teachers in Scotland has decreased. Table 43.1 shows this decline with data collected through Freedom of Information requests from all thirty-two local authorities (thirty satisfactory responses, one did not break down the figures by school and one is thought to be inaccurate). This was cross-referenced with information provided by the Scottish Qualifications Authority (SQA), the General Teaching Council for Scotland (GTCS) and the Scottish Government. In 2015, there were only 598 FTE teachers, which is lower than any other specialist area in the sciences, other Technologies or Mathematics. This has major implications for the health of the subject going forward, with some local authorities having fewer teachers than schools, particularly in rural or remote areas.

Table 43.1   Computer Science teachers in Scottish Schools, from 2005 to 2015

|                              | 2005 | 2007 | 2009 | 2011 | 2013 | 2015 |
|------------------------------|------|------|------|------|------|------|
| Number of FTEs               | 802  | 779  | 726  | 675  | 649  | 598  |
| Change compared to 2005 (%)  |      | −3   | −9   | −16  | −19  | −25  |

Source: Computing at School Scotland, 2016.

It's interesting to note that although the total number of pupils on the secondary school roll has fallen by 11 per cent, since 2005 there has been a 25 per cent decrease in the number of Computing teachers. By comparison, the numbers of teachers of English, Mathematics and Physics decreased by 4 per cent, 6 per cent and 10 per cent respectively. This suggests that pupils' access to Computing education in general, and CS in particular, narrowed. Over the last decade we have reached a position where nearly one fifth of Scottish schools (as at 2016), spread over half of the local authorities, have no computing specialist actively teaching classes. With a further quarter of secondary schools having only one Computing teacher, it is clear that guaranteed access to a coherent experience of Computing Science in the formal curriculum is less certain now than it was before the introduction of CfE.

It would be tempting to assume that schools, local authorities and the wider educational establishment no longer consider access to Computing Science education as a priority for pupils. However, nearly half of local authorities reported difficulties recruiting suitable candidates for CS teacher vacancies. Even where a post has been filled, there have been many instances where only one or two suitable candidates applied. Over half of local authorities have also had difficulties sourcing suitable Computing supply cover. The number of new teachers entering the profession is down by 67 per cent on 2006. As a further illustration of the lack of supply, only twenty newly qualified teachers in total joined the teacher induction scheme in 2014 and 2016. The Scottish Government has set specific and increased targets for Computing teachers since 2014, but with only two initial teacher education institutions in Glasgow able to recruit enough suitable applicants, more will have to be done to attract new entrants into the profession.

## COMPUTING QUALIFICATIONS

Historically, Computing education has centred on developing problem-solving skills by encouraging learners to apply knowledge, understanding and practical skills. Computing included the study of the professional, social, ethical and legal implications of its use, as well as the clear and concise communication of computing concepts using appropriate terminology. Starting at Intermediate 2 level (SCQF level 5) and upwards, options were provided in Artificial Intelligence, Computer Networking, and Multimedia Technology. The Higher qualification (SCQF level 6) in Computing also encouraged awareness of technological developments and progress, factors affecting system performance, and issues of syntax and semantics. Mandatory topics of study included data representation, computer structure, peripherals, networking and software. Learners also acquired knowledge and skills in developing software using a high-level programming language. The course encouraged them to make judgements, assess and compare ideas, and evaluate data. In Advanced Higher Computing, these ideas and skills were extended through investigation and analysis. It aimed to equip learners with skills to design and implement a solution to a significant computing problem of the learners choosing. The course focused on the software development process, looking at software development languages and environments, high-level programming languages, and standard algorithms with Computer Architecture replacing the Multimedia Technology optional unit. Students were assessed using both written and practical assessment instruments.

Running in parallel to the Higher Still Qualifications in Computing was 'Computing Studies' (introduced in 1984 and phased out in 2013). This was offered at Standard Grade

(SCQF levels 3–5) and Intermediate 1 level (SCQF level 4). The key aim of this course was to provide knowledge and experience of the technology that lies at the heart of modern society. It covered information technology concepts, the practical operation of hardware and software, and the awareness of how computers affect our work, home and leisure activities.

The new subject that was developed as part of CfE was called 'Computing Science' and combined concepts and skills from both the previous Computing and the Information Systems suite of qualifications. This emerged in response to a build-up of concerns with both Computing and Information Systems and Computer Studies in Scottish schools (see below). It was designed to combine the best aspects of both current subjects. Computing Science develops a range of computing and computational thinking skills, including skills in analysis and problem solving, design, as well as modelling, developing, implementing and testing digital solutions, across a range of contemporary contexts. In addition, the developers claim that it takes account of modern technologies and development methodologies related to software and information systems. The revised versions of these qualifications, currently being phased in, have been reorganised around four areas of application of Computing Science: Software, Web Development, Database Development, and Computer Architecture. A timed practical task carried out in class that samples skills across Software, and Web and Database Development will contribute to 30 per cent of the overall award with another 70 per cent from the written exam set by the SQA. At Advanced Higher level, this will change to a 40 per cent weighting for the practical task and 60 per cent for the final written exam.

## RATIONALE FOR COMPUTING SCIENCE

There has been a developing consensus that courses in Computing and Computer Studies needed substantial revision to meet the needs of students and educators for the twenty-first century in Scotland. For example, one point which was made by teachers was that this suite of subjects did not concentrate enough on the main concepts of Computing Science, and concentrated too much on hardware and systems that dated quickly and became obsolete. Similar issues were raised about the English qualifications by the Computing at School Working Group in 2012, before the establishment of separate groups in Scotland, Wales and Northern Ireland. In many ways, both of these criticisms echoed the more detailed range of concerns raised by the Royal Society of London (2012) about the state of Computing in schools across the UK. While the data and evidence presented in that report was based significantly on the English context, it also aligned with findings from interviews (conducted for this chapter) with other leading and informed figures in the field of Scottish education and teacher education.

Another issue that prompted the move was the confusion between 'Computing' – the science discussed above – and the use of computers in a wide range of settings to manage a vast array of activities and communications – often referred to more recently as digital literacy or digital skills. This has been widespread amongst parents and pupils, schools, local authorities, teaching colleagues and government ministers. One of the consequences is that Computing Science itself has been often overlooked in this confusion. This had implications in the past for policy, teacher education, and pupils' future lives and careers. This confusion has been more firmly addressed, with the new Technologies experiences and outcomes and benchmarks in the broad general education phase (nursery to third year of secondary school) and the Computing Science qualifications in the senior phase (fourth to sixth year of secondary school). However, it is important to continue to 'disaggregate' the term from wider notions of digital literacy, so that 'Computing Science' can achieve some distinctive recognition as a central scientific discipline in its own right. Although members of the Computing community are more keenly aware of the distinction, further work will need to be carried out to develop understanding more widely both within education and in public life generally.

## LEARNING FROM INTERNATIONAL PERSPECTIVES

Looking at Computer Science teaching internationally, it is still clear that other countries with a similar population size and gross domestic product (GDP) to Scotland have undertaken initiatives in the field of school Computing Science education from which Scotland could learn as it develops its Curriculum for Excellence. Israel, for example, undertook a major review of Computing in school in the 1990s. It now has one of the most rigorous Computer Science high school programmes in the world. Stephenson et al. (2005) consulted an international panel of Computer Science educators, including those in Scotland, Israel and Canada. They concluded that when a country is developing a new curriculum it is essential to ensure that it meets key criteria. These include ensuring that: there is a link between the outcome required and the strategies used; change is driven by 'real learning needs and not politically manufactured needs'; and the context of larger social and economic forces is considered. Furthermore, stakeholder agreement, adequate resources and a long-term vision were also cited as being central to success in curriculum improvement. Hazzan et al. (2008) developed a model to encapsulate the current high school Computer Science curriculum in Israel that is built on these criteria. Their 'Four Key Elements' are: a well-defined curriculum (including written course textbooks and teaching guides); a requirement of a mandatory formal CS teaching licence; teacher preparation programmes (including at least a Bachelor's degree in CS and a CS teaching certificate study programme); and research in CS education (Hazzan et al., 2008 p.281). The new curriculum has been in place since 1995, and is taken by 10,000–20,000 students.

New Zealand is another successful 'Computer Science country' with a population size and GDP comparable to Scotland. In 2008 two influential reports appeared (Grimsey and Phillipps, 2008; Carrel et al., 2008) that influenced a revamping of its school curriculum in Digital Technologies. The curriculum from 2011 has an explicit strand called 'Programming and Computer Science'. Having established the importance of programming skills, the curriculum designers are now shifting their focus to the infrastructural issues of creating suitable materials and developing teacher education. All seven of the major Computer Science university departments have been involved in the process, as well as in the revised teacher education that will support it. These examples help to provide a 'template' for some of the issues and challenges that Scotland still faces as it strives to implement and support its new Computing Science qualifications in Curriculum for Excellence.

## CONCLUSIONS

We are now over six years on from the centenary of Turing's birth, and Computing Science education has passed a turning point in Scotland. There is good reason for optimism, with the new Centre for Computing Science Education in Glasgow striving to promote the subject in new and innovative ways. Revisions and improvements to the existing Computing Science qualifications are coming on stream, and the new emphasis on the rigour of the scientific aspects of the discipline will help young people to establish the foundations of successful careers. Educating new generations in Computing Science will assist in creating more informed citizens and help to develop Scotland's economy in changing and challenging global conditions. However, the challenges of meeting specialist teacher supply, developing suitable innovative continuing professional development (CPD) with a pedagogical focus, and creating new and exciting teaching and learning materials remain. All these need to be addressed if Scotland is to truly bring its Computing Science education on to the world stage in the twenty-first century. Turing, we hope, would have been proud of the progress that has been made in Scotland. We hope to honour his memory by continuing the pace of improvements in the coming years.

## ACKNOWLEDGEMENTS

We would like to thank all those experts in the Computer Science field in Scotland who gave their time to answer our questions about the current state of developments and future prospects. However, in interpreting and analysing their very helpful responses, errors and omissions may have occurred. These are entirely our own.

## REFERENCES

BCS, The Chartered Institute for IT (2016) 'Barefoot boost for computing science in Scottish primary schools'. Online at www.bcs.org/content/conWebDoc/56541

Carrel, T., Gough-Jones, V. and Fahy, K. (2008) *The Future of Computer Science and Digital Technologies in New Zealand Secondary Schools: Issues of 21st Teaching and Learning, Senior Courses and Suitable Assessments*. Online at http://dtg.tki.org.nz/content/download/670/3222/file/Digital%20Technologies%20discussion%20paper.pdf

Computing at School Scotland (2016) *Computing Teachers in Scotland*, BCS, The Chartered Institute for IT. Online at www.cas.scot/wp-content/uploads/2016/08/ComputingTeachersinScotland-CASSReport2016.pdf

Computing at School Working Group (2012) *Computer Science as a School Subject: Seizing the Opportunity*. Online at http://community.computingatschool.org.uk/files/6708/original.pdf

Education Scotland (2016) *How Good Is Our School?* Fourth edition. Online at https://education.gov.scot/improvement/frwk2hgios

Education Scotland (2017) *Revised Technologies Experiences and Outcomes*. Online at https://www.education.gov.scot/Documents/Technologies-es-os.pdf

Grimsey, G. and Phillipps, M. (2008) *Evaluation of Technology Achievement Standards For Use in New Zealand Secondary School Computing Education*. Wellington: NZCS.

Hazzan, O., Gal-Ezer, J. and Blum, L. (2008) 'A model for high school computer science education: The four key elements that make it', 39th Technical Symposium on Computer Science Education, SIGCSE Bulletin, 40 (1), 281–5. New York: ACM.

Royal Society of London (2012) *Shut Down or Restart? The Way Forward For Computing in UK Schools*. London: Royal Society (Education Section). Online at http://royalsociety.org/education/policy/computing-in-schools/report/

Scott, J. (2013) The Royal Society of Edinburgh/British Computer Society Computer Science Exemplification Project. Proceedings of the 18th ACM Conference on Innovation and Technology in Computer Science Education. ACM, p. 315.

Scottish Qualifications Authority (2017) Computing Science qualifications overview. Online at https://www.sqa.org.uk/sqa/48477.html

Skills Development Scotland (2015) *A New Marketing Campaign Encouraging More People to Consider a Career in Scotland's Digital Sector is Being Launched*. Online at www.skillsdevelopmentscotland.co.uk/news-events/2015/october/new-campaign-to-promote-careers-in-the-digital-sector/

Stephenson, C., Gal-Ezer, J., Haberman, B. and Verno, A. (2005) *The New Educational Imperative: Improving High School Computer Science Education, Final Report of the CSTA, Curriculum Improvement Task Force*. Online at http://csta.acm.org/Publications/CSTAWhitePaperNC.pdf.

# 44

# Design and Technology

*David Morrison-Love*

> Technology – the application of knowledge and skills to extend human capabilities and to help satisfy human needs and wants – has had profound effects on society. (Education Scotland, 2009)

While 'educational technology' (or information and communication technology (ICT)) can be employed within any subject area, Technology Education (or Design and Technology) is itself a discrete subject area wherein its concepts, knowledge, processes and outcomes form a locus for pupils' learning. The earliest curricular incarnation of Design and Technology in Scotland appeared in the late 1800s when the Royal Society of Arts formalised the development of technical skills and knowledge in response to fast growing agricultural needs. Since that time, technology subjects have evolved to retain a valuable place within Scottish schools. This is not least insofar as they continue to foster knowledge, understanding, creativity, skills and dispositions related to real-world issues, processes and problems that are of considerable value to industry, business and society more widely. This evolution, however, has not been without challenge. Design and Technology is, in many senses, an educational construct with ongoing efforts to characterise better and cohere its underlying epistemology (Morrison-Love, 2017). The complex nature of technology in different contexts – curricular and otherwise – results in variations in how it is viewed and understood as a subject. Encouragingly, historical perceptions of technology education as simply woodwork, or as a less 'academic' pathway, appear to be lessening in Scotland.

The current suite of Scottish Design and Technology subjects can be characterised as drawing largely upon engineering and historically vocational roots (Doherty and Canavan, 2006). Collectively, they allow pupils to foster a wide range of skills and capacities in such things as: design thinking, research, concept development, manufacture and making, electronics, structures, control systems, graphics, computer modelling as well as technological effects and impacts. This builds technological capability and, within Curriculum for Excellence, is argued as essential for young people to embrace technological developments and play a major role in the global economy. Though not vocational by definition, these subjects offer unique and valuable points of departure for pupils into the world of work.

## DESIGN AND TECHNOLOGY IN THE SCOTTISH CURRICULUM FRAMEWORK

Historical, teacher workforce, political and socio-technological influences have, over time, shaped the accommodation of Design and Technology subjects in the Scottish curriculum. Pupils can engage with technology subject content from early years, through National level courses to Higher and Advanced Higher. The structure of this content differs between educational phases with pupils able to study more specialised areas of technology through subject choice as they move from the broad general education into the senior phase. In 2016/17, the drafting of subject benchmark statements was an attempt to better support progression through the general phase and on into the more specialist areas of study. Broad general education courses internally developed by departments necessarily introduce a spread of content and thinking but have, in the past, been recognised as disproportionately craft heavy by Her Majesty's Inspectorate of Education (HMIe). Benchmarks for Design and Technology are exemplified around the areas of design and construction, uses of materials, graphical representation and application of engineering that articulate with content across senior phase subjects. Until recently, pupils who opt to specialise further in Design and Technology would have chosen one or two core technology options from Design and Manufacture, Graphic Communication, Engineering Science, or practical subjects in Woodworking, Metalworking and Electronics. Additional modules and skills for work courses that some departments offer could provide additional possibilities, with 'Design and Technology' also available as a discrete subject option (though only at National 3).

Though this is a significantly greater number of possible subjects than for any other school department, resources and capacity within a school will typically allow for between two and four subjects to be offered within a range of Scottish Credit and Qualifications Framework (SCQF) levels. The landscape, however, has grown more complex with the emergence of new tensions concerning uptake. A slackening of the requirement that all schools run the broad general education up until the end of S3, and an increased flexibility in school timetabling, ultimately vary the points at which pupils undertake senior phase subjects. Simultaneously, a narrowing by schools of the number of subject choices at this transition point – for example, from eight to five – is growing in prevalence. This can amplify competition and make it more difficult for pupils to study more than one technology subject. In the first year of Design and Manufacture, there was a 47 per cent drop in pupil uptake when compared with the number of pupils sitting Intermediate Product Design and Standard Grade Craft and Design in the final year they ran (McLaren et al., 2014). Typically, Design and Technology is grouped in faculties alongside subjects such as Home Economics, Art and Design, Physical Education and Computing. Departments of between two and six teachers deliver courses from within the four main subject streams typically found across Scottish Design and Technology departments. These are characterised in the following sections.

## GRAPHIC COMMUNICATION SUBJECTS

This subject centres on the development of visual interpretation, representation, reasoning and literacy among learners. Here, pupils develop skills, knowledge and understanding in graphics and drawing types, conventions, equipment and technologies, graphic production and wider societal impacts. Historically, this subject evolved from 'Technical Drawing' which first appeared in the early 1970s alongside 'Building Drawing' as a core technical subject. Aspects of both were present within Standard Grade Graphic Communication, first introduced in 1992–3, and continue to be reflected in current courses. The addition of more presentation-based graphical approaches in Standard Grade marked a point of departure from the more engineering-influenced nature of its technical and building predecessors. Though these presentation approaches were procedural rather than artistic, it was sometimes felt, by both teachers and pupils, that an artistic predisposition was nonetheless advantageous. The opportunity for pupils to learn using commercial computer aided drawing (CAD) and three-dimensional (3D) modelling software is a distinct strength and the subject continues to respond to advances in them.

Currently, pupils can study Graphic Communication from SCQF levels 4 to 7. From National 4 to Higher, subjects are structured around '2D Graphics' and '3D and Pictorial Graphics'. In the first of these, learning focuses with increasing sophistication and demand on, for example, orthographic/geometric drawing, illustration and desktop publishing. The second encompasses pictorial drawings such as perspective sketches and isometric as well as 3D computer modelling using platforms such as Autodesk Inventor. In Advanced Higher, content is divided between units on commercial and visual media, and technical graphics with pupils able to extend their learning to include moving media.

Pedagogy involves individual, group and whole class approaches, and process modelling targeted at developing procedural knowledge and visual interpretation. E-learning solutions are often employed in relation to 3D modelling which increasingly foster pupils' self-directed learning. Assessment draws upon project work, an assignment and exam, though the decision to remove manual drawing from the latter of these places a stronger emphasis on visual interpretation.

## ENGINEERING SCIENCE SUBJECTS

For all of the same reasons articulated by de Vries (1996), Design and Technology in Scotland does not constitute applied science. This being said, Engineering Science reveals the closest overt proximity to Science and Maths of any of the subjects in this suite. With its roots tied to the 1960s subject 'Applied Mechanics', Engineering Science developed through a number of stages. In the 1970s, Applied Mechanics was replaced with Engineering Science which, to meet the shifting requirements of industry at that time, was considerably revised to form Technological Studies in 1988. It provided pupils with the opportunity to engage in largely top-down, systems-driven problem solving in which solutions draw understanding from a number of areas such as electronics and structures. Pupils had to move beyond just learning about concepts, laws and principles, and functionally use them.

Curriculum for Excellence saw Technological Studies revised once again, re-adopting the name Engineering Science. This was partly in response to the University of Glasgow's Engineering the Future project, which also gave rise to the STEM Central website. Available at SCQF levels 4 to 7, this subject draws heavily upon its predecessor. National 4, 5 and Higher courses comprise of units in 'Electronics and Control', 'Mechanisms and Structures' and 'Engineering Contexts and Challenges'. In the former two, pupils learn to analyse problem situations, simulate, develop, test and evaluate solutions. They build their understanding of analogue and digital electronics, and microprocessor control, as well as material properties, mechanical and structural concepts such as moments and nodal analysis. In contrast to Technological Studies, the latter unit engages pupils more explicitly with what engineers do and the social and environmental impacts which engineering has in the world. At Advanced Higher level, this unit evolves to focus learning on the management and development of real-world engineering projects. With schools no longer required to use Basic Stamp, several are introducing pupils to more contemporary processor platforms such as Arduino.

The systems approach and comparatively structured problem-solving heuristics shape subject pedagogy with an emphasis on deductive approaches to learning. Whole class, group and individual approaches to fostering conceptual understanding are often set within project and problem-based contexts. Course assessment takes place through exams and pupil assignments.

## DESIGN AND MANUFACTURE SUBJECTS

This subject evolved from a synthesis of Craft and Design, and Product Design. The former of these, first introduced in 1985 (revised in 1992), evolved from what was Integrated Craft which, for the first time, introduced plastic work to woodwork and metalwork, following the recommendations of the Scottish Examination Board's (SEB's) Curriculum Paper 10 in the early 1970s. Craft and Design further developed this in promoting a continuous rather than compartmentalised learning experience around designing and making that linked knowledge and understanding with project work. Notably popular with pupils, the subject provided opportunities for individualisation and a sense of ownership. Product Design, first introduced in 2004 at SCQF level 5 and above, offered pupils a strong insight into design and modern manufacturing, though was recognised in practice as having a greater emphasis on design over making in the sense that was often evident in Craft and Design. Challenges for some pupils lay with the level of English necessary for reasoning with complex design concepts.

Design and Manufacture, first introduced in 2012–13, offers pupils a similarly rich insight into the designed and made world but with more streamline curricular progression from SCQF levels 4 to 7. Structured around 'Design', and 'Materials and Manufacture' from National 4 to Higher, this subject seeks to develop capacities in design thinking, problem solving, analysis, creativity, ideation, prototyping and evaluation. Pupils develop knowledge and understanding of design concepts, tools, processes and manufacture from 3D printing and laser cutting, through to larger scale industrial production technologies. Considerations of ethical, environmental and societal implications deepen understanding through setting decisions in a wider context. Units in Advanced Higher focus on product analysis, development and evolution, allowing deeper examination of the historical and socio-technical influences on commercial products.

The varied nature of content engenders a range of whole class, group and individual learning and teaching approaches. These involve modelling, problem and project-based learning as well as design thinking. The most successful pedagogies explicate process over content and enable pupils to better transfer learning to individual project work whilst mitigating against fixation effects during idea generation.

## PRACTICAL SUBJECTS

In contrast to other subjects such as Design and Manufacture, this group of three subjects emphasises the development of practical skills in artefact manufacture over written understanding or design. Practical Woodworking and Practical Metalworking, available at SCQF levels 4 and 5, retain many of the more traditional hand and machining skills found in the technical subjects of the early 1970s. Practical Electronics differs insofar as it is structured around a design, fabricate and test process and has a nominal national annual uptake of just over 100 at National 5. At the same level, 4,366 pupils were presented for Practical Woodwork in 2016 but, reflective of resourcing, demand and the profile of teacher expertise, the uptake of Practical Metalwork is normally around one quarter of this (https://www.sqa. org.uk/sqa/files_ccc/2016-sqa-attainment-summary.pdf). These subjects are distinct in that they are not available beyond National 5 and are internally assessed.

Practical Woodworking and Metalworking are structured around three units. Success requires significant levels of practical problem solving, visual interpretation, and resilience in realising high quality material artefacts from construction drawings. In Practical Woodworking, pupils develop skills in frame and carcase construction, machining and finishing. Permeating skills include measuring marking out and cutting with an expectation that pupils work towards achieving practical tolerances of +/– 1 mm. This is also true of Practical Metalworking where pupils develop bench skills, machining, methods of fabrication and thermal joining. There has been an erroneous tendency to associate the practical nature of these subjects with a lower level of challenge, but this fails to recognise that challenge in learning exists in multiple forms. Many pupils find these subjects to be highly demanding due to the expected level of craftsmanship and sustained levels of concentration required.

Modelling and cognitive apprenticeship-style pedagogies dominate these subjects with significant demand on the classroom teacher to manage pupils and resources in a way that simultaneously maximises learning, health and safety. Pupils' grades are based on their value-added project.

## RECENT DEVELOPMENTS IN DESIGN AND TECHNOLOGY

Over the last few years, significant change in Design and Technology has been felt by departments across Scotland with some of the most notable being in Design and Manufacture and Graphic Communication. Teachers recently welcomed a dramatic reduction by the Scottish Qualifications Authority (SQA) in the number of assessment standards in Design and Manufacture from over thirty to just eighteen. Combined with new progression thresholds in all technology subjects, this eased both evidence gathering and better aligned the subject with the philosophy of Curriculum for Excellence. With subject content, a less linear conceptualisation of design activity enhances authenticity, though difficulty remains for many pupils in distinguishing between analytical and evaluative processes. In Graphic Communication, manual drawing with instruments was removed from SQA examinations. This prompted a tectonic shift in the nature of assessment for this subject which is now characterised far more by visual interpretation and reasoning. Pupils subsequently require quite different cognitive skills and changes to subject pedagogy for which teachers have received little support. Further change is likely following the government's decision to remove the requirement for unit assessments for all subjects.

## MOVING FORWARD

Design and Technology has made a robust contribution to the education of Scottish schoolchildren with continued opportunities and challenges. There are exciting opportunities for innovation with new and emerging digital technologies, but access to facilities such as laser cutting, 3D printing and high-end computing – whilst greater than ever – remains inconsistent across Scotland. Though design and technology provides a tremendous context for interdisciplinary learning, this sits largely untapped with Scotland yet to embrace more integrative approaches to science, technology, engineering and mathematics (STEM).

Finally, continued efforts to encourage highly capable teachers into Design and Technology are essential. Protection of disciplinary expertise forms a critical part of this within a growing culture of 'genericisation' in initial teacher education. Notably, of those students at the University of Glasgow working towards a teaching career in Design and Technology, around 58 per cent are female. This will grow the number of role models in an important, but still male-dominated, subject area.

## REFERENCES

de Vries, M. J. (1996) 'Technology education: beyond the "technology is applied science" paradigm', *Journal of Technology Education*, 8 (1).

Doherty, R. A. and Canavan, B. (2006) 'Mapping reform in Scotland's technology education curriculum: change and curriculum policy in the compulsory sector', in M. J. de Vries and I. Mottier (eds), *International Handbook of Technology Education: The State of the Art*. Rotterdam: Sense Publishers, pp. 347–75.

Education Scotland (2009) *Curriculum for Excellence: Experiences and Outcomes*. Online at https://www.education.gov.scot/Documents/all-experiences-and-outcomes.pdf

McLaren, S. V., Dunn, L. and Murdoch, G. (2014) *The TE of STEM: Recruitment issues. A Report to the Science, Technology, Engineering and Maths Education Committee*. Online at www.gov.scot/Resource/0045/00459939.docx

Morrison-Love, D. (2017) 'Towards a transformative epistemology of technology education', *Journal of Philosophy of Education*, 51 (1), 23–37.

# 45

# Drama

*Will Barlow*

## DRAMA WITHIN THE BROAD GENERAL EDUCATION

Learners in Secondary 1–3 work towards the third level of Curriculum for Excellence (CfE), while more able pupils study fourth level experiences and outcomes (Es and Os) (Education Scotland, 2009). Drama third and fourth level Es and Os develop learners' devising, presentation and reflective skills. However, it would be a limited view of Drama to suggest that it simply teaches acting or production skills. Drama is also a pedagogical approach that takes abstract curricular ideas, often focused on skills and concepts, and provides a learning context based on human experience. Winston and Tandy (2009) suggest that Drama education establishes a connected curriculum which deepens learners' curricular knowledge and understanding by creating a less fragmented educational experience. The Scottish Government (2008) asked educators to create interdisciplinary studies, thus interdisciplinary learning (IDL), to help learners establish links between Es and Os. Nevertheless, there remain schools which have little or no Drama provision. Therefore, it might be argued that the Scottish Government's request for an integrated curriculum cannot be established until equal weighting is given to curricular subjects.

## BROAD GENERAL EDUCATION DRAMA BENCHMARKS

Each broad general education (BGE) level has been expanded, with examples of Drama terminology and practice, to furnish learners and educators with the expectations of the national standards. The benchmarks map learners' engagement with practical and theoretical Drama throughout the levels by linking specific skills to individual Es and Os. Consequently, one might question whether the benchmarks have created a framework for skill assessment over an aesthetic pedagogy (see 'Drama and Aesthetic Education' below).

## NATIONAL 3 DRAMA

National 3 Drama builds upon the skills developed within the BGE and consists of two units, Drama Skills and Production Skills. Drama Skills develops learners' understanding of basic dramatic structures; Production Skills develops learners' understanding of theatre arts. Assessment might include observational checklists and video recordings.

## NATIONAL 4 DRAMA

National 4 Drama has three internally assessed units: Drama Skills, Productions Skills and an Added Value Unit. *Drama Skills* develops learners' understanding of form, genre, style and structure; *Production Skills* develops learners' abilities in the application of design roles; and the Added Value Unit requires learners to specialise in acting or a design role and present a devised or scripted Drama. Assessment might include evidence of learners' skills and knowledge developed during the first two units and a production support log for the final unit.

## NATIONAL 5 DRAMA

The updated National 5 Drama course develops learners' practical and reflective skills while advancing their knowledge and understanding of the social and cultural influences on Drama. Learners develop skills in: acting; responding to stimuli; using form, structure, genre and conventions; production areas; and presenting texts using a range of production areas. The course assessment consists of a question paper and a performance. The question paper has two sections, with the first requiring learners to answer questions based on a production in which they have participated. Section two requires learners to respond to stimuli by suggesting ideas on how to devise, rehearse and present to an audience. The performance assesses learners in either an acting or a technical production role and includes a written preparation for performance. Additionally, learners can be assessed against the standalone units of Drama Skills and/or Production Skills.

## HIGHER DRAMA

The current Higher Drama course structure includes two internally assessed units (Drama Skills and Production Skills) and an externally assessed Added Value Unit. Drama Skills develops learners' response to stimuli, and ability to apply and evaluate complex dramatic structures. Production Skills develops learners' knowledge and understanding of complex production skills (including directing) to enhance and evaluate presentations. The Added Value Unit consists of two components – a performance (including a written preparation for performance) and a question paper. Actors present two contrasting extracts from published scripts; directors direct two pages of a chosen text; and designers create a set design including an additional production role. The question paper consists of two essays which include an analysis of a studied text and a live performance.

## ADVANCED HIGHER DRAMA

The current Advanced Higher Drama course consists of Drama Skills, Production Skills and an Added Value Unit. Drama Skills develops learners' skills in creating, presenting and evaluating a devised performance using the methodologies of a key theatre practitioner. Production Skills develops learners' knowledge and understanding of complex production skills by exploring and analysing the influences, theories and practices of a key theatre practitioner. The final unit consists of a performance (including a written preparation for performance) and project dissertation. Actors perform two acting roles: one interactive and one monologue. Directors direct a key scene of their chosen text and designers produce a set design for a play, including a scale model set, and two production concepts. The project dissertation consists of an area of specialist study involving the research of relevant performance theories and practice.

## CURRENT TRENDS IN DRAMA – NATIONAL 5, HIGHER AND ADVANCED HIGHER DRAMA

Tables 45.1–45.3 give data for National 5, Higher and Advanced Higher Drama awards.

### National 5 Drama

Band A awards have declined yearly. There has been an increase in band B awards from 2014 to 2015 (however, this remains steady between 2015 and 2016). Awards at bands C and D have increased yearly as has candidates achieving a 'no award'. Candidate numbers increased between 2014 and 2015, however, in 2016 there was a 2.7 per cent decrease in candidates compared to 2015. Female candidates outnumber males and consistently achieve

Table 45.1    National 5 Drama candidate awards between 2014 and 2016

| Year, candidates and gender | Band A (%) | Band B (%) | Band C (%) | Band D (%) | No award (%) |
|---|---|---|---|---|---|
| 2014, candidates = 4,146 | 56.8 | 24.1 | 12.8 | 2.9 | 3.4 |
| Female = 2,941 | 61 | 22.5 | 11.4 | 2.4 | 2.7 |
| Male = 1,205 | 46.6 | 27.8 | 16.2 | 4 | 5.4 |
| 2015, candidates = 4,716 | 54.4 | 24.5 | 13.2 | 3.1 | 3.8 |
| Female = 3,282 | 58.2 | 23.8 | 12.3 | 2.7 | 3 |
| Male = 1,434 | 49.1 | 26.2 | 15.2 | 3.9 | 5.6 |
| 2016, candidates = 4,589 | 52.5 | 24.5 | 14.8 | 3.9 | 4.3 |
| Female = 3,113 | 57.3 | 22.5 | 13.1 | 3.8 | 3.3 |
| Male = 1,476 | 42.5 | 28.6 | 18.4 | 4.1 | 6.4 |

Table 45.2    Higher Drama candidate awards between 2015 and 2016

| Year, candidate and gender | Band A (%) | Band B (%) | Band C (%) | Band D (%) | No award (%) |
|---|---|---|---|---|---|
| 2015, candidates = 2,425 | 38.6 | 28.5 | 21.9 | 5.4 | 5.6 |
| Female = 1,732 | 40.9 | 28.1 | 21.6 | 5.1 | 4.3 |
| Male = 693 | 33.0 | 29.5 | 22.5 | 6.1 | 8.9 |
| 2016, candidates = 3,117 | 45.8 | 24.6 | 18.4 | 4.8 | 6.4 |
| Female = 2,213 | 49.8 | 24.5 | 16.7 | 4.4 | 4.6 |
| Male = 904 | 36.2 | 24.6 | 22.8 | 5.7 | 10.7 |

Table 45.3    Advanced Higher Drama candidate awards 2016

| Year, candidate numbers and gender | Band A (%) | Band B (%) | Band C (%) | Band D (%) | No award (%) |
|---|---|---|---|---|---|
| 2016, candidates = 537 | 28.1 | 28.9 | 24.6 | 8.9 | 9.5 |
| Female = 381 | 29.7 | 28.8 | 23.7 | 8.6 | 9.2 |
| Male = 156 | 24.4 | 28.8 | 26.9 | 9.6 | 10.3 |

more band A awards. Male candidates outperform females at bands B to D and are more likely to gain a no award banding (SQA, 2016a).

### Higher Drama

A 22 per cent increase was seen in 2016 in candidate numbers and a 7.2 per cent growth in band A awards in comparison to 2015. However, awards gained at bands B to D have decreased compared to those in 2015. There was a 1.2 per cent increase in candidates receiving no award between 2015 and 2016. Female candidates outperform males at band A awards and outnumber them in representation. Males outperform females at bands B to D and are more likely to gain a no award banding (SQA, 2016a).

### Advanced Higher Drama

The bandings of A–C were achieved by 81.6 per cent of candidates, while 18.4 per cent gained the lower bands of D and no award. Female candidates outperformed males at band A and tie at band B. Males statistically outperform females at B and D and are more likely to gain a no award banding (SQA, 2016a).

### Summary of Current Trends in Drama

Band A awards have declined since the introduction of National 5 Drama. However, since 2014 over 50 per cent of candidates have achieved a National 5 band A. Band A awards at Higher level have increased with a reduction in bandings B–C. There has been a yearly increase in candidates receiving no awards at National 5 and Higher. This suggests that the advancement between Drama courses might be too challenging for some candidates. In addition, questions might be asked of Education Scotland and the SQA as to how they can support educators in rectifying the yearly increase in no awards across Drama qualifications. In addition, there is an imbalance in the number of female compared to male candidates. Female candidates tend to achieve more band A awards than males, whereas male candidates are more likely to achieve a no award banding than females.

## DRAMA DEPARTMENTS AND FACULTIES

Drama departments, over recent years, have become subsumed in faculty structures with non-promoted colleagues frequently assuming additional responsibilities that were once the remit of principal teachers, often without financial reward. Additionally, a number of Drama departments have been created with probationary teachers who often operate without Drama support from faculty colleagues. This has the potential to cause additional pressure on inexperienced Drama teachers and possibly impact upon young people's attainment. However, faculty structures have the potential for IDL across faculty subjects to create a relevant and enriched pedagogy.

## TENSIONS WITHIN THE SCOTTISH DRAMA CURRICULUM

The Drama curriculum might be summarised as the *process versus product* debate. This debate centres on whether learners are taught the external skills of performance, or the development in understanding of self and others (Anderson, 2012). The Drama Skills and Production Skills units attempt to establish O'Toole and O'Mara's (2007, p. 213) suggestion of a 'unifying paradigm'. They suggest that a 'unifying paradigm' establishes tripartite learning based on making, performing and evaluating. This approach identifies the understanding and making of the art form as central components of the learning process (ibid.). However, the Added Value Units focus on theatre-making of a published script and critical appreciation, or aesthetic judgement, of theatre performances, texts and key practitioners' methodologies. Two potential issues arise from this focus. First, learners are becoming consumers of Drama and are possibly taught to appreciate it for its 'civilizing influences and [potential] to generate audience for adult theatre' (O'Toole et al., 2009, p. 129). Second, Drama might attempt to mirror professional theatre with learners being judged by adult standards. Judging learners by such standards might be confirmed if we consider the SQA's (2016b, p. 4) suggestion that candidates are sometimes cast in roles that are too demanding and, 'at times, direction of blocking and movement was weak, with lack of consideration to character interaction or understanding of character motivation'.

However, Theatre and Drama Education, while interrelated, are not the same and do not, nor should they, attempt to achieve similar outcomes (Anderson, 2012). Indeed, there are limited opportunities, with the National Qualifications, to assess learners who wish to study solely applied or devised theatre. Currently, only the National 4 Drama Added Value Unit enables learners to be assessed through either a devised or scripted performance. However, in practice, National 4 candidates tend to be co-assessed in the National 5 Drama Added Value Unit – a scripted performance.

### Drama Education is Not Professional Theatre – Schools Are Not Theatres

Drama education should not attempt to carbon copy professional theatre nor should it seek primarily to train actors, directors, designers or any other kind of Theatre/Drama worker (Anderson, 2012). Instead, Drama should engage learners with the aesthetic of the subject and develop their understanding of self and others, while advancing their understanding of theatre (Neelands and Nelson, 2015). Currently, only one E and O, at early level, centres on helping learners understand their world: 'I use drama to explore real and imaginary situations, helping me to understand my world (EXA 0–14a) (Education Scotland, 2009). Subsequent Es and Os and learning outcomes focus on performance skills. Therefore, one might argue that external skill development, which places the needs of audiences over learners, is central to the curriculum. Granted the Es and Os and learning outcomes are written from a learner's perspective; however, young people are predominantly being taught skills leading to a performance that assesses their interpretation of text, complex drama and production skills and impact on audience. The missing curricular link is for learners to be assessed in using these skills to devise performances in the Added Value Units.

## DRAMA AND AESTHETIC EDUCATION

Neelands and Goode (2015) support a view of Drama education that challenges the narrow, or exclusive, set of culturally bound forms of theatre. These forms often emphasise the separation of spectator and actor, through the performance of a playwright's work to an audience, or the studying of texts and teaching of acting skills. Instead, Neelands and Goode (2015) promote a 'conventions' approach where learners fuse the roles of spectator and actor, in the symbolic and real dimensions of the action, to develop the skills of sensitivity, perception and understanding of theatre itself. If we consider Anderson's (2012) suggestion that theatre and Drama education are not the same thing, this then enables practitioners to draw upon the aesthetics of theatre to create a form that places learners at the centre of the curriculum. Anderson (2012) indicates that this form empowers learners to devise and analyse work that is meaningful to them while engaging aesthetic control (the way learners develop skills and engage with drama over time) and understanding of the art form. Aesthetic control and understanding blur the lines of creating, performing and evaluating to create deeper engagement with dramatic meaning. This is because learners critically engage with stimuli to create, and be assessed on, devised performances which carry a social, historical and political meaning relevant to their lives (Anderson, 2012).

## THE BENEFITS OF DRAMA AND AESTHETIC EDUCATION – THE UNIQUENESS OF DRAMA

Discussions often abound regarding the motivational benefits of Drama to increase learner attainment and achievement. However, while not wishing to detract from the merits of these discussions, it is the uniqueness of Drama which might be missing from this discourse. Drama is unique within the curriculum as it enables learners to consider their understanding of the world afresh through the process of *enacted fiction*. Consequently, learners can manipulate people, place and time, within the safety net of symbolic dimension, giving them *permission to stare*. By holding both real and symbolic dimensions simultaneously in their heads, learners are empowered to create 'real-life' scenarios by suspending their disbelief and engaging their dramatic imagination to live in other people's shoes. In turn, learners attempt to understand others' perspectives and actions without ever suffering the long-term consequences accrued in the real world. This creates a 'here and now' curriculum that values participants' thoughts, feelings and fantasies and recognises the importance of the individual and collective human perspective. Therefore, the uniqueness of Drama is that it empowers learners to become the subject rather than object of their experiences.

## CONCLUSION

The CfE attempts to develop learners' practical knowledge and appreciation of Drama. However, in doing so, the opportunities for assessment in dramatic forms, other than a traditional Western view of theatre, is limited. As such, it could be argued that the uniqueness of Drama education is being missed and learners are systematically becoming the objects rather than the subjects of their learning. Therefore, the future of Scotland's Drama curriculum should involve a detailed discussion and debate as to what extent, if any, the curriculum is child centred.

## REFERENCES

Anderson, M. (2012) *MasterClass in Drama Education Transforming Teaching and Learning*. London: Bloomsbury.
Education Scotland (2009) *Curriculum for Excellence: Experiences and outcomes*. Online at https://edu cation.gov.scot/scottish-education-system/policy-for-scottish-education/policy-drivers/cfe-(building-from-the-statement-appendix-incl-btc1-5)/Experiences%20and%20outcomes#arts

Neelands, J. and Goode, T. (2015) *Structuring Drama Work*, third edition. Cambridge: Cambridge University Press.

Neelands, J. and Nelson, B. (2015) 'Drama, community and achievement: together I'm someone', in M. Anderson and J. Dunn (eds), *How Drama Activates Learning. Contemporary Research and Practice*. London: Bloomsbury, pp. 15–29.

O'Toole, J. and O'Mara, J. (2007) 'Proteus, the giant at the door: drama and theatre in the curriculum', in L. Bresler (ed.), *International Handbook of Research in Arts Education*. The Netherlands: Springer, pp. 203–18.

O'Toole, J., Stinston, M. and Moore, T. (2009) *Drama and Curriculum: A Giant at the Door*. Springer: Dordrecht.

Scottish Government (2008) *Curriculum for Excellence: Building the Curriculum 3: A Framework for Learning and Teaching*. Online at www.gov.scot/Publications/2008/06/06104407/0

SQA (2016a) Attainment statistics. Online at www.sqa.org.uk/sqa/64717.html.

SQA (2016b) *National 5 Drama Course Report*. Online at www.sqa.org.uk/sqa/47390.html

Winston, J. and Tandy, M. (2009) *Beginning Drama 4–11*, third edition. London and New York: Routledge.

# 46

# English and Literacy

*Hugh Gallagher and Linda Harris*

English, like all other subjects, has its own specialised curriculum content and terminology. In contrast to literacy, it affords a discrete focus on knowledge about and appreciation of literature. Simultaneously, the development of children's language use arises from their own reiterations and creations of a variety of text genres following the study of these in English classrooms. Pivotal skills such as the ability to analyse and to recreate features of narrative, character, theme, setting, structure and style remain central in the English curriculum. Learners are also, rightly, expected to: communicate their thoughts and opinions effectively; explain their understanding; synthesise ideas; debate their views; and develop critical literacy skills (Stevens, 2014). Scots literature and language, as in years past, have a renewed focus with a set-text list of Scots texts from which teachers may choose. In some departments, the incorporation of drama techniques in English teaching is facilitated by a Drama department complete with Drama studio, whereas in others media education is studied, up to and including Higher level. Young people, for whom English is an additional language, have the opportunity in some areas to gain National Qualifications (NQs) in English for speakers of other languages. Literacy encompasses a different skill set. It, of course, remains at the centre of educational discourse, is a priority in education in all sectors and subjects, and has become a well-established responsibility of all teachers; in this text it is dealt with separately in Chapter 58.

## FROM BRAVE NEW WORLD TO ILLUSION

In spite of the potential for a totally innovative curriculum with freedoms almost impossible to imagine twenty years ago, the inception of the Curriculum for Excellence (CfE), its course specifications and related documentation were widely criticised for lacking detail, whilst a CfE assessment structure was notably absent. The subsequent plethora of documentation created to address these perceived shortcomings have required teachers to retrieve (from websites), read, assimilate and put into practice a range of more or less extensive changes to practice. This has inevitably led to confusion and frustration in some quarters with substantial and grievous voicing of teachers' concerns in a range of public fora.

In January 2017, the Deputy First Minister announced the removal of the units in the English course framework beginning with National 5 in 2017–18 followed by Higher and Advanced Higher in subsequent years. While a welcome reduction in teacher workload, the change smacks of a 'knee-jerk' response to teachers' concerns in addition to necessarily reducing assessment for the young people in question. What was, in recent years, deemed to be robust assessment in the CfE framework has been discarded without a backward glance. The course assessment of National 5, Higher and Advanced Higher will be strengthened, it is claimed, to maintain twenty-four Scottish Credit and Qualifications Framework (SCQF) credit points and protect the integrity, breadth and standards of the NQs. Since this development may also raise questions about the value and credibility of National 4, there are also plans to reconsider the possibility of external assessment of the National 4 qualification. The earlier scepticism about the robustness of assessing through internal unit assessments need perplex no more; their removal was swift and decisive.

Part of the initial problem, it seems, was the fact that the assessments were compiled by various teams of personnel, each with what appeared to be different briefings. This naturally led to disharmony in the messages conveyed to teachers. It seemed that when the writing component was removed from the Higher and Intermediate 2 exam papers from 2010 onwards and placed instead in the folio, it was being relegated to a position of lesser importance; after all many of us who have worked with folios since back in the days of Standard Grade are well aware of the dangers to validity that can arise with folio work that contributes to overall course assessment. This major development has somewhat dashed the hopes of the authors of this chapter; it has not quite brought Armageddon but provides a curriculum that certainly falls short of the Brave New World envisioned when CfE was first tabled in 2004. Additionally, at the time of writing, the national press claim that the current exam system is failing Scotland's young people. Far more are failing National exams than before, and where in previous systems there was a compensatory 'O' grade or Intermediate level was awarded, with CfE the result is outright failure. It is claimed that these pupils have been entered for exams for which they are not adequately prepared; no excuse, though, for the resulting course assessment being quite so demoralising. A recent development, however, is the reintroduction of grade D as the mechanism for recognising positive achievement where a candidate has not achieved a pass.

## CREATIVE CLASSROOMS

It is to be hoped that the workload furore does not obscure the excellent work that abounds where it matters most: in classrooms. While time is built into learning programmes for preparing pupils for the summative assessment phase, the main emphasis should be, undoubtedly, on pupils' learning. This was, after all, one of the original aims of CfE – the decluttering of the curriculum resulting in more time for learning and teaching.

Notwithstanding the multitude of developments in most secondary English departments, teachers' innovation along with their determination to create positive learning experiences prevail. They continue to provide motivating, engaging, even inspiring experiences for young people as they develop knowledge, skills and competence in talking, listening, reading and writing and spanning the full spectrum of experiences and outcomes. As distinct from the changing curricular landscape, what effective learning looks like in the current English classroom is much the same as always. Some of the features, like the need for a respectful ethos, dialogic teaching, the effective use of formative assessment strategies, involving pupils wholly and actively in learning, using cooperative or collaborative and independent pedagogies, and enhancing learners' abilities to voice their thinking (Vygotsky, 1986), could be found in any classroom. The most notable key specifics relating to the effective teaching of English include:

- developing pupils' language skills in ways that show their interconnectedness, rather than allowing pupils to see them as discrete skill sets or knowledge areas;
- using a range of strategic approaches to develop pupils' writing including: exemplification, modelling, scaffolding, process and genre approaches, real contexts and purposes for real audiences, and collaborative writing as a developmental stepping stone;
- using Directed Activities Related to Texts (DARTS) approaches to engage pupils actively and practically in the process of meaning-making.

In the best English departments, young people benefit from imaginative activities that enable them to develop critical and creative thinking. They experience a broad and whole-some selection of challenging and enriching texts, classic and contemporary, media and Scots as well as blogs, texting and social media platforms. Children are reading, writing and talking in Scots and perceiving it as having parity of esteem with English. The existing Scottish text list will be updated for session 2018–19 onwards and the first National 5 and Higher English exams to feature content from the new list will take place in May 2019; this development is something that will be welcomed by many English teachers dispirited with the previous version and its preponderance of modern texts.

In a few English departments, good practice manifests in the form of electives or short courses, thus aligning well with the CfE principle of choice. In some schools learners are being supported in the use of learning logs or portfolios. In others, personal learning plans are used to record progress over time and support children and young people to reflect on their learning. The most effective learning often arises out of young people being given more autonomy, thus ensuring target-setting and profiling processes are purposeful and take learning forward, rather than simply being tokenistic. Bill Maxwell, the chief education inspector, in his review of education in all sectors between 2012 and 2016, found examples of 'outstanding and innovative practice' (Education Scotland, 2017, p. 3). In many schools, particularly secondary schools, positive arrangements have been made with partners to extend learning and enhance skills. These can involve arts organisations, local digital media initiatives, employers and local community projects. In most of these projects, young people work on practical activities with a high level of autonomy and they enjoy their learning (Education Scotland, 2013).

It is to be hoped that secondary teachers will focus predominantly on effective teaching and learning in their classrooms, but it has to be acknowledged that they would be doing a disservice to their pupils were they not to engage in preparation prior to examinations. Reading good quality non-fiction, for example broadsheet journalism, will support candidates effectively to prepare for Paper 1 (Reading) of the course assessments. Likewise, focusing effectively on the *key areas* of study in the texts and ensuring that learners are well versed in the texts' main literary concerns is paramount for Paper 2 (Critical Essay).

## RECENT DEVELOPMENTS

English courses, for many a decade, have organised learning in ways to develop children's ability in listening, talking, reading and writing, now known as the significant aspects of learning in English. Details are provided in the associated professional learning paper which should be used in conjunction with the Literacy and English progression frameworks and the benchmarks when assessing learners' progress.

National 1 and 2 courses, now in place, were created for pupils who formerly would have followed access courses in the previous curriculum and National 3, for the same pupils, has also been published. Nationals 4 and 5 and Higher have some common elements. Immediately recognisable are the knowledge, skills and processes that feature in the outcomes. In reading for example, pupils will learn how to elicit main ideas and specific information, how to use their knowledge of language to explain meaning and effect: this is the business of learning in English, reaching back to Standard Grade and beyond.

To date, there has been no publication or details provided on the standardised assessments promised in the National Improvement Framework (NIF) in 2016. The First Minister's Reading Challenge of 2016 is generally considered a positive step, in part owing to government visibly driving reading attainment. The arbitrary nature of the judgements, that will undoubtedly occur, do not appear to deter; the need to develop children's language skills is not in question. The Organisation for Economic Co-operation and Development's (OECD's) Programme for International Student Assessment (PISA) study indicates that not only do Scotland's children read less than their OECD counterparts but the UK reading test results are only around average compared to those of other countries (OECD, 2012).

## ASSESSMENT

Draft benchmarks for assessing learning at all levels were published in 2016 for Literacy and English, with other subjects being added in time until the final iteration in June 2017. It is essential that a shared understanding of expectations is reached, although moderation has not yet been publicly aired. Benchmark results for Literacy and English and Numeracy are those that will subsequently feed into NIF results and, doubtless, be judged. Higher English continues to have a high uptake with its peak in 2014, when English had the highest uptake of all Highers with 31,589 entries, an increase from 30,436 in 2013. Performance over time in Higher English has improved. In recent times, the pass rate increased from 70 per cent in 2010 to 76 per cent in 2014 (https://www.sqa.org.uk/sqa/74829.html). However, as before, relatively few pupils progress from Higher to Advanced Higher in English.

In S1–3, the broad general education (BGE) part of learning, young people participate regularly in self- and peer-assessment activities, a technique well documented as beneficial to progress. They also speak positively about the feedback received from their English teachers. In particular, written feedback on their writing aids them in understanding their strengths and next steps. There is scope, however, for teachers to improve the quality of feedback on reading and group discussion skills. At the senior phase, most young people are clear about their progress in English and set their own targets for improvement within the context of NQs. Scottish texts are widely used at Higher in all the main areas of the critical essay paper in addition to the textual analysis. Across all sectors, most schools are developing approaches to monitoring and tracking learners' progress and achievement in English (Education Scotland, 2015); this will be most beneficial if the knowledge gleaned is then used to inform teachers how best to support future progress. Closing the poverty-related attainment gap has been a main focus of the Scottish Government's agenda for the past several years and the government's Scottish Attainment Challenge has brought a major investment of resources.

## THE WAY AHEAD

As previously stated, Deputy First Minister, John Swinney, announced on 31 January, 2017 the removal of unit assessments at National 5 to Advanced Higher starting with National 5 in 2017–18 and the others following in the two ensuing years. With the course units being removed, revised course documentation was published in April 2017, in order to retain the original robustness of the course. The documentation for this change is to result in one single document for each subject.

A new mandatory 'Spoken Language (combined speaking and listening)' component is to be introduced at all levels that will be internally assessed as 'achieved' or 'not achieved' and will be based on existing standards. It will not contribute to the overall weightings (percentage) of the course assessment but candidates will need to achieve a pass in this component to gain the course award. There will be no change to the existing writing portfolio, which will continue to include one text of a broadly discursive nature and the other of a broadly creative genre (Higher and National 5). Question paper one will continue to focus on reading for understanding, analysis and evaluation of two non-fiction passages. Question paper two, entitled Critical Reading, will assess candidates' abilities to read and analyse a Scottish text as well as write a critical evaluation of a text of Scottish or other origin.

Inspectors have observed that, as yet, opportunities for interdisciplinary learning, work-based learning, creativity and personal achievements were not always being planned well enough to ensure that all young people could apply their learning and progress with sufficient pace and challenge (Education Scotland, 2017); this will undoubtedly provide food for thought for English teachers.

There is much rhetoric in the air; neologisms pepper the recently revised documents. Yet, the aspiration to develop connectedness in exploring and developing literacy skills may empower learners to hone skills, and acquire the knowledge that will lead them to be literate, critical, analytical, linguistically and culturally aware, well-read people. Once again, the English teachers of Scotland need to have the professional confidence and courage to believe that they can make that happen in the face of a shifting landscape.

## REFERENCES

Education Scotland (2013) *Creativity across Learning 3–18*. Livingston: Education Scotland.
Education Scotland (2015) *3–18 Literacy and English Review*. Livingston: Education Scotland.
Education Scotland (2017) *Quality and Improvement in Scottish Education 2012–16*. Livingston: Education Scotland.
English Excellence Group (2011) *English Excellence Group Report*. Edinburgh: Scottish Government.
Organisation for Economic Co-operation and Development (2012) *PISA 2012 Results in Focus. What 15-year-olds know and what they can do with what they know*. Paris: OECD.
Stevens, D. (2014) 'Critical literacy through initial teacher education in English', *Changing English*, 21 (1), 32–41, doi: 10.1080/1358684X.2013.875752
Vygotsky, L. [1934] (1986) *Mind and Language* (A. Kozulin, Trans.). Cambridge, MA: MIT Press.

# 47

# Geography

*Ashley Fenwick*

> The deceptively simple word 'geography' embraces a deeply contested intellectual project of great antiquity and extraordinary complexity. (Heffernan, 2003, p. 3)

Geography has been described as an 'awkward discipline' (Bonnett, 2008), spanning both physical and human environments and their interactions. Interdisciplinary themes such as space, place and environment connect to a multitude of subject areas, traversing both science and art-based disciplines. This might be viewed as both a curse and a strength. While some claim that this multiplicity fragments the discipline (Johnston, 2005), others would argue that Geography opens up a diversity of knowledges and perspectives on viewing the world (Castree et al., 2005). What is clear is that the purpose, content, organisation and place of Geography within the curriculum is, and always has been, contested and negotiated. Key characteristics and issues relating to Curriculum for Excellence, introduced in 2010, and how it is shaping Scotland's current Geography curriculum, are discussed in this chapter.

## BROAD GENERAL EDUCATION

Within the first three years of secondary school Scottish pupils will experience a broad general education (BGE). There is greater scope for teachers to exercise autonomy within this curricular stage and to develop units of work which are current, context specific and tailored to the interests and needs of pupils. Geography courses, termed People, Place and Environment, include enduring topics such as natural regions and earth forces, as well as new areas such as globalisation and fashion. Social, political, environmental and economic issues are examined through a range of local, national, European and global contexts.

Increasingly, interdisciplinary opportunities highlight natural links with a wide range of subject areas. Themes relating to learning for sustainability such as global citizenship and outdoor learning may be explored. Literacy, numeracy, health and wellbeing links are embedded. A strong Scottish emphasis is encouraged through exploration of the local environment and the development of partnerships. This has created opportunities to reintroduce fieldwork into the secondary curriculum and develop international links. Investigation work, discussion, debate and presentation of ideas are promoted. A range of formative assessment practices is utilised. Education Scotland (2013) reported that staff are developing their confidence in judging when a learner is secure at a curriculum level and developing their understanding of how to assess progress in regard to breadth, challenge and application through the use of pupil profiles.

The delivery model for BGE Geography varies from school to school. Traditionally, subject specialist teachers have delivered this stage discretely; however, a recent trend towards a more integrated multidisciplinary teaching approach is evident (Fenwick et al., 2013). This is often in conjunction with a structural shift from discrete Geography departments to Social Studies faculties. Faculty managers have in some instances created greater synergy across Geography, History and Modern Studies departments. However, in some schools, there is still resistance to the concept of a faculty manager who is not a subject specialist. There is also a sense that decisions relating to integrated courses and the timing of pupil choices have been imposed without sufficient understanding or discussion (Education Scotland, 2013). In some schools, pupils make option choices relating to Social Studies as early as the end of S1. In other schools, this is deferred to S3. Early decision making seems to contradict the idea of a BGE and narrows pupils' opportunities to engage with Geography. Concerns have been mooted about how well this phase equips students for the demands of the senior phase. The senior phase consists of Nationals, Higher and Advanced Higher. Benchmarks for Social Studies were published in August 2016 with the purpose of supporting subject specialist teachers in making robust assessments of learners' progress, the standards they should achieve, and to ensure that pupils are presented at an appropriate senior phase level. There has been little comment on benchmarks from the Geography community but concerns relating to reinforcement of instrumentalist and reductionist approaches to teaching and learning which are over-simplistic, undemanding of pupils, and dismissive of teachers' professional judgement and autonomy, have been raised (Priestley, 2016).

## NATIONAL QUALIFICATIONS

For most pupils, National courses begin in fourth year and are available at three levels (N3, N4, N5). Pupils begin at the level most appropriate for them. Courses build on the knowledge and skills introduced within the BGE phase and are divided into three units of study: physical environments, human environments and global issues (see Table 47.1). Themes relating to global citizenship and education for sustainability are explored and pupils are encouraged to reflect, debate and engage critically with these issues. Fieldwork, map work and investigative skills provide a real world context to develop essential numeracy and literacy skills.

Outcomes for each of these areas detail the skills and knowledge which should be covered. The structure and broad content is similar across National 3–5, enabling bi-level teaching. However, there are key differences in course assessment requirements, for example, National 3 and 4 are not graded and have no external exam (Table 47.2). One of the main changes associated with Nationals has been the introduction of greater internal assessment – unit passes must be evidenced to show all course outcomes have been met. There are on average five outcomes per unit. National 4 incorporates an 'Added Value Unit' (AVU) and National 5 an assignment. The purpose of the AVU is to allow for pupils to apply skills, knowledge and understanding whilst researching a geographical topic of their choice. This has increased teacher workload substantially and created an assessment-driven course. The National 5 assignment is completed under exam conditions and requires pupils to write up findings based on primary (e.g. river study, inner city changes) or secondary

Table 47.1   Geography: National course content summary

| Units of study | Content |
| --- | --- |
| Physical environments | Glaciated and coastal landscapes of the UK *or* |
| | Limestones and rivers |
| | Weather patterns within the UK |
| Human environments | Population and development |
| | Urban change |
| | Rural change |
| | Developed *and* developing country case studies are used to explore urban and rural change |
| Global issues | Schools select two global issues to study from the list: |
| | Climate change |
| | Trade and globalisation |
| | Tourism |
| | Health |
| | Impact of human activity on the natural environment |
| | Environmental hazards |

Table 47.2   Geography: National course assessment summary

| Nationals | Unit passes assessed internally | Course work | Final exam | Outcome |
| --- | --- | --- | --- | --- |
| 3 | Physical environment Human environment Global issues | | No | Course award |
| 4 | Physical environment Human environment Global issues | Internally marked Added Value Unit | No | Course award |
| 5 | Physical environment Human environment Global issues (No longer required as of August 2017) | Externally marked assignment completed in 60 minutes and worth 20 marks | Yes 140-minute exam worth 80 marks | Course grade A–D awarded |

data. Support materials have been described as vague and confusing (Scottish Qualification Authority (SQA), nd a). Clarification of the conditions for assessment of the assignment were provided in April 2017 and several key changes will be introduced in August 2017: the internal unit assessments for National 5 will no longer be a requirement to achieve an overall course award, the external exam will be worth 80 per cent and include more questions, mark allocation will rise from 60 to 80 and the duration of the exam will increase.

## HIGHER

The new Higher Geography course was introduced in 2014. Generally, pupils having successfully completed National 5 progress to Higher. The course is usually completed over one year. This was not a radical departure from the previous course. The unit structure echoes that of the National courses and skills retain a strong emphasis. The course aims to

Table 47.3   Higher Geography content

| Units | Content |
|---|---|
| Physical environments | Atmosphere |
| | Hydrosphere |
| | Lithosphere |
| | Biosphere |
| Human environments | Urban |
| | Rural |
| | Population |
| Global issues | Two of the global issues listed below are studied: |
| | Global climate change |
| | Development and health |
| | River basin management |
| | Trade and aid and geopolitics |
| | Energy |

develop understanding of the human and physical aspects of the contemporary world and the ways in which people and the environment interact and change in response to physical and human processes at a local, national and international level – Table 47.3 summarises Higher Geography content.

As part of the new qualification, students carry out an assignment completed under exam conditions in school, worth one third of their final grade. Candidates choose a topic to investigate, gather data and then analyse their findings. Students must pass internal assessments for all learning outcomes within each unit in order to be permitted to sit the external exam which equates to two thirds of their final grade.

The new Higher course has not been without controversy. Issues raised relate to: the removal of key content, such as river features from the physical environments unit; repetition across National and Higher courses; and time and assessment pressures limiting scope for personalisation and choice. The Scottish Association of Geography Teachers (SAGT) expressed concerns relating to the internal assignment and differentials in the support received at school and home, increased teacher workload and related fieldwork. The external exam has been heavily critiqued based on its literacy demands, imbalance between human and physical topics, and its short nature. Following the changes to National 5, the Higher exam paper is now twenty marks fewer. A review will take place in 2018.

## ADVANCED HIGHER

There are two components which make up the one-year Advanced Higher course – the project folio accounts for two thirds of the overall mark allocation and an external exam the remainder. The folio requires pupils to complete a fieldwork-based geographical study which is written up as a report. A critical evaluation essay on a controversial topic is the second element of the folio. This is written up as an essay. Pupils are required to pass two internal unit assessments which are based on each of the folio pieces. The exam tests map interpretation, data handling and processing questions. A study (SQA, nd a) completed for the SQA endorsed the Advanced Higher Geography course – in terms of its general principles, approaches and methods as appropriate and satisfactory.

## CURRICULUM FOR EXCELLENCE AND GEOGRAPHY

Curriculum for Excellence appears to have negatively impacted on Geography education in Scottish schools. A Royal Scottish Geographical Society and SAGT survey concluded that the current system was 'in danger of both letting young people down and undermining some of our most vital subjects' (Robinson, 2015). The nature of the National 4/5 courses, where pupils study on average six subjects in one year, has reduced Geography numbers. The majority of teachers (87 per cent) reported a 'large drop' in take-up. The delivery of Geography by non-specialist teachers, budget cuts, and poor resourcing of the new curriculum were highlighted as key concerns. Geography numbers and attainment results perhaps reflect some of these concerns. However, this trend is not reflected in other Social Studies. Fieldwork has always been a distinctive and memorable element of the Geography curriculum. Curriculum for Excellence has seen a strong policy focus on 'Learning for Sustainability'. This has provided a strong foundation for teachers to embed and justify a coherent and progressive approach to fieldwork. A wider acknowledgement of not just the cognitive benefits of fieldwork, but the social, emotional and health benefits, has been articulated more clearly. The introduction of the AVU has ensured that all departments undertake some fieldwork.

## ATTAINMENT STATISTICS

Attainment statistics although widely used as a measure of educational success must be viewed cautiously and the wider purposes of education acknowledged. Trends relating to subject uptake and grade comparisons based on 2016 Social Studies data are outlined below (SQA, nd b).

History continues to present the largest number of candidates at National level (15,942 compared to Geography 11,018), Higher (11,165 compared to Geography 8,157) and Advanced Higher (1,578 compared to Geography 900), followed by Modern Studies. Advanced Higher Geography is the exception, presenting a larger number of candidates than Modern Studies (900 compared to 851). Geography candidates perform well in relation to the other Social Studies at National 5. In 2016, 36.4 per cent of students received an A pass compared to 36.1 per cent of History and 34 per cent of Modern Studies. The number of Higher A passes have declined since the introduction of the New Higher from 33 per cent in 2015 to 26.9 per cent in 2016. History (37.6 per cent) and Modern Studies (31.8 per cent) students achieved an A pass in 2016. Advanced Higher Geography A passes reflect a small decrease from 23.2 per cent to 22.3 per cent. Other Social Studies similarly show slight decreases in A passes – History 32.7 per cent to 30.4 per cent and Modern Studies 26.8 per cent to 24.6 per cent. A downward trend in uptake is thus observed and a slight decrease in A passes gained. This may be a consequence of some of the concerns outlined earlier, linked to course choices, internal assessment requirements and course repetition.

## THE FUTURE

In the second decade of the twenty-first century we live in a world that is more interconnected and more uncertain than ever before. In understanding this complex mosaic, Geography has a critical role to play. Teaching Geography in what has been dubbed 'post-truth times' calls for a curriculum that allows students to critically question complex contemporary environmental, social, cultural and economic issues, to think creatively about the future, and support their development as aware and participating citizens.

Digital media can portray landscapes and convey human stories in powerful and absorbing ways, data and global events can be beamed into classrooms in real time, and Geographic Information System (GIS), tablet technology and computer apps can enhance Geography and engage young people. Dawkins encapsulates eloquently what Geography has the potential to achieve, thus awakening in pupils a curiosity, desire to question and appreciation of their world.

> There is an anaesthetic of familiarity, a sedative of ordinariness which dulls the senses and hides the wonder of existence. ... What is the best way of countering the sluggish habituation brought about by our gradual crawl from babyhood? We can't actually fly to another planet. But we can recapture that sense of having just tumbled out to life on a new world by looking at our own world in unfamiliar ways. (Dawkins, 1998, p. 11)

Passionate, committed teachers have always done this; however, changes in delivery models and staffing, and a narrowing of content and assessment-dominated courses, may have diverted attention and debate away from a focus on what is taught and why it is relevant to young people. Lambert (2011) calls for an approach to curriculum making that permits greater teacher engagement with subject knowledge and current academic developments – opening up dynamic, innovative and creative curricular possibilities and conversations that highlight the relevance and uniqueness of place. This perspective positions teachers as active agents who continually negotiate their role in making curricular decisions. This has significant long-term implications for policymakers, teacher professional development and initial teacher education programmes.

## REFERENCES

Bonnett, A. (2008) *What is Geography?* London: Sage.
Castree, N., Rogers, A. and Sherman, D. (eds) (2005) *Questioning Geography: Fundamental Debates*. Hoboken, NJ: Wiley-Blackwell Publishing
Dawkins, R. (1998) *Unweaving the Rainbow*. Boston: Houghton Mifflin.
Education Scotland (2013) *Social Studies 3–18*. Online at http://dera.ioe.ac.uk/18517/7/SocialStudies3to182013Update_tcm4-817061_Redacted.pdf
Fenwick A., Minty, S. and Priestley, M. (2013) 'Swimming against the tide: a case study of an integrated social studies department', *Curriculum Journal*, 24 (3), 454–74.
Heffernan, M. (2003) 'Histories of geography', in S. Holloway, S. P. Rice and G. Valentine (eds), *Key Concepts in Geography*. London: Sage, pp. 3–22.
Hopkin, J. (2011) 'Progress in geography', *Geography*, 96 (3), 116–23.
Johnston, R. (2005) 'Geography coming apart at the seams', in N. Castree, A. Rogers and D. Sherman (eds), *Questioning Geography: Fundamental Debates*. Hoboken, NJ: Wiley-Blackwell Publishing, pp. 9–25.
Lambert, D. (2011) 'Reframing school geography: a capability approach', in G. Butt (ed.), *Geography, Education and the Future*. London: Continuum.
Priestley, M. (2016) 'The endless quest for the Holy Grail of educational specification: Scotland's new assessment benchmarks'. Blog, Professor Mark Priestley. Online at https://mrpriestley.wordpress.com/?s=bench+marks

Robinson, M. (2015) 'A "perfect storm" in Scottish education', *RSGS Exploring Geography*, 27 July. Online at https://rsgs.org/a-perfect-storm-in-scottish-education/

Scottish Qualifications Authority (nd a) *Geography SQA*. Online at www.sqa.org.uk/sqa/45627.html

Scottish Qualifications Authority (nd b) Statistics archive. Online at www.sqa.org.uk/sqa/57518.4241.html

# 48

# History

*Joe Smith*

Previous editions of this book have opened by referring to the ongoing public interest in History and the History curriculum. Given this popular interest, this chapter has a challenging purview: to provide an introduction to History in Scottish schools, while also conveying something of the debates that take place within the subject community. This chapter, therefore, draws on two main sources: policy documents which provide much of the factual description of History in Scottish schools, while commentary on these policies is offered by a recent survey of Scottish History teachers undertaken by the University of Stirling working with the Scottish Association of Teachers of History (SATH). At the time of writing (2017) this survey had not been published.

## HISTORY IN THE PRIMARY AND JUNIOR SECONDARY PHASES

In common with long-standing practice in Scotland, History does not feature as a distinct subject in primary schools or the junior phase of secondary schools; instead it is one of three subjects known collectively as 'Social Studies'. Within Social Studies, 'people, past events and societies' (History) sits alongside 'people, place and environment' (Geography) and people in society, economy and business. It is expected and anticipated that teachers will draw out similarities and connections between these subjects.

How this works in practice differs from school to school. A minority of schools have downplayed the idea of three separate subjects, preferring instead to teach a fully integrated Social Studies curriculum. At the other end of the spectrum, some schools maintain sharp distinctions between the three subjects and ensure that each is taught by a subject specialist. Most schools adopt some sort of hybrid between these two models, perhaps having a specialist teacher delivering each subject to a different class for half a term at a time. Unfortunately, in most schools the decision about how Social Studies should be delivered is determined more by the strictures of the budget and the demands of the timetable than by educational considerations. Similarly, the adoption of a 'faculty' management structure in many schools means that many have a single principal teacher with responsibility for all the social subjects. In some schools, there is no teacher nominally in charge of History creating both creative opportunities and additional responsibility for unpromoted History teachers.

The relative merits of an integrated or discrete approach to teaching subjects is a matter of fierce but possibly irresolvable debate. Recent research implies that any such generalisations at a policy level are impossible (Brant et al., 2016), since the quality of a child's educational experience is determined far more by his or her teachers than by government policy. That said, it would be remiss not to point out the legitimate concerns that some have raised about the teaching of History in Curriculum for Excellence (CfE).

Concerns about the approach were first raised by the Royal Society of Edinburgh (RSE) which expressed concern that 'History is in danger of being diluted under the CfE framework' (RSE, 2011, p. 1). Although the RSE was writing speculatively, five years since implementation there is some evidence that classroom teachers share these concerns. Emerging findings from the SATH/University of Stirling survey of History teachers ($n = 101$) suggests that less than half of teachers felt that 'the aims of History in Curriculum for Excellence are clear' and only slightly more agreed that 'CfE was good preparation for studying History at the next level'.

However, the picture is not entirely bleak. Although around half of History teachers expressed concerns about the aims and rigour of History in Curriculum for Excellence, some 70 per cent agreed that the curriculum 'gave children a good historical education'. How might we explain this apparent paradox? One explanation might be the squeezing of History by competing curriculum demands in the junior phase of secondary. The survey revealed that over two fifths of schools teach History for less than an hour a week and that, in three quarters of schools, pupils can choose to discontinue their study of History at the end of second year. This does not compare well with much of Europe, where the study of History is compulsory until the age of 15.

## HISTORY AT CERTIFICATION LEVEL

History is offered at National, Higher and Advanced Higher levels. The aim of these courses is to give children a secure knowledge of their national History as well as a broader sense of the past. Bi-level teaching (i.e. the teaching of different qualifications in the same classroom) is a feature of many Scottish schools in S4, S5 and S6 and to make this possible there is considerable commonality between the topics studied at all levels of certification.

At both National 5 and Higher level, students study three units entitled 'Scottish contexts', 'British contexts' and 'European/World contexts'. Within each of these units, schools have a considerable degree of choice with five options for the Scottish contexts (including 'The Wars of Independence', 'The Scottish Reformation' and 'The Treaty of Union'); five options for the British contexts (including 'War of the Three Kingdoms', 'The Atlantic Slave Trade' and 'The Making of Modern Britain') and ten options for the European and World context. There are, therefore, 250 possible permutations that schools can offer (though inevitably some courses are more popular than others). While the breadth of the course, both in terms of chronology and geography is admirable, 'European and World contexts' is arguably something of a misnomer: of the ten options, only one (The Crusades), focuses substantially on the world beyond Europe and the modern United States.

At Advanced Higher, students study just one topic, chosen by their teacher from a list of eleven options. Once again, these topics are chosen to allow multilevel teaching and so there is significant crossover with the topics available at other levels. However, there is a broader chronological and geographic scope with some topics such as, 'Northern Britain: From the Iron Age to 1034' and 'Japan 1840–1920' only examined at Advanced Higher.

Despite the pressures on History in the junior phase, History at certification level is in rude health. In 2016, History was the third most popular non-compulsory subject at

National 5 level with some 16,000 entrants. Achievement at National 5 in History in 2016 was broadly in line with the averages across all subjects, with 36 per cent achieving an A in History and 77 per cent achieving a C or better (https://www.sqa.org.uk/sqa/80674.html).

However, these impressive figures for uptake conceal some major concerns for teachers of History at National Level. Over half of teachers profess themselves 'dissatisfied' with National level qualifications in their current form according to SATH/University of Stirling research. Complaints are varied but some are heard repeatedly: excessive content, the low status accorded to National 4 and a prescriptive examination mark scheme at National 5. National level qualifications are now so established that these problems can no longer be dismissed as teething problems; the move towards the removal of unit assessments implies that the Scottish Qualifications Authority (SQA) and the Scottish Government are taking some of these concerns seriously.

Despite misgivings about the National course, continuation rates are impressive: History is the third most popular subject at Higher grade after English and Maths. Encouragingly, History has even been increasing in popularity, with the number of entrants improving year-on-year from 9,193 entrants in 2010 to 11,168 in 2016 (https://www.sqa.org.uk/sqa/80674.html). Furthermore, History students achieve significantly better than in other subjects: while the overall pass rates are broadly similar, 37 per cent of History students received an A grade against an average of 29 per cent across all entries. This high attainment is mirrored in a 75 per cent teacher satisfaction rate with the course, explained in large part by the fact that Highers are an established and familiar part of the landscape of Scottish education, unlike the relatively new Nationals and CfE courses.

## BALANCE OF SCOTTISH HISTORY

Before the adoption of Curriculum for Excellence in 2011, there were widespread concerns about the presentation of Scottish History in the schools. The *5–14 Guidelines* which preceded Curriculum for Excellence mandated the study of 'ONE British context, ONE European context and ONE world context', but said only that there should be 'attention to Scottish contexts' (SOED, 1993, p. 34, all emphases in original). The result was extremely patchy coverage of Scottish History, an over-reliance on English textbooks and the persistence of unhistorical national mythologies. The only major empirical work in this area (Wood and Payne, 1999) gave children twenty-nine multiple-choice questions about significant events in Scottish History; only two questions saw more than half the respondents answer correctly.

Whether this troubling deficit of knowledge has been addressed since Curriculum for Excellence remains an open question. There has, so far, been no study undertaken which is directly comparable to Wood and Payne's, but there is little doubt that curricular changes have greatly increased the profile of Scottish History. The *Principles and Practice* document for social subjects now opens with a statement that children will 'develop their understanding of the History, heritage and culture of Scotland, and an appreciation of their local and national heritage within the world' (Scottish Government, 2006b, p. 1).

While it is encouraging that Scottish History is now foregrounded in curriculum planning, its framing has been criticised as problematic. An important criticism has been the conflation of 'history' and 'heritage' in Curriculum for Excellence (RSE, 2011; Smith, 2016). Although all historians would agree that children are entitled to a working knowledge of their own nation's history, care must always be taken that this does not lapse into parochialism. Most troubling in this respect is, perhaps, the National 5/Higher unit on 'Scotland and the Great War'. While no one would seek to diminish the impact of this conflict on Scotland, one cannot help but wonder whether a narrow national focus is the best way to teach about a war which saw naval engagements off the Chilean coast, Bengal lancers in Palestine and Japanese marines supressing a mutiny of Indian soldiers in Singapore.

## ASSESSING HISTORY

Assessment is an essential but controversial dimension of all curricula: essential because it scaffolds children's progression; controversial because it necessarily simplifies that progression. It is, perhaps, even more difficult to achieve a consensus around assessment in those subjects, like History, where 'getting better' means something other than 'getting more questions right'. Since there is not a totality of historical knowledge against which our knowledge can be cross-checked, we cannot simply ask closed questions and award a percentage. Instead of trying to judge the 'completeness' of a child's understanding of the past, we aim to judge its sophistication.

How exactly one measures the sophistication of a child's historical understanding is an educational Gordian knot. In its original incarnation, Curriculum for Excellence addressed this not by cutting it, but by ignoring it completely. The nearest approximation to an assessment framework was the *Experiences and Outcomes* document (Scottish Government, 2006a) which attempted to describe the outcomes that one could expect from a child at each level. For example, a child at first level might 'understand that evidence varies in the extent to which it can be trusted and can use this in learning about the past', while one at second level can 'use primary and secondary sources selectively to research events in the past' (p. 2). Given that the latter of these two outcomes is simply a description of the modernist historical method, it is difficult to know how a teacher might use these effectively to scaffold progression.

At the time of writing, the 'National Improvement Framework' and its attendant 'benchmarks' dominated discussion in Scottish Education. The need to develop benchmarks for Social Studies has brought the question of assessing historical understanding once more into focus. Early drafts of these benchmarks have been worryingly undemanding: with children of eleven years challenged to 'Describe and discuss at least three similarities and differences between their own life and life in a past society.'

Curriculum planners who are hoping to gain inspiration from assessment at certification level are likely to be disappointed. At National level, teachers have criticised the way that the syllabuses have distorted their teaching and, in turn, children's historical understanding to meet the narrow demands of the examination mark scheme. A common complaint has been the coining by SQA of neologisms such as 'analysis plus' which feature in the mark scheme, but have no parallel in the discipline of History.

## PROFESSIONAL ASSOCIATIONS

Some of these questions around assessment are being tackled by SATH which has grown as an organisation since it scrapped its subscription fee in 2014. Most of SATH's income now comes from its annual conference in November which is invariably well attended. The conference is both an opportunity for professional updating from academic historians and innovators in History education, and a chance to share practice with colleagues from across

Scotland. In 2016, SATH was bequeathed an enormous library of online resources by Education Scotland, as the latter chose no longer to host curriculum development materials on its website. This means that the SATH website will soon be the most comprehensive collection of History classroom materials in Scotland. There are various other less formalised communities of practice within Scottish education, not least a proliferation of Facebook groups, through which teachers offer each other help and support.

The proximity of government in a small nation like Scotland means that SATH boasts good working relationships with Education Scotland and SQA. These relationships ensure that SATH is consulted on changes in policy and allow SATH's members to be kept informed of high-level discussion about the future of their subject. At the time of writing, Education Scotland was consulting with SATH about the shape of the benchmarks for assessing History in the primary and junior phases. (The current version of the Social Studies benchmarks (as of 2017) can be found at https://education.gov.scot/improvement/Documents/Social%20StudiesBenchmarksPDF.pdf.)

## TEACHING AND LEARNING APPROACHES

Scottish History teachers remain committed to developing innovative and engaging ways of teaching the past. The use of enquiry questions to frame learning is an increasingly important aspect of practice, with children investigating questions like, 'Why did they ask to leave? St Kilda as a case study of emigration.' In the junior phase of high school, seven in ten teachers encouraged their pupils to form their own ideas about the past in every lesson, while nine in ten made use of primary sources with children at least once a month.

However, the time constraints at certification level have militated against more active forms of learning in the senior phase. While three quarters of teachers said that their children took part in role plays and simulations at least once a term during the broad general education (BGE) phase, this fell to just over half for certification courses. Conversely, while 48 per cent of BGE teachers reported that their students made notes from the board every week, this leapt to 87 per cent in the senior phase. While no one would dispute the importance of note-taking in certificate classes, these figures do imply that teachers are struggling to balance their instincts for pedagogical innovation with the demands of examination preparation.

## CONCLUSION

In common with all subjects (and all education systems), History in Scotland presents a mixed picture. History teachers have still not found the best way to navigate recent changes in policy, but they are committed to continuing the search. This commitment is born of a shared conviction that a rigorous and engaging historical education is the entitlement of every child in Scotland.

## REFERENCES

Brant, J., Chapman, A. and Isaacs, T. (2016) 'International instructional systems: social studies', *The Curriculum Journal*, 27 (1), 62–79.

RSE (2011) *The Teaching of History in Scottish Schools – Advice Paper 11–01*, Royal Society of Edinburgh. Online at https://www.rse.org.uk/cms/files/advice-papers/2011/ad11_01.pdf

Scottish Government (2006a) *Curriculum for Excellence: Social Studies Experiences and Outcomes.* Edinburgh: Scottish Government.

Scottish Government (2006b) *Social Studies: Principles and Practice.* Edinburgh: Scottish Government. Online at https://education.gov.scot/Documents/social-studies-pp.pdf

Smith, J. (2016) 'What remains of history? Historical epistemology and historical understanding in Scotland's Curriculum for Excellence', *The Curriculum Journal*, 27 (4), 500–17.

SOED (1993) *National Guidelines: Environmental Studies 5–14.* Edinburgh: Scottish Office Education Department.

Wood, S. and Payne, F. (1999) 'The Scottish school history curriculum and issues of national identity', *The Curriculum Journal*, 10 (1), 107–21.

## Website

Scottish Association of the Teachers of History (SATH) at www.sath.org.uk/

# 49

# Home Economics

*Agnes Macintosh*

Walk into a Home Economics (HEc) department today and what are you likely to encounter? In the more recently built schools you will find a department with facilities which are up to date and purpose-built; however, a great many departments are still struggling in difficult-to-manage rooms in older buildings. When considering the content being taught, there is such a wide range of courses which can be offered by a department that some schools try to provide most of the range whilst others limit themselves to a smaller selection. One thing, still commonplace, is that you will often find your way to the HEc department by your sense of smell because a significant amount of the classroom teaching time still involves large amounts of practical cooking.

Dedicated rooms are required to run the subject effectively. Specialist food rooms equipped with ten cookers and sinks, work areas and other specialised equipment are essential to give the practical experience required in the food discipline. Ideally, for health and safety reasons, a separate room is required for textile work – equipped with sewing machines, ironing boards and other essential smaller equipment.

Staff numbers have reduced in departments over the last thirty years. Gone are the days when it was possible to encounter seven or eight HEc teachers within one school. Some departments are now operating with one full-time member of staff and, worryingly, an increasing number of schools are removing HEc from the curriculum altogether due to skilled staff shortages. It is now more common to see a department with two or three teachers and often not all of those will be full-time. Scottish Government (2015) statistics show that there were 826 HEc teachers working in Scottish schools. Of these, 97 per cent were female, 3 per cent male and their average age was 45 years.

The importance of Home Economics to pupils is more than the sum of its parts. It is vastly more than learning how to cook and sew. Through this subject children are equipped with essential life skills underpinned by knowledge and understanding – crucial for their basic, healthy functioning in tomorrow's world. It can provide them with real-life connections to almost every other subject on the school curriculum, bringing relevance to the theory. It has a role to play in developing confident adults, able to make considered and wise choices in the operational tasks of daily living. To neglect its contribution to children's educational development would be to deprive them of numerous opportunities to make sense of an often confusing world.

## BROAD GENERAL EDUCATION

In the junior school (S1–3) a broad general education (BGE) as stipulated by Curriculum for Excellence (CfE) is on offer to pupils. In these early years of secondary schooling, it is usual that at least 50 per cent of teaching time is devoted to giving children practical experiences of food and textiles whilst the remaining time is spent delivering related theoretical content that supports and extends the practical learning. BGE courses are designed around the learning *experiences* and achievable *outcomes* (E&Os) and the significant aspects of learning (SALs) found primarily in the CfE documentation for: Technological Education; Health and Wellbeing (HWB); Literacy; and Numeracy. In departments' courses the E&Os found at levels 3 and 4 are usually cited as the criteria being addressed and assessment is focused on the ones pertaining to any particular unit of work. Within these units there are often numerous opportunities for pupils to exert choice, including in areas of design, materials and ingredients. Most of these teaching units have been designed and produced internally by each individual department; some teachers consider this unnecessary, repetitive workload, whilst others enjoy the flexibility afforded by the non-rigid course specifications of CfE allowing local adaptation in contexts chosen to suit pupils.

SALs are a more recent introduction to make the assessment of pupils' progress and achievement more manageable and trackable, by grouping the learning into six coherent bodies of knowledge, understanding and skills: the Food Experience; Developing Healthy Choices; Nutritional Needs; Keeping Safe and Hygienic; the Journey of Food; and Food and Textile Technologies. Five of the six SALs focus specifically on food studies whilst the remaining one includes food studies but is extended to cover textile studies. If both textiles and food are taught within a school, this heavier weighting towards food education is usually reflected, with at least two thirds of the curriculum time being devoted to food studies. This higher weighting is understandable as it is generally taught within the context of healthy eating, partly in response to the obesity epidemic that has engulfed the whole of Western society including Scotland. The most recent Scottish Government statistics state that

> in 2015, 65% of adults aged 16 and over were overweight, including 29% who were obese. There has been an increase in the proportion who are overweight or obese among both sexes (aged 16–64) since 1995, from 52% to 62%. Most of this increase was seen between 1995 and 2008, with figures remaining broadly stable since then. (Scottish Government, 2016)

The majority of schools still offer textile lessons within their BGE courses, even where it is not possible to continue progression through to Scottish Qualifications Authority (SQA) exam level. However, a small but significant number of schools have now removed it from their curriculum for a variety of reasons, including a lack of staffing and appropriate accommodation.

'Benchmarks' are the latest guidelines for teachers issued by Education Scotland to aid the planning of learning, teaching and assessment. They are designed to assist teachers in recognising the different progression levels that students will pass through on their journey towards achievement and excellence. The same E&Os are grouped under the six recognisable SAL headings and alongside each grouping appear descriptions of what learning within that area might look like.

'Problem-solving' tasks set within the context of both food and textile experiences are relatively commonplace in the BGE curriculum. 'Design and make a cushion' and 'design and make a pizza' are the types of learning experiences that might be on offer. This type of learning provides ideal opportunities for meaningful group work as well as individual creativity. A five-step process, or something similar, might be used in the classroom where the pupils are encouraged to approach the problem through analysis, research, planning, execution of the design, and finally reviewing the end result by testing the product, evaluating the process and reporting back. These activities, whilst developing a wide range of subject-based knowledge and practical skills, also involve useful, transferable, life skills including: active research; creativity; organisation and management; decision making; and innovative and critical thinking.

## NATIONAL COURSES

There are so many different SQA courses that can be run by a HEc department that choices are inevitable, as it is difficult and, certainly for most departments, inadvisable to deliver every possible option. In part due to the numbers of pupils coming into a department being split between different course options, bi-level and tri-level classes (where pupils are studying at multiple SQA levels) are common, with the challenges to good teaching and learning that this entails.

In food studies, most schools opt to offer either Hospitality: Practical Cookery (HPC) or Health and Food Technology (HFT) because few departments have sufficient staffing to cover both strands. HPC is the more popular option, as it provides more experiential practical cookery with related knowledge, whilst the HFT option, although containing a significant amount of practical cooking, does cover a larger amount of theory including consumer education and product development. Only the HFT course continues to Higher and Advanced Higher levels. Hospitality: Practical Cake Craft (HPCC), which is only available at National 5 level, has become an increasingly popular addition to the HEc curriculum in the last ten years. It is a stand-alone course which can be an option for any pupil having already completed another SQA HEc course, or it is often delivered to seniors in S5/6 who have had no experience of HEc since the completion of their BGE in the early years of secondary education.

Fashion and Textile Technology (FTT) is offered in a number of schools, often where the principal teacher (PT) has a particular interest or specialism in that subject; and when it appears on the curriculum it is usually very popular. It does require to be delivered in a specialist, or at least a dedicated, room; and classroom space is often at a premium, particularly in the modern Public–Private Partnership (PPP) schools built over the last decade. When decisions were made as to the design of these schools, often the PT and staff in post at the time had the final say as to whether their rooms would be kitchens or textile rooms and so any resurgence in this area of the subject is likely to be dependent upon the teaching space available.

The SQA (2016) statistics in Tables 49.1 and 49.2 are an indication of the popularity of the courses. In the summer of 2016 over 12,000 pupils were presented for courses in HPC, over 4,000 pupils were presented for HFT and over 1,000 pupils were presented for FTT. In total, for the mainstream HEc courses, almost 18,000 presentations were made.

Table 49.1  SQA results for 2016, grouped according to level of presentation

|  |  | Entries | Passes (A–C) | Passes (A–C) as a percentage of the total |
|---|---|---|---|---|
| Advanced Higher | HFT | 25 | 18 | 72 |
| Higher | FTT | 305 | 270 | 88.5 |
|  | HFT | 1,448 | 1,020 | 70.4 |
| National 5 | FTT | 572 | 529 | 92.5 |
|  | HFT | 1,904 | 1,573 | 82.6 |
|  | HPCC | 1,785 | 1,556 | 87.2 |
|  | HPC | 6,257 | 5,320 | 85 |
| National 4 | FTT | 189 | 165 | 87.3 |
|  | HFT | 829 | 770 | 92.9 |
|  | HPC | 3,862 | 3,681 | 95.3 |
| National 3 | FTT | 14 | 12 | 85.7 |
|  | HFT | 46 | 41 | 89.1 |
|  | HPC | 539 | 462 | 85.7 |
| National 2 | Food HWB | 196 | 128 | 65.3 |

Source: https://www.sqa.org.uk/sqa/80674.html

Table 49.2  SQA results for 2016, grouped according to subject area

|  |  | Entries | Passes (A–C) | Passes (A–C) as a percentage of the total |
|---|---|---|---|---|
| FTT | Higher | 305 | 270 | 88.5 |
|  | Nat 5 | 572 | 529 | 92.5 |
|  | Nat 4 | 189 | 165 | 87.3 |
|  | Nat 3 | 14 | 12 | 85.7 |
| HFT | Advanced Higher | 25 | 18 | 72 |
|  | Higher | 1,448 | 1,020 | 70.4 |
|  | Nat 5 | 1,904 | 1,573 | 82.6 |
|  | Nat 4 | 829 | 770 | 92.9 |
|  | Nat 3 | 46 | 41 | 89.1 |
| HPCC | Nat 5 | 1,785 | 1,556 | 87.2 |
| HPC | Nat 5 | 6,257 | 5,320 | 85 |
|  | Nat 4 | 3,862 | 3,681 | 95.3 |
|  | Nat 3 | 539 | 462 | 85.7 |
| Food HWB | Nat 2 | 196 | 128 | 65.3 |

Source: https://www.sqa.org.uk/sqa/80674.html

## STAFFING

Staffing is one of the biggest areas of concern for both HEc teachers and their schools. It is now a crisis which, if not resolved, could see the demise of the subject over a relatively short period of time. Already there are schools that are no longer offering the subject on their curriculum due to an inability to recruit and retain appropriately qualified teachers. Universities offering post-graduate teacher education courses are struggling to recruit sufficient students to fill their quotas. For session 2016–17 the overall target set by the government for the recruitment of HEc students in Higher Education Institutions was fifty-five – split between

Aberdeen, Dundee and Strathclyde universities, with Strathclyde hosting the largest student contingent. However, the final numbers recruited for all three universities was forty-seven students. Although only eight students short, this decline in numbers is now an established trend. Part of the problem is that there has not been a dedicated undergraduate training course for HEc teachers since the demise of the Bachelor of Arts (BA) HEc offered by institutions in the 1980s such as Caledonian University in Glasgow and Queen Margaret College (now Queen Margaret University), Edinburgh. Nowadays, students are accepted for post-graduate teaching courses with degrees in the areas of nutrition, health, food science, consumer science or textile design and construction. Often the universities offering these degrees are channelling students towards industry and it becomes difficult to recruit from this pool of expertise for education. Additionally, practical skills can be limited or missing entirely from these courses so that, when these students are recruited, they have experience in only parts of the subject content currently being delivered in schools. Thus, they may be required, by some teacher education institutions, to follow additional certificated courses of study to reach the standard of expertise necessary to allow them to competently teach all aspects of the subject.

A recent announcement by the Scottish Government has indicated that a new undergraduate degree to train HEc teachers is to be offered by the University of the Highlands and Islands through Perth College. This will be a four-year degree, starting in September 2018. It will commence with a Higher National Certificate (HNC) in Professional Cookery, and teacher education will be embedded with students ready to begin their probationary year in Scottish schools at its conclusion. This may be a much-needed boost to the profession but as yet there are not enough details regarding the content of the course to evaluate its likely contribution.

## WORKLOAD: TECHNICAL SUPPORT

Lack of support from a dedicated subject technician is a major issue amongst teachers of HEc. In most schools, around half of the units of learning involve practical, hands-on experience of food or textiles and many would see this as one of the most important contributions of the subject, particularly to HWB. However, it is now common to find no dedicated personnel support for staff to assist with the significant additional workload which accompanies such a practical, experiential learning environment. If indeed there is any support given, it is likely to be an allocation of someone from the school's auxiliary support team for one to two hours per day, and this support is not usually guaranteed; the auxiliary staff member can be withdrawn at no notice to attend to other administrative duties as deemed important by the school. Departments want to know why this is the case, and why some other subject areas such as Craft and Design and the sciences have dedicated members of staff to support their work whilst HEc does not. They question why the health and safety issues surrounding food (its acquisition, transportation, storage, preparation, handling and consumption) are not deemed an important enough risk factor to warrant dedicated, appropriately trained personnel support.

## WORKLOAD: EMERGENCE OF FACULTY HEADS

The emergence of more non-HEc specialist faculty heads has been creating problems in recent years. The concept of faculty heads can work well when the appointments are across areas which have similarities, but an increasing number of HEc teachers are finding themselves managed by non-HEc specialists. They do not have the training to deal with the specific requirements of a food and textile department with all its health and safety risks and the additional physical workload that accompanies the subject. As a result, what often happens is that the complex managerial, administrative and practical tasks peculiar to the subject are by necessity subsumed into the workload of the existing HEc teaching staff in the department, and this is not usually a welcome development. It is not unknown for these non-HEc specialists to undertake class teaching in the subject, with no training, and this is of significant concern.

## THE FUTURE

If the government is serious about tackling the obesity epidemic, and about 'closing the attainment gap' through having a healthy school population which is physically fit to receive the most from their learning, then it should consider the benefits to be acquired by making HEc a *core* HWB subject, giving an entitlement to every child at secondary (and even primary) school. Indirectly, the CfE ethos of interdisciplinary learning would also benefit by this move. The connections are wide-ranging: applied mathematics is to be found in both food and textile courses; a useful and engaging form of the English language is embedded in the specialist technical vocabulary; transferable life skills are the essence of problem solving and critical thinking; and social subjects and modern languages find a link with studies of foods around the world and the cultural history of the foods we eat today. Additionally, HEc finds a role in unveiling the sensitivities of religious observance surrounding specialist diets; it deals with the nutritional needs of a healthy body to perform normal daily and sporting tasks; and it provides an avenue for creativity in the decoration and presentation of both food and textile products.

For a long time, Scottish HEc teachers have had no strong, representative voice at a national level lobbying for their subject and bringing their issues to the attention of those with the power to change them. There is a Facebook interface called 'Home Economics and Food Education Scotland' which is proving to be a useful forum for encouraging teacher exchanges although, as is often the case with social media, reliability of data can be a problem. However, it is understandably not a recognised body on the national scene in the way that the representative associations for other subjects are, such as the Scottish Association for Music Education which states on its website that it is 'contributing to the creation of a strong, unified voice for music education nationally' (www.same.org.uk). There is a need for HEc teachers to become more politically active if the subject is not to be lost or adversely altered. Change is certainly coming to the subject for a variety of reasons, tight budgets not being the least of them. There is a danger that changes will be imposed upon staff, so HEc teachers urgently have to find a way to become proactive at a national level in order to have their voice heard before it is too late.

Finally, what's in a name? The debate on whether to change the subject's name and what that change should be has raged on now for more than a quarter of a century. Certainly the name is changing by degrees as individual departments opt for their own preferred choices. The SQA has dropped its use from all official exam papers but as yet there is no general consensus as to what the new name should be. Whatever the name, 'Applied Food and Textile Science', 'Home Economics' or some other designation, nothing will change its popularity amongst schoolchildren, the essential life skills and knowledge content it delivers, and its importance within the Scottish Curriculum for Excellence.

## REFERENCES

Scottish Government (2015) *National Statistics Publication 'Summary Statistics for Schools in Scotland –* *No.6: 2015 Edition*', 9 December. Online at www.scotland.gov.uk/stats/bulletins/01187

Scottish Government (2016) *Obesity Indicators: Monitoring Progress for the Prevention of Obesity Route* *Map – December 2016 Report*. Online at www.gov.scot/Publications/2016/12/3526

Scottish Qualifications Authority (2016) Annual Statistical report. Online at www.sqa.org.uk/sqa/61717.html

# 50

# Mathematics

*Ian Hulse and John Winter*

The development of Curriculum for Excellence (CfE) was governed by the following constraint: 'To face the challenges of the 21st century, each young person needs to have confidence in using mathematical skills, and Scotland needs both specialist mathematicians and a highly numerate population' (Scottish Executive, 2006). With CfE well established in secondary schools, this chapter considers central aspects of mathematics provision, aiming to identify the ongoing challenges facing secondary mathematics education.

## COURSES IN S1 TO S3 – BROAD GENERAL EDUCATION

CfE views Mathematics as a rich and stimulating activity, vitally important in life, work and learning but also rewarding in and of itself. It splits Mathematics into successive levels, learning at each of which is described by a collection of experiences and outcomes. The organisers for these are 'Number, Money and Measure', 'Shape, Position and Movement' and 'Information Handling'. Some of the Mathematics experiences and outcomes are also used to describe learning in numeracy, which thus appears as something like a traditional subject. But, whereas traditional subjects in secondary education are delivered by subject specialists alone, in CfE, 'all teachers have responsibility for promoting the development of numeracy' (Scottish Executive, 2006).

CfE originally anticipated that pupils begin level 3 as they enter S1. However, the mathematics involved here is too advanced for a significant proportion of new pupils, so most S1 and S2 pupils begin a school-designed programme of work at the appropriate level based on information received from feeder primary schools and, in some cases, from departmental testing early in S1. In schools following the intended curricular model, pupils will progress through these courses (and, for some, courses at level 4) until their broad general education comes to a close at the end of S3. CfE is not complemented by a suite of national assessments with which to assess, record and report on pupil progress. Not only the experiences and outcomes, but also the standards and expectations associated with them, are to be interpreted by those delivering the new curriculum. Pupils are regularly tested at an appropriate stage determined by individual departmental policy, and the results of these tests are used to measure attainment and also to ensure that the pupil will start the correct course in their senior phase. Initial criticisms that teachers required more guidance on how to deliver the curriculum and measure attainment led to what amounts to the unpacking of the original experiences and outcomes to produce a set of benchmarks (see Chapter 68). The document also includes a set of numeracy and mathematics skills:

- interpret questions;
- select and communicate processes and solutions;
- justify choice of strategy used;
- link mathematical concepts;
- use mathematical vocabulary and notation;
- use mental agility;
- reason algebraically;
- determine the reasonableness of a solution.

In 2016, Education Scotland's numeracy team also produced the National Numeracy and Mathematics Progression Framework (NNMPF) designed to support staff in their under-standing and importance of progression within the experiences and outcomes.

## COURSES IN S4 TO S6 – SENIOR PHASE

In 2013–14, new qualifications were introduced in secondary schools. A sketch of the structure, content and administration of these new qualifications is described for all levels in the senior phase. These qualifications concentrate on the development of mathematical language and techniques and the exploration of mathematical concepts. Qualifications in Applications of Mathematics (formerly known as Lifeskills Mathematics) are also available to develop mathematical skills in applications arising in personal life and work. The new national qualifications preserve the modular structure of the old ones. Updated Access 2 and 3 qualifications, renamed National 2 and 3, are available in Applications of Mathematics. National 2 consists of two compulsory units: 'Number and Number Processes' and 'Shape, Space and Data', and two optional units selected from 'Money', 'Time' and 'Measurement'. National 3 consists of three prescribed units: 'Manage Money and Data', 'Shape, Space and Measures' and 'Numeracy'.

National 4 and 5 qualifications are available in both Applications of Mathematics and Mathematics, and consist of three prescribed units and a course assessment. For Applications of Mathematics, the units at National 4 and National 5 cover 'Managing Finance and Statistics', 'Geometry and Measures' and 'Numeracy'. For Mathematics, prescribed units cover 'Expressions and Formulae', 'Relationships' and either 'Numeracy' (at National 4) or 'Applications' (at National 5). Higher Mathematics will cover 'Expressions and Functions', 'Relationships and Calculus' and 'Applications'. There is no Higher in Applications of Mathematics. Currently under development is a Statistics award at Scottish Credit and Qualifications Framework (SCQF) level 6 to address the gap in the syllabus of arguably the most practical and used of all applied mathematics topics. (Statistics is available at Advanced Higher level, along with the Mathematics of Mechanics).

The unit assessment element for National 5 and above is to be phased out gradually from 2017. Units were internally assessed and externally verified. In 2017–18 and beyond, National 5 courses will be assessed only by 'a strengthened' external examination – see Chapter 68 for a discussion of these changes. At National 4, the course assessment consists of, in addition to unit assessments, an examination (Added Value Unit), set and marked internally but along Scottish Qualifications Authority (SQA) guidelines (which stipulate inclusion of non-calculator items). These will be subject to internal verification by centres and external verification and certification by the SQA. National 4s will not be graded. At National 5, Higher and Advanced Higher, external examinations consist of two papers, in one of which a calculator may be used, and which are set, marked and graded A to D by the SQA. It should be noted that the units in Applications of Mathematics from National 3 to National 5 occur in a hierarchy, as do the units in Mathematics from National 4 to Advanced Higher. This means that skills and knowledge are cumulatively built through these units so that successfully completed units from a higher level constitute (typically incomplete) evidence in favour of a course award at a lower level.

While the transition to National 4 and 5 Mathematics from their predecessors has been a relatively smooth one, Applications of Mathematics is still developing its place in schools. The number of candidates sitting the external examination for it at National 5 remained steady in the years 2015 and 2016 (roughly 2,500 entries) but just over half of the candidates received no award (https://www.sqa.org.uk/sqa/77198.html). Concerns have also been raised over the number of students who have successfully completed National 4 Mathematics but are not able to cope with the work at National 5 level. The syllabuses of this subject at Nationals 4 and 5 are roughly the same as General/Intermediate 1 and Credit/Intermediate 2, with a few slight additions to the National 5 from the former Higher syllabus (simple vectors, quadratic theory). Higher and Advanced Higher Mathematics has remained roughly the same with only a slight realignment of the order of the topics. The final examination for National 5 is similar in structure to Credit/Intermediate 2 and Higher Maths has dropped multiple choice questions in paper one and has returned to a more traditional arrangement – however, there have been several public outcries over the content and appropriateness of some of the questions in the new Higher (the infamous crocodile question of 2015) which lead to considerably lower grade boundaries.

The streamlining of the system of assessment pre-Nationals – described in the third edition of this book as 'impossibly difficult to understand' for members of the public and employers alike (Bryce, 2008, p. 591) – has definitely been advantageous in some respects. However, some concerns have been expressed about the inclusiveness of the new qualifications, especially as National 4 has no external examination and pupils are wrongly perceived to have no qualification to show for their work on completion of the course. Increased workload for hard-pressed teachers administering a complicated pathway of internal unit assessments has been alleviated to a certain extent by the phasing out of these assessments from the National 5 and Higher maths courses but there have been concerns expressed by some that this may further reduce inclusivity.

Standard Grade may have had its faults but at least the vast majority of S4 pupils gained an award of some sort. These issues are discussed further in Chapter 68.

## ATTAINMENT

Some years ago the Organisation for Economic Co-operation and Development (OECD) stated that, 'Scotland performs at a consistently very high standard in the Programme for International Student Assessment (PISA). Few countries can be said with confidence to outperform it in mathematics, reading and science' (OECD, 2007, p. 16). This statement was borne out by the results from PISA 2009 where the mean pupil performance at S4 significantly exceeded that of the rest of the UK and OECD, whilst the 2007 *Trends in International Mathematics and Science Survey* (TIMSS) ranked Scotland seventeenth out of fifty-nine participating countries for mathematical attainment at S2 (Scottish Government, 2007). However, comparison of these studies with their predecessors and subsequent PISA surveys in 2012 and 2015 show that mathematical performance in Scotland has declined over recent years, that the gap between the highest and lowest attainers in mathematics is getting wider, and that there is a persistent gap in achievement in mathematics between boys and girls at S4.

The Scottish Government's (2016b) executive summary of PISA 2015 highlighted that Scotland's score in mathematics remained similar to the OECD average from 2012 to 2015, whereas science and reading had declined. However, and more tellingly, Scotland's relative performance compared to the other countries (including some in the UK) had declined. Also, the proportion of pupils performing at level 5 and above (the higher end of the OECD's proficiency level) and pupils performing at level 2 and below (the lower end) was below the OECD average.

From 2012, data on attainment has been available from the Scottish Survey of Literacy and Numeracy (SSLN). These surveys have been developed to complement CfE (replacing the Scottish Survey of Achievement, SSA), monitoring performance in literacy and numeracy in alternate years. The results from SSLN 2011, 2013 and 2015, which appraises numeracy, have produced some interesting results. The survey, which samples the work of over 10,000 pupils in P4, P7 and S2 from volunteer schools across Scotland, confirms that deprivation remains a significant factor for attainment in numeracy; pupils living with higher levels of deprivation were *half as likely* to be performing well or very well at the respective level as pupils with lower levels of deprivation (see www.gov.scot/Topics/Statistics/Browse/School-Education/SSLN). Gender imbalances were found at P4 and P7, though by S2 the difference between boys' performance and girls' performance was no longer significant. Attainment across transitions remains an issue, although the gap between P7 and S2 pupils performing well or very well at the relevant level is narrowing (from 72 per cent in P7 and 42 per cent in S2 in 2011 to 66 per cent and 40 per cent in 2015). These results, however, compare unfavourably with SSA findings before CfE was implemented, where it was shown that the proportion of pupils exhibiting adequate skills at the expected level declined from 70 per cent in P7 to 55 per cent in S2. Despite having identified the problem for many years now and great efforts being expended by local authorities, transitions from primary through early secondary are still associated with decreased mathematical attainment.

Some studies also provide data about attitudes to mathematics. Scottish Government (2007) put the proportion of S2 pupils enjoying mathematics in Scotland at 33 per cent. Although the 2008 SSA showed that close to 80 per cent of S2 pupils want to do well at mathematics, it reported the proportion to be less than 20 per cent for enjoyment of mathematics and finding mathematics interesting (see www.gov.scot/Topics/Statistics/Browse/School-Education/SSA2008). Attitudes to numeracy learning were investigated by SSLN. Although the percentage of pupils reporting to 'enjoy working with numbers' is lower than those asked if they usually do well working with numbers (66 per cent and 83 per cent respectively), the number of pupils that agreed with the statement, 'I learn things quickly when working with numbers' decreased significantly in S2 between 2013 and 2015. The largest decrease was from 70 per cent in 2013 to 64 per cent in 2015 (Scottish Government, 2016a).

The confidence that S2 pupils perceive they have in the various numeracy organisers range from 82 per cent for 'Money' and 'Rounding and Estimation', to 'Chance and Uncertainty' at 47 per cent. These roughly correlate with the findings for P4 and P7 pupils.

However, there was a statistically significant decrease between 2013 and 2015 in what the pupils perceived their abilities were in the organisers 'Measurement', 'Data and Analysis' and 'Time'. However, 'Fractions', 'Chance and Uncertainty' and 'Number and Number Processes' have recorded increases in confidence between 2011 and 2015.

Not surprisingly, the findings of the SSLN surveys have provoked ongoing criticism of CfE. Education Scotland has responded by creating national numeracy bodies consisting of organisers from local authorities and schools who have met frequently and produced teaching resources to address numeracy and mathematics attainment and progression across primary and secondary levels. Mathematics and numeracy attainment at secondary in Scotland thus presents a mixed picture, having once compared well with international norms but now exhibiting some decline and certain inequalities. The efficacy of CfE to address these issues is still debatable.

## PEDAGOGY

In 2005, Her Majesty's Inspectorate of Education (HMIE) reported that staff in most secondary schools 'had yet to consider the impact that different learning and teaching approaches and contexts for applying mathematical skills could have for developing pupils' learning skills, confidence, individual responsibility and effectiveness in contributing to group tasks and success' (HMIE, 2005, p. 9). The intervening years have seen a great deal of critical reflection on teaching approaches amongst mathematics teachers. Continuing professional development (CPD) opportunities have helped teachers to build their knowledge of newer methods. Guidance and support has been made available through national bodies such as HMIE and Education Scotland and at local authority level. Moreover, new teachers have been trained in courses designed with more contemporary pedagogy in mind and this has been complemented by a 'world class' system of teacher induction (OECD, 2007, p. 15). This ongoing professional development has resulted in positive changes to mathematics pedagogy. HMIE (2010, p. 9) noted with approval certain teaching methods, which included Assessment is for Learning (AifL) techniques and good use of information and communication technology (ICT), that are 'presently contributing particularly well to successful learning in mathematics'. It also noted the presence of further 'strong characteristics of effective teaching' (p. 8) such as maximised learner-to-learner interactions, explicit drawing of cross-curricular links, responsive planning and the use of plenary sessions.

Mathematics teachers continue to embrace innovative teaching methods such as collaborative/cooperative learning, blended learning and the use of ICT and online technology. Some schools have adopted excellent examples of blended approaches. Encouraged by whole school and local authority initiatives, great strides have been made towards integrating whole school numeracy and literacy approaches and the creation of meaningful cross-curricular programmes in numeracy. However, in a climate of perceived declining achievement in numeracy and mathematics it is incumbent on teachers to continually explore new approaches and pedagogies.

## REFERENCES

Bryce, T. (2008) 'Assessment in Scottish schools', in T. G. K. Bryce and W. M. Humes (eds), *Scottish Education, Third Edition: Beyond Devolution*. Edinburgh: Edinburgh University Press.

HMIE (2005) *Improving Achievement in Mathematics in Primary and Secondary Schools*. Livingston: HMIE.

HMIE (2009) *Improving Scottish Education: A Report by HMIE on Inspection and Review 2005–2008*. Livingston: HMIE.

HMIE (2010) *Learning Together: Mathematics*. Livingston: HMIE.

OECD (2007) *Reviews of National Policies for Education: Quality and Equity of Schooling in Scotland*. Paris: OECD Publishing.

Scottish Executive (2006) *A Curriculum for Excellence: Building the Curriculum 1*. Online at https:// www.education.gov.scot/Documents/btc1.pdf

Scottish Government (2007) *Trends in International Mathematics and Science Survey (TIMSS) 2007*. Online at www.gov.scot/Publications/2009/10/13150724/1

Scottish Government (2012) *Scottish Survey of Literacy and Numeracy 2011 (Numeracy)*. Online at www.scotland.gov.uk/Publications/2012/03/5285/0

Scottish Government (2014) *Scottish Survey of Literacy and Numeracy 2013 (Numeracy)*. Online at www.gov.scot/Publications/2014/04/5692

Scottish Government (2016a) *Scottish Survey of Literacy and Numeracy 2015 (Numeracy)*. Online at www.gov.scot/Publications/2016/05/2836

Scottish Government (2016b) *PISA (2015) Highlights from Scotland's Results*. Online at www.gov. scot/Publications/2016/12/7252

SQA (2017a) *Mathematics*. Online at www.sqa.org.uk/sqa/45750.html

SQA (2017b) *Course Report National 5 Lifeskills Maths*. Online at www.sqa.org.uk/files_ccc/ MathematicsIntermediate2EAR2015.pdf

# 51

# Modern Foreign Languages

*Do Coyle*

> Language plays a crucial role in ensuring cultural diversity, democratic citizenship and
> social inclusion. It thus has a key role to play in promoting social cohesion. (Council of Europe,
> 2006, p. 4)

## THE CHANGING LANDSCAPE

In 2015, the Organisation for Economic Co-operation and Development (OECD) report, *Improving Schools in Scotland: An OECD Perspective* commissioned by the Scottish Government, described recent Scottish education reforms as being at a 'watershed' (p. 10). The report was positive with regards to the enthusiasm for learning which young people generate as well as political patience embedded in the 'key transitions' and the potential take-off of the 'new' Curriculum for Excellence over a thirteen-year period. However, the report was less positive about achievement levels and a skilled workforce, emphasising the need for a more ambitious theory of change and a more robust evidence base available across the system.

Learner engagement is a prerequisite of powerful learning and improved outcomes, and that argues for innovating learning environments, especially in secondary schools, beginning in the most deprived areas (ibid., p. 19). The OECD report emphasised the need to create a *new narrative* for Curriculum for Excellence. It is against this backdrop that such a narrative will be explored focusing on key aspects of learning languages which include the selection and nature of languages to be learned, pedagogic approaches and pupil achievement in secondary schools. This chapter will consider a *new narrative* with respect to the teaching and learning of languages in secondary schools.

The study of modern foreign languages (ML) in Scottish secondary schools has had a chequered history over recent decades and is constantly in a state of flux. Set within an uncertain and rapidly changing sociopolitical landscape, national and global factors impacting on the nation's linguistic capital generate contradictory outcomes which present increasingly fundamental challenges for Scottish education. On the one hand, according to ScotCen's Scottish Social Attitudes (SSA) survey in 2016, 89 per cent of people in Scotland believe that learning a language other than English is important (see www.ssa. natcen.ac.uk/read-the-reports/scottish-social-attitudes-2016.aspx). On the other hand, a paucity of language teachers and fewer school leavers studying for language specific degrees at university, alongside budgetary constraints and the realities of restricted curriculum time allocation, have contributed to an overall decline in the uptake of young people opting for the new ML National Qualifications in S4 and S5. By 2016, French, German and Spanish entries had declined, yet with a rise in Spanish at S5. At the same time, of those choosing to continue their language studies to Advanced Higher (level 6) there have been increases since 2012, e.g. 8 per cent for French, 3 per cent for German, with a significant increase in Spanish. Data from the Higher Education Statistics Agency (SCILT, 2015) also indicate an 11 per cent increase in the number of graduates, if those taking a language component as part of their degree are included. The trends are mixed.

The 2016 survey also reports that there are over 39,000 children in Scotland in mainstream schools whose first language is not English, suggesting that an increasingly multilingual and multicultural population is not having a significant effect on the language learning ethos in schools (www.ssa.natcen.ac.uk/read-the-reports/scottish-social-attitudes-2016.aspx). Moreover, in 2012, at the time of the introduction of the Scottish Government's aspirational 1 + 2 language initiative, of the 47,741 pupils aged 15 and 16 in Scottish schools, only 12.1 per cent were studying a foreign language (Scottish Government, 2012). In 2012, the pathway to a positive national languages strategy aligned with European models was laid out with an initial focus on the teaching and learning of two additional languages in the primary school. The Scottish Government pledged to:

> introduce a norm for language learning in schools based on the European Union 1 + 2 model – that is we will create the conditions in which every child will learn two languages in addition to their own mother tongue. This will be rolled out over two Parliaments, and will create a new model for language acquisition in Scotland. (Scottish Government, 2011)

The notion of building linguistic capital and ensuring young people in Scotland have an entitlement to develop a useful range of language skills make a fundamental contribution to developing successful learners, confident individuals, responsible citizens and effective contributors. These attributes, which lie at the core of Curriculum for Excellence, are outlined in the chapters on early years and primary education. However, the context in which the ambitious 1+2 programme has been introduced in the primary sector and which will soon have significant impact on the secondary languages curriculum, is set for unprecedented change. Whilst Scotland's schools are under increasing pressure to ensure all pupils learn languages, the UK's exit from the European Union will undoubtedly have far-reaching consequences in terms of linguistic and cultural integration in a plurilingual, pluricultural Europe. The unknown short- and long-term effects of such political imperatives add an increasing urgency to all stakeholders involved with language teaching and learning to ensure that the underpinning values and beliefs which promote equality and social cohesion for global citizenship continue to be transparent and coherent to all learners, their families and communities.

## PERSISTENT CHALLENGES

According to the SSA 2016 survey (www.ssa.natcen.ac.uk/read-the-reports/scottish-social-attitudes-2016.aspx), it is generally considered useful for young people in Scotland to learn Western European languages such as French and German in schools. This reflects a traditional view of historical practices. Despite the government's 'push' to promote Mandarin and expand Gaelic-medium education, the position of languages in the curriculum continues to pose well-rehearsed challenges: choice of languages available in different secondary schools; the pupil experience in terms of progression and depth of understanding in two other languages; competition with other subjects for curriculum time and dealing with the commonly held belief that languages are 'difficult'; the cultural impact on individual and community identities associated with the promotion of different languages; attitudes towards and perceived usefulness of different languages; links with countries and regions where those languages are used; continued financial support for language assistants; and significant funding for expanding the supply of language teachers and actively supporting experienced practitioners to develop alternative approaches in keeping with evidence from within and outside Scotland – all of which impact on pedagogic approaches and what goes on in classrooms. These challenges raise specific questions, for example about the role of the first language for second languages speakers of English such as Polish; the impact of heritage languages beyond Gaelic-medium such as Scots and Doric; the positioning of more 'exotic' languages such as Mandarin and Arabic; the inclusion of British Sign Language and Latin in the mix; the growing popularity of Spanish – the list is complex. Moreover, implicit in questions about the choice of languages for learning lies the availability of teachers, sustainability of language provision over several years, prior experiences in different languages in the primary school and the entitlement to learn a third language in already 'stretched' allocated curriculum time. Young people are also entitled to an L3 experience within their broad general education (BGE). In the senior phase, young people should be able to study more than one additional language to National Qualification (https://education.gov.scot/Documents/modern-languages-pp.pdf).

A range of key educational organisations, government agencies and cultural institutes offer constant support. Community groups are active, and technology goes some way to providing pathways for language learning, cultural linking and opportunities for exploring shared learning spaces. However, the current realities of other subject disciplines in secondary schools such as science, technology, engineering and mathematics (STEM) subjects also making claims about the importance of their associated disciplines, bring into question the sustainability of building on primary experiences for learning two languages in secondary school in ways which inspire and genuinely raise the nation's linguistic capital. The *new narrative* has to address urgently critical factors such as teacher availability, appropriate and extensive professional learning and initial teacher education to face up to current challenges, longer term planning and sustainable outcomes rather than 'quick-fix' solutions.

## PEDAGOGIES AND PRACTICES

Over the last two decades, international language research into the theories and practices of language learning and teaching in a wide range of schools and contexts has generated fundamental re-visioning and advancement in conceptualising the 'what' and 'how' of language learning. In Europe, the *Common European Framework of Reference* (CEFR, Council of Europe, nd) builds on promoting plurilingualism, linguistic diversity, mutual understanding, democratic citizenship, lifelong learning and social cohesion – all of which align with the capacities of Curriculum for Excellence. The CEFR provides guidance for teaching, learning and assessing language skills according to six levels of language proficiency from beginner to advanced: A1 and A2 (Basic), B1 and B2 (Independent), C1 and C2 (Proficient). Whilst the UK has been slow to adopt the framework in practice, there are clear indications that the alignment of CEFR levels with Scotland's broad general education and beyond raise some important questions – being mindful of course that the CEFR is built on recommended rather than prescriptive levels. The Scottish Curriculum for BGE (ages 3–15) provides descriptors for each of the four levels of attainment in the national framework which focus on pupil experiences and learning outcomes. These descriptors emphasise learning progression across different ages and stages. However, given that pupils are now entitled to language learning experiences for seven years in their primary school and three years in their secondary school, current expectations of pupils after ten years of language experiences for the majority according to the CEFR *remain* at A2 (Basic Level). Without placing a 'glass ceiling' on higher levels of achievement, this is an achievable target in modern languages, provided we establish a solid basis in primary, have an appropriate gradient of progression in S1 to S3, and motivate our learners through relevant and stimulating learning experiences.

Arguments which suggest that primary language learning is about 'breadth as well as depth' impact on learner experiences in the secondary school. It is well documented that a lack of challenge in the languages curriculum acts as a demotivator (Jones and Doughty, 2015), which may raise further challenges in terms of adapting and experimenting with different teaching approaches that not only build on previous experiences but transparently advance linguistic progression, sustain motivation and make visible the contribution that language experiences make to the government's education agenda of 'raising attainment'. It puts increasing pressure on transition between primary and secondary stages, demanding language planning in the secondary curriculum which assures learner development and a sense of achievement, practical language skills and an understanding of the role that language (including first language) plays in deeper learning and intercultural understanding shared by teachers, pupils and the community.

It is imperative that secondary schools and centres take into account children's prior learning in the modern language(s) they have acquired at primary school. Secondary modern languages teachers should work closely with primary colleagues to ensure that learners continue to build on the language learning skills they acquired throughout their primary experience (Scottish Government, 2009).

Enabling and supporting secondary languages teachers to assure continuity, work collaboratively with their primary school colleagues, and be convinced of the tangible benefits of sustained language study for all pupils remains in the balance. Christie et al. (2016, p. 6) noted that:

> The engagement of secondary schools in the initiative is variable. In 'best practice' secondary language staff are engaged in anticipating the L2 and L3 abilities of learners as they progress to secondary school and in planning courses for the development of these languages. In other authorities, we saw little evidence of active forward planning.

A *new narrative*, incorporating the principles and practices associated with the CEFR, provides, however, *trans-European language level descriptors* and introduces the practical use of a Learners' Language Portfolio. The portfolio encourages individuals to celebrate their own languages profile from birth and set language goals based on individual interests and identities. Crucially it raises awareness in learners to document and evidence their achievements. This aligns with another key European concept for language education referred to as the Languages of Schooling, which adopts a holistic view of language in the school curriculum and community that not only acknowledges multilingual contexts but genuinely celebrates and uses them to learner advantage. As the Council of Europe report stated:

> 'language as subject' and 'language across the curriculum' (the idea that all subjects are involved in teaching and developing language) as part of a broad concept of 'languages of education which also incorporates foreign language learning. Thinking about language education in this way as a broad, all-embracing notion rooted in a policy of plurilingualism, is a departure from a more traditional approach which treats these different components of language in isolation from each other. (Council of Europe, 2006, p. 8)

Adopting and promoting a more holistic and 'joined-up' approach to language experiences works towards nurturing authentic connectivity based on real-world issues to encourage learners to continue their language studies into the upper school phase. In the secondary sector, this necessitates that greater collaboration between modern language teachers, heritage language-medium teachers and English as an additional language (EAL) specialists develops so that language and languages are normalised in 'language rich' classrooms; transfer between languages and communication skills are transparent; and high expectations are prevalent for pupils to use languages in relevant situations supported by the use of digital tools, social media and virtual spaces. Providing professional learning programmes which equip teachers to move from 'broad language experiences' to designing tasks and activities in the classroom which balance language *learning* and language *using* through problem solving, creative outputs and higher order thinking, thereby providing *relevant and motivating learning experiences* in S1–3, are a 'must' for secondary teachers. Drawing on the successful rejuvenation of language learning in other countries with similar linguistic profiles to that of Scotland such as Australia (Hancock, 2014) suggests that at the core lies a commitment towards the teaching workforce and career-long professional learning which challenges some current practices and inspires ownership and confidence to do things differently.

In addition, when teachers of English and other subjects connect with language classes, potential pathways for developing subject literacies and interdisciplinary learning emerge. Links between language learning and literacy development in the primary school are consistently made in curriculum guidelines. However, planning for the development of academic literacies which are essential for deeper and high-quality learning in the secondary school is absent. So too is making visible the interrelationship between first and other languages in terms of raising awareness, transferability of skills and the development of communicative competence in the broadest sense underpinning Curriculum for Excellence attributes. In other words, secondary schools are well placed to provide pupils with experiences of how language can be used as a learning tool across disciplines, topics and projects which encourage creativity and higher order thinking, but the implications for investment in supporting teachers to accomplish this through initial teacher education and career-long professional learning are urgent. A *new narrative* suggesting a 'rethink' in ways of designing a more *integrated* approach to languages at secondary level – yet one which safeguards fundamental principles of language learning – could well transform 'Languages' into a Curriculum for Excellence exemplar for more innovative ways of dealing with challenges of time, staffing, professional development and raising pupil attainment.

## BEYOND THE 'WATERSHED'

The SCILT (2011) *Modern Languages Excellence Report* highlighted the importance of maximum exposure to the language, the *use* of the language by the learners, an insistence on good pronunciation and application of grammatical structures across all four skills and the *integration* of languages and cultures. All of these remain fundamental to high-quality language teaching and learning. However, in the changing landscape, new factors such as accountability, international comparators such as PISA and a politically driven educational agenda impact significantly on approaches to language learning in secondary schools. This suggests that experimenting with alternative approaches to curriculum learning may lead to the emergence of a more integrated teaching and learning agenda, such as Content and Language Integrated Learning, which explicitly encourages and enables learners to *use* their language skills more broadly and connect with other language speaking communities. It also embraces global imperatives such as sustainability where language learning (communicative competence, intercultural understanding and identity formation) plays a fundamental role. The General Teaching Council for Scotland states: 'Learning for Sustainability is a priority. ... In schools, sustainable development education, global citizenship, outdoor learning and health and well-being are firmly embedded within Curriculum for Excellence. Learning for Sustainability weaves together and builds upon these themes' (www.gtcs.org.uk/professional-standards/learning-for-sustainability.aspx). So where is language learning? Why is it not visible in such discourse? What pedagogic changes are needed for it to be core to curriculum development in schools?

There are many outstanding examples of successful language learning in secondary schools and links with the business community are to be lauded. Language teachers strive to motivate learners and celebrate successes through initiatives which are too numerous to mention here. The Languages Network Group Scotland (LANGS), SCILT, the Scottish Association for Language Teaching (SALT), University Council for Modern Languages Scotland (UCMLS) and the cultural institutes and universities, to name but a few, showcase excellence across languages. The OECD acknowledges an enthusiasm for learning by young people. And yet current evidence suggests that unless some of the fundamental questions raised in this chapter are addressed, teachers are supported by senior leaders in school and languages become more prominent in the wider curriculum agenda, then change will be slow, multilingual voices will remain unheard and our young people will be disadvantaged. 'Unintended consequences' resulting from recent educational shifts indicate a sense of urgency to co-create a *new shared narrative*.

## REFERENCES

Christie, J., Robertson, B., Stodter, J. and O'Hanlon, F. (2016) *A Review of Progress in Implementing the 1+2 Languages Policy*, a report for Scottish Government published by the Association of Directors of Education in Scotland (ADES). Online at www.research.ed.ac.uk/portal/files/26719327/1_plus_2_report_Final.Published_version..pdf

Council of Europe (nd) *Common European Framework of Reference for Languages: Learning, Teaching and Assessment*. Online at www.coe.int/en/web/common-european-framework-reference-languages/

Council of Europe (2006) *Languages of Schooling: Towards a Framework of Reference for Europe*, DGIV/EDU/LANG (2007) 2, Intergovernmental Conference, Strasbourg, 16–18 October. Online at www.coe.int/t/dg4/linguistic/Source/LE_Conf06_Report_May07_EN.doc

Hancock, A. (2014) 'Language education policy in multilingual Scotland: opportunities, imbalances and debates', *Language Problems and Planning*, 38 (2), 167–91.

Jones, L. and Doughty, H. (2015) '(Turning Our) back to the future? Cross-sector perspectives on language learning', *Scottish Languages Review*, Issue 29, Spring/Summer, 27–40.

OECD (2015) *Improving Schools in Scotland: An OECD Perspective.* Online at www.oecd.org/education/school/Improving-Schools-in-Scotland-An-OECD-Perspective.pdf

SCILT (2011) *Modern Languages Excellence Report.* Online at www.scilt.org.uk/ResourceView/tabid/1092/articleType/ArticleView/articleId/191/Modern-Languages-Excellence-Report.aspx

SCILT (2015) *Language Trends 2014–2015.* Online at www.scilt.org.uk/Portals/24/Library/statistics/Language%20Trends%202014-15.pdf

Scottish Government (2009) *Curriculum for Excellence Modern Languages: Principles and Practice.* https://education.gov.scot/Documents/modern-languages-pp.pdf

Scottish Government (2011) Scottish National Party Manifesto. Online at http://votesnp.com/campaigns/SNP_Manifesto_2011_lowRes.pdf

Scottish Government (2012) *Language Learning in Scotland: A 1+2 Approach.* Online at www.scotland.gov.uk/Publications/2012/05/3670

# 52

# Modern Studies

*Sarah Proctor*

## VALUE AND PURPOSE

Modern Studies was devised in the 1960s against the backdrop of the Cold War. The need to consider political and domestic issues, as well as world events, led to the creation of a subject that was to be an amalgam of History and human Geography. It would look at political, economic and social factors, both at home and further afield, and give an understanding of life and decision-making processes relevant to pupils in the secondary classroom. When it began, Modern Studies was aimed at pupils who were less able and it has taken time and effort on the part of the profession to shake off this image and gain reputation as a subject which is challenging, thought provoking and worthy of certification. The course remains up to date and is constantly in a state of evolution. Today, with a continuing rise in pupil uptake for the subject at National level and beyond, Modern Studies is in a very healthy position. This has seen an increasing demand for the teachers required.

The subject is now at the heart of the curriculum, no longer on the periphery as an 'also-ran' study, indeed seeing growth in its popularity at Higher level. The reason for that expansion is arguably due in part to the greater politicised nature of young people. The Scottish independence referendum of 2014 galvanised youth in taking an interest in their future and led to 86 per cent of the population exercising their democratic right to vote (Electoral Commission, 2014). This rise in active participation was evident in the recent Scottish and Westminster elections and has produced a set of young people with the desire to learn more about governance and the democratic process. The 2017 election to the UK Parliament saw a rush with young people registering to vote in large numbers. Increased political literacy and knowledge of the institutions of government have stimulated young people to take an interest in their future.

## IMPORTANT CONTENT

The Modern Studies curriculum is based around important concepts and themes:

- studies of local, national and international issues from a socio-economic and political perspective;
- key issues – equality, needs, rights and responsibilities, participation and power, and representation;

- key skills – decision making, detecting bias, application of knowledge, interpreting statistics, supporting opinion.

In short, the subject supports an understanding of the world which young people inhabit today. It adds a relevance, realism and contextualises their lives; indeed requiring some sensitivity by classroom teachers. Refugees, poverty or matters related to crime and the law are particularly delicate subject matters and may affect young people in the classroom. The debated issues are often provocative and thought-provoking yet teach young people to form reasoned opinions backed by evidence. Preconceived ideas can challenge and leave pupils thinking about issues related to them.

Technological advances have made the world smaller and the plurality of social media ensures that information, misinformation and biased opinion dominate the lives and routines of youth today. Thus Modern Studies has become more relevant as the years have passed. Recent terror attacks in Barcelona, Manchester, London and Paris motivate young people to use social media to condemn and comment accordingly. The rise of 'fake news' has become strikingly apparent. With this, the need for Modern Studies, notably the enquiry skills element, is more crucial than ever before. Modern Studies teaches pupils to look for bias and exaggeration in all areas; the detection of accuracy in newspaper stories and beyond is of prime concern. These core skills are becoming increasingly required in the twenty-first century and probably account for the continued rise of the subject. Modern Studies also provides a platform to look at issues relevant to individual local areas. Hospital closures, environmental concerns and housing are all relevant to communities today. The political flux associated with austerity measures are currently of great concern.

## SEVEN CURRICULUM AREAS IN MODERN STUDIES

The principal areas for consideration focus on:

- *Representation.* Actions and decisions on behalf of others, for example politicians in Parliament/ class representative.
- *Rights and Responsibilities.* Freedoms given (and carried out within the parameters of law), for example work of a pressure group, newspapers, in society.
- *Participation.* Involvement, for example voting, pressure group, political party, campaign, fundraising
- *Ideology.* Ideas and beliefs of a political or economic society, for example capitalism, communism, often USA/China or North Korea or Russia.
- *Equality.* Wealth/status/wellbeing – local, national and international perspectives, for example elderly, those in poverty.
- *Need.* Requirements of individuals/groups/nations, for example health inequalities, women and ethnic minority representation, the developing world.
- *Power.* Actions affecting others. Often manifests in a conflict unit that can incorporate, for example, North Korea, Syria, terrorism, USA.

Given the broad nature of these issues we are left with the quandary of making each area relevant, accessible to all and, importantly, interesting. These are all areas which are of significance to pupils at all ages and stages.

## PRIMARY–S3

As part of the Social Studies family, Modern Studies content and skills is readily apparent in the section entitled People in Society, Economy and Business. Business remains a bit of a 'bolt-on' and is not generally related to the Social Subjects disciplines you move into at the third level. The experiences and outcomes at primary level (early to second level) lend themselves to more interdisciplinary work and as such could be termed as objectives concerned with global citizenship; thus Modern Studies teaching, for example fair trade, is more about the links across learning.

When moving to S1–3, topics present themselves. The Scottish Parliament, although considered at upper primary, is covered in more depth. It should be noted that to keep topics fresh and more engaging, teachers engage with Parliament differently, looking at devolved versus reserved powers, as well as engaging in the many issues that present themselves, thus keeping it relevant to today. There has been a variety of interpretations of the experiences and outcomes. Topics such as the Westminster Parliament, poverty, the media, and crime and the law are covered in part. Internationally, terrorism, the USA, China, the developing world and the United Nations Convention on the Rights of the Child are relevant and prevalent in many schools. Caution has to be met as, in the spirit of Curriculum for Excellence, any topic may be covered. Of note, the comparison of nation states to that of Scotland must also be included. Arguably, the curriculum is becoming overtly Scotland-centric as it would make more sense to compare say the politics of East and West (North Korea and USA or Britain).

## GREATER INTEGRATION ACROSS THE SOCIAL SUBJECTS?

In S1/S2 the principles of CfE lend themselves to several interpretations. For some, the social subjects should be fully integrated as a curriculum area; for others, the individual subjects of Geography, History and Modern Studies remain extant in the curriculum framework (with an occasional dalliance with Religious and Moral Education in some schools). The creation of faculties as a concept emerged in the post-McCrone era of Scottish education following the agreement reached in 2001 (www.gov.scot/Publications/2001/01/7959/File-1). The issue of curriculum modelling and 'innovative' methods of delivery is under scrutiny at present. Fenwick et al. (2013) explore the resistance of shifting towards a greater integration of core subjects in the delivery of Social Studies. This paper builds upon Priestley's earlier work which explored this issue in the early days of CfE ('there are no compelling reasons for subject separation' according to Priestley (2009)). There is a continuing trend to create faculty structures in Scottish schools, which arguably should create the conditions important to a curriculum that allows pupils to explore key themes, deepen their learning and enhance their subject-specific skills. Despite the existence of these homogenised broad faculty structures, there is, however, a continued resistance to the delivery of integrated approaches to this curricular area in many schools.

The recent *Social Studies 3–18* report (Education Scotland, 2013) identified clear issues with the delivery of integrated learning in Scottish schools. Two clear messages were given to schools: a warning about the dilution of individual subjects and a loss of identity: 'In planning across areas of learning, staff need to be mindful of ensuring knowledge, understanding and skills in social subjects are not lost' (Education Scotland, 2013). The meaningful learning which will allow pupils to solve real-world issues (Leopp, 1999) can be fulfilled naturally through an integrated model of delivery of Social Studies, if departments make the commitment to work together to show the importance of making connections in learning, thus enriching their knowledge.

In terms of linking Modern Studies to the wider curriculum, there are many overarching themes. Links to Religious Education, History and Geography are made effortlessly. Links are made to Mathematics, through the use of statistical data and analysis; Literacy and English to the detection of bias in the use of persuasion in the media. Home Economics can bring budgeting, food, diet and lifestyle to common courses and themes, making it easier to draw areas of the curriculum together. Following an integrated Social Studies course, Modern Studies is arguably at risk of being subsumed by History and Geography. Yet it can easily stand on its own due to the continued relevance and the enjoyment it can bring to the lives of young people today.

## ASSESSING AT BROAD GENERAL EDUCATION LEVEL

Benchmarks were introduced in 2017 stemming from the literacy and numeracy concerns which came towards the end of 2016 (see Chapter 68). They marked the introduction of some form of assessment but without prescribing an actual examination. It is of note that it is intended that both the experiences and the outcomes are covered in conjunction with the benchmarks. It is supposed that the latter give markers to when pupils should be at a particular juncture in their educational journey. What should not be ignored is the need for the skills of Modern Studies. These must be covered in depth as pupils must exhibit them when moving towards certificate classes.

## NATIONAL QUALIFICATIONS

National qualifications are in the midst of significant changes. Teachers frequently assert that the profession has not had time to catch breath and review content; it has been a rolling programme of change for many years. At Nationals 3 and 4 there are no formal external final examinations, with all assessments marked and recorded internally in schools and verified on an annual basis, albeit now on a reduced scale. With these new qualifications came the Added Value Units. Not since the investigation at Standard Grade had the examination process allowed for personalisation and choice. Allowing for the investigation of key themes, it saw pupils writing on a range of issues, often pertinent to them, and permitted them to draw their own conclusions. At Nationals 3 and 4 investigations were internally marked with some verification. At National 5 level it was arguably more robust where it was externally marked in conjunction with a final examination. The write-up at National 5 was to be under examination conditions. 2017 saw the reduction of the worth of the Added Value Unit, which places greater emphasis on the final examination. The figures shown in Table 52.1 suggest that the qualification is stable with 800 more students taking the exam in 2017 and the results only slightly down on the year before.

At Higher level, an integrated paper, offering a mixture of extended answers and source questions, has figured for several years. There is a replacement to the decision-making exercise (DME) in paper 2. Arguably the DME provided a platform for weaker candidates to gain marks. The assignment at this level reflects the National 5 exam, using similar skills and with the candidate having to write in more depth. With the current review of

Table 52.1  Numbers of passes in National 5 Modern Studies in 2016 and 2017

|      | A     | %    | A–B   | %    | A–C   | %    | A–D    | %    | Overall |
|------|-------|------|-------|------|-------|------|--------|------|---------|
| 2016 | 3,989 | 33.6 | 6,456 | 55.7 | 8,615 | 74.3 | 9,497  | 81.9 | 11,594  |
| 2017 | 3,980 | 32.1 | 6,790 | 54.8 | 9,415 | 76   | 10,737 | 83.5 | 12,385  |

Source: https://www.sqa.org.uk/sqa/80674.html

Table 52.2  Numbers of passes in Higher Modern Studies in 2016 and 2017

|      | A     | B     | C     | D     | Overall |
|------|-------|-------|-------|-------|---------|
| 2016 | 3,058 | 5,141 | 7,243 | 8,006 | 9,851   |
| 2017 | 2,974 | 5,823 | 6,928 | 7,688 | 9,319   |

Source: https://www.sqa.org.uk/sqa/80674.html

the Higher exam it is likely that the final paper will in future be longer and worth a greater number of marks. Table 52.2 shows the number of Higher passes in 2016 and 2017.

Advanced Higher has also seen an increase in the numbers of pupils studying for it in recent years. There is the trend in smaller schools to utilise expertise and to pull resources together, sending pupils to other establishments to continue their studies. 2017 saw a slight increase in the number of passes to 861, of which 239 gained an A pass (https://www.sqa.org.uk/sqa/80674.html). This continues to grow from the year before; the lure of carrying out a piece of research and enquiry-led teaching keeps the number of candidates studying at Scottish Credit and Qualifications Framework (SCQF) level 7 relatively stable and helps to bridge the gap from school to university.

What is worthy of note is that there will be changes to the assessment procedure in the coming years. Unit assessments will be removed as follows:

- from National 5 from session 2017–18;
- from Higher from session 2018–19;
- from Advanced Higher from session 2019–20.

In all of these, greater emphasis will be placed on the final exam, thus putting the onus on young people to recall information and knowledge and to apply it in specific skill areas.

Owing to the popularity of Modern Studies at Higher and Advanced Higher level, the Higher in Politics is becoming a growth subject. It is able to build on the practical examples cited and give a more theory-based paper. The pupils who embark on this level of study are very successful.

## MODERN STUDIES AS PART OF THE LEARNING FOR SUSTAINABILITY AGENDA

There is no doubt that Modern Studies meets the agenda for global citizenship, arguably more so than the sustainable environment. Global citizenship can be subsumed by Learning for Sustainability (LfS – see Chapter 65); however, Modern Studies plays a vital role looking at our place in the world and to the future of societies. The notion of looking at the world through a critical world vision lens is of paramount importance. Fair Trade, for example, allows young people to examine all aspects of life – from the growers and manufacturers, to the consumers. A subject as complex as this allows for exploration through debates, knowledge exchange and critical thinking. It very satisfactorily meets the criteria for education in sustainability. Nevertheless, we should never lose sight of the global citizenship agenda where topics such as modern slavery and child soldiers are relevant and make our pupils question.

## THE FUTURE?

Modern Studies is certainly relevant today. The numbers of candidates are rising year-on-year and there are few schools who do not have it as core subject. This situation is projected to continue to remain healthy. With the increased political engagement of young people, the desire to understand the world becomes greater therefore making the argument that there should be a greater emphasis on political literacy, putting Modern Studies teaching at the heart of this.

## REFERENCES

Education Scotland (2013) *Social Studies 3–18*. Online at https://education.gov.scot/improvement/Documents/SocialStudies3to182013Update.pdf

Electoral Commission (2014) *Scottish Independence Referendum: Report on the Referendum held on 18 September 2014*. Online at www.electoralcommission.org.uk/__data/assets/pdf_file/0010/179812/Scottish-independence-referendum-report.pdf

Fenwick, A. J. J., Minty, S. and Priestley, M. (2013) 'Swimming against the tide: a case study of an integrated social studies department', *The Curriculum Journal*, 24 (3), 454–74.

Leopp, F. L. (1999) 'Models of curriculum integration', *The Journal of Technology Studies*, 25 (2), 21–5.

Priestley, M. (2009) 'Social studies in Scotland's school curriculum: a case for a more integrated approach', *Education in the North*, 17 (November).

SQA (2017) Attainment Statistics (August). Online at https://www.sqa.org.uk/sqa/80699.html

# 53

# Music

*Allan Hewitt and Andrew Dickie*

Music has been a consistent presence within the Scottish educational system and current configurations are grounded in historical context. From the 1960s the subject was characterised by a curriculum that drew on the established division of music in the universities and conservatoires into performance, theory/rudiments and history. Pupils were expected to be able to read and write standard musical notation; performance repertoire was sourced from the Western classical tradition. Studies in music history and theory privileged pitch and rhythm perception, a knowledge of important composers and events, and the ability to deconstruct well-known items of the Western classical canon. Creative music making and ensemble performances were almost entirely absent, though much excellent work took place in extra-curricular contexts. This was ideal preparation for entry to advanced study in the tertiary sector but, consequential to the emphasis on technical performance and notation skills, large numbers of young people were excluded who had a keen interest in music but lacked the traditional skills and expertise necessary to access the curriculum at certificate level.

The unpopularity of Music as a subject choice provided the context for the comprehensive overhaul of Music within the secondary curriculum, stimulated by the publication of 'Music in Scottish Schools' (SED, 1978). The impact of the philosophical and practical shift it represented was felt immediately in the early 1990s with the development of the Standard Grade Music assessment documentation, followed in time by the content of the revised Higher Grade syllabus. The principles embodied in these developments continue to underpin Scottish Music education in the twenty-first century.

## CHARACTERISTICS OF SECONDARY MUSIC EDUCATION

Three underlying philosophical imperatives have shaped Music education in Scotland. While these are broadly reflective of wider trends internationally, Scotland can reasonably claim to have been at the forefront of innovation in Music education.

### Accessible To All

The threat to Music's continued place within the formal curriculum in the 1980s stimulated a concerted effort among curriculum planners to remove any barriers to study that were embedded in the existing award structure. While accessibility may be a given at the early stages of secondary education where Music is usually compulsory, it is intentionally applied also at the upper stages where studying Music is a choice. In the recent past this ambition towards accessibility is most obvious in the progressive decrease of minimum requirements for performance in terms of technical difficulty and duration of recital. This makes it possible for pupils who do not possess relatively advanced levels of performing skill to take the subject.

## Integrative

One of the distinguishing aspects of Music education in Scotland is the extent to which pupils engage in the full variety of musical activities rather than the class band ensemble-type activity that is the core of Music education, notably in the USA, but is only one component of the curriculum in Scotland. The embrace of the three elements of performing, understanding and creating music, and the deliberate attempt to transfer learning across these activities, reflects an acceptance of a particular school of music education philosophy, notably Thomas Regelski's 'Comprehensive Musicianship' model (Regelski, 1981). The central tenet is that musical learning is achieved through application and experimentation in performance, composition and analysis, rather than simply 'playing music'. More recently, music technology has formed a fourth 'pillar' of this integrative approach to Music education.

## Active Learning

Music education in Scotland has a focus on active learning: a belief that Music education is about doing things – playing and creating music – rather than learning about music (Hewitt, 1995). Rooted in the Vygotskian concept of socially situated learning (Hewitt, 2008), the emphasis is on the practical aspects of music making and in particular on developing pupils' conceptual learning rather than the abstractions of factual knowledge of music theory or history. The introduction of the concept list, which forms the basis of teaching and assessment in Understanding Music within the National Qualifications framework and infuses learning across all areas of school music making, exemplifies this approach.

## CURRICULUM

As noted previously (Hewitt, 2013), creative technologies such as digital audio workstations began to feature significantly in Music classrooms during the late twentieth and early twenty-first centuries. With the introduction of Curriculum for Excellence, Education Scotland and Scottish Qualifications Authority (SQA) took the decision to delineate Music and Music Technology as separate subjects within the awards framework. This reinforced the importance of Music Technology and its prevalence in the production and consumption of music in the twenty-first century. However, many schools lack the skills and resources to deliver the subject at the time of writing. There are increasing efforts to train teachers in Music Technology and there is evidence that more schools are introducing units in Music Technology in the junior phase.

## CURRICULUM – MUSIC

Music is taught by specialist subject teachers, usually located within a broader faculty structure (e.g. 'Expressive Arts'), alongside Art and Drama. Music is generally compulsory for all pupils in the early stages of secondary school and optional thereafter. At all stages, the Music curriculum comprises the three elements of performing, composing and understanding music.

## Performing

In performing, pupils are introduced in the early stages of secondary school to a range of instruments including electronic keyboard, guitar, drum kit, bass guitar and in some cases voice. Pupils are generally expected to develop a basic competence on at least two instruments with an emphasis on playing these in individual and group settings. For those who choose to continue with Music in the middle stages of secondary school, National 3 requires the performance of two difference pieces or sections of music at a minimum of Associated Board (AB) Grade 1 level. National 4 requires the performance of an eight-minute recital at AB Grade 2 level, while National 5 requires the performance of an eight-minute recital at AB Grade 3 level. The recital at National 5 takes place in front of a visiting assessor, while the other levels are recorded and assessed internally. At all levels, the recital involves two instruments. Pupils in the senior stages usually study Music at Higher level. In performance this requires the performance on two instruments of a twelve-minute recital at a minimum of AB Grade 4 level, in front of a visiting assessor. Advanced Higher requires a recital of eighteen to twenty minutes at a minimum of AB Grade 5 level.

## Composing

Composing activities during the early stages of secondary vary widely between schools. Music technology has increasingly provided an accessible and attractive platform for musical creativity; software such as Logic Pro allows pupils to explore different musical ideas and combinations that would otherwise be unavailable. In the middle and senior phases, composing is a mandatory part of the Music curriculum.

## Understanding Music (Listening)

Conceptual learning continues to be the foundation by which pupils develop their understanding and appreciation of Music. Most schools organise conceptual learning around a series of topics that may be based on a recognised musical style (e.g. 'classical' or 'jazz') or a more thematic aspect of music (e.g. 'opera', 'Scottish music'). At the upper stages, the Music: Listening unit further extends pupils' conceptual understanding of music and supports learning within the composing and performance/technology units. At Higher level this involves the detailed study of a number of prescribed works that encourage pupils to work at a broader/longer scale, assessed via a one-hour examination at the end of the unit.

## CURRICULUM – MUSIC TECHNOLOGY

Music Technology is a separate subject from Music, and is organised around three units of work.

## Music Technology Skills

In this unit pupils work through a series of tasks designed to equip them with the necessary skills to effectively utilise digital recording and production software. Tasks might include microphone placement and recording techniques, processing audio and Musical Instrument Digital Interface (MIDI) information, use of software plugins and production techniques, and creating a signal chain between input hardware, mixing desks and digital interfaces.

## Music Technology in Context

This builds on the skills learned in the Music Technology Skills unit, with pupils encouraged to apply their practical skills in an applied context, for example recorded live performance, radio broadcast, or composing and/or sound design for film, TV themes, adverts and computer gaming.

## Understanding Twentieth- and Twenty-first-century Music

The aim of this unit is to enable pupils to develop their knowledge and understanding of twentieth- and twenty-first-century musical styles and genres. Pupils gain an understanding of how music technology has influenced, and has been influenced by, wider developments in twentieth- and twenty-first-century Music.

## TRENDS IN UPTAKE AND ATTAINMENT

### Uptake

One of the principal objectives of curriculum reform in Music in the 1980s and 1990s was to arrest the significant decline in numbers taking the subject in the mid- and late stages of secondary education. Presentations at National 4 and 5 in Music are strong; assuming the number of presentations in English is representative of the total National 4 and 5 populations, National 4 presentations in 2016 were around 7 per cent ($n = 1,325$) and National 5 presentations around 16 per cent ($n = 7,542$; https://www.sqa.org.uk/sqa/80674.html). These uptake levels are similar to uptake of Standard Grade Music (Hewitt, 2013), indicating the stability of Music as a subject within the middle secondary stages.

Uptake of Higher Music decreased somewhat between 2015 and 2016 from around 21 per cent ($n = 4,340$) of those presented for Higher English in 2015 to around 14 per cent ($n = 5,181$) of those presented for Higher English ($n = 36,356$) in 2016. However, this still represents an increase on the uptake of Higher Music from the earlier part of the decade (Hewitt, 2013). Advanced Higher presentations remain stable, with 1,583 candidates presented in 2015 and 1,675 presented in 2016 compared to 1,299 in 2011 (https://www.sqa.org.uk/sqa/80674.html).

In Music Technology, numbers at National 4 have been very low ($n = 143$ in 2015 and $n = 126$ in 2016). At National 5 level, Music Technology also attracted a relatively low uptake in 2016 of around 2 per cent ($n = 745$), although this represented an increase from 1 per cent ($n = 498$) in 2015 and $n = 250$ in 2014 signifying an increased interest in this new subject. In Higher Music Technology presentations in 2016 represented around 1 per cent ($n = 486$) of the numbers presented for Higher English. Again, this represented an increase from 280 presentations in 2015 and should be interpreted in light of the discussion of Music Technology elsewhere in this chapter (https://www.sqa.org.uk/sqa/80674.html).

## Attainment

It was previously noted (Hewitt, 2013) that there was significant number of 'no award' grades made at Intermediate 1 and 2 level in Music. At Standard Grade, the seven-point grading scheme produced a fairly broad distribution across the upper grade levels. With a consistent five-point grading scheme across all National Qualification levels, the trend is towards the top grade point.

At Higher level, 59 per cent of candidates presented in 2016 achieved an A grade (compared to 44 per cent in 2011) and 25 per cent achieved a B grade (compared to 30 per cent in 2011). C grades reduced from 17 per cent in 2011 to 11 per cent in 2016, while the number of no awards reduced from 4.4 per cent to 2.8 per cent. As with National 5, this suggests that candidates' performance was either markedly improved from the previous version of the Higher or that grading procedures produced a more defined skewness in grade distribution. At Advanced Higher, 62 per cent achieved an A grade, similar to achievement levels reported in 2011 (https://www.sqa.org.uk/sqa/80674.html).

In Music Technology, at National 5 candidate attainment at the top level reduced from 54 per cent in 2014 to 50 per cent in 2016. Awards of B ranged from 26 per cent in 2014 to 24 per cent in 2016 while awards of C and D ranged from 13–14 per cent and 4 per cent respectively. The number of no award grades in 2016 was significantly higher in 2016 (7 per cent) compared to 2015 (3 per cent). At Higher level, A grades increased from 48 per cent in 2015 to 55 per cent in 2016. There were fewer C and D grades achieved in 2016 compared to 2015, while no award grades in both years were 7 per cent and 8 per cent respectively (https://www.sqa.org.uk/sqa/80674.html).

## CURRENT DEBATES AND CHALLENGES

Scotland boasts a rich and varied musical heritage with a proud record of producing world-class artists and composers across classical, jazz, rock, pop and traditional music. Accommodating this diversity within a formal curriculum has been challenging, especially for a teaching profession whose musical background and expertise has often been in the Western classical tradition. The desire to incorporate the rich diversity of musical experience within the classroom has stimulated some tension between delivering the building blocks of the classical tradition, such as notation, tonal harmony and technical skill in performance, and the desire (often from teachers themselves) to incorporate more contemporary approaches, or those drawn from a wider stylistic pool.

Similar challenges pertain to traditional Scottish music. The indigenous musical traditions of Scotland are now embedded into the formal music curriculum, most noticeably in the requirement for pupils to develop their knowledge and understanding of concepts based in those traditions (particularly the vocal and instrumental types of repertoire) and in the ability of pupils to sit performance exams on traditional instruments such as clarsach and bagpipes. However, traditional music often relies on a different form of pedagogy, one that is based on learning by ear, sharing repertoire and greater focus on the social aspects of music making. There is therefore more commonality with rock, pop, jazz and world music than the Western classical tradition. Embedding these approaches in the formal music curriculum is challenging but essential if authenticity of practice is valued (Hewitt, 2009).

## TECHNOLOGY AND TRAINING

The use of music technology, whether desktop-based or mobile, has transformed the creation and consumption of music. Young people have access to an unprecedented range of music and a multiplicity of platforms upon which to create their own music. In Scotland, music educators have readily adopted technological innovation within their classrooms and there is general recognition of the advantages that it can bring, especially to creative work. However, this requires equipment and up-to-date, effective and classroom-focused training. Otherwise, the danger is that classroom music and out-of-school musical experience will remain dichotomous for many young people in Scotland. In recent years, staff development and teacher collaboration in Music has increasingly moved online. A recent survey of 1,650 members of the Music Teachers Scotland Facebook forum indicated that all thirty-two authorities and most independent schools are represented by active members who regularly share resources and teaching strategies online.

## INSTRUMENTAL TEACHING

Finally, special mention should be made of the pivotal role of local authority-based instrumental teaching in Scotland. While the design of the curriculum was based on opening access to all pupils who wish to study music, there can be no doubt that the support of peripatetic instrumental staff, who are usually responsible for delivering small-group instruction within a cognate instrumental family (e.g. woodwind), is vital. Such provision caters for pupils who wish to pursue development of advanced skills that would simply be impossible within the classroom setting, and who lack the financial resource to access private instrumental tuition. Current threats to the local authority funding pose very real challenges to the continued high-quality provision of Music.

## REFERENCES

Hewitt, A. (1995) 'A review of the role of activity-based learning experiences in the music curriculum, and their current implementation in the Standard Grade Music course in Scotland', *British Journal of Music Education*, 12 (3), 203–14.

Hewitt, A. (2008) 'Children's creative collaboration during a computer-based music task', *International Journal of Educational Research*, 47 (1), 11–26.

Hewitt, A. (2009) 'Musical styles as communities of practice: challenges for learning, teaching and assessment of music in Higher Education', *Arts and Humanities in Higher Education*, 8 (3), 329–37.

Hewitt, A. (2013) 'Music education', in T. G. K. Bryce, W. M. Humes, D. Gillies and A. Kennedy (eds), *Scottish Education, Fourth Edition: Referendum*. Edinburgh: Edinburgh University Press

Regelski, T. A. (1981) *Teaching General Music: Action Learning For Middle and Secondary Schools*. New York: Schirmer Books.

SED (1978) Music in Scottish Schools, Curriculum Paper 16. Edinburgh: HMSO.

# 54

# Physical Education and Sport

*Andrew Horrell and Shirley Gray*

There have been long-standing concerns that Physical Education, as a subject area, is on the margins of the school curriculum. However, recently there have been a number of developments following the introduction of Curriculum for Excellence (CfE) in 2010 which have led to an increased focus on the contribution made by Physical Education to the curriculum provided in schools (Thorburn and Horrell, 2011). There have also been a number of research studies, leading to new insights about teachers' engagement in the policy process, their professional values, curriculum development and the practice of Physical Education in schools (Craig et al., 2016). CfE and the associated policy guidance actively encourage teachers to create curricula that attend to learners' needs and local conditions of practice. Therefore, although there are some similarities between schools, there are also notable differences, thereby making it difficult to make definitive statements about current practice in schools. In this chapter we do, however, draw on recent research and experiences to provide a selective exploration of contemporary and current issues pertinent to Physical Education in Scotland.

## PHYSICAL EDUCATION'S NATURE AND PURPOSE

The debates engaged in by analytical philosophers about whether or not Physical Education merits inclusion in the school curriculum on educational grounds may appear to be of little consequence for the day-to-day practice of teachers (Reid, 2013). Physical Education teachers in Scotland can point to the subject's prominent position within Health and Wellbeing (HWB) in CfE, an increase in teacher numbers, and its continued inclusion in the suite of national qualifications, as evidence that questions about its contribution have been overtaken by events. Nevertheless, there are implications for learners and teachers when the focus of Physical Education within CfE is on developing skills and attributes so that people can lead a physically active and healthy lifestyle. Recent research suggests that teachers have adopted a variety of pragmatic approaches, in many cases skilfully negotiating the potential tension between the intrinsic educational value of physical activities versus the instrumental use of them as vehicles for learning and the promotion of HWB (Horrell, 2016).

Prior to 2010, the emphasis on HWB within Physical Education was less explicit. Teaching and learning in Physical Education tended to focus on the acquisition of movements and skills necessary to develop performance in activities such as games, dance and gymnastics. Furthermore, the ways in which this might be achieved varied across the primary and secondary contexts. For example, in primary schools, Physical Education was organised according to the Expressive Arts curriculum. Rather than emphasising the role that Physical Education could play in terms of increasing pupil's physical activity levels and improving their health, a more aesthetic discourse was adopted, making reference to concepts such as space, dynamics and relationships (Thorburn and Horrell, 2011). By contrast, secondary Physical Education teachers tended to adopt a more activity specific and skill-based approach, applying concepts from the various domains within the field of sports science to support their practice and pupil learning. The introduction of examination courses, developed in the late 1980s and early 1990s (Standard Grade and then Higher Still Physical Education), presented a new set of challenges for teachers. Within both courses, learning experiences were focused on the acquisition, development and refinement of perceptual motor skills, with an emphasis on improvements in performance. In addition, pupils had to engage with and were assessed on a body of knowledge relating to the scientific theories, principles and practices associated with, for example, exercise physiology and motor learning. To be consistent with the rationale for these courses, teachers were expected to create workshops so that pupils could integrate and enhance their conceptual understanding through practical experiential learning. For many teachers, this particular challenge was overcome by including specific lessons in classrooms so that pupils could prepare for the written elements of the examinations (Thorburn, 2007). On the one hand, certificated courses may have assisted in securing curriculum time and providing parity with other subjects accepted by universities for entry on to degrees, but the 'academic' status presented pedagogical challenges, brought new concerns about attainment in examinations, and challenged the teachers' values about the practical nature of the subject.

These changes and challenges presented by certificated courses featured prominently in the professional lives of Physical Education teachers throughout Scotland, brought competing demands for their time, and perhaps restricted the scope for curriculum development in core Physical Education in the middle years (Thorburn and Horrell, 2011). Indeed, in the era of the 5–14 curriculum, teachers had the autonomy to determine the aims and content of the curriculum and, as a result, both the form and the quality of provision of core Physical Education varied across schools. Research highlighted that during this time, short blocks of activities with a focus on developing competence and competition contributed to pupils reporting negative experiences of core Physical Education. Whilst Physical Education may be popular among physically able pupils (boys in particular), for many pupils (especially girls), it lacked relevance and meaning (Mitchell et al., 2015).

## CURRICULUM FOR EXCELLENCE AND PHYSICAL EDUCATION

The introduction of CfE appeared to signify a move towards a process curriculum for all subjects and a focus on the development of 'capacities' that would prepare young people for life, work, and learning. The 'experiences and outcomes' statements provided teachers with a framework to inform planning and provision with three areas 'numeracy, literacy and HWB' identified as a 'responsibility of all' teachers (Scottish Government, 2009, p. 6). The growing concerns about the physical health of young people in Scotland has been identified as a strong driver for HWB, featuring as a responsibility of all and as one of the eight curriculum areas (Horrell et al., 2012). The guidance indicated that, as a responsibility of all teachers, learning environments conducive to HWB needed to support, skills and attributes such as self-awareness, relationships, confidence, mental wellbeing, and the ability to assess and manage risk and challenge discrimination (Scottish Government, 2009). The experiences and outcomes for Physical Education are presented as three lines of development: movement skills, competencies and concepts; cooperation and competition; and evaluating and appreciating. Teachers were expected to provide learning experiences for pupils that would enhance 'their physical wellbeing in preparation for leading a fulfilling, active and healthy lifestyle' (Scottish Government, 2009, p. 84).

A guiding principle of CfE has been that teachers should place the learner at the heart of their decision making, ensuring that mental, emotional, social and physical wellbeing are supported, and that learners develop the skills necessary to plan for choices and change. Initially, teachers reported that the introduction of CfE led to them focusing on their approaches to teaching and learning, with only limited changes required of the content of existing curricula (Gray et al., 2012). Recent research has sought to understand how teachers made sense of the policy guidance and enacted school-based responses (Horrell, 2016). The curriculum design principle that seemed to generate the greatest effect was 'personalisation and choice'. For some teachers, it reinforced the provision of a multi-activity model rather than signalling that a radical transformation of the curriculum orientated around HWB would be required. However, a complex picture emerges where the freedoms afforded by a flexible curriculum framework have led to a variety of different interpretations of what constitutes the promotion of HWB within Physical Education. Some schools have created more connected curricula, providing pathways within Physical Education, for example making links to the activities available in the wider community, aligning the courses planned for S1–3 with the National Qualifications offered in S4–6, and supporting the wider ethos of the school through interdisciplinary learning and events to support civic engagement. The inclusion of leadership courses to support those seeking to develop vocational qualifications also points to the pluralistic approach adopted in many schools where multiple aims are skilfully pursued to create rich learning opportunities for young adults.

## CHALLENGES AND DEVELOPMENTS

In the early stages of CfE, teachers indicated that although they were broadly supportive of its aims and purposes, engaging with and interpreting curriculum documentation had been challenging. Their expectations for clear guidance on matters of content and assessment were not met, the documentation associated with CfE required interpretation and the time available for professional development activities had been limited. The reorganisation of school management and curriculum leadership, to create less hierarchical structures, may have also contributed to differences in interpretation of CfE across and between schools. Many schools replaced single subject departments with a more streamlined structure of eight 'faculties'. The faculty of HWB may comprise Physical Education, Personal and Social Education, and Home Economics, but this not the case in all schools, as some have grouped subjects across curriculum areas of CfE to promote interdisciplinary working. An outcome of these changes is that, for many teachers, the previous arrangements for subject leadership for Physical Education have been disrupted and, although there is some indication that teachers view faculty structures positively, there is also evidence to suggest that teachers feel less supported and have fewer opportunities for career progression (Anderson and Nixon, 2010).

During this period of curriculum development, teachers appear to have engaged in a variety of self-directed and organised professional development activities, within and across schools, to develop their knowledge and understanding of the expectations of the curriculum. The formation of the Scottish Association of Teachers of Physical Education, in 2013, has provided an important forum for professional debate and dialogue. In addition to the informal and formal professional networks, resources and initiatives have sought to support policy enactment. Education Scotland and sportscotland provided £5.8 million to support local authorities; teachers were seconded and took up 'lead officer' roles to support colleagues in schools to improve the quality of Physical Education. It was also possible, through an open bidding process, for individual schools or clusters of schools to apply for grants of up to £3,000 from Education Scotland to improve the quality of Physical Education experiences. Other initiatives included the development of a teaching approach designed to develop links between moving and thinking (Better Movers and Thinkers), the appointment of a national development officer for gymnastics and dance, and investment in Scottish Disability Sports' inclusive Physical Education programme.

Challenges and developments related to assessment have had an impact on teachers' practice. This is to be expected given the powerful influence of assessment and the concerns about the attainment of pupils. Guidance on assessment appeared late in the development of CfE and teachers had sought more information on how to interpret the outcomes and use these productively to inform teaching and enable meaningful reporting to parents. Concerns related to assessment led to further guidance from Education Scotland, initially, 'significant aspects of learning' and more recently 'benchmarks' for each curriculum area with the intention that these will support teachers' professional judgements. These statements about specific skills and attributes all pupils may develop through a broad range of relevant learning experiences appear to be having quite an impact on teachers' practice. The development of new National Qualifications (NQ) in Physical Education at National 4, National 5, Higher and Advanced Higher are also likely to have an impact on the way teachers and pupils view the role of assessment and shape the way they interpret the focus of HWB. In the NQ courses in the senior phase (15–18), the promotion of a holistic view intersects with the increasing focus on the role of HWB to support sporting performance. The number of entries at Higher (6,404 in 2015 and 9,714 in 2016), placing Physical Education fourth in rank order after History, Maths and English, is an indication of the popularity of the subject and the possibility of new challenges for teachers managing this workload (https://www.sqa.org.uk/sqa/77198.html).

## SPORT IN SCHOOLS

Sport features prominently in the senior phase of CfE, where the focus of the new National Qualifications for Physical Education is on developing and improving practical and performance skills. In the Higher course, candidates will be assessed on their ability to perform in two different physical activities which must be challenging, competitive and/or demanding. The practical performance is worth 50 per cent, the other 50 per cent being based on a 2.5-hour exam paper, which assesses a candidate's ability to demonstrate knowledge and understanding of factors that impact on performance, an evaluation of their development plans and their response to a scenario based question. However, outwith the context of the National Qualifications, the role of sport within the Physical Education curriculum is perhaps less significant. The experiences and outcomes for physical activity and sport are largely the responsibly of the Active Schools coordinator. Even then, while there is some reference to creating opportunities for pupils to perform at the highest level, much of the policy text in this area focuses on how pupils should enjoy physical activity and sport and take part in physical activity to improve their physical health.

A more recent enterprise that aims to provide pupils with opportunities to develop and excel in a sports context is the School of Sport programme. This is funded by the Scottish Government's Cashback for Communities initiative, a scheme that uses money retrieved from crime to develop rugby, football or basketball with S1 and S2 pupils in schools. However, although these programmes are developed in line with CfE and pupils can have up to five periods of their curricular time devoted to the 'School of Sport', they are provided by the sports' national governing body representatives rather than the Physical Education teachers in each school. An important sports initiative that does involve the Physical Education teachers is the School Sport Award. With this award, schools can apply for a gold, silver or bronze award, a process that encourages them to put Physical Education and sport at the heart of their planning and practice, recognising and celebrating success. While the School of Sport programme and the School Sport Award clearly emphasise the value that sport and elite performance hold in education and life settings, there does appear to be a greater emphasis by the Scottish Government in grass roots participation and the personal and social development of all young people. This is somewhat in contrast to the UK Government more generally, which continues to invest in sport, primarily to increase their gold medal count in the next Olympics (UK Sport, 2017).

## WHAT MIGHT THE FUTURE BE?

As this chapter has outlined, the introduction of CfE had the potential to transform Physical Education and teachers could have focused more explicitly on aspects of HWB. However, although teachers are broadly supportive that the subject is located within the HWB area of CfE, as subject specialists they have worked to ensure that Physical Education would address its broader aims and purposes, rather than explicitly focusing on 'health' (Horrell, 2016). There remains a pluralistic approach within schools as teachers seek to balance and keep in view a wide range of aims for the subject (Craig et al., 2016). Teachers are seeking to make productive connections between the guidance of CfE which emphasises a holistic approach to the development of HWB and the senior phase where the focus of NQ requires learners consider 'factors impacting on performance'. There are some uncertainties about how teachers will negotiate the challenges that these new courses present because, although significant numbers of candidates are presented for assessment, there are a far greater number of children and young adults for whom the two hours/two periods each week is their primary and formative experience of Physical Education. The recent investments by Education Scotland and sportscotland indicate their intentions to support quality Physical Education for all children and young adults to promote learning and provide increased opportunities for engagement in physical activity. It would appear that in the current economic and political climate, sustaining funding will be challenging; however, Physical Education teachers are likely to continue to balance their provision of school sport, the support they provide for those electing for NQ courses, and learning experiences to promote HWB across the 3–18 age range.

# REFERENCES

Anderson, C. and Nixon, G. (2010) 'The move to faculty middle management structures in Scottish secondary schools: a case study', *School Leadership & Management*, 30 (3), 249–63.

Craig, M., Thorburn, M., Mulholland, R., Horrell, A. and Jess, M. (2016) 'Understanding professional issues in physical education – a Scottish insight', *Scottish Educational Review*, 48 (2), 80–100.

Gray, S., MacLean, J. and Mulholland, R. (2012) 'Physical education within the Scottish context: a matter of policy', *European Physical Education Review*, 18 (2), 258–72.

Horrell, A. (2016) *Pragmatic Innovation in Curriculum Development: A Study of Physical Education Teachers' Interpretation and Enactment of a New Curriculum Framework*. Unpublished doctoral thesis, University of Edinburgh, Edinburgh.

Horrell, A., Sproule, J. and Gray, S. (2012). 'Health and wellbeing: a policy context for physical education in Scotland', *Sport, Education and Society*, 17 (2), 163–80.

Mitchell, F., Gray, S. and Inchley, J. (2015) 'This choice thing really works … ' Changes in experiences and engagement of adolescent girls in physical education classes, during a school-based physical activity programme', *Physical Education and Sport Pedagogy*, 20 (6), 593–611, doi:10.10 80/17408989.2013.837433

Reid, A. (2013) 'Physical education, cognition and agency', *Educational Philosophy and Theory*, 45 (9), 921–33.

Scottish Government (2009) *Curriculum for Excellence*. Edinburgh: Scottish Government.

Thorburn, M. (2007) 'Achieving conceptual and curriculum coherence in high-stakes school examinations in physical education', *Physical Education & Sport Pedagogy*, 12 (2), 163–84, doi:10.1080/17408980701282076

Thorburn, M. and Horrell, A. (2011) 'Power, control and professional influence: the curious case of physical education in Scotland', *Scottish Educational Review*, 43, 73–85.

UK Sport (2017) *How Sport Funding Works*. Online at www.uksport.gov.uk/our-work/investing-in-sport/how-uk-sport-funding-works

# 55

# Physics

*Morag Findlay*

The history of Physics teaching in Scotland over the last fifty years or so reflects the changes in approach to the curriculum and teaching and learning over that period. The alterations from the introduction of O-Grades in the 1960s to the introduction of Curriculum for Excellence (CfE) in 2004 and new National Qualifications in 2012 via Standard Grades in the late 1980s; and the 5–14 Curriculum and the Higher Still Programme in the mid- to late 1990s, with the first examinations in 2000 (McVittie, 2008, p. 4), reflect a move from qualification for the top 30 per cent of a cohort to qualification for all. The merger of the Scottish Examination Board (SEB) and the Scottish Vocational Education Council (SCOTVEC) to form the Scottish Qualifications Authority (SQA) in 1997 also reflected a concern to provide certification for all pupils, not only those who would go on to university.

As detailed in Chapter 68, the introduction of the CfE programme culminated in the introduction of new National Qualifications to replace the Standard Grade and Intermediate 1 and 2 examinations. With regard to Physics, this process was completed with the introduction of the new National Qualifications Higher Physics examination in 2015 and Advanced Higher Physics in 2016. It is likely that the full implementation of the National Qualifications, the Scottish National Party (SNP) Government's drive to close the attainment gap, and to simplify the National Qualifications point towards the introduction of a new curriculum in the next few years.

The background to Physics teaching currently is the introduction of Curriculum for Excellence (CfE) and the implications which this has had for the National Qualifications. CfE has a focus on active learning (Scottish Government, 2008) which has changed the way Physics is taught by introducing more emphasis on conceptual thinking. Another influence is the ongoing emphasis on formative assessment as an integral component of teaching and learning, a legacy of the Assessment is for Learning programme in the 2000s.

## PHYSICS TEACHING IN SCHOOLS

Physics teachers work in the context of a science department or faculty. A head of science is replacing the role of the specialist principal teacher of physics who was responsible for the teaching of physics. He/she has responsibility for all of the science teaching within a science faculty. This may also include responsibility for subjects other than the sciences. A faculty head of science is more likely to be a biology or chemistry teacher than a physics teacher, based on the typical number of science teachers in a school (see Table 55.1). As a

Table 55.1    Number of science teachers in 364 Scottish secondary schools, from 2008 to 2015

| Subject | 2008 | 2009 | 2010 | 2011 | 2012 | 2013 | 2014 | 2015 |
|---|---|---|---|---|---|---|---|---|
| Biology | 1,177 | 1,177 | 1,162 | 1,157 | 1,169 | 1,190 | 1,179 | 1,165 |
| Chemistry | 989 | 963 | 936 | 928 | 935 | 935 | 937 | 932 |
| General Science | 153 | 137 | 143 | 141 | 143 | 116 | 129 | 128 |
| Physics | 887 | 865 | 868 | 850 | 837 | 822 | 823 | 807 |

Source: Scottish Government, 2015.

result, managing curricular change in Physics following the introduction of the National Qualifications is more likely to be distributed among the physics teachers in a department rather than led by a specialist principal teacher of physics. However, the implications of the change from specialist principal teachers to faculty heads for the implementation of curricular change are not being reviewed (Brown, 2014).

What are the implications of the larger number of biology than chemistry or physics teachers for the uptake of these subjects in schools? Data from the annual teacher census showed that in 2015, the average number of science teachers per secondary school was 3.2 biology teachers, 2.6 chemistry teachers and 2.2 physics teachers (see Table 55.1). Therefore the average secondary school has one fewer physics teacher than biology teachers. As a result, it is probable that in most secondary schools, fewer physics teachers are likely to take science classes in the first two or three years of the broad general education (BGE) than chemistry or biology teachers, with fewer choosing to take physics as an examination subject as a result. One way to interpret the smaller average number of physics teachers per school than biology or chemistry teachers is that there is a hidden shortage of physics (and to a lesser extent chemistry) teachers. This is likely to have an impact on the uptake of physics, particularly for Higher examinations.

Table 55.2 shows the number of entries for these examinations from 2007 to 2016. Over this period, the approximate mean number of Higher Biology and Human Biology entries was 13,300; for Chemistry there were 10,100 entries; and for Physics 9,300 entries. Comparing Tables 55.1 and 55.2 shows that there is a correlation between the number of science teachers for each subject and the number of Higher examination entries for each subject. This suggests that it may be possible to increase the number of pupils choosing to study Higher Physics by increasing the proportion of physics teachers in science departments so that pupils in the BGE phase are taught by more of them. This raises the question of how to increase the number of physics teachers. Government initiatives to recruit more draw on the existing pool of physics graduates – who have a wide range of attractive career options beyond teaching. So perhaps one answer to recruiting more physics teachers is to somehow make physics teaching a more (financially) attractive proposition.

## SCHOOL PHYSICS

What *is* (school) physics? According to Yates and Millar (2016, p. 303) university physicists and school physics teachers in Australia agree that the distinctive characteristics of the subject are 'learning a particular form of "stripping a problem to its fundamentals," "using mathematics to solve it," dealing with the "fundamental problems of the physical universe"'. It is likely that Scottish physics teachers would have a similar opinion. These

Table 55.2 Number of entries for Higher science subjects, from 2007 to 2016

| Subject[1,2] | 2007 | 2008 | 2009 | 2010 | 2011[3] | 2012 | 2013 | 2014 | 2015 | 2016[4] | Mean number of entries/year |
|---|---|---|---|---|---|---|---|---|---|---|---|
| Biology | 9,169 | 9,132 | 9,107 | 9,308 | 9,771 | 9,359 | 9,935 | 1,0161 | 9,739 | 7,362 | 9,304 |
| Chemistry | 9,490 | 9,505 | 9,582 | 10,179 | 10,293 | 10,301 | 10,356 | 11,125 | 10,597 | 9,862 | 10,129 |
| Human Biology | 3,712 | 3,755 | 3,992 | 4,078 | 4,269 | 3,656 | 3,541 | 3,449 | 4,107 | 5,499 | 4,006 |
| Physics | 8,582 | 8,765 | 9,002 | 9,018 | 9,447 | 9,470 | 9,492 | 10,071 | 9,611 | 9,038 | 9,250 |

Notes
1 The table contains the total numbers of Higher entries in a particular year. Revised Highers ran from 2012 to 2015 in parallel with the National Qualification (Higher Still) Highers; the first National Qualification (CfE) Highers were introduced in 2015.
2 2016 was the first year when only the National Qualification (CfE) Higher was examined.
3 The data from 2007 to 2011 are the number of entries for all centres.
4 The data from 2012 to 2016 are the number of entries for schools.

Source: https://www.sqa.org.uk/sqa/77198.html

statements are in agreement with some of the rationales for studying Physics in the course specifications for the National Qualifications. For example, the Higher Physics rationale explicitly links learning physics to the four capacities in Curriculum for Excellence, but also 'gives learners a deeper insight into the structure of the subject' (SQA, 2015, p. 4), which links to the first and last characteristics of physics identified above. 'Using mathematics to solve it' is implicitly one of the aims of Higher Physics as exemplified in the requirement for 'solving problems' in the unit specifications.

One of the ways in which physics teachers differ from chemistry or biology teachers is that physics teachers have learned how to 'think like a physicist' (Yates and Millar, 2016) and part of what they teach pupils is how to think in that way. How does learning to think like a physicist link to the main characteristics of physics identified in the previous paragraph? More broadly, how does learning to think like a physicist link to one of the perennial debates in education in general and physics in particular about the role of disciplinary knowledge versus skills and processes in education? The National Qualifications allow pupils to learn how to think like a physicist in several ways: through the use of mathematics in physics; applying physics concepts to problem solving; and the introduction of topics such as the Standard Model of particle physics.

One of the strengths of the subject in Scotland has always been teaching pupils to solve numerical questions. This has been recognised in reports about how well pupils have done in particular examinations (see for example SQA, 2016a). This finding is also supported by physics education research (Docktor et al., 2015) which suggests that students are good at numerical calculations, probably because they have been taught which relationship to choose to answer a particular question and drilled in its use. Nevertheless, pupils may find using mathematics in physics difficult because physicists and mathematicians – and by implication physics teachers and mathematics teachers – think about mathematics in different ways (Redish and Kuo, 2015).

The level of mathematics used in physics courses is noteworthy. The SQA policy is that the mathematics used should be at the level *below* the physics being studied. This means that pupils are not hampered learning physics because the mathematics involved is too difficult. Nevertheless, liaison between physics and mathematics departments to ensure that pupils have been taught particular areas of mathematics (such as the use of scientific notation for numbers (MTH4-06b) or the relationship between distance, speed and time (MNU 3-10a)) before the mathematics is used in physics lessons can be challenging.

Conversely, one of the challenges for physics teachers has been helping pupils to *apply* their conceptual understanding to new or unfamiliar situations (Docktor and Mestre, 2014; Docktor et al., 2015). Learning how to solve problems in physics is more difficult than selecting and then using a relationship. Applying conceptual understanding or analysing unfamiliar situations is a perennial challenge for candidates here (see for example SQA, 2016a). Docktor et al. (2015) suggest a solution where pupils are taught to explicitly identify the physics principle or concept they will use; justify the choice of this principle; and then plan how they will solve the problem. This approach is broader than picking a relationship and substituting numbers into the relationship because it requires pupils to draw on their conceptual knowledge *before* choosing the correct relationship. This approach is promising, but needs more research.

One of the changes to the new Physics courses has been the introduction of topics such as Special Relativity and the Standard Model of particle physics (Higher level) and General Relativity and Stellar Evolution (Advanced Higher level) to enthuse pupils about the subject. One of the challenges of this approach is that it moves teachers away from their comfort zone – preparing pupils to answer numerical questions about physics – to thinking about the frontiers of physics. However, the frontiers are a challenging place to be because the mathematics required to conceptualise, say, the Standard Model of particles is far beyond school-level mathematics (Yates and Millar, 2016). As a result, pupils are asked to accept these concepts on the word of the teacher rather than (in theory) being able to check ideas for themselves (for example to confirm that the acceleration of a body is directly proportional to the force applied and inversely proportional to its mass). This discrepancy raises issues about pupils' understanding of the nature of science and the difference between teaching physics to future physicists and teaching physics to citizens (the majority).

The current curriculum change is the introduction of the National Qualifications National 4 and National 5 to replace Standard Grade and Intermediate Physics and the new versions of Higher and Advanced Higher Physics. This change was completed when the first cohort sat the National Qualification Advanced Higher Physics examination in 2016.

The structure of the documentation for the National Qualifications is complex. Instead of a single arrangements document for each course, the Higher Physics documentation now consists of a mandatory course specification, course assessment specification and unit specifications, as well as course and unit support notes (SQA, 2016b). The unitary course and unit support notes contain 'mandatory course key areas', as well as 'suggested learning activities' and 'exemplification of key areas' which consist entirely of the relationships which appear on the separate relationships sheet for Higher Physics.

One of the ongoing challenges for teachers and pupils with these qualifications is the number of internal unit assessments which must be completed along with an externally assessed assignment and a pass in the external examination to complete the course. The unit assessments are a legacy of the merger of SCOTVEC and SEB to form the SQA. Pupils need to pass unit assessments for all units and complete a report of an experiment within one of the units to fulfil the internal assessment. In addition, there is a research-based assignment which must be completed in schools and marked externally. As a consequence of the intervention of the Deputy First Minister and Education Secretary, John Swinney, internal assessment will be phased out over the three years from 2016 for all National 5, Higher and Advanced Higher courses, including Physics (Scottish Government, 2016; see Chapter 68). It is to be hoped that the current review of National Qualifications will streamline the documentation needed for each course as well as removing the internal assessment.

Physics remains one of the most popular subjects in school at Higher level, but there are challenges for all science, technology, engineering and mathematics (STEM) subjects. One of the key approaches suggested by CfE is interdisciplinary learning (IDL) which encourages pupils to make connections between two or more different subjects. However, true IDL requires good basic knowledge in each of the disciplines and their different ways of thinking before links can be made.

Earlier, this chapter discussed the difficulties of liaising between physics and mathematics departments about the mathematics required for physics. However, there are also challenges in harmonising the approaches to data analysis among the science subjects, where graphs in physics are typically analysed using a best fit straight line or curve because there is a relationship between the variables; whereas in biology it is often uncertain if there is a link between the variables, and data points are joined with straight lines. This difference can be confusing for pupils, but arises out of the different types of data used in both subjects.

The number of girls choosing to continue with Higher Physics remains less than the number of boys. The National Qualifications have introduced subjects such as Special and General Relativity, the Standard Model and Stellar Evolution which have appeal to both sexes. However, perhaps considering the introduction of topics such as Medical Physics – which was found as Health Physics in the Standard Grade syllabus – would help to increase the number of girls choosing to continue with the study of physics.

## REFERENCES

Brown, S. (2014) 'The "Curriculum for Excellence": a major change for Scottish science Education', *School Science Review*, 95 (352), 30–6.

Docktor, J. L. and Mestre, J. P. (2014) 'Synthesis of discipline-based education research in Physics', *Physical Review Special Topics – Physics Education Research*, 10 (2), doi:10.1103/ PhysRevSTPER.10.020119

Docktor, J. L., Strand, N. E., Mestre, J. P. and Ross, B. H. (2015) 'Conceptual problem solving in high school physics', *Physical Review Special Topics – Physics Education Research*, 11 (2), doi:10.1103/PhysRevSTPER.11.020106

McVittie, J. (2008) *National Qualifications: A Short History*. Online at www.sqa.org.uk/files_ccc/ PNP_ResearchReport3_NationalQualificationsAShortHistory.pdf

Redish, E. F. and Kuo, E. (2015) 'Language of physics, language of math: disciplinary culture and dynamic epistemology', *Science & Education*, 24 (5–6), 561–90, doi:10.1007/s11191-015-9749-7

Scottish Government (2008) *Curriculum for Excellence: Building the Curriculum 3 – A Framework for Learning and Teaching*. Online at https://www.education.gov.scot/Documents/btc3.pdf

Scottish Government (2015) Teacher Census: Supplementary data. Online at www.gov.scot/Topics/ Statistics/Browse/School-Education/teachcenssuppdata

Scottish Government (2016) *Refocusing National Qualifications*. Online at http://news.gov.scot/ news/refocusing-national-qualifications

SQA (2015) *Higher Physics Course Specification*. Online at www.sqa.org.uk/files/nq/CourseSpec HPhysics15_16.pdf

SQA (2016a) *Higher Physics Course Report 2016*. Online at www.sqa.org.uk/files_ccc/HPhysics CourseReport2016.pdf

SQA (2016b) Higher Physics home page. Online at www.sqa.org.uk/sqa/47916.html

Yates, L. and Millar, V. (2016) '"Powerful knowledge" curriculum theories and the case of Physics', *The Curriculum Journal*, 27 (3), 298–312, doi:10.1080/09585176.2016.1174141

# 56

# Religious and Moral Education

*Leon Robinson and Leonardo Franchi*

Religious Education (RE) in Scotland is unique amongst the eight curricular areas of Curriculum for Excellence (CfE) in as much as it has two completely different iterations, one for Catholic Schools (Religious Education for Roman Catholic Schools, RERC), another for non-denominational schools (Religious and Moral Education, RME). In the former, a faith-based approach is taken (which while controversial to some, has an admirable clarity of purpose), while in the latter, the nature and purpose is increasingly contested, for reasons which will be become clear below. Only by being strong and well-informed advocates of the subject, in terms of its unique and distinctive contribution to pupils' education and development, can those interested in the continuation and development of RE hope to leverage adequate time and other resources.

## RELIGIOUS AND MORAL EDUCATION IN NON-DENOMINATIONAL SCHOOLS

The foundational document for RME is *Principles and Practice: Religious and Moral Education* (Scottish Government, 2017), which outlines the nature and the purpose of the curricular area in the context of the non-denominational school. This is supported by the *Experiences and Outcomes* document which outlines the required coverage in three discrete sections, namely 'Christianity', 'World Religions Selected for Study' and 'Development of Beliefs and Values' (https://www.education.gov.scot/Documents/rme-eo.pdf). There have been growing divisions between schools and practitioners in how these documents are understood and implemented, as noted in the *Impact Report* (Education Scotland, 2014) on Religious Education. This lack of consistency has led to young people in many schools not having a sound grasp of significant aspects of learning within RME: 'In most secondary schools, young people are not receiving their entitlement to religious and moral education in the senior phase' (Education Scotland, 2014, p. 4). The benchmarks for the subject, published in March 2017, are an attempt to 'draw together and streamline a wide range of previous assessment guidance (including significant aspects of learning, progression frameworks and annotated exemplars) into one key resource', and it remains to be seen whether these will help to support a more consistent interpretation of the aims of RME (Education Scotland, 2017a).

The non-statutory guidance document for RE in English schools (Department for Children, Schools and Families, 2010) has a clear statement on the purpose of RE, identifying it as being 'important in its own right and [making] a unique contribution to the spiritual, moral, social and cultural development of pupils'. In CfE there is nothing quite comparable to this unequivocal support for the subject in non-denominational schools. Although it is stated in CfE that 'subjects are an essential feature of the curriculum [and] provide an important and familiar structure for knowledge, offering a context for specialists to inspire, stretch and motivate' (Scottish Government, 2008, p. 20), there is no mention of the unique contribution that Religious Education can and should make to the 'spiritual, moral, social and cultural development of pupils'. There is a lack of clarity as to what is expected and required of a subject specialist in Religious Education.

In a recent study, *Does Religious Education Work?*, Conroy et al. (2013, p. 220) identified that 'the terms of reference within which Religious Education operates and its consequent objectives are so multiple, diffuse and fluid as to make it well-nigh impossible to offer anything like a comprehensive answer'. The sources of disagreement and difference are manifold. The entirely appropriate move away from largely uncritical, confessional Christian RE (a move which started shortly after the Second World War) has not so much evolved or developed the subject into a critical exploration of religion as an important phenomenon of human cultures and societies, but rather shattered it into countless, often poorly considered iterations of 'RE', many of which, significantly, shun the very label of 'religious' education, in favour of 'philosophy, ethics and citizenship studies' or some combination of these and other, variously and tenuously related, terms. A similar line of thought is found in the Scottish Government's *Impact Report*: 'The current variation in levels of support for the subject area are leading to inequity within the quality of delivery and in the amount of time given to the subject across Scotland' (Education Scotland, 2014, p. 4).

It is clear that within the teaching profession there are those who might prefer there not to be an 'R' in 'RE', preferring, perhaps, a move towards 'philosophy'. One senses advocacy for this idea, for example in Nixon (2008). The supposed increase in status conferred by these reconfigurations masks what could be described as an evangelical secularisation, which may just be as questionable a project as the old forms of religious confessionalism. This leaves a significant gap in the distinctive aims of RE:

> In a significant number of schools, children and young people need more opportunities to develop their own beliefs and values through learning about a range of religions and other beliefs. A clarification of beliefs and values which underpin and inform the non-denominational approach to RE is needed in order to support pupils in this important area of their education and development. (Education Scotland, 2014, p. 4)

There remains, however, an 'R' in the curriculum. It is the 'R' that makes the subject unique, distinctive and valuable. Without the 'R', the case for RE vanishes. The unique perspectives of religions, demonstrated specifically by the religiously literate (as distinct from the other, secular perspectives on religious matters), are dimensions of human experience and wisdom which are inaccessible and incomprehensible to those unwilling or unable to explore religions on religious terms. While the other social subjects aim to develop pupils' understanding of their 'own values, beliefs and cultures and those of others', RME is unique in its exploration of 'questions about the nature and meaning of life' (https://www.education.gov.scot/Documents/rme-eo.pdf, p. 1). While other areas refer to making 'meaningful' contexts for, and connections between, curricular areas, only RME refers to meaning in a teleological sense.

Levels of religious literacy, amongst teachers as well as pupils, are lamentably low. Even in the Conroy et al. (2013) study, focusing exclusively on schools in which RE was seen as strong, there was too often a lack of sophistication in teachers' understanding of religion. Notwithstanding A. C. Grayling's questionable critique of the subject's defenders, that 'Those who defend religious studies do so only because of vested interests' (Grayling, 2015), there remains a unique value to the subject, which is only contained in its religious dimension.

Unlike the situation in England, both religious and non-religious views are included in the Scottish curricular guidelines. The aim is that pupils will 'recognise religion as an important expression of human experience [and] learn about and from the beliefs, values, practices and traditions of Christianity and the world religions selected for study, other traditions, and viewpoints independent of religious belief' (Scottish Government, 2017, p. 1).

It is a fundamental principle that all children and young people throughout Scotland will consider a range of faiths and views, whatever their own situation and local context. In an increasingly secular Scotland, 'an ability to understand other people's beliefs' and to 'sensitively take account of and value the religious and cultural diversity within their own local communities, using relevant contexts which are familiar to young people' is part of the RE project, which should 'actively encourage children and young people to participate in service to others' (ibid.).

In order effectively to achieve these aims, religious literacy is required. Unfortunately, according to Conroy's team, 'there was minimal evidence of the use of primary religious texts as a resource for understanding the claims and experiences of religious communities, their histories and theologies' (Conroy et al., p. 221). Where secondary and even tertiary sources are used, to the exclusion of original, primary religious sources, there is a great danger that pupils will be exposed to inaccurate or even biased accounts of religious perspectives, beliefs and practices. While there is diversity within every tradition, care must be taken with how any tradition is represented and interpreted (Jackson, 2012).

The structural incentives which mark the 'success' of a school subject in terms of its achievements in public examinations highlight the sometimes irreconcilable tensions in RE, between the 'soft skills' of 'respect', 'reflection, discernment, critical thinking and deciding how to act when making moral decisions' articulated in the *Principles and Practices* document (Scottish Government, 2017) and the requirements of an examinable subject discipline. This tension 'is not self-evidently conducive to effective education or to the cultivation of religious literacy' and 'ambition is certainly frustrated by the performative imperatives of an examination-driven curriculum' (Conroy et al., p. 220ff.).

While children and young people often have good opportunities to develop literacy, numeracy and health and wellbeing through RME, it is important not to justify the continued existence and support of RE solely on its contribution to the development of knowledge and skills which could be learned elsewhere. Only by focusing on the distinctive contribution of RE can it be preserved as a meaningful subject on the school curriculum.

In RME, a clear focus is needed. What is it trying to achieve? How will the learning be organised? How will success be measured? These are the questions which need clear answers if firm grounds are to be established on which to base a defence of the subject. As the IR notes, 'Not all children and young people experience high-quality teaching and learning. There is scope in many schools for children and young people to engage in more active, independent and collaborative learning' (Education Scotland, 2014, p. 4). While children and young people need more learning that supports them to develop higher order thinking skills, this raises the question as to how well RE practitioners are applying their understanding of these skills in the work pupils are asked to complete. Having 'high expectations' in the abstract is not much use. Clearly structured approaches are needed, which will support pupils in developing these skills, through requiring responses from them which cannot be met without employing these skills. Too often, children and young people are not clear enough about the purposes of their learning and how to improve their achievements. Sharing 'learning intentions' is not the same as communicating the purposes of learning.

## RELIGIOUS EDUCATION IN CATHOLIC SCHOOLS

Catholic schools in Scotland are part of the state system and hence supported by the wider educational provision offered by the apparatus of government. Alongside this national system of support, Religious Education is rooted in the Church's own theological and educational traditions. This arrangement seeks to accommodate universal guidelines with local cultural dynamics. Such balancing acts are a feature of Catholic school systems across the world.

The Congregation for Catholic Education in Rome oversees the Church's educational initiatives. It offers guidance and support for Catholic schools throughout the world. Interestingly, the Congregation has said very little about the nature of Religious Education as a curriculum subject, focusing instead on the wider cultural and identity issues which surround Catholic education. Only one document deals specifically with RE. The Circular Letter to the Presidents of Bishops' Conferences on Religious Education in Schools (Congregation for Catholic Education, 2009) brings together various strands of thought which had appeared in its wider guidance on education published since the Second Vatican Council, which ended in 1965.

The provision of RE in Scotland is overseen by the Bishops' Conference of Scotland, composed of all eight of Scotland's bishops. Normally one member of the conference is responsible for overseeing educational matters on behalf of the conference although each bishop retains responsibility for provision in his own diocese. The Scottish Catholic Education Service (SCES), an agency of the Bishops' Conference, has responsibility for all matters pertaining to Catholic education, and is now recognised by the Scottish Government and local authorities as the 'one stop shop' for issues regarding Catholic schools.

The dedicated *Principles and Practices* document for RE in Catholic schools summarises neatly the purpose of the subject: 'Religious education in Catholic schools takes place within the context of the wider Catholic faith community, in partnership with home and parish. It is an integral part of the Catholic school, which is itself a community of faith.' The Scottish Government's commitment to CfE allowed the Church to develop a new syllabus for RE which would be in line, broadly, with the principles of CfE but consonant with the doctrinal and educational traditions of the Church. This was no easy task given CfE's commitment, in theory at least, to some local construction of curricula.

To make the most of this opportunity, SCES brought together a range of education professionals to write the curricular documents now known as *This is Our Faith* (TIOF). The version for P1–S3 was issued in 2011 (Scottish Catholic Education Service, 2011) and the senior phase edition (S4–6) was published in 2015 (Scottish Catholic Education Service, 2015). Both syllabi have been given approval (*recognitio*) by the Pontifical Council for Promoting New Evangelisation in Rome, the body responsible for confirming the suit-ability of programmes of Religious Education for Catholic schools. The arrival of TIOF in Catholic schools has encouraged some schools/clusters to create their own planners as road maps through the necessarily detailed curricular guidance. TIOF, while set within the overarching structure of CfE, proposes a body of core knowledge to be taught across the stages. This approach is supported by a host of resources on SCES's website, as well the relevant documentation from the Scottish Government. Such dual guidance again signals the extent of the educational partnership in Scotland between the Catholic Church and the Scottish Government.

## *THIS IS OUR FAITH:* STRUCTURE AND IMPLEMENTATION

Scotland, of course, is not immune to the advance of secular ways of thinking. This is not the place to analyse the causes of a perceived drop in religious commitment but it is worth noting that in TIOF we see a hope that a robust approach to RE will go some way to addressing the challenges raised by the phenomenon of low levels of religious practice in society. TIOF is grouped around eight Strands of Faith. These serve as the axes around which all teaching and learning revolve. The Strands of Faith are as follows: Mystery of God; In the Image of God; Revealed Truth of God; Son of God; Signs of God; Word of God; Hours of God and Reign of God. In using the eight themes as the core of the cur-riculum, RE is playing a key role in supporting the aims and purposes of Catholicism as a community rooted in a faith tradition. Each strand sets out in considerable detail the core knowledge and skills pupils should attain at each stage of their journey through primary and secondary school. The introduction of relevant subject benchmarks in 2017 offered a summary of the key topics for study while retaining the framework of the Strands of Faith (Education Scotland, 2017b).

One of the principal issues for curriculum reform in any subject is that of teacher exper-tise. In this respect, TIOF is ambitious in scope: the material presented for study, especially in the senior phase of secondary education, requires teaching staff to be well grounded in Catholic theology. Much RE in Catholic secondary schools is taught by 'generalist' teachers working alongside specialist teachers of RE. Although those invited to become generalist teachers will normally be in possession of the Catholic Teacher's Certificate in Religious Education from the University of Glasgow, the high level of specialist knowledge proposed in TIOF, especially in the material in the senior phase, might be an argument for rethinking ways of preparing teachers to teach this material. SCES and the School of Education at the University of Glasgow are collaborating to devise fresh approaches to the theological formation of prospective and serving teachers.

Clearly a considerable amount of staff development is needed for TIOF to be imple-mented successfully. It is worth noting that, thanks to the work of SCES, there is a substan-tial amount of guidance for teachers in TIOF itself:, as such, TIOF could be categorised as a form of teacher's manual. Nonetheless, SCES has recognised the need for ongoing theological development for teachers and, in partnership with other stakeholders in Catholic education, has set up a coordinating group to oversee and develop a more coherent and robust approach to 'professional learning' for teachers in Catholic schools. In time this welcome move should provide a sufficiently strong pipeline of theologically qualified teach-ers for service in Catholic schools.

## CONCLUSION

The introduction of subject Benchmarks (Education Scotland, 2017a) in RME/RERC, part of a wider initiative in Scottish education, is an attempt to give further clarity to teachers in the planning/teaching/assessing cycle. It remains to be seen what effect, if any, this will have on attainment in RE but the benchmarks should offer solid curricular signposts to teachers. How healthy is the subject? This is a wider issue but available data on the number of pupils presented for national qualifications shows a reasonable level of interest: 2,479 pupils sat the Higher Religious, Moral and Philosophical Studies (RMPS) exam in 2015 and this increased to 4,384 in 2016 (Scottish Qualifications Authority, 2015; 2016). Nonetheless, the ongoing development of RE in both denominational and non-denominational schools still requires some form of solid base. Currently, RE is located in a complex mesh of faculties and stand-alone departments with varying levels of academic qualifications in those who lead the discipline. It is the task of the Scottish Government and its partner agencies to address these issues and take the steps necessary to underpin the subject with sure and lasting foundations.

## REFERENCES

Congregation for Catholic Education (2009) Circular Letter to the Presidents of Bishops' Conferences on Religious Education in Schools. Online at www.vatican.va/roman_curia/congregations/ccatheduc/documents/rc_con_ccatheduc_doc_20090505_circ-insegn-relig_en.html

Conroy, J. et al. (2013) *Does Religious Education Work? A Multi-Dimensional Investigation*. London: Bloomsbury.

Department for Children, Schools and Families (2010) Religious Education in English Schools: Non-statutory Guidance 2010. Online at https://www.gov.uk/government/uploads/system/uploads/attachment_data/file/190260/DCSF-00114-2010.pdf

Education Scotland (2014) *Religious and Moral Education 3–18 Impact Report*. Online at https://education.gov.scot/improvement/Documents/rme30CurriculumImpactReviewRME.pdf

Education Scotland (2017a) *Benchmarks: Religious and Moral Education*. Online at https://education.gov.scot/improvement/Documents/RMEBenchmarksPDF.pdf

Education Scotland (2017b) *Benchmarks: Religious Education in Roman Catholic Schools*. Online at https://education.gov.scot/improvement/Documents/RERC_BenchmarksPDF.pdf

Education Scotland (nd a) *Curriculum for Excellence: Religious and Moral Education Principles and Practices*. Online at https://education.gov.scot/Documents/rme-pp.pdf

Education Scotland (nd b) *Curriculum for Excellence: Religious Education in Roman Catholic Schools Principles and Practices*. Online at https://education.gov.scot/Documents/rerc-pp.pdf

Grayling, A. C. (2015) 'Those who defend religious studies do so only because of vested interests'. Online at https://www.tes.com/news/school-news/breaking-views/ac-grayling-'those-who-defend-religious-studies-do-so-only-because

Jackson, R. (2012) *Studying Religions: The Interpretive Approach in Brief*. Online at www.theewc.org/Content/Library/Research-Development/Literature/Studying-Religions-The-Interpretive-Approach-in-Brief

Nixon, G. (2008) *From RE to RMPS: The Case for the Philosophication of Religious Education in Scotland*. Online at https://www.abdn.ac.uk/eitn/journal/55/

Scottish Catholic Education Service (2011) *This is Our Faith*. Glasgow: Bishops' Conference of Scotland.

Scottish Catholic Education Service (2015) *This is Our Faith – Senior Phase*. Glasgow: Bishops' Conference of Scotland.

Scottish Government (2008) *Curriculum for Excellence: Building the Curriculum 3: A Framework for Learning and Teaching*. Online at http://www.gov.scot/Publications/2008/06/06104407/0

Scottish Government (2017) *Principles and Practice: Religious and Moral Education*. Online at https://education.gov.scot/scottish-education-system/policy-for-scottish-education/policy-drivers/cfe-(building-from-the-statement-appendix-incl-btc1-5)/curriculum-areas/Religious%20and%20moral%20education

Scottish Qualifications Authority (2015) Attainment statistics. Online at www.sqa.org.uk/sqa/77197.html

Scottish Qualifications Authority (2016) Attainment statistics. Online at http://www.sqa.org.uk/sqa/64717.html

# 57

# Social Sciences

*John Gould*

Bertrand Russell (2004, p.4) once observed that: 'The fundamental concept in social science is Power, in the same sense in which Energy is the fundamental concept in physics.' Perhaps it is of little surprise then that those who study the Social Sciences are also the most likely to establish leadership roles in their subsequent careers. In 2015 a widely published study commissioned by the British Council found that a Social Sciences degree was one of the two most common prerequisites of professional leaders from around the world (the other being international study or work experience). After surveying 1,709 leaders across thirty countries, the empirical evidence demonstrated that studying the Social Sciences was the most likely academic route into leadership positions, ahead of graduates from Business or Engineering (British Council, 2015).

It is perhaps therefore fortuitous that – beyond the traditional Social Subject trinity of History, Geography and Modern Studies – the enhanced range of subject choices now available at Higher level in Scottish education has facilitated a great degree of consumer choice in S5 and S6. This trend is reflected in the incremental growth in uptake of the Social Sciences Highers: Philosophy, Politics, Psychology and Sociology.

When considered holistically, such Scottish Credit and Qualifications Framework (SCQF) level 6 activity also corresponds neatly with national priorities in education. For example, the roll-out of the Curriculum for Excellence (CfE) and its embedded principles within the Social Sciences Higher frameworks provide an appropriate platform for Scottish pupils to evaluate alternative modes of democracy (Higher Politics), incorporate a code of ethics into their own research design (Higher Psychology), challenge their own ethnocentric cultural bias (Higher Sociology) and continue the Scottish tradition of evaluating moral theories (Higher Philosophy).

The previous generation of pupils, generally commanded by their superiors to only take one social subject at Higher level, may have a tinge of envy at the wealth of options now available throughout many Scottish secondary schools. Are we therefore encountering a new era of youth Enlightenment? Or is this the simple consequence of supply meeting the demands of curious young minds?

It is little surprise that Scotland's youth is embracing the Social Sciences more readily. After all, the Scottish educational curriculum does not interface with its client base within a cultural vacuum; instead, in a zeitgeist where we have a pumped-up volume in political discourse (*Yes* or *No? Leave* or *Remain?*), where 16 and 17 year olds enter polling booths, and where an abundance of psychology-flavoured TV shows and films, and mind, body and spirit bookstore sections now occupy significantly more floor space, it is perhaps little surprise that young people in Scotland are more amenable to pursuing an academic interest in the Social Sciences.

Such consumer demand – over 6,000 Higher examination entrants in 2015/16 – remains comparatively modest when compared to the more established subjects on offer (Scottish Qualifications Authority, 2016). This is principally due to supply-side restraint such as schoolteachers lacking the eighty credits of qualifications and classroom experience to offer a Social Sciences curriculum, and peripheral perceptions of the Social Sciences as belonging to the domains of further or higher education. In something of a breakthrough, Psychology is now recognised as a Professional Graduate Diploma in Education (PGDE) discipline in its own right. However, no separate PDGE qualification in Scotland yet exists within the disciplines of Philosophy, Politics or Sociology. In practice therefore, it has been Modern Studies and Religious, Moral and Philosophical Studies (RMPS) teachers who have expanded the boundaries and embellished the curriculum portfolios on offer in various individual schools (with a piecemeal national picture consequently emerging).

Despite recent developments in professional recognition for teachers, the Social Sciences remain where the tectonic plates of secondary schools and local colleges often come into regular contact for the purposes of delivery. This symbiotic relationship between school and college allows for a more varied curriculum and learning experience, especially for S6 pupils. Colleges retain their core competencies of Higher National Certificate/Diploma (HNC/D) delivery, whilst the secondary schools provide their pupils with an augmented curriculum and better prepare them for articulation to a range of programmes in further and higher education.

## THE CFE HIGHER FRAMEWORKS AND SCHOOL/COLLEGE ACTIVITY

In academic year 2014/15, a dual system of 'old' and 'new' Highers were offered for one transitional session only. Academic year 2015/16 saw the final completion stage of the roll-out of the new Curriculum for Excellence Higher frameworks. This unified system – within which all entrants undertook the same course – is therefore more favourable for a meaningful analysis of the national picture.

The new CfE Social Sciences Highers were split across two separate 'curriculum areas': Social Studies (Politics) and Health & Wellbeing (Philosophy, Psychology and Sociology). Only fifteen candidates across the country sat examinations within the umbrella award of 'The Scottish Baccalaureate in Social Sciences'. However, activity across individual Higher level was much more vibrant, as Scottish Qualifications Authority (2016) examination data for session 2015/16 illustrates (Table 57.1).

The colleges continue to dominate provision of Higher Psychology and Higher Sociology. Behind the figures, this is even more pronounced as many schools still depend upon further education (FE) practitioners to deliver on their premises via Schools Link arrangements. The rationale for such partnerships can be found embedded within college strategic plans in the form of allocated percentages of curriculum activity for delivery in schools. Despite effectively providing a free service, colleges remain involved in such partnerships for three other strategic and operational reasons: a deep-rooted, traditional 'community' college ethos (despite the process of college regionalisation, local schools are still perceived by colleges as key stakeholders), a willingness to nurture partnerships with potential recruits, and the ability to claim Funding Council credits for each learner enrolled onto their system

Table 57.1   Higher Social Science awards for 2015/16

| Subject | Number of final examination candidates | From secondary schools (%) | From colleges (%) | From other types of institution (%) |
|---|---|---|---|---|
| Higher Philosophy | 1,008 | 94 | 6 | 0 |
| Higher Politics | 782 | 86 | 11 | 3 |
| Higher Psychology | 3,591 | 33 | 67 | 0 |
| Higher Sociology | 954 | 42 | 58 | 0 |

Source: Data adapted from Scottish Qualifications Authority, 2016.

(currently four credits per Higher pupil enrolled). It is not uncommon therefore for a college lecturer to visit a school under an arrangement whereby the college claims credits for the enrolments, yet the pupils never actually cross the threshold of the college and sit the final exam at their school.

On a practical level, school/college Social Sciences partnerships therefore usually follow one of the following formats:

- The secondary school pupils visit their local college as day release students (sometimes forming a composite group made up from several different schools).
- The college lecturer provides an outreach service and visits the local secondary school.

As Scotland's colleges continue to adapt and internally adjust to their post-merger operating environment, these Schools Link partnerships often provide them with additional logistical challenges. For example, local schools may indicate servicing requests in the spring – which do not actually materialise due to insufficient numbers in August (with the knock-on effect on college timetabling at the most critical time of the year); schools also sometimes request three classes per week on three different days – therefore, in practice, encouraging colleges to utilise part-time temporary lecturers due to the travel time involved and the subsequent inability to timetable regular, permanent tutors for other classes for large portions of the day. Colleges also have to adapt to parallel timetabling – whereby their own Social Sciences Higher students have a different amount of teaching time per week. By way of illustration: North Lanarkshire Council currently requests three separate classes of one-hour-and-forty minute duration per week per Higher, while New College Lanarkshire internally operates a three-hour and a two-hour class format per week for their internal Highers programme. An initial look at pre-appeal Scottish Qualifications Authority (2016) data for Social Sciences Highers performance in 2016 produces Table 57.2.

The Victorian-era Prime Minister, Benjamin Disraeli, once famously pointed out that there are lies, damned lies and statistics. Several mitigating factors may therefore be at work behind these divergent performance indicators. For example, many school pupils undertaking Social Sciences Highers are likely to be S6 entrants who have already achieved a number of Higher passes in S5 and are therefore looking for diversity and a broader curriculum range within their Universities and Colleges Admissions Service (UCAS) applications. In contrast, a significant number of college students undertaking Highers often have an initial lower attainment profile, or in many cases are mature returners with few qualifications at level 5 or level 6. Furthermore, the figures are obscured by the fact that a significant percentage of those listed as college entrants are actually S6 school pupils

500

Table 57.2   School and College Higher passes in the Social Sciences

| Subject | Pass rate in secondary schools (%) | Pass rate in colleges (%) |
| --- | --- | --- |
| Higher Philosophy | 70.6 | 40.7 |
| Higher Politics | 83.8 | 46.6 |
| Higher Psychology | 74.6 | 61.1 |
| Higher Sociology | 69.6 | 56.6 |

Source: Scottish Qualifications Authority, 2016.

on day release visit to their local college, particularly for Higher Psychology (perhaps partly explaining why Higher Psychology is the best performing Social Sciences Higher in the college sector).

## ADDED VALUE: DEVELOPING THE NEW SOCIAL SCIENTIST

The 'Science' element of the Social Sciences can be found within each discipline's inherent research foundations. Before the CfE Highers frameworks were implemented, some of these subjects, such as Higher Sociology, based the final grade exclusively on final examination performance. As a curriculum leader working in further education, it is particularly helpful therefore that the CfE Highers in the Social Sciences now lean heavily upon research assignments in the form of added value. Such tasks perform a key role in developing the tools and mindset of the early social scientist and, as instruments of summative assessment, they also contribute a significant element to an individual's overall final grade.

Table 57.3 outlines the percentage of respective final marks now assessed by means of an externally assessed, coursework research assignment.

Embedding the importance of research skills within the Social Sciences lays the formative foundations for further study at HN or degree level – where Research Methods units are usually compulsory features within SCQF level 7 curriculum frameworks. The associated techniques in identifying and evaluating relevant information, drawing reasoned conclusions and referencing sources are all key attributes of the social scientist. Component mark breakdowns for the 2016 diet provide further encouragement regarding the early nurturing of this skill set, with national mean data as shown in Table 57.4.

## CHALLENGES

Due to mergers and regionalisation, Scotland's colleges often have to work across several local authorities. In practice, this means servicing Social Sciences provision in secondary

Table 57.3   Research assignment final marks in the Social Sciences

| Subject | Final mark assessed via the research assignment (%) |
| --- | --- |
| Higher Philosophy | 33 |
| Higher Politics | 33 |
| Higher Psychology | 40 |
| Higher Sociology | 33 |

Source: Scottish Qualifications Authority, 2016.

Table 57.4    Research assignment: national mean data in the Social Sciences

| Subject | Research assignment: national mean mark |
|---|---|
| Higher Philosophy | 18.4/30 |
| Higher Politics | 20/30 |
| Higher Psychology | 25.9/40 |
| Higher Sociology | 19.4/30 |

Source: Scottish Qualifications Authority, 2017.

schools across a variety of catchment councils – many of whom have differing modi oper-andi with regard to the timetabling of their Highers programmes.

As well as the logistical aspects of further education practitioners servicing local schools, the new frameworks are not without scrutiny with regard to matters such as employing unlimited time and open-book approaches to the component unit assessments. The CfE Higher frameworks are also subject to ongoing scrutiny in the form of subject reviews, therefore effectively creating a moving target for deliverers. Such tweaking and refining of curriculum content can lead to a high turnover in assessment writing and the need for principal teachers, internal verifiers and quality managers to stay closely attuned to a raft of bureaucratic directives emanating from the centre (via Scottish Qualifications Authority, SQA). Despite this, the willingness to fine-tune the curriculum and amend 'live' instruments of assessment is generally to be applauded. Such moves, however, are themselves likely to be superfluous as unit assessments are phased out by 2018 (the 'old' unit assessments may, in practice, morph into useful formative tasks).

As with the other Highers, working with limited past papers provides a challenge to the classroom practitioner; likewise, the fact that many Social Sciences Highers are taken in sixth year ('crash' Highers) – as evidenced by the low uptake of National 5 programmes in 2016 shown in Table 57.5.

The 1,190 examination candidates at National 5 were less than a fifth of the 6,335 at Higher level in the Social Sciences. Furthermore, SQA do not currently offer a National 5 in Politics, and none of the Social Sciences is available at National 4 level. Perhaps as a consequence of the 'standing start' nature of many Social Sciences candidates, a key practical challenge for the deliverer is to develop their pupils' lexicon of terms and key concepts. Developing critical thinking and intrinsic confidence in using, for example, sociological language and philosophical language is a core development challenge for the classroom practitioner. With little foundational knowledge to build upon, internalising Social Science concepts and terminologies are an early pedagogical challenge for the tutor. It is also clear that Social Sciences Highers uptake is somewhat gendered as shown in Table 57.6.

Table 57.5    Uptake of National 5 in schools and colleges

| Subject | Number of final examination candidates | From secondary schools (%) | From colleges (%) |
|---|---|---|---|
| National 5 Philosophy | 300 | 97 | 3 |
| National 5 Psychology | 631 | 51 | 49 |
| National 5 Sociology | 259 | 45 | 55 |

Source: Adapted from Scottish Qualifications Authority, 2016.

Table 57.6    Uptake of Social Science Highers by gender

| Subject | Female entrants (%) | Male entrants (%) |
|---|---|---|
| Higher Philosophy | 61 | 39 |
| Higher Politics | 59 | 41 |
| Higher Psychology | 76 | 24 |
| Higher Sociology | 71 | 29 |

Source: Adapted from Scottish Qualifications Authority, 2016.

This trend is also manifest within the HNC/D Social Sciences programmes at Scotland's colleges. It also worth noting that there are currently no Advanced Highers available in any of the four Social Sciences subjects (Advanced Higher Sociology, for example, was removed from SQA's portfolio in 2007). This lack of SCQF level 7 provision is in sharp contrast to the upward demand trajectory that Scotland's colleges have been experiencing for their HNC/D Social Sciences programmes.

## PROGRESSION TO FURTHER EDUCATION

The Social Sciences are currently undergoing box office appeal across Scotland's colleges where HNC/D Social Sciences programme are often oversubscribed and hundreds of aspiring applicants have to be turned away each year. By 2015, the HNC Social Sciences programme had become the third most popular HNC award in Scotland, trailing only Early Education & Childcare and Social Care. There were 950 further education students enrolled on the programme across Scotland (66 per cent of whom were female). The HNC award had steadily increased in popularity in preceding years, overtaking Accounting, Computing, Engineering and even the traditionally popular college courses in Beauty Therapy, Music and Sport (Scottish Qualifications Authority, 2015).

In 2015, a further 440 students enrolled on the HND Social Sciences in Scotland (71 per cent of whom were female). However, colleges were essentially acting as feeders to universities and consequently the HND Social Sciences was only the eleventh most popular HND programme in Scotland (Scottish Qualifications Authority, 2015).

The HNC Social Sciences is an umbrella award that provides students with a taste of SCQF level 7 units such as History, Psychology, Sociology, Politics and Research Methods. The range of subjects facilitates university progression to a broad spectrum of degree programmes; thus partly explaining the tapering off between HNC and HND numbers. This trend is beginning to change, however, as some universities (particularly the post-1992 institutions) are now articulating an explicit preference for HND graduates directly into Year 3 of their degree programmes in Social Sciences. There is perhaps an economic rationale here: recruit students with 240 credits and top up the extra 120 credits to create an ordinary degree graduate. The SCQF, after all, is designed to facilitate direct entry to level 9 on the completion of 240 appropriate credits at college.

## CONCLUSION

Although long established and integral to many college portfolios, the Social Sciences subjects will perhaps continue in a peripheral and irregular orbit around the curriculum of many secondary schools (occasionally on offer … sometimes only available through college day release … or sometimes perceived as curious and intriguing but – in a rather Pluto-esque fashion – not being quite mainstream). Indeed, the traditional social subjects of History, Geography and Modern Studies still accounted for over 29,000 examination candidates in 2016 (almost fivefold the number in the Social Sciences; Scottish Qualifications Authority, 2016).

Despite this, the implacable growth in Social Sciences uptake within Scotland's schools is likely to continue as more in-house provision flows from an expanding, appropriately qualified, new generation of schoolteachers in subjects such as Psychology (now on offer as a PGDE specialism for those with eighty relevant degree credits). The increase in the number of schoolteachers with a minimum of SCQF level 8 in relevant subjects is likely to be incremental, therefore school–college partnerships will evolve, albeit in a more piecemeal nature cross Scotland. For example, the absence of Advanced Highers has already led to some schools taking a tentative interest in college Professional Development Awards (PDA) at SCQF level 7 in the Social Sciences. Enthusiasm for classroom study of the Social Sciences should not occur, either, in the absence of broader reflection and critical scrutiny. Indeed, those who highlight our national problems in recruiting science, technology, engineering and mathematics (STEM) students may have reservations about this curriculum trend.

In conclusion, two famous contributors to twentieth-century culture and thought perhaps encapsulate and sum up the dichotomous view of this subject area. Reflecting upon his six-year tenure in Scottish education as Rector of the University of Dundee in the late 1960s/early 1970s, the Academy Award winning actor and dramatist, Peter Ustinov, dryly concluded that the Social Sciences were for those who had not yet decided what to do with their lives. However, if education is really about empowerment, then perhaps our secondary schools should more readily embrace the sentiments of philosopher and Nobel laureate, Bertrand Russell, outlined in the introduction. After all, those who think differently are often the very same people who go on to change the world.

## REFERENCES

British Council (2015) *Educational Routes to the Top Revealed*. Online at https://www.britishcouncil. org/organisation/press/educational-routes-success-revealed

Russell, B. (2004) *Power: A New Social Analysis*. Routledge Classics Edition. New York: Routledge.

Scottish Qualifications Authority (2015) Statistics 2015. Online at www.sqa.org.uk/sqa/77197.html

Scottish Qualifications Authority (2016) Statistics 2016. Online at http://www.sqa.org.uk/sqa/64 717.4239.html

Scottish Qualifications Authority (2017) Information 2017. Online at www.sqa.org.uk/sqa/6300 2.4240.html

# VII

# CROSS-SECTORAL
# AND INTERDISCIPLINARY ISSUES

# 58

# Literacy across Learning

*Linda Harris and Hugh Gallagher*

A definition of Literacy: 'the set of skills which allows an individual to engage fully in society and in learning, through the different forms of language, and the range of texts, which society values and finds useful' (Education Scotland, 2009).

## INTRODUCTION

Over recent years, the teaching of Literacy has again become a priority in education and, simultaneously, there is a renewed focus on, and a more definitive acceptance of, literacy being the responsibility of all teachers rather than the province of English teachers alone. Being literate is central to our identity, our thinking and our learning. Literacy provides access to learning in all subjects, to communication, lifelong learning and, given its social and cultural relevance, all other aspects of our lives. At the time of writing, approximately 20 per cent of Scotland's children are living in poverty, many of whom have low attainment scores in literacy (www.cpag.org.uk/scotland/child-poverty-facts-and-figures). The understanding that literacy is so fundamental to children's learning is not new. That bedrock of literacy teaching, *A Language for Life* (commonly known as the Bullock Report; Department for Education and Science, 1975), is seminal in that it advanced similar views over four decades ago. The link between poverty and poor literacy attainment has, therefore, given rise to the plethora of, often government funded, discourses and policy initiatives currently in place, all charged with: addressing the gap in literacy attainment between the least and most disadvantaged learners; raising attainment; reducing inequity; and increasing life chances and employment prospects, whilst improving the literacy skills of *all* our children. This remains a national priority.

## THE STATE OF THE NATION

One of the early government interventions in the recent raft of papers was the *Literacy Action Plan* (Education Scotland, 2010) which was introduced as a means to tackling literacy problems in practical and proactive ways. The Plan highlighted the need for local authorities to develop their own literacy improvement strategies and advocated that the development of literacy skills was embedded in working with partners charged with implementing *Getting it Right for Every Child* (GIRFEC); highlighting the importance of literacy to parents; and ensuring the smooth transition of literacy attainment information between primary and secondary stages. In these approaches, teachers were to be supported in literacy development across all curricular areas and assessment would focus on identifying individual learning needs, progressing learning and raising standards. Teachers were to be encouraged to share their practice through collegiate working to develop effective approaches to literacy teaching, which were to include quality assurance and moderation of assessment to ensure consistency of standards across the system. The 2009 Programme for International Student Assessment (PISA) had already indicated that teachers' intervention could affect results and that increasing the reading engagement of learners, for example, could mitigate 30 per cent of the attainment gap associated with socio-economic disadvantage (https://www.oecd.org/pisa/pisaproducts/46619703.pdf).

The Action Plan also led to the development of inter-authority Literacy Hubs supported by the Education Scotland Literacy Team. These Hubs were to create opportunities for teacher collaboration, the sharing of best practice and networking. They are said to be succeeding with a total of twenty-two local authorities (of the thirty-two) involved to date. The Literacy Team also focuses on improving learning and teaching in line with Scottish Survey of Literacy and Numeracy (SSLN) findings (www.gov.scot/Topics/Statistics/Browse/School-Education/SSLN) and the *3–18 Literacy and English Review* (Scottish Government, 2015). Education Scotland's online professional learning communities also aim to support professional learning in literacy and English by providing an online space on which users can share resources and engage in dialogue.

Additionally, the Education Scotland-led National Literacy Network, which meets twice a year, provides a forum for sharing future developments with the hubs more widely and brings local authority literacy representatives and others together to share effective practice around the country. An additional focus of Education Scotland in the present day is in improving teachers' skills, including their own knowledge and skills in literacy. This focus is also supported by the National Implementation Board, responsible for implementing the Donaldson recommendations.

The curriculum itself (Curriculum for Excellence, CfE), emphasises the key role language and literacy skills play in gaining access to all learning and the need for these skills to be developed across all contexts by every teacher in all curriculum areas (Scottish Executive, 2006). CfE offers cross-cutting themes such as literacy, numeracy and health and wellbeing, all of which are the responsibility of all subject teachers, and are specifically directed at enhancing learning for disadvantaged learners.

The first Scottish Survey of Literacy and Numeracy to report on literacy only was that of April 2013, but a decline was already apparent by 2014 where top scorers among primary and secondary students decreased and there were larger numbers of low performers in secondary schools (www.gov.scot/Topics/Statistics/Browse/School-Education/SSLN). In the data, a pattern quickly and clearly emerged indicating that where low literacy attainment featured, poverty levels were higher. The final publication of literacy attainment will take place in 2017.

Literacy is also one of five key themes of the Raising Attainment for All (RAfA) programme launched across Scotland in June 2014. Two of RAfA's key 'stretch aims' were: to ensure that 85 per cent of children within each school cluster successfully experienced and achieved CfE second level literacy, numeracy and health and wellbeing outcomes in preparation for secondary school by 2016; and to ensure that 85 per cent of children within each school cluster successfully experienced and achieved CfE third level literacy, numeracy and health and wellbeing outcomes in preparation for the senior phase of school by 2019 (www.gov.scot/Topics/Education/Schools/Raisingeducationalattainment/RAFA). Additionally, the government launched the Scottish Attainment Challenge in 2015, a four-year programme aimed at tackling educational inequality by closing the gap in attainment between the most and least advantaged learners, including the appointment of attainment advisors for each local authority to support local improvement activity by creating local and national networks (see www.gov.scot/Topics/Education/Schools/Raisingeducationalattainment).

A range of positive results was reported to emanate from the developments above, including a record number of Higher English passes (23,972) being achieved in 2014 (Scottish Government, 2015a). Additionally, the hub approach resulted in improved focus on literacy enhanced practice; more robust evaluation; and increased inter-authority working, including the sharing of best practice.

Important research findings about ways to address literacy attainment were presented in *Closing the Attainment Gap in Scottish Education* (Sosu and Ellis, 2014) which indicates an average difference of 21 percentage points between learners from the least and the most deprived backgrounds across the P4, P7 and S2 stages. Consequently, a range of school and classroom strategies were recommended to support the development of literacy education. In 2013/14 the Scottish Qualifications Authority (SQA) created new National Literacy Units at Scottish Credit and Qualifications Framework (SCQF) levels 3, 4 and 5 to confirm standards and recognise literacy achievement for young people and adults. New SQA dashboard data was introduced to provide national, local authority, school and student-level information linked to economic deprivation factors about literacy and numeracy attainment, the quality and quantity of attainment, and school-leaver destinations. The data will be in a form useful to inspectors, local authorities and schools to focus on how to mitigate the poverty attainment gap (Sosu and Ellis, 2014). The tariff score data for national qualifications and the SSLN reveal a negative and persistent effect of poverty and disadvantage on literacy performance.

Curriculum guidance documentation combines the guidelines for Literacy with that of English. The *3–18 Literacy and English Review* (Scottish Government, 2015) framework, replaces the *Literacy and English Experiences and Outcomes* and is to be used in conjunction with the Significant Aspects of Learning paper (detailed in the associated Professional Learning paper, see https://highlandliteracy.files.wordpress.com/2014/06/literacyand englishupdate012014_tcm4-744807.pdf). These supporting documents are intended to provide a solution to the frequently voiced concerns about the nebulous nature of assessment in CfE and alleviate some of the anxieties teachers have experienced on this aspect since its inception. Notwithstanding, the authors of this paper are of the firm belief in the superlative importance of learning over assessment and were consequently less perturbed by these.

*How Good is Our School? Version 4* (Education Scotland, 2015) advocates a clear focus on developing skills in literacy, numeracy, health and wellbeing, creativity, digital and employability skills in a progressive way across the curriculum, indicating a concerted focus on improving literacy attainment. In fact, in the PISA study, a major three-yearly international study by the Organisation for Economic Co-operation and Development (OECD), Scotland featured unspectacularly across results in 2003, 2006 and 2009, remaining in broadly the same position in comparison with other countries. Scotland appeared only by 2009 to have reversed a decline since the 2000 study, with a score higher than the OECD mean. Unfortunately, it has been noted that this improvement is significantly attributable to the inclusion of new countries in the 2009 study as, without them, no improvement would have been reported. Nevertheless, it is worth noting that at the top levels, students are able to locate information in texts that are unfamiliar in form or content, demonstrate detailed understanding, and infer which information is relevant to the task assigned. They are also able to critically evaluate such texts and build hypotheses about them, drawing on specialised knowledge and accommodating concepts that may be contrary to expectations. Around 9 per cent of students in the United Kingdom are top performers. In England, 10 per cent of students are top performers, while 6 per cent of top performing students live in Scotland (www.oecd.org/pisa/pisaproducts/pisa2009keyfindings.htm).

The most recent publications regarding attainment are the *National Improvement Framework* (www.gov.scot/Publications/2016/12/9340/1) and *Delivering Excellence and Equity in Scottish Education* (www.gov.scot/Publications/2016/06/3853). The aim of the framework is to drive improvements in Scottish education, thereby closing the attainment gap. It promises excellence and equity based on standardised testing at P1, P4, P7 and S3 and will include a related training pack for schools. Another goal is that all new teachers will become experts in literacy teaching and this will, interestingly, aid government in evaluating the success of initial teacher education and the teacher induction scheme in supporting newly qualified teachers in literacy, numeracy and health and wellbeing. A further goal is to determine how effective learning, teaching and assessment are across Scotland, including the moderation of achievement of CfE levels in literacy and numeracy. There are no new fears presented here. In the same year *Delivering Excellence and Equity in Scottish Education* (2016) advocated a range of literacy strategies and supported Education Scotland in providing more practical advice on assessing achievement in literacy and making clear the expected benchmarks.

## IN SCHOOLS

Literacy has featured on many schools' improvement plans and has been a main focus of development for around the past decade. The formality of addressing literacy challenges in this way offers undisputed benefits since, as with all desirable developments, when there is a clear strategy at whole school level, improvements are more likely to be effected. Additionally, across all sectors, many schools now have designated literacy leaders or coordinators who are tasked with driving forward literacy strategies. In the best practice, young people have been consulted on their views about progressing learning more effectively through pupil focus groups or pupil councils.

Alternatively, many schools have organised whole school 'literacy groups', often led by a literacy leader, who may be an interested staff member from within or outwith the English department. These groups are working to identify, promote and monitor the implementation of key policy and practice in literacy across learning. Practitioners from a range of subject areas focus on specific aspects of learning in the course of the year, and aim to create consistency in the teaching of Literacy, often along with Numeracy and Health and Wellbeing. Few secondary teachers, even English teachers, have received any training in *literacy teaching* and if they are to respond positively to adopting responsibility for the teaching of literacy in their subjects, they need substantial support (Lewis and Wray, 2014). In the absence of externally provided support, more and more schools are adopting such in-house approaches.

It is widely recognised that the use of active and engaging methodologies, for example cooperative learning strategies, can be effective in the promotion of literacy development.

Teachers also recognise the benefits of using a shared language and common approaches and resources across the school. There exist other opportunities to engage in enquiry-based approaches where staff research, trial and discuss practice and these often lead to sustained improvements in practice. Examples include teacher learning communities with a focus on feedback to improve literacy teaching, and staff working in small groups to act as critical friends as they implement, for example, reciprocal reading strategies in the classroom. Staff, as part of a whole school agreement, are engaging in practices such as highlighting literacy in their learning intentions and sharing literacy-based success criteria to aid pupils in transferring and developing their skills. Many secondary schools have developed common success criteria for talking, writing and, to a lesser extent, reading and research skills to encourage a consistent approach across the curriculum.

Other links have been found between literacy gains and pupils' positive attitudes to social, emotional and behavioural competencies. Consequently, a number of schools are engaging in these and other approaches such as: effective collaborative work in small groups; peer tutoring; teaching metacognitive awareness; individual tutoring by qualified teachers; literacy teaching (as opposed to testing, which is more common); use of effective pedagogies; a focus on improving and monitoring attainment; high-quality professional development; and after-school activities such as study support (Ellis, 2015).

Approaches such as the use of learning logs, portfolios or personal learning plans are being used to record progress over time. In some schools, these learning profiles support children and young people to reflect on the skills they are developing and make connections across their learning, a beneficial outcome more often sought after than achieved.

## IN CLASSROOMS

An effective pedagogy pertinent to the development of literacy, and widely used in England, is dialogic teaching (Alexander, 2008), which combines a range of demanding skills and abilities of teachers to the benefit of learners. More advanced literacy skills can be progressed through effective questioning, by both teacher and learner, and through activities that require them to analyse and evaluate texts, explore language and literary techniques as well as explain the effects of these. Teachers also use genuine questions, as opposed to pseudo-questions, that generate the richest gains for learners rather than encouraging learners to repeat someone else's ideas. Teachers may even reformulate the learner's response to check that understandings align while also clarifying and developing thinking. There may well be challenges to justify assertions, followed by an offer of the teacher's own hypotheses for the purpose of providing alternative routes of thinking. Learners in turn challenge teachers, showing that classroom dialogue involves real argument. Simultaneously, the lesson continues to progress purposefully towards the learning intentions. Classroom climate throughout is supportive, challenging and cumulative. The complexity of the dialogue and thought is consequently deepened. Teachers may develop extended dialogue with a few pupils rather than brief exchanges with many, an approach considered more effective (Alexander, 2008; Alexander et al., 2014).

Another effective approach for addressing the attainment gap in literacy within classrooms is genre pedagogy. This pedagogy is based on Halliday's systemic functional linguistics which offers a metalanguage enabling teachers and pupils across the various subjects a method of conversing about the texts they use and approaches they may adopt to support learners to tackle these texts. From Halliday's work, Rose and Martin (2011) devised a programme entitled Reading to Learn, which employed both reading and writing strategies to support learners. The programme highlighted the role of the teacher as paramount in the literacy and learning process. While the authors acknowledged that all students benefited from the Reading to Learn programme, 'they stressed the significance of the additional gains that accrued to disadvantaged learners when teachers used this systematic literacy pedagogy to carefully select key texts and thoroughly prepare for focused teaching in all curriculum areas' (Rose and Martin, 2011; see also Acevedo, 2010). Academic texts in secondary subjects are constructed in different ways that present barriers for those other than subject experts. Subject specialists are, therefore, best placed to support students in meaning-making in their own disciplines; literacy development cannot be left to the English department alone. Basic literacy skills acquired at primary school are insufficient to cope with the increasing demands of secondary subjects brought about by the burgeoning body of knowledge that constantly takes school subject areas into new levels of complexity. Such teaching is particularly important to deliver equity for disadvantaged children because disciplinary literacy is where they often encounter problems (Ellis, 2015).

The linkage between literacy development and higher order thinking skills has also been capitalised upon in a large number of schools recently, following endorsement by Education Scotland. The development of communication skills such as the ability to communicate thoughts and opinions effectively and to explain learning is almost impossible without the ability to synthesise ideas and debate thinking. Literature in this area asserts that higher order thinking skills lead to deep learning and the ability to apply one's knowledge (Bloom, 1956; Fisher, 2013). Teachers have become more aware of visible thinking and many have used some of the visible thinking techniques such as Think, Pair, Share, and I see, I think, I wonder (Ritchhart et al., 2009).

In general, as teachers, we should be planning lessons in which literacy approaches are taught in a structured way so that learners are instructed into what actions to take with language whether in reading a text, actively listening and talking or in creating their own texts. In the latter, particular genres require to be analysed and deconstructed in order to equip learners with the tools they need to comprehend and to write their own. Teachers in all subjects require support with literacy teaching so that they, in turn, may more effectively support learners. Subject teachers need to reinforce any new subject specialist language in a systematic way through being acutely aware of our own language use and discussing new and unfamiliar vocabulary as it arises. The ultimate goal in these endeavours, though, must always be first and foremost a response to *what* the child has communicated rather than solely a response to *how* it was communicated.

There is without doubt, therefore, a resounding need to teach reading strategies such as prediction, skimming a text for main ideas and scanning for key words and content. Group discussion skills require to be taught progressively in secondary schools in *all* subjects so that learners can work collaboratively in a purposeful way. Children and young people need to be able to read for information, but they also need to be able to analyse and evaluate texts, consider the level of trust they should place in the information, and identify when and how others are aiming to persuade or influence them. Teachers are mindful of the importance of their role as protectors and guides for young people within a torrent of dangers, especially those who struggle to read and write and are, unwittingly, positioned by the texts they read. They are the ones who risk social isolation or worse, owing to the challenges of using the Internet, email, texting and social networking. Teachers navigate these currents skilfully in addition to supporting *all* pupils to progress through the notional learning milestones represented by the framework of CfE levels. The impressive aspirations Scottish teachers have always held for their pupils are testament to that.

## REFERENCES

Acevedo, C. (2010) *A Report on School-based Action Research: Will the Implementation of Reading to Learn in Stockholm Schools Accelerate Literacy Learning for Disadvantaged Students and Close the Achievement Gap?* Stockholm, Sweden: Multilingual Research Institute.

Alexander, R. J. (2008) *Towards Dialogic Teaching: Rethinking Classroom Talk*, fourth edition. Cambridge: Dialogos.

Alexander, R. J., Lefstein, A. and Snell, J. (2014) 'Triumphs and dilemmas of dialogue', in A. Lefstein and J. Snell (eds), *Better than Best Practice: Developing Dialogic Pedagogy.* London: Routledge.

Bloom, B. S. (ed.) (1956) *Taxonomy of Educational Objectives. Vol. 1: Cognitive Domain.* New York: McKay.

Department for Education and Science (1975) *A Language for Life.* Online at www.educationengland. org.uk/documents/bullock/bullock1975.html

Education Scotland (2009) *Curriculum for Excellence: Principles and Practice.* Online at https:// education.gov.scot/scottish-education-system/policy-for-scottish-education/policy-drivers/ cfe-(building-from-the-statement-appendix-incl-btc1-5)/Principles%20and%20practice

Education Scotland (2010) *Literacy Action Plan: An Action Plan to Improve Literacy in Scotland.* Online at www.gov.scot/Publications/2010/10/27084039/0

Education Scotland (2015) *How Good is Our School? Fourth edition.* Online at https://education. gov.scot/improvement/Documents/Frameworks_SelfEvaluation/FRWK2_NIHeditHGIOS/ FRWK2_HGIOS4.pdf

Ellis, S. (2015) *Improving literacy in Scotland: Four Policy Proposals.* Online at https://strathprints. strath.ac.uk/

Fisher, R. (2013) *Teaching Thinking: Philosophical Enquiry in the Classroom*, fourth edition. London: Bloomsbury.

Lewis, M. and Wray, D. (2014) *Literacy in the Secondary School.* London: Routledge.

Ritchhart, R., Turner, T. and Hadar, L. (2009) 'Uncovering students' thinking about thinking using concept maps', *Metacognition and Learning*, 4 (2), 145–59.

Rose, D. and Martin, J. R. (2011) *Learning to Write/Reading to Learn: Genre, Knowledge and Pedagogy in the Sydney School.* Sheffield: Equinox Publishing Ltd.

Scottish Executive (2006) *A Curriculum for Excellence: Building the Curriculum 1.* Online at https:// www.education.gov.scot/Documents/btc1.pdf

Scottish Government (2015a) *School-aged Literacy.* Online at http://www.gov.scot/Publications/ 2015/04/4553/4

Sosu, E. and Ellis, S. (2014) *Closing the Attainment Gap in Scottish Education.* York: Joseph Rowntree.

# 59

# Numeracy across Learning

*Tom Macintyre*

The Scottish Government's flagship Curriculum for Excellence (CfE) that has been implemented across schools and local authorities has a commitment to breadth of learning in the school curriculum. This curricular guidance is notionally split, with an entitlement for a 'broad general education' (BGE) covering five levels of learning from early through to fourth level up to the end of secondary 3 (year 10); a senior phase that leads to national qualifications follows this BGE. Throughout this curricular provision, there is a commitment to enable and facilitate the highest possible levels of literacy, numeracy and cognitive skills. The purpose of this chapter is to focus on *numeracy across learning* and to discuss how this aspect of learning can best be supported by the profession, noting that all registered teachers in Scotland have a responsibility for numeracy (as well as literacy and health and wellbeing), as part of the General Teaching Council for Scotland's (2012) *Professional Standards*. This chapter will first outline key features of CfE that pertain to a numeracy across learning agenda, before discussing how practitioners can meet the numeracy needs of learners. The chapter concludes with some suggestions to inform a whole school strategy for numeracy across learning.

## RESPONSIBILITIES OF ALL

In considering *numeracy across learning*, the focus lies on the needs of learners rather than on content, arrangements and syllabi, as would be the case for numeracy across the curriculum. The CfE policy framework argues that learning needs to have 'suitable breadth and challenge and be capable of wide application' (CfE Briefing 2 from Education Scotland, 2017) and that: 'All teachers have responsibility for promoting the development of numeracy. With an increased emphasis upon numeracy for all young people, teachers will need to plan to revisit and consolidate numeracy skills throughout schooling' (Scottish Executive, 2006, p. 20) from Education Scotland, 2017). This shared responsibility of all teachers to promote a wide application of numeracy skills in a wide range of varied contexts will support the oft-quoted *four capacities* that enable children and young people to be 'successful learners, confident individuals, responsible citizens and effective contributors' (Education Scotland, 2017). A deeper analysis of those capacities highlights attributes and capabilities contained therein, reflecting much of what has been gleaned from recent research on learning theories, including a strong emphasis on active and collaborative learning within a constructivist learning environment. In terms of *numeracy across learning*, specific capabilities cited in the framework include the ability to:

- (as successful learners) use numeracy skills; make reasoned evaluations; link and apply different kinds of learning to new situations
- (as confident individuals) assess risk and take informed decisions; achieve success in different areas of activity;
- (as responsible citizens) make informed choices and decisions; evaluate environmental, scientific and technological issues
- (as effective contributors) apply critical thinking in new contexts; create and develop; solve problems.

These policy aims can be addressed through effective interdisciplinary study but also through clearly focused and supported development of numeracy as witnessed through different subject specialisms.

## NUMERACY

Various attempts have been made to define *numeracy* and to capture what makes it distinct from mathematics. For many non-education observers and practitioners unfamiliar with mathematics and numeracy, the historical association of numeracy with competence in basic calculation is still prevalent. Within the published materials for the BGE phase in Scotland, a detailed set of experiences (I have …) and outcomes (I can …) are identified for numeracy as a subset of the wider study within mathematics. The numeracy experiences and outcomes (Es and Os) go beyond the historical emphasis on calculation to embrace aspects of 'measure' and 'information handling' as components of numeracy; Figure 59.1 shows the eight numeracy organisers in the framework.

These numeracy components are the responsibility of all practitioners and form the basis of the curriculum for numeracy across learning within CfE. The Es and Os provide some insight to what is expected of learners but practitioners need to interpret what the statements intend; often this can only be achieved where there is an in-depth appreciation of development and progression within a particular organiser. For instance, the third and fourth level Es and Os for 'estimation and rounding' rely on practitioners' knowledge extending to when, why and where one is reasonably expected to work to 'decimal places' or 'significant figures' and the impact those decisions will have on accuracy and error, including the concept of tolerance in problem-solving contexts. The documentation does not spell out all of those features or nuances:

> I can round a number using an appropriate degree of accuracy, having taken into account the context of the problem. (MNU 3-01a)

> Having investigated the practical impact of inaccuracy and error, I can use my knowledge of tolerance when choosing the required degree of accuracy to make real-life calculations. (MNU 4-01a)

Explicit documentation on numeracy across learning is not provided for studies in the senior phase, but the national qualification course support notes for each subject (Scottish Qualifications Authority, 2017) make reference to the development of numeracy skills, identifying cross-curricular learning and teaching opportunities within National 4 (N4) and

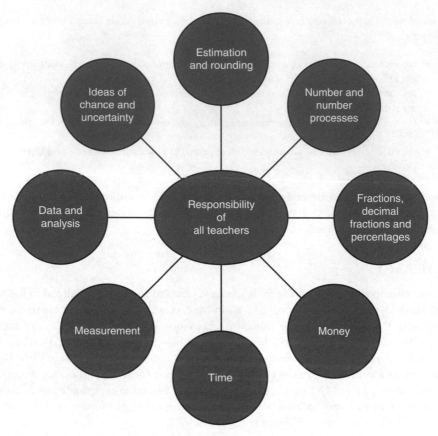

**Figure 59.1    Numeracy organisers identified in CfE's *Numeracy across Learning***

Source: https://education.gov.scot/Documents/numeracy-across-learning-pp.pdf

National 5 (N5) courses, as well as highlighting where key skills can be progressed within Higher (H) and Advanced Higher (AH) programmes of study.

Other sources of information for numeracy across learning in the senior phase are the course support notes (Scottish Qualifications Authority, 2017) for Mathematics at N4 and N5 and Applications of Mathematics at N4 and N5 (formerly named Lifeskills Mathematics). The majority of learners will study one or more of those courses during their senior phase. One unit from each of the Mathematics courses at N4 and N5 directly supports numeracy across learning, where Numeracy (N4) and Applications (N5) units make clear and explicit reference to the application of numeracy appropriate to the level of study. In the Applications of Mathematics courses there is a strong emphasis on using real-life or simulated environments and associated materials to develop skills in context. Another compelling feature is the prominence of reasoning and explanation within the learning and teaching experiences. Those emphases place high demands on learners to have conceptual understanding (Skemp, 1976) of the content covered, so that they can apply their knowledge in new and unfamiliar situations and are confident and secure in their knowledge to present, analyse and interpret evidence that leads to appropriate conclusions. The hierarchical structure from N4 to N5 essentially moves learners from 'straightforward' real-life contexts to those that may be less familiar and more demanding, as befits the descriptors for level 5 of the Scottish Credit and Qualification Framework (SCQF Partnership, 2017). At the time of writing there is no explicit progression for Applications of Mathematics at N5, although there is an award in Statistics at SCQF level 6 that may form part of a future Higher course within Applications of Mathematics.

Much as all practitioners should familiarise themselves with numeracy across learning Es and Os within BGE, they should also be acquainted with the relevant expectations and standards outlined in the Mathematics and Applications of Mathematics national qualification frameworks, insofar as they relate to numeracy development within their subject specialism. In so doing, practitioners will be well placed to support numeracy across learning and development of numeracy skills at the appropriate level throughout schooling.

Of the eight numeracy organisers set out in Figure 59.1, those that offer greatest progression and further development in the senior phase lie within information handling, that is, data and analysis; and ideas of chance and uncertainty. Statistical literacy is very much to the fore in that senior phase for a range of subjects. As far as the other numeracy organisers are concerned, a major focus in the senior phase will be on consolidation, breadth and application of the number and measure numeracy skills.

## STATISTICAL LITERACY

Much of what is studied and pursued by learners in their handling of data will come under the banner of statistical literacy, a broad term that has been defined as an ability to '[have] the confidence to engage with data, and the competence to be able to interpret them' (Porkess, 2013, p. 2). This definition of statistical literacy primarily concerns learners as *consumers* of data, where there are opportunities to explore numeracy across learning in a data-rich society, utilising their wider studies and definitely not solely relying on a mathematics environment. A mathematics subject specialist may have a role to play in helping learners understand the underlying mathematics, but it cannot be overemphasised that statistical literacy is more than working with numbers; contexts are at the heart of statistics as highlighted by Cobb and Moore (1997, p. 801), as they note: 'data are not just numbers, they are numbers with a context'. For this reason, the contexts afforded by across learning settings are central to learners' experiences as they seek to make sense of data and to communicate findings from investigations and problems set within a range of disciplines: 'To be statistically literate is to be able to make sense of statistics, i.e. to think critically about the information being presented; to understand the context; and to be able to tell the story in the data' (Australian Bureau of Statistics, 2013). A sound knowledge and understanding of the context being investigated, in tandem with necessary statistical skills, is essential in order to tell that story. Given that emphasis on context, this positions all practitioners to contribute and to 'tell their stories' on the basis of data collected and their insightful interpretation of information gathered in the statistics cycle (Figure 59.2).

However, there are gaps and insecurities reported in teachers' knowledge of, and confidence in, current pedagogical practices for numeracy and in developing the statistical skills required of them. Poor teacher knowledge can result in over-reliance on textbooks and often ends up being limited to the reproduction of facts and following recipe-style rules without

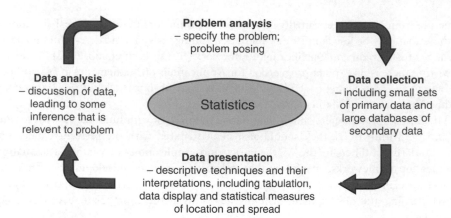

**Figure 59.2    Statistics cycle**

Source: Adapted from Porkess, 2013.

recourse to conceptual foundations or justification of practices. This continues to be seen in many Scottish secondary schools where textbook tasks can focus on computational aspects, at the expense of conceptual or relational understanding. For instance, this can be witnessed through blindly computing the 'mean, median and mode' of sets of abstract data with no serious attempt to interpret the findings or relate them to real contexts. Yet, in a society where 'open data' is increasingly available, there are numerous opportunities for learners as consumers of statistics to access real data for analysis and interpretation within a range of contextual sources.

## MEETING THE NUMERACY NEEDS OF LEARNERS

The *Principles and Practice* paper for numeracy across learning (Education Scotland, 2017) sets out a rationale for promoting and supporting numeracy skills throughout schooling. This resource also suggests pedagogical practices for a rich and stimulating learning envi-ronment, including 'developing mental agility' and 'frequently asking children to explain their thinking', but stops short of detailing any specific approaches that are recommended or currently perceived to be effective for learners. The lack of detail in either the experiences and outcomes or the principles and practice documentation can present difficulties for practitioners and school managers in pursuit of a whole school policy for numeracy across learning. Some of the challenges for teachers implementing cross-curricular numeracy, include:

- a limited personal confidence and understanding of numeracy;
- teachers' lack of awareness of learners' knowledge and skills in numeracy;
- teachers' inadequacy in enabling learners to apply skills in different contexts.

Much has been documented on the different dimensions of teacher knowledge, summa-rised and updated in Baumert et al. (2010) where distinctions are drawn between content knowledge (CK), subject specific pedagogical content knowledge (PCK) and generic peda-gogical knowledge. Their evidence and conclusions identify PCK as providing the greatest contribution to explaining student progress, that is, CK of itself is necessary but insufficient without the knowledge of teaching that underlies 'the development and selection of tasks, the choice of representations and explanations, the facilitation of productive classroom discourse, the interpretation of student responses, the checking of student understanding, and the swift and correct analysis of student errors and difficulties' (Baumert et al., 2015, p. 139).

So it will be with numeracy and numeracy across learning, where teachers' personal knowledge, confidence and understanding of numeracy may be in need of support and encouragement for a variety of reasons. For example, many teachers who have good numeracy skills themselves are perhaps unaware of current teaching methods and appropriate expectations of pupils; others who are confident about their mathematical ability but perhaps unaware of mathematical errors they make; and of course some may seriously lack confidence or have an inner fear of numeracy and mathematics that, if left unsupported, could be detrimental to learners in their care. Carter et al. (2015, p. 595) identifies comparable barriers for Australian teachers and concludes that to successfully embed numeracy in all learning areas, practitioners require: 'the commitment and support of school leaders, a review of school curriculum documents and pedagogical practices, professional development of teachers, and adequate funding to support these activities'.

In reviewing pedagogical practices and processes for numeracy with initial teacher education (ITE) students, we regularly find it necessary to focus on early numeracy and counting skills that inform mental strategies and written calculation processes. This review, engagement and development of alternative strategies for those students, requires a serious investment from them as they immerse themselves in currently promoted methods and gradually replace prior practices with those more suited to twenty-first-century skills. Such a review and engagement with current approaches in numeracy would begin to redress the challenges cited above and would be invaluable professional development for across learning practitioners.

The end goal for numeracy across learning is not necessarily to have common methods or single solutions – even if such agreement could ever be found – but rather for practitioners to be comfortable in supporting and extending a range of approaches that acknowledge how learners learn. In meeting the numeracy needs of learners, learners must be at the centre of the numeracy debate, recognising that confidence flows from personal achievement and conceptual understanding of processes and practices. The opposite is true if learners are expected to conform to using 'traditional' standard algorithms that they struggle to understand, or if presented with methods of practice that they are unaccustomed to when using numeracy in different settings, seeing those as the teacher's way and often getting confused and losing confidence to the extent that subsequent studies are adversely affected.

Those three strands of teachers' knowledge and skills, teachers' awareness of students' knowledge and skills, and teachers' ability to enable students to apply skills in different contexts, can come together to inform a whole school strategy for numeracy across learning. Supporting and developing teachers' pedagogical content knowledge in numeracy would appear to be key in reversing current trends of declining achievement in numeracy. Appropriately funded professional development will provide opportunities for collaboration, mutual sharing and support to ensure all practitioners can promote numeracy with confidence in the context of their own specialisms. Mathematics specialists should seek out opportunities to use topics and problems that are realistic to learners and that provide links to other areas of study. Teachers of other subjects should strive to meet the numeracy needs of learners by using correct mathematical language, notation, conventions and techniques that relate to learners' experiences as well as relating to their own subject. Above all, it is about looking for opportunities to promote numeracy in the widest sense, using the most appropriate method, embracing technology where necessary, but also placing high expectations on mental and written methods as students are encouraged to use their core numeracy skills with confidence.

## REFERENCES

Australian Bureau of Statistics (2013) *Understanding Statistics – Why Understanding Statistics Matters.* Online at http://bit.ly/1r2pFqg

Baumert, J., Kunter, M., Blum, W., Brunner, M., Voss, T., Jordan, A., Klusmann, U., Krauss, S., Neubrand, M. and Tsai, Y.-M. (2010) 'Teachers' mathematical knowledge, cognitive activation in the classroom and student progress', *American Educational Research Journal*, 47 (1), 133–80, http://pubman.mpdl.mpg.de/pubman/item/escidoc:2099380/component/escidoc:2099379/JB_Teachers_2010.pdf

Carter, M. G., Klenowski, V. and Chalmers, C. (2015) 'Challenges in embedding numeracy throughout the curriculum in three Queensland secondary schools', *Australian Educational Researcher*, 42 (5), 595–611.

Cobb, G. W. and Moore, D. S. (1997) 'Mathematics, statistics, and teaching', *The American Mathematical Monthly*, 104 (9), 801–23.

Education Scotland (2017) *Curriculum for Excellence.* Online at https://education.gov.scot/scottish-education-system/policy-for-scottish-education/policy-drivers/cfe-(building-from-the-statement-appendix-incl-btc1-5)/What%20is%20Curriculum%20for%20Excellence

General Teaching Council for Scotland (2012) *Professional Standards.* Online at www.gtcs.org.uk/professional-standards/professional-standards.aspx

Porkess, R. (2013) *A World Full of Data: Statistics Opportunities across A-level Subjects.* London: Royal Statistical Society and the Institute and Faculty of Actuaries.

Scottish Credit and Qualification Framework Partnership (2017) *The Framework.* http://scqf.org.uk/the-framework/

Scottish Qualifications Authority (2017) National Qualification subjects. Online at http://www.sqa.org.uk/sqa/45625.html

Scottish Executive (2006) *A Curriculum for Excellence: Building the Curriculum 1.* Online at https://www.education.gov.scot/Documents/btc1.pdf

Skemp, R. R. (1976) 'Relational and instrumental understanding', *Mathematics Teaching*, 77, 20–6.

# 60

# Digital Education in Schools

*Judy Robertson*

## INTRODUCTION

Digital education in Scotland should be informed by the excitement, ambition and innovation of computer science as an intellectual endeavour, and by a critical understanding of the social implications of computation and data science. The ability to *use* digital technology is insufficient at present: education for the digital age needs to be broadened to encompass computational thinking and to enable learners to understand and critique the effects of technology on society and individuals. This chapter briefly reviews recent developments in digital education in Scotland, including the new Scottish Government strategy. It then reports what we know about what access children have to technology at home and school. A review of the evidence about the benefits of digital learning follows, before focusing on the importance of computational thinking and how this is included in the new experiences and outcomes for Computing.

## NEW DEVELOPMENTS IN SCOTLAND

Digital education in Scottish Schools is in a period of change. Revisions to national qualifications at secondary level, a new national strategy for digital learning and teaching, and the introduction of new experiences and outcomes relating to computing in nursery and primary schools have been introduced within a period of three years.

At secondary level, three new national Computing qualifications for 16–18 year olds (National 5, Higher and Advanced Higher) have recently been revised. This redesign was initiated in 2010 with the first running of the National 5 course in academic year 2013/14.

In March 2015, Education Scotland produced a report called *Building Society* on learners' experiences and outcomes in the technologies area of Curriculum for Excellence (Education Scotland, 2015). It found that there was considerable variation in young people's experiences across the age ranges and between schools and local authorities. The report noted that:

> For too many young people, experiences in the technologies are not always strong enough. We believe that the position needs to be improved, at a time when Scottish young people are emerging into a world which is changing, educationally, economically and socially at an unprecedented rate. (Education Scotland, 2015, p. 5)

Following the publication of *Building Society*, the Scottish Government ran a stakeholder consultation about digital learning in schools, followed by the publication of a national strategy for learning and teaching through the use of digital technology (Scottish Government, 2016). The strategy aims to increase attainment and reduce inequalities through the appropriate use of digital technology: 'If used effectively and appropriately, digital technology can enhance learning and teaching, equip our children and young people with vital digital skills and crucially, it can lead to improved educational outcomes' (Scottish Government, 2016, p. 1). It has four key objectives:

- develop the skills and confidence of teachers;
- improve access to digital technology for all learners;
- ensure that digital technology is a central consideration in all areas of curriculum and assessment delivery;
- empower leaders of change to drive innovation and investment in digital technology for learning and teaching.

Achieving these objectives will require cooperation between universities which offer initial teacher education, the General Teaching Council Scotland, local authorities and schools. Changes will be required to both initial teacher education and continued professional learning provision to ensure that teachers are educated and supported in the effective use of digital technologies for learning.

Education Scotland released new significant aspects of learning (SALs) for the technologies within Curriculum for Excellence in 2016, including three new SALs for computing which is discussed later in the 'Learning about Concepts Underlying Technology' section of this chapter. This represents a major change in computing education at primary schools, and will therefore require additional support and education for teachers.

## CHILDREN'S ACCESS TO TECHNOLOGY

Children's access to technology has increased dramatically since the first computers were used in schools in the 1980s. A large proportion of children can now access educational materials at home using a desktop, laptop or tablet computer (see Table 60.1 for UK-wide figures). It is worth noting that this is by no means universal – up to 20 per cent of children may not have access to these devices at home, and it is important that teachers do not assume that children automatically know how to use computers or that they are all 'digital natives'.

As purchasing of digital technology for schools is the responsibility of the thirty-two local authorities, it is difficult to find definitive information about the service provision in the country as a whole. However, access to technology in schools is described as 'inconsistent' by the Scottish Government in their strategy for digital learning and teaching, which is why an aim of the strategy is to improve access for all learners. However, the Pathfinder project

Table 60.1  Percentage of children with access to technology at home

|                              | 5–7 years | 8–11 years | 12–15 years |
|------------------------------|-----------|------------|-------------|
| Desktop computer or laptop   | 80        | 79         | 86          |
| Tablet computer              | 79        | 86         | 83          |

Source: Ofcom, 2016.

(funded by Scottish government) has ensured that every school in Scotland has high-speed Internet access (Royal Society of Edinburgh, 2010).

Since tablet computers became popular consumer devices, various local authorities have purchased large numbers of them to support classroom learning. Figures from the Scottish Government indicate that to the end of December 2015, 66,090 devices had been purchased through the Scottish Government National Procurement Framework at a cost of £17.3 million. The framework offering includes a range of Android, Windows and Apple tablets as well as a notebook device. Approximately 75 per cent of purchases have been from the tablet offering (72 per cent iPads, 3 per cent Android, 1 per cent Windows) with the remaining 25 per cent being notebooks (Scottish Government, 2015, personal communication). Other local authorities (such as Falkirk) have introduced Bring Your Own Device (BYOD) policies to enable children to learn in school using devices from home while still offering devices to those who do not own them.

## USING TECHNOLOGY TO LEARN

Over the years there has been a tendency for evangelical learning technologists (such as myself) to inflate the promise of new technologies for schools. But it is worth considering how much technology actually does support learning. Large-scale international studies and articles which consider many studies over time (meta-analyses and systematic reviews) are very helpful to give us a broad picture. Based on a large survey and standardised test data set of 15 year olds across many countries, a recent Organisation for Economic Co-operation and Development (OECD) report concluded that 'the reality in our schools lags considerably behind the promise of technology', 'even where computers are used in the classroom, their impact on student performance is mixed at best' and 'technology is of little help in bridging the skills divide between advantaged and disadvantaged students' (OECD, 2015). These rather demoralising comments are in fact consistent with Higgins et al.'s review of educational technology which concluded that: 'Taken together, the correlational and experimental evidence does not offer a convincing case for the general impact of digital technology on learning outcomes' (Higgins et al., 2012). An advantage of reviewing large numbers of quantitative studies over time is that advanced statistical techniques enable researchers to estimate *how much* of a difference a new technique can make in the classroom. This makes it easier for busy teachers to decide whether the improvements in learning offered will be worth the effort and time spent introducing it. The term *effect size* refers to a measurement of how much change is introduced by an intervention, and *Cohen's d* is a commonly used standardised statistic which enables comparison of effect sizes across studies. As a guide to understanding what $d$ means, $d = 1.0$ is one standard deviation increase in an outcome measurement (such as a score in a maths test). This is equivalent to increasing learners' achievement by two to three years or improving rate of learning by 50 per cent. According to John Hattie, the author of a book which statistically reviews the results of 52,637 educational studies, educational interventions should have at least an effect size of $d = 0.4$ before they are introduced into the classroom (Hattie, 2009). This is because at least half of teachers can and do achieve this size of effect in their normal classroom practice. Hattie's review of eighty-two studies of computer-assisted learning found an effect size of $d = 0.37$, which falls slightly short of his recommended threshold for adoption. Of course, 'computer-assisted learning' refers to a wide range of possible hardware, software and topic combinations, so we should look at this in more depth.

The Scottish Government commissioned a literature review on the impact of digital technology on learning and teaching as part of developing the new national strategy. The review found that digital learning is helpful for numeracy ($d = 0.71$), modestly helpful for science ($d = 0.38$) and has variable usefulness for literacy – here the effect size is $d = 0.18$ but it rises to 0.56 when teachers have training and support. The key benefits of technology for supporting numeracy are for areas such as problem solving, practising number skills, exploring patterns, and increasing learner motivation and interest. The evidence suggests that shorter interventions work better for maths learning (six months or less) because the novelty effect which improves learner engagement does wear off.

It is important to remember that technology by itself rarely improves learning – the teacher has a key role to play. Research indicates that the effect sizes for learning technology interventions are highest when:

- technology is used as a supplement to teaching rather than a replacement (Cheung and Slavin, 2013);
- teaching is learner centred, and problem based (ICF Consulting Services Ltd, 2015);
- technology is used collaboratively (Higgins et al., 2012); the learner is in control (Hattie, 2009);
- teachers have been educated about computers as teaching and learning tools (Hattie, 2009);
- technology is used among a diversity of teaching strategies and multiple opportunities for learning (Hattie, 2009);
- feedback is optimised (Hattie, 2009).

From this we can conclude that the teacher's pedagogical expertise, and the extent to which they have been educated in the use of technology to support learning, is at least as important as the features of the technology itself. As the OECD report put it: 'In the end, technology can amplify great teaching, but great technology cannot replace poor teaching' (OECD, 2015).

## LEARNING ABOUT CONCEPTS UNDERLYING TECHNOLOGY

Using technology effectively to support learning in our schools would be a start, but we need to be more ambitious. Scotland has a rich history of scientific and engineering break-throughs, and in the future many such scientific breakthroughs will rely on underpinning computer science. To support scientific and medical advancements, we will need a genera-tion of learners with powerful, creative computational approaches to problem solving, and an ability to understand the wider implications and effects of the societal shift towards computation and data. This requires a focus on understanding process and information through the development of a set of cognitive skills referred to as *computational thinking*. This view is reflected in the Royal Society's influential review of computing in schools in the UK which recommended that 'Every child should have the opportunity to learn concepts and principles from Computing (including Computing Science and Information Technology) from the beginning of primary education onwards' (Furber, 2012, p. 6). In the last decade, there has been an international shift towards improving computer science edu-cation: countries including the US, Israel, New Zealand, Germany, India and South Korea have reformed their curricula to emphasise computer science as an intellectual discipline (Furber, 2012). The study of computational thinking from early primary school is now mandatory in England (Department for Education, 2013).

The new computing strand within the Technologies section of the Curriculum for Excellence is designed to teach learners about the fundamentals of information and process from an early age (Education Scotland, 2017). The conceptual knowledge gained when working towards the first significant aspect of learning (SAL), 'understanding the world through computational thinking', is required to then understand computing languages and technologies in the second SAL, before learners then 'design, build and test computing solutions' in the final SAL, using those technologies. The three SALs should be interwoven and approached as a spiral curriculum – one lesson might cover aspects of all three SALs. An important aspect of the three SALs is that they deliberately separate understanding core computing concepts as they crop up in everyday life (e.g. randomness in a board game which relies on dice), from how the concepts can be represented within computer systems (e.g. how to read code which has randomness built in), from actually writing the code from scratch (e.g. programing a new game which simulates dice). This separation is a response to findings from computer science education research which indicate that learners typically struggle with the cognitive complexity of trying to perform the difficult task of creating a new program if they only have a shaky grasp of underlying computing concepts or the programing language they have been asked to use. An online resource to support teachers with the computing strand of Curriculum for Excellence can be found at www.teachcs.scot.

## SUMMARY

Technology changes rapidly, and after a period of inertia, Scottish Government, Scottish Qualifications Authority (SQA) and Education Scotland have introduced a number of changes which will have a large impact on how technology is used to support learning in Scottish classrooms. Although all schools have Internet access, provision of other equipment is patchy – something which the new Scottish Government strategy aims to address. We have seen from research evidence that technology *can* be used to support learning, particularly in maths, but it is perhaps not such a positive picture as is sometimes claimed. Computational thinking – cognitive abilities required for innovation in computer science and technology – will increasingly be part of children's experiences from early years onwards, as seen in the new significant aspects of learning in technology. The teacher's role is key in unlocking the promise of digital learning and computational thinking. Teachers require education and support in both initial teacher education and continued professional development.

## REFERENCES

Cheung, A. C. K. and Slavin, R. E. (2013) 'The effectiveness of educational technology applications for enhancing mathematics achievement in K-12 classrooms: a meta-analysis' *Educational Research Review*, 9, 88–113, doi:10.1016/j.edurev.2013.01.001

Department for Education (2013) *National Curriculum in England: Computing Programmes of Study*. London: Department for Education.

Education Scotland (2015) *Building Society: Young People's Experiences and Outcomes in the Technologies*. Livingston: Education Scotland.

Education Scotland (2017) *Benchmarks: Technologies*. Online at https://education.gov.scot/improvement/Documents/TechnologiesBenchmarksPDF.pdf

Furber, S. (2012) *Shut Down or Restart? The Way Forward for Computing in UK Schools. Echnology*. Online at http://royalsociety.org/education/policy/computing-in-schools/report/

Hattie, J. (2009) *Visible Learning*. New York: Routledge.

Higgins, S., Xiao, Z. and Katsipataki, M. (2012) *The Impact of Digital Technology on Learning: A Summary for the Education Endowment Foundation*, November. Online at https://pdfs.semantic-scholar.org/d26b/b59f2536107b57f242b8289b1eb6f51d8765.pdf

ICF Consulting Services Ltd (2015) *Literature Review on the Impact of Digital Technology on Learning and Teaching*. Online at www.gov.scot/Publications/2015/11/7786

OECD (2015) *Student, Computers and Learning: Making the Connection*. Online at www.oecd.org/publications/students-computers-and-learning-9789264239555-en.htm

Ofcom (2016) *Children and Parents: Media Use and Attitudes Report*. Online at http://stakeholders.ofcom.org.uk/binaries/research/media-literacy/media-use-attitudes-14/Childrens_2014_Report.pdf

Royal Society of Edinburgh (2010). *Digital Scotland*. Online at http://www.rse.org.uk/wp-content/uploads/2016/09/Digital-Scotland-Final-Report.pdf

Scottish Government (2016) *Enhancing Learning and Teaching Through the Use of Digital Technology*. Online at www.gov.scot/Publications/2016/09/9494

# 61

# Health and Wellbeing

*Jennifer Spratt*


In response to the Schools (Health Promotion and Nutrition) (Scotland) Act 2007, Curriculum for Excellence has given high priority to *health and wellbeing*, framing it, alongside literacy and numeracy, as a cross-curricular area that should be supported in all aspects of learning. As such, health and wellbeing is seen to be the 'responsibility of all'. Unlike literacy and numeracy, Health and Wellbeing is seen both as a curricular area (learning *in* health and wellbeing), and as a more diffuse element of school life involving aspects such as ethos, relationships and rights (learning *through* health and wellbeing). Hence, teachers' responsibilities to health and wellbeing involve both curricular content and school environment. This chapter will focus on those aspects of health and wellbeing that are deemed to be a universal responsibility, rather than those areas such as physical education or nutrition that may require specialist knowledge.

Whilst the requirement for local authorities, schools and teachers to promote and support the health and wellbeing of children is now widely accepted in Scotland, it should not be forgotten that this is still relatively new territory. At the start of the twenty-first century, Mayall (2001) described the Cartesian divide between mind and body whereby schools focused on learning whilst paying scant regard to the health of pupils. At this time, the responsibilities for the health and the education of children resided in different government departments, with implications for the experience of children in schools. Policy initiatives such as the Health Promoting Schools movement (Scottish Government, nd a) coupled with the drive towards multi-professional working led to a changed understanding of the role of teachers in the health of children. This is articulated in the Curriculum for Excellence Health and Wellbeing policy (Scottish Government, nd b; nd c) which is closely linked to the interagency policy, *Getting it Right for Every Child* (GIRFEC) (Scottish Government, 2012). As well as redrawing professional boundaries, these policies legitimate intervention by schools and teachers into personal aspects of children's lives that may, previously, have been seen as the private concerns of families. Hence these policies merit some critical scrutiny.

Wellbeing is often portrayed as an alternative to an attainment-driven curriculum, removing the focus from learning outcomes to the holistic development of the 'whole child' (e.g. McLaughlin, 2015). However, one notable feature of Scottish policy is the way that health and wellbeing is presented as being interlinked with learning. The use of phrases such as *health and wellbeing across learning* and *learning through health and wellbeing* imply a close relationship. The sections that follow will firstly consider how Scottish policy conceptualises health and wellbeing in the school context, and will then discuss how this relates to teaching and learning.

## POLICY REPRESENTATION OF HEALTH AND WELLBEING

A key advantage of wellbeing as a policy term is that it conveys a universally positive con-notation and it is a concept that would appeal to professionals in the fields of health, social work, psychology and education. Perhaps, then, it is no surprise that that was chosen as the central concept around which the multi-professional policy GIRFEC is based. According to this model, childhood wellbeing can be judged against eight overlapping 'indicators of wellbeing': safe, healthy, achieving, nurtured, active respected, responsible and included (often abbreviated with the acronym SHANARRI). To convey a holistic notion of the 'whole child' at the centre of a 'shared vision' of wellbeing across the different children's services, the eight indicators are portrayed as a circle with eight sections – the 'wellbeing wheel', as shown in Figure 61.1.

Looking at the wording of each of the indicators, wellbeing is expressed in terms of the provision that is made for children by adults. For example, 'achieving' is articulated as 'being supported' in learning and 'included' is portrayed as 'having help' to overcome challenges. GIRFEC presents a rights-based model of wellbeing that focuses on the care of and provision for children. When children are identified as experiencing difficulties, they are assessed against the eight indicators of wellbeing and where provision is thought to be inadequate in one or more areas, an appropriate interagency response is developed. The GIRFEC understanding of wellbeing is a property of the care of children, rather than a description of the state of the children themselves.

In Curriculum for Excellence, the caring approach of GIRFEC is evidenced in *Health and Wellbeing across Learning: Responsibilities of All. Principles and Practice* (Scottish Government, nd b) which conveys the role of the teacher in developing a happy, supportive environment in which children can learn. For example, echoing some of the terms in the SHANARRI model: 'Children and young people should feel happy, safe, respected and included in the school environment and all staff should be proactive in promoting positive behaviour in the classroom, playground and the wider school community' (p. 1).

However, the *Health and Wellbeing across Learning: Responsibilities of All. Experiences and Outcomes* (Scottish Government, nd a) takes a somewhat different perspective on wellbeing when describing how this approach might impact on the lives of children themselves. Here health and wellbeing is portrayed as an individualised condition of children and young people. It can be seen as a set of skills of physical, emotional and social, self-understanding, self-management, risk awareness and risk management. For example, pupils can expect to be supported to 'understand and develop my physical, mental and spiritual wellbeing and social skills', to 'develop my self-awareness, self-worth and respect for others' and to 'expe-rience personal achievement and build my resilience and confidence'. Health is portrayed as a personal responsibility as young people are supported to 'understand how what I eat, how active I am and how decisions I make about my behaviour and relationships affect my physi-cal and mental wellbeing' and to 'participate in a wide range of activities which promote a healthy lifestyle'. In navigating their pathways through the risk infused world, young people are taught how to seek help as they 'understand that adults in my school community have a responsibility to look after me, listen to my concerns and involve others where necessary' whilst they 'assess and manage risk and understand the impact of risk-taking behaviour'. As

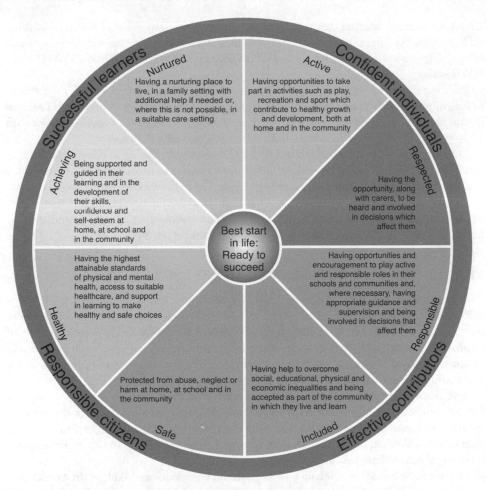

**Figure 61.1 The GIRFEC indicators of wellbeing (GIRFEC wellbeing wheel)**

Source: www.gov.scot/Topics/People/Young-People/gettingitright/wellbeing

Watson et al. (2012) have described, the school focus on health and wellbeing is very much about 'responsibilisation' of young people as they learn how to operationalise health-related competencies.

It could be argued that health and wellbeing is also communally situated, through the focus on social wellbeing. However, on close inspection, those items included in the experiences and outcomes under 'social wellbeing' appear to retain an individual focus. For example, the following item encourages scrutiny of one's own feelings and behaviour in a social setting: 'I understand that my feelings and reactions can change depending upon what is happening within and around me. This helps me to understand my own behaviour and the way others behave' (Scottish Government, nd a, HWB 0-04a/HWB 1-04a/ HWB 2-04a/HWB 3-04a/HWB 4-04a).

Similarly, the example below itemises some of the ingredients of friendship in functional terms, with a focus on teaching the individual how to 'build relationships': 'I know that friendship, caring, sharing, fairness, equality and love are important in building positive relationships. As I develop and value relationships, I care and show respect for myself and others' (Scottish Government, nd a, HWB0–05a/HWB1–05a/HWB2–05a/HWB3–05a/HWB4–05a).

Fielding (2011) has suggested that the contemporary focus on social skills is on learning to function in socially acceptable ways. He argues this has reduced the complexity of human interactions to 'doing relationships' rather than 'having friends', with a focus on successful social performance, rather than the enjoyment of the company of others.

Overall, then, we can see that whilst GIRFEC conveyed wellbeing as being cared for and cared about, Curriculum for Excellence links this to a strong sense of being able to look after oneself. This resonates with an argument published in the *British Medical Journal* that we should replace the classic World Health Organization (1948) definition of health as a state of physical, emotional and social wellbeing with a new twenty-first-century formulation of health as 'the ability to adapt and to self-manage' (Huber et al., 2011 p. 3).

## THE RELATIONSHIP BETWEEN WELLBEING AND LEARNING

The justification for the focus on health and wellbeing in Curriculum for Excellence is made in terms of benefits to learning. Health and wellbeing is consistently and repeatedly construed as a prerequisite to learning and, as such, enhancing wellbeing is seen as a way of improving children's capacity to successfully access the educational opportunities available in schools: 'Good health and wellbeing is central to effective learning and preparation for successful independent living' (Scottish Government, nd b, p. 2).

The functional role ascribed to health and wellbeing in supporting successful learning can be seen in its inclusion alongside literacy and numeracy as a key focus in the government's 'attainment challenge', aimed at reducing the socio-economic disparities in school attainment, although, unlike literacy and numeracy, it is not subject to benchmarking as a measure of national improvement.

Of course, 'learning' in Scotland goes beyond the knowledge and skills of the taught curriculum, to include the development of particular personal attributes (the four capacities), which the Scottish Government views as the desirable features of its citizens. The central purpose of Curriculum for Excellence continues to be, 'successful learners, responsible citizens, effective contributors and confident individuals', and as such is very much focused on shaping the characters of children and young people. The policy justification for the duty of every teacher towards health and wellbeing is framed in terms of fostering 'positive' personal attitudes and dispositions. The following phrase is repeated in several Curriculum for Excellence documents (in spite of the second sentence being a non-sequitur): 'Learning through health and wellbeing promotes confidence, independent thinking and positive attitudes and dispositions. Because of this, it is the responsibility of every teacher to contribute to learning and development in this area' (Scottish Government, nd a, p. 1).

Similarly, the appearance of the four capacities running around the rim of GIRFEC's SHANARRI wheel (see Figure 61.1) confirms the close relationship that is conceived between childhood wellbeing and the policy vision of the 'good citizen'. Thus, health and wellbeing is not simply valued in its own right, it is valued for the contribution that it makes to the education and development of children, and is seen as a vehicle through which to shape the characters and subjectivities of children in ways that are seen as desirable by the state. I have argued elsewhere (Spratt, 2016) that this view of wellbeing draws from the fields of psychology (wellbeing as social and emotional skills), health promotion (wellbeing as lifestyle choices) and social care (wellbeing as being cared for). Arguably, through the health and wellbeing policies, the discourses of other professional groups have migrated into classrooms as is it has become a 'taken for granted' aspect of teachers' responsibilities to pay attention to issues such as confidence, resilience, social skills and so on. What has been overlooked in this inter-professional policy arena is the contribution that learning itself makes to childhood wellbeing. Where teaching and learning are invoked in discussions of wellbeing it is through a sense of achievement, reaching milestones and, importantly, being recognised for that achievement. Little is said about the intrinsic value of learning for childhood flourishing.

Bringing a different perspective to bear, philosophers of education tend to conceptualise wellbeing in terms of the way in which a life is lived, rather how a person feels. Drawing from Aristotle, wellbeing is evaluated through an outward looking frame. For example, White (2011) considers the opportunities for doing the kind of things that a person considers to be valuable or meaningful. When wellbeing is considered in this way, then it becomes clear that education has a great deal to offer to wellbeing in terms of providing opportunities to undertake and choose activities and roles that people feel brings value to their lives. In terms of both content and pedagogy, meaningful learning enhances opportunities to lead a valuable life in the present and in the future. At a basic level, human experience is enhanced immeasurably by learning to read and write, and at a more sophisticated level, learning feeds the mind and the imagination and helps us to recognise and pursue those things that are of value to us. If our understanding of wellbeing is expanded to include human flourishing in the Aristotelian sense, then we can see that meaningful learning is a prerequisite of wellbeing, introducing a two-way relationship. I would argue that, although the Scottish Government is to be commended in highlighting wellbeing in schools as an important aspect of development, it has allowed other professional discourses to overshadow educational discourses in this area, and could place a stronger emphasis on the intrinsic value of education to childhood flourishing (Spratt, 2017).

## CONCLUSION

The Scottish curriculum emphasises the role of physical, social and emotional health and wellbeing in providing a basis from which to access what is offered in the school curriculum. Where children need support in this level of care, it is important that schools work with partners to address difficulties. However, much of what is badged as health and wellbeing can be seen as an effort to shape skills, attributes and, arguably, the subjectivities of children, in order to support other educational policy aims (such as attainment or development of the four capacities). In taking this approach, I have argued that health and wellbeing policies have drawn on the discourses of other professional groups whilst overlooking the contribution that education itself makes to wellbeing. This is not an argument against paying attention to the emotional needs of children in schools, but the contribution that teachers, uniquely, make to childhood flourishing through high-quality teaching and learning should not be forgotten.

## REFERENCES

Fielding, M. (2011) *Radical Education and the Common School: A Democratic Alternative*. London: Routledge.

Huber, M. et al. (2011) 'How should we define health?' *BMJ*, 343 (d4163), 1–3.

McLaughlin, C. (2015) *The Connected School: A Design For Well-being*. Online at https://www.sussex.ac.uk/webteam/gateway/file.php?name=the-connected-school.pdf&site=26

Mayall, B. (2001) 'Children's health at school', in P. Foley, J. Roche and S. Tucker (eds), *Children in Society: Contemporary Theory, Policy and Practice*. Basingstoke: Palgrave, pp. 195–201.

Scottish Government (2012) *A Guide to Getting it Right for Every Child*. Online at www.scotland.gov.uk/Resource/0041/00419604.pdf

Scottish Government (nd a) Schools (Health Promotion and Nutrition) Scotland Act: Health promotion guidance for local authorities and schools. Online at www.gov.scot/resource/doc/222395/0059811.pdf

Scottish Government (nd b) *Curriculum for Excellence: Health and Wellbeing across Learning: Responsibilities of All. Experiences and Outcomes*. Online at https://www.education.gov.scot/Documents/hwb-across-learning-eo.pdf

Scottish Government (nd c) *Curriculum for Excellence: Health and Wellbeing across Learning: Responsibilities of All. Principles and Practice*. Online at https://www.education.gov.scot/Documents/hwb-across-learning-pp.pdf

Spratt, J. (2016) 'Childhood wellbeing: what role for education?'. *British Educational Research Journal*, 42 (2), 223–39.

Spratt, J. (2017) *Wellbeing, Equity and Education: A Critical Analysis of Policy Discourses of Wellbeing in Schools*. Cham, Switzerland: Springer International Publishing.

Watson, D., Emery, C. and Bayliss, P. (2012) *Children's Social and Emotional Wellbeing in Schools: A Critical Perspective*. Bristol: The Policy Press.

White, J. (2011) *Exploring Well-being in Schools. A Guide to Making Children's Lives More Fulfilling*. Abingdon: Routledge.

World Health Organization (1948) Constitution. Geneva: World Health Organization.

# 62

# Citizenship Education

*Alan Britton*

In this chapter, I will illuminate the particular model of citizenship education that has emerged in recent times in Scotland. I will question whether there is sufficient clarity about the purpose and place of citizenship education in the Scottish schools system. I will also note the ongoing uncertainty around questions of responsibility for the provision and oversight of citizenship education, and whether it retains the necessary prominence and policy visibility to be enacted effectively. Given the rapidly evolving nature of society, the dynamic nature of national and global politics, and the emerging challenges to fundamentals of democracy itself, the need for clarity around such issues is greater than ever.

The idea that we ought to educate for citizenship is one of the oldest political and pedagogical propositions in the Western world. In ancient Greece, both Plato and Aristotle advocated citizenship education as a means towards building a society populated by a well-informed and articulate citizenry. Similar aspirations emerged in Rome, albeit mainly to be accomplished within the confines of the family, rather than through a public system of education. In both Greece and Rome the nature of the 'citizen' was of course rather different to the modern ideal of universal enfranchisement, nonetheless these early attempts at framing the relationship between the state, the citizen and education served as a template that retains echoes in the modern era.

In the twentieth century, the notion that the state, through its schools, should explicitly educate *about* and *for* citizenship fell variously in and out of fashion. In times of national crisis, some 'citizenship' curricula equated to little more than appeals to patriotism and a duty of unquestioning obedience. At its most extreme, this approach culminated in systematic attempts in Nazi Germany and the Soviet Union, for example, to indoctrinate young citizens into a life as mere objects subordinate to the will of the State. At other points in time, and in different places, including the UK and Scotland, there was less heed paid to the importance of citizenship education, despite some attempts to introduce what was known as 'political education' in England in the 1980s and 1990s. In Scotland the picture was muddied somewhat by the existence of Modern Studies (see Chapter 52) which addressed some, if not all, elements of citizenship.

A new formulation of citizenship education emerged in many countries across the world around the time of the millennium. The emphasis in this version of citizenship education was on providing young people with the knowledge and skills to function more effectively in society, and to contribute to, or actively participate in, political life. This widespread, more or less simultaneous, adoption of citizenship education in a broad spectrum of countries was presented as a response to the perceived disengagement and alienation of young people from the political and civic domains. There was certainly strong evidence that young people in the 18–25 category were less likely to vote than their older fellow citizens, although this was sometimes counterbalanced by the enthusiasm among younger people for single issue campaigning. The ideological thrust behind this new wave of citizenship education was broadly communitarian, with its explicit attempts to re-engage young people in society.

Perhaps due to the sometimes problematic (and indeed dark) legacy of historic attempts by the state to impose forms of citizenship education, even these more recent, apparently benign moves, provoked criticism from some commentators. These concerns sometimes related to the apparent danger of indoctrination, or the view that educating for citizenship was a needless distraction from the core business of education. Others argued that the kind of citizenship now being promoted was rooted in a passive consumerism and a non-critical, 'soft' citizenship that implicitly promoted conformity.

Further challenges arose from questions around the definition and purpose of citizenship education. Given that citizenship alone is potentially such an imprecise idea, by extension, 'citizenship education' may be even harder to delineate. If we are unclear about the kind of citizen we are trying to mould, it will be similarly difficult to provide a 'curriculum' that can achieve this. Indeed, the wider question would be about the kind of democracy we are building our citizens for (see Biesta, 2008 for a detailed discussion of these issues in relation to Scotland). Even if we achieve clarity around the aims of citizenship education, in practice a great deal can be lost in translation from policy to practice. In Scotland, for example, teachers have been encouraged at various times to focus on 'global citizenship education', 'international education', 'character education', 'values education' and 'political literacy'. All of these seem to be connected to, but not entirely synonymous with, citizenship education, and this demonstrates the potential complexity and confusion involved in making citizenship education work.

Yet another challenge relates to evaluating the outcomes of citizenship education. Are there any useful measures we could use as a proxy for effective citizenship education? Would it be sufficient to observe a longitudinal growth in young people's turnout at elections, and parallel growth in their pro-social behaviours? Is it possible or even ethical to assess the capacity for citizenship through tests and exams? Alternatively, for those averse to such crude metrics, are there other more nuanced ways of assessing the impact of citizenship education? However, if these other evaluative methods are too vague, and there is no accountability associated with the provision of citizenship education, will it even be taught?

The challenges highlighted above go some way towards explaining, if not excusing, the rather peculiar contemporary status of citizenship education in Scotland. At the time of writing, the positioning of citizenship education in Scotland is confused at best. It carries no statutory curricular weight in Scotland, yet appears as one of the four core capacities of *A Curriculum for Excellence* (as *Responsible Citizens*). For a spell, it was one of the national priorities in Scottish education, which were quietly put out to grass in the mid-2000s. Citizenship in Scotland is not a discrete subject, as it is in England (Davies, 2012, p. 37). Nor is there yet any persuasive evidence that it has been embedded within and beyond the curriculum in all of Scotland's schools as originally envisaged. The last truly comprehensive policy statement and guidance issued within Scotland on citizenship education was in 2002 (Learning and Teaching Scotland, 2002). This followed from an initial consultation document in 2000. It is noteworthy that the 2002 document was entitled 'Education for citizenship: a paper for discussion and development', which reflected its light touch, advisory status. For a decade or so thereafter, education for citizenship was promoted by a dedicated team within Learning and Teaching Scotland and supported by a network of named local authority advisors across Scotland. This professional development capacity has largely disappeared in recent years.

The *Learning for Sustainability* framework (One Planet Schools Working Group, 2012) revisited some aspects of citizenship, and recommended that 'education for global citizenship' should be an *entitlement* for all pupils, albeit within an interconnected matrix with 'education for sustainable development' (see Chapter 65) and 'outdoor learning' (see Chapter 63). The Scottish Government endorsed this recommendation but thus far has not made the substantial investment required to realise such an entitlement across the system. The revised General Teaching Council for Scotland (GTCS) standards locate citizenship within the broader set of values that all teachers are required to demonstrate in their professional capacities. The extent to which this can act as a lever specifically to promote citizenship education relies, however, on there being sufficient knowledge and understanding amongst beginning and well-established teachers alike. It also remains to be seen if the values and citizenship dimension becomes central to professional update and accreditation processes.

Given that the 2000 and 2002 documents remain the clearest articulation yet of the Scottish approach to citizenship education, it is perhaps worth revisiting the context from which they emerged, and the broad principles and practices that they promoted. They were certainly products of their time, having been influenced both by the advent of devolution in Scotland in 1999, and by the publication of the Crick Report in England in 1998 (Qualifications and Curriculum Authority, 1998). As noted previously they also reflected the concern at the time around the disengagement of young people from the political process and the more general malaise around diminishing 'social capital'. They reflected these rather pessimistic political and moral concerns, while at the same time capturing the contemporary optimism in Scotland around the possibility of democratic renewal following devolution.

The documents conspicuously avoided defining *citizenship* itself; instead, they sought to describe what the *capability* for effective citizenship should be. While this compromise avoided potentially endless terminological debate, for the reasons described previously it contributed to the subsequent imprecision in policy implementation, and the lack of a truly critical and interrogative stance on the nature of citizenship itself. Biesta (2008) highlighted the lack of a 'structural' approach to citizenship in this documentation, that is, the failure to prescribe an education in citizenship that encouraged young people to critique the very nature of their citizenship. Instead, he characterised the thrust of the proposed model as 'good deeds citizenship' focused on responsibilities, rather than a truly critical, active citizenship.

In more practical terms, the Learning and Teaching Scotland (2002) paper for discussion and development described four key ways in which schools might help to develop the capability for citizenship: through cross-curricular activities; subject specific delivery; school–community links; and a focus on pupil participation. It also asserted that young people should be regarded as citizens now, and not as citizens in waiting. This was one of the bolder assertions in the paper, implying that the full panoply of citizenship rights (as set out in the UN Convention of the Rights of the Child for example – see Chapter 64) ought to be enacted in all schools. Many aspects described in the 2002 paper were already evident in some Scottish schools, indeed a number of 'good practice' case studies featured in the document. In some senses, the model being proposed was not new; the challenge was in encouraging schools to see that often-unconnected initiatives ought to be understood as contributing to an education for citizenship.

The 2002 paper acknowledged the presence of Modern Studies in many Scottish secondary schools, as well as the people in society theme within the 5–14 curriculum. It noted that Modern Studies could make a potentially significant contribution, notably in relation to political literacy, but was insufficient on its own to deliver citizenship education. As Frazer (2003, p. 74) noted, however, there is a danger that 'insufficiency entails non-necessity'. In other words, in stating that the political dimension to citizenship is not enough, there is a danger that it is regarded as a non-essential component of citizenship education. Frazer ascribed this to a broadly anti-political culture across the UK, although the fact that around 20 per cent of Scottish secondary schools (HMIE, 2013) have no Modern Studies specialists may equally explain why the authors of the policy document felt unable to note its centrality.

Despite the sometimes confusing and rather problematic policy framework described above, many primary and secondary schools across Scotland have undertaken a range of initiatives that are consistent with the four mechanisms for building citizenship from the 2002 paper. Despite the inconsistent policy messages, and the succession of linked initiatives with the potential to confuse, there is a great deal of effective practice and activity in the broad domain of citizenship. Any of the following can be construed as 'citizenship education': authentic pupil councils, fair trade tuck shops, litter picks, visits to the Scottish Parliament, global connections and partnerships, John Muir awards, Eco Schools, Rights Respecting Schools, and engagement with local communities. One could legitimately add dozens of actions and curriculum areas to this list, which illustrates both the strength and the weakness of a vision for citizenship education that is so broad.

The more critical dimensions, where pupils might have a voice in relation to aspects of learning and teaching, or with regard to fundamental questions of power, inequality and participation in society, are less widely spread. However, even these are evident in some inspirational primary and secondary schools. The challenge is to gather evidence of impact, and to disseminate this outstanding practice in a system that has lost an entire 'middle' cadre of advisers and development officers. Another challenge is to persuade schools that educating for citizenship need not conflict with other priorities, such as literacy and numeracy. However, they are only likely to believe and respond to this if there is a strong reaffirmation of this fact across the system.

The present confluence of factors suggests that the time is ripe for a reappraisal of the place of citizenship education in Scotland. There are potential voters aged 16 in our secondary schools who deserve the educational foundation both to make independent informed choices, and to recognise the importance (and genealogy) of enfranchisement (see the introduction to Chapter 29). Recent evidence suggests that the passage of time since the democratic crises and associated bloodshed of the twentieth century has diminished younger generations' appreciation of democracy and increased their appetite for authoritarianism (Foa and Mounk, 2016). The question of what it means to be a citizen has therefore rarely been more pertinent or pressing, nor so complex, being bound up with issues of identity, constitutional flux and a sense of belonging in a globalised environment. The recent emergence of the 'post-truth' phenomenon, notably in political life, provides a further imperative to furnish young people (and indeed all citizens) with the 'epistemological literacy' (Britton, 2012) to appraise information critically and sceptically. In Scotland, the question of identity is often obfuscated, despite, or perhaps because of, the ongoing constitutional debate. However uncomfortable many schools and local authorities might feel about addressing such issues head on (see Head et al., 2015), we surely owe it to our young people to educate them for the complexities, challenges and opportunities of citizenship in the twenty-first century.

## REFERENCES

Biesta, G. (2008) 'What kind of citizen? What kind of democracy? Citizenship education and the Scottish Curriculum for Excellence', *Scottish Educational Review*, 40 (2), 38–52.

Britton, A. (2012) 'The citizenship teacher and controversial issues', in J. Brown., H. Ross and P. Munn, (eds), *Democratic Citizenship in Schools: Teaching Controversial Issues, Traditions and Accountability*. Edinburgh: Dunedin Academic Press.

Davies, I. (2012) 'Perspectives on citizenship education', in J. Arthur and H. Cremin (eds), *Debates in Citizenship Education*. Abingdon: Routledge.

Foa, R. S. and Mounk, Y. (2016) 'The democratic disconnect', *Journal of Democracy*, 27 (3,) 5–17.

Frazer, E. (2003) 'Citizenship education: anti-political culture and political education in Britain', in A. Lockyer, B. Crick and J. Annette (eds) *Education for Democratic Citizenship. Issues of Theory and Practice*. Aldershot: Ashgate.

Head, G., Hill, M., Lockyer, A. and MacDonald, C. (2015) *Schools, Political Literacy and the 2014 Scottish Referendum*. Glasgow: Stevenson Trust for Citizenship.

HMIE (2013) *Social Studies 3–18 Curriculum Impact Study*. Online at https://education.gov.scot/improvement/Documents/SocialStudies3to182013Update.pdf

Learning and Teaching Scotland (2002) Education for citizenship: a paper for discussion and development. Dundee and Glasgow: Learning and Teaching Scotland.

One Planet Schools Working Group (2012) *Learning for Sustainability*. Edinburgh: Scottish Government.

Qualifications and Curriculum Authority (1998) *Education for Citizenship and the Teaching of Democracy in Schools. Final Report of the Advisory Group on Citizenship*. (The Crick Report). Online at http://dera.ioe.ac.uk/4385/1/crickreport1998.pdf

# 63

# Outdoor Learning

*Peter Higgins and Robbie Nicol*

Recent conceptual arguments and policy developments have led to a change in the title of this chapter compared to previous editions of *Scottish Education*. Whilst the term 'outdoor education' is still in widespread use (and employed where appropriate below, primarily to preserve historical accuracy) the increasing use of 'outdoor learning' emphasises the value in using the school grounds or local areas, as well as residential outdoor settings. Although education outdoors can contribute to many curricular areas, 'outdoor learning' is widely conceptualised as based on three integrated areas of 'outdoor activities', 'environmental education' and 'personal and social development'. Whatever the focus, an experiential, adventurous and interdisciplinary approach to learning is a central pedagogical theme.

## EARLY DEVELOPMENTS

In the 1960s Scotland became one of the first places in the world where outdoor education became formalised (Higgins, 2002). Baker (2015) has traced various historical strands, including the remarkable antecedent of some forms of current provision; the 'Adventure Schools' (essentially meaning they had an 'open' curriculum) for the poor of the late-sixteenth century to mid-nineteenth century. He also described the early philosophical influences and practical experiments of Geddes, Reddie and Hahn who until the mid-twentieth century railed against monolithic approaches to learning whilst emphasising the benefits in health, personal development and environmental understanding. However, Baker argues, contemporary educational policy support for these initiatives was not forthcoming, and was probably subsumed under policy debates over academic, practical and vocational curricula – essentially that 'Scottish education did not have the educational cultural capacity to engage in outdoor education' (p. 106) and did not capitalise on the 'opportunities for a progressive and alternative educational philosophy' (p. 106), epitomised by the 'Progressive Schools Movement'.

Change came in the 1960s through the development of residential centres (Higgins, 2002; Baker, 2015), and the recent emphasis on local outdoor learning experiences and related policy developments has significantly increased opportunities.

## DEFINITIONAL ISSUES

As interest in outdoor learning has grown it has become an increasingly nuanced concept. More subtle understandings in practice and formal Scottish educational policy have emerged, as evidenced by *Curriculum for Excellence through Outdoor Learning* (CfEtOL), which asserts that:

> The core values of *Curriculum for Excellence* resonate with long-standing key concepts of outdoor learning. Challenge, enjoyment, relevance, depth, development of the whole person and an adventurous approach to learning are at the core of outdoor pedagogy. The outdoor environment encourages staff and students to see each other in a different light, building positive relationships and improving self-awareness and understanding of others. (Learning and Teaching Scotland, 2010, p. 7)

This serves as a useful indication of experiential outdoor pedagogy, and provides the basis of the interdisciplinary learning facilitated outdoors. In terms of location, it is useful to consider a concentric circles model with the school in the centre where outdoor learning opportunities are available in the immediate vicinity of the school grounds, through day trips and residentials, to multi-day expeditions. These approaches are described in detail by Beames et al. (2012).

Ultimately this and related philosophical and practical arguments, alongside policy developments such as CfEtOL, have paved the way for greater inclusivity of educational practice. It has also required shifts in conceptual thinking because the increased variety of places now available for learning had to be matched by appropriate pedagogical approaches. These views are consistent with 'place-based education' which immerses learners in local places familiar to them but which offer unique opportunities for interdisciplinary studies (see Beames et al., 2012).

## POLICY AND CURRICULUM

Policy interest has grown since the Scottish Parliament was established, and in the ten years until 2016, specialist fixed-term Development Officers at Education Scotland were employed to advise practitioners, develop and maintain resources and work with advisory groups. Through the period 2008 to 2010 considerable progress was made, culminating in *Curriculum for Excellence through Outdoor Learning*, which, as far as we know, was the first government document anywhere in the world specifically to link a national curriculum with outdoor learning. The statement that '[t]he journey through education for any child in Scotland must include a series of planned, quality outdoor learning experiences' (Learning and Teaching Scotland, 2010, p. 6) is remarkable as it both legitimises outdoor learning and emphasises that it must be progressive. The document was a cornerstone of a range of subsequent policy developments.

Since 2010, CfEtOL has been supported by growing Scottish Government Internet-based resources (some have been relocated to the National Improvement Hub, https://education.gov.scot/improvement/searchresults?k=outdoor learning) to support teachers to deliver formal and informal curricula outdoors, and also to understand and communicate reasons for doing so. These have been supplemented by those developed by charities, trusts and commercial providers.

An important recent policy development is that of Learning for Sustainability (LfS – Chapter 65). The Scottish Government established an 'LfS Advisory Group' in 2011, and in 2013 ministers accepted all thirty-one recommendations from its report (see www.scotland.gov.uk/Topics/Education/Schools/curriculum/ACE/LearningforSustainability).

Empirical research that led to the concept of LfS highlighted the significance of experiences in nature in developing positive attitudes to sustainability (Christie and Higgins, 2012), and supports the emphasis on outdoor learning in LfS policy, alongside the traditional elements of 'education for sustainable development' and 'global citizenship'. This provides an additional firm policy context for outdoor learning, and many schools and specialist providers are embracing this in their work.

## RECENT RESEARCH

In the past thirty years, research interest has grown substantially and much of the momentum has been built in Scotland. Whilst the University of Edinburgh has had a major role there are now academics and doctoral students with an interest or specialism in the area in most Scottish universities. Published output can be found in specialist and mainstream educational journals and related fields such as sociology, psychology, philosophy and the sciences. Further, academics in these 'mainstream' fields are taking an interest in the outdoors as a 'space' for research, and to explore interdisciplinary issues, for example the relationship between 'greenspace', health and wellbeing, physical activity and environmental understanding and values development. Increasingly these broader environmental aspects have been studied (e.g. Mannion et al., 2015; Natural England, 2016), and this has influenced policy and provision.

The impact of outdoor learning on educational performance has become increasingly evident (e.g. Christie et al., 2016; Natural England, 2016). The former study investigated the impact of structured outdoor learning experiences on Geography and Mathematics – and found that pupils enjoyed learning this way, and that such experiences provided opportunities for pupils to develop critical thinking skills that can be overlooked in early secondary education. This is significant as it relates both to curricular learning and broader pedagogical benefits. Mannion et al. (2015) followed up a 2006 empirical study to detail changing national outdoor learning provision since the introduction of Curriculum for Excellence (CfE). They reported similar findings to Christie et al. (2016) regarding positive learner engagement and educational experience. Many of their findings on national provision show increases in participation as below, and that, across the sector, schools are using the outdoors to address many aspects of CfE, 'Health and Wellbeing' and 'Learning for Sustainability'.

The study by Mannion et al. (2015) was funded by Scottish Natural Heritage (SNH), who have maintained their interest in outdoor learning in general, and specifically biodiversity and health, including supporting the idea of a '*Natural* Health Service' (see www.snh.gov.uk/land-and-sea/managing-recreation-and-access/healthier-scotland/). This is an area of growing interest and relevance across a number of policy areas. Other agencies such as the National Parks, sportscotland and the Forestry Commission have also supported research in these facets of outdoor learning, and related issues such as the impact on attitudes to sustainability (see Chapter 65).

## CONTEMPORARY ISSUES IN OUTDOOR EDUCATION

### Current Provision

The comparative (2006 to 2014) study by Mannion et al. (2015) noted that in preschool and primary, opportunities and average duration of summer-term outdoor learning events (mostly within grounds) increased, with the percentage of time outdoors as a proportion of the preschool day up to 36 per cent in 2014 (compared to 23 per cent in 2006), and in primary schools to thirty minutes per week (up from nineteen minutes in 2006). In secondary schools the increase was marginal, and primarily due to greater commitment to residentials. There were particular challenges for schools in areas of deprivation – arguably where outdoor learning may be most needed and potentially most beneficial.

Relatively few council owned and run outdoor centres continue to operate, but those that do are heavily used. Most receive little or no central funding and many have become charitable trusts. They, like independent commercial or charitable providers, are essentially in a competitive market, where schools select on the basis of a traditional relationship, cost and 'offering'. The educational merit of the residential may or may not be a factor, a paradoxical situation considering these visits take place primarily in the school academic terms.

Provision is uneven with some pupils being taught regularly outside the classroom whilst others may experience a few residential days of outdoor education in their whole school career. Families are expected to pay for residentials and field trips, raising issues over equity, willingness and ability to pay. Whilst some schools and councils have hardship funds to support pupils in need, many do not. This raises ethical issues that are rarely challenged.

## Cost and Time

The increases noted above seem to be a practical outcome of the conceptual arguments for more local outdoor provision (Beames et al., 2012; Christie et al., 2015). However, the variability from school to school, and the relative lack of provision at secondary level, certainly beyond the period of 'broad general education' is unfortunate given the research evidence of impact on pupil learning (Christie et al., 2016; Kuo Ming et al., 2018).

As Mannion et al. (2015) suggest, there remains significant scope for growth across all areas of provision, and doing so requires more teachers to decide to take their classes outdoors and to undertake local journeys which do not incur high costs (and sometimes none). The study by Christie et al., 2016) found evidence that teachers are seeing the potential for teaching subjects outdoors, and dealing with these and issues such as weather and teaching ratios by using school grounds, and the local environment, and capitalising on the links with learning for sustainability.

Opportunities for 'real-world' outdoor learning experiences provide a valuable counterpart to classroom subject-based learning, and can be linked closely to the expectations and delivery of CfE. Hence, outdoor learning should not be seen as a demand on curricular time but more an issue of the teacher choosing the most appropriate location to realise the curricular potential of CfE (Beames et al., 2012).

## Safety, Licensing and Regulation

Whilst accidents in outdoor learning are rare, specific legislation (Activities Centres (Young Persons' Safety) 1995 Act) and a dedicated licensing and inspection agency – the Adventure Activities Licensing Service (see www.hse.gov.uk/aala/aals.htm) – provide the legal framework for safety in the field. This is effective and reassuring, and the inspectors have been a source of valuable advice to practitioners. This has contributed to a conceptual shift from a focus on 'risk assessment' towards 'risk–benefit analysis'. The service has been subject to a UK review (2011–12) when Scotland decided to retain the service, and a further national consultation (2017–18) is underway.

If the curricular potential of CfE is to be more fully realised then local authorities will need to adopt a more enabling approach to support teachers in overcoming perceived barriers. Many of Scotland's councils have adopted online registering of local and residential school trips called 'Evolve' (see http://edufocus.co.uk/pages/evolve/visits.asp). Whilst this requires central coordination at council and school level, it provides both reassurance and useful data on outdoor learning activities and other school visits.

## Representation and Management of Outdoor Provision

There is no national framework for outdoor education in Scotland. The Scottish Advisory Panel for Outdoor Education is a forum for those who hold an advisory position within the thirty-two Scottish councils, whilst the Association of Heads of Outdoor Education Centres is similar but for centre managers. National Governing Bodies (NGBs) regulate outdoor instructional awards which, although useful to benchmark quality teaching of outdoor activities, are not intended to meet broader educational and curricular ambitions. A number of other agencies have specific interests, such as non-governmental organisations (NGOs; Field Studies Council, Royal Society for the Protection of Birds, John Muir Trust) and government agencies (SNH, Forestry Commission), most of which collaborate through the 'Real World Learning' partnership. Whilst this demonstrates the breadth of the 'sector' there is no representative body, nor organisation for teachers who teach outdoors. Consequently, it can be difficult for policymakers to gain an overview of provision, training needs or effectiveness of delivery (see below). One of the important roles of Education Scotland's Development Officers has been to convene a National Implementation Group for Outdoor Learning which brings together most of the parties listed above. However, with the discontinuation of Development Officer post, the future of this group is uncertain.

## Teaching Qualifications

Whilst the GTCS recognises outdoor education as a teaching subject and also through its professional recognition scheme (see www.gtcs.org.uk/professional-update/research-practitioner-enquiry/professional-recognition/professional-recognition.aspx), there is no requirement for teacher education institutions to deliver initial teacher education outdoors, and none offers formal qualifications. (There are Master of Science (MSc) programmes at the University of Edinburgh, but these are not specific teaching qualifications.) This is paradoxical given the status of CfEtOL and the Learning for Sustainability policy which established that 'outdoor learning should be a regular, progressive curriculum-led experience for all learners' (www.scotland.gov.uk/Topics/Education/Schools/curriculum/ACE/LearningforSustainability).

Similarly, the lack of a nationally coordinated in-service training for education outdoors leaves appropriate training/qualification open to interpretation. As noted above, the widespread acceptance of outdoor activities qualifications seems inappropriate as these focus on safe and professional practice in skill development rather than 'education'. Similarly, specialist qualifications such as 'forest school leader' are unnecessary for most teachers to take their classes out to a local wood, beach and so on. Rather, what is needed is a means of helping teachers (who are curricular experts) to be confident in local outdoor learning.

## Quality Assurance

The absence of a coherent understanding of the nature of outdoor learning and its benefits by education authorities and teachers continues to limit the quality and quantity of young people's experiences. Development Officers in Education Scotland have been central in liaising with the professional community and facilitating progress. However, recent changes in educational policy mean that in common with many other aspects of education, such posts are no longer deemed necessary. Whilst CfEtOL and LfS are positive developments, the lack of formal teaching qualifications and quality assurance processes limit the consistency of outdoor learning experiences, though the expectations included in *How Good is Our School? Version 4* (Education Scotland, 2015) go some way towards this.

## FUTURE PROSPECTS

Taken together, Scotland's knowledge base, culture, education system, infrastructure, climate and outdoor environment mean it is well placed to continue to develop outdoor learning as a legitimate, interdisciplinary, pedagogical approach that impacts upon personal, social and ecological/environmental domains within all sectors of formal education. In short, outdoor learning in the broad sense as well as in its contribution to learning for sustainability should be an everyday experience for all children who pass through the Scottish education system.

## REFERENCES

Baker, M. (2015) *Policy Development of Outdoor Education in Scotland*. Unpublished PhD thesis, University of Edinburgh.

Beames, S., Higgins, P. and Nicol, R. (2012) *Learning outside the Classroom: Theory and Guidelines for Practice*. New York: Routledge.

Christie, E. and Higgins, P. (2012) *The Impact of Outdoor Learning on Attitudes to Sustainability*. Edinburgh: Field Studies Council/University of Edinburgh.

Christie, B., Beames, S. and Higgins, P. (2016) 'Culture, context and critical thinking: Scottish secondary school teachers' and pupils' experiences of outdoor learning', *British Educational Research Journal*, 42 (3), 417–37.

Christie, B., Higgins, P. and Nicol, R. (2015) 'Curricular outdoor learning in Scotland: from practice to policy', in C. Henderson, B. Humbersone and H. Prince (eds), *International Handbook of Outdoor Recreation*. London: Routledge, pp. 113–20.

Education Scotland (2015) *How Good is Our School? Fourth edition*. Online at https://education.gov.scot/improvement/Documents/Frameworks_SelfEvaluation/FRWK2_NIHeditHGIOS/FRWK2_HGIOS4.pdf

Higgins, P. (2002) 'Outdoor education in Scotland', *Journal of Adventure Education and Outdoor Learning*, 2 (2), 149–68.

Kuo, M., Browning M. H. M. and Penner M. L. (2018) Do Lessons in Nature Boost Subsequent Classroom Engagement? Refueling Students in Flight. *Frontiers in Psychology*, 8, 2253. https://www.ncbi.nlm.nih.gov/pmc/articles/PMC5758746/

Learning and Teaching Scotland (2010) *Curriculum for Excellence through Outdoor Learning*. Glasgow: Learning and Teaching Scotland.

Mannion, G., Mattu, L. and Wilson, M. (2015) *Teaching, Learning, and Play in the Outdoors: A Survey of School and Pre-school Provision in Scotland*. Scottish Natural Heritage Commissioned Report No. 779. Online at www.snh.org.uk/pdfs/publications/commissioned_reports/779.pdf

Natural England (2016) *Natural Connections Demonstration Project, 2012–2016: Final Report*. Natural England Commissioned Report NECR215. Online at http://publications.naturalengland.org.uk/publication/6636651036540928

Scottish Government (2012) *Learning for Sustainability*. Report of the One Planet Schools' Ministerial Advisory Group. Online at www.scotland.gov.uk/Topics/Education/Schools/curriculum/ACE/OnePlanetSchools

# 64

# Children's Rights

*John I'Anson*

## INTRODUCTION

Since its formal inauguration in 1989, the United Nations Convention on the Rights of the Child (UNCRC) (United Nations, 1989) has become the most ratified of all conventions. Although the outcome of some ten years of deliberation immediately prior to formal agreement being reached, the beginnings of the process that led to the convention can be traced back to the Second World War. The implications of the UNCRC are indeed far-reaching since, as Cleland and Sutherland (2009, p. 2) observe, the convention:

> enshrines not only familiar social rights, such as the rights to health and education, but also civil and political rights, in the provisions for children's rights to freedom of expression, thought, conscience and religion and to be heard in all matters affecting them.

Clearly such a broad agenda involves multiple intersections with legal, policy and professional agendas at a national level, and with different theoretical traditions of inquiry too. This chapter is specifically concerned with the educational implications of children's rights in Scotland. Consequently, having outlined some of the key features of the UNCRC as an international legal text that aims to set minimum standards for children, together with a survey of key themes and theoretical orientations that have characterised its translation within the field of children's rights more generally, we will then consider the distinctive legal and policy context in Scotland, and explore how children's rights are refracted within a Scottish educational context.

## THE UNCRC AS INTERNATIONAL LEGAL TEXT

The UNCRC is part of an extensive legal framework of human rights, and as such it relates to a number of conventions and covenants that also have a bearing upon the lives of children and young people. Its fifty-four articles are not set out in any particular order of importance since each right is intended to be both inalienable and indivisible. That said, a number of key principles that variously inform their construction can be discerned, and Tisdall (2015, p. 810) has summarised these as:

non-discrimination (Article 2); a child's best interests must be a primary consideration in all actions concerning children (Article 3); a child's rights to survival and development (Article 6); and a child's right to express views freely in all matters affecting the child (Article 12).

It is worth noting at the outset that the UNCRC is a legal text; as such, it has certain advantages, such as its universal appeal and especially its authority to insist upon certain obligations. So, for example, states that are signatories to the convention are required to report every five years on how they have complied with rights and obligations under that requirement. However, the fact that the convention is a legal text also means that it has to be *translated* into other-than-legal modes of discourse. Such a translation is necessary if the articles of the convention are to be mobilised in ways that might impact the multiple cultures, spaces and relations that have a bearing upon children and young people's lives.

Foregrounding the issue of translation is important for several reasons. Once a translation has been achieved it usually becomes invisible and hence no longer thought about. There is a translation involved from the language used in Article 12, for instance, that speaks of 'the views of the child' and 'the right to express those views freely in all matters affecting the child' to the notion of 'children's voice', that is usually regarded as equivalent or as making the same kind of sense. As we will see below, the notion of 'voice' brings with it a particular set of assumptions that foreground certain aspects and not others, and these may differ according to context. Only if we notice such translations does it become possible to raise questions as to whether a given translation remains appropriate for a particular context and purpose, and, in the light of this, to consider whether some alternative response is desirable. Of course, the issue of who decides what is, or should be, the case in a given circumstance is a moot point that is often glossed over. Another way in which issues of translation can be surfaced is through international comparison, as this can help to surface a number of cultural assumptions – and elisions – that might otherwise go unnoticed. Thus, for example, studies have compared the approach taken in New Zealand, where equality in terms of biculturality is privileged, with Sweden, where the focus is upon induction into explicitly social democratic values and practices. A comparison of these different cultural contexts therefore gives insight into how children's rights are interpreted and mobilised differently and enables questions to emerge that might otherwise remain unconsidered.

So in what ways has the legal text of the UNCRC been translated into practice to date? Here, three key themes are identified that have had a significant presence in this work of mediation both within Scotland and more broadly. The dominant theoretical account within which these approaches have been framed will then be outlined. We will then be in a position to explore the distinctive shape that this translation work has taken in Scotland before raising questions as to possible future directions of travel that build upon this trajectory, that also ask questions about the educational implications of taking children's rights seriously.

## KEY THEMES IN THE TRANSLATION OF CHILDREN'S RIGHTS FROM LEGAL TEXT TO PRACTICE

### Children's Voice

Perhaps the most familiar translation in the case of children's rights is that of 'voice', which is no doubt prompted in large part through the incorporation of 'the child's view' in Article 12 of the UNCRC, as we have already seen. The very familiarity of the 'child's voice' in connection with children's rights discourse, can lead this translation to be regarded as unproblematic. However, in recent years there have been a number of critical investigations that have inquired into how the 'voice' presented in a given text has been produced: the extent to which contextual features, that are usually regarded as 'background', have informed this; and the ways in which adults have, perhaps unwittingly, circumscribed the agenda for discussion, and have had the final say in the redaction of texts that purportedly represent the views of children, for example. In these circumstances it is easy for a decontextualised presentation of themes and illustrations to support a particular writer's narrative, rather than this necessarily being what the children and young people might otherwise have said.

Furthermore, the notion of 'voice' might itself be regarded as somewhat problematic, since it appears to assume – as well as produce – precisely the kind of Western autonomous individualism that has been criticised in a number of studies. Whilst such an individualism might be characteristic of ideals associated with Minority World childhoods, it may not fit Majority World childhoods where different values and ideals are in play. Moreover, the complicity of 'voice' with the conditions and disciplinary logics associated with market economies has also been subject to trenchant critique. And so, while there may well be strategic reasons for promoting such autonomy as a means of presenting the child as a competent actor, this runs headlong into a number of theoretical and practical difficulties. Not the least of these is its tendency to create a series of binary oppositions, that include installing competition between children and other rights bearers, such as parents and educators, and a tension between a child's voice given in the immediate present, and that developed through time (which is sometimes indexed as a tension between 'being' and 'becoming'). Here, a translation of the UNCRC into practice that at first appears as benign and unproblematic, begins to unravel, raising some disquieting questions in the process.

## Children's Participation

The theme of children's 'participation' has also become a common means through which children's rights have been translated into practice. One of the advantages of this theme is the links this affords with sister fields of study such as inclusion, social justice and work on children's civic participation. An early, but still influential framework for thinking about children's participation in practice was Hart's (1992) 'ladder of participation' that ranged from forms of non-participation such as 'tokenism', all the way to 'child-initiated and shared decision making with adults' at the other. The foregrounding of participation (which is also aligned with Article 12 of the UNCRC) reflects a relational focus that has been a significant concern within both research and practice.

Such studies tend to foreground relations within a particular site and focus upon the qualities of relations that enable children and young people to thrive – in some cases, in ways that exceed what might otherwise have been expected from the demographic data available. The theme of participation also orients attention to the different spaces of children's participation, with a recognition that children's geographies are complex and cannot be assumed or known in advance of empirical investigation (e.g. Holt, 2011).

## Intergenerational Perspectives

Linked to the relational focus associated with participation, intergenerational relations has also emerged as a key theme in recent years, especially in relation to the translation of children's rights into policy. Thus in their research, Mannion and Gilbert (2015, p. 229) noted: 'the idea that intergenerational learning is made possible through responding to differences which are found in the relations between generations and the relations between people and the places they inhabit'. The theme of intergenerational relations includes discussion of some of the professional dilemmas that are surfaced within specific contexts, such as in Physical Education (PE). According to Öhman and Quennerstedt (2017): 'The avoidance of intergenerational touch is increasingly justified by referring to the children's rights agenda. Here, arguments for "no-touching" are linked to children's right to be protected from harm.' Following this principle, however, can lead to tensions both with pedagogical imperatives within PE, and with other rights. In this study, therefore, the authors explore some of the professional dilemmas that accrue from taking an intergenerational perspective, and outline an alternative approach that is responsive to the complexities encountered in actual practice.

Relational perspectives that foreground both intergenerational dimensions and place are also linked with more recent work in children's rights that takes an explicit ecological stance, especially as regards the values that inform sustainability. In such accounts, people and place are regarded as reciprocally co-emergent. Intergenerational relations are also acknowledged as having significant consequences for thinking about citizenship, especially as regards implications for multigenerational citizenship and its relevance for children.

## THEORETICAL TRANSLATIONS

Much of this work of translation in relation to children's rights remains strongly influenced by theories associated with the New Sociology of Childhood (e.g. James and Prout, 1997). The New Sociology of Childhood emerged at much the same time as the UNCRC and was immediately to hand as a theoretical framing that legitimised a concern with children's agency and expression, especially as regards children's present lives as worthy of concern. This approach to theorising has become – and remains – highly influential, especially in Scandinavia, UK, Central and Southern Europe, and Australia, where, for many theorists and practitioners, it is the default understanding and legitimation.

The New Sociology of Childhood challenged deep-seated assumptions that childhood was simply a preparation for the attainment of adulthood and that consequently the views of children – as children – had little value or traction. The foregrounding of children and young people's present views has promoted innovative practice, greater consultation and children's involvement in research practices. However, where this results in *an exclusive focus upon the present*, eliciting children and young people's preferences in the 'here and now', may well be educationally limiting if this does not include children's becomings as well. For to privilege what is currently the case over a longitudinal framing through time, may inadvertently neglect educational questions as to how new critical capacities are attained; induction into such practices may be necessary for 'reading' situations and imagining alternative horizons of possibility that are more inclusive of the views of children and young people. In other words, an exclusive focus on an *immediate present* may foreclose inquiry into the complex issues that arise as a young person's narrative, and powers of expression, change through time.

This is to raise critical questions as to how a children's rights agenda might connect with education, since the question of education (raised in Articles 28 and 29 of the UNCRC), can only fully arise once the issue of children and young people's change through time is addressed. To raise the question of education is, therefore, to enquire into the kinds of critical capacities that children and young people might draw upon so as to meaningfully contribute towards – and shape – the kind of society to which they belong, both now and in future. This was a key point raised by David Harvey (2006, p. 88) in his Amnesty Lecture at Oxford, 'The Right to the City', given back in 2003, when he observed that:

> The right to change the city is not an abstract right, but a right that inheres in daily practices, whether we are conscious of that right or not. ... How can I hope for an alternative possible urban world, even imagine its contours, its conundrums, and its charms, when I am so deeply immersed in the experience of what already exists?

To create moments 'in which our imaginations can wander and wonder about alternative possible urban worlds' (Harvey, 2006, p. 88), and to engage seriously with these kinds of questions, is to raise fundamental questions about the intersection of children's rights with education: as to the kinds of educational purpose and practice that might support this.

Whilst the New Sociology of Childhood remains a dominant theoretical framing, some commentators have argued that much research work in children's rights has become theoretically unadventurous and somewhat limited. In recent years, there is evidence in the literature of studies that draw upon a wider range of theorising, such as capabilities theory, relational ethics, together with an acknowledgement of other European educational traditions, such as *Bildung* and *Didactics* and, albeit much less frequently, other-than-European traditions. A number of studies have drawn upon Freire and, more frequently still, Foucault, so as to exercise a critical reading of sites and texts, whether this be an analysis of relational dynamics in a classroom, or an investigation of gendered images within school textbooks, for example. Having outlined some of the contours that characterise work in the field of children's rights more generally, how is this specifically refracted within the Scottish context?

## SCOTTISH TRANSLATIONS

The themes and theoretical translations that we have surveyed above, have also had a considerable impact upon children's rights research and practice within Scotland. However, in recent years one translation in particular has been foregrounded within the Scottish policy context, where children's rights have become associated with children's health and wellbeing. The pairing of children's rights with children and young people's wellbeing is a key feature of the 'landmark' legislation passed by the Scottish Parliament in 2014 – the Children and Young People (Scotland) Act 2014 (CYPA). This effectively puts much of the *Getting it Right for Every Child* (GIRFEC) approach onto a legal footing. GIRFEC identifies eight indicators of wellbeing, and these are often summarised under the acronym SHANARRI, that stands for: safe, healthy, achieving, nurtured, active, respected, responsible and included. An influential publication that provides guidance for practitioners, describes GIRFEC as the 'bedrock' for all children's services (Scottish Government, 2012, p. 6). A wide range of curricular initiatives draw upon this framing, and it is particularly evident in recent curriculum policy such as *Building the Ambition: National Practice Guidance on Early Learning and Childcare* (Scottish Government, 2014). The GIRFEC approach has been valuable in providing a shared language between different professionals working with children and young people, such as teachers and social workers.

Be that as it may, according to Tisdall (2015, p. 807), children's rights and children's wellbeing 'differ conceptually, methodologically and politically' and should not, therefore, be regarded as equivalent concepts. The different genealogies of wellbeing and rights need to be acknowledged rather than simply conflated into a single discourse. The strong association of children's rights with a wellbeing discourse in Scotland also runs the risk that other, specifically educational, imperatives become sidelined. This raises a number of critical educational issues, especially in regard to the intersection of children's rights discourse with that of education per se. And so, whilst acknowledging the bold steps that Scotland has taken thus far in translating a children's rights agenda in terms of health and wellbeing, we might, nevertheless, still wish to question 'how good is our translation'? In other words, to what extent does a translation aligned primarily with a discourse of health and wellbeing address specifically educational issues, and, if not, what are the implications of keeping the question of the *educational* intersection of children's rights and education live?

Here, it is worthwhile recalling that education derives from the Latin *educere*, which means, quite literally, 'to lead out'; from this root, it then becomes possible to trace a number of significant lines along which a distinctively educational approach might be articulated. One such approach characterises an educational account as consisting in three elements: the critical, experimental and ethical elements, respectively (I'Anson and Jasper, 2017). Although distinct, each of these three elements is, in practice, mutually constitutive and so each is a necessary dimension of education. Within these terms, therefore, a distinctively educational translation of children's rights will seek to develop policies and pedagogies that actively keep in play the critical, experimental and ethical elements. Conversely, a translation that neglects one or more of these elements would, within these terms, be regarded as lacking in these respects.

And it is here that one might wish to raise a series of educational questions concerning the translation of a children's rights agenda within a health and wellbeing framing. For this, it might be argued, is to foreground the ethical element over the other educational elements, the capacities for critique and experimentation. Within these terms, we might wish to ask how, for example, a child or young person might acquire critical literacy practices, or be afforded opportunities for trying things out empirically so as to learn from such experiences. These opportunities might be crucial for meaningful and creative involvement in the kinds of re-imagining society, towards which David Harvey gestured, above.

Important though a health and wellbeing translation is, this does not fully encompass the educational implications of children's rights: whilst this addresses the ethical element of education, an exclusive focus upon wellbeing may lead to a forgetfulness of the critical and experimental elements. Consequently, such a translation may neglect the kinds of critical capacity that the intersection between education and children's rights might otherwise engender. In this connection, it is noteworthy that the two other crosscutting educational themes in the Scottish 3–18 curriculum – those of numeracy and literacy – tend to be presented as separate and at some remove from a children's rights perspective, which, as we have seen, is linked primarily with health and well-being.

Within a Scottish educational context, therefore, significant steps have been taken as regards the translation of a children's rights agenda within the terms of an ethics of care, but wider questions remain vis-à-vis ways in which broader educational implications and translations might be realised. One such issue concerns the extent to which children are educated about their rights as such. Research undertaken by BEMIS (2013), in relation to both teachers and children's knowledge of their human rights in Scotland, for example, found that children's understandings were weak, and that teachers often felt ill-equipped and uncertain when teaching about rights perspectives. This points up a need for such issues to be taken up both within initial teacher education (ITE) and within the context of continuing professional development for teachers (Struthers, 2015). The foregrounding of a dynamic understanding of education in terms of critical, experimental and ethical elements also opens up questions as to the role that specific subjects might play in relation to a broader rights-informed education. This is to raise a series of educational questions as to which knowledges and which practices are implicated in thinking more fully about the implications of a children's rights agenda. Thus, the role of media literacy, for instance, might be considered vital at a time when untruths are peddled as 'post truth' and the reiteration of negative and one-sided representations of 'Islam' are commonplace. Likewise, a more extended educational discussion of rights might include within its purview some of the ethical implications of taking the complex issues raised by acts of cultural appropriation seriously.

The educational implications of taking a children's rights approach are therefore far-reaching indeed, with ramifications that cut across all subject areas and activities. This raises a challenge to many settled areas of practice, with the pedagogical implications extending to how routine activities – such as lesson planning – are carried out. In this connection, for example, most lesson planning approaches that students on ITE programmes are inducted into are behaviourist and teacher-centred in approach. The introduction of rights-based approaches is typically grafted upon such underlying orientations, rather than beginning with rights-informed questions that might foreground consultation and the promotion of children's capacities to meaningfully engage in pedagogical issues. This is just one issue that is illustrative of the kinds of pedagogical rethinking that the intersection of children's rights and education might provoke.

Of course, the question then emerges as to how a children's rights-based approach is evaluated: at what point is a professional's ethical responsibility to children discharged, how is this determined and by whom? At the present time, professional codes of conduct typically resolve such questions in terms of lists of performance indicators that an individual professional is expected to evidence in particular ways. Whether this results in a more radical educational questioning (in terms of, for example, the three elements of education), is a moot point. As far as institutions are concerned, within Scotland, the uptake of the Rights Respecting Schools Award (RRSA) initiative has been high. This approach, organised by the United Nations Children's Fund (UNICEF), designates schools as 'rights respecting' in response to a series of requirements that schools have to fulfil. Such initiatives undoubtedly raise the profile of children's rights and offer schools guidance in relation to how they might more effectively translate the articles of the UNCRC into everyday practice. Although no comparable research in relation to this has been carried out in Scotland, research carried out in England has raised a number of critical questions apropos whose voice tends to be listened to and the extent to which consultation with children and young people extends to a school's core educational priorities and pedagogical practices (Robinson, 2014).

## CONCLUSION

This chapter has mapped some of the distinctive contours that characterise the translation of children's rights into practice within Scottish Education. It has been argued that significant steps have been taken in Scotland to engage a children's rights agenda, not least through new statutory requirements and the follow-through into policy enactments. All such work involves translations, and, in the case of Scotland, this has been under the sign of children and young people's health and wellbeing. This, as we have seen, has raised the profile of rights and the responsibilities of adults in regard to children and young people's care and wellbeing, and has in turn inaugurated a shared language, via the GIRFEC framework, for inter-professional cooperation and dialogue. However, significant issues remain if the question of the intersection of children's rights with education is raised.

Whilst the importance of children and young people's wellbeing cannot be overstated, a more fully *educational* response to children's rights will require further translations that impact across even broader horizons of concern. In particular, the potential contribution of the other two cross-cutting themes of literacy and numeracy, together with the distinctive contributions of different subject areas will be necessary if children and young people are to be encouraged to engage critically, ethically and experimentally in practice. The intersection of children's rights with education, in short, involves the development of critical capacities that enable children to engage more fully in educational dialogues that concern their own becomings. Such work is to welcome the incoming of the new, whether this be through critical readings of current situations, opportunities to think otherwise, or an acknowledgement of the rights and responsibilities that come from all relational engagements.

## ACKNOWLEDGEMENT

I am grateful to Dr Andrea Priestley for conversations in relation to children's rights in a Scottish context.

## REFERENCES

BEMIS (2013) *A Review of Human Rights Education in Schools in Scotland*. March. Online at http:// bemis.org.uk/documents/BEMIS%20HRE%20in%20Schools%20Report.pdf

Cleland, A. and Sutherland, E. E. (2009) 'Children's rights in Scotland – where are we now?' in A. Cleland and E. E. Sutherland (eds), *Children's Rights in Scotland*. Edinburgh: W. Green/ Thomson Reuters, pp. 1–22.

Hart, R. (1992) *Children's Participation: From Tokenism to Citizenship*. Florence: UNICEF International Child Development Centre. Online at https://www.unicef-irc.org/publications/ pdf/childrens_participation.pdf

Harvey, D. (2006) 'The right to the city', in R. Scholar (ed.), *Divided Cities*. Oxford and New York: Oxford University Press, pp. 83–103.

Holt, L. (ed.) (2011) *Geographies of Children, Youth and Families: An International Perspective*. Abingdon and New York: Routledge.

I'Anson, J. and Jasper, A. J. (2017) *Schooling Indifference*. London and New York: Routledge.

James, A. and Prout, A. (1997) *Constructing and Reconstructing Childhood: Contemporary Issues in the Sociological Study of Childhood*. London and New York: Routledge.

Mannion, G. and Gilbert, J. (2015) 'Place-responsive intergenerational education', in R. Vanderbeck and N. Worth (eds), *Intergenerational Space*. London: Routledge, pp. 228–41.

Öhman, M. and Quennerstedt, A. (2017) 'Questioning the no-touch discourse in physical education from a children's rights perspective', *Sport, Education and Society*, 22 (3), 305–20.

Robinson, C. (2014) 'Developing mutually respectful adult-child relationships in schools: is this a reality experienced equally by all pupils?' *Research Intelligence*, British Educational Research Association (BERA), issue 125, pp. 18–19.

Scottish Government (2012) *A Guide to Getting it Right for Every Child*. Online at www.scotland.gov. uk/Resource/0039/00394308.pdf

Scottish Government (2013) High resolution GIRFEC diagrams. Available at: www.gov.scot/ Topics/People/Young-People/gettingitright/resources/girfec-diagrams

Scottish Government (2014) *Building the Ambition: National Practice Guidance on Early Learning and Childcare*. Online at https://education.gov.scot/improvement/Pages/elc1buildingtheambition. aspx

Struthers, A. (2015) *Building Blocks for Improving Human Rights Education within Initial Teacher Education in Scotland*. A Report by the Centre for Human Rights in Practice, Warwick Law School, University of Warwick. Online at https://www2.warwick.ac.uk/fac/soc/law/research/ centres/chrp/publications/building_blocks_report.pdf

Tisdall, E. K. M. (2015) 'Children's rights and children's wellbeing: equivalent policy concepts?' *Journal of Social Policy*, 44 (4), 807–23.

United Nations (1989) *The United Nations Convention on the Rights of the Child* (*UNCRC*), General Assembly resolution 44/25, 20 Nov. 1989. U.N. Doc. A/ RES/44/25. Online at: www.ohchr. org/en/professionalinterest/pages/crc.aspx

# 65

# Learning for Sustainability

*Peter Higgins and Beth Christie*

## INTRODUCTION

It is clear that the long-term future of our planet cannot be taken for granted. This, and the associated notion of education that takes this responsibility seriously, is a long-standing implicit and, more recently, explicit value of the Scottish education community. The concept of 'sustainability', within a Scottish educational context, arose from these values.

Whilst there are many historical antecedents, there can be little doubt that the work of the Scots polymath Sir Patrick Geddes (1854–1932) contributed significantly to our awareness. His educational philosophy, his approach to community planning, his contribution to our understanding of our dependence on ecological processes, and his conceptual 'Think global, act local' message which, although it resonates through his writings, does not appear as a distinct phrase within his work (Higgins and Nicol, 2011), all remain influential. Similarly, the Scottish émigré John Muir's championing of the national parks movement has been central to the global recognition of the value of biodiversity. More recently, a Scot, Professor John Smyth was one of a small team who wrote a significant part of the declaration of the 1992 Earth Summit in Rio de Janeiro (Agenda 21) and, in particular, Chapter 36 on 'Education, training and public participation'. Whilst these may be disparate figures, their combined work and that of others has provided Scottish 'sustainability educators' with a legacy to build on which has local, and perhaps even more international, credibility and respect.

Characteristic of a contested field there has been ongoing definitional and terminological discussions surrounding these ideas for much of the past century. Such debate has influenced changing awareness of our impacts on, for example, biodiversity and climate change, our perspectives on our global responsibilities, and a range of moral, philosophical and practical dimensions. Recently, the internationally significant national educational concept of 'Learning for Sustainability' (LfS) has become part of Scottish educational policy. This development builds on a number of factors such as: a greater awareness of the scale of our impacts and significance of 'sustainability'; challenging and supportive developments by the General Teaching Council for Scotland (GTCS), the 'third sector' and academia; a range of United Nations (UN) and other international initiatives; and changes in government policy focus. Learning for Sustainability offers a holistic pedagogical approach that seeks to build the values, skills and knowledge necessary to develop practices within schools, communities and, at governance levels within teacher education, accord with the collective aim of taking action for a sustainable future.

## THE EMERGENCE OF LfS: A TERMINOLOGICAL DISCUSSION

A description of an educational approach to 'sustainability' demands a prior discussion of this term. In international policy statements the most commonly used variant is 'sustainable development' (SD). This term was coined at the World Commission on Environment and Development as a pragmatic approach to bridging the gap between the need for 'sustainability' (as an ecological imperative that demonstrates that growth cannot be unlimited, and the imperative to establish a human/ecosystem equilibrium), and the need for 'development' in many human communities around the world. This responsibility was succinctly defined in *Our Common Future*, generally known as the 'Brundtland Report' (World Commission on Environment and Development, 1987), as 'the ability to make development sustainable to ensure that it meets the needs of the present without compromising the ability of future generations to meet their own needs' (p. 16). While this definition has been both elaborated and critiqued (e.g. for not defining terms such as 'development', 'needs', 'generations'), it has stood the test of time and is generally accepted to imply human current and intergenerational social equity. However, though it is rarely cited, the report's final statement that 'in its broadest sense, the strategy for sustainable development aims to promote harmony among human beings and between humanity and nature' (para 81) somewhat redresses the balance. Recently, Martin et al. (2013) emphasised the significance of human/ecosystem equilibrium in describing education for sustainable development (ESD) as 'a process of learning how to make decisions that consider the long-term future of the economy, ecology and equity of all communities' (p. 1523), where '*all* communities' is intended to signal our interdependence by including all living communities on the planet.

Nonetheless, despite its wide adoption internationally and by the UN and United Nations Educational Scientific and Cultural Organization (UNESCO), the Scottish education community was uneasy about the implicit direction of 'education for sustainable development'. A preference for an approach that built knowledge and skills to support decision making, and a term that invited critique – 'sustainable development education' (SDE) – arose in the 1990s. The fortunes of the field in the period 1993–2007 have been traced by Lavery and Smyth (2003) and McNaughton (2007). In the following account these terms (ESD and SDE) and its current variant, LfS, are used in their contemporary context. This foregrounding is necessary as it maps the philosophical and pragmatic development that has led to the current concept of LfS.

## THE EMERGENCE OF LFS: THE POLITICAL CONTEXT

The United Nations Decade of Education for Sustainable Development (UNDESD) during the period 2005–2014 served as a stimulus for SDE, building upon both Scotland's rich tradition and the introduction of Curriculum for Excellence (CfE). A number of these achievements are recorded in the mid-decade and final reports (Higgins and Lavery, 2013); however, as the end of the decade approached there was concern that momentum would be lost and prospects of curricular inclusion of SDE would recede. In the final years of the decade several independent but connected initiatives proved to have a telling impact on the future development of what became known as 'Learning for Sustainability'.

## A Broad Policy Context

Successive Scottish Governments have made a commitment to renewable energy and 'green employment', and since 2007 there has been a move to meet all of Scotland's demand for electricity by renewables by 2020, with the associated expectation of employment opportunities. In this context it was (and continues to be) advantageous for relevant technological and social aspects of SD to be considered in schools and further education (FE)/higher education (HE) institutions. In essence, aspects of sustainability have become accepted as a national ambition.

## Learning for Sustainability Scotland: A United Nations Recognised Regional Centre of Expertise on ESD for Scotland

As early as 2010, the SDE community began to discuss ways to maintain the momentum beyond the end of the decade. In 2012 an application went forward to the United Nations University to establish a UN recognised Regional Centre of Expertise in ESD for Scotland (RCE Scotland – see http://learningforsustainabilityscotland.org/). This was approved later that year, and since then its role has been to act as a central conduit for information, develop projects through working groups and support a range of third sector organisations and a broader membership community. It has also added to Scotland's international profile in the field.

## The General Teaching Council for Scotland's Professional Standards

In December 2012 the GTCS published its revised 'professional standards' which became part of a national framework for teachers' professional learning and development. Learning for sustainability is now embedded in the professional values and personal commitments sections of the three new Professional Standards relating to Registration, Career-long Professional Learning, and Leadership and Management, and every teacher and education professional is expected to demonstrate LfS in their practice. Whilst the standards are under review in 2018, LfS looks set to remain, as currently, a central focus.

## A Manifesto Commitment

As early as 2010 various agencies began to lobby political parties to include commitments to SDE in their manifestos for the 2011 Scottish parliamentary elections. Perhaps most significant was the World Wide Fund for Nature Scotland's success in persuading the Scottish National Party (SNP) to include a commitment to exploring 'One Planet Schools' (in the context of our current use of three planets' worth of resources) in their manifesto.

## The One Planet Schools Group

In 2011 the SNP government established several ministerial advisory groups with relevant remits. The remit of the 'One Planet Schools' Advisory Group was to explore the concept of 'One Planet Schools' within the context of Curriculum for Excellence, and reflect the general thrust of *Learning for Change* (Scottish Government, 2010; see also www.gov. scot/Topics/Education/Schools/curriculum/ACE/OnePlanetSchools). This signalled the government's intent to encourage schools to gradually reduce their use of resources and develop a values orientation that addresses sustainability through a whole school approach. The ministerial advisory group report (titled *Learning for Sustainability*) was published in December 2012 (Scottish Government, 2014) and established a model of LfS that integrated three equally important facets – Sustainable Development, Global Citizenship Education and Outdoor Learning with an overarching aim to develop: 'a whole school approach that enables the school and its wider community to build the values, attitudes, knowledge, skills and confidence needed to develop practices and take decisions which are compatible with a sustainable and more equitable future'. The 'Scottish Studies' group focused on culture, history, language and the Scottish landscape, and this provides rich opportunities for helping students to understand issues central to climate change, biodiversity and community development (see www.scotland.gov.uk/Topics/Education/Schools/curriculum/ACE/ScottishStudies).

The advisory group report made five high-level recommendations (and thirty-one sub-recommendations) for Scotland's schools, as part of CfE:

1. All learners should have an entitlement to learning for sustainability.
2. In line with the new General Teaching Council of Scotland's Professional Standards, every practitioner, school and education leader should demonstrate learning for sustainability in their practice.
3. Every school should have a whole school approach to learning for sustainability that is robust, demonstrable, evaluated and supported by leadership at all levels.
4. School buildings, grounds and policies should support learning for sustainability.
5. A strategic national approach to supporting learning for sustainability should be established.

## The Scottish Government Response

In March 2013, Dr Alastair Allan (then Minister for Learning, Sciences and Scotland's Languages) accepted all thirty-one recommendations (almost all in full: see www.gov.scot/Topics/Education/Schools/curriculum/ACE/OnePlanetSchools/GovernmentResponse). Whilst 'the ground had been prepared' through the developments above, and alignment had been secured via the inclusion of LfS in the GTCS Professional Standards, the Scottish Government's acceptance of the report was nonetheless remarkable. The combination of the five main recommendations, the inclusion of outdoor learning (to provide sensitising experiences in nature – see Chapter 63) as a key feature of LfS, and the acknowledgement of the central role of values/action combine to make this an internationally unique policy.

## A STRATEGIC NATIONAL APPROACH: THE DEVELOPMENT OF *VISION 2030+*

### The LfS Implementation Group

Acceptance of the fifth recommendation of the *Learning for Sustainability* report (Scottish Government, 2014) led to the establishment of an LfS Implementation Group. The remit and membership of the group was to ensure that LfS policy was implemented and that momentum was maintained through existing agencies such as Education Scotland, GTCS, Scottish Qualifications Authority, local authorities and Scottish Futures Trust (commissioning and funding school buildings), and that support was provided for the many non-governmental agencies involved in this field. The secretariat was provided by the Scottish Government and the UN RCE Scotland. The group met regularly through the period from 2013 to March 2016 when their final report, *Vision 2030+*, was submitted (see https://education.gov.scot/improvement/lfs1vision).

## The Role of Education Scotland

During this period Education Scotland had a significant role through a seconded Development Officer who supported existing staff, Scottish Government officials and the implementation group. The key outcomes of this were (a) the development of an extensive website to support education professionals, (b) an LfS whole school self-evaluation framework and, crucially, (c) significant inclusion of LfS in *How Good is Our School? Version 4* (HGIOS4; see Education Scotland, nd; 2015; 2017). This is the framework that underpins effective self-evaluation for practitioners and school leaders at all levels. It now includes 'increase learning for sustainability' as an overarching aim. This makes LfS development a visible and high priority in Scottish education.

## The UN Sustainable Development Goals

Concurrent with these developments, the UN was consulting on and developing the 2015–30 UN Sustainable Development Goals (SDGs; see https://sustainabledevelopment.un.org/?page=viewandnr=1021andtype=230andmenu=2059). Following their agreement and announcement, the First Minister (Nicola Sturgeon) made an immediate pledge to implement them in Scotland. These differ from their predecessors, the Millennium Development Goals, in that they refer to the domestic policy agenda of all nations. Alongside the obvious message in their title, most of the SDGs signify directly the international community's concern with sustainability – notably those demanding action, for example to combat global climate change, and conserve terrestrial and marine biodiversity and productivity; achieving other SDGs is clearly dependent on these.

## The *Vision 2030+* Report

The LfS Working Group took the view that this global agenda was also Scotland's agenda and that their final recommendations to Scottish ministers should reflect this; hence the report's title: *Vision 2030+*. The report takes account of the local and global context, and the wider policy dimensions of sustainability, and is essentially a route map for the further embedding of LfS in Scottish education. It was submitted in March 2016 and accepted in full by three ministers: Education, Sciences and Scotland's Languages; Environment, Climate Change and Land Reform; and International Development and Europe. Whilst, again, this is a remarkable indication of the strategic place of LfS, the recent (2016) manifesto commitments of the re-elected SNP have had a significant effect on the education policy landscape. The implications for LfS are discussed below.

## LEARNING FOR SUSTAINABILITY AND THE CROSS-CURRICULAR CONTEXT

Sustainable development education claimed a place in schools alongside traditional disciplines as a cross-curricular or interdisciplinary theme. As with SDE, perhaps, uniquely, LfS presents several distinct challenges to the curriculum: its interdisciplinarity, its political content and a values/action dimension.

### Interdisciplinarity

An interdisciplinary topic is difficult to place in a discipline-based curriculum. As this was one of the challenges CfE was designed to meet, SDE's early accommodation in the curriculum is perhaps no surprise but is worth noting as an achievement; all the more so for its continued inclusion and the emergence of LfS as an important aspect of education policy development in the period 2011–16.

### Political and Values/Action Dimensions

Implicit and explicit in discussions of global sustainability challenges is that personal, collective and political actions are required to address them. Though it was a strong theme in SDE it is now more explicit in 'Learning *for* Sustainability', the pedagogy of which is discussed below. This is a rarity in the curriculum, and one that not all education professionals will be comfortable with as it may challenge their own norms and behaviours, and indeed those of the school; similarly policymakers may feel unsettled when examining their professional practice and political agendas.

### Outdoor Learning

As noted above, outdoor learning is one of the three key components of LfS. The justification comes from empirical research (summarised in the *Learning for Sustainability* report (Scottish Government, 2014), and also here in Chapter 63), but it is also a manifestation of previous policy commitments established through *Curriculum for Excellence through Outdoor Learning* (Learning and Teaching Scotland, 2010). Whilst providing learning opportunities outdoors is a passion for some teachers, for others it is challenging, and likewise some local environments are less suitable than others. Appropriate pedagogies may be unfamiliar to some, and whilst the affordances of outdoor environments foster interdisciplinary learning, considerations such as the weather, the uncertainty and serendipity of events and outcomes make teaching outdoors challenging for some individuals and some schools.

Advocates of LfS recognise that it provides opportunities to challenge curricular norms; to focus on addressing complex interdisciplinary issues that develop critical thinking skills and an action orientation (and attention can be paid to the role of the school within local community and local governance). Such skills position LfS as offering significant contributions to formal and broader community-relevant education; moreover such skills have application in a broad range of contexts beyond sustainability.

## LEARNING FOR SUSTAINABILITY AND ATTAINMENT

Whilst the focus of LfS is not overtly disciplinary, its approach and content should support disciplinary and, of course, interdisciplinary learning. Evidence is increasingly emerging that commitment to LfS correlates with a wide range of formal and curricular educational benefits. For example, a recent Scottish study, led by Education Scotland and prepared in response to the end of the UN Decade of Education for Sustainable Development in 2014 (see https:// education.gov.scot/improvement/Pages/lfs3-conversations-about-learning-for-sustainabili ty.aspx), asked, 'Does an orientation towards sustainable development make a difference at classroom level and has it improved outcomes for learners, their families and school communities?' The concluding report comprised studies of twenty schools/centres (early years, primary, secondary and additional support needs, across differing geographical and socio-economic contexts), selected due to their 'interesting approaches or long-standing commitment to learning for sustainability'. The schools reported consistently positive outcomes in:

- confidence and skills of learners;
- innovative teaching, learning and assessment;
- learning experiences and motivation of learners;
- the reputation of the centres;
- staff morale, wellbeing and motivation (including commitment to ongoing professional learning);
- ethos of the school, community partnerships and community spirit.

The study was included in an eighteen-nation UNESCO project which showed similar consistent results across all nations (Laurie et al., 2016). Further, in many high-scoring Programme for International Student Assessment (PISA) countries, academic performance increased in schools committed to ESD and gave more meaning to curricula, leading students to be more engaged, committed and self-confident. In these schools, ESD promoted acquisition of additional relevant knowledge and skills, as well as perspectives and values, and helped to prepare students for an uncertain future by instilling flexible competencies, empathy and creativity. These schools also engaged more with local communities by opening opportunities for students, parents and others to be involved in meaningful ways (Laurie et al., 2016). In essence, where schools commit to ESD/LfS, a wide range of educational benefits ensue, in particular the development of higher-order skills including critical thinking and interdisciplinary understanding.

## LEARNING FOR SUSTAINABILITY IN SCHOOLS – CAMPUS AND COMMUNITY

Learning for sustainability is not confined to the curriculum. It encompasses all aspects of a school's work and can be conveniently organised in terms of curriculum, campus and community. The inclusion of the headline recommendation in the *Learning for Sustainability* report (Scottish Government, 2014) that 'School buildings, grounds and policies should support learning for sustainability' was an acknowledgement that there is a direct sustainability benefit relating to government and local authority targets on carbon emission reduction following the Climate Change (Scotland) Act 2009, as well as the pedagogical benefit of students, staff, parents and the wider community seeing demonstrable institutional commitments. Similar considerations apply to biodiversity obligations and the educational potential of school grounds, covering outdoor teaching and play. The inclusion of the reference to the pedagogical significance of buildings, grounds and practices in the LfS report is evidence based but the effectiveness of such an approach for the broader community is worthy of research attention.

## LEARNING FOR SUSTAINABILITY IN HIGHER EDUCATION AND FURTHER EDUCATION

Exposure to LfS in schools is significant as a context for the development of an interest and technical skills appropriate to a wide range of academic and practical aspects in HE, FE and in related careers. Universities and colleges have a role in the general understanding of sustainable development-related issues in almost all if not all disciplinary areas in the sciences and engineering, the arts, humanities and social sciences, and in medicine. As such they are a natural destination for school graduates with an interest and training in these areas, and provide much of the scientific evidence, social science and related material that continues to develop our understanding of sustainability in schools.

## LEARNING FOR SUSTAINABILITY IN TEACHER EDUCATION AND CAREER-LONG PROFESSIONAL LEARNING

There is no current requirement for Scottish teacher education institutions (TEIs) to include LfS in their programmes. This is paradoxical given that it is a GTCS requirement for the profession and a Scottish Government policy commitment. Nonetheless, many TEIs are now addressing this issue with optional courses and some inclusions in the core elements of programmes. One development that should aid progress is the recent award of funding by the Gordon Cook Trust for a collaboration between the RCE Scotland and the GTCS, to support the implementation of LfS in Scotland's TEIs. The core of the work is to develop a 'self-reflection tool' which TEIs and the GTCS will use to review the content and approach of any teacher education programme to ensure that the GTCS professional values and standards, specifically in LfS, are being met.

Despite its policy status, the Scottish Government has provided no specific career-long professional learning (CLPL). A range of charitable trusts and commercial agencies have developed training programmes on specific aspects of LfS, but the most prominent and comprehensive is the Learning for Sustainability course funded by the British Council through their 'Connecting Classrooms' programme. This collaboration between the University of Edinburgh, the RCE Scotland and the British Council is based on a UK-wide 'core-skills' (e.g. critical thinking) development programme which is delivered in Scotland through a focus on LfS. The course is free to participants and delivered several times a year (2015–18) in a blended-learning (face-to-face and online) ten-week block, in various locations across Scotland. It has been validated by the GTCS for 'professional recognition', and Scottish College for Educational Leadership (SCEL) endorsement is currently being sought. A fully online version has been developed and, if funding is available, will enable all Scottish teachers and education professionals to access the course. One further opportunity for GTCS accreditation is available through an online Masters level course in LfS offered by the University of Edinburgh, and other organisations offer similar programmes that focus on, for example, LfS and outdoor learning.

## FUTURE PROSPECTS

The process that introduced LfS into Scottish Education involved all relevant parties in the conceptual and policy development, crucially alongside the GTCS Professional Standards. The support of Education Scotland has also been significant in both resource development and structurally through, for example, HGIOS4. Similarly, and despite the lack of state funding, ways to capitalise on the commitment of interested teachers through a range of CLPL provisions have been found; these approaches are reaping rewards in terms of professional development and the emergence of whole school approaches to LfS. Further, every opportunity has been taken to align developments with other national (e.g. climate change) commitments and international (e.g. UN SDGs) agendas. Little wonder then that Scotland's leadership role has been applauded by UNESCO (Martin et al., 2013; UNESCO, 2014) and the European Parliament, and greeted with interest in a number of other countries.

The international significance of LfS (ESD) is evident across a range of sources; for example the UN SDG 4.7 (as agreed to by the Scottish Government) states:

> By 2030, ensure that all learners acquire the knowledge and skills needed to promote sustainable development, including, among others, through education for sustainable development and sustainable lifestyles, human rights, gender equality, promotion of a culture of peace and non-violence, global citizenship and appreciation of cultural diversity and of culture's contribution to sustainable development. (United Nations, 2016)

Similarly, the 2016 UNESCO Global Education Monitoring Report has aligned with the UN SDGs in focusing on the central significance of this agenda.

However, the overt and overriding focus of the new (2016) Scottish Government on *bridging the attainment gap* has led to a reprioritising of many aspects of educational policy and provision. Whilst LfS has a broader purpose than the core features of this agenda – 'literacy, numeracy and health and wellbeing' – educational attainment and success in adult life is clearly built on additional skills that LfS does encourage, in particular, and as evidenced by the Connecting Classrooms CLPL programme and the Scottish and UNESCO studies, higher order skills in critical thinking and interdisciplinary understanding. Taking this broad view of 'attainment' and with a long-term vision in mind, the formal process of embedding the LfS recommendations has continued, particularly through the *Vision 2030+* report. However, making substantial change is a demanding ongoing process, and this requires central policy commitment and coordination to ensure that momentum is maintained and Scotland meets its international commitments.

The work of recent decades and specifically the development of LfS has been absolutely necessary but not sufficient to bring about the deep reorientation necessary to address sustainability. The following represent key actions for the future:

- *Scotland needs an education action plan for the SDGs.* LfS can shape educational thinking and practice to help interpret and implement the UN SDGs by 2030. This requires a supported and monitored SDG education action plan. This is a multidimensional project requiring collaboration across a wide range of government policy areas.
- *All Scottish schools must be sustainable schools.* Recent progress needs to be consolidated and integrated to fully embed the entitlement to LfS for all learners. This requires concerted effort by government and related agencies, schools and teachers, third sector providers and others to include LfS in curricula and inspection regimes, to support teachers and education

leaders through professional development, and to ensure LfS is a central focus in any review of Curriculum for Excellence.

- *Ongoing support and monitoring is necessary*. To ensure progress on all thirty-one recommendations of the 'Learning for Sustainability Ministerial Advisory Report' (www.gov.scot/Topics/Education/Schools/curriculum/LearningforSustainability), and the developments outlined in the *Vision 2030+* report (Education Scotland, 2016) requires designated staffing in government agencies. Further, enactment of the *Vision 2030+* report requires all the key educational agencies 'to include LfS in their corporate plans, strategies, processes and communications to promote on-going engagement, reflection and advancement of LfS at all levels' (Scottish Government, Education Scotland, GTCS, Scottish Qualifications Authority (SQA), SCEL, and other key agencies and bodies). This is unlikely to happen unless it is monitored.

- *Learning for sustainability needs to be integrated in the delivery of key educational initiatives*. These include the Scottish Attainment Challenge, the National Improvement Framework, Developing the Young Workforce Programme and the ongoing review of Curriculum for Excellence.

- *The SDGs and LfS must be integrated with other Scottish Government policy priorities*. Whilst these educational issues are global and national educational imperatives in their own right, they have a broader context which relates to many, if not all, Scottish Government policy areas. Issues such as the management of Scotland's landscapes and seas, dealing with climate change, community development, renewable energy, countryside tourism, health and well-being and others are all intimately connected to sustainability. Introducing integrated policy approaches to these issues in the next Parliament would demonstrate both commitment and 'joined-up' government.

- *Teacher education programmes must include LfS*. Every local authority, TEI, school and individual teacher is required to demonstrate LfS in their relevant educational context. Teacher education programmes are accredited by the GTCS and must reflect the values and expectations within the Professional Standards Framework. These changes will take time to become fully embedded and will require concerted ongoing support and monitoring. Any revision of such GTCS Professional Standards and guidelines, for example those for initial teacher education, must include a commitment to LfS. This process is in line with the work and aspirations of the UNESCO international project on Reorienting Teacher Education to Address Sustainable Development (www.unesco.org/new/en/education/themes/leading-the-international-agenda/education-for-sustainable-development/partners/educators/teacher-education/)'

In summary, the narrow focus on specific forms of attainment misses the far broader perspective that includes higher-order skills, interdisciplinarity and values/action competences. It also overlooks the structural and political inequities, such as poverty and deprivation, that a narrow view and measure of attainment fails to take account of; consideration of such justice issues requires a concerted and holistic approach which positions education as part of community. For many, such social justice issues are fundamental to any notion of 'sustainability'. The Scottish Government commitment to LfS provides an opportunity to take a holistic, long-term approach towards 'closing the attainment gap' and in doing so meet a variety of strategic policy and practical ambitions; such a coherent aspiration has significance for the imperative to address sustainability and enhance the developmental and educational prospects of school pupils. The evidence is plain and the need is urgent.

## REFERENCES

Education Scotland (nd) *Whole School and Community Approach to Learning for Sustainability (LfS): Self-Evaluation and Improvement Framework*. Online at https://education.gov.scot/improvement/Documents/Frameworks_SelfEvaluation/FRWK11-LfS-framework.pdf

Education Scotland (2015) *How Good is Our School? Fourth edition*. Online at https://education.gov.scot/improvement/Documents/Frameworks_SelfEvaluation/FRWK2_NIHeditHGIOS/FRWK2_HGIOS4.pdf

Education Scotland (2016) *Vision 2030+: Concluding Report of the Learning for Sustainability National Implementation Group*. Online at https://education.gov.scot/improvement/documents/res1-vision-2030.pdf

Education Scotland (2017) *Conversations about Learning for Sustainability*. Online at https://education.gov.scot/improvement/practice-exemplars/Conversations%20about%20learning%20for%20sustainability

Higgins, P. and Lavery, A. (2013) 'Sustainable development education', in T. G. K. Bryce, W. M. Humes, D. Gillies and A. Kennedy (eds), *Scottish Education, Fourth Edition: Referendum*. Edinburgh: Edinburgh University Press, pp. 337–42.

Higgins, P. and Nicol, R. (2011) 'Professor Sir Patrick Geddes: *"Vivendo Discimus"* – by living we learn', in C. Knapp and T. Smith (eds), *A Sourcebook for Experiential Education: Key Thinkers and Their Contributions*. New York: Routledge, pp. 32–40.

Laurie, R., Nonoyama-Tarumi, Y., McKeown, R. and Hopkins, C. (2016) 'Contributions of ESD to quality education: a synthesis of research', *Journal of Education for Sustainable Development*, 10 (2), 1–17.

Lavery, A. and Smyth, J. (2003) 'Developing environmental education, a review of a Scottish project: international and political influences', *Environmental Education Research*, 9, 361–83.

Learning and Teaching Scotland (2010) *Curriculum for Excellence through Outdoor Learning*. Glasgow: Learning and Teaching Scotland.

Martin, S., Dillon, J., Higgins, P., Peters, C. and Scott, W. (2013) 'Divergent evolution in education for sustainable development policy in the United Kingdom: current status, best practice, and opportunities for the future', *Sustainability*, 5 (4), 1522–44, www.mdpi.com/2071-1050/5/4/1522/htm

McNaughton, M.-J. (2007) 'Sustainable development education in Scottish schools: the sleeping beauty syndrome', *Environmental Education Research*, 13, 621–35.

Scottish Government (2010) *Learning for Change: Scotland's Action Plan for the Second Half of the UN Decade of Education for Sustainable Development*. Online at www.gov.scot/Publications/2010/05/20152453/2

Scottish Government (2014) *Learning for Sustainability: The Scottish Government's response to the Report of the One Planet Schools Working Group*. March. Online at *www.gov.scot/resource/0041/00416172.docx*

UNESCO (2014) *Shaping the Future We Want: The UN Decade of Education for Sustainable Development (2005 – 14) Final Report*. Paris: UNESCO.

UNESCO (2016) *Education for People and Planet: Creating Sustainable Futures for All*. The Global Education Monitoring Report. Online at http://unesdoc.unesco.org/images/0024/002457/245752e.pdf

United Nations (2016) Goal 4 targets. Online at www.undp.org/content/undp/en/home/sustainable-development-goals/goal-4-quality-education/targets/

World Commission on Environment and Development (1987) *Our Common Future: Report of the World Commission on Environment and Development* (the Brundtland report). United Nations. Online at www.un-documents.net/our-common-future.pdf

# 66

# The Scots Language in Education

*Anne Donovan and Liz Niven*

## THE SCOTS LANGUAGE – ITS HISTORY AND DEVELOPMENT

Scots is an Indo-European language descended from a northern form of Anglo-Saxon. By the seventh century AD, this Germanic branch of the language had reached the south-east of what is now Scotland and by the eleventh century AD was firmly established across central and southern Scotland. In addition to such Anglo-Saxon vocabulary as *bairns*, *thrawn*, *bide* and *byre*, strong Scandinavian, French and Dutch influences can still be heard in words such as *lass*, *lug*, *lowse*, *braw*, *douce*, *fash*, *scone* and *redd*. Latin remains in, for example, *janitor* and *dux*; Irish and Scots Gaelic have provided further lexical items such as *bens*, *glens* and *straths*. Thus, as with the English language, contact with other countries and the legacy of loan words from several nations have contributed to the formation of the Scots language.

Much written Scots was produced in the late fourteenth-century court of James IV by the King's commissioned poets and dramatists and, by the early sixteenth century, Scots was developing as an all-purpose national language. This was the nearest point at which Scots came to adopting a written standard, accepted, on equal terms, with other European languages. However, English began to wield greater influence around the time of the Reformation in 1560 when the Geneva Bible was translated into English rather than Scots. Anglicisation increased after the departure of James VI to London and the Union of the Crowns in 1603, particularly among the Scots nobility. Finally, after the Treaty of Union in 1707, English became the official language of government and the court, even though Scots was almost universally spoken throughout lowland, central and North-East Scotland, and Gaelic in the Highlands and Islands.

## CONTEMPORARY SCOTS

Contemporary spoken Scots embraces a wide variation in language on a continuum from Scottish Standard English to broad Scots. The possible range of pronunciation, vocabulary, grammar and idiom is wide, and nuances can be so subtle that its speakers are unaware that they are not actually speaking English. While examples of overt Scots might be demonstrated in vocabulary such as *aye* or *wee*, *kye* or *yowe*, covert Scots might be employed in the use of words such as *pinkie* or *outwith*.

In some situations words have different meanings in English than in Scots. For example, 'a chap at the door' or 'going for the messages' are common Scottish phrases with a different meaning when spoken by English speakers. Similarly, grammatical constructions such as the use of the definite article and possessive pronoun ('I have the flu and I'm away to my bed' rather than 'I have flu and I am going to bed') are typically Scottish while the use of 'yous' as a second person plural pronoun emulates the *vous* of French grammar. Yet these are often regarded as 'bad grammar' rather than examples of legitimate Scots. A good description of contemporary Scots is explained in *Understanding Grammar in Scotland Today*:

> Broadly speaking, we can argue that it involves contact between two distinct language varieties – Broad Scots and standard Southern English – a contact that eventually created a third variety: Scottish English. Language users in Scotland can make use of any of these three varieties. (Corbett and Kay, 2009, p. 3)

Frequently, speakers will codeswitch and shift between speech forms depending on their current audience and purpose. The Scottish writer Andrew Greig succinctly expresses this in his novel *Electric Brae*:

> His accent was moving in and out of focus like his finger. Who are we? I wondered. We don't even speak consistently. We'll say 'yes' and 'aye' in the same conversation, alternate between 'know' and 'ken', 'bairn' and 'wean' and 'child' and not even know why … We're a small country with blurry boundaries. (Greig, 1992, p. 56)

## SCOTS – LANGUAGE OR DIALECT?

As stated in the Mercator-Education Dossier, *The Scots Language in Education in Scotland*:

> One of the greatest barriers to Scots being acknowledged as a distinct language in Scotland is its close proximity to English. As both are Germanic languages, from a common root and sharing much vocabulary, modern Scots tends to exist on a continuum with broad Scots at one end and Scottish Standard English at the other. This situation is roughly similar to the continuum that exists in Dutch/German and Danish/Norwegian. No controversy exists with these languages in establishing whether they are dialects or languages. (Niven, 2002, p. 6)

The Scottish Language Dictionaries list ten dialect areas. All have their own particular pronunciation and dialect variations. For example, 'good' might be written and pronounced as *guid* or *geed* or *gweed*. Opinions vary widely as to whether an agreed written standard is desirable; some creative writers and readers fear a dilution of individuality, while some language activists would prefer an agreed written language, not necessarily spoken by any particular region of the country. The argument as to whether Scots is a language or a dialect frequently provides a diversion from productive discussion about Scots language issues.

However, several factors contribute to the widespread belief that Scots is indeed a language: it is widely spoken throughout Scotland, it has all the elements of a language (that is, accent, dialects, grammar, idiom), it has a clear geographical boundary within a nation state and it has a centuries-old pedigree of literature. The only missing element is the lack of a standardised written form.

## COMMON PERCEPTIONS OF SCOTS

The perception of Scots as an inferior version of English has led to its lack of official recognition, as well as confused and conflicting attitudes. Though the introduction of policies from official bodies such as the Scottish Government and Creative Scotland is gradually having some impact on these views, worryingly, it is often those who are themselves Scots speakers who perceive their voice as less acceptable. When interviewed, a vast number refer to their speech as slang rather than Scots. The implications of these beliefs for Scottish national identity are considerable. In a university study of Glasgow dialect it was noted that:

> To move into the realms of 'proper' speech holds national significance as well as class significance for the Scot. Even if the English dialect speaker takes lessons to perfect an RP [Received Pronunciation] accent, he will still be English. If the Scot does this, he may throw away more in the loss of an outward, recognisable national identity ... both may disguise their regional origins but only one belies his national identity. Yet many Scots speakers continue to feel inferior about their voice thus perpetuating the phenomenon kent as The Scottish Cringe. (Menzies, 2004, p. 3)

The gathering of accurate statistics has, until recent years, been unsatisfactory and inadequate. Only since 2011 have official statistics on the number of people defining themselves as Scots speakers become available from the census. Despite the belief on the part of many Scots speakers that their speech is not in fact Scots, but an inferior form of English, the 2011 Census figures revealed that 1.6 million people responded 'Yes' to the question, 'Do you speak Scots?' The inclusion of Scots for the first time in the Language section alongside Gaelic and English was a watershed moment, indicating a greater commitment to the status of the Scots language.

## OFFICIAL POLICY

Official bodies have become noticeably more positive towards Scots in recent years. The Scottish Government's aims and objectives for Scots and the practical steps to achieve these, with specific reference to the inclusion and development of Scots in the curriculum, can be found at https://beta.gov.scot/policies/languages/. It has also been stated that:

> Education Scotland will make siccar that a team within the organisation haes specific responsibility for promotin a coherent approach tae the plannin, lairnin, teachin an assessment o Scots within the context o relatit national policy an the Curriculum for Excellence implementation plan. (http://media.scotslanguage.com/library/document/ScotsLangPolicy.pdf)

Education Scotland's Policy on Scots is similarly supportive and positive about Scots language:

> With its various dialects, Scots forms an integral part of Scotland's heritage and cultural life, playing a vital role in children's and young people's learning about Scotland. It can also make a strong contribution to the development of children's and young people's literacy skills. (https://education.gov.scot/Documents/cfe-briefing-17.pdf)

Official support for the Scots language has also been demonstrated by the Statement of Linguistic Rights for Scots, compiled by the former Cross Party Group on Scots Language, and the ratification of the European Charter for Scots at Part II. Another positive development is that Creative Scotland, the Scottish Government's arts funding body, has launched a Scots language policy promoting the use of the language across art forms, stating, 'We support the status of Scots, alongside Gaelic and English, as one of the three indigenous languages of Scotland' (www.creativescotland.com/__data/assets/pdf_file/0018/31590/ Scots-Language-Policy-June-2015.pdf).

## SCOTS IN EDUCATION – POLICY

Official attitudes have certainly altered since an early schools inspector observed that Scots 'is not the language of educated people anywhere' (Scottish Education Department, 1946, p. 75). The 1990s saw the growth of support for Scots in the curriculum, particularly in the 5–14 documents, primarily in English Language. In the section devoted to Scottish culture published in 1992 it was stated that the first tasks of schools were to enable pupils to be confident and creative in this language. This recognition of Scots as a language to be fostered and developed in schools led to its greater visibility in the curriculum and to the preparation of high-quality Scots language resources. Curriculum for Excellence (CfE) replaced the 5–14 National Guidelines, with phased implementation required by 2010. Scots language is now included in the Languages section of the curriculum areas, which states that 'The Scots language provides a rich resource for children and young people to learn about Scotland's culture, identity and literature' (Education Scotland, 2017). Studying Scots enables learners to develop transferable literacy skills, and can enhance engagement in language and literacy.

However, while CfE makes positive statements about Scots, there is still an overall sense of the need to 'sell' its inclusion in the curriculum, rather than treat it in the same way as the English language. For example, the entry for English lists 'parts of speech, punctuation, grammar and syntax', while the one for Scots is concerned with 'its history, dialects, role in education and how to incorporate Scots into teaching across the curriculum' (Education Scotland, 2017). Perhaps the next updated documents on CfE should contain similar references to the language features of Scots, indicating that Scots has achieved parity with English and does not require justification of its 'role in education'.

Scottish language and literature feature in the curriculum at secondary level, though it has not always been compulsory to study a Scottish text for Scottish Qualifications Authority (SQA) examinations. From 2012, the study of a Scottish text at Higher and National 5 has been mandatory and assessed. Some texts in Scots are included in the choice of Scottish texts and the study of literature in Scots is recommended by Education Scotland, but it has never been compulsory to study a text written in Scots. The Scottish Language Paper at Advanced Higher level has now been discontinued. In 2014, the SQA introduced the Scottish Studies Award, which provides students with opportunities to study a range of Scottish topics including Scots language, and the Scots Language Award, which enables them to study the history and development of the Scots language and to develop their ability to understand and communicate in the Scots language. While these two awards should increase the study of Scots language use in the senior phase, they do not provide Universities and Colleges Admissions Service (UCAS) points. Very few students were ever presented for the Scottish Language paper at Advanced Higher level and teachers have indicated that this was due to lack of knowledge and confidence about Scots language issues. Unless this situation is addressed, not many students are likely to study towards the Scottish Studies or the Scots Language awards. To match the shifts in attitude by official examination bodies, there needs to be professional development to bring about similar shifts in practical action. A professional award is available through the General Teaching Council (GTC) for Professional Recognition for Scots Language. To date, fifteen have been applied for and successfully awarded.

## SCOTS IN EDUCATION – PRACTICE

In spite of positive policies, the experience of children varies greatly from school to school. In some primary schools, Scots permeates the curriculum, with signs around the school in Scots as well as English, and classes compiling local dictionaries of Scots. It is still not uncommon, though, to be welcomed at a school entrance by a list of languages spoken by pupils which does not include Scots. In some primary schools, children experience a varied selection of texts in Scots, while in others they may learn a poem for Burns night but see no other Scots throughout the year. Furthermore, the increased provision of nurseries and playgroups for Scottish children, welcome though it is, has provided an earlier opportunity for children to fail to develop their home language. Without Scots speakers in the nurseries and Scots materials such as stories, songs and nursery rhymes, the anglicisation of children's speech is likely to start at an even earlier age than previously. This issue is being addressed by statements in CfE and occasionally resources are being made available.

Variation in practice is also found at secondary level where there is little evidence of whole school approaches to Scots. However, many teachers across Scotland have reported improvements in levels of attainment and attitude among their pupils as a result of building more Scots language into their programmes of study. The Scottish Attainment Challenge, introduced to achieve equality in education outcomes, provides opportunities to include Scots language in its activities.

One of the difficulties in ensuring that policies on Scots are implemented in practice is that many teachers feel less than expert in the subject. Although the study of Scots exists at undergraduate level in Aberdeen, Glasgow and Edinburgh universities, little or no Scots is offered during initial teacher education at these institutions. As long as there is no compulsory study of Scots language and literature for all teachers in training, practitioners with limited knowledge about and confidence in these areas will continue to appear in the classroom, thus perpetuating the current anomalous situation.

## SCOTS LITERATURE

One area where Scots is alive and vigorously kicking is in contemporary literature. As has been stated previously, Scotland has a rich literary heritage, much of it in Scots. In the early part of the twentieth century, the so-called 'Scottish Renaissance' is well represented by poets such as MacDiarmid, who observed in 1958 that if Scottish writers use English, they must be content to play a very subordinate role, and prose writers like Nan Shepherd and Lewis Grassic Gibbon, who stated that Scots would 'adorn his meaning with a richness, a clarity and a conciseness impossible in orthodox English' (Gibbon, 1980). In the later part of the twentieth and into the twenty-first century a similar resurgence has been noted, resulting in a clear confidence in the way that writers use the languages of Scotland in whatever ways they choose, whether these languages are English, Scots, Gaelic, Punjabi or a mixture of these or other languages heard in Scotland. Also there is increasing interest in and respect for writing in Scots (though it may not necessarily be called that). James Kelman's Booker Prize for *How Late It Was, How Late*, and the international reputation of *Trainspotting* by Irvine Welsh are two of the most obvious examples of this, but there is an appetite by publishers, reviewers and translators furth of Scotland for Scots writing.

Poetry in Scots is highly popular across the world and Scotland has produced many award-winning poets in Scots, including Kathleen Jamie; her work has received many prestigious awards, including the T. S. Eliot Prize which she has won on three occasions. Since 2004, the Scottish Government has appointed a Scottish Makar, with the remit to create new work and promote poetry throughout the country, particularly encouraging young people to engage with the art form. The appointment of such highly distinguished and well-kent writers as Edwin Morgan, Liz Lochhead and Jackie Kay, all of whom have written eloquently in Scots, can only have an effect on the perceptions of the Scottish people especially, perhaps, young people.

## EDUCATIONAL RESOURCES

Suitable resources with which to teach Scots language and literature are crucial. Commercial or centrally produced resources have tended to favour English; the production of and maintenance of Scots language materials has been an ongoing problem due to its relatively small market. This has led to many excellent materials going out of print or becoming unavailable after a relatively short time. A major example of this is *The Kist/A Chiste* which, despite having been awarded the TES/Saltire Education prize, can now only be purchased second-hand and whose excellent teaching materials and audio recordings are no longer available. A shorter online version of *The Kist* on the Education Scotland website has currently been removed; it should soon be available on the Scots Language Centre site. Other examples of out-of-print high-quality resources are the Channel 4 series, *Haud Yer Tongue*, and the TES/Saltire Award-winning textbook *Turnstones 1*, published by Hodder and Stoughton. Copies of all these resources are still available in some schools and worth making use of. Though it is to be hoped that some of these resources may become available online, there is still a value in print books for the classroom.

The need for public subsidy to counteract this trend is shown by the successful model of the Itchy Coo project. Founded by writers Matthew Fitt and James Robertson (with Edinburgh-based Black & White Publishing), it publishes high-quality books in Scots for all age ranges. It also developed an intensive outreach and education programme in schools and libraries and acted as consultants for policy development. The outreach ended in 2011, but publication continues. Itchy Coo has shown the great demand for Scots books with high production values. However, it must be emphasised that without substantial public subsidy this would never have happened.

The Internet has good materials for Scots in education. Matthew Fitt's Scots Hoose is an excellent online resource designed to support creativity in the Scots language and Susan Rennie, who was also involved in Itchy Coo, has a website with information on her own books and other resources for Scots language. Children's books in Scots are available from the Scottish publisher, Kelpies. BBC2's Scots Scuil brought together six young Scots from across the country for a week of Scots language workshops. Clips from the programme, available online, are a valuable resource; as well as dealing with the language itself, they also explore attitudes to Scots within families and allow extensive time to the ideas of the young folk themselves.

Many organisations and official bodies provide a rich source of information and resources. Some regions are reprinting resources, including high-quality work from local authorities such as Tayside and Dumfries and Galloway. The latter has relaunched Scots resources realigned to CfE and delivered free copies to every school in the region, an excellent use of Scots coordinators working regionally to support teachers. The Elphinstone Kist, provided by Aberdeen University's Elphinstone Institute is also an excellent resource for poetry and prose in the Scots of the North-East.

The Association of Scottish Literary Studies (ASLS) has supported and published texts in Scots for many years; they produce *Scotnotes* on a wide variety of Scots texts suitable for use in schools. ASLS also published John Corbett's *Understanding Grammar in Scotland Today*, an excellent textbook for teachers and pupils seeking an informative linguistic analysis of the language.

The Scots Language Centre (SLC) supports and encourages Scots. SLC focuses on the use of Scots as a spoken language. The Education section of the SLC website contains the most comprehensive list of Scots language education resources online as well as material aimed at teachers, students and interested members of the public.

The Scottish Language Dictionaries (SLD) are government-funded and produce Scots dictionaries, classroom-related materials, interactive language activities and a grammar workbook. Scuil Wab, an education website, is also maintained. An education officer has a remit to maintain and develop resources as well as run workshops for staff and pupils.

Education Scotland developed and provided teaching materials to support Scots language texts in the curriculum. Scots language education coordinators created a substantial increase in online Scots materials as well as delivering in-service to support them. However, during the revamp of Education Scotland's website, few Scots resources are currently available.

In 2015 the National Library of Scotland appointed a Scots Scriever whose remit is to produce original, creative work in Scots and to raise the profile, understanding and appreciation of creative work in the Scots language, particularly in education. The first Scriever, Hamish MacDonald, initiated the Wee Windaes website, which makes available some of the Scots resources of the National Library (http://wee-windaes.nls.uk/).

Support from publicly funded bodies or the ring-fencing of funds for Scots language resources (paralleled in other countries with minority languages) would still seem to be necessary if Scots language books and resources are to compete fairly in the marketplace against English language books with their vastly greater economies of scale. With the possibilities of digitisation, it is to be hoped that some out-of-print materials may be resurrected and updated; the need for wider distribution of resources to render publications viable may therefore be reduced.

## CLASSROOM PRACTICE

Poetry in Scots is often a starting point for many reading, writing and talk activities in Scots, while the use of dictionaries and word-banks shows pupils that Scots words are not simply corruptions of English; grammatical and linguistic concepts can be taught in the medium of Scots. An excellent animated film, created by the Scots language coordinators based at Education Scotland, is a popular introduction to the history of the language (see https://www.youtube.com/watch?v=tdmj3E1dmkk).

Writing in Scots may lead to anxiety about spelling. The use of a dictionary may help, offering various spellings from which a pupil may choose; for some pupils, however, it is more of a hindrance, preventing them from hearing their own voice. The process of writing in Scots itself provides opportunities for discussion of linguistic and cultural issues which arise. Models of increasing sophistication may be used at later stages and greater opportunities offered for reading in a variety of genres. The SQA's inclusion of some set texts in Scots encourages more use of Scots.

## SCOTS LITERATURE VERSUS SCOTS LANGUAGE?

In spite of supportive policies and good educational materials, is it still the case that Scots language is less acceptable in the classroom than Scots literature? The perception that Scots is suited to personal rather than formal communication prevails, leading to few lessons taught in Scots and even, on occasion, the correction of pupils who speak in Scots. It is still questioned whether teaching Scots impedes pupils' ability to communicate in English and uses time that would be better spent in teaching standard English. Research suggests that those who are fluent in their mother tongue and whose linguistic competences are developed in that language are more easily able to learn other languages. This applies to speakers of Scots as well as other languages. As Gordon Gibson says in *The Scots Language: Its Place in Education*:

> Evidence from research seems to all point in one direction, telling us that familiarity with a range of languages and dialects enhances the language development of children, extends their metalinguistic awareness and is of positive benefit to them in their education. (Niven and Jackson, 1998, p. 102)

This is applicable to Scots speakers as well as speakers of community languages such as Urdu and Punjabi, and to other bilingual children. Research suggests that failure to develop children's skills in both languages can be detrimental. In the UK, bilingual education for Welsh and Gaelic speakers is well established but has never been a serious proposition for bilingual children from minority ethnic backgrounds. Not only has Scots medium education never been seriously considered, many parents and some teachers seem to feel that teaching pupils in their own language and about their own language will actually disadvantage them. The cultural and historical reasons for this have been discussed above.

## PROSPECTS

It is difficult to predict the future prospects for the Scots language in education. On the one hand they seem positive, given the publication of highly supportive policies from the country's major official bodies: the Scottish Government, Education Scotland and Creative Scotland. While this excellent development suggests an optimistic future for the language in society, education and the arts, it remains to be seen to what extent these policies are put into practice and, more importantly, to what extent and for how long they are supported.

The 2010 Ministerial Working Group on Scots Language noted that development in the area of education required urgent action because the lack of resources and priority for Scots in education 'endangers all recent progress' (see Executive Recommendations at www.gov.

scot/Publications/2010/11/25121454/0). The fact that progress can be short-lived remains a threat to the planning and maintenance of the language in education. The report stated that CfE provided a promising environment for Scots, but also suggested that there was now an opportunity for the development of a permanent dedicated Scots language bureau to meet the growing demand for training and resource development. The report called for Scots language coordinators and an educational website and indicated that regional dialect diversity should be integral to education policy. Though most of the working group's recommendations were implemented, several have by now have been diluted. For example, four national Scots language coordinators were appointed (rather than the six recommended by the Ministerial Working Group) and only one now remains in post; the prospect of further appointments is uncertain.

The recent 'updating' of Education Scotland's website shows how easily things can change. This has resulted in virtually all its excellent Scots resources (many of which were produced by the coordinators) becoming currently unavailable. Most Scots resources are to be allocated to partner organisations or archived for future review, but it is uncertain when this will happen. At time of writing, the archived material is unavailable; searching for Scots language on the site produces very limited results and previous links no longer work. Furthermore, the endorsements of Scots which were prominent on the website are currently invisible.

It is now more difficult for teachers, parents and other interested parties to find information on and resources for Scots. Even if these eventually become available on the sites of partner organisations such as the Scots Language Centre, the fact that they are not on the official website of the executive agency of the Scottish Government, tasked with improving the quality of the country's education system, seems to suggest a downgrading of the subject. Greater visibility of Scots resources and policy statements on Education Scotland's website and the reappointment of Scots language coordinators are necessary to ensure that government policy is implemented, while the enshrining of Scots policy as an Act of Parliament would guarantee its continuing status.

Some consider the lack of standardisation of the written language to be a drawback and its non-inclusion in the judiciary or in parliamentary documents prevents its ratification at Part I to the European Charter of Minority Languages, which would give it greater status and protection. The public visibility of the written language is limited, though there are signs of progress in the popularity of the Itchy Coo publications and the fact that one Scottish newspaper, *The National*, now publishes a weekly column written in Scots. Creative Scotland's commitment to increasing the use of Scots in their communications, promotions and events and on their website and social media is helping to raise the profile and status of Scots and the launch of the National Library of Scotland's Wee Windaes project in 2016 was conducted by Holyrood's Minister for Education, indicating the importance of the project. The Scottish Government also has an official Twitter account for *aw things tae dae wi the Scots leid*. That teachers across Scotland have reported improvements in levels of attainment and attitude among their pupils as a direct result of building more Scots language into programmes of study augurs well for the language's future in schools. Some parents, however, still need to be convinced before there is anything equivalent to the pro-Gaelic movement.

For many Scots families – including strong Scots speakers – the language's status remains problematic; its greatest hope of survival might be in its proximity to the English language and thus its adaptability to contemporary needs. Greater public awareness of Scots in its twenty-first century forms and clearer support from the Scots-speaking public might be required to bring about increased inclusion in education. Conversely, the more status that is conferred on the language by government and official bodies, the greater acceptance and respect might develop amongst the Scottish people.

In a typically democratic manner, the fate of Scots language will probably be decided by the Scottish people and not imposed from above. Unlike English dictionaries which are prescriptive, Scots dictionaries are descriptive. However, many educationalists and activists, aware of the implications of language repression, would prefer to see a more concerted structured approach, with language maintenance and planning debated at a national level. It would seem that the Scottish Government and education system, as well as teachers, pupils and parents, are still uncertain as to how to proceed with their treatment of twenty-first century Scots language. On the one hand, there is widespread support for the inclusion (though not necessarily compulsory) of Scots literature in the curriculum. On the other hand, there is still unease about the encouragement of spoken Scots in education and in formal society. The puzzle remains: why is there such reluctance about the value or the consequences of 'allowing' a nation to hear its own voice? Meanwhile between 1.5 million and 3 million Scottish people continue to speak the language at some point on the linguistic continuum. Most remain illiterate in this language, a somewhat unusual situation in a nation with a highly developed educational system.

## REFERENCES

Corbett, John (1997) *Language and Scottish Literature*. Edinburgh: Edinburgh University Press.
Corbett, John and Christian Kay (2009) *Understanding Grammar in Scotland Today*. Glasgow: ASLS
Creative Scotland (2016) Scots Language Policy. Online at www.creativescotland.com/what-we-do/
     latest-news/archive/2015/06/scots-language-policy-published
Education Scotland (2010) *Curriculum for Excellence*. Online at https://education.gov.scot/scottish-
     education-system/policy-for-scottish-education/policy-drivers/cfe-(building-from-the-state
     ment-appendix-incl-btc1-5)/What%20is%20Curriculum%20for%20Excellence
Education Scotland (2017) *Scots Language in Curriculum for Excellence: Enhancing Skills in Literacy,
     Developing Successful Learners and Confident Individuals*. Online at https://education.gov.scot/
     improvement/Documents/ScotsLanguageinCfEAug17.pdf
Gibbon, L. G. (1980) *Smeddum: Stories and Essays*. London: Longman.
Greig, A. (1992) *Electric Brae*. Edinburgh: Canongate.
Kay, Billy (2006) *Scots: The Mither Tongue*. Edinburgh: Mainstream.
McClure, J. Derrick (1997) *Why Scots Matters*. Edinburgh: Saltire Society.
Menzies, J. (2004) *An Investigation of Attitudes to Scots and Glasgow Dialect Among Secondary School
     Pupils*. Online at www.arts.gla.ac.uk/STELLA/STARN/lang/MENZIES/menzie1.htm
Niven, L. (2002, 2017) *The Scots Language in Education in Scotland*. Netherlands: Mercator-Education:
     European Network for Regional or Minority Languages and Education.
Niven, L. and Jackson, R. (eds) (1998) *Scots Language: Its Place in Education*. Newton Stewart: Watergaw.
Scottish Education Department (1946) *Primary Education: A Report of the Advisory Council
     on Education in Scotland*. Edinburgh: Scottish Education Department.
Scottish Government (2015) *Scots Language Policy*. Online at www.gov.scot/Resource/0048/00484561
Scottish Government (nd) *Policy: Languages*. Online at https://beta.gov.scot/policies/languages/

### Websites

BBC2's Scots Scuil at www.bbc.co.uk/programmes/p00mrwbh/clips
Elphinstone Kist at www.abdn.ac.uk/elphinstone/kist/

Matthew Fitt's Scots Hoose at www.scotshoose.com/contact.html
*Scotnotes* at http://asls.arts.gla.ac.uk/Scotnotes.html
Scottish Language Dictionaries at www.scotsdictionaries.org.uk
Scots Language Centre at www.scotslanguage.com
Scottish Language Dictionaries at www.scotsdictionaries.org.uk/
Scuilwab at www.scuilwab.org.uk/
Susan Rennie at https://susanrennie.co/sweetieraptors/

# 67

# Gaelic Education

*Boyd Robertson*

Gaelic is the longest-established of Scotland's languages and became, for a brief period, the language of Crown and government. From the twelfth century, the status of the language was eroded by anglicising influences and it became increasingly marginalised. Today, only 1.1 per cent of Scots speak Gaelic. These 57,600 Gaelic speakers are found mostly in the Western Isles and on the western fringes of the mainland but there are also significant communities of Gaelic speakers in urban centres such as Glasgow, Edinburgh and Inverness. The last forty years have seen a remarkable renaissance of the language and culture which is reflected in the census figures for younger age groups.

## EARLY YEARS EDUCATION

It is appropriate to begin an overview of Gaelic education with the preschool sector because this has been the seedbed for much of the regeneration and growth in Gaelic. Increasing exposure to the English language and to Anglo–American cultural influences caused parents and activists to become concerned about the detrimental effect this would have on young children's fluency in, and attitude towards, Gaelic. It was considered essential to counteract that trend by seeking to associate the minority language with positive and enjoyable experiences and this led in the late 1970s to the formation of the first Gaelic playgroups and to demands for children's television programmes in Gaelic.

A national association, Comhairle nan Sgoiltean Àraich (CNSA), was set up in 1982 to promote the development of Gaelic-medium playgroups. Despite being a voluntary sector provider with limited resources, CNSA was instrumental in setting up a network of preschool groups across Scotland. However, the introduction by the government of an entitlement to funded nursery education for 4 year olds and subsequently for 3 year olds led to a mushrooming of nursery school provision and a reduced role for CNSA. Over 1,000 children now attend fifty-four Gaelic nurseries, most of which are located in schools with Gaelic-medium streams. The government's official agency for the language, Bòrd na Gàidhlig, is developing a new early years service in partnership with local authorities and the Parental Advisory Scheme and there are currently sixty-five 0–3 groups throughout the country.

## PRIMARY EDUCATION

Provision for Gaelic in primary has been transformed in the last four decades. Before the reorganisation of local government in the 1970s, Gaelic had a minor role in the primary curriculum. Even in schools in strong Gaelic-speaking communities, the teaching medium was almost exclusively English, the home language of most of the pupils being reduced to the status of a subject for study. The position of Gaelic changed radically in 1975 with the launch of a bilingual education project by the newly formed local authority for the Outer Hebrides, Comhairle nan Eilean. This was the first time that Gaelic as a medium of instruction was officially sanctioned in state schools and represented a major advance for the language in education. There was a favourable parental response to the project initially but, by the early 1980s, concerns were being expressed about the level of fluency in Gaelic being attained by pupils in some schools after several years of bilingual schooling.

Doubts about the ability of bilingual models to deliver fluency in Gaelic comparable to that in English and a growing awareness of the erosion of the language amongst the school age population made parents, educationalists and language activists realise that another approach was needed. Developments in Welsh and other minority languages were studied and the findings suggested that use of the minority language as the medium of education had to be maximised to ensure language maintenance and transmission. Highland and Strathclyde Regional Councils responded to parental pressure for Gaelic-medium education (GME), setting up units in schools in Inverness and Glasgow in 1985. The success of these units, and the continuing spread of the playgroups, fuelled demand for provision in other areas. By 2015–16, fifty-nine schools and 3,009 pupils were engaged in Gaelic-medium education. Most schools are in the Highlands and Islands but there are several in non-Gaelic-speaking areas such as Aberdeen, Cumbernauld, Edinburgh, Kilmarnock and Stirling. Gaelic-medium units or streams are generally located in local schools in which the majority of pupils are educated in English but 1999 saw the beginning of a new phase in GME with the opening of Scotland's first all-Gaelic school in Glasgow and the designation of five schools in the Outer Hebrides as Gaelic schools. The first purpose-built, all-Gaelic primary school opened in Inverness in 2007 and dedicated Gaelic schools have been established subsequently in Edinburgh, Fort William and Portree. A further five schools have been classified as Gaelic schools by Comhairle nan Eilean Siar.

In virtually all Gaelic-medium classes there is a mix of fluent speakers and learners. The proportions vary depending on the type of community the school serves. In rural, island schools, several of the pupils come from Gaelic-speaking homes while in urban, mainland schools, few pupils have that home background. The Gaelic-medium curriculum adheres to the principles of Curriculum for Excellence. The framework for Literacy and Gàidhlig is formulated along similar lines to that for English. It sets out 'broad descriptions of the range of learning opportunities which will contribute to the development of literacy' in the language and recognises that there are significant differences in the development of certain linguistic skills between English and Gaelic (https://education.gov.scot/Documents/literacy-gaidhlig-pp.pdf). This arises from the fact that GME begins with a period of total language immersion.

Education Scotland issued guidance to local authorities and schools on the implementation of GME in 2015 in its *Advice on Gaelic Education*. The Advice describes total immersion as being 'the early stage of learning through the medium of Gaelic … where no other language is used'. This phase normally continues until late in P3 but may be extended into

P4 in multi–composite classes. The stage beyond P3/4 is known as the immersion phase in which the curriculum across all four aspects of learning from Building the Curriculum 3 is taught through the medium of Gaelic. The Advice acknowledges that some schools and authorities have referred to the stage beyond total immersion as the bilingual stage and have thus allowed English 'to be too dominant in the learning process'. Education Scotland asserts that 'There is a substantial body of evidence from inspection that partial immersion is not effective in developing fluency.'

A 2011 HM Inspectorate of Education report, *Gaelic Education: Building on the Successes, Addressing the Barriers*, defined two outcomes for GME 3–18, one being that children and young people 'are equally confident in the use of Gaelic and English' and the other that they 'are able to use both Gaelic and English in a full range of situations within and outwith school'. The 2015 Education Scotland guidance recognises that because of the initial concentration on language development, children in GME 'will not be working at the same rate of learning and progress as their peers in English medium education through the Curriculum for Excellence Experiences and Outcomes across the curricular areas', but avers that they will 'demonstrate equal competency, if not better, by the end of P7'. There is little doubt that GME has been a success. Research into the attainments of pupils receiving Gaelic-medium primary education found that Gaelic-medium pupils often out-performed their English-medium peers even in English language (Johnstone, 1999). Similar results were reported in a more recent Edinburgh University study (O'Hanlon et al., 2010).

Gaelic features in the curriculum of primary schools in another two forms. In the Outer Hebrides, some schools which do not have Gaelic-medium streams, offer pupils a form of bilingual education developed from the earlier programme. Schools which have GME streams also provide a measure of bilingual education to pupils outwith the Gaelic stream. Gaelic also features as a language subject in English-medium primary schools in various parts of the country including areas of the Highlands where the language was once widely spoken. This Gaelic Learner Education (GLE) builds on a Gaelic Language in the Primary School scheme (GLPS) which ran from 2000 and also operates in areas where there is a Gaelic-medium school or unit in the locality. GLE is delivered, in conjunction with other modern languages, as part of the national 1+2 languages initiative which seeks to give pupils exposure to two languages over and above their first language. In 2013–14, around 8,000 primary pupils were learning Gaelic as part of the GLPS programme.

## SECONDARY EDUCATION

The use of Gaelic as a medium of education in secondary schools has not kept pace with developments in primary. The language was first used in the teaching of secondary subjects in 1983 when Comhairle nan Eilean set up a pilot project as an extension to its primary bilingual programme. The first Gaelic-medium unit on the mainland opened at Hillpark Secondary in Glasgow in 1988. Further provision was established in 1992 in Millburn Academy, Inverness and Portree High School, thus ensuring continuity of Gaelic-medium education for pupils of the three largest primary units. By 2015–16, GME was operating in seventeen secondary schools. August 2006 saw the opening of the first all-through Gaelic-medium school in Scotland in Glasgow affording pupils education through the language from age 3 to 18. By 2016–17, the school roll was 841. The use of Gaelic as a medium in secondary is restricted to two or three subjects in most schools. History is the subject most widely taught through Gaelic. Candidates may elect to sit Gaelic versions of National 5 examinations in History, Geography, Mathematics and Modern Studies and Higher Mathematics may be taken in Gaelic.

The development of Gaelic-medium education in secondary has been hampered by various factors. One is the fragmented nature of the secondary curriculum with its specialist subject structure. The typical primary school with one teacher per class lends itself more readily to a smaller cohort and the level of funding required is significantly less. Various attempts have been made to ameliorate this situation and the related one of the shortage of subject specialist teachers in GME. The most recent initiative, e-Sgoil, provides an online learning portal which gives pupils across the Western Isles and other parts of Scotland access to lessons and resources from a base in Stornoway.

Pupils in Gaelic-medium classes also study the language as a subject. They take the Gàidhlig course which is designed for fluent speakers and leads to certificate examinations at Nationals 3, 4 and 5, Higher and Advanced Higher. In 2016, 158 candidates sat the National 5 Gàidhlig examination while 132 took Higher and thirty-one sat Advanced Higher. The fluent speakers category includes pupils who have been in bilingual programmes in primary, and a small number who may not have had access to Gaelic-medium education and had little or no exposure to the language in primary, but come from Gaelic-speaking homes and begin formal study of the language in secondary.

A Gaelic (Learners) course leading to separate certificate examinations was instituted in 1962. This followed a campaign by prominent Gaelic teachers highlighting the inequity of asking learners of Gaelic to sit the same examination as native speakers. The new course brought provision for pupils learning Gaelic broadly into line with that for pupils learning other modern languages. Less than 10 per cent of state schools offer the Gaelic (Learners) option. Most of these are located in the Highlands and Islands. The number of schools has reduced through amalgamations and closures from forty to twenty-seven and there have been regional fluctuations with expansion in the Inverness area and contraction in Glasgow. Some schools in the independent sector occasionally present pupils for National Qualification examinations. The number of presentations for the Gaelic (Learners) exams in 2016 was 145 at National 5, eighty-four at Higher and twenty-four at Advanced Higher.

In schools in the Outer Hebrides, Skye and the West Highland mainland, it is council policy that all first and second year pupils study Gaelic and another modern language. In most other parts of Scotland, pupils typically have to choose between Gaelic and French, or German, from first year or take Gaelic as a second language option in second or third year. These option arrangements militate against a large uptake of the subject. The teaching of Gaelic has changed radically in the last thirty years. Where it was once a subject of study and analysis using English as the medium of instruction, the methodology deployed today aims to produce learners with communicative competence in the language and uses the target language extensively in the classroom.

In addition to the long-term courses outlined above, the Scottish Qualifications Authority (SQA) has a range of National units available for Gaelic learners. These cover the four key language skills and can be built into National courses, National Progression Awards and National Certificates. There are only a few units specifically designed for fluent speakers but any units on the SQA catalogue may be delivered and assessed through the medium of Gaelic.

## SUPPORT STRUCTURES

Recent developments have been facilitated and sustained by the creation of enabling mechanisms and support structures. Chief among these has been the Scheme of Specific Grants for Gaelic Education initiated in 1986. Under this scheme, local authorities submit project proposals to the Scottish Government and receive up to 75 per cent funding for approved projects. Grants are awarded for new or additional provision and authorities are expected to meet the full costs of initiatives after five years. The scheme's initial budget of £250,000 had risen to £4.482 million in 2015–16. Authorities can bid for funding on an individual or collective basis, but authorities are expected to allocate a proportion of total funding to collaborative projects. The specific grants scheme and the impulse to collaborate created a need for coordinated action by local authorities and led to the formation of an inter-authority network. Although the network made substantial progress in addressing the main areas of need, it was clear that a more permanent arrangement for the production of resources was required. This led to the establishment by the government of a national resource centre for Gaelic on Lewis in 1999. The new centre, Stòrlann, has delivered an extensive publishing programme but resources are still needed in most curricular areas.

National agencies such as the SQA and Education Scotland (ES) play significant roles in supporting Gaelic education. The SQA has a Gaelic Assessment Panel which nominates setters, examiners, moderators and markers for national examinations and provides advice relating to syllabus and assessment. The panel has produced revised and extended guidelines on Gaelic orthography which update and further exemplify the Gaelic Orthographic Conventions published in 1981 by the Scottish Examination Board. SQA and ES representatives participate in working parties which prepare subject guidelines and advice for national curriculum development programmes.

Curricular resources for GME and for Gaelic as a subject are to be found on the Education Scotland National Improvement Hub and on the Stòrlann website. Stòrlann operates a dedicated site for Gaelic learning materials. There is provision for Gaelic in the Scottish Schools Digital Network (GLOW) and facilities such as GLOW Blogs and GLOW Meet are particularly helpful in the Gaelic context where many teachers are located in rural and islands schools and can feel professionally isolated. An online GME resource database, e-Stòras, developed by Comhairle nan Eilean Siar, furnishes teachers with a catalogue of resources for use at all stages. The BBC produces radio and television programmes which cater for learners and fluent speakers and address various stages within primary and secondary. MG ALBA which administers the Gaelic Broadcasting Fund sponsors Film G, an annual short film competition for schools, and is involved in other initiatives such as a website for learners of all ages (LearnGaelic.scot).

Language development bodies and other agencies also play an important part in supporting and promoting Gaelic in education. The language development agency, Comunn na Gàidhlig (CnaG), performed a vital role in community animation and in the development of many aspects of Gaelic education in the 1980s and 1990s and was instrumental in setting up Comann nam Pàrant (Nàiseanta), a national association of parents, which has branches in most places where there is GME and in the formation of the Association of Secondary Gaelic Teachers (CLAS). A government agency for the language, Bòrd na Gàidhlig, was established in 2002 and continued CnaG's advocacy of official recognition for the language. This was finally achieved in 2005 with the passing of the Gaelic Language (Scotland) Act. The Act seeks to secure 'the status of Gaelic as an official language of Scotland' and to create the conditions for a sustainable future for the language by providing direction to Gaelic development activities through a strategic language planning approach. Under the Act, Bòrd na Gàidhlig became a statutory body with responsibility for advising the government on all matters relating to Gaelic language and culture. It is charged with devising a National Gaelic Language Plan that specifies strategies and priorities for future development. The third National Plan covers 2017–22. Bòrd na Gàidhlig has set up an advisory national body for Gaelic education that brings together local authorities, universities, colleges and national education agencies and the Bòrd funds a range of projects and initiatives designed to develop Gaelic education.

## TEACHER EDUCATION

Initial teacher education (ITE) in Gaelic is provided in four universities. The universities of Strathclyde and Aberdeen have traditionally been the main providers but the University of Edinburgh and the University of the Highlands and Islands (UHI) now offer training for Gaelic teachers. Primary ITE is provided mainly within four year Bachelor of Arts (BA) courses and the one year Professional Graduate Diploma in Education (Primary) (PGDE(P)) courses. There are Gaelic pathways in the BA course which enable Gaelic-speaking students to receive tuition in linguistic skills and teaching methods. Periods of school experience in a Gaelic unit are built into the pathway and into the training of students on the PGDE(P) course. Most of the training in Gaelic is optional and outwith core elements of the course. ITE arrangements for secondary teachers are more established. Gaelic is one of the subject specialisms in which students undertaking the PGDE (Secondary) course can qualify and they receive training in Gaelic teaching methods as a core part of the course. Their training prepares them to teach both the Gàidhlig and Gaelic (Learners) courses. There has been little pre-service provision for trainee teachers of other subjects intending to teach their specialisms through the medium of Gaelic but a recent collaborative venture by UHI and Comhairle nan Eilean Siar is designed to address that deficiency. Dissatisfaction has been voiced about the nature and extent of training provided for Gaelic-medium teachers. Surveys have shown that newly qualified teachers are critical of pre-service arrangements and feel inadequately prepared for the Gaelic-medium classroom with its additional demands and specialised requirements, notably immersion teaching.

Most in-service training in Gaelic is organised and delivered at local authority and school level with occasional input from university staff. An t-Alltan, a large-scale event open to all Gaelic teachers, is organised annually by Stòrlann and there are training events as part of national curriculum development initiatives. Teachers wishing to convert from secondary to primary or to gain a qualification to teach another secondary subject can do so by means of a one-term additional teaching qualification (ATQ) course at a university. Several teachers have entered Gaelic-medium teaching by this route and the ATQ has helped authorities address staffing shortages in particular places. Bòrd na Gàidhlig commissioned the universities of Strathclyde and Edinburgh to develop a Gaelic Immersion Course for Teachers (GIfT) which provides qualified teachers who have an interest in Gaelic with an opportunity to take the initial steps towards becoming Gaelic-medium teachers. A longer-established partnership between the Gaelic College, Sabhal Mòr Ostaig (SMO), and the University of Aberdeen led to the provision of another in-service course, Streap, designed to equip serving teachers with sufficient linguistic competence and confidence to be able to transfer to the Gaelic-medium sector.

A number of other steps have been taken to increase the supply of Gaelic-medium teachers. Recruitment drives have been mounted by Bòrd na Gàidhlig and the Scottish Funding Council (SFC) has funded places specifically for Gaelic-medium students. A collaborative venture by the University of Strathclyde and Lews Castle College saw a distance-learning PGDE(P) with Gaelic course developed which was subsequently extended to other colleges of the UHI. Another UHI partner, Sabhal Mòr Ostaig, collaborated with Aberdeen University on a joint Honours Master of Arts (MA) in Gaelic with Education which from 2017 will be run wholly through UHI and will be almost entirely delivered in Gaelic. The University of Edinburgh entered the field of Gaelic teacher education in 2015 with a twin-track four- or five-year MA Gaelic and Primary Education course. These measures have helped to reduce the gap between supply and demand but the throughput of trained personnel is still not sufficient to allow expansion of the Gaelic-medium sector.

## FURTHER AND HIGHER EDUCATION

The use of Gaelic as a medium of education extends into the tertiary sector and is indeed at its most comprehensive in one college. Sabhal Mòr Ostaig was founded in 1973 as a Gaelic College in Skye. Initially, the college ran a programme of short courses in Gaelic language and culture but, ten years on, it embarked on full-time provision. Today, the college, which has received government recognition as the National Centre for Gaelic Language and Culture, offers a range of certificate, diploma, degree and postgraduate courses in Gaelic language and culture. Many of these courses can be undertaken by distance learning. All courses are delivered and assessed in Gaelic. The college campus houses several national projects including a historical Gaelic dictionary project, a Gaelic place names project, and a large-scale project, Tobar an Dualchais/Kist o' Riches, to digitise and catalogue the extensive folklore and music archives of the School of Scottish Studies at Edinburgh University, the Gaelic Department of BBC Scotland, and the Campbell Collection in Canna. These archives of folksong and folklore are now available online and are a treasury which yields a rich resource of Gaelic and Scots material for exploitation in the Curriculum for Excellence.

Sabhal Mòr Ostaig, Lews Castle and other colleges in the north joined forces to form the University of the Highlands and Islands. UHI, a federal, collegiate institution embracing thirteen academic partners, gained full university title in 2011. Traditionally, students wishing to study Gaelic at university had to go to Aberdeen, Edinburgh or Glasgow, each of which has a Celtic department. These departments offer a range of undergraduate courses in Gaelic and Celtic Studies and students can take an honours degree in Celtic or a joint honours in Celtic and another subject. Provision is made for those wanting to learn the language and Celtic Civilisation classes cater for those with an interest in cultural heritage. Postgraduate study opportunities are also available in the discipline. The Royal Conservatoire of Scotland in Glasgow offers a degree course in Scottish Music which has some Gaelic components.

## COMMUNITY EDUCATION

Time spent in school is but a fraction of the time spent in the home and community, and the contribution of these domains to the education of the child is being recognised increasingly in the development of Gaelic education. A number of local authorities arrange evening classes for parents wishing to learn Gaelic in order to assist, and keep in step with, the linguistic progress of their offspring. A website for parents and children engaged in GME run by Stòrlann offers a homework helpline and learning aids. Some authorities also provide language packs for parents who are not Gaelic speakers so that they can help their children with homework. Reinforcement of the language beyond the school is regarded as a vital part of the GME strategy, especially for children from non-Gaelic-speaking homes, and a nationwide network of Gaelic youth clubs for children aged 5 to 12 was established by CnaG.

Another community initiative, Fèisean nan Gàidheal, seeks to reinforce the link between the language and culture. A *fèis*, or festival, is typically a week-long event which offers children tuition in Gaelic and in a variety of Gaelic arts including drama, storytelling, song and music. The *fèis* movement began in Barra and has evolved into a national agency which assists with the organisation of forty-six separate *fèisean* in communities in, and beyond, the Highlands and Islands. Fèisean nan Gàidheal also provides a Gaelic theatre in education service to schools and a *Fèisgoil* programme of lessons for learners in primary schools where the language is not yet part of the curriculum. A number of agencies run classes and short courses for adult learners. The community education departments of local authorities and colleges continue to be the principal providers. University departments of continuing education also offer Gaelic classes. Intensive short courses for learners are organised by a number of public and private agencies.

## RESEARCH

Although much research has been conducted on linguistic, socio-linguistic, demographic and literary topics by university departments, agencies such as the SMO Lèirsinn Research centre and by individuals such as Professor Kenneth MacKinnon, research on Gaelic education has been sparse until comparatively recently. Some of the most important research projects into aspects of Gaelic education have been conducted by Stirling University. The first of these was an evaluation of the Western Isles Bilingual Project, published in 1987. The findings were generally favourable to the project and supportive of the bilingual scheme. Professor Richard Johnstone's 1994 review of research on the *Impact of Current Developments to Support the Gaelic Language* gave a comprehensive account and perceptive analysis of developments in education and other fields of Gaelic activity. The third government-funded Stirling project was a three-year programme of research into the attainments of pupils in Gaelic-medium primary education in Scotland. The research, published in 1999, confirmed that pupils educated in Gaelic 'were not being disadvantaged in comparison with children educated through English' and were, in many instances, outperforming English-medium pupils, while also gaining the advantage of proficiency in two languages (Johnstone, 1999). These findings have been echoed in a 2010 study conducted by a team of researchers (O'Hanlon, McLeod and Paterson) from Edinburgh University.

Socio-linguistic research in Gaelic received a major boost in 2009 with the advent of the Soillse research network, a partnership of the universities of Aberdeen, Edinburgh, Glasgow and UHI. The SMO-based Soillse programme, which had an initial £5.29 million budget and was 50 per cent externally funded, has helped to increase research capacity in the language and has focused on Gaelic in education, language policies and language in the community. Research undertaken in education has included a study of patterns of Gaelic and English use in Gaelic-medium preschool, primary school and secondary school settings, an analysis of choice and attainment in Gaelic-medium primary and early secondary education, and a study of language use, ideologies and attitudes in young adults educated in Gaelic. A major conference on Gaelic research, Rannsachadh na Gàidhlig, is held biennially in one of the universities with a Celtic or Gaelic department. Papers on linguistic, literary, educational and cultural topics are published in conference proceedings.

## PROSPECTS

There have been several highly significant developments in Gaelic in Scotland in the past thirty years. These have included the introduction and expansion of GME, the establishment of a government agency for the language, the passing of a Gaelic Language Act, and the creation of a Gaelic television channel, BBC ALBA. The growth in GME from 1985 has been remarkable and justifies the claim that it has been 'one of the success stories of Scottish education' (General Teaching Council for Scotland, 1999). The 2011 Census recorded a modest, but nevertheless significant, increase in the number of children able to speak Gaelic, an uplift that can be attributed largely to GME. However, the demographic challenge which the language faces remains formidable with one estimate suggesting that 1,500 new Gaelic speakers are needed each year to offset the attrition in the number of older Gaelic speakers.

Spectacular as the development of GME has been, significant challenges lie ahead. One of these will be the attainment of the 2012 National Plan target of a 15 per cent year-on-year increase in the number of children entering Gaelic-medium education from a baseline of 400 in 2011–12. The growth experienced by the all-Gaelic schools in Glasgow, Inverness and Edinburgh and the opening of similar schools elsewhere will go some way towards that goal. A concern remains that the advances made in urban areas have not been matched in rural parts of the Highlands and Islands. The creation of Gaelic schools in dispersed and thinly populated rural areas remains more problematic than in urban centres. It is an issue which Bòrd na Gàidhlig will have to seek to resolve in its engagement with local authorities during production of their language plans and in fulfilling the terms of the statutory guidance issued in respect of the Education (Scotland) Act 2016.

A particular challenge facing GME is that of meeting demand. There have been instances where local authorities have sought to cap enrolment because of a failure to plan adequately and timeously for expansion and to provide sufficient capacity in schools. In other cases, uncertainty as to teacher recruitment has been cited by authorities as the reason for not offering additional GME provision. A number of steps have been taken to address the shortage of GME teachers but a more coherent, sustained and effective strategy is required.

The seepage of pupils from GME at the primary–secondary interface and at other transition points in secondary school is another issue. A key factor affecting this is that GME in secondary school has not been properly planned and fully developed. The number of subjects available through Gaelic is limited and access needs to be enhanced and made more consistent. It is expected that recent initiatives in distance learning will go some way to addressing the current deficiencies.

The *Advice on Gaelic Education* (Education Scotland, 2015) sets strong expectations about the use of Gaelic for learning, teaching and assessment in all aspects of the 3–18 curriculum and should allay parental concerns about the variability in language models that have been adopted by local authorities. It is to be hoped that the new guidance will lead to more uniform implementation of the good practice that does exist in maximising the use of the language as the vehicle of instruction. That, in turn, should allow the target of attaining communicative competence in both Gaelic and English by the end of primary school to be achieved more readily. It should also instil more confidence in pupils in their use of the language beyond the confines of the classroom. Research has indicated that youngsters who have been educated in Gaelic do not use the language regularly after leaving school.

Access to the language and culture should not be confined to the Gaelic-medium sector. Over 90 per cent of secondary school children in Scotland are denied the opportunity to learn Gaelic in their local school. Research, attitudinal surveys, audience figures for learners' programmes on television and the uptake of learners' classes in continuing and higher education all suggest that there is considerable potential for the development of provision for learners within secondary schools. It is anticipated that a report on adult learners commissioned by Bòrd na Gàidhlig will lead to more structured pathways and more bespoke resources which will enable greater numbers of learners to progress to fluency.

Despite the overdue introduction of a Scottish Studies option in the curriculum, Celtic and Gaelic elements of Scottish heritage, life and culture continue to be neglected in most Scottish schools. It is an indictment of the education system that so few pupils have any awareness, let alone knowledge, of Celtic civilisation or Gaelic culture. This defect manifests itself in singularly ill-informed varieties of public discourse and in negative attitudes to the language and culture in certain quarters.

## REFERENCES

Bòrd na Gàidhlig (2017) *The National Gaelic Language Plan 2018–2023*. Inverness: Bòrd na Gàidhlig.

Curriculum for Excellence (2011) Gaelic Excellence Group Report. Edinburgh: Education Scotland.

Education Scotland (2015) *Advice on Gaelic Education*. Online at https://education.gov.scot/improvement/Documents/Gael3-Advice-on-Gaelic-Education-Eng.pdf

General Teaching Council for Scotland (nd) *Teaching in Gaelic Medium Education: Recommendations for Change*. Online at www.gtcs.org.uk/web/FILES/FormUploads/teaching-in-gaelic-medium-education1659_221.pdf

HM Inspectorate of Education (2011) *Gaelic Education: Building on the Successes, Addressing the Barriers*. Livingston: HM Inspectorate of Education.

Johnstone, R. (1994) *The Impact of Current Developments to Support the Gaelic Language*. Review of Research, Stirling: Scottish CILT.

Johnstone, R. (1999) *The Attainments of Pupils Receiving Gaelic Medium Primary Education in Scotland*. Stirling: Scottish Centre for Information on Language Teaching and Research.

O'Hanlon, F., McLeod, W. and Paterson, L. (2010) *Gaelic medium Education in Scotland: Choice and Attainment at the Primary and Early Secondary Stages*. Inverness: Bòrd na Gàidhlig.

O'Hanlon, F., McLeod, W. and Paterson, L. (2012) *Language Models in Gaelic-medium Pre-school, Primary and Secondary Education*. Edinburgh: University of Edinburgh.

Robertson, B. (2018) *Gaelic: The Gaelic Language in Education in the UK*. Leeuwarden: Mercator-Education.

### Websites

e-Sgoil at www.gtcs.org.uk/News/teaching-scotland/67-e-sgoil.aspx

GLOW at https://glowconnect.org.uk/

Stòrlann at www.storlann.co.uk/beurla/index.html#Content

# VIII

# ASSESSMENT, CERTIFICATION AND ACHIEVEMENTS

# 68

# Assessment in Scottish Schools

*Tom Bryce*

## ASSESSMENT: WHAT FOR AND WHEN?

Assessment is *multifunctional*. It serves a number of purposes in education, the most important being argued here is its influence upon learning. Hence the chapter begins with the nature and use of *formative* assessment, looking at strategies which teachers have been encouraged to use, the research evidence favouring quality feedback to pupils (making it *feedforward*), and the importance of addressing the substance of pupils' thinking in what is assessed. Assessment is also required for *summative* purposes and at key points throughout schooling it is necessarily judgemental and used for a variety of predictive functions, requiring care, assurances and comprehensible reporting of what has been attained by pupils. These functions dominate public discourse as well as pupils' lives, with assessment figuring regularly in reports to parents throughout the primary and secondary stages; annually in school reports (to central government) of teachers' judgements of pupils' attainments of Curriculum for Excellence (CfE) levels in literacy and numeracy at P1, P4, P7 and S3; and periodically through international surveys (Organisation for Economic Co-operation and Development (OECD)/Programme for International Student Assessment (PISA)) of reading, maths and science. The most recent of these (both the school reports to government and the international comparisons) have raised concerns about worsening performances by Scottish pupils. At the upper stages of secondary schools there is annual interest – and, for the young people concerned as well as their parents, concern and anxiety – in the Scottish Qualifications Authority (SQA) results of National, Higher and Advanced Higher courses. Each year, the national press makes much of these results, generating league tables of schools' performances. Government focuses on results in another sense, that is, not only on improvements in award numbers overall, but upon the backgrounds of applicants whose results count for university places. Lower entry requirements are being set for students from poor backgrounds (by all Scottish universities by 2019) and ever increasing, additional demands are being made of able students – such are current government obsessions with social engineering in the interests of equality, no matter the effects on quality and excellence. The chapter looks at how criteria for assessment are specified, via grades and levels and the recently published CfE *benchmarks*. Attention is paid to recent decisions taken by Scottish Government concerning assessment in reaction to concerns expressed by teachers regarding workload. Comments are made regarding the relationship between formative and summative aspects of assessment and the constraining (distorting?) effects of reporting formats upon formative assessment.

Assessment for teachers is conventionally thought of as something to be carried out *after* teaching has taken place. Simply put, it is to check on the learning that has taken place. For other professionals however – in medicine, dentistry, social care and so on – assessment means something rather different. In the work of these professionals it is conventionally thought of as something to be carried out *before* treatment takes place. With ever increasing public (as well as professional) scrutiny and accountability, the care with which such specialists carry out assessments tries to ensure that the treatments they pursue correspond closely and effectively: treatment leads to reassessment and the resulting cyclic arrangement is beneficial to clients and professionals alike. There is some merit in teachers seeing comparisons in their own field and having equal concerns for rigour and *connection* in the relationship between teaching and assessment (and therefore being professionally accountable for it). Assessment should have a close and effective link with the teaching which led to its conduct: assessments which reveal inadequate learning should pointedly lead to the re-teaching required. The expression characterising the process in this way is *formative* assessment. Defined formally, it is 'all those activities undertaken by teachers, *and by their students in assessing themselves*, which provide information to be used as feedback to modify the teaching and learning activities in which they are engaged' (Black and Wiliam, 2001, p. 2, emphasis in the original).

For the best part of ten years, prior to and overlapping with the start of Curriculum for Excellence, Scottish teachers were persuaded through a national initiative to develop their practices in this way: to alter how they conducted assessment so that it has maximum impact on pupil learning and encouraging pupils to see how they can improve their current understandings and skills. The thrust of that Assessment is for Learning (AifL or just AfL) movement was to supply meaningful feedback *for* learning to occur, helping individuals to move forward from their current position. It contrasted with the traditional and widespread view of assessment, the assessment *of* the learning that has taken place: that is, looking backwards, checking what pupils have learned from their schoolwork – said to be 'summative' for it purports to summarise the pupil's learning, knowledge and capabilities up to that point. The purposes of assessment described in CfE documentation stress both of these (in that order, but without any recognition of possible tensions). Information from assessment serves several important purposes: to support learning; to give assurance to parents and others about learners' progress; to provide a summary of what learners have achieved, including through qualifications and awards, and to inform future improvements (www.gov.scot/resource/doc/341834/0113711.pdf). And the August 2016 documentation states that: 'Assessment is integral to learning and teaching. It is an ongoing process' (https://education.gov.scot/improvement/Documents/cfestatement.pdf).

Summative assessment using predetermined criteria, often 'level related' or 'grade related' (more of which in due course), is very much an established regime and gathered strength when the development of the Standard Grade curriculum in secondary schools in the 1980s began the idea of spelling out objectives and criteria nationally. However, it figures everywhere on the ladder of education, and assessment is a preoccupation of teachers' lives, such are the demands it makes. There are positive and negative factors associated with the use of criteria to record grades or levels as indications of assessment: positive in that it helps to ensure that everyone does the same thing and exercises judgements against the same standards; negative when everything and anything is considered 'grade-able' – which invites the uncomplimentary term, 'assessment-is-for-grading'; or, less pejoratively, level checking or reaching the benchmark. An important issue is the relationship between formative assessments and those summative assessments which are used for key decisions such as permitting entry to a course (for example, in using S3 attainment results to allow pupils entry into particular courses in S4) or certificating exit from a course ('He got a B in his Higher English'). Whether it is possible to compromise constructively between assessing the learning that *has* occurred and assessing in the interests of *future* learning/relearning will be considered later in the chapter. First, formative assessment itself will be looked at more closely.

## ASSESSMENT FOR LEARNING AND STRATEGIES FOR ITS IMPROVEMENT

The AfL movement concentrated upon developing the quality of formative classroom assessment throughout the country. It derived considerable benefit from the impressive efforts by Dylan Wiliam of the London Institute of Education to disseminate the messages emanating from research on comparisons between summative and formative assessment in real classroom situations (see Black and Wiliam, 1998; 2001; Black et al., 2002). These comparisons showed that where teachers, in the course of their assessment feedback, emphasise what pupils have done well and, more importantly, what they need to do to tackle the improvements required, the process is much more effective than simply grading the work. The argument turns on practicable, innovative strategies to change what teachers actually do. For many years, government (notably through Education Scotland and its predecessor curriculum body), local authority continuing professional development (CPD) providers, and schools who became convinced of the effectiveness of more formative versions of assessment, all gave testimony to the benefits of *raising the quality of classroom interactions* in order to connect assessment and learning more explicitly. The emphasis was upon: the use by teachers of thoughtful questions, listening carefully to how pupils try to explain things and commenting reflectively on what they say or write; on helping pupils, staff and parents to be clear about what is to be learned and what success would be like; on giving timely feedback about the quality of pupils' work and how to make it better; and involving pupils in deciding the next steps in their learning. The AfL principles, intended to get pupils to take more responsibility for their own learning, have been a central plank in Curriculum for Excellence developments nationally and their adoption has been evaluated during Her Majesty's Inspectorate of Education (HMIE) inspections of both schools and local authorities (Hutchinson and Young, 2011).

There is a fair amount of research evidence to show that teachers can be encouraged to give qualitatively better feedback by instigating strategies like:

- allowing longer 'wait' times during classroom questioning (to better ensure that pupils think about what is being pursued) and adopting a 'no hands' strategy (to keep everyone alert and allow teachers to selectively target learners);
- incorporating 'traffic-light' systems to target help more readily – where pupils use coloured pens, cards, stickers and so on to say what they are comfortable with and don't need going over (green), what they are rather uncertain about (amber) and what they can't do and need help with (red), all of which help teachers to target their help more readily;

- using 'two stars and a wish' strategies (where teachers try to ensure that they concentrate in a marking exercise on finding two things to comment on favourably and one weakness (only) which needs addressing in such-and-such a way, thereby shifting the balance of demotivation/motivation that can arise from corrective feedback);
- making use of 'self-' and 'peer-assessment' (pupils being trained to assess each other's work, enabling them to gain access to more reaction and discussion of their efforts and understandings, rather than waiting on the teacher's feedback);
- exploiting apps like Showbie on iPads to handle assignments, provide check tests and give feedback (or, in a less sophisticated environment, using mini-whiteboards whereby pupils show their thinking to a teacher during class sessions).
- encouraging senior pupils to mark a copy of their own test efforts using marking instructions (cf. SQA exemplar material), then comparing them to their teacher's marks;
- refraining from the use of grades when marking pupils' work (working with written comments instead) to prevent the 'What did you get?' phenomenon which blinds learners to what the advice is.

## EVIDENCE FOR THE EFFICACY OF GOOD FEEDBACK (MAKING IT *FEEDFORWARD*)

The last item is perhaps the most significant and demanding recommendation from researchers – actually *refraining* from the use of grades when marking. The argument here, borne out by a number of studies, is that pupils normally pay little or no attention to written feedback when grades are attached to their homework exercises, test results and so on. They simply engage in comparisons of grades with each other. Proponents of formative assessment urge teachers to take the uncomfortable step (given the prevailing regime) of *not* using grades and to operate with written comments only, these designed to focus upon what the pupil should do next and differently. Very many teachers say it is nigh impossible to get round the distracting 'What did you get?' phenomenon, even where pupils are familiar with strategies used to formatively assess their efforts; teachers say that a school's requirements to submit grades overwhelms their efforts. However, the evidence that the quality of teacher feedback really matters does figure in research. For example, Hattie's scrutiny of the effects of various influences upon pupil (student) learning has involved him in determining 'effect sizes' in numerous studies of the relationships between a host of school variables and pupil attainment (see, for example, Hattie and Timperley, 2007). 'Teacher feedback' is the first item on the list of the score or more of potential variables built into these researches. Good feedback (according to Petty, commenting on Hattie's findings) includes:

telling students what they have done well (positive reinforcement), and what they need to do to improve (corrective work, targets etc.), but it also includes clarifying goals. This means that giving students assessment criteria for example would be included in 'feedback'... High quality feedback is always given against explicit criteria, and ... as well as feedback on the task, Hattie believes that students can get feedback on the processes they have used to complete the task, and on their ability to self-regulate their own learning. All these have the capacity to increase achievement. Feedback on the 'self' such as 'well done you are good at this' is not helpful. The feedback must be informative rather than evaluative. (www.geoffpetty.com/research.html)

For teacher feedback, the effect size amounts to advancing a pupil's traditional grade at fourth year by two levels or so, or by advancing him/her by one year or more in attainment.

However, it must be remembered that an important issue is that surface or rote learning (see Chapter 23) can yield effect sizes, too, and there should be concerns about the extent to which school and SQA assessments tap that kind of learning.

## ASSESSING *WHAT* LEARNERS ARE THINKING

All of the advice listed above refers to *strategies* which teachers can use to make formative assessment better. They cut across topics, subject matter and the very substance of what learning is about. Wait time, no–hands–up and so on have in themselves nothing to say about what it is *in pupils' thinking* about the ideas at the core of learning which teachers must pay attention to. Some researchers have suggested that, important and successful though the AfL movement has been, it has distracted researchers (and professional learning providers) from focusing teachers' attention on *what* they should attend to in the process of formatively assessing. In the words of Coffey et al. (2011), looking at science teaching: 'Strategies should be in the service of ... what and how students' are thinking and participating' (p. 4). Perhaps it is a matter of balance. Coffey et al. readily concede the valuable emphasis there has been on how good descriptive feedback on pupils' work offers guidance on improvements to be made (feedforward), on how it should be task focused and timely. But they do stress that assessment should give more weight to the *substance* of what learners seem to be saying.

> we propose that it is essential for teachers to frame what is taking place in class [in terms of] students' ideas and reasoning ... Formative assessment, then, becomes about engaging with and responding to the substance of those ideas and reasoning, assessing with discipline-relevant criteria, and, from ideas, recognizing possibilities along the disciplinary horizon. (Coffey et al., 2011, p. 23)

Researchers concerned with the assessment of children's writing have raised similar concerns. Ellis (2012) found that Scottish primary teachers frequently determined success criteria before lessons took place rather than negotiating them with pupils. Often the criteria presented a narrow view of a successful piece of writing, focusing upon the technical/syntactic aspects of the work rather than the communicative purposes served by it. Headteachers did check that 'two stars and a wish' were being operated but did not monitor the content of the comments being noted by teachers. Interestingly, and of concern, a comparison of the comments given to pupils revealed that the more able writers were more likely to receive comments about what they had said, whereas less able writers were more likely to be given comments about technical and syntactic features. As Ellis (2012) noted:

> writing is about communicating ideas. If those who find it hardest to write fail to get feedback on *what* they have said, they may begin to view writing, not as a means of communication, but as a task involving a set of rules and procedures to be applied correctly. The lack of intrinsic purpose will impact on the quantity of writing, on how they feel about it, on their understanding of why learning to write is important and on the potential that writing has to empower the writer. (p. 10)

## ENCOURAGING OR DISCOURAGING MORE FORMATIVE ASSESSMENT?

With respect to encouraging teachers across Scotland to carry out more formative assessment, progress has been slow and somewhat uneven. The national evaluation of the AfL programme conducted in 2003 and 2004 (Condie et al., 2005) noted that greater movement had taken place in primary schools over secondary schools and that further impacts would be long term. In that context, in the fourth edition of *Scottish Education*, the present writer therefore lamented the removal from the Education Scotland (ES) website of the extensive positive testimonies and advice from teachers and schools regarding AfL: classroom assessment focusing on formative intentions came off the official agenda. That happened during the run-up to the introduction of the National 4 and 5 qualifications which, rather unconvincingly, claimed formative benefits to be had from unit tests formally required en route to, and as a prerequisite of, sitting final examinations (see a later section in this chapter regarding their recent withdrawal). Testing and everything connected with the examination of pupils had long been associated with specified criteria, much of it having been of a behavioural nature thus identifying the endpoints of learning. Significantly, Wiliam himself, in the late 1990s, had stated that 'we must refuse to accept the incompatibility of SA [summative assessment] and FA [formative assessment]. Instead we must find ways of mitigating the tension, by whatever means we can. Of course, this is a vast undertaking ...' (Wiliam, 2000, p. 16). Writing in 2011, he continued to press that a behavioural focus must be avoided and that feedback mechanisms need to take into account the wider circumstances of pupils' responses and the particular learning context in classrooms. In Scotland, that advice has been largely ignored. Furthermore, Hutchinson and Young (2011) explicitly acknowledged that the AfL programme did *not* address the link with students aged 15–18 studying for National Qualifications. Citing the report of a pilot study, they acknowledged that the mood among many secondary teachers meant reluctance to change their practice.

To explore this, it is worth considering the whole argument about SA and FA the other way round. One theoretician, Taras (2005), has argued that all assessment necessarily *begins* with SA, because it involves judgement, and that FA is SA plus feedback. She rationalises what happens educationally by distinguishing between the *form* and the *function* of assessment (the instructional *process* is the same for both but SA is *multifunctional*) stating that: 'Currently, FA is the antiseptic version of assessment and SA has come to represent all the negative social aspects' (Taras, 2005, p. 469). In other words, Taras recognises that beyond the place of assessment during learning, other factors figure in what may (or should) be done with the summarising judgements of assessment. These admittedly, and realistically, go way beyond scores and grade levels into how well schools can convince pupils, and their parents, that further progress is possible. Necessarily, teachers must find effective ways of encouraging young learners to believe in themselves that mid-term grades which fall short of those desired or required by the end of a course of study *are* improvable and that current judgements are not 'terminal'. Little of that is technical: much of it lies in the art of teaching and rests upon good working relationships between teachers and learners. A little more about this will be said later but a first consideration is to look briefly at how assessment criteria have developed in the Scottish system over recent decades and are shaped by the operations of summative assessment and course levels.

## SUMMATIVE ASSESSMENT: GRADES, LEVELS AND QUALIFICATIONS

For the last forty years or so, successive changes to the curriculum of Scottish schools have brought increasing specification to both content and assessment criteria. According to official advice, standardisation and 'good practice' in assessment have been encouraged through Standard Grade (in the 1980s), Scottish Vocational Education Council (SCOTVEC) modules (later in the 1980s), 5–14 (1990s), Higher Still (National Qualifications, 2000s), then Curriculum for Excellence (later in the 2000s). Grade-related criteria began with Standard Grade's three levels (credit, levels 1 and 2; general, levels 3 and 4; and foundation, levels 5 and 6; no award, 7); hence the notion of a scale of final achievement was reconfirmed. SCOTVEC modules required all of a module's outcomes to be met to earn a pass. With 5–14 there was an attempt to better connect primary and secondary schooling and bring a (st)age dimension with ascending targets to the specification of Scotland's national curriculum (stopping short of S4 and S5 because of the existence of Standard Grade which had taken so long to get in place). The curriculum specification was far from an assessment blueprint, which pleased some but not others in the professional communities of Scottish education. Higher Still, launched in 1999–2000, brought together academic and vocational qualifications into one multilevel framework for S5 and S6 and beyond into further education, essentially a big brother to Standard Grade. The range of qualifications (Access, Intermediate 1, Intermediate 2, Higher and Advanced Higher) extended the ability/attainment levels significantly and they became referred to as National Qualifications (NQs). Detailed outcomes defined each course and its level, and grades A, B and C were accorded to the achievement of a course. The new system did extend opportunities for attainment, especially for middle- and lower-attaining 16 year olds and for students with special needs, according to Raffe et al. (2005).

## Curriculum for Excellence Levels

In 2004, a major overhaul of the whole school curriculum was signalled in the government paper *Ambitious, Excellent Schools – Our Agenda for Action* (www.scotland.gov.uk/library5/education/aesaa-00.asp). From this, Curriculum for Excellence was evolved (and formally commenced nationally in session 2010–11). Other chapters of this book deal with the attempted 'decluttering' of the curriculum, the attempts to give schools more flexibility in what they teach children, and provide critical appraisals of the current state of play. With regard to assessment, what should be taught was specified at four levels for preschool up to 16 years (with further changes to post-16 qualifications, as discussed below). The assessment criteria for CfE tend to emphasise skills rather than content and the experiences and outcomes (the Es and Os or E&Os) for the various levels, take the form of 'I can ...' statements, it being judged by the curriculum developers that, by expressing intentions in first-person, pupil terms should be clearer, more useful and understandable by those on the receiving end. The Es and Os are not content-free however and the contextualisation for each does convey what should be learned. They provide a means whereby focused discussion can take place (particularly with older pupils) regarding what has been learned/not learned/needs revision or further practice, and so forth. Figure 68.1 illustrates some examples for the topic of electricity in Science.

Levels 1 and 2 are those for lower and upper primary respectively; levels 3 and 4 are those for lower and middle secondary respectively. By desiring such statements to express what should be experienced (the Es) *and* simultaneously what should be the outcomes (the Os), the latter seem diminished in detail. It remains for empirical research and fieldwork to ascertain whether assessment is blunted or not as a result.

However, the picture has been made more complex by the specification of benchmarks. These are discussed below. With the change from the previous curriculum, it was readily apparent that the four levels for CfE correspond closely to the *key stages* in the curriculum for England and Wales – a step towards commonality across the countries of the UK, despite

**Early**

I know how to stay safe when using electricity. I have helped to make a display to show the importance of electricity in our daily lives.

**Level 1**

I can describe an electrical circuit as a continuous loop of conducting materials.
I can combine simple components in a series circuit to make a game or model.

**Level 2**

I have used a range of electrical components to help to make a variety of circuits for differing purposes. I can represent my circuit using symbols and describe the transfer of energy around the circuit.

**Level 3**

Having measured the current and voltage in series and parallel circuits, I can design a circuit to show the advantages of parallel circuits in an everyday application.

**Level 4**

Through investigation, I understand the relationship between current, voltage and resistance. I can apply this knowledge to solve practical problems.

By contributing to investigations into the properties of a range of electronic components, I can select and use them as input and output devices in practical electronic circuits.

Using my knowledge of electronic components and switching devices, I can help to engineer an electronic system to provide a practical solution to a real-life situation.

**Figure 68.1   CfE experiences and outcomes for Science electricity**

Source: https://www.education.gov.scot/Documents/all-experiences-and-outcomes.pdf

the proudly held distinctiveness of Scottish education? (Scotland's 'early' stage, preschool to the end of the reception year in primary, is 'foundation' south of the border; Scotland's 'first' stage, 5–7 years, is level 1; 'second', 7–11 years, is level 2; 'third', 11–14 years, is level 3; and 'fourth', 14–16 years, is level 4.) All of the experiences and outcomes for CfE can be found at https://www.education.gov.scot/Documents/all-experiences-and-outcomes.pdf

## Beyond S2: National Awards

Following a national consultation conducted in 2008, Scottish Government announced in June 2009, that:

- From 2013/14 onwards, there would be a new qualification at Scottish Credit and Qualifications Framework (SCQF) levels 4 and 5, called National 4 and National 5, to replace both Standard Grade (General and Credit) and Intermediate 1 and 2 whilst reflecting the best features of the then present arrangements (Standard Grade Foundation level would be removed, with Access 3 providing an appropriate replacement).
- New qualifications in literacy and numeracy at SCQF levels 3, 4 and 5 would be introduced from 2012/13, to be called National Literacy and National Numeracy, based on a portfolio

of work across the curriculum. (Note that this was changed in 2010 when the then Cabinet Secretary, Mike Russell, announced that these would be backed into English and Maths respectively in the form of tests.) The literacy experiences and outcomes across learning can be found at www.ltscotland.org.uk/learningteachingandassessment/learningacrossthecurriculum/responsibilityofall/literacy/experiencesandoutcomes/index.asp

• The existing Access, Higher and Advanced Higher qualifications would be retained as points of stability, and reviewed to ensure they fully reflect CfE.

The government was clearly pressurised by industry and commerce to put tests of literacy and numeracy in place, despite teaching unions, parents (the Scottish Parent Teacher Association) and several university faculties of education being against the proposal. A concession was granted that these be in S3, not S4, to allow more examinable subjects than five to be taken in S4. National 4 is internally assessed in schools, but not graded, that is, coursework is used with some quality assurance by SQA. National 5 has internal and external graded assessment (the latter an exam), akin to the practice that had been in place for Intermediates. The external examinations figure in S4 +, clearly an attempt to revert to consistency across authorities. National Assessment Bank (NAB) tests were used for some years, then discontinued in 2010, being replaced by National Assessment Resources (NARs) – an online set of resources (see www.gov.scot/Topics/Education/Schools/curriculum/assessment).

Candidates who failed unit assessments could retake them, a consequence which added complexity to the considerable workload pressure upon subject departments as well as candidates. It takes little arithmetic to see that a pupil taking, say, five courses in S5, would have been undertaking very many formal tests long before they reached the May diet of examinations, fifteen at least, with some schools requiring 'graded NABs' as well as 'prelim' examinations to be sat. A department had to fit in NABs for absentees and resits for those who failed them. Pupils and teachers were truly said to be 'NABed to death'. Subsequently, unit assessments were judged to be just too demanding for teachers and their removal was announced by government in 2016, as described at the end of this chapter.

The new National Levels 4 and 5 were phased in by session 2015–16. Following the introduction of CfE in session 2010–11, the last certification of Standard Grades took place in 2012–13. The new Highers and Advanced Highers were introduced in sessions 2014–15 and 2015–16 respectively. Overall, the government's preferred option was for a 3 + 3 model for secondary education – the broad general education of pupils should continue from primary and span S1 to S3, with subject choice for upper school taking place at the end of S3. Many schools and authorities sought to retain a 2 + 2 + 2 model, one which reflected the traditional pattern of pupils choosing their subjects for specialisation at the end of S2. In a 3 + 3 model, some schools opted to run two tracks in the upper school: pupils starting either National 4 or 5 in S4, with the more able (level 5) candidates commencing Highers in S5 and Advanced Highers in S6. In a 2 + 2 + 2 model, some schools also ran two tracks: National 4 and 5 courses spanning S3 and S4, with the more able (level 5) candidates taking Highers in S5 and Advanced Highers in S6.

## Reconciling Formative and Summative Assessments: Reporting

With regard to reporting assessment results to pupils and parents, for primaries, written comments are accompanied by CfE grades 1 and 2 (or 3+, as the case may be). For secondaries, written comments accompany CfE grades at levels 3–4 (or lower levels, as the case may be). The actual formats of current pupil reports vary by authority, the government having earlier decided not to insist upon a national format. However, a fair number have capitalised on electronic systems (such as those of SEEMIS). These have the advantage that, as well as generating reports for pupils and parents, the system lets teachers/senior management teams carry out detailed monitoring of individual pupils, with user-friendly, visual formats of progress being made (or not). Flexible electronic formats for monitoring pupils' progress also mean that senior management have increasingly powerful ways of monitoring subjects and teachers too. 'Could do betters' won't do! Nevertheless, grades dominate everywhere, so 'aggregating' them sensibly is often problematic. Treating every recorded grade as if it was summative, and somehow merited arithmetical averaging, when in fact it was earlier intended to be formative, will not advance the assessment process usefully. Much more subtle judgements are necessary in many cases, especially those where pupils are making steady gains and their earlier low grades should be ignored. The present context for teachers, one that is dominated by accountability and pressures to ensure that pupils will achieve the best possible final results, alas means that there is considerable pressure on them to treat recorded grades as if they were *all* summative. The system is in a predicament: genuinely formative assessment and grading are mutually contradictory and pupils and parents are part of 'the problem'. Not long into certificate courses they do ask how well they/their offspring are faring in respect of likely outcomes at the end of the course.

But some teachers do live with the grading regime and find it possible to get their pupils to take advice and improve their understandings. One has to reason that it all depends upon the integrity of the processes which teachers deploy, long term, with their pupils, with how genuine they are themselves (and can make themselves in the particular settings within which they teach). Teachers who turn pupils on to realistic prospects of advancement and how to make the best out of prevailing circumstances seem to be able to get pupils to face predictions as challenges, rather than as forecasts of certainty or defeat. As with everything in learning, it all turns on motivation. Good teachers know that the deep personal messages that they convey to pupils, day in and day out, through all their statements, both deliberate and casual, are crucial to what pupils take out of learning. In this sense the educational process is more important than the product. An effective process shifts the responsibility for learning from the teacher to the pupil. In recognition of this, some secondary schools have delayed the effects of grading, encouraging staff to use written commentary for assessment for a good part of a certificate course, only later combining comments and grades.

Parent education and persuasion is a necessary aspect of any innovations in formative assessment. The use of electronic systems for reporting *with grades* as the main entries, desirable as it is, runs essentially counter to the main intention. Ironically, the technological advancements in reporting schemes now permeating the system tend to be undermining all the efforts which have been made to improve the quality of formative assessment. Teachers *must* be effective assessors and convincing in the discharge of their duties to pupils and parents. The reporting system requires to be tailored accordingly. (See further discussion in Chapter 71.)

## Assessment and the Transition between Primary and Secondary

The *Assessment at Transition Report* (Hayward et al., 2012) contains the findings of a Scottish Government-funded project which looked at teachers' understandings of the assessment they made of pupils' work around the time of transition from primary to secondary school. Although much good practice was reported to be in place, both primary and secondary teachers felt that it was difficult for secondary planning to use both broad 'levels' information *and* detailed information about the progress of individual pupils. CfE levels information was only used for setting and secondary teachers expressed the need for more detail on content coverage, portfolios of pupil work and conversations with individual pupils prior to the start of S1. In the (international) literature, difficulties in smoothing the transition between sectors is often reported as partly due to the lack of detailed information applicable to different subjects and partly because of differing priorities in the two sectors. The development of professional relationships and cross-visits between primary and secondary teachers is emphasised as being helpful to promote understanding, as are formative approaches to learning and assessment. The practitioners interviewed in this Scottish research indeed valued professional interaction across the primary–secondary interface and wanted more of it in 'protected time'. With respect to the recording of assessment information, there were significant variations – across and between school clusters and within secondary schools. Teachers wanted greater clarity about P7 profiles and reporting, for many believe that, in practice, the former merely duplicates the latter. The interpretation of standards evidently concerned teachers, there being uncertainty about how to come to a judgement about the CfE level reached by each pupil. The report stated (on page 13) that:

> Some teachers used an inappropriate 'grading' approach (grading each single task) rather than a 'best fit' judgement – this was in effect encouraged in some LAs [local authorities] by the requirement to record very frequently levels and 'Developing, Consolidating, Secure' within levels (for tracking individual progress), despite teachers' expressed concerns that the information being recorded lacked validity and consistency across teachers and schools and was not helpful for planning future learning.

With such serious findings, the writers of the report concluded that there must be a better alignment between the policy aspirations for CfE and what was then happening in schools; exemplifications are much needed of how teachers can decide upon a level of attainment through scrutiny of the profile of a pupil's work to yield a 'best fit'. In intimating the publication of this report, the *Times Educational Supplement Scotland* (*TESS*) of 3 August 2012 emphasised 'how fragile progress in this area [transition from primary to secondary] has been under Curriculum for Excellence'.

## CONCERNS ABOUT FALLING STANDARDS OF ACHIEVEMENT

### Teacher Reports on CfE Level Achievements

An annual return of data from all publicly funded schools now provides information concerning pupil performance in literacy (reading, writing and talking) and numeracy at P1, P4, P7 and S3, thus giving an indication of young people's achievements during their broad general education. It consists of reports based on teacher judgements of the proportion of pupils who have achieved the expected CfE level. The report for data pertaining to June 2016 showed that

- the proportion of pupils achieving the CfE level relevant for their stage *fell* throughout the primary stages;

- the proportion of S3 pupils achieving CfE third level or better was *between 84 and 87 per cent* for each curriculum area;
- there was a marked *attainment gap* between the least and most deprived areas of Scotland;
- the gap *widened* throughout the primary stages;
- *females* consistently outperformed males across all stages and curriculum areas;
- children of White-Scottish background were *outperformed* by children of Asian, African and mixed ethnic backgrounds;
- achievement varied markedly by *local authority* (Scottish Government, 2016).

The opening paragraph of *The Times* article of 14 December publicising the 2016 data commenced with the emphatic summary: 'More than a quarter of children in Scotland cannot read, write or count to an acceptable standard by the time they finish primary schools, according to teachers.' Reacting to the findings, the government 'recognised that teachers were not confident in applying [expected standards for attainments appearing in the experiences and outcomes documentation] to assessment'. As a result, Education Scotland published new *Benchmarks for Achievement* of CfE levels in literacy and numeracy in August 2016 in order to provide a more explicit and clear statement of standards and stated that benchmarks for other areas of the curriculum would be published in due course (Scottish Government, 2016) (see below).

## Worsening Scottish Performance in International Rankings

Months prior to the publication of these survey results in 2016 came other concerns about falling standards of achievement. The PISA surveys, set up in the year 2000, permit comparisons to be drawn among the participating seventy-two OECD countries every three years, there being controlled testing of some half a million 15 year olds in reading, maths and science. Surveys like these are part of the 'global testing culture' which Smith (2016) notes has spread around the world, concomitant with the expansion of accountability measures in all societies. For him, it worryingly makes testing synonymous with accountability and therefore synonymous with education quality. Figure 68.2 shows the worsening performance of Scottish pupils for the six PISA surveys in question. The most recent figures saw Scotland fall from 'above average' in reading and science to 'average' in world rankings in the PISA 2016 report. In reading, Australia, Germany, the Netherlands, New Zealand, Norway and Slovenia had all moved ahead; in science, England, New Zealand, Slovenia, Switzerland and the Netherlands had all surpassed Scotland.

(See also discussion in Chapter 71.)

The 2016 report made 'uncomfortable reading' for the Scottish National Party (SNP) Cabinet Secretary for Education, John Swinney, not least because the First Minister had previously stated that 'she wanted to be judged on her record in education'. Political reactions were unsurprisingly critical of the government, the Conservative spokesman describing them as 'shocking statistics' and 'a damning indictment of a decade of failure under the SNP'. The Labour spokesman stated that 'SNP ministers should be ashamed of these results' and the Lib Dems criticised them for overwhelming schools with '20,000 pages of guidance given to teachers' in respect of CfE implementation. The Scottish Greens sought more investment in staff and a simplified workload for teachers, 'so that they have more time to connect with their students'. Much of the professional debate has focused on CfE itself, with Lindsay Paterson of Edinburgh University – a long-term critic of the

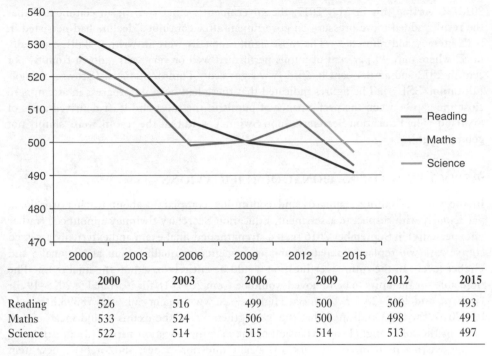

| | **2000** | **2003** | **2006** | **2009** | **2012** | **2015** |
|---|---|---|---|---|---|---|
| Reading | 526 | 516 | 499 | 500 | 506 | 493 |
| Maths | 533 | 524 | 506 | 500 | 498 | 491 |
| Science | 522 | 514 | 515 | 514 | 513 | 497 |

**Figure 68.2    Mean scores for Scotland in OECD surveys**

Source: www.gov.scot/Resource/0051/00511095.pdf

current curriculum, which he considers has devalued the intellectual demands of traditional knowledge – describing the PISA results as 'shocking'. Mark Priestley of Stirling
University who has always been in support of the broad direction of CfE for its local
flexibility, pupil-centred approaches and greater teacher autonomy, shared some of these
concerns about knowledge. However, he disagreed that CfE was to blame; rather that it had
been, thus far, inadequately developed (for a range of reasons – see Chapter 96). On this
count he agreed with OECD's Andreas Schleicher who reasoned that Scotland needed to
move from an *intended* curriculum to an *implemented* curriculum. Walter Humes has argued
that there are deep-rooted causes for the PISA results, not least the strong central direction
by government and its agencies which have pressed ahead on CfE matters, paying little heed
to concerns and criticisms from practitioners and researchers alike. For him, independent
thinking 'should not be thought of as a crime against the state'. Keir Bloomer pointed the
finger at how Education Scotland was operating, judging its inspection remits and its curriculum leadership to be in serious conflict, thus failing to implement CfE as it had been
intended (*The Sunday Times*, 8 January 2017).

### Falling Standards in Literacy and Numeracy, Especially in Writing

Further evidence of declining standards emerged from the most recent Scottish Survey
of Literacy and Numeracy (SSLN). The survey conducted in 2016 (of 10,000 pupils)
revealed that the standard of reading and writing in primary schools had dropped since

2012. Reporting this in May 2017, the government's chief statistician commented that the results added more pressure on government after continued decline had persisted in both literacy and numeracy. The most significant falls were in writing skills, especially in S2 where only 49 per cent of pupils performed well or very well – down from 64 per cent in 2012 and 55 per cent in 2014 (www.gov.scot/Topics/Statistics/Browse/School-Education/SSLN). The figures indicated that there had been no progress in attempts to close the gap between the performance of pupils in the most and least deprived areas of Scotland. The Education Secretary, John Swinney, said that the results were 'simply not good enough'.

## 'REFOCUSING THE NATIONAL QUALIFICATIONS'

In the wake of falling standards and continuing complaints about teacher workload, particularly with respect to assessment, Education Secretary Swinney announced (rather unexpectedly) in September 2016 that 'a strengthened final exam and externally assessed coursework will replace mandatory unit assessments for qualifications at National 5 and Higher level'. In the future, certification would be entirely based on the final exam. The timetable for the units to be removed would be from 2017–18 for National 5; 2018–19 for Highers; and 2019–20 for Advanced Highers (see www.sqa.org.uk/sqa/78398.html). In late 2016, the SQA indicated that the 'strengthening' of the exams would mean one or more of the following: (1) an extension of the existing question paper; (2) an extension of the existing item of coursework; (3) a new question paper; and/or (4) a new item of coursework. Details pertaining to individual subjects are now given in the spread-sheet accompanying the aforementioned SQA website. A consequence of the change would mean that candidates who fail National 5 will *not* achieve National 4 retrospectively. However, Mr Swinney was forced into a U-turn on the decision, following representations from teachers, and introduced emergency measures in April 2017. These indicated that 'Schools will be able, in exceptional circumstances, to continue presenting candidates for both National 5 Units and the course assessment' (www.parliament.scot/S5_Education/General%20Documents/20170330INCabSecEducReChangesNationalQualifications.pdf). All of the changes, whether expedient and temporary or long term, present challenges to schools regarding their progression arrangements in the upper school. The official line from central government in March 2017 on these matters was that: 'Decisions about progression pathways and curriculum models for learners through the Senior Phase remain a matter for local authorities and schools in order to ensure they best meet the needs of young people' (www.gov.scot/Resource/0051/00516166.pdf). Furthermore,

> These decisions, which should be reached during S3, must be informed by effective tracking and monitoring of learners' progress through the Broad General Education (BGE). A clear understanding of the curriculum level achieved in each subject area at the end of BGE is a critical piece of information to inform this decision …

## THE NEW BENCHMARKS OF ACHIEVEMENT

In August 2016, Education Scotland published a new CfE document entitled, *A Statement for Practitioners from HM Chief Inspector of Education* (https://education.gov.scot/improvement/Documents/cfestatement.pdf). This introduced benchmarks, stating that:

The purpose of the Benchmarks is to set out very clear statements about what children and young people need to learn to achieve each level of the curriculum. Benchmarks streamline and embed a wide range of existing assessment guidance (significant aspects of learning, progression frameworks and annotated exemplification) into one key resource to support teachers' professional judgement.

One reason for the new nomenclature was presumably an attempt by government to be seen to be simplifying the experiences and outcomes laid out for the National Qualifications. Certainly 'benchmarks' appeared during a marked period of teacher complaints about assessment workload and the Depute Minister seemed anxious to get on the side of teachers. The expression 'streamlining' does seem a giveaway and the preface to the report concedes that: 'There is currently too much support material and guidance for practitioners.' Information about the new Numeracy and Mathematics benchmarks and the Literacy and English benchmarks has been provided (see https://education.gov.scot/improvement/Pages/Curriculum-for-Excellence-Benchmarks-.aspx; see also discussion of benchmarks in Chapter 71).

The key messages in the 2016 document include the following statements in respect of what teachers should do:

- Periodically (from time to time) use assessments to sample and pull together learning in a joined-up way.
- Plan an appropriate balance between on-going and periodic assessment – this will vary from stage to stage.
- Moderate assessment judgements by taking account of a sample of evidence from different sources to discuss standards and the progress of learners.
- As a school, develop simple and effective approaches to monitoring and tracking learners' progress particularly in literacy and numeracy.
- Tracking needs to be as easy to use as possible.
- Regularly discuss tracking information with colleagues to plan additional support and interventions to help improve learners' progress.
- Evaluate learners' progress on an on-going basis and keep short concise notes to help planning for next steps in learning. This will include identifying where additional support and challenge may be needed.
- Use the benchmarks to help monitor progress and support overall professional judgement of when a learner has achieved a curriculum level.
- Involve children and young people in leading their own learning and involve them in profiling their achievements.
- Reporting to parents should highlight latest progress, identify next steps in learning and build on profiling. Discussions should highlight ways in which parents can support their child's progress.

One can certainly see that the language of official guidance now attempts to be persuasive and rather commonsensical: *Do it this way and it won't be so hard.* To this writer, it does not look as though the ways in which formative assessment can be conducted are being advanced. Grades, as checks of levels to be marked off – or benchmarks to be reached – seem to be the system's order of the day. The tick-box mentality, which teachers despise, looks here to stay.

# REFERENCES

Black, P. and Wiliam, D. (1998) 'Assessment and Classroom Learning', *Assessment in Education*, 5 (1), 7–74.

Black, P. and Wiliam, D. (2001) *Inside the Black Box*. London: King's College.

Black, P., Harrison, C., Lee, C., Marshall, B. and Wiliam, D. (2002) *Working Inside the Black Box: Assessment for Learning in the Classroom*. Slough: NFER-Nelson.

Coffey, J. E., Hammer, D., Levin, D. M. and Grant, T. (2011) 'The missing disciplinary substance of formative assessment', *Journal of Research in Science Teaching*, http://onlinelibrary.wiley.com/doi/10.1002/tea.20440/full

Condie, R., Livingston, K. and Seagraves, L. (2005) *Evaluation of the Assessment is for Learning Programme: Final Report*. Glasgow: University of Strathclyde, Quality in Education Centre.

Ellis, S. (2012) 'Teaching writing: reconciling policy and pedagogy'. Paper presented at the American Educational Research Association annual conference (Non Satis Scire: To Know is Not Enough) held in Vancouver, British Columbia, 13–17 April.

Hattie, J. and Timperley, H. (2007) 'The power of feedback', *Review of Educational Research*, 77 (1), 81–112.

Hayward, L., Menter, I., Baumfield, V., Daugherty, R., Akhtar, N., Doyle, L., Elliot, D., Hulme, M., Hutchinson, C., MacBride, G., McCulloch, M., Patrick, F., Spencer, E., Wardle, G., Blee, H. and Arthur, L. (2012) *Assessment at Transition Report*. Glasgow: University of Glasgow. School of Education.

Hutchinson, C. and Young, M. (2011) 'Assessment for learning in the accountability era: empirical evidence from Scotland', *Studies in Educational Evaluation*, 37 (1), 62–70.

Raffe, D., Howieson, C. and Tinklin, T. (2005) 'The introduction of a unified system of post-compulsory education in Scotland', *Scottish Educational Review*, 37 (1), 46–57.

Scottish Government (2016) *Achievement of Curriculum for Excellence (CfE) Levels 2015/16: Experimental Statistics – Data under Development*. 13 December. Online at www.gov.scot/Resource/0051/00511579.pdf

Smith, W. C. (ed.) (2016) *An Introduction to the Global Testing Culture*. Oxford: Symposium Books.

Taras, M. (2005) 'Assessment – summative and formative – some theoretical Reflections', *British Journal of Educational Studies*, 53 (4), 466–78.

Wiliam, D. (2000) Integrating summative and formative functions of assessment. Keynote address to the European Association for Educational Assessment, Prague: Czech Republic, November. Online at http://eprints.ioe.ac.uk/1151/1/Wiliam2000IntergratingAEA-E_2000_keynoteaddress.pdf

Wiliam, D. (2011) 'What is assessment for learning?' *Studies in Educational Evaluation*, 37, 3–14.

# 69

# The Scottish Qualifications Authority

*Tom Bryce and Walter Humes*

## PURPOSE, RESPONSIBILITIES AND STRATEGIC PRIORITIES

The Scottish Qualifications Authority (SQA) is a statutory non-departmental public body (NDPB) created under the Education (Scotland) Act 1996 as amended by the Scottish Qualifications Authority Act 2002. The organisation has two main responsibilities. The larger part of its operations, and the one for which it is best known in teacher/further education lecturer circles, is as an awarding body: devising, developing, validating and awarding qualifications other than degrees, the best known of which are National Qualifications. Its smaller role is concerned with the approval and quality assurance of awarding bodies that plan to enter people for qualifications, including customised awards to meet the needs of individual companies and organisations.

In its corporate plan for 2016–19, SQA defines its mission in the following terms:

- Purpose: SQA's purpose is to provide products and services in skills, training and education which positively impact on individuals, organisations and society.
- Vision: We will digitally transform our organisation to offer customers better service by delivering efficient, scalable and new enabling approaches.

The statement of purpose is clear and appropriately ambitious. By contrast, the vision statement is an example of the kind of professional jargon that sometimes gives education a bad name. What exactly is meant by 'scalable and new enabling approaches'? It is the sort of statement that might be meaningful to those working within the organisation but seems obscure and pretentious to outsiders. That said, SQA is not the only NDPB to make statements like these on websites and in public communications.

Eight strategic goals are set out in the corporate plan:

1. Develop, deliver and maintain a portfolio of qualifications and services to support the needs and aspirations of Scotland, its people and its economy.
2. Provide leadership and expertise in a range of areas including assessment, qualification development and quality enhancement.
3. Support the Scottish Government's agenda to maximise the benefits of international engagement and co-operation.
4. Ensure our culture and values support the engagement and wellbeing of our staff and foster their commitment to the success of SQA.

5. Deliver high-quality, continually improving, efficient and responsive services to our customers.
6. Continue to develop SQA as a leading public body and key player in the skills, training and education landscape.
7. Continue to pursue a business model that would enable SQA to reduce its dependency on the public purse, and invest in and improve the Education and Skills system.
8. Independently accredit, quality assure and regulate approved Awarding Bodies and qualifications thereby safeguarding the interests of learners, employers, parents, funding bodies, providers and the Scottish Government.

These are similar, but not identical, to the goals in previous corporate plans. They are mapped against a series of rather boastful national outcomes set out by the Scottish Government (e.g. 'We have tackled the significant inequalities in Scottish society.' 'Our children have the best start in life and are ready to succeed', www.gov.scot/Publications/2016/01/8314/2). The economic context is a major driver of SQA's operations. In the corporate plan, there are several references to the need for skilled workforces to promote economic growth, the impact of technology on the types of learning that are valued, and the consequences of globalisation for services, industry and job prospects.

The explicitness of the SQA's commitment to government priorities is striking. Given that a substantial proportion of its income comes from government, this is perhaps not surprising. It may also be a continuing legacy of the examinations crisis of 2000 when central government had to intervene following serious operational failures which attracted adverse publicity and necessitated formal inquiries. Since that time SQA has been perceived as a rather compliant organisation, anxious not to attract criticism from politicians and prepared to follow central direction. Ironically, it is perhaps for this very reason that it now finds itself subject to the charge that it has failed to consult sufficiently with teachers or to listen to their concerns over Curriculum for Excellence and National Qualifications (which is discussed more fully below).

Information about the precise nature of contacts between government and non-departmental public bodies is hard to come by: informal exchanges and telephone calls may be just as significant as the reports of formal meetings with agendas and minutes. It would be interesting to know, for example, what kind of dialogue takes place between senior civil servants and SQA officials. Who meets with whom on a regular basis, and at what level do they operate? Is it always a matter of the former saying: 'Here is what the government wants – it's your job to help to deliver it', or is there scope for the latter to make substantive input into the policy process? This becomes particularly important when innovations are being planned. Successful innovation depends on a number of factors: a well-thought-out policy, informed by evidence; adequate resources for development work; opportunities for teachers and lecturers to contribute to the process; and leaders who can win the hearts and minds of the front-line staff responsible for implementing the changes. Concerns about confidentiality mean that it is hard for outsiders to gain a good understanding of the way assessment policy is initiated, developed and refined. This raises questions about the structure and management of SQA.

## ORGANISATIONAL STRUCTURE AND MANAGEMENT

The chief executive of SQA since 2007 has been Dr Janet Brown, who was formerly managing director of industries with Scottish Enterprise and before that worked in business management in the private sector. This background perhaps explains the strong 'corporate' character of the organisation. Dr Brown works with an executive team of six directors whose remits cover Finance, Operations, Business Development, Business Systems and Transformational Change, Qualifications Development and Corporate Services. Overall policy and strategy is determined by a board of management, which consists, in addition to the chief executive, of ten members drawn from schools and colleges, and public and private sector organisations. Board minutes are available on the SQA website. As an indication of the close links with Scottish Government, the May 2016 meeting was attended by the then Cabinet Secretary for Education and Lifelong Learning, Angela Constance, as well as by two senior government officials. Ms Constance spoke of the government's focus on reducing the attainment gap between children from rich and poor families and members of the board fully supported initiatives designed to achieve this objective.

SQA also has an advisory council. Its role is to advise SQA on the needs and views of stakeholders in relation to qualifications and awards. The membership of thirteen (as listed in February 2017) includes representatives of schools, colleges, parents, employers and trades unions, all of whom will have perspectives to offer on the fitness for purpose of SQA's qualifications and the efficiency with which the processes of conducting examinations and awarding qualifications are carried out. As its name suggests, the advisory council does not have executive power to make decisions but, given the need to retain the confidence of clients, SQA would be unwise to disregard the representations of council members. Just as private sector companies are now expected to pay more heed to the views of shareholders at annual general meetings, so public sector organisations emphasise the value attached to partnerships with stakeholders.

## THE SCALE OF ANNUAL OPERATIONS: STANDARDS, PASS RATES AND APPEALS

Much of the day-to-day activity of SQA is carried out by teams working in particular areas of specialism, whether in relation to traditional school courses (in English, History, Mathematics, Chemistry, etc.) or in vocationally oriented college courses (in Construction, Engineering, Retail, Hospitality and Tourism, etc.). A great deal of work is involved in the development of assessment instruments and in trying to ensure that standards are maintained from year to year. Occasionally there are criticisms of particular examination papers (e.g. Higher Geography and National 5 Maths in 2016) but, given the scale of SQA operations, these are relatively rare. When new qualifications are planned, design teams, consisting of experts drawn from local authorities, colleges, universities and employers, are involved in the process. Implementation events, led by curriculum development specialists, and aimed at the teaching staff in schools and colleges, are held in different parts of the country. What is clear, however, is that the intentions behind new courses are not always communicated as effectively as they might be and this can lead to confusion and frustration on the part of teachers and students. As many research reports have shown, introducing change in curriculum and assessment rarely proceeds entirely smoothly and the controversies which do arise affect all examination bodies – and are more than technical in nature. Press and public attention is always focused on the marking of papers, the delivery of certificates on time and, of course, on pass rates. The changes from Standard Grades, through Intermediates to National 4 and 5 courses, plus the revisions to the Highers during recent years (fully documented in Chapter 68) have not made for easy comparisons of standards

Table 69.1   Pass rates for National Qualifications

| Level | Pass rate in 2015 (%) | Pass rate in 2016 (%) | No. of entries in 2016 |
|---|---|---|---|
| National 4 | 93.3 | 93.2 | 122,961 |
| National 5 | 79.8 | 79.4 | 295,083 |
| Higher | 79.2 | 77.2 | 197,774 |
| Previous Higher | 76.7 | – | – |
| Advanced Higher | – | 81.7 | 23,795 |
| Previous Advanced Higher | 80.9 | – | – |
| Scottish Baccalaureate | 80.3 | 73.6 | 140 |

Note: Based on passes at National 4 and grade A–C awards at National 5, Higher and Advanced Higher.

over time. These are matters of concern, annually, to teachers and the public alike, and to the press, who thrive on them.

The *SQA Annual Review for 2015–16* (SQA, 2016) highlights the main services, projects and initiatives carried out by SQA staff and the wider community of professionals who work alongside them. An indication of the scale of operations is that over 1.1 million National Qualification (NQ) exam scripts for 142,862 candidates were marked in that year and 180 subject-based training sessions were run for the nearly 6,000 teachers employed as markers. Table 69.1 shows the pass rates for the several NQ course levels studied at school (and beyond) for the years 2015 and 2016. To take examples: the average of the two National 5 pass rates (79.6 per cent) is little different from the Intermediate 2 figures of earlier years (which averaged 79.1 per cent between the years 2008 and 2012); the average of the two new ('Revised') Higher pass rates (78.2 per cent) shows an increase from the 'old' Higher figures which averaged 74.9 per cent between the years 2008 and 2012 (https://www.sqa.org.uk/sqa/77716.html). Drawing attention to the data for the Highers, *The Guardian* of 4 August 2015 commenced its coverage of the 'new-look' exams (the Revised Highers) with 'A record number of Scottish teenagers have passed their Higher exams, prompting calls for SNP ministers to investigate whether the qualifications have been made easier.' The pass-rate increases were just over 3 percentage points (though the Maths paper proved to be harder than expected and prompted much attention in the press and on social media).

The organisation operates a post-results appeal procedure – full details of possible appeals against decisions taken by SQA valid from August 2016 are given in *The Appeals Process: Information for Centres* (SQA, 2017). In brief, a school headteacher can appeal decisions regarding assessment arrangements for disabled candidates and/or those with additional support needs (ASN); exceptional circumstances affecting external examinations of NQ subjects; and cases of malpractice regarding internal or external assessments. Pupils (or teachers) who think they should ask for an appeal to be triggered might usefully explore the details now set out on the website cited above (most recently dated July 2017), though they should note that appeals can only be made by schools/colleges.

Appeals are charged for if the grade remains unchanged following a requested clerical check or marking review of a candidate's examination paper(s) and/or other externally assessed components. Currently (2017), the charges are: £10 for a clerical check, £29.75 for a marking review, and £39.75 for a priority marking review. Clearly these act as a disincentive for irresponsible action on the part of candidates or their families, though over recent years concerns have been expressed that this disadvantages pupils living in more deprived circumstances. It has been shown that appeals on behalf of pupils attending independent schools are proportionately higher than those from comprehensive schools, suggesting that cost may act as a disincentive. There is no charge for the Exceptional Circumstances Consideration Service. The post-results service for the 2016 diet of examinations dealt with 13,908 requests, most of which were for a review of marking, of which 2,688 (19.3 per cent) resulted in a change to a pupil's grade. The corresponding figures for the 2015 diet were 12,077 requests of which 2,378 (19.7 per cent) resulted in a grade change.

The mention of pupils with additional support needs in the previous paragraph highlights the fact that the SQA has to take account of changes in the general school population. As more youngsters with a range of conditions (autism, dyslexia, language problems, physical disability, visual and hearing impairment, etc.) have their special needs recognised and catered for within mainstream education, so suitable arrangements to enable them to take examinations and gain qualifications have to be made. These may take various forms – for example having a scribe, allowing short breaks or extra time. Ensuring such provision is both fair and adequately tailored to the specific needs of candidates is evidence of the system adapting in an inclusive way to allow youngsters to achieve their potential. A report in 2017 by the campaign group the Scottish Children's Services Coalition estimates that a quarter of children in Scotland now require some form of additional support.

## DIGITAL, ONLINE SERVICES AND E-ASSESSMENT

Electronic forms of assessment constitute an important challenge for examination bodies in many countries at the present time. In the drive to make its resources more reliable and efficient, and also more responsive to the needs of users (whether candidates, presenting centres, employers or universities), SQA has continued to develop electronic assessment and support materials online. Straightforward examples include the Understanding Standards part of the website where teachers and lecturers can find exemplifications of mark allocations for the questions in exam papers. PDFs of pupil scripts can be explored in conjunction with commentary from the marking team. These offer subject-specific guidance to teachers seeking to familiarise themselves with what should be expected of pupils/students in exam answers. For an example, regarding questions sat in the 2016 Higher Physics paper, see https://www.understandingstandards.org.uk/Subjects/Physics/Higher/2016.

The aforementioned Annual Review for 2015–16 also describes its operations in respect of online and digital services. Web pages for National Qualifications were recorded as having nearly 20 million page views and more than 3 million downloads of past papers. Apps continue to be made available on various platforms and SQA notes their growth in popularity (stating them to be 'a great success'). Young people are evidently following the services on LinkedIn, Twitter and Facebook. More generally, scrutiny of the SQA website shows that the organisation does try to make information accessible. For example, the section providing Frequently Asked Questions (FAQs) has information categorised under headings: Centres, Learners, NQs, Results Services and so on, there being as many as fifteen FAQs per heading, each of which offers a paragraph or so of guidance. One cannot know what encouragement teachers give to pupils to explore the website but the organisation is clearly making determined efforts to assist a range of users who have queries about different aspects of SQA's operation.

SQA was a partner in five European Social Funded projects between 2007 and 2013. To instance one, the Transforming Scottish Education Through Technology (TranSETT)

Project used funding to create new qualifications and support materials across a number of curriculum areas. The detail of these areas and resources are listed at SQA (2012). Reports of the project record a high uptake of the pre-vocational and professional qualifications (National Certificates and National Progression Awards) resulting from the e-assessments which were developed. Prior to that work, Scottish Government had invested £95 million in 129 projects across Scotland 'to develop the national workforce, create and safeguard jobs, and regenerate communities' (see investment preparations historically reported in 2014 at SQA, 2014).

In general, many claims are made for e-assessment including: (1) increases in teaching time with the automatic marking of questions and quick return of results to students; (2) online analysis of learners' responses permitting feedback (tailored to an extent); (3) the use of social software technology (including blogs and wikis) by students to share views and information, leading to possibilities for group assessment; and (4) the storage of extended response answers for later scrutiny by teachers. Anyone familiar with *closed* test items of the standard fixed response kind (say the basic 'choose one from four alternatives' in a simple multiple-choice format) will appreciate that it is easy to work up their complexity to make guessing less likely, thus enhancing the quality of the test. Modern forms of e-assessment easily lend themselves to attractive and interesting possibilities: drop-down lists with animations; combining different demands in the question stem in multimedia displays; drag and drop pictures or symbols in order to answer queries; 'connect' tasks where information has to be linked together by the examinee from two lists or a matrix of possibilities; and so forth. However, *open* response questions can now be formatted electronically, the simpler versions requiring the student to type into designated sections of the computer screen ('free text' items), more complex ones incorporating simulations (generally called 'simulation items'). An 'experiment and respond' item, for example, would require the student to move icons on screen and respond to instructions and questions accordingly. On-screen diagnostics can be made adaptive, that is they can be made to change according to the responses given by the person undertaking the assessment. If test material is being used formatively, then a sophisticated e-assessment format can supply feedback item by item. If it is being used summatively, then summary screens can provide feedback overall, as well as scores and grades. The makers of e-assessment materials claim that a central advantage is that, since the speed of interacting with test content is learner driven, the feedback that can be supplied is given exactly where and when it is needed – at the point of any cognitive conflict the learner is experiencing. There are a number of commercial manufacturers of e-assessment materials, including Surpass, the E-Assessment Platform and TAG Developments, all of whom believe that their products hold out the prospect of transforming learning, not just assessment. Blended e-assessment consists of combinations of traditional pen-and-paper examination formats (which are often said to be convenient) with grading, reporting and statistical analysis all done electronically. Research reported by Llamas-Nistal et al. (2013) indicates that such combinations can be cost-effective, enabling both formative and summative assessments to be carried out.

SOLAR is SQA's free online assessment tool for formative and summative assessment (see www.sqa.org.uk/sqa/8165.744.html). It consists of banks of quality-assured test items of various types spanning SCQF level 2 to level 8 – that is, up to Higher National Diploma, Diploma of Higher Education and Technical Apprenticeship Scottish Vocational Qualification (SVQ) 3 awards. Hence for pupils in senior school, they span National 4, 5,

Higher and Advanced Higher. Browser-based software allows access on Macs, PCs, tablets and iPads and yields analyses of performances, scores and so on. Presenting centres (i.e. schools and colleges) which choose to use summative e-assessments are guaranteed by SQA that they are quality assured (questions are randomly produced from pre-verified item banks) and that scores generated by SOLAR are correct. Secure log-in arrangements, passwords and so forth enable the software to run the assessments. Pupils who choose to use SOLAR for formative assessments of their progress in learning course material can access the system at any time. They can familiarise themselves with test material of comparable standards and obtain feedback on their answers to questions.

Another significant source of online materials is the programme developed and maintained at Heriot-Watt University known as SCHOLAR. This is an online portfolio of interactive learning material for Scottish schools suitable for National 5, Higher and Advanced Higher level courses. All but one of the thirty-two local authorities in Scotland subscribe to it, as do some thirty independent schools (figures at 2017). The subjects include science, technology, engineering and maths (STEM), Business and Languages and are all aligned to the SQA framework. The SCHOLAR material (http://scholar.hw.ac.uk/) contains an abundance of interactive multimedia, quizzes and assessments and can be used both as a study aid and for revision. Teachers can access SCHOLAR courses and assessments via the Scottish Schools Digital Network (GLOW), the national intranet for education in Scotland. The programme can be downloaded on a mobile phone or tablet using suitable apps, rendering flexibility for pupils to work with it at times and in locations of their choice. Web-based learning allows teachers to set pupils work and track how they are managing it. That is, formative assessment is integrated within it, there being sophisticated interactivities and simulations to bring about the learning and ongoing diagnostic assessment of errors and mistakes in thinking. Enthusiasts speak well for the interactivity and engagement which can be achieved. The home page of SCHOLAR refers to its forum as

> a legal not-for-profit partnership between the University and ADES, the Association of Directors of Education in Scotland, with the Education Authorities as members paying an annual subscription. Key stakeholders, including Education Scotland, SQA and School Leaders Scotland, are part of the Forum's consultation framework.

In summary, and from a research perspective, Stodberg's (2012) review of seventy-six research articles on the use of e-assessment scrutinised the three leading journals in the field (*Assessment & Evaluation in Higher Education*, *British Journal of Educational Technology* and *Computers & Education*). He concluded that in most cases e-assessment works well for both formative and summative assessment, and that 'computerised marking can be as accurate as human marking and sometimes even more consistent' (p. 602). Furthermore, the prospects for skills and competences traditionally difficult to assess continue to be promising. Stodberg thinks that the focus for e-assessment should be driven by pedagogical rather than by technological considerations.

## RECENT CRITICISMS OF THE SQA

In 2017, the Education and Skills Committee of the Scottish Parliament published a report on the *Performance and Role of Key Education and Skills Bodies* (Scottish Parliament, 2017). The four public bodies scrutinised by the committee with evidence sessions carried out in

November 2016 were Skills Development Scotland (SDS), the Scottish Funding Council (SFC), Education Scotland (ES) and the SQA. In respect of the SQA, evidence was taken predominantly from teachers but also from academics and the chief executive herself. Several criticisms and recommendations were thereby made to the Parliament concerning SQA operations, particularly in respect of its core function as an awarding body. In this role, the report notes that SQA (essentially summarising *some* of the organisation's strategic goals stated at the start of this chapter):

- devises and develops qualifications other than degrees;
- validates qualifications (makes sure they are well written and meet the needs of learners and tutors);
- reviews qualifications to ensure they are up to date;
- arranges for, assists in, and carries out, the assessment of people taking SQA qualifications;
- quality-assures education and training establishments which offer SQA qualifications; and
- issues certificates to candidates.

The committee concluded that the clear evidence it had received from teachers 'should give the SQA serious cause for concern' (paragraph 22). That evidence diverged seriously from what teachers felt comfortable in reporting to SQA itself and so the committee considered that the authority should review its consultation processes in order to 'enable candid communication from those with criticisms to make' (also paragraph 22). The committee stated that, through further monitoring of SQA performance, it would expect to see speedy improvements in the design, delivery, supporting documentation and marking of National Qualifications. With respect to the Curriculum for Excellence (CfE) itself, a 'disconnect' was said to be apparent between its design principles and the implemented curriculum. So much so that the committee considered learners to have been let down and teachers subjected to onerous workloads, leading to a breakdown in trust and threats of industrial action. While Education Scotland was also criticised for its responsibilities in this connection (the committee accepting that design responsibilities for CfE qualifications were diffuse), responsibility for communicating changes, in the eyes of the Parliament, lay 'squarely with the SQA' (paragraph 27). The errors figuring in recent national exam papers and their marking (SQA 'core business') were judged to be unacceptable. It was thought that the long-term aim of the SQA to be self-financing, and therefore ongoing associated commercial work, should not dilute its focus on its core business.

Further evidence as to dissatisfaction with SQA is apparent in the pre-budget scrutiny by the committee. An online survey in receipt of 1,171 responses to questions about the perceived connection between the functions of SDS, SFC, ES and SQA and national outcomes was carried out in October 2016. The Scottish Parliament Information Centre (SPICe) briefing paper notes that more than half of the responses were concerned with the SQA. While 73 per cent of respondents agreed or agreed strongly that SQA qualifications enabled learners to access and progress within further education and higher education, respondents expressed little trust in the SQA. With the statement, 'our customers and users trust us to get it right for them', 67 per cent disagreed or disagreed strongly. Around half of the respondents disagreed or disagreed strongly that SQA qualifications 'deliver a comprehensive and high quality school qualifications system' (48 per cent) and a further 16 per cent were undecided. Similar opinions were expressed about whether SQA provides qualifications that prepare young people for work (SPICe, 2016).

A particular example of disquiet arose early in 2017 following proposals to change assessment arrangements for National 5 examinations, to take effect from 2017–18 (changes to other courses would follow in later years). In response to complaints from teachers about excessive workload and over-assessment, the Cabinet Secretary for Education, John Swinney, had decided to scrap unit assessments (making this announcement during the Scottish Learning Festival in September 2016). To ensure that courses were properly assessed, the SQA was asked to come forward with revised arrangements, further details of which are given in Chapter 68. In a number of courses these involved strengthening final examinations. A survey by the *Times Educational Supplement Scotland* found that, in twenty-eight out of forty-two National 5 subjects, pupils would be required to sit longer exams, while in nine practical subjects they would have an exam where none previously existed. The five other subjects would have new or increased coursework to cover. Critics complained that for most pupils the changes would involve a return to 'high stakes' final examinations, an approach that ran counter to progressive thinking about learning and assessment. This was denied by Mr Swinney. An SQA spokeswoman said that the changes would have a positive impact on teacher workload 'while maintaining the integrity and credibility of the national qualifications' (http://mailer.sqa.org.uk/Archive/Content/921067d9-fcf3-4e38-b2eb-a70c012ae92d). This episode served to illustrate the professional and political pressures to which SQA staff are often subject.

## CONCLUSION

As the national qualifications agency in Scotland for awards below degree level, SQA carries substantial responsibilities. At an operational level, these involve managing complex arrangements for a diverse portfolio of courses, regular communication with schools, colleges and other bodies, and the provision of up-to-date information and support for teachers and learners across Scotland. To this can be added the need to ensure public confidence that the standard of SQA awards is maintained from year to year and that the whole process is perceived as fair and reliable. As has been shown, some concerns have been expressed about how well SQA has been discharging these responsibilities. These have arisen in a context of political sensitivity. The 2016 Programme for International Student Assessment (PISA) results raised uncomfortable questions about the quality of Scottish education, particularly compared to other parts of the UK. Instead of being 'above average' in reading, mathematics and science, Scottish secondary pupils were judged to be only 'average'. This represented a decline from previous performance, as described more fully in Chapter 68. The political reaction has taken several forms. A review of the governance of Scottish education was initiated, which included the role and function of national organisations such as the SQA. Politicians tend to think in a short time frame and are inclined to favour high-visibility responses to perceived crises, such as institutional restructuring. That is not always the best strategy. With something as important as the credibility not only of the examination system but of Scottish education as a whole, a more thoughtful and measured programme of reform may be required. Perhaps that should include the degree of government control and ministerial direction to which SQA has been subject in recent years.

## REFERENCES

Llamas-Nistal, M., Fernandez-Iglesias, M. J., Gonzalez-Tato, J. and Mikic-Fonte, F. A. (2013) 'Blended e-assessment: migrating classical exams to the digital world', *Computers & Education*, 62 (2013), 72–87.

Scottish Parliament (2017) *Performance and Role of Key Education and Skills Bodies*. SP Paper 59. 2nd Report, 2017 (Session 5). Online at: www.parliament.scot/S5_Education/Reports/ESS052017R02.pdf

SPICe (2016) *SPICe Briefing*. 3 November. Online at: www.parliament.scot/S5_Education/General%20Documents/20161104ESCtteeSPICeSurveyResults.pdf

SQA (2012) E-assessments and learning resources. Online at www.sqa.org.uk/sqa/files_ccc/SQATranSETTLeaflet.pdf

SQA (2014) *Centre Readiness to use E-assessment*. Project report jointly prepared by CCEA, SQA and the Welsh Government. Online at https://www.sqa.org.uk/files_ccc/Centre_readiness_to_use_E-Assessment-17-12-14.pdf

SQA (2016) *SQA Annual Review 2015–16*. Online at www.sqa.org.uk/sqa/77353.html

SQA (2017) *The Appeals Process: Information for Centres*. Online at https://www.sqa.org.uk/files_ccc/Appeals_Process.pdf

Stodberg, U. (2012) 'A research review of e-assessment', *Assessment & Evaluation in Higher Education*, 37 (5), 591–604.

### Websites

SCHOLAR at http://scholar.hw.ac.uk/

SQA Corporate Plan 2016–19 at www.sqa.org.uk/sqa/files_ccc/SQA-Corporate-Plan-2016-19.pdf

SQA SOLAR Online at www.sqa.org.uk/sqa/8165.744.html

SQA: The Appeals Process: Information for Centres at https://www.sqa.org.uk/files_ccc/Appeals_Process.pdf

SQA TranSETT Project at www.sqa.org.uk/sqa/files_ccc/SQATranSETTLeaflet.pdf

SQA: Understanding Standards at www.understandingstandards.org.uk/Subjects/Physics/Higher/2016

# 70

# SQA Findings on Scottish Attainments

*James Morgan*

## INTRODUCTION

The Scottish Qualifications Authority (SQA) develops, assesses and awards qualifications taken in workplaces, colleges and schools. It provides qualifications across Scotland, the UK and internationally. Separately, as SQA Accreditation, it accredits vocational qualifications (other than degrees) delivered in Scotland, including Scottish Vocational Qualifications, and approves awarding bodies that wish to award them.

As an awarding body, SQA works with schools, colleges, universities, industry and government, to provide high quality, flexible and relevant qualifications. It strives to ensure that its qualifications are inclusive and accessible to all, that they recognise the achievements of learners, and that they provide clear pathways to further learning or employment. SQA also provides qualification attainment data to the Scottish Government which is used to support schools and educational authorities and for policy.

The Scottish Credit and Qualifications Framework (SCQF) is a way of comparing Scottish qualifications. It covers achievements such as those from school, college, university and many work-based qualifications. It does this by giving each qualification a level between one and twelve and a number of credit points. The level of a qualification shows how difficult the learning is. The credit points show how much learning and assessment is involved for the average learner in achieving that qualification. This includes face-to-face teaching, self-directed learning and assessment. Each credit point represents ten hours of learning. Throughout this chapter SCQF credit and level have been used to describe qualifications. Most SQA qualifications are designed to a set SCQF level and number of credit points. The position of SQA qualifications in the Scottish Credit and Qualifications Framework is outlined in Figure 70.1.

This chapter sets out to report on trends in attainment of SQA qualifications from 2012 to 2016. Additionally, this chapter will mention some of the issues which were important in the last five years and which are expected to become important in the next five years.

## ATTAINMENT IN NATIONAL QUALIFICATIONS

National Qualifications are predominantly offered in the 'senior phase', that is, the fourth (S4), fifth (S5) and sixth year (S6) in Scottish secondary schools. In the period 2012–16 SQA developed and administered examinations and other summative assessments for three

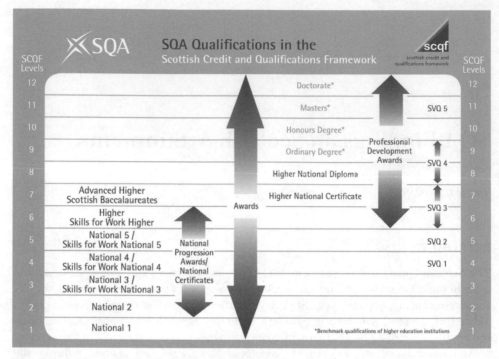

**Figure 70.1   Scottish Credit and Qualifications Framework**

Source: Courtesy SQA.

sets of National Qualifications developed under various curricula reforms over the past thirty years. These are outlined below.

## Standard Grades

Standard Grades were National Qualifications introduced progressively from the late 1980s to be taken at the end of compulsory education, in S4. The last diet of Standard Grade examinations took place in 2013. Standard Grades were generally taken over the third and fourth year at secondary schools. Learners often took seven or eight subjects. There were three levels in Standard Grade: Credit (Grades 1 and 2), General (Grades 3 and 4) and Foundation (Grades 5 and 6). Learners usually attempted examinations at two levels – Credit and General, or General and Foundation. This made sure that learners had the best chance of achieving as high a grade as possible. Only the highest level a learner achieved was certificated. All Standard Grade qualifications attracted twenty-four SCQF credit points at SCQF levels 3, 4 and 5 for Foundation, General and Credit respectively.

## National Courses (1999–2015)

National Courses were National Qualifications introduced in 1999 as part of the 'Higher Still' reforms. The last diet of examinations for these National Courses examinations took place in 2015. National Courses were usually made up of three National units and an external assessment (which could be an exam or a piece of coursework). They were originally developed as one-year courses for use in post-16 education, for those who had achieved a Standard Grade and for adults. They were available at Access 1 to 3, Intermediate 1 and 2, Higher and Advanced Higher. Some schools offered Intermediate units and courses as alternatives to Standard Grade in S3 and S4. Access 1, 2 and 3 courses attracted SCQF credit points at SCQF levels 1, 2 and 3, respectively. Intermediate 1, Intermediate 2 courses and Higher courses all attracted twenty-four SCQF credit points at SCQF levels 4, 5 and 6, respectively. Advanced Higher courses attracted thirty-two SCQF credit points at SCQF level 7.

## National Courses (Current)

The current National Courses were introduced on a phased basis, by level, as learners experiencing Curriculum for Excellence moved through the school system. The first qualifications were assessed in 2014. In session 2015–16, with the introduction of the new Advanced Higher, all National Courses were fully in place for all learners. There is now a single suite of qualifications available – National 1 to National 5, Higher, Advanced Higher and the Scottish Baccalaureate.

Highers are normally needed for entry into university or college to study for degree or Higher National Certificate or Diploma courses (HNCs or HNDs). Advanced Highers are aimed at students who have passed Highers, and are usually taken in S6 or at college. These courses extend the skills and knowledge gained at Higher level and are useful for entry to university or employment.

The current National Courses have been designed to reflect the purposes and principles of Curriculum for Excellence and involve the assessment of different skills and knowledge, for example deeper learning and higher-order thinking skills and application of learning. Learners will have undertaken different approaches to assessment of the new qualifications. National 4 qualifications are internally assessed and quality assured by SQA. Almost all of the National 5, Higher and Advanced Higher courses include three internally assessed units, a course assessment of coursework and an examination. This allows valid assessment of a wider range of skills and knowledge. In the majority of courses, a learner's final grade is based on a combination of coursework assessment and a final examination.

Table 70.1 outlines the various types of National Qualifications assessed by SQA over the past five years.

Table 70.1  National Qualification examinations, 2012–16

| Year | SCQF level 4 | SCQF level 5 | SCQF level 6 |
|---|---|---|---|
| 2012 | Standard Grade General<br>Intermediate 1 | Standard Grade Credit<br>Intermediate 2 | Higher (previous) |
| 2013 | Standard Grade General<br>Intermediate 1 | Standard Grade Credit<br>Intermediate 2 | Higher (previous) |
| 2014 | Intermediate 1<br>National 4 | Intermediate 2<br>National 5 | Higher (previous) |
| 2015 | National 4 | National 5 | Higher (previous)<br>Higher (current) |
| 2016 | National 4 | National 5 | Higher (current) |

Source: Courtesy SQA.

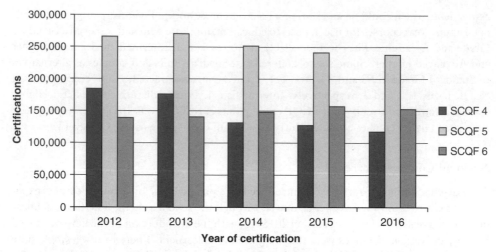

Figure 70.2    Attainment in National Qualifications, 2012–16

Source: Courtesy SQA.

Table 70.2    Attainment in Advanced Higher, 2012–16

|                  | 2012   | 2013   | 2014   | 2015   | 2016   |
|------------------|--------|--------|--------|--------|--------|
| Advanced Higher  | 17,299 | 18,162 | 18,171 | 18,899 | 19,443 |

Source: Courtesy SQA.

Figure 70.2 outlines attainment in National Qualifications at aggregate SCQF levels 4, 5 and 6. This presentational approach has been adopted due the fact that different qualification types at the same SCQF level were being assessed in each year.

Over this period the number of qualifications attained at these SCQF levels decreased from around 592,000 qualifications in 2012 to around 510,000 qualifications in 2016. Over this period qualifications attained at SCQF level 4 decreased by over 66,000 and qualifications attained at SCQF level 5 decreased by around 27,000. In contrast, there was an increase in attainment of qualifications at SCQF level 6 of around 13,000.

Table 70.2 shows the increase in attainment of Advanced Higher qualifications over the past five years. Attainment figures for 2016 are the revised Advanced Higher developed as part of the Curriculum for Excellence qualifications development.

## SCOTTISH BACCALAUREATES

Scottish Baccalaureates in Science, Languages, Expressive Arts and Social Sciences were introduced from 2009. The Scottish Baccalaureate consists of a coherent group of current Higher and Advanced Higher qualifications with the additional requirement of an interdisciplinary project. The interdisciplinary project is an internally assessed unit at SCQF level 7 which attracts sixteen SCQF credit points in which learners apply their subject knowledge in realistic contexts. This involves carrying out an investigation or practical assignment. This is likely to involve working outwith the learner's school, for example in a college or

Table 70.3   Attainment in Scottish Baccalaureates, 2012–16

|                 | 2012 | 2013 | 2014 | 2015 | 2016 |
|-----------------|------|------|------|------|------|
| Expressive Arts | –    | 5    | >5   | 5    | 6    |
| Languages       | 26   | 28   | 19   | 18   | 24   |
| Science         | 122  | 120  | 111  | 71   | 67   |
| Social Sciences | –    | 12   | 12   | 5    | 13   |
| Total           | 148  | 165  | 145  | 99   | 110  |

Source: Courtesy SQA.

university, or in a community or workplace setting. Scottish Baccalaureates are awarded at Pass and Distinction at SCQF level 7.

Table 70.3 outlines the attainment of Scottish Baccalaureates over the five years from 2012 to 2016.

## HIGHER NATIONAL CERTIFICATES AND DIPLOMAS

Higher National Certificates and Diplomas provide preparation for a vocational career or for further study. They are normally delivered by further education colleges. Higher National Certificates and Diplomas have a long and proud history as the leading higher education qualifications for technician, technologist and first-line management occupations. In 1925, twenty-four engineers and chemists attained the first Higher National qualifications in Scotland. The changing nature of skills and industry requirements has been the constant driving force to continually develop and refine these qualifications. The proof has been generations of Higher National graduates with long and successful careers.

HNCs, if taken as a full-time study, usually take one year to complete. They attract ninety-six SCQF credit points at SCQF level 7. HNDs, if taken as a full-time study, usually take two years to complete. They attract 240 SCQF credit points at SCQF level 8.

HNCs and HNDs are developed by SQA in partnership with further education colleges, universities and industry. They provide both the practical skills and the theoretical knowledge for employment. Many of the qualifications allow articulation to the second and third years of Scottish four-year degree programmes. Qualifications developers are advised that relating their design and structure to National Occupational Standards (NOS) will ensure that the qualifications are fit for purpose and serve the needs of candidates, employers and the economy. There are around 300 HNCs and HNDs covering subject areas ranging from accounting, business administration, childcare, computing, engineering, and hospitality to social sciences, trade union skills and water operations.

Figure 70.3 shows that attainment of both Higher National Certificates and Diplomas has been relatively static between 2012 and 2016.

## SCOTTISH VOCATIONAL QUALIFICATIONS

Scottish Vocational Qualifications (SVQs) are developed by representatives from industry, commerce and education. SVQs are offered by various awarding organisations accredited by SQA. The figures in this chapter only show SVQs awarded by SQA itself. SVQs have been offered by SQA for over twenty-five years. SVQs are an integral part of most of Scotland's

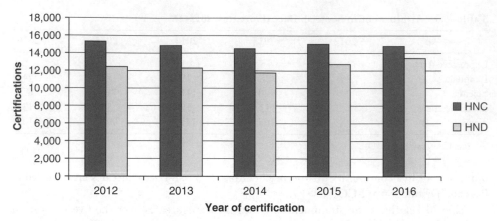

**Figure 70.3    Attainments in Higher National Certificates and Diplomas, 2012–16**

Source: Courtesy SQA.

range of modern apprenticeship frameworks, which are a key way of getting young people into skilled and meaningful employment. Examples of Modern Apprenticeships include Social Services and Healthcare; and Food and Drink Operations. SVQs are wholly based on NOS developed by sector skills bodies. They assess the application of skills, knowledge and understanding as specified in the standards through performance evidence in the workplace or a realistic working environment (RWE) as appropriate. They also show how the content of the NOS refers to the relevant core skills. Previously, there were five levels of SVQs, from level 1 (approximately SCQF 4) to level 5 (approximately SCQF 11). SCQF levels have been progressively introduced to describe SVQs. The number of SCQF credit points varies depending on the needs of the industry sector responsible for developing the occupational standards on which the qualifications are based. Figure 70.4 shows that attainment in SVQs has fallen by around 8 per cent between 2012 and 2016. 'Unlevelled' are qualifications which have not as yet been allocated SCQF level and credit points.

## ATTAINMENT IN NATIONAL QUALIFICATIONS GROUP AWARDS

While SQA's annual diet of National, Higher and Advanced Higher examinations attracts a great deal of interest, SQA also has a wider portfolio of more vocationally oriented National Qualification Group Awards. These provide more flexible combinations of internally assessed units for vocational purposes and are mostly delivered by further education colleges.

National Qualification Group Awards include National Certificates (NCs), National Progression Awards (NPAs) and Awards (AWDs). National Certificates and National Progression Awards are designed to prepare learners for employment, career development or progression to more advanced study at HNC/HND level. They also aim to develop a range of transferable knowledge including core skills. Each one has specific aims relating to a subject or occupational area. The qualifications are aimed at 16–18 year olds or adults in full-time education. They are aligned to National Occupational Standards or other professional or trade body standards, as appropriate to the group award. Awards are characterised

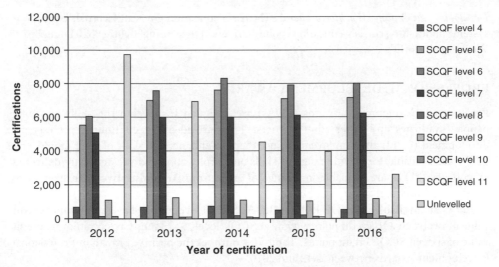

Figure 70.4    Attainments in Scottish Vocational Qualifications, 2012–16

Source: Courtesy SQA.

by their flexible nature and are designed to develop and provide recognition of specific skills, for example an Award in Volunteering is available at SCQF levels 3, 4 and 5.

At SCQF levels 2 and 3, a National Certificate requires fifty-four SCQF credit points while at SCQF levels 4, 5 and 6, seventy-two SCQF credit points are required. National Progression Awards require a minimum of twelve SCQF credit points and are available at SCQF levels 2 to 6.

Figure 70.5 outlines the positive increase in the uptake of this portfolio during 2012–16. These qualifications will form an important element of the Scottish Government's

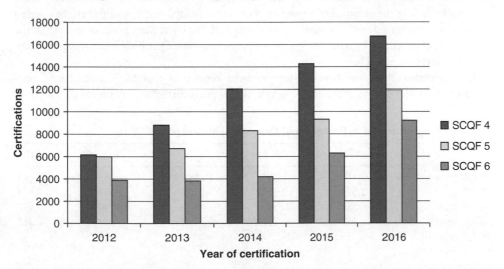

Figure 70.5    Attainment in National Qualifications Group Awards, 2012–16

Source: Courtesy SQA.

*Developing the Young Workforce* agenda (https://education.gov.scot/scottish-education-system/policy-for-scottish-education/policy-drivers/Developing%20the%20Young%20Workforce%20(DYW).

## PROFESSIONAL DEVELOPMENT AWARDS

Professional Development Awards (PDAs) are designed to develop the skills of young people, graduates and other adult learners. They are ideal for continuing professional development (CPD) and employers can use them to enhance the skills of their employees. PDAs are available for a wide range of skills and professions and are generally delivered by colleges. PDAs are available in a range of areas from Administrative Management to Workplace Coaching.

PDAs are available at SCQF levels 6–12. At SCQF level 6 they have a minimum credit value of twelve SCQF credit points, while at SCQF levels 7–12 they have a minimum credit value of sixteen SCQF credit points. Table 70.4 outlines the positive growth in Professional Development Awards between 2012 and 2016.

## DEVELOPMENTS AND OPPORTUNITIES

Over the period 2012–2016 there has been a noticeable reduction in the number of National Courses attained. The introduction of new National courses to support the wider Curriculum for Excellence reforms resulted in existing qualifications being phased out and the new qualifications in most cases being delivered and assessed in the same years. This makes comparisons problematic.

However, two variables may have contributed to this decrease in the overall number of qualifications attained. Firstly, a drop in the S4, S5 and S6 school roll over this period. Secondly, as a result of a reduction in the number of qualifications undertaken by learners in S4, due to changing presentation patterns informed by wider Curriculum for Excellence reforms including the removal of almost all S3 entries. Additionally, while there has been a reduction in the number of National Courses attained there has been positive growth in the attainment of other SQA qualifications, for example National Qualifications Group Awards, at SCQF levels 4, 5 and 6.

In September 2016, the Scottish Government requested that SQA undertake a programme of activity to review the assessment in the recently introduced National courses over

Table 70.4    Attainment in Professional Development Awards, 2012–16

|               | 2012  | 2013  | 2014  | 2015  | 2016  |
|---------------|-------|-------|-------|-------|-------|
| SCQF level 6  | 1,409 | 1,295 | 904   | 648   | 1,361 |
| SCQF level 7  | 2,398 | 2,516 | 2,577 | 2,909 | 3,534 |
| SCQF level 8  | 351   | 249   | 458   | 530   | 498   |
| SCQF level 9  | 152   | 217   | 225   | 399   | 412   |
| SCQF level 10 | 55    | 51    | 61    | 73    | 55    |
| SCQF level 11 | 17    | 14    | 9     | 0     | 0     |
| Unlevelled    | 1,118 | 738   | 617   | 546   | 290   |
| Total         | 5,500 | 5,080 | 4,851 | 5,105 | 6,150 |

Source: Courtesy SQA.

a three-year period. This will involve the removal of internal unit assessment at National 5, Higher and Advanced Higher and a strengthening of course assessment largely as a result of stakeholder concerns, principally trade unions, over the contribution which internal unit assessment was making to teacher workload. Internal unit assessment was introduced during the late 1990's 'Higher Still' reforms. Additionally, in the coming years the Scottish Government is committed to closing the attainment gap, that is, achieving equity in educational outcomes with a particular focus on closing the poverty-related attainment gap.

# 71

# The National Improvement Framework and the Return of National Testing

*Chris McIlroy*

## INTRODUCTION

There is considerable agreement about sound principles for effective strategic leadership of educational improvement which are applicable to a small country like Scotland.

- Engage with research, the profession and the public to develop a clear vision, clear guidance and a small number of priorities.
- Stick to the vision and the priorities, keeping to the high ground nationally and leaving education authorities, clusters and schools to develop the detail of ideas in practice.
- Engage all levels of the system in making improvements, focusing strongly on teacher professional learning, and stimulating and challenging learning and teaching.
- Manage the pace of change and avoid being sidetracked where the gain isn't worth the pain.
- Maintain a set of indicators of success showing trends but don't be panicked by ups and downs in a single year or set of data.

In practice, successive education ministers supported by national agencies have struggled to achieve effective strategic management. In this chapter an account is given of the recently devised National Improvement Framework and the proposed use of national standardised testing to improve standards: readers are invited to reflect on the application of these principles as the text unfolds.

The National Improvement Framework (NIF) was published by Scottish Government in December 2016 following widespread consultation on a draft version (see Scottish Government, 2017 which combines NIF and the Improvement Plan). It aimed to improve the strategic management of educational change in Scottish schools by setting a small number of continuing priorities for improvement within the vision for Curriculum for Excellence (CfE). This would help schools to concentrate on essential conditions for the educational success of children and for the nation, and bring more continuity and stability to the improvement process.

Improving achievement for all learners has been the dominant aim in educational policy over recent decades. In the last ten years 'achievement' has been fleshed out in CfE to refer to standards in literacy, numeracy and health and wellbeing, together with the skills needed for learning, life and work in the twenty-first century, including personal and social skills, creativity, problem solving, critical thinking, reasoning and understanding. There remains a broad political and educational consensus that the CfE vision is worthwhile. The questions surrounding it are about how clearly it has been articulated, communicated, understood and realised in practice.

The NIF restated the broad aim of raising achievement for all whilst giving special emphasis to reducing educational disadvantage for children living in poverty ('closing the gap'). The framework's subtitle of 'achieving excellence and equity' signalled the emergence of twin aims: to raise achievement for all and to address poverty-related disadvantage.

Improved strategic management of educational change, the moral crusade to reduce educational disadvantage and the drive to improve overall standards are all important and worthwhile agendas for Scottish education. However, many of the headlines surrounding the launch of the NIF related to its proposal to improve the consistency of data through nationally standardised testing and reporting of children's progress. Although some of the purposes avowed for national testing are different from those of the 1990s and practice in standardised testing had become commonplace in Scottish education authorities, there remained sufficient concern that a high stakes' testing system would emerge to reignite debates from the Michael Forsyth era (the late 1980s and early 1990s).

The NIF made a range of other proposals, for example on school governance and the roles of education authorities and national bodies and research. Although this chapter will touch on some of these issues, it will mainly analyse the contribution of the NIF as *a strategic approach* to educational improvement and evaluate two key projects within the strategy, that is addressing educational disadvantage and introducing national testing. (The First Minister and senior figures in Education Scotland have claimed, disingenuously, that the tests are not 'national tests'. They are clearly tests and they will be designed, standardised, collated and used at national level.)

## THE NIF AS A STRATEGIC APPROACH TO EDUCATIONAL IMPROVEMENT

Programme for International Student Assessment (PISA) data tells us that the Scottish approach to school improvement in recent decades has resulted in lower rates of achievement than other countries that would be regarded in Scotland as comparators. To rub salt into the wound, in the most recent PISA survey published in December 2016 by the Organisation for Economic Co-operation and Development (OECD), Scotland recorded its worst performance since 2000 with scores for mathematics, reading and science all showing patterns of decline (see Chapter 68 for fuller details). This matters to Scotland's international competitiveness. It also suggests that many Scottish children could achieve more across a range of aspects of learning which affect the quality of their learning and their lives. The PISA results attracted alarmed media headlines and vociferous criticism from opposition parties of the Scottish National Party (SNP) government's ten years of leadership of education. The strategic management of improvement didn't seem to be working.

Moreover, the strategic leadership of education has been unsuccessful in engaging teachers in a change process that they feel that they can manage, lead and control, that focuses on outcomes for learners and contributes to their school's needs and to the national agenda. In the fourth edition of *Scottish Education* this writer commented on some of the issues facing schools in improvement planning and argued for a better alignment between national and school priorities for improvement:

> The explanation for this lack of alignment between the improvement priorities for the nation and for individual schools lies in the many competing interests which shape school improvement. National developments, education authority and cluster priorities are considered alongside the priorities emerging from a school's own self-evaluation. The process is pressured, the big picture can get lost in the detail and the timeframe is often too short to address difficult long-term issues.
>
> This raises the wider issue of the effectiveness of national agencies and education authorities in working with schools to present a coherent and steady picture of change and avoiding requiring them to consider too many fragmented and specific developments. It should be an aspiration for Scotland to achieve a new consensus in our political and educational leadership on the more effective management of educational change. (McIlroy, 2013)

A new National Improvement Framework was badly needed! Other organisations, notably the increasingly influential OECD, gave impetus to the need to improve the strategic management of education. Andy Hargreaves, a key contributor to *Improving Schools in Scotland: An OECD Perspective* (OECD, 2015), has contrasted the key features of the approach to change in the USA with those of Ontario and found that reforms in the USA were unable to achieve deep and lasting changes in practice because:

- they focused on things that were too distant from the instructional core of teaching and learning;
- they assumed that teachers would know how to do things they actually didn't know how to do;
- too many conflicting reforms asked teachers to do too many things simultaneously;
- teachers and schools did not buy in to the reform strategy (OECD, 2011).

At least some of these features resonate with the Scottish experience.
    Ontario's national improvement approach encompassed:

- a small number of continuing broad priorities;
- space (though limited) by self-denying ordinance from politicians for local priorities based on self-evaluation;
- engagement of all the layers in leadership, enquiry and problem solving;
- schools often differing in the detail and in the 'how' they make changes.

Michael Fullan's work in Ontario also stresses the value and manageability of focusing on a small number of continuing priorities for improvement. Priorities should be 'memorable' so that they become clear in teachers' thinking, 'sticky' so that they endure and 'actionable' in their impact on learners in the classroom (Hargreaves and Fullan, 2012). The priorities in the National Improvement Framework can sit comfortably with this advice:

- improvement in attainment, specifically in reading, writing and numeracy;
- closing the attainment gap between the most and least disadvantaged children;
- improvement in children and young people's health and wellbeing;
- improvement in sustained school leaver destination for all young people.

OECD fingerprints are evident in these priorities. The NIF has adopted an approach to change, which is based on OECD evidence of success and has many strengths. It enables a relentless focus on key areas of children's development and learning with the intention of raising achievement for all and closing poverty-related gaps. The Scottish Attainment Fund and, more recently, the Pupil Equity Fund target additional resources towards these priorities. Arrangements for accountability in *How Good is Our School? Version 4* (Education Scotland, 2015) were also aligned with the NIF priorities. Scottish Government seemed to be adopting a coherent approach. The prospects for strategic management were looking good.

To make this sound strategic approach work requires politicians and government to stick to the high ground of strategy and the broad agenda of improvement and avoid becoming prescriptive or enmeshed in detail. Sadly, the emphasis by government on setting strategic priorities and leaving detail and choice of approaches to authorities and schools was almost instantly undermined by their publication of a delivery plan. This was very detailed, with over a hundred actions, some of them prescriptive, and far too tightly paced in its timescales. Its tone resonated of one-directional flow of messages and instructions rather than of professional engagement, debate, dialogue and leadership at every level, which are fundamental aspirations of CfE.

An immediate example was in the publication of benchmarks. *Improving Schools in Scotland: An OECD Perspective* (OECD, 2015) had criticised the lack of clarity in teachers' understanding of CfE levels: 'Too many teachers are unclear what should be assessed in relation to the Experiences and Outcomes, which blurs the connection between assessment and improvement.' In response, Education Scotland hastily prepared and published sets of new 'benchmarks', aiming to increase the clarity and shared understanding of what is meant by 'achieving a level' in different aspects of the curriculum. On their return for a new school year in August 2016, teachers were welcomed with numerous pages of 'benchmarks'. Well intentioned to support the consistency of assessments, these shifted signals about what is important in the curriculum. Specific and easily checked fragments of learning were highlighted as assessments for the rich and sometimes open-ended learning opportunities indicated in the experiences and outcomes.

It is difficult to achieve clarity and shared understanding of curriculum advice. Two broad approaches are possible. One route is to increase the specificity of advice as in the benchmarks. This risks distorting the richness of curriculum and pedagogy as what is assessed is privileged over other aspects of learning. The other aims at teachers 'unpacking', understanding and critiquing the advice. This fits well with CfE philosophy and with what we know is likely to lead to durable educational improvement. It requires considerable time for professional learning, dialogue and moderation. The direction taken by Education Scotland for a 'quick fix' to clarity through benchmarks adds another layer of complexity and tension to advice rather than simplifying the guidance. (See also the discussion of benchmarks in Chapter 68.)

The broad strategy for improvement in the NIF had been soundly based and informed by research and experience. It had been quickly endangered by tactics based on an anxiety to control and the political desire under pressure to communicate a greater sense of urgency in addressing issues. Since then, there have been efforts to reassert the big picture and play down the detail. Time will now tell whether the potential of the NIF to improve strategic management in setting and communicating priorities is achieved.

## CLOSING POVERTY-RELATED GAPS IN ACHIEVEMENT

A challenging project for strategic leadership based on the NIF was to promote greater equity through the 'Scottish Attainment Challenge' (SAC) while continuing to stress the Raising Attainment for All programme (see www.gov.scot/Topics/Education/Schools/Raisingeducationalattainment/RAFA). The latter aims to help all learners to achieve higher educational standards, bringing advantages for learners, society and the economy. The recent PISA results underlined its importance. The SAC aims to benefit individuals disadvantaged by poverty, bring greater fairness to educational outcomes and assist social cohesion. Evidence of the powerful link between poverty and educational outcomes has accumulated over the last fifty years (see Chapter 12). More recently, national concerns about 'austerity' and the failure to improve poverty-related outcomes were highlighted in the influential reports, *Improving Schools in Scotland: An OECD Perspective* (OECD, 2015) and *Closing the Attainment Gap in Scottish Education* published by the Joseph Rowntree Foundation (Ellis and Sosu, 2014). There is both synergy and potential conflict in developing practice to achieve these 'twin' aims. Early on, the team providing strategic leadership to the SAC realised that clarity about purpose and differentiated approaches was needed to ensure that each aim supports rather than undermines the other.

The NIF drew heavily on the OECD publication *Synergies for Better Learning* (OECD, 2013) to construct a useful summary of broad 'drivers' to raise attainment based on international research. Improved attainment is often promoted internationally using 'universal approaches' aimed at benefiting all learners. The drivers include increased parental involvement and support for children's learning, development of teacher professionalism, assessment and the use of performance information, and school leadership. However, the single set of drivers used by OECD and the NIF did not distinguish those which are more effective in raising attainment for all learners from those that help to reduce poverty-related attainment gaps.

Some universal approaches to improve general standards are also effective in reducing poverty-related gaps. For example, research presented by the Educational Endowment Foundation indicates that improvements in the quality of feedback to learners, in collaborative learning, and in promoting certain types of thinking (metacognition and making inferences) promote both general improvements in achievement for all learners and bring particular benefits to disadvantaged learners. It is clear, therefore, that all teachers can focus profitably on these aspects within their classrooms to address both of the aims.

In contrast, other effective universal approaches to raising attainment may raise overall standards without leading to greater equity. Figure 71.1 using SQA exam data shows that making use of these broad drivers in recent years has achieved some improvement in overall standards but the gap has remained fairly constant. Why does this happen? Research tells us that, just as some universal approaches narrow gaps between learners from disadvantaged backgrounds, others may widen them. For example, there is evidence that parental involvement and *general* provision of preschool education and homework often increase gaps because parents with greater 'cultural capital' in education make a stronger impact on their children's achievements than parents in poverty. Recognising this, the government has started to differentiate provision, for example providing more teachers in nurseries in disadvantaged communities.

Within the classroom, too, teachers' actions may widen or decrease gaps through the ways that they respond to children's language and out-of-school experiences, set expectations and

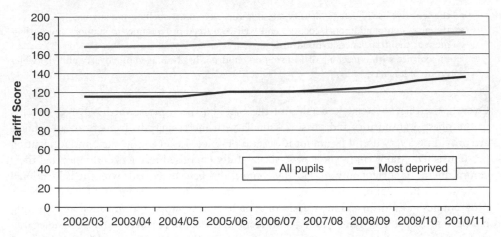

**Figure 71.1    Tariff scores for SQA across successive years**

Note: Tariff scores are explained at http://insight-guides.scotxed.net/support/InsightTariff.pdf

levels of challenge, develop inclusion, form groups and allocate their time and attention to meet different needs. Increasing levels of challenge and awareness of needs, careful day-to-day assessment of response and progress, and the use of focused or targeted additional or enriched support for periods of time can all help to reduce achievement gaps.

Although the impact of individual teachers is significant, actions at whole school, community and wider social levels can maximise impact on many poverty-related achievement issues. Harnessing the skills of teachers in working and learning together to promote well-planned innovation is one route to success. Developing consistency of good practice is another. Using the time and resources of the wider team in the school and community, engaging school leadership and additional staff in targeted additional or enriched support, including for parents who need help in supporting learning outwith school, all maximise impact. At a wider level, the way government and councils use resources is important. The Pupil Equity Fund is a brave and well-resourced example of harnessing the ideas and energy of schools and clusters to stimulate approaches that reduce the impact of poverty on achievement. It locates change at the level that it takes place to release the ideas and energies of teachers in the school and classroom in partnership with education authorities. The approach is right even though some headteachers are currently uncertain of the best uses of the funding.

The NIF agenda involves teachers and schools in doing some things differently to achieve the twin aims. Bringing these aims together in practice is a new challenge for teachers and schools. It requires a different focus to differentiation and support for pupils. Teachers are currently less clear, experienced and confident in blending successful approaches to meet the needs of all learners with specific approaches that target the needs of economically disadvantaged individuals or groups. In particular, teachers will need more clarity and support on:

- ways of promoting inclusion in all aspects of children's experience and learning where disadvantage creates barriers to learning, for example identifying and addressing differential participation in classwork, visits, clubs, home learning and supported study;

- the sensitive use of data to identify target groups, avoiding labelling and stigma;
- the provision of additional, focused and well-resourced programmes of support and enrichment as counterbalances to disadvantage;
- the balance within teaching of focusing on children disadvantaged by poverty and the wider group of learners.

Overall, the early strategic leadership of the SAC has been praiseworthy. Developments in the phase 1 authorities and phase 2 schools with increasing involvement of all schools are providing a very useful forum for ideas and practice. Local engagement and innovation has flourished. Major conferences have successfully energised teachers and increased their commitment. Important outward looking connections have been made with the Educational Endowment Foundation and with key figures in the London Challenge and City Challenge programmes in England and in Wales. Some high-quality support for professional learning has been provided. Decisions within parameters on the use of resources have been delegated to partnerships of education authorities and schools. Education Scotland has a clear and appropriate role in accountability.

But this is a long-term development, which will require continuity and persistence. Evidence from other countries and from past Scottish experience suggests that gaps are more likely to be reduced than closed. Across different social groups, variation in cultural capital, influence and resources such as tutoring and extra-curricular activities to support their children's educational success will generate challenges to greater equity across social groups. The educationally advantaged will not cede their advantage easily and will compete actively for scarce resources. Pressures on government spending may come to bear down on resources. The jury will remain out, therefore, on the success of the very worthwhile SAC until it is sustained over time and evidence of impact and improved outcomes emerges.

## ASSESSMENT AND TESTING

*Improving Schools in Scotland: An OECD Perspective* (OECD, 2015) encouraged improvements to data and its use in Scottish schools. This chimed with the recommendations of the Joseph Rowntree report (Ellis and Sosu, 2014) for better data to monitor the effects of poverty on achievement. Improvements to data and its uses, therefore posed a key challenge for Scottish Government.

Following the discontinuation of 5–14 national testing in 2003, Scotland had developed a 'low stakes' assessment system for the 'broad general education' phase of CfE. This relied mainly on teachers' professional judgements about learning and progress, with periodic use of standardised tests in almost all schools and education authorities – though authorities used different tests. What were its strengths and weaknesses?

The sound principles of 'Assessment is for Learning' (AifL) provided a framework for assessment practice in the classroom as described in Chapter 68. These principles emphasise, for example, teachers and learners sharing learning intentions and success criteria; asking thoughtful questions; and engaging teachers and learners in providing effective feedback. This emphasis on good formative assessment improved practice in many schools though its impact was superficial in others. It remains an important long-term development with benefits to national outcomes anticipated rather than yet achieved.

CfE levels of experiences and outcomes provided useful general advice for planning and pedagogy. Teachers found them to be less easily applied in summarising progress through the levels because they require discussion and interpretation to clarify their meaning. As a result, a shared understanding of CfE levels was, and remains, relatively weak at the primary and early secondary stages, notwithstanding some very good but insufficient support for moderation. Teachers sometimes used test results alongside classwork in reporting to parents. Headteachers and education authorities varied in their development of assessment practice and in their use of data to promote improvement.

A key strength was that the assessment system provided scope for teachers to encourage 'basic skills' alongside wider outcomes and dispositions. This sat well with the CfE aspiration to promote a range of important attributes and capabilities as well as a broad and challenging set of understanding and skills, including for example social skills, creativity and critical thinking. Some of these aspects can be tested but in many cases development is better judged through observing and evaluating signposts of progress. Barack Obama captures the relative importance of preparation for standardised tests and for a broad and stimulating education:

> When I look back on the great teachers who shaped my life, what I remember isn't the way they prepared me to take a standardised test. What I remember is the way they taught me to believe in myself. To be curious about the world. To take charge of my own learning so that I could reach my full potential. They inspired me to open up a window into parts of the world I'd never thought of before. (https://obamawhitehouse.archives.gov/blog/2015/10/26/open-letter-americas-parents-and-teachers-lets-make-our-testing-smarter)

The Joseph Rowntree report (Ellis and Sosu, 2014) had advocated better data to track learners' progress in relation to poverty. Although attainment data was widely available from teacher assessments and standardised tests, data indicating socio-economic circumstances was rarely used to investigate connections between learners' background and their progress. Information on standardised tests was not collated nationally and did not lead to 'league table' comparisons of schools. National monitoring of standards and changes over time was based on sampling using PISA, the Scottish surveys of literacy and numeracy, and, at the secondary stages, data on qualifications and leaver destinations. Despite some specific criticisms, this generally met this function well. The following are some key proposals for assessment practice at school and national level:

- A new Scottish standardised test will be introduced on aspects of literacy and numeracy within CfE to increase consistency.
- Teachers' professional judgement will continue to be valued and supported. Teachers can override test results if they jar with their professional judgement.
- Data from teacher judgement of CfE levels for literacy and numeracy, informed by the new tests, will be collated nationally alongside 'metrics' relating to Health and Wellbeing.
- Better information and increased moderation will help teachers 'to support individual children's progress and to identify where improvement is needed'.
- Tracking of learners' attainment in relation to poverty will be improved by analysing attainment data alongside Scottish Index of Multiple Deprivation (SIMD) information. Better data will help in evaluating initiatives to address poverty-related attainment.
- Assessment information will be used by headteachers to 'guide improved planning and self-evaluation'. Data on CfE levels will be collected and published nationally and used for teacher and school accountability.
- Collated data on all pupils' achievement of CfE levels will be used to monitor national standards. The Scottish surveys of literacy and numeracy will be discontinued as a means of tracking national standards and changes over time.

However much the language values teacher professional judgement and diagnosis, these proposals create a 'high stakes' assessment and testing system. Two of the major changes were the introduction of standardised tests and their use, alongside professional judgement, in accountability. What does the research tell us about the likely impact of these changes?

International research about the advantages and disadvantages of testing in raising attainment gives some inconsistent messages. Some studies report that the tests have little or no influence on what teachers do in the classroom. Some provide support for the role of testing in driving up standards in aspects of literacy and numeracy, arguing that this is because testing encourages an emphasis on important basic skills, with accountability reinforcing the attention given to them.

However, the greater weight of evidence indicates that standardised testing linked with accountability has undesirable effects on learners and learning, and on achievement. Once testing becomes linked to accountability, it often distorts the curriculum so that what is tested becomes what matters. It can lead to teaching to the test and focus teaching on aspects of learning that are easily measurable, risking, for example, the broad aspirations for CfE. An Australian survey of the literature on testing highlights some of the concerns:

> A range of concerns regarding the impact of high stakes testing is evident in the international literature. These range from the reliability of the tests themselves to their impact on the wellbeing of children. This impact includes the effect on the nature and quality of the broader learning experiences of children which may result from changes in approaches to learning and teaching, as well as the structure and nature of the curriculum. (Polesel et al., 2012, p. 4)

Some studies show that testing can lower expectations and reduce motivation for children who don't 'perform' well relative to norms via practices in labelling and grouping children, making it even more difficult to close gaps for disadvantaged learners.

A specific and important warning for the NIF proposals from research and experience in England highlights the dangers of using one tool or test to serve too many purposes. A select committee of the Westminster Parliament reflected on this mistake. Recommendation 2 of its report (House of Commons, 2008) states:

> The evidence we have received strongly favours the view that national tests do not serve all of the purposes for which they are, in fact used. The fact that the results of these tests are used for so many purposes, with high-stakes attached to the outcomes, creates tensions in the system leading to undesirable consequences, including distortion of the education experience of many children. In addition, the data derived from the testing system do not necessarily provide an accurate or complete picture of the performance of schools and teachers, yet they are relied upon by the Government, the QCA and Ofsted to make important decisions affecting the education system in general and individual schools, teachers and pupils in particular. In short, we consider that the current national testing system is being applied to serve too many purposes. (House of Commons, 2008)

The challenge for Scotland was to improve the quality and use of assessment data whilst avoiding the negative effects of high stakes testing. Being 'data rich' is undoubtedly helpful to school improvement, and schools are increasingly using a range of data including surveys, evidence of participation, engagement and positive attitudes as well as on attainment, attendance and exclusions. Research links teachers' active use of data to improvements for learners. However, the NIF strategy on data did not take sufficient account of the body of research and experience of high stakes testing, placing the achievement of its own aims at risk.

Effective use of data is more readily achieved in a localised 'low stakes' environment where three conditions are met. They are that:

- it should be managed, used and interpreted at the level closest to practice;
- it should be used to raise questions (e.g. 'Have I underestimated this child's skills?', 'Does s(he) need more support or challenge?', 'Have I got the pace of learning right?') not to provide conclusions;
- individual sets of data should not be inflated beyond the weight that can be placed on them.

Each condition is considered in turn.

## It Should Be Managed, Used and Interpreted at the Level Closest to Practice

The Scottish Government promotes ideas of subsidiarity: seeking to maintain its strategic role but devolving responsibility to the levels closest to communities and practice. An appropriate strategic role for government in national monitoring is to *sample* the achievements of Scottish learners and evaluate whether there is evidence of improvement or declining standards. Monitoring national standards requires a survey, which repeats sufficient assessment items from previous surveys to justify comment on changing standards over time. (Changes to survey arrangements have been a shameful feature of Scottish education over the last fifty years, making it almost impossible to track standards over time.) To maximise its impact on improvement, monitoring should promote dialogue with authorities, agencies, clusters and schools on links between standards and classroom practice. Although, improvements to PISA and the national surveys have been suggested by research, these surveys already provided reasonable tools for national monitoring and avoided disruption to teaching and assessment practice.

Strategic monitoring does not require gathering information on each school, classroom and pupil – a huge and wasteful bureaucratic process and the antithesis of strategic national monitoring. Arrangements for the *national* collation and publication of attainment data on CfE levels from every school based on professional judgements that are 'informed' by standardised tests unhelpfully raise the stakes without adding value for learners. Whereas it is legitimate for government to ensure that there is a system in place to ensure good data, collation and use (including a Scottish standardised test if that is desired), the management of arrangements sit better locally with those managing schools and authorities. National monitoring through sampling facilitates a devolved, low-key and more effective assessment system and resolves the problems of one assessment tool serving too many purposes.

## It Should Be Used to Raise Questions Not to Provide Conclusions

Standardised tests are designed so that an individual's performance on a test can be compared with a reliable picture of the population as a whole on a set of items. To achieve 'reliability' they focus on a narrow subset of skills. The tests can, therefore, contribute to diagnosis but only in a limited way and alongside a range of other evidence of progress. Where teachers use this information alongside their professional judgements about a child's performance in a low stakes environment to raise questions about learners' progress, the result can be positive.

Accountability which explores issues and improvements and 'gives an account' to children, parents and communities from the teams managing schools is also more effectively and intelligently located at local level in schools, clusters and education authorities where it can be accompanied by an understanding of context and based on a range of evidence.

Instead Scottish Government published data on individual schools on the achievement of CfE levels in December 2016. The data was poor: some was moderated, some was not, and some was influenced by local standardised tests. More generally, the proposal in NIF to gather data intends to mix together evidence gathered for different purposes and in different ways, combining more and less reliable and more and less valid data into a single data set. It increases the probability of the media presenting raw data and league tables, data that has little meaning, without an understanding of the context of the schools and the differences in cohorts in socio-economic factors, gender and prior learning which influence attainment. To use this as a basis for judgements about schools and the performance of teachers would inevitably cause unfairness and confusion.

### Individual Sorts of Data Should Not Be Inflated beyond the Weight That Can Be Placed on Them

Unfortunately, where high stakes assessment develops, teachers tend to defer to test results as 'scientific', 'objective' and 'accurate' – providing conclusions rather than questions and theories to be tested. Standardised test data becomes regarded as a reliable proxy for achievement, with results inflated beyond the weight that can be placed upon them. Despite the rhetoric accompanying the NIF that tests should 'inform' or 'confirm' a teacher's professional judgement, in practice they dominate it. We know from Scottish experience of national tests that when teachers were faced with a test result, which differed from their professional judgement, they usually gave weight to the test.

### CONCLUSION: HOPES, DREAMS OR GOLDFISH?

The advent of the Scottish Parliament in 1999 changed the intensity of educational leadership and policymaking in Scottish education. It increased the engagement of politicians in educational decisions, bringing politicians closer to the views, values and experiences of learners, parents and carers, teachers, the public and the media. This positive shift was accompanied by increased tendencies for ministers to make hasty decisions, to be prescriptive and try to micro-manage change. Frequent ministerial changes added to volatility and to variation in their assertiveness. The formation of Education Scotland with responsibilities for leading development and for evaluation embedded a fundamental conflict of interest. This weakened its independence in evaluation and the strength of its professional advice to ministers. As a result, the political–professional balance was sometimes distorted.

The NIF has provided an opportunity to restore the balance by developing a culture and framework for partnerships and continuity in strategic leadership and devolved responsibility. It has offered the potential to improve standards through continuity and clarity of purpose and increased professional engagement. It has strong foundations in the consensus for developing high standards in literacy, numeracy and health and wellbeing alongside twentieth-century skills. Although political differences have been much more evident recently and the Scottish Conservatives have placed CfE 'on probation', differences largely focus on means rather than aims: on the management of education and qualifications, and the clarity of advice and support to teachers, resources and finance. Thus the potential for shared priorities is still present.

However, clear messages that the government was occupying the high ground of strategy were undermined by the detailed and unrealistically paced delivery plan and the introduction of new national tests with heavy central involvement. The framework now needs to return to the high ground of strategy in setting and focusing relentlessly on priorities, on professional engagement and responsibility, and high-quality learning and teaching because these are key ingredients of success. The response in June 2017 (Scottish Government, 2017) to the consultation on school governance offered a golden opportunity for government to restore the balance to reinforce the NIF strategy and the broad agenda of improvement.

This opportunity has been missed. The aspirations to empower teachers and schools in leading improvement; to increase partnership working across clusters and networks; to 'strengthen the middle'; to widen the focus on improvement reaching into communities; the 'offer' of improved professional learning for teachers and leaders; and greater devolution of resources and staffing to schools are all worthwhile. The review's main problem is its advocacy of extensive and turbulent structural change. This will divert energy into changing organisations, linkages, roles and personnel and away from a focus on changing culture, achievement, and learning and teaching.

Education Scotland will grow additional arms in 'regional improvement collaboratives', compounding existing conflicts of interest and purpose and adding to the churn that has constrained its impact in recent years. The role of local authorities in promoting quality and improvement will be correspondingly truncated on the basis that their effectiveness varies and some are small. Published inspection reports on education authorities, though a little dated, found no apparent link between effectiveness and size of education authority. They do support the claim of variation but evaluated most authorities as positive forces for improvement through their ongoing engagement with local schools and clusters. In 2015, Estyn reported at least as great a variation in the effectiveness of regional improvement bodies in Wales (see http://democracy.blaenau-gwent.gov.uk/aksblaenau_gwent/images/att2796.pdf).

Despite the review's concern to empower teachers and schools, its tone is often of command, prescription and control. For example, partnerships will be prompted by 'a duty' and organised within the new regional structure. Teachers, leaders, education authorities and agencies are instructed what they 'will' do and there is a density of detailed actions for change. Government influence on professional issues is overt. The First Minister and Depute First Minister will chair key committees – the International Council of Education Advisers and a Scottish Educational Council.

An alternative way forward was to adopt an evolutionary approach. Building on existing good practice in Scotland and beyond, informal partnerships within and across schools and within and across education authorities could have been more actively fostered and resourced. This could harness enthusiasm to improve practice and give clear purposes for self-evaluation. It would align well with better provision for professional learning for teachers and school leaders. A return to more rigorous evaluation of education authorities and their arrangements for self-improvement and partnerships (with consequent reshaping of their roles) alongside increased frequency of improvement-focused school inspections could provide a more measured, managed and successful agenda for change.

Far from developing its strategic role and empowering the profession, the review takes Scotland towards a centrally and politically managed education system which goes well beyond the democratic responsibility to set broad priorities. Power brings the obligation to avoid the temptation to overuse it. Restricting political intervention to strategy and empowering and trusting others to make their contribution could yet bring stability to the system and facilitate a clear focus on improvement to achievement. It is never too late to change tack!

The challenge of poverty-related disadvantage has been persistent in many areas of life over the fifty years from *Cathy Come Home* to *I Daniel Blake*. The impact of poverty on educational outcomes has been clear throughout this period as differences in health, housing, attendance, family pressures and morale, educational capital and school responses influenced learning and achievement. The track record of previous Scottish initiatives to address disadvantage from 'Areas of Priority Treatment' through 'Circular 991' to 'Early Intervention' illustrate examples of success as well as the need for a long-term, sustained programme, as each was discontinued following recession or the emergence of other priorities.

No one should underestimate the task of the SAC in tackling powerful social factors influencing educational success and changing culture, priorities, attitudes and behaviours in schools. Although its successes will make a relatively small impact on raising overall standards, SAC is a worthwhile and determined development. It strikes a chord with Scottish values for equity and fairness. Its determination is reflected in strong political and financial support. It is worthwhile because of the difference that it can make to individuals' lives and educational success and to the development of a more cohesive and fairer society.

If the early strategic management of the SAC has been commendable, the proposed use of national standardised tests to improve standards finds little justification in research. It will absorb emotional and professional energy that could be better directed to improvements in learning and teaching. The need to reduce adverse effects of standardised testing by involving central government only at a strategic level was emphasised above. In addition, several specific features should be mentioned as illustrations of issues related to the tests. Computer-based tests are designed to reduce workload but, unsurprisingly, some teachers report that some children perform better with pencil and paper, thus questioning their reliability. Proposed timetables have been delayed for piloting tests and to trial 'adaptive' tests that stop when a child has difficulty. Testing children in their early years is counterproductive: it increases unreliability and is inferior to observing the young child in a range of contexts, giving weight to oral language development and to emotional maturity. In searching for improvement, we should take care not to flush away what we value and have learned from the past.

## REFERENCES

Au, Wayne (2007) 'High-stakes testing and curricular control: a qualitative metasynthesis', *Educational Researcher*, 36 (5), 258–67, www.jstor.org/stable/30137912

Education Scotland (2017) *Conversations about Learning for Sustainability*. Online at https://education.gov.scot/improvement/Documents/lfs3-conversations-about-LfS.pdf

Ellis, S. and Sosu, E. (2014) *Closing the Attainment Gap in Scottish Education*. Joseph Rowntree Foundation. Online at https://www.jrf.org.uk/report/closing-attainment-gap-scottish-education

Hargreaves, A. and Fullan, M. (2012) *Professional Capital: Transforming Teaching in Every School*. New York: Teachers College Press, Columbia University.

House of Commons (2008) *Testing and Assessment: Government and Ofsted Responses to the Committee's Third Report of Session 2007–08*. Online at https://publications.parliament.uk/pa/cm200708/cmselect/cmchilsch/1003/1003.pdf

McIlroy, C. (2013) 'The Scottish approach to school improvement: achievements and limitations', in T. G. K. Bryce, W. M. Humes, D. Gillies and A. Kennedy (eds), *Scottish Education, Fourth Edition: Referendum*. Edinburgh: Edinburgh University Press, pp. 434–45.

OECD (2011) *Lessons from PISA for the United States, Strong Performers and Successful Reformers in Education*. Online at https://www.oecd.org/pisa/46623978.pdf

OECD (2013) *Synergies for Better Learning: An International Perspective on Evaluation and Assessment: Pointers for Policy Development*. Online at https://www.oecd.org/edu/school/Synergies%20for%20Better%20Learning_Policy%20Pointers.pdf

OECD (2015) *Improving Schools in Scotland: An OECD Perspective*. Online at https://www.oecd.org/education/school/Improving-Schools-in-Scotland-An-OECD-Perspective.pdf

Polesel, J., Dulfer, N. and Turnbull, M. (2012) 'The experience of education: the impacts of high stakes testing on school students and their families'. Literature review by Whitlam Institute, University of Western Sydney.

Reay, D. and Wiliam, D. (1999) '"I'll be a nothing": structure and agency and the construction of identity through assessment', *British Educational Research Journal*, 25 (3), 343–354.

Scottish Government (2017) *2017 National Improvement Framework and Improvement Plan for Scottish Education: Achieving Excellence and Equity*. Online at www.gov.scot/Resource/0051/00511513.pdf

# IX

# FURTHER AND HIGHER EDUCATION

# 72

# Knowledge, Skills and Pathways in Further Education

*Gary Husband*

The industrial heritage of Scotland is long, proudly upheld and (at the time of writing) becoming increasingly important in these times of enhanced political uncertainty, both nationally and internationally. Over the last century, further education (FE) has played a consistent and important role in both supporting and shaping the industrial and economic landscape of Scotland. You need look no further than the names of some of the colleges that existed pre-regionalisation (which I will return to shortly), Stevenson, Telford, Adam Smith, James Watt and Carnegie to name a few, to get a flavour of the historical connections with commerce and industry and its captains. As the post-1970s and 80s decline in manufacturing, heavy engineering (more recently), offshore oil production and mining has taken its toll on the social and economic prosperity of the industrialised belt of Scotland and the north-eastern coast, the fortunes of many FE colleges have also changed. The FE sector in Scotland today is a much changed arena to that of thirty years ago, in fact, to that of five years ago, and is still very much in a state of continuous flux. This chapter explores the current situation with regards to knowledge, skills and pathways within the changing FE sector in Scotland today. These headings are used to scrutinise policy and practice in relation to both students and the professional community working within the sector. Specific attention is drawn to the socio-economic drivers emanating from policy and the purpose and perceived values of FE and the related tensions therein. The amorphous nature of the sector is unpicked in some detail with the aim of understanding the effect of the proliferation of the dichotomy of vocational and academic knowledges underpinning the commentary on the impacts of sector reform and the experiences of students. The chapter goes on to explore the values and purpose of FE in Scotland and the recent pressures brought about through restructure, changing legal and corporate identity, and the many faces that this diverse and heterogeneous sector wears.

## THE CHANGING FACE OF FURTHER EDUCATION IN SCOTLAND

Further education is often characterised as being the vocational sector, in fact beyond the shores of the United Kingdom, vocational education and training (VET) is frequently the title it carries. Although holding true for a significant part of the curriculum offered in many colleges, it is not a description that covers the full scope of provision of FE in the

UK and, specifically, Scotland. A significant proportion of courses offered across all aspects of FE are not focused on the vocational acquisition of a practical skill set but are academically focused. (I will come back to this problematic dichotomy in more detail later in this chapter.) In describing FE as a sector, we are also frequently guilty of assuming that FE means colleges of further education. However, once again this is an insufficient description or definition as it fails to take into account the many private training, community education, third sector and charitable providers of education and private business offerings that also fall under the banner. FE is a complex, multifaceted, often disparate grouping of provisions that finds itself described as a sector, where in reality it is perhaps better thought of as a group of smaller sectors filling the gaps in educational provision across society; FE does not simply fill the gap between school and university. The diversity of the sector is no more evident than within colleges themselves which act as a microcosm of learning, covering an enormously diverse curriculum. This in itself can be problematic for leadership and management as policy is frequently devised and implemented in something of a blanket fashion and consequently frequently fails to tailor to the specifics and nuances of the differing subject areas and specialisms.

The amorphous cohesion constructed by policy and described as FE, suffers (understandably) from both an identity crisis and a crisis of prestige. It is repeatedly described in terms that fail to take into account every aspect of the provision under its very large umbrella and, as such, its perceived association with only providing vocational learning has given it a reputation as a second choice or lower standard offering. Subsequent governments across the whole of the UK have struggled repeatedly to fully capture FE's purpose, place, value, remit and scope, leading to a period of benign neglect that has only in the last few years begun to be addressed, albeit rather contentiously. There can be little surprise at this outcome as much of the policy and funding reform has been aimed at the college provision, while the rest of the 'sector' has not gone untouched by repeated and constant reform. Where the economy has been through boom and (dramatically) bust, training provision for trades, industry and commerce has seen similar meteoric peaks and troughs in numbers, engagement and uptake. The knock-on effect to funding, student numbers and sector-specific skills has been dramatic.

The introductory paragraphs to this chapter purposefully paint a picture of a sector beset with challenges in order to highlight the shifting context and complex background in which its successes are still evident, many and growing. FE is the sector that supports a broad scope of industry, promotes equity in and access to adult education, whilst offering a haven for second chance learning and creative industries. There are few areas of our lives where FE graduates are not playing vital roles (construction, retail, childcare, industry, transport, public health – the list goes on). It is important to acknowledge early on in this discussion that the current situation in Scottish FE is challenging but, nevertheless, FE is now attracting the significant attention of local and national government, policymakers and the broader educational community in an intensity not seen in over twenty-five years, much of which will form the basis of the ongoing discussions and analysis in the coming pages.

In a previous edition of this book, Canning (2013) opens by highlighting the tensions and related debate associated with the differences between vocational and academic types of knowledge. In his detailed epistemological analysis, Canning highlights the historical and deep-rooted tendency of scholars to elevate liberal knowledge and denigrate the vocational. As highlighted by Fisher and Simmons (2012), the culturally deep-seated and institutional divisions leading to the imbalance in parity of esteem between vocational and academically associated routes to learning has never been effectively addressed. This is in part down to the cultural heritage of the UK and the national drive for attainment at higher education level, but also in part to the vocational sector itself. The dichotomy between academic and vocational knowledge is essentially false, as any engineer, chef or health care professional (to name a few) will attest to. You cannot effectively practice in a skilled profession without a comprehensive skills base *and* an accompanying thorough understanding of the underpinning theories that give depth and transferability. However, the increasing focus on a competitive globalised economy and commodification of education (for profit) has seen the stripping away of some of the previously present academic or (theoretical) knowledge and supplanting it with performative assessment-focused, modular learning with skills-based, narrow quantifiable outcomes (Wheelahan, 2010). Crucially, underpinning theoretical ideas that broaden understanding beyond motor reproduction have been given reduced space in many curricula and are frequently taught separately (where at all) and given clear delineation in provision. The divide between academic knowledge and vocational knowledge is not just evident between the higher education and further education sectors, but very much present within the FE sector itself, enacted through practices partially due to both stringent funding reform and an emphasis on quantifiable accountability strategies.

The theoretical underpinnings in academic practice that support the development of acquired and practiced skills are arguably one of the defining factors when considering the development and deployment of tacit artisan skills. The combination of skills mastery and theoretical understanding allows for predictive, diagnostic and analytical use of 'vocational' abilities, and it is this combination upon which much of our economy, social practice, health care and leisure industries are based. There is a problem however: employers now increasingly identify that FE graduates from both full-time and apprenticeship courses are not 'work ready' and require further extensive on the job training. As highlighted by Education Scotland (2016), very few colleges have dedicated strategies for developing employability in students. Lacking in transferable and core essential skills (literacy, numeracy and IT as examples), graduates of vocational routes in both schools and colleges are showing signs of falling victim to the narrowing of curriculum and specific outcomes-based assessment regimes. This, within the Scottish context (and indeed the wider UK), has now drawn significant attention from government policymakers to further and vocational education, the like of which has not been seen since the early 1990s and, consequently, the process of reform has begun in earnest. I will return to this in further discussion regarding pathways and skills within FE but the analysis would be incomplete and lacking in context without first discussing the significant changes made to the governance and structure of the FE sector in Scotland between 2010 and 2017.

## REGIONALISATION AND GOVERNANCE

In 2011, the Scottish Government published *Putting Learners at the Centre: Delivering Our Ambitions for Post-16 Education* (Scottish Government, 2011). The review outlines the Scottish Government's position (at the time) as being focused on the economic growth and prosperity of Scotland. The post-16 education sector was to be restructured, funded and managed with this as a primary purpose and objective. Although this review covered (in part) both universities and colleges of further education, the strongest effects of this document and its related recommendations would have a greater impact on FE. Subsequent reviews would act on these recommendations and several significant changes in the form of regionalisation would go on to dramatically shape FE in the following five years. Taking a focus on jobs and economic growth meant that the government were now in a position to ensure that the training provisions for industry and the wider economy were in place, that access to courses was equitable, standards measurable and colleges accountable. Interestingly, an implicating factor in shaping significant changes imposed on the FE sector was the economic crash of 2008 and subsequent austerity measures across funding for all public sectors. The government at the time was quick to announce that spending on compulsory education was protected and ring-fenced; however, this did not apply to the FE sector.

2012 saw the submission and publication of the *Report of the Review of Further Education Governance in Scotland* (Griggs, 2012). Known colloquially as the Griggs report, after its author, the enacted recommendations contained within would prove to be the most far reaching and significant changes to the FE system in Scotland since the passing of the Further and Higher Education Act (Scottish Government, 1992; Government UK, 1992) and known as incorporation, which took place in 1992. The 1992 Act brought about several significant changes to funding regimes and the governance of the FE sector, effectively giving colleges their independence from government control. The initial findings of the 2012 Griggs review were concerned primarily with the structure of the FE sector, its governance and funding. Although issues of equality and innovation are cited as being of primary importance and the driving factors behind the review, it is telling that in the summary outlining the most pressing problems to be addressed (as seen by Griggs) within the FE sector, the review focused on issues of funding, outlining that colleges were not sustainable in their current form. Whilst the subsequent regionalisation agenda was enacted in 2013 under the auspices of equitable access and continuity of provision, the coinciding cuts to funding – 18 per cent between 2011 and 2014 (Audit Scotland, 2015) – were a significant factor in the reduction in both provision and teaching staff as the curriculum was rationalised and refocused on younger learners in full-time courses. Between 2011 and 2014 part-time course places were reduced by 43 per cent, funding for short courses (ten hours or fewer) was removed completely, and teaching staff within the sector were reduced by 9.3 per cent (full-time equivalent), mainly achieved through voluntary severance schemes (Audit Scotland, 2015). Some of these schemes, shortly after completion, came under significant scrutiny for reported, and subsequently investigated, irregularities with some payments to senior staff being reclaimed. These problematic redundancies and related rationalisations of staff and provision across the sector had far-reaching implications and prompted the Education Secretary at that time (Angela Constance) to put together a task group to investigate and report on practice. The resulting report carried with it specific recommendations for good governance and practice across the FE sector in Scotland and represent a significant recognition by the Scottish Government that problems with mergers had been encountered (Scottish Government, 2016a).

In practical terms, several of the forty-two existing colleges were merged to form a mixture of twenty-six unaffected existing colleges and several new larger organisations operating within thirteen regions (see Table 72.1). The rationale for the regionalisation was multifaceted but in essence was promoted as a way of ensuring a strategic regional curriculum focused on the needs of the wider community (including business, infrastructure and industry). The regionalisation process also aimed to rationalise the provision by promoting the creation of centres of excellence where resource in a region could be focused into one

Table 72.1 Post-regionalisation colleges of further education

|  | Region | College |
|---|---|---|
| **Single college regions** | Dumfries and Galloway | Dumfries & Galloway College |
|  | Scottish Borders | Borders College |
|  | Forth Valley | Forth Valley College |
|  | West Lothian | West Lothian College |
|  | Ayrshire | Ayrshire College |
|  | Edinburgh & Lothians | Edinburgh College |
|  | West | West College Scotland |
|  | Fife | Fife College |
| **Multi-college regions** | Aberdeen and Aberdeenshire | North East Scotland College |
|  | Tayside | Dundee and Angus College |
|  | Glasgow | Glasgow Kelvin College |
|  |  | Glasgow Clyde College |
|  |  | City of Glasgow College |
|  | Lanarkshire | New College Lanarkshire |
|  |  | South Lanarkshire College |
|  | Highlands and Islands | Grouped as University of Highlands and Islands (UHI)* |
|  |  | Perth College |
|  |  | Lews Castle College |
|  |  | Orkney College |
|  |  | Shetland College |
|  |  | Inverness College |
|  |  | Moray College |
|  |  | North Highland College |
|  |  | Argyll College |
|  |  | Sabhal Mòr Ostaig |
|  |  | West Highland College Highland Theological College NAFC Marine Centre |
|  |  | Scottish Association Marine Science |

*Although granted university status in 2011, the UHI is the umbrella organisation for the multiple colleges operating within the Highlands and Islands region

hub providing a higher quality of provision as opposed to several smaller providers offering a dispersed curriculum across several centres.

The opportunities of regionalisation were interesting in that they reportedly offered increased access to a higher quality provision in bespoke locations with direct links to industry, offering a broader basis for work-based/influenced support for learning. However, much of this rationalisation is still ongoing and several of the new colleges are still in the process of building new bespoke premises to house newly formed centres of excellence. The merger process was not without its issues as several organisations reported problems with rationalisation of management structures, estates, curriculum and support functions and associated staff (Scottish Funding Council, 2016). Indeed, both during and since the merger process, there have been several rounds of industrial action staged by both academic and support staff who have been separately trying to negotiate and secure nationally agreed terms and conditions. Although several local disputes have been resolved, national bargaining and protection of jobs are still issues that may well lead to further withdrawals of labour. This has also impacted students who have faced challenges such as, in many instances, the removal of access to localised provision and increased distance to travel to rationalised curriculum offerings. These issues are outstanding and have yet to be fully addressed in many of the newly formed regions and related colleges (Scottish Funding Council, 2016).

Although merger and restructure have been an outcome of the review carried out by Griggs (2012), one of the main instigating factors of the merger process was the changes to governance recommended by Griggs within the subsequent report of findings following the review (see Scottish Parliament, 2013). A centralising of governance practice and homogenisation of process was to be introduced which would be overseen by ministerial appointments of regional chairs for regional boards of governance. Instead of each institution having a separate board, a regional board would be introduced to oversee all colleges within the designated geographical regions. In a further change to practice, the appointed regional chairs would also receive pay in remuneration for their time, a significant change in policy. In practice this has not been without its issues, as college chief operating officers (principals) are now answerable to a paid regional chair appointed directly by the Minister for Education. This has set up an unusual power dynamic at the senior level of leadership within colleges, as principals are not only answerable to the board but also directly to the Minister of Education via the remunerated and directly appointed regional chair. The system has yet to have had sufficient time in operation to determine fully the potential implications, but it is of interest and noteworthy when considering the source and basis for decision making and leadership vision in the newly formed large regions and related colleges in Scotland.

Given that Scottish FE is undertaking to implement all of these changes across the country, the implications and impact on students should be central to the ongoing debate. Having discussed the implications of the regionalisation agenda on the structure and governance of the sector, it is important to now review the policy revisions introduced regarding the knowledge, skills and pathways of the students accessing the sector.

## SKILLS, KNOWLEDGE AND PATHWAYS

In his chairperson's report, introducing a personal perspective, Sir Ian Wood (Scottish Government, 2014), citing the labour force survey of 2014, draws attention to the problem of post-2008 youth unemployment in Scotland. At 18.8 per cent, Wood points out that nearly one fifth of youth in 2014 awoke each morning and wondered if their country needed them. Beyond the hyperbole, Wood raises an important and stark statistic which is deftly set against an image of a country failing to fully support its young people, including those who don't go straight to university from school (according to the cited data, 50 per cent). Given the previous discussion, related to parity of esteem of vocational learning with academic attainment, Wood's observations are both laudable and to be welcomed as they draw attention to the FE sector that, as previously highlighted, has suffered two decades of declining attention and interest from government. As such, significant tension exists within the opening of the report, entitled *Education Working for All*, in that it draws a direct link between FE and its (assumed) sole purpose in promoting employability through vocational pathways and learning. There is no mention of the purpose or role of FE (or indeed education) beyond economic prosperity and in supporting personal development for reasons other than employment. For the moment, this will be accepted and explored as there are many courses and students in FE who *are* engaged with developing the required skills to secure or continue in employment. However, as the discussion moves towards tackling the purpose of FE and equitable access, these issues will be addressed.

As highlighted in the introductory paragraph of this chapter, FE has a long-standing tradition of supporting transitions from school into employment through the provision of courses validated by industry itself. It was recognised a number of years ago that, along with colleges offering vocational-based routes to employment, schools also had a significant role to play. School/college partnership agreements are highly individual to local authority, college and sponsoring employers and, as such, are difficult to discuss in individual detail; however, the core purpose is to introduce young people to the specific skills and knowledge related to a particular trade or role. The benefits of such school/college partnerships were reviewed in 2008 in a report commissioned by Education Scotland and Her Majesty's Inspectorate of Education (HMIE), *Expanding Opportunities* (Scottish Government, 2008). The report highlighted strengths in engagement of disaffected learners, expanding curriculum, increased confidence and successes in attainment, particularly in practical sessions. The report also highlighted areas requiring improvement and chose as an initial point to raise the issue of good results being achieved in practical lessons but a lack of engagement in theory classes. As raised earlier in this chapter, this is a persistent and ongoing issue related to the false dichotomy created that differentiates knowledges related to practical application and to theoretical understanding. It is surely a more difficult task to deliver a practical lesson devoid of theoretical underpinning knowledge than to provide a rich background of knowledge supporting the practical application of skills development? In the writer's experience, and as a lecturer of mechanical and automotive engineering in the FE sector for several years, I struggled with this for a large part of my career. I frequently found removing this false dichotomy to be highly productive. Teaching theory in the automotive workshops of several colleges, I dispensed with over 50 per cent of classroom-based 'theory' and concentrated on enriching practical classes with theory-based discussions. Where better to teach how an engine works than in a workshop with engines?

The *Expanding Opportunities* (Scottish Government, 2008) report does, however, highlight an important point about diversification of choices for young people and the need to remove prejudice against vocational routes. Signalling that a vocational route is a viable and acceptable option for those in the latter years of compulsory education offers broader choices to those who might not have the desire to attend university. Whether attendance leads to a full-time place or the opportunity to secure an apprenticeship (a task broadly accorded insufficient credit for its difficulty) or leads to another avenue entirely, the diversified curriculum and exposure to an adult learning environment in itself could possibly go some way to preparing individuals for self-directed practice, whether in work or education. The choices faced by many people wishing to enrol on a course in FE in Scotland are influenced by many factors. FE provides much more than just vocational skills training. Although individual colleges often have either specialist focus or areas of expertise, most (if not all) offer a curriculum that goes beyond the vocational. The purpose of the FE sector is debated and contentious (largely due to its diversity) but certainly goes some way beyond just providing training for economic engagement and preparation for work. Until recently, it was possible to attend FE colleges in Scotland and enrol in one of several different models of course. Full-time, part-time, day release, evening, community, short, endorsed and recognised or hobby (to identify a few) courses graced the pages of the bulging prospectus of each college. This cuts to the heart of the purpose of FE: community learning and repeated opportunities to engage with a course or line of interest. Sadly, the budget cuts to FE in Scotland (as detailed previously) have disproportionally affected part-time study and those courses not leading to a qualification or certificate, such as hobby courses and community education programmes. Access to part-time learning opportunities has nationally almost been halved (since 2012) and, as a consequence, those most affected are frequently now not able to attend college as full-time study is not possible due to the requirement to support families and earn a living (single parents, those rehabilitating, and low income families, to name but a few). As part-time courses are withdrawn, the opportunities for those most disadvantaged or those requiring the greatest support are reduced as the focus of FE is forced by funding regimes to narrow and concentrate on courses that lead to employment, or, certainly, the increased chance of securing it. This is incongruous with the traditional model of FE that was seen very much as a hub of community learning provision where access to education was not dependent on the expressed desire to improve your income earning potential. Desires to learn could easily also be focused on personal interest, community work, rehabilitative and supportive activity, or social engagement. The desires within communities are still there but the colleges are increasingly less able to support this sort of provision as the funding does not allow for it. Apprenticeships as a mean to earn while learning (albeit as low as £3.40 an hour for some indentured trainees receiving the minimum wage for apprentices) are scarce and increasingly hard fought as access to and choice of part-time study continues to fall.

The progressive developments that have been made in the provision of FE are to be found in the transitional boundaries between sectors, or, more accurately, the increasingly blurred boundaries. In discussing school/college partnerships it was possible to review the benefits to schools and school pupils in attending FE colleges for part of their study; similar benefits can be found for FE students wishing to progress to university. The word progress in the last sentence is perhaps misleading and a hangover from the belief that university offers a superior learning experience to FE colleges; the courses, focus and pedagogies are unique and frequently tailored to different ends. Transitions between FE and higher education (HE) are changing as increasing numbers of degree courses are taught in partnership between collaborating organisations. 2+2 (two years in college and two years in university) degrees are increasingly provided to capture the required vocational expertise of the staff in FE and the research-focused teaching of partners in HE. This is not seen as progressing from FE to HE as it is one qualification taught and provided in partnership. Where previously it was frequently considered that HE partnerships with FE colleges were in a supportive role from the university, increasingly the vocational expertise within colleges is seen as critical for the teaching of a valuable industry-focused degree and the support is bilateral (Husband and Jeffrey, 2016).

## FUTURE PATHWAYS AND THE CONTINUED DEVELOPMENT OF FURTHER EDUCATION IN SCOTLAND

In the context of Scottish, British and international political landscapes, we are standing on the cusp of potentially the most significant changes to national governance and political philosophy since the mid-1940s. Writing this in early 2017 and looking back to a year ago, it was then difficult to conceive of the UK leaving the European Union and the forty-fifth President of the United States of America being Donald Trump. However, in this newly dubbed 'post-truth' era, the deep and far-reaching impacts of the 2008 financial crisis, increasing conflict in the Middle East and related refugee crisis, and the accelerating glo-balisation of the knowledge economy have all filtered through into popular politics. Poised on the threshold of a new era of international political wrangling in which, for many millions of displaced people, the future is at best uncertain, new alliances are being forged, national and devolved governments are trying to legislate, and skills requirements are being assessed. The Scottish Government is not alone in its efforts to design and impose reform on FE but is amongst the most proactive in its approaches.

The UK-wide apprenticeship levy comes into force in the spring of 2017 which will see larger companies (those with an annual pay bill of over £3 million) having to pay into a national fund for the support of apprenticeships. The levy will be set at 0.5 per cent of total pay bill with an initial allowance of £15,000 deducted. As an example, a £5 million pay bill would mean a levy of £25,000, and when the £15,000 allowance is deducted the final sum owed would be £10,000. The levy is an example of national policy set in Westminster that has an impact on the devolved education of Scotland. The levy will still be paid in Scotland but will go to the Scottish Government for use in supporting Scottish apprenticeship placements (it will replace existing funding, and not add to it). In response, the Scottish Government has promised to increase the number of apprenticeship places annually, by 2020, to 30,000 (Scottish Government, 2016b). It remains to be seen if these changes will have an impact on the availability and quality of apprenticeships but it certainly demonstrates a national willingness to address the importance of cross-sector skills training.

Thomas and Gunson, (2017), in a research project drawing on qualitative data collected in Scotland, draw attention to several critical factors (as they see them) for skills develop-ment and FE over the coming years. These factors include embedding an outcome approach and setting a clear national purpose of the skills system, regional integration of the skills system, clarifying roles of learning routes within the skills system, learners and employers co-designing a responsive skills system, improving flexibility of learning, and increasing transferability of learning. These points, although some possibly contentious, again draw attention to the importance of the role of FE in shaping the national response to the dynamic needs of the national economy. Given the current opportunities for schools, colleges and universities to take on these identified points, it is possible to see how a parity of esteem in provision can be achieved through integrated working and partnerships. Indeed, substantial work would be needed to clarify exactly how these points would or could be implemented, but they certainly offer some substance and a starting point to continue to develop collabo-ration with all sectors of Scottish education.

However, and as promised, I must return to the point raised earlier about the role of FE in Scotland beyond the part it has in supporting industry and the economy. In Husband (2016) I claimed that if we do not (as a nation) start to publicly support FE, colleges would start to disappear. I was criticised for engaging in hyperbole, a point I am willing (in part) to concede but also offer no apology for. The continued cuts to FE funding over the last seven years have had a disproportionate impact on already marginalised groups in our society. Part-time courses in Scottish colleges have been halved and for those unable to support themselves and without someone on which they can rely for support, full-time study is frequently not an option. So, for those who can no longer access their chosen area of study because of cuts and the requirement to study full-time, FE has, in effect, disappeared. The building is still there but of little use if you cannot access its provision. Although Thomas and Gunson (2017) offer laudable suggestions for the development of the skills sector (which was their remit), this does not offer a full picture of the changes required to

FE in order to make it once again a sector for all. A re-imagining of the possibilities of the sector beyond the focus of preparation for work or as a bastion for 'last chance' learning will in many ways mitigate many of the negatives of the last seven years of policy change and restructure. Regionalisation with a focus on community development, and school and university partnerships with a dual focus on equity and social justice in partnership with employability, would not detract from promoting economic sustainability, but as part of a broader national educational focus on citizenship, would enhance all aspects of FE. Scottish FE stands at the threshold of significant change over the next five years; the opportunities for positive change, to both counter previous mistakes and further develop a sector for all are boundless. As with academic and vocational knowledge, a focus on inclusion, equity, social justice, the national economy, along with the support and development of industry, are not mutually exclusive but could quite easily be, and should be, mutually inclusive.

## REFERENCES

Audit Scotland (2015) *Scotland's Colleges*. Edinburgh: Scottish Government.

Canning, R. (2013) 'Liberal, academic and vocational knowledge exchange', in T. G. K. Bryce, W. M. Humes, D. Gillies and A. Kennedy (eds), *Scottish Education, Fourth Edition: Referendum*. Edinburgh: Edinburgh University Press.

Education Scotland (2016) *The Development of Learner Employability in Scotland's Colleges*. Edinburgh: Scottish Government.

Fisher, R. and Simmons, R. (2012) 'Liberal conservatism, vocationalism and further education in England', *Globalisation, Societies and Education*, 10 (1), 31–51.

Government UK (1992) Further and Higher Education Act, 1992. London.

Griggs, R. (2012) *Report of the Review of Further Education Governance in Scotland*. Edinburgh: Scottish Government.

Husband, G. (2016) Learn to love colleges – before they disappear. *The Conversation*. London.

Husband, G. and Jeffrey, M. (2016) 'Advanced and higher vocational education in Scotland: recontextualising the provision of HE in FE', *Research in Post- Compulsory Education*, 21 (1–2), 66–72.

Scottish Government (2014) *Education Working For All!* Edinburgh: Scottish Government.

Scottish Funding Council (2016) *Impact and Success of the Programme of College Mergers in Scotland*. Edinburgh: Scottish Government.

Scottish Government (1992) Further and Higher Education (Scotland) Act 1992. Edinburgh.

Scottish Government (2008) *Expanding Opportunities*. Edinburgh: Scottish Government.

Scottish Government (2011) *Putting Learners at the Centre: Delivering Our Ambitions for Post-16 Education*. Edinburgh: Scottish Government.

Scottish Government (2016a) *Good College Governance*. Edinburgh: Scottish Government.

Scottish Government (2016b) *Scottish Government Response to the UK Government Apprenticeship Levy*. Edinburgh: Department of Employability and Training.

Scottish Parliament (2013) *SPICe Briefing: College Regionalisation*. Online at www.parliament.scot/ResearchBriefingsAndFactsheets/S4/SB_13-73.pdf

Thomas, R. and Gunson, R. (2017) *Equipping Scotland for the Future: Key Challenges for the Scottish Skills System*. Edinburgh: Scottish Government.

Wheelahan, L. (2010) *Why Knowledge Matters in Curriculum: A Social Realist Argument*. London: Routledge.

# 73

# Teaching and Learning in Further Education and Higher Education

*Velda McCune*

## INTRODUCTION

In Scotland, further education (FE) qualifications are often strongly vocational, emphasising what is needed to perform well in specific roles in the workplace. Teaching in FE also encompasses more basic learning such as literacy and life skills and programmes of instruction are generally perceived as offering high levels of student support. Scottish FE encompasses a broad range of learning opportunities including Higher National Certificates and Higher National Diplomas (HNC/HND) (see Chapter 75). It therefore covers the levels of the Scottish Credit and Qualifications Framework (SCQF) up to level 6 and professional development awards beyond that. Most further education is provided to participants over the age of sixteen within Further and Higher Education Colleges. Further education can also be provided in high schools and workplace or community settings. HNCs and HNDs bring together practical and theoretical learning with an emphasis on employment. They are equivalent to the first two years of higher education (HE) and degree arrangements increasingly now straddle colleges and universities in coordinated arrangements between the institutions concerned (as Chapters 72 and 75 explain). Universities award bachelors and masters degrees, postgraduate diplomas, postgraduate masters degrees and doctorates, thus spanning SCQF levels 7 to 12. Degrees in HE emphasise scholarship and transformation through critical and informed engagement with diverse perspectives. HE is generally perceived as requiring greater student autonomy than FE. While degrees in HE are often seen as less directly vocationally focused than FE, there are exceptions to this general trend such as law, medicine, dentistry, architecture and business. Thus FE and HE do have some areas of similarity despite the different cultures and foci of these institutions. Both FE and HE in Scotland prepare students for all aspects of life including global citizenship, complex problem solving, autonomous and ethical professionalism and many forms of further study and employment (QAA, 2011). As such, it is important that they support students to develop a broad range of capacities and attributes. Both need to prepare students to make use of their learning in contexts where uncertainty, complexity and competing value positions are common.

## THE CONTEXT FOR LEARNING AND TEACHING
## IN FE AND HE IN SCOTLAND

Teachers in both FE and HE in Scotland have been operating in contexts characterised by constant change shaped by policymakers, economic pressures and the impacts of globalisation. The introduction of Curriculum for Excellence in Scotland has had important implications for both FE and HE, some of which will be discussed later in this chapter. The policy and structural changes in FE have been particularly extensive in recent years (as explained in Chapter 72). The current political upheaval – which has begun with the UK voting to leave the European Union – will shape further changes in both sectors. While some of the impacts of the wider social and political contexts remain uncertain, there are some challenges for teachers which seem likely. The much-discussed diversity of students in FE and HE classrooms in Scotland will certainly increase in FE in response to the impact of greater austerity leading to further economic disadvantage for students. For HE, unpredictable shifts in the participation of EU and other international students is already a growing concern.

The developing audit cultures, managerialism and resultant work intensification in both FE and HE frame what is possible for teachers in these contexts (see Chapters 6 and 7); it is typically much more extensive and established in FE than in HE in Scotland. In HE, the National Student Survey (NSS) has been influential in placing pressure on teachers to focus on certain themes such as the timeliness of assessment feedback. There has also been concern that the focus on student satisfaction in the NSS may distract from other aims – such as challenging students and providing opportunities for their world views to expand. The impact of the Teaching Excellence Framework in HE in Scotland is somewhat uncertain but likely to be significant. Quality assurance and enhancement in Scottish HE is lauded for its developmental focus and lack of excessive audit. In FE there is a more formal inspection regime including observation of teaching. FE also has a longer history of teaching qualifications for staff. The experiences of teachers on short-term and part-time contracts has been an important theme in recent discussions of FE and HE in Scotland. While well-supported part-time roles can be very valuable, there is concern that part-time teachers may work more hours than they are contracted for and therefore miss out on development opportunities. Short-term contracts may be useful for some teachers – for example, in working as doctoral students – but raise concerns about casualisation of teaching and job insecurity.

## LEARNERS AND LEARNING IN FE AND HE IN SCOTLAND

### Learner Diversity

Learners in both FE and HE in Scotland are characterised by multiple and intersecting forms of diversity which interact with their identities as learners. These include socio-economic conditions, gender, age, lesbian, gay, bisexual and transgender+ (LGBT+) identities and orientations, disability, ethnicity and country of origin. Institutions in Scotland show strong and stable differentiation in their status, and students with socio-economic advantage tend to attend the high status institutions (Croxford and Raffe, 2015). Students also bring varied prior experiences of education, which are key to understanding how they learn. Meaningful learning experiences must be designed from the outset to be inclusive.

FE typically includes students from more diverse socio-economic backgrounds than HE, and HE institutions also differ markedly from one another in this regard. FE in Scotland tends to involve more students who have had more troubled prior learning experiences, complex needs, and who may be starting their learning at a very basic level (Curzon and Tummons, 2013; Duckworth, 2014). Students in FE are also younger than those typically accepted into HE. HE in Scotland tends to bring together more students from different countries across the world, although this varies markedly with institution and subject area. Some Scottish universities have a strongly global focus. Part-time study is possible in both sectors but more common in FE, although the proportions of part-timers is now shrinking as a consequence of policy decisions taken at government level (as explained in Chapter 72).

## Learners' Background Knowledge and Beliefs about Learning

Learners of course come to their learning experiences in FE and HE with different levels of knowledge and understanding of their subject areas. Students' prior learning may include misconceptions and misunderstandings which need to be challenged in new learning situations (Ashwin et al., 2015). These misconceptions may relate to the subject content or to the practices of the subject area, such as how to write assignments. Learners will also bring quite different beliefs about learning and teaching, which will shape how they react to particular learning experiences (Ashwin et al., 2015). If a student believes, for example, that learning involves the teacher as 'authority' telling them the correct answers so that they get customer satisfaction then the student would be very unlikely to see any benefit in group work or peer feedback. Such perspectives are sadly common in the discourses around learning and teaching in both sectors in Scotland and elsewhere. By contrast, a student who believes that their role in learning is to actively construct their own understanding by critically engaging with the subject area is likely to value a wide range of learning experiences.

## Learning as Acquisition and Participation

One useful way to understand the broad processes of learning which take place in FE and HE is to consider the metaphors of *acquisition* and *participation* (Sfard, 1998). She points out that both of these metaphors are valuable in understanding how learning goes forward. Acquisition can involve anything from rote memorisation of important factual information to students actively engaging in the process of constructing new personal understandings of key concepts in their subject areas. The emphasis, however, is always on students acquiring knowledge which they can carry forward to other situations. Participation metaphors, by contrast, emphasise the situated nature of learning. Thus the focus is on participating in shared processes of knowing and understanding situated within particular communities, rather than on students retaining the acquired understanding. The sense is that the knowing and understanding are contextualised ongoing processes which are situated within particular communities. Sfard challenges the idea of discrete packages of knowledge and understanding belonging to students and easily transferred to other settings. These metaphors shed some light on the challenges which students may face in learning in FE and HE in Scotland and elsewhere. The acquisition metaphor draws attention to whether students are spending sufficient time on task, engaging in appropriate learning processes which will allow them to acquire knowledge, or to surface and challenge any misconceptions they may hold. The participation metaphor can explain why students struggle to understand how to construct successful assignments, even when they have succeeded well in prior learning experiences. It reminds us that that it is not as simple as knowing what a good examination answer, essay or report should be like. Rather, the nature of high-quality work will be constructed differently through the norms and practices of different subject area communities, different institutions and different work groups within and beyond institutions. Scottish HE may present particular challenges for some students in this regard, as the four-year degree has more breadth and flexibility in subject choice than in some other countries, particularly in the early years of study. Thus students in transition to university will need to come to terms with a broader range of tacit practices and expectations about what makes for high-quality work.

The participation metaphor emphasises how learning is a process of identity development for students, something which is often challenging and fraught, particularly if other core aspects of learners' identities are challenged or undervalued. A common concern in both FE and HE is the extent to which students are engaged with and identify with their subject areas and how this shapes their will to participate actively in learning opportunities (Duckworth, 2014; Ashwin et al., 2015). While students have choices about whether and what to study, these choices arise in the context of societal, community and family discourses about learning, which can make certain choices seem more possible or necessary and others seem unreachable. Socio-economic status and power also shape students' choices and the meaning they are able to find in their studies. All of this being the case, many students in both FE and HE in Scotland experience some doubts about the value of what they are learning for their imagined futures and often bring a complex mix of intrinsic and extrinsic motivations to their studies. Additionally, study in FE can be treated in society as having lower status, and college learners in Scotland and elsewhere are more likely to have had prior negative learning experiences which contribute to how they respond to current learning situations. The flexibility of the Scottish HE system may make it more possible for students to shape the direction of their future studies to suit their imagined futures, although this flexibility is not always available in practice due to concerns such as timetabling and oversubscribed popular courses.

Students' skill in learning is often raised as an issue by teachers in both sectors. Depending on the context, the challenges may relate to: numeracy and mathematical capabilities; diverse aspects of language; approaches to learning and studying; and the capacity to monitor, organise and manage learning. These challenges often relate to the norms, practices and power of particular learning communities. Students may be seen, for example, as having problems in literacy because they are unpractised in the forms of literacy required in particular learning contexts. They may simultaneously be highly skilled in the literacy practices of their other communities (Curzon and Tummons, 2013). These challenges are not restricted to students who have struggled in their learning in the past. Students with highly successful and straightforward learning trajectories are often challenged by enacting effective learning within the practices of new communities when they make transitions (Ashwin et al., 2015). The participation metaphor for learning – which emphasises how the nature of high-quality learning is always situated – makes it clear that such challenges would be expected. Knowing how to learn effectively in high school, for example, does not straightforwardly prepare students to learn effectively in the context of a particular subject area in higher education. This may become easier in future to some extent, for students coming into Scottish FE and HE from Scotland, as Curriculum for Excellence emphasises applying learning and critical thinking in new contexts. The four capabilities from Curriculum for Excellence do not, however, explicitly focus on the metacognition and self-regulation of learning which would be required to manage transitions more smoothly. The full nature of the implementation of Curriculum for Excellence is still to be seen and analysed and its implementation will likely vary considerably between schools.

## THE DESIGN OF LEARNING EXPERIENCES IN SCOTTISH FE AND HE

### Who Sets Curricula and Course Designs?

In FE in Scotland, curricula are quite tightly defined by the Scottish Qualifications Authority while teachers in some areas of HE have considerable freedom over what and how they teach and assess. There are, however, some subject areas in HE in Scotland – such as engineering, veterinary medicine and psychology – in which professional bodies exert a powerful influence on curricula. Whereas teachers in HE generally only have to specify broad outlines of their topic areas, the teaching and assessment practices for module and programme approval, teachers in FE are typically required to produce plans for individual lessons. In Scottish HE the design of modules and courses is generally taken forward by individual academics, or teams of academics sometimes with input from educational developers and learning technologists.

### What Shapes Curricula and Course Design?

Teachers' perspectives on course and programme design in FE and HE are also often influenced by their participation in educational development experiences. Quality assessment and enhancement processes are also significant. Relevant legislation – such as the 2010 Equality Act – also shapes teaching and assessment decisions. In HE in particular, the choices made about course and programme design are strongly influenced by the traditional practices of departments and subject areas. One theme that has been highly influential in course and programme design in Scottish HE and FE has been the importance of working backwards from well-conceived learning outcomes or objectives. Once objectives have been specified, teachers align their curricula and assessment practices closely to them. Learning outcomes can be referenced against the SCQF to ensure that learning is at the appropriate level for the qualification awarded. In HE the subject benchmark statements in the UK quality code are also important reference points.

The choices made about teaching approaches in the design of courses in Scottish HE can be traditional at times, with lecturing, tutorials and laboratory work having been common for many years. In FE, classes tend to be smaller and staff spend a greater proportion of their time teaching so students tend to be supported more closely and directly. The importance of students' active engagement in the learning process has been a common theme in both colleges and universities in Scotland for many years. That being the case, designing teaching approaches which require students to take a stronger role in the learning process is becoming more common. One example of this in HE is 'flipped' classroom approaches – where students prepare core knowledge and understanding in advance and teachers use class time for surfacing misconceptions and active learning. There is also growing interest in student involvement in course design, or student co-creation of learning opportunities. Some of these approaches give the student considerably more power over the design of learning experiences than has typically been the case in the past.

## Assessment in FE and HE

Assessments in FE and HE are designed to encourage and evaluate the forms of learning sought in the learning outcomes. Assessment and related feedback to students has become a particular concern in Scottish HE recently as this is the area in which institutions tend to receive the lowest scores in the NSS. Both FE and HE in Scotland use a wide range of assessment formats including oral presentations, practical activities, reports, essays, examinations, online assessments and authentic assessments (which emphasise students engaging with the complexities of professional practice). There is emphasis in both sectors on developing assessments which are reliable and also valid measures of the desired outcomes.

As assessment and related guidance and feedback on assessments are centrally important drivers of learning, designing assessments which are good learning experiences and which prepare students well for their future roles are key concerns (Ashwin et al., 2015). A distinction is often made between the formative and summative functions of assessment (see Chapter 68). Formative aspects of assessments provide information to learners and teachers on how well learners are doing and how they can improve. Formative assessment might be very informal, such as comments to learners about the quality of their understanding during classroom discussion. More formal formative feedback would include comments on students' draft writing. The summative aspect of assessment in FE and HE is concerned with formally judging students' progress and awarding credit. Further important concerns are the coherence of assessments across whole programmes of study, the integration of assessment with other aspects of curricula, and how assessments prepare students for later assessments and their future lives. Self- and peer-assessment processes are often seen as important for preparing students to be effective lifelong learners (Medland, 2016).

## Supporting Student Transitions in FE and HE

The design of learning experiences in the earlier years of FE and HE often emphasises that students are in transition from prior learning situations with different norms and practices and require guidance in aspects such as new forms of assessment and managing independent learning. This often relates to efforts to improve learning in the context of performance measures (Christie et al., 2016). Other forms of transition – such as between the earlier and later years of degree programmes and the transitions into postgraduate programmes – have not been emphasised as strongly. This interest in transitions has led to the development of a wide variety of induction experiences for students across institutions, and 'student transitions' was the focus of the Scottish Enhancement Theme for HE in the years 2014–17, supported by the Quality Assurance Agency for Higher Education, Scotland. (The new theme for 2017–21 is 'evidence-based enhancement'.) Historically, some of the transition support for students in Scotland has involved stand-alone events or guidance materials. There is now a growing emphasis on longitudinal support either through programmes prior to or alongside students' day-to-day studies or embedded ongoing induction within subject area teaching. The transitions between colleges and universities have been in focus in part due to their importance for successful widening of participation (Christie et al., 2016). Students in colleges typically have fewer socio-economic advantages compared with students from the more prestigious universities. So, where students make a successful transition from college to university study this can be an important vehicle for making HE student populations more diverse, especially in the more research-intensive universities.

## Digital Education

The possibilities enabled by digital education in FE and HE have developed at a remarkable rate in recent years. Virtual learning environments have become almost ubiquitous, potentially bringing together multi-modal course content, opportunities for synchronous and asynchronous online discussion, quizzes, assessment submission, Web 2.0 tools and more. People interact with these digital tools in complex ways and settings, seeding the emergence of diverse forms of learning. Some of the opportunities arising may be particularly positive, such as enhanced participation from students with caring responsibilities or disabled students who struggle to attend class in person. The use of Web 2.0 tools such as wikis – which are designed for broad participation rather than teaching from the front – could support more active roles for learners in constructing learning opportunities. There are potential concerns, however, about the new opportunities thus made available for collecting data about students and plagiarism detection contributing to the surveillance culture. The structure of virtual learning environments and the metaphors used within them can also constrain possibilities for learning. Further, virtual learning environments in Scottish FE and HE are still regularly used as repositories for resources, or to replicate face-to-face teaching online, without realising the unique, new possibilities of digital environments. Beyond the virtual learning environments for particular local groups of students, many institutions in Scotland are now offering wholly online courses and massive open online courses (MOOCs). These originated in prestigious North American universities, offering free online education to anyone able to access the Internet. MOOCs have been offered from Scottish universities since 2012 with many thousands of students participating, according to Sinclair (2013). Courses and programmes offered online are sites of possibility for reconceptualising Scottish FE and HE on a global scale and for the evolutions of new identities for learners and teachers.

## TEACHERS AND TEACHING IN FE AND HE

### Teachers' Roles and Identities

In this section, teaching is defined broadly to include anything a teacher may do to promote learning, including assessment and feedback. For teachers in both FE and HE in Scotland, it is common that being a teacher is not their first and not necessarily their main professional identity. Many teachers in FE will have been successful specialists in other areas of work who are now passing on their experience to others (Duckworth, 2014). In HE, it is common to begin with qualifications and a career focused on research in the subject area before taking on more teaching responsibility. In FE in Scotland teachers are expected to have a Teaching Qualification Further Education (TQFE) accredited by the General Teaching Council for Scotland, or substantial professional experience. In HE in Scotland, teaching qualifications are not required across the board but universities are increasingly encouraging or requiring academics who teach to participate in provision which leads to professional recognition in the form of Fellowship of the Higher Education Academy (FHEA).

Teachers in FE and HE in Scotland therefore often have complex professional roles and identities relating to their different communities of practice. As is common in professional roles, teachers in these areas often engage with complex problems where the solutions cannot be easily specified in advance. These challenges often involve stakeholders with diverse perspectives and frequently have emotional and moral as well as cognitive dimensions (Duckworth, 2014). That being the case, the importance of ongoing reflection in and on practice is often emphasised for these roles and typically forms an important focus in teaching qualifications and continuing professional development.

## Educational Development and Teaching Qualifications

In HE, reflective practice in professional development for teaching is typically focused around the UK Professional Standards Framework against which Higher Education Academy (HEA) accreditation is achieved. This framework addresses: areas of activity, such as teaching and assessment; core knowledge, such as knowledge about learners; and professional values, including promoting equality of opportunity. In FE, TQFE qualifications address what teachers need to know about learners as well as teaching and assessment practices and professionalism in teaching. The TQFE also includes assessed teaching practice, which is uncommon in HE, although HEA-accredited provision is now required to include either observation of teaching or references, as verification of teaching practice.

Teaching in both sectors involves balancing the needs of diverse learners through a range of teaching and assessment methods. Making strong connections with learners' prior experiences and current knowledge and understanding is emphasised as being crucial for students' learning. Empathic interest in students, good relationships and classroom climates, and the teacher sharing enthusiasm for the subject are also key. These aspects can present significant challenges for teachers, particularly in large classes and where the learners are highly diverse. FE often allows closer engagement over time with smaller groups of students but the diversity in students' preparedness for study is much greater than in HE. Engaging all learners in active learning processes where their own ideas are surfaced, explored and tested is also core to effective teaching in colleges and universities throughout Scotland.

## Inclusive Practice

Inclusive practice is emphasised in Scotland. At its most basic, this involves teachers taking the time to make standard certain practices – such as always wearing a microphone where it is available and providing teaching materials in advance of classes. At its best, inclusive teaching in FE and HE involves consistently designing and enacting teaching and assessment to optimise the learning of all students and to value all students' backgrounds and perspectives.

## Teachers' Choices about Assessment and Feedback to Students

Assessments and the guidance and feedback related to these assessments are among the most important drivers of student learning across FE and HE in Scotland and elsewhere (Ashwin et al., 2015). As mentioned earlier, particular attention is currently being focused in HE on the quality and timeliness of feedback, as the NSS tends to show lower scores in these areas than in other aspects of teaching. There is ongoing concern that students often either misunderstand feedback or do not engage with it deeply, and teachers are exploring methods to create formative feedback opportunities which engage students and enhance their learning. Teaching in colleges typically involves closer engagement with students and their assessed work than is common in universities, something that students can find challenging in transition between the different types of institution (Christie et al., 2016). Tutors in FE, for example, will often comment on drafts of student work which is relatively unusual in HE.

## Interactive Technologies and Teaching

In HE in Scotland – where classes are often larger than in FE – there has been considerable interest in using technologies to allow more interactive learning in large classes. The use of electronic voting systems, for example, is becoming more common. These systems involve the teacher posing a question to the class and the participants then use an electronic device to vote on the correct answer (or perhaps the option they agree with in a debate). The students' answers can then be displayed anonymously to the class as a whole. After this, a common strategy is for the teacher to allow the students to debate and discuss their answers, then another round of electronic voting takes place. At this point, more students usually get the correct answer and then the teacher can then explain the correct answer for those students who are still stuck. These methods have a strong underpinning in constructivist perspectives on learning and have been shown to enhance students' conceptual under-standing (Nicol and Boyle, 2003). They are sometimes combined with 'flipped' classroom methodologies where students learn core content independently before class and then class time is focused on more active learning opportunities.

## Working with Students' Behaviour

As in other countries, teachers in FE and HE in Scotland sometimes struggle with some aspects of students' behaviour. This requires teachers to exercise careful moral, emo-tional and practical judgement. In HE there has been ongoing concern with students misunderstanding – or deliberately not following – good academic practice in terms of citing the sources of the words and ideas in their work. Advice for teachers in this area emphasises making sure that students are supported to learn good academic practice, which is often tacit and difficult to understand. Considerable use is made of plagiarism detection software, with the intention of both educating students and identifying those who continue with bad practice. Many teachers are concerned about the ways in which using such software could be seen as surveillance and displaying a lack of trust in students. In FE, classroom behaviour is discussed more explicitly as an issue. Students in further education are more likely to have had negative prior learning experiences and some behave in disruptive ways in class (Curzon and Tummons, 2013; Duckworth, 2014). Classroom management practices and the importance of building relationships with students therefore feature strongly in guidance to teachers in FE.

## CONCLUSIONS AND FUTURE DIRECTIONS

This is a time of extraordinary opportunity, challenge, complexity and change for teaching and learning in FE and HE in Scotland. Scottish institutions can connect with more learn-ers locally and globally than ever before with the potential to shape learners as critically aware professionals ready to meet the challenges of complexity, uncertainty and competing value positions in a globalised world. Balancing the perspectives of diverse learners and stakeholders in a time of resource constraint and political uncertainty is a great challenge but a crucially important one to Scotland and the wider world.

Resisting discourses of consumerism and managerialism to keep creating worthwhile experiences for all learners is key. The student learning experience will be greatly diminished if students come to see themselves as simply buying a service with which they should be satisfied rather than having transformative learning experiences. These meaningful learning experiences may feel uncomfortable and disturbing at first and are not well represented by satisfaction surveys. If teaching comes to be managed simplistically through the blunt use of numerical data alone then many of the excellent teachers in FE and HE will be undervalued and may become demoralised. Can we continue to counteract the simplistic approaches and surveillance which can arise in online education to work with the exponential changes in available technologies to shape novel, creative and inspiring learning experiences?

## REFERENCES

Ashwin, P., Boud, D., Coate, K., Hallett, F., Keane, E., Krause, K.-L., Leibowitz, B., MacLaren, I., McArthur, J., McCune, V. and Tooher, M. (2015) *Reflective Teaching in Higher Education*. London: Bloomsbury.

Christie, H., Tett, L., Cree, V. and McCune, V. (2016) '"It all just clicked": a longitudinal perspective on transitions within university', *Studies in Higher Education*, 41 (3), 478–90.

Croxford, L. and Raffe, D. (2015) 'The iron law of hierarchy? Institutional differentiation in UK higher education', *Studies in Higher Education*, 40 (9), 1625–40.

Curzon, L. and Tummons, J. (2013) *Teaching in Further Education*, seventh edition. London: Bloomsbury.

Duckworth, V. (2014) *How to Be a Brilliant FE Teacher: A Practical Guide to Being Effective and Innovative*. London: Routledge.

Medland, E. (2016) 'Assessment in higher education: drivers, barriers and directions for change in the UK', *Assessment & Evaluation in Higher Education*, 41 (1), 81–96.

Nicol, D. and Boyle, J. T. (2003) 'Peer instruction versus class-wide discussion in large classes: a comparison of two interaction methods in the wired classroom', *Studies in Higher Education*, 28 (4), 457–73.

QAA (2011) *Graduates for the 21ˢᵗ Century: Integrating the Enhancement Themes, Outcomes and Achievements*. Glasgow: QAA.

Sfard, A. (1998) 'On two metaphors for learning and the dangers of choosing just one', *Educational Researcher*, 27 (4), 4–13.

Sinclair, C. (2013) 'Teaching and learning in further and higher education', in T. G. K. Bryce, W. M. Humes, D. Gillies and A. Kennedy (eds), *Scottish Education, Fourth Edition: Referendum*. Edinburgh: Edinburgh University Press.

# 74

# Higher Education in Turbulent Times

*Terry Brotherstone and Murdo Mathison*

## CONTEXT AND ISSUES

In mid-2016, shortly before this chapter was commissioned, the basic questions to be dealt with in a discussion about Scottish higher education (HE) seemed reasonably clear. However the decision that the UK should withdraw from the European Union (EU) – so-called 'Brexit' – upset many assumptions, and the volatility of the situation was only increased by the May 2017 UK general election campaign.

First on the agenda before the disturbance of Brexit was the anticipated publication of Audit Scotland's first-ever report on higher education (Audit Scotland, 2016), with its potential to promote both analysis of the state of Scottish universities after seventeen years of devolution – including almost a decade of Scottish National Party (SNP) government – and informed public debate about the challenges ahead. A second issue was that there would clearly be implications for Scotland from the then projected Westminster Higher Education and Research Bill (in the event passed at Westminster in April 2017). The white paper on which it was to be based was already the subject, south of the border, of a fierce campaign of opposition by academics concerned at its privatising tendency: they had produced an 'alternative white paper', *In Defence of Public Higher Education*, published by the Convention for Higher Education (Holmwood et al., 2016). Third, the Higher Education Governance (Scotland) Act (Scottish Government, 2016a), which marked a modestly but distinctively innovative approach to university governance in Scotland, had been passed by the Holyrood Parliament in April for implementation between 2017 and 2020. Fourth, government was expressing heightened concerns about the need to enhance training in workforce skills. A report had been commissioned to appear in October, which, while this did not directly concern HE, had potentially controversial implications for the sector. Finally, in May, the Sutton Trust published important research (Hunter Blackburn et al., 2016) concerning the vexed question of how to widen access to HE, taking into account the effect of the 'no-fees' offer to Scottish-resident students in home universities – a signature SNP policy by then generally accepted by all Holyrood parties except the Conservatives. Government action was signalled in March 2016 when its Commission on Widening Access, chaired by Dame Ruth Silver, published *A Blueprint for Fairness* (Silver, 2016), to be followed in December by the appointment of Professor Peter Scott as Commissioner on Fair Access.

All these remain important issues. As a clearly defined agenda for analysis, however, they were overtaken – a fortnight before the Audit Scotland Report (2016) appeared – by the 23 June Brexit referendum result. The unexpected outcome – opposed by over 60 per cent of all Scottish voters and overwhelmingly by the HE sector across the UK – threatened to upset the assumptions on which the Audit Scotland Report had been based. In addition to major concerns about access to EU research resources, continued Scottish Government funding for EU students (not guaranteed beyond 2018) could no longer be relied on, and uncertainty surrounded the right to remain of academics who are EU nationals and who comprise 16 per cent of the total in Scottish universities, including as many as 23 per cent of research staff. At a meeting of the UK Parliament's Scottish Affairs Select Committee in October, Professor Sir Tim O'Shea – the then Principal (vice-chancellor) of the University of Edinburgh and a leading figure in the principals' lobbying body, Universities Scotland (US) – said that the consequences for HE could be disastrous.

O'Shea also commented intriguingly (though in another context) that universities north of the border were now more determinably describing themselves as *Scottish* rather than as UK universities. He was referring specifically to the provision in the Westminster Higher Education and Research Bill extending the right of institutions with no research credentials to university status, creating a danger to the international reputation of Scotland's universities if they were seen as part of what might be perceived as a thereby diminished UK HE system. That this could be said by such a senior figure, however, potentially has wider significance. Since the publication of G. E. Davie's *The Democratic Intellect* (Davie, 1961) – cogently criticised as objective historical analysis though it has often been – Scotland's historically distinctive HE system has played its part in sustaining discourse about post-Second World War national identity. The Scottish Government's advisory panel to review university governance, chaired in 2011–12 by the Robert Gordon University Principal, Professor Ferdinand von Prondzynski, opened its report by quoting the Scottish metaphysician Sir William Hamilton, who in 1835 defined a university as 'a trust confided by the State to certain hands for the common interest of the nation' (von Prondzynski, 2012). The Scottish HE tradition, the report declared (p. 2), 'is a distinctive one, rooted, before the twentieth century, in its commitment to social mobility and social responsibility; and, since World War II, in the northern nation's particularly strong commitment to the principles of the welfare state …'. The argument that this distinctive tradition could – if deployed critically rather than nostalgically – play a significant part in discourse about meeting the real challenges of the twenty-first century informed the von Prondzynski report's recommendations.

Public debate about the future trajectory of HE in the UK as a whole and not merely within Scotland, it might be argued, could be enriched were ideas generated in the context of Scottish distinctiveness to be addressed within the wider discourse. As the intellectual historian Professor Stefan Collini, a prominent opponent of the neoliberal trajectory of higher-education reform under successive UK governments, told a conference of university trade unionists in Edinburgh in 2011, what was particularly 'dispiriting' about it was the way it involved a changed conception of the relationship between university education and society (Collini, 2017). The retreat from funding from general taxation signals 'a loss of belief in the public, as opposed to the individual, value of higher education', and reduces discourse about universities to the proposition that they 'need to justify getting more money … by showing that they help to make more money'. This alleged 'realism' means the substitution of the collective social aspiration to have 'an educated population' with the crudely economistic demand for 'an employable workforce'. While Collini warned that much of the language informing Scottish Government HE policy was little different from that south of the border, and he eschewed the crude romanticism often attending references to Davie's *Democratic Intellect*, he welcomed the fact that Scottish HE at least has 'a tradition to appeal to' – one, moreover, 'with built-in democratic purchase'. In contrast to Westminster policy statements, it had allowed a Scottish Government, equally conscious of electoral considerations, to state in its post-16-education policy paper, *Putting Learners at the Centre* (Scottish Government, 2011) that 'the prime responsibility' for funding HE 'should lie with the state'.

Discussion about Scottish universities and their future, therefore, can contribute to a much-needed wider debate about HE. The underlying issues in Scotland are essentially no different from those in the rest of the UK (rUK), and the immediate problems on campuses north of the border are no less acute. Systemic underfunding since the late 1970s and particularly since the expansion of the 1990s; the threat to collegiality and academic freedom from strategies involving compulsory redundancies; deteriorating relations between lecturing and research staff and senior management, fuelled by rocketing salary differentials; and a sense that staff are excluded from meaningful decision making, these things are as apparent in Scotland as elsewhere.

It is not within this chapter's remit to make particular policy proposals, nor is it our intention to exaggerate Scottish difference and its possibilities. Discussion about Scottish answers to the challenges ahead – whatever the country's political future is to be – will still have to take place in the context of the now crisis-ridden and increasingly questioned, but still hegemonic system of globalised capital. It seems clear, however, that the electoral surprises of 2016 in the UK's EU referendum and the US presidential vote – and the unexpected degree of support shown for the relatively left-wing policies of the Labour Party in the May 2017 general election – were not simply conjunctural events: they marked a new period of political turbulence and unpredictability. This perhaps creates the discursive space for the radical rethinking of the assumptions underlying economic and social policy since the late 1970s – decades during which UK universities have been increasingly subject to the idea that they must serve, and be judged by their compliance with, a trajectory underpinned ideologically by Thatcherite neo-liberalism. The somewhat different outlook informing HE policy north of the border could provide an opportunity for new initiatives by those Hamilton saw as entrusted by the nation to work in universities – both in the interests of the Scottish people and in line with the needs of science and the promotion of human knowledge internationally.

However negative the immediate impact on universities of Brexit turns out to be, the new situation creates possibilities for expanded terms of debate, positive rethinking and reform. But this is not to suggest an abstractly futuristic discourse: immediate practical problems need to be confronted. Tony Bruce's 2012 Higher Education Policy Institute (HEPI) report, *Universities and Constitutional Change in the UK: The Impact of Devolution on the Higher Education Sector* (Bruce, 2012), confirmed that devolution has led in the UK to the existence of four HE systems with divergent trajectories, and that Scotland's approach represents the most striking difference from, at the other extreme, England's. Arguments about the relative merits of these models will of course continue. The electoral success of Labour's 'abolition of fees' promise in May 2017, for example, put back on the agenda an issue that seemed settled in England, with Scotland's 'no tuition fees' policy orthodoxly dismissed as eccentric. This is a development reinforcing the argument that Scottish HE has the opportunity to play an important part in a much wider public debate.

## THE AUDIT REPORT

The much-anticipated report of Audit Scotland (2016) highlighted that, although the sector overall, at the time of the EU referendum, appeared financially healthy, there were large and potentially damaging differences in the resource available to particular higher education institutions (HEIs). Such imbalances, moreover, are likely to be accentuated, both by the continuation of austerity economics leading to further public spending cuts, and by the possibility that larger, research-led HEIs will be able to attract increased fee income from students from rUK. The commission saw these institutional differentials as a potential challenge to the sector. Its report noted that, while Scottish HE as a whole, in 2014–15, had income of £3.5 billion, a surplus of £146 million and reserves of £2.5 billion, the University of Edinburgh and the three 'ancients' (St Andrews, Glasgow and Aberdeen) accounted for 54 per cent of the total income – and Glasgow and Edinburgh alone for 41 per cent. Five universities, moreover, relied on the Scottish Funding Council (SFC) for more than 50 per cent of their income, making them more vulnerable to economies in public spending. In the financial year 2016–17, there was a 3 per cent cut to the revenue budget, which was followed by a further 1.3 per cent announced in the Scottish Budget for 2017–18.

The uneven ability of Scottish HEIs to generate income compounds the danger of the Scottish HE sector losing coherence, not because different universities have different 'missions' which is potentially positive, but because they have different finance-driven, institutional cultures imposed on them. Already universities north of the border – and some more than others – have been seeking to reduce staff on grounds of financial shortfalls or the desirability of increasing surpluses. Threatened and actual compulsory redundancies in a quarter of Scotland's HEIs create insecurity and a breakdown in management–union relations. This, along with the growing use of zero-hours contracts and the fact that, at the time of writing, 54 per cent of all academic staff, including 49 per cent of teaching staff, are subject to insecure terms of employment, is doing potentially irreparable damage to the collegial culture on which universities for long relied.

## THE WESTMINSTER ACT IN SCOTLAND

Although HE policy is the business of Scotland's Parliament, the fact that universities compete on a UK basis for research funding, students and staff means, as O'Shea indicated, that what happens in the rUK impacts north of the border. The Westminster Government's Higher Education and Research Act changes the infrastructure of UK research investment, and, in paving the way for the introduction of a Teaching Excellence Framework (TEF) – linking it, certainly in England, to further increases in tuition fees – it encourages new HE providers, including private ones, to set up institutions with university status. This was the danger that led O'Shea to suggest speaking of *Scottish* rather than UK universities. Since – through the work done by HE teaching and research staff – Scotland (according to the 2015–16 *The Times Higher* international tables, https://www.timeshighereducation.com/world-university-rankings/2016/world-ranking#!/page/0/length/25/sort_by/rank/sort_order/asc/cols/stats) has, per head of population, more universities in the world-ranked top 200 than any country other than Luxembourg; performs relatively well in UK research assessments; and attracts a disproportionately large share of UK research funding, he was able to make the point with some authority.

As long as Scotland remains part of the UK – even were there to be greater devolved powers – its HEIs will be affected by the student tuition-fee regime south of the border. Since the 2017 UK general election, the drive for ever-growing student contributions has come under question, but, unless the Labour Party's promise to follow Scotland in abolishing fees is fulfilled, Scottish universities – in their desire to remain within the still-dominant 'competitive', commercial discourse, and not to be perceived as offering an 'inferior product' – are likely to seek to maximise income from their rUK students. This possibility underlies the concern that the Scottish Parliament passed what is known as a legislative consent (or Sewel Convention) motion allowing for aspects of a Westminster law to take effect in Scotland – in this case, the clauses that refer to the UK research infrastructure and to participation, if HEIs so decide, in the TEF. Despite the fact that the TEF is not generally regarded as a better quality assurance system than Scotland's Quality Enhancement Framework and enhancement-led institutional review, some HEI managements have bowed to pressures to submit to what is, in effect, market-driven *force majeure*, rather than a concern for standards. The fear is that rUK students may opt for English universities of equivalent prestige that promote themselves with 'marketing' labels like 'Gold graded'. In June 2017 the latest TEF results were published, showing that five Scottish universities had participated in the TEF – Dundee, Robert Gordon University, St Andrews, Abertay and Heriot-Watt (https://www.timeshighereducation.com/news/teaching-excellence-framework-tef-results-2017).

Amongst many concerns about the TEF, a University and College Union (UCU) analysis suggested that its proposed metrics are deeply flawed and would lead to many otherwise successful and highly rated Scottish HEIs performing comparatively poorly. Allowing students' grading of teaching to play a part, moreover, could lead, under managerial pressure, to a reduction in marking standards; and there is evidence that female lecturers and those from Black and minority ethnic backgrounds tend to be scored lower by students than their white male counterparts. More than that, allowing for Scottish HEIs to participate in the TEF also raised a fundamental issue of democratic accountability. The TEF did not appear in the Higher Education and Research Bill itself – the Act only allows for its introduction via the formation of a new Office for Students, and this is a body with no remit in the Scottish HE system. Because the Sewel Convention process allows for only limited parliamentary scrutiny at Holyrood, a technical device, rather than serious political debate, was used to introduce to Scotland a measure conceived in the context of a policy agenda at odds with the democratically endorsed value system informing the university system north of the border. It was certainly the case that as universities began, in early 2017, to discuss their positions with regard to participation in the TEF it became clear that, at best, the measure was creating divisions within the Scottish HE system, even if not always along predictable lines.

## GOVERNANCE REFORM

The fact that a reform with ill-publicised but potentially far-reaching implications can be introduced with little parliamentary scrutiny highlights the importance of campus democracy – particularly in a case like the TEF, the introduction of which requires individual HEIs to decide on participation – and university governance has been a live issue north of the border since at least 2011. Soon after it was elected with an overall majority, the SNP Government responded to pressures – including a strong trade-union campaign – by commissioning the von Prondzynski panel to review HE governance and propose reforms. It reported in 2012 and, in the spring of 2016, the issue dominated Scottish public policy discourse about HE, as the Higher Education Governance (Scotland) Act (Scottish Government, 2016a) made its way through the Holyrood legislative process.

The von Prondzynski review was the source of the Act, but was far from fully implemented by it, leaving a number of recommendations for further debate. What was most striking about the panel appointed was that the Scottish Government signalled its intention to seek advice on an important HE matter from representatives of different campus interests (a principal, a chair of governors, a university rector, an academic trade unionist and a student leader) rather than – as had become the usual practice at Westminster – figures from the business and financial worlds. The concerns the review panel addressed derived from two widely held perceptions. First, that, despite the acknowledged excellence of Scotland's universities, the trend within the system away from collegial governance towards *managerialism* (as opposed to necessary, good management) had gone too far. And second, universities – while remaining what the review called 'autonomous public institutions' committed to the core value of academic freedom – should be more open and transparent in their relationship with society as a whole.

Principal amongst the reforms enacted – in some cases after strong resistance from Universities Scotland in particular – involved the addition of new student association and trade union positions on governing bodies; a slight widening of the definition of academic freedom; and the introduction of election by all staff and students of the chair of the governing body. This last reform (the most controversial along with trade union nominations to governing bodies) was proposed as a way of extending to all HEIs the long-standing Scottish practice by which – in the University of Edinburgh, the three 'ancients' and later Dundee – students (and, in the case of Edinburgh, staff) elect rectors with (except in Dundee) the right to chair the governing body. (In the event, following a rather confused campaign of opposition, this was modified in the Act to allow for 'elected chairs' to work alongside, rather than in the place of, existing rectors in ways that remained to be determined.) The Act came into force early in 2017. An approximately four-year transitional period has been allowed to avoid requiring existing governors to step down before the end of their term. Universities have begun to implement the Act with varying degrees of alacrity or reluctance, but it has to be fully implemented by the end of 2020.

Amongst the proposals not enacted were, first, that there should be a government-funded but independent institute of higher education to enhance the evidence base for ongoing reform, mitigating the tendency for public debate to descend from well-based argument into *parti pris* polemic. Second, von Prondzynski proposed repatriating the role of the Queen's Privy Council in reviewing university ordinances to an ad hoc Scottish body subject to oversight by the Scottish Parliament. A third outstanding proposal was that staff and student representatives should sit on university remuneration committees, and this was supported by many Members of the Scottish Parliament (MSPs) concerned at the adverse publicity annually surrounding reports of university principals, already in some cases on salaries of well over a quarter of a million, receiving well-above-inflation pay rises, far in excess of offers to other staff. Fourth, it was recommended that university governing bodies should meet in public except in respect of genuinely confidential matters: since HE receives over £1 billion of public money annually, the public should have at least the opportunity to observe their general decision making.

A fifth proposal was for at least 40 per cent of the members of HE governing bodies to be women. A Holyrood amendment to enact this was rejected on the grounds that, at the time, this issue was ultra vires. Subsequent adjustments in devolved powers, however, mean that the Scottish Government has introduced a more general Gender Balance on Public Boards Bill, and in anticipation of how opinion is moving, many HEIs have already brought about real increases in the number of women acting as lay members on governing bodies, indeed as chairs, substantially changing the 2011–12 situation, when there were no female chairs in Scotland and only a quarter of members were women.

## FUNDING, UNIVERSITY EDUCATION AND THE SKILLS AGENDA

HE funding in Scotland comes from a number of sources. The Scottish Government, through the Student Awards Agency, pays the tuition fees for Scottish and (at present) EU students, with universities charging rUK students up to £9,000 annually, paid with deferred-till-in-employment loans. Fees for students from other parts of the world range from £8,880 to £47,200 per annum. Public money also reaches HEIs through the SFC as teaching grants, research funding, and resource for capital projects. Universities, too, receive outside research grants and have charitable, endowment and investment income – some institutions far more so than others. The Audit Scotland (2016) report showed that discrepancies in dependence on SFC funding ranged from, at one end, St Andrews (only 20 per cent of income from the SFC) to, at the other, the University of the Highlands and Islands (83 per cent). These growing divergences threaten the idea of Scotland as a small nation with a distinctively integrated HE system – one that comprises universities widely perceived as public bodies, theoretically at least of equal standing, fulfilling diverse roles and meeting a collective need as central to the wellbeing of civil society as socially funded health care.

The SFC – formed in 2005 by amalgamating the Scottish Higher Education Funding Council and the Scottish Further Education Council – is the arm's-length body responsible for distributing government-allocated funds to both sectors. From the point of view of universities this status allows the council to ensure that they receive public funding without compromising their institutional autonomy. Although the many pressures there now are on HEIs to supplement income with business-like activities mean that autonomy is no longer the sufficient-in-itself condition for the protection of the core value of academic freedom it was once assumed to be, it remains an essential one.

This needs restating because the SFC's responsibility to work within Scottish Government policy – and particularly the perceived imperative to redress deficiencies in necessary workforce skills, harnessing the expertise available in HE to this end – potentially challenges the idea of institutions free to determine their own academic agendas. Autonomy of course must be exercised responsibly and it is reasonable to call for greater transparency and internal campus democracy to ensure that it is. But HE in Scotland has never been conducted in 'ivory towers' isolated from socio-economic and business needs, and the idea that one key object of a university education is to provide a path to socially necessary – but also productive and fulfilling – employment lies at the heart of a Scottish tradition in which the preparation of a professional class of clergy, lawyers and teachers (and indeed scientists and engineers) was central to the good society.

A university education, however, cannot be simply about creating paths to employment or meeting immediate economic demands. Universities must remain distinctive institutions providing higher education in a research environment, and instilling in students the value of learning and scholarship for their own sake. They contribute indispensably to social objectives by creating the conditions in which students can develop as critical and concerned citizens, not merely economic agents equipped with specific expertise deemed necessary at a particular time by a particular government. Promoting a skills agenda, if the SFC is not allowed, or chooses not, to recognise the special nature of the HE sector, could lead, by a different route, to diminishing the reputation of the Scottish university system in the way that O'Shea feared the Westminster bill would do by granting university status to institutions without research credentials.

These comments were prompted by concerns about the direction of policy that grew in the summer of 2016 when the SFC, along with the various Scottish enterprise agencies, came under scrutiny in the Scottish Government's *Enterprise and Skills Review* (www. gov.scot/Publications/2016/10/4372). Charged to consider how these bodies could better work together to meet government enterprise and employment targets, it was commissioned by the Cabinet Secretary for the Economy and Jobs, Keith Brown, rather than by education ministers. Amongst the initial recommendations was the proposal that the SFC and enterprise agencies sit under a national board with a remit more closely to coordinate their work. The danger perceived lay not in this aim in itself, rather in the implication that, in practice, this would result in a new type of board, perhaps chaired by a government minister, which would replace all the existing bodies. In the event, after sustained pressure from the sector, the SFC was retained as an independent body, albeit operating under a new strategic board. The review, however, is ongoing and will continue to be taken note of by the sector.

## WIDENING ACCESS AND PROMOTING FAIRNESS

The most obvious differentiating feature amongst the four divergent UK national HE systems identified in the Bruce (2012) report lies in their approach to the financing of student tuition, with the Scottish 'no-fees' and the English 'high-fees-financed-by student-loans' prescriptions (largely unquestioned by the Westminster political establishment until the electoral popularity of Labour's May 2017 abolition-of-fees pledge) the outliers in the range. Although tuition in Scottish universities was historically financed by student payments, the 'no-fees' policy (in reality a continuation of the UK-wide, welfare-state principles largely abandoned at Westminster) was seen as in tune with the 'democratic' emphasis in the 'democratic intellect' tradition. However, recent research at the Edinburgh-based Centre for Research in Education Inclusion and Diversity – reported in the aforementioned Sutton Trust publication (Hunter Blackburn et al., 2016) and elsewhere – showed that the 'no-fees' policy has not, in itself, increased the access to HE amongst students from disadvantaged backgrounds, on which Scotland's current record is, arguably, relatively poor. It does, however, contribute to the perception that the system is, by and large, 'fair' (see Chapter 85).

The English high-tuition-fee system – mitigated to some extent in different ways in Wales and Northern Ireland – rests on the neo-liberal premise that higher education is primarily an individual, positional, rather than a social, good, which should substantially be paid for by those whose life prospects benefit from it. In Scotland the political consensus supporting the 'no-fees' policy is broken only by the Conservatives, who, although since the 2016 election the official opposition at Holyrood, were supported by less than a quarter of voters, and whose much-proclaimed breakthrough – from one MP to thirteen – in the 2017 UK election was substantially attributable to the party's campaign against an immediate second Scottish independence referendum rather than to any shift in social policy.

However, the evidence that, in the short term at least, there has been greater advance in widening access in England than in Scotland obviously gives a measure of superficial credibility to the argument that the 'no-fees' policy, and providing the resource to tackle the access problem, are incompatible.

Historically, however, the *idea* of a unified and unifying educational system providing opportunity for the lower classes (the so-called 'lads o' pairts') to progress to university, and the *fact* that a slightly higher percentage of disadvantaged boys in the nineteenth and early twentieth centuries than in England *did* gain access, remain factors sustaining a greater measure of commitment to social-democratic values in Scotland than in England taken as a whole (a difference, for the time being at least, of political significance, though some social-attitude surveys suggest the gap is statistically marginal). To introduce a funding model like England's would have implications going beyond a pragmatic response to a particular problem. The longer-term success of the English experiment – flawed and risk-attended as the leading *Financial Times* commentator, Martin Wolf, amongst others, has argued – is in any case far from assured and is already jeopardising the stability of less 'competitive' HEIs south of the border (Wolf, 2017). The challenge in Scotland must be to meet the targets set by the 2016 Silver Commission on what is now increasingly referred to as 'fair' rather than simply 'widened' access – to which the Scottish Government, its new Commission for Fair Access under Peter Scott, and, amongst others, the Scottish Labour Party, are all committed – in ways that retain the allegiance of Scottish students, potential students and their families, who believe that, at some fundamental level, the Scottish policy provides an essential basis of fairness from which to start.

The Silver Commission set an initial target: by 2030, 20 per cent of all students should be from the 20 per cent most deprived backgrounds: in 2015–16 the figure published by the SFC was only 14 per cent, having improved by only 0.3 per cent over the previous two years. The task of accomplishing this without compromising the integrity of the Scottish university system poses a challenge that can only be met by treating the Silver goals not simply as major challenges in themselves, but rather as targets that have to be contextualised within a more general discussion about societal futures. This will require – of government and all those in HE and in wider society committed to the idea of Scotland as a working social democracy – collaboration in some radical rethinking. A progressive answer to the question of fair access to HE will involve a break from the mindset that treats the education budget as a fixed pot, which can only be added to – if at all – by commodifying the 'product', and seeing it rather as the funding of a social necessity that has to be publicly paid for. In Scotland, government policy reflects this aspiration somewhat more strongly than the Westminster approach, but the nettle of how the need can be met, and the resource provided, has yet to be collectively grasped.

## IN CONCLUSION

The decision that the United Kingdom should leave the EU means that Scottish HE faces a new, economically and culturally challenging situation, within which many current and upcoming problems have to be confronted. They include the dangers inherent in the institutional resource imbalances identified by Audit Scotland; the threats or potential threats to the special character of HE posed by the Westminster Higher Education and Research Bill and the methods chosen to overcome the skills deficit; and the development of fair-access opportunities for students from deprived backgrounds. The new situation, however, has created an opportunity for some radical rethinking about the sector's future and about its relationship to the nation's democracy. This chapter has offered no blue-print for further reform, but underlying it is the argument that problems should be addressed and challenges met, not simply with a view to pragmatic solutions, but, more profoundly, by also paying explicit attention to the underlying trajectory of policy and its social implications.

During the coming period there will be continuing dispute about Scotland's future rela-tionships with the UK and the EU (or 'Europe'). It will be taking place amidst the ongoing crisis in the global economic order. Against that background, the distinctive HE system north of the border – in some respects, historically at least, more in tune with continental Europe than England – faces an important choice. It can either be orientated towards building on and developing its distinctiveness, offering an alternative path to the one cur-rently being followed at Westminster (and perhaps even influencing substantial changes in Westminster's HE policies), or it can follow the current Westminster model – perhaps with modifications – increasingly opening universities to competition, the profit motive and the financing of access to university (for all but the most disadvantaged) in line with the idea that, rather being a social necessity, it is a positional good to be paid for by individual 'consumers'.

In 1885 the Liberal peer, and Rector of St Andrew's University, Lord Reay, declared that:

> The development of brain-power on a wide scale is what a Scottish statesman has to look to. If we had a Scottish Parliament sitting in Edinburgh, I have no doubt that the organisation of the uni-versities would be the first number on the legislative programme. (Reay, in Knight, 1894, p. 302)

Now that that Parliament exists, it is appropriate to be reminded that, *mutatis mutandis*, higher education still has a key part to play in the future of Scottish society and in how its social values are defined.

## NOTE

This chapter was completed well before a dispute over the pension scheme (USS), which covers most academic and academic-related staff in the older ('pre-92') universities, erupted UK-wide in February 2018 that led to historically unprecedented industrial action involving 10 Scottish HEIs.

## REFERENCES

Anderson, R. (2011) 'History', in University and College Union Scotland, *Intellect and Democracy: A Report Submitted to the Cabinet Secretary for Education and Lifelong Learning*. Edinburgh: UCUS.

Anderson, R. with Wallace, S. (2015) 'The universities and national identity in the long nineteenth century, c. 1830–1914,' in R. Anderson, M. Freeman and L. Paterson (eds), *The Edinburgh History of Education in Scotland*. Edinburgh: Edinburgh University Press, pp. 265–85.

Audit Scotland (2016) *Audit of Higher Education in Scottish Universities*. Edinburgh: Scottish Government. Online at www.audit-scotland.gov.uk/report/audit-of-higher-education-in-scottish-universities

Bruce, T. (2012) *Universities and Constitutional Change in the UK: The Impact of Devolution on the Higher Education Sector*. London: Higher Education Policy Institute. Online at www.hepi.ac.uk/wp-content/uploads/2014/02/Devolution-Summary-Report.docx

Collini, S. (2017) 'The English problem and "the Scottish solution"', in *Speaking of Universities*. London: Verso.

Davie, G. E. (1961) *The Democratic Intellect*. Edinburgh: Edinburgh University Press.

Forde, C. and McKinney, S. (eds) (2016) Special edition on widening access to higher education in Scotland, *Scottish Educational Review*, 48 (1).

Holmwood, J., Hickey, T., Cohen, R. and Wallis, S. (eds) (2016) *In Defence of Public Higher Education: Knowledge for a Successful Society. The Alternative White Paper for Higher Education*. Online at https://heconvention2.files.wordpress.com/2016/06/awp1.pdf

Hunter Blackburn, L., Kadar-Satat, G., Riddell, S. and Weedon, E. (2016) *Access in Scotland: Access to Higher Education for People from Less Advantages Backgrounds in Scotland*. Online at https://www.suttontrust.com/research-paper/access-in-scotland/

Kerevan, G. (2013) 'Democratic intellect or degree factory? The changing civil and cultural place of the university in Scotland', in T. G. K. Bryce, W. M. Humes, D. Gilles and A. Kennedy (eds), *Scottish Education, Fourth Edition: Referendum*. Edinburgh: Edinburgh University Press, pp. 755–69.

Knight, W. (ed.) (1894) Rectorial Addresses Delivered at the University of St Andrews, London.

Paterson, L. (2015) 'George Davie and the democratic intellect', in G. Graham (ed.), *Scottish Philosophy in the Nineteenth and Twentieth Centuries*. Oxford: Oxford University Press, pp. 236–69.

Riddell, S., Weedon, E. and Minty, S. (eds) (2015) *Higher Education in Scotland and the UK: Diverging or Converging Systems?* Edinburgh: Edinburgh University Press.

Silver, R. (2016) *A Blueprint for Fairness: The Final Report of the Commission on Widening Access*. Edinburgh: Scottish Government. Online at www.gov.scot/Resource/0049/00496535.pdf

Scottish Government (2011) *Putting Learners at the Centre: Delivering Our Ambitions for Post-16 Education*. Edinburgh: Scottish Government. Online at www.gov.scot/resource/doc/357909/0120943.pdf

Scottish Government (2016a) The Higher Education Governance (Scotland) Act 2016. Norwich: The Stationery Office. Online at www.legislation.gov.uk/asp/2016/15/pdfs/asp_20160015_en.pdf

Scottish Government (2016b) *Enterprise & Skills Review: Report on Phase 1* Edinburgh: Scottish Government. Online at www.gov.scot/Topics/Economy/EntandSkillsreview

von Prondzynski, F. (2012) *Report of the Review of Higher Education Governance in Scotland*. Edinburgh: Scottish Government. Online at www.gov.scot/resource/0038/00386780.pdf

Weedon, E., Kadar-Satat, G., Hunter Blackburn, L. H. and Riddell, S. (eds) (2016) *Access in Scotland*. London: Sutton Trust. Online at www.suttontrust.com/researcharchive/access-in-scotland/

Wolf, M. (2017) *The Use and Abuse of Economics in the Debate on Universities*. Annual Lecture of the Council for Defence of British Universities, London, CDBU, 26 January.

75

# Access, Progression and Retention in Further Education and Higher Education

*Cristina Iannelli*

## INTRODUCTION

Widening access to higher education (HE) has been high in the policy agenda of the Scottish Government for a number of years. Recently a new impetus to achieve this goal has been given by the recommendations formulated by the Commission on Widening Access (CoWA). This commission, chaired by Dame Ruth Silver, was set up in 2015 to advise the Scottish Government on ways in which social inequality in HE could be eradicated. In 2014, in her presentation of the Programme for Government to the Parliament, the Scottish First Minister Nicola Sturgeon declared:

> I want us to determine now that a child born today in one of our most deprived communities should, by the time he or she leaves school, have the same chance of going to university as a child born in one of our least deprived communities. That means we would expect at least 20% of university entrants to come from the most deprived 20% of the population.

Following this announcement, CoWA was established and, after extensive consultations with practitioners, academics, various associations and the wider public, published two reports. The interim report (www.gov.scot/Publications/2015/11/9302) examined the main barriers to widening access and identified some systemic issues that may work against the achievement of equal access in Scotland. In the final report (https://beta.gov.scot/publications/blueprint-fairness-final-report-commission-widening-access), thirty-four recommendations were made to tackle the individual and systemic barriers identified in the interim report. Among them, the commission endorsed the appointment of a Commissioner for Fair Access to lead system-wide efforts to drive fair access and to coordinate the gathering of more substantial evidence for the development of effective policies.

The government target of 20 per cent from the most deprived areas to attend HE by 2030 is an ambitious one; the current rate of HE entrants from these areas being 16 per cent and having increased only by 1 per cent in the last ten years (Scottish Funding Council, 2016, Tables 25a and 25b). This is also only one aspect of the wider governmental agenda aimed at promoting an equalisation of educational opportunities among students with different gender, ethnicity, age, disabilities (i.e. people with 'protected characteristics' in the

Scottish policy context) and socio-economic backgrounds. In Scotland, HE is provided by both universities and colleges. The provision of sub-degree qualifications in colleges is an important feature of the Scottish HE system, which shapes the way in which the widening access agenda has progressed until now (see next section). For this reason the two sectors, university and college, are discussed together and the term HE in this chapter refers to both unless otherwise stated.

How far is Scotland from achieving the target of improving opportunities to enter HE for less advantaged social groups? To answer this question, we need to take a step back and establish what has been achieved until now by looking at patterns in HE entry over time and the role of different HE sectors, the extent of contemporary inequalities, issues of progression and retention, current policies aimed at increasing HE participation of under-represented groups, and discuss present and future challenges.

## EXPANSION OF HIGHER EDUCATION – A STORY OF INCLUSION AND DIVERSION

### Patterns of Expansion

In the last fifty years, Scotland (like the rest of the UK) has witnessed an unprecedented expansion of HE. The main periods of expansion followed the publication of three important documents:

- the Robbins Report in 1963 which recommended the expansion of universities and widening participation to all people qualified by ability and attainment to pursue university studies;
- the 1992 Further and Higher Education Act which upgraded the polytechnics (central institutions in Scotland) to university status, granting them the ability to award degree-level qualifications, and established separate funding councils for universities and colleges in England, Scotland and Wales; and
- the Dearing Report and the associated Garrick Report for Scotland in 1997 which, among the many policy issues addressed, stressed the importance of supporting expansion and widening participation. The Garrick report also recommended enhanced collaboration between further education (FE) colleges and universities to facilitate the transition of students from colleges to universities (referred to as 'articulation routes' into degree programmes).

In Scotland, HE expansion took place through the foundation of new universities and the extension of HE provision in colleges. In the 1960s, adding to the four ancient universities (St Andrews, Edinburgh, Glasgow and Aberdeen) established in the fifteenth and sixteenth centuries, another four were established – the Universities of Dundee, Strathclyde, Heriot-Watt and Stirling (from now on referred as the old universities). In the 1990s, following the abolition of the binary system which distinguished between universities and polytechnics, new universities were created at Abertay, Glasgow Caledonian, Napier, Paisley and Robert Gordon. In the same years the provision of HE in FE colleges substantially increased. These colleges, originally established to provide vocational education and training for apprentices, technicians and administrative staff, assumed an important role in the provision of sub-degree-level qualifications, Higher National Certificates (HNCs) and Higher National Diplomas (HND) (Gallacher, 2014).

A key factor for HE expansion was the large increase in the number of people who became eligible to attend HE over time. The expansion of secondary education and the rise

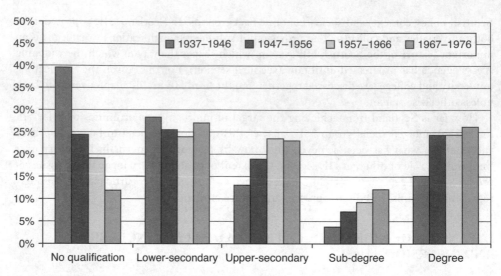

**Figure 75.1   Educational attainment by birth cohort**

Source: Iannelli (2011) – Figure 1 (p. 255) – 2001 Scottish Household Survey data. Reprinted with permission Iannelli (2011) © Cambridge University Press

of school attainment were essential for this expansion to take place. Figure 75.1 provides an illustration of the extent to which educational attainment improved across different generations in Scotland. It shows the highest educational attainment achieved by people born in four different decades between 1937 and 1976. Apart from the striking decline in the percentage of people who left education with no qualification, the data show a substantial increase in the percentages of people who gained a post-compulsory school qualification, that is, an upper-secondary or tertiary qualification (from 32 per cent to 61 per cent). In particular, while only 19 per cent of people born between 1937 and 1946 achieved a higher qualification, this percentage doubled (38 per cent) in the youngest cohort born between 1967 and 1976. Particularly noticeable is the growth in the percentage of people who gained a sub–degree-level qualification (mainly offered in FE colleges). This percentage tripled, from 4 per cent to 12 per cent.

Regarding the increase in secondary school attainment, Paterson et al. (2004) reported data from governmental sources showing that the percentages of young people achieving three or more Highers (the Scottish upper secondary qualifications) grew from 20 per cent in 1981 to 32 per cent in 1999 (Table A7.4). The latest data available show they reached 43 per cent in 2015 (Scottish Government, 2016, Table 5). Three or more Highers is usually considered the minimum requirement for entering university in Scotland. Thus, the increase in the proportions of pupils achieving this outcome denotes a substantial increase in the number of eligible candidates for university entrance.

Data from the Scottish School Leavers Surveys provide information on the proportions of secondary leavers who entered HE shortly after leaving school (at age 18–19) between the end of the 1980s and the beginning of the twenty-first century (Figure 75.2). These data confirm the rapid growth in the percentages of school leavers who made the transition to HE in the 1990s. Moreover, these percentages are presented broken down by the four HE sectors (the residual category 'other' representing HE institutions outside Scotland). The

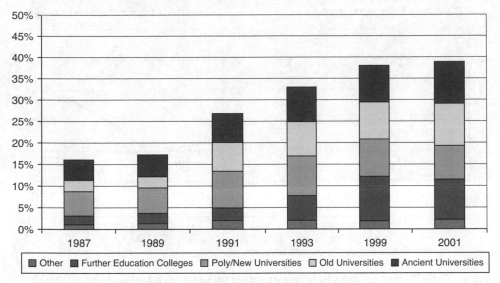

**Figure 75.2   Expansion of tertiary education by institution type**

Source: Iannelli (2011) – Figure 4 (p. 258) – Scottish School Leavers Survey data. Reprinted with permission Iannelli (2011) © Cambridge University Press

HE expansion in Scotland has been uneven: even though the growth occurred in all sectors, old universities and FE colleges witnessed the largest increase. As noted by Iannelli et al. (2011):

> As a share of those attending higher education, what began as two large and two small sectors (ancient universities and polytechnic colleges compared to old universities and further education colleges) became four sectors of relatively equal shares by 2001: for example polytechnic colleges fell from 35% of entrants (i.e. 5.6/15.9) to 21%, whereas FE colleges rose from 13% to 25%. (p. 724)

According to the most recent data, in 2014/15, the Scottish HE Initial Participation Rate for those aged between 16 and 30 was 55 per cent (Scottish Funding Council, 2016). A significant majority of them continue to be less than 20 years of age. About 21 per cent studied in FE colleges, 32 per cent in universities in Scotland and another 2 per cent in institutions outside Scotland (Hunter Blackburn et al., 2016).

## Expansion and Widening Access

The large increase in the overall proportion of people attending HE was accompanied by the inclusion of groups of the population who were largely under-represented, in particular women, people from less advantaged social backgrounds and mature students. Thus, at the end of the 1980s gender differences in HE entry disappeared and, at the beginning of the 1990s, for the first time, the proportion of women gaining access to HE exceeded the proportion of men. Moreover, although participation rose in all age groups, between 1984 and 1993, it rose most sharply among mature students. In 1993 nearly a quarter of entrants to full-time undergraduate courses were aged 25 or over (Paterson, 1997, Table 1). The doors

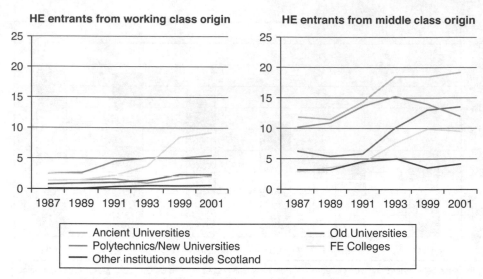

Figure 75.3    Patterns of expansion by institution type and social origin (percentages)

Source: Scottish School Leavers Survey data, https://discover.ukdataservice.ac.uk/catalogue?sn=5143

of HE also opened up for people from lower socio-economic groups. However, acquiring a degree remained a rather infrequent experience among the most disadvantaged. Figure 75.3 presents data from the Scottish School Leavers Surveys, which compare the percentages of young HE entrants among children of professional/managerial and working class origins over time and by HE sector (Iannelli et al., 2011). The first impression emerging from these data is of persistent stark differences in overall participation between the two groups. Although the HE entry rate of young people from working class origin tripled between 1987 and 2001, in 2001 only 20 per cent of them succeeded in entering HE compared to 58 per cent of young people from a professional/managerial class of origin (percentages calculated by adding up the percentages of HE entrants of the five sectors shown in Figure 75.3). The expansion benefited all social groups and this is why the gap between children of more and less advantaged social groups has remained large.

The second interesting point relates to the disaggregation of these data by HE sector. While the growth in HE entry of children of professional classes occurred mainly in the ancient and old universities, the most prominent sectors of expansion for children from working classes were the new universities and the FE colleges. Iannelli et al. (2011) comment: 'Higher education expansion led to significant improvements in the participation of young people from the most disadvantaged background (and also for the intermediate social background) but that this occurred through a process of diversion towards lower-status institutions' (p. 736). The 'process of diversion' referred to here highlights how social inequalities in HE were maintained by channelling the new entrants to less prestigious institutions, thus preserving the places in the most prestigious institutions (i.e. ancient and old universities) for students from more advantaged social classes.

Of course, for those students who lacked the necessary qualification for university entry, FE colleges have represented the only opportunity to access HE since entry requirements for sub-degree courses were (and still are) lower. In Scotland, as in the rest of the UK, each university and each subject area decide their entry requirements. The most prestigious universities are highly selective not only in terms of school attainment (only applicants who achieve the top grades in their final school exams are considered) but also in terms of school subjects required to access certain disciplines within these institutions. These universities have identified eight academic subjects (among them English, maths, languages and sciences) as 'facilitating' entry to their institutions. Recent research has shown that 'facilitating' subjects are studied to a larger extent by children from more advantaged social backgrounds, while vocationally oriented subjects are mainly taken by pupils from more disadvantaged backgrounds. This ultimately perpetuates social inequalities in pupils' chances of entering the most prestigious universities.

Apart from the school factors mentioned above, there are other aspects which influence people's likelihood to study at college. Colleges' regional locations make them easily accessible and a less costly study option; their outreach work in communities facilitates access to information about their courses; the flexibility of teaching provision (e.g. evening classes and part-time courses) allows students from less advantaged social backgrounds and mature students to combine work and study; and flexible routes to HE courses in university (i.e. 'articulation') facilitate entry into the second or third year of a university degree programme, after having acquired HNC/HND qualifications (Gallacher, 2009). In summary, overall the large provision of sub-degree courses in Scotland (mainly HNC and HND qualifications in FE colleges) has allowed access of non-traditional students, that is, students from working class origin, mature students and also women, to HE (even though in the case of women, their growth in participation occurred at both degree and sub-degree levels).

## THE EXTENT OF INEQUALITIES IN THE TWENTY-FIRST CENTURY

In 2005, the newly established Scottish Funding Council (SFC), which emerged from the unification of the Scottish Further Education Funding Council and the Scottish Higher Education Funding Council, published its first *Learning for All* report. This report and the following ones, published on an annual basis, aim to summarise the progress made towards widening participation through the presentation of a series of indicators measuring how successful the HE sector has been in tackling inequalities in HE access, retention and achievement (see the 2016 report at www.sfc.ac.uk/publications-statistics/statistical-publications/statistical-publications-2016/SFCST062016.aspx).

The 2005 report acknowledged that progress towards widening access had been slow in both the FE and university sectors and 'educational participation and achievement is highly skewed, particularly by socio-economic background, geography and gender'. The report particularly noted *men's disadvantage* in relation to participation, retention and achievement in HE; *social disadvantage* with those from the least deprived areas being about twice as likely to be participating in HE as people from the most deprived area; and *area disadvantage* with people living in certain areas of the country (e.g. Lothians, Lanarkshire, Highlands and Islands) having lower participation in HE in both FE and universities. Regarding other categories of people with protected characteristics, the report documented that people with disabilities were likely to participate broadly in proportion to their numbers in the general population and people from ethnic minorities were more likely to participate than the general population. However, access and outcomes for people with disabilities varied hugely depending on the nature of their disability and there were variations between ethnic groups in the field of study chosen in HE. HE participation of mature students has seen a decline in recent years. Thus their participation in first degree programmes dropped from 23 per cent in 2005–6 to 18 per cent in 2014–15 and in sub-degree level from 58 per cent to 43 per cent (Scottish Funding Council, 2016). Current policies on widening access have mainly targeted young people and this may have had a negative impact on other students, in particular the adult learners.

## Social Inequalities in Access

At present, a lot of effort and public funding has been invested in reducing social inequalities in education. However, there is some controversy on how 'social disadvantage' is identified in the Scottish policy context. The main indicator of social disadvantage used by the SFC in its reporting is the Scottish Index of Multiple Deprivation (SIMD). This measure is also used to target interventions to improve educational achievement and progression to HE of children and young people who live in the areas of the greatest material deprivation (see next section). SIMD identifies almost 7,000 small areas across all Scotland (called 'data zones') and ranks them according to their level of concentrations of multiple deprivation. The 2012 index is a weighted sum of thirty-eight indicators across seven domains: income, employment, health, education, skills and training, housing, geographic access and crime. The areas with different degrees of social disadvantage are usually identified by dividing the index into quintiles, the first quintile including the 20 per cent most disadvantaged areas.

This indicator has been subject to criticism because, being an area-level indicator, it fails to capture people in socio-economic disadvantage who do not live in particularly deprived areas (as defined by SIMD) and, on the other hand, people may live in deprived areas and not be disadvantaged. This is obviously important when designing policies aimed at tackling inequalities between individuals from different socio-economic backgrounds, the risk being that interventions may advantage non-deprived people living in deprived areas and miss out a large number of socially disadvantaged people who live in parts of Scotland which are not deprived.

Based on this measure, in 2013–14 the proportion of Scottish-domiciled full-time first degree entrants to universities from the 20 per cent most deprived areas (SIMD20) was 14 per cent while the same proportion for the least deprived areas (SIMD80) was 29 per cent (www.gov.scot/Publications/2015/11/9302). This proportion varied widely among institutions, from 4.3 per cent (University of Aberdeen) to 24.4 per cent (University of West of Scotland). In the same years, the proportion of full-time students from the 20 per cent most deprived areas studying HE courses in colleges was 25 per cent (Scottish Funding Council, 2016). It is clear from these data that the institutional differentiation of the HE sector continues to play a major role in differentiating opportunities among people from different social backgrounds. Reducing social inequalities in access to HE to reach the government's target of '20% of university entrants to come from the most deprived 20% of the population' has proved to be problematic for most universities in Scotland, with the exception of the University of Glasgow Caledonian and the University of West of Scotland, which exceed this target. Considering that the great majority of undergraduate programmes is delivered by universities (about 78 per cent in most recent years), increasing the proportion of people entering these institutions from the most deprived 20 per cent of the population is a major task.

## PROGRESSION FROM COLLEGE TO UNIVERSITY

Over the last few years, the Scottish Government has encouraged the expansion of progression routes from sub-degree programmes at college to four-year degree programmes at university. 'Articulating' students are defined as those students who, after having acquired a Higher National (HN) qualification at college, gain entry into the second (for HNC qualified) or third year (for HND qualified) of a degree programme. The articulation route is seen as a means through which to achieve widening access in HE since many of the HNC/HND students are from more disadvantaged backgrounds and had not achieved the minimum requirements to directly enter university from school. It is also seen favourably due to their lower costs for the public finance because the costs related to the years spent at college are lower than the costs associated with university attendance.

About 47 per cent of HNC/HND students in Scotland progress to degree-level study at university (Hunter Blackburn et al., 2016). This percentage is not evenly spread across all universities and all fields of studies. Indeed graduates from colleges mostly gather in the new universities (post-1992) and enter disciplines such as business, computing and social sciences (Gallacher, 2014). The links between colleges and new universities have been strengthened by the creation of six articulation hubs across Scotland, five of which are based in new universities. These hubs received funding to increase the number of students progressing from HNC/HND programmes to degree courses, and to support this transition. Even though this policy has been beneficial in increasing the number of college graduates entering university, it has also continued to 'divert' students from more disadvantaged backgrounds away from the most prestigious universities.

Another important issue is that, among HNC/HND graduates who progress to university, only 22 per cent are awarded full credit, that is, a full recognition of prior learning (Hunter Blackburn et al., 2016). Thus, many college graduates will have to start from year one or two of a degree programme, spending five or six years of study in total to obtain a degree. This ultimately does not reduce costs for the public finance and increases costs for the students by prolonging their studies beyond the usual length, thus delaying entry into the labour market. The reason why some universities (in particular the ancient universities) may not recognise in full, or recognise only in part, prior learning in college is that those students are considered not prepared enough to engage with the content of a second- or third-year degree-level programme. Evidence suggests that indeed some college students find the transition to university difficult and that retention rates for articulating students in university are lower than the corresponding second- and third-year students (Kadar-Satat et al., 2016).

## HE RETENTION

Inequality in HE access is only one aspect of the wider goal aimed at promoting equal opportunities in HE among different social groups. Another important part is related to students' ability to complete their course of study after entering HE. Dropping out from HE has adverse personal implications for the student as well as negative effects on the institutions. It generates additional financial costs for both students and HE institutions. Thus reducing the risk of student dropout is a key aspect of the widening participation strategy. Compared to other countries, Scotland (and the UK more generally) has high retention rates and these rates have been improving. Thus, in 2014–15 retention rates at university and at college were 91 per cent and 83 per cent respectively (these latter figures include partial completion of the programme). As for access, there are differences in the retention rates by gender, age and social background. Men, mature students and people from disadvantaged backgrounds are more likely to drop out from their studies. Thus, in 2014–15, the retention rate at university was 90 per cent for men and about 88 per cent for mature students and people from the 20 per cent most deprived areas. With the exception of mature students (who are more likely to complete their programme of study in college), men and people living in the most deprived areas also have lower retention rates at college.

While no significant differences have been found in drop-out rates among first-year students from different social backgrounds studying in the new universities, significant differences emerge in the ancient and old universities (Kadar-Satat et al., 2016). However, the differences in the probability of dropping out of more disadvantaged socio-economic groups are in large part explained by their lower attainment at the time of university entry. This highlights the importance of school attainment not only for access to, but also for succeeding in, university. It also highlights the need for academic support before and after university entry. Unfortunately, in Scotland empirical evidence on inequalities in progression and retention is still scarce. The existing research is often patchy, mainly focusing on the experience of a single institution, and the analysis conducted is purely descriptive. There is a clear need to gather more information at national level which would allow us to analyse inequalities at different stages of the HE experience, from application and access to progression and achievement, and to link the institutional provision of teaching and student support to student learning experiences.

## CURRENT POLICIES AIMED AT PROMOTING WIDENING ACCESS

Over the last ten years, a series of policies have been implemented at national and institutional levels aimed at encouraging entry and progression to HE for socially disadvantaged students. In addition to the expansion of the articulation route from college to university discussed above, other important policies include the abolition of tuition fees, the introduction of outcome agreements between the SFC and the HE institutions, targeted places for widening access students, and interventions in schools such as the 'Schools for Higher Education Programme' (SHEP).

### Free Tuition

In 2007, when the Scottish National Party (SNP) came to power and started a minority government, undergraduate education in Scotland became free for Scottish and EU students. The strong commitment of successive SNP governments to free tuition fees is well illustrated by the famous words that the former First Minister Alex Salmond pronounced in 2011: 'The rocks will melt with the sun before I allow tuition fees to be imposed on Scottish students' (see, for example, www.telegraph.co.uk/news/politics/SNP/11238554/Alex-Salmond-unveils-tuition-fees-tribute-as-he-resigns.html). Indeed, the policy of 'free tuition fees' has become one of the pillars of the social justice agenda of the SNP even under the current First Minister, Nicola Sturgeon. Although in principle providing 'free HE tuition for all' is an appealing idea, the evidence suggests that simply abolishing tuition fees has not produced the expected result of equalising opportunities. This is due to the fact that, to finance the system, the government has imposed a cap on students' places and reduced their maintenance grants. The unintended consequence of this policy has been a socially regressive system which has benefited more socially advantaged students than less advantaged ones (Hunter Blackburn et al., 2016). This is because maintenance costs are high and, given the limited availability of grants supporting these costs, to be able to afford studying at university, people from lower social backgrounds need to borrow money, ending up with large debts which need to be repaid at the end of their studies.

## Outcome Agreements

Since 2012, universities in Scotland were required by the SFC to achieve improved outcomes in HE, including in the area of widening access, through outcome agreements. The 2013 Post-16 Education (Scotland) Act which followed strengthened the accountability of institutions through the introduction of statutory widening access agreements and introduced the possibility for the SFC to impose financial penalties on institutions which did not make good progress in relation to widening access. Even though financial penalties have yet to be applied for those institutions which fail to achieve their targets, HE institutions have been subject to close scrutiny from the SFC and more widely from the public through press coverage which follows the publication of *Learning for All* reports. As a result, growing efforts have been made by each university to create or participate in existing widening access programmes which include outreach activities, summer schools, access and bridging courses, and various support systems for those in HE such as peer mentoring.

An important means used by the Scottish universities to improve access by people in the most disadvantaged social groups to their institutions is the use of *contextualised admission criteria*. Universities take into account applicants' contextual information which may have hampered their ability to achieve high grades at school and offer them a place using less stringent entry criteria than normally applied (for example, accepting them at the minimum entry requirement). The contextual information considered at the application stage includes: having attended a school where the level of performance in examinations is below the national average, having been in foster care, having participated in access programmes, and living in the most deprived areas of the country.

## Targeted Places

In recognition of the difficulty of accommodating new entrants in selective universities where the competition for places is fierce and the number of places is capped, the SFC has funded the creation of additional places to be allocated to students from disadvantaged backgrounds. Starting from 2012–13, the SFC reserved 727 undergraduate places in the most selective universities in Scotland for students from disadvantaged backgrounds and 1,020 undergraduate places for students articulating from college to university in fourteen universities. This policy did positively impact on recruitment of students from the most disadvantaged backgrounds (SIMD20) to the ancient universities, in particular to the University of Glasgow. Unfortunately, as a consequence of funding cuts, the SFC decided to cancel funding for these additional places in the academic year 2016–17. The success of this policy testifies that additional places at university are needed to push the widening access agenda.

## Interventions in Schools

There is a general agreement that policy interventions aimed at tackling inequalities should start early and that the transition to HE is only the last link in a chain which sees the accumulation of disadvantage from childhood onwards. Funding has been made available to support targeted initiatives aimed at improving attainment in the local authorities of Scotland with the highest concentrations of deprivation (£750 million for the Attainment Scotland Fund) and for supporting schools with low rates of progression to HE, such as SHEP. SHEP is a national-level programme which aims to encourage progression of pupils from disadvantaged backgrounds to HE. SHEP activities mainly target S3 to S6 students and include individualised support and guidance, as well as participation in summer schools and open days, delivered by Scottish colleges and universities. Policies targeting low progression schools have been successful but have not yet produced the step change required to substantially reduce inequalities in access to HE.

## PRESENT AND FUTURE CHALLENGES

Although some progress has been made to widen access to HE in Scotland, opportunities to attend university and to acquire a degree are still significantly different among different social groups. In particular, the gap between the most and the least advantaged people continues to be large in the most prestigious universities, and has its origins in school. There are a number of reasons which may explain the lack of substantial impact of current policies in combating inequalities in HE.

The first issue which is largely overlooked is that 54 per cent of poor children do not live in the 20 per cent most deprived areas (Hunter Blackburn et al., 2016) and many of them do not attend low progression schools. Thus, interventions solely focusing on deprived areas or specific schools inadvertently exclude a large number of people who would benefit from them. Recent research has shown that Scottish cities are becoming less segregated and this calls for an individual-based approach (such as the Pupil Premium in England).

The second issue is that a myriad of interventions are implemented in schools (sometimes in the same schools and at the same time) and in HE institutions but it is difficult to establish which interventions are the most effective since no robust evaluation has been carried out. In a time of limited funding, a cost-effectiveness evaluation of the different interventions is essential to decide which intervention should be retained. The strong commitment of the Scottish Government to free tuition fees has led to the imposition of a cap in student numbers and this has reduced the universities' capacity to expand to accommodate non-traditional students. As stated above, the targeted places made available by universities through the additional funding provided by the SFC have proved to be successful. However, due to cuts, this extra funding has been withdrawn. Furthermore, it should be recognised that the articulation route from college to university has its limitations. HNC/ HND programmes were originally designed to provide vocational, practical education and training and not to prepare students for university. There is a risk that they will become a hybrid which will not serve well either their original function to prepare for employment or their new function to facilitate entry to university. Finally, another important issue is related to what happens after widening participation students enter HE. Contextualised admission criteria, progression to degree-level courses of articulating students, access and bridging courses help to get disadvantaged students through the door but do not eliminate the other hurdles they encounter to successfully complete their HE degree. A more consistent, coordinated and effective support system is needed within all HE sector.

These are some of the challenges ahead that the education sectors and policymakers will need to tackle if they want to widen HE opportunities to all those who have the ability and aspirations to study in HE. The newly appointed Commissioner for Fair Access, Professor Peter Scott, will have a key role in providing strategic leadership and driving substantial progress towards this ultimate goal. However, his action will need to be supported by coordinated efforts from all those involved in schools, colleges and universities. Only in this way will a substantial improvement in the education experience and in the life chances of many disadvantage people be achieved.

# REFERENCES

Gallacher, J. (2009) 'Higher education in Scotland's colleges: a distinctive tradition', *Higher Education*, 63 (4), 384–401.

Gallacher, J. (2014) 'Higher education in Scotland: differentiation and diversion? The impact of college-university progression links', *International Journal of Lifelong Education*, 33 (1), 96–107.

Hunter Blackburn, L., Kadar-Satat, G., Riddell, S. and Weedon, E. (2016) *Access in Scotland: Access to Higher Education for People from Less Advantaged Backgrounds in Scotland*. Online at www.suttontrust.com/wp-content/uploads/2016/05/Access-in-Scotland_May2016.pdf

Iannelli, C. (2011) 'Educational expansion and social mobility', *Social Policy and Society*, 10 (2): 251–64. © Cambridge University Press, reproduced with permission.

Iannelli, C., Gamoran, A. and Paterson, L. (2011) 'Scottish higher education, 1987–2001: expansion through diversion', *Oxford Review of Education*, 37 (6): 717–41.

Kadar-Satat, G., Iannelli, C. and Croxford, L. (2016) *Beyond Access to HE: Widening Access Initiatives and Student Retention in Scotland*. Edinburgh: AQMeN, University of Edinburgh. Online at www.research.aqmen.ac.uk/files/2017/07/Beyond-Access-to-HE-FINAL_2.pdf

Paterson, L. (1997) 'Trends in higher education participation in Scotland', *Higher Education Quarterly*, 51, 29–48.

Paterson, L., Bechhofer, F. and McCrone, D. (2004) 'Education and life chances', in *Living in Scotland: Social and Economic Change since 1980*. Edinburgh: Edinburgh University Press.

Scottish Government (2016) *Summary Statistics for Attainment, Leaver Destinations and Healthy Living*. Online at www.gov.scot/Publications/2016/06/4523/downloads

Scottish Funding Council (2016) *Higher Education Students and Qualifiers at Scottish Institutions 2014–15*, Edinburgh: SFC. Online at www.sfc.ac.uk/communications/Statisticalpublications/2016/SFCST052016.aspx

## Websites

Dearing Report at www.educationengland.org.uk/documents/dearing1997/dearing1997.html

Garrick Report at www.leeds.ac.uk/educol/ncihe/scottish.htm

Robbins Report at www.educationengland.org.uk/documents/robbins/robbins1963.html

# 76

# From Adult Education to Lifelong Learning

*Janis Davidson*

## INTRODUCTION

In this chapter differing perspectives are identified on the role and purpose of the provision of learning opportunities for adults that are reflected in research and practice as well as policy. The development of provision is described, beginning with the outcomes of a review of adult education in the 1970s (Scottish Education Department, 1975), and concluding with an overview of current policy statements on adult and lifelong learning. I suggest that the move from adult education to adult and lifelong learning is more than simply a change in terminology. These are not interchangeable expressions and do represent varying views about the potential contribution of adult learning opportunities to positive outcomes for individual learners and their families, as well as wider Scottish society.

The potential for a range of positive outcomes from the provision of learning opportunities for adults has been recognised in current research and policy, by adult education practitioners, and of course by learners themselves. However, despite a stated ambition that 'the outcomes that learners achieve will be world-leading' (Education Scotland and Scottish Government, 2014, p. 6), this aspect of Scottish education remains the smallest, at least in terms of government funding. Due in part to changing government priorities since the latter half of the last century, the way in which learning opportunities for adults are organised and supported is specific to the Scottish context. Here, there have been tensions that arise from contrasting perspectives on the role and purpose of provision that stress the importance of the economy, the individual learner and society (Cooke, 2006), although it could be argued that, since the financial crash in 2008/9 and subsequent challenging fiscal times, there has been greater emphasis on the economy. In Scottish policy terms, adult education lies between two main policy strands: that which affects informal and community-based adult learning and that which has the development of skills at the heart of its agenda. However, it is connected to a wide range of government priorities including health, adult literacies, family learning and community empowerment.

The educational provision that is the focus of this chapter does not include formal further and higher education that is addressed elsewhere in this text (principally Chapters 1, 6 and 7 in Section I, but see also in the other chapters in this Section IX and Chapter 100 in Section XII), and it is separate from in-service professional and continuing training and development opportunities provided by employers. However, these organisations are often partners in the provision of a variety of learning opportunities for adults, sometimes as part of outreach activities.

## FORMAL, NON-FORMAL OR INFORMAL?

It is not easy to clarify the terms that are being used in any discussion of the education of adults, given debate concerning the various contexts in which learning can take place. The term 'adult' is itself contested, but this chapter addresses learning provision that is outside the compulsory education system and is targeted to learners aged 16+. In some of the literature, the terms used to describe education are formal, non-formal and informal. Tight (1996) suggests that what we think of as *formal education* is the system that is sponsored by the state. It is delivered within educational institutions such as schools, further education colleges and universities, and the learning is often accredited. In this categorisation, formal education is associated with a curriculum that is designed in advance, and has explicitly stated learning outcomes. *Non-formal* learning is delivered outside formal education institutions, by a range of organisations that are not bound by the constraints of the system. Nonetheless, *non-formal education* is a planned activity that sets out to facilitate learning. Without the regulation associated with the formal system, there is greater scope for aspects of the curriculum to be negotiated with participants. Tight identifies *informal* as describing all kinds of education not included in the formal and non-formal categories. It refers to the kind of incidental learning that arises from everyday events and experiences and occurs throughout our lives. Examples are learning from travel, from interactions with friends and family, from television and the Internet, and it encompasses both planned and unintended learning. Using this categorisation, many learning opportunities for adults that are discussed in this chapter could be described as non-formal, but there are overlaps among the categories. For example, some non-formal adult learning opportunities include an option to be accredited by the formal system. Also, non-formal and informal education can take place within the buildings of formal institutions. Furthermore, education both within and outside the formal system is sometimes described as informal, because the teaching makes use of less formal participatory, or student-centred methods. In Scotland, there is a particular type of community-based adult learning (CBAL) that is sometimes referred to as informal learning but is planned and organised activity, with associated learning outcomes. Key features of this type of provision are that it is targeted to those that have been excluded or disadvantaged for a range of reasons, that the curriculum or content is negotiated with learners and it aims to address issues that are of concern to them. It is difficult therefore to provide a single definition of adult education, as boundaries between different types of provision are often blurred. Furthermore, terminology has changed over time, reflecting, to an extent, changing views about the purpose and potential contribution of provision.

## EARLY ADULT EDUCATION

The roots of adult education can be seen in the commitment to the provision of education for religious discipline and spiritual reform following the Scottish Reformation (Cooke, 2006). Later, in the early eighteenth century, religious concerns continued to serve as the impetus for the provision of organised learning opportunities for adults. Examples are the library scheme and the 'night schools for servants and adults' in the Highlands sponsored by the General Assembly of the Church of Scotland (Cooke, 2006, p. 16). During the nineteenth and early twentieth centuries two traditions developed that arose from differing perspectives. One was a 'respectable' tradition in which education for the poor was promoted by wealthy members of society. This tradition had its base in Calvinist ideas of self-improvement, but can be linked also to the increasing need for a skilled workforce brought about by industrialisation (Tett, 2010). The second tradition was a radical adult education that grew from working-class movements that sought to educate men and women in order to better understand their circumstances, with the aim of effecting social change (Tett, 2010). Although these can be seen as conflicting traditions, Cooke (2006) has noted that notions of self-improvement and a 'desire to "get on" in life' (p. 1) have been an incentive for radical adult education as well as the motivation for individual development seen in the 'respectable' tradition. Throughout the first half of the twentieth century, adult education in this tradition developed through university extramural provision and evening classes provided by local authorities. At the same time, radical education for working men continued to be provided by socialist educators (Tett, 2010). The Workers' Educational Association (WEA) was another provider of adult education during this period, and there was some rivalry between it and providers of more radical socialist education in Scotland, rooted in ideological differences (Cooke, 2006). Despite these developments, it has been observed that there was relatively little organised adult education provision in Scotland until the middle of the twentieth century. A report produced by the Committee of Inquiry that carried out a review of adult education (Scottish Education Department, 1975) observed that: 'Scotland was very much slower than England to develop adult education in an organised way' (p. 2). Nonetheless, the development of a range of learning opportunities for adults has continued since the time of the review to today.

## ADULT EDUCATION IN SCOTLAND: DIFFERING PERSPECTIVES

Learning opportunities for adults encompass a diverse and complex array of provision. Some examples are small discussion groups, courses that support individuals to return to learning or employment, provision that aims to develop literacy and basic skills, as well as a range of interest-based and some accredited provision. The variety of providers is equally diverse, ranging from small, self-constituted groups to local authorities, and the third sector. In some instances, these providers work in partnership with further and higher education institutions with the aim of widening access to more formal types of learning and creating routes for learner progression. Within this range, various views on the role, purpose and potential contribution of provision can be identified. Cooke (2006) has described these as: 'serving the needs of the economy, the interests of the individual, or fostering the democratic society' (p. 172). In this chapter, I make use of these categories in order to compare and contrast them but, in practice, there are overlaps for learners, providers and policymakers.

In the first view, the role for adult learning is to contribute to *economic outcomes both for the individual learner and for society*. The context for this perspective is the emergence of the idea of a 'knowledge society' that places increasing importance on knowledge and information for economic growth. Developments in information and communication technologies and the economic and social effects of globalisation are part of this landscape (Field, 2006). It can be argued that adult learning opportunities that aim to develop learners' vocational skills benefit individuals through improved access to employment and potential for increased income. In addition, there is a potential contribution to society as a whole through increased competitiveness in business leading to a stronger economy. However, Tett (2010) has questioned the assumed link between participation in vocational training and economic benefits, observing that any connection is complex and may not lead to prosperity for all. There is potential for inequality if opportunities are targeted to and taken up by those who are already highly skilled. A further issue is whether the responsibility for updating the skills of the workforce is seen as lying with adult learners themselves, with the risk that individuals are criticised for not participating in continuous learning to meet the needs of their employers and society in general (Field, 2006). A problem with emphasising the economic benefits arising from adult learning provision is that the focus is on the workforce, leaving out the many adults that for a variety of reasons are not in employment.

A contrasting perspective on adult learning is that the purpose is *individual personal development*. The aim here is to facilitate learners' achievements, in relation to their own goals and interests. Potential outcomes of participation from this standpoint include better health, increased confidence, improved family relationships, or simply the personal satisfaction derived from increased knowledge of a particular subject of interest. Learning opportunities for adults in this perspective might provide scope for individuals to develop knowledge and skills that improve their employability, but this is not the main aim. A report of three-year longitudinal research that was undertaken across the UK, supports the idea 'that learning "means" and "does" much more in the lives of adults' (Biesta et al., 2011, p. 11) than the narrow economic view sometimes prioritised in policy. This large-scale research project found evidence of the 'ubiquity and variety' (p. 11) of adult learning as well as the value some adults place on the process of learning, rather than any specified outcome. In Scotland, research undertaken into learners' perceptions of their participation in community-based adult learning (Macintyre, 2012) found that this type of provision was linked to educational, social and personal progression for participants, but did not lead directly to economic gain in terms of improved access to employment or promotion at work. In this research, CBAL had supported participants to achieve personal development in a range of ways and was linked closely to individual learners' motivation and ambitions. Within the personal development perspective, a stated aim is sometimes to support participants to become self-directed learners, in order to explore and understand alternative views of the world. This can be seen as one of the main goals of participation in learning for individuals, or it can be seen as contributing to a third perspective on adult learning: social change.

In this third view, learning provision for adults has *a social purpose*. It offers an opportunity for learners to develop their knowledge and skills with the aim of supporting collective action to bring about social change. The beliefs of Paulo Freire, a Brazilian revolutionary educator working with adults living in poverty in the last century, have been influential in this idea of adult education. For Freire, a key role for adult education was to facilitate the development of participants' understanding of the society in which they lived, with the explicit aim of changing it. Tett (2010) has observed that although this is a strongly held view for some, there are relatively few educators working within this radical tradition of adult education in the Scottish context. One explanation could be that radical approaches are not always encouraged by providers, perhaps because they can involve community activists making demands for change that challenge those holding power in relation to local decision making. Where this approach *is* found, often in the voluntary sector, the role and purpose of learning provision is to address inequality and disadvantage. Tett has highlighted how social movements, such as the women's movement, disability rights campaigns and environmental action organisations, provide opportunities for learning that challenge dominant views and change how we think about the world. Social movements offer the possibility of building knowledge around a single issue with the aim of revising understanding. Tett suggests that those working within community education (see also Chapter 81) could work effectively with social movements to promote critical thinking and support action for social change.

It is important that these perspectives on adult learning are not seen as mutually exclusive. In practice there are overlaps in terms of the aims of providers, the motivations of learners and the outcomes of participation. For example the skills and knowledge gained from provision that aims to bring about individual development or social change might also improve participants' employment prospects. Similarly, vocational skills-based learning might also lead to increased confidence, or renewed social networks, leading to personal development or social action. Within their research, Bicsta et al. (2011) found that there are varied opinions about what counts as important in learning, and that the views of individual learners might contrast with those expressed in policy. It should be acknowledged too that participation in learning is not always a positive experience, with all learners achieving their goals. In the research carried out in Scotland (Macintyre, 2012), progression was closely connected to the learners' individual circumstances and was influenced by events in their lives. New caring responsibilities, unemployment or ill health, for example, could create barriers to positive outcomes for learners. Within Scottish policy, there are contrasting perspectives on the role and potential contribution of adult learning. As government priorities have changed, so too has the view of how and why learning opportunities for adults should be provided.

## POLICY: ADULT EDUCATION

An early policy document that shaped the way in which adult learning was organised and delivered in Scotland was *Adult Education – The Challenge of Change*, the report from the Committee of Inquiry, chaired by Kenneth Alexander (Scottish Education Department, 1975). Known as the Alexander Report, this document was the outcome of a review of adult education that was to consider 'the aims appropriate to voluntary leisure time courses for adults which are educational but not specifically vocational' (Scottish Education Department, 1975, p. vi), so the focus was local authority provision and was explicitly not learning for work. The Alexander Report described four aims for adult education: to enable adults to achieve a fulfilling personal and social life; to help individuals to access information such as health and consumer information more readily; to encourage acceptance and tolerance in a pluralist society; and to support adults to become involved in decision-making processes (Scottish Education Department, 1975). The view of the purpose of provision that underpinned these aims was linked to personal and social development, and it recognised a role for adult education in supporting adults to manage the challenges of rapid social change. The Alexander Report noted that: 'those to whom adult education should be of most value are least involved' (Scottish Education Department, 1975, p. 15). The committee advocated an expansion of provision, but this was to be targeted to specific groups such as young mothers, the elderly, and adults who worked unsocial hours, as well as others identified as experiencing disadvantage. A further concern was that adult education should more closely meet the needs and aspirations of adults that had not participated in the past. This represented a change for local authority adult education that had comprised mostly traditional evening classes, towards provision more closely linked to learners' interests (Tett, 2010). These twin concerns of *targeting resources towards disadvantaged adults* and *developing provision that was rooted in the interests of learners* reflect an important shift in adult education and remain strong themes in current policy. There was to be a move away from subject-based provision most often accessed by middle class learners towards opportunities for adults experiencing disadvantage in order to address issues identified by them. The Alexander committee recommended that adult education should be brought together with youth and community work, to form a new community education service (Scottish Education Department, 1975, p. 35). The aim here was to strengthen adult education by aligning it with larger and better-resourced youth and community provision (Cooke, 2006). One outcome was that the organisation and delivery of adult education provided by local authorities came to be influenced by a strand of Scottish policy as it applied to community education and later community learning and development (CLD), the term used in current policy to describe learning and development work with young people, adults and communities. CBAL, then, came to be viewed as one aspect of this broader field of practice (see Chapter 81 for more on community education and CLD).

For the next two decades, some adult education, and CBAL in particular, was addressed in policy as part of community education, with professional training being developed that emphasised the features that adult education had in common with the youth and community service. During the same period, other providers such as the Workers Educational Association, voluntary organisations and university extramural departments continued to offer opportunities for adults to learn across a range of subjects and issues. Local government reorganisation in 1996, whereby thirty-two authorities were formed from the regional and district councils, saw reductions in funding and staffing for local authority adult education provision. Thereafter, successive policy developments moved community education towards the realisation of key government priorities of social inclusion, lifelong learning and active citizenship. The purpose of community education, and CBAL as part of that, was linked to both personal development and building 'community capacity', the latter term being associated with groups' abilities to become involved in local decision making to address specific issues. However, the extent to which the status quo is likely to be challenged through participation in learning provision that is funded by the state is open to debate. At the same time, a role was beginning to be established for CBAL to contribute to a lifelong learning agenda, with 'achievement through learning for adults' (Scottish Executive, 2004, p. 8) identified as one of three national priorities for CLD work.

Since the publication of the Alexander Report, the perspective in policy on the role and purpose of adult education has evolved. While acknowledging a social purpose for adult education, the report emphasised its role in individual personal development. Subsequent policy documents have continued to focus on this, but have emphasised the development of groups' capacities to participate in local decision making and contribute to social inclusion as well. A further shift in policy is an increasing focus on identifying measurable outcomes for government-funded adult learning provision, with a requirement that providers are accountable to funders and that their work is available for scrutiny. Since 2002, CBAL has been included in inspections of CLD work that make use of a framework that focuses on the outcomes and impact of provision. While it is important that providers are able to account for the finances they receive from the public purse, one consequence has been that aspects such as qualifications attained by learners, as well as progression (defined largely as moving to other learning opportunities or employment) are prioritised and reported. Other positive outcomes of participation such as self-confidence, sometimes leading to an increased sense of agency (Biesta, et al. 2011) or improved family relationships (Macintyre, 2012), can be more difficult to measure and there is a risk that these are not acknowledged in policy. The focus on learning opportunities that address learners' concerns established by the Alexander committee was continued in later policy documents (see, for example, Scottish Executive, 2004). So too was the prioritisation of funding for disadvantaged and excluded groups.

## POLICY: LIFELONG LEARNING

The way in which adult learning is organised and delivered in Scotland has been influenced by another strand of policy: that which addresses *lifelong learning and skills*. The idea of lifelong learning can be traced to the publication of a report by United Nations Educational Scientific and Cultural Organization (UNESCO) in the early 1970s that discussed the need for lifelong education and focused on personal and social development aims. However, it was the production of a number of policy documents in Europe and the establishment of the European Year of Lifelong Learning in 1996 that led to the term becoming widely used in the UK (Tett, 2010). The phrase first appeared in Scottish policy two years later in *Opportunity Scotland*, a document that included higher and further education, vocational training and informal learning within the definition (Scottish Office, 1998). While *Opportunity Scotland* described a range of individual and societal goals for lifelong learning, preparing adults for work 'to keep pace in the jobs market and ensure Scotland is equipped to compete in the global economy' was seen as an important role (Scottish Office, 1998, p. 4). It has been noted that the move from 'adult education' to 'lifelong' or 'continuing' education in policy was more than a simple change in terminology: 'It signified the end of a tradition and the dismantling of an adult education *movement* which was to be gradually subsumed into a general education and training system (Fieldhouse, 1996, p. 68, emphasis added). In the UK context, Fieldhouse highlighted a shift in policy away from adult education as a way of addressing inequality and disadvantage towards a role for lifelong learning in achieving economic goals. However, as we have seen, some adult education provision in Scotland has continued to be targeted towards specific disadvantaged groups to support individual personal development and achieve the government's goals for social inclusion and active citizenship. A further issue arises from the use of the word 'education' instead of 'learning'. The former suggests the presence of an educator, or at least organised activity with some support for learning. The latter can encompass learning undertaken by individuals alone, thereby placing the responsibility for learning on the individual and potentially removing the need for state support.

Since the beginning of this century there have been several policy statements about lifelong learning in Scotland. In one, a definition of lifelong learning was provided that took account of personal and social development goals as well as economic aims. Priority areas of provision were literacy, numeracy and information technology and other learning related to both work and personal life. The theme of addressing the learning needs of specific groups, such as those with disabilities and retired adults was continued, and the role and potential contribution of provision was linked to personal development as well as vocational skills. In contrast, a different document described the necessity for a lifelong learning system that responded to the needs of employers, defined as a well-educated and highly skilled workforce. Here, again, it was suggested that improving the skills levels of adults is likely to lead to economic outcomes both for individuals and the wider economy. The role of lifelong learning in this strategy is explicitly to develop participants' skills and confidence for work. In this respect, the Scottish approach to lifelong learning echoes the position across the

UK and beyond. Field (2006) suggests that 'public policy tends to be driven, globally, by largely economic concerns: competiveness, rather than citizenship, is the primary focus of policy (p. 11), and he notes that acceptance of this approach to policy on lifelong learning is 'virtually universal' (p. 29), at least in Organisation for Economic Co-operation and Development (OECD) member states. However, policy can reflect the range of government priorities, and these shift with the influences of changing values and global events. The Scottish Government has continued to view lifelong learning as a way of addressing the dual problems of the need for competitiveness in a global economy and tackling social exclusion (Cooke, 2006), perhaps making the assumption that, as adults develop skills for employment through participation in lifelong learning, they will access a range of other opportunities as a result of their inclusion in the workforce.

## FROM ADULT EDUCATION TO ADULT AND LIFELONG LEARNING

Currently, learning opportunities for adults in Scotland are provided by agencies such as local authorities, trades unions, colleges, third sector groups, national organisations and employers (Education Scotland and Scottish Government, 2014). The policy context is complex. Indeed one current document (Education Scotland and Scottish Government, 2014) identifies thirty-one policy priorities associated with CBAL. These are wide-ranging and include: sustainable development; financial capability; health and community empowerment as well as literacies; English for Speakers of Other Languages (ESOL); family learning; and Gaelic. Employability and strategies designed to increase the numbers of young people (post-16) in education, training or employment are an important part of this environment. More specifically, learning for adults has continued to be driven by two main policy strands that affect adult learning, lifelong learning and skills. For example, in the post-recession updated skills strategy (Scottish Government, 2010), the aim is 'a skilled and educated workforce' (p. 9) that will improve productivity and support economic recovery. The policy takes account of the contribution of higher education to the development of skills, through the focus on graduate attributes, and it makes links with a proposed review of post-16 education and vocational training that later identified a key role for further education in developing skills to meet the needs of employers. There is a role for CLD in engaging adults in lifelong learning and to 'establish sustainable programmes for workforce development' (p. 28). Both the skills strategy and the review of post-16 opportunities acknowledge the wider benefits of skills enhancement such as reductions in crime, improved health and greater social cohesion, and there is discussion of how to balance the economic and social benefits of skills development. Nonetheless there is an emphasis on the economy, with the role and purpose of lifelong learning connected strongly to the development of vocational skills to support sustainable economic growth.

In another current document, the terminology used is adult learning (Education Scotland and Scottish Government, 2014). In this 'statement of ambition', adult learning is important for health, family and community but is vital for employability also (p. 4). Adult learning is to be informed by three core principles. The first is that learning should be lifelong, blurring the boundaries between adult and lifelong learning terminology. The theme of addressing the needs of specific groups is continued and adults are to be supported to overcome barriers to engagement with learning associated with age, ability and social background. Second is the principle that adult learning should be life-wide, addressing personal, work, family and community concerns and therefore 'not restricted by vocational imperatives' (p. 6). This statement demonstrates a continued acknowledgement of a role for adult learning beyond the economic. The third principle is that provision should be learner-centred, focused on the needs and interests of learners, continuing this theme in Scottish policy, especially in community-based provision. This document is explicit about the government's ambitions for adult learning in Scotland, stating that learners should be involved in the development of provision, that there should be good quality support and guidance, and that learning opportunities should be widely available, both in local communities and online.

During the ten years of SNP Government in Scotland, learning opportunities for adults have been acknowledged in a range of policy and guidance documents. However, this element of education remains marginal in comparison with formal education, in terms of both visibility and funding. Furthermore, there is a risk that the potential contribution of adult learning to adults' own interests and aspirations will not be recognised, especially if it is discussed solely in relation to government priorities (Crowther, et al., 2014). The importance of measurable outcomes of adult learning has continued to be underlined, with less emphasis on the processes of learning. The statement of ambition is clear: there must be 'strong evidence of personal impact as a result of learning' (Education Scotland and Scottish Government, 2014, p. 10). An unknown factor is the extent to which the various stakeholders in adult learning can be brought together to deliver the high-quality, lifelong and life-wide provision identified in the statement. Providers are likely to hold some of the differing perspectives on the roles and purpose of adult learning discussed in this chapter, presenting a challenge for developing a shared commitment and view about what is needed (Crowther et al., 2014). A potential response is the framework of professional development opportunities for adult learning practitioners to enhance their skills, recommended in the statement of ambition. However, it is not yet clear how this will be enacted.

## CONCLUSION

In this chapter I have tried to provide a flavour of the complex and diverse environment in which learning opportunities for adults are provided. It is difficult to define this aspect of Scottish education that usually takes place outside the formal education system, but includes formal institutions as part of the wide range of organisations that offer learning opportunities for adults. There are contrasting perspectives on the role, purpose and potential contribution of adult learning and these too are not clearly defined, with overlaps and contradictions among the views of the various stakeholders. To an extent developments could be seen as a move from a focus on adult education to support individual personal development and social change, towards an emphasis on the potential contribution that learning for adults can make to economic growth in current policy on lifelong learning and skills. However, as I have argued, the situation is more ambiguous. There has been continued acknowledgement of the various roles and purposes of adult learning within policy, with different emphases reflecting the various priorities for government. This creates potential tensions in the context of competition for funding for this already very under-resourced part of Scottish education.

The publication of the statement of ambition (Education Scotland and Scottish Government, 2014) suggests that adult learning that aims to achieve a range of positive outcomes for individuals, families and communities will continue to be supported in Scotland. An implementation plan and the establishment of a strategic forum demonstrate an intention at least to ensure this type of provision remains part of the adult learning landscape.

However, in a policy context in which sustainable economic growth is a stated priority (Scottish Government, 2010), it will be important that these initiatives are well funded and supported in future policy, if the ambition for adult learning in Scotland is to be achieved.

## REFERENCES

Biesta, G. J. J., Field, J., Hodkinson, P., Macleod, F. J. and Goodson, I. F. (2011) *Improving Learning through the Lifecourse*. Abingdon: Routledge.

Cooke, A. (2006) *From Popular Enlightenment to Lifelong Learning. A History of Adult Education in Scotland 1707–2005*. Leicester: NIACE.

Crowther, J., Gallacher, J. and Osborne, M. (2014) 'A distinctive vision: adult learning in Scotland', *Adults Learning*, 25 (4), 26–31.

Education Scotland and Scottish Government. (2014) *Adult Learning in Scotland: A Statement of Ambition*. Edinburgh: Scottish Government.

Field, J. (2006) *Lifelong Learning and the New Educational Order*, second revised edition. Stoke on Trent: Trentham Books.

Fieldhouse, R. and associates (1996) *A History of Modern British Adult Education*. Leicester: NIACE.

Macintyre, J. (2012) 'Lifeline work: community-based adult learning and learners' personal progression', *Studies in the Education of Adults*, 44 (2), 186–203.

Scottish Education Department (1975) *Adult Education – The Challenge of Change*. Edinburgh: HMSO.

Scottish Executive (2004) *Working and Learning Together to Build Stronger Communities. Scottish Executive Guidance for Community Learning and Development*. Edinburgh: Scottish Executive.

Scottish Government (2010) *Skills for Scotland: Accelerating the Recovery and Increasing Sustainable Growth*. Edinburgh: Scottish Government.

Scottish Office (1998) *Opportunity Scotland. A Paper on Lifelong Learning*. Edinburgh: Stationery Office.

Tett, L. (2010) *Community Education, Learning and Development*. Edinburgh: Dunedin.

Tight, M. (1996) *Key Concepts in Adult Education and Training*. London: Routledge.

# X

# SCOTTISH SOCIETY:
# EDUCATION FOR ALL?

# 77

# Inclusion for All?

*Lisa McAuliffe*

## THE INCLUSION DEBATE

Inclusion is a complex and multidimensional concept. Ongoing debates about inclusion have attempted to address the following key questions: Who is to be included, where, and how? Some scholars (e.g. Ainscow et al., 2006) have differentiated between narrow conceptualisations of inclusion, which equate it with the mainstreaming of children and young people with disabilities, and broad conceptualisations which widen the focus to include all children and young people at risk of marginalisation and exclusion. Broad conceptualisations of inclusion also embrace the adults in and around the school, from staff to parents/carers and the wider community.

A milestone in the inclusion movement was the 1994 Salamanca statement which proclaimed that 'regular schools with [an] inclusive orientation are the most effective means of combating discriminatory attitudes, creating welcoming communities, building an inclusive society and achieving education for all' (UNESCO, 1994, p. ix). However, in order for regular schools to welcome and respond appropriately to diversity in learners, their families and the wider community, a paradigm shift is necessary whereby regular schools are transformed from institutions whose main focus is to serve the needs of dominant groups to spaces that embrace diversity and promote social justice. This is the important difference between integration, where the school remains aligned to dominant norms, and inclusion where the school is flexible, responsive, supportive and accommodating of all learners, staff and visitors. The move from integration to inclusion is a complex and demanding process requiring strategic planning and commitment. Where this process is not supported adequately, the consequences can be detrimental for all involved. Some of the submissions to a recent consultation on additional support for learning (Scottish Parliament Education and Skills Committee, 2017) raise concerns that a number of learners in Scottish schools are set up to fail as a result of being in mainstream classrooms that lack the infrastructure required to meet their needs. These concerns are reminiscent of the 2006 National Association of Schoolmasters/Union of Women Teachers (NAS/UWT) report (MacBeath et al., 2006) which pointed out that, without systematic efforts to transform mainstream schools into inclusive schools, many learners and their teachers are caught in a very challenging and often damaging struggle.

Research (see Topping, 2012 for a recent discussion) has attempted to answer the question: Does inclusion work? Unsurprisingly, no definitive answers have emerged. This is due to methodological issues such as the variation in the definitions of inclusion used in different studies, the differences in the criteria used to determine whether inclusion works, and the difficulty in isolating the impact of other factors on the targeted outcomes. In other words, whether inclusion works or not depends on how it is conceptualised, what outcomes are used to judge its effectiveness, and the extent to which any identified impact can be attributed to it and not to other factors. One conceptual tool that can help us to view inclusion holistically is the presence–acceptance–participation–achievement framework suggested in Farrell and Ainscow (2002). Here, each stage is a prerequisite for the next and all are required for successful inclusion: children and young people must be *present*, *accepted* and valued for who they are, enabled to *participate* in the educational and social experiences the school offers, and empowered to *achieve*. Although this framework is typically used to examine the inclusion experiences of learners, it could also be used to explore the experiences of adults such as staff, parents/carers, and members of the wider community. From this perspective, *presence* can refer to the extent to which diversity is reflected in the staff working in the school and in the parents/carers and members of the wider community contributing to its operation. *Acceptance* can refer to the extent to which all adults are recognised and valued for who they are. *Participation* can refer to the extent to which all adults are enabled to participate in the life of the school. For staff this could involve participating in decision-making groups. For parents/carers and members of the wider community, in addition to contributing to school development in this way, participation could also involve opportunities and experiences which are mindfully planned and sufficiently flexible to include parents/carers who work full-time or have language-related difficulties, perhaps associated with low literacy levels or limited command of the English language. *Achievement* for staff could refer to advancement to promoted posts while for parents/carers and members of the wider community it could involve serving as officers in bodies such as parent councils and parent–teacher associations.

The presence–acceptance–participation–achievement framework provides a helpful structure for understanding inclusion and will be used as a lens through which to examine the current state of inclusion in Scottish education.

## INCLUSION IN SCOTTISH EDUCATION

The conceptualisation of inclusion that is found in current Scottish education policy discourse is broad. The code of practice which provides guidance on the implementation of the Education (Additional Support for Learning) (Scotland) Act (the ASL Act; amended in 2009 and most recently in 2017) points out that the Act aims to ensure that *all* learners receive the support that will enable them to take full advantage of educational opportunities available in Scottish schools. 'Included' is one of the wellbeing indicators listed in *Getting it Right for Every Child* (GIRFEC), the national policy aiming to improve outcomes for all children and young people in Scotland. According to GIRFEC, inclusion means being a full member of the community in which one lives and learns, and having access to the support required to overcome social, educational, physical and economic inequalities. Inclusion is one of the quality indicators in the latest edition of *How Good is Our School? Version 4* (HGIOS4), the self-evaluation framework supporting Scottish schools in their efforts to develop and improve. According to this document, schools must strive to ensure that all learners are included, engaged, supported and involved fully in the life of the school. In addition, HGIOS4 points out that, in an inclusive school, all learners, parents/carers, staff and partners feel respected and are treated in a fair and just manner; the inclusive school values diversity and challenges discrimination. Characteristics such as age, disability, gender reassignment, marriage and civil partnership, pregnancy, race, religion or belief, sex and sexual orientation are not barriers to participation and achievement, while effective strategies are in place to improve attainment for learners facing challenges. Furthermore, children and young people in the inclusive school are knowledgeable about equalities and inclusion, and feel able to challenge discrimination, xenophobia and intolerance. A number of Curriculum for Excellence experiences and outcomes provide schools with opportunities to help learners develop the knowledge and understanding required to think and act as envisaged by HGIOS4. For example, the Health and Wellbeing experiences and outcomes (E&Os) focus on the development of self-awareness and respect for others, the Religious and Moral Education (RME) E&Os address values such as fairness and equality in the context of human rights, while the Social Studies E&Os cover discrimination and its impact on people's lives.

In order to support Scottish schools' efforts to achieve the inclusion aims of education policies, and to implement the inclusion and equality E&Os, the General Teaching Council for Scotland (GTCS) has listed social justice as a core value that must inform and guide teaching and all other professional tasks performed by teachers. According to the GTCS professional standards, teachers must value diversity and show commitment to the principles of democracy and social justice through fair, transparent, inclusive and sustainable practices in relation to: age, disability, gender and gender identity, race, ethnicity, religion and belief, and sexual orientation.

We can conclude, therefore, that an appropriate policy framework is in place to ensure that Scottish education is inclusive for all. However, anecdotal evidence from Scottish educators who are sharing their concerns through various networking platforms, and a number of recent reports, suggest that inclusion at all four levels proposed by the presence–acceptance–participation–achievement framework still remains elusive for some. Using the framework as point of reference, the remainder of this section provides examples that highlight gaps between the rhetoric of inclusion and the reality of inclusion as experienced by some individuals and groups.

Scottish education is doing very well in respect of the first level of the presence–acceptance–participation–achievement framework, as highlighted in a recent Organisation for Economic Co-operation and Development (OECD) report (2015) which characterised Scottish schools as highly inclusive based on the degree to which learners from different socio-economic backgrounds attend the same school. Scottish Government data show that nearly 96 per cent of learners attend mainstream schools and there is a continuing decline in exclusion rates, which currently stand at just under 3 per cent, although it is a concern that this figure includes a disproportionate number of learners with certain characteristics such as additional support needs (Scottish Government, 2017). However, a big challenge to inclusion as presence for all arguably comes from the persistently limited diversity in the teaching profession (see Chapter 87 on ethnicity).

Statistics relating to the second level of the presence–acceptance–participation–achievement framework also give cause for concern. Of the 116 learners with a disability who participated in a recent survey commissioned by ENABLE Scotland (2016), 67 per cent reported that they have been bullied, 62.5 per cent stated that they do not feel understood, and 60 per cent said that they feel lonely. Research exploring the experiences of the lesbian, gay, bisexual and transgender (LGBT) community has also highlighted acceptance and recognition issues. Three quarters of LGBT respondents to a recent study (Equality Network, 2015, sample size: 1,052) stated that they never (39 per cent) or only sometimes

(33 per cent) feel able to be open about their sexual orientation at school, while, according to another study, 90 per cent of LGBT people have experienced homophobia, biphobia and transphobia at school and 64 per cent have been directly bullied because of their sexual orientation or gender identity (Time for Inclusive Education, 2016, sample size: 287; see Chapter 86 on lesbian, gay, bisexual, transgender and intersex (LGBTI)). A 2011 study by the GTCS exploring the experiences of probationary teachers (Matheson and Morris, 2011) found that half of the respondents had not disclosed their disability to GTCS or their authorities due to fears of stigma and concern that disclosure might affect their prospects of employment on completion of the probation. This was a small-scale study with only sixty-six respondents and hence the generalisability of the findings is limited, yet it provides a valuable insight into the perceptions of newly qualified teachers about attitudes towards disability in Scottish schools. The 2010 Scottish Social Attitudes Survey (Ormston et al., 2011) found that 46 per cent of the respondents (sample size: 1,495) considered people from the Gypsy/Traveller community to be unsuitable to work as primary teachers, with 41 per cent feeling the same way about people who experience depression from time to time, 31 per cent giving this answer for people who have had a sex change operation, 18 per cent responding in this way for people who identify as gay or lesbian, and 15 per cent having this attitude towards people who identify as Muslim. Although some improvement was noted in comparison to the responses given to the same question in the 2006 Scottish Social Attitudes Survey (Bromley et al., 2007), and notwithstanding the hope that attitudes have become even more positive since the 2010 (Ormston et al., 2011) survey, taken together the figures in this paragraph suggest that inclusion as acceptance of all still has some way to go in Scottish education.

The picture is not more encouraging with regards to the third level of the presence–acceptance–participation–achievement framework. The 2016 survey commissioned by ENABLE Scotland mentioned above revealed that 46 per cent of the 116 participating learners with disabilities reported that they do not get the same chances to take part in games in the playground as everyone else, 25 per cent do not get to participate in sports at school, and 23 per cent do not get to go on school trips. These figures echo the findings of a 2013 study by Moscardini et al. which showed that learners with additional support needs are under-represented in instrumental instruction in music, and reported the striking finding that from the 5,122 learners who were considered for the purposes of this study, not even one child with a physical disability received instrumental instruction. A further illustration of the gap between rhetoric and reality in respect of inclusion as participation comes from the ENABLE Scotland study which reported that the words or phrases the participating parents/carers (sample size: 503) most commonly used to describe their experiences of the school system were 'stressful' (77 per cent), 'battle' (67 per cent), 'lack of information' (57 per cent) and 'alone' (44 per cent). These figures, coupled with the finding of a 2012 survey by Black and Ethnic Minority Infrastructure in Scotland (BEMIS) showing that 77 per cent of the 328 parent councils who participated in the survey had no ethnic minority members, suggest that more needs to be done to ensure that parents/carers participate as partners in the education of their children, as envisaged by the ASL Act and GIRFEC.

Perhaps the most concerning example in respect of the final level of the presence–acceptance–participation–achievement framework is the persistent gap in the attainment between learners from the most and least advantaged areas in Scotland (defined as such according to the Scottish Index of Multiple Deprivation). For example, in 2015/16, 55 per cent of learners from the least advantaged areas performed well or very well for their level in the P4 Scottish Survey of Numeracy (SSLN) compared to 76 per cent of learners from the most advantaged areas, while 79 per cent of S3 learners from the least advantaged areas achieved Curriculum for Excellence (CfE) third level or better compared to 93 per cent of learners from the most advantaged areas (Scottish Government, 2016). The differences in the attainment levels of specific groups are more pronounced. The 2014/15 Scottish Government data show that only 86 per cent of learners who are looked after left school with at least one qualification at Scottish Credit and Qualifications Framework (SCQF) 3 compared to 98 per cent of all school leavers, while a 2015 report on the attainment of learners with sensory impairments commissioned by the Scottish Parliament showed that learners with visual or hearing impairment leave school with fewer qualifications than their peers who do not have any additional support needs. For example, in 2012/13, 91.7 per cent of school leavers without additional support needs had positive destinations, compared to 85.3 per cent of school leavers with visual impairment and 89.4 per cent of school leavers with hearing impairment – and the figures for school leavers with physical or motor impairment and language or speech difficulties are even lower (81.9 per cent and 80.2 per cent respectively). Efforts to understand and address the reasons for these gaps are ongoing; however, it can be helpful to consider these figures alongside findings of research such as the ENABLE Scotland survey (2016) which pointed out that fewer than 12 per cent of the 204 participating educators felt satisfied that they can meet the educational and developmental needs of learners who have a learning disability, while 62 per cent of the eighty-two participating class/subject teachers said they have experienced stress and professional anxiety, due to not having the right support to meet the needs of these learners. The statistics show that despite the inclusive spirit of education policies and pledges to address inequalities in Scottish education, steep challenges still exist and impede progress. The figures give cause for concern and pose important questions. If the policy framework is inclusive, why is there a gap between policy and practice? If we intend to make Scottish education truly inclusive, as is deserving of the children and young people who attend Scottish schools, their families and the communities to which they belong, then we must ask what stands in the way and what can be done to address the issues. It is to these questions that we will turn next.

## BARRIERS TO INCLUSION

Allan (2013) has highlighted three types of barriers to inclusion: environmental, structural and attitudinal. *Environmental* barriers refer to the physical environment. Although as a result of equality legislation it is now a legal requirement that schools are accessible to users with mobility constraints or other access issues, environmental barriers do not end here. The physical environment includes wall displays, the books in the book corner and school library, the resources used for teaching and learning, and the content of the curriculum. The presence–acceptance–participation–achievement framework can be used here, too, to help us understand what counts as an inclusive environment. Questions to consider include the extent to which the diversity in the community and in society more generally is present in the displays, books and other resources, and in the content of the curriculum. In addition, consideration must be given to how diversity is portrayed – is the message one of acceptance and recognition or is it one that creates a dichotomy between the dominant and minoritised groups and gives the latter 'outsider' status? Are members of diverse backgrounds and with diverse abilities and skills depicted as full participants and achievers? If our intention is to 'get it right for every child', it is important to ensure that every child develops a sense of belonging and attachment to the school as this is a necessary condition for effective learning and participation (Slaten et al., 2016). Cooley's (1902) 'looking glass' theory suggests that our sense of self grows out of our perceptions of what others think of us. Children (and adults) who do not see themselves reflected in the displays, resources or content of the curriculum, or who see their cultures, backgrounds, abilities or skills misrepresented, are unlikely to feel included and this will inevitably affect the extent to which they invest in the school and participate in what takes place in it.

*Structural* barriers can arise from the way schools are organised and operate. Consideration should be given to the extent to which practices, rules, norms, traditions and other organisational patterns are mindful of and proactively responsive to diversity. For example, attention should be focused on what counts as achievement, how it is measured and recorded, and in what ways it informs progression and post-school destinations. Mechanisms for capturing and acting on the views of the school community should ensure that no individual or group is excluded through, for example, lack of flexible tools to capture different voices or dismissal of what may be perceived as 'outsider' perspectives. Processes and procedures associated with the identification of needs and provision of support should enable a fair and responsive allocation of resources. Teaching and learning practices should acknowledge different ways of acquiring and communicating knowledge and the value of different perspectives. Using a relevant and responsive curriculum and pedagogy, and promoting respectful and nurturing relationships can go a long way towards creating supportive infrastructure that can enable all learners to engage and succeed.

*Attitudinal* barriers refer to the values and beliefs about ability, difference, diversity, development and the learning process. Deterministic views about what children can achieve based on their backgrounds, 'labels' or other characteristics can limit their achievements and growth (Florian, 2009). Seeing some children as more worthy of support and resources than others is equally damaging. Attitudinal barriers arise from unexamined assumptions and misconceptions. In many cases, they are the result of the blinding power of one's own privilege which makes it difficult to acknowledge and consider other perspectives and possibilities. Attitudinal barriers are entrenched in one's value system and can have far-reaching implications. As Ainscow (2005, p. 117) aptly put it:

> Even the most pedagogically advanced methods are likely to be ineffective in the hands of those who implicitly or explicitly subscribe to a belief system that regards some students, at best, as disadvantaged and in need of fixing, or, worse, as deficient and, therefore, beyond fixing.

## PROMOTING INCLUSION FOR ALL

Scotland's efforts to provide inclusive education have attracted international recognition (OECD, 2015). However, as the statistics mentioned earlier show, we are still not 'getting it right' for every child or adult in our schools. The previous section highlighted some of the reasons why this may be so. In this section, some suggestions are made that could help us move forward. Rouse (2008) has argued that inclusive practice is developed through knowing, believing and doing. Knowledge about teaching, learning and assessment strategies, classroom organisation and management, child development, the contribution of the family and wider community to education, and what may stand in the way of learning and participation is pivotal to the development and implementation of inclusive practice. However, it is important to remember that knowledge is not fixed but dynamic. Keeping up to date with developments in the field of inclusive education is vital as it can help to challenge outdated notions about development and learning, and replace them with forward thinking that can transform beliefs and actions.

Consideration of action brings us to the issue of pedagogy and the skill set required to identify and remove barriers to learning and participation, and to eliminate discrimination and disadvantage. The argument that there is no one-to-one correspondence between types of pedagogy and specific conditions or 'labels' is well rehearsed and the evidence in support of it is compelling (Florian, 2009). The principles of effective teaching and learning apply to all children, regardless of diagnoses or characteristics. The skills that teachers need to teach all children effectively are the skills associated with high-quality general teaching and include the ability to set high expectations for all, provide appropriate scaffolding, develop thoughtful assessments, be both proactive and responsive, facilitate the active engagement of all learners, promote positive relationships and cooperation, and recognise and build on prior learning and experience (James and Pollard, 2006).

Teachers teach children, not 'labels', not least because no two learners with the same diagnosis are the same. By reducing children to their diagnoses we deny the complexity of human nature and personhood. This is not to trivialise the importance of expertise. In the field of inclusion, expertise refers to the advanced knowledge, understanding and skills some educators have as a result of their practice and engagement with relevant scholarship. However, the role of these educators should not be to take children away to teach them in a particular way that matches their diagnoses or characteristics. Although from time to time it may be necessary for educators with specialist expertise to work with individual children or groups, their role should mainly be to help classroom teachers understand why a child with a specific condition or characteristic may be experiencing barriers to learning and participation and what evidence-based responses may be appropriate in their context. In this way, educators with specialist expertise scaffold the development of classroom teachers and enable them to be teachers of all children.

Much research focusing on teachers' attitudes towards and experiences of inclusion has highlighted the need for more pre- and in-service education about diversity in the classroom (e.g. OECD, 2010). Such findings are often followed by calls for 'more training'. While professional development in the area of inclusive education is key to effective inclusive practice, it is important not to reduce this development to training in the use of specific approaches and tools. *Know-how* is necessary but, arguably, not very useful if separated from *know-why*. As the debate around specialist pedagogy has highlighted, educators' efforts to develop the knowledge, understanding and skills that will enable them to be effective teachers of all children should start with an examination of the values and beliefs that inform their pedagogy, and with a deconstruction of outdated notions about how children learn and develop. In addition, consideration must be given to how the principles of effective pedagogy identified through research such as the Teaching and Learning Research Programme (James and Pollard, 2006) or Learning without Limits (Hart et al., 2004) can be applied across teaching and learning situations and contexts. Once this important foundation is in place, specialist professional development focusing on the barriers that may be linked to particular features of specific conditions or learner profiles can build onto it. Arguably, the most effective professional development combines the latest scholarship on a topic with insights arising from practical experience in the field and an inquiry approach to enhancement. Much useful professional development can occur through collegial interactions within and across learning communities. Coming together to pool expertise, share experiences and develop evidence-informed, context-appropriate solutions to inclusion dilemmas can be enriching, empowering and mutually beneficial. A number of resources are available to help educators explore inclusion issues through professional dialogue. The National Framework for Inclusion (Scottish Teacher Education Committee, 2014), which is mapped onto the GTCS professional standards and invites practitioners to consider key questions in relation to inclusive practice, can be a powerful tool for collegial professional learning and enquiry but also for individual professional update.

A final point concerns resources. Reports that educators feel they need more 'training' in the area of inclusion tend to also note concerns about lack of resources (Topping, 2012). An important question here is: What type of resources are both effective and efficient? If resources refer to commercial packages offering 'off-the-shelf' solutions, then a critical approach is required. Although many of these can be very useful, before schools invest in them questions should be asked about the philosophy that underpins them and the evidence that supports their claims. If resources refer to additional staff such as learning support assistants, consideration must be given to their deployment. Research has shown that in some cases learners with additional support needs become the responsibility of the learning support assistants and have less contact with the class teacher than learners without additional support needs which can affect negatively their academic progress (Blatchford et al., 2011). Although in principle having more adults in the classroom can be beneficial, it is important to consider the type of contribution each adult makes to ensure that learners receive maximum benefit.

## CONCLUSION

Scotland's inclusive education policy is considered one of the country's greatest strengths. However, as suggested by the concerns shared during the recent consultation on additional support for learning held by the Scottish Parliament Education and Skills Committee (2017), and as shown in a number of recent reports such as the ones mentioned earlier, there is still much scope for improvement. In this chapter, a number of barriers that can hamper efforts to get it right for every child and adult member of the school community were identified and some ways to overcome them were proposed. There is genuine commitment in Scotland to promote inclusion for all. Working together within education and across children's services, and drawing on assets available at local and national level, we can ensure that Scottish schools provide the truly inclusive educational experiences that all learners and the communities around them deserve.

## REFERENCES

Ainscow, M. (2005) 'Developing inclusive education systems: what are the levers for change?' *Journal of Educational Change*, 6 (2), 109–24.
Ainscow, M., Booth, T. and Dyson, A. (2006) *Improving Schools, Developing Inclusion*. London: Routledge.
Allan, J. (2013) 'Inclusion for all?' in T. G. K. Bryce, W. M. Humes, D. Gillies and A. Kennedy (eds), *Scottish Education, Fourth Edition: Referendum*. Edinburgh: Edinburgh University Press, pp. 787–95.

BEMIS (2012) *Ethnic Minority Parental Involvement within Parent Groups: (PTAs and Parent Councils)*. Online at http://bemis.org.uk/documents/Outline%20Report%20-%20BEMIS%20SPTC.pdf

Blatchford, P., Russell, A. and Webster, R. (2011) *Reassessing the Impact of Teaching Assistants: How Research Challenges Practice and Policy*. London: Routledge.

Bromley, C., Curtice, J. and Given, J. (2007) *Attitudes to Discrimination in Scotland: 2006 Scottish Social Attitudes Survey*. Online at http://mywf.org.uk/uploads/projects/borderlines/Archive/2007/0054713.pdf

Cooley, C. H. (1902) *Human Nature and the Social Order*. New York: Charles Scribner's Sons.

Farrell, P. and Ainscow, M. (eds) (2002) *Making Special Education Inclusive*. London: Fulton.

Florian, L. (2008) 'Special or inclusive education: future trends', *British Journal of Special Education*, 35 (4), 202–8.

Florian, L. (2009) 'Towards an inclusive pedagogy', in P. Hick, R. Kershner and P. T. Farrell (eds), *Psychology for Inclusive Education – New Directions in Theory and Practice*. Abingdon: Routledge.

ENABLE Scotland (2016) *#IncludED in the Main?!* Online at https://www.enable.org.uk/wp-content/uploads/2017/08/IncludED-in-the-Main-22-Steps-on-the-Journey-to-Inclusion.pdf

Equality Network (2015) *The Scottish LGBT Equality Report: Lesbian, Gay, Bisexual and Transgender (LGBT) People's Experiences of Inequality in Scotland*. Online at www.equality-network.org/wp-content/uploads/2015/07/The-Scottish-LGBT-Equality-Report.pdf

Hart, S., Dixon, A., Drummond, M. J. and McIntyre, D. (2004) *Learning without Limits*. Maidenhead: Open University Press.

James, M. and Pollard, A. (2006). *Improving Teaching and Learning in Schools. A Commentary by the Teaching and Learning Research Programme*. London: Institute of Education, University of London.

MacBeath, J., Galton, M., Steward, S., MacBeath, A. and Page, C. (2006) *The Costs of Inclusion: A Study of Inclusion Policy and Practice in English Primary, Secondary and Special Schools*. Online at https://www.educ.cam.ac.uk/people/staff/galton/Costs_of_Inclusion_Final.pdf

Matheson, I. and Morris, P. (2011) *Reflecting on Experiences of People with Disabilities Participating in the Teacher Induction Scheme: Report on Survey Responses*. Online at www.gtcs.org.uk/web/FILES/FormUploads/reflecting-on-experiences-people-with-disabilities-in-tis.pdf

Moscardini, L., Barron, D. and Wilson, A. (2013) 'Who gets to play? Investigating equity in musical instrument instruction in Scottish primary schools', *International Journal of Inclusive Education*, 17 (6), 646–62.

OECD (2010) *Educating Teachers for Diversity. Meeting the Challenge*. Online at https://www.oecd.org/edu/ceri/educatingteachersfordiversitymeetingthechallenge.htm

OECD (2015) *Improving Schools in Scotland: An OECD Perspective*. Online at https://www.oecd.org/education/school/Improving-Schools-in-Scotland-An-OECD-Perspective.pdf

Ormston, R., Curtice, J., McConville, S. and Reid, S. (2011) *Scottish Social Attitudes Survey 2010: Attitudes to Discrimination and Positive Action*. Online at www.equalitiesinhealth.org/public_html/documents/SASFindings_000.pdf

Rouse, M. (2008) 'Developing inclusive practice: A role for teachers and teacher education?' *Education in the North*, 16 (1), 6–11.

Scottish Government (2016) *National Improvement Framework for Scottish Education: 2016 Evidence Report*. Online at www.gov.scot/Resource/0051/00511488.pdf

Scottish Government (2017) *Statistics: School Education*. Online at http://www.scotland.gov.uk/Topics/Statistics

Scottish Parliament (2015) *10th Report (Session 4): Attainment of Pupils with a Sensory Impairment*. Online at www.parliament.scot/parliamentarybusiness/CurrentCommittees/92452.aspx

Scottish Parliament Education and Skills Committee (2017) *Additional Support Needs in School Education*. Online at www.parliament.scot/parliamentarybusiness/CurrentCommittees/103397.aspx

Scottish Teacher Education Committee (2014) *National Framework for Inclusion*. Online at www.frameworkforinclusion.org/pages/index.php?category=0

Slaten, C. D., Ferguson, J. K., Allen, K., Brodrick, D. and Waters, L. (2016) 'School belonging: a review of the history, current trends, and future directions', *The Educational and Developmental Psychologist*, 3 (1), 1–15.

Time for Inclusive Education (2016) *Attitudes towards LGBT in Scottish Education*. Online at www.tiecampaign.co.uk/research

Topping, K. (2012) 'Conceptions of inclusion: widening ideas', in C. Boyle and K. Topping (eds), *What Works in Inclusion?* Maidenhead: Open University Press, pp. 9–19.

UNESCO (1994) *World Conference on Special Needs Education: Access and Quality*. Paris: UNESCO.

# 78

# Additional Support Needs

*Lio Moscardini*

## INTRODUCTION

The concept of additional support needs has provided a framework, in theory at least, for the recognition of all children requiring additional support. Traditionally, responses to difference have been based on a medical model of identifying a deficit within individual children and categorising and segregating on the basis of this diagnosis. The adoption of the term *additional support needs* in the early 2000s represented a significant conceptual departure from the construct of *special educational needs* by taking into account broader social and contextual factors that give rise to the need for support. While policy and legislation set out the underlying principles of support and their application in practice, arguably weak understandings of the concept of additional support needs has led to the term being used as a proxy for special educational needs. Consequently, there is a risk that these principles become applied primarily to specific groups of children based on categories of disability or models of deficiency. The move towards a broader interpretation of educational support should be seen within the context of inclusion. Since its establishment in 1999, the Scottish Parliament has introduced laws relating to education that are concordant with the United Nations Convention on the Rights of the Child and with European human rights legislation. These developments reflect a shift from the needs-driven agenda of the latter decades of the twentieth century towards a recognition of rights and entitlement of all children to a quality education.

The Education (Additional Support for Learning) (Scotland) Act (the ASfL Act) was passed in 2004 and the Code of Practice published the following year. Amendments to the Act in 2009 and revisions by Scottish Government to the Code of Practice (Scottish Government, 2010), saw educational support frameworks situated alongside Curriculum for Excellence and within the overarching national policy of *Getting it Right for Every Child* (GIRFEC), now enshrined in law in the Children and Young People (Scotland) Act 2014. Through the legislative frameworks and related policies, which have taken into consideration factors relating to disadvantage and social deprivation, Scotland has adopted a broad, inclusive stance on educational support that reflects the position outlined by the Organisation for Economic Co-operation and Development (OECD), as indicated in Chapter 77. The extent to which the rhetoric of inclusion and the translation of policy into practice have been realised in the experiences of children requiring additional support continues to engender debate. A progress report on the implementation of the Act concluded that 'more needs to be done' for children from disadvantaged circumstances (Scottish

Government, 2012, p. 26). In February 2015, Scottish Government initiated the Scottish Attainment Challenge and underpinned this with the National Improvement Framework that was launched in January 2016 with the key aim of closing the poverty-related attainment gap. The Education (Scotland) Act 2016 has incorporated the reporting procedure for that framework into statute.

The narrative of vulnerable and disadvantaged children in the educational system predates the establishment of compulsory education in 1872. The challenge presented by particular learners who stress the educational system and defy categorisation has existed since Victorian times, their underachievement even then recognised as related to social deprivation. Once labelled as 'backward' children, the perceived requirements for them at various times have included treatment following a designation of handicap; education-based diagnosis; a response to an identified need; and, most recently, the recognition of the 'reasons for support'. There is an underlying pattern that resonates with current issues and practices, which remain unresolved either by individual pathologising or by systemic approaches. The discussion in this chapter is situated against a background of the ongoing narrative of children who, while recognised within the construct of additional support needs, are not generally recognised within the discrete category of disability.

## THE CONCEPT OF ADDITIONAL SUPPORT NEEDS

The statutory definition set out in the Education (Additional Support for Learning) (Scotland) Act 2004, amended 2009, is:

> A child or young person has additional support needs for the purposes of this Act where, for whatever reason, the young person is, or is likely to be, unable without the provision of additional support to benefit from school education provided or to be provided for the child or young person. (www.gov.scot/Publications/2009/11/03140104/0, Section 1.1)

This provision means that many children, who might not have been identified within the previous framework of special educational needs, are now recognised through statute as being entitled to additional support. The need for support may be short term or long term and may include:

- having motor or sensory impairments;
- being bullied;
- being particularly able or talented;
- having experienced a bereavement;
- experiencing interrupted learning;
- having a learning disability;
- being looked after by a local authority;
- having a learning difficulty;
- living with parents who are substance abusers;
- living with parents who have mental health problems;
- having English as an additional language;
- not attending school regularly;
- having emotional or social problems;
- being on the child protection register;
- being a young carer. (Scottish Government, 2010, p. 13)

This list is not exhaustive, nor are the circumstances assumed to mean that additional support will be necessary.

The legislation also imposes a duty on education authorities to identify and keep under review any additional support needs of children and the adequacy of any support provided. The term 'additional support' is defined in the 2009 legislation as something that is 'additional to, or otherwise different from provision (whether or not educational provision) made generally for children' (Section 1.3). This is an important point of law, which helps to clarify a misconception expressed by some practitioners, that 'all children have additional support needs'. To suggest that all children require additional support implies that no child requires support that is in any way additional or different to the support that all children receive.

## THE LEGISLATIVE FRAMEWORK

The amendments to the 2004 Act which came into force in November 2010 included: a broadening of the concept of 'additional support' to include support from services outwith the school and beyond education; further requirements in relation to children who are looked after by a local authority; an extension of the rights of parents relating to placing requests; and access to Additional Support Needs Tribunals for Scotland.

An important development in the chronology of Scottish legislation was the Standards in Scotland's Schools etc. Act 2000. Section 15, which took effect in August 2003, set out the requirement of mainstream education for all children in what is frequently referred to as 'the presumption of mainstream'. Exception to this requirement can be made on the grounds of suitability of such placement based on: the child's ability or aptitude, unreasonable public expenditure and any detrimental effect on other children with whom the child may be educated. Notwithstanding this provision and following recent campaigns by lobbying groups, Scottish Government has committed to a review of this aspect of the legislation (at the time of writing). In October 2002, the Disability Strategies and Pupils' Educational Records (Scotland) Act 2002 took effect, placing responsibility on education authorities and schools to recognise the rights of children with disabilities and to meet their needs effectively by developing better communication, increased participation of the child and improvements to the physical environment. These Acts underlined further the shift away from a recognition of need and towards the rights and entitlements of children.

More recently, the Children and Young People (Scotland) Act 2014 has made provision for a single planning framework, the Child's Plan, which should be available for children who require extra support that is not generally available. The Act also makes provision for all children from birth to 18 to have a 'named person', a single professional point of contact for children and young people, parents and relevant professional agencies to provide support and facilitate access to any services that may be required. The introduction of a named person for every child was seen as controversial by some and challenged by representative groups. Both the Outer and the Inner House of the Court of Session rejected petitions contesting its introduction. A subsequent judgement by the UK Supreme Court in July 2016 determined that the provision of a named person for every child is compatible with European Union law and does not breach human rights. At the time of writing, the implementation of this provision has been delayed and the revision process is ongoing.

It is worth recalling that in 1978 the Warnock Report, a UK-wide report, famously recognised that about 'one in five' children could experience difficulties in learning at some point in their school career. In Scotland in the same year, a report by Her Majesty's Inspectorate (HMI) and published by Her Majesty's Stationery Office, 'The Education of Pupils with Learning Difficulties in Primary and Secondary Schools in Scotland', sometimes referred to as the PWLD report, stated that up to 50 per cent of children in the educational system might experience difficulties in learning at some point. Two fundamental themes emerged from the PWLD report: the need to recognise educational support as a whole school responsibility and the recognition of the curriculum as a barrier to learning. Forty years later, we are still wrestling with the idea of the learning environment as a contributing factor to learning difficulties for a large group of pupils. In recent years, there has been a rise in the number of children recorded as having additional support needs with considerable variation across local authorities. In 2015, 22.5 per cent of the school population were recorded as having additional support needs, which represents an increase of 4.5 per cent since 2005. This is more likely to be accounted for by changes in the recording process rather than by changes in the actual pupil population (Riddell and Weedon, 2016)

## SUPPORTING CHILDREN'S LEARNING: CODE OF PRACTICE

The current Code of Practice (Scottish Government, 2010) provides guidance on the legislation. It outlines the following four factors, which give rise to additional support needs: the learning environment; family circumstances; disability or health need and social and emotional factors. Additional support needs arising from the *learning environment* relate to barriers to learning created by, amongst other things, inflexible curricular arrangements and inappropriate approaches to learning and teaching. *Family circumstances* include a home life that is disrupted by poverty, domestic abuse, parental alcohol or drug misuse, homelessness and parental health problems. Issues relating to *disability or health need* are most closely related to previous special educational needs categories: for example, sensory impairment, autism spectrum conditions, learning difficulties and mental health problems. *Social and emotional* factors may be related to behavioural difficulties as well as issues such as bullying or racial discrimination (Scottish Government, 2010, pp. 24–5). This elaboration of factors that give rise to additional support needs takes into consideration social issues, which arguably are less explicit in more traditional constructions of special education needs and reflects the position taken by the OECD (2007).

### Support Frameworks

The revised Code of Practice recognises Curriculum for Excellence as an inclusive and flexible curriculum for all learners. It also sets out a framework that connects the process of staged assessment and support to the integrated services approach outlined in the policy *Getting it Right for Every Child* (GIRFEC). GIRFEC is a national programme underpinned by the principles of the United Nations Convention on the Rights of the Child; it aims to ensure that all children receive the help they need, when it is needed, through a coordinated approach across all agencies. The Code of Practice does not prescribe a specific model for assessment and support procedures to be adopted by all authorities, rather it sets out guidance on the Act's provisions and a framework for a staged approach to identifying and supporting children with additional support needs that each of the thirty-two education authorities should develop. Arguably, this is respectful of the diversity and range of provision across Scotland. However, it has resulted in variations of practice and a bewildering array of terminology relating to individualised support planning across education authorities.

## Staged Intervention

All education authorities have put this staged approach in place with most authorities typically setting out about four stages. At the initial stage, identification and support takes place within the classroom. At the next stage this moves beyond the classroom but remains within the school, for example other members of staff may help in the assessment and support process. Beyond this stage, support goes outwith the school but remains within educational services, for example referral to psychological services. At the highest level, support is required from agencies outwith education, for example social services or the health board. These stages are not necessarily sequential or hierarchical and some children may require high tariff support to be put in place immediately because of the complexity of their support needs. Parents, carers and the child should also be involved in the process.

The process of staged intervention takes into consideration the responsibility every teacher has in supporting learners. However, there is a lack of clarity surrounding the earliest phase of staged intervention, usually referred to as Stage 1, which is problematic. Classroom-based levels of support occur regularly within the context of the routine, ongoing support from the class teacher. If a child were deemed to require additional support within the classroom, then it would seem appropriate that information about the child and the support processes involved should be communicated. The extent to which this should be formalised presents a dilemma. Formalisation may constrain this process. On the other hand, the assumption that communication will occur effectively through informal mechanisms may result in some children not receiving the support they need. The problem is compounded further by the distinction between 'Universal Support' and 'Targeted Support' as set out by Education Scotland (see, for example, at https://blogs.glowscotland. org.uk/glowblogs/eslb/category/supporting-learners/universal-support/page/2/) whose online definition of the first of these is not consistent with that set out in the Code of Practice, which implies a more individualised response (Scottish Government, 2010, p. 38). At the time of writing, Education Scotland documentation states that every child is entitled to 'Universal Support' with all staff having a responsibility in this. 'Targeted Support' is described as 'additional focused support ... usually co-ordinated by staff with additional training and expertise through a staged intervention process.' This raises the issue of the role and responsibility of the class teacher in providing support, particularly through the process of staged intervention at the earliest stage (Stage 1). The distinction as set out by Education Scotland is problematic for two reasons. First, it undermines the teacher's role and responsibility in providing targeted support in the classroom by suggesting this is the role of a more qualified 'expert' from outwith the classroom. This is not to suggest that deeper knowledge and understanding may not be required to support particular learners. The second problem relates to the process of staged intervention. Most local authorities' guidelines make clear that, at the earliest stage, the process starts in the classroom with the class teacher. This is particularly significant given that not all children identified at Stage 1 are recorded formally. The Education Scotland account of targeted support seems to reflect a higher level of staged intervention, thus negating the purpose of Stage 1. This is a cause for concern particularly if one considers which children are at risk of being overlooked in this process. It does not seem unreasonable to suggest that appropriate pedagogical responses within the context of the learning environment of the classroom are an appropriate Stage 1 strategy within the scope of the class teacher.

Although the 'learning environment' is recognised within the Code of Practice as a factor that gives rise to additional support needs, there is a worrying reluctance to recognise this as a significant barrier to learning for many children. Contrary to HMI recommendations in the 1978 PWLD report, deficit indicators, redolent of remedial and within-child deficit models, continue to be prevail. At the time of writing, information available online through Education Scotland continues to display this deficit model with barriers to learning being described in terms of within-child deficits. The process of staged intervention has been linked to GIRFEC where at each level the need for further support is described as 'situation not resolved and need for further action identified' (Scottish Government, 2010, p. 38). For some children the need for ongoing support will be lifelong, some children in fact possibly requiring multi-agency support from birth. To view children and young people as 'situations to be resolved' flies in the face of fundamental principles of inclusion and support. It would be more appropriate to consider whether further additional support is required.

## Coordinated Support Plans

The coordinated support plan (CSP) is the highest tariff individual support plan relevant to all local authorities. It is the only individualised plan that is statutory and is intended for those children who require support from a range of different services and whose additional support needs arise from complex or multiple factors deemed to have a significant and ongoing effect on the education of the child. There is evidence that the low-incidence group of children who require high levels of support are not assured statutory CSPs, with some local authorities employing non-statutory additional support plans (ASPs) in their place. In relation to the high-incidence group of children who require lower levels of support, issues revolve around identification, recognition and ultimately agency.

The Code of Practice sets out the relationship between the Child's Plan (referred to above) and the CSP in paragraphs 104–5. While the CSP is a multi-agency educational plan, the Child's Plan potentially covers a wider range of issues related to promoting a child's wellbeing and may refer to matters not contained in the CSP.

## ADDITIONAL SUPPORT NEEDS TRIBUNALS SCOTLAND

The Additional Support Needs Tribunals for Scotland (ASNTS) was established in November 2005 following the 2004 Act. The function of the ASNTS is to hear appeals, known as references, made by parents and young people against the decisions of education authorities relating to the provision of educational support. References can relate to CSPs, placing requests and post-school transitions. In March 2011, the jurisdiction of the ASNTS was extended and, consequently, they may also consider references relating to claims of disability discrimination within education. A requirement of the 2009 amendments to the 2004 ASfL Act was a legal duty on the Scottish Government to provide a national advocacy service to parents and young people to support them through the ASNTS process. The providers of this service are known as Let's Talk ASN, a joint initiative of Govan Law Centre and Kindred Advocacy. At the time of writing, the current tribunal system is under revision. It is anticipated that the ASNTS will transfer into the Health and Education Chamber in October 2017.

## ISSUES OF CLASSIFICATION AND REPRESENTATION

In the landmark book, *A Sociology of Special Education*, Sally Tomlinson distinguished between normative and non-normative categories of disability (Tomlinson, 1982): normative categories being those conditions about which there is a general (normative) agreement usually through diagnosis or known aetiology. The non-normative group is comprised of children whose difficulties have no known aetiology; it consists largely of children with general (as opposed to specific) learning difficulties and/or behavioural and emotional difficulties. Tomlinson considered the existence of the group from a sociological perspective arguing that social class has a significant bearing on the identification and response to this particular group of learners. It is the largest group of children with additional support needs in the system and is characterised by disadvantage and low socio-economic status. This group has been recognised within post-Warnock categories of learning difficulties (Norwich and Kelly, 2005) although the extent to which children within this group now come to be identified and supported through the process of staged intervention is unclear.

HMIe identified a 'lack of clarity and consistency' in the collation of data around pupils with additional support needs (HMIe, 2010, p. 9). By definition, the concept of additional support needs implies a fluctuating group, which presents a challenge in quantifying certain groups of learners, most notably those who would be considered with non-normative categories. This relates directly to how (and whether) these children are identified and recorded through a process of staged intervention and how any resultant data come to be inputted statistically. Arguably, the children being counted are those that are most easily identified within what Tomlinson describes as normative categories. An analysis of Scottish Government *Statistical Bulletins* and Pupils in Scotland records from 2004 to 2016, suggests that this may be the case.

Data presented in the *Statistical Bulletins* are problematic in terms of providing a clear picture of the representation and proportionality of particular groups. Scottish Government statisticians work with the various and varied categories and terms presented by local authorities, which have been gathered from schools. For example, in some local authorities, schools inform the authority of those children who are at the higher levels of staged intervention, with children who are supported within the classroom and the wider school not necessarily being recorded beyond the school. It would appear therefore that the figures are largely dependent on how schools and subsequently local authorities interpret and apply the recording processes. This may also explain why children who generally experience difficulties in their learning and who would be considered to have additional support needs may be overlooked in the formal recording process, particularly at the earliest phase of staged intervention, while those children whose difficulties would be considered within normative categories are more readily quantifiable. There appears to be no mechanism within data collection procedures for recognising the potentially large group of learners for whom the learning environment is the source of difficulty. Although the enumeration of non-normative groups is problematic, the prominence of the learning-disabled category is a cause for concern; it is regressive in both overlooking social and environmental factors and in situating the difficulty within the child. Given the expansion of the additional support needs population and the current focus on closing the attainment gap, it is important to apply a more critical analysis from a sociological perspective to explore the underlying processes, which might help to explain this phenomenon.

## TEACHER EDUCATION

The General Teaching Council for Scotland has responsibility for regulating the teaching profession in Scotland. The Standard for Full Registration specifies that registered teachers must effectively identify and respond appropriately to pupils who require additional support. There is also a requirement under the Standard for Initial Teacher Education that programmes of initial teacher education should prepare student teachers in their capacity to support all pupils. Under the Requirements for Teachers (Scotland) Regulations 2005, teachers working with children with visual impairment, hearing impairment or dual-sensory impairment are required to have an additional qualification. There is no legal requirement for an additional qualification for teachers working with any other groups of children or young people with additional support needs. All of the Scottish teacher education institutions offer post-graduate courses to Masters level in the area of inclusive education/educational support. This is within the context of teachers' continuing professional development and is recognised as such by education authorities who identify a qualification in this area as desirable.

While universities have a duty to ensure that students undertaking courses in initial teacher education learn about additional support needs, and this requirement is fulfilled, there are concerns expressed by some third sector organisations that this aspect of teacher professional development is inadequately covered at both pre-service level by universities and post-service by education authorities. The 2010 report of the Donaldson review team, *Teaching Scotland's Future*, also identified a need for increased teacher professional development in the area of additional support needs. It is noteworthy that of the six explicit references to additional support needs within the document, four are qualified by specific reference to dyslexia and autism. There are two issues related to these recommendations: the first is a concern with the notion of 'training' as something that is separate from the teachers' ongoing professional development; the second relates to the conceptualisation of additional support needs being applied. If the call is for further teacher development in additional support needs, then there is a need to be specific about what is meant by additional support needs – implicitly the call seems to be for teachers to know more about particular disabilities and impairments. Donaldson makes this explicit in relation to the two high-profile and important fields of dyslexia and autism. It is worth perhaps reflecting on the need for professional development that focuses on the development of teaching approaches that support the participation of all children.

The National Framework for Inclusion (www.frameworkforinclusion.org) was commissioned by Scottish Government and developed by the Scottish Teacher Education Committee Inclusion Group, now the Scottish Universities Inclusion Group, a working group of academics from each of the Scottish initial teacher education institutions. It aims to support students and teachers in developing their knowledge and understanding of inclusive education and emphasises the need to focus on values and beliefs for inclusion in advance of considering professional knowledge and understanding and skills and abilities. This relates to the findings of Norwich and Lewis's (2005) systematic review that found no evidence of distinct pedagogies for children with learning difficulties. The significance of this is that it challenges the notion that there are specific pedagogies for groups of learners in which teachers require 'training'. There are some areas in which specific pedagogies do exist, for example in the teaching of children with autistic spectrum conditions. However, this does not negate the view that by making the learning environment more accessible for particular children, all children benefit. For many teachers, it may be about recognising and extending what they are already doing and on developing the kind of pedagogical content knowledge required to support all learners.

Rather than viewing teacher expertise in educational support as being primarily about individualistic responses to specific categories of disability, greater emphasis needs to be placed on the development of teachers' knowledge and understanding of pedagogical practices that support the inclusion of all learners. This focuses on establishing a learning environment for all children instead of one that is intended for most children, with individual responses to those identified as different. This argument does not propose the same response for everyone; rather it recognises the response to particular children in terms of the degree or intensification of support that is required and how this support might be structured. However, there is a significant concern about a loss of expertise and the capacity within the system to support teacher learning in the field of additional support needs and the development of inclusive practice. This is particularly notable when considering low-incidence learners who require high levels of support; there is no longer any university in Scotland providing courses specific to this group. In some situations, lack of a critical perspective has led to the promotion of regressive practice involving remedial approaches driven by deficit models. When coupled with a diminishing capacity to challenge unreconstructed views of what constitutes inclusive practice, the promotion of inclusive education through a more considered and nuanced focus on the child's learning environment becomes more arduous. Put bluntly, we appear to be moving backwards.

## FUTURE PRIORITIES

Scotland has much to be proud of in its adoption of the concept of additional support needs and the translation of this into policy. Legislation and policy frameworks underpin an educational support system designed to facilitate a dynamic response to identifying and responding to the needs of all children. Future priorities should lie in continuing to develop a consistent and equitable approach to ensure that all children receive the support to which they are entitled. This may require more careful consideration of who comes to be identified as requiring additional support and why they are being identified.

This chapter began by outlining a concern about the high-incidence group of vulnerable and disadvantaged children recognised within the construct of additional support needs, but in reality often overlooked in practice (Scottish Government, 2012). Given that many children are identified as requiring additional support for the first time in school, class teachers have a key responsibility in recognising and responding to children requiring support through a clear and coherent model of staged intervention. This support should be recognised as a dynamic process situated within the context of an inclusive learning environment. The development of inclusive pedagogical approaches provides a context for the support of all learners. In this way vulnerable children, who might be recognised in non-normative categories, come to be recognised and supported rather than being overlooked or misrepresented within a disability category. The real concern is that a continued and narrow focus on normative categories fuels a persistence with individualised responses to difference, resulting in the term additional support needs continuing to be used as a proxy for special educational needs, with those children who have been a source of tension in the educational system for over a century failing to receive the support to which they are entitled.

## NOTE

As this book was going to press, the Code of Practice referred to in this chapter underwent a further revision and appears at:
Scottish Government (2017) *Supporting Children's Learning: Statutory Guidance on the Education (Additional Support for Learning) Scotland Act 2004 (as amended) Code of Practice (Third Edition).* Online at www.gov.scot/Resource/0052/00529411.pdf

## REFERENCES

Donaldson, G. (2010) *Teaching Scotland's Future: Report of a Review of Teacher Education in Scotland.* Edinburgh: Scottish Government.
HMIe (2010) *Review of the Additional Support for Learning Act: Adding benefits for learners. A Report by HMIE to Scottish Ministers*, November. Online at http://dera.ioe.ac.uk/2009/1/raslaabl.pdf
Norwich, B. and Kelly, N. (2005) *Moderate Learning Difficulties and the Future of Inclusion.* London: Routledge-Falmer.
Norwich, B. and Lewis, A. (2005) 'How specialized is teaching pupils with disabilities and difficulties?' in A. Lewis and B. Norwich (eds), *Special Teaching for Special Children? Pedagogies for Inclusion.* Maidenhead: Open University Press.
OECD (2007) *Students with Disabilities, Learning Difficulties and Disadvantages Policies, Statistics and Indicators.* Paris: OECD.
Riddell, S. and Weedon, E. (2016) 'Additional support needs policy in Scotland: challenging or reinforcing social inequality?' *Discourse: Studies in the Cultural Politics of Education*, 37 (4), 496–512, doi: 10.1080/01596306.2015.1073012
Scottish Government (2010). *Supporting Children's Learning: Code of Practice (Revised edition).* Online at www.gov.scot/resource/doc/348208/0116022.pdf
Scottish Government (2012) *Supporting Children's and Young People's Learning: A Report on Progress of Implementation of the Education (Additional Support For Learning) (Scotland) Act 2004 (As Amended).* Online at www.scotland.gov.uk/Resource/0038/00387992.pdf
Tomlinson, S. (1982) *A Sociology of Special Education.* London: Routledge & Kegan Paul.

## Website

Warnock Report at http://webarchive.nationalarchives.gov.uk/20101007182820/http://sen.ttrb.ac.uk/attachments/21739b8e-5245-4709-b433-c14b08365634.pdf

# 79

# Psychological Services and Their Impact

*Tommy MacKay*

Educational psychology services in Scotland are unique (MacKay and Boyle, 2016). In setting out their unique aspects, this chapter discusses the history of the profession from the early days of child guidance services, the effects of legislation, the qualifications and training of staff, the range and source of referrals and the contribution made to the Children's Hearings and social work. Consideration is also given to the impact of the profession on local and national policy, and to current issues and challenges, with a particular focus on the contribution of educational psychology to closing the attainment gap and addressing the mental and physical wellbeing of all children and young people. The uniqueness of Scottish educational psychology services may be demonstrated in relation to four aspects of their history and development: their statutory foundation; the role and functions of psychologists; the development of nationally agreed quality standards; and the establishment of post-school psychological services.

## A UNIQUE STATUTORY FOUNDATION

The first aspect of the uniqueness of Scottish services is that they are built on a statutory foundation that is broader than for any other country in the world (MacKay, 1996). Their functions are prescribed in Section 4 of the Education (Scotland) Act 1980, with subsequent amendments, as follows:

> It shall be the duty of every education authority to provide for their area a psychological service, and the functions of that service shall include: (a) the study of children having additional support needs; (b) the giving of advice to parents and teachers as to appropriate methods of education for such children; (c) in suitable cases, provision for the additional support needs of such children; and (d) the giving of advice to a local authority within the meaning of the Social Work (Scotland) Act 1968 regarding the assessment of the needs of any child for the purposes of any of the provisions of that or any other enactment. (https://www.legislation.gov.uk/ukpga/1980/44/contents)

These duties have much in common with the work done by psychologists elsewhere in the UK, but there are several important differences. First, while sharing many aspects of professional practice and development with services in England and Wales, Scottish services are fundamentally different in that all of the above duties are mandatory and not discretionary. While, for example, the contribution of the educational psychologist in England and Wales is generally wide-ranging, the duties provided by law are narrow, and are limited to assessments of children with special educational needs and disabilities for the purposes of education, health and care (EHC) needs assessments.

Second, the term 'additional support needs' when used to describe the functions of psychological services is intended to be of very broad interpretation. It replaced the term 'special educational needs', which in its turn was a direct replacement for the older term 'handicapped, backward and difficult children', which it was an attempt to modernise. The population embraced by this description has been defined in statutory instruments and official guidance, and includes the full range of psychological problems of children and young people, whether educational, behavioural or developmental, and whether occurring in the context of school or elsewhere. Indeed, the single most important legislative statement that can be made about educational psychology in Scotland is that it is not a school psychological service, but provides such a service as part of a wider statutory remit.

Third, the statutes governing Scottish educational psychology require services to give advice not just to the education authority but to the 'local authority', that is, to the council as a whole, in relation to areas beyond schools and education. The breadth of that function beyond education is seen in the reference to the Social Work (Scotland) Act 1968, by which the psychologist has a duty to provide assessment and advice in relation to the Children's Hearing system, in addition to wider advice regarding 'any other enactment'.

## DEVELOPMENT OF CHILD GUIDANCE SERVICES

Educational psychology is a relatively young profession, and its development in Scotland dates from the 1920s. The context in which it developed was set by its parent discipline child psychology, which had become an established subject in the universities by the end of the nineteenth century. In 1884, Francis Galton opened in London his anthropometric laboratory for the study of individual differences, and advocated the scientific study of children. James Sully, a founder member of the British Psychological Society and convenor of its first meeting in 1901, opened a psychological laboratory in 1896. In his classic *Studies of Childhood* (1896), he outlined the importance of 'the careful, methodic study of the individual child', and teachers and parents were invited to take difficult children to his laboratory for examination and advice on treatment. Sully paved the way for a new kind of specialist to work with children in the educational sphere, and in 1913 Cyril Burt became the first educational psychologist in the UK on his appointment to London County Council.

These events had a significant influence on the development of child guidance in Scotland (Boyle and MacKay, 2010). In 1923, the first appointment of a child psychologist was made when David Kennedy Fraser was appointed jointly by Jordanhill College to train teachers for schools for the mentally handicapped and by Glasgow Education Committee as a psychological adviser. Meanwhile the Bachelor of Education degree (the EdB, not to be confused with the recent/current pre-service degree qualification, BEd) was established in all four universities, and this provided the background to training in educational psychology for many years. In 1925, Professor James Drever set up a 'psychological clinic' at Edinburgh University, followed in 1926 by the establishment of an 'educational clinic' at Glasgow University by Dr William Boyd.

While these were the forerunners of the Scottish child guidance clinics, the first establishment to bear this name was the independent Notre Dame Child Guidance Clinic, founded in Glasgow in 1931. It was also the last to use such a description, since the term 'child guidance service' was replaced by 'psychological service' in subsequent educational legislation. The Notre Dame Clinic was established on an American model with a three-member team of psychologist, psychiatrist and social worker, and its main focus was on emotional and behavioural problems. Renamed the Notre Dame Centre in 1994, it continues to provide a therapeutic service to children and young people in cooperation with health, social work and education services.

## THE EFFECTS OF LEGISLATION

The statutory period for child guidance began with the Education (Scotland) Act 1946. Glasgow had established the first education authority child guidance service in 1937, to which it appointed a full-time psychologist, and by the outbreak of the war several authorities had clinics in operation, mainly operating on a voluntary basis on Saturday mornings. In recognition of these developments, the 1946 Act empowered education authorities to provide child guidance services, with functions expressed in almost identical terms to the present statutory duties. The Special Educational Treatment (Scotland) Regulations 1954 which stemmed from the Act had important implications for psychologists, who developed a central role in determining which of these children required special education. The functions of the child guidance service became mandatory in 1969, while the Education (Mentally Handicapped Children) (Scotland) Act 1974 led to an extended role for psychologists in working with pupils with complex learning difficulties. The Record of Needs legislation in 1981 extended the psychologist's role further. Its replacement by the Education (Additional Support for Learning) (Scotland) Act 2004 gave parents a new right to request a psychological assessment of additional support needs.

Several other pieces of legislation have had important implications for the development of psychological services. Until the early 1970s, psychologists worked almost exclusively with children, the main thrust being with those of primary school age and to a lesser extent with preschool children. Work in secondary schools developed extensively and, following the Disabled Persons (Services, Consultation and Representation) Act 1986, services were renamed 'regional or island authority psychological services', with a remit for the population aged 0–19 years. This new term was also soon rendered obsolete and, following the Local Government (Scotland) Act 1994, psychological services faced a period of major reorganisation under the thirty-two new unitary authorities established in 1996. The Children (Scotland) Act 1995 with its increased focus on children's rights again provided a changing context for the work of psychologists. The Standards in Scotland's Schools etc. Act 2000 made provisions for promoting social inclusion and raising attainments in core skills, and in doing so highlighted areas in which the future contribution of educational psychology would be vital. Finally, the Children and Young People (Scotland) Act 2014 framed in legislation the *Getting it Right for Every Child* (GIRFEC) 'SHANARRI' indicators – the aim that the child should be 'safe, healthy, achieving, nurtured, active, respected, responsible and included'. Although educational psychologists are not specified in the Act, the GIRFEC framework forms an important area of their required functions within children's services.

## QUALIFICATIONS, TRAINING AND STAFFING

The training of educational psychologists has changed dramatically over the years in structure and in content. Prior to the 1960s, psychologists were first and foremost teachers. Indeed, they were frequently listed in education department records as 'teachers employed as psychologists', and it was usually recommended that they should have a minimum of two years' teaching experience. Entry to the profession was through the Master of Education (Med) Honours degree (formerly the EdB), specialising in Educational Psychology. In 1962, a postgraduate course in educational psychology was established for graduates with a first degree in psychology and, to meet the demands for recruitment following services becoming mandatory in 1969, postgraduate courses of this kind were soon operating in Aberdeen, Edinburgh, Glasgow, Stirling and Strathclyde Universities. They offered the degree of Master of Science (MSc) or the Diploma in Educational Psychology (later Master of Applied Science, MAppSci).

Considerable debate ensued about whether teacher training and experience were necessary qualifications for entry to educational psychology, although many employing authorities continued to demand full General Teaching Council for Scotland (GTCS) registration. It was the profession itself that recommended new approaches to training. Now the only route into the profession is through an honours degree in psychology, or equivalent, and a professional postgraduate degree in educational psychology. This training recognises that it is the study and practice of psychology itself that best informs the assessment and intervention strategies used by psychologists, and that best equips them to give appropriate advice to teachers, parents and others. A broader experience of the education system than was provided under the former teacher training arrangements is an essential aspect of training, and this is provided for within the structure of the postgraduate programmes. Most entrants to the profession take the four-year single honours degree in Psychology at one of the Scottish universities and proceed to the two-year MSc in Educational Psychology at either Dundee or Strathclyde University.

Trainees must spend at least two years following (or prior to) their first degree gaining additional qualifications or experience in fields relevant to educational psychology. This may be, for example, in children's homes, teaching, research or the voluntary sector. As a result, entrants to the profession have for many years been very highly qualified and experienced in their preparations for beginning work as educational psychologists. Practice tutors from the field are centrally involved in supervising placements in psychological services throughout the two postgraduate years.

The final steps in reaching independent professional status involve a probationary year working under the supervision of an appropriately qualified psychologist in a psychological service, to meet British Psychological Society (BPS) requirements for eligibility to become a chartered psychologist and for registration with the Health and Care Professions Council (HCPC), a statutory requirement for all practitioner psychologists since 2009. Psychologists may proceed to undertake the degree of Doctor of Educational Psychology (DEdPsy), but their existing qualifications are already recognised as being at the doctoral level required for HCPC registration. Quality and standards of training and induction into employment are monitored by the training committee of the BPS Scottish Division of Educational Psychology. For psychologists in service, local arrangements for further study and training are supplemented by a national action enquiry initiative led by Education Scotland.

Staffing levels in services vary, but on average they provide a ratio of approximately one psychologist to 3,000 of the 0–19 population. Each of the thirty-two local authorities either has its own psychological service or shares one jointly with a neighbouring authority. In almost every case services are under the direction of a principal educational psychologist, who may have additional roles within the authority's senior management team, supported by senior psychologists except in smaller services.

## THE ROLE AND FUNCTIONS OF PSYCHOLOGISTS

The second aspect of the uniqueness of Scottish services relates to the role and functions of psychologists. These include research as a core function agreed at government level. MacKay defined three levels of work and five core functions for the profession, together with the quality standards that represent good practice (MacKay, 1999). Following a national review of educational psychology in Scotland, these were endorsed by Scottish ministers as the basis on which services would operate (Scottish Executive, 2002). The three levels are: the level of the individual child or family; the level of the school or establishment; and the level of the local authority. Psychologists have a key role in facilitating interactions between these levels. They also cover the entire age range of children and young people in both mainstream and special sectors in relation to a full spectrum of educational and clinical difficulties in learning, behaviour and development. In addition, they frequently occupy the central role in coordinating the work of a multidisciplinary team from health, education, social work and the voluntary agencies. The breadth of this work gives psychological services a pivotal role in assisting the local authority in the management and development of resources in the field of additional support needs.

In relation to each of the three levels of work, the five core functions are consultation, assessment, intervention, training and research. All of these operate within an interactive context in which the problems of individual children and young people are assessed as part of a wider environment such as classroom or school. While assessment and intervention therefore may involve direct work with the individual, including use of standardised assessment instruments, a central part of the psychologist's role is in assisting parents and teachers in supporting children with difficulties. This leads to considerable involvement by psychologists in parenting skills, classroom management strategies and staff training, and in the development of new methodologies for helping young people who experience problems in their learning, behaviour or development. Some services focus on a 'consultation model' of service delivery in which the educational psychologist works largely through others rather than with individual children and young people. However, there will always, of course, be those whose difficulties require the expert assessment and intervention of the psychologist carrying out direct work with the individual.

Although acting frequently in a liaison capacity between the education authority, the school and the child or parent, the psychologist in giving advice and making recommendations must always act in the best interests of the child or young person. This is required by the Code of Conduct and Ethics of the BPS and the Standards of Conduct, Performance and Ethics of the HCPC, both of which set nationally recognised professional standards in relation to psychological practice. A key skill of the psychologist therefore in giving independent advice is the ability to negotiate arrangements that will best meet children's needs, and to handle tensions that may arise from the perspective of the school or other agencies, or indeed between the child and the parent.

## QUALITY STANDARDS

The third aspect in which Scottish services are unique relates to quality standards. The profession in Scotland has been proactive in the promotion of quality services and maintenance of professional standards. It has done this in three main ways. First, the performance indicators published by the Scottish Executive (MacKay, 1999) were the first nationally endorsed quality standards in the world for educational psychology services. They were fully supported and developed throughout the entire process by an extensive consultation exercise involving all staff in all services. These were developed further as a comprehensive self-evaluation toolkit in the standard format used by Her Majesty's Inspectorate of Education (2007). Second, through the BPS Scottish Division of Educational Psychology, psychologists campaigned for a fully chartered profession, and became the only branch of UK psychology to be fully regulated in this way several years before regulation became a statutory requirement. Third, the profession requested that the education functions of psychological services should be included in the HMIE inspections of education authority services, so that they would be subject to the same process of scrutiny as other branches of education. This resulted in an inspection of all services, undertaken from 2006 to 2010 (Her Majesty's Inspectorate of Education, 2011). In turn, the inspection process has been replaced by a system of validated self-evaluation (VSE), with psychological services working in partnership with Education Scotland as part of the authority's own cycle of self-evaluation and improvement planning.

## RANGE AND SOURCE OF REFERRALS

The foundation of a psychological service and its predominant activity is casework. This is based on interactive assessment and intervention involving both the children or young people who are referred, and the local contexts, such as school or family, in which they function. The range of problems referred is almost certainly wider than for any other branch of psychology. Reasons for referral include all of the traditional groupings within the field of additional support needs – moderate, severe and complex learning difficulties, visual and hearing impairments, physical disability, emotional and behavioural disorders, autism spectrum disorders and language disorders – together with a full range of mental health issues including anxiety, depression and post-traumatic stress. Referrals arise in discussion with various agencies, and in some cases are made directly by parents. Older children and young people have a right to make a confidential self-referral, and this is treated in a way that takes account of age and maturity, and the nature of the problem referred. Nevertheless, since problems do not generally occur in isolation but within a family, social or educational context, the small group of self-referrals would normally be guided towards a position that encouraged liaison with other agencies.

It is the schools themselves that have always accounted for perhaps 80 per cent of referrals to services across Scotland, and much of the backbone of the work arises from referrals of pupils with educational difficulties or behaviour problems in the classroom. While this may be the most routine aspect of the work of the psychologist, it is often the contribution that is most valued by teachers and others who are seeking to support children with difficulties.

## CHILDREN'S HEARINGS AND SOCIAL WORK

Since 1969, one of the statutory functions of psychological services has been to provide reports to the social work department or the Reporter to the Children's Panel in cases where psychological advice may be helpful. The pattern of referrals from the Reporter varies, and in some services accounts for a significant proportion of the total workload. The problems referred may occur mainly in relation to the home, the school or the community, and may centre on issues of childcare and protection, criminal offences or school attendance issues. In addition, a large number of other situations require joint working between psychological services and social work, including the needs of children who are looked after or accommodated by the local authority. The effect of more recent legislation has been to increase the involvement of the psychologist with social work and the Reporter in a wide range of childcare issues.

## POST-SCHOOL PSYCHOLOGICAL SERVICES

The fourth aspect in which Scottish services are unique is in their history of provision of post-school psychological services (MacKay, 2009). The Beattie Report on post-school education and training for young people with special needs (Scottish Executive, 1999) recommended that educational psychology services should be extended to provide a service to young people in the 16 to 24 age group who had left school. Following a period of preparatory work to develop a structure and role for such services, the Executive funded a pilot project in twelve Pathfinder authorities for the period 2004–6. On the basis of the evaluation of this initiative (MacKay, 2006), the government extended the provision of post-school psychological services to all thirty-two authorities. The main thrust of these services has been strategic rather than at the individual level, with psychologists working in partnership with a range of post-school providers in further education, training and employment.

The establishment of post-school services represented a significant challenge to educational psychology in terms of the structure and role of services, additional recruitment requirements, continuing professional development for staff, the curricula of university training programmes, and finding field placements for trainee psychologists. It also required educational psychologists to provide services beyond education, and to work with agencies that have a national rather than a local authority structure, such as Skills Development Scotland. More fundamentally, provision of services to adult age groups raised issues regarding the nature and scope of educational psychology itself, as a profession with a focus on children and adolescents and on models drawn from developmental psychology.

## IMPACT ON EDUCATIONAL POLICY AND DEVELOPMENT

As well as fulfilling their central task of assisting children and young people with additional support needs, educational psychology services have made a substantial impact on education authority policy and development, not only in the field of additional support needs but also in relation to education in general. This may be illustrated by reference to four areas.

First, the role of psychologists in shaping policy for additional support needs at national and local authority level has been a crucial one. Most authorities have relied heavily on psychological services in planning and developing their provision, and in a national context psychologists have contributed substantially to government circulars and guidance in this area. Psychologists have also been a dominant force in promoting a philosophy of inclusive education, and in developing the context that enables pupils with additional needs to be educated along with their mainstream peers.

Second, through research, training, promotion of good practice and production of resources, educational psychologists have had a significant influence on classroom management strategies, anti-bullying policies, parent partnership, child protection procedures, learning support, and school organisation and ethos. It is probably the case that virtually every educational establishment in Scotland at nursery, primary, secondary and special level uses strategies or resources developed by psychological services.

Third, psychologists have been central in highlighting the importance of socio-economic disadvantage as a major dimension in Scottish education. Through published research they have not only emphasised its significance as the principal correlate of educational underachievement but have also developed a range of interventions for tackling its effects. Examples include the research on nurture groups in fifty-eight Glasgow schools (Reynolds et al., 2009) and the development of resources to promote nurturing schools (Glasgow City Council, 2014). In addition, in many education authorities psychologists have been instrumental in developing a policy framework that targets additional resources on disadvantaged populations.

Fourth, the work of educational psychologists in Scotland in designing projects for improving children's achievement in literacy has been internationally recognised (see, for example, Burkhard, 2006) and has had a major impact on national practice in the setting up of the National Literacy Commission. This contribution has been acknowledged in the design and development of literacy initiatives in almost all of the education authorities in Scotland.

## CURRENT ISSUES

The national review of services (Scottish Executive, 2002) envisaged a future in which the educational psychologist would provide holistic services across the contexts of home, school and community, and would contribute to the 'well-being of all children and young people, and not only to those with special educational needs' (paragraph 2.30). Since that time, the commitment of the profession to universal psychology services for the benefit of all has been a central theme. Three areas are highlighted here as key priorities: closing the attainment gap; the mental health agenda; and the physical health agenda.

### Closing the Attainment Gap

Educational psychologists view themselves as playing a central role in relation to the Scottish Attainment Challenge, launched by the Scottish Government in 2015 with a view to promoting equity in educational outcomes, and focusing on those areas of socio-economic disadvantage where attainment is lowest. The *National Improvement Framework for Scottish Education* (Scottish Government, 2016) emphasised a 'particular focus on closing the poverty-related attainment gap' (p. 3). The whole question of understanding how children learn and achieve, and what barriers they may face in doing so, is at the heart of educational psychology, and a key contribution to this field nationally is crucial if the profession is to be seen as relevant to the government's educational priorities.

## The Mental Health Agenda

The Scottish Government (2017) launched its ten-year vision for the nation's mental health in its *Mental Health Strategy: 2017–2027*. The vision includes a key focus on early intervention and work in schools. For a number of years, there has been a well-documented rise in the prevalence of mental health problems in children and young people. This includes depression, suicide rates, anorexia nervosa and other serious eating disorders, alcohol problems, drug abuse, and emotional and behavioural difficulties in general. Educational psychologists represent a key therapeutic resource for young people, especially in educational contexts such as schools. They are the professionals most thoroughly embedded in educational systems; they have the widest training in child and adolescent psychology; and they are therefore best placed to be generic child psychologists. Appropriate and evidence-based educational psychology practice can play a crucial role in bringing about positive change in the lives of children and young people, not only through expert individual therapeutic work, but also through preventative programmes at whole school and authority level to build young people's resilience and to promote mental wellbeing.

## The Physical Health Agenda

The promotion of physical health has been a central priority of the Scottish Government for more than a decade. Its *Better Health, Better Care: Action Plan* (Scottish Government, 2007) commits it to supporting good health choices and behaviours amongst children and young people. It has determined that 'health promotion will permeate every aspect of school life' (p. 30). However, the *State of Child Health 2017* report (Royal College of Paediatrics and Child Health, 2017) has highlighted Scotland's health record as being among the worst in Europe, with a crisis in terms of obesity and major issues relating to smoking and other health-risk behaviours. The subject of health and educational psychology remains essentially a 'greenfield site' (MacKay, 2011, p. 7), but one in which educational psychologists are well positioned to play a central role, by drawing from health psychology models that focus on the links across awareness, attitudes, intentions and behaviour, and by applying these models to supporting schools in their health promotion agenda.

## THE FUTURE

All of these priority areas – closing the attainment gap and the mental and physical health agendas – fall in the very heartland of the psychologist's expertise and role in relation to learning, development and behaviour. Educational psychology in Scotland is a vibrant and confident profession which has successfully embraced major changes and challenges and which anticipates a positive future. At the same time, the profession faces a range of pressures and challenges from both internal and external sources. Within the profession there are continuing tensions between 'old' and 'new' models of educational psychology. The old model was of the expert working with the individual child and relying on the widespread use of psychometric tests, particularly the intelligence test. The new model is of the collaborative professional working in consultation with schools and organisations at systemic level. These, of course, are caricatures, and the process of change towards wider and more dynamic ways of working has been of long duration. It has been marked, however, by vast diversity of philosophy and practice between individual psychologists and across services, seen in conflicting views on the place of standardised assessments, now used in fewer services, on the extent to which there should be a focus on working directly with the individual child, and on the position of the profession in relation to the 'medical model', with some services, for example, playing no central role in autism diagnostic teams, while others are an integral part of the process.

In terms of external pressures, an issue likely to have longer-term impact is the reduction in the number of educational psychologists, the numbers expected to retire in a short period, and the great reduction in trainee placements on university programmes since 2012, following withdrawal of the previous funding arrangements. However, future training arrangements are under discussion between the government and the professional organisations and a positive way forward is anticipated. Post-school psychological services have also become marginalised in many authorities because of shortages of staff and lack of capacity, and this in turn has raised difficulties in providing relevant placement experiences for trainees.

In relation to the mental health agenda, an educational psychology service is available to every school in the country, whether primary, secondary, nursery or special. Yet there is not a single mention of educational psychology in any of the key government documents in this field. This is a challenge for which the profession itself must take responsibility if it intends to establish a central role in relation to the national priorities for children and young people.

Although facing these and other tensions and challenges, educational psychology, as an integral and vital element in the local authority structure, has made a significant impact on educational policy and practice nationally. The inspection of educational psychology by HMIE (2011) concluded that across Scotland services had made important contributions to the implementation of key national priorities, including the Education (Additional Support for Learning) (Scotland) Act 2004 and its 2009 amendments, and the GIRFEC agenda. They were meeting the needs of parents and families effectively, were working to the benefit of individual children and young people through intervention programmes and therapeutic approaches, and they had contributed to improving their achievement and transition into education, training and the world of work. It is not only in the national but also in the international arena that the profession in Scotland has established its place (Topping et al., 2007). In looking to the future, Scottish educational psychology is poised to provide an extended range of universal services in contributing to the Scottish attainment challenge and in promoting physical and mental health in schools and in the community.

## REFERENCES

Boyle, J. M. and MacKay, T. A. W. N. (2010) 'The distinctiveness of Scottish educational psychology services and early pathways into the profession', *History and Philosophy of Psychology*, 12 (2), 37–48.

Burkhard, T. (2006) *A World First for West Dunbartonshire – The Elimination of Reading Failure*. London: Centre for Policy Studies.

Glasgow City Council (2014) *How Nurturing is Our School?* Glasgow: Glasgow City Council.

Her Majesty's Inspectorate of Education (2007) *Quality Management in Local Authority Educational Psychology Services: Self-Evaluation for Quality Improvement*. Livingston: HMIE.

Her Majesty's Inspectorate of Education (2011) *Educational Psychology in Scotland: Making a Difference*. Livingston: HMIE.

MacKay, T. A. W. N. (1996) 'The statutory foundations of Scottish educational psychology services', *Educational Psychology in Scotland*, 3, 3–9.

MacKay, T. A. W. N. (1999) *Quality Assurance in Educational Psychology Services: Self-Evaluation Using Performance Indicators*. Edinburgh: Scottish Executive.

MacKay, T. A. W. N. (2006) *The Evaluation of Post-School Psychological Services Pathfinders in Scotland*. Edinburgh: Scottish Executive.

MacKay, T. A. W. N. (2009) 'Post-school educational psychology services: international perspectives on a distinctive Scottish development', *Educational and Child Psychology*, 26 (1), 8–21.

MacKay, T. A. W. N. (2011) 'The place of health interventions in educational psychology', *Educational and Child Psychology*, 28 (4), 7–13.

MacKay, T. A. W. N. and Boyle, J. M. (2016) 'The development of educational psychology in Scotland', in C. Arnold and J. Hardy (eds), *British Educational Psychology: The First Hundred Years*, revised edition. Leicester: British Psychological Society, pp. 156–69.

Reynolds, S., MacKay, T. and Kearney, M. (2009) 'Nurture groups: a large-scale, controlled study of effects on development and academic attainment', *British Journal of Special Education*, 36 (4), 204–12.

Royal College of Paediatrics and Child Health (2017) *State of Child Health Report 2017*. London: RCPCH.

Scottish Executive (1999) *Implementing Inclusiveness – Realising Potential*. Edinburgh: Scottish Executive.

Scottish Executive (2002) *Review of Provision of Educational Psychology Services in Scotland* (The Currie Report). Edinburgh: Scottish Executive.

Scottish Government (2007) *Better Health, Better Care: Action Plan*. Edinburgh: Scottish Government.

Scottish Government (2016) *National Improvement Framework for Scottish Education: Achieving Excellence and Equity*. Edinburgh: Scottish Government.

Scottish Government (2017) *Mental Health Strategy: 2017–2027*. Edinburgh: Scottish Government.

Sully, J. (1896) *Studies of Childhood*. London: Longmans Green.

Topping, K., Smith, E., Barrow, W., Hannah, E. and Kerr, C. (2007) 'Professional educational psychology in Scotland', in S. Jimerson, T. Oakland and P. Farrell (eds), *The Handbook of International School Psychology*. Thousand Oaks, CA: Sage, pp. 339–50.

# 80

# The 'People' People: The Many Roles and Professional Relationships of Social Workers

*Ian Milligan*

## A CONTROVERSIAL BUSINESS

This chapter will offer an introduction to the social work profession and an overview of some key principles and factors that shape social work practice – 'a controversial business' (Horner, 2012, p. 2). Social work is controversial perhaps because it involves highly sensitive areas of work and the exercise of power, such as intervening in family life to protect children, providing reports for courts and children's hearings, or assessing people who want to foster or adopt. Making recommendations or decisions in these circumstances is difficult, not least because social workers have to continue to deal with those who may be unhappy or critical of their findings. Indeed, according to Horner, social work 'inevitably attracts opprobrium' because of its location 'at the interface between the rights of the individual and the responsibilities of the state towards its citizens' (Horner, 2012, p. 2). It is widely accepted that social work as a whole is complex and challenging: 'Social workers undertake some of the most demanding tasks society asks of any group of staff … Over many years, society has come to expect more of social work and has asked social work to do more' (Scottish Executive, 2006, p. 1).

Hence, this chapter is written in order to promote inter-professional understanding; to help other professionals, especially education personnel, understand how social workers approach their work. Social workers undertake their work through building relationships with the 'service users' they work with, and working with other professionals is also an important part of the job. In broad terms, social work is required to carry out two contrasting types of function: personal support and advocacy (the care function) on the one hand, and 'social control' (the protection function) on the other. 'What is apparent is that society expects social workers – and their colleagues engaged in the broader related field of social care – to both protect and care for those citizens deemed in need of such protection and care' (Horner, 2012, p. 7).

## PUBLIC CRITICISM

At regular intervals – or so it seems – social workers and their profession have become the target of a great deal of public criticism associated with the deaths of young children who were 'known' to social services. The apparent failure of social workers to protect children from neglectful or abusive parents, and especially when they return children to abusive parents, leads to criticism in the media and then to responses from government and other politicians. Responses to two deaths, those of 'Baby P' (Peter Connelly) and Brandon Muir, display contrasting 'treatment' of social workers from respective UK and Scottish ministers. This may reflect a more respectful view of social workers in Scotland and an 'official' recognition of the difficulties they face. Peter Connelly was 17 months old when he died in London in August 2007, and Brandon Muir was 23 months when he died in Dundee in March 2008. Both children had been severely assaulted by the partners of their mothers, and in both cases the social workers and health professionals were criticised for failing to act timeously or effectively. It is not the intention to examine these cases here but rather to consider the respective governmental responses in the immediate aftermath. In the 'Baby P' case, under pressure from the tabloid press which had named and vilified the social workers involved in the case, the UK Minister for Children, Ed Balls, made scathing criticisms of the social workers concerned and the Director of the Children's Services Department was forced to resign. When Brandon Muir died in Dundee – only shortly after the 'Baby P' case – there was a different reaction from the Scottish Minister for Children, Adam Ingram. The response of the Scottish Government was to recognise the difficult nature of the social workers' job. Both governments did require the respective local authorities to take action to improve their child protection services and they also set in train various reviews. When the Scottish inquiries reported in August 2009, the Education Secretary announced the creation of a new national centre to support local child protection activity and rejected calls for legislation to ensure that more children were taken into care, but instead emphasised the need for more support for 'frontline professionals' (Scottish Government, 2009).

## SOCIAL WORK AS A PROBLEM-SOLVING PARTNERSHIP

Social work is commonly seen as a 'helping' profession, usually working with individual 'cases' rather than groups, and local authority social work departments have long been established to provide help to those in need or difficulty, including people with disabilities. While the intention may be to *help* people in difficulty, of course many people may be very unhappy to be required to 'work with' social workers. While social workers are indeed expected to offer 'support, guidance and assistance' – in the words of the Social Work (Scotland) Act 1968 – the question of *how* that help is offered is central to understanding the roles of social workers. Social workers are trained to engage, assess and intervene in people's lives but not in the belief that they should have the answers, or access to all the resources, required to solve people's problems. Rather, the emphasis is on respect for people as individuals, with their own strengths and qualities as well as difficulties, and social workers will always be keen to avoid dependency of service users on them. They may well act as advocates for their clients to help them get rights and entitlements, in terms of welfare benefits, for example. This commitment to working *with* people rather than doing things *for* them or *to* them has been reinforced in recent years by changing terminology from 'client' to 'service user'. The adoption of the term has been associated with notions of not 'labelling' people and 'empowerment', which has become a central way of thinking about work with people who are often socially excluded or marginalised (Adams et al., 2009). Some writers have criticised the term as symptomatic of a 'managerialist' turn in social work in which individuals with complex difficulties or troubled circumstances are viewed as if they were consumers of services with a range of choices (Wilson et al., 2008, p. 7). On a more positive reading, the aspiration behind its use is that people should not be categorised because of their disability or addiction or family problem – which could lead to disrespect or discrimination – but only by the fact that they are 'using services'. The international definition of social work, accepted by the British Association of Social Workers, prefers the term 'problem solving' to 'helping' and includes the promotion of a social justice function of social work: 'The social work profession promotes social change, problem solving in human relationships and the empowerment and liberation of people to enhance well-being … Principles of human rights and social justice are fundamental to social work' (International Federation of Social Workers, 2000).

This definition emphasises a wider, community-development function which may apply more in low-income or developing countries than in wealthier countries. Nevertheless, wherever social work is practised the focus is on individuals in need, their family relationships and resources, *and* their social context. Thus when it comes to the professional task of making an assessment of an individual's situation, the social worker will always include the wider community aspects and the social circumstances of the individual child or adult. In practice this often means not attributing blame to an individual but seeking to understand the context and reasons for the behaviour or circumstances they are in. In one widely used social work textbook, the authors review debates about the definition of social work and claim: 'All these definitions suggest that at the heart of social work is the need for change. People come to social work agencies, either willingly or reluctantly, because they want something or someone to change for the better' (Coulshed and Orme, 2012, p. xix).

Since the Regulation of Care Act (2001), social work is now a fully regulated profession with a 'protected title', meaning that someone can only be called a social worker if he or she is registered with the Scottish Social Services Council (SSSC) or its equivalent across the UK. Like nurses and teachers, social workers must adhere to professional codes of conduct and meet registration requirements. They may also be prevented from working as a social worker if, following an investigative process, they are found to have seriously breached the rules and ethics of their profession. The following extract from the Code of Conduct for workers gives an indication of the multiple responsibilities that social workers have and the strong emphasis on a rights-based approach to practice. Part of the Code states that social service workers must:

- protect the rights and promote the interests of service users and carers;
- strive to establish and maintain the trust and confidence of service users and carers;
- promote the independence of service users while protecting them as far as possible from danger or harm;
- respect the rights of service users whilst seeking to ensure that their behaviour does not harm themselves or other people. (Scottish Social Services Council, 2009, p. 23)

## RELATIONSHIP-BASED WORK

From the time of its growth and development as a generic service in the late 1960s (Hothersall, 2014), social work was described as a 'personal social service', and the main tool at the disposal of the social worker is their relationship with the 'service user'. This is a professional relationship oriented around addressing specific issues or problems. Sometimes the relationship will be very short term, for example while carrying out an initial assessment. Where social workers have a longer-term relationship with their service users, the latter may sometimes refer to their social worker as a friend. Social workers are usually very uncomfortable about being described as a friend, and certainly do not think of themselves in that way – but nevertheless the notion of being a 'friendly professional' (Wilson et al., 2008, p. 2) is apposite to relationship-based practice. Social workers form relationships in order to gain a non-judgemental insight into their service user's situation with a view to carrying out assessments that include client strengths as well as difficulties. While always seeking to form empathic and respectful relationships with service users, social workers will nevertheless have working relationships with many people who are not happy to be 'working' with them. On occasion, social workers will be threatened with violence and, in some cases involving child protection matters, social workers will be expected to visit a family in pairs. They are trained to recognise the pervasiveness of prejudice, to understand situations non-judgementally and assess needs professionally – no small task even with training: 'Relationship-based practice involves practitioners developing and sustaining supportive professional relationships in unique, complex and challenging situations' (Wilson et al., 2008, p. 8).

Social workers also have important roles as 'gatekeepers' to services. For example, they need to make the community care assessments which determine whether an older person receives care in his or her own home or a place in a residential home. In children's services, social workers write reports for courts and children's hearings, recommending when a child should be taken into care or returned home and, in relation to criminal justice, social workers act as probation officers monitoring compliance with court decisions. So it is clear that social workers have statutory functions and act on behalf of society in challenging situations. Nevertheless, in all these differing aspects – providing support, assessing eligibility for services or undertaking abuse investigations – the importance of relationship-based practice continues to be affirmed by many within the profession: 'It [social work] is above all about relationships. We see at the heart of social work the provision of a relationship to help people (children, young people and adults) negotiate complex and painful transitions and decisions in their lives' (Wilson et al., 2008, p. xiii).

Social workers also have to operate in multiple settings and the ability to initiate constructive relationships with professionals as well as service users is another key aspect of the social work role. Other professionals generally operate in one main type of environment: the school, the clinic, or perhaps an office or centre of some kind. Social workers, while being office based, are expected to engage alongside others in *their* domains: the service users' homes, the school, clinic, residential home and so on. Even in situations where they are the 'lead professional' with unique roles and statutory responsibilities, such as child protection investigations or community care assessments, social workers are usually working alongside others. In child protection investigations, they will often work with the police and when making care assessments they have to draw on the contributions of various others, including the general practitioner (GP), service user and their family. Thus it is clear that establishing effective relationships with all sorts of people constitutes a large part of the social work role. In consequence, communicating effectively and honestly about serious and sensitive matters, both verbally and in writing – while preserving confidentiality – is a key challenge demanding high-level communications skills.

## TRAINING

In recent years there has been an increasing emphasis on involving service users and carers very directly in the training of social workers (Coulshed and Orme, 2012). The 'user and carer' formula denotes the fact that social workers usually have to engage with the child or adult who is the subject of their intervention *and* that person's immediate relative or carer. These carers have sometimes banded together and campaigned for better services and for their perspectives to be listened to. 'Carer' voices have been especially prominent in areas such as learning disabilities and kinship care of children. Similarly, the 'user' voice has been particularly prominent among adults with physical disabilities and those with mental health problems. People in these situations have formed self-help groups and campaigning organisations seeking to influence social policy, and they are often critical of the way that social work services are provided. The influence of such voices can be seen in the fact that the regulations governing the training of social workers now require the involvement of 'users and carers' in all aspects of the training, from involvement in student selection to contributions to the curriculum (Scottish Executive, 2003). Social work training includes, of course, specific theories and practice skills related to work with people of all ages and with a wide range of difficulties, needs and rights. However, it also includes a considerable emphasis on inter-professional or collaborative working, which is considered further below. Knowledge of the law, human rights and the application of formal guidance is also major focus of training. Other public sector professionals may be surprised by the extent to which social workers in their daily work will have familiarity with specific pieces of legalisation and will often be following detailed policies and procedures: 'Law and social policy affect practice at almost every turn' advises a recent textbook for social work students (Hothersall, 2014, p. 1).

## SERVICE INTEGRATION AND INTER-PROFESSIONAL PRACTICE

> Research shows that integration is a flexible and at times poorly defined concept; despite this it has been highly influential in rhetoric, policy and practice. (Welch et al., 2014, p. 5)

As already noted, social workers often spend a considerable portion of their time interacting with other professionals, including police officers, housing officials and early years workers, as well as school teachers and health personnel. While each profession has its distinct identity and focus of work, it is important for professionals to have a basic understanding of each other's roles so that shared work can be undertaken on the basis of up-to-date knowledge of the other and not just out-of-date impressions or even prejudices. Since 2014, there has been a major push, underpinned by legislation, to integrate health and social work adult services (Welch et al., 2014), and children's services through the *Getting It Right For Every Child* (GIRFEC) approach. Governments have been pushing for more inter-agency and inter-professional collaboration because it is believed that no one department or service can successfully tackle some of the persistent and serious social problems such as drug and alcohol addiction and protecting children from parental neglect. In the current economic climate where public spending is reducing, governments are also pushing for increased efficiency from public services and service integration is seen as one way of achieving this. Nevertheless despite the obvious appeal (to policymakers) of encouraging professionals to work together, there is less clarity about what this means in practice in the face of the continuing existence of separate professions each with their own focus of work. There are many possible models of integration, each of which will be disruptive of existing structures and patterns of service delivery: 'Whilst the drivers of integration and the potential benefits are becoming clearer, it is not always easy to know exactly how to go about integration in order to realise these benefits most effectively' (Welch et al., 2014, p. 7).

GIRFEC has been a long-term approach and policy framework by which the Scottish Government has sought to improve outcomes for children across a broad range of 'wellbeing' indicators. While the aspiration is to support families and promote early intervention for those in need of help, it has linked the service delivery aimed at those most vulnerable children to a framework of service delivery for all children and families, causing some controversy in the process. It is an approach which seeks to promote integrated working among all professionals working with children but did not seek to force services – such as education and social work – to become organisationally merged.

GIRFEC is an approach that recognises the rights of children, as enshrined in the United Nations Convention on the Rights of the Child (UNCRC), and seeks to give those rights practical expression. The GIRFEC approach is about how practitioners across all services for children and adults meet the needs of children and young people, working together where necessary and supporting families to ensure children and young people can reach their full potential (Scottish Government, 2015, p. 8).

Whether it is a first referral or an ongoing case, social workers are usually involved in a process of assessment, intervention and then reassessment. To do this properly they need to get a rounded picture of a child or adult's difficulties and so typically they will be in phone contact with health visitors, where there is concern about a baby or toddler, or teachers in the case of older children. The health visitors and teachers may in fact have been the ones who raised the child's welfare concern in the first place. Social workers often have two contrasting aspects to their engagement with school staff. On the one hand they will be seeking information – perhaps requesting a report – about the child's behaviour or educational progress; on the other hand they may be giving some information about the child's family situation or perhaps advocating for the child following a period of absence or exclusion.

One area where teachers and social workers are expected to work together is to improve the educational outcomes of children who are in care. In recent years there has been a considerable effort to improve the educational attainment of looked after children, who have often been doing very badly, with few achieving Standard/National grades or Highers or going on to university. Social workers were told that they must have higher aspirations for the children in their care and not just write off their educational chances because they faced major personal and family problems. The residential and foster carers were also expected to do much more to provide 'educationally rich environments' in their homes and actively support homework and encourage children's learning through the provision of wider social and educational opportunities. Similarly, schools were told that they must not have low expectations of children simply because they were in care and had very difficult backgrounds. Rather, they were expected to know who the looked after children were in school, and then to monitor their progress providing such additional support as might be needed (Scottish Government, 2008).

However, there is one key difference between social work and health or education, in that the latter two are universal services – they actually serve the whole population and are for the most part valued. Generally speaking, using these services does not carry any stigma, apart perhaps from the mental health field. Social work, by contrast, is not a universal service. It is open to anyone who needs a service but its remit is a targeted or selective one. It is a service that protects *vulnerable* children and adults, and channels services to them with the aim of helping them to the point where they no longer need assistance. Social work services also play an important role in other areas of child welfare such as the provision of regular 'respite care' for children with complex or multiple disabilities. Services such as respite care, or 'short-break' services as they are now known, are generally popular with families and much in demand. However, when social workers intervene in family life there is usually considerable stigma associated with the process. Social workers are expected to counter stigma and discrimination and must show respect for, and offer support to, vulnerable, difficult and sometimes dangerous people. They bring this with them to the work of professional collaboration. While not denying for a moment that teachers and nurses too have professional obligations not to discriminate, it is often the social-worker's job to advocate on behalf of people whom other professionals find difficult.

## WORKING WITH CHILDREN AND FAMILIES

At one level, the whole area of dealing with child abuse and neglect is a highly regulated and formalised state activity with formal mechanisms (broadly referred to as 'child protection procedures') in place, underpinned by legislation to be adhered to by all professionals, particularly those with statutory responsibilities (social workers).

> On the other hand, dealing with a child who has been abused or neglected, whose parents may deny involvement in this, and who are angry and frightened is a very personal, 'in your face' experience which is fluid, subjective, messy and scary; something very difficult to regulate. (Hothersall, 2014, p. 129)

Where a child's wellbeing is the focus of concern, the social worker will seek to work with the parent(s) to identify the issues that are leading to the child being neglected or abused, and the quotation above gives an excellent sense of what that can involve for the social worker in a child protection 'case', and why it is such a demanding task. Many troubled families will be affected by drug or alcohol addiction, mental illness or domestic violence. Other parents may be vulnerable because of a learning disability and lack of family or community support. Sometimes parents are willing to work voluntarily with a social worker, but often social workers have to compile reports which are submitted to the Children's Hearing system for consideration as to whether 'compulsory measures of supervision' may be required. In these situations the Children's Hearing may decide either to place a child in care or keep him or her at home, but require the social worker to provide supervision, through regular visits. Supervision orders imposed by the Children's Hearing will run for a maximum of one year though they can be, and often are, renewed. When working with a child and his or her family, the social worker will aim to increase the capacity of the parent(s) to provide good enough care for their child. If parents are willing and able to acknowledge the problem, the social worker tries to identify strengths and resources that the parents have and the network they might be able to draw on. So social work is always seeking to find a way to strengthen the family and, when it is assessed, that the child is safe and the family are providing appropriate levels of care, then social work will withdraw. They may help them access resources, such as drug counselling or benefits advice, or practical help in terms of replacing furniture and so on. Social workers can also provide service users with small cash payments in emergency situations. This is justified when the provision of a small payment – typically for food or electricity – can prevent an admission to care of a child or sibling group with all the disruption, distress and costs associated with even a short stay in care.

Although they have a child protection function and can in extreme cases take a child into care against the parents' wishes, the aim of social work intervention is to keep children within their birth family and to provide parents with the support that will enable them to keep their child safe. Thus social workers will usually try hard to keep families together, even when other professionals might feel that things are going seriously wrong and children are suffering the effects of neglect or inadequate parenting. While some children are relieved to be taken away from intolerable circumstances, others often say that they want to remain with their parents and only for the abuse or neglect to stop.

Nevertheless it is important to note that significant numbers of children *are* taken into care or, in the official jargon, become 'looked after away from home'. The numbers of children 'looked after' have increased since the early 2000s and the most recent statistics show around 15,000 children in Scotland are 'looked after' at any one time, approximately 1.3 per cent of the population aged 0 to 18 (Scottish Government, 2016). Out of these children, 4,000, or 26 per cent, will be in the 'looked after at home' category. Of the remainder, around 5,700 children are in foster care, with a further 4,000 placed, on the decision of the Children's Hearing, with family or friends (kinship care). There will be a further 1,500 children in residential care, either a children's home or special residential school, and another small group of children are adopted each year. It is difficult to summarise the 'care journey' of these children. They are in fact a very heterogeneous group; some are young babies, but many are teenagers. Some will only have a short period of time in care before being reunited with their family, while others will spend many years in care. For a small number of young children, the local authority is faced with the difficult problem of finding a permanent placement when it is decided by the court that they are to be placed for adoption against their parents' wishes. Traditionally, this option has been pursued for a small number of children, but in recent years, particularly with regard to the impact of heroin addiction on some parents with young children, it has been necessary to make more decisions to find permanent alternative families via adoption or long-term fostering.

## CONCLUSION

Social work is a challenging profession and commonly involves working with members of society who are affected by poverty and social exclusion, combined with significant health difficulties or serious family problems. The UK continues to be a very unequal society and the effects of inequality confound policymakers in many fields including health, education, housing and social welfare. Governments have made the reduction in child poverty a priority but progress has been slow and targets are not being met. Many of the previous societal responses to chronic disability, mental ill health and child maltreatment involved separation of people from the mainstream – in long-stay hospitals, day centres or special schools. These types of 'solution' have been rejected in favour of maintaining people within families and communities whenever possible, and retaining only a small number of separate centres or institutions to deal with exceptional circumstances. There is widespread agreement that people with disabilities and disadvantages should not be segregated from society if at all possible and should have their needs for care and support, health and housing, education and employment met in 'normal' or mainstream environments. Even when children do need to be removed from their own home on child protection grounds, the alternative is to be used for as limited a time as possible. Similarly, for older people, the greatest emphasis in terms of service development is on services that allow people to remain in their own homes for as long as possible. While these trends present huge challenges for those such as community nurses and GPs, in the area of health, and for school staff, in terms of the presumption of mainstreaming, social work has a critical contribution to make. The social work role involves assessing need and acting both as a gatekeeper and a monitor of service delivery for some of the most disadvantaged or 'challenging' people in society.

In all these arenas, professionals are likely to find that they are expected to work together in the support of people in need and to provide services in an inclusive and non-stigmatising way. Wherever this is happening you will find social workers. They have a unique role, but they cannot usually achieve good results on their own and they are often accountable in multiple directions – to clients, to managers, to other professionals in collaborative work. They are acting as agents of the local state, on behalf of society as a whole, to assess risk and meet crisis situations, while they are also seeking to help their service users to claim their rights and access services to which they are entitled. The job cannot be made easy but it can be made easier and more effective if other professionals take the time to understand their role and work collaboratively with them.

## REFERENCES

Adams, R., Dominelli, L. and Payne, M. (2009) *Social Work: Themes, Issues and Critical* Debates, third edition. Basingstoke: Palgrave Macmillan.

Coulshed, V. and Orme, J. (2012) *Social Work* Practice, fifth edition. London: Palgrave Macmillan/ BASW.

Horner, N. (2012) *What is Social Work? Context and Perspectives*, fourth edition. London: Sage/ Learning Matters.

Hothersall, S. (2014) *Social Work with Children, Young People and their Families in Scotland*, third edition. London: Sage/Learning Matters.

International Federation of Social Workers (2000) Definition of social work. Online at www.ifsw.org/ policies/definition-of-social-work/

Scottish Executive (2003) *The Framework for Social Work Education in Scotland*. Edinburgh: Scottish Executive.

Scottish Executive (2006) *Scottish Executive Response to the 21st Century Social Work Review: Changing Lives*. Edinburgh: Scottish Executive.

Scottish Government (2008) *Core Tasks for Designated Managers in Educational and Residential Establishments in Scotland*. Edinburgh: Scottish Government. Online at www.gov.scot/Publications/ 2008/09/09143710/0

Scottish Government (2009) 'Death of Brandon Muir'. Press release 19 August. Online at www. scotland.gov.uk/News/Releases/2009/08/19130947

Scottish Government (2015) *Children and Young People (Scotland) Act 2014: Revised Draft Statutory Guidance*. Edinburgh: Scottish Government. Online at www.gov.scot/Resource/0049/00490013. pdf

Scottish Government (2016) *Children's Social Work Statistics Scotland, 2014–15*. Online at www.gov. scot/Publications/2016/03/5133/326276

Scottish Social Services Council (2009) *SSSC Codes of Practice for Social Service Workers and Employers*. Online at www.sssc.uk.com/about-the-sssc/multimedia-library/publications/37-about-the-sssc/information-material/61-codes-of-practice/1020-sssc-codes-of-practice-for-social-service-workers-and-employers

Welch, V., McCormack, M., Stephen, J. and Lerpiniere, J. (2014) *Integrating Health and Social Care in Scotland: Potential Impact on Children's Services.* Glasgow: CELCIS. Online at https://www.celcis.org/knowledge-bank/search-bank/integrating-health-and-social-care-scotland-potential-impact-childrens-services/

Wilson, K., Ruch, G., Lymbery, M. and Cooper, A. (2008) *Social Work: An Introduction to Contemporary Practice.* Harlow: Pearson.

# 81

# Community Education and Community Learning and Development

*David Wallace and Annette Coburn*

## INTRODUCTION

Community education and its Scottish incarnation as community learning and development (CLD) systematically engages informal and non-formal education processes in the interests of achieving a wider social purpose with participants. Though the capabilities that grow through this process may attract accreditation and transfer to the world of work, the primary intent is to contribute to learning in groups as part of a community development process. Community education embodies an explicit engagement with social justice objectives through participation in community programmes in which participants learn together.

This chapter explores founding principles to show the underpinning philosophy and value base for contemporary community learning and development practice. Offering some overview of the policy environment, and the strong emphasis given to CLD by the Scottish Government, we will also reflect on the economic and political context to illustrate the evolution of Scottish Government strategy. We will emphasise the educative practice and potential in CLD and highlight its unique locus in achieving governmental priorities for learning and for social justice. In analysing these aspirations we question whether policy rhetoric is being matched with appropriate levels of resourcing to afford sustainable development of relevant services. Our analysis shows an urgent requirement for intellectual, material and political renewal if CLD is to meet the challenges set by prevailing structural inequality, a rapidly changing political climate, including Brexit (and the likelihood of a further referendum on Scottish independence), and Scottish Government priorities for community planning and community empowerment. Evidence of success, even in straitened times, leads us to firmly advocate for a more sustainable CLD service that has at its core the pursuit of social justice and empowerment in communities.

## COMMUNITY EDUCATION BECOMING COMMUNITY LEARNING AND DEVELOPMENT

The practice of community education is deeply principled and has a focus on collaborative educational work with groups sharing community interests. Founded on a canon of educational theory located predominantly in the progressive works of John Dewey, Antonio

Gramsci and Paulo Freire, community education is informed by an appreciation of the educational nature of politics and by the political nature of education. Core and overlapping conceptions of community development, popular education, critical pedagogy, the emphasis on new literacies (see Education Scotland, 2016a) and informal education exemplify this philosophical underpinning. Working collaboratively, the concern to embrace and develop experience, for dialogue and for mutual engagement around shared concerns, provides a cornerstone for grassroots democratic educative processes.

Organisationally, community education services existed in Scotland from 1975 following the publication of *Adult Education – The Challenge of Change* by the Scottish Education Department. As a result of this seminal report, community education departments were created in all of the then regional councils in Scotland and saw the amalgamation for the first time of the three core domains of practice in adult education, youth work and community development. For a time, across the majority of the country, there was relative consistency in operational structures, professional qualification routes, and in contractual and career pathways. Over time this pattern has become more disparate.

A move away from this fairly uniform service provision was initiated on local authority reform in 1996 and accelerated by the inception of the new Labour Government in 1997. Disaggregation of community education services from the former structures, on the creation of the current unitary authorities, saw a prolonged period of destabilisation and disruption. Reprioritisation and reorganisation, often involving amalgamation of community education services with other council service departments, saw shifts in staffing from existing roles and movement away from existing duties in neighbourhoods and projects. Scottish devolution shortly thereafter, though validating practice principles in a range of policy initiatives, saw a further and extended period of review and development in which the *process* of community education was reconfigured in policy as an *approach* to community learning and development.

Ideals in community practice are countered by dominant assumptions about the economic purpose, commodification and expression of a functional utility of learning. However, community-based education is seen as a communitarian enterprise through which education represents a democratising process. An engagement with and extension of social practices, learning in the community at its purest is explicitly situated (located within the lives of participants) and sociocultural (responsive to the cultural milieu of participants), as evinced in the ethos underpinning Scottish adult literacies policy and practices from 2001. More generally, these principles are evidenced in successive developments in the profession and in particular through the governance of community learning and development. Policy and governance frameworks have taken ethical practice values and further advanced philosophies of empowerment, self-determination, participation, partnership and inclusion and equality (Scottish Government, 2014). The social purpose and democratic ethos of practice is central to these ideals and is consequently a founding principle for community education.

In Scotland, the term community learning and development has largely succeeded community education and is now predominantly used to describe a wide range of informal learning and development activity that engages individuals and groups of all ages in their communities. This activity is developed and implemented by a diverse range of paid staff and volunteers in organisations across the public and third sectors. Despite having a variety of differing job roles and job titles, what they have in common is a distinct set of dispositions underpinned by a recognised set of principles and philosophies. In professional terms, CLD competences, standards and values articulated by the CLD Standards Council provide for a defined community of practice that exemplifies an explicit and shared educational mission.

Representing an amalgam of discrete and loosely coupled practices – in youth work, community-based adult learning and community development work – community learning and development is organised predominately through local authorities and third sector voluntary and charitable organisations (Education Scotland, 2015). A graduate profession since the early 1990s, it evolved from earlier professional qualifying courses in youth and community work offered by colleges of education from 1964 (notably at Moray House in Edinburgh and Jordanhill in Glasgow). Since 2009, the Community Learning and Development Standards Council for Scotland has overseen standards, training and registration for the profession. Validated degree and Master's programmes in community education and community learning and development are now offered by a number of Scottish universities.

Bringing together community education and community development traditions, the sector might reasonably be described as embryonic, finding its first expression in Scottish educational policy in 2002. The consequent move to define CLD as an 'approach' has seen a range of disparate agencies such as community development trusts, housing associations, training companies and social enterprises also contributing to the breadth of fieldwork, though operationally their primary focus may not be centrally connected to the CLD value base.

Thus, accurately defining and accounting for the CLD workforce remains a recurring problem. Education Scotland undertook the most recent national workforce survey in 2015 that resulted in 308 organisational responses (which compares with smaller responses obtained in 2007 (79), 2008 (92) and 2010 (64)). Though confirming it remained incomplete, the survey consequently identified 6,899 paid staff deployed in 245 discrete organisations. Of responding organisations 62 per cent were third sector, 24 per cent were local authorities and 14 per cent listed as other. CLD is distinctive in that there is a reliance on part-time and volunteer staff as evidenced by the 141 organisations (66 per cent) that reported volunteers as part of the workforce and recording just over 44,000 volunteer staff – 80 per cent of whom operating in the third sector.

## COMMUNITY LEARNING AND DEVELOPMENT – PRINCIPLES AND PRACTICE

The scale of the challenges for community learning and development and the importance attached to such programmes are encompassed by the Scottish Government's National Performance Framework through which the function of community learning and development was identified as:

1. improved life chances for people of all ages, through learning, personal development and active citizenship; and
2. stronger, more resilient supportive, influential and inclusive communities. (See also Scottish Government, 2016a.)

The legislative context for CLD was strengthened by the enactment of The Requirements for Community Learning and Development (Scotland) Regulations 2013. These place a duty on local authorities to secure the delivery of CLD in their area, working with other providers and communities to put in place a process to assess CLD need and develop three-year plans. The official guidance to local authorities (Scottish Government, 2014) states that CLD should empower people, individually and collectively, to make positive changes in their lives and in their communities, through learning. The regulations go further in prescribing five core principles that underpin practice, vis:

- *empowerment* – increasing the ability of individuals and groups to influence matters affecting them and their communities;
- *participation* – supporting people to take part in decision-making;
- *inclusion, equality of opportunity and anti-discrimination* – recognising some people need additional support to overcome the barriers they face;
- *self-determination* – supporting the right of people to make their own choices; and
- *partnership* – ensuring resources, varied skills and capabilities are used effectively. (https://education.gov.scot/Documents/cld-regulations-la-guidance.pdf, p. 3)

However, these core principles may be interpreted in widely divergent ways and result in radically differing responses in practice. The focus in programmes emerging in response to the five principles may necessarily be shaped by available resources in staffing, disparate agency priorities and by prevailing economic context. At one end of the practice continuum, the focus may be on the interests of the individual and instrumental learning for certification, while on the other, the engagement process is centred on supporting the collective and working toward a democratic society. Tett (2010) identified three approaches to practice in CLD that were universal, reformist and radical. In the *universal* model, the CLD worker provides learning and development opportunities open to the whole of the population. The scarcity of resources for CLD has, however, weighed against such a universalist approach. Instead, the priority has been to ensure that scarce resources are targeted to particular disadvantaged and excluded groups, an approach supported in policy and characterised by Tett as reformist. The key purpose for CLD in the *reformist* model is the provision of learning opportunities for targeted individuals, families and groups (routinely identified through the Scottish Index of Multiple Deprivation) with the aim of supporting personal development that may lead to individual, social or economic gains. Here, the role identified for the CLD worker is in supporting participants to develop skills and self-confidence in order to combat disadvantage or exclusion. As the recent CLD workforce survey shows (Education Scotland, 2015) there is not an even distribution of CLD staffing across the country. Where there has been stability in staffing and a sustainable focus for practitioners, it is evident that strong community networks and traditions of practice are possible. However, it is equally evident that in some local authority areas there are fewer qualified staff than required and this restricts the capacity of practitioners to address core principles meaningfully.

CLD continues to be strongly influenced by the work of Brazilian educator Paulo Freire whose seminal empowering approach was to support learners to understand their world critically – developing new levels of critical consciousness in order to be able to work for change (Freire, 1970). Freire's approach was to work alongside learners, building a curriculum with them that was rooted in their lived experience. In this *radical* tradition, the practitioner holds a structural view of injustice and inequality and engages with individuals and groups to develop critical consciousness and initiate action on inequality to effect change in society. Although a strong underpinning for practice generally, the numbers of practitioners working predominately within the radical perspective in Scotland are relatively small – the trend has been for practice traditions to grow away from such open and critical practices to more regulated learning programmes and courses. In terms of Taylor's classification (Taylor, 2011, p. 187), the core focus in practice may be expressed as the development of social capital (networks and norms established through building relational capacity) with an increasing emphasis on human capital (located in the development of individual skills and knowledge). Organisational capital (expressed through the habits of organising and the willingness to take action) appears still to be a strong principle (Scottish Government, 2016a) but seems to be afforded least priority in audit and inspection regimes, CLD fieldwork discourse and staff deployment.

Whichever perspective is held, CLD practice is underpinned by a theoretical analysis of informal education. It has been argued that both informal and formal educators share a common aim in seeking to foster learning. Whilst informal educators sometimes adopt formal methods in their work, their concern with fostering learning in everyday social situations marks them out as informal educators. Reflecting a core value base drawn from the works of John Dewey, the purpose of informal education involves working with people to encourage them to learn from and build on their experiences. The emphasis here is on *working with* people, as opposed to *working on* them, calling for a core empathy and concomitant democratising value base. Implicit in and central to these theories of informal education is a Freirean commitment to the sharing or equalising of power between educators and learners.

CLD operates at the meso-level between the individual and the state, the local and the global, the personal and the wider society (Tett, 2010). CLD activity consistently serves as a catalyst for engagement in learning, cultivating trusting relationships as a mechanism for creating and building participation. Primarily operating in teams or project groups, CLD practitioners are often deployed to a particular geographical area (a locale) or have a particular catchment area (covering a number of locales). Like teachers or lecturers, they have expertise in adopting a range of educational methodologies. Distinctively, the CLD worker will network in a community, develop a profile of interests and issues, aim to build working relationships and negotiate learning activities in partnership with its constituents. Practitioners may also be involved in partnership work with schools and learning communities and with agencies such as housing associations, health boards and further education colleges. Routinely, there is engagement with forums established to ensure interdisciplinary practice and to coordinate local community and neighbourhood policy priorities. Further, practitioners network and engage at neighbourhood level with a wide range of volunteers and community leaders, supporting and resourcing community-based learning which is connected to forms of activism, local needs assessment, service planning and implementation, and to addressing the issues and interest of local residents. Practice may take place in community centres, in other public facilities such as libraries, schools, youth centres and in neighbourhood project bases – occasionally in purpose built premises, but more typically in borrowed or shared premises converted for open access or general community use. Although imbued with universal and egalitarian purposes, CLD is not currently organised as a universal service. Rather, fieldwork practitioners are remitted to enact social justice priorities and engage with those for whom structural inequality and discrimination shape their lived experiences (Scottish Government, 2016b). Characteristically, the confidence and knowledge gained from this process represents a transformational experience for participants. Voice and agency that may have been dormant or suppressed become activated (Taylor, 2011, p. 210). Where realised, this provides the embodiment of government priorities in social justice and empowerment and in turn offers the potential for community development.

## COMMUNITY LEARNING AND DEVELOPMENT – POLICY AND PRACTICE

The implementation of Curriculum for Excellence has become an overarching concern for educational practitioners in and out of school. Indeed it is a fairly straightforward proposition to successfully map CLD youth work and family learning outcomes with the curriculum's priorities. The articulation of Curriculum for Excellence aspirations – developing capacities as successful learners, confident individuals, responsible citizens and effective contributors to society – closely aligns with CLD practices and principles. Practitioners' expertise in experiential, situated and informal forms of community-based education mean they are well placed to advance Curriculum for Excellence priorities. Whether this becomes a nascent border pedagogy (Coburn and Wallace, 2011, p. 42), bridging formal and informal education, depends heavily on whether the confines and values of formal education are truly being made more permeable through the Curriculum for Excellence. Our reading of the trend in schools-based youth work and in CLD-led family learning programmes is that the partnership process, though productive for young people and families, is weighted toward CLD workers operating in the interest of school protocols. The degree to which school protocols are modified to align with youth work curriculum values or CLD principles is much less evident. Other social and educational policies also place community learning and development at the heart of government responses – though the context for this is often provided by adverse economic measures that impinge on the poorest people in the poorest communities. As a result of the 2008 financial crisis, the United Kingdom Government embarked upon and is maintaining an austerity economic policy that hits the poorest who are dependent most on social welfare and public services the hardest. While the Scottish Government has sought to ameliorate the worst effects of this, the impacts on the poorest in society are still strongly felt by and disadvantage some communities; a manifestation of structural inequality remains entrenched. The report of the Christie Commission on the future of public services in Scotland, published in June 2011, called for radical reform of Scotland's public services, in both delivery and culture. It identified unprecedented challenges to the public sector in terms of sharply reduced budgets and increased demand from a changing demography and growing social need. The commission concluded that nothing less than an urgent and sustained programme of reform embracing a new collaborative culture was required.

CLD has therefore never been more strategically important, positioned at the forefront of meeting community priorities across key Scottish Government policy areas. In renewing its commitment to CLD, it was noted in the *Strategic Guidance for Community Planning Partnerships* (2012) that,

> building a learning culture is central to the well-being, resilience and dynamism of our communities ... [and called for public services to] ...build on the assets and potential of the individual, the family and the community ... to involve people everywhere in the redesign and reshaping of their activities. (www.gov.scot/resource/0039/00394611.pdf)

This guidance offered a moment of promise and optimism for the future development of CLD in finally realising its full potential for engaging communities in organising their own affairs. Developing inclusive communities by this means aims to enable human flourishing and a contribution to a fairer, stronger and more equitable Scotland.

Yet, such optimism was short-lived. Since the Community Empowerment (Scotland) Act 2015 (www.gov.scot/Topics/People/engage/CommEmpowerBill) was passed and the statutory regulations on the Requirement for Community Learning and Development (https://education.gov.scot/Documents/cld-regulations-la-guidance.pdf) came into force, the promise of reduced inequality and community-managed services has been compromised by a continuing series of cuts in public spending. A Joseph Rowntree funded report (Hastings et al., 2015, p. 21) provides a context by showing that, between 2010 and 2015, real expenditure change per capita for every local authority (with the exception of Shetland) showed cuts averaging -5.7 per cent. The report also demonstrated that such cuts are felt disproportionately by those in the poorest communities as defined by the Scottish Index of Multiple Deprivation (SIMD1 (poorest) = -9.4 per cent; SIMD2 (second poorest) = -9.1 per cent). This trend clearly diminishes the kind of powerful learning infrastructure that is required for all communities to realise their aspirations through asset transfer, community empowerment and community learning as expressed in successive policy documents.

As part of a public service reform agenda in Scotland, flowing from the Christie Commission, a key aim of reform is to improve the capacity of services to reduce inequalities as well as deliver innovative solutions. This is seen to rest on four 'pillars': prevention, partnership, people and performance, all of which may equally be pillars of CLD. There has been a strong advocacy of social democratic tradition in Scotland that has in turn championed the role of the state in the lives of ordinary Scots. The underlying principles of community learning and development, the processes of co-production and emphasis on community planning all reflect this agenda. Arguably, co-production signalled that policy would now be seen in terms of negotiated outcomes between a range of stakeholders including users and other members of the community. Ostensibly, community learning and development through the community planning process represented a core part of a state response to engage local people in shaping policy decisions and outcomes for services that affect them. An influential and developing policy initiative is a move towards consideration of assets, as an approach to 'salutogenesis' (focusing on factors that support positive attributes like human health and wellbeing, rather than concentrating on a pathologising stance). Some policymakers and CLD practitioners are undoubtedly able to focus on asset transfer models of practice as a means of renewing Scottish democracy through an engagement with the five CLD principles. However, there is a concern that social experience is being converted to private troubles (Tett, 2010) and that responses to inequality, poverty and discrimination are 'sub-contracted' to the people who experience disadvantage. This risks obscuring structural issues and shifting the responsibility for social problems from the state onto individuals and communities. Critically, asset transfer and approaches to co-production come at a time when Education Scotland (2015) reported local authorities' comments about this being a period of great change for them and that 'service redesign, offers of voluntary redundancy, early retirement and non-filling of vacancies were all highlighted as reasons for declining staff numbers'. In the same report the apparently concomitant growth in third sector volunteering further hints at a shift from full-time staffing commitment in community learning and development services and therefore an apparent scaling back of state involvement in resolving issues.

## COMMUNITY LEARNING AND DEVELOPMENT – FUTURE CHALLENGES

As we have shown in this chapter, CLD is strongly supported in Scottish Government policy and legislative instruments. However, the overall position of CLD infrastructure is patchy and in some local authority areas is depleted at best. Since the restructuring of Scottish local authorities in 1996, community education and community learning and development has been in an almost continuous process of review and reorganisation. There has been a recent trend in some local authorities to effect savings through restructuring and through a process of facilitating senior staff (who are most experienced and most expensive) to leave the service. In general terms, though the need for CLD principles has never been greater, the national infrastructure is diminished and stressed – squeezing the principles, practices and staffing resources required to meet demands made in policy. In some areas, the CLD organisations have economy of scale and are more resilient and adaptable enough to survive current challenges. Our reading of the position is that this is not the case nationally. As we enter further uncertain, possibly even epochal times, there is therefore a need to consider future-proofing the community learning and development service.

With regard to wider uncertainty, the UK referendum that resulted in a vote to leave the European Union (subsequently known as Brexit) is significant to public service continuity and in particular to CLD practice. A cross-party report of the Scottish Parliament published in January 2017 confirmed substantial concerns about the adverse impact of leaving the European Single Market and the Customs Union. This uncertainty is amplified in a sector-wide survey conducted by the Scottish Council of Voluntary Organisations (SCVO) in February 2017 in which only 6 per cent of 400 third sector representatives thought Brexit would bring significant positive opportunities; 81 per cent felt that it would have a negative impact on poverty and social exclusion (www.scvo.org.uk/long-form-posts/third-sector-forecast-for-2017/). The detail and process toward Brexit remains to be negotiated and at the time of writing cannot be determined with any accuracy – indeed Jonathan Freedland (2017) writing in *The Guardian* referred to the number of sovereign states with whom Brexit requires negotiation and alluded to a game of twenty-seven dimensional chess for which the UK Government was singularly unprepared. At this juncture, projecting forward, the prospect of responses required to trade tariffs, custom restrictions, ageing population, the necessity of migration; and the rewriting of rights, standards and norms currently existing under EU laws suggests at the least a rebalancing and reframing of the social and economic circumstances in which Scottish education takes place. There is a likelihood through the process of negotiating Brexit that there will be a period, till 2019 (and possibly beyond), of economic uncertainty and the possibility of a significant period of restabilising in which the economy will be adversely affected and employment and social rights potentially weakened.

In the event of such a 'hard' Brexit, as appears to be planned by the Conservative Government, the economic shock will push many of the least well off in our society in to even greater hardship. As SCVO point out in their survey of 2017, this will lead to a rise in demand for community and other services provided through already hard-pressed third sector organisations. We endorse the views consequently expressed by SCVO that communities must be resilient enough to withstand the impact of any rise in inflation and subsequent fall in living standards. Indeed it is our estimation that the time is right now for the Scottish Government to complement their contemporary legislation for community learning and development and put in place a national restructuring programme to boost training and recruitment to the profession and to ensure that there is an equitable distribution across the country of CLD agencies and practitioners.

## FINAL COMMENTS

As a communitarian concern at a time when the failures of capitalism and neo-liberalism undermine social solidarity, community learning and development practices appear to be all the more vital. The gathering places for citizens (the agora, which is a profoundly democratic space for participation, collaboration and dissent) are increasingly threatened, marginalised or dismantled (Standing, 2016 p. 186).

'Community Learning and Development is at the heart of our community, and the community cannot function without its heart.' This column headline appeared in the *Falkirk Herald* of 19 January 2017 and was connected to the Unison Trades Union campaign against job losses in the sector and the proposed cuts by the local council in 2017 that would stop all CLD adult education services and result in reduced CLD youth services to selected council areas. The newspaper piece is instructive in that it contains the essence of the dilemma facing CLD services in local authorities across the country. On the one hand, CLD is seen, rightly, as essential to the lifeblood of a community; on the other, it is caught in a vicious cycle of budgetary restraints impinging on local authorities and which across the country results in service stasis or depletion. In some local authorities this results also in restructuring of CLD into disparate and often ideologically unsympathetic service departments (including schools). The effect, happening here and throughout the country, is a threat to the realisation of Scottish Government social justice and community learning policies. The Scottish Government's statement of ambition (adult education), adult literacies strategy, youth work strategy, lifelong learning strategy, community-planning agenda and community empowerment legislation all require the infrastructure of sustainable community learning and development services if they are to be enacted in a meaningful way. The increasing importance placed on the contribution of CLD to this range of policies and priority concerns has emerged at the same time as worries being expressed that CLD 'may have been disproportionately affected by constraints on public spending' (Education Scotland, 2015, p. 5). This structural depletion, in the context of austerity and tight settlements for local authorities is indeed deeply worrying.

Despite the aspiration for social and economic inclusion through education, the gap between the richest and the poorest in our society is growing. Scotland's independent advisor on poverty reported to the First Minister in 2016 that Scotland still suffers 18 per cent poverty amongst all individuals (22 per cent of children, 19 per cent among working age adults and 12 per cent of all pensioners) (Eisenstadt, 2016). Social class continues to be the main indicator of success or failure in schools and the sense of failure post-school for some is compounded by a profoundly deterministic lesson that learning is not for them. The Scottish Attainment Challenge (SAC) and the associated Pupil Equity Fund, designed to support schools in interventions to assist in tackling the poverty-related attainment gap, focuses on accelerated targeted improvement in literacy, numeracy and health and wellbeing. However, while £750 million is targeted at this programme (and £120 million Pupil Equity Fund devolved directly to headteachers), CLD colleagues in the field have expressed regret that no funding is provided directly to CLD services that have a proven track record in bridging community and school, sustaining and developing community involvement in learning and that draws parents, family and the community into the wider community empowerment process through community-based learning programmes in the SIMD priority areas. Keying directly into humanitarian concerns about structural inequality and discrimination, we must open up education funding to build a more socially just and inclusive vision. A common pursuit of social purpose education whose key values are a commitment to social justice, greater social and economic equality, and a more participatory democracy appears to be a means to realising education for empowerment, participation, inclusion and equality, self-determination and partnership (Education Scotland, 2016b).

In some instances, the articulation of CLD through instruments and practices akin to schooling can be hierarchical, bureaucratic and inimical to meaningful democratic participation of the most marginalised groups. We believe the solution to this problem is to find more creative ways to reclaim democratic learning, drawing on philosophical and activist traditions that help participants to think and learn collectively about the nature of social problems and as a means of developing practical tools to take collective action for social justice. We argue here that it is this Freirean process that represents the distinctive and core value base of community learning and development and its constituent domains of informal education practice in youth work, adult learning and community development. It is this value base that remains a crucial element of Scottish education especially as we journey forward into uncharted waters.

## REFERENCES

Coburn, A. and Wallace, D. (2011) *Youth Work: In Communities and Schools*. Edinburgh: Dunedin.

Education Scotland (2015) *Working with Scotland's Communities: A Survey of Who Does Community Learning and Development*. Livingston: Education Scotland.

Education Scotland (2016a) *Scotland's Adult Literacies Curriculum Guidelines: Learning, Teaching and Assessment*. Online at https://www.education.gov.scot/Documents/adult-literacies-curriculum-framework.pdf

Education Scotland (2016b) Overview of Education Scotland's priorities for 2016–17. Online at https://education.gov.scot/improvement/Documents/gael2-Education-Scotlands-Priorities-201617.pdf

Eisenstadt, N. (2016) *Shifting the Curve – A Report to the First Minister by the Independent Advisor on Poverty and Inequality*. Edinburgh: Scottish Government.

Freedland, J. (2017) 'Brexit is about to get real. Yet we are nowhere near ready for it'. *The Guardian*, 11 March. Online at https://www.theguardian.com/commentisfree/2017/mar/10/brexit-real-triggering-article-50

Freire, P. (1970) *Pedagogy of the Oppressed*. New York: Herder and Herder.

Hastings, A., Bailey, N., Bramley, G., Gannon, M. and Watkins, D. (2015) *The Cost of the Cuts: The Impact on Local Government and Poorer Communities*. York: Joseph Rowntree Foundation.

Scottish Government (2014) *The Requirements for Community Learning and Development (Scotland) Regulations 2013: Guidance for Local Authorities*. Edinburgh: Scottish Government.

Scottish Government (2016a) *Community Learning and Development Plans 2015–18: Planning for Change in Scotland's Communities*. Online at https://education.gov.scot/Documents/cld-plans-2015to18.pdf

Scottish Government (2016b) *Delivering Excellence and Equity in Scottish Education: A Delivery Plan for Scotland*. Online at www.gov.scot/Publications/2016/06/3853

Scottish Parliament (2017) *Brexit – What Scotland Thinks: Summary of Evidence and Emerging Issues*. Online at www.parliament.scot/parliamentarybusiness/CurrentCommittees/103135.aspx

Standing, G. (2016) *The Corruption of Capitalism: Why Rentiers Thrive and Work Does Not Pay*. London: Biteback.

Taylor, M. (2011) *Public Policy in the Community*, second edition. Basingstoke: Palgrave Macmillan.

Tett, L. (2010) *Community Learning and Development*, third edition. Edinburgh: Dunedin Academic Press.

### Website

Christie Commission report at www.gov.scot/resource/doc/352649/0118638.pdf

# 82

# Multi-agency Working

*Joan Forbes*

Co-working across child sector agencies and professional groups has become a central tenet in governance, policy and practice in Scotland, other UK countries and internationally. The shift from mono- to multi-(many) or trans-(cross-cutting) forms of professional work is premised on the benefit to children and families in locating children's assessed needs being 'at the centre' of agencies' co-work (Forbes and Watson, 2012). Equally, the shift towards multi-agency working is economically driven, premised on more cost-effective public sector service delivery. Recognised elsewhere, the discourses of 'social justice' and 'economic efficiency' closely intertwine in multi-agency working policy and its enactments in practice (Forbes and McCartney, 2015).

In Scotland, 'joined-up' public services aimed to prevent children failing in the school system – and more broadly in life and society, cut across education and other children's sector services, such as health and social care. More broadly, in relation to particular complex needs and circumstances of children and their families, co-work may where necessary, for example, for 'at risk' children unlikely to enter the workforce, potentially being socially excluded (Levinas, 2005), include other public agencies such as housing and policing. A shift to the concept of the prevention of children's educational and social exclusion has been developed since the 1990s as a central aim for social care, education, health and allied professions, and public agencies more broadly. Relatedly, a shift has occurred in agencies' strategies and practitioners' practices towards collaborative support for children in receipt of several services. A series of policy and practice changes have viewed multi-agency co-work as a – *the* – key strategy for 'better outcomes' on children's assessed needs and educational and social inclusion. Over time, shifts to co-working models of collaboration have effected major re-conceptualisations, and reconfigurations of children's services, and concomitant remodelling of the sector workforce (Forbes and McCartney, 2012; Forbes and Watson, 2012; Hill et al., 2012).

Increasing attention to service integration in children's services' policy and governance requires that different agencies' practitioners work together to provide timely, 'seamless' service, ensuring that all necessary specific expert knowledge and skills are brought together and applied for the benefit of the child. Co-professional working is increasingly expected across child sector practice with the concomitant expectation that a positive impact will be made on children's experiences and outcomes. However, limited attention has been paid as to how (on what governance and policy bases) professionals collaborate, why (on what research evidence), and with what effects (what child workforce remodelling and practice reconfigurations are involved).

Reviewing policy and drawing on policy research and theory to understand how multi-agency working works in Scotland, the chapter critically comments on the categories and terminology applied; it then examines issues relating to types and models of multi-agency co-practice; and goes on to delineate previous and current key policy and governance developments and their effects in and for multi-agency practice, including the 'flagship' *Getting it Right for Every Child* approach (hereafter, GIRFEC). In closing, the concept of 'wicked' issues – complex issues that persistently challenge society and current policy and practice orthodoxies – is examined. It is argued that such endemic and occasionally 'startling developments' – societal 'game-changers' beyond the boundaries of any single agency – necessitate a joined-up, multi-agency, trans-professional (professionally cross-cutting) response (Lawson, 2016).

## SPECIFYING CATEGORIES: UNTANGLING THE CONCEPTS AND TERMINOLOGY

Since the inception of 'multi-agency working' in the UK countries and other places, the 'guddle' (a confused and confusing mess) of terms involved has frequently been highlighted. However, authors have less commonly emphasised the effects of such terminological fuzziness. The effects of careless and imprecise, or 'sloppy' (Lawson, 2016, 3.1), usage involve loss of conceptual clarity, categorical purchase and understanding of each concept and exactly what is involved in using each term (Forbes and Watson, 2012; Forbes and Sime, 2016). Understanding of 'multi-' and related terms, and of 'agency' and related terms, demands particular care about their use in policy, governance and research. Drawing on a number of prior definitions used in research and, for example, by Scottish Government agencies, distinctions relevant in this chapter may be understood in relation to the key terms 'multi-' and 'agency-':

- *multi-agency working*: where more than one agency works with a young person, family or a project;
- *inter-sectorial working*: where two or more public sectors and their agencies or services such as education, health and social care work together.

Other key terms, salient in the conceptual and terminological map of 'multi-agency working' and used here are:

- 'Mono-' which is most frequently used with 'professional' or 'disciplinary' – where a single professional practitioner group or subject discipline, such as social work practitioners, is involved and/or works singlehandedly in a job role task, for example, a class teacher with a child in their class.
- 'Trans-' used to conceptualise relations that 'cut across', used with 'sector' or 'agency', 'professional' and 'disciplinary'. Trans-sectorial: (a) work across two or more public sector agencies (e.g. education, health, social work) on cross-cutting issues; (b) co-working across the child and adult public sectors on cross-cutting issues. Trans-professional: work across professional groups on cross-cutting engagements, remits or responsibilities. Transdisciplinary: collaborative working across (academic) subject disciplinary areas (such as sociology, economics, linguistics, spatial planning, housing studies) on cross-cutting research, policy and practice issues and engagements.

To understand 'working' relations amongst agencies, it is helpful to distinguish the category of 'agency' and of the concept of professional working relations that are 'cross-cutting' (see e.g. Percy-Smith, 2005). The following understandings of what exactly is involved in any particular model of 'multi-agency working' are pertinent in this chapter:

- *Holistic government or governance*: integration and coordination of the work of different agencies or services at all levels and in relation to all aspects of policy-related activity – policymaking, regulation, service provision and scrutiny. (For example, the 2013 merger of eight police forces and related agencies such as the Scottish Crime and Drug Enforcement Agency into a single 'Police Scotland'.)
- *Cross-boundary working*: agencies working together beyond the area of any one service on issues beyond the scope of any one agency.
- *Cross-cutting*: issues that are not the 'property' of a single organisation or agency, for example child poverty, child protection, new arrival families.
- *Integration*: agencies working together in a single, often new, organisational structure. (For example, the restructuring of Scottish Police and Fire and Rescue public agencies into single national services since the relevant 2012 legislation.)

Transformations of Scotland's children's policy, governance and institutional-level practice on multi-agency working mirrors shifts globally in child and adult sector public services. In Scotland, noted above, the recommendations of a government commissioned report, *The Future Delivery of Public Services*, 2011, known as the 'Christie Report', heralded police and fire services' mergers, a structural redesign and workforce remodelling towards integration, each now a single service in Scotland. Relevant in this chapter, the Christie Report explicitly called for new inter-agency training for the public services, envisaging that such training would reduce professions' 'silo mentalities', drive 'service integration', and build up a 'common public service ethos' across the sector (p. ix).

## MULTI-AGENCY WORKING: GLOBAL POLICY AND GOVERNANCE DRIVERS

Focusing the attention and resources of governments globally on the holistic wellbeing of children, the publication of the 1989 United Nations Convention on the Rights of the Child (UNCRC) may be viewed as a 'watershed' moment that necessitated subsequent shifts to multi-agency working. Since 1989, UNCRC has prompted the production of holistic (whole child) 'child strategies' and accordingly the deployment of resources (economic, including the children's workforce) in new approaches and programmes underpinned by the UNCRC policy goals. The UNCRC specifications were recognised in the Children and Young People (Scotland) Act 2014, thereby giving children's rights, as realised in GIRFEC policy, a statutory basis in Scots law.

Incremental policy 'step change' towards collaboration 'in the round' between children's agencies and professions that puts the welfare and wellbeing of the child 'at the centre' has been mirrored in child strategy policy and approaches elsewhere. Such cultural transformations have occurred in the USA, England – the Every Child Matters framework led the changes in other UK countries in putting 'the child at the centre' of multi-agency working, in Northern Ireland, Wales, Ireland and other places (see Forbes and Watson, 2012; Hill et al., 2012).

Investigation by Coles and colleagues (2016) shows clear correspondences between the children's system policy models and principles of European countries and those of Scotland. Like Scotland, UNCRC-based children's rights are central in Nordic countries' social justice models. More broadly, and highly pertinent in this chapter, child strategy policy in (Western continental) European countries pursues *collaborative* solution-focused support embedded within public services. In Scotland, like these other places, major incremental policy, legislation, strategy and practice shift requires professionals and agencies to collaborate (engage as appropriate in multi-professional and multi-agency working) and coordinate, or integrate as required, to work effectively together, putting the child at the centre of their co-work.

Other world-level agencies endorse the pivotal call by UNCRC in 1989 for countries worldwide to put in place child strategies and programmes, including changes to remodel the children's sector workforce and redesign the knowledge and skills needed in children's practitioners' education and training. In a seminal 2010 report, *Framework for Action on Interprofessional Education and Collaborative Practice*, the World Health Organization (WHO) recognised the need for co-working to transform the co-working practice of health with other public sector agencies (such as education). Seeking systems-level change that would produce an appropriately skilled (health) workforce that could work effectively with other agencies, the WHO *Framework for Action* calls for cross-cutting initial professional education of health workers and other professional groups (p. 13, inverted commas original): 'Interprofessional education is essential to the development of a "collaborative practice-ready" health workforce.'

In Scotland, co-responsibility for multi-agency working that places the child at the centre has become a practice reality for all agencies working with children and young people and their families. The requirement for multi-agency coordination across agencies' organisational boundaries unequivocally underpins all practice prescriptions given in, for example, the *Guidance on Partnership Working between Allied Health Professions and Education* (Scottish Government, 2010). Published in the context of work on the WHO *Framework for Action* directives, and premised on Allied Health Professionals' long-term experience of working with education and other agencies, the *Guidance on Partnership Working* establishes the co-responsibility of allied health professions and education for co-working. The partnership working approach is informed, too, by the principles of GIRFEC (www.gov. scot/Publications/2005/06/20135608/56098), the Scottish national multi-agency 'child strategy' approach since 2005.

A number of the current Scottish Government national outcomes pertain to the GIRFEC agenda and to public services reform premised on multi-agency working. National Outcome 16 states that 'Our public services are high quality, continually improving, efficient and responsive to local people's needs.' Further:

> The achievement of this outcome will be determined by the ability of public services to develop and deliver person centred services and to contribute effectively to Scotland's future prosperity. Public services must also prioritise the issues that matter most to people, ensuring the focus of public spending and action builds on the assets and potential of the individual, the family and the community. *Collaboration across public services will underpin the Government's efforts to reform public services.* (www.gov.scot/About/Performance/scotPerforms/outcome/pubServ, emphasis added)

## MULTI-AGENCY WORKING: KEY SCOTTISH CHILD POLICY AND LEGISLATION

Since the UNCRC (1989), a marked shift towards forms of co-working that bridge and link professionals' practice across child sector agencies has characterised policy in Scotland. The institution of the New Community Schools programme (1998), the aspirational model delineated in *For Scotland's Children: Better Integrated Children's Services* (Scottish Government, 2001), and the ensuing 'flagship' GIRFEC policy agenda (2005) sought to institutionally embed and subsequently remodel multi-agency working in schools and other agencies.

A landmark policy statement, *New Community Schools: The Prospectus* (1998, www. sehd.scot.nhs.uk/publications/fm30/fm30.pdf), signalled a major shift. *The Prospectus* viewed the school as 'the hub' for integrated delivery of education and other services to children. It mandated co-location of services in 'multi-agency hubs' in schools to improve the educational outcomes for children; improve the life chances for young people; tackle the opportunity gap; introduce a more holistic approach to children's needs; address social, emotional and health problems; and ensure that children achieve.

*The Prospectus*, published almost twenty years ago, explicitly recognised that 'the gap' between children that was key, was the gap between the *opportunities* (and related socio-economic resources) available to children, linking *the lack of opportunity and living in conditions of relative poverty and disadvantage for some*, with *educational outcomes*. Ahead of its time, *The Prospectus* recognised that *educational outcomes* – attainment – depend more on the availability to children of broader opportunities and a holistic approach to the particular life-wide problems a child may experience, than what a teacher, school or education alone can do.

*The Prospectus* introduced school-site, multi-agency working as the mechanism to ensure that the different, diverse or multiple needs of all children were met in the round (ibid., Foreword). *The Prospectus*, moreover, introduced the concept of service integration: changed systems, structures and practices. Stating unequivocally that the 'integration of services is essential' (ibid., Introduction, Section 2), it called for: integrated provision of school education; informal as well as formal education; social work and health education and promotion services; integrated management; integrated objectives (for service delivery arrangements and measurable outcomes); and multidisciplinary training and staff development (ibid., Framework, Section 3, parentheses added).

In 2002, *Count Us In – Achieving Inclusion in Scottish Schools* re-emphasised the school-as-hub in a twin strategy on social inclusion and raising educational standards (see note at http://archive.scottish.parliament.uk/business/committees/education/inquiries/pmi/HMIe.pdf). To provide a more *integrated* and holistic support service, it plainly stated that 'inclusive education relies on schools working in partnership with others'; and made a number of clear recommendations on education and other agencies' (health, social work and others) co-work relations:

- shared understanding of aims and objectives and a clear understanding of the contribution that each agency can make towards achieving them;
- true partnership – all partners are prepared to share decision making and the leadership of specific pieces of work in appropriate ways;
- ways in which staff from schools and other agencies relate to each other and to pupils have to be flexible and managed responsively to meet the needs of individuals and groups;
- good opportunities for joint training between professional groups are crucial.

Invoking '*inter-*' work relationships between separate agencies and 'their' practitioners, *Count Us In* also enjoins better structural integration of agencies' work in a holistic service; coordinated planning of services; and reformed relationships between agencies' practitioners in support of the 'inclusion agenda'.

In parallel, the Scottish school curriculum programme, *Curriculum for Excellence* had been implemented from 2010. The CfE policy ambition was for Scotland's children to be: successful learners, confident individuals, responsible citizens and effective contributors. Beyond narrow academic attainment, the CfE programme focus on young persons' full engagement and participation in community and society, regardless of dis/ability, gender, ethnicity or social class, constituted a step change in education policy. Germane here, charging all schools and teachers with broader citizenship learning to develop high levels of educational and societal participation and agency for students, predicated new ways of working for schools and other agencies. Consonant with the GIRFEC child strategy, the aims of CfE prompted new 'extended' forms of professionalism in the child sector. Two high-profile programmes now decree co-working as required across the children's workforce – statutory services, other public agencies, and relevant voluntary and private agencies.

## MULTI-AGENCY WORKING IN LAW

The Children and Young People (Scotland) Act 2014 enshrines children's rights in law, constituting the statutory basis for the GIRFEC policy programme. In relation to multi-agency working, the 2014 Act rules that, from 2015, all relevant Scottish Government ministers (not solely education) issue reports on how their directorate has taken into account the UNCRC (1989) specifications. Relevant here, the Act also requires local authorities and health boards to develop joint children's plans, in cooperation with a range of other service provider agencies. Further, it establishes in law the concept of a statutory universal 'named person' for all children in Scotland, placing a duty on relevant public bodies to share information with a child's named person. Following a UK Supreme Court judgement in August 2016 that the proposal's information sharing provisions related to data protection law were insufficiently clear, the introduction of the named person scheme has been delayed from 2016 until autumn 2017. Certainty on the legality of the information sharing systems and processes is patently of concern for children's agencies and practitioners undertaking cross-agency communications and information transfer to support children (Forbes and Watson, 2012).

## INTEGRATING INSPECTORATES: RETAINING SEPARATE REGISTRATION BODIES

Applying to all children's services, the GIRFEC approach mandates effective integrated co-working by all children's practitioners and agencies, driving

> the developments that will improve outcomes for children and young people by changing the way adults think and act to help all children and young people grow, develop and reach their full potential. *It requires a positive shift in culture, systems and practices across services for children*, young people and adults. (Scottish Government, 2008, p. 6, emphasis added)

In tandem since 2005, a joint cross-agency inspection regime has driven a culture and practices of multi-agency working. Key inspection prescriptions integrating agencies' practice include: *A Common Approach to Inspecting Services for Children and Young People* (HMIE, 2006), which introduced generic quality indicators; and the *Code of Practice for the Joint Inspection of Services to Protect Children and Young People* (Scottish Government, 2006) aimed to put in place integrated inspections, the related necessary powers to share records and information provided in the Joint Inspection of Services for Children and Inspection of Social Work Services (Scotland) Act (Scottish Parliament, 2006). Two further policies emanating from education embed a coherent multi-agency service self-evaluation and inspection framework: *A Guide to Evaluating Services for Children and Young People Using Quality Indicators* (Scottish Government, 2007) and *Improving: Services for Children* (HMIE, 2007). Taken together, service inspection policy has effected ever closer agency integration on strategic and operational levels.

Multi-agency working is now a requirement of registration and maintenance of professional registration status. Co-working is mandatory for teachers in General Teaching Council for Scotland (the Scottish teacher registration body) standards requirements, and also for other children's agencies. Issues remain: while co-practice is now routine at the school–clinic (institutional) level and practitioners at the individual professional level are more regularly acquiring the necessary context-specific, co-problem-solving, soft skills and practices for good 'multi-' working, governance structures remain 'mono-' professional.

Equally, Scotland child strategy policy on multi-agency working, now unequivocally ordained in GIRFEC, CfE, other education and public agencies' policy, and made statutory in law has not, to date, been realised in redesigned, realigned forms of practitioner preparation for co-work. Practitioners continue to learn mainly 'mono-' disciplinary 'home agency' knowledge (for example, linguistics, education professional studies) in mainly 'mono-' professional university departments. Practitioners, clinics and schools remain accountable to their 'home' agency professional registration and institutional management structures. Managerial structures are not routinely  shared, and separate professional registration bodies and professional associations (trade unions) operate (Forbes and McCartney, 2012). The product of these disconnects being practitioners not best equipped to act in multi-agency work contexts.

## MULTI-AGENCY WORK: GIRFEC – SCOTLAND'S CURRENT CO-PRACTICE MODEL

The current overarching 'flagship' educational and social policy and related legislation pertaining to all services to children in Scotland, wheresoever 'delivered' – schools, clinics, homes, community – is the GIRFEC strategy. The *GIRFEC: Proposals for Action* (Scottish Government, 2005) policy highlights that key ideas in the wellbeing approach derived from child welfare and protection developments and specifically a consultation paper on the children's hearing system (www.gov.scot/Topics/People/Equality/18507/EQIASearch/ChildrensHearings). The GIRFEC child strategy constitutes a sector overarching whole child approach to meeting needs and improving wellbeing. Applying to all agencies' work, it obliges practitioners and agencies to optimally coordinate – join-up – their work, spanning previous mono-professional and mono-agency boundaries. Specified in *A Guide to GIRFEC* (Scottish Government, 2008, p. 6), the approach:

> builds from universal health and education services and drives the developments that will improve outcomes for children and young people by changing the way adults think and act to

help all children and young people grow, develop and reach their full potential. It requires a positive shift in culture, systems and practices across services for children, young people and adults.

The approach introduced eight wellbeing indicators (informally, the 'SHANARRI' indicators), viz., that Scotland's children are: safe, healthy, achieving, nurtured, active, respected, responsible and included. The GIRFEC approach, accepting that all children shared these childhood-long and life-wide needs, rights and expectations, has from the start been underpinned by the core idea that no one agency or service, or profession, has the breadth and scope of knowledge and skills to address all of these. Therefore, no single agency could be solely responsible – or made, or expected to be singly responsible for addressing all of these needs. Coles et al. (2016, p. 342) elaborate:

> The GIRFEC proposals for the improvement of children's services encouraged improved integration of policy and practice at both national and local levels, so that agencies and practitioners could work together around children's needs, to ensure that children received the help they needed when they needed it.

Most recently (2017), the Scottish Government GIRFEC site (www.gov.scot/Topics/People/Young-People/gettingitright) describes the GIRFEC strategy in the following terms:

- GIRFEC is the national approach in Scotland to improving outcomes and supporting the wellbeing of children and young people by offering the right help at the right time from the right people. It supports them and their parent(s) to work in partnership with the services that can help them.
- It puts the rights and wellbeing of children and young people at the heart of the services that support them – such as early years services, schools and the National Health Service (NHS) – to ensure that everyone works together to improve outcomes for a child or young person.
- Most children get all the support and help they need from their parent(s), wider family and local community, in partnership with services like health and education. Where extra support is needed, the GIRFEC approach aims to make that support easy to access and seamless, with the child at the centre.
- It is for all children and young people because it is impossible to predict if or when they might need extra support.

A number of key principles have incrementally come to underpin the GIRFEC approach, including: early intervention, and attention to children's early years; local responses, such as the 2006–9 Highland (region) Pathfinder Project, which centrally informed subsequent local and national policy guidance on multi-agency working; the role of the 'lead professional' – not a statutory requirement, but delineated in policy and guidance as good practice where a child has particularly complex needs that may necessitate more tightly linked multifaceted multi-agency working; and the now contested role of a named person, legislated for in the 2014 Act. This is a professional role taking responsibility for a child as single point of contact to provide support and advice to families, including on all necessary children's services, and to raise and appropriately pass on to the correct agencies and authorities concerns about the child's wellbeing, aiming to ensure the child's overall wellbeing – that all eight SHANARRI indicators are being met for that child.

The Scottish National Practice Model (NPM) brings together the current language and GIRFEC approach to identify and respond to concerns for a child. The NPM language and approach now pertain to all relevant, responsible agencies. All children's practitioners, from the stage of co-assessment of concerns and needs for a child onwards, therefore, as appropriate, use: the GIRFEC 'Well-being Wheel' (the eight SHANARRI indicators and the concept of wellbeing legislated in the 2014 Act); and the 'My World Triangle' and the 'Resilience Matrix' (not statutory in law, but recommended in guidance and policy). Together, as appropriate, these tools constitute a shared approach across agencies and practitioners. This 'stepped approach' by all practitioners and agencies to the organisation of all information on a child has established a joint system and processes for gathering, recording, discussing and deciding how identified and assessed child wellbeing concerns should be addressed. An important effect of the introduction of the NPM and its principles, approaches and tools, therefore, has been to align the processes used by all child sector agencies. The Scottish Parliament Information Centre (2013, p. 7) briefing on the provisions for the NPM notes, for example, that: 'It is recommended that it is used by all agencies, including when recording routine information.' GIRFEC therefore has an emphasis on the way that information is shared and recorded by different professions.

For children's agencies' and relevant adult services' practitioners, GIRFEC demands particular shifts on assessment, recording, child data sharing and so forth that, together, as top-down, cross-sectoral directives, fundamentally realign and essentially redesign previous and 'naturally evolving' co-working principles and practices. The current (2016) Scottish Government website (www.gov.scot/Publications/2016/03/9481/3) states that that for 'people working in children's and adult's services' GIRFEC means:

- The child or young person is at the centre of your work, understanding what their unique needs are and how you can help.
- You use common tools, language and processes to consider a child or young person's wellbeing, working closely with them, their parent(s) and other professionals, supporting them where appropriate.
- You feel confident that you have the right information to provide the best support you can to a child or young person and their parent(s).

The integrated approach introduced through GIRFEC, locating the child at the heart of multi-agency working, is key to effective cross-agency collaboration. The focused purpose of GIRFEC model co-practice is to effectively ensure shared assessment of needs and, from 2017, a single child's plan.

## MULTI-AGENCY WORKING: ORTHODOXIES, CHALLENGES AND GAME-CHANGERS

Scotland like other countries faces a number of challenging problems, viz., child wellbeing and protection, looked after children and young people, new migrant children, child poverty and disadvantage. Such challenges demonstrably cut across the expertise and resources of a number of public agencies at all levels: institutional level (school, clinic, youth care and youth justice institutions); the level of policy and governance; and at the level of practitioners' knowledge and skills acquisition for co-practice (Forbes and Sime, 2016). None of these complex, 'wicked' problems (see e.g. Forbes and Watson, 2012), emergent social and economic realities, 'startling developments' (such as the unforeseen number of new arrival migrant children and families from the extended European Union countries), and the post-2015 arrival of asylum-seeking refugee children and families, can be adequately addressed within a traditional twentieth-century style, 'mono-' working education system.

That such major societal challenges cannot be ameliorated solely by education is an insight that needs to be understood in any policy and governance response. For example, current policy tightly couples 'child poverty' and 'academic attainment', whereby the responsibility for solving the 'wicked' intergenerational problem of the educational outcomes of poor children is placed on schools and teachers. In a different framing, causes for the under-attainment of children living in poverty may be viewed as an effect of their lack of economic capital and concomitant lack of full sociocultural access. Such reframing of the issues immediately 'changes the game', demanding a public sector systems-wide multifaceted multi-agency response (Forbes and Watson, 2012; Forbes and Sime, 2016; Lawson, 2016).

Augmenting government policy directives that prescribe sectoral 'multi-' and 'trans-' working, part of the responsibility for the 're-culturing' of agencies in the child sector towards 'multi-' working must lie with professional standards bodies and with those responsible for children's practitioners' initial professional education. Necessary developments to support separate professional registration bodies' multi-agency working 'standards' statements would be the following:

1. the production of agreed aligned standards for cross-agency and cross-professional working and leadership;
2. restructuring to realign university departments which educate and prepare practitioners to enter, continue to develop professionally, and exercise leadership and management functions in children's agencies;
3. ensuring that all child sector practitioners acquire – and practice – the necessary cross-professions, cross-disciplines and cross-agency knowledge and skills to achieve what GIRFEC characterises as necessary.

That is: to get it right for every child in and through a universal approach applying to all Scotland's children.

This chapter has shown that future hard questions on child/person-centred multi-agency working towards the twin drivers of better outcomes for children and social justice must carefully and fully frame issues and solutions with a clearer regard to practitioners' and agencies' intellectual resources. These should strengthen trans-agency connections and trans-professional work relations, and in particular look 'upstream' to the transformational redesign of all inappropriate 'mono-agency' thinking in initial education and professional registration bodies' standards. The multi-agency universal approach envisaged in the GIRFEC strategy must be pursued.

## REFERENCES

Coles, E., Cheyne, H., Rankin, J. and Daniel, B. (2016) 'Getting it Right for Every Child: a national policy framework to promote children's well-being in Scotland, United Kingdom', *Milbank Quarterly: A Multidisciplinary Journal of Population Health and Health Policy*, 94 (2), 334–65, doi/10.1111/1468-0009.12195/full

Forbes, J. and McCartney, E. (2012) 'Leadership distribution culturally? Education/speech and language therapy social capital in schools and children's services', *International Journal of Leadership in Education*, 15 (3), 271–87.

Forbes, J. and McCartney, E. (2015) 'Educating child practitioners: a (re)turn to the university disciplines', *Discourse: Studies in the Cultural Politics of Education*, 36 (1), 144–59.

Forbes, J. and Sime, D. (2016) 'Relations between child poverty and new migrant status, academic attainment, and social participation: insights using social capital theory', *Education Sciences*, 6 (24), doi: 10.3390/educsci6030024

Forbes, J. and Watson, C. (eds) (2012) *The Transformation of Children's Services: Examining and Debating the Complexities of Inter/professional Working*. London: Routledge.

Hill, M., Head, G., Lockyer, A., Reid, B. and Taylor, R. (eds) (2012) *Children's Services: Working Together*. Harlow: Pearson.

HMIE (2006) *A Common Approach to Inspecting Services for Children and Young People Consultation Document*. Online at www.gov.scot/Publications/2006/03/29100307/26

HMIE (2007) *Improving: Services for Children*. Online at http://dera.ioe.ac.uk/241/1/ischgiocp.pdf

Lawson, H. (2016) 'Categories, boundaries, and bridges: the social geography of schooling and the need for new institutional designs', *Education Sciences*, 6 (32), doi: 10.3390/educsci 6030032

Levinas, R. (2005) *The Inclusive Society? Social Exclusion and New Labour. Second edition*. Basingstoke: Palgrave MacMillan.

Percy-Smith, J. (2005) *What Works in Strategic Partnerships for Children?* Basingstoke: Barnardo's.

Scottish Government (2001) *For Scotland's Children: Better Integrated Children's Services*. Online at www.gov.scot/Publications/2001/10/fscr

Scottish Government (2005) *Getting it Right for Every Child: Proposals for Action*. Online at www.gov.scot/Publications/2005/06/20135608/56144

Scottish Government (2006) *The Code of Practice for the Joint Inspection of Services to Protect Children and Young People*. Online at www.gov.scot/Publications/2006/05/16175644/0

Scottish Government (2007) *A Guide to Evaluating Services for Children and Young People Using Quality Indicators*. Online at http://dera.ioe.ac.uk/6481/1/evaluating%20services.pdf.pdf

Scottish Government (2008) *A Guide to Getting it Right for Every Child*. Online at www.gov.scot/resource/doc/238985/0065813.pdf

Scottish Government (2010) *Guidance on Partnership Working between Allied Health Professions and Education*. Online at www.gov.scot/Publications/2010/05/27095736/0

Scottish Parliament (2006) Joint Inspection of Services for Children and Inspection of Social Work Services (Scotland) Act. Online at www.parliament.scot/parliamentarybusiness/Bills/24785.aspx

Scottish Parliament Information Centre (2013) *SPICe Briefing. Children and Young People (Scotland) Bill*. Online at www.parliament.scot/ResearchBriefingsAndFactsheets/SB_13-38.pdf

World Health Organization (2010) *Framework for Action on Interprofessional Education and Collaborative Practice*. Online at http://apps.who.int/iris/bitstream/10665/70185/1/WHO_HRH_HPN_10.3_eng.pdf

## Websites

Christie Report at www.gov.scot/resource/doc/352649/0118638.pdf

Every Child Matters framework at https://www.gov.uk/government/uploads/system/uploads/attachment_data/file/272064/5860.pdf

Highland (region) Pathfinder Project at www.gov.scot/resource/doc/1141/0117449.pdf

United Nations Convention on the Rights of the Child at https://www.unicef.org.uk/what-we-do/un-convention-child-rights/

# 83

# Disaffection with Schooling

*George Head*

Disaffection, as far as it can be identified through non-attendance in schools, is problematic, to varying degrees, in all 'Western' countries. In the UK, the US and most of Europe, for example, the state provides free education in nursery, primary and secondary schools. In common with the rest of the UK, the law in Scotland requires children between the ages of 5 years and 16 years to be in education, normally in schools, thereby entitled to eleven years of compulsory education. Disaffection with schooling is notoriously difficult to 'define' and is often associated with disengagement, which is equally complex, entailing notions of non-cooperation, non-participation and non-attendance. A number of studies in both Scotland and England have focused on pupils identified by their teachers as disaffected, usually based on their (mis)behaviour in school. Almost inevitably, school disciplinary procedures lead to such behaviour resulting in exclusion or pupil self-withdrawal from school, referred to, in Scottish Government statistical publications, as unauthorised absence including truancy. Whilst truancy may be seen as a negative and irresponsible reaction to school and learning, exclusion is often seen as a socially and legally acceptable decision on the part of schools as a means of addressing pupil disruption and poor behaviour. Absence, truancy and poor behaviour (leading to exclusion), therefore, have been considered as markers of pupils' disaffection with schooling and, historically, the Scottish Government's published statistics on exclusions and unauthorised absence have been used to identify the extent of pupil disaffection in Scottish schools. This chapter explores the complexities of what is considered as disaffection with schooling, the extent of the problem, the factors that contribute to pupil disaffection and the measures chosen by schools and local authorities to address it.

## DEFINITION AND TERMINOLOGY

Defining what exactly constitutes problematic non-attendance and hence disaffection in school is complex and complicated by a number of factors, some of which pertain to schools and others lying beyond the school. Consequently, this leads to difficulty in how levels of absence are calculated and how research and literature are interpreted. For example, some authorities and schools consider term-time holidays as absence, which, whilst it can be considered non-attendance, is not necessarily a marker of disaffection. In June 2003, the then Scottish Executive Education Department (SEED) issued a circular on non-attendance that included definitions of what constituted attendance, disaffection with schooling, authorised absence and unauthorised absence in Scotland. Attendance was defined as, 'participation in a programme of educational activities arranged by the school' (Scottish Executive Education Department, 2003, p. 2). In addition to attendance at school itself, this definition allowed for work experience, educational visits, study leave during exam times, other events organised in conjunction with the school, and education through outreach services or hospital teachers.

Unauthorised absence in Scotland, therefore, remains simply any unexplained absence, truancy and family holidays during term time. The one context that remains within a 'grey' area is absence as a result of exclusion. Whilst it is recognised that exclusion is 'imposed by the school and not the action of a pupil or parent' (Scottish Executive Education Department, 2003, p. 4) and therefore does not constitute unauthorised absence, it nevertheless remains a contested area and is reported separately from other absence. Within a schools context, Charlton et al. (2004) argue that there is a close relationship between exclusion and truancy and their negative impact on behaviour and the relationships among pupils and teachers. Hilton's (2006) Scottish study found similar relationships among long periods of truancy, exclusion from school and pupil disaffection.

Shute and Cooper (2015, p. 66) point out that the fifteenth-century etymology of truancy refers to 'one who wanders from an appointed place', which provides a generally understandable working definition that allows for nuances and variation in recent and current studies. In Scotland, truancy is described as 'unauthorised absence from school for any period as a result of premeditated or spontaneous action on the part of pupil, parent or both' (Scottish Executive Education Department, 2003, p. 4). This definition was confirmed in subsequent bulletins on attendance and absence statistics for Scottish schools up to and including December 2011. Recent literature has widened the scope of truancy research to include in-school truancy (Shute and Cooper, 2015) and truancy and wellbeing (Attwood and Croll, 2016). Indeed, in order to reflect children and young people's experiences, there is recognition that truancy is variable from casual (infrequent, less than e.g. three days, skipping single classes), to moderate (four to nine days) and chronic (frequent, longer, e.g. ten or more days).

The range of terms used to identify or describe young people who are not in school reflects the complex nature of non-attendance in schools. Terminology can be as obvious and transparent as, for example, 'absentee', most likely to be used to described someone who is not at school for a short period. Where unauthorised absence or periods of non-attendance are more persistent and long term, the terminology applied to young people becomes more sophisticated, with connotations of deficit in social, psychological and learning aspects of their make-up. The choice of term for young people who are persistently absent from school depends on how the problem of non-attendance is perceived and the way in which schools and teachers deal with the pupils concerned. They may differentiate, for example, between truants on the one hand and school refusers on the other, with the former attracting perceptions of being harder working and less badly behaved than the latter. The label assigned to students is not just a matter of semantics, as the explanations for and subsequent management of persistent absence is dependent on the perceptions that underpin the terminology.

The term 'school refuser' may be chosen in preference to other common usages such as 'truant' and 'school phobic' for two principal reasons. First, the terms 'truant' and 'phobic' carry with them connotations that can serve as distractions when considering the learning of the young people involved. Truants are often characterised as being disaffected or disengaged with schooling and the approach suggested is one of alternative, usually vocational, education. Consequently, young people considered in this way are likely to find themselves attending further education colleges for at least part of their education. Phobic, on the other hand, carries connotations of a quasi-medico-psychological deficit.

Whilst there is a tendency in some of the literature to equate the terms 'phobic' and 'refuser', in both cases the student's problem is constructed as not belonging to the school, curriculum or pedagogy, and responsibility for creating the context in which the young person can learn is located outwith the mainstream classroom. However, 'refuser' does not carry the psychological weight as 'phobic'. The common experience of young people in Scotland considered phobic is referral to an educational psychologist (see Chapter 79) and, in extreme cases, removal from mainstream to segregated education in a special school. 'School refuser', on the other hand, simply describes what happens and makes no social, psychological or moral judgement on the young person or his or her behaviour. All school refusers are simply that: they refuse, for whatever reason or none, to go to school. The decision whether a student is described as phobic or truant is subjective, dependent on the opinions of teachers and others who work with the pupil. The description may well be accurate but can limit the approach adopted and act as a distraction from the main goal of education and prime focus of schools and teachers, that is, the young person's learning. In such cases, the terms 'truant' and 'phobic' suggest a deficit approach, assuming that the disaffection or phobia has to be 'fixed' before learning can be addressed.

## EXTENT AND VARIATION

The Scottish Government publishes biannual statistics on school attendance that indicate that overall absence rates are under 7 per cent and falling, the actual figure for 2014/15 being 6.3 per cent (Scottish Government, 2015). These figures cover attendance at mainstream primary and secondary schools as well as special schools and there is considerable variation among the sectors. Scottish Government statistics indicate, for example, that the level of absence in primary schools is consistently lower than in other sectors. The figures for December 2015, when percentage attendance is taken into account, indicate absence in primary schools at 4.9 per cent whilst the levels in secondary and special schools were 8.2 per cent and 9.3 per cent respectively. Whilst these percentages might seem low, they represent a significant number of pupils in Scotland who are absent from school on any one day. In addition, children with additional support needs, looked-after children, children whose first language is not English and children from urban areas of deprivation are likely to be over-represented in these statistics.

Research literature and other documents provide data that allows elaboration of government statistics. The Scottish Government (2007) document, *Included, Engaged and Involved*, estimated that one in five pupils had been involved in casual truancy, although less than 2 per cent were responsible for half of casual truancy. Furthermore, Shute and Cooper (2015) argue that 62–71 per cent of students truant *at some point*. Similarly, Attwood and Croll (2016) indicate that in their longitudinal study in England, one in five students reported truanting, though the most serious cases were limited to less than 1 per cent of their sample over the period of their research.

## FACTORS AFFECTING DISAFFECTION

Research has highlighted the connections between poverty, deprivation, low socio-economic class and non-attendance at school. Relationships between attendance and a number of other general educational factors such as the negative correlation between absence and attainment are suggested as significant, although no causal link has been established. It can also be argued that reasons for absence and the main barriers to regular attendance depend on the individual perspectives of pupils, parents, teachers, social workers and paraprofessionals, and research has established three sets of influences that encompass the range of reasons for non-attendance. These are home influences, school influences and pupil influences. Bimler and Kirkland (2001) speculate that there may be eight 'styles' of truanting that accounted for each of the individual reasons that young people offered for their non-attendance. The reasons themselves were identified as belonging to five clusters of truanting, two of which were associated with parental influences and three related to delinquency. Regarding non-attendance in terms of these clusters in turn suggests interventions based on school factors, family factors and factors related to teenage rebellion and delinquency. Broadhurst et al. (2005) similarly identify the relationship between home and school as significant, but discriminate between 'enduring' and 'discontinuous' forms of disengagement with school.

Home influences include family problems, attitudes towards school, and cultural and neighbourhood influences. In a range of studies, teachers and schools also identify home background as a crucial influence on attendance. In addition, depending on family history and academic performance, teachers may hold low expectations of some students. For example, Reid (2004a) found that the vast majority of unauthorised absences in primary schools were parentally condoned and that teachers believe that a pattern of parentally condoned absence, related to poor parenting skills and drug and alcohol abuse, is the reason behind most non-attending behaviour and disaffection.

School factors include ethos, leadership, curriculum and systems. Perhaps surprisingly, however, whilst teachers may have considered the academic aspect of school as a factor precipitating truancy, it was not universally deemed problematic by young people (Davies and Lee, 2006; Attwood and Croll, 2016). In those studies where pupils cited schoolwork as an influencing factor, it was not so much the curriculum itself but how it was taught that was identified as being an issue. In these instances, pupils identified teaching as instruction and teachers' perceived lack of interest in them as individuals as contributing towards feelings of disaffection and subsequent truancy. Moreover, assessment-driven learning, league tables and lack of adequate support for learning were considered significant influencing factors (Hilton, 2006; Reid, 2006). In Hilton's (2006) study, difficulties with schoolwork included large class sizes, the formal academic nature of the curriculum and lack of support for learning. Moreover, she reported that the constant focus on assessment undermined enjoyment of practical and creative activities. In Reid's (2006) study of educational social workers, his participants also identified the inflexibility of the national curriculum in England and Wales and the consequent lack of an appropriate alternative curriculum with an emphasis on practical activities as significant.

School factors considered to have a strong influence on pupils' decisions to truant were mostly related to school ethos, management and systems that left pupils feeling alienated. In each of the studies discussed in this chapter, pupils cited bullying (especially being bullied) as a reason for absenting themselves from school. This appears to have been exacerbated by a perception that some schools' pastoral care systems were inadequate for dealing with issues between pupils.

Closely related reasons given for non-attendance were illness (particularly in cases where the school was perceived to be unconcerned) and exclusion or suspension, which was equally interpreted as a sign of lack of concern on the school's part. 'At the heart of the disaffection the young people expressed was their sense of alienation from the key adults who embodied the values and priorities of mainstream school' (Hilton, 2006, p. 307).

Pupils with high levels of non-attendance acknowledge school-based factors as influencing decisions to absent themselves from school, but from their perspective, other factors were more significant. For example, in Attwood and Croll's (2016) study, they found that there was little complaint about the nature of the curriculum, but the general school atmosphere and poor relationships with teachers were the main reasons for non-attendance. Relationships with other pupils were also cited as significant factors. Bullying, lack of friends, unruly behaviour and peer-group pressure were cited in a number of studies as having a strong influence on pupils' decisions to truant (Hilton, 2006; Attwood and Croll, 2015). Indeed, the school as a social setting, rather than its role as an academic institution, would appear to be a much more noteworthy factor. Davies and Lee's (2006) study particularly highlighted the social nature of school.

The young people involved in studies considered in this chapter were clear that the social aspects of schooling were the major factors affecting their attendance and were able to project the impact of these factors on their lives beyond school. For them, their relationships with teachers depended on their and their friends' perceptions of the professional stance and personal traits of individual teachers, how they taught and their attitudes towards young people. Appropriate classroom interaction for them was based on mutual respect and being treated in an adult fashion, and teaching was about generating insight and understanding rather than instruction. Neither the subject nor the content of the curriculum was problematic for them.

Similarly, peer relations were powerful factors, especially for girls. In addition to negative relationship factors such as bullying and behaviour in classes and around the school, friendship was also a factor taken into consideration prior to absenting from school. For example, a significant number of participants in Attwood and Croll's (2006; 2016) studies were able to identify a negative precipitating event or series of events such as bullying or behaviour in class prior to withdrawing from school, but also reported going with friends as influencing a decision to truant.

This is similar to Head and Jamieson's (2006) finding, where the 'perceived constant surveillance by school, teacher and peers' (p. 38) contributed towards the creation and reinforcing of an identity related to students' reasons for not attending school. Hilton's (2006) study revealed a similar focus on relationship issues, especially those between pupils and teachers, rather than curricular matters. In addition, there was a perception among her participants that where relationships among pupils were difficult and problematic, teachers were unwilling to interfere. When pupil relationships were dealt with as a matter of school discipline, this was perceived as a mechanistic response that did not attempt to address the root of the problem and was considered symptomatic of teachers' and schools' lack of real concern for their pupils' welfare. Even when school was spoken of in educational terms, participants expressed dissatisfaction with the problems of obtaining adequate support. This led to a growing sense of isolation and not being valued, which in turn affected students' behaviour, including non-attendance. For these young people and those in other studies, there was a real sense of disappointment with school and school systems, and they perceived them to have failed them as people. For pupils, therefore, in contrast to the perceptions of their teachers and other professionals, it is school as a social setting and especially the relationships between pupils and teachers that are the most persuasive and powerful factors precipitating a decision not to attend school.

In addition to the set of three influences discussed above, Attwood and Croll (2006) also identified two sets of factors that impact on truancy: those that render young people vulnerable to truancy, mostly what could be described as environmental factors; and those that precipitate truancy, or what could be termed causal factors. Whilst Attwood and Croll assign factors to each of these categories, it may be that what constitutes environmental or causal factors depends on the perspective of the individuals involved. For example, most of the adults in each of the studies appear to have interpreted school-based factors such as curriculum, assessment and exams, and young people's 'failure' to perform to a high level as causal factors. Other factors such as school ethos, pedagogy and matters of pastoral care and support for learning, almost by definition, would be construed as environmental factors.

The young people themselves, however, held an opposing view. Hilton's (2006) participants, for example, considered the academic challenge of schools as non-causal but the factors that precipitated truancy were related to school as a social setting, especially relationships with teachers and other pupils. Moreover, there also appears to be a possible dichotomy between the views of parents and those held by teachers, social workers and other adults. Parents see the main causes of non-attendance as in-school matters including bullying and teachers' attitudes towards children. Teachers and other professionals, by way of contrast, appear to view the home environment and the influence of parents as having a greater influence on attendance (Davies and Lee, 2006).

Whilst non-attendance may be a problem for schools, self-withdrawal, that is, a pupil deliberately and possibly openly choosing not to attend school may, in fact, be a solution for some non-attenders who find school difficult for a number of reasons, some of which are discussed below. In these instances, Davies and Lee (2006) and Attwood and Croll (2016) argue that pupils' decisions to disengage with school amount to the articulation of a critique of school and the educational system. Attwood and Croll (2016) argue that young people choose to truant not because they cannot cope intellectually with school but because they choose to absent themselves from a context which they consider irrelevant and where they feel they do not belong. Similarly, Hilton (2006, p. 310) argues that in some instances, the problem may lie with teaching and the curriculum and not the pupil: 'the narrowed academic focus of the current curriculum and formalized pedagogy has led some scholars to interpret truancy as an entirely rational and understandable choice for pupils who see little relevance in it for their own working lives'.

Truancy is also a social problem with social costs and therefore cannot be considered in isolation. Several studies since the turn of the millennium cite evidence that indicates that the majority of crime committed in shopping centres during daytime can be attributed to young people who should otherwise have been at school. Truancy is also associated with other social issues such as drinking, taking drugs, minor crime and other forms of anti-social behaviour. Reid (2006) also points out that longitudinal studies indicate that there may be links between poor attendance and a range of social factors that have an impact on later adult life. Attwood and Croll (2006) also highlight that levels of truancy become more marked in secondary school. Truancy and attendance figures for Scotland (Scottish Government, 2011) reflect that trend and also suggest that additional support needs and social deprivation, such as that indicated by registration for free school meals and the Scottish Index of Multiple Deprivation, exacerbates the extent to which children and young people from disadvantaged backgrounds are likely to be absent from school.

## ADDRESSING TRUANCY AND DISAFFECTION

Within the four UK countries, parents can be prosecuted if their children do not attend compulsory education either in school or at home. In England and Wales, there is an emphasis on the regulation of parents' and young people's behaviour with regard to attendance at school: a range of procedures are followed beginning with the issue of an attendance order and, if parents do not make appropriate arrangements for their child's education, fines can be imposed or they can be sent to prison. In Scotland, local authorities have statutory responsibilities to provide appropriate education for children and young people. Pupils who do not attend school can be referred to a children's panel (the hearings system in Scotland for supporting children and young people at risk – see Chapters 79 and 80) and sent to segregated provision, for example a special school or unit. In addition, under the terms of the Education (Scotland) Act 1980, parents of children who do not attend school and who have not made other appropriate arrangements for their education can be reported to the Procurator Fiscal. Indeed, the regulatory philosophy may be so ingrained in approaches to dealing with attendance that even some measures intended to support rather than punish, such as guidance teams and support bases, have been nevertheless interpreted by young people as forms of punishment (Hilton, 2006). However, issues of non-attendance at schools are complex and confusing, and measures taken to address pupil absence have been largely ineffective and lacking in coherence, coordination and a common understanding of the problem.

Whilst overall the problem of truancy remains consistently at a relatively low level, there is nevertheless an enduring issue to be addressed for the small core of pupils responsible for most incidences of truancy. One appropriate way of addressing non-attendance for this group may be to consider the experiences of young people from the two perspectives suggested by the reasons cited for truancy, namely environmental factors and causal factors, which relate closely to Attwood and Croll's (2006) duo of precipitating events and school as a social setting. The combination of people and setting has been highlighted as the crucial mix in considering matters of non-attendance. For example, Broadhurst et al. (2005, p. 106) argue:

> At the heart of debates about education and participation is the intractable debate around agency and structure ... Who or what is at fault in relation to the persistent disengagement of children and young people from schooling? There is concern that discourses associated with The Third Way place greater emphasis on strategies to enhance individual agency and are more punitive than pupil-centred or family-centred methods (Blyth, 2001), failing to account for the deeply intractable nature of school disengagement and alienation from formal systems.

Punitive measures, however, have not been the sole means of addressing disaffection, behaviour and non-attendance; what could be described as a more pastoral or holistic approach has also been adopted. In a pastoral model, agency is not conceptualised as a citizen's responsibility to participate in a social contract, but is considered more in terms of a human capability to be nurtured and developed and an entitlement that is to be fostered and met. Holistic approaches, therefore, mostly centre on measures aimed at reducing school exclusions and absences through addressing the educational and social needs of young people. For example, Charlton et al. (2004) evaluated an alternative curriculum approach and found that inter alia the young people involved appreciated and responded to being treated like adults, the more relaxed atmosphere, better relationships with teachers and, most importantly, having control over their lives. They reported that some participants in the scheme chose to start attending school again as a direct result of their experience on the programme. Davies and Lee (2006) similarly argue that responding to non-attendance requires addressing the quality of relationships between teachers and pupils.

Holistic perspectives recognise that there can be a circular effect among the various factors affecting reasons for truanting and disaffection. Addressing non-attendance at school, therefore, may begin with an acknowledgement that for the student, it is often seen as a positive step to remove themselves from an uncomfortable, alien or even threatening context. In Scotland, for example, government advice recommends that where pupils are absent from school for no otherwise satisfactory reason, then schools should invoke a series of supportive procedures, including home visits by members of the school's pastoral care team or a home–school link worker and, where necessary, seeking the involvement of other children and family services in a multi-agency approach. In such cases, referral to more formal agencies, such as the Reporter to the Children's Panel, is seen as a last resort.

## DISCUSSION

The way in which disaffection and non-attendance in schools is addressed depends, there-fore, on how absence is conceptualised. Whilst some factors are suggestive of the breakdown of social networks requiring intensive, long-term and probably multi- and inter-agency intervention, others, especially those related to casual or moderate truancy, imply disrup-tion rather than breakdown and that short- to medium-term intervention would suffice. Regardless of the conceptualisation, however, certain factors emerge as common. These can be thought of as belonging to one or more of three strands: the relationships between home and school; what happens in school itself; and school as a social institution, especially the relationships between pupils and teachers. Each of these strands can be addressed in terms of systems, with, for example, schools having policy statements on dealing with learning, behaviour, non-attendance and sharing information, and working towards greater cohesion in multi- and inter-agency initiatives (see Chapter 82 for multi-agency working). Consequently, in an overtly holistic and ecosystemic approach, some local authorities are encouraging better attendance at schools as part of strategies to address social inclusion (Reid, 2004a). However, the same author points out that his research reveals that where multidisciplinary measures are in place, it is often the case that teachers are unaware of the other professionals involved and that headteachers may in fact prefer resources to be entirely school based rather than belonging to the central authority (Reid, 2004a), and that the processes involved have come to be seen as problematic and frustrating (Reid, 2004b; 2006). In Scotland, initiatives to address behaviour in schools through Curriculum for Excellence and *Getting it Right for Every Child*, intended to develop greater coherence and collaboration among children's services, may also be taken into account when considering levels of absence, truancy and exclusion and hence indications of disaffection with school.

Addressing school disaffection in a holistic way entails, in the end, a pedagogical approach (in its widest sense). It concerns the values and beliefs that teachers, schools and the wider community hold regarding young people, their learning and their place in society. Ultimately, it includes the values and beliefs held by young people themselves and how they play out in the complex relationships and interactions between teachers and pupils in schools. The environment in which they grow up, including school, lays the foundations of children and young people's development, learning and behaviour. Pastoral measures to address disaffection, therefore, recognise and affirm children and young people as members of the school community within the wider community with the rights, capabilities and entitlements that membership entails. Whilst in a punitive context, disaffection and its manifestations are seen as obstacles and barriers to learning and participation in schooling, in a pastoral approach these same features form the conditions that allow for the exploration and nurturing of pupil identities related to their sense of themselves as learners. Thus, these same young people cease to be 'disaffected pupils' and become instead young people whose relationships, behaviour and attendance indicate that they might be experiencing disaffection with schooling.

## REFERENCES

Attwood, G. and Croll, P. (2006) 'Truancy in secondary school pupils: prevalence, trajectories and pupil perspectives', *Research Papers in Education*, 21 (4), 467–84.

Attwood, G. and Croll, P. (2016) 'Truancy and well-being among secondary school pupils in England', *Educational Studies*, 41 (1–2), 14–28, doi: 10.1080/03055698.2014.955725

Bimler, D. and Kirkland, J. (2001) 'School truants and truancy motivation sorted out with multidimensional scaling', *Journal of Adolescent Research*, 16 (1), 75–102.

Blyth, E. (2001) 'The impact of the first term of the New Labour Government on social work in Britain: the interface between education policy and social work', The British Journal of Social Work, 31 (4), 563–77.

Broadhurst, K., Paton, H. and May-Chahal, C. (2005) 'Children missing from school systems: exploring divergent patterns of disengagement in the narrative accounts of parents, carers, children and young people', *British Journal of Sociology of Education*, 26 (1), 105–19.

Charlton, T., Panting, C. and Willis, H. (2004) 'Targeting exclusion, disaffection and truancy in secondary schools', *Emotional and Behavioural Difficulties*, 9 (4), 261–75.

Davies, J. D. and Lee, J. (2006) 'To attend or not to attend? Why some students choose school and others reject it', *Support for Learning*, 21 (4), 204–9.

Head, G. and Jamieson, S. (2006) 'Taking a line for a walk: including school refusers', *The Journal of Pastoral Care in Education*, 24 (3), 32–40.

Hilton, Z. (2006) 'Disaffection and school exclusion: why are inclusion policies still not working in Scotland?' *Research Papers in Education*, 21 (3), 295–314.

Reid, K. (2004a) 'The views of head teachers and teachers on attendance issues in primary schools', *Research in Education*, 72, 60–76.

Reid, K. (2004b) 'A long-term strategic approach to tackling truancy and absenteeism from schools: the SSTG scheme', *British Journal of Guidance & Counselling*, 32 (1), 57–74.

Reid, K. (2006) 'The views of education social workers on the management of truancy and other forms of non-attendance', *Research in Education*, 75, 40–57.

Scottish Executive Education Department (2003) *Circular no. 5/03: School Attendance and Absence*. Edinburgh: Scottish Executive.

Scottish Government (2007) *Included, Engaged and Involved Part1: Attendance in Scottish Schools*. Edinburgh: Scottish Government.

Scottish Government (2008) *Attendance and Absence in Scottish Schools 2007/08*. Edinburgh: Scottish Government.

Scottish Government (2011) *Summary Statistics for Schools in Scotland no. 2: 2011 Edition*. Edinburgh: Scottish Government.

Scottish Government (2015) *Summary Statistics for Schools in Scotland no. 6: 2015 Edition*. Edinburgh: Scottish Government.

Shute, J. W. and Cooper, B. S. (2015) 'Understanding in-school truancy', *Kappan*, March, 65–8.

# 84

# Educating Migrant and Refugee Pupils

*Daniela Sime*

Migration is now a feature of an increasingly globalised world and a central issue for political and public debate. This chapter focuses on the education of young people who have migrated to Scotland from other countries. According to the United Nations (2013), 15 per cent of the world's estimated 232 million migrants are children and young people. Family migration affects children's education, their relationships and potentially their wellbeing. Educators need to be aware of how migration, as a major life event, can affect children's ability to learn, to ensure provision is adequate and all young people achieve their potential. Access to education is a right for all children, stipulated in the United Nations Convention on the Rights of the Child (1989), and migrant children are entitled to education as soon as they arrive. The aim of this chapter is to provide a better understanding of the effects of migration on young people's everyday experiences, with a focus on how schools can best support them.

## SCOTLAND AND GLOBAL MIGRATION

Migration is not a new phenomenon, although there has been a recent increase in migration flows worldwide. The majority of migrants are pushed away from their home countries by poverty and conflict and tend to move internally (i.e. from rural to urban areas) or to neighbouring countries. The current refugee crisis has seen millions of Syrians resettled in neighbouring countries, Turkey, Greece and Jordan. Only a minority of migrants undertake long-distance migration. The United States has been for centuries the largest industrialised country attracting migration, although over the last decades, new immigration destinations have emerged. Within Europe, better work opportunities have seen many migrating from East to West. Many countries which traditionally had more emigration are now becoming mainly 'receiving' countries and need to adapt to an increasingly diverse population. This is also the case for Scotland. Migrants' lives and decisions to settle in another country are often linked to available employment and children play a key role in these decisions (Sime and Fox, 2015a). Children's safety and precarious employment opportunities may make parents decide to leave children behind.

Increasing mobility has made migration an issue of political and media debate. The last decade has seen considerable tensions between advocates of the economic benefits of migration and the perception of migrants as a threat to national identity and social stability. A rise in the anti-immigration sentiment across the United Kingdom was also linked to the Brexit vote. In a context of predominantly anti-migrant attitudes across Europe, the public in Scotland seems less opposed to migrants than in England. Scotland has, however, a relatively low migrant population (4 per cent against over 10 per cent in England). The Scottish Government has identified immigration as a driver for population and economic growth, advocating policies of attracting migrants and promoting an inclusive and multi-cultural Scotland (see www.onescotland.org). The Scottish independence referendum in 2014 brought to the fore the debates on national identity and what it means to be Scottish (as opposed to, or in addition to, being British). The debates around Scotland's position in the UK and Europe will continue in the context of Brexit.

## CATEGORIES OF CHILD MIGRANTS

In Census 2011 (https://www.ons.gov.uk/census/2011census), the percentage of foreign-born people residing in Britain was 13.1 per cent (up from 7 per cent in 1983), which represents 7.5 million people; over half have arrived since 2004. In Scotland, the minority ethnic population has doubled from 2 per cent in 2001 to 4 per cent in 2011. These demographic changes have also meant an increase in the number of migrant children in Scotland, and the number of children born to recent migrants (the so-called 'second generation'). Across the UK, there are now over 1 million children with English as an additional language (National Records of Scotland, 2013). Children from a migrant background should not be considered as one group, because they vary in terms of country of origin, social class, gender, religion, ethnicity and so on. As migration is frequently seen in terms of ethnicity, certain groups become more visible, while others are invisible. White migrants from the old Commonwealth countries such as Australia, Canada and South Africa are one of the largest immigrant groups, though rarely mentioned in media debates on migration. White Europeans have recently attracted media attention in the Brexit debate, although they are all counted under the 'White – Other' category in ethnic monitoring exercises, while representing several nationality groups.

The ways in which states categorise different migrant groups impacts not only on indi-viduals' rights to work and participate fully in society, but also on the ways they are perceived by their communities and their sense of belonging. Most migrants are economic migrants, who come to pursue better work opportunities or careers. Other categories include asylum seekers and groups less 'visible' in the media, such as international students, tourists and retirees. Since 1951, refugees have been protected by the United Nations Convention Relating to the Status of Refugees (www.unhcr.org/3b66c2aa10.pdf). The Convention, ratified by 145 countries, defines a refugee as a person who is unable or unwilling to return to their country of origin 'because of a well-founded fear of persecution on account of race, religion, nationality, membership in a particular group, or political opinion'. Asylum seekers are seeking protection under the Convention, and they become refugees once granted this status by countries where they apply for protection. Most countries restrict asylum seekers' access to work and some public services, on the basis that access to work would act as an incentive for others to make the journey and claim asylum under false pretences. This means that asylum seekers are mostly living in poor-quality social housing and on a minimal income, making them vulnerable to poverty and exploitation.

While many children migrate as part of a family group, increasing numbers make perilous journeys across several countries alone. As migration can be expensive, families make tough decisions to send children alone to safety. This category of 'unaccompanied asylum seeking children' poses significant challenges for public services. In addition to the significant emotional and psychological trauma that many experience during their journey, the absence of a family member post-arrival means that the state becomes their corporate parent. There are also issues in terms of access to support and rights. As children, their age entitles them to full access to services such as education; as migrants, however, their access to services differs between local authorities. Also, while as children they might receive support, such as access to education, accommodation and health care, their entitlements change when they turn 18, meaning that they live with the anxiety of an unknown future and are vulnerable to trafficking and exploitation.

## MIGRANT PUPILS IN SCOTLAND

The counting of migrant pupils is not straightforward. The *Summary Statistics for Schools in Scotland* (Scottish Government, 2016a), which relies on data submitted by Scottish local authorities and schools, puts the number of pupils who have English as an additional language (EAL) at 39,342. For comparison, there were 26,131 EAL pupils in Scotland in 2012, then 29,532 pupils in 2013 and 32,504 in 2014. Scotland has seen thus a significant increase in the number of EAL pupils since 2007 when records began (when only 741 EAL pupils were recorded). The majority of the newly arrived pupils since 2004 are Polish. Ethno-linguistic diversity is clearly a permanent feature of Scotland's education system and teachers have to support the needs of pupils at different stages of learning English as an additional language. The Scottish Refugee Council estimates that around 250 young people, aged under-18, have arrived in Scotland unaccompanied by a legal guardian. They are recorded as 'unaccompanied asylum seeking children' (UASCs).

The geographic distribution of migrant children across Scotland is also of interest. Pupils' experiences will be different in cities to rural areas, which may experience less diversity. Families tend to migrate to urban areas, where work opportunities are more readily available, which means that Scotland's cities are currently reporting the highest numbers of EAL learners. The ten local authorities with the highest numbers of EAL learners and the top three languages spoken by pupils in each of these are given in Table 84.1. Not all of these pupils are newly arrived migrant children. The main three languages recorded in each area reflect the successive waves of migration to the UK, with groups who arrived from the old Commonwealth states in previous waves (Urdu, Punjabi, Arabic speakers) and more recently established communities, like Polish or Lithuanian.

## KEY ISSUES IN THE EDUCATION OF MIGRANT CHILDREN AND YOUNG PEOPLE

Schooling raises several challenges for migrant pupils, including adapting to a new language, curriculum and school system, but also emotional challenges, such as coping with loneliness, separation from family members left behind, and establishing new friendships. Schools need to acknowledge the significant life transition which migrant pupils experience and consider the issues which may impact on their academic and personal development. Family migration clearly has an emotional toll, especially as children are rarely involved in decisions to migrate (Sime and Fox, 2015a). For young people who migrate alone, the concerns for the safety of the families they left behind and their own future are significant factors, with risks for mental health and emotional wellbeing.

Table 84.1  Scottish local authorities with the highest number of EAL learners

| Local authority | Number of pupils whose home language is not English, Gaelic, Scots, Doric nor sign language | Number of pupils who have English as an additional language (EAL learners) | Number of languages | Main three languages after English |
|---|---|---|---|---|
| Glasgow City Council | 14,355 | 12,743 | 115 | Urdu, Punjabi, Polish |
| Edinburgh City | 8,272 | 6,096 | 102 | Polish, Arabic, Urdu |
| Aberdeen City | 4,383 | 3,459 | 81 | Polish, Arabic, Malayalam |
| Fife | 1,975 | 1,336 | 60 | Polish, Punjabi, Urdu |
| Aberdeenshire | 1,935 | 1,671 | 54 | Polish, Scots, Lithuanian |
| North Lanarkshire | 1,844 | 1,428 | 51 | Polish, Scots, Urdu |
| West Lothian | 1,761 | 1,414 | 56 | Polish, Scots, Urdu |
| Dundee City | 1,750 | 1,195 | 62 | Polish, Urdu, Punjabi |
| Highland | 1,660 | 1,352 | 60 | Polish, Scots, Latvian |
| East Renfrewshire | 1,305 | 886 | 49 | Urdu, Punjabi, Polish |

Source: Scottish Government, 2016.

## The Migration Experience and Implications for Pupil Support

Access to education is a human right stipulated in the United Nations Conventions on the Rights of the Child (1989). The Scottish Government has expressed its commitment to deliver equality of opportunity to all and to ensure that education promotes their safety and wellbeing. The Standards in Scotland's Schools Act (2000) expects schools to meet the needs of all pupils and support them to achieve their full potential. Existing legislation specifies that all children have a right to additional support, if they require it. The Additional Support for Learning (Scotland) Act (2004) provides a broad definition of what may count as additional support; migrant pupils may require support with learning English, but also support in other areas, for example disability or emotional support. It is important that language does not act as a barrier and children are adequately assessed, using interpreters whenever needed, to ensure adequate provision is put in place at the earliest opportunity. Schools can adopt several measures to support pupils new to the country to cope with this transition. These may include: a thorough initial assessment which involves the family, providing additional support with language and other curricular areas; a buddying system; and a welcoming environment which is reflective of the diverse cultures in the school. Schools are often 'hubs' for parents to meet other families and to find out about local services available. Children become facilitators of social capital and social networks for their parents. Their agency in the process is significant (Sime and Fox, 2015b).

Evidence suggests that minority status and poverty combine with underlying issues of racism and class, placing certain groups at a disadvantage in terms of opportunities for education, employment and participation, with impact on their integration. Children from families with lower levels of employment or education may thus experience poverty and marginalisation, especially in the absence of extensive networks of support. One group which suffers ongoing discrimination, racism and marginalisation is that of Roma migrants. Roma remain the lowest achievers in schools across Europe, discriminated against in schools and through other services, and likely to suffer from extreme poverty (Sime et al., 2017).

As language may be a barrier to communication with families, it is important that teachers and schools are alert to signs of neglect, abuse or exploitation, and follow processes of child protection. Cases such as those of Daniel Pelka, a four-year-old Polish boy who died in West Midlands in 2012 from neglect and physical abuse inflicted by his parents, show that practitioners need to ensure that child protection procedures are followed and language is not a barrier to children's safety. Some migrant children may be vulnerable to other risks, such as trafficking and exploitation, female genital mutilation and physical punishment. These may be cultural practices legal in some countries, while they are criminal offences in the UK. Educators need to work with other services to ensure families are aware of children's rights to integrity and protection and ensure their safety.

## The Attainment of Migrant Pupils

The Additional Support for Learning Act (2009) emphasises the support needed for migrant learners' achievement as it specifies that schools 'should be proactive in addressing the learning needs, and learning achievement of bilingual learners' (2004, p. 27). It recognises the links between the development of literacy in children's home language and the development of literacy in English, which might mean that some young people may require additional support to ensure that bilingualism is an asset in education rather than a barrier to academic achievement. Further guidelines to support the learning of bilingual pupils, in line with the four capacities of the Curriculum for Excellence, were developed in a document called *Learning in 2(+) Languages* (2005; see Scottish Government, 2011). This report recognises that bilingualism is a clear asset with proven cognitive benefits and schools should encourage it and build on family-based learning.

The attainment of migrant pupils is an issue of worldwide concern. Across most Western countries, on average, migrant children have significantly lower levels of attainment than their non-migrant peers. The Organisation for Economic Co-operation and Development (OECD) Programme for International Student Assessment (PISA) is a triennial international survey of 15-year-old pupils near the end of their compulsory education. The assessment focuses on science, reading and mathematics (see Chapter 68). The results from the 2015 survey (OECD, 2015a), which included over 500,000 pupils from seventy-two countries, highlighted that the academic success of pupils from an immigrant background differs across countries. In most countries, first-generation migrant pupils performed worse than students without an immigrant background, with a gap of about forty-three points. Second-generation migrant pupils performed somewhat better than first generation, but they were still behind pupils without an immigrant background. While the OECD report acknowledges that the cultural capital and education pupils have acquired in their country of birth are important factors, it states that 'their performance is even more strongly related to the characteristics of the school systems in their host countries' (OECD, 2015b, p. 2). The PISA results for migrants from the same country of origin and similar socio-economic backgrounds showed considerable differences in scores across destination countries, suggesting that educational policies and mechanisms of support available can make a significant difference to their attainment. The results also show that migrant pupils do better in mathematics and problem-solving tests than in reading, suggesting that a minority home language puts migrants at disadvantage in standardised tests. In addition to the language penalty, migrant pupils suffer from structural disadvantages in school, with teachers' attitudes and low expectations of migrant success as key factors (Janta and Harte, 2015).

In the UK, the attainment gap of children from an ethnic minority background has been an issue of ongoing concern. In particular, the low attainment of young people from Black Caribbean background, many second-generation migrants, and Gypsy Travellers, has been highlighted. In England, data on attainment at age 16, using the threshold of achieving five or more General Certificate of Secondary Education (GCSE) passes at A*–C grades, indicates that performance of Travellers of Irish heritage (17.1 per cent) and Gypsy/Roma (11.6 per cent), Black Caribbean (58.6 per cent), Pakistani (61.6 per cent) groups is below that of their White British peers (65.1 per cent). At the same time, the achievement of Bangladeshi (70.6 per cent) and Indian (81 per cent) and Chinese (85.5 per cent) students is higher (Department for Education, 2015). In Scotland, the latest Scottish Credit and Qualifications Framework (SCQF) level 4–6 data (2015) suggests that Gypsy Travellers are the lowest achievers, with Polish young people slightly behind their White – Scottish peers. The Asian minority ethnic pupils in Scotland are doing better than their White peers (see Table 84.2).

Table 84.2  Percentage of school leavers by attainment at SCQF level 4 to 6 by pupil ethnicity, 2014/15

| | 2014/15 | | |
| --- | --- | --- | --- |
| | 1 or more at SCQF level 4 | 1 or more at SCQF level 5 | 1 or more at SCQF level 6 |
| White – Scottish | 96.3 | 85.0 | 59.8 |
| White – Other British | 96.0 | 85.0 | 60.0 |
| White – Irish | 100.0 | 87.1 | 54.8 |
| White – Polish | 88.8 | 76.0 | 42.3 |
| White – Gypsy/Traveller | 61.4 | 40.9 | 15.9 |
| White – Other | 95.7 | 87.0 | 63.0 |
| Mixed or multiple ethnic groups | 96.5 | 89.5 | 68.0 |
| Asian – Indian | 98.6 | 92.1 | 71.6 |
| Asian – Pakistani | 97.9 | 89.7 | 71.1 |
| Asian – Chinese | 99.4 | 95.4 | 88.0 |
| Asian – Other | 96.6 | 90.9 | 77.7 |
| African/Black/Caribbean | 98.9 | 93.8 | 74.6 |
| All other categories | 96.3 | 85.1 | 62.1 |
| Not disclosed/Not known | 93.0 | 81.5 | 53.2 |
| All leavers | 96.2 | 85.2 | 60.2 |

Source: www.gov.scot/Topics/Statistics/Browse/School-Education/TrendAttainmentS4S6

Poverty is directly linked to attainment. It can impact children's learning, for example through limited access to learning materials or after-school activities, with an increased risk of ill health and developmental problems. Research on migrants' living conditions post-migration suggests that many tend to settle in poorer neighbourhoods, where housing is usually cheaper. Risk factors such as exclusion through poor access to educational services and the language barrier can combine in the case of migrants to create multiple disadvantages. While the presence of migrant pupils in schools does not have a negative effect on student performance in these schools, according to PISA analysis referred to above, the presence of large numbers of pupils with low educated parents in one school has a far greater negative impact on the overall school achievement. This suggests that educational policies need to concentrate on the distribution of migrant children across schools and across classrooms within schools. It is also clear that, across Europe, poor educational achievement puts some migrant pupils at risk of long-term underachievement, unemployment and marginalisation. Children from a migrant background are disproportionately represented among early school leavers. However, there are countries (Belgium, Germany, Switzerland) which have combined successful education and social policies to buffer the negative effects of poverty and migration among young people and increase their achievement, according to the 2015 PISA analysis (OECD, 2015a).

## Language and Literacies Diversity, Identities and Belonging

Increasingly, individuals around the world operate in two or more languages. This increasing linguistic diversity is cultural capital for future generations and an asset for Scotland's schools. While the curriculum in Scotland is delivered mainly in English, teachers have become more alert to the literacy skills that bilingual pupils develop outside the classroom, through family-based learning. This means that teaching needs to become more reflective of the multiple literacies that young people operate in across the home and school, and local, transnational and virtual spaces. Young people increasingly use literacies in email, podcasts, videos and other forms of visual media. This calls for a multilingual approach in the classroom, reflective of the diversity of cultures and languages, but also of the diverse modalities young people experience as texts. While the focus in schools remains on English language skills, it is important that young people's competencies in other languages are acknowledged and featured more prominently in curriculum practices.

Languages, cultures and one's sense of identity are closely linked. The processes of identity construction are complex and young migrants navigate several social, cultural and linguistic spaces. If curriculum materials reflect a single, monolingual culture, young people may feel alienated, excluded and uncertain about their place in their new country. Educators may think that their lack of competence in other languages is a barrier to creating an inclusive linguistic and cultural school environment. Research with EAL pupils shows that aspects such as multilingual signage, use of words in other languages in the classroom, encouragement of young people to use other languages between themselves and an interest from staff and pupils in children's home languages, histories and cultures give a clear message that other identities matter and are part of the school culture.

In teaching, the use of pupils' other languages through careful differentiation of curricular activities which do not rely on English support can motivate EAL learners. As previously mentioned, formal assessments such as national tests are not equitable to EAL learners and do not always give an accurate assessment of their attainment and may disincentivise them to achieve. Teachers must be careful not to take EAL learners' level of competence in English as an indicator of attainment in other subject areas. With increasing diversity, new assessment mechanisms are needed, which do not penalise migrant children. Currently, young people in Scotland can take English for Speakers of Other Languages (ESOL) qualifications (National 2–5 and Higher); however, few schools offer these qualifications. ESOL Highers are, however, recognised as entry to Scottish universities. For newly arrived pupils, teachers must also be aware that while young people's conversational English may develop in a matter of months, they may take several years to acquire subject-specific jargon and reach full linguistic competence. It is important therefore that their access to curriculum is not impaired by their developing competence in curricular English or writing skills, and teachers must find ways to make curriculum tasks accessible, for example by translating instructions.

Moving to another country also raises issues of identity and belonging for young people, who may encounter difficulties in finding new friendships while missing family and friends left behind (Sime and Fox, 2015a). Young people may also become alienated by schools, either through the curriculum if unrepresentative of their cultural identities, or through social isolation and loneliness. These are significant risks for young people's motivation and wellbeing. Research also shows that schools are places in which young people experience everyday racism, such as name calling or being mocked or laughed at for their accent, misunderstanding of colloquialisms or slang words, clothing or culture-specific customs. Teachers' own attitudes have also been highlighted by research. Some teachers hold anti-immigrant attitudes, which may interfere with their duties to ensure all learners are treated equitably. It is important that teachers ensure their actions, verbal and non-verbal, indicate they are treating all learners fairly and do not inadvertently exclude migrant learners. Teachers may unintentionally send the wrong message, for example by avoiding to call on pupils thinking they do not have the language competence. In 2016 the Scottish Government legislated the duty of public services to promote race equality and fairness of opportunities through the *Race Equality Framework*, which reaffirms the government's commitment to race equality, treating individuals as equal, and actively tackling discrimination (Scottish Government, 2016b).

Young people may also feel alienated in their communities; a sense of belonging takes time to develop and depends on young people's opportunities to know about services available and make friendships locally. Schools can be instrumental in facilitating young people's access to networks of support by working with local agencies to increase initiatives for cultural dialogue and inter-ethnic collaborations. Pupils often become brokers for families, who may not know of services available or may be new to English. Factors such as parents' own education, language competence and social class are key factors in their involvement with schools. Scottish education policy documents refer often to 'young people's aspirations' and parents' aspirations as closely linked to issues of attainment and school performance. Parental aspirations among migrant groups vary. Parents who show 'low' aspirations may have experienced inequalities in their own education, such as the case of Roma, and may think that it is unrealistic for their children to stay in school. It is important that schools find ways to make the curriculum and school structures accessible to migrant families in their children's learning, as parental involvement is a strong predictor of educational achievement.

## FUTURE ISSUES FOR POLICYMAKERS AND PRACTITIONERS

In the context of intensifying migration worldwide, the inclusion of migrant pupils will remain a key priority for schools. The ongoing debates over Scotland's position in the UK and Europe increases the uncertainty over the status of some migrants and over the future immigration regulations. This means that in future, schools are likely to see ongoing mobility of young people, and uncertainty over their future plans and their families' decisions to remain in the UK. This raises issues for educators not only in terms of supporting migrant pupils' attainment, but increasingly in terms of emotional support and the need to ensure that young people are not victims of racism or discrimination in schools or communities, as anti-immigration rhetoric permeates public debates.

Three sets of policies can be implemented for effective support of migrant pupils and to reduce the risks of their low attainment and marginalisation (Nusche, 2009). System-level policies refer to structural features of education systems, such as the mechanisms through which migrant families can choose the schools their children attend, how schools monitor children's progress, issues of resource for schools in areas where migrants settle, and policies of selection and assessment. For example, the segregation of migrant children across socio-economic characteristics reduces their probability of continuing to secondary education and increases their risk of underachieving. Educational policies need thus to consider factors such as the geographical distribution of migrants and school catchment areas, choice of schools and ability grouping. In addition to system-level policies, school-level policies and individual-level policies can reduce migrant children's disadvantage. Individual-level policies focus on student characteristics, such as socio-economic background and language proficiency. These can depend on the level of resource allocated to schools, such as additional funding for individual pupil support. School-level policies shape the school organisation and classroom environments, such as teachers' attitudes towards migrant children and expectations of them, and value given to family–school relationships. With financial austerity, teachers' ability to provide a supportive curriculum that recognises migrant pupils' identities, languages and cultures is likely to be affected by inadequate funding to EAL services and additional support needs provision. Policies of supporting schools with migrant pupils include allocation of additional resources with flexibility on how funds are spent to cater best for pupils' needs. Funding strategies can either adopt an integrated approach, targeting areas of disadvantage where many migrants might live, or target the specific needs of migrant pupils, for example through EAL services. Investment in early years, for example, leads to better long-term attainment and lower costs in remedial services later on.

Other measures can be taken at school level to reduce the inequity which might impact on migrant pupils' attainment. Migrant pupils tend to be over-represented in low ability groups and special schools, which may suggest that educational systems tend to favour non-migrant pupils. Curriculum and teacher routines tend to be modelled on the majority culture values, norms and experiences, which may seem alienating to migrant pupils. The bias in school materials, for example through the absence of migrant experiences or ethnic diversity, can have a negative impact on children's self-esteem and sense of belonging. It is important that teachers consider these aspects in designing curricular activities and make the curriculum content relevant to all. Teachers also need to be aware of their potentially negative bias towards migrant students, for example through lower expectations or marking bias, when assigning them to lower ability groups or not entering them for exams. Schools need to ensure effective mechanisms for EAL assessment, where teachers use assessment tools that take into account linguistic and cultural differences. Teachers' awareness of the challenges migration poses to pupils' ability to learn and wellbeing can help their practice, by giving them the confidence and knowledge required to identify best support. The fact that migrant pupils are often victims of racism and discrimination means that teachers have a duty to support their integration and fair treatment in school, but also beyond the school gates. This means teachers need to be prepared to tackle issues of racism and discrimination and be more aware of their own actions as potentially discriminatory.

Evidence suggests that migrants are not always aware of support available and schools can signpost families. Apart from funding at school level, pupils may qualify for additional means-tested support. In addition to ensuring families are aware of entitlements, work with families should focus on addressing their linguistic and cultural needs in order to enable them to engage in their children's education. This may include making information about the education system available in minority languages, using interpreters when meeting parents or using family liaison officers. Working with parents to build on children's family-based learning and to ensure parents are enabled to support their children's learning may require time to build relationships. It is important that teachers feel confident in interacting with families and do not think of language differences as a major barrier. Families should not be disadvantaged by language and they should have equitable access to the curriculum and school activities. The major challenge for an equitable education is ensuring that pupils receive the best support to enable them to achieve to their potential, while not losing sight of the particular barriers to equality associated with their migrant status. The very low proportion of teachers who are from an ethnic minority or migrant background is also an issue for future policy in Scottish education.

# REFERENCES

Anderson, C., Foley, Y., Sangster, P., Edwards, V. and Rassool, N. (2015) *Policy, Pedagogy and Pupil Perceptions: EAL in Scotland and England*. Online at www.ceres.education.ed.ac.uk/wp-content/uploads/Policy-Pedagogy-and-Pupil-Perceptions-Final-full-report.pdf

Department for Education (2015) *GCSE and Equivalent Attainment by Pupil Characteristics: 2014*. Online at https://www.gov.uk/government/statistics/gcse-and-equivalent-attainment-by-pupil-characteristics-2014

Janta, B. and Harte, E. (2015) *Education of Migrant Children: Education Policy Responses for the Inclusion of Migrant Children in Europe*. Santa Monica, CA, and Cambridge, UK: Rand Corporation.

National Records of Scotland (2013) *Census 2011: Population and Household Estimates for Scotland Release 1C*. Online at https://www.nrscotland.gov.uk/news/2013/census-2011-population-and-household-estimates-for-scotland-release-1c

Nusche, D. (2009) 'What works in migrant education? A review of evidence and policy options', *OECD Education Working Papers* 22, doi.org/10.1787/227131784531

OECD (2015a) *PISA 2015*. Online at https://www.oecd.org/pisa/pisa-2015-results-in-focus.pdf

OECD (2015b) *Helping Immigrant Students to Succeed at School – and Beyond*. Online at https://www.oecd.org/education/Helping-immigrant-students-to-succeed-at-school-and-beyond.pdf.

Scottish Government (2011) *Language Learning in Scotland: A 1+2 Approach*. Online at www.gov.scot/resource/0039/00393435.pdf

Scottish Government (2016a) *Summary Statistics for Schools in Scotland, No: 7-2016*. Online at www.gov.scot/Publications/2016/12/9271

Scottish Government (2016b) *Race Equality Framework for Scotland 2016–2030*. Online at http://dera.ioe.ac.uk/25928/1/00497601.pdf

Sime, D. and Fox, R. (2015a) 'Home abroad: Eastern European children's family and peer relationships after migration', *Childhood*, 22 (3), 377–93.

Sime, D. and Fox, R. (2015b) 'Migrant children, social capital and access to public services: transitions, negotiations and complex agencies', *Children & Society*, 29 (6), 524–34.

Sime, D., Fassetta, G. and McClung, M. (2017) '"It's good enough that our children are accepted": Roma mothers' views of their children's education post-migration', *British Journal of Sociology of Education*, 39 (3), 316–32.

United Nations (2013) Number of international migrants rises above 232 million. Online at www.un.org/en/development/desa/news/population/number-of-international-migrants-rises.html

## Websites

Here to Stay? project at www.migrantyouth.org
Scottish Refugee Council at www.scottishrefugeecouncil.org.uk/news_and_events/news

# 85

# Gender and Scottish Education

*Sheila Riddell and Elisabet Weedon*

Gender inequality in Scotland has, until relatively recently, been understood in terms of male domination of educational space and resources. There is now a greater awareness of the nature and extent of gender divisions in Scottish education, as evidenced by the publication of the *Equalities Action Plan* (Skills Development Scotland, 2016) and the Scottish Funding Council's *Gender Action Plan*, also published in 2016. There has also been a shift in the discourse, so that the problem of gender inequality now tends to be viewed in terms of male underachievement, as official statistics point to girls attaining better grades in school, leading to higher rates of female participation in further and higher education.

This chapter attempts to offer a more nuanced analysis, suggesting the need to take into account social class as well as gender in order to understand patterns of school attainment, where girls from disadvantaged backgrounds are doing much worse than their more advantaged peers, and only marginally better than boys from similar backgrounds. We point out the persistence of gender divisions in subjects taken at school, college and university, where boys dominate the field of science and technology, leading to ongoing gender gaps in labour market outcomes and earnings. We also highlight the need to examine the position of women and men not just in education and employment, but also in other key social spheres such as political participation.

Following the recent focus on male disadvantage in overall attainment, key bodies such as the Scottish Funding Council and Skills Development Scotland have decided to set targets in order to counteract gender inequalities. We argue that change will only occur when social audit approaches are combined with efforts to understand the circumstances which lead to gender divisions in the first place. Finally, there is a need to examine the unintended, as well as intended, outcomes of target setting to avoid the possibility of perverse effects. For example, well-intended measures meant to equalise male and female educational and occupational participation might have the perverse effect of limiting women's access to areas of the labour market where they have traditionally tended to do well, without opening up new opportunities.

## UNPACKING THE NOTIONS OF EQUALITY AND SOCIAL JUSTICE

There are different ways in which educational equality and inequality may be understood. Drawing on the work of the political scientist Nancy Fraser (2005), an equality of outcome approach, framed within a discourse of (re)distribution, suggests that it is important to identify and reduce disproportionalities in school attainment linked to variables such as gender and social class. By way of contrast, other versions of educational equality, framed within discourses of recognition and representation, emphasise the importance of ensuring that children from different backgrounds are assured equal levels of respect and representation in decision-making processes within education systems and the outside world. If children, young people and adults experience fair and respectful treatment as they progress through the education system, they are likely to be able to participate fully in the political, cultural and economic life of their society. A central argument of this chapter is that while there has been considerable emphasis on identifying and remedying gender differences in participation and attainment, there has been less focus on the way in which diverse masculine and feminine identities are shaped within education systems, with different consequences for various social groups.

## GENDER, SOCIAL CLASS AND ATTAINMENT IN SCOTTISH EDUCATION

Over the past fifty years, there have been major shifts in patterns of school attainment in Scotland, particularly in relation to gender. Researchers at the Centre for Educational Sociology (CES), University of Edinburgh, used longitudinal data to compare girls' and boys' examination performance with the passage of time. They found that, whereas in the early 1970s there were no gender differences, by 1984 there was a considerable female advantage in overall attainment (see, for example, Howieson and Iannelli, 2008). Explaining these changes, CES researchers maintained that comprehensive reorganisation in Scotland was associated with a general improvement of standards of attainment, with girls and pupils of low socio-economic status being the main beneficiaries.

The improvement in girls' relative attainment is linked to the influence of second wave feminism, which emphasised the importance of women's participation in education and employment. Major economic changes from the late 1970s onwards had a significant impact on young people's job prospects. Young working class men found that traditional jobs in manufacturing and heavy industry, such as coalmining and shipbuilding, disappeared. The expansion of the service sector led to an increase in female employment, although the jobs on offer in areas such as social care, beauty and call centres were often poorly paid and insecure. Households increasingly depended on women's as well as men's wages to cover household expenditure. Middle class women increasingly entered the legal and medical professions which had been traditional male preserves, although they continued to fall behind in seniority and earnings after the birth of the first child (Hills et al., 2010). Overall, the confluence of feminist ideology and labour market changes contributed to a much greater emphasis on girls' educational attainment and labour market participation.

The higher educational attainment of girls relative to boys has continued since the trend was first noted in the 1970s. Croxford et al. (2001) showed that in 1999, girls gained more Standard Grade awards than boys and the largest differences in performance were found at the highest levels of attainment, with more girls than boys gaining five or more awards at 1–2 (Credit level) and 1–4 (General and Credit level). A similar pattern was found at Higher grade. In 1999, 55 per cent of young men compared with 61 per cent of young women completed S5 and S6 with three or more Higher grade passes at A–C. Scottish Qualifications Authority (SQA) data from 1999 showed that female candidates performed better than males in every subject they entered, apart from Physical Education, Economics and General Science.

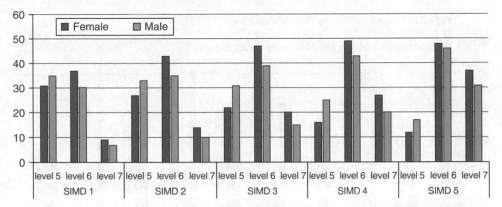

**Figure 85.1** **Percentage of school leavers by highest qualification achieved at SCQF level 5, SCQF level 6 and SCQF level 7, by SIMD 2012 quintiles and gender, 2014–15**

Source: Data provided by the Scottish Government in 2016.

A decade and a half later, Scottish Government data for 2014/15 showed a similar pattern, with girls doing better than boys overall (see Figure 85.1). However, Figure 85.1 also shows that differences associated with neighbourhood deprivation (as measured by the Scottish Index of Multiple Deprivation (SIMD)) are much larger than gender differences. Girls tend to leave school with slightly higher qualifications than boys overall, but pupils from the most advantaged areas in Scotland (SIMD 5) are roughly four times as likely to gain at least one advanced Higher compared with pupils from the least advantaged neighbourhoods (SIMD 1). This in turn feeds through to different post-school destinations, as shown in Figure 85.2. More girls than boys go on to higher education, but differences associated with neighbourhood deprivation are far more significant than gender differences. About three times as many pupils from the most advantaged neighbourhoods enter higher education compared with those from the least advantaged.

A number of points are suggested by these data. First, it is evident that the relative difference in the performance of the most advantaged and least advantaged social groups is considerable and has not significantly eroded over time. Whilst gender differences persist, social class differences are much greater, so a major concern of Scottish educators should be to narrow the attainment gap between those from more and less socially advantaged backgrounds. These differences in attainment are strongly associated with inequality in household income and, as noted by Hills et al. (2010), relative to other European countries, both the UK and Scotland have high levels of economic inequality which act as a brake on social mobility. Successive Scottish governments have attempted to tackle inequality, including the present Scottish National Party (SNP) administration through the Attainment Challenge Initiative and the National Improvement Framework. Despite these efforts, levels of economic and educational inequality in Scotland and England are broadly similar and highly problematic because of their association with many other social problems including diminished life chances and adverse social problems ranging from domestic violence to drug and alcohol abuse (Hills et al., 2010).

Since inequalities related to social class are clearly much greater than those related to gender, the question arises as to whether gender issues still require attention. As argued below, it is essential to understand the ways in which gender intersects with social class at all levels and in subtly different ways. In order to illustrate aspects of this intersection, we

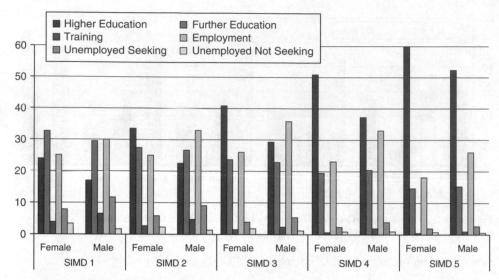

**Figure 85.2   Destinations of school leavers from publicly funded schools by SIMD 2012 quintiles and gender, 2014–15**

Source: Data provided by the Scottish Government in 2016.

Note: Three categories with entries at 1 per cent or below have been omitted (Voluntary Work, Activity Agreements and Unknown)

discuss gender and the curriculum in school, college and university, as well as differences in the identification of additional support needs.

## GENDER AND THE CURRICULUM

It is evident that gender differences in subject uptake have proved remarkably resistant to change, with major implications for the labour market position of women and men. Croxford et al. (2001) noted gender differences in subjects within curriculum modes. Since science is such an important subject in an increasingly technological age, it is worth looking closely at male and female participation in this area. Croxford (1997) analysed such patterns over a fifteen-year period in the context of the introduction of the common curriculum in the 1980s and the implementation of equal opportunities legislation. The proportion of girls aged 14–16 studying Physics slowly but steadily climbed from 10 per cent in 1976 to just over 20 per cent in 1990. In Biology, the proportion of boys studying the subject has also increased, from 12 per cent in 1976 to 28 per cent in 1990, although the pattern here is less smooth, with small declines in 1986 and 1988. Croxford concluded that even though the common curriculum in Scotland is presented in gender-neutral terms, the opportunities for choice within it result in girls and boys opting for different routes, with their attendant messages about appropriate concerns and future occupations for males and females. This, she suggests, may be attributed to 'deep-seated attitudes that some subjects are more appropriate for girls or boys' (Croxford, 1997). She commented: 'Gender differences in post-compulsory courses and careers would be reduced if there was a larger common entitlement and less choice of subjects for the final two years of each national curriculum' (Croxford, 2000).

To what extent has the curriculum become more gender neutral over time? Data for 2016 published by the Scottish Qualifications Agency show that traditional gender differences are still firmly entrenched within the Scottish curriculum and become more marked as pupils move through the education system (see Figures 85.3 and 85.4). At levels 5 and 6, nearly twice as many girls are entered for Biology compared to boys. A similar pattern is found in French, where girls outnumber boys, while in Physics the reverse pattern is evident. Computing Science is heavily male dominated, with boys making up around 80 per cent of all those entered at levels 5 and 6. It should be noted, however, that even though many subjects are dominated by either boys or girls, pass rates are relatively high for those of the minority group, presumably indicating a high level of motivation amongst those going against the gender grain.

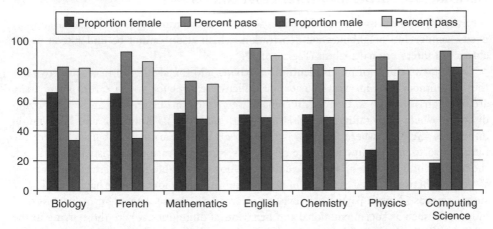

**Figure 85.3 Proportion of female and male entries at SCQF level 5 by selected subjects, and percentage pass rates A–D, 2016**

Source: https://www.sqa.org.uk/sqa/64717.html

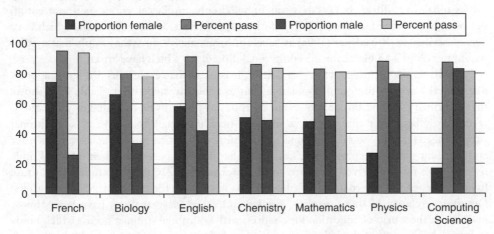

**Figure 85.4 Proportion of female and male entries at SCQF level 6 by selected subjects, and percentage pass rates A–D, 2016**

Source: https://www.sqa.org.uk/sqa/64717.html

Evidence from across Europe suggests that the best way of avoiding stark gender differences is to delay subject choice for as long as possible – see, for example, the European comparative report published in 2009 (www.nesse.fr/nesse/activities/reports/gender-report-pdf). Some European countries, such as Sweden, where subject choice is deferred until upper secondary stage, have less marked gender divisions in science compared with Scotland. The strongly gendered curriculum in Scotland continues to send out clear messages to girls and boys about appropriate constructions of masculinity and femininity, underlining the point that our concerns need to go beyond addressing the problem of boys' underachievement.

## GENDER AND ADDITIONAL SUPPORT NEEDS

A further persistent issue in Scottish education is the association between additional support needs, gender and neighbourhood deprivation, which again cannot be understood in the absence of intersectional analysis (Figure 85.5).

Overall, two thirds of pupils identified as having additional support needs are boys and they outnumber girls in every category of difficulty except for young carer, where there are more girls than boys. Gender differences are greatest in the areas of autistic spectrum disorder, where boys outnumber girls by five to one; social, emotional and behavioural difficulties (SEBD), where the ratio is three to one; and learning disabilities, where the ratio is two to one. In low incidence disabilities, such as hearing and visual impairment, the number of boys and girls is more equal. As shown by Table 85.1, there is also a strong association between living in an area of deprivation and being identified as having additional support needs. This is particularly evident in areas which are dependent on professional judgement such as social, emotional and behavioural difficulties, where those living in the most deprived areas are more than 2.6 times as likely as likely to be placed in this category compared with those living in the least deprived areas. As well as being the largest category of difficulty, being identified as having social, emotional and behavioural difficulties carries a strong social stigma and is associated with exclusion from school. The label is attached by professionals to children, but is rarely sought by parents, unlike categories such as attention deficit hyperactivity disorder (ADHD), autistic spectrum disorder or dyslexia, which have been described by Roger Slee (1995) as 'labels of forgiveness', since they imply that neither parent nor child is to blame for the educational difficulties which have arisen.

As with pupils identified as having SEBD, it is clear that exclusions are not randomly distributed amongst the pupil population, but are socially structured. Table 85.2 shows that at primary school, boys are over eleven times as likely to be excluded as girls and at secondary school over three times as likely to be excluded. Pupils who have additional support needs (mainly social, emotional and learning difficulties, autistic spectrum disorder and learning disabilities) are about four times as likely to be excluded as others. Pupils living in the most deprived areas are seven times more likely to be excluded than those living in the least deprived areas. Disabled pupils have twice the rate of exclusion of others. Despite the clarity of these patterns, gender and social class analyses have been almost invisible in the world of education for children with additional support needs, which tends to focus on the needs of the individual pupil in isolation from his or her social context.

Disproportionalities in the field of additional support needs and exclusions highlight the social and educational marginalisation of boys from disadvantaged backgrounds. Scottish Government statistics on the prison population (one of the highest in Western Europe

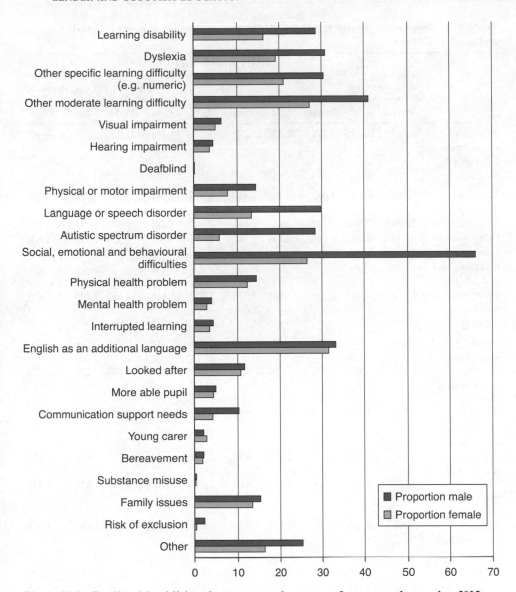

**Figure 85.5   Pupils with additional support needs: reasons for support by gender, 2015 (rate per 1,000 pupils)**

Source: http://www.gov.scot/Topics/Statistics/Browse/School-Education/dspupcensus/ dspupcensus15

at 153 per 100,000 population) show that 95 per cent of prisoners are men aged under 25 from socially disadvantaged backgrounds (www.gov.scot/Resource/0049/00491398.pdf). Half were previously excluded from school and the majority have literacy and numeracy skills below the level that would be expected for an 11-year-old child. Given the 'school to prison pipeline' also identified in other developed countries, there is clearly an economic as well as a social imperative to address the educational failure of economically and

Table 85.1   Number of pupils with different types of reason for support by SIMD and gender, 2014–15

| | SIMD 2016 Quintile | | | | | | | | | |
|---|---|---|---|---|---|---|---|---|---|---|
| | Most deprived | | 2 | | 3 | | 4 | | Least deprived | |
| | Female | Male | Female | Male | Female | Male | Female | Male | Female | Male |
| Pupils for whom reason for support is reported | 19,952 | 28,896 | 14,571 | 22,252 | 12,258 | 19,113 | 11,241 | 17,820 | 9,025 | 14,463 |
| Learning disability | 1,580 | 3,023 | 1,082 | 2,166 | 816 | 1,618 | 787 | 1,449 | 771 | 1,274 |
| Dyslexia | 1,349 | 2,146 | 1,309 | 2,049 | 1,433 | 2,302 | 1,510 | 2,518 | 1,451 | 2,326 |
| Other specific learning difficulty (e.g. numeric) | 1,748 | 2,540 | 1,647 | 2,334 | 1,565 | 2,455 | 1,708 | 2,524 | 1,238 | 1,836 |
| Other moderate learning difficulty | 2,752 | 4,047 | 2,376 | 3,481 | 2,056 | 3,233 | 1,835 | 2,870 | 1,105 | 1,809 |
| Visual impairment | 424 | 578 | 370 | 493 | 318 | 451 | 312 | 431 | 316 | 409 |
| Hearing impairment | 318 | 405 | 265 | 304 | 253 | 297 | 262 | 310 | 229 | 273 |
| Deafblind | 5 | * | 7 | 9 | * | 7 | * | * | 6 | * |
| Physical or motor impairment | 582 | 1,091 | 553 | 1,025 | 508 | 994 | 523 | 1,037 | 459 | 960 |
| Language or speech disorder | 1,166 | 2,806 | 1,012 | 2,366 | 950 | 2,164 | 820 | 2,055 | 732 | 1,588 |
| Autistic spectrum disorder | 587 | 2,807 | 514 | 2,483 | 469 | 2,052 | 398 | 1,941 | 329 | 1,749 |
| Social, emotional and behavioural difficulty | 3,042 | 7,950 | 2,236 | 5,725 | 1,936 | 4,694 | 1,676 | 4,412 | 1,184 | 3,015 |
| Physical health problem | 1,190 | 1,425 | 913 | 1,221 | 861 | 1,121 | 929 | 1,015 | 788 | 943 |
| Mental health problem | 269 | 381 | 239 | 344 | 250 | 316 | 246 | 320 | 183 | 279 |
| Interrupted learning | 437 | 581 | 287 | 393 | 231 | 321 | 223 | 304 | 131 | 158 |
| English as an additional language | 4,906 | 5,423 | 2,893 | 3,255 | 2,016 | 2,236 | 1,493 | 1,689 | 1,420 | 1,519 |
| Looked after | 1,459 | 1,531 | 867 | 985 | 630 | 674 | 507 | 626 | 355 | 393 |
| More able pupil | 270 | 294 | 252 | 290 | 306 | 316 | 318 | 427 | 307 | 482 |
| Communication support needs | 454 | 1,154 | 351 | 931 | 337 | 801 | 267 | 715 | 239 | 590 |

| | SIMD 2016 Quintile | | | | | | | | | |
|---|---|---|---|---|---|---|---|---|---|---|
| | Most deprived | | 2 | | 3 | | 4 | | Least deprived | |
| | Female | Male | Female | Male | Female | Male | Female | Male | Female | Male |
| Young carer | 350 | 226 | 283 | 192 | 263 | 201 | 200 | 155 | 86 | 81 |
| Bereavement | 259 | 303 | 166 | 209 | 129 | 146 | 136 | 152 | 104 | 120 |
| Substance misuse | 62 | 90 | 22 | 47 | 14 | 22 | 17 | 22 | 8 | 14 |
| Family issues | 2,109 | 2,536 | 1,316 | 1,475 | 872 | 1,095 | 736 | 870 | 388 | 509 |
| Risk of exclusion | 68 | 359 | 34 | 213 | 17 | 134 | 22 | 144 | 10 | 59 |
| Other | 1,885 | 2,623 | 1,347 | 2,082 | 1,003 | 1,659 | 970 | 1,608 | 660 | 1,253 |

* Less than five.

Source: Data provided by the Scottish Government.

Table 85.2  Cases of exclusion and rate per 1,000 pupils by gender, additional support needs, disability and Scottish Index of Multiple Deprivation (SIMD 2012), 2014–15

| | Cases of exclusion | | Rate per 1,000 pupils | |
|---|---|---|---|---|
| | Primary | Secondary | Primary | Secondary |
| Boys | 3,197 | 10,734 | 16.2 | 75.0 |
| Girls | 281 | 3,364 | 1.5 | 23.8 |
| Pupils with additional support needs | 1,926 | 6,957 | 25.9 | 117.4 |
| Pupils with no additional support needs | 1,543 | 7,095 | 5.0 | 31.5 |
| Assessed or declared disabled | 787 | | 52.6 | |
| Not assessed or declared disabled | 16,373 | | 24.7 | |
| Lowest 20% of SIMD (most deprived) | 7,579 | | 52.0 | |
| Highest 20% of SIMD (least deprived) | 1,005 | | 7.9 | |

Source: www.gov.scot/Topics/Statistics/Browse/School-Education/exclusiondatasets/exclusionsdataset2015

socially disadvantaged young men. However, this is not to imply that girls from socially disadvantaged backgrounds have a smooth passage through the school system. Those who experience mental health or behavioural difficulties may simply absent themselves from school. The minority who become involved in the formal exclusion process may be allocated to units where staff are used to dealing with the problems of violent young men rather than depressed young women and therefore receive little help.

## GENDER DIVISIONS IN POST-SCHOOL EDUCATION

As noted earlier, girls' performance in Highers has improved more rapidly than that of boys since the late 1970s and they now make up the majority of students in higher education. In addition, the growth in female university participation is explained by the redesignation of initial teaching and nursing education as degree-level subjects. At college level, women and men are fairly equally represented, albeit in different curricular areas. As part of its *Gender*

**Table 85.3    Subject areas in colleges and universities with severe gender imbalances**

| Colleges | Universities |
|---|---|
| **Female under-representation** | |
| Construction (general) | Architecture, Building and Planning |
| Building/Construction Operations | Engineering |
| Building Services | Technologies |
| Engineering/Technology (general) | Computer Sciences |
| Mechanical Engineering | |
| Electrical Engineering | |
| IT: Comp Science/Programming/Systems | |
| Vehicle Maintenance/Repair | |
| **Male under-representation** | |
| Child Care Services | Social Studies |
| Hair/Personal Care Services | Nursing |
| | Training teachers |
| | Psychology |

Source: www.sfc.ac.uk/web/FILES/Corporate_publications_SFCCP052016_GenderActionPlan/
SFCCP052016_Gender_Action_Plan.pdf

*Action Plan*, the Scottish Funding Council has identified the subject areas where there are severe gender imbalances (see Table 85.3). The aim is that by 2030, no college or university course will have more than 75 per cent of one gender, suggesting that serious efforts will be made to recruit women into Computing Science and men into Education and Nursing.

Skills Development Scotland has also recently expressed concern about the stark gender divisions evident within its Modern Apprenticeships training programmes (see Tables 85.4 and 85.5). Virtually all programmes are differentiated along gender lines, with females

**Table 85.4    Top five frameworks by participation and gender, 2014/15**

| Frameworks | Female | Male | Total |
|---|---|---|---|
| Hospitality | 1,572 (56%) | 1,221 (44%) | 2,793 |
| Business & Administration | 1,744 (71%) | 707 (29%) | 2,451 |
| Retail | 1,094 (55%) | 909 (45%) | 2,003 |
| Freight Logistics | 85 (5%) | 1,505 (95%) | 1,590 |
| Engineering | 61 (5%) | 1,303 (95%) | 1,364 |

Source: https://www.skillsdevelopmentscotland.co.uk/media/40691/2869_sds_equalities_action_plan_
digital_v7.pdf

**Table 85.5    Top five segregated frameworks by participation and gender, 2014/15**

| Frameworks | Female | Male | Total |
|---|---|---|---|
| Glass Industry Operations | 0 | 198 | 198 |
| Achieving Excellence in Sports Performance | 0 | 182 | 182 |
| Heating, Ventilation, Air Conditioning and Refrigeration | 0 | 94 | 94 |
| Power Distribution | 0 | 41 | 41 |
| Land-based Engineering | 0 | 34 | 34 |

Source: https://www.skillsdevelopmentscotland.co.uk/media/40691/2869_sds_equalities_action_plan_
digital_v7.pdf

concentrated in those leading to less well-paid areas of the labour market. As shown in Table 85.5, five programmes are entirely male preserves, and these are the ones leading to better-paid jobs. Like the Scottish Funding Council, Skills Development Scotland has set targets for tackling these inequalities. For example, the Skills Development Scotland (2016) *Equalities Action Plan* states that by 2021, the aim is to reduce to 60 per cent the percentage of Modern Apprenticeship frameworks where the gender balance is 75:25 or worse. As already noted, although the target is clear, little attention is paid to the actions which might be needed to bring about the intended changes.

## LABOUR MARKET OUTCOMES

Women do not translate their success in school and higher education into labour market advantage and, since the economic crash of 2008, conditions have deteriorated particularly for those with few or no school qualifications. The Equality and Human Rights Commission (2016) noted that between 2008 and 2013, there was a significant increase in unemployment rates of 2.4 percentage points for women (to 6.4 per cent) and of 2.9 percentage points for men (to 7.7 per cent). Men are more likely to be self-employed than women, but female self-employment increased from 76,000 in 2007 to 101,600 in 2014, an increase of 34 per cent. Male self-employment over this period increased by 6 per cent. It should be noted that many people who are self-employed would rather be in more secure employment, but have taken this route in preference to being unemployed. As in other parts of the UK, in Scotland men were significantly more likely to be in manager, director or senior official occupations than women – 10.4 per cent of men in employment compared with 5.9 per cent of women.

Young people aged 16–24 have been particularly adversely affected by the consequences of the economic crisis. They have the lowest employment rate (51.5 per cent) of any age group and the highest unemployment rate (20.1 per cent; see Scottish Government, 2013). Employment rates for this group significantly decreased and unemployment rates increased between 2008 and 2013, with higher rates of educational participation only partly explaining these changes. Pay declined in real terms in Scotland between 2008 and 2013, with young people, particularly those with few or no qualifications, experiencing the largest fall. Overall, women were paid less than men. In 2013, the median hourly earnings (excluding overtime) for men were £12.66 compared with £10.45 for women. Men's average pay fell slightly more than women's between 2008 and 2013, leading to a small narrowing of the gender pay gap from 17.7 per cent to 17.5 per cent. Howieson and Iannelli (2010) demonstrated that girls with low levels of qualification at school have much worse labour market outcomes than their male peers.

## GENDER AND POLITICAL REPRESENTATION IN SCOTLAND

Given the emphasis on equality in the Scotland Act 1998, it is worth considering the extent to which the Scottish Parliament, established in 1999, has succeeded in delivering greater gender equality. As noted by Anne Phillips (1998), fair representation of women in the public sphere is extremely important because of the attendant messages about whose voices should be heard and which agendas should be addressed. In the case of the Scottish Parliament, progress towards fair representation of women and men appears to have halted, despite the three main political parties having female leaders (at the time of writing). In 2003, the high point of female representation, women made up 39.5 per cent of

Table 85.6    Scottish Parliament 2016 by party and gender

| Party | Female | Male | Total | % Female |
|---|---|---|---|---|
| SNP | 27 | 36 | 63 | 42.9 |
| Conservative | 6 | 25 | 31 | 19.4 |
| Labour | 11 | 13 | 24 | 45.8 |
| Green | 1 | 5 | 6 | 16.7 |
| Lib Dem | 0 | 5 | 5 | 0 |
| Total | 45 | 84 | 129 | 34.9 |

Members of the Scottish Parliament (MSPs), but in 2011, this proportion declined to 34.9 per cent (forty-five women MSPs). As shown in Table 85.6, in 2016 there was no change in the proportion of women MSPs. The two parties operating quota systems, the SNP and Labour, had much higher female representation than the others (42.9 per cent and 45.8 per cent respectively). The Conservatives gained ground in 2016, but had a low proportion of female MSPs (only 19 per cent of the total), while women made up only 17 per cent of Green MSPs. The Liberal Democrats had no female MSPs (https://www.holyrood.com/articles/inside-politics/analysis-representation-women-scottish-parliament).

## FUTURE ISSUES FOR POLICYMAKERS AND PRACTITIONERS

At the time of writing (early 2017), it seems likely that the next few years will see major political, social and economic change in Scotland, the rest of the UK and the developed world, as the UK proceeds with Brexit despite the economic and social uncertainties. Looking back over two decades, it is clear that girls and women have made great progress in terms of participation and attainment. However, it is equally important to remember that educational outcomes are strongly differentiated by both social class and gender and these divisions persist within the school and post-school curriculum, leading to marked inequalities in the labour market and in political representation. The economic fallout of the 2008 economic crash continues to be felt by large sections of the population, with particularly adverse consequences for those with few or no qualifications, particularly young people and women. The 'failing boys' discourse, highlighted by Jackson et al. (2010), does not capture the complex implications for different social groups, and tends to ignore the fact that male and female young people from socially advantaged backgrounds have been relatively protected.

It is interesting to note that the Scottish Government, the Scottish Funding Council and Skills Development Scotland have begun a systematic analysis of gender divisions in educational participation and attainment, with targets seen as the means of reducing gender inequalities. Phillips (2004) has argued that disproportionalities in social outcomes should always be critically analysed, and overall these initiatives are to be welcomed. However, they may easily lead to oversimplified understandings of the problem and the types of action which are needed. Targets generally treat groups, such as girls and boys, as homogeneous, failing to recognise that gender is always interconnected with other variables such as social class, ethnicity and age, and these should be taken into account in data analysis and action. Furthermore, there is a need to understand the social conditions which lead to particular patterns of participation and attainment. For example, young women may be deterred from different types of engineering by sexist attitudes and unwelcoming environments, and these need to be addressed. Similarly, young men may be deterred from pursuing careers in caring because of low pay and lack of social recognition. Targets alone will not address these problems. Finally, there is a need to be aware of the perverse outcomes which may arise if the impact of targets are not carefully monitored. For example, it may well be a good thing to have a better gender balance in teaching and nursing. However, it is also important to recognise that these have traditionally been routes to social mobility for women from less advantaged social backgrounds. If the proportion of men in these areas increases, it is likely that there will be fewer opportunities for women, unless new opportunities open up in traditionally male spheres. We need to be careful that targets are set and monitored in a way which promotes greater gender and class equality, rather than diminishing opportunities for already disadvantaged groups.

## ACKNOWLEDGEMENT

We would like to thank Dr Aisling Spain of the Scottish Government for providing us with unpublished data, enabling us to examine various aspects of the relationship between gender and deprivation.

## REFERENCES

Croxford, L. (1997) 'Participation in science subjects: the effects of the Scottish curriculum framework', *Research Papers in Education*, 12 (1), 69–89, 1997.

Croxford, L. (2000) 'Gender and national curricula', in J. Salisbury and S. Riddell (eds), 2000, *Gender, Policy and Educational Change: Shifting Agendas in the UK and Europe*. London: Routledge.

Croxford, L., Tinklin, T., Ducklin, A. and Frame, B. (2001) *Gender and Pupil Performance* Interchange 70. Edinburgh: Scottish Executive.

Equality and Human Rights Commission (2016) *Is Scotland Fairer? The State of Equality and Human Rights 2015*. Glasgow: Equality and Human Rights Commission.

Fraser, N. (2005) 'Reframing justice in a globalized world', *New Left Review*, 36, 69–88.

Hills, J., Brewer, M., Jenkins, S., Lister, R., Lupton, R., Machin, S., Mills, C., Modood, T., Rees, T. and Riddell, S. (2010) *An Anatomy of Inequality in the UK*. London: London School of Economics.

Howieson, C. and Iannelli, C. (2008) 'The effects of low attainment on young people's outcomes at age 22–23 in Scotland', *British Educational Research Journal*, 34 (2), 269–90.

Howieson, C. and Iannelli, C. (2010) 'The effects of low attainment on young people's outcomes at age 22–23', *British Education Research Journal*, 34 (2), 269–90.

Jackson, C., Paechter, C. and Renold, E. (eds) (2010) *Girls and Education 3–16: Continuing Concerns, New Agendas*. Maidenhead: Open University Press.

Phillips, A. (1998) *The Politics of Presence*. Oxford: Oxford University Press.

Phillips, A. (2004) 'Defending equality of opportunity', *Journal of Political Philosophy*, 12 (1), 1–19.

Scottish Funding Council (2016) *Gender Action Plan*. Edinburgh: Scottish Funding Council.

Scottish Government (2013) *Local Area Labour Markets in Scotland – Statistics from the Annual Population Survey 2013*. Online at www.gov.scot/Publications/2014/05/4201/3

Skills Development Scotland (2016) *Equalities Action Plan: For Modern Apprenticeships in*. Glasgow: Skills development Scotland.

Slee, R. (1995) *Changing Theories and Practices of School Discipline*. London: Routledge.

# 86

# Addressing LGBTI Issues in Scotland's Schools

*Ian Rivers*

Lesbian, gay, bisexual, transgender and intersex (LGBTI) inclusion is a hot topic in Scotland today. The Time for Inclusive Education (TIE) Campaign has, in recent years, garnered significant support from the key political parties at Holyrood in its efforts to promote LGBTI inclusive education in Scotland's schools. In March 2017, it saw Resolution 11 passed by the Scottish National Party at its spring conference which resulted in the Scottish Government agreeing to establish a group to work towards LGBTI inclusion in all schools. TIE along with other third sector organisations such as LGBT Youth Scotland, Stonewall Scotland and the Equality Network have been at the forefront of supporting schools and further and higher education institutions in tackling homophobia, biphobia and transphobia (HBT). They currently provide resources for teachers to combat bullying in these areas.

This chapter explores the history and context surrounding LGBTI inclusion. It provides an overview of the research on the experiences of LGBTI young people in Scotland and examines the policies that underpin inclusion in Scotland's schools. The focus of the chapter then turns to research looking at HBT bullying, its long-term implications and the ways in which denominational schools can work proactively to support LGBTI pupils. The chapter concludes by providing signposts to resources that can be used by teachers in the classroom. Throughout this chapter, references to LGB, LGBT and LGBTI are made. Some studies and policies have focused on sexual orientation only (LGB), some have referenced transgender or trans young people as well as those who are LGB (LGBT) and some have referred to another group of young people who identify as intersex (LGBTI). Some basic definitions are provided below:

- *Heterosexual/Straight*: someone who is attracted to people of the opposite sex.
- *Gay/Lesbian*: someone who is attracted to people of the same sex.
- *Bisexual*: someone who is attracted to people of the opposite and same sex.
- *Transgender/Trans*: identifying as a trans man, trans woman, trans non-binary or as a cross-dressing person. Trans includes those who have undergone surgical transition as well as those who may be considering it. Surgery is not a requirement for trans identity. Increasingly we are seeing children identify as trans in primary school.
- *Intersex*: identifying as an intersex man, intersex woman or intersex non-binary person. Intersex people include those who are born with physical attributes (including genitalia)

or chromosomal variations that do not 'fit' typical definitions of 'male' and 'female'. Some undergo surgical procedures to conform (often during childhood), others do not.

The Scottish Trans Alliance points out on its website that intersex status is distinct from trans status and the two should not be confused. Since 2014, the Scottish Government has used the acronym 'LGBTI' in order to ensure that intersex people are acknowledged as being distinct in terms of identity and experience from trans people.

Other identities that can be found in the literature include gender-queer, gender non-binary and queer. These terms are used to denote a desire not to be limited in terms of human expression by cultural expectations of what it is to be 'male' or 'female'. The term cisgender is also increasingly used when referring to individuals whose gender identity matches the gender they were assigned at birth.

## HISTORY

Homosexuality was decriminalised for men over the age of 21 years in 1980 in Scotland (it was 1967 in England and Wales). While successive governments have reduced the age of consent from 21 to 16 years for all young people, the Conservative Government led by the late Margaret Thatcher introduced a piece of legislation that became synonymous with LGB discrimination in schools – Section 28 (or 2a in Scotland). In 1988 the UK Government introduced an additional clause (Section 2a) to Section 28 of the 1986 Local Government Act which stipulated that local authorities in England, Wales and Scotland, 'shall not intentionally promote homosexuality or publish material with the intention of promoting homosexuality'. Additionally they could not, 'promote the teaching in any maintained school of the acceptability of homosexuality as a pretended family relationship'. Here 'maintained schools' referred to public, nursery or special schools as defined by the Scotland Act (1980). Although no successful prosecutions were ever brought by individuals or organisations against local authorities, schools or teachers who ignored Section 28, it remains one of the most widely cited reasons why schools and local authorities failed to combat HBT bullying and support LGBTI pupils and teachers. Section 2a was eventually repealed in Scotland on 21 June 2000; however, it was not repealed in England and Wales until November 2003. It never applied to Northern Ireland.

## YOUNG PEOPLE IN SCOTLAND

In 2012, LGBT Youth Scotland undertook a study of the lives of LGBT young people aged 13–25 years. The resulting reports, published in 2012 and 2013 (LGBT Youth Scotland et al., 2012; 2013), offered a useful insight into the progress Scotland had made since the repeal of Section 2a. Overall, it was found that LGBT young people who reported feeling accepted by their communities were more likely to be in employment or education. They were also more confident in reporting hate crime to the police and were less likely to consider themselves as having mental health issues. Over 70 per cent of the young people surveyed (350) said that they believed Scotland was a good place to be LGBT and 68 per cent said they were accepted and included by their families. Those that had attended an LGBT-specific youth group were also more likely to report being 'very happy' with their lives when compared to those who had not attended such a group (LGBT Youth Scotland et al., 2013). However, other findings from this study indicated that Scotland still had a significant journey to make towards full LGBTI inclusion:

- 88.2 per cent thought that homophobia remained a problem in Scotland;
- 83.9 per cent thought transphobia was also a problem for Scotland;
- 67.3 per cent thought that biphobia was a problem for Scotland;
- 47.5 per cent felt there were enough places where they can safely socialise and be open about their sexual orientation and gender identity.

Not all of the young people who participated in this survey had experienced discrimination; however, the fact that so many felt that homophobia, biphobia and transphobia remained an issue suggested that many of the initiatives introduced by the Scottish Government were not well understood and there was a lack of evidence relating to the actions that were being taken to combat such discrimination.

## THE POLICY CONTEXT

In 2004 Scotland introduced its charter for children entitled *Protecting Children and Young People* following a review of the Children's Hearings System and pledged that those at risk of abuse or neglect could expect the following:

- to get the help they need when they need it;
- to be seen by a professional such as a teacher, doctor or social worker to make sure they are alright and not put at more risk;
- to be listened to seriously, and professionals will use their power to help them;
- to be able to discuss issues in private when, and if, they want to;
- to be involved with, and helped to understand, decisions made about their life; and
- to have a named person to help them. (www.gov.scot/Resource/Doc/1181/0008817.pdf)

Supporting the charter, and building upon various pathfinder projects in the Highlands and Lanarkshire, the Scottish Government subsequently introduced its national approach to improving outcomes and supporting the wellbeing of all children and young people which it entitled *Getting it Right for Every Child* (GIRFEC; see Chapter 78 for an overview). GIRFEC – which is now enshrined in law (see the Children and Young People (Scotland) Act 2014, www.legislation.gov.uk/asp/2014/8/contents/enacted) – has eight indicators of wellbeing at its heart: safe, healthy, achieving, nurtured, active, respected, responsible and included (collectively known by the acronym SHANARRI). The principles underpinning GIRFEC include better integration and information sharing among services for children and young people. Both GIRFEC and the Curriculum for Excellence (CfE) are inclusive and require those supporting children and young people to take into account the needs of those who identify as LGBTI. As the then Minister for Children and Young People, Aileen Campbell, wrote in 2013 for LGBT Youth Scotland's *Impact Report*:

> Our ambition is to give children and young people the best opportunities in life to thrive and develop into healthy, confident individuals, ready to succeed. Through legislative and policy developments, the Scottish Government is committed to ensuring that the United Nations Convention on the Rights of the Child is a reality in Scotland. And we will continue to work with partners to ensure that children and young people are listened to, respected and have their views taken into account. (Cameron et al., 2013, p. 2)

Along with the development of GIRFEC, in 2006, the Scottish Executive asked representatives of LGBT community organisations and universities to form a working group to look into ways of addressing negative and discriminatory attitudes towards LGBT people in Scotland. The LGBT Hearts and Minds Agenda Group identified five key areas for consideration: workplaces and public services; religion and belief; education and family; media and leadership; citizenship and social capital (Scottish Government, 2008a). The working group reported back with seven key recommendations relating to education:

- LGBT inclusion in the curriculum;
- Her Majesty's Inspectorate of Education (HMIE) to develop a good practice framework for schools in addressing the needs of LGBT young people, inspectors are trained on LGBT issues, and the General Teaching Council for Scotland (GTCS) includes a section of LGBT equality within their information for teachers on professional conduct;
- pastoral care of LGBT young people to be incorporated into professional standards;
- LGBT issues to be included in adult learning provision;
- LGBT awareness training to be included in teacher education;
- Scottish Government and local authorities take a lead in anti-homophobic bullying work in schools;
- commission further research into the experiences of trans young people and LGBT parents.

In responding to the report, the Scottish Government demonstrated a commitment to the majority of recommendations, citing the work it had already undertaken jointly with key stakeholders. However, it was clear that local authorities also had a role to play in ensuring that legal obligations to LGBT young people were met in terms of their wellbeing as well as their pastoral care needs. Education authorities were also identified as having the primary responsibility for ensuring that teachers' continuing professional development (CPD) or career-long professional learning (CLPL) included LGBT awareness raising (Scottish Government, 2008b). This has since been included in the GTCS standard for registration as a teacher in Scotland and the standard for CLPL. Specifically, teachers should demonstrate ways in which they are: 'Committing to the principles of democracy and social justice through fair, transparent, inclusive and sustainable policies and practices in relation to: age, disability, gender and gender identity, race, ethnicity, religion and belief and sexual orientation' (GTCS, 2012a, p. 5). Additionally, the code of professionalism and conduct (5.1) requires teachers to: 'engage and work positively with pupils, colleagues, parents and carers in an open, inclusive and respectful way, in line with the law and with a non-judgemental approach whatever their background, personal circumstances, cultural differences, values and beliefs' (GTCS, 2012b, p. 12).

In terms of inspection, the fourth edition of the *How Good is Our School?* (HGIOS4; Education Scotland, 2015) guide to self-evaluation and improvement asks staff to reflect upon the ways in which their school celebrates diversity and challenges discrimination (see Indicator 3.1: Ensuring Wellbeing, Equality and Inclusion):

We ensure inclusion and equality leads to improved outcomes for all learners. All learners are included, engaged and involved in the life of the school. All children and young people feel very well supported to do their best. Learners, parents and carers, staff and partners feel that they are treated with respect and in a fair and just manner. We understand, value and celebrate diversity and challenge discrimination. In our school age, disability, gender reassignment, marriage and civil partnership, pregnancy, race, religion or belief, sex and sexual orientation are not barriers to participation and achievement. We have effective strategies in place which are improving attainment and achievement for children and young people facing challenges such as those from our most deprived areas, young carers, those who are looked after and those with additional support needs.

Despite its long history of promoting inclusion, the Scottish Government continues to be concerned about the prevalence of HBT bullying in its schools as research suggests that their efforts to promote LGBTI inclusion have not had an effect on rates of bullying and discrimination experienced by LGBTI young people.

## HBT BULLYING IN SCOTTISH SCHOOLS

The very first studies of HBT bullying in Scotland's schools were retrospective; adults were asked to recall their experiences of being bullied because of their actual or perceived sexual orientation. From an initial sample of 190 LGB adults, only 7 per cent of respondents came from Scotland (Rivers, 2001). The results from this study indicated that participants recalled being called names most frequently at school. Being ridiculed publicly and rumour mongering were also frequently cited as was being hit or kicked. Only 22 per cent of participants said they had told a teacher about the bullying they experienced with only 16 per cent telling their teacher why they were bullied. Later studies conducted by LGBT Youth Scotland and Stonewall Scotland suggested that very little had changed in Scottish schools. For example, in LGBT Youth Scotland's 2006 report entitled, *Promoting Equal Opportunities in Scotland*, just over half the respondents to the online survey (seventy-seven) reported being subject to homophobic bullying at school (O'Loan et al., 2006). In its 2012 study of 350 LGBT young adults (many of them still in education), LGBT Youth Scotland et al. found that nearly 70 per cent reported experiencing homophobic or biphobic bullying at school, with four out of five saying that they were aware of it happening to others. Incidents of homophobic and biphobic bullying were also reported by students attending Scottish colleges (24.6 per cent) and universities (13.8 per cent). For trans participants (who made up 10 per cent of the sample), results indicated that rates of bullying were even higher: 76.9 per cent in schools, 69.2 per cent on colleges and 37.5 per cent in universities (LGBT Youth Scotland et al., 2012).

Stonewall Scotland's (2012) research also suggested that the bullying of LGBT pupils was endemic in Scottish schools. Based upon their sample of 158 young people aged between 12 and 19 years, it found that 52 per cent reported experiencing homophobic bullying with 99 per cent reporting having heard anti–LGBT epithets such as 'poof' or 'lezza'. Only 11 per cent of LGB participants indicated that teachers intervened when homophobic bullying occurred and 26 per cent reported that teachers never challenged homophobic language.

In a report commissioned by the Scottish Government, Black et al. (2012) reported that of the 4,898 school staff they surveyed from thirty-one local authorities, 8 per cent of teachers and 12 per cent of support staff reported having been aware of homophobic, biphobic and transphobic behaviour in their schools. More recently Lough Dennell and Logan (2015) reported that of the local authorities they surveyed only twenty-two had policies that refer to bullying on the grounds of sexual orientation, seventeen gave advice on recording such incidents and only eleven provided further explanatory notes or guidance on the subject. Yet, 50 per cent of the teachers surveyed said they were of aware of pupils being bullied because of their actual or perceived sexual orientation.

Finally, in 2016 the TIE Campaign published its own report entitled *Attitudes towards LGBT in Scottish Education*. Using data drawn from 287 pupils and recent school leavers and 479 teachers, this report highlighted the fact that, for many pupils and teachers, HBT bullying remains a concern. Of those pupils and school leavers who identified as LGBT, 64 per cent had experienced bullying as a result of their sexual orientation or gender identity. Additionally, 86 per cent reported that LGBT issues were never discussed in their schools. Among those who identified as heterosexual (36 per cent), 73 per cent said that HBT bullying was never challenged at school and only 7 per cent felt that teachers were appropriately trained to tackle the issue. Of the 479 teachers who took part in TIE's survey, 87 per cent reported hearing homophobic, biphobic and transphobic comments at school. Additionally 80 per cent of teachers felt that they had not been adequately trained to tackle HBT bullying at school and 91 per cent said they would attend further training or CLPL (TIE, 2016). Currently there is very little information on the experiences of intersex pupils in Scotland's schools.

## 'THAT'S SO GAY'

Recently researchers have considered whether phrases such as 'that's so gay' are in fact homophobic. McCormack (2013) has argued that it is important to understand the context in which peers interact (hostile versus friendly environments) when challenging what might be thought to be homophobic language. In contexts where there is intent to harm another, where the environment is considered anti-LGBT and where LGBT pupils feel unsafe then comments such as 'that's so gay' are indeed likely to be homophobic. However, in contexts where there is no intent to marginalise others and where there is little evidence of anti-LGBT sentiments, phrases such as 'don't be gay' may be part of social banter. McCormack has argued that while schools in the 1980s and 1990s may well have been anti-LGBT, this is not the case today and thus it is important to understand the nature of relationships young people have. However, two caveats should be added here. First, the use of the word 'gay', regardless of context, has a negative connotation (e.g. being worthless or without value). Second, phrases such as 'that's so gay' continue to privilege heterosexuality – no one ever got detention for saying, 'you're so straight'. Ultimately, hearing pupils use phrases such as 'that's so gay' offers an opportunity for teachers to explore the use of language and how this phrase can impact upon how LGBTI people feel about themselves and how others may view pupils who use such language.

## HBT BULLYING, MENTAL HEALTH AND ACADEMIC ATTAINMENT

Research has consistently shown that those who experience HBT bullying at school are at an increased likelihood of reporting depression, anxiety, post-traumatic stress and suicide ideation. In TIE's (2016) study, 95 per cent of LGBT participants reported that they believed bullying had a lasting, negative impact upon their lives. One in four participants said that they had attempted suicide as a result of the bullying they experienced at school, while 15 per cent of the sample indicated they had attempted suicide more than once. In terms of deliberate self-harm (e.g. cutting), 13 per cent of LGBT participants indicated that they had self-harmed once and 45 per cent indicated that they regularly self-harmed whilst being bullied. In Stonewall Scotland's (2012) *School Report*, 26 per cent of the LGB young people it surveyed said that they had tried to take their own lives at some point, with 54 per cent reporting that they had deliberately self-harmed (cutting or burning).

In terms of attainment, Stonewall Scotland found that 49 per cent of the young people it surveyed felt that they were not achieving their best at school. These findings are echoed in LGBT Youth Scotland et al.'s (2012) report: over 50 per cent of LGB young people who had experienced HBT bullying felt that their academic work had suffered. This rose to 88 per cent among trans young people. Overall, 45 per cent of the young people surveyed indicated that their academic work had been affected by the presence of homophobia, biphobia and transphobia within educational institutions (regardless of whether or not they had experienced bullying directly).

## DENOMINATIONAL SCHOOLS

It is often claimed that denominational schools are opposed to LGBTI inclusion and do not support pupils and teachers who identify as LGBTI. In Scotland, Catholic schools have faced significant criticism from some LGBTI organisations because they must also take into account matters of doctrine. Following the 1918 Education (Scotland) Act denominational schools were brought under the control of local authorities and are thus publicly accountable (Education (Scotland) Act, 1980). However, the Equality Act (2010) confirms that denominational schools within local authorities are given certain exclusions which relate to the appointment of staff and pupil admissions (i.e. they may preference pupils who practice a particular faith or belief). However, they cannot lawfully discriminate against pupils on the grounds of their religion, or treat one or more pupils less favourably because of their religion or a lack of religion.

## RELIGION AND LGBTI ISSUES

In terms of LGBTI inclusion, while Holy Scripture may condemn sexual behaviour among members of the same sex because it is not procreative, leaders of many of the world's religions have also condemned the discrimination of LGBTI people. For example, in 1986 the Prefect of the Congregation for the Doctrine of the Faith, Cardinal Joseph Ratzinger (later Pope Benedict XVI), wrote in a letter to bishops: 'It is deplorable that homosexual persons have been and are the object of violent malice in speech and action. Such treatment deserves condemnation from the Church's pastors wherever it occurs.'

Echoing this statement, in 1997 the Dalai Lama's spokesperson similarly condemned violence perpetrated against lesbians and gay men:

> His Holiness was greatly concerned by reports made available to him regarding violence and discrimination against gay and lesbian people. His Holiness opposes violence and discrimination based on sexual orientation. He urges respect, tolerance, compassion and the full recognition of human rights for all.

While the Qur'an describes sexual relationships between men as 'deviant' and 'excessive', potential punishments for homosexuality depend entirely upon the ways in which religious laws draw upon the Hadith (a collection of sayings from the Prophet Muhammed and other religious leaders) and are interpreted and applied in a particular country.

## SAME-SEX MARRIAGE DEBATE: DIFFERENT PERSPECTIVES

Perhaps one of the best resources to garner the views of the different faith groups in Scotland can be found in the written submissions to the Scottish Government's (2013) consultation on same-sex marriage. Here faith communities have voiced a range of opinions with respect to the recognition and solemnisation of same-sex relationships on religious premises. For example, the response by the Scottish Council of Jewish Communities noted differences in opinion among its own followers of Judaism. The Muslim Council of Scotland stated unequivocally: 'From the Islamic perspective we totally oppose same sex marriage in any shape or form. This view is very clear and straightforward within the teaching of Islam, as is the case with the very large majority of the world religions.' The Baptist Union of Scotland affirmed that it: 'Gives thanks to God for creating man and woman in his image and seeks to follow the witness and teaching of scripture for any expression of human sexuality.' The Church of Scotland, whilst in broad agreement with the government's proposals, stated that:

> The Church believes that teachers should not be forced to support same sex marriage or civil partnerships in the course of teaching under threat of job loss or disadvantage. Teachers should be entitled to equivalent protections to celebrants. This is particularly so for teachers who are already in post.

The Free Presbyterian Church of Scotland wrote:

> We do not believe that the Scottish Government has or will give adequate protection to Christian teachers and to Christian parents who have most serious moral and religious objections to any promotion of homosexuality in schools. We most strenuously resisted the removal of previous legislation which prohibited the promotion of homosexuality in schools and call for it to be reinstated immediately to prevent moral degeneracy in the rising generation. We will continue to resist educational practices in schools which treat homosexual unions as if they were marriages and will recommend and urge parents to withdraw children from any class in any subject where this moral iniquity is to be advanced in any form.

The Catholic Head Teachers Association (CHAS) responded with the following key statement condemning discrimination while also upholding the belief that opposite- and same-sex marriage cannot be considered equitable and that civil partnerships provide sufficient legal recognition:

> Catholic teaching condemns unfair discrimination on the basis of sexual orientation. We recognise that legislation provides for civil partnerships which entitle same sex couples to equivalent legal benefits and rights as heterosexual couples and we cannot see how the proposed legislation will provide any additional legal protections.

## CURRENT GUIDANCE FOR CATHOLIC SCHOOLS

In response to the Scottish Executive's guidance to education authorities on the Equality Act 2006 (a precursor to the 2010 Equality Act), the Scottish Catholic Education Service briefed its schools on the issue of sexual orientation. Its briefing (issued in November, 2009) stated:

> Schools must not discriminate against pupils on grounds of their sexual orientation, or that of their parents. This includes actions in terms of admissions to school, exclusions from school, the treatment of bullying and the provision of extra-curricular activities.
>
> The guidance explicitly refers to Catholic schools having the right to deliver religious and moral teaching in accordance with guidance provided by the Scottish Catholic Education Service.
>
> The Catechism of the Catholic Church teaches that homosexual persons 'must be accepted with compassion, respect and sensitivity' and that 'every sign of unjust discrimination ... should be avoided'. (http://sces.org.uk/briefing-on-equality-act/)

Furthermore, in 2016, a spokesperson for the Catholic Church in Scotland said that the Church had committed itself to ensuring that LGBTI issues were addressed appropriately and sensitively: 'The Church is working with the Catholic Head Teacher association to ensure that all teachers have adequate knowledge, understanding, and training and feel confident in addressing all aspects of relationships education, including LGBTI matters, in an appropriate and sensitive way' (Hayes, 2016).

Some concerns do remain however. References to same-sex attraction being 'objectively disordered' may be seen as irreconcilable with LGBTI inclusion. In its document entitled, *The Pastoral Care of Homosexual Persons*, the Roman Catholic Church does describe attractions to people of the same sex as, 'ordered toward an intrinsic moral evil; and thus the inclination itself must be seen as an objective disorder' (Roman Catholic Church, 1986, paragraph 3). However, the claim that attraction to a person of the same sex is an 'objective disorder' is, as Arland Nichols (President of the John Paul II Foundation for Life and Family) wrote in *Crisis Magazine* (Nichols, 2014), one that is in need of further explanation. He argues that the 'objective disorder' in this case *does not* relate to the person or the attraction (he goes on to state that the Church has reiterated that every human being is 'wonderfully made' in the 'image of God'), but to the fact that, in its eyes, same-sex attraction is not naturally *ordered* towards one or more 'goods' (e.g. heterosexual marriage and procreation). Nichols points out that phrases such as 'intrinsic moral evil' and 'intrinsically disordered' should be understood principally in terms of being 'gravely contrary to chastity' and what the Church believes to be natural law.

Notwithstanding the above, the phrase 'objective disorder' or any variant of it has no basis in modern psychiatry or psychology. Homosexuality was declassified as a mental illness in 1973 by the American Psychiatric Association and in 1990 by the World Health Organization – both organisations publish the diagnostic manuals we use today to identify mental disorders.

## RESOURCES AVAILABLE FOR TEACHERS

Creating an LGBTI inclusive school environment means acknowledging and celebrating the diversity that exists within the school community. It means celebrating LGBT History Month and using images that demonstrate that there is more than one family configuration. We know that families come in all shapes and sizes, but do the images in school brochures, handbooks and guides illustrate such diversity?

It is also possible to bring LGBTI issues into the curriculum. For example, in England, Schools Out UK has developed a resource for teachers called 'The Classroom' which includes lesson plans for Art, Design and Technology, English, Geography, History, ICT and Computing, Mathematics, Modern Foreign Languages, Music, Physical Education, Religious Education, and Science. These lesson plans can be adapted for use in any class. Additionally, LGBT Youth Scotland, the TIE Campaign and Stonewall Scotland have produced resources and workshops for primary and secondary teachers which include lesson plans and ideas for tackling homophobic bullying, trans inclusion and celebrating LGBT History Month. The Scottish anti-bullying service, respect*me*, currently provides a range of resources and training on tackling all forms of bullying. Key resources in the LGBTI field can be found at the web addresses listed in References.

Together these organisations have trained thousands of teachers and student teachers. Their resources ensure that all pupils, regardless of their current or future sexual orientation or gender identity, feel safe and supported at school. There can be no room for discrimination in Scotland's schools.

# REFERENCES

Black, C., Chamberlain, V., Murray, L., Sewell, K. and Skelton, J. (2012) *Behaviour in Scottish Schools 2012: Final Report*. Edinburgh: Scottish Government, IPSOS Mori Scotland.

Cameron, A., Coates, A. and Anderson, T. (2013) *Transforming Lives: Youth Work at LGBT Youth Scotland: An Impact Report*. Online at https://www.lgbtyouth.org.uk/files/documents/Trans forming_Lives.pdf

Education Scotland (2015) *How Good is Our School? Fourth edition*. Online at https://education. gov.scot/improvement/Documents/Frameworks_SelfEvaluation/FRWK2_NIHeditHGIOS/ FRWK2_HGIOS4.pdf

GTCS (2012a) *Standards for Registration: Mandatory Requirements for Registration with the GTCS*. Online at www.gtcs.org.uk/web/FILES/the-standards/standards-for-registration-1212.pdf

GTCS (2012b) *Code of Professionalism and Conduct*. Online at www.gtcs.org.uk/web/FILES/ teacher-regulation/copac-0412.pdf

Hayes, K (2016) 'The Catholic Church in Scotland wants to help tackle homophobia in schools'. Online at www.pinknews.co.uk/2016/07/20/the-catholic-church-in-scotland-wants-to-help-tackle-homophobia-in-schools/).

LGBT Youth Scotland, Lough Dennell, B. L. and Logan, C. (2012) *Life in Scotland for LGBT Young People: Education Report*. Online at https://www.lgbtyouth.org.uk/files/documents/ Life_in_Scotland_for_LGBT_Young_People_-_Education_Report_NEW.pdf

LGBT Youth Scotland, Lough Dennell, B. L. and Logan, C. (2013) *Life in Scotland for Young LGBT People: Community & Identity*. Online https://www.lgbtyouth.org.uk/files/documents/ Research_/LGBTYS_Life_-_Community_and_Identity_-_new_version.pdf

Lough Dennell, B. L. and Logan, C. (2015) *Prejudice-based Bullying in Scottish Schools: A Research Report*. Online at https://www.equalityhumanrights.com/sites/default/files/prejudice-based_ bullying_in_scottish_schools_research_report_0.pdf

McCormack, M. (2013) 'Mapping the boundaries of homophobic language in bullying', In I. Rivers and N. Duncan (eds), *Bullying: Experiences and Discourses of Sexuality and Gender*. London: Routledge, pp. 91–104).

Nichols, A. K. (2014) 'The meaning of "objectively disordered"'. *Crisis Magazine*. August. Online at http://www.crisismagazine.com/2014/objectively-disordered

O'Loan, S., McMillan, F., Motherwell, S., Bell, A. and Arshad, R. (2006) *Promoting Equal*

*Opportunities in Education: Project Two: Guidance on Dealing with Homophobic Incidents: Phase 1 Report and Recommendations.* Online at www.gov.scot/Publications/2006/05/25091604/0

Rivers, I. (2001) 'The bullying of sexual minorities at school: its nature and long-term Correlates', *Educational and Child Psychology*, 18 (1), 33–46.

Roman Catholic Church (1986) *The Pastoral Care of Homosexual Persons.* Online at www.familieslink. co.uk/download/sept07/Pastoral%20care%20of%20homosexual%20persons.pdf

Scottish Government (2008a) *Challenging Prejudice: Changing Attitudes Towards Lesbian, Gay, Bisexual and Transgender People in Scotland.* Online at www.gov.scot/Publications/2008/02/19133153/5

Scottish Government (2008b) *Scottish Government Response To 'Challenging Prejudice: Changing Attitudes towards Lesbian, Gay, Bisexual and Transgender People in Scotland'.* Online at www.gov. scot/Publications/2008/11/04154235/0

Scottish Government (2013) *Responses from Organisations to the Scottish Government's Consultation on the Registration of Civil Partnership and Same Sex Marriage.* Online at www.gov.scot/ Publications/2012/07/9221/0

Stonewall Scotland (2012) *The School Report: The Experiences of Young Gay People in Scotland's Schools 2012.* Online at https://www.stonewallscotland.org.uk/sites/default/files/scottish_ school_report_cornerstone_2012.pdf

TIE (2016) *Attitudes towards LGBT in Scottish Education.* Online at www.tiecampaign.co.uk/research

## Websites

Education (Scotland) Act 1980, Chapter 44, at www.legislation.gov.uk/ukpga/1980/44/pdfs/ ukpga_19800044_en.pdf

LGBT Youth Scotland at https://www.lgbtyouth.org.uk/schools-and-education

Respect*me* at http://respectme.org.uk/

Stonewall Scotland at www.stonewall.org.uk/our-work/education-resources

The Classroom at www.the-classroom.org.uk

TIE Campaign at www.tiecampaign.co.uk/

# 87

# 'Race' Equality in Scottish Education

*Rowena Arshad*

It is helpful to start by acknowledging that the term 'race' is highly problematic. It has no scientific basis and this is why some authors place the word 'race' in inverted commas. It is nevertheless a term that is enshrined in law, such as in the Equality Act 2010, and is often used as a shorthand term to capture discussions related to different ethnicities, cultures, colours and languages. Given the non-scientific basis of the term, some policymakers and researchers prefer to use the term 'ethnicity' rather than 'race'. The term 'ethnicity' was defined by the House of Lords (*Mandla v Dowell Lee* [1983] UKHL 7). They defined an ethnic group as people who have some long shared history (ancestral or geographical) and characteristics arising from a range of factors that include social and cultural conventions, a common language, literature and religious observance. As educators, our priority is to be aware of the contested nature of terms.

It is also helpful to reflect on how racial equality has been approached in education. Robin Richardson (2003), an experienced adviser in equalities work, suggests the concept has largely been used in two ways: first, as a measurable outcome. Achieving racial equality in education would mean reducing any gaps in attainment and achievement between different ethnic groups. Second, the term as a moral value, aspiration and principle so we would educate people not to discriminate on racial grounds. The two are connected concepts and there is a need to be mindful of both definitions.

The demography of Scotland, in terms of ethnic diversity, has been changing in direction and at a pace which has not been witnessed since the migration of Irish people to the West of Scotland in the latter half of the nineteenth century. The pupil census of 2016 recorded 684,206 pupils, whose ethnic backgrounds were known, with 11,939 not disclosing (Scottish Government, 2016a). Of those that declared, 91 per cent recorded themselves as White (Scottish, Other British, Gypsy/Traveller, Polish, Irish or Other) and approximately 5.8 per cent of pupils recorded themselves as from a minority ethnic group (including the category Mixed and Other). Of those who recorded as not White, the largest group was of Asian Pakistani background (1.9 per cent) followed by African (1 per cent). The pupil census shows a higher proportion of minority ethnic pupils in schools than the share of the minority ethnic population at large, as the age profile of minority ethnic people tend to be from the younger age profile.

There has also been increasing linguistic diversity in recent years. In 2009, there were 138 different languages reported as being the main home language for pupils attending Scottish schools – with 15,411 pupils identified as having English as an additional language.

This figure rose to 24,555 in 2011 and 26,921 in 2016. There are now 144 languages recorded as being spoken daily in homes across Scotland (https://www.scilt.org.uk/ Library/StatisticsonlanguagesinScotland/tabid/2914/Default.aspx).

The teaching workforce in Scotland remains predominantly white, female and monolingual, and this profile has remained fairly constant over the years. The latest Scottish Government statistics for teachers in 2016 record that 94 per cent were 'White UK', 'White British' or 'White Other', 1 per cent 'Minority Ethnic', and 5 per cent 'Not Disclosed' – with little variation among sectors (Scottish Government, 2016b).

Statistics can of course be read and grouped in different ways. So, while the 'White' category includes Gypsy/Travellers, this information needs to be positioned within a context that understands that many Gypsy/Traveller pupils face disproportionate experiences of racist harassment and bullying, experience more school exclusions, and, when they attend school, their experiences are more likely to encounter unequal access to an appropriate curriculum or cultural support as compared with majority White groups.

Also, while research into the experiences of minority ethnic pupils evidence a range of common experiences including experiences of racism, discrimination and language barriers, it is important to recognise that minority ethnic pupils are not a homogenous group. For example, school leavers who identified as Asian-Chinese had the highest levels of attainment as compared to all other ethnic groups with 97.1 per cent indicating a positive follow-up destination compared with 91.9 per cent for those who recorded as White Scottish (www.gov.scot/Resource/0050/00501962.pdf). It should also be noted that the categories used to collect ethnicity and national identity data changed in 2011 to bring the pupil and teacher census categories in line with the categories used in the main population census. This means it may not always be possible to make direct comparisons to previous years as some categories have been expanded to capture more accurate data. For example, the category African/Black/Caribbean has been broken down to capture those who record as African, African-Other or Caribbean/Black, and in the White category, a new category, White-Polish, has been added in recognition that, in Scotland, numbers of Polish people have increased significantly.

What is stark is that the teacher demographics for Scotland do not match the increasing diversity of the pupils they are teaching. On one hand, this should not matter if we focus on improving each teacher's capacity and ability to respond to individual pupil needs (e.g. being able to extend the academic experiences of bilingual pupils and being more confident to tackle subtle everyday forms of racism or discrimination). However, research has shown repeatedly that teachers at all levels of education report a lack of confidence in tackling racism or even recognising how subtle forms of racial inequalities might be occurring. Many still indicate that they are not well equipped to support pupils who are multilingual (Hick et al., 2011).

Research has also shown that having a teacher who looks like you can matter, as these teachers can serve as role models, mentors, cultural bridges and advocates. One of the more interesting pieces of quantitative data that adds weight to the importance of having a more diverse teaching workforce in an increasingly diverse classroom is a study conducted in 2015 by Egalite et al. They followed the progress of 2.9 million public school students in Florida over a seven-year period, examining the test scores of the pupils in relation to teacher ethnicity. They factored in other variables that might impact on achievement such as the pupil poverty status, proficiency in English, teacher quality, and gender, but still found that pupils did benefit from being taught by a teacher that looked like them. When there was ethnic or colour congruence between teacher and pupil, the pupil test scores went up marginally as compared to other years. They found the impact on results was most pronounced in primary schools and for the pupils who were labelled as most 'low performing'. While this is one study, albeit very large scale, the authors are mindful that to really test their findings, further similar studies should be carried out in other parts of the United States. Nevertheless, what cannot be ignored is that as the diversity of the pupils in Scottish schools continues to grow, there is now a pressing need to identify effective strategies to attract and retain a more diverse set of teachers. There is also a need to hear what teachers have repeatedly asked for, which is continued professional learning to better equip them to meet their twenty-first-century obligations.

The next part of the chapter traces in brief key developments on multicultural and anti-racist education to the establishment of the Scottish Parliament. It then moves to looking at developments post-devolution and concludes with some issues for teachers and educators to consider in the future.

## RACIAL EQUALITY PRE-DEVOLUTION

The dominant approach in Scottish education in the 1970s was 'assimilationist'. The emphasis was on assisting children, for whom English was a second language (referred to as 'ESL children'), to 'catch up' with indigenous English-speaking peers in their adopted country. The response in some Scottish educational authorities was the establishment of language centres to which children could be withdrawn from mainstream schools for full- or part-time education. Community languages such as Punjabi, Urdu and Cantonese were deemed of less value and indeed potentially harmful to the cognitive development of the 'ESL child'. Eager for their children to achieve in their 'adopted' country, minority ethnic parents listened in good faith to teachers, crediting them with knowing best, and, as English was to be given priority, they often refrained from speaking their mother tongue to their children at home. The focus was on the 'problem' of not being able to speak English and the many positives of diversity were in the main not recognised.

Multicultural education, when it was introduced, focused on celebrating differences and finding out about minority cultural traditions. This approach focused on finding out about the traditions, customs and beliefs of those who were different, with the aim of promoting better understanding and good relations. There was generally a silence or simply non-recognition of barriers at institutional level or of the impact of racial discrimination.

The most significant initiative to prompt the shift to adopting a more critical approach to multicultural education was the Swann Report, *Education for All* (Swann, 1985). Originally set up to investigate the problems of minority ethnic children, it concluded by drawing attention to the growing underachievement of African-Caribbean pupils in mainstream schools and highlighted the impact of social and economic factors. It was the first government report to mention 'institutional racism' as a problem in British society and urged all schools, irrespective of ethnic composition, to confront the issue of racism as part of political education. It led to an extension of the multicultural approach to be combined with explicit acknowledgement and challenging of racism. This approach has sometimes been referred to in Scotland as multicultural and anti-racist education (MCARE). MCARE recognised the value of cultural diversity but went further to examine how power impacted on the life experiences of black and minority ethnic people, arguing for basic changes in the social structures of society. This period saw a plethora of courses on MCARE to develop teacher understanding of the issues.

For much of that period of pre-devolution, the education community was divided on whether to adopt multicultural education or anti-racist education, or both, and on whether to incorporate MCARE within a generic equal opportunities policy or to retain discrete policies for each equality dimension. The Centre for Education for Racial Equality in Scotland (CERES), in preparing this chapter for the first edition of this book in 1999, carried out a survey with all thirty-two local authorities to find out how local authorities and schools were meeting their obligations in the area of race equality. The survey found that:

- Schools (particularly primary schools) tended to verge on playing 'safe' rather than challenging racism; their curriculum approach reflected multiculturalism in the choice of resources and an emphasis on festivals and global-development education.
- Compartmentalisation and 'bolt-on' approaches predominated, particularly in the secondary sector, where the responsibility for MCARE in the curriculum was often located within specific subject areas, and mainly within social subjects.
- Visible minority ethnic pupils were tacitly viewed as 'incomers'/'foreigners' or alternatively were endowed with an assimilated 'Scots' or 'New Scots' identity; how they defined themselves was not given much attention by curriculum developers and researchers.
- Bilingualism, apart from Gaelic, was perceived as a problem by teachers; the provision of community language teaching (for example, Urdu, Punjabi, Bengali, Cantonese or Arabic) was sparse, despite the well-documented research evidence on the cognitive benefits of bilingualism and the maintenance of mother tongue.
- Few authorities had effective policies for dealing with racial harassment, despite the evidence of racial bullying; some appeared to be reluctant to see the relevance of such policies, particularly for early-years or special-education sectors.
- The rhetoric of 'parental power, choice and diversity' had remained marginal to the interests of minority ethnic parents, who were invisible in many of the policy documents in Scottish education and, more seriously, in decisions about their children's education.

Meanwhile, at general and education policy level, it was widely assumed that Scotland had 'good race relations' and that there was 'no problem' here. Consequently, racism did not become an issue in Scottish political and policy discourse or, by extension, in teacher education institutions or schools. Gradually, due to the pressure placed on policymakers and education institutional leaders by activist teachers, teacher unions, minority ethnic organisations, parents and communities, there was a shift from a stance of total complacency to one that accepted, albeit grudgingly, that racism was a phenomenon not confined to urban areas where high numbers of minority ethnic people resided, such as Birmingham. The research in Scotland by three Central Region primary teachers, Donald, Gosling and Hamilton, *'No problem here'? Children's Attitudes to Race in a Mainly White Area*, despite being over twenty years old, is an excellent example of the kind of study that starkly addresses the importance of pursuing an active anti-racist agenda, particularly for schools with low numbers of minority ethnic pupils. Their research remains as relevant today as it did then, possibly more so as developments globally are indicating a need for informed literacy on matters of diversity.

## 'RACE' EQUALITY POST-SCOTTISH DEVOLUTION

Around the time of devolution, three events occurred which prompted a step change to how race issues were addressed in Scotland. The first was that Scotland was on the cusp of having its own Parliament, a Parliament that dared to be different and placed social justice and human rights at the heart of its agenda. The second was the publication of the Stephen Lawrence Inquiry report (Macpherson, 1999). This report challenged those in power to address the matter of institutional racism, a concept previously not acknowledged in any real sense in Scotland. The report discussed the central importance of organisational culture and suggested that norms, assumptions, expectations and culture were powerful influences in shaping the ethos of a workplace. The third was the enactment of the Race Relations (Amendment) Act 2000 (RR(A)A, 2000). The then Scottish Executive responded by publishing an action plan for Scotland in 2000 and creating two Scotland-wide groups to take forward its recommendations. One of these groups, the Race Equality Advisory Forum (REAF), prepared a 'race' equality strategy for Scotland, which included a section on education. Among the key recommendations were:

- the introduction of a presumption that all data collection and reporting should be done on an ethnically disaggregated basis and, where appropriate, by religious affiliation, belief and languages used;
- the development and publication of a strategy in which English as an Additional Language (EAL – this term replaced the previous expression, English as a Second Language, ESL) – and bilingual provision could be maintained, developed and resourced in Scotland;
- providers of continuing professional development courses for teachers should include 'race' equality issues as both permeative and discrete strands;
- the upcoming review of initial teacher education should incorporate an analysis of equality issues, including 'race' equality; the General Teaching Council for Scotland to ensure that consideration of 'race' equality issues form part of the quality control during validation reviews of teacher education courses/institutions and in the setting of teacher competences (see Scottish Executive, 2000, paragraph 3.16).

The Scottish Executive Central Research Unit (CRU) commissioned an audit of research on 'race'-related issues within Scotland in the previous ten years. The CRU report, *Audit of Research on Minority Ethnic Issues in Scotland from a 'Race' Perspective* (Netto et al., 2001), also included an education chapter. That chapter documented over 100 pieces of research related to 'race' and education. Her Majesty's Inspectorate of Education (2005) conducted an inspection of how 'race' equality was being taken forward in Scottish schools. The Scottish Executive also commissioned the first study on minority ethnic pupils' experiences of school in Scotland (MEPESS). The MEPESS research (Scottish Executive, 2005) involved interviews with ninety-four pupils, eighty-two teachers and thirty-eight parents across four authorities. The study found that schools had a strong stance on tackling overt racist incidents as well as commitment to the promotion of multiculturalism through the celebration of faiths and festivals.

However, while parents and pupils appeared comfortable with the terms 'race equality' and 'anti-racism', even though their interpretations varied, many teachers acknowledged unease with the vocabulary of 'race'. There was a marked avoidance of terms such as 'anti-racist' or 'race equality'; instead, teachers tended to use words such as 'inclusion' and 'diversity'. The report found that many teachers identified the promotion of 'race' equality as working with minority ethnic pupils, particularly regarding how well the school was supporting bilingual pupils through its interaction with the EAL service. Few teachers focused on how they might use the curriculum to take forward anti-racist issues or on what the benefits of 'race' equality work might be for majority ethnic pupils or for themselves as teachers. Another study in that same time period of secondary pupils in Glasgow schools by Caulfield et al. (2005) found that while teachers did show respect for different customs and religious practices, young people were more likely to seek support from fellow pupils when faced with racism or racial bullying.

For the period 2007–15, there was less direction and clarity of how Scotland wanted to address issues of racial equality in education. Policies and initiatives, developed to support multicultural and anti-racist work, went into abeyance in other than in the most committed schools and local authorities. Austerity measures were beginning to appear and posts that would have supported equalities work started to disappear or become merged with other areas of work. Many curriculum resources produced in the period 1999 were lost due to organisational changes, for example when Learning and Teaching Scotland became Education Scotland in 2011.

## IMPACT OF LEGISLATION AND POLICIES

The first major piece of legislation for education since 1980, the Standards in Scotland's Schools etc. Act 2000, included equal opportunities in its schedules. It required each education authority to include an account 'of the ways in which they will, in providing school education, encourage equal opportunities and in particular the observance of the equal opportunity requirements' (section 5.2b). However, the key legislation that was to bring the most wide-ranging change in 'race' equality in Scotland was, as previously mentioned, the Race Relations (Amendment) Act (RR(A)A) 2000. This pioneering Act was introduced to strengthen the framework for ensuring that all public authorities provided services in a way that is fair, accessible and non-discriminatory on the grounds of 'race', ethnicity or colour. As a result of the RR(A)A 2000, Scottish pupil attainment was disaggregated according to ethnicity and we are now far more able to obtain ethnicity-based statistics. The RR(A) A 2000 was replaced by the Equality Act 2010. The Equality Act, which has its home in the Westminster Parliament, brought together a range of older equality-related legislation relating to 'race', gender and disability, while adding three new areas – sexual orientation, religion and belief, and age – into a single framework.

After a decade of inactivity on policy direction on race equality, in late 2016, the Scottish Government launched a fifteen-year Race Equality Framework for Scotland (Scottish Government, 2016a). There is an entire section in this framework on education and lifelong learning. In relation to improving the lives of all children, the government has underpinned their framework to the United Nations Convention on the Rights of the Child. A key policy vehicle for providing an inclusive environment and supporting race equality is via the National Improvement Framework for Education. The focus is on creating supportive learning environments, using curriculum as a way of informing and shaping responsible global citizens (for example, in tackling racism), improving career guidance for minority ethnic pupils as a way of tackling occupational segregation related to 'race', ensuring minority ethnic pupils' needs are recognised within *Getting it Right for Every Child*, embedding issues of race into the health and wellbeing agenda, and clearly tackling race-related bullying as part of Scotland's overall prejudice-based bullying initiatives. The government is also committed to improving teacher competency and capacity in tackling racism and supporting diverse learners, as well as improving the diversity of teachers in the workforce. This framework is welcomed and the test will be in whether the aspirations are converted into clear action targets with deadlines.

A concern is that much of the framework's work is dependent on key organisations, which have proven to date to be somewhat reticent and not proactive, in taking race equality issues forward in any systematic and critical way. Another concern is that the framework strategy relies quite significantly on 'mainstreaming' as a primary approach to embedding race equality. Mainstreaming is an approach adopted by the European Union to promote gender equality. The Scottish Government defines mainstreaming as 'a social justice-led approach to policy making in which equal opportunities principles, strategies and practices are integrated into the everyday work of government and other public bodies' (www.gov. scot/Publications/2003/05/17105/21754). The concept can only work if those that have to embed race equality issues into policy and practice have a good understanding of how racism might exclude equal access and participation, and what therefore needs to be done to ensure genuine inclusion.

Two significant areas of policy since 2009 need also to be considered in relation to racial equality in education, not least because both these policies have the potential of sidestepping issues of racial equality. The first is the Additional Support for Learning (ASL) Act (2004), amended in 2009 and the second is the *Language Learning in Scotland: A 1+2 Approach* published in 2012.

The ASL Act was seen, on its introduction, as a key vehicle for promoting inclusion (and racial equality) for all pupils. This Act placed a duty on every local authority in Scotland to meet the 'additional need' of any pupil in its care. 'Needs' as defined by the Act are wide-ranging and cover pupils who are being bullied and those with different ability or learning needs (gifted, with learning difficulty, those who require EAL support), as well as particular categories of pupils, such as those from Gypsy/Traveller backgrounds. It remains the Scottish Government's flagship policy for achieving inclusion in schools. Matters associated with 'race' such as ethnicity, linguistic diversity, faith and belief are therefore ostensibly covered by the ASL Act. However, it is prudent to interrogate the possibilities and limitations of the ASL Act in relation to the addressing and promotion of 'race' equality. It can be argued that the ASL Act, by focusing attention on individual pupil needs, has enabled Scottish education to disengage from considering institutional forms of discrimination, as suggested by the Stephen Lawrence Inquiry report (Macpherson, 1999). The ASL Act's main focus is to ensure that learning and teaching provision is adjusted to ensure every child is included. This may or may not require adjustments at institutional level or for system-wide factors impacting on a range of pupils to be captured. The Lawrence Inquiry report emphasised the need for institutional change, which required vigorous promotion of the ethical/ideological values of 'race' equality within services and institutions, to recognise the existence of racism at different levels (personal, cultural and institutional) and to make changes accordingly. The ASL Act potentially falls short of meeting these requirements.

*Language Learning in Scotland: A 1+2 Approach* was introduced in recognition that Scottish pupils needed to develop language capabilities. This ambitious policy drew on the European Union 1+2 model which aspires to create opportunities for each child to learn two languages in addition to their home language. Each pupil would be offered the opportunity to learn one additional language when they start school with the introduction of a third language four years on. A survey of the Scottish public, conducted in 2016 by the

Scottish Government, found that 89 per cent of those surveyed were in favour of Scottish pupils learning more languages and for that to start from the age of 5 (https://www.scilt. org.uk/Library/StatisticsonlanguagesinScotland/tabid/2914/Default.aspx). Again, it would be prudent to examine the possibilities and limitations of the Act in relation to racial matters. The benefits of being able to speak one or two different languages do not need to be rehearsed. There is research, large and small scale over decades, that evidence that bilingualism can raise standards of literacy, numeracy and general cognitive capacity. Being fluent in different languages enhances communication across communities and countries, and having an emerging workforce that can speak different languages will enhance Scotland's position within a global economic community and the employability of each individual.

The challenge is how we avoid the emergence of a hierarchy of languages where languages viewed as part of 'our' heritage, or for economic purposes, are given status, and languages which are perceived to have less value or lower status are marginalised, even though some of these languages are ones spoken daily by pupils. For example, there is an assumption that the 1 of 1+2 would be English plus two further languages. While that might be the norm in Scotland, we must ask what consideration is being given to the many pupils for whom L1 is not English and that English would be L2 or even L3.

The Scottish Government (2010) in their code of practice for supporting children's learning to accompany the ASL Act clearly recognises the linguistic capital that bilingual pupils bring to the school (Hancock, 2014). Hancock suggests that the challenge for schools is to decide which languages to offer, and how to validate and build on the linguistic resources that children already possess, including the language of migrants and those with British Sign Language (BSL). It is therefore important that Scotland's teaching workforce, still largely monolingual, embraces the ambitions of 1+2 while working to avoid an emergence of a hierarchy of languages, where the positioning of some languages as less valuable is likely to impact on pupil identity and how minority communities feel in the wider school community. A key question then is to reflect on how can the 1+2 initiative assist the promotion of racial equality and recognition of languages in Scotland such as Polish, Urdu, Scots and Arabic?

## LOOKING AHEAD

It is important to acknowledge that in every local authority in Scotland there will be examples of good practice promoting racial equality. The stimulus for successful work has tended to be the presence of energetic and visionary teachers, headteachers and authority staff who interact with pupils, parents and community members to broaden and deepen work on racial, ethnic and religious activity.

Recent large-scale research on the views of minority ethnic young people in Scotland found that young people are acutely aware of everyday racism on the basis of accent, skin colour, faith, dress, nationality and ethnicity (Hopkins et al., 2015). They were often strategic cultural negotiators able to employ complex, sophisticated and multiple strategies to ensure they felt safe, valued and recognised. Young people (both majority and minority) wanted more opportunities to discuss contemporary issues, such as racism, Islamophobia, anti-immigration attitudes and religious intolerance. The challenge for schools is how to open up such opportunities via the flexibility that the Curriculum for Excellence affords and in a way where pupils are engaged in shaping such learning.

Another theme, emerging from the above study, is the level of misinformation and misrecognition that exists about people labelled as 'ethnic minorities'. For example, there is misrecognition as a result of skin colour, as this quote from Donald, a young Asian boy who is Catholic, demonstrates:

> Most people actually do [think I am Muslim]. Like, and our RE [Religious Education] teacher once thought I was a Muslim because of my skin colour. Then, yeah and when I first came to this school some of my friends now were shocked that I was a Catholic. They thought I was Muslim as well. (Donald, male, 12–15, Greater Glasgow)

Another young person, Renuka, shares similar experiences:

> the way I speak and the way I act, I think is Scottish, but it is my skin colour … people think that I am not Scottish. (Renuka, female, 16–18, Glasgow)

The energy it takes to counter constant misrecognition is unlikely to be fully understood by those who do not experience such daily invalidations. A key question then for educators is how do we understand or engage with the concept of misrecognition? More importantly, how can we harness the curriculum as a tool for tackling such misrecognition?

*How Good is Our School? Version* 4, section 3:1 highlights the importance of wellbeing in the context of maximising learner successes and achievement. As classrooms become more diverse, it is vital for teachers to develop an understanding of what wellbeing would mean for pupils from diverse cultural, ethnic and religious backgrounds. Howard's 'three sides of the Achievement Triangle', familiar to many teachers who aspire to be reflective and reflexive practitioners, suggests that it is important to (1) to know yourself, (2) to know your pupils and (3) to know your practice (Arshad, 2012, p. 215). Finally, while racial equality work is generally understood to be framed around supporting minority ethnic pupils, real progress on tackling racism and promoting racial equality can only be made when teachers recognise that racial equality is beneficial for *all* pupils.

## REFERENCES

Arshad, R. (2012) 'The twenty-first century teacher needs to engage with race and racism', in R. Arshad, T. Wrigley and L. Pratt (eds), *Social Justice Re-examined*. Stoke-on-Trent: Trentham Publications.

Caulfield, C., Hill, M. and Shelton, A. (2005) *The Transition to Secondary School. The Experiences of Black and Minority Ethnic Young People*. Online at https://www.researchgate.net/profile/Malcolm_Hill2/publication/242766263_The_transition_to_secondary_school_the_experiences_of_black_and_minority_ethnic_young_people/links/5443b8d50cf2a6a049ab02ad.pdf

Egalite, A. J., Kisida, B. and Winters, M. A. (2015) 'Representation in the classroom: the effect of own-race teachers on student achievement', *Economics of Education Review*, 45, 44–52.

Hancock, A. (2014) 'Language education policy in multilingual Scotland', *Language Problems and Language Planning*, 38 (2), 167–91.

Her Majesty's Inspectorate of Education (2005) *Working Together for Race Equality, 2005: The Scottish Executive's Race Equality Scheme*. Online at www.gov.scot/Publications/2005/11/29152513/25163

Hick, P., Arshad, R., Watt, D. and Mitchell, L. (2011) *Promoting Cohesion, Challenging Expectations: Educating the Teachers of Tomorrow for Race Quality and Diversity in 21st Century Schools*. ESCalate. Online at http://dera.ioe.ac.uk/14759/1/8666.pdf

Hopkins, P., Botterill, K., Sanghera, G. and Arshad, R. (2015) *Faith, Ethnicity, Place: Young People's Everyday Geopolitics in Scotland*. Online at http://eprint.ncl.ac.uk/file_store/production/217632/D009B06B-42B9-47C7-AA00-6329E1312F4A.pdf

Macpherson, Sir William (1999) *The Stephen Lawrence Inquiry: Report of an Inquiry by Sir William Macpherson of Cluny*. London: The Stationery Office. Online at www.archive.official-documents. co.uk/document/cm42/4262/4262.htm

Netto, G., Arshad, R., de Lima, P., Almeida Diniz, F., MacEwen, M., Patel, V. and Syed, R. (2001) *Audit of Research on Minority Ethnic Issues in Scotland from a 'Race' Perspective*. Edinburgh: Scottish Executive Central Research Unit.

Richardson, R. (2003) 'Removing the barriers to race equality in education: ten points to think and talk about'. Paper presented at conference 'Steps for Promoting Race Equality in Education', Brunei Gallery, London, 10 June.

Scottish Executive (2000) *Working Together for Race Equality – The Scottish Executive's Race Equality Scheme*. Online at www.gov.scot/Publications/2002/11/15866/14292

Scottish Executive (2005) *Insight 16: Minority Ethnic Pupils' Experiences of School in Scotland (MEPESS)*. Edinburgh: Scottish Executive. Online at www.scotland.gov.uk/Publications/2005/03/mepess/1

Scottish Government (2010) *Supporting Children's Learning Code of Practice*. Online at www.gov.scot/resource/doc/348208/0116022.pdf

Scottish Government (2013) *Scottish Government Equality Outcomes: Ethnicity Evidence Review*. Online at www.gov.scot/Publications/2013/06/1953/3

Scottish Government (2016a) Pupil census 2016 supplementary data. Online at www.gov.scot/Topics/Statistics/Browse/School-Education/dspupcensus/dspupcensus16

Scottish Government (2016b) Teacher Census, supplementary data. Online at www.gov.scot/Topics/Statistics/Browse/School-Education/teachcenssuppdata/teachcensus2015/teachercensus2016

Scottish Government (2016c) *Race Equality Framework for Scotland: 2016–30*. Online at www.gov.scot/Resource/0049/00497601.pdf

Scottish Government (2016d) *Summary: Ethnicity and School Education*. Online at www.gov.scot/Topics/People/Equality/Equalities/DataGrid/Ethnicity/EthSchEd

Swann, M. (1985) *Education for All*. Online at http://www.educationengland.org.uk/documents/swann/swann1985.html

# 88

# Religious Intolerance: Sectarianism

*Stephen J. McKinney*

## INTRODUCTION

The subject of contemporary sectarianism in Scotland has been prominent in government, media and, increasingly, academic discussion since the beginning of the third millennium. It is linked to historical manifestations of sectarianism, but there is a developing acknowledgement and recognition of the ways in which it has evolved in a changing religious and socio-economic landscape. The first part of this chapter offers an overview of the recent history of the phenomenon and the government's response to it. The discussion in this part focuses on three main issues that have remained problematic in the debates on sectarianism in the twenty-first century. First, there is the continuing challenge of establishing conceptual clarity when discussing sectarianism in Scotland. Second, there are often unhelpful comparisons drawn between sectarianism in Scotland and Northern Ireland. Third, there has been, until recently, very limited research evidence about the subject in Scotland. A number of important research reports have been published in the last few years and some of these will be examined and evaluated.

The second part of the chapter explores the role, or perceived role, of education, particularly school education, in debates on sectarianism. It offers an analysis of the possible relationship between denominational schooling and sectarianism, drawing from the evidence that has been provided by recent research. This will be followed with a review of some experiences of discrimination and the importance and value of anti-sectarian education, especially in schools.

## CONTEMPORARY SECTARIANISM IN SCOTLAND

This chapter is primarily focused on contemporary sectarianism and education. If readers wish to pursue the history of sectarianism in more detail, they are referred to the corresponding chapters in previous editions of *Scottish Education*: Finn (1999), (2003): Conroy (2008); McKinney (2013) and to works such as Brown (1991); *The Innes Review* (volume 42); Bruce et al. (2004); Devine (2006); and McKinney (2015a).

A series of events in the late twentieth century and the early twentieth-first century prompted the then First Minister, Jack McConnell, into organising a highly publicised Summit on Sectarianism on 14 February 2005. These events included the murder of two Celtic fans (1995 and 1999), the Donald Findlay incident in 1999 (a prominent Scottish

Queen's Counsel (QC) who was filmed telling anti-Catholic jokes), the James MacMillan lecture of 1999 and the reaction to this lecture, and increased hostility between some supporters of Celtic and Rangers football clubs (Gallagher, 2013). *The Record of the Summit on Sectarianism* (Scottish Executive, 2005) fails to express any clear definition of sectarianism, but it does identify and discuss 'four key themes central to tackling bigoted and sectarian attitudes and behaviours'. These four key themes were: interfaith work; education; sport; and marches and parades. These would later become distilled to three: football-related violence, marches and parades, and education. The Scottish Executive also published *Sectarianism: Action Plan on Tackling Sectarianism in Scotland* (2006a) and *Building friendships and strengthening communities* (2006b). Both documents highlighted the importance of education. Education, then, has been consistent as one of the fundamental components of the Scottish Government strategy to address sectarianism in modern Scotland.

Further football-related hostility led a subsequent First Minister, Alex Salmond, to call a meeting of police and representatives of football clubs and associations on 8 March 2011. A joint statement was produced condemning violence, bigotry and alcohol misuse in relation to football-related activity. The Scottish Government commissioned a poll on sectarianism (published 2 September 2011). The results indicated that 89 per cent of Scots agree that sectarianism is offensive; 89 per cent agree that sectarianism is unacceptable in Scottish football; 85 per cent agree that sectarianism should be a criminal offence; and 91 per cent agree that stronger action should be taken to tackle sectarianism and offensive behaviour associated with football (see www.gov.scot/Resource/Doc/925/0120664.pdf). It was claimed that these statistics were based on the opinion of the Scottish people and they were used to expedite the progress of the Offensive Behaviour at Football and Threatening Communications (Scotland) Act. This Act was passed by the Scottish Parliament on 14 December 2011 and came into force on 1 March 2012. The Act includes coverage of sectarian chanting and threatening behaviour related to football matches. Statistics on religiously aggravated crimes began to be published annually from 2011. While these must be treated with caution, they indicate a steady level of crimes against Catholics and Protestants. The majority of crimes are committed against Catholics and this imbalance is exacerbated when correlated with the percentage of Catholics in the Scottish population (15.9 per cent recorded in the census data of 2001 and 2011).

Roseanna Cunningham, Member of the Scottish Parliament (MSP), established an Advisory Group on Tackling Sectarianism (AGoTS) in Scotland on 9 August 2012. The aim of the advisory group was to answer two questions: What is sectarianism in Scotland now? and How would we best deal with its consequences? The advisory group has published two reports: Scottish Government (2013) *Advisory Group on Tackling Sectarianism in Scotland. Independent Advice to Scottish Ministers and Report on Activity 9 August 2012–15 November 2013. (November 2013)* and Scottish Government (2015) *Tackling Sectarianism and Its Consequences in Scotland. Final Report of the Advisory Group on Tackling Sectarianism in Scotland. (April 2015)*. These two reports aimed to clarify the nature and scope of contemporary sectarianism and outline the most effective ways to tackle it. The *Final Report* (Scottish Government, 2015) produced some key conclusions that can be summarised as follows (section 7). First, there is a gap between the perception that sectarianism is widespread and a problem in society, and the evidence to substantiate this perception. Second, there is limited evidence of structural sectarianism. Third, there is evidence that a minority have been affected by sectarianism, but many people have not been affected or have been able to avoid it. Fourth, there are patterns in the perceptions about the 'seriousness and extent of sectarianism' and the contributors to the continuing existence of the problem. Fifth, there is 'considerable evidence of social integration between Protestants and Catholics'. Sixth, there is 'little evidence of sectarianism at the heart of Scottish Politics'. Seventh, there is a lack of robust knowledge about the nature and extent of sectarianism in some key areas.

## TERMINOLOGY

As has been suggested above, the definitions or descriptions of the terms used in the debate about sectarianism are of crucial importance; there is a continuing requirement for greater conceptual clarity. Sectarianism is not a word that is exclusive to Scotland, nor is it a word that refers exclusively to interdenominational Christian hostility. It is closely related to prejudice and bigotry. Prejudice is preconceived opinion that has no foundation in reason or actual experience. Bigotry is an intolerance of others who have different. Contemporary sectarianism refers to intolerance between a number of different groups within the same religious faith that could lead to hostility and possibly even violence. In the Scottish context the term has historically been used to refer to a commonly perceived Catholic–Protestant divide within the Christian tradition. It has emerged that forms of sectarianism exist within other faith groups in twenty-first-century Scotland, for example sectarianism between different Muslim groups in Glasgow. This chapter is restricted to the interdenominational Christian divide.

The *Final Report* of the AGoTS (Scottish Government, 2015) warns of the dangers of oversimplification and overgeneralisation in trying to understand sectarianism (section 1.8.1). A more nuanced understanding of the labels 'Catholic' and 'Protestant' is required, and also of the variety of models and interpretation of Catholic and Protestant identity that exist in contemporary Scotland, sometimes with very little or no discernible religious affiliation. Similarly, the *Community Experiences of Sectarianism* (Goodall et al., 2015) reports that the terms 'Loyalist' and 'Irish Republican' are used to refer to types of processions, but these terms are far from homogenous and are rather simplistically used for complex varieties of organisations that arrange processions.

Trying to establish an adequate definition of sectarianism for the contemporary Scottish scene is highly problematic because of the complexity of the territory and the challenge of referencing its historical and contemporary manifestations. The following is a more detailed working definition that can be applied to the different manifestations of sectarianism in contemporary Scotland (adapted from various sources: Leichty and Clegg, 2001; Bruce et al., 2004): sectarianism consists of intolerant beliefs and attitudes that may be translated into actions. These can be expressed in interpersonal, communal and possibly institutional ways. Sectarianism involves some exclusivist and intransigent understanding of religious beliefs and attitudes and typically is in the form of a shared or group identity that fosters a sense of belonging. This is sometimes more of a quasi- or nominal religious identity, with very loose connections to mainstream religion. Sectarian groups tend to claim that their identity is founded on authentic historical roots and shared memory – roots and memory that may be selective, self-serving or semi-mythical. The group is configured such that other groups which hold contrasting beliefs and attitudes can be perceived to threaten the identity and history of the group and are stigmatised as the 'others'. In a sense, it is a claim for belonging and communal identity that is partly defined by affirming an 'authentic' identity but also partly defined by opposition to the threat of the 'inauthentic' – the others. Sectarianism, thus, justifies the marginalisation, alienation and possible demonisation of the 'others'. This can lead to hostility, verbal abuse, intimidation and even violence.

## COMPARISONS BETWEEN SECTARIANISM IN SCOTLAND AND NORTHERN IRELAND

Any attempt to draw comparisons about contemporary sectarianism between Scotland and Northern Ireland must be exercised with extreme caution. The *Final Report* of the AGoTS (Scottish Government, 2015) states that events in Northern Ireland after 1969 have emphasised the differences between Northern Ireland and Scotland, rather than the similarities (section 1.8.5). There are, in fact, some quite striking differences between the history, development and manifestation of sectarianism in these two parts of the UK (McKinney and Conroy, 2015). It is important for an understanding of contemporary sectarianism in Scotland to draw out some of the salient differences.

First, according to Bruce (2000), there is no strong, unified Protestant culture in Scotland that could support a consistent opposition or even hostility towards Catholics. The Protestant churches can at times be divided among themselves in Scotland. We can add to this that the Protestant churches in Scotland do not have any anxiety about the encroaching influence of a bordering (ostensibly Catholic) country as they do in Northern Ireland. Second, Scotland does not have sets of political parties that are strictly divided on nationalist/Catholic (Social Democratic and Labour Party, and Sinn Fein parties) and unionist/Protestant lines (Ulster Unionist Party and Democratic Unionist Party parties) that attract the Catholic and Protestant votes (Beaudette and Kirkpatrick, 2017). Perhaps some comparison could be made with the traditional, though not exclusive, Catholic vote for the Labour Party in Scotland. However, this trend has witnessed fairly dramatic changes in recent years: a marked increase in the Catholic vote for the Scottish National Party (SNP) in recent elections: 2003 (17 per cent); 2007 (24 per cent); 2015 (possibly as high as 48 per cent), and support for independence: 57 per cent of Catholics voted *yes* in the independence referendum in 2014 (Curtice et al., 2009; Wilkinson and Lamb, 2015). Third, there has been no sustained armed conflict in Scotland to parallel the Troubles in Northern Ireland, which lasted from 1968 to 1998 and caused approximately 3,500 deaths (Isaacs, 2017). Fourth, there is no segregation in housing in Scotland, along Christian denominational divisions, as there is in some of the major areas of Northern Ireland, including Belfast where there are examples of strictly demarcated areas. Carrigan (2010) states that this creates serious problems for communication between the different communities and that the communities lack knowledge and understanding of each other. In Northern Ireland, contact theory is being used to address this social problem and recent interventions in schools include programmes of shared education (e.g. children from different schools being educated together in certain school subjects) which have been introduced in some areas (Hughes et al., 2012).

The last difference, and the one most pertinent for this chapter, is that the state school systems in Northern Ireland and Scotland are very different. The forms of schooling in Northern Ireland are much more complex than Scotland. There are selective and non-selective schools (grammar and secondary schools) and a far greater number of single-sex schools than in Scotland. There are maintained schools (attended primarily by Catholics); controlled schools (attended primarily by Protestants); and a small number of integrated schools (attended by children of all faiths and none). There is evidence that Catholic children in Northern Ireland are more likely to attend a controlled school (5.4 per cent at primary level; 2.1 per cent at secondary level; and 7.7 per cent at grammar level) than Protestant children attending a maintained school (1 per cent at primary level; 0.8 per cent at secondary level; and 0.9 per cent at grammar level), but the numbers in both cases, as can be seen, are still very low (Borooah and Knox, 2015). The controlled and maintained schools are frequently located in denominationally segregated areas. This creates debates about whether the different types of schools are symptomatic of the sectarian divisions, help to create the divisions or contribute to the divisions.

## RECENT RESEARCH REPORTS

The AGoTS interim report of 2013 called for 'in-depth research to monitor sectarian attitudes and activity' to be increased to provide evidence (Scottish Government, 2013). This research would be able to progress earlier research that was examined in two important previous reviews: *Religious Discrimination and Sectarianism in Scotland: A Brief Review of Evidence (2002–2004)* (McAspurren, 2005) and *An Examination of the Evidence on Sectarianism in Scotland* (Scottish Government Social Research, 2013). The Scottish Government commissioned new research, and three reports were published in 2015 that did provide further evidence. A concise overview of these three reports is provided below.

The *Scottish Social Attitudes Survey 2014: Public Attitudes to Sectarianism in Scotland* (Hinchcliffe et al., 2015) was conducted by the independent research organisation ScotCen Social Research and involved 1,501 interviews. One of the findings was that Catholics are more likely to preserve a sense of religious identity (72 per cent) than Protestants (45 per cent) (section 2.15). Catholics and Protestants appear to be well integrated in Scotland. Independent research provides evidence of an increasing level of intermarriage between Catholics and Protestants, especially in the younger generations (Raab and Holligan, 2012). A large majority of people believe that sectarianism is a problem (88 per cent); many see it as a problem in specific areas (69 per cent); and a smaller percentage believe it is widespread in Scotland (19 per cent). Around a third believe the problem is focused in Glasgow and the West of Scotland. The perceived causes of sectarianism will be discussed in the section on sectarianism and education.

Goodall et al. (2015) conducted qualitative research in 2014–15 that focused on public perceptions and experiences of sectarianism in five case study sites across Scotland. In total, the research team conducted thirty-eight semi-structured interviews and eight moderated focus groups. The sites chosen were: Glasgow City; North Lanarkshire; Edinburgh; Dundee; and the Western Isles. The main themes discussed in the report are: the discursive deficit; where sectarianism happens; gender; generations and families; memory and the power of 'exceptional' events; jokes, banter, music and other signifiers; football; Loyalist and Irish Republican processions; and strengthening communities. Some of the findings from this research will be used to inform the discussion on sectarianism and education.

Hamilton-Smith et al. (2015) carried out a mixed methods study into the community impact of public processions in Scotland in 2013. In stage one, the researchers used publicly available data to quantify the processions that occurred throughout Scotland in 2010–12 and the range and characteristics of these processions. In stage two, they selected six processions and conducted interviews with procession organisers and those involved in the authorisation and policing of the procession. Stage three selected three sites and included: observations of processions; on-street mini-surveys of those who were present at the time of the procession; short surveys of businesses near the route of the procession; and interviews with local residents before and after processions. This last dimension of the research – the interviews with local residents – had the potential to provide important information, but the research team faced significant challenges in accessing local residents for the pre-procession interviews and they adopted on-street surveys. There was some success with the post-procession interviews but the interviews recorded no change in residents' attitudes. The researchers realised that this was an understandable response to one procession. It would possibly have been more appropriate to assess the cumulative effect of a number of processions.

Some important points emerge from this report. The (limited) results of their pre-procession survey indicate that a majority of respondents held 'generally negative views' about Loyalist (53 per cent) and Irish Republican processions (56 per cent). The post-procession residential surveys (low response rate) revealed increased negativity towards the processions. Interestingly there is no real evidence of an increase in criminal incidents as recorded by the police, in the period of time around the processions. There are clear indications that Loyalist and Irish Republican processions have become better organised and the stewarding has improved. This has been confirmed by an independent report commissioned by the Scottish Government on the organisation, administration and policing of marches and parades (Rosie, 2016). Nevertheless, there are still concerns about the behaviour of supporters and observers of the processions, rather than those processing, and some of the band members who have been hired for the day. It is noted that some organisations have taken responsibility for the stewarding of supporters.

## SECTARIANISM AND EDUCATION: THE EXISTENCE OF DENOMINATIONAL SCHOOLS

A recurring theme of this chapter is the lack of robust evidence to substantiate claims about the nature and extent of sectarianism. The lack of evidence is also a feature of discussions about the putative role of denominational schools in causing or contributing to sectarianism (McKinney (2015a) provides a full discussion of the ambiguous position adopted by the Church of Scotland on denominational schools; McKinney (2015b) provides a detailed and critical examination of sectarianism and denominational education in the AGoTS's *Final Report* (Scottish Government, 2015)). The question of the position of denominational schools in Scottish society and possible connection they may have with sectarianism is discussed in a number of reports. These will be considered in relation to the following issues: public attitudes on what contributes to sectarianism; discrimination against people who are perceived to be Catholic because they have attended a Catholic school; the description of segregated communities in the 1970s; and, finally, questions about the discontinuation of denominational schools and the end of their (presumed) contribution to sectarianism.

Hinchcliffe et al. (2015) reported on what was perceived to contribute to sectarianism in Scotland. These can be viewed in three groups: highest contributors (67–100 per cent); medium contributors (34–66 per cent) and lowest contributors (0–33 per cent). The first group (perceived highest contributors) consists of football (88 per cent); Orange Order marches (79 per cent); and Irish Republican marches (70 per cent). The second group (medium contributors) consists of: events in Ireland (51 per cent); denominational schools, and the Internet and social media (both 37 per cent); and newspapers, television and the radio (34 per cent). The factors in the third group (lowest contributors) includes: churches (27 per cent); non–denominational schools (8 per cent); and the police (8 per cent). At first sight, this might appear to be an indictment of denominational schools but the data must be compared with the results for what are considered to be the factors that contribute most to sectarianism. If we adopt a similar three-group approach, there is a marked difference between the sets of statistics. There are no factors in the highest contributor group of between 67 and 100 per cent. There is only one contributor in the medium contributor group: football (55 per cent). In the third group, all of the contributors are 13 per cent or below. This includes: Orange Order marches (13 per cent) and Irish Republican marches (3 per cent). Denominational schools are considered to contribute most to sectarianism by 5 per cent of the research sample.

There is some limited evidence from the research reports that people can be disadvantaged because they can be identified as Catholic, or presumed to be Catholic, when they reveal the name of the school they attended. In a section in the *Community Experiences of Sectarianism* (Goodall et al., 2015), one of the men interviewed stated that the name of the school that people attended was a signifier of group identity – he qualified this, 'for 90% of the time' (section 13.1). This conflation of perceived Catholic identity with attendance at a Catholic school was mentioned by other respondents (section 13.6). Another man stated that he had been refused employment in the Govan shipyards two years previously because he had been identified as a Catholic by his Irish Catholic name and by the school he had attended (section 14.1). Two interviewees stated that they had been denied membership of golf clubs because of their names and the schools they had attended (section 14.1). There is a reference to one member of Focus Group 1 who describes being brought up in Glasgow in a very divided neighbourhood. She states that when she was growing up in Glasgow in the 1970s, it was 'something like your Northern Ireland situation, really'. She could not remember the names of the Catholic schools but she did not play with Catholic children and did not talk to them (section 8.3). She draws a comparison with Northern Ireland where people walk down different sides of the street or are not allowed to walk down some streets – 'that is the way it used to be near enough here as well'. The difficulty with this evidence about Glasgow is that, while describing an unwelcome and insidious segregation, the claims would be stronger if corroborated by supporting evidence and if it were not so time restricted (the 1970s), which means that even if this was the case the situation could have changed in the last forty years.

One of the solutions proposed for reducing sectarianism in the *Community Experiences of Sectarianism* (Goodall et al., 2015) in local areas was ending 'separate schooling for children of different religious backgrounds' (section 16.3). In a wonderful example of contradictory views, *continuing* separate schooling was perceived by some in the same report to be a solution to sectarianism. The same polarisation of views is presented in the AGoTS's *Final Report* (Scottish Government, 2015) where it is reported that some argued strongly that 'the existence of choice in schooling relating to denominational schools was sectarian in and of itself', while others argued that 'targeting one sort of school (presumably denominational) as a contributor to sectarianism was itself sectarian' (section 1.9.8). The question of the discontinuation of denominational schools ultimately remains inconclusive. The questionable and, at times, conflicting nature of the evidence concerning denominational schools and the perceptions of the low level of their importance as contributors to sectarianism are probably among the factors that led to the conclusion in the *Final Report*, consistent with its position in the interim report (Scottish Government, 2013), that closing schools would not help to eradicate sectarianism (section 4.41). It is also unlikely that any political party in Scotland would suggest a policy of closure because of the amount of controversy it would provoke.

## SECTARIANISM AND EDUCATION: ANTI-SECTARIAN EDUCATION IN SCHOOLS

The efforts of schools to tackle sectarianism can be considered under two headings: what schools already do to address the problem and what they might do to provide leadership that might influence wider social and cultural attitudes. The AGoTS's *Final Report* (Scottish Government, 2015) emphasises that most of the sectarian behaviour that is exhibited and experienced by young people is in their communities outside school time (section 4.36). It does state that sectarianism can at times 'spill into hostility between young people or in schools' (section 1.9.2). However, the topic of sectarianism is addressed in youth and community organisations and in schools (section 4.52). The document advocates a 'strong emphasis' on the need to engage with the issue of sectarianism with young people in schools (section 1.9.8) and proposes that this is conducted in an age-appropriate way. It also emphasises the importance of inter-school relations (recalling the recommendations of Scottish Executive, 2006b). Schools can be supported in this work by organisations such as Nil by Mouth, Sense over Sectarianism, and Show Bigotry the Red Card. Goodall et al. (2015) report that many respondents considered sectarianism and sectarian values to be derived from families and social contacts (section 16.2). The intervention is best focused on the young, as it is questionable if other generations could be reached. The use of education in schools and community programmes for the reduction of sectarianism in local areas is recommended (section 16.1). In schools, this is promoted in some areas through a 'push on tolerance'. One respondent commented that her nephews were being taught about sectarianism in school in Aberdeen: they had previously known nothing about this topic. She questioned if this was in fact counterproductive as it appeared to generate some low level sectarian behaviour in the children.

The *Final Report* (Scottish Government, 2015) states that some key areas of Scottish culture have a responsibility to lead proactively in anti-sectarianism and in the promotion of good relations. These areas include education (also churches, football and local government) (section 1.15.3). The report advises that educationalists, among others, have identified social media as a major new conduit for disseminating sectarian ideas and this has to be addressed (section 3.12). It seeks greater leadership by Scottish football in engagement with schools in concerted anti-sectarian intervention (section 4.24.2). Education Scotland is charged with ensuring that the topic of sectarianism is appropriately addressed in the school curriculum, whether treated as a stand-alone issue or integrated into the wider equalities issue (section 4.42). When it is treated as a stand-alone issue it should be 'integrated into the curriculum in a clear, locally appropriate way' (section 4.43): schools can use local histories to inform the lessons (section 4.44). The *Final Report* states that every school should be able to demonstrate how it has addressed the issue of sectarianism (section 4.45). The recommendations on the role of education consolidate the position of schools as key agencies for tackling sectarianism.

## CONCLUDING COMMENTS

Arguably, the AGoTS's *Final Report* (Scottish Government, 2015) did not have the impact on Scottish society and public perception that it deserved. This may have been due to the contemporaneous publication of the three research reports discussed above which may have pre-empted some of the findings of the *Final Report*. It may also be due to a growing awareness of deeper issues that can be discerned from closer analysis of the figures for religiously aggravated crimes in Scotland over the last few years. In recent years there has been a slow, but steady, decrease in the number of reported religiously motivated crimes against Catholics and Protestants in Scotland. There has, however, been a marked increase in the recorded number of religiously aggravated crimes towards the Muslim population and a relatively high level of crimes towards members of the Jewish community, per head of population. This development has caused considerable distress to these two religious groups and signifies an invidious trend that requires urgent attention. It suggests that it may be time to reconceptualise sectarianism as one manifestation of a wider issue, religious intolerance and discrimination in Scotland, and to ensure that all forms of religiously aggravated crime in Scotland receive sufficient attention.

# REFERENCES

Beaudette, D. M. and Kirkpatrick, A. B. (2017) 'Zero-sum of all fears: intergroup threat, contact, and voting behaviour in Northern Ireland', *European Political Science Review*, 9 (1), 51–71.

Borooah, V. K. and Knox, C. (2015) 'Segregation, inequality, and educational performance in Northern Ireland: problems and solutions', *International Journal of Educational Development*, 40, 196–206.

Brown, S. J. (1991) '"Outside the covenant": the Scottish Presbyterian Churches and Irish immigration, 1922–1938', *The Innes Review*, 42 (1), 19–45.

Bruce, S. (2000) 'Comparing Scotland and Northern Ireland', in T. M. Devine (ed.), *Scotland's Shame? Bigotry and Sectarianism in Modern Scotland*. Edinburgh: Mainstream Publishing.

Bruce, S., Glendinning, T., Paterson, I. and Rosie, M. (2004) *Sectarianism in Scotland*. Edinburgh: Edinburgh University Press.

Carrigan, S. (2010) *The Real Peace Process*. London: Equinox.

Curtice, J., McCrone, D., McEwan, N. and Ormston, R. (2009) *Revolution or Evolution?* Edinburgh: Edinburgh University Press.

Devine, T. M. (2006) *The Scottish Nation 1700–2007*. London: Penguin.

Gallagher, T. (2013) *Divided Scotland. Ethnic Friction and Christian Crisis*. Glendaruel: Argyll Publishing.

Goodall, K., Hopkins, P., McKerrell, S., Markey, J., Millar, S., Richardson, J. and Richardson, M. (2015) *Community Experiences of Sectarianism*. Edinburgh: Scottish Government Social Research.

Hamilton-Smith, N., Malloch, M., Ashe, S., Rutherford, A. and Bradford, B. (2015) *Community Impact of Public Processions*. Edinburgh: Scottish Government Social Research.

Hinchcliffe, S., Marcinkiewicz, A., Curtice, J. and Ormston, R. (2015) *Scottish Social Attitudes Survey 2014: Public Attitudes to Sectarianism in Scotland*. Edinburgh: ScotCen Social Research.

Hughes, J., Lolliot, S., Hewstone, M., Schmid, K. and Carlisle, K. (2012) 'Sharing classes between separate schools: a mechanism for improving inter-group relations in Northern Ireland?' *Policy Futures in Education*, 10 (5), 528–39.

Isaacs, M. (2017) 'Faith in contention: explaining the salience of religion in ethnic conflict', *Comparative Political Studies*, 50 (2), 200–31.

Leichty, J. and Clegg, C. (2001) *Moving beyond Sectarianism*. Dublin: The Columba Press.

McAspurren, L. (2005) *Religious Discrimination and Sectarianism in Scotland: A Brief Review of Evidence (2002–2004)*. Edinburgh: Scottish Executive Social Research

McKinney, S. J. (2015a) 'The historical and contemporary debate about the relation of Catholic schools in Scotland and the social problem of sectarianism', *Ricerche di Pedagogia e Didattica – Journal of Theories and Research in Education*, 10 (1), https://rpd.unibo.it/article/view/4680

McKinney, S. J. (2015b) 'Sectarianism and state funded schooling in Scotland. A critical response to the final report of the advisory group on tackling sectarianism in Scotland', *Scottish Educational Review*, 47 (2), 20–36.

McKinney, S. J. and Conroy, J. C. (2015) 'The continued existence of state-funded Catholic schools in Scotland', *Comparative Education*, 51 (1), 105–17.

Raab, G. and Holligan, C. (2012) 'Sectarianism: myth or social reality? Inter-sectarian partnerships in Scotland, evidence from the Scottish Longitudinal Study', *Ethnic and Racial Studies*, 35 (11), 1934–54.

Rosie, M. (2016) *Independent Report on Marches, Parades and Static Demonstrations in Scotland*. Edinburgh: Scottish Government.

Scottish Executive (2005) *The Record of the Summit on Sectarianism*. Online at www.gov.scot/Publications/2005/04/2193329/33313

Scottish Executive (2006a) *Sectarianism: Action Plan on Tackling Sectarianism in Scotland*. Online at www.gov.scot/Publications/2006/01/26134908/0

Scottish Executive (2006b) *Building Friendships and Strengthening Communities: A Guide to Twinning between Denominational and Non-denominational Schools*. Online at www.gov.scot/Publications/2006/12/07092739/0

Scottish Government (2013) *Advisory Group on Tackling Sectarianism in Scotland. Independent Advice to Scottish Ministers and Report on Activity 9 August 2012–15 November 2013. (November 2013)*. Online at www.gov.scot/Publications/2013/12/6197/0

Scottish Government (2015) *Tackling Sectarianism and Its Consequences in Scotland. Final Report of the Advisory Group on Tackling Sectarianism in Scotland. (April 2015)*. Edinburgh: Scottish Government.

Scottish Government Social Research (2013) *An Examination of the Evidence on Sectarianism in Scotland*. Online at http://www.scotland.gov.uk/Publications/2013/06/8109/0

Wilkinson, P. and Lamb, C. (2015) *The Tablet*, 15 May.

# XI

# TEACHERS AND TEACHER EDUCATION

# 89

# Scottish Teachers: Then and Now

*Aileen Kennedy*

## INTRODUCTION

Education has long been seen as central to Scottish identity, and of course, that places teachers centre stage. As early as 1696, there existed an Act of Parliament which laid the foundation for 'parish schools' (the Act for Settling of Schools) in Scotland, characterising the early development of the teaching profession as one intimately tied with religion, and focused on providing education for all, at least in principle. Chapter 9 provides more detail on the wider significance of this, and other Acts of Parliament, but it is important to note that this legislative demand that each parish provide and pay the salary for a 'school master' made Scotland one of the first countries in the world to legislate for a national system of schooling staffed by salaried teachers.

So, we have a long and proud history relating to the development of the teaching profession, and while its shape and context has undoubtedly changed significantly over the past 300 or so years, there is a general sense in which teaching has been, and is still, seen as a worthy and honourable profession in Scotland (Gray and Weir, 2014). Bill Gatherer's chapter on 'Scottish Teachers' (Gatherer, 2013), published in all four previous editions of this volume, provided a detailed historical account of Scottish teachers. What this present chapter seeks to do is to provide a brief overview of that historical context, but then to explore in some detail the demographics and characteristics of the contemporary profession in Scotland, exploring how the profession is shaped and governed. It does this with reference to the wider international context in seeking to provide a comparative perspective on teachers in Scotland.

## TEACHERS IN SCOTLAND: A BRIEF HISTORICAL OVERVIEW

The notion of 'education for all' has long roots in Scotland, with parish and burgh schools set up throughout Scotland to comply with the 1696 Education Act. This emphasis on education for all Scottish children was a Calvinist attempt to connect citizens with the word of God; literacy was therefore seen as central to religion. The parish schools were funded by a combination of local landowners and the Church of Scotland, who paid the school master's salary and provided him with a house. These school masters were men who had had some university education, but who were most likely not from rich families themselves and did not have the means or support to go on to other professional positions. They were able to introduce their pupils to the classics, literature and philosophy, and above all, provided religious mentoring to their pupils.

However, as Gatherer (2013) points out, there was a dark side to this too, with these 'virtually second-hand clergymen' (p. 976) imposing strict Calvinist values on their pupils, which included corporal punishment. The parish leaders and parents alike were supportive of the school master adopting this stance, as it was commonly believed that to 'spare the rod' would 'spoil the child'. These school masters delivered education to pupils in a didactic way, expecting their pupils to rote learn, mainly in silence.

In addition to the mandated parish schools, many urban towns also had burgh schools, which enjoyed slightly higher status and were staffed by school masters who received higher salaries than their parish counterparts. These school masters were intellectually engaged, both teaching and writing scholarly papers, and had close links with universities, some of them going on to become professors. They had a clear view of the purpose of schooling, and served this well: to transmit historically situated educational values and to promote and sustain Scottish national culture.

While the provision of a parish school became mandatory, attendance at school was not made compulsory until the Education (Scotland) Act of 1872. However, while this national focus on providing education for all was seen as progressive, uptake was patchy, something highlighted in George Lewis' 1843 book, descriptively entitled *Scotland, a Half-educated Nation*. Teachers' jobs were very much to drill the pupils before them in the basic subjects. Their role was not to attend to the 'whole child', to promote children's voice or rights, or to explicitly adopt inclusive practices which might attract a wider pupil population to school.

## Teaching as Liberation for Women?

Women were not taken seriously as teachers until later in the nineteenth century, when the need for mass production of teachers, together with the implications of men going to war, led to women being allowed to teach 'important' subjects. Prior to this some women (widows or spinsters, as teaching was not a job for married women) taught in so-called local parish 'dame schools', teaching children reading, writing, spinning, knitting, scripture lessons and other valuable homemaking skills. For a long time, the education of girls reflected a limited and defined social role, with little opportunity to undertake advanced study.

As more teachers were needed for public schools as a result of the 1872 Act, and the need to 'train' teachers became recognised, women, mainly from the middle classes, began to see teaching as a possible route to a professional career. While in some ways this proved liberating, women were still not given parity of esteem with men, being paid less, being less likely to become promoted, and being subject to the 'marriage bar' until 1945, meaning women had to leave their posts as teachers upon getting married. In the late nineteenth century, male teachers were paid between £121 and £145 per annum, while female teachers were paid between £62 and £72 per annum (https://files.eric.ed.gov/fulltext/ED104864.pdf). Despite the differential pay and conditions, the early part of the twentieth century, for a variety of reasons, saw a massive change in the gender balance of teaching (see Table 89.1).

The gender dimension in teaching remains a pressing issue today, as will be discussed later in this chapter.

Table 89.1  Percentage of male/female teachers in the late nineteenth and early twentieth centuries

| Date | Male teachers | Female teachers |
|---|---|---|
| By 1851 | 65% | 35% |
| By 1911 | 30% | 70% |

Source: Corr, 2009.

## Emerging Professionalisation

As teaching moved steadily from being an extension of the work of the church, to being seen as a fundamental public service, and indeed a profession in its own right, not only did the composition of the profession change, but so too did the processes for educating and governing teachers.

Scotland has a long history of providing 'training' or education for its teachers, with David Stow (1793–1864) being a pioneer in the field. Following the mass production of teachers in the late 1800s/early 1900s, teacher education was located in specialist colleges of education, which subsequently merged with local universities to become faculties or schools of education. The academic demands of teacher education became a marker of teacher quality in Scotland, something envied by other countries where this was/is not necessarily the case. This fundamental principle regarding how teachers should be educated is once more under scrutiny as the Scottish Government seeks to address pressing workforce challenges in specific subjects and certain geographical areas of the country.

Part of the reason for Scotland's ability to hold on to the premise that teacher education should be located in the universities is the existence and prominence of two particular bodies, the Educational Institute of Scotland (EIS) and the General Teaching Council for Scotland (GTCS). The EIS, now seen principally as a teacher 'union', was initially established in 1847 for the purpose of 'promoting sound learning and of advancing the interests of education in Scotland' (www.eis.org.uk/About/our_history.htm), achieving a Royal Charter from Queen Victoria in 1851. By the start of the twentieth century it had begun to take a more prominent role in relation to teachers' pay and conditions, and to this day, it continues its dual role in attending to both the quality dimension in Scottish education and the more traditional 'trades union' dimension. (See Chapter 93 for more detail on the current work of teacher associations in Scotland.)

In 1965 the GTCS was formally established by an Act of Parliament, following extensive discussion prompted by concerns about a proliferation of unqualified teachers post-Second World War. Amongst other things, the GTCS has powers to register teachers, to accredit programmes of initial teacher education (ITE) and to oversee professional standards, thereby acting as a significant force in shaping how teachers are perceived, how they are educated and how their ongoing professional conduct and learning are governed. (See Chapter 94 for more detail on the GTCS.)

With the EIS and GTCS firmly established for some considerable time, teachers in Scotland have had a comparatively stable professional existence when considered alongside teachers in other countries where teacher voice has less chance of being heard. That said, the existence of such strong and stable organisations can arguably also serve to limit creativity, change and diversity.

Since the 1980s, when primary teaching became a degree-only route, all teachers in

Scotland are required to be graduates, and to hold registration with the GTCS in a specific sector/subject. Hulme and Menter's chapter on 'The evolution of teacher education and the Scottish universities', in the fourth edition of this volume (published in 2013), provides an overview of the introduction and historical development of teacher education in the university sector. Teachers, and the processes that educate and govern them, have changed significantly since the earliest days of the parish schools; the following section provides a summary of the composition of the teaching profession in contemporary Scotland.

## TEACHERS IN SCOTLAND: A CONTEMPORARY OVERVIEW

The Scottish Government's (2016) annual school census shows that there were 50,970 teachers working in Scottish schools, a figure up by 253 from the previous year. Interestingly, while little more than ten years ago there were concerns over an ageing teacher population, with a majority of teachers at that time in their late 40s/early 50s, the 2016 figures show a relatively flat age profile between the ages of 23 and late 50s. Of more concern at the moment are the gender and ethnicity profiles, neither of which adequately reflect the pupil population. Statistics on gender show an overwhelmingly female teaching population in every school sector (Table 89.2).

Interestingly, however, the gender profile of headteachers does not match the gender profile of the teaching population as a whole: 86 per cent of primary headteachers are female, compared with 90 per cent of the teacher population, while only 41 per cent of secondary headteachers are female, compared with 63 per cent of secondary teachers. While these figures are perhaps not surprising to anyone who has lived or learned in Scotland, the UK or even Europe more generally, it is important to understand that the feminisation of the teacher workforce is undoubtedly a cultural phenomenon. Drudy (2008) reports that 'while the proportion of women in primary teaching increased in all geographical regions worldwide in the latter part of the twentieth century (the period 1970–1997), in the least developed countries they remained in a minority' (p. 311), going on to suggest that 'the proportions of women in teaching in the different regions world-wide could reasonably be taken as indicators of the stage of economic development in various regions' (p. 312). As well as the important influence of the stage of economic development in a country, the purpose and structure of schooling arguably also has an influence. In countries where secondary education is seen as distinctively more 'academic' than primary education, there still remain differentials in the requirements of teachers' qualifications, with resulting differentials in pay. So, while teachers in Scotland are paid on a common scale, regardless of the sector in which they work, in many other countries teachers are paid differently depending on the level of schooling they teach at:

Table 89.2   Percentage of female/male teachers

|        | Early learning and childcare | Primary | Secondary | Special |
|--------|------------------------------|---------|-----------|---------|
| Female | 95%                          | 90%     | 63%       | 76%     |
| Male   | 5%                           | 10%     | 37%       | 24%     |

Source: Scottish Government, 2016.

the salary of an upper secondary school teacher with 15 years of experience and typical qualifications in Belgium, Denmark, Finland, Mexico and the Slovak Republic is at least 25 per cent higher than that of a pre-primary school teacher with the same experience and typical qualifications. (OECD, 2016, p. 406)

It is interesting to note that in Scotland, in times when schooling was perceived as an elite, academic activity, teaching was dominated by men, but as the purpose of schooling has become more socially oriented, the more it has become dominated by women.

Whether the feminisation of the teacher workforce is problematic remains a moot point. Drudy (2008) points out that 'there is little support in the research for any contention that boys' performance would necessarily improve with male teachers' (p. 319), and she also queries the evidential basis of the notion that boys need more male role models. So, if there is little empirical evidence to show that a more gender-balanced teacher workforce would improve pupil outcomes, is there any other reason to consider the gender imbalance problematic? For women, the answer is most definitely 'yes'. Drudy (ibid.) points to research that suggests 'the more feminised any occupation is, the more likely it is to be poorly paid' (p. 319), going on to illustrate that Organisation for Economic Co-operation and Development (OECD) figures in 2007 demonstrated that in the four countries in which upper secondary teaching was dominated by men (Korea, Switzerland, Germany and the Netherlands), teachers' pay was more likely to be proportionally higher than elsewhere.

This has interesting implications for what has traditionally been seen as a positive aspect of teacher education – its ability to attract 'widening participation' (WP) students; students who have been disadvantaged in terms of social and cultural capital. The University of Edinburgh describes the aim of WP as being 'to address the discrepancies in the take-up of higher education opportunities between different social groups'. Teaching, and primary teaching in particular, appear to attract considerably more WP students than other more traditional, elite university disciplines, suggesting that teaching perhaps serves to mask the wider problem of equity of access to higher education and to the professions.

Of course, gender is not the only factor worthy of exploration in terms of the teacher workforce: the latest Scottish Government (2016) school census reports 149 languages being spoken in Scottish schools, by 39,342 pupils for whom English is not their first language. While corresponding figures for teachers, that is, the languages they speak, are not available, figures on teacher ethnicity show an overwhelmingly white Scottish or British population, indicating a very limited languages profile. In the 2016 census figures, 93 per cent of primary teachers and 89 per cent of secondary classed themselves as white Scottish or white British. This is problematic in two regards: first, the teacher population appears to be nowhere near as diverse as the pupil population it teaches, and second (if we are prepared to accept that ethnic diversity is likely to be correlated with linguistic diversity) the Scottish Government's 1+2 languages policy (www.gov.scot/resource/0039/00393435.pdf) looks to be particularly challenging if we do not have linguistically competent teachers. The 1+2 approach states that from 2020 every child in Scotland will be entitled to learn one additional language from primary 1 and a further additional language from primary 5 (see Chapter 33 for further discussion on the 1+2 approach). The current lack of linguistic diversity in the teaching profession suggests either compromise of the 1+2 policy, or a serious change to the entry requirements for teachers and to ITE programmes themselves, particularly in the primary sector. Currently, GTCS entry requirements state (General Teaching Council for Scotland, 2013, p. 7):

> In line with the Scottish Government Languages Working Group report *Language Learning in Scotland: A 1+2 Approach* (2012) all students undertaking a programme leading to a teaching qualification for Primary education must have attained a languages qualification at Higher level or equivalent (SCQF level 6) either on entering the programme of initial teacher education or on its completion. (At a future date, within the next five years, consideration will be given to making this a requirement which must be met prior to entry to a programme of Initial Teacher Education.)

While upping the language entry requirements might seem like a reasonable response to the 1+2 demands, it must be acknowledged that languages are not the only area where teachers' knowledge is being questioned. There have been calls, most notably from the Royal Society of Edinburgh, to make a Higher science (or equivalent) a prerequisite for entry to primary ITE. In addition, the current national emphasis on literacy and numeracy has led to increased scrutiny of required entry qualifications in English and Maths for teachers across the preschool/secondary spectrum.

The discussion so far suggests that there are issues to be considered in terms of the composition of the teacher population, and the specific knowledge requirements of entrants, but perhaps more pressingly, recent times have seen a shortage of teachers per se, and this is particularly acute in specific subjects and in certain geographical areas of Scotland. This led, in May 2017, to the Scottish Parliament Education and Skills Committee holding an enquiry on teacher workforce planning. The enquiry brought into sharp focus the issue of teacher quality and teacher preparation, but also shone light on issues around the status of the profession. This is partially acute in terms of the status and perception of teaching for science, technology, engineering and mathematics (STEM) teachers vis-à-vis alternative STEM-focused careers. The growing emphasis on Masters-level learning, evident in the significant Scottish Government funding for post-qualification programmes, together with the first full Masters ITE route, provides some hope that this policy direction will serve to enhance the status of teachers, as well as providing more knowledgeable and able teachers. That said, despite a growing global political focus on Masters-qualified teachers, there is limited empirical evidence to support the taken-for-granted assumption that Masters-level teachers necessarily result in better pupil outcomes (Brooks et al., 2012). Yet OECD figures (OECD, 2014, p. 506) point to a growing tendency for countries to require teachers to have a Masters degree, particularly in secondary education:

> In 11 of the 35 countries with available data a masters degree is required to teach at the primary level, and in 17 and 22 countries, respectively, it is required to teach general subjects at the lower secondary and upper secondary levels. (p. 502)

It looks likely that this upward pressure for teachers to have higher and more diverse entry qualifications, and to undertake ITE at Masters level, is going to remain on the agenda for the foreseeable future. What we really need, therefore, is greater investment in good empirical research that will help us to understand more carefully the factors in teacher education that facilitate better outcomes for pupils.

## CONCEPTUALISING THE 'GOOD' TEACHER IN SCOTLAND

The foregoing discussion focuses on the composition of the teacher workforce, and the knowledge-demands expected of them. In seeking to understand this context more deeply, it is important to consider the ways in which the 'good' teacher is conceptualised in Scotland. The historical overview at the start of the chapter portrayed the teacher in nineteenth-century Scotland as authoritarian and didactic, with schooling privileging boys over girls and rarely rising above the 'elementary' stage for the poor, regardless of policy moves to provide schools in every parish and then to make schooling compulsory. It wasn't until the 1872 Education Act which gave parents legal responsibility for their children attending school, that compulsory schooling really took hold. With this move, the pupil population changed to include a wider cross-society range of pupils. More recently, the pupil population demographics have shifted again as migration becomes more commonplace. Alongside these changes which have led to greater ethnic and linguistic diversity, the presumption of mainstreaming, which gained legal standing through the Standards in Scotland's Schools etc. Act 2000, has led to a much wider range of additional support needs being met in mainstream classrooms. The teacher in twenty-first-century Scotland is required to work with an increasingly diverse range of pupils, and to strive to increase attainment for all pupils as part of a global competition to increase economic productivity and enhance national status, hence the growing focus on Masters-level teacher education in Scotland.

However, despite a seeming commitment to viewing teaching as a Masters-level profession, recent policy suggests some conceptual confusion over what constitutes 'good' teacher education. The package of 'new and innovative routes' demanded of teacher education universities by the Cabinet Secretary for Education in 2016 included a range of responses: Masters-level routes, STEM-specific routes, routes for returning to teaching, as well as what have been termed 'fast-track' routes which combine ITE and the induction year. And controversially, it was reported in June 2017 that a fast-track route into teaching, designed to tackle teacher shortages, would be put out to tender by the Scottish Government. Reaction to this news focused on the expectation that such a route would allow the social enterprise charity known as Teach First into Scotland for the first time. The Teach First route, as currently operating elsewhere, gives graduates limited contact with universities, setting the scene for a potentially very different conceptualisation of the Scottish teacher. Under existing versions of such routes operating in priority areas and subjects in England and Wales, graduates receive university input for only five weeks before beginning work in primary and secondary schools where they deliver 80 per cent of a teacher's timetable and start working towards a Professional Graduate Diploma in Education (PGDE) over two years. While considerable debate exists about the merit and value of such a route into teaching, reactions to the Scottish Government's intentions from academics and unions alike were hostile. Ian Menter (University of Oxford) voiced the view that any proposal to introduce a route into teaching that marginalised universities would be a 'tragedy', their contribution providing 'the critical edge that 21$^{st}$-century teachers desperately needed in order to undertake their challenging work successfully' (TES Scotland, 2017). Rowena Arshad (University of Edinburgh) declared that Scotland should aim for *more qualified* teachers, supporting the Finnish model of a Masters-level profession 'to create professionals able to adapt to complexity and diverse circumstances' (also TES Scotland, 2017). Larry Flanagan, General Secretary of the EIS, stated in *The Scotsman* of 2 June 2017 that allowing organisations such as Teach First into schools would be a 'betrayal of the high professional standards we operate in Scotland'. In October 2017 the tender was released, dubbed the 'Tartan Teach First'. It invited proposals for 'an ambitious and innovative programme for high-quality graduates … that will provide them with an opportunity to develop their leadership skills' (https://jmcemedia.wordpress.com/2017/10/10/tartan-teach-first-a-look-inside-scottish-government-plans/). The programme is to be GTCS accredited, offer a Masters-level academic award, and is to deploy students in schools with high levels of deprivation. As noted above, the Scottish teacher universities have been vocal on their resistance to a Teach First-type approach, many publicly declaring that they would not enter into such a partnership. However, the tender has made clear that, provided the programme has connection with a university able to offer a Masters-level award, this does not have to be a Scottish university. Interestingly, the tender seeks a provider to develop the programme which will then be handed over to the government in its entirety, resulting in a significant change in the hitherto unchallenged position of universities as sole providers of ITE in Scotland.

At the same time, the Cabinet Secretary for Education announced at the Scottish National Party (SNP) annual conference in October 2017 that government intended to address the teacher shortages in STEM subjects by offering £20,000 bursaries (from the start of academic year 2018–19) to help people working in these areas to change career, and undertake a teaching qualification. The use of such incentives has been mooted before in Scotland, but has always been resisted in an attempt to show equal value to all subjects. This bursary, together with the development of some radically different ITE routes, suggests that the essence of what it means to be a 'good' teacher in Scotland is being challenged by conflicting policy directions. Thus, we sit at a crossroads whereby a future version of this chapter might detail a much more diverse view of who contemporary teachers are in Scotland, and what their motivations, qualifications and career aspirations might be.

The official expectations of teachers are currently laid out in the GTCS's professional standards (see www.gtcs.org.uk), and alongside detailing knowledge and skills expected of teachers, they also place considerable emphasis on values, leadership and sustainability. The standards also privilege a conception of teacher as enquirer, stating in the Standard for Full Registration that teachers must 'know how to engage critically in enquiry, research and evaluation individually or collaboratively, and apply this in order to improve teaching and learning' (General Teaching Council for Scotland, 2012, p. 12) and that they should 'adopt an enquiring approach to their professional practice and engage in professional enquiry and professional dialogue' (p. 19). This stance is supported actively by the GTCS through, for example, their provision of access to education journals. This view of the teacher fits with what Menter et al. (2010, p. 24) would classify as a 'transformative' orientation towards professionalism, one which 'brings an 'activist' dimension into the approach to teaching', and a perspective that has gained considerable admiration internationally.

However, the picture is not straightforward, as Scottish Government education policy is increasingly shaped by the National Improvement Framework (NIF), the latest version being the '2017 National Improvement Framework and Improvement Plan', published in December 2016 (see Chapter 71). The NIF privileges numerical measurement of progress, including the introduction of standardised testing for pupils, and an increasingly prominent view that teaching should be 'data-led'. It highlights 'teacher professionalism' as one of the key drivers fundamental to improvement in education, thereby placing considerable responsibility on teachers to 'deliver' improvements identified and measured by government. So, the transformative orientation discussed above in relation to the enquiry stance in the Standard for Full Registration is therefore not the only way that teaching is being conceptualised in Scotland. Rather, the NIF, and related policy developments, position teaching much more clearly within what Menter et al. (2010) would classify as the 'effective' paradigm, with its emphasis on technical accomplishment and measurement: 'it is the model for an age of accountability and performativity' (p. 21).

Elsewhere in this volume, discussion of initial teacher education (Chapter 90) demonstrates further ideological confusion, where current government policy is simultaneously supporting the development of Scotland's first two-year Masters route (the University of Edinburgh's Master of Science (MSc) in Transformative Learning and Teaching) while at the same time supporting the development of 'fast-track' PGDEs and calling for school-based routes which may be led by organisations outwith the university sector. What does this all convey about the current vision of the teacher in Scotland? It is fair to say that while there is considerable emphasis on the transformative orientation, increasing importance being given to Masters-level learning and explicit policy statements about the need for teachers to be enquiring, there is also a more managerial, technicist discourse at play, driven in part by teacher supply concerns, and in part by a political desire to impose more easily measurable, externally imposed accountability measures. However, as Menter et al. (2010, p. 21) point out:

> From a political perspective it is difficult to reject this model because it prioritises value for money for taxpayers and emphasises the opportunity for all pupils to achieve to their best potential and subsequently to contribute to the economy and society.

Teacher 'quality' is measured in a number of different ways. The most overt expression of teacher quality is through the GTCS suite of professional standards which describe three key elements: professional skills and abilities; professional knowledge and understanding; and professional values and personal commitment required or expected of teachers at different stages in their careers. Yet these standards themselves display a range of different purposes and different underpinning conceptualisations of teacher professionalism (Kennedy, 2016), with some performing a more managerial, technicist function and others, particularly the Standard for Career-long Professional Learning, supporting a more activist conception of professionalism. Interestingly, however, in the 2012 revision of the standards, three themes were prioritised which serve to shape formally how teachers are expected to carry out their work. These themes are: values (particularly pertaining to social justice); sustainability; and leadership, and these three themes appear as central in each of the standards within the suite (see www.gtcs.org.uk for further detail on the standards). While teachers in many countries now have their work shaped by sets of professional standards, these standards vary in how they are structured, what they prioritise and how they are used. Importantly, they are not a neutral description of uncontestable aspects of a teacher's practice, rather they are socially and culturally constructed and their interrogation can reveal a lot about how a nation views its teachers in terms of both what teachers 'should' be doing and the extent to which they are trusted (that is, whether the standards are used to support professional learning and teacher autonomy, or to impose externally driven narrow measures of accountability). See Kennedy (2016) for further discussion on how standards shape perceptions of teachers and their work across the UK and Ireland.

While professional standards are a useful signifier for how the profession is shaped and governed for the general public, the media is a much more powerful conveyer of messages about teachers. Articles about teachers in the media in Scotland tend to be reports of individual teachers doing interesting things, or teachers who have done very bad things: local news stories. The discussion of teachers as a profession is less commonly seen, especially when compared to nursing, medicine, social work and so on. Recent reporting has focused on teacher shortages, prompted by the Scottish Government teacher workforce enquiry and recruitment campaign. The teacher-bashing of years gone by has turned more directly to SNP-bashing, where perceived falling standards are laid at the door of the Scottish Government, accused of 'taking its eye of the ball' and focusing on the fight for independence rather than the 'day job'. While this has perhaps masked some of the potential blame that might otherwise have been laid at the door of teachers, it also suggests a lack of professional presence in general public discussion. Surely, with a now fully independent GTCS, the teaching profession should have more of a proactive presence in the Scottish media? Individual teachers have taken to social media much more readily in recent years, but these discussions tend to be within the education realm rather than in the general political/societal realm.

An international study of teacher status in 2013 revealed some interesting observations about how the status of teachers in the UK compare with that of teachers in twenty other countries (Dolton and Marcenaro-Gutierrez, 2013). It should be noted, however, that these data refer to the UK as a whole rather than Scotland in particular. When asked which other professional teachers were most like (social workers, nurses, local government managers, librarians or doctors) the majority of respondents likened teaching to social work and nursing. Yet in China, respondents were more likely to equate the status of teachers with that of doctors, whereas in Brazil and the US the most common association was to librarians. These data demonstrate how powerful cultural understandings of professions are, but also give us 'permission' to consider that the status of teaching is not necessarily permanently fixed. What makes these observations on status and equivalent professions even more interesting is that respondents in all countries in the study, except Japan, also estimated teachers' pay to be less than it actually is. So, this means that the professional equivalence perceptions were based on inaccurate views of teacher salary, demonstrating that teacher status is not always based on accurate knowledge of teachers' work. This suggests an even greater need for a more overt and proactive media presence for teachers.

## FINAL WORDS

The teaching profession has changed significantly over the past 300 years or so since the 1696 Act for Settling of Schools, but what can be seen throughout this period is how the teaching profession is constantly subject to the influence of particular social and political events. Now, more than ever, with social media at our disposal, and with an increase in access to Masters-level learning which actively promotes criticality and agency, teachers have the opportunity to play a more active role in the decisions being made about them. If teachers take up this challenge seriously, then the next few years could bring exciting challenge and debate among the key stakeholders in education.

## REFERENCES

Brooks, C., Brant, J., Abrahams, I. and Yandell, J. (2012) 'Valuing initial teacher education at masters level', *Teacher Development: An International Journal of Teachers' Professional Development*, 16 (3), 285–302, doi: 10.1080/13664530.2012.688674

Corr, H. (2009) *Changes in Education Policies in Britain, 1800–1920. How Gender Inequalities Shaped the Teaching Profession*. Lampeter: Edwin Mellen Press.

Dolton, P. and Marcenaro-Gutierrez, O. (2013) *2013 Global Teacher Status Index*. London: Varkey.

Drudy, S. (2008) 'Gender balance/gender bias: the teaching profession and the impact of feminisation', *Gender and Education*, 20 (4), 309–23.

Gatherer, B. (2013) 'Scottish teacher', in T. G. K. Bryce, W. M. Humes, D. Gillies and A. Kennedy (eds), *Scottish Education, Fourth Edition: Referendum*. Edinburgh: Edinburgh University Press.

General Teaching Council for Scotland (2012) *The Standards for Registration: Mandatory Requirements for Registration with the General Teaching Council for Scotland*. Online at www.gtcs.org.uk/web/FILES/the-standards/standards-for-registration-1212.pdf

General Teaching Council for Scotland (2013) *Memorandum on Entry Requirements to Programmes of Initial Teacher Education in Scotland*. Edinburgh: GTCS.

Gray, D. and Weir, D. (2014) 'Retaining public and political trust: teacher education in Scotland', *Journal of Education for Teaching*, 40 (5), 569–87.

Hulme, M. and Menter, I. (2013) 'The evolution of teacher education and the Scottish universities' in T. G. K. Bryce, W. M. Humes, D. Gillies and A. Kennedy (eds), *Scottish Education, Fourth Edition: Referendum*. Edinburgh: Edinburgh University Press, pp. 905–14.

Kennedy, A. (2016) 'Standards and accountability', in Teacher Education Group (eds), *Teacher Education in Times of Change: Responding to Challenges across the UK and Ireland*. Bristol: Policy Press.

Menter, I., Hulme, M., Elliot, D. and Lewin, J. (2010) *Literature Review on Teacher Education in the 21st Century*. Edinburgh: Scottish Government.

OECD (2014) 'Indicator D6: What does it take to become a teacher?', in *Education at a Glance 2016: OECD Indicators*. Paris: OECD Publishing.

OECD (2016) *Education at a Glance 2016: OECD Indicators*. Paris: OECD Publishing.

Tes Scotland (2017) *New Route into Teaching in Scotland Could Bypass Universities*. Online at https://www.tes.com/news/school-news/breaking-news/new-route-teaching-scotland-could-bypass-universities

Scottish Government (2016) *Summary Statistics for Schools in Scotland, No: 7-2016*. Online at http://www.gov.scot/Publications/2016/12/9271

# 90

# Initial Teacher Education in Scotland

*Ann MacDonald and Ann Rae*

Globally, there are many and varied routes to qualifying as a teacher: this chapter offers an exploration of the uniqueness of that process in Scotland. Beginning with a historical summary outlining the positioning of initial teacher education (ITE) within universities, there then follows an outline of the policy landscape influencing ITE at the time of writing. National ITE provision is then briefly considered, followed by a case study analysing the philosophy informing one undergraduate programme developed in one Scottish university, in response to recent Scottish Government (SG) policy on ITE. The chapter concludes by considering future possibilities for teacher education in Scotland.

## HISTORY OF INITIAL TEACHER EDUCATION IN SCOTLAND

Scotland claims pride in its long tradition of education achieved, in part, through its distinctive education system. Yet, bespoke ITE, programmes of study designed specifically to provide initial teacher education, is a relatively modern concept. Up until the mid-nineteenth century, 'school masters' were sometimes educated at university, in classics, literature, philosophy and theology. Teachers in the rural parish schools, however, were more often high-achieving working-class young men. Such teachers had no higher education, either academic or professional, though they often aspired to it. Neither group had undergone 'teacher training' nor professional higher education (HE) specifically tailored to equip them to teach (see Chapter 89 for a more detailed history of teachers in Scotland).

A significant increase in the population of Scotland during the nineteenth century meant that a major recruitment drive was required to increase the number of teachers and schools. At this time 'Normal' schools were set up, administered by the Church of Scotland in urban areas and they formed the beginnings of 'teacher training'. David Stow opened the first of these, the Dundas Vale Normal Seminary in Glasgow in 1837 (the first such institution in Europe and forerunner of Jordanhill College of Education). Later, new teacher training establishments were put in place, such as Moray House, purchased by the Free Church of Scotland in 1848 for this purpose. Both denominations continued to provide teacher training over the ensuing decades, with a measure of state cooperation and support. The need for a steady and reliable output of teachers became more urgent in 1872 when the Education (Scotland) Act made primary schooling compulsory for all children between the ages of 5 and 13. At the same time, responsibility for providing schooling was gradually handed over by the Presbyterian churches into state control (though the Roman Catholic Church retained theirs) with teacher training centres all under government control by 1907. This marked a significant turning point for teacher education in Scotland and paved the way for the training colleges model (later colleges of education) which remained in place until the late twentieth century.

The 'universitisation' of colleges of education in Scotland took place in the 1990s. By this time, undergraduate ITE had already achieved degree status, the final intake to the three-year Diploma in Education having taken place in 1983, after which the Diploma was replaced with Bachelor of Education (BEd) degree programmes. These, along with existing Postgraduate Certificate in Education (PGCE) programmes, established teaching as a graduate-only profession in Scotland. At the time of writing, this continues to be the case, and indeed, there are now new programmes offering ITE at Masters level. Teacher education institutions (TEIs) initially sought accreditation of their degrees through bodies such as the Council for National Academic Awards (CNAA), or from neighbouring universities, but gradually colleges of education merged with local universities to form faculties or schools of education such as those which now exist in the universities of Aberdeen, Dundee, Edinburgh, Glasgow, Highland and Islands, Stirling, Strathclyde and the West of Scotland. These mergers, while rationalised in terms of the desirability of locating teacher education within the academy and a desire for research-informed teacher education, also owed something to the ongoing struggle to finance colleges of education as separate institutions (Hulme and Kennedy, 2016).

For our discussion below, therefore, it is important to note that the 'universitisation' of colleges of education at the close of the last century did not represent the first engagement of teacher education with the academy. Rather, before the mid-nineteenth century, where teachers held qualifications at all, it was an academic university degree rather than a professional qualification which was deemed appropriate preparation for a career in teaching. Furthermore, educationists like Simon Laurie (first holder of the Bell Chair at the University of Edinburgh in 1876) successfully argued for education as a university discipline, and TEIs like Moray House maintained links with the university over the following century, with some student teachers taking combined degrees between the university and the college of education. However, the 'practical turn' in teacher education, a move toward models which elevate 'practical' knowledge over theoretical and pedagogical knowledge (Furlong and Lawn, 2011, p. 6), and the introduction of the CNAA-accredited BEd in 1984, saw a withdrawal from universities in favour of bespoke professional degree programmes. It is, perhaps, ironic that when Scottish Office policy dictated that teaching be an all-graduate profession, teacher education distanced itself from universities in favour of college-based programmes.

## RECENT POLICY INFLUENCES ON INITIAL TEACHER EDUCATION IN SCOTLAND

In 2001, in a review of teachers' pay and conditions, *A Teaching Profession for the 21st Century* (Scottish Government, 2001), Professor Gavin McCrone highlighted the importance of continuing professional development (CPD), clearly indicating that it was neither possible nor desirable for ITE to meet all the learning needs of prospective teachers. In 2011, in a review of the McCrone report, *Advancing Professionalism in Teaching* (Scottish Government, 2011), Professor Gerry McCormac drew attention to the notion of progressively building knowledge and professional understandings over time, rather than the adoption of an 'empty vessel' approach to ITE. In 2011, Professor Graham Donaldson, formerly Her Majesty's Senior Chief Inspector of Education, published a Scottish Government-commissioned review of teacher education in Scotland, *Teaching Scotland's Future*. While careful to highlight that there was much to be proud of in Scottish teacher education, Donaldson subjected it to scrutiny, prompting change nationally to ITE programmes. Recommendations promoted coherent career-long teacher education based on a rationale of lifelong learning, stressing the need for more effective partnerships between schools and universities. Additionally, changes to ITE provision were recommended, including the discontinuation of BEd programmes for primary teachers, to be replaced with programmes in which students were to be afforded the opportunity to study elsewhere in the university outwith schools of education.

Drawing, in part, on traditional conceptions of professionalism and discourses of intellectualism, Donaldson recognised the complexity of teaching, and the necessity of investing in a system that values and supports intellectual challenge during ITE and in career-long professional learning (CLPL). It can be argued that his former role as head of Her Majesty's Inspectorate of Education from 2002 to 2010 equipped Donaldson well to carry out such a review of teacher education. However, this may also explain why school effectiveness discourses of quality assurance and accountability also prevail throughout the report.

Inevitably, in the wake of Scotland's relatively poor ranking in the 2015 Programme for International Student Assessment (PISA) and the drop in writing performance in the 2016 Scottish Survey of Literacy and Numeracy (SSLN), focus on accountability in teacher education sharpened. In 2016, the *National Improvement Framework for Scottish Education: Achieving Excellence and Equity* (NIF; Scottish Government, 2016a) set out the areas thought to be the most important in bringing about improvements in children's attainment by employing six drivers of improvement, including teacher professionalism. Later in 2016, *Delivering Excellence and Equity in Scottish Education: A Delivery Plan for Scotland* (Scottish Government, 2016b) followed, charging teachers in Scotland with driving continuous improvement. Rather than adopting an authentically transformative approach that acknowledges education as a critical, socially constructed act, NIF, and the subsequent guidance, signalled a reductive input/output model of teaching. It further suggested that statistical information gathered on the time spent studying literacy during ITE would allow evaluation of student teachers' preparedness to teach literacy to a high standard. In May 2017, the Cabinet Secretary for Education and Skills indicated that the Scottish Government would provide teachers with the resources to improve literacy. However, as Menter (2017) highlights, resources supporting the practical turn in the absence of professional knowledge are unlikely to bring about sustainable change to the attainment gap.

The role of the General Teaching Council for Scotland (GTCS) and the early introduction by the GTCS of 'competences', later revised as the Standards for Initial Teacher Education, then further revised as Standards for Professional Registration, and now in the process of yet another review, can on the one hand be argued as cementing the practical turn. On the other hand, the 2012 standards take account of the thinking of many leading international educationalists, and can be argued to be an attempt to resist reductive, technicist, training discourses by offering a conceptualisation of teaching as a reflective, enquiring, potentially transformative act. At the time of writing, and in contrast to the understanding of teacher education laid out in NIF, the Scottish Government has also funded a study titled *Measuring Quality in Initial Teacher Education* (MQuITE). The study aims to investigate how quality in ITE can be measured in a Scottish, context-appropriate way, whilst considering what such measures tell us about quality in different ITE routes. The GTCS are co-investigators along with representatives from Scotland's eight TEIs. The study will run from 2017 to 2022, with findings published annually, giving the sector itself a welcome opportunity to contribute to developing an appropriate accountability framework.

## INITIAL TEACHER EDUCATION IN SCOTLAND: CONSIDERING THE PRACTICAL TURN AND THE INTELLECTUAL TURN

Given the complexity of the historical and policy evolution of ITE in Scotland, it was inevitable that differing and competing conceptualisations of the nature and purpose of initial teacher education would emerge. This leads us to ask, what is ITE for? What are we, as teacher educators, trying to achieve? What is valued and by whom? From a philosophical perspective, the dichotomy of 'what is valued' versus 'what is valuable' in teacher education leads to a consideration of the practical turn and the intellectual turn.

Academia has long been an area of dissonance for teachers, and this dichotomy is often seen in attitudes to ITE. There is a popular discourse that ITE course content is irrelevant and that it fails to prepare adequately for the practice of teaching. This discourse of relevance is a marked feature of debate on teacher education across the UK, and one which was challenged in the Donaldson review. 'The "discourse of relevance" is a powerful part of the (re)turn to the practical in that it brings an intensification, re-orientation and simplification of professional knowledge to focus – in the main – on *contemporary* practice in schools' (Beauchamp et al., 2015, p. 161). Even where ITE learning is valued by practitioners, that value tends to be regarded as 'professional' rather than as educationally fulfilling at a personal level. Few describe their experience of ITE as transformative, as offering any intellectual awakening or liberation. It seems that ITE has traditionally failed to provide that transitional space which leads prospective teachers to reflect upon themselves and their lives in ways that are transformative.

The current practice on the part of Scottish TEIs of referring to 'teacher education' rather than 'teacher training' indicates a commitment to the intellectual turn, challenging the 'discourse of relevance'. Qualification to teach is granted following successful completion of either a four-year undergraduate programme or a one-year postgraduate programme with many programmes now including Masters-level credits. However, in common parlance, the term 'teacher training' is still in frequent use, including, at times, by Scottish Government. Conceptually, continually drawing attention to the distinction between teacher education and teacher training is important. Thus far, supported by the rigour of the GTCS accreditation process, ITE in Scotland has resisted importing on-the-job training routes such as School Direct and school-centred initial teacher training (SCITT). However, in 2014 the GTCS accredited the University of Northampton's Postgraduate Certificate in Education top-up course. Questions can be raised as to whether this could be an early indication that Scotland may be moving from its distinctive approach: this is the first time the GTCS has accredited a course designed and taught outside Scotland.

Teach First, based on Teach for America, is an accelerated teacher training programme delivered during a five-week residential summer institute, which claims to provide trainees with the skills and knowledge required for teaching. The training is delivered by Teach First trainers in partnership with universities, and exemplifies the practical turn. However, in the absence of a partnership with a Scottish university, Teach First has been unable to gain a foothold in Scotland, despite the fact that Scottish universities are subject to the same neo-liberal influences as those in England and other parts of the United Kingdom. Under recent pressure from the Scottish Government to demonstrate speedy responses to work-force planning, increased recruitment to programmes for teachers of science, technology, engineering and mathematics (STEM), as well as the demand that teachers should be able to do more to impact outcomes for literacy and numeracy, it seems reasonable to speculate that Scottish higher education institutions (HEIs) will have to work cooperatively to resist enticement into business with Teach First.

Across the eight TEIs in Scotland there were various responses to the Donaldson report. Professional Graduate Diploma in Education (PGDE) programmes came in for little criticism in the report and TEIs continue to offer a one-year PGDE route, with some providers offering elements of these programmes in online or blended modes. Some TEIs, notably Stirling and Aberdeen, were already offering alternative models of undergraduate ITE before the publication of the report and, since 2014, all other TEIs have replaced BEd primary programmes. The resulting Scottish landscape for undergraduate provision in ITE is now much more varied than previously, when programmes differed little from one TEI to another. A variety of four-year primary education programmes are now offered across Scotland, some entitled Master of Arts (in the ancient universities) and others Bachelor of Arts. All offer some opportunity for study outwith education, some with 'outside' courses, and others (concurrent degrees) with more sustained models of study in disciplines other than education. The pattern of embedded school experience (placement) is also more varied, with some TEIs concentrating this in particular years of the programme and others retaining the 'block' placement model across all four years. Flexible pathways are more frequently offered, with some TEIs allowing students to defer decisions on whether to enter ITE until after year one, while others afford students the opportunity to opt out of the ITE element of their degree mid-programme. While most undergraduate ITE is in primary education, specialist undergraduate routes remain for Physical Education (in Edinburgh) and for Technology and Music (in Glasgow). At the time of writing, two TEIs also offer undergraduate degree programmes in Gaelic-medium education (GME).

Notwithstanding this more diverse picture, we are still some way from achieving the coherent innovative framework for ITE for which Smith (2013) called in the previous edition of *Scottish Education*. Universities have been slow to challenge the primary/secondary divide and to offer programmes which qualify teachers to straddle this divide and teach across sectors (as noted by Smith, 2013). There is some movement in this respect, however, in postgraduate Masters programmes which are being developed at the time of writing. That said, there is little clarity around the move towards the Masters-level profession which Donaldson hinted at, and a lack of strategy about how this might be achieved, if indeed it is valued at all.

## A CASE STUDY: ONE SCOTTISH UNIVERSITY'S RESPONSE TO DONALDSON

In order to explore questions on the nature and purpose of ITE, we offer below a case study of the response of one university – the one in which we, the authors, are employed – to Donaldson's proposal to replace BEd Primary. Thus, turning from a national perspective to a local one, this case study is offered, not as an archetype, nor as an ideal, but as a lens through which to examine the complexities of the endeavour of ITE. Whilst the structure of the response is explained for ease of understanding, our interest is more in the principles underlying the response, principles which might be applied equally to many other forms of ITE provision, present and future.

In September 2014, the Moray House School of Education, University of Edinburgh (UoE) launched a suite of programmes known as the 'MA [Master of Arts] in Primary Education with ...' as a replacement for the previous BEd Primary Education (Hons) programme. The new suite was named to combine the traditions of a distinctively Scottish teacher education, established at Moray House in the mid-nineteenth century, with the historic tradition of the four-year honours programmes in the Humanities in UoE. The programmes comprise four strands of study over four years, namely Educational Studies, Primary Studies, Professional Experience and Practice (PEP) and an outside (or 'with') subject taken from the wider university provision to honours level. This combination was to provide students with the opportunity for in-depth study in a subject discipline outwith Education, alongside the study of Education and Educational Practices, leading to the award of an academic degree along with a teaching qualification in primary education. The 'with' subject is offered primarily as an opportunity for students to acquire what Donaldson termed 'deep knowledge' in a subject discipline. Instead of the block placement model traditionally used in ITE, the programmes incorporate a year-long experience in one school in year 3. Whilst innovative for ITE, this year-3 model is well established in other vocational programmes, such as Architecture, across Scottish universities.

## The UoE Philosophy for Undergraduate ITE

The MA programmes are premised on the importance of regarding teacher education as a lifelong process. Following Donaldson, we regarded our task as to offer a first stage in a process of lifelong learning – a deliberate challenge to the notion that ITE ought to deliver teachers as 'classroom ready' (Beauchamp et al,, 2015), the finished product fully equipped for all the rigours of teaching. The programmes aim to enhance and broaden the academic aspirations and achievements of students, and reflect an unapologetic attempt to raise the bar academically. Our endeavour in creating the suite of MAs was to provide degrees which took ITE to Russell Group standards of undergraduate study; degrees which were, first, degrees in the academic discipline(s) of education, and, second, professional qualifications in teaching. The programmes deliberately challenged what others have termed 'the practical turn' in teacher education (Furlong and Lawn, 2011, p. 6). In contrast to school-based training schemes such as those mentioned above, we set out to offer academically robust, research-led degrees. We wanted the most academically able young people to aspire to teaching, as previous undergraduate programmes had not always succeeded in attracting many such school leavers. We wanted to eschew the notion that good primary teachers were those with a sunny personality and a love for children – laudable though these qualities are. Rather, we wished to establish that the best teachers are those who understand the processes of learning and teaching, who understand the nature of knowledge, have the ability to problematise and deconstruct knowledge, and who understand the complex nature of society.

In planning these programmes, UoE consciously adopted a sociocultural approach to teacher education, one which recognises the 'craft' of teaching as only one element of the desirable preparation of future teachers. In the design and development of the suite of MAs, central to our approach was the belief that teachers should develop deep understandings of the nature of reality, and of human reflection on it, and that this is best achieved through the lenses of the academic disciplines of Sociology, Philosophy, Psychology and Policy Studies.

Students are encouraged to interrogate the policies and practices of schooling through these disciplinary lenses with a view to developing critical understandings of the political nature of schooling and teaching, and the contested nature of knowledge and its production and reproduction in educational settings. For example, student teachers are encouraged to understand the social and cultural worlds which pupils inhabit, and the indices of difference (e.g. gender, class, race, religion, disability, sexuality) which may influence their participation in schooling and which might present barriers to learning. Further, we aim to produce teachers who are disposed to reflect on the nature of knowledge, and to understand knowledge as socially and culturally produced. An exploration of how knowledge is constructed, and how this in turn produces tensions between different conceptualisations of curriculum, enhances students' understanding of how such constructions impact on policy and practice. Through this study, students develop an understanding of teaching as political work, and are encouraged to inhabit identities as activist teachers in a changing world.

In terms of curricular knowledge, a new approach was taken from the outset. Instead of dividing available space and time between curricular areas (which fails to problematise the notion of disciplines and their boundaries), notions of curricula are introduced by contextualising the study of subject disciplines within a philosophical interrogation of the nature of knowledge. Unlike previous approaches, students are introduced to the complexities of the nature of knowledge *before* considering approaches to learning and teaching in curricular areas. Similarly, they are enabled to consider knowledge within discrete disciplines, with a particular emphasis on literacy and numeracy, *before* being asked to explore learning within interdisciplinary contexts. To some extent, this design addresses the problem of what Donaldson refers to as the 'quart into pint pot' issue – the difficulty of 'covering' the entire curriculum in preparing 'generalist' primary teachers (see Smith, 2013), in that the emphasis is on the principles of curriculum rather than on the delivery of content. Further, the MA degrees consciously position current curriculum policy, Curriculum for Excellence (CfE), as *one* approach rather than as *the* approach to learning and teaching, encouraging students to reflect on and critique curriculum policy, and to situate it both historically and geographically, taking cognisance of the various contexts of power, and of the political and societal pressures and influences which bring policy into being. For this reason, we deliberately resisted Smith's (2013) suggestion that ITE programmes might be structured around CfE.

Such an approach is not without its tensions, however. Inevitably issues arise between the academic freedom of universities and the competing demands of structures, bureaucracy and hierarchy within Scottish schooling. These tensions play out in differing conceptualisations of the nature and purpose of ITE and the competing and complex ways in which knowledge and power operate. For example, the 'with subject' could be regarded as an imprudent use of limited time, exacerbating the 'quart into pint pot' issue, and too remote from the primary classroom and curriculum to be of service in teacher development. We might have chosen to locate the 'with subject' within the School of Education, so that students could gain a specialism which would translate directly into classroom practice: to study, say, Mathematics Education, rather than pure Mathematics. The notion that the in-depth study of a subject is of value to student teachers in its own right, or for the intellectual stimulation and development of the student, is not necessarily universally recognised. Concerns linger around the lack of time devoted directly to individual curriculum areas within the degree programmes, and around what this implies about how these areas are valued, and how prepared teachers will be for induction year. This exemplifies the tension between the conceptualisation of ITE as a space in which to learn the specifics of curriculum, and the conceptualisation of it as a springboard from which the tools of intellectual discovery and agentic inclination are launched.

There are further complexities. As observed by Smith (2011), the provision of such concurrent degrees for students of education may in itself perpetuate the perception that education is not in itself a robust academic discipline. Donaldson's (2011) concern that the traditional BEd did not provide ITE students with 'the values and intellectual challenges which underpin academic study' could surely be answered by ensuring robust academic enquiry *within* Education Studies and in curriculum theory, without giving over significant proportions of ITE degree programmes to additional disciplines. On the other hand, the opportunity for students to study outwith departments of education does address the cultural 'separateness' of TEIs, which, before Donaldson, had tended to operate in isolation from the wider university, even after the initial 'universitisation' of the 1990s.

## The UoE Approach to Programme Development in Partnership

In an attempt to encourage improvement in partnership working, Donaldson invited universities to innovate and reconstruct partnerships in order to strengthen and enhance existing relationships and develop improved structures, resulting in the collaborative development of a national partnership framework. In relation to school experience, Donaldson (2011) recommended that university and school-based learning 'should be interlinked, with connections being the means of developing educational theory through practice' and that 'new models of joint staffing should be developed to enhance the quality and impact of the placement experience'.

Looking to enact systemic change, the UoE Teacher Education Partnership (TEP) moved to an organising structure that enabled 'practice-based courses [to] involve the integration of the expertise of university and school-based educators' (Zeichner, 2012). This was a significant undertaking. In keeping with many other TEIs, the general effectiveness of the 'duplication model' (Smith, 2013) had inhibited the development of enhanced models of partnership in Scotland. Looking beyond a model concerned mainly with student placements and the assessment of students during placements, UoE became concerned to find ways to work authentically with local authority and school partners.

Making use of a number of short-life working groups, the professional experience and practice components of 'MA in Primary Education with ...' programmes were purposefully developed in partnership with school-based colleagues who were positioned as teacher educators. This model was crucial for the development of the year 3 courses, comprising the year-long, school-based course and the educational studies and primary studies courses. Working together, school colleagues led the school perspective on practice while university colleagues led on theoretical perspectives for practice. Taking into account the ongoing challenge of how to equip students who will be confident and competent as they embark on their probationary year, UoE eschewed the practical turn, looking instead to the paradigms of the reflective teacher, the enquiring teacher and the transformative teacher (Menter et al., 2010).

However, while those involved with course design and development were enthusiastic, deeply interrogating what it is to be a teacher, and developing structures that could ensure students were provided with enhanced opportunities for learning, not all school colleagues, nor indeed university colleagues, embraced opportunities to reconstruct what it is to be a student engaged in developing understanding through practice, or what it is to be a teacher educator. Donaldson's prompt that all teachers should view themselves as teacher educators can be interpreted as positively blurring the theory/practice dichotomy. However, setting aside debate on the dichotomy itself, merely stating that all teachers should consider themselves as teacher educators is, in itself, unlikely to bring about systemic change. It seems unlikely that the above will be matters for only the University of Edinburgh Teacher Education Partnership to consider.

A less anticipated strengthened partnership has come in the shape of the Scottish Council of Deans of Education (SCDE), the body which represents Scottish schools of education located in the universities which offer ITE, previously known as the Scottish Teacher Education Committee (STEC). In 2017, strongly signalling a united front and the reinvigorated intentions of schools of education to shape the future of teacher education, Professor Ian Menter (2017) was commissioned by SCDE to write a literature review on the role of universities in teacher education. In summary, his report argues that while there may be a need to respond to current workforce demands, standards in teacher education should not be compromised, and the place of the university in teacher education is crucial in this respect.

## LOOKING AHEAD

Writing as we are at a time of flux for ITE, some reflections and concerns emerge. Policy on teacher education in Scotland reflects some of the distinctiveness of Scottish education more widely, focusing on democracy, social justice, academic rigour and integrity. Indeed, even as recently as the Donaldson (2011) report, the rhetoric around teacher education was academic and values-driven, with a commitment to social justice and to challenging discrimination. The language of marketing has been relatively absent in Scotland until now.

However, recent Scottish Government announcements herald further innovation for ITE in Scotland. Prompted by workforce concerns, government is currently working with Scotland's TEIs to develop a range of new ITE routes including: fast-tracking that combines ITE with the induction year, concurrent first degrees in education with a secondary-school subject, distance learning programmes, and dual primary/secondary qualifications. These innovations are proposed along with assurances of maintained 'high standards'. Yet, with the clearly felt need to look beyond the local to national and international influences and development, there is a danger of future innovations operating as 'policy as spectacle' (Humes, 2013): changes which have superficial, market appeal, rather than changes built on a sound rationale. There is also a danger of concentrating on systems and structures (whether national or international) rather than on ideas and, by doing so, developing practices which are devoid of sound philosophical basis and therefore in themselves are anti-intellectual, even whilst appearing to call for a re-intellectualisation of ITE.

There have long been questions around the place of undergraduate ITE within universities, with the implication that such vocational degrees lack academic rigour (although it is too early to appraise this in respect of degrees developed post-Donaldson) or that teaching in the twenty-first century requires more life experience than most undergraduate students can bring. The implication here is that such degrees should be discarded in favour of a narrowing to postgraduate-only routes. Consequently, at the time of writing, the University of Edinburgh is preparing to launch a two-year postgraduate ITE route, which will offer, for the first time in Scotland, the opportunity to achieve a full postgraduate Masters degree and cross-sector teaching qualification combined. This can be seen as an attractive and positive addition to the nation's ITE portfolio when understood in terms of academic rigour and challenge, and the post-Donaldson commitment to aim towards a Masters-level teaching profession. However, this innovation can be seen as shaped by neo-liberal influences, and the case for the place of undergraduate ITE remains open for debate.

As can be seen, significant tensions continue to arise between academic freedom for universities and the demands of structures, bureaucracy, hierarchy and workforce planning within Scottish schooling. Education as an academic discipline remains both contested and vulnerable. Preserving the place of teacher education in the university as a rigorous, respectable area of study reliant on intellectual curiosity and interrogation of bodies of knowledge has become increasingly difficult, not least because teacher education is publicly funded. Tensions arising from Scottish Government expectations for ITE can be seen in the demand that ITE should be agile in responding to workforce planning. A managerial, technicist perspective informs this belief that, upon joining the profession, probationer teachers should be: competent in teaching literacy and numeracy; capable of making effective judgements about children's learning; equipped with the skills to address the attainment gap; and able to evidence impact quickly from professional learning. On the other hand, the expectation endures that Scottish universities should design and deliver teacher education programmes that will cultivate a 'reinvigorated' teaching profession: a research-informed, intellectually curious, adaptive profession prepared to adopt a critical enquiring approach to meet collectively the challenges of teaching Scotland's increasingly diverse population. A balanced approach is, therefore, required to reconcile expectations based on 'what a good teacher looks like' with 'what the government expects from ITE'. We, therefore, hope for an approach to ITE in the future which contextualises teacher education in Scottish society, builds on the previous successes of Scottish teacher education and, importantly, resists panic stimulated from either internal or external sources. This will be important in reshaping both ITE and education policy so as to maintain a distinctive Scottish approach to preparing new teachers.

## REFERENCES

Beauchamp, G., Clarke, L., Hulme, M. and Murray, J. (2015) 'Teacher education in the United Kingdom post devolution: convergences and divergences', *Oxford Review of Education*, 41 (2), 154–70.

Donaldson, G. (2011) *Teaching Scotland's Future – Report of a Review of Teacher Education in Scotland*. Online at www.gov.scot/Publications/2011/01/13092132/0

Furlong, J. and Lawn, M. (eds) (2011) *Disciplines of Education: Their Role in the Future of Education Research*. London: Routledge.

Hulme, M. and Kennedy, A. (2016) 'Teacher education in Scotland: consensus politics and the Scottish policy style' in G. Beauchamp, L. Clarke, M. Hulme, M. Jephcote, A. Kennedy, G. Magennis, I. Menter, J. Murray, T. Mutton., T. O'Doherty and G. Peiser (eds), *Teacher Education in Times of Change: Responding to Challenges across the UK and Ireland*. Bristol: Policy Press.

Humes, W. (2013) 'Political control of educational research', *Scottish Educational Review*, 45 (2), 18–28.

Menter, I. (2017) *The Role and Contribution of Higher Education in Contemporary Teacher Education*. Edinburgh: Scottish Council of Deans of Education.

Menter, I., Hulme, M., Elliot, D. and Lewing, J. (2010) *Literature Review on Teacher Education in the 21st Century*. Edinburgh: Scottish Government.

Scottish Government (2001) A *Teaching Profession for the 21st Century: Agreement Reached Following Recommendations Made in the McCrone Report*. Online at www.gov.scot/Publications/2001/01/7959/File-1

Scottish Government (2011) *Advancing Professionalism in Teaching*. Online at www.gov.scot/Publications/2011/09/13091327/0

Scottish Government (2016a) *National Improvement Framework for Scottish Education – Achieving Excellence and Equity*. Online at www.gov.scot/Publications/2016/01/8314

Scottish Government (2016b) *Delivering Excellence and Equity in Scottish Education: A Delivery Plan for Scotland*. Online at www.gov.scot/Publications/2016/06/3853

Smith, I. (2011) 'Revisiting the Donaldson review of teacher education: is creative innovation secured?' *Scottish Educational Review*, 43 (2), 17–38.

Smith, I. (2013) 'Initial teacher education', in in T. G. K. Bryce, W. M. Humes, D. Gillies and A. Kennedy (eds), *Scottish Education, Fourth Edition: Referendum*. Edinburgh: Edinburgh University Press, pp. 915–26.

Zeichner, K. (2010) 'Rethinking the connections between campus course and field experiences in college- and university-based teacher education', *Journal of Teacher Education*, 61 (1–2), 89–99.

Zeichner, K. (2012) 'The Turn Once Again Toward Practice-Based Teacher Education', Journal of Teacher Education, 63 (5), 376–82.

# 91

# Teacher Professional Learning

*Aileen Kennedy and Anna Beck*

## GLOBAL CONTEXT

Since the first edition of *Scottish Education* was published nearly twenty years ago, the world of professional learning for teachers in Scotland has changed hugely, and terminology has evolved alongside this changing policy and practice. What was originally seen in rather simplistic terms as 'in-service education', became known as 'continuing professional development' (CPD), but is now more commonly referred to as 'professional learning', as the purpose becomes more explicitly focused on teacher learning rather than development in a more general sense. These changes in terminology reflect the ongoing debate about teacher professional learning across the globe. Indeed, the trajectory of many professional learning policies worldwide can be seen to reflect ideas promoted in globally influential documents such as those produced by the Organisation for Economic Co-operation and Development (OECD) and the European Union (EU).

This global move is driven by increasing competitiveness as nation states seek to strengthen their own economies by improving the educational attainment of their citizens. Thus, global measures of pupil attainment such as the Programme for International Student Assessment (PISA), Trends in International Mathematics and Science Study (TIMSS) and Progress in International Reading Literacy Study (PIRLS) have become indicators of the success of nation states' school systems. They are part of a cultural movement that Biesta (2017) refers to as the 'age of measurement' (p. 315); a powerful movement which Stronach (2010, p. 10) contends is resulting in a 'global homogenizing effect'. This competitive environment has resulted in nation states seeking to replicate the policies and practices of the countries seen to be the best 'performers', and organisations such as the OECD have played their part in this by sharing evidence of 'what works'. At the root of this narrative is the influential pronouncement in the 2005 OECD report *Teachers Matter* which stated that 'raising teacher quality is perhaps the policy direction most likely to lead to substantial gains in school performance' (p. 23). More than a decade later, the global meta-narrative of professional learning continues in this vein, with the OECD background report for the 2017 International Summit on the Teaching Profession, stating that 'The education systems that have succeeded in improving student outcomes in our rapidly evolving landscape point the way forward: teachers must be the top priority' (p. 11). However, while the message that 'teachers matter' persists, the demands on teachers appear to be growing; not only are they expected to engage in lifelong professional learning, but they must be able to prepare students to face technologically-driven change, to work in different jobs and fields or create their own work environment, to distinguish the quality of sources of information, to become critical thinkers, to adapt to change, to relate to people with different cultural background and beliefs, to persevere when confronted with adversity and to learn throughout their lives. (Ibid.)

There is an explicit recognition here that the pupil population is becoming increasingly diverse, and that teachers require critical and relational skills in addition to excellent professional knowledge. The global meta-narrative has moved from simply expecting excellence, to an unequivocal position that the best education systems in the world focus on 'excellence and equity'. Readers familiar with the Scottish education policy context will recognise this mantra from our national policy documentation, but it would appear that the 'excellence and equity' panacea has crept into global discourse, with concomitant expectations on teachers in relation to their professional learning.

This twin-pronged emphasis on excellence and equity brings with it a number of challenges, both practical and conceptual. In terms of professional learning, it challenges the relative importance of gathering evidence of excellence, often equated with competition and a managerial conception of professionalism, vis-à-vis an emphasis on values and local solutions, often equated with collaboration and a democratic conception of professionalism. As global trends aspire to this twin-pronged focus, so the challenges for teacher professional learning policy and practice intensify.

Scotland, of course, has responded in its own way to this wider context and this chapter focuses on the 'glocalisation' of the global discourse: it begins by giving an overview of the current Scottish policy context. Thereafter it outlines the current structures of professional learning in Scotland, exploring the forces which shape it, before drawing to a close with discussion of some contemporary tensions and challenges.

## SCOTTISH POLICY CONTEXT

At the time of writing, we are now almost seven years from the publication of *Teaching Scotland's Future* (Donaldson, 2011). The Donaldson Report, as it is more commonly known, contained fifty recommendations for the improvement of teacher education across the early, career-long and leadership phases. Given the broad scope of this policy and the ambitious nature of some of its recommendations, the Donaldson Report was heralded as one of the most radical reforms in the history of Scottish teacher education. The extent to which we can say that radical change has actually occurred is unclear; however, the report has played a fundamental part in shaping the nature of teacher professional learning in Scotland today.

Of specific relevance to this chapter is the way in which this policy attempted to reconceptualise teacher professionalism, thereby promoting particular forms of professional learning. The core of the report hinges on the development of teacher professionalism, referred to throughout the report as 'twenty-first century professionalism', 'extended professionalism', 'enhanced professionalism' and 'reinvigorated professionalism', with no definition of what 'professionalism' actually means (Kennedy and Doherty, 2012).

The report entertains a vision of teachers as 'expert practitioners' who are 'engines of professional progress' and distinguished by their capacity for self-determination and judgement. It also highlights the intellectual nature of teaching, positioning it as 'complex' and 'challenging' and promoting the importance of Masters-level learning. Central to this vision is the belief that teachers should take responsibility for identifying their own professional learning needs and locating the relevant provision required. This was significant as it suggested a move away from top-down local authority funded 'CPD events', and a move towards grass-roots teacher-led learning. This sort of transition required a fundamental shift in the culture of the teaching profession and undeniably raised a number of issues around engagement and motivation.

The implementation of the Donaldson Report recommendations was in the hands of two partnership groups, the National Partnership Group (NPG) and the National Implementation Board (NIB). Both of these groups were comprised of representatives from key organisations in Scottish education, including the Scottish Government, General Teaching Council for Scotland (GTCS), Education Scotland, local authorities, universities and individual classroom teachers. The combined work of these partnership groups, and wider networks, resulted in a number of changes to the content and structure of teacher education. The most obvious examples in relation to professional learning are: the development of partnerships between local authorities and universities to support student and classroom teachers; increased uptake of Masters-level learning; the revision of the suite of professional standards, including the introduction of the 'Standard for Career-Long Professional Learning'; the establishment of a system of reaccreditation, later to be conceptualised as 'Professional Update'; and, the establishment of the Scottish College for Educational Leadership (SCEL).

While some academics have carried out small-scale, unfunded analyses of aspects of the Donaldson Report and its implementation, there has been very limited planned, systematic research. To date, the only piece of research that evaluates the impact of the Donaldson Report as a whole is a Scottish Government commissioned evaluation carried out by a market research company in 2015: *Evaluation of the Impact of the Implementation of Teaching Scotland's Future* (for the full report see www.gov.scot/Publications/2016/03/5736). The evaluation provides some insightful information into the landscape of professional learning, suggesting that there has been a significant cultural shift amongst the teaching profession in relation to their engagement in professional learning with a greater willingness to try new approaches. Possible reasons for this shift included an increased focus on professional learning; increased ownership of professional learning with acceptance that it is now teachers' responsibility; a greater awareness of activities leading to professional learning; and the decline of 'CPD events'. Although the evaluation points to the beginning of a reconceptualisation of professional learning, the authors warned that there was still a considerable distance to be travelled before Donaldson's 'vision' could be realised. It is important to note that the findings of this evaluation might not be a direct reflection of the impact of the Donaldson Report, but of a wider shift in the landscape in which this report has played a part.

This wider policy landscape extends beyond Scotland, and across the globe there has been a significant shift in the nature of curriculum policy discourse from prescriptive curriculum, testing and inspection to policies that seek to reprofessionalise teaching, highlighting the importance of teacher professionalism and teacher judgement. These policies position teachers as active agents of change in curriculum development and appear to recognise teacher agency, the ability to critically shape our own response to perceived change, as an important feature of teacher professionalism (Priestley et al., 2015).

In line with this wider global shift, the original discourse around Curriculum for

Excellence (CfE) in Scotland emphasised the role that teachers should play in forming and shaping policy, positioning teachers as 'agents of change' and 'co-creators' of the curriculum. On the surface, this move appeared to provide a degree of flexibility to schools, providing teachers with opportunities to use their professional knowledge and judgement to adapt the key principles from CfE into classroom practice. In reality, it led to concerns being raised about the lack of guidance and the potential time commitment required of classroom teachers, and raised issues about the type and amount of teacher professional learning required to implement CfE as originally conceived.

In 2014, the Scottish Government commissioned the OECD to conduct a review of the implementation of CfE and related impacts on quality and equity in Scottish schools. The report, *Improving Schools in Scotland: An OECD Perspective* was published in 2015. It made a set of recommendations to improve the continued implementation of CfE, the impact of which are fairly significant for teachers and the context in which they work and learn. Increased evaluation of teaching practice and a move to measure individual pupil learning place the classroom teacher in a vulnerable position. Furthermore, the enforcement of stricter curriculum guidelines removes the flexibility and opportunity for teacher autonomy that the original intentions of CfE created.

The OECD review also suggested that the proposed National Improvement Framework (NIF) had the potential to provide the robust evidence base that CfE lacked. As the NIF was under development during the time that this review was conducted, this recommendation might be read as more of an endorsement. Given the increasing influence of the OECD on national education reforms, it is perhaps unsurprising that this suggestion was followed by a succession of policy documents supporting the NIF and plans for its delivery.

The NIF and the subsequent *Delivering Excellence and Equity in Scottish Education* (DEESE; see www.gov.scot/Publications/2016/06/3853) set out the Scottish Government's vision for education, listing six key drivers of improvement, one of which was teacher professionalism. A succession of NIF-related documents has been released, including detailed 'delivery plans', all of which draw on the OECD rhetoric around 'teacher quality' and its role in achieving 'excellence and equity'. Each of these documents contains statements about the importance of improving teacher professionalism and professional learning and it is clear that professional learning is being used as a tool to drive change (Sachs, 2016). There is some indication as to how the government plans to do this, but a number of claims are made about the skills that teachers should possess in order to deliver this plan. They should develop as enquiring professionals and as experts in teaching literacy, numeracy and health and wellbeing while increasing their participation in Masters-level learning. They suggest that school inspection, local authority self-evaluation reports, information about teacher engagement in Professional Update (see at www.gtcs.org.uk/professional-update/professional-update.aspx) and the collection of teacher views should assist in this. With the subsequent parliamentary focus on gathering evidence around teacher workforce planning and teacher education (see records for the Education and Skills Committee business in May 2017, at www.parliament.scot), it has become clear that teachers, and teacher professional learning, have become an increasingly more prominent part of the 'age of measurement' (Biesta, 2017). This has important implications for the ways in which teacher professional learning is made accountable.

Of course, this whole context is made even more precarious in the wake of the outcomes of the governance review, *Education Governance: Next Steps* (Scottish Government, 2017). The 'excellence and equity' mantra is found throughout the report, and the argument for change draws heavily on OECD publications. In terms of professional learning, there is a clear call for greater coherence and 'streamlining', under the auspices of a 'renewed and revitalised Education Scotland' (p. 38) which will support new 'regional improvement collaboratives'. These regional collaboratives, the government argues, are 'best placed to co-ordinate hands-on professional learning and leadership development to teachers in line with a focus on developing methods of improvement that work for local circumstances' (ibid.).

Teacher professionalism, teacher leadership and professional learning are all positioned as key drivers in the government's plan to deliver their vision of 'excellence and equity'. The use of the term 'empowering our teachers' in the review title suggests that the reform might align with a democratic model of teacher professionalism. However, this appears less likely when a case is made for a system based on 'effective accountability' where individuals can be held 'responsible for their actions'. A further tension emerges when professional learning is positioned as an 'expectation' as well as an 'entitlement', pointing to divergent conceptions of professional learning and professionalism. The aftermath of the governance review represents a time of uncertainty around the future of school education, and it is likely that the significant changes proposed will change the way that professional learning is structured, funded and supported, and potentially influence the types of professional learning that are valued.

Around the same time as the governance review was open to consultation, the most recent results of the PISA were published (see Chapter 68 for details). PISA, a product of the OECD, is a triennial assessment of mathematics, reading and science that evaluates education systems by testing the skills and knowledge of a sample of 15-year-old students. Despite being the subject of much methodological criticism, PISA data is a key driving force of policy and is often used by governments to compare education systems within what is becoming an increasingly competitive space. Its most dominant use in Scotland tends to be as a policy tool: it appears and reappears in political discourse to justify educational reform, despite the criticisms and concerns that surround it.

In a similar vein, the results of the Scottish Survey of Literacy and Numeracy (SSLN;www.gov.scot/Topics/Statistics/Browse/School-Education/ScottishSurveyOfLiteracyNumeracy) were published in May 2017 and showed a decline in literacy, leading to panic about 'falling standards' and a knee-jerk response which lay the blame, in large part, at the feet of teachers, and teacher education. Given the globally assumed link between teacher quality and student attainment, recent PISA and SSLN results have further increased expectations on teachers to improve 'excellence and equity', with a consequent focus on teacher professional learning.

## THE STRUCTURE OF PROFESSIONAL LEARNING AND THE FORCES THAT SHAPE IT

This section outlines the key structures that currently shape and govern teachers' professional learning in Scotland. In line with the move from 'in-service education' to 'professional learning', there has been a gradual diversification of different types of professional learning with informal teacher-led events such as TeachMeet, live discussions on Twitter and collaborative blogging growing in popularity. Traditional forms, such as one-off CPD events, still exist, alongside more formal accredited Masters-level CPD, and these activities also now often interweave new technologies into their existing format (e.g. using hashtags to share events and stimulate discussion). With the emergence of new technologies and new platforms, CPD is not restricted to the local, but can involve teachers engaging internationally. This brings enormous possibilities, but also interesting challenges and a need to reconceptualise where the control of professional learning lies.

There are a number of organisations involved in the delivery and support of professional learning, including Education Scotland, local authorities, charities, private providers, professional associations such as the Educational Institute of Scotland (EIS) and, of course, the SCEL, established as a result of the Donaldson Report. Some of these can be considered as shaping forces in their own rights, and make important contributions to the overall professional learning narrative, but the organisation that arguably plays the most significant role in shaping and governing teacher professional learning is the GTCS (see also discussion in Chapter 94). Alongside the development of policies and standards, the GTCS supports and promotes the development of high-quality professional learning in Scottish education through a number of different platforms and tools. It provides a range of resources and systems to encourage teachers to engage with various aspects of professional learning. For example, it provides access to a catalogue of academic journals and e-books for all registered teachers in Scotland and has developed 'Education Hub', an online space to promote discussion around research. It also has the capacity to award 'professional recognition' to individual teachers, acknowledging formally their enhanced learning in specific areas, and, soon, to bestow 'professional learning awards' to institutions which demonstrate organisational commitment to professional learning. However, its formal functions in relation to post-qualification professional learning focus on two interlocking areas: professional standards and Professional Update.

## Professional Standards

The GTCS maintains a 'suite' of professional standards for all registered teachers. However, the standards within the suite perform a range of both mandatory and developmental functions, rendering it, arguably, a suite in name only (Kennedy, 2016). The current version of the standards was introduced in 2012, and they are currently under review again, with the revised suite due to be launched in August 2019. The current suite comprises the following:

- *The Standards for Registration*, encompassing the Standard for Provisional Registration (SPR) and the Standard for Full Registration (SFR). These are mandatory for all registered teachers in Scotland. Student teachers are expected to meet the SPR on completion of their initial teacher education (ITE) course, and the SFR on completion of their induction year. The SFR provides the baseline for career-long competence, and therefore performs a significant regulatory function (Watson and Fox, 2015).
- The *Standard for Career-long Professional Learning* (CLPL) replaces the Standard for Chartered Teacher, which underpinned the Chartered Teacher Programme, prior to its abolition in 2012. The Standard for CLPL is

> not designed as a benchmark of teacher competence; rather it is distinctive in that it is designed to inform and support teachers to develop and improve their learning and practice in a systematic way which reflects their growing expertise and their ability to work in different contexts. http://www.gtcs.org.uk/web/FILES/the-standards/standard-for-career-long-professional-learning-1212.pdf, p. 6)

- *The Standards for Leadership and Management* supersede the 2005 Standard for Headship and include both the Standard for Middle Leadership and the Standard for Headship. They were 'developed to support the self-evaluation and professional learning of those in, or aspiring to, formal leadership roles in schools' (GTCS, 2012b, p. 2).

Each of the standards is built around three interrelated categories: (1) professional values and personal commitment; (2) professional knowledge and understanding; and (3) professional skills and attributes. Although the content and format of the second and third categories differ between each standard, the list of professional values remains the same throughout the entire suite: social justice, integrity, trust and respect, and professional commitment to lifelong enquiry, learning, professional development and leadership.

The importance of educational research and an enquiry-based approach to professional learning is built into the standards from the very beginning. For example, to 'achieve' the SFR teachers must be able to engage critically with literature, educational research and policy; engage in reflective practice to enhance professional learning; and contribute to the professional learning of colleagues.

## Professional Update

In 2012, the Scottish Government tasked the GTCS with developing a system of active registration within which all teachers would be required to participate. Following a consultation process and a two-phase pilot, the GTCS introduced 'Professional Update' (PU) in 2014. In order to maintain registration with the GTCS, all teachers are required to engage with PU and participate in a 'sign-off' process every five years where their participation is confirmed officially to the GTCS. Two key purposes of PU as stated by the GTCS on its website are to:

- Maintain and improve the quality of our teachers as outlined in the relevant GTCS Professional Standards and to enhance the impact that they have on pupils' learning.
- Support, maintain and enhance teachers' continued professionalism and the reputation of the teaching profession in Scotland. (www.gtcs.org.uk/web/FILES/professional-development/professional-update-presentation.pdf)

PU is promoted as an ongoing process that brings together two pre-existing elements of professional learning: a system of self-evaluation against appropriate GTCS professional standards and participation in the professional review and development (PRD) process. As such, PU might be recognised as the driving regulatory force behind professional learning. Watson and Fox (2015) highlight a tension here between divergent functions of the process. On one hand, it is promoted to teachers as an 'entitlement' to help and support in various aspects of their professional learning journey, while on the other, it has the potential to be used as an accountability tool to measure teacher professionalism as a condition of ongoing licensing.

## A Framework for Professional Learning

At the time of writing, the GTCS was developing a new framework for professional learning, which articulates an enhanced model of teacher professionalism. The purpose of the model is to outline the core purposes and principles of professional learning. Essentially, it will provide a rich and detailed description of the type of learning perceived to have impact on student learning. The framework is intended to work alongside the current professional standards and PU, serving as a conceptual umbrella under which the various aspects of professional learning sit.

Reflecting the shift from 'teacher development' to 'teacher learning', the central focus of the model is the teacher as *learner* and the relationship between teacher learning and student learning. The development of this model is underpinned by educational research and theory and the theoretical element of the model is promoted as one of its driving features. Although the development of professional standards and PU were informed by research, the links to theory were less clear.

Drawing on work by Hargreaves and Fullan (2012), the model promotes the importance of *professional capital*, suggesting that it can only develop when teachers have access to the following:

1. high-quality, career-long professional learning that helps to develop deep knowledge and critical understanding about learning, teaching and education (human capital);
2. the development of relationships and partnerships through collaborative practice: learning with and from others (social capital);
3. effective and informed professional judgement driven by an 'enquiry stance' and shaped by professional values (decisional capital).

Another body of research that this model draws on is the literature around teacher agency (Priestley et al., 2015), claiming that teacher agency is an important and necessary element of teacher professionalism. Teachers are viewed as 'active agents of change' and the model recognises that the development of agency requires the appropriate support structures to be put in place.

Given the timing of the development of the model, it could be assumed that it has been developed in response to the NIF and subsequent DEESE. The increased focus on the 'impact' of teacher learning might be seen as an attempt to better align the agendas of improved professional learning and the development of a system characterised by 'excellence and equity'. The GTCS explicitly states that teacher professionalism is the most important driver out of the six drivers listed by the NIF for closing the attainment gap. Although this framework appears to empower teachers by highlighting the importance of teacher agency and professional capital, it also positions individual teachers as fundamental to change, and therefore central to delivering government's policy objectives. The extent to which this overarching conceptual framework will impact on practice remains to be seen.

## Teacher-led Professional Learning

There has recently been a significant shift towards teacher-led forms of professional learning in Scotland: informal events or collaborative spaces that encourage teachers to promote or share ideas, enquiry or research. The most important feature of this kind of learning is that it is organised by teachers for teachers, although is sometimes supported by organisations such as GTCS and SCEL.

Perhaps the most well-known example of teacher-led professional learning is 'TeachMeet'. This began in Scotland, but can now be found across the globe. TeachMeets are described as 'unconferences' and are organised as informal meetings for teachers to share ideas and good practice. Although grass-roots professional learning existed before the publication of the Donaldson Report, it is possible that its increasing popularity is partly due to the increasing narrative promoting the importance of teachers to take responsibility for their own professional learning.

Social media platforms, such as Twitter, have continued to grow in popularity as online spaces for collaborative professional learning. An increasing number of teachers are engaging in online discussion groups, which are accessed through shared hashtags. One example of this is #ScotEdChat, which is a weekly online discussion on Twitter on various topics in Scottish education. This can be seen as a form of collaborative professional learning, where a network of teachers can connect with other teachers across Scotland and internationally.

Another form of online professional learning that has recently increased in popularity is teacher blogging, one example of which is Pedagoo. This is a growing community of teachers who support each other in a collaborative way, encourage each other and share innovative and effective approaches to education, taking the form of a collaborative blog, which is promoted and discussed through Twitter.

The focus on teacher professional learning in Scotland appears to have intensified in the past twenty years since it first became a policy priority. The foregoing discussion has sought to provide an outline of the current structure and policy context. The chapter now concludes with some observations about challenges and the potential future direction of professional learning.

## CONCLUSION

The current policy context, both nationally and internationally, provides a number of significant challenges for teacher professional learning. Internationally, the continued heralding of a meta-narrative which links teacher quality to pupil outcomes sets a high-stakes agenda for teachers and for those who shape and support their learning. The importance of this agenda to governments globally serves to further support the principles underpinning the 'age of measurement'. Nationally, this global agenda is playing out explicitly in the Scottish Government's 'National Improvement Framework' with its growing emphasis on identifying and employing tools for performance measurement. There is a danger that the 'evidence' arising from these performance measurements (which are not always able to measure what counts) will be used to suggest that teachers are not appropriately equipped to carry out the demands of the role, and that a culture of blame will ensue. While not denying the link between great teachers and good pupil outcomes, the age of measurement appears to bypass issues of ideology, values and the fundamental purpose of education.

The performative measures valued in this age of measurement could, of course, be balanced to an extent by the existence of a wider range of research evidence focusing on teacher professional learning. This should include high-quality policy studies which focus not simply on measurable outcomes of professional learning, but on the unintended or unplanned outcomes, on the policy process itself, and on developing more nuanced and sophisticated ways to identify and evaluate the impact of teacher professional learning. This would require two things in particular (Kennedy, 2017, pp. 580–1): policy research which is planned at the outset of policy developments; and teacher education/professional learning policy to be deemed to be of significant enough value to be granted funding. With a Western university research culture which tends not to value 'local' or 'insider' research, this could prove to be a significant challenge.

In calling for greater value and investment in policy research which focuses on teacher professional learning, it is important also to acknowledge that such research is not without its conceptual challenges. Measuring 'quality' in professional learning would require us to define more clearly and accurately what such quality looks like, and to be able to understand causal conditions, even if they are at the level of broad contextual features. When we consider the range and type of activities that might be considered to constitute professional learning, we can begin to see the size of this challenge. For example, this chapter highlights a growth in teacher-initiated professional learning, and yet this is happening alongside an increased focus on the importance of Masters-level, and increasingly, formal, Masters-accredited learning. The challenge of identifying factors within each of these two spheres that lead to 'good' professional learning is not insignificant.

In conclusion, we suggest that in order for Scottish professional learning to continue to be seen as world-leading, we need to reconsider the balance between externally imposed accountability, and teacher-initiated accountability which provides space for individuals and school communities to drive the nature and priority of professional learning activities. Above all else, this should not be a discussion which exists only among senior policymakers, it must include teachers and the wider education community in talking together about what constitutes valuable and worthwhile professional learning, and how we might best account for our actions in this sphere.

## REFERENCES

Biesta, G. (2017) 'Education, measurement and the professions: reclaiming a space for democratic professionality in education', *Educational Philosophy and Theory*, 49 (4), 315–30.

Donaldson, G. (2011) *Teaching Scotland's Future: Report of a Review of Teacher Education in Scotland*. Edinburgh: Scottish Government.

GTCS (2012a) *The Standard for Career-Long Professional Learning: Supporting the Development of Teacher Professional Learning*. Online at http://www.gtcs.org.uk/web/FILES/the-standards/standard-for-career-long-professional-learning-1212.pdf

GTCS (2012b) *The Standards for Leadership and Management: Supporting Leadership and Management Development*. Online at www.gtcs.org.uk/web/Files/the-standards/standards-for-leadership-and-management-1212.pdf

Hargreaves, A. and Fullan, M. (2012) *Professional Capital: Transforming Teaching in Every School*. New York: Teachers College Press.

Kennedy, A. (2016) 'Standards and accountability in teacher education', In G. Beauchamp, L. Clarke, M. Hulme, M. Jephcote, A. Kennedy, G. Magennis, I. Menter, J. Murray, T. Mutton., T. O'Doherty and G. Peiser (eds), *Teacher Education in Times of Change*. Bristol: Policy Press, pp. 143–60.

Kennedy, A. (2017) 'Researching teacher education policy: a case study from Scotland', in M. Peters, B. Cowie and I. Menter (eds), *A Companion to Research in Teacher Education*. Heidelberg: Springer, pp. 569–81.

Kennedy, A. and Doherty, R. (2012) 'Professionalism and partnership: panaceas for teacher education in Scotland?' *Journal of Education Policy*, 27 (6), 835–48.

OECD (2005) *Teachers Matter: Attracting, Developing and Retaining Effective Teachers*. Online at https://www.oecd.org/edu/school/34990905.pdf

OECD (2015) *Improving Schools in Scotland: An OECD Perspective*. Online at www.oecd.org/education/school/Improving-Schools-in-Scotland-An-OECD-Perspective.pdf

OECD (2017) *Empowering and Enabling Teachers to Improve Equity and Outcomes for All*. Online at http://talis2018.nl/gfx/content/ISTP%202017.pdf

Priestley, M., Biesta, G. J. J. and Robinson, S. (2015) *Teacher Agency: An Ecological Approach*. London: Bloomsbury.

Sachs, J. (2016) 'Teacher professionalism: why are we still talking about it?' *Teachers and Teaching: Theory and Practice*, 22, 413–25.

Scottish Government (2017) *Education Governance: Next Steps – Empowering Our Teachers, Parents and Communities to Deliver Excellence and Equity for Our Children*. Online at www.gov.scot/Publications/2017/06/2941

Stronach, I. (2010) *Globalizing Education, Educating the Local: How Method Made Us Mad*. Abingdon: Routledge.

Watson, C. and Fox, A. (2015) 'Professional re-accreditation: constructing educational policy for career-long teacher professional learning', *Journal of Education Policy*, 30, 132–44.

# 92

# Teacher Leadership

*Margery McMahon*

## INTRODUCTION

Over the last two decades a programme of education reform has resulted in considerable changes for the teaching profession and to understandings of what it means to be a teacher in Scotland in the twenty-first century. Much of this of has been driven by major government policy initiatives, notably the agreement reached between the government and the teaching profession through *A Teaching Profession for the 21st Century* (SEED, 2001, known as 'the McCrone Agreement' and the *Teaching Scotland's Future* (TSF) report on teacher education (Scottish Government, 2011), known as 'the Donaldson Report'. Underpinning both of these reform programmes was a new conceptualisation of the teacher as leader, as an educational professional who leads learning within and beyond their classrooms, for pupils and colleagues.

This new model of teacher leadership, its adoption by the teaching profession, the issues engendered by its promotion, and the ways in which the profession has engaged with it, form the focus of this chapter. The chapter begins by exploring, first, understandings of teacher leadership in Scotland and as considered in the wider and expanding international literature. Next, the chapter considers the ways in which teacher leadership has become manifest in Scottish education, considering its early antecedents in the Chartered Teacher programme. The final section of the chapter looks at more recent developments and conceptualisations which have emerged through policy-led discussions at the international summits on the teaching profession and more informal networks such as Pedagoo and Research-Ed, which, as 'teacher-led' grass-roots initiatives, serve as important indicators of the way in which the notion of 'teacher leadership' has been embraced by the teaching profession.

## TEACHER LEADERSHIP IN SCOTLAND

The set of professional standards, overseen by the General Teaching Council for Scotland (GTCS), provides guidance on the role and work of teachers and school leaders in Scotland. To be fully registered as a teacher with GTCS, teachers must demonstrate how they have attained (at the end of a one-year induction programme) and are maintaining (through a Professional Update scheme) the Standards for Registration. In the professional standards, the leadership expectations of all teachers are clearly stated from the outset:

All teachers should have opportunities to be leaders. They lead learning for, and with, all learners with whom they engage. They also work with, and support the development of, colleagues and other partners. The Standards for Leadership and Management include a focus on leadership for learning, teacher leadership, and working collegiately to build leadership capacity in others. (General Teaching Council for Scotland, 2012, p. 2)

Specifically, within the Standard for Headship, headteachers are expected to 'establish and sustain teacher leadership and collaborative working to support the enhancement of teaching and learning' (General Teaching Council of Scotland, 2012, p. 21).

The embedding of teacher leadership within the professional standards reflects the ways in which various education agencies and bodies responded to the recommendations of the TSF report (Scottish Government, 2011). Within that report, the success of Curriculum for Excellence was seen to be dependent on 'the quality of leadership at all levels and on the ability and the willingness of teachers to respond to the opportunities it offers' (Scottish Government, 2011, p. 4).

The implementation (in part or in full) of the fifty recommendations from this report had significant consequences for teaching and teacher education in Scotland. The report called for changes in the initial preparation of teachers and their ongoing professional development. Allied to this was a strengthening of leadership and leader preparation across the system, structurally, through the establishment of a new Scottish College for Educational Leadership (SCEL).

The aim of Scotland's new leadership college was to oversee and coordinate provision for leadership development for teachers and school leaders in Scotland from early career through to headship and system-level leadership. This involved the development of a series of leadership initiatives and programmes in collaboration with a range of partners including universities. The early work of the college focused on a new 'Into Headship' programme for aspiring headteachers; an 'Excellence in Headship' programme for headteachers in post for more than two years, and a Fellowship Programme for experienced, senior headteachers. A teacher leadership programme was also prioritised as an important initiative so that the new college was accessible to the full profession and not just those seeking leadership posts.

## UNDERSTANDINGS OF TEACHER LEADERSHIP

The promotion of 'leadership at all levels' and 'teacher leadership' in the years since the publication of the TSF report has revealed some of the challenges that can arise from efforts to advance approaches which are not fully defined in the policy and guidance documentation but which cut across formal structures of positional leadership in schools. There is the risk also that advocacy for such approaches assumes the culture and conditions needed for leadership exists in schools (such as distributed leadership), when the reality on the ground may be very different.

With a brief to build 'leadership at all levels', SCEL has sought to provide greater clarity around teacher leadership. Part of this entailed a national engagement exercise across Scotland, undertaken in 2016. Through workshops with over 1,000 teachers and stakeholders, it provided a useful weather-check on how teachers perceive teacher leadership in Scotland. A key message from it was the need for a culture shift across the education system, where prevailing hierarchies could stifle creativity, innovation and leadership (Scottish

College for Educational Leadership, 2016, p. 27). Barriers to developing teacher leadership were seen to be time, workload and confidence; and a lack of opportunities for experience, appropriate professional learning, recognition, support, encouragement and trust. Questions of equity and equality of opportunity were seen as issues to be tackled (Scottish College for Educational Leadership, 2016, p. 12).

In seeking to define and describe teacher leadership, the report summarised responses to provide a typology of a teacher leader as first and foremost an effective teacher, who could also work well with, and influence, their colleagues. They are:

> passionate about learning and teaching. Through informed and innovative practice, close scrutiny of pupils' learning needs and high expectations they play a fundamental role in improving outcomes for children and young people. Teacher leaders are effective communicators who collaborate with colleagues, demonstrate integrity and have a positive impact on their school community. They model career-long professional learning. (Scottish College for Educational Leadership, 2016, p. 18)

The report concluded with a recommendation that 'a culture change in Scottish education is required to ensure that teacher professionalism and autonomy is equitably valued and nurtured across the system' (Scottish College for Educational Leadership, 2016, p. 27). In taking this forward there is a growing body of international literature on teacher leadership to draw from, but with a degree of 'muddiness' (Wenner and Campbell, 2017, p. 135), given the variance within and across systems as to how teacher leadership is defined and conceptualised. Wenner and Campbell's (2017) systematic review sought to examine 'how teacher leadership is defined, how teacher leaders are prepared, their impact, and those factors that facilitate or inhibit teacher leaders' work' (p. 134). The aim was to build on York-Barr and Duke's (2004) literature review on the topic. Would the largely theoretical considerations still hold?

For the purposes of their study, Wenner and Campbell (2017) defined teacher leadership as 'teachers who maintain [K–12] classroom-based teaching responsibilities, while also taking on leadership responsibilities outside of the classroom' (p. 140), a definition that for them empowers teachers but implies that they somehow go above and beyond their typical duties not just influencing individual teachers, but also having the capability to influence the entire school, community and profession. Features of teacher leadership identified from the literature, studied as part of their review included: working beyond the classroom walls, supporting professional learning in their schools, and being involved in policymaking and decision making at some level, with the ultimate goal of improving student learning and success and seeking improvement and change for the whole school organisation (p. 157). Their review of the literature found that the research relating to teacher leadership is not always theoretically grounded; that principals, school structures, and norms are important in empowering or marginalising teacher leaders; and that very little teacher leadership research examines issues of social justice and equity (p. 134).

The Organisation for Economic Co-operation and Development (OECD) report *Improving Schools in Scotland* (2015) presented a broad understanding of teacher leadership, outlining what such practitioners do. Drawing from Lieberman and Miller's definition of teacher leadership as initiating improvement and innovation practices within and beyond their schools (Lieberman and Miller, 2011 in OECD, 2015, p. 130), the OECD report saw teacher leadership as a means for developing teachers' competence and confidence as educators; one that 'advances their professional learning, promotes change and improvement in schools, encourages professional collaboration and collegiality, and boosts professional status and recognition' (OECD, 2015, p. 130).

While acknowledging that teacher leadership includes but extends beyond distributed leadership (OECD, 2015, p. 130), the OECD report did not elaborate on the role of school culture and climate in promoting or inhibiting teacher leadership. Such questions and issues are not unique to the Scottish context, and around the world education systems, grappling with ways to promote, and indeed regulate teacher quality, are encountering the challenges of 'trying to shape a new paradigm in which teacher leadership is expected and considered an opportunity to improve schools, despite the fact that it risks prompting clashes between bureaucratic and professional orientations to change' (Talbert, 2010 in Lieberman, 2015, p. 3).

In their critique of the discourse of educational leadership, Torrance and Humes (2015) argue that leadership has been deliberately given prominence within the policy context to assist the process of workforce reform, through enhanced expectations placed on teachers (Torrance and Humes, 2015, p. 793). Within contemporary theoretical and policy rhetoric, they argue, the term 'teacher leader' is used for specific purposes and teacher leadership is promoted for the purpose of engaging teachers in a bottom-up approach to school improvement (Torrance and Humes, 2015, p. 794). There is a focus, they suggest, on what teacher leaders *do* and 'the teacher leadership role emerges through teachers' actions through a *stance*, a mind-set, a way of being, acting, and thinking as a learner within a community of learners with shared accountability' (Darling-Hammond et al., 1995, p. 95 in Torrance and Humes, 2015, p. 794).

This view accords with a recent study which constructs leadership as *practice* and leadership as *identity development* (Hanuscin et al., 2016, p. 357) *and within these two constructs sees a* 'teacher leader' to be one who not only engages in the practice of leadership, but who also identifies his/herself as a teacher leader (ibid.). Sinha and Hanuscin's (2017) study explores the development processes involved in becoming a teacher leader, which they found to be an emergent process of development involving 'a synergistic interplay of an individual's views of leadership, engagement in leadership practices and identity development' (p. 368).

In examining the contested nature of the discourse of educational leadership in Scotland, Torrance and Hume (2015) also find the way in which teacher leadership has been conceptualised to be problematic. This is due in part to lack of clarity and precision within a multiplicity of definitions, citing Murphy's thirteen differing definitions (p. 798). It is due also to the absence of an evidence base to support assertions, acknowledging that while 'such principles are commendable in many respects, evidence of their translation into school practice remains limited' (p. 794).

As teacher leadership has evolved in recent years, the definition may continue to lack precision, though arguably there is greater consensus about what teacher leaders do. Questions remain, however, as to whether all teachers are teacher leaders and how teacher leadership can be differentiated from what is expected, routinely, from all classroom practitioners. Rather, can this be seen as a form of accomplished or exemplary practice for which the term 'pedagogical leadership' might be more appropriate, raising further questions about the accordance of teacher leadership with 'leadership for learning'?

Defining teacher leadership also requires more critical consideration of what is understood by 'leadership,' and as the SCEL report noted, for some the term 'leadership' can in itself be seen as a barrier (Scottish College for Educational Leadership, 2016, p. 12). This can occur when leadership is conceptualised only as positional or role related, without recognising the cultures and practices which ensue when more distributive approaches to leadership are adopted, and where leadership is seen as both influence and relational, effected and experienced, in part through networks, within and beyond the school. Thus, teacher leadership cannot be understood without consideration of power and hierarchy but also teacher agency and autonomy, with the potential for these to elide or clash. The Chartered Teacher initiative in Scotland is one example where such a clash occurred and it is to this we now turn.

## APPROACHES AND MODELS OF TEACHER LEADERSHIP

In many respects the Chartered Teacher initiative was the first formal attempt to promote a model of teacher leadership as a part of a major education reform initiative in Scotland. The status of Chartered Teacher was one of the outcomes of the 2001 teachers' agreement which sought to enhance the status of the teaching profession by formalising teachers' professional learning through a mandatory requirement of thirty-five hours of continuing professional development (CPD) each year. While a flattening of structures within schools resulted in the removal of some leadership posts, the introduction of the new status of Chartered Teacher aimed to support a new model to reward teachers who wished to pursue their career without having to leave the classroom. The issue of 'reward' (through salary incentives and professional recognition) and 'without having to leave the classroom' were, however, to prove problematic in how the Chartered Teacher initiative evolved. In the latter case, 'leaving the classroom' was more generally understood at the time as the choice to be made in relation to career progression, where a decision to pursue a leadership role meant 'leaving the classroom.'

The new *Standard for Chartered Teacher* (published in 2002) was explicit in the expectation that Chartered Teachers would be leading the learning of others within and beyond their classrooms. As well as being exemplary practitioners in their own classrooms, they were expected to support the professional learning and development of their colleagues. They should be committed to influencing and having a leading impact in team and school development, and to contributing to the professional development of colleagues and new entrants to the profession.

A revised *Standard for Chartered Teacher* in 2009 strengthened the leadership role further, with Chartered Teachers expected 'to be at the forefront of critically engaging with practice and to take a leading role in its development and implementation of change in current and future educational initiatives' (Scottish Government, 2009, p. 1). Within this, the potential for teacher agency was more explicit, with Chartered Teachers expected to contribute to enhancing the quality of the educational experience provided by the school and to the wider professional context of teaching, and by articulating a personal, independent and critical stance in relation to contrasting perspectives on educational issues, policies and development (Scottish Government, 2009, pp. 7–10).

A *Code of Practice on the Role and Contribution of the Chartered Teacher* accompanied the 2009 revised *Standard for Chartered Teacher*. The need for such a role and contribution to be defined had arisen in the years since the introduction of the Chartered Teacher initiative, where lack of clarity, for both Chartered Teachers and school leaders, about how Chartered Teachers might contribute in schools could potentially cause frustration and tension. The significant salary enhancement attached to the status added to such tensions, particularly at a time of growing accountability in an era of financial austerity. The Code of Practice acknowledged and endorsed 'the growing movement away from the traditional concept of leadership within schools simply being the responsibility of the head teacher and senior managers to the view that every qualified teacher has, by definition, a leadership role to play' (ibid.). How this might be done was exemplified in the Code of Practice, through, for example, leading and/or contributing to projects to initiate change; and working as a leading member of a team, inside and/or outside the classroom, to share good practice, improve teaching and learning, and develop a range of appropriate resources with a view to enhancing attainment and achievement across the school and/or educational community. It could involve supporting, advising and mentoring colleagues and also entail developing aspects of the curriculum and leading curricular change and assessment in the school.

The attempt to formalise and provide clarity was short-lived and the Chartered Teacher programme was ended in 2011. While a number of factors contributed to its final demise, the lack of clarity around a role attributed with leadership responsibilities but without a leadership position was important, particularly in a system where schools were evolving towards more distributed forms of practice but where, nevertheless, existing hierarchies still prevailed.

There are important insights to be gained from initiatives such as Chartered Teacher particularly in relation to identifying and creating the conditions in which they might flourish, engage the profession and have positive impact for schools and learners and how such conditions can be sustained. The role of incentivisation is also important, as the initiative showed that even the significant salary enhancement attached to the scheme was not sufficient to attract the number of teachers originally anticipated. It may be the case that the motivation to become involved with teacher leadership and networks is greater than the official status and financial reward that formal schemes accrue. It also raises questions about how leadership is understood and constructed in schools, placing a greater emphasis on leadership as relational and leadership as influence.

## TEACHER LEADERSHIP – FOR AND BY TEACHERS

In recent years there has been growth of more informal, teacher-led initiatives which appear to be attractive to teachers, and bottom-up initiatives such as Research-Ed, Pedagoo and TeachMeet which have emerged as informal teacher leadership networks. With loose structures and effective use of social media, these teacher-led networks emphasise their grass roots and space (virtual and real) for teachers to collaborate, share, connect and network. While these exist outside formal structures, there has been a move also to provide more formal teacher leadership programmes and a number of postgraduate programmes at Masters level are now available for teachers in Scotland. Similarly in other systems such as in the USA and Canada there have been efforts to provide formal professional learning opportunities that promote teacher leadership.

On the global stage, teacher leadership has become more firmly established on the agenda of the international summits on the teaching profession which have taken place annually since 2011. A key focus of the summits has been the coming together of policymakers, representatives of the teaching profession and teachers' professional associations, to identify and support key features of effective education systems. At each summit there is a clear focus on school leadership and teacher quality. Teacher leadership featured highly in the discussions at the 2015 summit held in Canada. The promotion of a 'collaborative model of school leadership involving teacher leaders who can participate in making decisions about the school and strengthen its pedagogy' was promoted and within this roles for leaders were identified, including mentoring new teachers, coaching teachers in specific subjects, observing other teachers and providing feedback on classroom practice, leading professional learning in schools, and working with poor schools to raise the quality of instruction and student achievement (Asia Society, 2015, p. 10). A clear focus on pedagogy was emphasised with teacher leadership seen as something that can strengthen the instructional core of the school, create career opportunities for talented teachers, and promote innovation and improved student outcomes (p. 11). There was recognition that the understandings and practices associated with leadership vary across education systems. In some systems it forms part of a structured career path while in others it is more informal. The report on the 2015 summit noted that in some systems teacher voice in decision making is the prime consideration, while in others teacher leadership is principally about working with teachers to strengthen the pedagogy of the school. A more informal approach to teacher leadership is taken in Finland where schools are much smaller, so all teachers are involved in curriculum development, assessment, introducing new pedagogies, leading teacher teams and mentoring new teachers, but without permanent or fixed roles or levels. In Estonia, leadership is regarded as something that is team based. However, the summit's report noted that while generally there is much interest in having teachers play expanded roles in schools, teacher leadership is not yet widespread in policy or practice (p. 11). The summit's report also noted that participants engaged in a sharp debate as to whether teacher leadership is a formal role versus an attitude or a practice, an aspect of professionalism. Some participants argued that leadership today is less about formal position than about a person's ability to move a group around a set of ideas. This debate encapsulates the contested nature of teacher leadership and reflects some of the struggles and challenges experienced, not least in the Scottish context. One such challenge is the role of teacher leadership at a time when there is a determined policy focus on closing the attainment gap amidst a discourse of social justice leadership which is considered below.

In their article on social justice and leadership development, Forde and Torrance (2016) found, from the literature consulted, the need for leaders who pursue a social justice agenda to engage fully with their specific context and adopt an advocacy role. In this, they argue, there is a strong political dimension (p. 109). While the assumption underpinning much of the literature is that this is a responsibility of the school leader/principal, Forde and Torrance emphasise that it is important that social justice leadership is not seen as a function solely of headship but is a facet of all leadership roles (p. 115). They propose that, if the intentions underpinning the policy articulations of equality and social justice are to be addressed, leaders need the understandings, skills and motivation to focus on shaping the conditions in schools and classrooms that foster inclusive pedagogies, and which engage constructively with issues of diversity (p. 107). They go on to demonstrate this through a development continuum, which maps leadership knowledge, dispositions and practices at key stages: pedagogical leadership, middle leadership, school leadership and systems-level leadership (p. 115).

It is argued that an important aspect underpinning each level in this framework is that a critical stance is built, where values are the basis of action and decisions, and where the tensions and dilemmas faced by leaders are acknowledged and ways of addressing them are explored (Forde and Torrance, 2016, p. 116). The building of a critical stance resonates with Wenner and Campbell's (2017) findings in relation to their review and concern about the lack of attention given to issues of equity and diversity (p. 164). In promoting a model of social justice leadership which encompasses advocacy and activism, the potential challenges that this form of teacher agency might bring for teacher leaders needs to be considered. This is not easy, given, as we have seen, the different understandings and enactments of teacher leadership that prevail. Wenner and Campbell raise concerns, too, about the need for initiatives to be grounded in high-quality research, particularly as teacher leadership is increasingly constructed as a key component of school reform (p. 135).

## CONCLUSION

In recent years teacher leadership has come to be seen as a measure of the extent to which the understanding and practice of leadership in schools has loosened, becoming more collegial, collaborative, democratic and shared. While many schools are moving towards more distributed approaches, the scale and impact of this cannot not be fully understood due to the variance in definitions and approaches and range of empirical evidence to draw from. The ways in which teachers may be empowered to lead might also be seen as an indicator of the extent to which a reprofessionalisation of teaching has occurred. In Scotland, the GTCS professional standards and SCEL's Framework for Educational Leadership provide some sort of road map for how this is understood and manifest. Looking more widely, however, forms of teacher leadership appear to be contingent upon context and culture, oscillating between teacher-led initiatives and system-driven approaches. The tensions and challenges that may result from this were seen to some extent in the Chartered Teacher initiative in Scotland where an emerging model of teacher leadership clashed with a system requiring accountability and evidence of impact. In the Scottish context, understandings about, and practices of, teacher leadership have continued to evolve, and the ambition of a 'school and teacher-led school system' in Scotland, announced in the government's governance review in June 2017, placed further emphasis on empowering teachers as leaders of learning. This may reflect the extent to which teacher leadership is coming to be seen as central to the realisation of wider policy goals for improving learning and teaching and closing the attainment gap as part of Scotland's National Improvement Framework.

## REFERENCES

Asia Society (2015) *Implementing Highly Effective Teacher Policy and Practice. The 2015 International Summit on the Teaching Profession.* Online at http://istp2015.org/Documents/ISTP-Asia-Society-report_Final_EN.pdf

Forde, C & Torrance, D 2016, Social justice and leadership development. *Professional Development in Education,* Vol 43, No. 1.

General Teaching Council of Scotland (2012) *Professional Standards for Teachers in Scotland.* Online at www.gtcs.org.uk/professional-standards/professional-standards.aspx

Hanuscin, D., Sinha, S. and Hall, M. (2016) 'Supporting teachers in (re)constructing identities as leaders: the role of professional development', in. L. Avraamidou (ed.), *Studying Science Teacher Identity.* Rotterdam: Sense Publishers.

Lieberman, A. (2015) 'Introduction to "creating the conditions for learning: teachers as leaders"', *The Educational Forum,* 79 (1), 3–4.

OECD (2015) *Improving Schools in Scotland: An OECD Perspective.* Online at https://www.oecd.org/education/school/Improving-Schools-in-Scotland-An-OECD-Perspective.pdf

Scottish College for Educational Leadership (2016) *Developing Teacher Leadership Report*. Online at www.scelscotland.org.uk/whats-happening/news/developing-teacher-leadership/

Scottish Government (2009) *Standard for Chartered Teacher*. Online at www.gov.scot/ Publications/2009/09/22144755/1

Scottish Government (2011) *Teaching Scotland's Future: Report of a Review of Teacher Education in Scotland* (Donaldson Report). Online at www.gov.scot/Publications/2011/01/13092132/0

SEED (2001) *A Teaching Profession for the 21st Century: Agreement Reached Following the Recommendations Made in the McCrone Report*. Edinburgh: HMSO.

Sinha, S. and Hanuscin, D. L. (2017) 'Development of teacher leadership identity: a multiple case study', *Teaching and Teacher Education*, 63, 356–71.

Torrance, D. and Humes, W. (2015) 'The shifting discourses of educational leadership: international trends and Scotland's response', *Educational Management Administration & Leadership*, 43 (5), 792–810.

Wenner, J. A. and Campbell, T. (2017) 'The theoretical and empirical basis of teacher Leadership: a review of the literature', *Review of Educational Research*, 87 (1).

York-Barr, J. and Duke, K. (2004) 'What do we know about teacher leadership? Findings from two decades of scholarship', *Review of Educational Research*, 74 (3), 255–316.

# 93

# Teachers' Professional Organisations

*Larry Flanagan*

Over the past few decades, general membership of trade unions has fallen in both the public and the private sectors; education, however, has maintained a high density of trade union membership, across the UK, with almost all teachers belonging to a professional association.

In Scotland, the predominant teacher union is the Educational Institute of Scotland (EIS), which represents around 80 per cent of teachers and lecturers. Founded in 1847, the EIS is the world's oldest professional association for teachers. It was granted a Royal Charter in 1851 by Queen Victoria and continues to exercise its power to award fellowships for outstanding service to education. The EIS recruits education professionals from all grades of post in all sectors of education: nursery, primary, special and secondary, as well as having networks for special categories such as Instrumental Music Instructors, Quality Improvement Officers (QIOs) and educational psychologists. It also has self-governing associations for both further and higher education: the Further Education Lecturers' Association (FELA) and the University Lecturers' Association (ULA). Overall membership of the EIS, based on its affiliation to the Scottish Trades Union Congress (STUC), is circa 55,000. It is Scotland's third biggest trade union. The EIS is affiliated, also, to the Trades Union Congress (TUC).

Whilst the EIS is the largest organisation, in the secondary sector there is also the Scottish Secondary Teachers' Association (SSTA), which was founded in 1944. Originally predicated on the premise of secondary teachers requiring to be organised separately when primary teaching was not a graduate profession, the SSTA has continued to attract some teachers in the secondary sector for a variety of reasons. During the industrial dispute of the 1980s, it was perceived, by some, as being less militant than the EIS and accordingly attracted some support from those who wished to limit their involvement in industrial action. The SSTA affiliates to the STUC based on 7,800 members but does not affiliate to the TUC. The third trade union is NASUWT (the name being derived from its anteced-ent organisations the National Association of Schoolmasters and the Union of Women Teachers), a UK-wide body, affiliating to the STUC on 7,000 members. Unlike the SSTA it recruits from primary as well as secondary. Although relatively small in Scottish terms, NASUWT has a significant membership furth of Scotland.

In UK terms the National Union of Teachers (NUT), which recruits in England and Wales, is the largest education union. The EIS and the NUT are partner unions, operat-ing collaboratively across common concerns. There is also the Association of Teachers and Lecturers (ATL), which no longer recruits in Scotland but which retains a historic membership, mainly in the independent sector. These unions have amalgamated to create the National Education Union (NEU) and are in the process of a phased transition from their existing structures to the fully merged operation of NEU, which will be the biggest education union in Europe, with over half a million members. It will be interesting to observe what new dynamics are brought into play by NEU, which clearly will have a prominent role in jurisdictions across the UK, although it will not be organising directly in Scotland.

Previous discussions in Scotland about uniting the teacher trade unions – at least the two main bodies of the EIS and the SSTA – have, however, made little progress, although there is partnership protocol between these two unions. This is perhaps surprising given the general trend towards amalgamation and merger amongst many other unions and the relatively few major policy differences that exist between the Scottish-based organisations.

Outwith the three STUC-affiliated teacher trade unions there exist a further three bodies worthy of note: Voice, the Association of Headteachers and Deputes in Scotland (AHDS) and School Leaders Scotland (SLS). Voice developed from the Professional Association of Teachers, which expanded into Scotland in the 1980s as a non-striking alternative to both the EIS and the SSTA, and it remains as such. Voice accepts membership from others involved in education such as child development officers. The AHDS and SLS represent headteachers in their respective sectors, primary and secondary, and have close links with similar bodies in England and Wales. Both recently opened their ranks to include depute heads and principal teachers as a means of boosting their membership. School Leaders Scotland (previously known as Headteachers' Association of Scotland, HAS) in particular regards itself as primarily a professional association and indeed it has been developing its profile along similar lines to the Association of Directors of Education in Scotland (ADES), seeking to influence government policy and acting as a forum for consultation. There is some evidence that both national and local government are keen to support this profile.

The final organisation to mention is the University and College Union (UCU), which was formed in 2006 following a merger between the Association of University Teachers (AUT) and the college lecturers' union, National Association of Teachers in Further and Higher Education (NATFHE). In Scotland, UCU is a predominantly higher education organisation, having only a relative handful of college lecturers in membership, as the EIS represents the vast majority (96 per cent) of this group of educators.

Most teacher organisations see themselves as having a dual function – to act in the traditional sense of a trade union in protecting their members and advocating on their behalf on employment issues such as conditions of service and salaries, but also to contribute, as a professional voice, to debate and the development of policy in the broader interests of Scottish education. This dual responsibility is not always evenly discharged as the political affairs of the day often create the context for union activity.

The trade union nature of teachers' organisations was shaped by the major disputes of the 1970s and the mid-1980s, when the EIS, and to a lesser extent the SSTA and NASUWT, were engaged in industrial action around conditions of service and salaries. The successful resolution of the two main campaigns of these periods created a legacy of loyalty from members which has helped to sustain the high level of unionisation prevalent in the profession.

A major consequence of the agreement entitled *A Teaching Profession for the 21st Century* (Scottish Government, 2001; often called the McCrone Agreement, although the final negotiated arrangements differed substantially in some areas from the McCrone recommendations) was an established consensus on the importance of continuing professional development (CPD) for teachers, and this opened the door for the development of the professional aspect of the work of the teaching unions. The EIS has been keen to involve itself in this area of work. It has worked in partnership with several universities, for example, to deliver professional development courses, and was involved heavily with the University of the West of Scotland around the development of the Chartered Teacher Programme. It currently receives funding from Scottish Government to deliver Masters-level training for members, in conjunction with City & Guilds.

The importance of teachers' professional learning was underlined by the Donaldson report (2010), *Teaching Scotland's Future*, which outlined a comprehensive approach around supporting teacher development from initial teacher education through to career-long learning – an approach echoed in the revised General Teaching Council for Scotland (GTCS) standards, which incorporate leadership and development frameworks within the three main standards (GTCS standards can be viewed online at www.gtcs.org.uk). It is worth noting that the general council of the GTCS has a teacher majority and that candidates for election are often, although not necessarily, endorsed by individual trade unions, notably the EIS.

A significant development within the EIS, since 2003, but not pursued by other unions, has been the creation of learning representatives (LRs) in support of the previous Labour Government's lifelong learning agenda. Learning reps, as they are known, are not trade union activists in the normal sense. Whilst some individuals may be involved in the broader work of the union, most are primarily focused on the professional learning agenda. Unlike a school rep, who would act as organiser/advocate for members in relation to conditions of service, for example, learning reps are supported professional development. Learning reps are trained by the EIS, in conjunction with TUC Learning and higher education partners, to develop an expertise in supporting colleagues in the pursuit of professional development. Where they have been established, they work cooperatively with local authority education departments to help deliver desired outcomes around the CPD agenda; over 100 joint EIS/ local authority events have been organised, for example, in support of a more collegiate approach to the delivery of professional learning. In the school sector, LRs would work across a number of establishments within a council area and in further education (FE) a rep would work across a single college. Although funded and developed by the EIS, learning reps offer their support service to all teachers. This area of activity bears testimony to the professional nature of teacher organisations in Scotland.

Developing a role around facilitating professional learning, as well as advocating for its provision, is likely to be a growing agenda for teacher unions. In referencing the importance of professional development, the Organisation for Economic Co-operation and Development (OECD, 2015) report, *Improving Schools in Scotland: An OECD Perspective*, talked of the opportunity for 'teacher unions along with GTCS to take on a more prominent role as leaders of effective learning' (p. 131). Stevenson and Bascia (2016), in their paper 'Changing unions in challenging times: international case studies in union renewal', explore how, across the globe, several teacher trade unions are engaging in professional learning as a tool for recruitment and retention of members, citing the EIS as one of their case studies.

The specific element of the EIS learning representatives network has also been examined in very positive terms by Alexandrou (2015): 'A learning odyssey: the trials, tribulations and successes of the Educational Institute of Scotland's further education and teacher learning'. Alexandrou noted how learning reps had evolved as leaders within their sector, 'more by accident than design', becoming experts in the field of post-compulsory education. He noted, in particular, the level of partnership working which learning reps facilitated between key stakeholder and the professional associations, and more broadly with the profession.

Fortunately, the refocusing on professional development afforded by the *Teachers' Agreement for the 21st Century* (www.gov.scot/Resource/Doc/158413/0042924.pdf) followed on from the timely establishment of the Scottish Parliament in 1999. The fact that education is a devolved matter has shaped the more consensual nature of education policy debate in Scotland than elsewhere in the UK, notably England. The previous Labour and Labour–Lib Dem Executives and the current Scottish National Party (SNP)-led Government have all been supportive of a process of engagement with the teaching profession, rather than one of confrontation which had certainly been the hallmark of the previous decade. However, the more straitened financial period in which we exist may well test the notion of collegial approaches more generally. A further tension is created by education having moved politically centre stage, with the consequence that the previous broad party political consensus around policy development and delivery has been replaced by a more adversarial approach which, perhaps, generates more heat than light. This is a reflection of the sharper political lines which have been drawn around the constitutional question of Scottish independence. The Conservative Party, for example, has spoken openly about withdrawing support for the Curriculum for Excellence programme. Recent statistics from the OECD Programme for International Student Assessment (PISA) and from the Scottish Survey of Literacy and Numeracy have both provoked politicking around the competency, or otherwise, of the Scottish Government on the issue of education.

The key forum for negotiations on salary and conditions of service for teachers and associated professionals is the tripartite Scottish Negotiating Committee for Teachers (SNCT), which involves Convention of Scottish Local Authorities (COSLA) (eight seats), as the umbrella organisation for local authority employers, Scottish Government (three seats) and the teachers' side (eleven seats), where the EIS holds a majority position. Because of its predominance over the teachers' side, in reality the EIS is the key decision maker for potential agreements, a position that sometimes leaves other trade unions free to agitate on sensitive matters without having to take responsibility for the eventual success or failure of negotiations. The current Teachers' Panel composition, from 2011, is based on respective memberships relating to those who are covered by SNCT arrangements: thirteen EIS; three SSTA; two NASUWT; one Voice. From this the negotiating team comprises eight EIS; one SSTA; one NASUWT; and one seat shared in rotation between Voice and the SSTA. SLS and AHDS have recently reactivated their membership of the Teacher's Panel.

The Scottish Government, which is represented by civil servants at the SNCT, maintains bilateral contacts with all the teacher organisations and is generally positive about working in a constructive manner on matters of policy. It is significant, for example, that the professional associations (the EIS, SLS, AHDS and SSTA, later joined by NASUWT) were all invited to take up places on the Curriculum for Excellence Management Board and have played a key role in shaping the direction and detail of this major programme, notwithstanding growing tension around the resourcing and rate of implementation that has been developing recently. In a similar vein the new bodies which have been established, the *Curriculum and Assessment Board* and the *Strategic Board for Teacher Education*, have extensive trade union representation, and the General Secretary of both the EIS and SLS are members of the overarching *Scottish Educational Council,* which is chaired by the Cabinet Secretary for Education.

Relationships between COSLA and the trade unions have tended to be more fraught as there is a direct employer/employee function in play and, in a period of austerity, significant budget pressures create challenges. The national agreement between the EIS and Scottish Government around the protection of teacher numbers, for example, has proved to be a source of contention. Generally speaking, however, COSLA, and within COSLA's structures, ADES, strive for a collaborative approach, also.

Within each local authority there exists a Local Negotiating Committee for Teachers (LNCT) operating under the general umbrella of the national body and with certain specifically delegated areas of responsibility, for example agreeing job-sizing arrangements for promoted posts. In some LNCTs, elected councillors meet directly with union representatives, but in most the management side is staffed by senior directorate members. LNCT agreements are co-signed and publicised as negotiated policy statements. In some authorities, the remit has been broadened so that the LNCT acts as a general consultative forum. Some LNCTs have a more collegiate approach than others but from a trade union perspective they are important, effective bodies which help to maintain a constructive working relationship between teachers and their employers.

Following a period of relative calm in terms of industrial relations, the financial crisis has precipitated several areas of dispute that threaten that stability; indeed, the issue of pensions sparked the first nationwide teachers' strike in over twenty-five years on 30 November 2011. There has, of course, been a significant level of industrial action in the further education sector, primarily involving the EIS which has a substantial membership in this sector, organised through FELA. The previous independent status of colleges, which have been faced with major financial challenges, led at times to an unfettered approach to industrial relations on the part of some college managements, and the institution-by-institution-based negotiations that arose became quite intense. The recent return to national negotiations on salaries and conditions, an element of the welcome reassertion of colleges as part of the public education system, may lead to a more positive framework moving forward.

Although unions organise matters slightly differently, a key aspect of the service offered to members is individual support to those who find themselves in difficulty in their employment. For many teachers, the main motivation to join a trade union remains the need to guarantee advice and support if things go wrong. All the teacher organisations, however, have been forced to broaden the range of services they provide to members to include areas such as insurance offers, discount purchases and professional development opportunities; the EIS, for example, is the principal shareholder of a company called EIS Financial Services.

An increasing pressure on the unions has been the volume of litigation they are now involved in, which is a costly demand on their resources. Tribunals and court proceedings are a staple aspect of modern union activity. However, despite the expansion of ancillary services by unions it seems certain that over the forthcoming decade teachers will have a renewed focus on protecting their conditions of service and restoring salary levels to previous equivalents, which may see a greater focus bearing on the trade union function of their representative bodies. Industrial action over Scottish Qualifications Authority (SQA)-generated workload and the first local authority level strike action since the 1980s (West Dunbartonshire, on the issue of faculties) may well be portends of a challenging period ahead.

Given the financial pressures that have arisen in the public sector and the consequent attacks on teachers' salaries and conditions; the potential challenge of governance changes following the Scottish Government's consultation; the creation of a National Improvement

Framework which places national government very clearly in the driving seat around school improvement; and the very public and correct focus on 'closing the attainment gap', it seems certain that teacher trade unions will continue to be centre stage in the landscape of Scottish education.

## REFERENCES

Alexandrou, A. (2015) 'A learning odyssey: the trials, tribulations and successes of the Educational Institute of Scotland's further education and teacher learning', *Research in Post-compulsory Education*, 20 (1), 113–26.

Donaldson, G. (2010) *Teaching Scotland's Future: Report of a Review of Teacher Education in Scotland*. Online at www.gov.scot/resource/doc/337626/0110852.pdf

OECD (2015) *Improving Schools in Scotland: An OECD Perspective*. Online at www.oecd.org/education/school/Improving-Schools-in-Scotland-An-OECD-Perspective.pdf

Scottish Government (2001) *A Teaching Profession for the 21st Century*. Online at www.gov.scot/Resource/Doc/158413/0042924.pdf

Scottish Government (2015) *A Draft National Improvement Framework for Scottish Education*. Online at www.gov.scot/Publications/2015/09/7802

Stevenson, H. and Bascia, N. (2016) 'Changing unions in challenging times: international case studies in union renewal'. Paper presented to Education International Executive Board, Brussels, Belgium, 26 October.

# 94

# The General Teaching Council for Scotland as an Independent Body – But For How Long?

*Tom Hamilton*

When *Scottish Education* was last published in 2013, the General Teaching Council for Scotland (GTCS) was a year into its new status as an independent body. Independent status had been granted by legislation from the Scottish Parliament (Scottish Government, 2011), coming into effect from April 2012. The new status showed Scottish Government and parliamentary confidence in the GTCS, building on its successful history since the mid-1960s when it was set up because of concerns about the quality of Scottish education and the employment of uncertificated teachers. In 1965 the General Teaching Council was to be the gatekeeper and guardian of the teaching profession and those twin ambitions continued in the 2011 legislation which gave as the principal aims of the GTCS that it should contribute to improving the quality of teaching and learning, and maintaining and improving teachers' professional standards.

So, in present circumstances when we still have concerns about the quality of Scottish education, how does the GTCS currently fare and what does its future hold in the light of the publication of *Education Governance: Next Steps Empowering Our Teachers, Parents and Communities to Deliver Excellence and Equity for Our Children* (Scottish Government, 2017)? The intention in this chapter is to:

- look at the format of the independent GTCS and its new powers;
- examine the GTCS model of the teacher:
- consider sources of influence on its thinking, and outline relevant issues within the Scottish educational context;
- identify various challenges;
- speculate on future developments.

## THE MAKE-UP OF THE COUNCIL

The move to independent status made few fundamental changes to the make-up of the Council. The number of council members was reduced from fifty to thirty-seven with mainly the same constituencies continuing: elected teachers, members nominated from various Scottish organisations and appointees. (The only organisation losing its nominee was the Directors of Social Work and the only group added was parents.) Teachers were still in the majority with nineteen. There were eleven from the universities, further education, local authorities, independent schools, parental organisations and the two main churches. The final seven were independent appointees who were to be laypeople, that is, explicitly not teachers.

The appointees increased from six to seven, so proportionally there was greater weight given to representing the public interest but there was quite explicitly no change to a teacher majority. This was surprising as the UK trend had been for the abolition of registrant majorities on regulatory bodies. Eyebrows were also raised that the opportunity was not taken to be more radical with a much smaller board rather than a large council. Council members now serve a four-year term and can complete a total of eight years in office over twenty years. There is also a two yearly 'refresh' of the council with members being replaced on a rolling basis. (However, the downside is the need for expensive two yearly elections and disruption to committees and their work.)

## NEW POWERS

The powers of the independent GTCS were enhanced by the 2011 Order. The GTCS was to set all the standards for school teachers. Rather than government, it was to be the body which 'determines' school teaching qualifications (TQs) and what needs to be in initial teacher education (ITE) programmes. It could also register other people working in educational settings. It was required to develop a reaccreditation scheme for registered teachers. All work was to be done in the public interest. The council immediately began reviewing the standards, the first occasion all had been looked at simultaneously. A steering group and three writing groups took forward the review of the existing standards and then drafted revised ones. These groups were led by council officers but had all relevant parties represented. An extensive public consultation was undertaken with open meetings across Scotland. There were opportunities to contribute views online and use was made of Glow Meets for those in remoter parts to contribute. Twitter was used to encourage debate – which led to robust exchanges with some who saw standards as 'yet another stick to beat teachers with'. However, over nine months this debate led to consensus and the standards were approved in December 2012. It was stressed by the unions that support materials should be provided for teachers using the new standards and hence various materials went onto the GTCS website.

As the standards were simultaneously considered there was an opportunity to ensure greater coherence and continuity. All standards now have at their core the same statement about values, so from student teacher to headteacher there is a shared set of values which should be at the heart of what teachers do within education. All standards have elements of leadership laced through them. Clearly it is central to the Standards for Leadership and Management but elements can be found in the others as they build leadership capacity. All standards also consider learning for sustainability, a crucial topic for education and society, which has attracted international recognition. Indeed the standards in general have been called both 'inspiring' and 'bold and supportive of high quality individual professional judgment' by the Organisation for Economic Co-operation and Development (OECD, 2015).

After such praise, should the GTCS just rest on its laurels regarding standards? No, as there will always be work needed to ensure the standards are at the heart of what teachers in Scotland do (emphasised by the OECD). All standards have a shelf life (about five years) after which they need to be revised to reflect changing educational priorities, practices and contexts. Comment on the future of the standards is provided below.

The new power to 'determine' teaching qualifications was taken to heart by the GTCS. Since the early 1990s the government had done this through occasional publication of guidelines for programmes of ITE qualifications in Scotland. The last Scottish Government version was 2006 – with GTCS involvement in the review and content. For decades the government had also steered ITE by publication of a Memorandum on Entry Requirements for Programmes of Initial Teacher Education in Scotland (the Entry Memo). Until fairly recently this had been an annual publication but latterly the Entry Memo had become an occasional publication. So, with its new powers, the GTCS set about a review of both these documents. The previous review of the guidelines undertook some public consultation, but in 2013 a much wider exercise was completed, making use of online responses and face-to-face meetings. The Entry Memo had never been consulted on publicly as government practice had been to meet privately with Her Majesty's Inspectorate of Education and the GTCS, then ask for university views on issues. The GTCS decided that, acting in the public interest, having public consultation was necessary, so there was significant open engagement with a wide variety of views expressed, particularly around the Entry Memo.

The ITE guidelines link closely with the standards (particularly Provisional Registration) and give a clear statement of the model of the teacher the GTCS wants to see developed in ITE. They give the aims and purposes of ITE and set parameters for programmes. They endeavour to ensure all key aspects of beginning teacher professional development are covered in ITE without being overly restrictive on universities in terms of innovation – which indeed is invited. They also form the basis for GTCS accreditation.

The Entry Memo sets minimum qualifications which candidates must have to gain entry. There are general requirements for all applicants, then specific requirements related to particular secondary subjects. Having Higher English (or an equivalent) continued to be required for all in the first revised Entry Memo. For primary it had long been a requirement to have at least a Scottish Credit and Qualifications Framework (SCQF) level 5 Maths qualification but this had never been required for secondary. Given that all teachers have a responsibility for numeracy, most respondents to the Entry Memo consultation saw this as anomalous so a similar requirement for secondary was introduced, meaning that from 2014 secondary ITE students also needed a Maths qualification. For some respondents this did not go far enough and they argued for Higher Maths. Given the government's 1+2 language policy, others argued for requiring a Higher Modern Language but the GTCS thought there was a danger of pricing ITE out of the market by being too specific in qualifications, so both points were resisted. (However, a commitment to revisit these points by 2020 was given.) A commitment to support the development of new TQs in Dance and Psychology was also given – both now developed.

Since 1965, the GTCS has registered teachers, but the 2011 Order gave the power to register other people working in educational settings. The one group who over several years had expressed a desire for registration was Instrumental Music Instructors (IMIs). They work in schools and their pay and conditions of service are decided by the Scottish Negotiating Committee for Teachers. They are able to be members of the Educational Institute of Scotland (EIS) – indeed the EIS has a network for them. Yet, they could not previously be registered. With its new powers, the GTCS set about developing an IMI registration system. Again a consultation exercise was conducted and views sought. Most were positive but initially both the Convention of Scottish Local Authorities (COSLA) and the Association of Directors of Education in Scotland (ADES) were negative, suspicious that this was a backdoor route for IMIs seeking pay parity with teachers, who are paid slightly more.

Both the Scottish Parent Teacher Council and the National Parent Forum Scotland were appalled to discover music instructors were not GTCS registered – and hence not regulated like teachers. Both bodies strongly supported IMI registration. This carried some weight with COSLA and ADES, both of which gradually accepted the professionalisation argument put forward by IMIs. It was also of influence on some of the more conservative GTCS members who saw the role of the GTCS as the registration of teachers and were concerned that registering others might risk diminishing the role of teachers. However, accepting the pluses of increased IMI professionalism and the positives that registration and regulation would bring to a group of staff who work in close proximity to children, IMIs are now eligible for GTCS registration.

The final new power granted to the independent GTCS was actually phrased as a requirement – to develop a reaccreditation scheme. The GTCS had been working on such a scheme but having it stated like this was advantageous as it gave the council (and teachers) no choice as it was legislation. Following normal practice the council had set up a working group with a wide range of stakeholders and after debate the scheme was entitled Professional Update (PU). An extensive piloting exercise was undertaken, supported by considerable research (see www.gtcs.org.uk/). PU requirements were trialled and support mechanisms and materials developed. Having decided employers had a key role in PU, the GTCS undertook validation exercises with all Scottish local authorities and other organisations which employed substantial numbers of teachers. Preparation for validation meant both employers and staff (normally through unions) working together to ensure each organisation's professional review and development (PRD) process was up to date and fit for purpose. This led to positive developments with staff regularly praising the process.

Not every registered teacher is working in schools or having day-to-day contact with children so the council decided to introduce two registration statuses with Full Registration (General) being required for teaching while Full Registration (Associate) would allow people to maintain registration if not teaching. Mechanisms to move between the two were also developed. General status teachers follow the full PU process, while it is modified for those with associate status.

While various challenges were met in the development of PU, GTCS research has been positive about both the development and the worth of the new system. This is in stark contrast to some other places (Ontario and Japan) where the introduction of similar schemes fell apart due to teacher perception that the systems were being imposed from on high. Scotland should be proud of how all the actors within education worked positively and consensually to bring about this potentially very significant development.

Since its launch in August 2014, the system has continued to be reviewed to ensure it is being used appropriately. Ongoing concerns are around finding time for PRD processes to be completed properly and the level of reviewer preparedness for using coaching and mentoring. GTCS research has also consistently found those directly involved in the PU process do not see it as particularly time-consuming or adding to workload and that any concerns about online recording systems have been effectively addressed by the GTCS. However, the real test will be to see if, over the years, Professional Update has any effect on the quality of education in Scotland and whether the potential of PU is being delivered.

## THE GTCS MODEL OF THE TEACHER

As noted above standards, guidelines and the Entry Memorandum all are based on the same GTCS model of the teacher, which is that teachers:

- have professional values;
- are reflective and innovative;
- are experts in pedagogy;
- are agents of change rather than recipients of it;
- are autonomous while recognising their place within systems;
- have commitment, resilience and high levels of self-efficacy;
- have appropriate subject content and pedagogic content knowledge;
- are accountable and consider the impact of their teaching on pupils and learners;
- know about research and scholarship and where appropriate actively practise research;
- are committed to their own ongoing professional development;
- are aware of education's links to other fields;
- are committed to working with other professionals within and beyond education.

Clearly such a model has not just appeared and hence a debt must be acknowledged to educationalists such as Lawrence Stenhouse, Judyth Sachs, Michael Fullan, Linda Darling-Hammond, Marilyn Cochran-Smith and Andy Hargreaves, whose work has been drawn on in developing this conceptualisation.

In terms of wider approaches to professionalism, the GTCS has also been influenced by the work of Evetts (2012) who argues for a new hybrid form of professionalism. In recent decades traditional occupational professionalism with its commitment to altruism, high standards and ethics (but subject to criticism for perpetuating a closed shop where self-interest and protectionism may flourish) has often been replaced with organisational professionalism emphasising standards, targets, accountability and managerialism (but subject to criticism that teachers are reduced to functionaries delivering the curriculum). Evetts suggests a new hybrid professionalism encompassing a professional wish for empowerment, innovation and autonomy but recognising the public interest need for quality assurance and accountability. For the GTCS this has attractions and fundamentally fits with its twin aims of contributing to improving the quality of teaching and learning and maintaining and improving teachers' professional standards.

In its thinking on the model of the teacher, the council was also influenced by other bodies such as the British Educational Research Association (BERA), the European Commission (EC) and the OECD. BERA and RSA (2014) suggested that in a research-rich, self-improving system teachers have a responsibility for developing research literacy to inform aspects of their professional practice. This responsibility should be stressed in ITE and career-long professional learning standards and registration requirements. BERA also argued that, for this to work, teachers needed to have opportunities throughout their careers to engage with and, where appropriate, practise research. Such ambitions feature in the standards and GTCS model of the teacher. They also chime with developments such as the GTCS providing all registered teachers in Scotland access to published research through the EBSCO platform.

Various EC publications have also been noted by the GTCS. For example, Piesanen and Välijärvi (2010) suggest that to further teachers' professional identity and improve practice there should be a continuum for teacher professional development and support should be given for lifelong learning. These two points are central to the standards and PU.

More recently, the European Commission (2015) has argued that teacher professionalism should incorporate collaborative practices, within a collaborative culture. Schools and ITE universities should be encouraged to engage in networks and professional learning communities. The GTCS encourages such approaches through its EducationHUB, having research suggested to teachers by a GTCS Research Engagement Group and its Teacher Researcher Programme.

While Scotland is not part of the OECD's Teaching and Learning International Survey (TALIS), it has noted various TALIS findings about successful education systems, for example:

> Teaching staff need to be able to innovate and adapt their practice continuously; this includes having critical attitudes which enable them to respond to students' outcomes, use of new evidence from research and practice, and professional dialogue. Results from TALIS suggest that teachers engaging in professional development are also more likely to use innovative teaching practices. (Organisation for Economic Co-operation and Development, 2014, p. 23)

OECD also argues for teachers to have a strong sense of agency, helping to encourage self-efficacy leading to increased job satisfaction and higher levels of resilience. Despite what some critics might claim, these features are exactly what the GTCS is endeavouring to develop in teachers as can be seen in professional recognition awards which encourage professional learning, sharing it with colleagues and then public recognition and celebration.

## SCOTTISH EDUCATION ISSUES IMPACTING ON THE GTCS

Curriculum for Excellence has impinged on the work of the GTCS in various ways. The place of subject teaching is one example and linked to it the development of interdisciplinary learning (IDL). As schools endeavour to be innovative (and deal with staffing issues), a frequent question to the GTCS has been about secondary headteachers insisting on teachers teaching outside their own subjects, thereby challenging traditional practices applied to subject teaching. What could be done within GTCS registration categories? The GTCS provided website guidance, indicating examples of good practice (different subject teachers working together, jointly planning, delivering and assessing programmes of study) but it also had to admit that the Scottish Government had largely sold the pass in 2005 in Circular No 4 which dealt with The Requirements for Teachers (Scotland) Regulations 2005 Repeal of the Schools (Scotland) Code 1956. The circular said:

> The repeal of … these regulations will allow education authorities and schools to deploy teachers according to the educational needs of children, rather than on the basis of their teaching qualification. From 30 September 2005, the appropriateness of a teacher for a particular post will be a matter for education authorities as employers. Prior to the placement of a teacher in a particular post, an employing local authority must be assured that the teacher has the appropriate professional skills and knowledge required for the post to which they are appointed.

The final sentence was the caveat allowing the GTCS to argue the importance of subject registration and also to stress the need for good cooperative practice amongst teachers to ensure non-specialist teachers were well prepared if teaching outside their subject.

Also related to the delivery of Curriculum for Excellence was the increasing number of school/college partnerships being developed. The use of college lecturers (who do not require GTCS registration) continues to be problematic. In response, the GTCS pressed forward with attempts to encourage greater levels of registration in the colleges but, admittedly, without huge success. Numbers remain disappointingly low.

The answer to these issues lies in the hands of the Scottish Government. The 2011 Order expressly says that the Scottish Government continues to determine the Teaching Qualification for Further Education (TQFE) (although civil servants had on one occasion to be reminded of this) and it also effectively still has overall control of the professional standards for lecturers in Scotland's colleges. Ironically, all programmes leading to the TQFE have to have GTCS accreditation but, while the colleges do largely encourage teaching staff to undertake TQFE, there is no mandatory requirement.

The government could (and should) solve these issues by taking two steps. The determination of the teaching qualifications for the college sector and the relevant standards should be passed to the GTCS and the government should also make GTCS registration mandatory for teaching in the colleges. This would enhance professionalism and regulation within the college sector and allow far greater educational flexibility in how pupils and students are taught. The Scottish Government has over recent years already made significant changes to the college sector and these further changes would be a force for good, bringing college and school staff under the same professional regulatory umbrella.

In terms of making GTCS registration mandatory for other teaching staff, the Scottish Government is doing this for independent schools. As a result, the GTCS has been working extensively with the Scottish Council of Independent Schools (SCIS) and schools to find ways to register all independent school teachers. Most were already registered as their schools had registration as a condition of employment but some were not, and the GTCS has been endeavouring to find mechanisms for those without TQs (or sometimes academic qualifications) to meet registration requirements. Such mechanisms have been to explore restricted forms of registration – that is, teaching only within a particular school – or the use of 'top-up' TQs.

Top-up programmes have also been used in addressing issues of teachers qualified outside Scotland (QOS), particularly some coming from England. England has (and has had) a plethora of routes into teaching some of which do not require a TQ. For example, the Graduate Teacher Programme (GTP) in the past, or some versions of the current School Direct model, simply do not award a TQ which means that those completing them are largely restricted to teaching in England as they have no recognised TQ.

For a short time, the University of Aberdeen offered a GTCS accredited top-up programme for such teachers wishing to move to Scotland but then withdrew the programme. The University of Northampton also offered a similar programme. It was brought forward for consideration by the GTCS which, since independence, was in a position to accredit programmes outside Scotland. That gained accreditation meaning that non-TQ holders from the English system had a potential route to GTCS registration. The University of Buckingham, a private university, also offered a form of TQ which SCIS schools were keen to use for their unqualified staff and this too gained GTCS accreditation helping to address the needs of some independent school staff.

The GTCS has also increased flexibility in gaining registration by reintroducing the possibility of applicants gaining Provisional Conditional Registration. This allows, for example, an applicant from England who has completed a GTP and gained considerable practical teaching experience to be provisionally registered while meeting a set condition such as gaining a top-up TQ. Given the shortage of teachers in some areas, this helps to address recruitment issues and criticism of the GTCS by some of inflexibility. However, we should note too that Brexit raises various registration issues!

## CHALLENGES

Education in contemporary Scotland sets the GTCS various challenges. Delivering on Professional Update, the registration of all teachers in independent schools and increasing the numbers registered in colleges have been mentioned but there are other challenges.

Fitness to Teach, the Code of Professionalism and Conduct (COPAC) and the Framework on Teacher Competence are all challenging. Teachers are human beings and as such, occasionally, individuals behave inappropriately. This might be dishonesty, unprofessional conduct or incompetence and the GTCS is charged with dealing with such matters. Given the number of teachers on the register (73,000 in May 2016) the number of complaints against teachers (200/300 annually) is low, the number proceeding to hearings even lower and those then subject to sanctions lower still – perhaps a couple of dozen each year. So why the challenge?

Cases appear to be ever more complex. Legal requirements must be met and be seen to be met. Fitness to Teach cases sometimes take lengthy periods and this is a concern to the GTCS, respondents, their representatives, witnesses and employers. Steps have been taken to try to streamline processes, while maintaining its integrity. There are case management discussions to identify timescales and a 'with consent' format introduced where the teacher admits whatever the issue is. These help but some cases are still lengthy – including the possibility of Court of Session appeal, itself a lengthy and expensive, but significant, process. The GTCS has endeavoured to supply teachers with support and advice materials in the Fitness to Teach area. There is COPAC, a student code, advice on social media and guidance for those attending hearings.

Another challenge is the relationship between the GTCS and other bodies. How does the GTCS work with the unions/Scottish Government/universities/local authorities/ Education Scotland/the Scottish College for Educational Leadership/the public/parents/ and so on? Such relationships present challenges and need to be developed and managed. Sufficient information needs to be made available and, where necessary, working relationships forged. Other bodies need to understand the role of the GTCS, be aware of its powers and know what it can and cannot do.

A particularly important relationship is of course with registrants. The GTCS has put considerable effort into building communications through its magazine (available on paper and electronically), the council website and much public speaking by GTCS staff. However, research in 2015 suggested the GTCS message does not always get across to registrants but also that teachers who had had direct involvement with the GTCS tended to rate it highly.

During the writing of this chapter the GTCS announced an increase its annual registration fee – a still low £65 – but from social media comment, this was clearly beyond the means of teachers. This illustrates two challenges: keeping registrants onside and living within the organisation's financial means.

Mentioned above was the relationship between the GTCS, unions and the Scottish Government. These links are vital within education, but if the GTCS is to maintain its independent body status, it must work at ensuring it is seen to be at arm's length from both unions and government. Until recently the usual response was the unions thought the GTCS too close to government, while government thought the GTCS too close to unions, suggesting it was probably just about right in its positioning. Now, with the Scottish Government putting such strong emphasis on closing the attainment gap and the formation of the National Improvement Framework with specific roles for the GTCS, council must be wary that it is not perceived as being too cosy with government and, in essence, becoming a government agency rather than independent. However, the recent Scottish Government's *Education Governance: Next Steps* publication (Scottish Government, 2017) brings other questions and speculations.

## SPECULATIONS ON FUTURE DEVELOPMENTS

*Education Governance: Next Steps* is very significant for the future of the GTCS. It proposes that legislation should be brought forward establishing a new Education Workforce Council for Scotland (EWCS) to replace the GTCS. The new body will 'take on the responsibilities of the GTCS, the Community Learning and Development Standards Council and register other education professionals' (Scottish Government, 2017, p. 37). It will 'support the professionals and provide confidence to parents and carers' (p. 7). So who are these 'professionals'? Clearly more than just teachers, as the government's publication explicitly mentions 'the wider education workforce such as early years practitioners, classroom assistants, additional support for learning assistants and school librarians' (p. 18) and then, in due course, Community Learning and Development Services (p. 19). Later it states that it 'will recognise the contribution of the whole school workforce by working with them to introduce professional standards for these staff, including classroom assistants' (p. 24). In its comparison of the responsibilities of existing bodies and what is proposed for the future, it suggests that professional standards, regulations and registration will be the domain of the new EWCS and the Scottish Social Services Council (SSSC), so it appears that the latter is to maintain its role in early education.

The timeline for consultation on the new EWCS is autumn 2017 as part of a wider consultation on an Education Bill. Work with the wider school workforce to introduce professional standards is scheduled to start in September 2017. At the time of writing, GTCS standards themselves are under review and the GTCS needs to ensure that the philosophy and approach of the current standards is not lost by turning them into narrow, mechanistic competences. It will also have to take into account comments made over recent times on the current versions, good as they are. For example, the OECD (2015, p. 159) said:

The strengths of the professional standards and appraisal processes for teachers and leaders in Scotland are that they are strongly developmental across career states and largely consistent with international practice .... However ... [the] standards are strongly process focused, rather than having improvement in outcomes for learners as a central component. While learner outcomes should not be the only focus of a standards or appraisal system, because these outcomes are impacted by many factors beyond the control of teachers and schools, stronger reference to learners' progress is more likely to create improvement.

So, the next iteration of the standards is likely to include a closer focus on learner outcomes and improvement – but even the OECD recognises they cannot be the sole focus. Biesta (2015) makes a similar point, arguing that standards have to avoid 'bureaucratic' accountability – meeting predetermined, top-down outcomes. Rather they should promote 'democratic' accountability – encouraging teachers to explore the very purposes of education. There will be many competing voices during the review and it will be interesting to see what the GTCS does for the continued betterment of Scottish education and how it either operates in conjunction with or in parallel to the development of standards for other groups within the education workforce.

Much of what is being suggested regarding the formation of an education workforce council follows on from steps already taken in Wales where GTC Wales was transformed into the Education Workforce Council for Wales (EWCW) in 2015. The EWCW registers and regulates a considerably wider range of education workers beyond teachers, notably including college lecturers. Surely this is a group which should be included within the remit of the new body for Scotland? If not, a real opportunity will have been missed. Also of note is that the EWCW is nominally an independent body but in various areas its legislation states that it is subject to the direction of the Welsh Government. The EWCW has a small council of fourteen whose members are entirely appointed by Welsh ministers so, if that is followed by the Scottish Government, where stands the current council model of the GTCS with various constituencies?

Nothing is stated in the *Education Governance* publication on the government's intention in these areas so it will be interesting to see what the autumn 2017 consultation has to say. Will the independence of the GTCS be short-lived before being put formally under the direction of the Scottish Government? How will the conservativism of Scotland's teacher unions react to such possible changes? Of course the current government is a minority administration and this needs legislation, which can never be guaranteed, but which other party would argue against this?

## REFERENCES

Biesta, G. (2015) 'What is education for? On good education, teacher judgement and educational professionalism', *European Journal of Education*, 50 (1), 75–87.

British Educational Research Association and Royal Society for the Encouragement of the Arts, Manufacturing and Commerce (RSA) (2014) *Research and the Teaching Profession: Building the Capacity for a Self-improving Education System*. London: BERA.

European Commission (2015) *Shaping Career-long Perspectives on Teaching: A Guide on Policies to Improve Initial Teacher Education*. Brussels: European Commission's Directorate-General for Education and Culture.

Evetts, J. (2012) 'Professionalism in turbulent times: changes, challenges and opportunities'. Keynote presentation to Professional Practice Education and Learning (ProPEL) Conference, University of Stirling 9 May.

Organisation for Economic Co-operation and Development (2014) *The OECD Teaching and Learning International Survey (TALIS) – 2013 Results*. Paris: OECD. Online at www.oecd.org/edu/school/talis-2013-results.htm

Organisation for Economic Co-operation and Development (2015) *Improving Schools in Scotland: An OECD Perspective*. Paris: OECD

Piesanen, E. and Välijärvi, J. (2010) *Education and Training 2010: Three Studies to Support School*

*Policy Development Lot 2: Teacher Education Curricula in the EU Final Report.* Brussels: European Commission's Directorate-General for Education and Culture.

Scottish Government (2005) Circular No 4/2005 10 October 2005: The Requirements for Teachers (Scotland) Regulations 2005: Repeal of the Schools (Scotland) Code 1956. Online at www.gtcs. org.uk/web/FILES/education-in-scotland/scottish-government-education-circular.pdf

Scottish Government (2011) *Public Services Reform (General Teaching Council for Scotland) Order 2011.* Online at www.legislation.gov.uk/ssi/2011/215/contents/made

Scottish Government (2017) *Education Governance: Next Steps Empowering Our Teachers, Parents and Communities to Deliver Excellence and Equity for Our Children.* Edinburgh: Scottish Government.

# 95

# Researching Education in Scotland

*Laura Colucci-Gray and Kirsten Darling-McQuistan*

## INTRODUCTION

This chapter aims to delineate key dimensions of the historical and political evolutions of educational research in Scotland which, over the course of a century, have both mirrored and made a significant contribution to wider theorisations of the role of research in education. We begin from the time of writing, February 2017, with the Scottish Government announcing provision of significant financial support for schools in a bid to 'close the attainment gap' (Swinney, 2017). At a time of austerity, with increasing pressures on public services, post-devolution Scotland focuses on a nationwide, 'improvement agenda' aiming to raise standards and performance for Scottish education. However, the expectation that research and related evidence-based practices would lead to 'amelioration' of schools and education, has been subject of a complex and lively debate, which has involved the Scottish educational community for some time.

## EDUCATION IN THE SPOTLIGHT

Two significant policy developments introduced in recent years – the Scottish Curriculum for Excellence (CfE) and the Donaldson review of teacher education (Donaldson, 2011) – were set out to promote greater autonomy for teachers, mentoring and professional inquiry undertaken by practitioners. More recently, however, the evaluation of CfE undertaken by the Organisation for Economic Co-operation and Development (OECD) in 2015 acknowledged the bold vision but called for a more ambitious theory of change, and a more robust evidence base, 'especially about learning outcomes and progress' (p. 21). Then, in January 2017, evidence from the Programme for International Student Assessment (PISA) results for literacy, science and maths, presented a picture of Scottish students lagging significantly behind neighbouring European countries (see Chapter 68 for details). Against this climate of doubt over the anticipated benefits of recent educational policies, debate over the role and purpose of research in Scottish education has acquired central position. Core to the analysis is the nature of research and the 'evidence' it produces: how it should be collected, by which methods and by whom? Traditions of inquiry diverge considerably across the natural and the social sciences, and more so for education, a gap often occurs between research sites (such as universities) and sites of practice (such as schools). Some forms of research may be of lesser or greater use depending on who performs the research, who is asking the questions and whose specific interests are being served.

With the title 'Researching Education' this chapter reviews traditions of educational research in Scotland and how they relate to broader societal shifts affecting the production of new knowledge in society. The historical and cultural context of Scottish education is signalled as a productive space to both reaffirming established views of educational research and signalling opportunities for new visions and new approaches. The chapter will conclude with a set of offerings and an open question: what opportunities might be available for research in Scottish education?

## THE CHANGING NATURE OF RESEARCH: TRADITION AND CRITIQUE

Central to the examination of the nature of educational research generally is the relationship between the knower and the known, that is, the researcher (and who may be conceived as one) and the extension of what may be conceived to be their research. Contestation and debate are inherently part of this discussion: far from being an abstract idea, research is both conceived and performed in communities of practice, but the boundaries of such communities, determining who is included and who is excluded, the criteria for good research, and how different groups communicate with each other in an unequal, social space are matters of cultural and political negotiation. To first approach discussion of the nature of educational research in Scotland, it is thus useful to consider some of the historical and philosophical developments which contribute to define the status of research in the evolving, global society.

The years comprising the First to Second World Wars saw the expansion of modern, scientific research as a professional activity for the generation of wealth. Research and development projects in the medical sciences, transport and agricultural applications developed in universities and, funded by governments, were first deployed during the European conflicts and subsequently for the re-establishment and growth of national economies in Europe. In an analysis of the Scottish political and historical landscape, Lingard and Sellar (2014) describe Scotland as a largely rural state, yet operating as a nation, within the technologically advanced, knowledge economy of United Kingdom. From a cultural point of view, we note two significant aspects: Scotland is the homeland of the enlightenment project with its emphasis on measure, technology, and power over nature; yet it is within the Scottish cultural fabric that we find the seeds of the democratic spirit, with its emphasis on discipline and practical reason. As Lingard and Sellar (2014) maintained, schools and teachers are highly regarded in Scotland. Located at the heart of the Scottish culture, schools and teachers are sites of symbolic and power reconstructions; they hold the mandate for society.

With these characteristics, researching education in Scotland is a complex affair, involving universities offering research services as well as public education, teachers' unions, and an emerging Scottish Government holding increasing economic and legislative power (Lingard and Sellar, 2014). It is an intricate and textured history, holding several cues to current questions and what may be the opportunities for the future.

### Tradition

As reported by Nisbet (1999), the first recognisably identified educational research project in Scotland traces back to 1931, when the newly founded Scottish Council for Research in

Education (SCRE), instigated by the teachers' union – the Educational Institute of Scotland (EIS) – was commissioned to describe the mental ability of Scottish children. The study was going to be Scotland's first and unique contribution to an International Examinations Inquiry, designed as a survey of the whole country, following an ongoing research focus on children's cognitive performance on tests, which started in Europe at the beginning of the nineteenth century (particularly Germany). In the early days, Nisbet (1999) reports, Scottish educational research was set out to reflect the analogy with research in industry and applied sciences:

> All the considerations which have led to a general recognition of the importance of scientific research as an aid to industry apply with equal force to education. ... What is wanted to raise the level of efficiency in school work is the ... constant examination of existing practice by scientific methods. (Nisbet, 1999, citing Wake 1988, p. 41)

Education would model itself upon the methods of the scientific experiment, exemplified by the medico-psychological model, and so it thrived as an approach well into the 1960s. Scottish educational research became established through the contributions of recognised figures, such as the brothers John and Stanley Nisbet themselves. In that period the Scottish Educational Research Association was founded (1974), alongside two research journals, *Education in the North* followed by *Scottish Educational Review*, as fora for researchers, and also teachers, to associate and share practices.

From the early psychological studies, the focus of Scottish educational research later moved to include, largely, studies of pedagogical effectiveness, by means of testing children's performances on reading and numeracy tasks. Notable examples are the four surveys of achievement in Science and Mathematics conducted from 1985 to 1997 under the auspices of the Assessment of Achievement Programme (AAP), funded by the former Scottish Executive. The surveys were conducted against a background of significant change at the time, with the introduction of the 5–14 curriculum, which preceded CfE. As Nisbet (1999) indicated, the drivers for research were mainly pedagogical: how achievement can be raised by means of changing practices. Notably, pedagogical experiments such as, for example, measures of practical assessment would aim to produce assessment resources to support the practice of teachers. However, after the last AAP survey, undertaken in 1996 (see Stark et al., 1997), we observe some interesting and subtle shifts in focus, context and audience for educational research.

## ... and Critique

AAP surveys were eventually resumed in 2005, rebaptised the Scottish Survey of Achievement (SSA) 'as a new and more robust tool' and introduced under the auspices of the devolved Scottish Government (www.gov.scot/Publications/2006/06/23121326/1). The SSA research was one of the first sets of quantitative research instruments, followed by studies such as *Growing up in Scotland* (GUS) and the 'Shifting the Curve Report', which have been used in recent years to inform the government's strategy, particularly with regard to tackling poverty and inequality. The acronym change however – from AAP to SSA – marked two more significant alterations; first, in the research subjects, changing from university researchers working in university departments of education, to government officers, availing themselves of specialist statistical units. Second, in focus, with a more specific emphasis on the encapsulation of evidence of children's progress 'within a level', as prescribed by the curriculum. Such shifts correspond to a variation of the driving questions behind the research, from an assessment of learning to 'evidencing' learning, where measures of human capital are taken as proxies for the fitness of pupils and the quality of schooling systems (Lingard and Sellar, 2014).

So, this brief account shows how the positivistic trend deployed to measure educational gains is well known and well established in Scottish education. Commonly with positivistic research, the researchers take a distant approach towards their object of study, with a view to produce objective and generalisable accounts. However, while the intention of the earlier surveys was to assess and inform educational practice, over time, the gap between the 'researchers' and their subjects, (i.e. pupils' learning and teaching practice) widened considerably. University staff came under increasing pressure to deliver teacher education and build research capacity, while lessening their role of privileged research interlocutors for the Scottish Executive (later, government). Perhaps more significantly however, large-scale changes in demographics, austerity measures and socio-environmental instability confronted governments across Europe, including Scotland, with new challenges, resulting in, for example, the government's current emphasis on wellbeing and sustainability agendas. Shifting away from the concerns of university researchers, educational research moved to the realm of public policy, whereby research deemed to be 'scientific' is expected to provide evidence for driving decisions, and 'speak truth' to power. Research became the tool for improvement in society, through enabling a system of accountability for successful management of resources, from industry through to school education and the work of teachers.

## THE RISE OF 'EVIDENCE-BASED' PRACTICE

In face of the mounting social inequalities, we can thus see the appeal of the current 'improvement' agenda, seeking to tighten monitoring of attainment, not simply based upon the characteristics of children, or the nature of pedagogical practice, but as a direct result of the actions and performance of teachers. Such approach follows a common, global trend which has gained considerable momentum and is particularly evident in some renderings in the USA and the UK, with the rise of 'evidence-based' practice in education. In the United States, following the reintroduction of the 'No Child Left Behind' policy, clear emphasis was given to systematic, empirically based forms of research measuring the outcomes of practices delivered by effective teachers.

Such developments have illustrious roots and are commonly traced back to 1997 with David Hargreaves' famous statement that education should be evidence-based and evidence informed; that teachers should maximise the utility of research findings (Elliott, 2007). Within the discourse of effectiveness however, teacher professionalism is narrowly construed to account for 'what works', requiring teachers to 'deliver' or 'produce' on the basis of stated measurement systems, such as PISA. The autonomy and professional judgement of teachers is reduced, and with it, also, the scope for educational opportunities suited to children with different needs and abilities. So, twenty years after the last survey of achievement in Scotland, we see how the pursuit of value-free research, aided by measurable outcomes and standardised tools, neither seemed to challenge nor enhance understanding of 'success' and 'ability' for different groups of learners. On the contrary, within a reduced frame of effectiveness, research evidence is also reduced to value the assumptions that 'work' for, and are held by, a restricted group of people.

In this view, inequality appears to be an inherent feature of measurement systems which separate educational research from context, and teachers from their relationship with pupils. Such separation occurs at many different levels, through the use of technical language (as set in curriculum documents), and monitoring by numerical accounts, which may not be suited to capture a plurality of contexts and voices. Notable in this regard was the case offered by Kennedy (1999) cited by Elliott (2007) of teachers disregarding the use of externally generated data sets focusing on student performance. Teachers found data of little use and felt they could not interpret it 'without more knowledge of what these students were actually doing' (ibid., p. 157). Further divisions occur through time, and the lack of opportunity for knowledge derived from research to be made available in practice. This problem is particularly prominent for large-scale studies, requiring cascading down of recommendations from experts to laypeople, across different sets of values, languages and expertise. Research and the evidence produced may thus not be responding to local needs.

## CRISIS AND OPPORTUNITY

Overcoming the unquestionable appeal of the 'what works' agenda entails reconsideration of the wider set of actors involved in education, including children themselves. In the first instance, we note the gap between the descriptions of the phenomenon under study, as it may be conducted through positivistic research, and the ongoing, in the moment experience of participants. Contributions from feminist theorists, cultural ecologists and phenomenologists foreground meanings in formation and the intentions guiding human activities, which may be ambiguous, charged with contextually bound, subjective and emotional connotations (Griffiths, 2014). This type of research is not concerned with producing accounts for external viewers, but mostly with finding meanings: research is a form of inquiry centred upon experiences and relationships, and it serves the needs of participants seeking to better understand their everyday life experiences. Hence, the meaning of 'improvement' – attracting current political focus – may look quite different for different traditions of inquiry: in one sense, it is progress measured against targets; in another sense, it is responsiveness to the needs of learners in relevant contexts. Acknowledging different methods and purposes for research can be productive to widen the scope for involvement of different actors, addressing a more extensive set of concerns. For example, the expectations placed upon research to generate 'improvement' may be left unattended if the research being produced does not relate, or feel relevant to, teachers and/or does not address the interests and concerns of learners.

Addressing the limitations of traditional, positivistic accounts could thus be a means for recovering a broader range of educational projects to suit different needs and communities. Such a shift, however, entails increased reflexivity on the side of researchers – in their various educational roles – operating at different levels, and across sites of multiplicity, diversity and contestation. A key aspect of the process lies with communication: not so much as transfer of information but as a form of corresponding, that is, becoming aware and conscious of what may be salient questions or important problems, and how one's way of conceiving an issue may be different from the way in which others would. Arguably, against the new wave of change in Scottish policy, Scotland may re-engage with a substantial question: what research? How could different approaches be effectively implemented to serve multiple needs? Answering such questions requires looking more closely at the relationship between teachers and research, as holding the 'mandate for society' in Scotland.

## WHAT RESEARCH FOR SCOTLAND?

As we noted earlier, while later than some other European countries in joining the educational research trend, Scotland is well recognised for being one of the first countries with 'practitioner inquiry' featuring largely within the identity of Scottish teachers. This identity-work can be traced back to the influential work of Lawrence Stenhouse, in the early 1960s, who by asking the question, 'What counts as educational research?' (Stenhouse, 1981, p. 113) established a role for teachers within educational research processes: valuing the unique contribution that teachers – who are part of the complex milieu of happenings within a classroom – can make to their own and our understandings of educational processes. Furthermore, Stenhouse believed that researchers should 'justify themselves to practitioners' (ibid., p. 113): a sentiment that engages with earlier critiques of 'objective', 'data-driven' forms of research, which do not engage, or connect with, the lived and varied experiences of teachers and learners. In this respect, Stenhouse might appear to presage Hargreaves' aspirations for educational research to inform the concrete activities of education. However, Stenhouse's insights promoted an 'expansive' view of educational research, as a process accounting for the subjective perspectives of practitioners involved in collaborative, knowledge-seeking and democratic forms of inquiry.

Fast-forwarding to current times, we recognise that a debate between different views of educational research still exists, with evidence-based approaches and practitioner research sharing the same space in Scottish policy. One of the most influential policy documents produced in Scotland in recent times, the Donaldson review of teacher education, foregrounds:

> the most successful education systems do more than seek to attain particular standards of competence and to achieve change through prescription. They invest in developing their teachers as reflective, accomplished and enquiring professionals who have the capacity to engage fully with the complexities of education and to be key actors in shaping and leading educational change. (Donaldson, 2011, p. 4)

Through the coordinating and regulatory influence of the General Teaching Council for Scotland (GTCS), policy recommendations have become incarnated into professional standards; the teachers' role is explicitly demanding engagement with practitioner inquiry, alongside an ongoing commitment to sustainability and social justice. Most notably, in 2013 GTCS enabled teachers to gain access to academic journals via EBSCO, one of the largest databases for educational research. However, it seems that such developments are being engulfed within a regressive policy agenda, morphed somehow into the narrower 'closing the attainment gap'. So, if the purpose and the intentions for research-informed practice cannot be disputed, what is less clear is the form this research or inquiry will take.

As a contribution to the Donaldson review, a literature review carried out by Menter et al. (2010) on behalf of the Scottish Government, identified 'four influential "paradigms" of teacher professionalism: the effective teacher, the reflective teacher, the enquiring teacher and the transformative teacher' (p. 21). Through this analysis, a continuum of levels of awareness of context and relationships emerges: from the reductive level of providing evidence of students' cognitive performance on predefined standards and outcomes; to gathering evidence on one's practice for the purpose of pedagogical innovation; through to the more textured analysis of practices developing collaborative and activist forms of learning, involving different ways of working. Each level of this continuum of professionalism has implications for the possible nature of research within Scottish education. The 'effective teacher' can deliver upon demand, concerned with gathering evidence of measurable outcomes. Such a view does not conceal the inclination to remove or certainly control diversity, subjectivity and contingency within educational research. Conversely, the space offered by the 'transformative' view of teacher professionalism, which is still visibly woven through Scottish history and recent policy, looks for a more textured expression of research; it moves beyond conceptions of practitioner inquiry aligned with the production of 'excellence' to evidencing, as proposed by Stenhouse, the extent to which teaching approaches 'are ethically consistent with educational ends' (Elliott, 2007, p. 146). This more expansive view of teacher professionalism encourages openness to dialogue and partnerships across domains, going some way to meet the recommendations of the OECD report in 2015: 'CfE needs to be less managed from the centre and become more a dynamic, highly equitable curriculum being built constantly in schools, networks and communities with a strengthened "middle" in a vision of collective responsibility and multi-layer governance' (p. 13).

However, while teachers are clearly given a voice and a key role in curriculum development, recent statements from the Scottish Government point to a possible reversal of this position, by explicitly providing 'key messages about what teachers and practitioners are expected to do to effectively plan learning, teaching and assessment for all learners' (Scottish Government, 2016). So, what will it be for teachers? How do research practices become part of their daily activity and their very being: what support and methods are available to teachers on this complex, transformative journey?

## FROM PRACTITIONER INQUIRY …

Arguably, supporting the development of teacher professionalism requires further exploration of the nature of teacher research, a view which shifts the emphasis from nouns, databases and solutions, to verbs. The verb in question is 'to research', with the prefix *re*, pointing to the recursive and ongoing process of searching, as probing, from different angles and perspectives in order to *re*consider practice through ongoing *re*flection, in dialogue with others. Exploring the notion of 'educational research' as '*re*search(ing)', and as an integral aspect of a teacher's professional identity, is critical, both in terms of engaging with the subjectivity of the teacher and avoiding technocratic interpretations of research as a disembodied practice, employed to support 'effective' learning and teaching. Within this space, the notion of 'activist professionalism' elaborated by Sachs (2000) supports the idea of 'transformative' practice considered by Menter et al. (2010), thus providing clear signals as to how such a role might not only be enacted, but developed and nurtured. Activist professionalism resists dominant, 'managerial' discourses of professionalism, which are geared towards individual teachers demonstrating their capabilities in relation to imposed goals. Activist professionalism is both collective and collaborative in nature, involving trust and reciprocal partnerships between professionals, *across sectors* – thus not only establishing the need for teachers to be engaged in research, but for them to work with teacher educators/ researchers, who are working *with* them, as opposed to *on* them. For Sachs (2000), practitioner research is a critical aspect of activist professionalism, involving practitioners and researchers in 'shared inquiry into patterns of practice' (p. 89). Activist professionalism therefore supports teachers in defining themselves as 'key actors in shaping and leading educational change' as per Donaldson's recommendations (2011, p. 4). Crucially, however, the fusion of research activity with professional practice is not simply a mechanical process, adding to the toolkits of language and mannerisms of a teacher. An important dimension requiring further consideration is the teacher's awareness of entering a wider inquiry process, involving ongoing self-disclosure, as teachers engage with questions and concerns about the meaning of 'being educators'. So, for the Scottish teacher/research practitioner, research is always and inherently carried out in the first person.

## … TO RESEARCHING IN THE FIRST PERSON

Understanding teacher research as an inquiry conducted in the first person is paramount to the process of acknowledging teachers' voices but also those of the pupils. Currently, methods such as action research attract greatest appeal within the Scottish education system, and they have been integrated as part of the continuum of professional learning endorsed by the General Teaching Council for Scotland. However, as indicated earlier, the extent to which these approaches give teachers the opportunity to speak in the first person, and reveal their voices, perspectives and experiences, which express their values, morals, cultures, histories, passions and interests, may be limited. The ambiguity of the term research and the ambitions of research to inform policy for excellence makes it possible for such methods to be adopted on a limited scope, with a focus on the *what works* – the formula for 'success' – and excluding teachers' own theorisations. For example, the downfalls of isolating and extracting specific strategies and approaches that 'work' for one teacher in one classroom were brought to the fore quite publicly, through the critique of 'We are learning to' (WALT) and 'What am I am looking for?' (WILF), memorable acronyms for supporting practice in a bid to 'raise attainment'. Such superficial 'shortcuts', often without critique or even evidence, continue to be exploited within a political context which has a firm eye on the products of schooling. The inquiring, reflective teacher often gives way to the effective one, in order to fulfil expectations of improvement, asserting positive impacts without a sound grasp of the implications and opportunities that new practices bring to the educational forum.

Going some way towards addressing such concerns, other methods, which are gaining ground in Canada, Australia and parts of the United States, assert the prime role of the teacher engaging with self-study: a practitioner-inquiry approach which, differently from the most common version of teacher as researcher, encourages the teacher to know themselves in amongst the noise and rhetoric of policy discourse, and which overshadows *who* they are, both in their being and becoming.

In this vein, self-study research should embody key characteristics, in order to achieve its overarching *raison d'être*, for example self-study research must: 'ring true', allowing others to connect with experiences, and in doing so, support *re*interpretation of these experiences; take an 'honest' and 'fresh perspective'; and demonstrate authenticity by clearly conveying the context of the study, including the *relational* nature of the space which teachers negotiate in their day-to-day practice. These characteristics of self-study research align well with writing and narrative forms of inquiry. Negotiating entry into self-study research is, in fact, beginning a 'new story' in our already storied existence. Watson (2007) draws attention to the need to engage with teachers' 'small stories': the stories that emerge because of the complexity of everyday action and interactions which, she suggests, enable the 'performance of identities and the construction of self (p. 371). Supporting the ongoing construction and *re*construction of self by engaging with teachers' 'small stories' is, therefore, a potentially powerful methodology for promoting *transformative* forms of teacher professionalism. Such insights bring the affordances of self-study and narrative methodologies to the fore for teachers in Scotland, who are navigating both the contradictions and the openings they have been given at a political level, to bring about change in practice.

Elaborating further, Griffiths (2014) discusses the value of supporting teachers' creative processes, in order for them to engage in the 'daunting, exciting, risky re-evaluation of themselves and their pedagogical relationships' (p. 117). Employing creative methods, such as stories, is not simply reporting of experience but it involves practitioners in 'symbolising' their experiences: 'symbolisation is the attempt to express something about experience, something about the subjective inner life ...' (ibid., p. 121). The act of symbolisation will thus be available to both teachers and students joining in together to offer a more nuanced and humanised enactment of educational research. Beyond 'hard data', and yet not excluding those, it is through story writing that the research process begins, allowing the surfacing of experience and memory, giving shape to questions, and allowing for the exploration of significant connections. Through story writing, the singular process of thinking acquires meaning, only to become overshadowed by the richness of the coming together of the collective voices of other writers: 'Not only are the arts valuable in themselves, but also they make it possible for people to build the common, public world ... For this people need to express who and what they are' (ibid., p. 121).

We suggest that such approaches, which originated to counter positivistic turns in educational research, are more explicitly concerned with the process of being and becoming an educated person. The usefulness of instrumental approaches to evidence-based practice is not denied. However, educational research is also, and foremost, sharing in the fundamental purposes of education, thus accounting for what may not be wished for, for what may go wrong and what might have been excluded from focus. Beyond achievement of specific goals, this view of research may grant scope for a more long-term, political and cultural reform.

## CLOSING REMARKS

Throughout this chapter, we have argued for the need to widen conceptions of research and methodologies, in order to enable all stakeholders involved in educational research to participate in critical dialogue over the processes and outcomes of research. This view of research inquiry engages with what we understand 'educational research' to be: a collective process, undertaken with awareness of the complexity of the relationship between teaching, learning and subject matter, both inside and outside the classroom. However, such shift also involves looking outwards and exploring possible ways of supporting teachers, researchers and policymakers onto this path.

Equally, acquiring reflexivity in research entails method, and ongoing professional learning: teacher research and inquiry – as we have suggested – are not simply an individualised act, they take place across multiple sites, hybrid spaces for collaborative inquiry. In April 2017, while this chapter was being finalised, the government published *A Research Strategy for Scottish Education* outlining key roles for schools, parents, local authorities and private providers in supporting the improvement agenda. Consideration for academic establishments is given in the form of funding to pursue 'independent' academic research. This model appears to perpetuate rather than challenge the old distinction between 'teaching on the ground' and academic research. If the 'improvement' agenda was truly seeking to make 'real' change in the lives of pupils through their time in schools, a significant challenge will be that of supporting educational models which bring communities together, to address common problems. Researching education may thus be part of this evolving picture: which way for Scottish education?

## REFERENCES

Donaldson, G. (2011) *Teaching Scotland's Future: Report of a Review of Teacher Education in Scotland*. Edinburgh: Scottish Government.

Elliott, J. (2007) *Reflecting Where the Action Is*. London: Routledge.

Griffiths, M. (2014) 'Encouraging imagination and creativity in the teaching profession', *European Educational Research Journal*, 13 (1), 117–29.

Lingard, B. and Sellar, S. (2014) 'Representing for country: Scotland, PISA and new spatialities of educational governance', *Scottish Educational Review*, 46 (1), 5–18.

Menter, I., Hulme, M., Elliot, D. and Lewin, J. (2010) *Literature Review on Teacher Education in the 21st Century*. Edinburgh: Scottish Government

Nisbet, J. (1999) 'How it all began: educational research 1880–1930', *Scottish Educational Review*, 31 (1), 3–9.

OECD (2015) *Improving Schools: An OECD Perspective*. Online at https://www.oecd.org/education/school/Improving-Schools-in-Scotland-An-OECD-Perspective.pdf

Sachs, J. (2000) 'The activist professional', *Journal for Educational Change*, 1 (2), 77–95.

Scottish Government (2016) *Curriculum for Excellence: A Statement for Practitioners from HM Chief Inspector of Education*. Online at https://education.gov.scot/improvement/documents/cfestatement.pdf

Scottish Government (2017) *A Research Strategy for Scottish Education*. Online at www.gov.scot/Publications/2017/04/8907

Stark, R., Bryce, T. and Gray, D. (1997) 'Four surveys and an epitaph: AAP science 1985–1997', *Scottish Educational Review*, 29 (2), 114–20.

Stenhouse, L. (1981) 'What counts as research?' *British Journal of Educational Studies*, 29 (2), 103–14.

Swinney, J. (2017) 'John Swinney: the improvement agenda requires all of our focus'. 6 March. Online at https://www.holyrood.com/articles/comment/john-swinney-improvement-agenda-requires-all-our-focus

Watson, C. (2007) 'Small stories, positioning analysis, and the doing of professional identities in learning to teach', *Narrative Inquiry*, 17 (2), 371–89.

# XII

# LOOKING FORWARD:
# THE FUTURE OF EDUCATION
# IN SCOTLAND

# 96

# Curriculum Reform:
# Progress, Tensions and Possibilities

*Mark Priestley*

## INTRODUCTION

The school curriculum is a hot topic in education. The recent introduction of new forms of national curriculum require a higher degree than formerly of teacher engagement in curriculum-making. And yet curriculum studies – the academic study of curriculum theory and practice – has been in decline for some years. Schwab, writing as long ago as 1969, described the field as moribund, decrying the poverty of curriculum theory. A more recent phenomenon is the decline in the capacity of teachers to engage in curriculum development; what Michael Apple described as a 'lost art' (personal conversation with author, 2016). This is a problem, because nationally mandated curriculum reform is now a fact of life for schools, requiring new forms of engagement by teachers. In common with many countries worldwide, Scotland's schools have witnessed successive waves of reform in the past twenty-five years. Modern curriculum reform can be understood to some extent in the context of globalisation, as a reaction to forces exerted on nation states: as a response to rapid social, economic and technological change; as an economic lever to ensure the creation of a more skilled and competitive workforce; and as the development of national narratives to counter perceptions of the nation at risk. In this context, it is hardly surprising that we have witnessed a burgeoning international economy of educational ideas, for example characterised by the work of the Organisation for Economic Co-operation and Development (OECD), including the Programme for International Student Assessment (PISA), the development of international frameworks of key competencies, and a continual recycling of what is seen as international best practice. A critical understanding of curriculum issues – by policymakers, policy developers and practitioners – is much needed in the face of these emerging trends.

Recent curriculum reform falls into two broad cycles of activity. The 1990s saw the development of highly specified curriculum frameworks – in Scotland's case the 5–14 Curriculum – with subject content typically articulated as learning outcomes, set out in linear and hierarchical levels. Such frameworks were indicative of a trend towards 'teacher-proof' curricula, and 5–14 was subsequently criticised for being over-prescriptive, cluttered with content and assessment-driven. The period since the turn of the millennium has seen what in many ways can be viewed as a radical departure in curriculum policy – what Priestley and Biesta (2013) have termed the 'new curriculum'. Scotland's Curriculum for Excellence (CfE) is a good example of this emerging international trend in curriculum policy (while also manifesting many local features). CfE has, in many respects, progressive credentials, although these directions have been far from unproblematic: for instance, learner-centredness; a focus on skills development (as opposed to learning facts); decluttered content; and an apparent (re)turn to teacher autonomy in curriculum-making. Nevertheless, CfE retains many of the features termed technical–instrumental by critics such as Young and Muller (2010), who have critiqued the 'new curriculum' for its apparent economic instrumentalism and its downgrading of knowledge. Technical–instrumental features include the continued recourse to setting out the content of the curriculum as learning outcomes expressed in levels. In the case of CfE, 1,820 experiences and outcomes statements are set out across five levels in eight curriculum areas and three interdisciplinary areas (OECD, 2015), with an assumption that students will progress through the levels in a neat linear fashion. CfE is notable, in that Scottish reforms have encompassed much more than an articulation of a curriculum framework. It has been accompanied by a raft of parallel and complementary policy initiatives, for example the reforms to teacher professional education following the 2010 Donaldson report, *Getting it Right for Every Child* (GIRFEC) and the National Improvement Framework (NIF).

Recent experience of cyclical curriculum reform would suggest that we can expect further policy innovation. Indeed, in Scotland, the OECD (2015) review of CfE has given the green light to further reform of the curriculum – a new simplified narrative, for example. In the foreseeable future, however, it seems likely that such reform will remain limited in scope; a great deal of political capital has been invested in CfE, which has been sold to the public as being 'Excellent', the be-all and end-all of curriculum policy, so to speak. This means that wholesale reform is easy to characterise as a climbdown following failure, and is thus politically risky. So what kind of curriculum reform might we expect within this political context? What type of reform might, additionally, be sensible, given the changing demands on schooling in the twenty-first century, and how might insights from the field of curriculum studies inform such advances? This chapter will address these issues. It first examines the changes that have followed in the wake of the CfE reforms since 2004, offering a critical analysis of the tensions that have shaped these developments. Then it offers some additional insights from the field of curriculum studies, which might inform those who seek to update Scotland's school curriculum, across the multiple fields of policy, support and practice.

## PROGRESS AND TENSIONS

Rhetoric surrounding CfE has often made the claim that the curriculum is transforming the educational experiences and outcomes of young people in Scotland's schools. For example, the 2016 Education Scotland Statement for Practitioners asserted that 'Curriculum for Excellence (CfE) is transforming learning experiences for children and young people across Scotland' (Education Scotland, 2016, p. 1). Such statements need to be treated with caution. The OECD review of the curriculum suggested that the picture is much more mixed, stating that 'CfE has been implemented in ways that do not align with the original intentions of an essentially uncluttered, professional curriculum' (OECD, 2015, p. 105). Furthermore, the OECD pointed to the paucity of research in this area, suggesting that 'there is a clear need to know how CfE is actually being implemented in schools and communities across Scotland' (OECD, 2015, p. 11). There is currently little research relating to the impact of CfE on children's and young people's learning and attainment, although there is more research around the degree to which CfE has been implemented in schools (e.g. see Priestley and Minty, 2013; Priestley et al., 2015). So, what does this research tell us?

First, there is widespread agreement that CfE articulates a largely coherent and progressive approach to modern schooling, particularly as set out in the earlier documentation. It covers the age range 3–18. It is rooted in a clear set of purposes (the attributes and capabilities comprising the four capacities), principles and values. As a macro-level curriculum framework, CfE has attracted widespread praise from overseas, and has been emulated by other jurisdictions, including Wales in recent years. According to the OECD, 'CfE represents an ambitious and important departure that has sought to develop a coherent 3–18 curriculum around capacities and learning, rather than school subjects, taking a different approach to assessment and national prescription from what was in place before' (OECD, 2015, p. 37). Moreover, its principles have been widely supported by the teaching profession in Scotland, at least in its early phase of development. For instance, Priestley and Minty (2013) reported that the majority of respondents in their Highland study were positive about CfE as a direction of travel. Nevertheless, it would be fair to assert that fourteen years on from the original vision of CfE, the curriculum remains a system-level construct rather than lived practice. Research suggests that CfE is at best only partially implemented in terms of the vision set out in 2004 (Priestley and Minty, 2013; Priestley et al., 2015), with considerable evidence in schools of strategic compliance and the relabelling of existing practices as CfE. These trends are supported in the OECD analysis, which states that 'implementation is proceeding at varying speeds' (OECD, 2015, p. 10).

This analysis raises the question of why CfE, despite its undoubted merits, can be characterised as only partially implemented after more than a decade of development. The OECD review has helpfully identified three broad areas that need to be further developed if CfE is to be fully realised. These are:

- The development of a new simplified narrative for the curriculum.
- A strengthening of the middle tier of educational governance (i.e. the development of meso-level capacity for the leadership of curriculum development).
- More comprehensive enactment of CfE in schools.

The ensuing analysis will be structured around these themes, which reflect curriculum development activity at the macro-, meso- and micro-levels of the educational system.

## A New Simplified Narrative

The sheer complexity of CfE has been widely recognised as an issue impeding implementation, and leading to bureaucracy and an intensification of teacher workload. According to the OECD, 'the complexity of the layers and dimensions, when all are put together, raises its own questions about how comprehensible is the Curriculum for Excellence' (OECD, 2015, p. 45). There are several aspects to this complexity. First, there is the structure of the curriculum, with content and pedagogy articulated through the specification of hundreds of experiences and outcomes. Priestley and Humes (2010) were critical of this approach, suggesting that it is fundamentally incompatible with the four capacities, in that CfE thus offers alternative starting points for curriculum development in schools. In practice, many schools have largely ignored the first principles set out in the four capacities, and focused instead on an audit approach, where each and every experience and outcome is separately evidenced through classroom practice. This approach has created the conditions where bureaucracy has proliferated, and encouraged strategic compliance with the curriculum (see Priestley and Minty, 2013). Furthermore, such tendencies have been well-documented in previous research literature (e.g. see CEDEFOP, 2009), which clearly shows the dangers of atomised learning, strategic compliance and teacher overload when outcomes or objectives are too tightly specified. The OECD review concurred, stating that 'the risk has been identified in curriculum design and teaching that the Experiences and Outcomes will be treated as a manual and the separate items followed separately and slavishly' (OECD, 2015, p. 43). It is clear that such dangers have been recognised in Scotland, where there has been work to group experiences and outcomes together into significant aspects of learning, and the establishment of a Tackling Bureaucracy working group by the government.

A second aspect of the complexity lies in the increasingly labyrinthine supporting documentation produced by Education Scotland and other agencies. According to the OECD, there is 'an "overwhelming perception" that there is "too much guidance and not enough time to look at it" and many reported that they found the Education Scotland and SQA websites hard to navigate' (OECD, 2015, p. 105). The 2016 *Statement for Practitioners* also acknowledged this issue, stating that: 'There is currently too much support material and guidance for practitioners. This is contributing to the growth of over-bureaucratic approaches to planning and assessment in many schools and classrooms across the country' (Education Scotland, 2016).

Curriculum guidance by Education Scotland has continued to reiterate (often with subtle changes) rather than replace previous guidance. Several clear tendencies are evident, all of which militate against clarity in curriculum development: (1) a tendency for meanings to change (for example the experiences and outcomes were not originally intended to be assessment standards, but subsequently came to be called this); (2) a tendency for certain terminology to become fashionable for a while, then to be replaced by other terms (e.g. 'achievement pathways', 'progression pathways', 'learning pathways'); and (3) a tendency for documentation to become more highly specified over time. The latest example of this last point – the specification of extremely detailed benchmarks for assessment – appears to have emerged as a response to calls by the OECD to provide a new simplified narrative. While these benchmarks have been accompanied by an apparent simplification of the experiences and outcomes, they add a new layer of complexity.

The preceding paragraphs focus on how CfE has specified the curriculum. It is, however, worth reflecting briefly on an interesting lack of specification: the lack of a clearly articulated process for curriculum development. The prevailing orthodoxy in many education systems is to steer practice through outcomes or performance indicators, and thus this lacuna in CfE is not surprising; however, the lack of progress in enacting CfE in schools might be attributed to it. As noted, advice emerging from around 2008 onwards was for schools to audit current provision against the experiences and outcomes, and this has led to often superficial, tick box approaches to curriculum development. Conversely, CfE would have benefited from a robust theory of change, underpinned by clear practical processes such as collaborative professional enquiry (see Drew et al., 2016). Presumably this is what the OECD had in mind when they stated:

> It needs an ambitious theory of change and a more robust evidence base, especially about learning outcomes and progress. CfE needs to be less managed from the centre and become more

a dynamic, highly equitable curriculum being built constantly in schools, networks and communities with a strengthened 'middle' in a vision of collective responsibility and multi-layer governance. (OECD, 2015, p. 11)

I shall further develop this issue in the final section of the chapter.

## A Strengthened Middle

The extract from the OECD report provides a neat bridge into the next area of analysis, namely that CfE would have benefited from the existence of a more effective middle tier (or meso-level) to support curriculum development. This would provide the necessary infrastructure for translating theoretical curriculum (i.e. policy) into practice (i.e. the lived curriculum in schools). In order to achieve this, the review recommended strengthening the middle tier of educational governance. Currently, meso-level governance is largely conducted by local authorities and the national agency, Education Scotland. These organisations have performed different functions. Local authorities have, since the 1990s, tended to focus on quality improvement processes (for example audits of school practice) rather than the provision of support for curriculum development (through, for example, subject advisors or generic curriculum development expertise). In addition to its school inspection role, Education Scotland (and its predecessor, Learning and Teaching Scotland) has tended to focus on the production of guidance, as noted already, rather than acting as a hands-on leader or facilitator of curriculum development in schools. This combined focus on challenge and guidance (often through the specification of performance indicators) is entirely consonant with the predominant approach to curriculum regulation through the specification of outcomes rather than processes, and it has had some important consequences. Foremost amongst these has been the often limited approach to curriculum development, based around evidencing outcomes and performance indicators. It is clear, from the research findings we have to date, that risk aversion in the face of accountability pressures, performativity and strategic compliance have been part of the picture leading to the current situation of incomplete engagement with and implementation of the curriculum (Priestley and Minty, 2013; Priestley et al., 2015). Missing from the process has been the sort meaningful system-level curriculum development activity, involving collaboration amongst teachers, that was evident in the Schools Council Projects in the 1970s, and which developed programmes for schools that could be adopted nationally.

## Curriculum Enactment in Schools

Strengthening the middle provides the infrastructure for supporting curriculum development. Nevertheless, a national curriculum can only be developed ultimately in schools through the enactment into practice of the official framework. In the words of the OECD, 'there is need now for a bold approach that moves beyond system management in a new dynamic nearer to teaching and learning' (OECD, 2015, p. 10). Teachers should be fundamental to this process as active agents of curriculum development. Earlier sections provide an analysis of structural/system issues shaping the development of CfE; however, there are also a number of reasons relating more directly to teachers' capacity, which help to explain why CfE has not moved beyond this theoretical phase to become an enacted practical curriculum. Missing from the early process of developing CfE in schools was a systematic sense-making phase along the lines of the first stage of the current Welsh curriculum reforms (Embedding the Four Purposes). Here, groups of schools, supported by meso-level regional consortia, are at the time of writing engaging with one another to develop understanding of the key tenets of what is a new approach to education for them, before actively implementing the curriculum. Research into the enactment of CfE in three Scottish local authorities suggests that this lack of sense-making has significantly shaped teachers' subsequent engagement with CfE (Priestley and Minty, 2013; Priestley et al., 2015; Drew et al., 2016). There are several aspects of this. First, while many teachers were seen to broadly welcome the principles of CfE (first order engagement), deeper understanding of the implications of these for practice was often found to be lacking (second order engagement). Second, there seems to have been a mismatch between the prevailing 'transmission' philosophy of many teachers and the implicit constructivist underpinnings of CfE. This stands in contrast to other countries introducing similar curricula, where the reforms have tended to either bring policy into line with teachers' beliefs about learning (e.g. New Zealand), or where substantive work has taken place to develop teachers' theories of knowledge before the enactment of reforms (e.g. Finland: see Sahlberg, 2011). Third, research suggests that teachers tend not to possess highly developed professional knowledge in the area of curriculum development. Recent development work in one Scottish local authority illustrates the liberating effect of developing such knowledge as part of a systematic programme of collaborative professional enquiry (Drew et al., 2016). Finally, and relating the issue of teacher agency to the structural/system issues outlined above, one can make the case that even high-capacity teachers will find it difficult to fully enact CfE in the face of tensions within policy, its complexity, the absence of structured support and leadership for curriculum development, and the perceptions of risk stimulated by heavy-duty accountability mechanisms (Priestley et al., 2015). This has been a particular issue in secondary schools, where CfE has become identified primarily with national qualifications in the senior phase, but is also an issue in primaries, where a common approach to curriculum development has been to evidence achievement of outcomes, and many teachers have sought to treat the CfE as if it were the previous assessment-driven 5–14 curriculum (Priestley and Minty, 2013; Priestley et al., 2015).

## FUTURE POSSIBILITIES

The critique offered in the previous sections may suggest that I am opposed to CfE. This is far from the case; despite some reservations about the coherence of the policy (e.g. Priestley and Humes, 2010), I remain committed to the direction of travel. My critique is largely aimed at the enactment of the curriculum, including the methodologies employed in its development. This final section of the chapter will consider some issues that might be considered if we are to make the most of the considerable potential of CfE, to enact it in the spirit in which it was originally conceived, and (in the words of the OECD) make the most of this 'ambitious and important departure' (OECD, 2015, p. 37) from the constraints of traditional schooling. These steps are both conceptual and practical, and involve new thinking about the formation of policy, support for its development and the enactment of school practices.

### Curriculum Development – Some Conceptual Issues

Some thinking about the concept 'curriculum' – what it means, how it functions in different fields of practice, what educational practices relate to it – is necessary as a precursor to undertaking curriculum development. In recent years, a rather narrow conception of curriculum has taken root. This is a view of curriculum as a set of items of content to be taught, often expressed as assessable outcomes and linked to accountability practices. It has been accompanied by the widespread use of the 'delivery' metaphor. In such a view, curriculum becomes little more than a product, developed by policymakers and uncritically 'delivered' by practitioners. Such thinking is inadequate for a number of reasons, not least because it fails to take account of the complex social processes in play as teachers translate policy into practice. These problems are amplified when one is developing a curriculum such as CfE, in that these curricula are set out in general terms as frameworks to guide educational practice, rather than as prescriptive recipes to be followed to the letter. It is therefore no surprise that teachers in countries such as Scotland, when faced with the new curriculum and when applying old thinking, have routinely called for further detail. Consideration of the following conceptual issues is helpful as we move forward.

## Curricular Strata

Curriculum is a multilayered set of practices, and these practices operate differently at different layers of the system. The conceptual map in Figure 96.1 is useful here.

This sort of thinking enables us to see that there are different practices and different functions within each layer, and helps us to develop clarity about what is involved in developing the curriculum at each level. If we see the function of the macro-level as setting out in broad terms the vision for the curriculum, its big ideas (principles, purposes and values) and to outline the sorts of resources and processes available to schools to develop

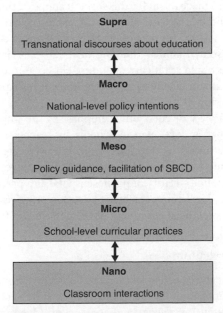

**Figure 96.1   Curriculum practices at different levels**

Note: SBCD = School-based curriculum development.

Source: Adapted from Thijs and van den Akker, 2009.

these into practice, then this opens up possibilities for the projected simplification of the narrative of CfE. There is a clear implication that it should not be the role of government to micro-manage curriculum development, and schools should not expect increasingly specified instructions for practice.

This conceptual model also raises significant questions about support for curriculum development. The meso-level is important here, as schools do not necessarily have the resources or capacity to develop the curriculum; nor is it reasonable to expect each school to reinvent the wheel. Meso-level support may be available in various forms, for example:

- The production of additional guidance for curriculum development (although Scotland should be wary of repeating its former experience of increasingly complex written guidance and a spiral of specification, which has in turn led to increasing bureaucracy in schools).
- The promulgation of curriculum development projects, where resources are pooled and course materials developed for use in schools.
- Leadership of practitioner enquiry and curriculum development in schools.

It seems reasonable to assume that, if such thinking is taken into account, then it will lead to the development of meso-level structures that fulfil these and other support functions, perhaps through the establishment of regional support structures. Regional structures might offer the availability of leaders for curriculum development processes, building system capacity – a cadre of expert teachers, for instance, who can work in their own schools and spend part of the week supporting colleagues in other schools.

As part of its reform of school governance, set out in a series of policy intentions in 2017, the Scottish Government plans to establish a number of regional improvement collaboratives, which may provide a mechanism for this form of support, though the details have still to be worked out. In addition, the large numbers of teachers currently undertaking funded Masters programmes are an obvious pool of expertise who might contribute to this process. The OECD has demonstrated similar thinking in its 2015 review of CfE: 'While being all-Scotland in reach, we would see it corresponding closely to the new "middle". Without specifying precisely who might belong to it, we would see it reshaped so that it is essentially about professional leadership' (OECD, 2015, p. 104).

Finally, this stratified view of curriculum emphasises the importance of viewing curriculum as something that is developed in schools by teachers. A curriculum does not happen in any real sense until it is translated from the principles outlined in policy into practice, and this can only be achieved in schools. This requires teachers to understand the principles set out in policy – clarity of purpose is vital as a precursor to purposeful curriculum development – and it requires teachers to develop practices that are fit for purposes; otherwise, the danger of superficial enactment of the new curriculum is very real.

## A Holistic View of Curriculum

A further implication is that we need to take a more holistic view of the curriculum practices developed in schools. Curriculum has traditionally been seen as comprising three message systems: curriculum (content), pedagogy and assessment. One might add a fourth dimension to this, namely provision.

- *Content*. Modern curricula have been criticised for privileging skills and downgrading knowledge. The policies have been criticised for failing to make explicit the importance of knowledge/content. The framing of many of these curricula around detailed lists of learning outcomes has led to a narrowing of curricular content in many cases. School-based curriculum development should account for questions around knowledge. What knowledge is valuable or powerful for young people if they are to become critically engaged citizens in a modern democracy? What knowledge should be acquired by an educated person? How do we determine what knowledge is relevant (and not just interesting and motivating)?

- *Pedagogy*. As well as addressing questions around knowledge, school-based curriculum development should also address questions about method. If part of becoming educated is to develop skills and dispositions, then it is important that teachers give due consideration to how pedagogy is fit for purpose, and how they structure classroom experiences to provide a rich and purposeful learning environment. One-size-fits-all solutions and off-the-shelf packages can be unhelpful. Cooperative learning has been widely adopted in Scotland to meet the needs of CfE, and has considerable merits; however, death by cooperative learning is every bit as painful for young people as death by a thousand worksheets. Effective pedagogy will be varied and fit for purpose, and will invariably include progressive student-centred approaches as well as more traditional didactic methods.

- *Assessment*. Assessment has had a bad press in recent years, as it has come to drive learning, often in quite instrumental ways. Nevertheless, assessment is a vital part of classroom practice. Good assessment should be embedded in classroom teaching, fulfilling multiple functions – summative, formative and evaluative – and more often than not is informal, occurring through classroom dialogue. Curriculum development should take account of assessment by building in assessment opportunities at the planning stage.

- *Provision*. This is the area often neglected during school-based curriculum development. There are several issues to account for, particularly in secondary schools, notably timetabling and the organisation of subjects. Experience in Scotland suggests that many secondary schools have struggled with the pedagogy for the new curriculum because they have not addressed these issues. The standard secondary school timetable is problematic because it does not easily allow for methodologies such as cooperative learning and other active approaches (e.g. field trips). Related to this are questions about how we structure the division of the corpus of knowledge into teachable chunks. The traditional subjects taught in schools in Scotland tend to encourage a fragmented school week, and do not easily allow for content to be updated. Where, for example, is the space to teach knowledge about society, or knowledge about the political system? The UK tends to be out of step with the rest of the world in this respect; elsewhere integrated subjects (e.g. social studies) are more common.

## A Process for Curriculum Development

The preceding discussion suggests that new ways of thinking about the curriculum are necessary if Scotland is to make the most of the promising directions set out in CfE policy. It does not, however, provide more than a general guide to the practical tasks involved in school-based curriculum development. In recent years, there has been considerable interest in collaborative enquiry methodologies for school-based curriculum development. One such approach has been developed in a Scottish local authority (Drew et al., 2016) in the context of CfE. It takes teachers and leaders through a process of making sense of new ideas, and developing fit-for purpose practices, before then undertaking school-based curriculum development projects with colleagues. A conceptual phase first stimulates thinking about the curriculum, and helps teachers to develop their theories of knowledge, through relevant academic reading, related to issues in their classroom practice. This comprises the following steps:

- *Engaging with purposes.* Exploration of the big ideas of the curriculum: the four capacities and principles of CfE; educational values; the big question 'what are schools for?'
- *Engaging with practices.* Identification of fit-for-purpose practices: what will such practices look like in terms of knowledge/content, pedagogy, assessment and provision?
- *Engaging in contextual audit.* Consideration of current practices and of barriers to and drivers of change: what are the barriers and drivers, and how might they be addressed?

A practice-based phase then follows:

- *Engaging in practice.* Critical collaborative professional enquiry: the systematic development and evaluation of an intervention or interruption to existing practices.

## CONCLUSION

This chapter starts from the premise that critical understanding of concepts from the field of curriculum studies is necessary to develop the new curriculum, as exemplified by CfE. It then illustrates how CfE has not been developed to its full potential, in a large part due to a lack of such understanding by key actors, including teachers. The chapter concludes by suggesting some theoretical concepts and practical steps which might be taken to maximise the considerable potential of CfE, at what the OECD (2015) has described in its recent review as a 'watershed moment'. The OECD also exhorted the Scottish Government to be 'bold', to grasp the nettle at this key stage in the development of Scotland's curriculum, and to enact a curriculum that truly represents the high aspirations set out in CfE. This will require some new thinking; it will also need political fortitude, as it will involve dropping some sacred cows, and taking steps that might be pilloried in the media as a climbdown, or past failure. This will prove to be less problematic than it might seem if underpinned by a robust theoretical base for action, and the articulation of a clear set of processes for putting this into practice. The ideas expressed in this chapter provide a contribution to this debate.

## REFERENCES

CEDEFOP (2009) *The Shift to Learning Outcomes: Policies and Practices in Europe*. Luxembourg: Office for Official Publications of the European Communities.

Drew, V., Priestley, M. and Michael, M. K. (2016) 'Curriculum development through critical collaborative professional enquiry', *Journal of Professional Capital and Community*, 1 (1), 92–106.

Education Scotland (2016) *Curriculum for Excellence: A Statement for Practitioners from HM Chief Inspector of Education*. Online at https://www.education.gov.scot/Documents/cfe-statement. pdf

OECD (2015) *Improving Schools in Scotland: An OECD Perspective*. Paris: OECD.

Priestley, M. and Humes, W. (2010) 'The development of Scotland's Curriculum for Excellence: amnesia and déjà vu', *Oxford Review of Education*, 36 (3), 345–61.

Priestley, M. and Biesta, G. J. J. (eds) (2013) *Reinventing the Curriculum: New Trends in Curriculum Policy and Practice*. London: Bloomsbury Academic.

Priestley, M. and Minty, S. (2013) 'Curriculum for Excellence: 'a brilliant idea, but …'', *Scottish Educational Review*, 45 (1), 39–52.

Priestley, M., Biesta, G. J. J. and Robinson, S. (2015) *Teacher Agency: An Ecological Approach*. London: Bloomsbury Academic.

Sahlberg, P. (2011) *Finnish Lessons: What Can the World Learn from Educational Change in Finland?* New York: Teachers College Press.

Schwab, J. L. (1969) 'The practical: a language for curriculum', *School Review*, 78 (1), 1–23.

Thijs, A. and van den Akker, J. (2009) *Curriculum in Development*. Enschede: Netherlands Institute for Curriculum Development (SLO). Online at www.slo.nl/downloads/2009/curriculum-in-development.pdf

Young, M. and Muller, J. (2010) 'Three educational scenarios for the future: lessons from the sociology of knowledge', *European Journal of Education*, 45, 11–27.

# 97

# A Pupil's Experience of Scottish Education

*Jonathan Tevendale*

In November 2004, a few months before I would desert the comforts of nursery and prepare to enter the horrifically big and horrifically bad world of primary school, a group of politicians published a document which would define my future. Not in the mind-blowingly profound 'we-are-changing-the-world' sense I imagine its creators would have liked, but through the constant creation of barriers and hindrances, disguised as progress.

That said, it's impossible for me to easily measure the importance of the Curriculum for Excellence (CfE) because I am a total and unchangeable product of its diktats. As my education began, the ideas of this new curriculum began seeping into schools around the country. While the old system remained and did, to some extent, shape me, it was little more than an ignored older brother living in the weeks following a new baby's birth, squawking (to much success) for everyone's attention. My education has been coloured by the introduction of CfE, and then CfE proper; nothing else.

Unlike the others writing in this book, I am no expert on education and approach it from an entirely biased and subjective perspective. Giving any under-18 the freedom to write about exams, school and education is dangerous, and balance will inevitably have to make way for the occasional polemic.

One last disclaimer should be made: there is no way of telling whether or not my experience of Scottish education, and the curriculum which underpinned it, has been in any way similar to those of the thousands of other children learning in its aftermath. My first primary school had forty pupils, my second sixteen, and the high school I currently attend (and which I will soon leave) is home to just over 100. I live in the remote Highlands of Scotland, and am sheltered from some of the things which colour the Scottish education system for others. There are, for example, few disciplinary issues, because the teacher will likely see your mum in the shop, and you can be sure she'll tell her everything. There is also the possibility, as in my case, that the teacher is your mum, and failure to submit homework will result in two unbearable lectures: one from the mouth of a teacher, and one from the (considerably less restrained) mouth of a parent.

My situation has hardly been typical, my perspective hardly objective and my knowledge of the system I've just been through anything but secure. That said, I would be hard pushed to find anything more life-affecting than my education, and I have much to say about it.

I find it fitting that my time in primary school should begin with frustration and a level of chaos which I feel has been sustained from P1 to S6. With a series of substitute teachers replacing the very ill woman who would educate me for the majority of my first three years of school, my early education lacked the security it might have benefited from. One of the more colourful experiences I had in primary school involved a fresh-faced trainee teacher whose lessons all focused on a stuffed camel toy, which became the subject of our reading, writing and Maths for weeks. As amusing and enthralling as this technique was, I couldn't help but feel sorry for the camel who found itself in the Highlands. In hindsight, this was perhaps my first experience of the Curriculum for Excellence approach, one which uses practical engagement as a means of reinforcing and propelling learning; I don't deny it was a fun and probably did make a positive impression on me, but it had an air of the Curriculum for Excellence ridiculousness which would characterise most future run-ins with the new system.

The excitement was short-lived and soon the rather more traditional teacher, with whom I would remain for the next few years, returned. Maths was Maths and writing was writing, something which pleased me no end, being more earnest aged 5 than I am now and will ever be. Despite these improvements, I found myself increasingly angry as the terms ticked by: when my partner in Maths went away on holiday in the middle of term time, I was told to stop doing Maths for two weeks, as it was inconvenient. We 'studied' books without words, despite the fact that a notable portion of the class could already read, and that the others might have benefited from learning how. When I completed a mathematical exercise I was told to 'colour in the apples' and wait patiently rather than being given something useful to do. I can understand how inconvenient I must have been, and how bizarre a 6 year old interested in Maths must have seemed, but it annoyed me. Perhaps the headmaster's characterisation of me as 'strange', and lacking a 'sense of humour' in a letter to my parents was accurate, but I felt my strangeness ought to have been accommodated, and the wit of a 6 year old irrelevant to the dispute. Certainly, there seems to have been much disparity between the government policy that learning should 'meet … individual interests and needs', and this educational practice, which made it clear that abnormality was okay, but only if you kept quiet about it, and provided it never became 'inconvenient'.

I managed to escape this school before I was forced to move into the class taught by that headmaster: I don't feel we would have got on. In my second school, teaching was traditional, with a shiny Curriculum for Excellence facade. We were brutally subjugated to the 'times table' while the 'smart board' inexplicably became a hugely important and much lauded part of education. This was perhaps because the latter was a physical manifestation of the twenty-first-century interactivity that modernists adore, or perhaps because the teacher (understandably) enjoyed all the new buttons she was suddenly allowed to press; certainly, it was a largely useless novelty.

For me, this school represented the best of both modernity and traditionalism. There was an almost total deference to arithmetic, reading and writing (where the CfE has encouraged the practice of 'vocational learning') but a more modern recognition that, as individuals, we should learn individually. There was not a single child working from the same page of a textbook. We worked from a reading website called Raz-Kids in which we received virtual furniture to kit out our spaceships in return for a successfully completed exercise, each focusing on something different, from the cycling career of Lance Armstrong to the migration of birds. While I regret the fierce materialism it must have encouraged in us, and the fact that it got 7–11 year olds competing ruthlessly for ownership of the biggest spaceship and coolest extraterrestrial dishwasher, there was no better introduction to our flawed society; and it certainly got us to read.

The vocational aspects of education emphasised in the new curriculum were not found in our academic teaching, but occurred separately. Every Tuesday afternoon we would knit, spurred on only by fear of the old lady who supervised us. Occasionally, we would take a break from school to tend to the garden, something that I hated but which was appreciated by many. In order to fund the annual skiing trip the school was temporarily transformed into a South-East Asian sweatshop, in which we helped produce candles, Christmas tree decorations and general tat to be sold to coerced parents, each working under the terrifying glare of our teacher. Never has forced child labour been so rewarding; and it makes sense that having been shown the workings of capitalism with Raz-Kids, we were shown what society might look like under socialism.

My happiness with this more liberal approach to modern education coincided with a notable increase in popularity of the 'cult of the curriculum'. Like something which might be found in Maoist China, the four-part description of the ideal pupil was painted across every other wall in the school: successful learners, confident individuals, responsible citizens, effective contributors, a mantra so outrageous in its meaninglessness that I'm certain it's yet to affect a single pupil. I still see this phrase today, and think it would be much improved by a Kim Jong un-esque portrait of John Swinney positioned proudly above it.

Nevertheless, my experience of primary school became positive, but only once I had been freed from the restrictiveness of my first school. The change in atmosphere is best reflected by my different roles in the schools' plays: in the first I played a shepherd, besotted by Jesus Christ; in the second I was a drag queen in our very own ABBA-inspired version of Cinderella. There was no need to be so earnest when I was content with my education, and I feel my 'sense of humour' was able to flourish in this environment, something I'm sure my previous headmaster would be delighted to hear.

Nevertheless, I wasn't there for long and I soon arrived at high school, removed from my comfortable position on the primary school hierarchy, and placed right at the bottom of the new one; I, a former chieftain, was revealed to be little more than a nervous, bespectacled child. In many ways high school was exciting and satisfied my desire to try new things, but this was contrasted by the sense that much of what I was doing was the useless by-product of a meeting during which men in suits tried hard to appear progressive, stopping before their grand visions could have any practical effect on the Scottish youth.

High schools Maths was no more difficult than that which I'd been marched through in primary school. Frequent sermons on the importance of 'revision' didn't change the fact that we were learning nothing new. This time, instead of being told to 'colour in the apples', I was told to 'wait patiently', and in many ways the former was a better use of my time. CfE pizzazz was used to disguise the insubstantiality of the education below, where it's supposed to enhance it. I was only able to escape the monotony of this by taking Intermediate 2 Maths early (something I was allowed to do given the laissez-faire atmosphere of my school), a radical solution to a problem which shouldn't have existed in the first place, and which reminded me all too much of my experiences aged 5.

Religious Studies consisted of videos and our teacher's repeated declaration that 'you die, get buried, and your corpse gets eaten by worms', a sentiment I happen to agree with, but which contributes nothing towards the attainment of a broad perspective on religion, particularly important in a village consisting only of Catholics and Protestants. Fortunately, I managed to withdraw myself from Religious Education to study Latin online, something I still study: swapping one useless subject for another, to much personal benefit. Online study has been difficult, but the independence it requires has been rewarding, and has occurred only by rejecting a subject the government says I should study in favour of one I approached entirely alone.

We studied global warming in Geography, General Science, Physics, Chemistry, Modern Studies, French, and Personal and Social Education (PSE), invariably going over the same basics again and again. I have only just begun looking at climate change again after years of boredom and repetition, my enthusiasm still muted by this experience. In S3 Geography I insisted for an entire year that climate change didn't exist, with the sole aim of sparking a little drama and making the lessons bearable. School should ignite a social and environmental conscience in its pupils, but not through incessant boredom.

PSE (an acronym which makes the title 'Personal and Social Education' only a little bit more tolerable) is perhaps the biggest disaster of my education. We were taught archaic pseudoscience pertaining to visual, auditory and kinaesthetic learners, needlessly shoe-boxed aged 13. We were told to rank the confidence of ourselves and those around us out of ten and discuss our justification, and when I unsubtly objected, I was sent to the deputy headmaster for 'disrespect and poor work ethic'. Surely disciplining pupils for scepticism is the trademark of a dictatorship, not the liberal education desired by the Scottish Government? As a young gay man, I found little value in sex education, and doubt I would have felt any differently about it even if I were straight. Discussion of alcohol and drugs invariably stemmed from a mid-1990s video clip, in which a helpless teenager is peer-pressured into snorting coke and dies. Teenagers do drugs, and if they don't they know people who have; hyperbole makes us laugh, not think. There was an absence of any debate – and we were ineffectually taught what to feel, rather than being encouraged to come to the appropriate conclusions ourselves. I sat through this compulsory subject for thirty-five minutes every morning from S1–3, several hundred hours I will never get back, and never had the choice of keeping. If an outline for PSE teaching is provided anywhere, then there seemed to be a clear disconnect between that set out in theory, and the utter pointlessness of reality.

Bizarrely, I found exams somewhat liberating. I enjoyed the ultimate objective they provided me with, and they allowed teachers to concentrate on the provision of knowledge, rather than the wishy-washy aim of 'making us better people', which often seemed to be the only goal provided by Education Scotland. I've been told that our education was organised around a set of so-called 'experiences and outcomes'. What was clearly designed to make us well-rounded individuals rather than exam machines often seemed little more than a series of box-ticking exercises: an obligation without purpose, an unnecessary necessity. Of course, individual and highly skilled teachers made learning worthwhile, but typically by gearing lessons in S1–3 towards the ultimate goal of passing exams; those who tried to improve us as people, however noble, floundered.

I was lucky to be allowed to take a number of early Highers, alongside several others in my year group. While frowned upon by the system, these have been of much benefit to me and to others. Pupils at other schools are forced to take a set diet of National 5s, Highers and, sometimes, Advanced Highers; we were allowed to enter at a level deemed appropriate, and received a much broader, much more general education as a consequence. I was able to try Chemistry, and quickly rule it out as something I didn't want to do again, but what's important is that I could if I wanted to, whereas most people's Highers are inevitably determined by what they studied at National 5.

Many of the new additions to exam courses, in my view, improved education. The 'assignments' I produced in Physics, Chemistry and History were rewarding and interesting and, despite making me more stressed than I have ever been before, made a welcome change from the more traditional approach to learning. Despite this, I felt we were working ahead of the Scottish Qualifications Authority (SQA): after we'd submitted our work, they would figure out what they wanted from it. Advice I heard being given to the year below me was not available to my class. Despite teachers and learners following the marking scheme requirements word by word, SQA examiners seem to have wanted something 'more', something which wasn't defined for me, for my teachers or, I'm starting to think, in the minds of the creators themselves. As the final exam rapidly approached, we were not so much concentrating on doing past papers, but wondering when example questions would be created, because as we learnt the course, it felt to me like the SQA were creating it. As a stressed and exasperated student, it was not encouraging to feel that those in charge had about as much idea about what to do as I did.

I am more than content with my exam performance, but believe I have done well in spite of a floundering system rather than because of it. Many of my teachers spent hours piecing together unclear directives, such that education began feeling more like an impossible sudoku than a cohesive and coherent system. Maybe this will change as the SQA comes to terms with the new exams it has created, but a whole generation of pupils has been treated as expendable lab rats, putting up with failed first attempts to secure the success of our successors.

Too often the government has tried to enforce modernity through unclear platitudes and wishy-washy descriptions of what pupils should be like, rather than making education genuinely individual and genuinely meaningful, giving us the tools to improve on our own rather than attempting to churn out perfect citizens. We learn not to be deceived by the 'system' rather than working alongside it towards success. This is the trademark of an educational authority too self-aggrandising and caught up in its own language to realise what matters to the pupils who actually have to follow the path they set for us.

# 98

# An Alternative Vocational Pathway: A Model for the Future

*Iain White*

## ORIGINS AND GOVERNANCE OF NEWLANDS JUNIOR COLLEGE

Newlands Junior College (NJC) exists to help young people aged 14 to 16 who are disengaged from education to re-engage and make a success of their lives, while contributing positively to society. It is a non-profit company that is registered as a charity and also as an independent school with the Registrar of Independent Schools in Scotland. As such, a board of trustees manages the college.

NJC was the brainchild of Jim McColl OBE, chairman and chief executive officer (CEO) of Clyde Blowers Capital. From 2003 onwards, McColl was extensively involved with the Glasgow Welfare to Work Forum and then its successor, Glasgow Works, as chair. During this time he became increasingly aware of the moral and economic tragedy of young people disengaging from the school system and failing to find a positive destination when they left. They then went into the welfare system and their talent and potential was wasted. McColl determined to do something about this and came up with the idea of establishing a different type of school which would cater for the disengaged, be linked directly to the workplace, prepare young people for a job or a place in further education, and nurture and develop their talent.

NJC evolved from this thinking. At the time of writing, the major part of its funding comes from sponsorship by Clyde Blowers Capital and a number of companies in the private sector, whilst there is also financial support from the public sector through the Scottish Government and three local authorities – Glasgow City Council, North Lanarkshire Council and Renfrewshire Council. Major donors are offered a place on the board of trustees. Local authorities with which the college works closely may also be invited to nominate members of the board. In addition, there is a capacity to co-opt other members with specific expertise considered essential for the good running of NJC.

Operational management is in the hands of the principal, who is responsible to the board of trustees for the effective management of NJC. The principal is required to work within the strategic framework established by the board, which sets out the broad purposes of NJC, defines the client group that it is designed to serve, and describes in general terms the nature of the curriculum that will be offered. Within these parameters, there is the freedom of action and approach that characterises the independent sector. The board expects the principal and staff to 'get on with it' and deliver success for the young people. The young person achieving a positive destination measures this success. The route to get there is by and large unimportant and left to the principal and the NJC staff.

The regular meetings of the board of trustees ensure accountability. The principal submits a progress report every six to eight weeks and its content is discussed. An annual standards and quality report is also produced. Internally, the principal meets all members of staff individually on a regular basis to discuss student progress in curriculum areas and, separately, to focus on their own personal development through the General Teaching Council Scotland's Professional Update programme. There is an acute awareness amongst the staff members of the ways in which they are accountable. The freedom of approach that they have is accompanied by the imperative of delivering success for the young people. This is taken very seriously by all concerned.

There has been a conscious effort to eliminate bureaucracy around the operation of NJC and this has brought huge benefits. Our ability to develop and make changes has been enhanced because we can do so extremely quickly. Opportunities can be seized and ideas implemented rapidly. When this is coupled with our willingness to take a chance on what might be seen as revolutionary approaches, we welcome the freedom that accompanies our independent status.

## WHAT IS DISTINCTIVE ABOUT NJC?

Scotland has excellent schools. Most young people leave well prepared for adult life and work. But some do not: 1,554 statutory leavers across Scotland were in activity agreements, unemployed or unaccounted for in 2015 (Skills Development Scotland, 2015), and among those are many young people with much to offer. However, for some reason, the normal school experience has not inspired them and they become demotivated and likely to fail. NJC has been specifically designed with these young people in mind. Its intensive individual support, emphasis on relationships and strongly vocational curriculum provide a different experience that can re-engage them and set them on the road to success. NJC is not for everyone: it provides a specialist service for a very specific group of students whose existing and latent potential is developed. With positive relationships as the key to success, the NJC experience provides a skills-based, personalised approach through which individual excellence is fostered in preparation for work.

There are two basic criteria for entry to NJC. Local schools are invited to identify pupils of around 14 years of age who are not currently benefiting from their education. The first criterion is that the nominee must be either disengaged, or disengaging from, regular secondary schooling. Low and sporadic attendance levels and a lack of enthusiasm and commitment to the learning process are indicators of this disengagement. The second criterion is that the nominating school must be able to give evidence of latent potential that is not being nurtured and developed currently. Students who successfully come through the nomination and selection process are awarded a fully funded scholarship.

The basic catchment for NJC is the Southside of Glasgow and its eleven secondary schools, although there are some exceptions to this general principle. In March 2017, there were students from North Lanarkshire, Renfrewshire and other areas of Glasgow making up one third of the NJC roll. The nominating school completes a form giving details of the young person and why they are considered suitable for consideration for a place. The way by which the school arrives at the decision to nominate is entirely a matter for its own internal arrangements. The next stage is that the nominee is invited to come to NJC to meet a couple of members of staff and see the facility. A carer and possibly someone like a pastoral care teacher from the school, or a social worker or other complementary professional, accompanies the nominee. There is an informal conversation during which NJC begins to consider the potential suitability of the nominee. Simultaneously, the nominee is able to consider whether NJC is an option that is attractive to them. The next stage is the assessment centre. This takes place over a more extended period of time in the summer term. Potential students are invited to come back to NJC, this time to meet other nominees and work with them on problem-solving exercises, teamwork activities and tasks that are designed to allow all present to get to know one another a little. These activities are all observed and, at the conclusion, the suitability of each candidate is considered on an individual basis. NJC and members of staff from schools work together to ensure that a different kind of opportunity is made available to those young people who seem most likely to gain from it.

NJC provides Scottish education with an additional resource. It is not in competition with comprehensive secondary schools. It aims to work closely with its partner schools to ensure that every young person receives the kind of education best suited to their needs. Once a young person moves to NJC, they transfer to its roll and the former school is kept informed of progress. Members of staff from the schools often visit to see for themselves how their former pupils are getting on.

## THE NATURE OF THE CURRICULUM

NJC is committed to achieving positive outcomes. Structures and processes are secondary. Every young person who leaves to enter a job or take on further study is a gain for society and a vindication of the NJC philosophy and approach. Young people are individuals and need to be treated as such. This belief is very important to NJC. However, in every case, NJC's priorities are:

- to build a positive relationship with the student and his/her home;
- to create an environment that will allow the student to be motivated to approach learning with renewed purpose and enthusiasm;
- to get a meaningful positive destination for each student.

Curriculum philosophy, although important, is subordinate to these aims.

Experience is teaching us that the most important thing that NJC does is to build positive relationships amongst all who are part of the NJC family: viz. students, carers, members of staff, partner professionals and business partners. Positive relationships are the key. Hard work is put into building these and everything else follows in its wake. Our experience further tells us that it is the very shortage of these relationships in the school lives of those who ultimately become our students that causes them to disengage. That is what our students tell us. They do not say that they disengaged because the curriculum in their previous school failed to meet their needs and aspirations.

Additionally, NJC is founded on the belief that many disengaged young people can be motivated by learning that is clearly linked to their future lives and, in particular, the possibility of success in earning a living. Vocational learning is thus central to the NJC curriculum and everything possible is done to have NJC mirror the workplace. While partners deliver the vocational courses, the soft skills linked to employment are further emphasised and developed by all that is done in NJC. Developing positive attitudes, skills for life and increased confidence are central too. Hence, personal development is also an indispensable element of the NJC approach. This combined emphasis on vocational education and personal development is the distinguishing feature of the NJC curriculum structure. It is seen as essential if our young people are to be motivated and encouraged to learn. As stated previously, the glue that holds it all together is the development of positive relationships. At the same time, formal academic learning is vital, because it leads to qualifications that are essential to the young person's progress. Improving examination performance has never been a stated purpose of NJC yet outcomes have demonstrated that great success in exams happens!

The curriculum of NJC thus consists of three strands: academic, vocational and personal development.

The *academic* curriculum focuses on four core subjects studied at National 4 or 5 – English, IT, Mathematics and Physics/Laboratory Science – but covering a much broader spread through the mechanism of interdisciplinary learning assessed through skills development. Emphasis is placed on basic skills of literacy and numeracy and on broader intellectual skills.

In 2017, *vocational* learning is offered in collaboration with partners such as City of Glasgow College, Riverside Music Complex and GTG Training. The students choose three options from a menu. In 2016–17, City of Glasgow College offered courses in engineering, construction, hairdressing, creative industries, hospitality/professional cookery, early education and childcare, sport and business administration. A further vocational option is offered through the Riverside Music Complex in Busby. As well as potentially giving access to an expanding area of employment, this music technology course serves to extend the range of the curriculum into the expressive arts. This menu of vocational courses changes from year to year to meet student needs. To complement the further education college-based vocational experiences, GTG provides work-based learning in vehicle systems maintenance to students in year 2.

*Personal development* runs through everything that is done at NJC. An extensive programme of personal and social development offers opportunities for a rich range of qualifications as well as building constructive attitudes and self-confidence. In particular, in 2017 NJC is working with SkillForce Scotland to deliver ASDAN personal development qualifications at bronze, silver and gold levels and the Duke of Edinburgh Award (Bronze). In addition, students study for the Scottish Qualifications Authority (SQA) Employability Award at level 4, Outward Bound Trust certification, the John Muir Environmental Award, National Navigation awards and courses in first aid and health and safety at work.

## THE LEARNING ENVIRONMENT

The small scale of NJC allows for great flexibility in the timetabling arrangements. This flexibility is used whenever required to accommodate special events and experiences and to assist students to progress to higher levels in their studies. A critical aspect of the NJC experience is the close personal support provided for each individual. The focus at NJC is very much on the individual and what can be done to provide the experience that will bring a successful outcome for that young person. NJC arrangements are made to fit around the needs of the individual student. The opposite can often be the case in regular schools where, too often, the young people are made to fit into a timetable. There are organisational and historical reasons for that situation being the case in schools and this further emphasises the validity of the role that NJC discharges.

Most of the young people who come to NJC arrive with a negative view of education. The key task is to re-engage their interest and make them believe they can have a worthwhile future if they put in the effort and work alongside us. The induction programme and the first few weeks are vital. During this time, residual perceptions amongst the new students that lead to members of the NJC staff being seen as the enemy are lost as the impact of the developing good relationships is seen and appreciated by the students. NJC is small and strongly supportive of the individual. Each year group contains only thirty students, so there is maximum number of sixty between year 1 and year 2. There is a small staff group. The people who make up that group all know each student as an individual and are committed to providing high levels of personal support. There is potential for varying the experiences of the individual student by altering the composition of the working week both in terms of content and length. In some cases a longer working week will come from a greater exposure to work experience in an area where the student has a career aspiration. This would be accompanied by a concentrated focus during in-house activities. Extended staff support would allow the student to learn in chunks, for example a morning of IT and an afternoon of English in a week otherwise filled with work experience.

This leads us to the different nature of curriculum delivery in year 2 because the NJC approach is designed to make flexibility easier as well as to better meet individual needs. When students enrol at NJC in year 1, they are assigned to a class group and, by and large, that group is taught the in-house subjects in a model that is fairly traditional. This is a deliberate strategy to help bring focus, rigour and direction that have previously been lacking in the students. However, as time goes on more flexibility develops until, by year 2, the approach is completely different. By that stage, learning in traditional class groups is abandoned in NJC. The whole concept of how learning is structured is approached to fully meet the needs of the individual. Within personal development, and the other curriculum areas delivered by NJC staff – English, IT, Maths and Science – individual students are not assigned to a specific number of sessions for each subject in each week at specific times. Rather, at any time, the student is aware of the adults who are available to work with and makes a choice based on personal need. Progress, and the hurdles between the student and successful course completion, determines the choice made. The student decides what subject to go to at what time. The student's overall progress is monitored by the NJC adviser system. To help students realise their full potential, they are assigned a personal adviser. The adviser is a member of the NJC staff who meets with the student on a regular basis, discusses progress, helps with goal setting and can advocate on the student's behalf.

The adviser is also responsible for communicating and sharing information with parents/carers, and fostering involvement and commitment on the part of the carers. While ensuring that young people are on target with learning, the adviser system is also designed to check that the student's skills are being developed and assessed. Everything is put in place for the student to set out on their future destination as well prepared as they can be. Each student's carer is able to communicate with the adviser, in a way, and at a time and place, that is convenient for the family. In addition parents/carers have the ability to access online reports at any time. This drive to maintain positive relationships, and regular communication with parents and carers, means that they know that NJC will be in touch regularly. When they see the NJC number on their phone it does not mean that it is going to be bad news!

At NJC every aspect of learning is assessed for the development of skills. In other words, when students get better at a particular area of their programme, it is recorded in the electronic skills log and used to build an accurate and useful outline of what each student is good at – their strengths – and areas for development. Our belief is that every young person has strengths and they all learn how to describe the skills they already have and those they are developing. The bespoke skills log system provides a skills taxonomy and each learner can use it to identify, describe and record skills development. It can also produce reports.

Although NJC differs from ordinary secondary schools in terms of size and curriculum, its approaches are also in line with some mainstream thinking in Scottish education. The emphasis on the individual is consistent with the idea of personalised education that runs through Curriculum for Excellence (Scottish Executive, 2004). At the same time, the strong focus on vocational education resonates with the recommendations of the Commission for Developing Scotland's Young Workforce (2014) chaired by Sir Ian Wood. Also, by bringing success in National Qualifications to previously disengaged students, NJC helps tackle the Scottish Attainment Challenge launched by the First Minister in February 2015. NJC is designed to contribute to Scottish education by pursuing national objectives in ways that are uniquely adapted to the needs of individuals in a very special client group. Working closely with other parts of the system, it has added something new and helps to address key issues of underachievement and inequity in the Scottish system. NJC doesn't look or feel like a school. Being located within an industrial site, it has the atmosphere of a place of work. The whole NJC culture and experience is deliberately mirrored on the workplace because NJC seeks to have young people work ready by the end of their two-year course. Students have access to up-to-date technology. NJC is equipped with mobile and desktop devices to allow learning to happen in a variety of ways and in a number of locations. The Apple platform is used throughout.

This environment allows NJC to meet head on the challenge that learning doesn't just happen in the classroom and it can happen anywhere. The use of excellent IT resources means that NJC students can go wherever there is an opportunity to learn. The college has the most advanced IT provision available so that students have a state-of-the-art learning experience. These resources also aid communication by allowing both students and parents to communicate with staff in a variety of ways using social media and mobile technology. The focus is on finding the method with which each family is most comfortable. NJC also has a college library that provides students with a mix of learning environments, including group and quiet study areas. In the library, students can access book-based materials and online resources that complement their formal coursework.

## STUDENT PROGRESSION AND WORK EXPERIENCE

NJC staff and students and their parents/carers communicate frequently with City of Glasgow College staff and partner companies to ensure progression to a meaningful future destination, be it a job or a place in further education. This system is supported and enhanced by NJC's close links with Skills Development Scotland whose advisers also provide one-to-one support for students. A key component in preparing for the future is work experience. Every student gains experience in the work sector they are interested in. Placements are flexible to fit in with the needs of our business partners. Work experience is an essential part of life at NJC and key to getting students work ready because it allows them to gain a first-hand knowledge of what the workplace is like. The frequency of work experience is another key difference at NJC. In most schools, the S4 work experience week is the extent of the direct engagement of students in the workplace. In NJC all students are able to access multiple work experience placements and, in some cases, these can go on for lengthy periods of time. Students are also encouraged to seek placements for themselves. There is also a scheme by which students are supported on a one-to-one basis by mentors from NJC's business partners and friends. These mentors provide support, coaching and act as role models for our students.

Students' destinations are carefully matched to both their potential and their strengths, by agreeing targets and reviewing them regularly to ensure success. Support for NJC students does not stop at graduation. With its emphasis on positive relationships, NJC operates like a big family. Once you are an NJC graduate, the college commits to being there for you in the weeks, months and years to come for coaching, advice and support as required. Already we work with graduates in this way.

## OUTCOMES AND LOOKING TO THE FUTURE

NJC opened in November 2014 and its first cohort of students graduated in June 2016 (fourteen males and five females). The successes of the group members were significant: 100 per cent went into positive destinations; 100 per cent had five awards at National 3 and 90 per cent had five awards at National 4; all had at least one National 5 award and some had multiple National 5 awards; 35 per cent achieved the ASDAN Personal Development Gold Award and all but one of the remainder succeeded at either bronze or silver levels. Success rates in other awards include Fearless (70 per cent), Heart Start (65 per cent), the National Navigation awards (80 per cent), the John Muir Discovery Environmental Award (70 per cent), Outward Bound Trust certificate (60 per cent), the Duke of Edinburgh Award (80 per cent) and the SQA Employability Award (95 per cent). These measures of achievement clearly put NJC in the 'best in the country' category – and all of this with young people who were previously disengaged!

The output from NJC against stated objectives has been extremely successful. If the proof of the pudding is in the eating, we were all able to feast on the successes of our 2016 graduate group and the expectation of further positive outcomes in June 2017. That leaves the big question – 'What now?' It is our belief that there is a compelling argument that junior colleges like NJC should be established across the country to bring success in education and positive destinations to young people who fall into the disengaged and disengaging group. The establishments should be tailored to respond to local needs and be free-standing within a national network. Crucial to their success would be a governance model that brings the freedom of the independent school alongside a governing body drawn from stakeholders and, importantly, the private sector. Funding should come from a redirection of money already in the public purse to be supplemented by private sector investment. The detailed case has been researched and there is clear evidence that the numbers of young people to form client groups do exist (Skills Development Scotland, 2015).

Furthermore, the moral imperative on the grounds of social justice brooks no debate. The return on investment is similar to mainstream education because the money spent up front from the public purse will be repaid many times over, as costs of welfare benefits, health provision and the criminal justice system are cut because the graduates enter the employment stream rather than the benefit stream. They would even be paying taxes! All that is required is for the political will to match the rhetoric and make it happen.

## REFERENCES

Commission for Developing Scotland's Young Workforce (2014) *Education Working for All! Commission for Developing Scotland's Young Workforce Final Report.* Online at www.gov.scot/Publications/2014/06/4089

Scottish Executive (2004) *A Curriculum for Excellence: Report of the Curriculum Review Group.* Edinburgh: Scottish Executive.

Skills Development Scotland (2015) *Scotland: Initial Destinations of School Leavers 2014/15.* Glasgow: Skills Development Scotland.

# 99

# A Journalist's Perspective on the Future of Scottish Education

*Henry Hepburn*

The pace of change in my industry really hit home on a hot summer's evening in Finland in August 2016. I was part of a gathering of international journalists, and we were rounding off the day with a few drinks in a beer garden under the looming whiteness of Helsinki Cathedral. A local reporter for Bloomberg, the business news specialists, had joined our group and chipped in as we talked about technology's potential to make many skilled jobs obsolete. 'It's already happening in journalism', he said – his employers were deploying algorithms that could rapidly convert a dense financial report into a crisp piece of prose without human intervention.

In *The Rise of the Robots*, the futurist Martin Ford (2015) shows how artificial intelligence could turn conventional notions of work on its head. Even skilled professionals such as lawyers and scientists will see opportunities eroded by rapidly advancing information technology, he argues. And while the companies that drove the industrial revolution were mass employers, the digital revolution is very different: the likes of Google and Facebook, for example, use powerful technology that fuels booming stock prices and global influence despite a relatively tiny workforce.

In his closing keynote speech to the 2015 Scottish Learning Festival, Chris van der Kuyl, an entrepreneur at the forefront of Scotland's burgeoning gaming industry, told the many watching teachers to brace themselves:

> We live in an age where you're experiencing the fastest change [in technology] you've ever experienced in your life. Things are changing today faster than they ever have in anyone's lifetime – and it'll be the slowest pace of change you'll ever experience again.

The implications for education are stark. As Ford (2015) puts it in his book: 'The unfortunate reality is that a great many people will do everything right – at least in terms of pursuing higher education and acquiring skills – and yet still fail to find a foothold in the new economy.' Seldom has the need for a nimble school system been more obvious – for a curriculum that can adapt to the rapidly changing demands of an uncertain future, of a digital revolution where technology could wipe out whole employment sectors and perhaps even displace work as a cornerstone of our lives. Surely, then, we should be thankful that in Scotland we have Curriculum for Excellence (CfE)? CfE, I have heard countless times since I started working as an education reporter in 2006, puts Scotland at the vanguard of educational reform: as much a philosophy as a curriculum, CfE would collapse artificial boundaries between subjects and sectors and emancipate the teaching workforce from the dispiriting requirement to cram pupils' heads with knowledge for exams. Instead, CfE would lead to a mutually rewarding dialogue between student and teacher, equipping the former with skills and a sense of resourcefulness that could be applied in myriad workplaces.

That sort of utopian rhetoric, however, has started dying away in recent times. Even fans of CfE are sounding jaded. Sir Tim Brighouse, who famously helmed the London Challenge and helped turn around the city's schools, has forged close links with Scotland and spoken warmly of what educators are trying to do here. In March 2017, at an event near Edinburgh that brought teachers from the four UK nations together to learn from each other, I asked him to sum up Scottish education. 'Lumbering along in the right direction' was his précis. That, if we set aside the windy rhetoric of politicians, is about as positive as most people in Scottish education are likely to get just now. Many recognise Sir Tim's 'lumbering' entity (after all, it's a decade-and-a-half since the genesis of CfE – should it still enjoy the benefit of doubt afforded to works in progress?). But the right direction? Not all international observers are convinced these days; others see Scottish education asleep at the wheel, at risk of hitting the verge.

The morning after Donald Trump was elected US president in November 2016, gallows humour was swirling about in Stirling as educationists from far and wide, attending an international conference to launch the Stirling Network for Curriculum Studies, slurped on their hotel coffee. Never had there been a more important time for education, said organiser Professor Mark Priestley, as the audience digested the implications of a president who proudly disavowed reason and deemed tolerance an 'Establishment' frippery. What might have come next was an injection of optimism, courtesy of CfE. I'd seen that plenty of times in the past, from both domestic and international observers: fans of CfE talking up a reform, fuelled by moral purpose, that would break with deadening education tradition, liberating teachers and perhaps even inspiring similar innovation around the world. Instead, I heard a lament – two of them, in fact. First, Anne Looney, director of the Republic of Ireland's Higher Education Authority, was a little apologetic (this was a room of mostly Scots, after all) but nevertheless pulled few punches. She harked back to the 'ripples of excitement' that CfE had caused around the English-speaking world, but regretted a 'very noticeable' change. CfE had gone from saying 'really powerful things about what we want for learners and what we want for Scotland to using much more generic language around "delivery" and "improvement"'. It had made a global impression by prioritising teachers' 'professional judgement', but now 'It sounds different – it sounds less expansive, it sounds less open.' Scotland was instead aping other countries, where conversations about curricular innovation were sidelined amid ever-growing demands for teachers to take on 'the delivery imperative, the quality imperative, the closing the [attainment] gap imperative'. Her assessment was tinged with sorrow: 'A generic policy language has robbed education of something, and I think there's a missing piece of the landscape.'

Another speaker had a similar but pithier take on Scottish education. Professor Jan van den Akker – introduced as a 'seminal thinker on the curriculum' – was 'a bit amazed and almost taken aback by this enormous emphasis all the time on "delivering" and "delivery"'. He was 'tired and discouraged' from reading jargon that made people working in Scottish education sound like 'a nation of deliverers' – or, as he also put it, 'postmen'. At the government level, emphasis has shifted subtly from high-minded rhetoric about transforming

Scottish education towards more utilitarian preoccupations, whether a review of school governance or the standardised national assessments scheduled for 2017–18. CfE is giving way to a more hard-headed approach from policymakers who feel the need to 'do something' amid the flak they have taken for declining performance of pupils in the international Programme for International Student Assessment (PISA) survey – which, despite many criticisms of its methodology, still carries considerable weight – and the Scottish Survey of Literacy and Numeracy (SSLN), which has since been scrapped.

It feels like there has been a failure of nerve with CfE, that the initial idealism never truly vaulted over a stubborn strain of conservatism in Scottish education. If, for example, we compare Scotland with Finland, the latter *has* been through truly radical change, such as the scrapping of a national inspection system several decades ago. For all that the Scottish inspection regime is now portrayed as a less confrontational affair – although not all would share that view – it is hard to imagine it ever being abolished.

There is another essential ingredient in Finland's genuinely progressive education system that Scotland lacks: chutzpah. In August 2016, @thisisFINLAND, a marketing arm of the Ministry for Foreign Affairs on the Twitter social network, sent out a surprisingly breezy message, in the knowledge that ongoing education reform would lead to a dip in PISA results later that year: 'The new core curriculum might knock #Finland off the top of the Pisa rankings for #education, but who cares!'

Such blithe disregard seems unlikely in Scotland, where ministers and the media are more in thrall to PISA. So more testing of children – starting with 5 year olds – becomes a reasonable course of action. Meanwhile, secondary schools still largely pivot around the short period when pupils cram for their Highers, as teachers were reminded in March 2017 when, after an Education Scotland review of inspections, they were admonished for failings in S1–3.

The optimism I often heard from teachers around CfE a decade ago is now in shorter supply. The profession bought in wholeheartedly to a reform that might have been called Curriculum for All, given its ambition to break with a tradition that prized the amassing of Highers – and the rite of passage into university – above other achievements. By 2017, however, Scotland's largest teaching union, the Educational Institute of Scotland (EIS), was bemoaning a 'narrowing of the debate around what achievement means' and a focus on 'CfE levels, SQA exam results and standardised assessment data [which] has not visibly taken account of the types of achievement that matter to pupils with additional needs' (www.eis. org.uk/public.asp?dbase=2&id=3611).

There were always some CfE refuseniks. I would often be surprised when I met teachers at parties or weddings and found some deeply sceptical about a reform that they felt was messing around with a high-quality education system. It made me wonder whether the keen-as-mustard teachers I encountered at conferences and professional development events were representative of the overall workforce. CfE has ended up betwixt and between – there's been enough change to alienate those who never liked it to begin with, but not enough for its champions. English teacher and author Kenny Pieper, a founder of Pedagoo, the popular online network for teachers, has railed against media doom-mongering about Scottish education. Yet writing in the *Times Educational Supplement* (TES) *Scotland* in March 2017, he poured out his frustration about an unwillingness 'to waver from the same rigid timetabling in secondary school' that denied 'freedom to innovate' and the realisation that 'we seem to be struggling to implement our flagship Curriculum for Excellence'. If CfE was only going to be implemented half-heartedly, he reasoned, Scotland should 'dump the idea'.

Yet the pervasive gloom should not obscure Scottish education's transformation in recent times. I do not recognise the picture of unmitigated failure painted by opposition politicians, and I marvel at progress in the quarter of a century since I left my school in Aberdeen. In March 2017, *TES Scotland* ran a hugely powerful article by Andrew Campbell, the son of the late Grace Campbell, who in the 1970s and 1980s fought a long legal battle to have corporal punishment banned in schools. He was at pains to underline just how different Scottish schools were back then, when teachers were 'inculcated into using physical punishment as part of their classroom routine' and parents dared not challenge them. Those who did, as the Campbell family discovered, risked ostracism – not to mention anonymous phone calls and bricks through their windows.

Schools have changed in myriad ways. In architectural design, for example, remorseless straight lines and tight, washed-out corridors once called to mind the Overlook Hotel in Stanley Kubrick's classic horror film, *The Shining*; now, airy atriums, blasts of colour and 'outdoor classrooms' are standard. The classical diet of subjects has been shaken up: there are schools that genuinely treat bicycle maintenance, care and dance with the same sense of importance as English, Maths and History. And I am struck by pupils' confidence and eloquence. My generation, in contrast, went to university largely unprepared for the idea of learning as dialogue: we would stare at our feet in tutorials, hoping no one caught our gaze, as students from other countries waxed lyrical.

Meanwhile, changing views of school leadership, far removed from the idea of heroic heads who drag their staff forward by sheer force of will, promise more democratic schools where all teachers can innovate. Initiatives such as TeachMeets and Pedagoo, as well as commercial online platforms like Twitter and Yammer, are allowing teachers to share ideas far beyond their own classrooms. Even an arch critic of the government, Labour education spokesman Iain Gray, said in *TES Scotland* in March 2017 that teachers were more professional than when he taught physics in the 1980s: they created an 'incredibly positive' atmosphere in schools because they strived to help all pupils, not just the high-fliers who took precedence in the past.

Despite such causes for optimism, many teachers say the mood of the profession is worsening. Recent concerns include bureaucracy, as reams of new 'benchmarks' appear. Standardised assessment raises the spectre of top-down accountability and school league tables, they say, while new qualifications and teacher shortages reduce the palette of subjects available to pupils. Even organisations not known for rocking the boat have concerns. The General Teaching Council for Scotland (GTCS), in its submission to the governance review, suggested that a fundamental tenet of Scottish education – equity – was under threat. Yes, the government points to record university entry rates from poorer areas and many more school leavers from those areas now gaining at least one Higher. But the GTCS said CfE and qualifications reform had been 'characterised by unjustifiable variations between local authorities'. This had 'undermined the principle that children have common entitlements to educational provision across Scotland, regardless of the school they happen to attend' (www.gtcs.org.uk/web/FILES/News-resources/GTCS_Response_to_Education_Governance_Review.pdf).

Education Secretary John Swinney made a striking statement of intent in a speech at Queen Margaret University in March 2017. Jutting through the usual ministerial murk of jargon and platitudes was a short but stark warning. The 1,100 submissions to the governance review, he said, clearly showed 'a strong body of opinion that does not accept the need to change. And what is perhaps most worrying is that this body of opinion is from within

Scottish education.' His message was uncompromising, even confrontational: 'Change is needed, change is happening and more change is coming.'

Swinney fleetingly resembled Michael Gove, the strident reformist who butted heads with teachers over four years as Westminster Education Secretary. Swinney may not have the same ideological zeal, but perhaps he is trying to achieve a delicate – some say impossible – balance by mollifying right-wing critics (assessments will drive up standards, schools will be liberated from the dead hand of local authorities) and encouraging progressive educationists (there will be no top-down interference in schools, breaking the poverty cycle is key). Some observers of Scottish education say Swinney is well-intentioned, but even they fear he is backfilling a reform that was never properly set out in the first place.

The governance reforms received a mixed response when the government published its plans in June 2017. The subsequent parliamentary debate highlighted a sometime Scottish National Party (SNP) knack for formulating policy (in education and beyond) that neuters the ire of opponents on all sides: the Conservatives' education spokeswoman, Liz Smith, welcomed the devolution of more power to headteachers while regretting that this idea was not fully followed through; Labour's Iain Gray, meanwhile, was initially rather subdued, as he welcomed Swinney's refusal to let schools opt out of local authority control.

What worked in party-political skirmishes, however, left many within Scottish education frustrated, as they felt the plans were vague and contradictory. Days after the SNP revealed its hand on governance – albeit with many details still to be worked out – a conference in Edinburgh gathered many key figures in Scottish education to ruminate on its implications. Some secondary headteachers expressed excitement at the prospect of being freer to decide on their school's priorities, although there was a widespread feeling that this sentiment would not be shared by all senior management teams in their sector. In contrast, education consultant and former council chief executive Keir Bloomer predicted that many primary heads – particularly in smaller rural schools – would be 'quaking in their boots' at the prospect of more responsibility for staff recruitment and curriculum design.

Some commentators argued the reforms were more of a power grab than an attempt to liberate schools. Many had predicted that the reforms would spell the end of government agency Education Scotland – a focus for constant criticism over its perceived lack of independence from ministers – or at least that its twin roles of inspection and curriculum would be split up; instead, in one of the reform's biggest surprises, Education Scotland emerged reinvigorated by the news that it would subsume the widely praised Scottish College for Educational Leadership (SCEL), which had only been set up in 2014. Meanwhile, the six or seven 'regional improvement collaboratives' envisaged by the government, critics argued, were less a common-sense move to pool resources across artificial council boundaries than an attempt to exert more control over local authorities. The governance reforms, a group of academics argued in a letter to *The Herald* newspaper on 9 July 2017, followed an essentially Conservative educational agenda.

Unions, meanwhile, argued that even if the reforms had some merit, they would be pointless without extra funding – beyond the £750 million Attainment Scotland Fund the government has promised to hand out over the course of the current Parliament – and that they were a distraction from poverty, the root cause of educational inequality. In attempting to alienate no one with its reforms, the government appeared in danger of pleasing no one.

Setting aside education governance reform, the worries of Scotland's teachers are piling up, including budget cuts, malfunctioning new qualifications and swelling numbers of children with additional needs. Meanwhile, the wider world is on shifting sands, from the breakneck advance of digital technology to populist movements that threaten the political order of recent times. Teachers must prepare students for a highly unpredictable and fast-changing world; rote learning and prescriptive curricula have never seemed less adequate. At the recent Four Nations event, teachers from Scotland, England, Wales and Northern Ireland found much in common. The structures they operated within were different, but all presented frustrations and, as one speaker put it, teachers had to 'duck and dive' around them.

Despite many changes for the better over recent decades, teachers in Scotland still work in an often rigid system. They will continue to duck and dive, with considerable success. The frustration is that, under CfE, they were told they wouldn't have to.

## REFERENCE

Ford, M. (2015) *The Rise of the Robots: Technology and the Threat of Mass Unemployment.* New York: Basic Books.

# 100

# The Direction of Post-school Education in Scotland

*Jean Barr*

In looking to the future a brief glance at the past is in order. It may help to orientate us to the direction of travel thus far of post-school education. It may also help us to gain some purchase on the road not travelled.

There was a huge expansion of post-school education in the late 1980s and 1990s in the UK and throughout most of the developed world. The UK's higher education (HE) system became a mass system amidst a flurry of government reports on post-school education: the Dearing Report, *Higher Education in the Learning Society* (1997); *Learning Works: Widening Participation in Further Education* (1997); *The Learning Age* Green Paper, England (1998); *Learning Is for Everyone: Widening Opportunity*, Green Paper, Scotland (1998). Two further reports from committees chaired by Alan Milburn were also significant: *Unleashing Aspiration: The Final Report of the Panel on Fair Access to the Professions* (2009) and *University Challenge: How Higher Education Can Advance Social Mobility* (2012).

During this period there was concern about the participation of non-traditional groups. Helena Kennedy, who chaired *Learning Works*, stressed *widening* – not just increasing – participation. By underlining the distinction, Kennedy was also challenging the political tendencies of the 1980s that privileged marketisation in education. Collaboration between providers was emphasised too – an acknowledgement that further education (FE) and informal adult education provide alternative routes into HE and that boundaries between educational providers are not always clear. Shared aims for economic, personal and social development were tempered by predictable claims that the access agenda was about 'dumbing down'.

## POST-DEVOLUTION INITIATIVES

Political changes in Scotland at the turn of the twenty-first century gave new powers over education and training to the Scottish Parliament. Expectations of increased divergence between Scottish and English education systems were countered by strong pressures towards convergence, such as the global market in higher education (see Gallacher and Raffe, 2012). The challenges facing Scotland, including an ageing population, economic recession and social polarisation, were the same problems that led governments elsewhere to promote lifelong learning. In Scotland too, in the early days of the devolved Scottish Parliament, there was a brief flirtation with this notion.

Thus one of the first acts of the first Labour-led Scottish Parliament of 1999 was to create a parliamentary committee on enterprise and lifelong learning, tasked with promoting a lifelong learning strategy to 'promote personal fulfilment and enterprise, employability and adaptability, active citizenship and social inclusion'. In keeping with this wide-ranging approach the new administration paid attention to community-based adult education, reviewed the training of community education staff and launched a new initiative in adult basic education. However, it pulled back from implementing the committee's most radical recommendation: to move towards an *entitlement* model of learner funding.

In any case, concern for 'learning through life' was short-lived. Policy on adult and continuing education shifted decisively (back) towards an instrumental agenda, with an emphasis on employability and narrowly conceived basic skills. When Labour lost the 2007 election to the Scottish National Party (SNP), the new administration's educational policies were focused firmly on full-time initial education. The SNP had three goals: reform of the school curriculum around 'capabilities'; removal of all tuition fees for Scottish domiciled undergraduates at Scottish universities; and, with the election of a majority SNP Government in 2011, reduction of the number of FE colleges through a process of mergers, to reduce costs and to form part of an overhaul of post-16 education. Community education became 'community learning and development' and the Enterprise and Lifelong Learning Committee excised 'lifelong learning' from itself, eventually settling on the 'Education and Culture Committee'. Adult learning policy returned to its default setting.

While the Scottish Funding Council was tasked with supporting widening access to university education, funding was simultaneously withdrawn from part-time learners in further education colleges (Field, 2015). Part-time provision in colleges has now declined substantially, and the Scottish Government's policy of 'free' full-time university tuition fees, seen as a self-evident good, has come to so powerfully frame the debate on post-school education as to block out many other concerns, including the impact of this policy on adult, further and lifelong education – and on poor students. How has this come about?

In 2001 the Labour-led government in Edinburgh removed up-front fees for Scottish university students, replacing them with a one-off graduate endowment of £2,000 (£2,700 at today's prices) to be paid after graduation. The Education (Graduate Endowment and Student Support) (Scotland) Act of 2001 defined the graduate endowment as 'a fixed amount that some graduates will be liable to pay, after they have completed their degree', adding that the funds raised are to be used to 'provide student support, including bursaries, for future generations of disadvantaged students' (https://www.legislation.gov.uk/asp/2001/6/contents).

The expectation was that around 50 per cent of undergraduates, including all those on Higher National-level courses as well as those moving from a Higher National course to a university degree and taking less than two further years to complete, would be exempt from paying the endowment. Some mature and disabled students were also exempt. It is worth pausing here to underline the fact that it was not the SNP who abolished up-front tuition fees but the first Scottish Executive, a coalition between Labour and Liberal Democrats. What the minority SNP administration abolished in 2008 was the graduate endowment scheme. Stefan Collini, one of the most persistent critics of the English university fees system, regards some kind of graduate endowment scheme as a great improvement on the arrangement in England where annual fees, met by loans, have reached £9,000. Writing in 2016 he says, 'If we are to fund HE by means other than a properly progressive form of general taxation then some form of graduate endowment or equivalent of national insurance contributions would be less damaging' (Collini, 2016).

## FUNDING – RHETORIC AND REALITY

The SNP has now been in power for a decade, since 2007 as a minority government, and from 2011 until 2016 as a majority government. In 2013, as a result of the rising costs of its university fees policy, it cut maintenance grants for the poorest students by 40 per cent without parliamentary scrutiny. Maintenance grants had already been cut in real terms since 2007 when the SNP came to power. They have now been halved. Young students from families earning less than around £30,000 per annum have lost out because grant cuts have more than outweighed any benefit to them from the abolition of the graduate endowment scheme.

Lucy Hunter Blackburn, the former civil servant responsible for implementing the graduate endowment scheme, points to mounting evidence that free university tuition represents a middle-class handout by stealth: 'It's superficially universal, but in fact it benefits the better-off most, and is funded by pushing the poorest students further and further into debt.' Such evidence is presented in *Higher Education in Scotland and the UK* (Riddell et al., 2016), a study of higher education policy across the UK. In the final chapter, Sheila Riddell concludes that free university tuition in Scotland has not produced the egalitarian, progressive outcomes claimed for it.

A critical analysis in the *New Statesman* on 15 December 2015 spells out the implications in blunt terms. As a result of prioritising universal free university tuition over targeted grants, says Tim Wigmore, the *worst* place for poor students in the UK is Scotland. Students here now leave university with an average debt of £21,000. This is more than in Wales and Northern Ireland, countries that have tuition fees. When less generous spending on bursaries by Scottish universities is taken into account (English institutions spend more than three times as much on bursaries, because of their student fee income), many disadvantaged Scottish students will graduate with larger debt burdens than equivalent students in England.

*Access in Scotland*, a report published in May 2016 by the Sutton Trust (Blackburn et al., 2016), warns that the free tuition fees policy has not improved application, acceptance or entry rates for the poorest in Scotland, as compared with countries that charge. It may even have backfired because of the need to cap the number of university places for home students in order to make the free tuition policy affordable. The failure of the Scottish university system to keep up with rising demand for places results in greater competition and the squeezing out of youngsters from deprived backgrounds. In England, where the cap on places has been removed and the system is expanding, students from less advantaged backgrounds are more likely to get a university place.

The report also finds that in Scotland the proportion of students from independent schools attending an ancient university rose from 19 per cent in 2004 to 26 per cent in 2014/15, and that the proportion of middle-class entrants in pre-1992 universities is increasing. Of the students who attended independent schools in Scotland, 71 per cent took up places at the ancient universities compared with only 29 per cent of students who attended state schools. Of the entrants to Scotland's pre-1992 universities, 67 per cent have parents with managerial and professional backgrounds.

## WIDENING ACCESS

A Commission on Widening Access chaired by Dame Ruth Silver was established in partial response to the Sutton Trust research and published its final report, *A Blueprint for Fairness*, in March 2016. In her submission to the Commission, Blackburn stressed the need to improve maintenance grants rather than increasingly relying on loans-based support for poor students. Her reasoning is clear:

> The Scottish arrangements are building up a regressive sharing of student debt in the Scottish graduate population. Those who started with least will end up owing the government most … and have to forego the most from their salaries in future, reducing their relative capacity to pay for housing, pensions, childcare and other costs. This is simply unfair It … raises the question of whether the cost of widening access is to [be met] disproportionately by deductions from the future earnings of those from poorer backgrounds. (Blackburn, 2015)

There is an assumption that devolution has caused Scotland and England to drift apart and change direction, especially in education policy, the best-known divergence being in university student fees. Yet the difference in student finance between Scotland and England does not mean, as conventional wisdom would have it, that someone from a working-class background in Scotland has a greater chance of attending university than someone in England from the same background. In reality, Scotland now has the UK's lowest number of school leavers from the poorest fifth of the population going to university: in England, the figure is 17 per cent, in Wales, 15.5 per cent whilst in Scotland it is just 9.7 per cent. Young people from the most advantaged areas are more than four times likelier to enter higher education than those from the least advantaged backgrounds (Blackburn et al., 2016).

Recent research on medical students in the UK should give further pause for thought. A study of 33,000 applications to twenty-two medical schools across the UK found that a disproportionate number of medical students come from the most affluent homes (https://www.theguardian.com/society/2016/jan/22/medical-school-students-wealthy-backgrounds). So far, so unsurprising. The sting in the tail is the differences *between* the nations of the UK. In England, 8.7 per cent of medical students were from the poorest 20 per cent of the population by postcode, against 4.3 per cent in Scotland. In Scotland, where private schooling is far more prevalent in some areas, particularly Edinburgh, 35 per cent of medical students came from fee-paying schools as against a UK average of 27 per cent. This is an uncomfortable finding for anyone who believes in Scotland's special concern for social justice, particularly in education.

Free university tuition seems to have blinded both government and the wider public to the broader picture. In Scotland most of the growth in the numbers of youngsters from poor families entering higher education has been through sub-degree courses in colleges. Working-class students traditionally use further education colleges, sometimes as a route to university via Higher National Certificate (HNC) and Higher National Diploma (HND). Since 2006, it is estimated that 90 per cent of growth in the higher education participation rate for disadvantaged students in Scotland has been via this route. Indeed 17 per cent of *all* Scottish higher education occurs in colleges, as compared with 6 per cent in England. Around 50 per cent of Higher National students go on to university, usually to post-1992 institutions (former polytechnics or colleges), often without receiving full credit for their further education work. It therefore takes them considerably longer to complete a degree (see www.hesa.ac.uk).

## FURTHER EDUCATION AND LIFELONG LEARNING

Cuts to the FE sector have undermined what was already a Cinderella service in our education system. The number of FE colleges in Scotland almost halved (from thirty-seven to twenty) between 2011/12 and 2014/15, in part as a result of college mergers. More significantly, between 2007/8 and 2014/15 the number of college *places* fell from 379,233 to 222,919. Worryingly, more than a third of FE students from the most deprived backgrounds fail to complete their courses; retention rates on longer courses have worsened and female enrolments have fallen (see www.hesa.ac.uk).

The Scottish Funding Council says the decline in numbers is a result of colleges being asked to prioritise more 'substantive courses' by the Scottish Government and to reduce the number of learners enrolled on leisure programmes and short courses. The Educational Institute of Scotland points out that the decision to prioritise full-time courses for younger learners, coupled with the change in government priorities, has a knock-on effect on part-time courses that often attract adults, carers, disabled learners and others. It has weakened the lifelong learning elements that have been a long-standing, if small, aspect of Scottish FE provision.

A major chunk of lifelong learning was once called 'second chance education' – that is, adult education designed specifically for those who did not do well at school, who may be daunted by formal education and need step-by-step commitments, or who have little time because of caring or other work commitments. Many participants in such provision are women who were not served well by school in the past. The kinds of flexible learning opportunities that are likely to suit them are now being discouraged.

This reduction of part-time college provision is taking place in a climate where local authority funding for adult and community education, including a rich and distinctive seam of community-based learning in some of Scotland's most deprived areas, has already all but dried up. Long-standing adult education providers such as the Workers Educational Association are also struggling to survive, and the higher education sector has made it clear that it, too, prefers to recruit young school leavers to full-time courses and to close down adult and continuing education departments and programmes.

Such cuts in student grants, reduced FE student places and an underfunded local adult education service are not the inevitable result of a reduced Scottish block grant from Westminster. The Scottish Government has choices. The most significant choice so far has been the decision to freeze council tax at a cost of £560 million in 2015–16 and £630 million the following year. This is a lot of money not available for FE colleges, student grants or community-based adult learning and it is a matter of political choice concerning what to prioritise.

## TAX CHOICES

An option that was not available in 2013, when maintenance grants were so drastically cut, became available in 2016–17: to use the new income tax-raising powers long sought by the SNP. The Scottish Rate of Income Tax (SRIT) is a progressive tax that hits harder as income rises because there is a tax-free personal allowance. However, the Scottish

Government has had more than a decade in power without exercising its already devolved tax-raising powers: since 1999 it has had the power to raise or cut income tax by 3p in the pound. That power has never been used. The new Scotland Bill devolves nearly full control over income tax bands and rates as well as a £2.5 billion welfare budget to Holyrood. It is the perfect moment for a wider debate about priorities.

In the lead-up to the Scottish Parliament election in May 2016 and as local councils were facing cuts of £350 million that year and £500 million the following year, First Minister Nicola Sturgeon announced a 'radical reform' of local government finance. Besides a 'more progressive council tax' (a tiny adjustment to the top bands E–H) she said that if local councils boosted economic growth and therefore income tax receipts, they would share in the benefits and have more to spend. Any such plan will take years to implement and will be too late to protect local services from the cuts to council budgets that are now in progress. The tweak in council tax bands E–H will raise just £100 million in 2017–18 when it comes into force to coincide with the end of the council tax freeze.

As for the new income tax-raising powers long sought by the SNP on a redistributive ticket, Scottish Finance Secretary Derek Mackay, setting out his budget for 2017–18 just before Christmas 2016, did nothing to change the basic rate of tax or to alter the tax bands. All he did was decline to emulate the UK Treasury's small tax cut for higher earners. This means that the 40 per cent top income tax rate will start at £43,430 in Scotland while in the rest of the UK it will start at £45,000. There could scarcely be a more modest use of Scotland's new income tax raising powers.

## THE LACK OF CHALLENGE

The question arises: Why has there been no deeper questioning of the SNP's policy record, particularly in education? Opposition is weak, not just in the Labour Party but in the wider polis. Few think tanks provide sources of criticism and new policy ideas, and the institutions that make up the warp and weft of Scottish civil society – trade unions, churches, professional associations, educational bodies, voluntary organisations and businesses – seem to lack the will to speak up. These institutions, which were once pivotal in preserving the Scottish nation within the union, now fail to hold their government to account. It is ironic that so much effort was expended on creating a devolved Scottish Parliament while there is now scant interest in what that government actually does.

Close-knit institutional connections and strong social, cultural and intellectual cohesiveness distinguished the much-vaunted eighteenth-century Scottish Enlightenment from the Enlightenment in England, which was a looser, more demotic, affair. The Scottish men of letters were involved in a collective project to improve the Scottish nation within the union and to demonstrate its worth in relation to its bigger sibling. The creatively critical and open discussion on education that might now hold government to account is notably absent in the present. Yet time and time again it has been shown that it is contestation and debate – together with a strong dose of doubt – rather than control and consensus that are the wellspring of creativity and innovation, as well as of compromise.

The debate over Scotland's future constitutional position might have been expected to foster developments in adult learning. Yet in the run-up to the independence referendum in 2014 there was a striking absence of civic adult learning opportunities. In the earliest stages some excellent community meetings with outside speakers fostered informed debate and adopted a critical stance towards both sides of the Scottish independence campaign. A few courses run by the Workers Educational Association and university adult and continuing education departments created space to deliberate on a range of views. But as the campaign bedded down, open-ended discussions virtually ceased.

Now, more than ever, in the wake of Brexit and the fragmentation of traditional political party loyalties and certainties, there is a need for informal adult education of the civic learning kind where people can debate questions of importance to them as citizens. Such opportunities for dialogue traditionally formed part of adult education programmes in universities, colleges and community settings. In the drive to credit-rate all learning such provision has been all but squeezed out.

## A BROADER CONCEPTION OF ACCESS

In September 2016 the Scottish Government confirmed its *Plan for Scotland*. In response to the aforementioned Widening Access Commission it affirms: 'We have set the Government and our universities, along with the wider education system, the challenge of ensuring that by 2030, 20 per cent of university entrants are drawn from the 20 per cent most deprived communities' (Scottish Government, 2016).

The Widening Access Commission was dominated by the question of university access and its remit was narrowly focused on school leavers' life chances, with no recognition given to second chance learners, or even to the key role that adult learning could play in the government's own strategy for widening access to higher education. Yet the wider context of adult learning provision remains critically important.

Public funding for adult learning has been slashed across the UK. In this, there are few differences between Scotland, England and Wales. Yet whilst there are strong collective voices for the adult, community and lifelong education sector in other European countries, including England and Wales, this is no longer the case in Scotland, where virtually no such lobby is apparent.

Traditionally the movement for public adult education depended on support from trade unions, co-operatives, women's institutes, voluntary organisations, community groups and churches. It required pressure 'from below' as well as support 'from above'. Any new strategy for lifelong education requires a similarly broad coalition of forces; otherwise, marketisation will squeeze out alternatives, and provision will be geared to profitability rather than social need.

With the election of a new minority SNP Government in 2016, its new brief for post-school education will encompass the appointment of a Commissioner for Widening Access, take forward other recommendations from the Widening Access Commission and pursue a review of student funding for those aged 16–24. Only one political party in Scotland, RISE (Respect, Independence, Socialism, Environmentalism), has mentioned the lower grant for mature students as a problem that needs to be addressed.

The government has also accepted the commission's recommendation to lower the entry threshold for students from deprived areas. This has to be achieved with no new money and a continuing cap on university places. The resulting displacement of candidates is unlikely to affect those from private schools but, rather, those not especially disadvantaged but 'ordinary Scots' from state schools.

In any event, such tinkering fails to address the real educational challenges facing us. A root and branch overhaul of the entire post-school/tertiary system is long overdue. In particular there has to be a radical shake-up of education for those who do not go to university.

This requires a reversal of the current overwhelming emphasis on higher education for 18–21 year olds towards a diverse system of post-school education underpinned by greater equity and less restrictive funding.

People from the adult and continuing education world have long sought radical change in post-school education, including a transformed higher education system based on the concepts and practices of continuing education and lifelong learning and where knowledge based on experience is valued as well as learning based on books (see Taylor et al., 2002).

Such a possibility and direction of change recedes ever further in Scotland, as education is more and more heavily weighted to initial and formal education on the one hand and narrow vocational skills training on the other. Historians of education in Scotland tend to write as if 'education' were synonymous with 'schooling and universities', says Tony Cooke in his history of adult education in Scotland (Cooke, 2006, p. 9).

This tendency has diverted attention away from the diverse range of popular education that once existed both inside and outside the universities here, and in which many women as well as men participated. The concept of 'popular enlightenment' had resonance in Scotland, but less so in England, observes Jonathan Rose, who points out that this rich tradition was often self-help in style and radical in motivation. 'Unsurprisingly', he comments, 'mutual improvement was Scottish in origin' (Rose, 2002, p. 59).

It is easy to forget in this so-called 'post-truth' era of politics that the development of knowledge was once a battleground in Britain, especially in the nineteenth century. Yet we may be going through a comparable period of struggle today. The progressive erosion and neglect of popular and liberal adult education in Scotland is particularly dispiriting in this context, as is the recent narrowing of horizons brought about by redefining progressive politics along a pro/anti-independence axis.

## AN ALTERNATIVE STRATEGY

The need for fundamental change in the direction of travel for post-school education is gaining support elsewhere in the UK. For example, Alison Wolf has recently proposed that at age 18 all adults should be given an individual entitlement to tertiary education, to be used as and when they see fit and, crucially, not restricted to pursuing a degree (Wolf, 2016). A similar funding model was put forward by the Scottish Parliament's Enterprise and Lifelong Learning Committee over a decade ago but was not implemented.

Much of Wolf's analysis relates to tertiary education in England, but her key observations apply equally to Scotland where, too, the only game in town is universities. All other post-secondary provision for age 19+, whether in FE or adult education, is in sharp decline. Under current conditions students are offered free tuition tied to a degree, once.

If entitlement were to a certain sum of money rather than to a degree then individuals could choose what sort of course they want to pursue and they might decide to 'bank' some money for future use. They would have good reasons to do 'sub-degree', part-time (perhaps, even, 'taster') courses, say, rather than as now, strong reasons and pressures not to. Those who choose additional education and training after they have been at work for some time or have raised a family tend to make more informed choices. As an economist, Wolf also points out that in a changing labour market it makes no sense to concentrate government expenditure almost exclusively on 18–21 year olds.

Publicly supported institutions have no incentive at present to offer anything other than degrees. If students held financial entitlements under their own control, institutions' incentives would change. There would be good reasons for them to make a diverse range of courses available, at various levels, delivered flexibly and part-time.

An individual financial entitlement system is a necessary, but not in itself, sufficient condition for a reformed tertiary education system – one that is, in the words of Alison Wolf's report 'fit for purpose' (Wolf, 2016, p. 10). After years of neglect we have created, almost by default, a denuded post-school/tertiary education sector with derisory levels of adult skills training and a paucity of adult/community education provision. Extremely low staff morale, especially in the further education sector, is the inevitable consequence.

A reversal of this trend requires addressing the whole population, embracing lifelong learning and developing technical/vocational education to a high standard supported by liberal adult education that helps to enable people to deal with problems related to both work and society. Universities, further education colleges and community-based adult education would all have a role in delivery, as, too, could study circles organised by voluntary groups, workplaces and trades unions. Such often locally based provision would be capable of responding to local needs and be accessible to students of all types, not just young full-timers.

Lower-income students are more likely to attend local, less selective, institutions such as those that are currently being starved of funds. Under the reforms proposed here – towards education and training that can happen at any time in people's adult lives – there would be a strong incentive for such institutions to offer a greater variety of courses and modes of delivery. In addition to stimulating the development of more varied provision, a shift to an entitlement model of funding would also help to reverse the downward trend in older, part-time students. Such outcomes would be strengthened if the entitlement model of funding were extended to groups as well as individuals.

In Scotland where university education (for which Scottish and non-UK European Union students pay no tuition fees) has been funded at the direct expense of further education, the effect of such a shift in direction would be especially far-reaching. This is because university education in Scotland is highly regressive in its beneficiaries, as this chapter has argued. Those with most gain the most. A shift to an entitlement model could transform this regressive system into a more progressive (more equitable) one.

The signs do not augur well for such devolved, responsive local provision in Scotland. Whilst there are some indications that the SNP minority government is beginning to be judged on its policies, its centralising trajectory continues. Thus, in a statement in the Scottish Parliament in November 2016 John Swinney announced the formation of a new Scotland-wide statutory board that will incorporate Scottish Enterprise, Highlands and Islands Enterprise, Scottish Development International, Skills Development Scotland and the Scottish Further and Higher Education Funding Council.

Such a single 'overarching board' would, he announced, 'replace individual agency boards while retaining the separate legal status of each of the bodies'. Whilst the nature and role of this super-quango was somewhat unclear, it seemed likely that it would be chaired by a Scottish Government minister and would exercise huge power and influence over large swathes of Scottish life. A further shrinkage in the influence of local, regional and independent voices was on the cards. However, the SNP intentions were thwarted when a vote by Members of the Scottish Parliament defeated the proposal on 1 March 2017 (see at https://www.holyrood. com/articles/news/scottish-government-defeated-over-scottish-funding-council-plans).

## REFERENCES

Blackburn, L. H. (2015) 'Student funding in Scottish higher education'. Paper presented to the Scottish Government's Commission on Widening Access, Moray House School of Education Centre for Research in Education Inclusion and Diversity, 2 September.

Blackburn, L. H., Kader-Satat, G., Riddell, S. and Weedon, E. (2016) *Access in Scotland*. Edinburgh: The Sutton Trust.

Collini, S. (2016) 'Who are the spongers now?' *London Review of Books*, 21 January.

Cooke, A. (2006) *From Popular Education to Lifelong Learning: A History of Adult Education in Scotland*, Leicester: NIACE.

Field, J. (2015) 'Policies for adult learning in Scotland'. In M. Milana and T. Nesbit (eds), *Global Perspectives on Adult Education and Learning*. Basingstoke: Palgrave Macmillan, pp. 15–28.

Gallacher, J. and Raffe, D. (2012) 'Higher education policy in post-devolution UK: more convergence than divergence' *Journal of Education Policy*, 27 (4), 467–90.

Riddell, S., Weedon, E. and Minty, S. (eds) (2016) *Higher Education in Scotland and the UK: Diverging or Converging Systems?* Edinburgh: Edinburgh University Press.

Rose, J. (2002) *The Intellectual Life of the British Working Class*. Yale, CT: Yale University Press.

Scottish Government (2016) *A Plan For Scotland: The Scottish Government's Programme for Scotland 2016–17*. Online at www.gov.scot/Publications/2016/09/2860

Taylor, R., Barr, J. and Steele, T. (2002) *For a Radical Higher Education: After Postmodernism*. Buckingham and Philadelphia: SRHE and Open University Press.

Wolf, A. (2016) *Remaking Tertiary Education: Can We Create a System That Is Fair and Fit For Purpose?* London: The Education Policy Institute, King's College London.

### Websites

*A Blueprint for Fairness: Final Report of the Commission on Widening Access* at https://beta.gov.scot/publications/blueprint-fairness-final-report-commission-widening-access/

*Learning Works: Widening Participation in Further Education* at https://core.ac.uk/download/pdf/9063796.pdf

*The Dearing Report* at http://www.educationengland.org.uk/documents/dearing1997/dearing1997.html

*The Learning Age: A Renaissance for a New Britain* at http://www.leeds.ac.uk/educol/documents/summary.pdf

*University Challenge: How Higher Education Can Advance Social Mobility* at https://www.gov.uk/government/uploads/system/uploads/attachment_data/file/80188/Higher-Education.pdf

*Unleashing Aspiration: The Final Report of the Panel on Fair Access to the Professions* at http://www.creativitycultureeducation.org/unleashing-aspiration-the-final-report-of-the-panel-on-fair-access-to-the-professions

# 101

# The Future of (Scottish) Education: An International Perspective

*Trevor Gale and Stephen Parker*

## INTRODUCTION TO THE FUTURE

We have been set an impossible task: to ponder the future of education in Scotland and to imagine what this might look like from the outside, looking in; that is, from an international perspective. Yet as philosopher Charles Taylor would counsel, no one knows the future, particularly in relation to the social world, and there is no sure way of predicting it (Taylor, 1985). This is because societies are open systems – they are always subject to external influence – and they are spaces of intersubjective meaning-making, including changes in how people think about themselves and about others (Taylor, 1985). Brexit, snap elections and posturing around Scottish independence are good examples of these external/internal influences at work to change relations and subjectivities, in ways we could not have imagined even a year ago. As examples of the fluidity of the 'social imaginary' (Taylor, 2004), of 'becoming' (Sotirin, 2005), they illustrate how:

> it is impossible to predict what new vocabularies of self-understanding people will adopt and because these interpretations form part of the reality that is to be explained, and because their action might be influenced by these, there is no sure way of predicting the future. (Abbey, 2000, p. 157)

What we can say about the 'functionings' (Sen, 2009) of the social world is 'what worked' (Biesta, 2007) and what did not. As Taylor explains:

> it is much easier to understand after the fact than it is to predict. Human science is largely *ex post* understanding. Or often one has *the sense of impending change*, of some big reorganization, but is powerless to make clear what it will consist in. (Taylor, 1985, p. 56, emphasis added)

It is this 'sense of impending change' or what Raymond Williams, the father of cultural studies, refers to as the 'structure of feeling' – that is, different ways of thinking, vying to emerge – which we seek to articulate in this chapter. The vocabulary to speak this future already exists if we are prepared to look beyond Scotland to what has emerged or is emerging elsewhere. Even with Taylor's caution, our confidence to use such vocabulary is based in the penchant for between-nation 'policy borrowing' (Lingard, 2010), propagated by the now global influence on education of the Organisation for Economic Co-operation and Development (OECD). What is happening elsewhere is now a useful guide to Scotland's future, particularly given the Scottish Government's invitation for OECD involvement.

In a similar vein, William Gibson – the 'noir prophet' of cyberpunk science fiction – muses that 'the future is already here – it's just not very evenly distributed'. We understand this to mean that education futures can be seen in the education presents of others. But Gibson was also suggesting that access to technological developments is mediated by wealth and location. This is certainly how Bourdieu (1990) understands the working classes in the mid-1900s and their aspirations for access to the material benefits of a secondary school education enjoyed by their upper class peers; aspirations he describes as 'false hope', with the benefits distributed long before. This too is the vocabulary we want to mobilise in relation to the future of Scottish education; to speak of economic dis/advantage and location, both social and spatial.

Drawing on this vocabulary, we make three tentative predictions:

1. With the introduction of standardised assessment and compared with students elsewhere, the academic attainment of school students in Scotland will stagnate and may even deteriorate, and the attainment gap between Scottish students from low and high socio-economic backgrounds will remain and may even widen.
2. The focus on 'what works' in schools seeking to redress this gap and on randomised control trials to determine how to identify what works will have limited success given the disregard for, or at least limited understanding of, the relevance of sociocultural contexts in educational achievement and of the limitations of cause–effect explanations of education 'interventions'.
3. The adoption of a medical model of teachers as 'clinicians' might foster greater collaboration among teachers in making judgements about their students' learning but will disconnect them from understandings of students' lived experiences, particularly the lives lived by students from disadvantaged communities, and from the broader purposes and achievements of education which characterised a previous Scottish Enlightenment.

The reference point for our predictions tends to be Australia, which is something of an experimental laboratory for much global education policy and practice, although not exclusively. We also make reference to England, Canada and the USA – other post-industrial anglophone nations attempting to navigate an increasingly uncertain economic and political future.

## IN THE FUTURE, PERFORMANCE IS EVERYTHING

In 2015, the Scottish Government (SG) announced the introduction of 'national standardised assessments' (Scottish Government, 2015) for school students in Scotland (administered at Primary 1, 4 and 7 and Secondary 3), with the catchy ambition to 'know the gap in order to close the gap' (Scottish Government, 2016a, p. 4) between the academic achievement of students from low and high socio-economic backgrounds. There is an implied expectation in this announcement that once the nature and extent of the gap is known, targeted interventions will be introduced aimed at improving educational outcomes for 'low performing' students and even that standardised assessment itself is one such intervention.

In introducing this standardisation of assessment, Scotland joins a long list of anglophone nations engaged in national testing; assessment regimes 'sharing a common logic and producing similar effects' (Lingard et al., 2016, p. 2). The similarities in logic are not lost on the Scottish Government, which has commissioned the Australian Council for Educational Research (ACER) to develop and administer standardised assessment in Scottish schools. So what kinds of effects can Scotland expect?

First, the distribution of Scottish students' academic achievement is unlikely to change very much and where there is change, we can anticipate overall student performance to decrease and the gap between students from low and high socio-economic backgrounds to remain and possibly even widen. This is certainly the experience in Australia. Introduced in 2008, the (Australian) National Assessment Program – Literacy and Numeracy (NAPLAN) is an annual census of the academic attainment of primary and middle years students (years 3, 5, 7 and 9). The tests concentrate on five main areas: reading, writing, spelling, grammar and punctuation, and numeracy. Through NAPLAN, the government seeks to 'drive increased competition between schools, as a means of achieving improvements in school quality and hence, gains in education outcomes' (Australian Productivity Commission, 2016, p. 30). Yet there has not been anything like this return on investment: 'Australia's performance on national and international student assessments has stalled or, in some cases, declined' (Australian Productivity Commission, 2016, p. 30). Recent Programme for International Student Assessment (PISA) results also show that the gap between high and low performing students in Australia has widened, now well above the OECD average (OECD, 2016). These results are not peculiar to Australia but are also evident in several other nations with national standardised assessment. National mandatory tests are beginning to lose their shine in post-industrial nations. For example, in England, PISA results have plateaued in recent years (Wyse and Torrance, 2009) and in the USA there is now an 'increased likelihood that students from disadvantaged contexts are less likely to graduate from high school than they were before the tests became mandatory' (Thompson and Harbaugh, 2013, p. 301).

Second, we can expect to see the publication in Scotland of school test results and comparisons made between Scottish schools. In Australia, each school's NAPLAN scores are published by the government on its https://myschool.edu.au website – freedom of information requests would ensure their public availability anyway. While My School does not produce league tables, it is possible to generate these from the public data and Australian media outlets have collated information from the website to produce and publish comparisons and rankings. This has increased both media and public interest, opening up possibilities for a range of effects beyond the use of test data for diagnostic purposes (Lingard et al., 2016).

For example, 'parents are encouraged to exercise choice in relation to their child's school enrolment based on NAPLAN data, thereby putatively contributing to school improvement through pursuing exit strategies where school performance is perceived to be poor' (Lingard et al., 2016, p. 5). The effect has been a 'residualisation' of government schooling with the flight of the middle classes to more affluent independent or government schools (Mills, 2015) as parents seek out classrooms for their children that produce higher NAPLAN scores. As a result, the student population of Australian schools is now far more homogenous, with 'like' students (with similar social, cultural, economic circumstances) tending to be enrolled in similar schools. Yet there has been a somewhat unexpected and negative flow-on effect for academic attainment. Comparative research between Australia and Canada – two nations of similar histories, populations and education systems, with the exception that student populations in Canadian schools are far more heterogeneous – has shown that homogenisation in Australian schools has led to greater disparities in academic attainment (Perry and

McConney, 2010); by comparison, in Australia there are fewer students at the upper ends of performance on PISA and the spread of student performance is greater.

Third, we can expect that Scotland will become a much more performative environment for students, teachers and schools. Student performance on standardised assessment will become a proxy for teacher effectiveness and for student engagement with Scotland's Curriculum for Excellence. This is because standardised assessment is premised on and indeed creates 'an imagined and clear line of sight from what teachers do and what students learn' (Gale, 2017). In nations where it has been introduced, student performance on standardised tests has become the measure for judging teacher effectiveness and the basis for new regimes of teacher accountability and school governance (Lingard and Sellar, 2013). In Australia, the imperative to improve student performance on standardised assessment is 'reshaping professional practices and relationships, and creating new understandings about what constitutes good literacy teaching and what counts as good leadership' (Kerkham and Comber, 2016, p. 86). Not all of this reshaping is beneficial for students' education. In the USA:

> a pattern seems to have emerged that suggests that high-stakes testing has little or no relationship to reading achievement, and a weak to moderate relationship to math, especially in fourth grade but only for certain student groups. ... This particular pattern of results (only affecting fourth grade math) raises serious questions about whether high-stakes testing increases learning or merely more vigorous test preparation practices (i.e., teaching to the test). (Nichols et al., 2012, p. 3)

As Comber cautions, 'mandated literacy assessments need scrutiny, in terms of both what they produce *and* what they remove' (Comber, 2012, p. 133, emphasis original) from the purposes of education. While assessment is meant to provide a check for teachers on what their students know and can do (summative assessment) and how they are progressing towards what they need to know and do (formative assessment), under national regimes assessment defines the sum of what is to be known (the lived curriculum) and prescribes approaches to knowledge formation (the lived pedagogy). Standardised assessment does not simply *monitor* student's academic achievement. It more fundamentally *determines* curricula and pedagogy.

In this performative environment, the stakes are high for students, teachers and schools. They are also high for governments. A sense of 'PISA shock' (Ertl, 2006) – 'the feeling among some OECD countries that they are falling behind the rest of the world in student achievement' (Gale and Parker, 2017, p. 523) – has fuelled a 'narrative of decline' (Sellar and Lingard, 2013, p. 478) of educational standards, and the fear of being left behind by other nations. Underpinning the drive for *national* standardised testing, then, are nations' relative performances on *international* testing such as PISA (Sellar and Lingard, 2013). The Scottish Government has confidently, almost defiantly, stated that its performance as a government will be judged at the next election (anticipated to be in May 2020) on the basis of how well it has performed in education. In relation to standardised assessment, it has also declared that:

> We are not introducing a national testing regime. The national standardised assessments are not 'high stakes tests'. The results will not determine any key future outcomes for students (such as which school they go to, or whether they can progress to the next level). There will be no pass or fail. (Scottish Government, 2016b, p. 1)

This alternative view of Scotland's education future might well come to pass but it is difficult to believe when glimpses of the future from around the world suggest otherwise. Moreover, it is hard to imagine that a government would introduce a test and then take no actions based on the results (see also Chapter 71).

## IN THE FUTURE, ALL THAT MATTERS IS WHAT WORKS

With student performance in mind, and in an attempt 'to avoid the disadvantages often associated with rigid systems of testing' (Scottish Government, 2015, p. 1), the Scottish Government (2017) has recently released its *Research Strategy for Scottish Education* (here-after, the *Research Strategy* or the *Strategy*). Its purpose is to develop 'the research infra-structure, knowledge base of "what works" and the capacity of the system to use evidence' (Scottish Government, 2017, p. 3) to improve the academic attainment of low performing students and thus close the gap with their higher performing peers. 'What works' is at the heart of the strategy: to identify whatever it takes to improve students' performance, measured on standardised tests.

It is not hard to see where this is going, given the mirroring of language mobilised in government policy and practice in England, including the involvement of the Education Endowment Foundation and of teachers as researchers, generating the evidence for 'inter-ventions that serve to reduce the gap' (Scottish Government, 2017, p. 10). Given this antecedent, we can expect to see the introduction in Scotland of randomised control trials (RCTs) of 'interventions' seen to have worked in other jurisdictions and tested with the involvement of Scottish teachers in implementing interventions and making evidence-based judgements on their local applicability.

RCTs have become the new 'gold standard' in education research (St. Pierre, 2006; Holmes et al., 2006), championed by English physician and medicine academic Ben Goldacre and increasingly by others. In his paper *Building Evidence into Education*, commis-sioned by the UK Department for Education, Goldacre declares an impending 'revolution in the production and use of evidence' (Goldacre, 2013), if only education was to take up the experimental methods of medicine, specifically RCTs. According to Goldacre, RCTs provide a better way of producing evidence of what works in redressing low student per-formance. And 'by collecting better evidence of what works best, and establishing a culture where this evidence is used as a matter of routine, we can improve outcomes for children, and increase professional independence' (ibid., p. 7). Unfortunately, this independence does not extend to determinations on ontological questions about the nature of education and of the social world more generally (Biesta, 2007; Gale, 2017).

As the new standard for education research, RCTs have also informed the creation of the Education Endowment Foundation (EEF), established in 2011 with funds from the UK's Department for Education and administered by the Sutton Trust. The EEF is explicitly named as a future partner in the Scottish Government's *Research Strategy* and will provide Scotland with a repository of Scottish-appropriate interventions for teachers to implement. EEF has amassed its bank of 'evidence-based' practice by funding 'robust trials of high-potential programmes and approaches which have yet to be tested' (https://educationen-dowmentfoundation.org.uk/) and which are aimed at raising the academic attainment of students particularly from disadvantaged backgrounds. RCTs are its preferred method for testing interventions, having funded RCT evaluations of 'Achievement for All', 'Growth Mindsets', 'Research Use in Schools' and so on.

What we can expect to see in Scotland, then, are RCTs in the order of the recent *Closing the Gap: Test and Learn* (CtG) project (Childs and Menter, 2017), commissioned by the UK's National College of Teaching and Leadership (NCTL). According to its report authors, the CtG project was 'the first programme in the world to trial multiple interventions simultaneously using a wholly collaborative approach across a large number of schools' (Churches et al., 2017, p. 34), 'the first nationwide randomised controlled trial in education' (Childs et al., 2017, p. 19) and 'the first large scale quasi-experimental study that aimed to be able to relate particular pedagogical innovations to student outcomes on a large scale' (Menter and Thompson, 2017, p. 69). The project report (Churches, 2016) and a recently published edited book (Childs and Menter, 2017) provide considerable detail about the CtG project RCTs, and a glimpse into Scotland's future. In the detail, it is worth noting that 'the majority of the interventions showed no effect greater than existing good practice' (Churches et al., 2017, p. 51). RCTs in Australia have reported more success (Gore, 2016), although their uptake as a method for education research is not as widespread and, as yet, their influence is not as great.

Irrespective of the success or otherwise of RCTs, there are conceptual and ideological flaws of varying severity in the Scottish Government's *Research Strategy*, which will have a bearing on navigating towards a brave new future for Scottish education. First, identifying 'what works' is not the same as identifying what will work – 'we cannot and should not expect that situations will stay the same over time, and we should definitely not expect this in the social realm' (Biesta, 2007, pp. 15–16) – which defeats the purpose somewhat of building a bank of interventions for future use; that is, evidence on interventions is time and context bound. There is acknowledgement of time-sensitivity in the *Strategy*, although a 'comprehensive evidence base' (Scottish Government, 2017, p. 9) still remains the goal. Second, what works in one context might not work in another. Again, the *Strategy* acknowledges this general point but only in so far as it highlights the need for 'translating international lessons into the Scottish context' (ibid., p. 4). That is, the imagination is of a homogenous student population in Scotland and it likens context to a language to be translated devoid of culture. Third, to the extent that differences are acknowledged, 'the impact of social background on performance is [to be] fully taken into account and ameliorated' (ibid., p. 13) by teachers. This is RCT speak for fancy statistical footwork to 'reduce between-participant variation' (Churches et al., 2017, p. 41). It is also a deficit account of communities: that amelioration (reduction of negative influence) is required. The perceived need for 'interventions' itself indicates an external imposition on the varying purposes of education within communities; the narrowness of these external purposes (to improve scores on standardised tests) is enough to call them into question. And fourth, RCTs on which the validity of these interventions depend are predicated on a social world that has the same characteristics as the physical world, specifically that the social world can be explained solely in terms of casual relations. But it cannot. RCTs belong to a different ontological realm (Gale, 2017).

In a 'what works' rationale, none of this matters. All that matters is what is seen to work. Scotland's past of 'progressive Scottish Enlightenment and educational heritage … [which] has been central to the construction of Scottishness' (Lingard, 2008, pp. 969, 971), is unlikely to be its future.

## IN THE FUTURE, JUDGEMENTS WILL BE CLINICAL

Going forward, teachers in Scotland will need to suspend judgement on these issues with the government's *Research Strategy* and develop a new set of *clinical* judgements (also see

Goldacre, 2013). Specifically, the *Strategy* proposes training to 'support practitioners to be able to act on lessons derived from research ... [and] to understand the lessons from data that they have gathered themselves' (Scottish Government, 2017, p. 13). In this it complements the aspirations of Scotland's most recent review of teacher education (Donaldson, 2011) for teaching to become 'a research-informed profession' (p. 31) and for the creation of 'hub teaching schools as a focus for research, learning and teaching' (p. 91) – 'a teaching hospital model' (p. 112).

This is not affirmation of or support for long traditions in education of promoting *critical* judgement (e.g. Tripp, 1993): of teachers as (action) researchers – advocated by Carr and Kemmis (1986) and many others – who are able to generate and interpret a full range of data to inform their teaching practice; or of the many teacher education and professional development programmes aimed at the preparation of *deliberative* professionals (Gale and Molla, 2017) able to make dialectic thought–action judgements. In fact, in a clinical model there is ignorance or denial that these even exist or at best a claim that they do not contribute (much) to teacher judgements, confined as they apparently are to 'the mechanics of teaching and unsubstantiated opinions' (McLean Davies et al., 2013, p. 101). This dismissive attitude seems to be common among 'what works' proponents who label education evidence that does not support their views as non-existent or 'false', after the 'fake news' phenomenon. Rather than being informed by 'bad' research, it is more likely that teachers' current professional judgements are not those seen to be required in the future – certainly not judgements about 'epistemological equity' (Dei, 2008), 'funds of knowledge' (Moll et al., 1992) and 'agency freedom' (Sen, 2009) in education (Gale et al., 2017) and definitely not judgements that call into question standardised assessment or test performance as the primary purpose of education. The arena of research-informed teacher professional judgement has been invaded and claimed as *terra nullius*, as if theory–research–practice relations in teaching had never been thought before and did not exist:

> the adaptation of a medical discourse to the preparation of teachers offers a new paradigm for teacher preparation learning which has at its centre the 'translation' and application of theory and research in the sites of practice. (McLean Davies et al., 2015, p. 515)

In the presumed absence of models of teaching informed by an education discipline and of teachers making research-informed judgements, the future for teachers and their judgements in Scotland looks decidedly medical, specifically clinical, the key characteristics of which are: *collaboration* (in so far as this requires judgements by groups of teachers, but not by or with students, parents or communities), *dispassion* (an objectification of students, and of parents and communities, through their reduction to statistical measures of performance) and *comparison* (in relation to other – sometimes 'like' – population groups but also pre- and post-intervention). Executed in this way, judgements are to be made on the evidence, which is typically derived from medical research methods, specifically RCTs, and which – as noted above – have become the new gold standard in education research. In the same way, we can expect to see the new gold-standard teacher in Scotland to be a clinician. This has already been foregrounded in *Teaching Scotland's Future* (Donaldson, 2011), which made explicit and favourable reference to the review of the preparation of *Tomorrow's Doctors*, highlighting that:

> It is not enough for a clinician [read 'teacher'] to act as a practitioner in their own discipline. They must act as partners to their colleagues, accepting *shared accountability* for the service provided to patients [read 'students']. They are also expected to offer leadership, and *to work with others to*

change systems when it is necessary for the benefit of patients. (General Medical Council, 2009, p. 4 in Donaldson, 2011, p. 42, emphasis added)

A clinical model of teacher education has already experienced some, albeit limited, traction in Scotland, with its introduction at the University of Glasgow in 2011, although its architects (Conroy et al., 2013) are at pains to emphasise new forms of theory–practice relations and partnerships as principles that characterise the Glasgow version of the clinical model. They caution that:

> the use of the term 'clinical' does not imply uncritical acceptance of the applicability of the 'medical model' to the professional education of teachers. We do not aim to supplant professional judgement with lessons extracted from scientific evidence of 'what works' conveyed by clinical educators in school settings. (Conroy et al., 2013, p. 564)

And yet this is exactly what their Australian collaborators intend (see McLean Davies et al., 2013) and what we are also likely to see in Scotland. As Abbey (2000) notes (see above), new vocabularies contribute to new self-understandings; they contribute to the formation of new realities and they influence actions. For example, the introduction in 2008 of a medical discourse to the preparation of teachers at the University of Melbourne, Australia, has produced a Master of Learning Intervention that 'sees teaching as a clinical-practice profession such as is found in many allied health professions' (McLean Davies et al., 2013, p. 93). From this starting position the programme aims to produce teachers 'who are interventionist practitioners', by which they mean teachers who 'manipulate the learning environment' and implement 'appropriate' interventions (i.e. pedagogies evidenced to have been successful elsewhere) and then 'evaluate their impact' on individual students (i.e. looking for 'a positive effect on student learning outcomes'), basing their judgement 'on "data" drawn from a range of "sources"' (McLean Davies et al., 2013, pp. 93–101). Interventionist teachers and student teachers 'work with others to assess, plan, and evaluate impact' (McLean Davies et al., 2013, p. 104), a collaborative process described elsewhere as 'quality teaching rounds' similar to the 'instructional rounds' experienced by doctors and interns 'doing the rounds' in hospital wards (Gore et al., 2015).

There are a number of variations to this clinical model of teaching evident in teacher education around the globe, particularly in anglophone nations (for an overview, see Burn and Mutton, 2013). What they appear to have in common 'is widespread acceptance that teacher quality is the major *in-school* influence on student achievement' (McLean Davies et al., 2013, p. 93, emphasis added) – reluctant recognition that out-of-school influences are far greater than teachers on students' academic achievements (cf. Hattie, 2009). Elsewhere (Gale and Parker, 2017) we have argued that this 'acceptance' is misplaced, on at least two fronts. First, the influence of homes, families and communities does not stop at the school gate or when students enter classrooms. We are not talking here just about students' different social and economic circumstances – variables to be controlled by interventionist teachers – but more significantly about classrooms, schools and education systems as sociocultural and political spaces of position and stance, of manoeuvre and struggle, which differently configure 'the logic of practice' (Bourdieu, 1990). Second, social interactions, including classroom interactions, are never entirely unilateral (Berliner, 2014) – students 'speak back' to teachers and they also interact with their peers – such that one can never fully predict the effects of teacher 'interventions' from one implementation to the next.

Teacher judgement needs to be exercised at the point of implementation not just at the point of evaluating intervention impact. If clinical judgements are to be the future for teachers in Scotland, as these glimpses of impending change suggest that they are, then the effect will be partial and uneven as clinical judgements are themselves partial and uneven.

## CONCLUSION

Of course, none of our predictions may come to pass. The future may have eluded us. Our best estimate of what the future holds for education in Scotland remains based on what has and has not happened elsewhere and on what might logically progress from Scotland's current policy settings. We are also aware that our predictions of the future have been partial in other ways, limited by space and sector.

For example, given more space we would have said more about the likely effects of the decision of the recent Commission on Widening Access (2016) in Scottish universities. As similar reviews of higher education in other nations have done before it, the Commission recommended that by the year 2030 'students from the 20% most deprived backgrounds should represent 20% of entrants to higher education' (CoWA, 2016, p. 13). Significantly, Scottish higher education is a closed system in which the number of university places are regulated and controlled by government. The *widening* of access (through participation targets) to include more people from deprived backgrounds without an *expansion* of the system overall will logically squeeze out other social groups. At first glance, one might think that this will affect lower middle class students with lower entry qualifications who might then seek entry to further education colleges or similar, but it just might be that students from higher socio-economic backgrounds will vacate Scotland's higher education system for universities elsewhere. Such students are typically more geographically mobile and are more willing and able to move to institutions abroad to maintain or enhance their social advantage (Marginson, 2006; Findlay and King, 2010; Sellar and Gale, 2011), which they may perceive to be threatened by an influx of differently positioned students. In a global higher education field, national boundaries are less important to those with the means of mobility.

We have also said nothing about the potential of Teach First to enter Scotland and diminish the commitment to teaching as a profession, rendering it an intermediary step towards another goal as it has done elsewhere in the world (Parker and Gale, 2016). We have said nothing of nursery and early childhood educators achieving a similar status as teachers, as is the ambition in Australia (Cutter-Mackenzie et al., 2014) and would seem to be the direction of travel in Scotland. And we have not aired our suspicions that further education colleges will make greater claims as destinations of distinction, as they have in Australia (Webb et al., 2017). There has already been movement in this regard with the introduction of the Higher Education and Research Bill, which seeks to make it easier for further education colleges to attain degree-awarding status (Fielden and Middlehurst, 2017), a logical next step in the evolution of the University of the Highlands and Islands. In Australia, degree-awarding technical and further education colleges (TAFEs) have become the choice for school leavers from high socio-economic backgrounds with lower university admission qualifications, muscling out their lower status peers (Gale et al., 2015). It would not be too much of a stretch to imagine that this too might happen in Scotland.

Crucially, what we have predicted is an education future for Scotland that is increasingly subjected to a medical discourse and of low performing students increasingly pathologised.

We see this future as reductive and limiting for some, uneven in its sociocultural distribution, and which seems counter to the ethos of a Scottish Enlightenment. We desperately hope that we have got it wrong. And yet, as Chris Patten (Chancellor, University of Oxford) has said, commenting on the developing terms of Britain's messy divorce (i.e. Brexit): 'The cliff beckons; the lemmings are lining up' (https://www.project-syndicate.org/commentary/britain-messy-brexit-divorce-by-chris-patten-2017-03).

## REFERENCES

Abbey, R. (2000) *Charles Taylor*. Teddington, UK: Acumen Publishing.

Amrein, A. L. and Berliner, D. C. (2002) 'High-stakes testing, uncertainty, and student learning', *Education Policy Analysis Archives*, 10 (18), 1–74.

Australian Government (2009) *Transforming Australia's Higher Education System*. Canberra: DEEWR.

Australian Productivity Commission (2016) *Report on Government Services 2016*. Online at https://www.pc.gov.au/research/ongoing/report-on-government-services/2016

Berliner, D. C. (2014) 'Exogenous variables and value-added assessments: a fatal flaw', *Teachers College Record*, 116 (1), 1–31.

Biesta, G. (2007) 'Why 'what works' won't work: evidence-based practice and the democratic deficit in educational research', *Educational Theory*, 57 (1), 1–22.

Bourdieu, P. (1990) *The Logic of Practice*. Trans. R. Nice. Stanford. CA: Stanford University Press.

Burn, K. and Mutton, T. (2013) *Review of 'Research-informed Clinical Practice' in Initial Teacher Education. Research and Teacher Education: The BERA-RSA Inquiry*. Online at https://www.bera.ac.uk/wp-content/uploads/2014/02/BERA-Paper-4-Research-informed-clinical-practice.pdf?noredirect=1

Carr, W. and Kemmis, S. (1986) *Becoming Critical: Education, Knowledge and Action Research*. Geelong: Deakin University Press.

Childs, A. and Menter, I. (eds) (2017) *Mobilising Teacher Researchers: Challenging Educational Inequality*. London: Routledge.

Childs, A., Firth, R. and Menter, I. (2017) 'Who, how and why? Motives and agendas for key stakeholders in Closing the Gap', in A. Childs and I. Menter (eds), *Mobilising Teacher Researchers: Challenging Educational Inequality*. London: Routledge, pp. 34–56.

Churches, R. (2016) *Closing the Gap: Test and Learn: Research Report*. London: Department for Education/National College for Teaching and Leadership. Online at https://www.gov.uk/government/uploads/system/uploads/attachment_data/file/495580/closing_the_gap_test_and_learn_full_report.pdf

Churches, R., Hall, R. and Brookes, J. (2017) '*Closing the Gap – Test and Learn*: an unprecedented national educational research project', in A. Childs and I. Menter (eds), *Mobilising Teacher Researchers: Challenging Educational Inequality*. London: Routledge.

Comber, B. (2012) 'Mandated literacy assessment and the reorganisation of teachers' work: federal policy, local effects', *Critical Studies in Education*, 53 (2), 119–36.

Commission on Widening Access (CoWA) (2016) *A Blueprint for Fairness: The Final Report Of the Commission on Widening Access*. Edinburgh: Scottish Government.

Conroy, J., Hulme, M. and Menter, I. (2013) 'Developing a "clinical" model for teacher Education', *Journal of Education for Teaching*, 39 (5), 557–73.

Cutter-Mackenzie, A., Edwards, S., Moore, D. and Boyd, W. (2014) *Young Children's Play and Environmental Education in Early Childhood Education*. Heidelberg: Springer.

Dei, G. J. S. (2008) 'Indigenous knowledge studies and the next generation: pedagogical possibilities for anti-colonial education', *Australian Journal of Indigenous Education*, 37(Supplementary), 5–13.

Donaldson, G. (2011) *Teaching Scotland's Future: Report of a Review of Teacher Education in Scotland*. Edinburgh: Scottish Government.

Ertl, H. (2006) 'Educational standards and the changing discourse on education: the reception and consequences of the PISA study in Germany', *Oxford Review of Education*, 32 (5), 619–34.

Fielden, J. and Middlehurst, R. (2017) *Alternative Providers of Higher Education: Issues for Policymakers*. Oxford: Higher Education Policy Institute.

Findlay, A. M., King, R., with, Geddes, A., Smith, F., Stam, A., Dunne, M., Skeldon, R. and Ahrens, J. (2010) 'Motivations and experiences of UK students studying abroad (Research Paper; No. 8). Dundee: Department for Business Innovation and Skills. Online at http://discovery. dundee.ac.uk/portal/files/1468641/BIS_RP_008.pdf

Gale, T. (2011) 'Expansion and equity in Australian higher education: three propositions for new relations', *Discourse: Studies in the Cultural Politics of Education*, 32 (5), 669–85.

Gale, T. (2017) 'What's not to like about RCTs in education?' in A. Childs and I. Menter (eds), *Mobilising Teacher Researchers: Challenging Educational Inequality*. London: Routledge, pp. 207–23.

Gale, T. and Molla, T. (2017) 'Deliberations on the deliberative professional: thought-action, provocations', in J. Lynch, J. Rowlands, T. Gale and A. Skourdoumbis (eds), *Practice Theory and Education: Diffractive Readings in Professional Practice*. London: Routledge, pp. 247–62.

Gale, T. and Parker, S. (2017) 'The prevailing logic of teacher education: privileging the practical in Australia, England and Scotland', in M. Peters, B. Cowie and I. Menter (eds), *A Companion to Research in Teacher Education*. Dordrecht: Springer, pp. 521–35.

Gale, T. and Tranter, D. (2011) 'Social justice in Australian higher education policy: an historical and conceptual account of student participation', *Critical Studies in Education*, 52 (1), 29–46.

Gale, T., Molla, T. and Parker, S. (2017) 'The illusion of meritocracy and the audacity of elitism: expanding the evaluative space in education', in S. Parker, K. Gulson and T. Gale (eds), *Policy and Inequality in Education*. Singapore: Springer Singapore, pp. 7–21.

Gale, T., Parker, S., Molla, T. and Findlay, K., with Sealey, T. (2015) 'Student preferences for bachelor degrees at TAFE: the socio-spatial influence of schools'. Report to the National Centre for Student Equity in Higher Education. Centre for Research in Education Futures and Innovation (CREFI), Deakin University, Melbourne, Australia.

Goldacre, B. (2013) *Building Evidence into Education*. Online at http://media.education.gov.uk/ assets/files/pdf/b/ben%20goldacre%20paper.pdf

Gore, J. (2016) 'Reform and the reconceptualisation of teacher education in Australia', in R. Brandenburg, S. McDonough, J. Burke and S. White (eds), *Teacher Education: Innovation, Intervention and Impact*. Singapore: Springer, pp. 15–34.

Gore, J., Smith, M., Bowe, J., Ellis, H., Lloyd, A. and Lubans, D. (2015) 'Quality teaching rounds as a professional development intervention for enhancing the quality of teaching: rationale and study protocol for a cluster randomised controlled trial', *International Journal of Educational Research*, 74, 82–95.

Hattie, J. (2009) *Visible Learning: A Synthesis of over 800 Meta-analyses Relating to Achievement*. London: Routledge.

Holmes, D., Murray, S. J., Perron, A. and Rail, G. (2006) 'Deconstructing the evidence-based discourse in health sciences: truth, power and fascism', *International Journal of Evidence-Based Healthcare*, 4 (3), 180–6.

Kerkham, L. and Comber, B. (2016) 'Literacy leadership and accountability practices: holding onto ethics in ways that count', in B. Lingard, G. Thompson and S. Sellar (eds), *National Testing in Schools: An Australian Assessment*. Abingdon and New York: Routledge, pp. 86–97.

Lingard, R. (2008) 'Scottish education: reflections from an international perspective', In T. G. K. Bryce and W. H. Humes (eds), *Scottish Education, Third Edition: Beyond Devolution*. Edinburgh: Edinburgh University Press.

Lingard, B. (2010) 'Policy borrowing, policy learning: testing times in Australian Schooling', *Critical Studies in Education*, 51 (2), 129–47.

Lingard, B. and Sellar, S. (2013) '"Catalyst data": perverse systemic effects of audit and accountability in Australian schooling', *Journal of Education Policy*, 28 (5), 634—56.

Lingard, B., Thompson, G. and Sellar, S. (2016) 'National testing from an Australian Perspective', in B. Lingard, G. Thompson and S. Sellar (eds), *National Testing in Schools: An Australian Assessment*, Abingdon and New York: Routledge, pp. 1–17.

McLean Davies, L., Anderson, M., Deans, J., Dinham, S., Griffin, P., Kameniar, B., Page, J., Reid, C., Rickards, F., Tayler, C. and Tyler, D. (2013) 'Masterly preparation: embedding clinical practice in a graduate pre-service teacher education programme', *Journal of Education for Teaching*, 39 (1), 93–106.

McLean Davies, L., Dickson, B., Rickards, F., Dinham, S., Conroy, J. and Davis, R. (2015) 'Teaching as a clinical profession: translational practices in initial teacher education – an international perspective', *Journal of Education for Teaching*, 41 (5), 514–28.

Marginson, S. (2006) 'Dynamics of national and global competition in higher Education', *Higher Education*, 52 (1), 1–39.

Menter, I. and Thompson, I. (2017) 'Closing the evidence gap? The challenges of the research design of the *Closing the Gap: Test and Learn* project', in A. Childs and I. Menter (eds), *Mobilising Teacher Researchers: Challenging Educational Inequality*. London: Routledge, pp. 57–72.

Mills, C. (2015) 'Implications of the MySchool website for disadvantaged communities: A Bourdieuian analysis', *Educational Philosophy and Theory*, 47 (20), 146–58.

Moll, L. C., Amanti, C., Neff, D. and Gonzalez, N. (1992) 'Funds of knowledge for teaching: using a qualitative approach to connect homes and classrooms', *Theory Into Practice*, 31 (2), 132–41.

Nichols, S., Glass, G. and Berliner, D. C. (2012) 'High-stakes testing and student achievement: updated analyses with NAEP data', *Education Policy Analysis Archives*, 20 (20), 1–35.

OECD (2016) *PISA 2015: Results in Focus*. Paris: OECD. Online at https://www.oecd.org/pisa/pisa-2015-results-in-focus.pdf

Parker, S. and Gale, T. (2016) 'Teach first, ask questions later: A summary of research on TF's alternative vision of teaching and teachers'. Briefing paper prepared for the Scottish Teacher Education Committee (STEC). Online at https://www.researchgate.net/publication/320705928_Teach_First_Ask_Questions_Later_A_summary_of_research_on_TF%27s_alternative_vision_of_teaching_and_teachers

Perry, L. and McConney, A. (2010) 'Does the SES of the school matter? An examination of socioeconomic status and student achievement using PISA 2003. *Teachers College Record*, 112 (4), 1137–62.

Scottish Government (2015) *Creating a Smarter Scotland: A Draft National Improvement Framework for Scottish Education*. Edinburgh: Scottish Government. Online at www.gov.scot/Resource/0048/00484452.pdf

Scottish Government (2016a) *Delivering Excellence and Equity in Scottish Education: A Delivery Plan for Scotland*. Edinburgh: Scottish Government.

Scottish Government (2016b) *Assessing Children's Progress: Questions and Answers*. Online at www.gov.scot/Resource/0051/00510563.pdf

Scottish Government (2017) *A Research Strategy for Scottish Education*. Edinburgh: Scottish Government.

Sellar, S. and Gale, T. (2011) 'Mobility, aspiration, voice: a new structure of feeling for student equity in higher education, *Critical Studies in Education*, 52 (2), 115–34.

Sellar, S. and Lingard, B. (2013) 'Looking East: Shanghai, PISA 2009 and the reconstitution of reference societies in the global education policy field', *Comparative Education*, 49 (4), 464–85.

Sen, A. (2009) *The Idea of Justice*. Cambridge, MA: Belknap Press.

Sotirin, P. (2005) 'Becoming-woman', in C. J. Stivale (ed.), *Gilles Deleuze: Key Concepts*. Quebec: McGill–Queen's University Press, pp. 98–109.

St. Pierre, E. A. (2006) 'Scientifically based research in education: epistemology and ethics', *Adult Education Quarterly*, 56 (4), 239–66.

Taylor, C. (1985) *Philosophy and the Human Sciences: Philosophical Papers 2*. Cambridge: Cambridge University Press.

Taylor, C. (2004) *Modern Social Imaginaries*. Durham, NC: Duke University Press.

Thompson, G. and Harbaugh, A. G. (2013) 'A preliminary analysis of teacher perceptions of the effects of NAPLAN on pedagogy and curriculum', *The Australian Educational Researcher*, 40 (3), 299–314.

Tripp, D. (1993) *Critical Incidents in Teaching: Developing Professional Judgement*. London: Routledge.

Webb, S., Bathmaker, A., Gale, T., Hodge, S., Parker, S. and Rawolle, S. (2017) 'Higher vocational education and social mobility: educational participation in Australia and England', *Journal of Vocational Education and Training*, 69 (1), 147–67.

Wyse, D. and Torrance, H. (2009) 'The development and consequences of national curriculum assessment for primary education in England', *Educational Research*, 51 (2), 213–28.

# 102

# The Funding of Scottish Education

*David Bell*

## INTRODUCTION

How is the amount of money spent on education in Scotland decided and by whom? These are vitally important questions for anyone seeking to understand the structure and performance of the Scottish educational system. The amount spent determines the quantity and quality of resources that can be deployed to impart learning and skills across the population: the *by whom* question identifies how officials at different levels of government control education spending and use this to make education providers comply with their policy priorities.

Thus, the purpose of this chapter is to explain how spending decisions are made at different levels of government and how these affect the resources provided to support education. One might (naïvely) assume that educational policies reflect the wishes of the electorate. The reality is much more complicated. Since governments are typically elected on a manifesto in which education policy plays a significant, but not dominant, role, references to education policy are probably those that candidates believe to be least damaging to their electoral prospects. These may lack strategic vision and have only a passing acquaintance with evidence on the success or failure of past policies. Nevertheless, once elected, if education providers are dependent on public funding, they may have little option but to comply with these manifesto commitments of the elected government. He who pays the piper calls the tune.

We begin by painting the big picture – how much we spend on education and how it is divided between different levels – preschool, school and higher and further education. To put these numbers in perspective, we draw comparisons with other parts of the UK and indeed other parts of the developed world. The Organisation for Economic Co-operation and Development (OECD) devotes much resource to the collection of a wide range of data on education and to make these available in a way that facilitates cross-country comparisons. These are the most reliable comparative data on education systems across the world, although there are differences in the organisation of education systems that may be concealed within the numbers.

Next, we consider how money is spent within Scotland and how education has fared within the Scottish budget over recent years. This has been a difficult time for the economy and economic policy has been characterised by *austerity* budgets – constraints on public spending that are intended to reduce the UK's fiscal deficit, which stood at an unsustainable

9.9 per cent of gross domestic product (GDP) in 2009–10. There is an acrimonious debate about how far this deficit should be reduced – but that argument is for another place.

Then we turn the spotlight on teachers' pay and conditions, which are normally the largest element in the educational budget. Attracting and retaining high-quality teaching staff is essential for a successful education system. In most countries, the majority of teachers are public sector workers and their pay and conditions are heavily influenced by budget decisions made by central and/or local government. Scotland is no exception: teachers' pay is a recurrent bone of contention between the Scottish Government and teachers' representatives.

Finally, having concentrated on the financial *inputs* to Scotland's education system, we examine some aspects of the *outputs* from the system. Measurement of the outputs of the Scottish education system has always been contentious. For example, there has always been strong resistance to publishing school league tables in Scotland, unlike England. And Scotland does not have a good track record in establishing evidence on how varying the inputs to the education system affects the outputs it produces. We touch on some of these issues in the final sections of the chapter.

## THE BIG PICTURE

All developed countries allocate resources to education. Although there are competing priorities for government support such as defence and health, education is such a fundamental building block for social and economic progress that it invariably receives resources from government to support learning and skills development. However, the extent of this support varies widely by country. The latest OECD data show the UK to be one of the highest spenders on education in the developed world (see bottom row of Table 102.1). Whereas the UK allocates around 6.6 per cent of its annual income (GDP) to education, at the other end of the spectrum Italy only devotes 4 per cent. The average education spend for OECD countries is 5.2 per cent of GDP, well below countries like Denmark, New Zealand, Korea, the United States and the UK. However, it is clear that there is no simple relationship between educational spending and economic success. Germany and Ireland have been amongst the most successful economies since the financial crisis of 2008, yet they typically spend a considerably smaller share of their GDP on education than the UK, whose economic recovery since 2008 has been relatively weak.

Table 102.1 contains another important metric, namely the shares of public and private expenditure within the overall allocation to education by each country. Here again there are significant contrasts. The OECD estimate is that the share of *private* spending on education in the UK (1.9 per cent) is only surpassed by the United States (2.1 per cent). Other OECD members tend to rely more heavily on public spending, financed by taxes, to support educational provision. The education systems in English-speaking and Asian countries are typically more dependent on private funding than is the case for countries on the European mainland.

The case for private funding rests on the argument that the benefits from education are both private and public and therefore costs should be shared between the public and those who directly benefit (for example, by earning more than they would otherwise have done). However, dependence on private funding may limit access to education to those with the ability to pay which in turn creates social division and may limit social mobility in the long run.

Table 102.1 Spending on education among developed countries (as a share of GDP)

| | United Kingdom | Denmark | New Zealand | Korea | United States | Norway | Canada | Portugal | Australia | Belgium | Finland | Netherlands | Sweden | France | OECD average | Ireland | Japan | Germany | Spain | Italy |
|---|---|---|---|---|---|---|---|---|---|---|---|---|---|---|---|---|---|---|---|---|
| Public expenditure on education institutions | 4.8 | 6.3 | 4.7 | 4.6 | 4.2 | 6.1 | 4.5 | 4.9 | 3.9 | 5.6 | 5.6 | 4.5 | 5.2 | 4.8 | 4.4 | 4.4 | 3.2 | 3.7 | 3.5 | 3.6 |
| Private expenditure on education institutions | 1.9 | 0.2 | 1.7 | 1.7 | 2.1 | 0.1 | 1.6 | 0.9 | 1.8 | 0.2 | 0.1 | 0.9 | 0.2 | 0.5 | 0.8 | 0.5 | 1.2 | 0.6 | 0.7 | 0.4 |
| Total expenditure on education institutions | 6.6 | 6.5 | 6.4 | 6.3 | 6.2 | 6.2 | 6.2 | 5.8 | 5.8 | 5.8 | 5.7 | 5.4 | 5.4 | 5.3 | 5.2 | 4.8 | 4.4 | 4.3 | 4.3 | 4.0 |

Source: www.oecd.org/education/skills-beyond-school/education-at-a-glance-2016-indicators.htm

The private contribution to the funding of education in Scotland is smaller than that in the UK as a whole. For example, Scotland has 29,600 private school pupils compared with 522,900 in the UK overall (see https://www.isc.co.uk/research/). The Scottish private school population therefore accounts for 5.7 per cent of the UK total, well below its share in the overall population (8.3 per cent). A further large element of private spending comes from tuition fees in higher education, which are almost universally levied by English universities at £9,000 per annum for each student. Scottish students studying in Scottish institutions are not charged for tuition. Their tuition costs are allocated to the public sector, whereas in England only unpaid loans to cover tuition fees are charges on the public sector.

The mechanism by which educational providers are allocated to the private or public sectors is controlled by the Office for National Statistics (ONS) and is based on strict accounting conventions. Thus, for example, further education colleges in England were deemed to no longer belong to the public sector as a result of changes in their governance arrangements made by the Education Act 2011. These changes do not apply to Scotland, Wales and Northern Ireland. Even though the Act does not significantly change how English colleges are funded, it makes comparisons of private and public education spending between the UK nations more difficult (see Scottish Parliament Information Centre, 2016).

## EDUCATION SPENDING IN SCOTLAND

As mentioned above, the UK Government's principal fiscal policy since 2010 has been to reduce the UK fiscal deficit. This policy has been implemented largely through cuts in spending rather than tax increases. Spending cuts at UK level are passed on to Scotland via the Barnett formula, which adjusts Scotland's block grant by Scotland's population share of the changes in spending set by the UK Government on 'comparable programmes' where the Scottish Government has a competence, such as health and education. Therefore, if the UK Government decides to cut spending on education, Scotland's block grant will also reflect that cut, though the Scottish Government is free to leave education spending untouched and reduce spending in one of its other responsibilities.

Most spending on education in England is known some time in advance. The UK Government carries out regular spending reviews which determine departmental budgets for the next three to four years. Its main outcome is a projection of spending (both current and capital) in each department (health, education, etc.). The Scottish Government budget is also determined by the spending review process through the Barnett formula. This means that the Scottish Government broadly knows the block grant it is likely to receive over the medium term, rather than for just the next financial year. There are annual adjustments following each UK budget, known as Barnett 'consequentials', which vary the amounts set by the most recent spending review, though rarely by a significant amount.

However, while historically correct, the above explanation of the determination of Scotland's block grant omits important newly acquired revenue sources. This is because the Scottish Government is in the process of acquiring new tax powers which result from the UK Government response to the 2014 independence referendum. These were set out in the 2016 Scotland Act. These new powers mean that the Scottish Government will soon control around 40 per cent of all tax revenue raised in Scotland, making it one of the most powerful sub-national governments in the world in terms of its ability to generate and then spend its tax revenues as it sees fit. However, since 40 per cent of tax revenues can only finance a minority of public spending, the remainder of the Scottish Government's funding will continue to come through the traditional Barnett formula route as described above.

The new tax arrangements mean that the Scottish Government is less sure how much it has to spend each year. This is because the yield from taxes can never be exactly predicted. In addition, because the transfer of tax-raising powers to Scotland means that the UK Government has less revenue, in return the Scottish Government has had to accept a reduction in its block grant from Westminster. Whereas this means that the amount that the Scottish Government has to spend overall is broadly unchanged, it will not be exactly the same. The calculation of the reduction in the block grant is extremely complex and will not be finally resolved until well after the end of the fiscal year to which it applies. Thus, with new tax powers comes greater uncertainty over revenue, which in turn increases the uncertainty over the amount that Scottish Government can spend on services, including education.

The most recent spending review was conducted in 2015 by George Osborne. It set departmental expenditure limits (DEL) for each spending department in the UK Government. It allocated £302 billion to the Education Department in England to spend between 2016–17 and 2020–1. While this may seem a large amount of cash, the settlement for day-to-day spending on education actually implies a 1.1 per cent cut during the period. Austerity will continue to have a negative effect on the education budget at UK level.

The Scottish Government received its DEL allocation as part of the 2015 Spending Review process. The 2015 Spending Review set this at £26.3 billion. But after the passage of the 2016 Scotland Act, with enhanced revenue-raising powers for the Scottish Parliament, including around £12 billion from income tax, the DEL allocation for Scotland for 2018–19 was reduced to £13.8 billion. As mentioned above, because Scotland is sending less tax to the UK Government, it is receiving a smaller block grant in return.

The Scottish Government will also continue to receive some annually managed expenditure (AME) from the Treasury. AME comprises those elements of spending that are difficult to manage other than on an annual basis. This is of some importance for the education budget as we shall see subsequently.

Recent outturns for the Scottish budget from 2012–13 to 2016–17 are shown in Table 102.2. Not all budget lines are shown, but those relevant to education or to comparisons with education are included. Amounts are converted into 2016–17 prices so that comparisons between years can be made with the effects of inflation removed. The rightmost column shows the percentage real change in spending between 2012–13 and 2016–17. The Health and Sport budget is not only the largest single budget in the Scottish Government portfolio, it also has grown steadily since 2012–13, having been largely exempt from the cuts that affected other budgets. The Scottish Public Pensions Agency pays for teachers' and other public sector pension schemes. Spending on this budget line, which is paid for by the UK Government as part of AME, has increased markedly during the last five years. Teachers' pensions are managed on a 'pay as you go' basis – current pensions are drawn from current contributions made by teachers' employers and teachers themselves. At present, the UK Government makes up the shortfall, should it arise, via AME spending. This contrasts with a 'funded' scheme, where individuals build up a 'pension pot' from which they can subsequently draw in retirement. As pensions have become more expensive to fund, due to low interest rates and increased longevity, so their costs to the public purse have risen.

Table 102.2    Scottish Government draft budget, 2018–19 (£m, real terms 2016–17 prices)

|  | 2012–13 | 2013–14 | 2014–15 | 2015–16 | 2016–17 | Cumulative change 2012–13 to 2016–17 (%) |
|---|---|---|---|---|---|---|
| Health and Sport | 12,404 | 12,484 | 12,566 | 12,782 | 13,261 | 6.9 |
| Scottish Public Pensions Agency | 2,723 | 2,765 | 3,718 | 3,504 | 3,301 | 21.2 |
| Learning | 186 | 166 | 161 | 177 | 183 | –1.4 |
| Children and Families | 96 | 100 | 99 | 91 | 81 | –15.6 |
| Higher Education Student Support | 684 | 699 | 833 | 902 | 907 | 32.5 |
| Scottish Funding Council | 1,779 | 1,756 | 1,762 | 1,731 | 1,781 | 0.1 |
| Local Government | 11,915 | 10,761 | 11,042 | 11,116 | 10,337 | –13.3 |
| Administration | 239 | 216 | 206 | 187 | 182 | –23.9 |
| Scottish Government Budget | 35,838 | 35,843 | 37,437 | 37,739 | 37,297 | 4.1 |

Source: www.gov.scot/Publications/2017/12/8959

The 'Learning' entry is intended to 'deliver targeted national programmes and related support to Scottish education'. It encompasses a variety of programmes that are outside local government control, such as support for Gaelic and 'Strategy and Performance'. The Children and Families budget is aimed at improving outcomes for children, young people and families. It includes some spending on early learning and childcare as well as support for children in care.

In 2016–17, more than £900 million was spent by the Student Awards Agency for Scotland (SAAS) on loans, grants and bursaries for students taking higher education courses. These funds were mainly distributed among 143,000 full-time undergraduate students. Only 18,000 part-time students were supported and at a much lower level than those studying full-time. Maintenance loans are made available to students from low-income households. In 2016–17 the total amount of these loans was £506 million, at an average of £5,300 per student. Around £380 million of the 2016–17 budget for student support was funded through UK AME, with the remainder coming from the Scottish Government. However, to add further complication, around £176 million has been charged to the Scottish Government for the estimated future costs of student loan non-repayment. This mirrors the procedure for charging the costs of non-repayment of loans that cover both tuition fees and maintenance in England to public spending. The higher education student support system, which is administered by SAAS, is certainly the most complex of the budget lines which support Scottish education.

The Scottish Funding Council (SFC) portfolio includes college and university education, which together account for about £1.7 billion of the Scottish Government's budget. While the SFC is tasked with implementing Scottish Government policy in relation to higher and further education, universities in particular have other sources of funding. They raise money from research and from tuition fees for students from outwith Scotland. These other sources of funding give them a degree of independence which they jealously guard and which gives them a measure of political leverage. SFC spending was largely static in real terms between 2012–13 and 2016–17. In contrast, the Scottish Government's own admin-istration budget has been savagely pruned, falling by almost 24 per cent over the period. While dramatic changes in spending allocations have occurred between spending priorities, the overall Scottish Government budget has grown modestly, by 4.1 per cent. In the UK as

956

Table 102.3   Real local government spending by function, 2011–12 to 2015–16 (£m at 2016–17 prices)

| | 2011–12 | 2012–13 | 2013–14 | 2014–15 | 2015–16 | Cumulative change 2011–12 to 2015–16 (%) |
|---|---|---|---|---|---|---|
| Education | 4918 | 4853 | 4779 | 4745 | 4839 | –1.6 |
| Cultural and related services | 664 | 647 | 640 | 662 | 611 | –8.0 |
| Social work | 3111 | 3141 | 3163 | 3199 | 3239 | 4.1 |
| Roads and transport | 498 | 485 | 455 | 432 | 427 | –14.2 |
| Environmental services | 700 | 684 | 687 | 685 | 699 | –0.2 |
| Planning and development services | 314 | 296 | 291 | 286 | 248 | –20.9 |
| Central services | 463 | 410 | 505 | 452 | 478 | 3.2 |
| Non-HRA housing | 350 | 325 | 336 | 352 | 301 | –14.1 |

Note: HRA = Housing Revenue Account

Source: https://www.gov.uk/government/uploads/system/uploads/attachment_data/file/539465/PESA_2016_Publication.pdf

a whole, total government spending increased by 0.84 per cent over the same period. This largely reflects UK Government decisions to cushion areas that happen to be 'comparable' under the Barnett formula (such as health) from the most savage spending cuts.

Perhaps confusingly, the largest budget line supporting education is that allocated to local government, since school education is the largest component of local authority spending. Within the Scottish budget, local government spending declined by 13.3 per cent in real terms between 2012–13 and 2016–17. Among the major services funded by the Scottish Government, local government has arguably been subject to the most severe budgetary discipline, which inevitably means that local authorities have had increasing difficulty in maintaining services. Table 102.3 shows local government spending by function from 2011–12 to 2015–16. Again, the data are presented in real terms, at 2016–17 prices.

Within local government, education budgets have been cut in real terms, but not by as much as some of the more discretionary services that local government provides, such as culture and related services, roads and transport, and planning and development. Increasing demand for social care for older people has led to real increases in social work spending, a pressure that will continue to grow. Nevertheless, a 1.6 per cent cut in real terms has placed significant pressure on school budgets, which in turn constrain the hiring of new staff and pay levels. In 2015–16, cash spending by local authorities on education was £4.9 billion, of which £3.4 billion (68 per cent) was allocated to employee costs. Teachers' pay cost £2.4 billion with other employees such as teaching assistants costing just under £1 billion. Increased spending on teachers' pay or additional staff is clearly difficult for local authorities within the current financial environment.

Table 102.3 gives the overall allocation to Scotland's local authorities. But how much does *each* authority receive to support its educational provision? The mechanism by which the Scottish Government allocates grants to individual local authorities is known as the Grant Aided Expenditure (GAE) system. GAE uses the 'client group' approach which means that funding allocations are based largely on the size of the relevant population (number of clients). In the case of education, the client group is largely the school-age population. However, there are important 'tweaks' which mean that the provision is not simply determined by pupil numbers. For example, island authorities receive significantly larger provisions presumably due to the greater cost of providing education in these areas. Second, various adjustments are made to increase provision in deprived areas due to the higher costs of providing education where there are a large number of families in difficult circumstances and in need of support, or where there are significant numbers of non-native English speakers and so on.

The GAE does not directly provide a stream of cash to local authorities. Rather it represents what is known as a spending *provision*. This is an estimate of the cost of providing a particular service. Once aggregated over all local authority services, the GAE is the basis for calculating the General Revenue Grant for each local authority and forms the major part of their annual income.

The simple reason that GAE does not represent actual funding is that not all support for local authority services comes from the Scottish Government: some funding comes from council tax and non-domestic rates. The GAE calculation takes the estimated revenues from these other sources into account. Table 102.4 gives GAE provisions for different education services aggregated across Scotland for fiscal year 2016–17. Implicitly, the table shows the relative priorities that the Scottish Government assigns to different types of education and to different parts of the educational process.

**Table 102.4   Grant aided expenditure, 2016–17**

|  | £000s |
| --- | --- |
| Nursery School Teaching Staff | 26,215 |
| Primary School Teaching Staff | 902,523 |
| Secondary School Teaching Staff | 1,141,745 |
| Special Education | 243,588 |
| School Transport | 54,853 |
| School Meals | 74,691 |
| School Non-Teaching costs including Property | 859,543 |
| School Hostels and Clothing | 26,998 |
| School Security | 15,173 |
| Gaelic Education | 5,570 |
| Teachers for Ethnic Minorities | 8,317 |
| Education Deprivation Assessment | 59,005 |
| Community Education | 122,207 |
| Residual Further Education | 2,317 |
| Residual FE Travel and Bursaries | 5,492 |
| Childcare Strategy | 44,556 |
| Sure Start Strategy | 59,912 |
| Adult Literacy and Numeracy | 12,482 |
| National Priority Action Fund | 248,828 |
| Former Excellence Fund | 66,600 |
| Pre-School Education | 162,695 |
| Teacher Pensions | 113,774 |
| **Total** | 4,257,085 |

Source: www.gov.scot/Topics/Statistics/18209/2016–17settlement

For example, adult literacy and numeracy received relatively small support in comparison with the funding allocated to preschool education. These aggregate amounts are divided between local authorities, programme by programme. Interestingly, these totals have remained unchanged since the 2008–11 settlement, perhaps due to a wish not to upset local authorities, though allocations to individual local authorities will vary if the size of its 'client groups' have changed.

Education spending by local authorities need not be exactly equal to the Scottish Government GAE allocation for education. Local authorities have some statutory functions in relation to education, but as long as these are met, they can choose to spend more or less than the GAE allocation and can use their other sources of income to do so. Average educational spending by local authorities between 2008–9 and 2015–16 has been £4.8 billion, which is higher than the GAE allocation for Scotland as a whole.

Local authorities are not immune from Scottish Government pressure to improve educational outcomes. Such improvements may not be possible without increased spending. As an example, Scotland's recent poor performance on the Programme for International Student Assessment (PISA) tests has been a catalyst for increased intervention in education by the Scottish Government, since it has borne much of the criticism for the poor outcomes. We return to this issue in the final sections of the chapter.

Although the overall distribution of GAE to different education services has not changed since 2008, *actual* spending by local authorities reveals interesting shifts in the distribution of spending between the different forms of education they provide. This is shown in Table 102.5.

In the last decade, local authority education spending has increasingly focused on early years and primary education. Provision for special education has also increased, taking an additional 0.7 per cent of the local government education budget by 2015–16. The services which have suffered relatively are secondary education and education provided outside the school. Support for community learning has fallen by almost 30 per cent, from 3.5 per cent to 2.5 per cent of the local authority education budget and in 2015–16 secondary schools accounted for only 39.4 per cent of the budget, compared with 41.5 per cent in 2008–9. The lack of statutory support for services such as community education make them vulnerable when resources are tight.

The GAE process leads to differences in levels of support between local authorities due to the adjustments made, for example, for deprivation and rurality. Local authorities have other sources of income and also have the ability to vary education spending provided they

Table 102.5 Shares of local government spending on education by type of provision

|  | 2008–9 (%) | 2010–11 (%) | 2012–13 (%) | 2014–15 (%) | 2015–16 (%) | Change 2008–9 to 2015–16 (%) |
|---|---|---|---|---|---|---|
| Pre-primary education | 6.5 | 6.6 | 6.6 | 7.2 | 7.8 | 1.2 |
| Primary education | 36.8 | 37.6 | 38.2 | 38.5 | 38.5 | 1.8 |
| Secondary education | 41.5 | 40.9 | 40.8 | 40.1 | 39.4 | −2.2 |
| Special education | 10.5 | 10.9 | 10.7 | 11.2 | 11.1 | 0.7 |
| Community learning | 3.5 | 3.1 | 3.0 | 2.4 | 2.5 | −1.0 |
| Other non-school funding | 1.2 | 1.0 | 0.9 | 0.5 | 0.7 | −0.5 |
| Total | 100.00 | 100.00 | 100.00 | 100.00 | 100.00 |  |

Source: www.gov.scot/Topics/Statistics/Browse/Local-Government-Finance

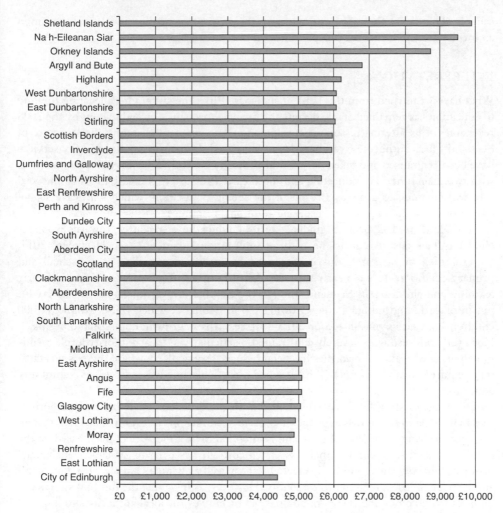

**Figure 102.1  Gross educational revenue expenditure per person aged 3–18, 2015–16**

Note: The table refers to 'revenue expenditure'; capital expenditure on buildings and so on is excluded.
Source: https://beta.gov.scot/publications/scottish-local-government-finance-statistics-2015-16/pages/9/

meet their statutory obligations. This leads to quite substantial variations in spending as shown in Figure 102.1, which shows gross educational spending in 2015–16 by local authority divided by the estimated population aged 3–18 in 2016. Local authority education spending is mainly concentrated on these ages, as is clear from Table 102.5.

Spending per head in this age group in Shetland (£9,896) is more than double that in Edinburgh City (£4,393). Some of the reasons for this wide difference are due to the GAE; others have different sources. The GAE gives special allowances for island communities. It also provides more resources to local authorities with smaller schools and where more children receive free school meals, features that are more likely in Shetland than in Edinburgh. Independently of the GAE calculations, almost all children in Shetland will attend state schools. That is not the case in Edinburgh, where private schooling is relatively common and which therefore reduces cost pressures on the state sector.

## INTERPRETATIONS

What have we learned from this mass of statistics? First, the system for allocating funding to education has remained stable despite the financial pressures brought about by the 2008 recession. In its aftermath, serious consideration was given to changing the structure of Scotland's local authorities; yet that has not happened. In contrast, police and fire services have been centralised and taken out of local authority control. This leaves local authorities with two main functions: education and social care. Pressure to increase funding on social care will continue to grow as a result of the ageing population, which will leave school education in a difficult position in seeking additional resources.

Second, there has been a gradual shift in educational resource towards younger children. This partly reflects the body of international evidence (see Heckman, 2017, for example). In Scotland, this is evidenced by increased spending on preschool and primary education. It is too early to assess the full impact of increased provision of early learning and childcare in Scotland, though the Scottish Government has, to its credit, put in place a longitudinal study, Growing Up in Scotland, which tracks around 14,000 children born either in 2004–5 or 2010–11 (see https://growingupinscotland.org.uk/). However, with resources severely constrained, particularly at local authority level, spending on other educational priorities has been reduced, particularly where there is no statutory requirement for provision. This has had a particularly adverse effect on community education.

Third, the existing GAE system coupled with the decisions made by local authorities lead to wide variations across Scotland in levels of spending on education. The GAE system has been unchanged for several years and is intended to be a measure of need based on the number of eligible clients and their associated costs. It has perhaps remained unchanged because a new system would likely create losers as well as winners among Scotland's local authorities and losers tend to protest loudly. However, as it stands, the funding system has no links to outcomes and there are no financial incentives for local authorities to improve schools' performance. Perhaps it is time for a rethink. This issue is taken up in the final sections of the chapter.

Fourth, although Scottish Government funding for further and higher education has remained stable in real terms, there has been some variation in the allocation between colleges and universities. Scotland's universities have a stronger political voice, partly because of their international reputation, but also because they claim that the introduction of tuition fees in England will put them at a competitive disadvantage unless they receive additional public funding. Colleges, in a weaker position, saw their share of the SFC budget fall from 36.7 per cent in 2009–10 to 31.4 per cent in 2013–14. Since then, following large-scale reorganisation of the sector, their share has modestly increased to 34 per cent (figures drawn from several Scottish Funding Council reports and accounts).

In the next section, we consider the largest element of educational costs – pay. We focus on teachers' pay, because not only has this been an ongoing bone of contention, but also because it is possible to derive reasonably accurate statistics for this group, given the large number of teachers compared with others employed in the education sector.

## TEACHERS' PAY

Since teachers account for a substantial majority of the educational workforce, teachers' pay dominates local authority education budgets. Local authorities wish to maintain a fully staffed and motivated workforce at a time when their financial resources are severely constrained.

We begin again with the big picture. Figure 102.2 compares salary scales for different types of teaching ranging from pre-primary to upper secondary. It shows starting salaries, salaries after 10 and 15 years' experience and finally salaries at the top of the scale. The data are presented for Scotland, England, the average for the OECD, the 22 EU States that are members of the OECD. They are also converted into dollars and adjusted for differences in purchasing power across countries, so they should represent real differences in standards of living. Note that overall, average wages in the UK rank fifteenth out of the thirty-five OECD member countries.

Given the UK's above average income ranking within the OECD, it is not surprising that for some types of teaching, wages in Scotland and England exceed the OECD and EU averages. This is most evident for mid-scale pre-primary and primary teachers. For other categories of teaching, the salary advantages are much smaller or indeed negative.

Recruitment into any profession depends on the costs of acquiring the necessary qualifications and the likely rewards for these, both present and future. In most countries, the qualifications required for teaching upper secondary pupils are more demanding than those required for pre-primary pupils. Rewards are therefore typically greater for upper secondary teachers. This is evident in the OECD and EU averages, which show a small increase

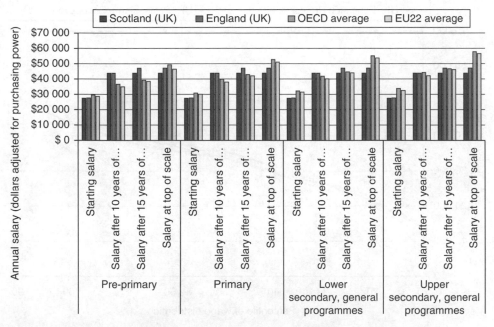

**Figure 102.2   Teachers' annual salary at various grades (measured in dollars and adjusted for differences in purchasing power)**

Source: www.oecd.org/education/skills-beyond-school/education-at-a-glance-2016-indicators.htm

for starting salary from pre-primary to upper secondary teachers and a much larger increase at the top of the scale.

The data for Scotland and England show relatively small differences, but slightly higher rewards at the top of each scale in England. However, in terms of standard of living, these may be offset by the lower costs of housing in Scotland which are not taken account of in the OECD purchasing power adjustment, which only operates at country level. Thus, although teachers at the top of the lower secondary scale may earn slightly more in England, their standard of living is not necessarily higher.

Compared with the OECD or EU averages, it appears that teachers' wages in Scotland are less progressive at the top end of the scale. That is, while Scottish teachers' wages increase sharply during their first ten years in the profession, subsequent increases in earnings are much slower. The same is true, albeit to a slightly lesser extent, in England.

The more rapid progression of teachers' earnings in the rest of the UK is confirmed by a completely different data set, the ONS Annual Survey of Hours and Earnings (ASHE). Data for the earnings of education professionals (which are dominated by teachers) and professional occupations in general are shown in Figure 102.3 both for Scotland and for the UK as a whole. It shows that for those education professionals who earn less than the median wage, those employed in Scotland earn slightly more than those in the rest of the UK, though the differences are relatively small and are also similar to earnings in professional occupations as a whole. However, above the median wage, differences in earnings

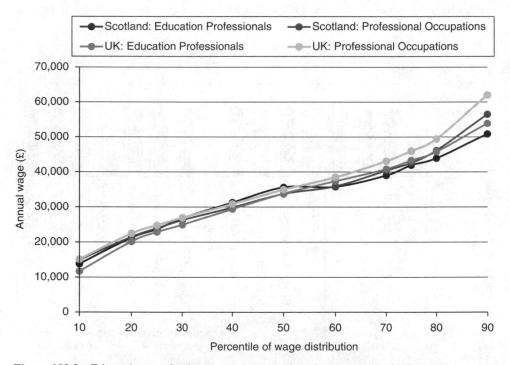

Figure 102.3   Education professionals: annual earnings by percentile, 2017

Source: https://www.ons.gov.uk/employmentandlabourmarket/peopleinwork/earningsandwork inghours/bulletins/annualsurveyofhoursandearnings/2017provisionaland2016revisedresults

increase, with better paid teachers in Scotland earning less than those in the rest of the UK, who in turn earn less than those in professional occupations as a whole. At the ninetieth percentile, education professionals in Scotland earn £51,000, while those in the rest of the UK earn £54,000. At the same point in the distribution, those in professional occupations in Scotland earn £56,000, while those in the UK as a whole earn £62,000.

Scotland appears to have a more egalitarian approach to setting teachers' pay than is evident in the rest of the UK. While this may be laudable, it should be realised that the potential downside may be an unwillingness to enter a profession where long-term rewards appear to be less attractive than in alternative occupations. And for those already employed, willingness to take additional responsibility (e.g. a headship) may be weakened if the rewards for so doing are considered inadequate.

Scottish teachers have experienced a drop in their real wages in recent years. Between 2011 and 2017 the ASHE data imply that both the median and mean wage of education professionals increased by 4 per cent. But inflation (as measured by the GDP deflator) increased by 9 per cent over this period, implying a 5 per cent fall in the real purchasing power of their salaries. The group with earnings just below the median (around £33,000) experienced the largest drop, given that their earnings declined even in money terms. In contrast, earnings growth was strongest among those in the top four deciles of the distribution of educational professionals' salaries. They therefore experienced a smaller drop in living standards.

Another important pay-related issue is the gender pay gap. This is illustrated in Figure 102.4. Again the data are drawn from ASHE. They show earnings between the twentieth and eightieth percentiles of the male and female education professional wage distributions. Estimates outwith this range are unreliable and therefore not shown. Average pay for male education professionals in 2017 working in Scotland was £37,348, while the

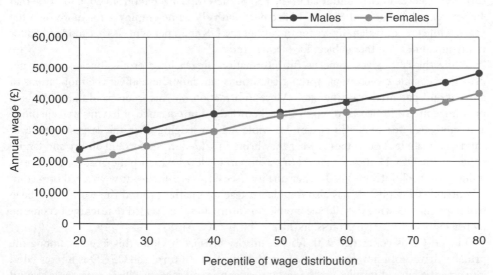

Figure 102.4   Education professionals in Scotland annual earnings by gender and percentile, 2017

Source: https://www.ons.gov.uk/employmentandlabourmarket/peopleinwork/earningsandwork inghours/bulletins/annualsurveyofhoursandearnings/2017provisionaland2016revisedresults

median wage was £35,709. The equivalent figures for females were £31,850 and £34,593. The gender wage gap measured at the mean is 14.7 per cent and at the median 3.1 per cent. Why the large difference between these measures? This is explained by Figure 102.4, which shows that male and female teachers' earnings do not differ by much around the middle of the wage distribution. This may reflect a large concentration at the top of one of the standard scales. Recall that Figure 102.2 showed that in Scotland, unlike other countries in the OECD, there is little earnings progression after ten years in the teaching profession.

However, male earnings exceed those of females both at the bottom and the top of the wage distribution. This explains the much larger difference in mean earnings. These estimates of the gender pay gap are not corrected for full-time or part-time working, nor for level of qualification. And it is the case that these estimates compare favourably with the 2017 estimates for the gender pay gap in professional occupations as a whole in Scotland which were 27.5 per cent at the mean and 21 per cent at the median. Nevertheless, they do show that there are significant differences in earnings by gender within education which certainly warrant further investigation.

What about aspects of employment other than wages? We have some limited data from the ONS Labour Force Survey (LFS) on working time (https://www.ons.gov.uk/employmentandlabourmarket/peopleinwork/employmentandemployeetypes/bulletins/uklabourmarket/latest). These, for example, show little difference in average paid hours of work between Scotland and the rest of the UK, and virtually no difference between primary and secondary teachers in Scotland. The LFS also shows that teachers in Scotland currently have around the same gender mix and age structure as those in the rest of the UK. One significant difference which does emerge is that teachers in the rest of the UK claimed to work an average of 14.1 hours per week *in addition* to their contracted hours in 2017, while in Scotland the equivalent figure was 11.4 hours a week. Another difference is that teacher turnover is lower in Scotland than in the rest of the UK. LFS data from 2016 indicate that 46 per cent of teachers in Scotland have been with the same employer for more than ten years, while the equivalent figure for the rest of the UK is 36 per cent. Is this good or bad for pupil outcomes? Another subject for further study.

While the LFS gives some useful information on teaching professionals, it does not provide a complete picture of working conditions and how these affect the motivations of current and potential teaching staff. More information on this issue would seem to be a pressing concern in Scotland, given the acknowledged importance of having well-qualified and motivated teachers. For example, while acknowledging that the largest source of variation in student outcomes is what they bring to school in the form of ability and family support, the OECD argues that the most important lever which policymakers can use to influence school outcomes is 'teacher quality' (see *Teachers Matter* at www.oecd.org/edu/school/34990905.pdf). It has also found that teacher salaries around the world have been frozen or cut following the 2008 economic downturn and this has led to teaching become an increasingly unattractive profession (http://bit.ly/2CEAus8).

The OECD is concerned with teacher quality because it views this issue as among the primary drivers of improved outcomes from education. In turn, the OECD is interested in outcomes because of its mission 'to improve economic and social wellbeing of people around the world' (www.oecd.org/about/). This chapter has thus far concentrated on the inputs to the educational process – how much resource Scotland has directed to education overall and to its various components, including teachers' pay. In the next section, we briefly discuss outcomes, their measurement and role in Scotland's education system.

## OUTCOMES

Scotland has long had its own qualifications linked to its own unique education system. These have generally been highly regarded and have served its social and economic development. They were supplemented by vocational training, often provided and funded by employers. However, economic change has forced many countries to reassess their education system and in particular to question whether it is producing students able to fulfil their potential both in society and in the workplace. These economic changes include globalisation, where international trade effectively pits workers in one country against those in another and which puts downward pressure on wages. This process is also at least partly responsible for a weakening of the vocational education strand, with employers increasingly expecting the public sector to provide suitable workers rather than train them themselves. Economic change has also involved the introduction of new technologies, which reduces the demand for unskilled labour but which places a premium on those with the skills to develop, adapt and utilise new technologies. Again, this process has led to increased expectations that the education system will provide the necessary skills to adapt to a more 'high-tech' economic environment.

Realisation that the education system may not be producing citizens best adapted to the 'new economy' has led to widespread pressure to monitor its outcomes and, in a world of scarce resources, to question how best to deploy resources to improve outcomes. And because each country has tended to have its own outcomes measurement system, international organisations have made the case for uniform systems of testing across countries. The best known of these is the Programme for International Student Assessment developed at the OECD, which tests students across the world on their science, mathematics and reading abilities.

There are many arguments against placing too great a weight on the outcomes of PISA tests. They may be culturally specific; they may not test the right kinds of skills and they may be subject to bias due to countries focusing resources to improve their PISA ranking. However, there are counterarguments which suggest that measurement of outcomes provide useful information, at least as far as indicating whether the economy has an adequate supply of skills to facilitate economic growth. The links between economic growth and skills have been extensively researched (Hanushek, 2017) and the conclusion that there is a strong connection between growth and skills development is generally accepted.

Against this background, Scotland's performance on these tests has been disappointing across all domains (see Figure 102.5) and has led to it slipping down the international PISA rankings. Although the educational establishment may be sceptical, there is little doubt that these objective tests carry political weight. And there is particular sensitivity to criticisms of educational performance, given that Scotland's economic growth has lagged behind other parts of the UK since the financial crash of 2008. It is therefore no surprise that there has been a rash of initiatives aimed at improving educational outcomes. For example, in October 2017 the Scottish Government announced the establishment of six regional improvement collaboratives (see Chapters 17 and 18) intended to concentrate expertise so that innovations to learning and teaching can be rolled out across local authorities. It has also announced reforms for 2018 intended to give schools more freedom to choose staff and to make curriculum choices.

What is absent from the Scottish debate thus far are significant attempts to link educational inputs with outcomes. Responsibility for this lacuna perhaps rests with the academic

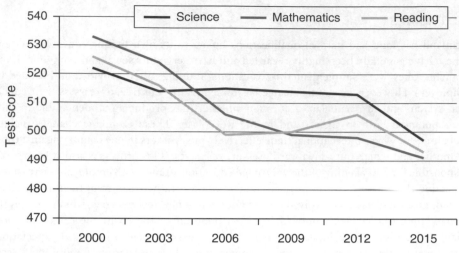

**Figure 102.5    Scotland's PISA scores, 2000–15**

research community in Scotland. In contrast, there has been extensive analysis of the potential causes of variations on educational outcomes in England. For example, explanations for the substantial improvement in schooling in London have been extensively researched (see '"London effect" in schools due to gradual improvements not policies, says report', *The Guardian*, 2015, https://www.theguardian.com/education/2015/sep/30/london-schools-success-gradual-improvements-not-policies-lse-ifs-report).

Further, given the focus of this chapter on how spending is allocated to Scotland's local authorities for education, analysis of the impact of spending on school outcomes is particularly relevant (see UK Parliament, 2014).

The recently introduced Curriculum for Excellence (CfE) is intended to be a transformative model of education that will 'help children and young people gain the knowledge skills and attributes needed for life in the 21st century' (see Education Scotland, nd). As the results from the new National Qualifications that are associated with the CfE are published, there will inevitably be pressure to understand the drivers of pupil outcomes within this new qualifications framework. The arguments involved in developing a deep understanding of these factors are necessarily highly technical. Nevertheless, it is essential that they are addressed. Scotland has not invested sufficiently in building the research capacity to carry out such studies.

As an example, Figure 102.6 shows the proportion of pupils achieving CfE Level II in reading by local authority plotted against spending on education per person aged 3–18 by local authority (from Figure 102.1). It is fairly clear that there is no simple relationship between spending and CfE outcomes, and it is not surprising that this is the case given the many other factors which influence pupil attainment. However, further exploration of this relationship and in particular the assessment of the effects of *changes* in the resources allocated to education would promote a better understanding of how spending and outcomes from the new National Qualifications interact. The main data resource that could adequately support such analysis is the Growing Up in Scotland study. But this evidence could also be supplemented by pilot studies to determine the impact and cost-effectiveness of specific interventions.

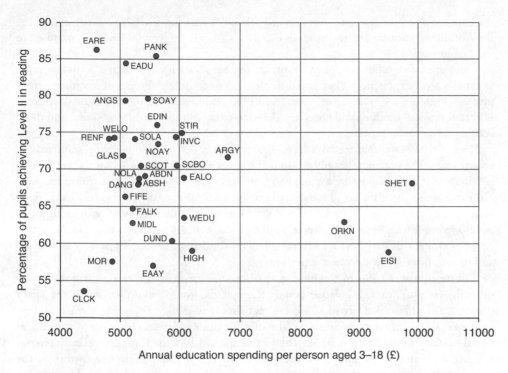

**Figure 102.6    Curriculum for Excellence Level II (Reading) results and spend per person by local authority, 2016–17**

Notes: ABDN = Aberdeen City; ABSH = Aberdeenshire; ANGS = Angus; ARGY = Argyll & Bute; CLCK = Clackmannanshire; DANG = Dumfries & Galloway; DUND = Dundee City; EAAY = East Ayrshire; EADU = East Dunbartonshire; EALO = East Lothian; EARE = East Renfrewshire; EDIN = Edinburgh City; FALK = Falkirk; FIFE = Fife; GLAS = Glasgow City; HIGH = Highland; INVC = Inverclyde; MIDL = Midlothian; MOR = Moray; EISI = Na h-Eileanan Siar; NOAY = North Ayrshire; NOLA = North Lanarkshire; ORKN = Orkney Islands; PANK = Perth & Kinross; RENF = Renfrewshire; SCBO = Scottish Borders; SHET = Shetland Islands; SOAY = South Ayrshire; SOLA = South Lanarkshire; STIR = Stirling; WEDU = West Dunbartonshire; WELO = West Lothian; SCOT = Scotland.

Sources: www.gov.scot/Publications/2017/12/5300; www.gov.scot/Topics/Statistics/Browse/Local-Government-Finance

## CONCLUSIONS

This chapter has examined how funding is allocated to Scottish education. The big picture is that attempts to control the UK fiscal deficit have resulted in a sequence of 'austerity' budgets at UK level that have had a negative effect on education funding for almost the entirety of the last decade. As in England, local government spending in Scotland has been particularly hard hit by budget reductions which have adversely affected education budgets, particularly in those areas not protected by statute. The mechanism which determines grants to individual local authorities has not changed for over a decade, though individual allocations vary as the size and other attributes of 'client groups' changes. In terms of actual spending, there has been some resource shift towards early years and primary education at the expense of secondary and community education. There has also been a small shift in the distribution of spending by the Scottish Funding Council in favour of higher as opposed to further education.

Compared with other developed countries, teachers' salaries in Scotland do not increase as rapidly with experience. They also differ less between different types of teaching – from primary to upper secondary. Pay is one feature that influences the relative attractiveness of different types of teaching and hence the decisions that entrants to the profession and those seeking advancement make.

Recent data show that teachers have experienced a real decline in living standards in recent years. They are not the only group that have experienced this outcome. Nevertheless, particularly for those just below median earnings, the decline has been more marked. Unfortunately, the data do not show whether this is the result of the relatively short salary scales within the profession. The OECD recognises that teachers' salaries in many developed countries have been adversely affected since the financial downturn in 2008. It is concerned that this may have an adverse effect on the attractiveness of teaching as a career and in turn on countries' economic performance.

The gender wage gap in teaching is smaller than in many other occupations but is nevertheless significant. It is larger among those at the lower and upper end of the salary distribution, and is relatively small around median earnings.

A chapter mainly devoted to financial issues inevitably focuses on inputs to the educational system. However, it is important to understand how such inputs affect outcomes because ultimately social and economic performance is determined by the quality of the nation's educational output, not by the inputs. For policy intervention intended to improve outcomes it is first necessary to measure these. In respect of at least one of these measures, the PISA assessments, Scotland's performance has been relatively poor. It is important that Scotland develops a better understanding of how changes to the delivery and resourcing of the educational system affect outcomes. It needs to up its game in this form of analysis to ensure that the substantial resources that are devoted to education efficiently deliver desirable social and economic outcomes.

## REFERENCES

Education Scotland (nd) *What is Curriculum for Excellence?* Online at https://education.gov.scot/scottish-education-system/policy-for-scottish-education/policy-drivers/cfe-(building-from-the-statement-appendix-incl-btc1-5)/What%20is%20Curriculum%20for%20Excellence

Hanushek, E. (2017) 'For long-term economic development, only skills matter'. Bonn: IZA, World of Labor. Online at http://stanford.io/2FdXFeA

Heckman, J. (2017) *Invest in Early Childhood Development: Reduce Deficits, Strengthen the Economy.* Online at https://heckmanequation.org/resource/invest-in-early-childhood-development-reduce-deficits-strengthen-the-economy

Scottish Parliament Information Centre (2016) *ONS Reclassification of Colleges.* Online at www.parliament.scot/S5_Education/Inquiries/20161216SPICeONSReclassification.pdf

UK Parliament (2014) *What Impact Does School Spending Have on Pupil Attainment?* Online at https://www.parliament.uk/documents/commons-committees/Education/Impact-of-school-spending-on-pupil-attainment.pdf

# 103

# The Future of Scottish Education

*Walter Humes, Tom Bryce, Donald Gillies and Aileen Kennedy*

Since the publication of the previous edition of this book in 2013, public confidence in the quality and direction of Scottish education has suffered a series of setbacks. Taken together, these have suggested that earlier official descriptions of the strengths and achievements of the system have been complacent and self-serving. This chapter will first review some of the evidence that has caused disquiet and the various efforts to address the problems. Particular attention will be given to proposals to reform the governance of the system. It will then go on to consider wider contextual issues which may affect the future distinctiveness of Scottish education: these include continuing uncertainties about the country's constitutional position and global pressures on all educational systems. The focus will be mainly on school education as that is the sector that has attracted most criticism. Reference to the future of preschool, further education, higher education and lifelong learning can be found in earlier sections of this volume.

## THE RISING TIDE OF CONCERNS

Although the reports highlighting areas of concern about Scottish education have attracted adverse publicity and given opposition parties in the Scottish Parliament an opportunity to attack the record of the Scottish National Party (SNP) Government, it is worth noting some continuities in relation to fundamental principles which are shared across the political spectrum. Education in Scotland is still widely regarded as a public good, a vital contributor to social progress and worthwhile employment, and an essential part of effective citizenship in a democracy. Furthermore, there is an honourable tradition in Scotland of regarding education as a means of promoting equality of opportunity, so that children from any background can progress to advanced levels of study and successful careers. Although this aspiration has never been fully achieved in practice, and there remains an intractable minority of pupils who underachieve, as well as a disturbing gap between the attainments of youngsters from advantaged and disadvantaged backgrounds, the ideal of equality of opportunity persists. It has been an important part of the dominant narrative of Scottish education, even if the reality has fallen short of the rhetoric.

Against this background, the evidence of failure has been particularly uncomfortable. One of the most disturbing findings came from the results of the Programme for International Student Assessment (PISA) published in 2016. As detailed in Chapter 68, these rated Scotland as only 'average' in reading, maths and science. In the previous survey, Scotland was rated as above average in reading and science, and average in maths. Within the UK, England and Northern Ireland achieved better results than Scotland. Sir Michael Wilshaw, outgoing head of Ofsted in England, said 'Scotland used to be a beacon of excellence – it's not any more' (quoted in *The Herald*, 7 December 2016). The top performing countries overall were Singapore, Japan, Canada, Finland and Estonia.

An educational system should not be judged solely on results in formal assessments but the PISA study involved 540,000 15-year-old students across seventy-two countries so its findings cannot be dismissed. Although Scotland still performs comparatively well in global terms, it is the direction of travel that is worrying: a pattern of decline has been evident since 2000. Of particular concern is the fact that Scotland has low numbers of very high-attaining pupils. In science, for example, fewer than 8 per cent of Scottish pupils perform at the highest level: in Singapore, it is 24 per cent. At a time when there is a drive to promote science, technology, engineering and mathematics (STEM) subjects, this must be a matter of serious concern.

Further bad news came from the Scottish Survey of Literacy and Numeracy (also described in Chapter 68) which, reviewing progress in literacy over the period 2012–16, reported in 2017 that standards had declined. The study found that fewer than half of 13 and 14 year olds were performing well in writing, a decline of 15 per cent from the previous survey. A less dramatic drop was evident in the final year of primary school: 65 per cent of pupils were performing well in writing, compared to 72 per cent four years earlier. In reading too, a pattern of decline (albeit small compared to that in writing) was apparent and there remained a significant gap between the achievements of children from the least and most deprived areas. A leader in *The Scotsman* had the headline 'Time running out to sort out education' (10 May 2017).

All educational reforms take time to bed in and be accepted by the teaching profession. Even so, it is remarkable that, more than a decade after Curriculum for Excellence (CfE) was first conceived in 2004, angry letters by experienced teachers should continue to be published. Alan Carroll, a recently retired secondary teacher, wrote in *The Herald* (10 May 2017), 'All secondary teachers ... are struggling under the weight of the badly thought out, disastrously introduced, woolly, vague and amorphous Curriculum for Excellence.' He continued: 'Teachers with decades of experience are drowning under a tsunami of bureau-cratic educational double speak, much of which was badly written, often contradictory and almost impossible to clearly understand.' Carole Ford, a former headteacher of Kilmarnock Academy and former president of School Leaders Scotland, has also been a persistent critic of Curriculum for Excellence. She has complained about the gulf in opinion between the educational establishment and classroom teachers and has asserted that 'Much of CfE runs counter to teachers' experience, training and intuition.' Most fundamentally, she has posed the question, 'Where is the solid evidential and intellectual basis for CfE developments?' (Ford, 2011).

Another aspect of disquiet about the current state of Scottish education is the adequacy of its institutional framework to bring about desired improvements. Both Education Scotland, the national advisory body on the curriculum and the agency which carries out school inspections, and the Scottish Qualifications Authority (SQA), which is responsible for the examination system, have been criticised for their stewardship of the curriculum reform programme. Questions have been raised about whether the dual function of Education Scotland – curriculum advice and inspection – is credible, since it effectively allows the organisation to assess the implementation of policies which it has itself helped to promote. It is argued that something more independent is required. Similarly, the SQA has come under attack for the quality of some its exam papers, its poor responsiveness to teachers' concerns and its hasty revision of assessment arrangements for some national examinations in 2017 (albeit acting under pressure from the Scottish Government). In 2017 the government introduced plans to reshape the governance of Scottish education, though not in the form some critics had expected (see below).

The role of the General Teaching Council for Scotland (GTCS) has also come under scrutiny. In 2017, the Education and Skills Committee of the Scottish Parliament initiated an enquiry into the recruitment and retention of teachers. Many of the submissions by student teachers, established teachers and headteachers were critical of their experiences, although a note of caution is important here in terms of how representative these views are of the teaching force as a whole. The comments by some student teachers were particularly disturbing, though again their representativeness might be questioned. They complained about inadequate courses in universities, variable support by mentors while on placement, overwork and stress. A few said they did not see their future in Scotland, citing better prospects and rewards overseas. Ratings of initial teacher education courses feature in the (UK university) National Student Surveys where those in Scotland are very high. The picture is, therefore, mixed. Nevertheless, in view of the comments received by the Education and Skills Committee, it was not surprising that that the chair wrote to the chief executive of the GTCS, which is responsible for setting standards and validating courses in universities, seeking a response to the issues raised. Two of the agencies which had some responsibility for existing provision felt obliged to make statements challenging the negative picture that had been presented. The chair of the Scottish Council of Deans of Education, Morag Redford, representing the university providers of teacher education courses, said that standards of entry qualifications were higher than for many other professional degrees. And Maureen McKenna, president of the Association of Directors of Education, representing local authorities which accept students for placement, claimed that the standard of new teachers entering the profession was impressive. The fact remains, however, that the recruitment and retention of teachers is a problem, with many vacancies remaining unfilled in particular subjects and particular geographical areas. Some observers attribute part of the blame to the loss of many principal teacher posts in secondary schools and the discontinuation of the Chartered Teacher scheme which allowed those experienced teachers with a strong track record in the classroom, who did not wish to move into management, to receive financial and professional recognition for their pedagogic skills. Teachers' unions also cite unattractive salary levels as a disincentive.

The cumulative effect of negative reports about the state of Scottish education has been damaging. Some of these deal with very specific aspects of provision but contribute to the overall picture of an educational service that is struggling to achieve its ambition to become (in the words of the First Minister) a 'world leading' system. For example, part of the explanation for the decline in standards of literacy has been attributed to the reduction in school libraries, staffed by trained librarians. The workforce has declined from 334 full-time posts in 2010 to 240 in 2017 (www.gov.scot/Topics/Statistics/). There has also been a decline in specialist staff supporting pupils with additional support needs (ASN). This has occurred at a time when the number of pupils recorded as having ASN has increased from 102.2 pupils per 1000 in 2010 to 248.7 per 1000 in 2016 (www.gov.scot/Topics/Statistics/Browse/School-Education/TrendSpecialEducation). What lessons can be drawn from the rising tide of concerns and what has been the official response?

## REQUIREMENTS FOR IMPROVEMENT

Effective educational policies require a number of conditions to be met: an honest assessment of existing provision based on reliable, independent evidence; a persuasive vision of future aims and priorities, supported by a well-articulated case; capable leaders able to win the hearts and minds of teachers who will be asked to implement changes; sound administrative structures capable of translating ideas into effective action; adequate support in the form of curriculum resources and professional learning opportunities to prepare the ground for the proposed reform; and clear documentation that provides both a rationale and a practical guide to the new arrangements.

Some of these conditions have been absent from Scottish education in recent years. The Scottish Government has frequently claimed that it wishes its policies to be 'evidence informed' but its record in this regard has, at best, been patchy. Lindsay Paterson, Professor of Education Policy at Edinburgh University, has said that 'Scottish education is now a data desert' (TESS, 12 May 2017), citing the decision to withdraw from international surveys such as the Trends in International Mathematics and Science Study and the Progress in International Reading Literacy Study. Even the national Scottish Survey of Literacy and Numeracy, cited above, will now be discontinued, raising the suspicion that officials are keen to make it harder to find out whether the quality of learning is improving, declining or standing still. More positively, the longitudinal study on Growing Up in Scotland carried out by ScotCen Social Research, which tracks the lives of several groups of Scottish children, has provided valuable information about such things as family circumstances, child health, parenting and access to services. In addition, from August 2017 schools and local authorities will have access to data and information from new standardised assessments on aspects of literacy and numeracy. How adequate this will prove be in the medium to long term remains to be seen, and it must be borne in mind that such data are only one type of 'evidence' on which to base policy decisions.

In the case of CfE, government for a long time resisted frequent requests by academics and bodies such as the Royal Society of Edinburgh for an independent evaluation of the programme. When, eventually, the Organisation for Economic Co-operation and Development (OECD) was commissioned to undertake a study, what it produced was a 'report' rather than a full 'evaluation', because some of the data needed for the latter was simply not available. More recently, the Scottish Government has asked an international panel of experts to offer advice on the best way forward. The panel undoubtedly contains some very distinguished people but one article (in the online journal *Sceptical Scot* in February 2017, http://sceptical.scot/2017/02/4771/) suggested that some of the members could not be regarded as genuinely independent since they had already expressed positive views about Scottish education or were recipients of the Robert Owen Award for 'inspirational educators', a prize introduced by the Scottish Government in 2013.

It is too early to assess what contribution the panel of experts has made but the Scottish Government could certainly not be accused of inaction in the face of mounting evidence of a decline in standards. Various initiatives have been launched. The Scottish Attainment Challenge was introduced in 2015, putting substantial new resources into education, followed by a National Improvement Framework (Scottish Government, 2017a). The National Improvement Framework (analysed in Chapter 71 by Chris McIlroy) has four priorities: raising attainment; closing the attainment gap between the most and least disadvantaged children; improving the health and wellbeing of children and young people; and improving employability skills and school leaver destinations. In February 2017, a Pupil Equity Funding scheme was announced, giving an additional £120 million to schools in an effort to reduce the poverty-related attainment gap. There are also plans to strengthen leadership training in the face of difficulties in recruiting headteachers, particularly (but not exclusively) in rural areas. This has resulted in twenty-three of Scotland's thirty-two councils employing headteachers who have responsibility for more than one school. Although this practice mainly affects the primary sector, there are two examples of combined secondary headships (one in Glasgow, the other in South Ayrshire). Figures reported in 2017 (TESS, 28 July) indicated that almost 10 per cent of headteachers in Scotland are now in charge of more than one school.

Leadership has been one of the buzzwords of the last decade. In 2014, the Scottish College for Educational Leadership (SCEL) was established following the recommendations of the Donaldson report. SCEL describes itself as 'an exciting and innovative resource for educational leadership in Scotland' (www.scelscotland.org.uk/) but, interestingly, despite garnering a very positive reputation in the sector, SCEL will come under the auspices of a refocused and expanded Education Scotland as a result of the 2017 governance review. In March 2017, the Scottish Government announced a new package of training support for headteachers. SCEL will run an Excellence in Headship scheme for existing head teachers over a period of four years, backed by £1.6 million of government funding. In addition, the Scottish Government, in partnership with the Hunter Foundation, plans to support leadership academies run by the social enterprise organisation, Columba 1400. This would be funded by £2 million of government money and £1 million from the Hunter Foundation.

Reactions to these initiatives from teachers' organisations have been mixed. Additional resources are always welcome but questions remain about the overall strategy which seeks to promote both 'excellence' and 'equity', a twin-pronged focus not exclusive to Scotland. The political strategy of pursuing both excellence *and* equity is premised on both being desirable when they can, in practice, each have unintended knock-on effects on the other. For example, some critics express concerns about the inequitable effects built in to modern curricula like CfE. Assignments and reports of personal investigations, 'homework', rather depends on the 'home' in which the work is carried out. The more educated, the more involved the parents (and the wealthier they are if inclined to make use of tutors to augment certificate examination practice), the better the attained grades for the young people concerned. Presentation patterns themselves, and therefore to some extent subsequent attainments, may reflect decisions taken at authority or school level: the more subjects a school permits during the senior phase of school, the more likely a candidate is to impress a university selector. Less able students who are unlikely to pass National 5 examinations take only records of their internal assessments to prospective employers, many of whom can be unconvinced of their merits. The soon-to-be-enforced lowering of university entrance requirements from less well-off applicants will raise the competition stakes overall: well-qualified students compete with each other and universities (and also employers) therefore increasingly deploy other measures to distinguish the able from the outstanding. Significantly, these measures (arranged relevant work experiences; educationally focused extra-curricular activities; culturally enhanced years-out) all favour children from more advantaged families. 'Excellence' and 'equity' are certainly worthwhile ambitions for an educational system; their joint pursuit is operationally complex in reality.

A significant omission from the responses to acknowledged problems has been any discussion of the importance and quality of *political* leadership in Scottish education. Since devolution in 1999 there have been no fewer than nine Ministers/Cabinet Secretaries for Education in Scotland (four during successive SNP administrations). This raises questions about the continuity and coherence of educational policy. New ministers like to make their mark quickly, inclining them to announce a series of high-profile 'initiatives', often at launch events marked by boastful rhetoric and extravagant promises. Political discourse (not just in education) has become inflated and the language of public relations has taken over from more measured forms of words. These tendencies are not helpful, when what is needed is honest appraisal, hard-headed analysis and proposals that have been carefully thought through. Part of the problem facing Scottish education is that the short time frame to which politicians work is geared to the next election, while it is known from past reforms (Standard Grade, 5–14, Higher Still and National Qualifications) that it takes much longer to embed effective changes in the educational system.

Professional resistance to change has been a feature of Scottish education for some time, which education ministers have often found frustrating. In the run-up to the Scottish Parliament elections in 2016, the Educational Institute of Scotland (EIS), the largest teachers' organisation, produced a manifesto entitled 'Standing up for Scottish Education'. It had quite a lot to say about financial cutbacks, inadequate resources and teacher workload, but offered nothing in the way of new ideas. Arguably, the EIS has lost touch with its own history, which dates back to 1847. In its earlier days, and particularly in the period after the First World War, it was often in the vanguard of innovation, encouraging research and putting forward policy proposals on the curriculum and better methods of assessment. Although it deserves some credit for encouraging partnership with other agencies in the field of continuing professional learning, nowadays it is largely a reactive organisation, responding to government plans, and too often adopting a negative, anti-intellectual stance. This does a disservice to its members and appears to put short-term self-interest above the longer-term needs of the system as a whole.


## GOVERNANCE REFORM

Perhaps the most significant government reaction to public concern about the quality of Scottish education was the set of far-reaching proposals to reform the governance of the system announced in June 2017: these raised sensitive questions about professional standards, institutional competence and democratic accountability (Scottish Government, 2017b). The rhetoric of the document appeared progressive and enlightened. It expressed a desire to reduce bureaucracy and devolve decision making to schools and teachers, while encouraging 'collaboration' and 'partnership'. The role of local authorities was to be reduced. New 'regional improvement collaboratives' would be established to provide better support for teachers. Headteachers would be able to appoint their own staff, though they would also be held directly responsible for reducing the attainment gap.

Will these changes begin to address the concerns that have been raised about the quality of Scottish education? They depend on the assumption that reconfiguring the structure of the system, creating new bodies and redefining the role of existing ones, will automatically bring benefits. For example, Education Scotland, the body responsible for inspection and advising the government on the curriculum, is to be 'renewed and revitalised'. This came as a surprise to many observers as that organisation was seen as bearing a fair degree of responsibility for the limited success of Curriculum for Excellence. There has also to be a Scottish Education Council and an Education Workforce Council, the precise remits of which have yet to be established. How this amounts to a reduction in bureaucracy is unclear. The governance review has been subject to widespread criticism over a perceived lack of willingness to take on board the evidence gathered during the consultation period, which showed overwhelmingly that the sector was not in favour of regionalised governance structures at the expense of local democracy. At a conference held in Edinburgh to discuss the proposals in June 2017, one critic, Keir Bloomer, an independent education consultant (and former chief executive of a local authority), described the regional collaboratives as 'top-down … authoritarian, unwanted, bureaucratic and hierarchical'. He added that 'they reinforce all the worst characteristics of the culture of Scottish education' (reported in *The Herald*, 23 June 2017).

The reference to culture is important. It can be argued that the fundamental problems of Scottish education are cultural rather than structural. They have deep historical roots which have encouraged teachers to be compliant and conformist in the face of policy directives from above. Independent critical thinking has not been encouraged in practice, either at the stage of initial teacher education or in the course of career progression, despite a growing rhetoric supporting the notion of teacher as inquirer. Evidence given to the Education and Skills Committee of the Scottish Parliament in 2017 by student teachers, experienced teachers and headteachers reinforced this point. Significantly, many of those giving evidence preferred to remain anonymous. Even if the new structural arrangements represented a genuine desire to devolve decision making to school and community level, to expect staff suddenly to start demonstrating real agency is rather optimistic. As many studies have shown, effecting change takes time and rarely fits in with the timetables of political leaders.

## RESEARCH PRIORITIES

In 2017 the Scottish Government published *A Research Strategy for Scottish Education* (Scottish Government, 2017c) with a set of priorities linked to the National Improvement Framework. The appearance of this document was welcome after years of tension between government and the research community (see Humes, 2013). Potential research projects are expected to relate to three key themes:

- supporting the research infrastructure through better access to data and training of researchers;
- effective commissioning and dissemination of evidence on 'what works' and improving system performance;
- improving the understanding and use of evidence at all levels of the school system.

As general principles, these statements would receive widespread approval but much will depend on the specific projects that are approved. It is instructive to set them alongside a list of research priorities drawn up by Douglas Weir, who has worked in Scottish education for more than fifty years, including a period as Dean of Education at the University of Strathclyde. In an unpublished valedictory address at the University of Aberdeen in 2017, he listed ten 'un- or under-researched issues' that he considered worth investigating. Several of them concerned aspects of teacher education including: new forms of preparation for teaching as a career; teacher retention and recruitment; school placements for student teachers; the gender balance of the teaching workforce; and the possibility of having teachers of general subjects up to S3 (thereby reducing the fragmented nature of the secondary curriculum).

What Professor Weir's list highlights is the critical importance of the quality of the teaching profession in any attempt to improve attainment and begin to reverse the downward trend of recent years. More than any other factor, it is the expertise of teachers and their ability to establish good relationships with learners, encouraging them to work hard and develop their knowledge and skills, that determines educational outcomes. But simply to say this does not address the scale of the problem. Budget constraints on local authorities have meant that the size of the teaching force in Scotland has declined. Even so, a GTCS study (reported in *The Herald*, 26 June 2017) found that in the summer of 2016 there were 730 unfilled vacancies across twenty-seven of Scotland's thirty-two local authorities. Furthermore, during the same year, 861 teachers between the ages of 21 and 45 left the profession. This indicates that teaching is not regarded as a particularly attractive career option, which creates difficulties for teacher recruitment and retention. Ken Muir, the chief executive and registrar of the GTCS, has suggested (at the same June 2017 conference referred to earlier) that a major cultural shift is taking place which is altering perceptions of occupational choices and pathways. The relative security of teaching is not enough to attract graduates who find the diversity and greater financial rewards of other fields more appealing. If this continues, then the prospects of an early reversal of recent trends are bleak.

There are many other aspects of Scottish education that merit research scrutiny. One of the suggestions made in previous editions of this book was the creation of a specialist centre for the study of the economics of education. It was argued that the constituency of informed opinion about this topic was small and that, at a time of economic constraints in local government, and plans to devolve more responsibility to headteachers, the case for a better understanding of educational finance was strong. At national level, difficult decisions have to be made about the distribution of resources among the various sectors (preschool, primary, secondary, further, higher, adult) and the costs and benefits of different types of intervention. For example, would devoting more resources to preschool education produce better outcomes (in terms of reducing the attainment gap) than efforts to widen access to higher education for socially disadvantaged groups? Again, when government announces that funds will be made available for favoured projects, it is sometimes not clear whether new money is involved or simply a reallocation of resources from existing budgets. Having a specialist centre for the economics of education would help professionals to understand the complexity of many policy options. So far, however, there has been no evidence of any desire to create such a centre. Central government can, of course, draw on the expertise of economic and statistical specialists within the civil service: politicians may prefer to rely on them rather than encourage external sources of analysis which may cast doubt on the wisdom of certain policy decisions. There may also be a fear that too much knowledge in the public domain could lead to fractious inter-sector tensions about the division of overall education budget. Continuing to operate in the rather murky world of historical allocations has certain political advantages. As this book was being written, reports of Scotland's economic position were of great concern, with recession seeming imminent. Written by an independent and much respected economist (David Bell), Chapter 102 in this section carefully and critically examines recent patterns of spending on education and the future prospects for the country. In the light of the very many changes which have been made to the education system in the last decade, we must note the imperative in his conclusion. From an economist's perspective: 'It is important that Scotland develops a better understanding of how changes to the delivery and resourcing of the educational system affect [its] outcomes.'

## WIDER CONTEXTUAL FACTORS

The 2014 referendum on Scottish independence produced a result in favour of remaining part of the United Kingdom. However, the issue remains on the political agenda, with the SNP Government still committed to holding a second referendum despite a retreat from its original timetable. That intention was given added impetus by the 2016 UK referendum vote on membership of the European Union (EU). There was a clear majority in Scotland in favour of remaining part of the EU, while the UK vote as a whole produced a narrow margin in support of leaving. This enabled the SNP to claim that the democratic wishes of the Scottish people were once again being ignored – an argument that had previously been used to highlight the anomaly that people in Scotland often found themselves being governed by a party at Westminster that had very little support north of the border. In the 2015 general election there was only one Conservative returned in Scotland, compared with fifty-six SNP Members of Parliament (MPs). The general election of 2017 did, however, see the SNP losing twenty-one seats (one third of the votes in three years), with gains by both the Conservative and Labour parties. Two senior members of the SNP, Alex Salmond and Angus Robertson, lost their seats. The First Minister's response was to put the call for a second referendum on hold – 'to reset the independence campaign'.

What is the significance of this continuing constitutional uncertainty for Scottish education? Education is a fully devolved matter under the control of the Scottish Parliament. Even before devolution in 1999, it had enjoyed considerable autonomy and, certainly at school level, had developed in different ways from education in England. Scottish secondary schools, for example, are more uniform in character, following the comprehensive model, than their counterparts in England, where a wide variety of types, including 'free schools' and 'academies', outside administration, has emerged. Before she called the surprise UK general election in 2017, the Prime Minister, Theresa May, indicated that she was in favour of giving approval for the setting up of new grammar schools in England, with selective entry at the age of 11 (the policy was subsequently dropped following the inconclusive outcome of that election). Policymakers in Scotland have not so far shown any inclination to move in these directions, and the SNP Government would be highly resistant to anything that smacked of 'anglicisation', but the perceived failings of Scottish education have opened up the possibility of some innovation. The independent 'think tank', Reform Scotland, has argued for some time that there is insufficient diversity of provision and that a 'one-size-fits-all' approach is no longer defensible.

What can be said about education in post-devolution Scotland is that it has been affected by the stronger sense of nationhood reflected in the greater creative output in literature and the arts. A more confident national 'voice' can be seen in the teaching of Scottish history, which for far too long hardly featured in the curriculum. English is no longer regarded as the sole medium of instruction to which all learners must conform. Scotland's two other native languages, Gaelic and Scots, are valued and celebrated as part of the nation's cultural heritage. But these developments, which seem to point towards greater divergence from England, coexist alongside a set of international pressures which tend in the direction of uniformity. Powerful international bodies, such as the OECD compare the strengths and weaknesses of educational systems, through such instruments as the PISA results referred to above. It has been argued that there is now a Global Educational Reform Movement pushing countries in a particular direction, emphasising skills, enterprise and adaptability. Critics (e.g. Ball, 2007) see this as following an agenda that suits the interests of multinational companies and global capitalism, while defenders regard it as an opportunity to learn from the experience of successful systems, adapting them to local circumstances. Politicians are extremely sensitive about their country's position on comparative league tables. Scotland is thus attempting to negotiate a delicate path between perceived imperatives deriving from a rapidly changing international environment, dominated by economic and technological forces, and a desire to remain true to national values and traditions such as those set out in George Davie's famous book, *The Democratic Intellect* (Davie, 1961). Trying to reconcile traditional conceptions of the individual scholar in pursuit of knowledge and truth as part of a civic contribution, with a much more focused and pragmatic view of learning, in which the corporate leaders regard education as a commodity in the marketplace, subservient to wider economic needs, is far from easy and may prove impossible. All the soothing language of public relations in the world cannot ultimately reconcile fundamentally different aspirations. Although Scotland has so far been fairly resistant to the intrusion of the private sector into mainstream education, its influence can be detected in various ways. The financing of many school buildings has been made possible through public–private partnerships, with some unfortunate consequences. In 2016, seventeen schools in Edinburgh had to be temporarily closed following the collapse of a wall in a primary school. Similar structural defects were found in seventy-one other schools across fifteen council areas. Parents who can afford to employ private tutors to increase their children's chances of performing well in exams do so in increasing numbers. Again, many learning packages can be accessed online, some free but others not.

Some years ago, the OECD outlined a number of future school scenarios. These were not offered as predictions but as a stimulus to thinking about how schools might respond to social, political, economic, demographic and technological changes. The scenarios ranged from minor variations of the status quo, through 're-schooling' options, in which schools were seen as either 'core social centres' or 'focused learning organisations', to rather alarming 'de-schooling' developments in which public trust in state provision declined and a flexible 'network society' emerged serving various 'communities of interest'. This would be socially divisive and greatly intensify inequalities. The most extreme de-schooling option was described as 'teacher exodus – the meltdown scenario'. (For a fuller discussion of these scenarios, see Chapter 115 in the second edition of this book.)

The debate has moved on and the OECD now has a project entitled the Future of Education and Skills: Education2030 (www.oecd.org/edu/school/education-2030.htm). 2030 is also seen as a key target date by the United Nations Educational Scientific and Cultural Organization (UNESCO), which has published a series of documents setting out principles and targets (see e.g. UNESCO, 2016; 2017). The OECD project starts from the belief that

> There are increasing demands on schools to prepare students for more rapid economic and social change, for jobs that have not yet been created, for technologies that have not yet been invented, and to solve social problems that have not been anticipated in the past.

The project has two strands. The first is to 'develop a conceptual learning framework relevant to 2030'. This seems to involve an attempt to produce a common language for educational debate, focusing particularly on the notion of 'competencies', a concept that has had a rather chequered history. Some people regard it as potentially bringing a degree of rigour and precision to the aims and outcomes of education. Others regard it as crudely reductionist, focusing narrowly on measurable skills and undervaluing the less tangible aspects of learning (reflection, divergent thinking, creativity, individual experience).

The second strand is described as an 'international curriculum analysis' to 'build a knowledge base that should contribute to making the process of curriculum design and development evidence-based and systematic'. It is hoped that this would support 'educational transformations' which too often are disrupted by 'competing objectives', poor 'sequencing of reforms' and 'political cycles'. The idea that a purely rational, technocratic approach to curricular reform could somehow circumvent the messy political aspects of educational and social change is, at best, idealistic and, at worst, anti-democratic. Moreover, education is inevitably a highly contested field, closely intertwined with alternative visions of the good society. What the OECD agenda shows, however, is that there are powerful global pressures at work, seeking for a variety of reasons (some self-interested, some more benign) to push educational systems in a similar direction. Scotland, like other countries, will have to decide how far it is prepared to cooperate in this process.

If the picture that has been presented in this chapter seems rather negative, that is a reflection of the climate of debate at the time of writing. Much good work still goes on daily in schools up and down the country and Scottish education needs advocates as well as critics, as contributors to this book amply testify. But if the system as a whole is to flourish and regain some of the standing it enjoyed for many years, it requires better political leadership, more honesty among professionals about areas of weakness, a stronger and more balanced evidence base on which to build future policies and, perhaps above all, greater openness to ideas which may challenge cherished orthodoxies but which hold out the possibility of moving forward constructively in new directions.

## REFERENCES

Ball, S. J. (2007) *Education Plc: Understanding Private Sector Participation in Public Sector Education*. London: Routledge.

Davie, G. (1961) *The Democratic Intellect: Scotland and her Universities in the 19th Century*. Edinburgh: Edinburgh University Press.

Ford, C. (2011) 'The trouble and truth about Curriculum for Excellence', *Times Educational Supplement Scotland*, 16 December.

Humes, W. (2013) 'Political control of educational research', *Scottish Educational Review*, 45 (2), 18–28.

Scottish Government (2017a) *National Improvement Framework and Improvement Plan for Scottish Education*. Edinburgh: Scottish Government.

Scottish Government (2017b) *Education Governance: Next Steps – Empowering our Teachers, Parents and Communities to Deliver Excellence and Equity for our Children*. Edinburgh: Scottish Government.

Scottish Government (2017c) *A Research Strategy for Scottish Education*. Edinburgh: Scottish Government.

UNESCO (2016) *Education 2030: Framework for Action*. Paris: UNESCO.

UNESCO (2017) *Education Transforms Lives*. Paris: UNESCO.

# Glossary of Abbreviations

| | |
|---|---|
| AAP | Assessment of Achievement Programme |
| AB | Associated Board |
| ACER | Australian Council for Educational Research |
| ACfE | A Curriculum for Excellence (also CfE) |
| ADES | Association of Directors of Education in Scotland |
| ADHD | Attention Deficit Hyperactivity Disorder |
| AGoTS | Advisory Group on Tackling Sectarianism |
| AH | Advanced Higher (NQ level) |
| AHDS | Association of Headteachers and Deputes in Scotland |
| AifL | Assessment is for Learning (also AfL) |
| AME | Annually Managed Expenditure |
| API | Age Participation Index |
| ASfL | Additional Support for Learning (also ASL) |
| ASHE | Annual Survey of Hours and Earnings |
| ASL | Additional Support for Learning (also ASfL) |
| ASLS | Association of Scottish Literary Studies |
| ASN | Additional Support Needs |
| ASNTS | Additional Support Needs Tribunals for Scotland |
| ASP | Additional Support Plan |
| ATL | Association of Teachers and Lecturers |
| ATQ | Additional Teaching Qualification |
| AUT | Association of University Teachers |
| AVU | Added Value Unit (in NQ assessments) |
| AWD | Award |
| BA | Bachelor of Arts |
| BB–BL | Better Behaviour – Better Learning |
| BCS | (1) Bishops' Conference of Scotland (2) British Computer Society |
| BEd | Bachelor of Education |
| BEMIS | Black and Ethnic Minority Infrastructure in Scotland |
| BERA | British Educational Research Association |
| BGE | Broad General Education |
| BPS | British Psychological Society |
| BR–BL–BB | Better Relationships, Better Learning, Better Behaviour |
| BSL | British Sign Language |
| BTC | Building the Curriculum |
| BYOD | Bring Your Own Device |

| | |
|---|---|
| CAD | Computer Aided Drawing |
| CAW | Chemistry at Work |
| CBAL | Community-based Adult Learning |
| CBT | Cognitive Behaviour Therapy |
| CEC | Catholic Education Commission |
| CEEC | European Committee for Catholic Education |
| CEFR | Common European Framework of Reference |
| CELCIS | Centre for Excellence for Looked after Children in Scotland |
| CEO | Chief Executive Officer |
| CERES | Centre for Education for Racial Equality in Scotland |
| CES | Centre for Educational Sociology |
| CfE | Curriculum for Excellence (also ACfE) |
| CfEtOL | Curriculum for Excellence through Outdoor Learning |
| CGI | Cognitively Guided Instruction |
| CHAPS | Catholic Head Teacher Association of Primary Schools Scotland |
| CHAS | Catholic Head Teachers' Association of Scotland |
| CK | Content Knowledge |
| CLAS | The Association of Secondary Gaelic Teachers |
| CLD | Community Learning and Development |
| CLPL | Career-long Professional Learning |
| CNAA | Council for National Academic Awards |
| CNAG | Comunn na Gàidhlig (also CnaG) |
| CNSA | Comhairle nan Sgoiltean Àraich |
| COPAC | Code of Professionalism and Conduct |
| COSLA | Convention of Scottish Local Authorities (also CoSLA) |
| CoWA | Commission on Widening Access |
| CPD | Continuing Professional Development |
| CRU | Central Research Unit |
| CS | Computing Science |
| CSP | Coordinated Support Plan |
| CYPA | Children and Young People Act (2014) |
| DARTS | Directed Activities Related To Texts |
| DEdPsy | Doctor of Educational Psychology |
| DEESE | Delivering Excellence and Equity in Scottish Education |
| DEL | Departmental Expenditure Limit |
| DES | Department of Education and Science |
| DHT | Depute Headteacher |
| DME | Decision Making Exercise |
| DWP | Department for Work and Pensions |
| DYW | Developing the Young Workforce |
| EAL | English as an Additional Language |
| EC | European Commission |
| E&CC | Education and Culture Committee (of the Scottish Parliament) |
| EdB | Bachelor of Education Degree |
| EEF | Education Endowment Foundation |
| EHC | Education, Health and Care |
| EIS | Educational Institute of Scotland |

| | |
|---|---|
| ELC | Early Learning and Childcare |
| ELIR | Enhancement-led Institutional Review |
| ELISA | Enzyme Linked Immunosorbent Assay |
| E&Os | Experiences and Outcomes (of CfE) (also Es and Os) |
| ES | Education Scotland (formed from the merging of HMIE and LTS |
| ESC | Education and Skills Committee |
| ESD | Education for Sustainable Development |
| ESL | English as a Second Language |
| ESOL | English for Speakers of Other Languages |
| EU | European Union |
| EWCS | Education Workforce Council for Scotland |
| EWCW | Education Workforce Council for Wales |
| FA | Formative Assessment |
| FAST | Families and Schools Together |
| FE | Further Education |
| FELA | Further Education Lecturers' Association |
| FERB | Further Education Regional Board |
| FHEA | Fellowship of the Higher Education Academy |
| FOI | Freedom of Information |
| FSM | Free School Meals |
| FTE | Full-Time Equivalent |
| FTT | Fashion and Textile Technology |
| GAE | Grant Aided Expenditure |
| GCSE | General Certificate of Secondary Education |
| GDP | Gross Domestic Product |
| GERM | Global Education Reform Movement |
| GIfT | Gaelic Immersion course for Teachers |
| GiRFEC | *Getting it Right for Every Child* (also GIRFEC) |
| GIS | Geographic Information System |
| GLE | Gaelic Learner Education |
| GLOW | Scottish Schools Digital Network |
| GLPS | Gaelic Language in the Primary School scheme |
| GME | Gaelic-Medium Education |
| GP | General Practitioner |
| GTCS | General Teaching Council for Scotland |
| GTP | Graduate Teacher Programme |
| GUS | *Growing Up in Scotland* |
| H | Higher (NQ level) |
| HAS | Headteachers' Association of Scotland (now School Leaders Scotland) |
| HBAI | Households below Average Income |
| HBT | Homophobia, Biphobia and Transphobia |
| HCPC | Health and Care Professions Council |
| HE | Higher Education |
| HEA | Higher Education Academy |
| HEc | Home Economics |
| HEI | Higher Education Institution |
| HEIPR | Higher Education Initial Participation Rate |

| | |
|---|---|
| HEPI | Higher Education Policy Institute |
| HFT | Health and Food Technology |
| HGIOS | *How Good is Our School?* |
| HGIOS4 | *How Good is Our School? Version 4* |
| HMI | Her Majesty's Inspectorate |
| HMIE | Her Majesty's Inspectorate of Education (also HMIe) |
| HMSO | Her Majesty's Stationery Office |
| HN | Higher National |
| HNC | Higher National Certificate |
| HND | Higher National Diploma |
| HPC | Hospitality: Practical Cookery |
| HPCC | Hospitality: Practical Cake Craft |
| HPV | Human Papilloma Virus |
| HWB | Health and Wellbeing |
| IB | International Baccalaureate |
| ICT | Information and Communication Technology |
| IDL | Interdisciplinary Learning |
| IEP | Individualised (or Individual) Educational (or Education) Plan (or Programme) |
| ILA | Individual Learning Account |
| IMI | Instrumental Music Instructor |
| IQ | Intelligence Quotient |
| IR | Impact Report |
| ISC | Independent Schools Council |
| IT | Information Technology |
| ITA | Individual Training Account |
| ITE | Initial Teacher Education |
| JRF | Joseph Rowntree Foundation |
| KPI | Key Performance Indicator |
| LA | Local Authority |
| LAAC | Looked After Accommodated Children |
| LAC | Looked After Children |
| LANGS | Languages Network Group Scotland |
| LFS | Labour Force Survey |
| LfS | Learning for Sustainability |
| LGBT | Lesbian, Gay, Bisexual and Transgender |
| LGBTI | Lesbian, Gay, Bisexual, Transgender and Intersex |
| LNCT | Local Negotiating Committee for Teachers |
| LR | Learning Representative |
| LTS | Learning and Teaching Scotland |
| MA | (1) Master of Arts (2) Modern Apprenticeship |
| MAppSci | Master of Applied Science |
| MCARE | Multicultural and Anti-Racist Education |
| MEd | Master of Education |
| MEduc | Master of Education with Teaching Qualification (Primary) |
| MEPESS | Minority Ethnic Pupils' Experiences of School in Scotland |
| MER | Managing Environmental Resources |

| | |
|---|---|
| MI | Multiple Intelligences |
| MIDI | Musical Instrument Digital Interface |
| ML | Modern Languages |
| MMT | Multiple and Multi-dimensional Transitions |
| MOOC | Massive Open Online Course |
| MP | Member of Parliament |
| MQuITE | Measuring Quality in Initial Teacher Education |
| MSc | Master of Science |
| MSP | Member of the Scottish Parliament |
| MTV | Making Thinking Visible |
| NAB | National Assessment Bank |
| NAPLAN | (Australian) National Assessment Program – Literacy and Numeracy |
| NAR | National Assessment Resource |
| NAS/UWT | National Association of Schoolmasters/Union of Women Teachers |
| NATAS | Network of Art Teachers Across Scotland |
| NATFHE | National Association of Teachers in Further and Higher Education |
| NC | National Certificate |
| NCTL | National College of Teaching and Leadership |
| nd | No date |
| NDPB | Non-Departmental Public Body |
| NEET | Not in Employment, Education or Training |
| NEU | National Education Union |
| NGB | National Governing Body |
| NGO | Non-Governmental Organisation |
| NHS | National Health Service |
| NIB | National Implementation Board |
| NIF | National Improvement Framework |
| NJC | Newlands Junior College |
| NNMPF | National Numeracy and Mathematics Progression Framework |
| NOS | National Occupational Standards |
| NPA | National Progression Awards |
| NPFS | National Parent Forum Scotland |
| NPG | National Partnership Group |
| NPM | National Practice Model |
| NQ | National Qualification |
| NSEAD | National Society for Education in Art and Design |
| NSS | National Student Survey |
| NS-SEC | National Statistics Socio-Economic Classification |
| NUT | National Union of Teachers |
| OECD | Organisation for Economic Co-operation and Development |
| Ofsted | Office for Standards in Education |
| ONS | Office for National Statistics |
| OSCR | Office of the Scottish Charity Regulator |
| PC | Parent Council |
| PCK | Pedagogical Content Knowledge |
| PCR | Polymerase Chain Reaction |
| PDA | Professional Development Awards |

| | |
|---|---|
| PE | Physical Education |
| Pedagoo | Online community of teachers sharing educational practices |
| PELO | Physical Education Lead Officer |
| PEP | Professional Experience and Practice |
| PERG | Physical Education Review Group |
| PGCE | Postgraduate Certificate in Education |
| PGDE(P) | Professional Graduate Diploma in Education (Primary) |
| PGDE(S) | Professional Graduate Diploma in Education (Secondary) |
| PIRLS | Progress in International Reading Literacy Study |
| PISA | Programme for International Student Assessment |
| PLAN C | Professional Learning and Networking for Computing |
| PPP | Public–Private Partnerships |
| PRD | Professional Review and Development |
| PSE | Personal and Social Education |
| PT | Principal Teacher |
| PTA | Parent Teacher Association |
| PTG | Principal Teacher of Guidance |
| PTPS | Principal Teacher of Personal Support |
| PU | Professional Update |
| PWLD | Pupils with Learning Difficulties |
| QAA(HE) | Quality Assurance Agency (for Higher Education) |
| QAMSO | Quality Assurance, Moderation of Standards Officer |
| QC | Queen's Counsel |
| QI | Quality Indicator |
| QIO | Quality Improvement Officer |
| QOS | Qualified Outside Scotland |
| QUIPE | Quality Improvement and Professional Engagement |
| RAfA | Raising Attainment for All |
| RCT | Randomised Control Trial |
| RE | Religious Education |
| REAF | Race Equality Advisory Forum |
| REF | Research Excellence Framework |
| RERC | Religious Education for Roman Catholic Schools |
| RIC | Regional Improvement Collaborative |
| RIF | Record of Inspection Findings |
| RISE | Respect, Independence, Socialism, Environmentalism (political party) |
| RME | (1) Religious and Moral Education (2) Realistic Mathematics Education |
| RMPS | Religious, Moral and Philosophical Studies |
| RP | Received Pronunciation |
| RR(A)A | Race Relations (Amendment) Act |
| RRSA | Rights Respecting Schools Award |
| RSC | Royal Society of Chemistry |
| RSE | Royal Society of Edinburgh |
| rUK | Rest of the UK |
| RWE | Realistic Working Environment |
| SA | Summative Assessment |
| SAAS | Student Awards Agency for Scotland |

| | |
|---|---|
| SAC | Scottish Attainment Challenge |
| SAGT | Scottish Association of Geography Teachers |
| SAL | Significant Aspect of Learning |
| SALT | Scottish Association for Language Teaching |
| SATH | Scottish Association of Teachers of History |
| SCCC | Scottish Consultative Council on the Curriculum |
| SCCORE | Scottish Central Committee on Religious Education |
| SCCYP | Scottish Commissioner for Children and Young People |
| SCDE | Scottish Council of Deans of Education |
| SCEL | Scottish College for Educational Leadership |
| SCES | Scottish Catholic Education Service |
| SCILT | Scotland's National Centre for Languages |
| SCIS | Scottish Council of Independent Schools |
| SCITT | School-centred Initial Teacher Training |
| SCOLA | Scottish Committee on Language Arts |
| ScotCen | Scottish Social Research Institute |
| SCOTVEC | Scottish Vocational Education Council |
| SCQF | Scottish Credit and Qualifications Framework (see also SQF) |
| SCRE | Scottish Council for Research in Education |
| SCT | Standard for Chartered Teacher |
| SCVO | Scottish Council of Voluntary Organisations |
| SD | Sustainable Development |
| SDE | Sustainable Development Education |
| SDGs | Sustainable Development Goals |
| SDS | Skills Development Scotland |
| SEAL | Stages of Early Arithmetical Learning |
| SEB | Scottish Examination Board |
| SEBD | Social, Emotional and Behavioural Difficulties |
| SED | Scottish Education Department |
| SEEAG | Science and Engineering Education Advisory Group |
| SEED | Scottish Executive Education Department |
| SFC | Scottish Funding Council |
| SFR | Standard for Full Registration |
| SG | (1) Scottish Government (2) Standard Grade |
| SHANARRI | Safe, Healthy, Achieving, Nurtured, Active, Respected, Responsible and Included (indicators of wellbeing in GIRFEC) |
| SHEEC | Scottish Higher Education Enhancement Committee |
| SHEFC | Scottish Higher Education Funding Council |
| SHEP | Schools for Higher Education Programme |
| SIF | Summarised Inspection Findings |
| SIMD | Scottish Index of Multiple Deprivation |
| SIPP | Scottish Improvement Partnership Programme |
| SJCRE | Scottish Joint Committee on Religious Education |
| SLC | Scots Language Centre |
| SLD | Scottish Language Dictionaries |
| SLS | School Leaders Scotland |
| SMO | Sabhal Mòr Ostaig |

| | |
|---|---|
| SNCT | Scottish Negotiating Committee for Teachers |
| SNH | Scottish Natural Heritage |
| SNP | Scottish National Party |
| SOEID | Scottish Office Education and Industry Department |
| SOLACE | Society of Local Authority Chief Executives |
| SP | Senior Phase |
| SPICe | Scottish Parliament Information Centre |
| SPR | Standard for Provisional Registration |
| SPTC | Scottish Parent Teacher Council |
| SQA | Scottish Qualifications Authority |
| SRIT | Scottish Rate of Income Tax |
| SRUC | Scotland's Rural College |
| SSA | Scottish Survey of Achievement |
| SSE | Scottish Standard English |
| SSERC | Scottish Schools Education Research Centre |
| SSLN | Scottish Survey of Literacy and Numeracy |
| SSSC | Scottish Social Services Council |
| SSTA | Scottish Secondary Teachers' Association |
| STEAM | Science, Technology, Engineering, Art and Mathematics |
| STEC | Scottish Teacher Education Committee |
| STEM | Science, Technology, Engineering and Mathematics |
| STUC | Scottish Trades Union Congress |
| SVDP | St Vincent De Paul Society |
| SVQ | Scottish Vocational Qualification |
| TAFE | Technical and Further Education College |
| TALIS | Teaching and Learning International Survey (OECD) |
| T-ASK | Technology Attitudes, Skills and Knowledge |
| TeachMeet | Organised but informal teacher-led events to share good practice |
| TEF | Teaching Excellence Framework |
| TEI | Teacher Education Institution |
| TEP | Teacher Education Partnership |
| TES | *Times Educational Supplement* |
| TESS | *Times Educational Supplement Scotland* |
| TGfU | Teaching Games for Understanding |
| TIE | Time for Inclusive Education |
| TIMSS | Trends in International Mathematics and Science Study |
| TIOF | *This is Our Faith* |
| TLRP | Teaching and Learning Research Programme |
| TQ | Teaching Qualification |
| TQFE | Teaching Qualification for Further Education |
| TSF | *Teaching Scotland's Future* (the Donaldson report) |
| TUC | Trades Union Congress |
| UASCs | Unaccompanied Asylum Seeking Children |
| UCAS | Universities and Colleges Admissions Service |
| UCU | University and College Union |
| UFC | Universities Funding Council |
| UGC | University Grants Committee |

| UHI | University of the Highlands and Islands |
| UKIP | UK Independence Party |
| ULA | University Lecturers' Association |
| UN | United Nations |
| UNCRC | United Nations Convention on the Rights of the Child |
| UNDESD | United Nations Decade of Education for Sustainable Development |
| UNESCO | United Nations Educational Scientific and Cultural Organization |
| UNICEF | United Nations Children's Fund |
| UoE | University of Edinburgh |
| US | Universities Scotland |
| UWS | University of the West of Scotland |
| VET | Vocational Education and Training |
| VSE | Validated Self-Evaluation |
| WALT | We are learning to |
| WEA | Workers' Educational Association |
| WHO | World Health Organization |
| WILF | What am I looking for? |
| WP | Widening Participation |
| WWF | World Wide Fund for Nature |

# Index

Note: tables are indicated by page numbers in *italics*, illustrations are indicated by page numbers in **bold**.